A CHILD'S WORLD

INFANCY THROUGH ADOLESCENCE

Diane E. Papalia and Sally Olds are also the coauthors of

Human Development, Fourth Edition (with Ruth Duskin Feldman)
Psychology, Second Edition

A CHILD'S WORLD

INFANCY THROUGH ADOLESCENCE

Diane E. Papalia
University of Pennsylvania

Sally Wendkos Olds

McGRAW-HILL PUBLISHING COMPANY

New York   St. Louis   San Francisco   Auckland   Bogotá   Caracas   Hamburg
Lisbon   London   Madrid   Mexico   Milan   Montreal   New Delhi   Oklahoma City
Paris   San Juan   São Paulo   Singapore   Sydney   Tokyo   Toronto

A CHILD'S WORLD
INFANCY THROUGH ADOLESCENCE

1234567890 VNH VNH 89432109

ISBN 0-07-048546-1

This book was set in Palatino by York Graphic Services, Inc.
The editors were Michael R. Elia, James D. Anker, and Susan Gamer;
the designer was Joan E. O'Connor;
the production supervisor was Salvador Gonzales.
The photo editor was Inge King;
the permissions editor was Elsa Peterson.
New drawings were done by Fine Line Illustrations, Inc.
Von Hoffmann Press, Inc., was printer and binder.

Library of Congress Cataloging-in-Publication Data

Papalia, Diane E.
  A child's world: infancy through adolescence/Diane E.
Papalia, Sally Wendkos Olds.—5th ed.
      p.   cm.
  Bibliography: p.
  Includes indexes.
  ISBN 0-07-048546-1.—ISBN 0-07-048547-X (pbk.)
  1. Child development.   2. Child psychology.
  3. Adolescence.
I. Olds, Sally Wendkos.   II. Title.
HQ767.9.P36   1990
305.23'1—dc20   89-8171

ABOUT
THE AUTHORS

DIANE E. PAPALIA is a professor who has taught thousands of undergraduates at the University of Wisconsin. She received her bachelor's degree, majoring in psychology, from Vassar College, and both her master's degree in child development and family relations and her Ph. D. in life-span developmental psychology from West Virginia University. She has published numerous articles in such professional journals as *Human Development*, *International Journal of Aging and Human Development*, *Sex Roles*, *Journal of Experimental Child Psychology*, and *Journal of Gerontology*. Most of these papers have dealt with her major research focus, cognitive development from childhood through old age. She is especially interested in intellectual development and factors that contribute to the maintenance of intellectual functioning. She is a Fellow in the Gerontological Society of America. She is currently affiliated with the University of Pennsylvania.

(© Thomas Victor)

SALLY WENDKOS OLDS is an award-winning professional writer who has written more than 200 articles in leading magazines and is the author or coauthor of six books addressed to general readers, in addition to the three textbooks she has coauthored with Dr. Papalia. Her books *The Complete Book of Breastfeeding* and *The Working Parents' Survival Guide* have both been issued in completely updated and expanded editions. She is also the author of *The Eternal Garden: Seasons of Our Sexuality* and the coauthor of *Raising a Hyperactive Child* (winner of the Family Service Association of America National Media Award) and *Helping Your Child Learn Right from Wrong*. She received her bachelor's degree from the University of Pennsylvania, where she majored in English literature and minored in psychology. She was elected to Phi Beta Kappa and was graduated summa cum laude.

To our parents,
Madeline and Edward Papalia
and Leah and Samuel Wendkos,
for their unfailing love, nurturance, and
confidence in us, and for their abiding conviction
that childhood is a wondrous time of life.

And to our children,
Anna Victoria
and Nancy, Jennifer and Dorri,
who have helped us revisit childhood
and see its wonders and challenges
with new eyes.

CONTENTS

MIDDLE CHILDHOOD

ADOLESCENCE

LIST OF BOXES

■ CHAPTER 15

■ CHAPTER 16

PREFACE

In the prefaces to the previous editions of *A Child's World*, we described how this book continues to develop—just as do Vicky and Jason, the "typical" children you will come to know well through these pages. In some ways, this fifth edition is much like the earlier editions—just as children of any age retain many of the characteristics they were born with. Yet there are some important differences. In addition to keeping up with the newest research in a rapidly expanding discipline, we have sharpened our focus in several areas.

The Fifth Edition

OUR AIMS FOR THIS EDITION

Our goal for this edition remains the same: to make the study of child development come alive for those of you with a professional interest in children, for those who have an intellectual curiosity about the way we all develop from conception through adolescence, and of course for those who will be raising or have already raised families.

One of the ways we work toward this goal is by telling stories about "Vicky" and "Jason"—incidents from the lives of real children (most of whom the authors know well) which illustrate important principles in child development. Another way is by offering many specific examples instead of vague or abstract generalities. And another is our continued treatment of the most important theories and research findings in the field, always with an emphasis on how they can be used. We are aware that you want to know how this information can help you deal with children—as a teacher, examiner, interviewer, tester, healer, counselor, or parent.

To meet our goal, we are also still asking the same basic questions: What factors influence children's development? What can adults do to help children realize their potential? How much control do children exert over their own lives? What aspects of development are typical for most children? In what ways is each child unique? What is normal? What is cause for concern?

In this edition, we are asking some new questions and coming up with some new answers. This revision represents a significant updating of the literature, as we discuss new research and new theories. Virtually every topic in this book has been updated with new information or new interpretations. Furthermore, we have expanded our efforts to synthesize research findings and to help students interpret them and think critically about controversial issues. Our continued work on two other college textbooks, *Human Development* (for courses in development throughout the life span) and *Psychology* (for introductory courses), has helped us refine and sharpen our thinking about child development. The changes in this revision, then, represent growth and development in our own ideas.

ORGANIZATION

There are two major approaches to writing about and teaching child development. The chronological approach looks at all aspects of development at different stages of life, such as infancy or adolescence; the topical approach traces one aspect of development at a time.

We have chosen the *chronological* approach, which provides a sense of the multifaceted nature of child development, as we get to know first the infant and the toddler, then the young child and the schoolchild, and finally the adolescent on the brink of adulthood. Accordingly, we have divided this book into five parts. The first part consists of the Introduction and Chapter 1. Then, we discuss physical, intellectual, and social and personality development during infancy and toddlerhood (the second part), early childhood (part three), middle childhood (part four), and adolescence (part five).

Readers who prefer a *topical* approach may read the book in this order: Chapters 1, 2, 3, and 4 (overall theories and issues, heredity and environment, prenatal development, and birth and the neonate); Chapters 5, 8, 11, and 14 (physical development); Chapters 6, 9, 12, and 15 (intellectual development); and Chapters 7, 10, 13, and 16 (social and personality development).

CONTENT

We continue to emphasize the crucial first 9 months of development, the prenatal period. We are more keenly aware than ever that children grow up in many different worlds and in many different kinds of families, and we talk about the influence of many family situations. As before, we include topics of contemporary social significance: ethics of research; effects of divorce, single parenthood, and parents' work; emotional disturbances in childhood and current treatments; development of moral judgment; changing sexual attitudes and behavior among adolescents (with special attention to teenage pregnancy); and other issues.

There is also much that is new. While we have retained the scope, emphasis, and level of previous editions, we have made many significant changes in this fifth edition. In addition to a greater emphasis on the interrelationships among the different stages of development and among various influences on children, we have updated material whenever new findings or interpretations have been available, reorganized material to make it more effective, and added completely new sections. Among the important changes are the following:

- *New sections.* Biographical sketches of Freud, Erikson, and Piaget; development of the brain; social referencing; development of self-control and self-regulation; Bem's gender-schema theory; childhood obesity; academic achievements of Asian children; how parents can teach children to think and influence their achievement in school; "self-care" (or "latchkey") children and adolescents; psychological maltreatment; and ways to keep students from dropping out of school.
- *Important revisions.* We have revised our discussions of Erikson's theory and the "virtue" to be achieved at every stage; low birthweight; implications of sensitivity to pain in newborns; memory in infancy and childhood; influence on language development and the controversy over "motherese"; how day care affects mother-baby attachment; dental health and care (emphasizing progress in recent years); self-concept and self-esteem; effects of divorce on children; and eating disorders in childhood and adolescence.
- *New introduction.* Our new Introduction provides an orientation to the book and discusses the authors' perspective and goals.
- *New tables and illustrations.* Many new tables, figures, and photographs reinforce and add to textual discussions. New visual presentations make it easier for students to compare major theories and important research methods, and to absorb information about birth defects, risk factors for low birthweight, childhood fears, and adolescents' use of drugs.

BOXES

In this edition, we have five categories of boxes:

- *The Research World.* These boxes, new to this edition, discuss up-to-date studies, with an eye to encouraging students to think critically about data and conclusions from "cutting-edge" research. In this category are such contemporary concerns as a possible genetic basis for shyness, what constitutes fetal abuse, the stress of being born, the implications of crawling for development in infancy, symbolic gesturing, how a mother's depression affects her baby, "benefits" of childhood illness, children's ability to distinguish appearance from reality, transition from elementary to junior high school, and psychological effects of early and late maturation.
- *The Everyday World.* Each developmental chapter includes one or more boxes showing practical ways to apply research findings. These boxes cover such topics as effects of a pregnant woman's use of alcohol, how to comfort a crying baby, dangers of infant walkers, dealing with negativism in toddlers, handling eating problems, guiding children's television viewing, helping children adjust to divorce, raising boys and girls without gender-role stereotypes, and preventing sexually transmitted diseases and pregnancy in adolescence.

- *Around the World.* These boxes present "windows" on child development in societies other than our own, showing that the world of children is indeed universal, and that children grow up in many different kinds of cultures, under many different influences. These discussions treat such issues as cross-cultural differences in motor development, impact of culture and technology, prenatal care in western Europe, immunization against childhood illnesses, implications of the one-child family in China, and an Asian perspective on moral development.

- *Professional Voices.* Statements from prominent researchers and theorists in child development, some of them from interviews conducted specifically for this book, include both classic and contemporary thought on a wide range of important issues. They offer more personal expressions of the beliefs of some of the most important people in the field.

- *A Child's World and You.* Questions in these boxes encourage students to think critically about controversial issues and to form opinions about the best course of action in a variety of situations.

LEARNING AIDS

We also provide a number of basic teaching and learning aids, several of which are new to this edition. These include:

- Part overviews
- Chapter-opening outlines
- Marginal glossary—definitions of key terms in the margins of the text
- End-of-chapter lists of key terms, in the order in which they have been discussed
- End-of-book glossary repeating the marginal definitions
- End-of-chapter summaries of major points
- Recommended readings (either classic or lively contemporary books)
- Bibliography
- Indexes for names and for subjects
- Full-color illustration program of photographs and art that underscores and expands on the textual discussions, with captions that emphasize important points.

Supplementary Materials

An extensive package of supplementary materials adds to the value of this book as a teaching and learning tool:

- Study Guide with Readings
- Instructor's Manual
- Test Item File (and a computerized test file for use with IBM, Apple, and Macintosh)
- Slide set
- Videotapes (instructors will be able to choose from a variety of videos)

Acknowledgments

We would like to express our gratitude to the many friends and colleagues who, through their work and their interest, helped us clarify our thinking about child development.

We are especially grateful for the helpful evaluations and suggestions given by the academic reviewers of the published fourth edition of *A Child's World* and the manuscript drafts of this fifth edition: Nancy J. Austin, Virginia Commonwealth University; Patricia L. Bell, Orange County Community College; Andrew Biemuller, University of Toronto-Institute of Child Study; Robert W. Bohlander, Wilkes College; Lyn Boulter, Catawba College; Maureen Callahan, Webster University; Joan Cook, County College of Morris; Donald R. Cusumano, St. Louis Community College; Lawrence A. Fehr, Widener University; Sallie J. Grant, Furman University; Hurst M. Hall, Northwestern State University; Robert Herrmann, Christopher Newport College; Ilene Hunter, Solano Community College; Eugene William Krebs, California State University; Michele Martel, Northeast Missouri State University; Nancy K. Moersch, University of Loyola at Chicago; Carmen H. Owen, York College; Gregory Pezzetti, Rancho Santiago Community College; Lillian M. Range, University of Southern Mississippi; Robert F. Rycek, Kearney State College; Carl Scott, San Jacinto College; Peggy Skinner, South Plains College; Paul Wellman, Texas A & M University; Sue Williams, Southwest Texas State University.

We appreciate the strong support we have had from our publisher and would like to express our thanks to Michael R. Elia, our editor for this edition; and to our production editor, Susan Gamer. Inge King, photo editor of all five editions of *A Child's World,* again used her sensitivity to children and her good eye to find outstanding photographs. Joan O'Connor and the artists working with her produced a cover and book design noteworthy for their esthetics, as well as their rendering of concepts. Kelly Koski and Andrew Hubsch provided valuable help with many phases of research. Finally, we'd like to give special thanks to the children in our lives who were the inspiration for incidents in the lives of ''Vicky'' and ''Jason.''

Diane E. Papalia

Sally Wendkos Olds

ABOUT
A CHILD'S WORLD

I'm like a child
trying to do everything
say everything
see everything
and be everything
all at once

John Hartford, 1971

IF YOU WERE TO MEET the child whom we call "Vicky," the first thing you would notice about her might be her cheerful, outgoing, humorous personality. She smiles and laughs often, greets the world like a friend, and would probably charm you with a joke or funny comment. The feature you might notice first about "Jason," a child of about the same age, is his physical agility. Wiry, flexible, and strong, he is usually in motion—and a joy to watch.

Both these children, of course, have many other characteristics that make up their personalities, and these characteristics result from a great many influences. Some of their traits—like Vicky's sense of humor and Jason's physical ability—are like those held by people closest to them: her father, his mother. Other traits seem to spring from nowhere. In any case, the blend of each child's physical, intellectual, and psychological characteristics is unique to that child. How did this blend come about? How did these children become the unique individuals they are? Which events in their lives have had the greatest influence? Which of their characteristics will persist into adulthood? Which will change? The answers to questions like these are what we seek when we study *child development,* the scientific study of normal changes in children over time.

We want to answer such questions for a host of reasons. First is basic curiosity: for most of us, nothing is more interesting than understanding ourselves and the people we care about. By examining how children develop—from conception through adolescence—we will come to know more about ourselves and our fellow human beings. Second, the answers have practical benefits. When we understand how development occurs, we can step in to help people live happier, more fulfilled lives. Finally, since no society can approach its potential unless its members fulfill their own, we help ourselves when we help others. Let us see, then, what this book is all about.

How This Book Presents the Study of Child Development

Each human being is like other people in some ways but unique in others. This book, too, is like other books about child development in some ways, but different in others—the topics it discusses, the way it treats them, how it illustrates and organizes them. Its singularity rests on how it reflects the point of view of each of its authors. To help readers assess what we say, we outline the perspectives from which we wrote this book. We start with our philosophical stance and go on to describe our more pragmatic concerns.

WE CELEBRATE HUMANITY

In a book about child development, it is not surprising that our emphasis is on what research and theory have to tell us about human beings. Whenever possible, we cite research that has been performed on children rather than animals. Sometimes we *need* to refer to animal studies—for example, where ethical standards prevent us from using children in research, as they would in explorations of possibly harmful consequences to the baby of a mother who takes drugs during pregnancy. When we do present conclusions based on animal research, we apply them with caution, since we cannot assume that they apply equally to humans.

Our primary interest, though, is in uniquely human qualities. Children are more adaptive than animals seem to be. They can imagine and pursue goals that animals cannot; they participate in a culture in ways that animals do not. These powers make the study of child development more complex than it otherwise would be. And we celebrate that complexity because it reflects the richness of humanity.

In keeping with this viewpoint, we have included a number of boxes titled "Around the World."* These boxes briefly explore the diversity and complexity of child development in other cultures. They pose a warning to us as scientists: when it comes to understanding humanity, we must look to its richness before we can find any unifying simplicity.

WE BELIEVE IN THE RESILIENCE OF CHILDREN

We do not believe that a passing event or experience can easily ruin the rest of a child's life. Yes, one especially traumatic incident or a pattern of deep deprivation in childhood may well have grave and long-lasting consequences. However, the stories of countless people, some of whom have been followed by researchers from childhood into middle or old age, teach us that later events can often transform the results of early experiences. In most cases, one experience is unlikely to cause irreversible damage, and a nurturing environment can often help a child overcome the effects of early deprivation. Studies of children on the Hawaiian island of Kauai, for example, have reinforced our belief in children's resilience by showing that even when children have been seriously injured at birth, the best predictor of development is the nature of the experiences the children have had while growing up (E. Werner, 1985).

WE RECOGNIZE THAT CHILDREN
HELP SHAPE THEIR OWN DEVELOPMENT

Children are not passive recipients of influences. They help shape their own environment, and then they respond to the environmental forces that they have helped bring about. In other words, influences are *bidirectional,* flowing from the outside world to the child—and from the child to the child's world. Beginning at birth, babies' inborn traits influence the ways parents and other people react to

---

*See the list of boxes on pages xvii–xx.

Children help shape their own world, and then they respond to that world. It is hard to tell from this picture who laughed first—mother or baby—but once the fun began, each affected the other. The same cycle can occur with other moods, too.

them. People have different ways of treating a cheerful baby and a cranky one, an active baby and an apathetic one, or a healthy baby and a sick one. The "fit" between parents and child—the degree to which the parents feel comfortable with the child—affects parents' feelings. Energetic, active parents may become impatient with a slow-moving, docile child, although more easygoing parents might welcome a child with such a personality (A. Thomas & Chess, 1977).

Language is a particularly striking area in which infants affect the world around them: when babies babble and coo, adults are more likely to talk to them, which then makes the baby "talk" more. This cycle of conversation helps children acquire the ability to use language—and to gain better control over their own lives.

WE ARE PRACTICAL

As two people who live in the real world, we examine research findings carefully to see how we or others can use them to solve practical problems. *Basic research*, the kind undertaken in the spirit of intellectual curiosity with no immediate practical goal, and *applied research*, which addresses an immediate problem, complement each other.

In fact, these two types of research often go together. Basic research into children's intelligence can reveal how a child of a particular age learns and thinks. Applied research can use that basic knowledge to develop age-appropriate education. If, for example, we wanted to know when children can grasp the concept of quantities and numbers, we might develop a program to test children of different ages on their ability to recognize and deal with number concepts. This would be *basic research*. If we then wanted to apply this research to teach number concepts in the classroom, we could design a program to try out different ways of doing this and see which way turned out to be most effective. This would be *applied research*.

Every chapter from Chapter 2 on includes a box titled "The Research World," which reports on new developments in either of these two kinds of research. Also, each of these chapters includes one or more boxes titled "The Everyday World." These boxes show how basic findings can be used to solve practical problems.

WE RESPECT ALL STAGES OF THE LIFE SPAN

Although this book is about the development of children, we are fully aware that development and growth do not end, as this book does, with adolescence. Throughout the book we refer to the long-term implications of many childhood experiences, and we discuss some of the ways in which children's development affects their parents. However, we are convinced that people continue to change, often in positive ways, as long as they live. Many of the changes that occur in adulthood cannot be predicted from childhood or even adolescence, since they occur as the result of experiences or relationships in adulthood.

As you read this book, you will see these various attitudes reflected again and again in our discussions. To bring some of these issues to life, we have created two fictional characters, Vicky and Jason.

Meet Vicky and Jason

Real children are not abstractions. They are living, laughing, crawling, crying, shouting, shrieking, jumping, whining, skipping, reaching, thumb-sucking, nose-picking, diaper-wetting, tantrum-throwing, question-asking human beings. To help you see children more as they really are and to personalize the statements we make about the way children develop, we introduce two leading characters who will grow up as their story unfolds in this text. We follow these personages, whom we have named Vicky and Jason, from conception to the time we leave them (or they leave us) in adolescence. We also come to know Vicky's parents, Ellen and Charles, and Jason's parents, Julia and Jess, as we see them interacting with their children. And as we trace these families' adventures, we are reminded that whenever we talk about children, we talk not about abstract concepts in imaginary space, but about real children in a real world.

Neither of these families, of course, exists in real life. And yet all these people exist in some way, since every anecdote in which they appear, and every fact that relates to them, is rooted in truth. Nothing about Vicky and Jason or their parents is made up. The stories about them are drawn from two sources. One source is the actual lives of real children, either our own children (four between the two authors) or children whom we have observed. The other source is reports of actual research; these give us a wider view of children, so that Vicky and Jason can represent the American "Everychild," developing normally.

NORMAL DEVELOPMENT

Normal development means proceeding through recognized developmental stages at a typical rate. Wide variations in normal development, however, allow for a great deal of individual difference. Throughout this book, we talk about *average* ages at which certain behaviors occur: the first smile, the first word, the first step. In all cases, these ages *are* only averages. No child is exactly average in every aspect of development. There is a wide normal spectrum of individual differences with respect to height and weight, walking and talking, understanding ideas, forming relationships, and so forth. Therefore, all the average ages we give should be regarded as flexible. Only when children deviate drastically from the norm is there cause for considering them either exceptionally advanced or retarded. The important point to remember is that all normal children go through the same general *sequence* of events, even though the *timing* varies greatly.

NO CHILD GROWS UP IN A VACUUM

Both Vicky and Jason are typical, normal children, who might be of any race, any religion, or any ethnic heritage. However, they share some characteristics that not all children possess. Both Vicky and Jason were wanted children; each is growing up in a home with two loving parents; each is healthy; each is free from financial want. Unfortunately, not all children grow up in such favorable circumstances.

When we study the development of children growing up the way Vicky and Jason are, then, we cannot generalize our conclusions to children born to malnourished teenagers, or children who do not get enough to eat, are rarely spoken to at any length, are neglected or abused, or receive a deficient education. These children are growing up in a world light-years away from the ideal. In this book we talk about what circumstances like these mean for children's development. We do not confine our discussions to either the ideal or the typical.

A Reminder: The Real World and Real Children

One item this book cannot provide is a living child. For that, you need to keep an eye on the real world and the children in it. Jason and Vicky can only begin to tug at you, to pull you from the laboratory into the real world. With their help, though, and with the new knowledge of children that you will gain as you proceed through your course in child development, you will look at every child you see with new eyes.

Observe the children about you—your sisters and brothers, nieces and nephews, daughters and sons. Observe the children you see in stores and restaurants, on buses and airplanes, in playgrounds and front yards. Pause to listen to and to watch children as they confront and experience the wonder of ordinary life.

Look, too, at the child you once were yourself. Recall some of your own earlier experiences, which may help to illustrate the various concepts discussed in this book. Look at the world through the eyes of a child, and the wonder you see will become your own.

A CHILD'S WORLD

INFANCY THROUGH ADOLESCENCE

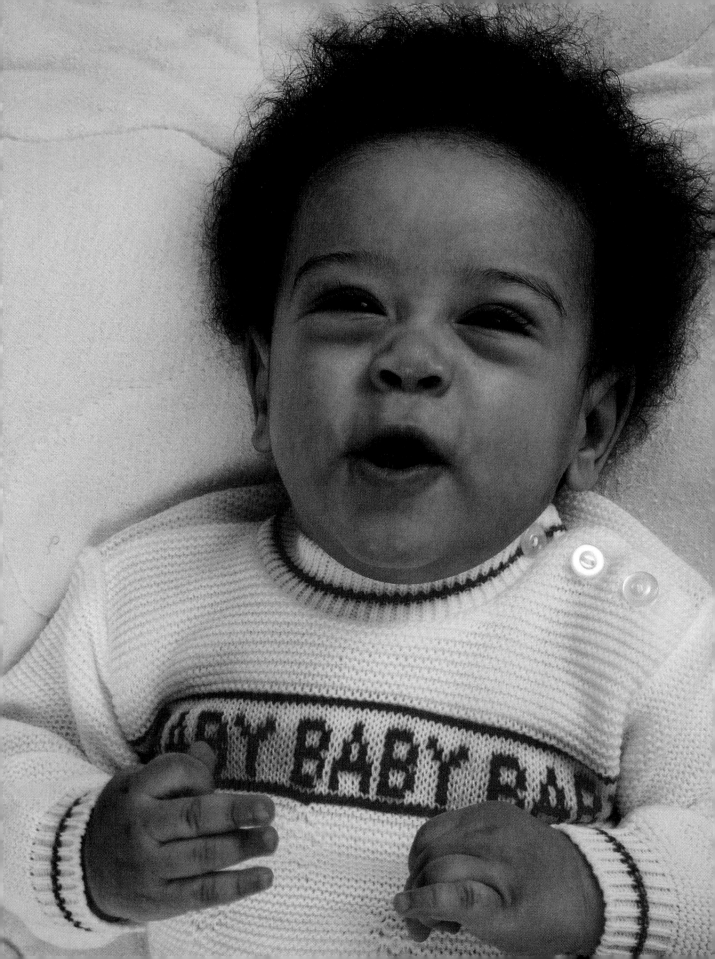

CHAPTER 1

A CHILD'S WORLD

Theories, Issues, and Methods for Studying It

C hildren have neither a past nor a future. Thus they enjoy the present—which seldom happens to us.

Jean de La Bruyère, *Caractères*, 1688

PREVIEW QUESTIONS

- Why is it important to study child development?
- What are the four major perspectives for looking at development?
- Who are the most important theorists in the field, and what are the main aspects of their theories?
- What are the main aspects and stages of children's development, and what are the main influences on it?
- How do researchers study children, and what are the advantages and disadvantages of each method?

AT 3 YEARS OF AGE, Vicky pipes up: "I can drive our car!" When Charles nods and says "Yes, when you're older you can drive it," Vicky starts to cry at the idea that he thinks she cannot drive it now. She needs to feel competent—and to show her competence, which she does by acting out her definition of driving: climbing into the driver's seat and twirling the steering wheel (which she calls the "tee-whee").

This scene is more complex than it seems. Underlying what Vicky says and does are such aspects of her development as how she learns what a car is and what physical actions driving involves, how she pronounces words, how she communicates with other people, how she feels about herself, and how she shows her feelings. Let us look at the ways developmentalists identify and study these and other aspects of children's development.

A Child's World: Concepts and Issues

WHAT IS DEVELOPMENT, AND WHY SHOULD WE STUDY IT?

child development
Scientific study of normal changes in children over time.

quantitative change
Change in amount, such as in height, weight, or size of vocabulary.

qualitative change
Change in kind, as in the nature of intelligence.

The study of *child development* is the scientific study of the normal quantitative and qualitative ways in which children change over time. *Quantitative change* involves changes in *amount*, such as in height, weight, and size of vocabulary. The study of *qualitative change* is more complex, since it involves changes in *kind*, such as the changing nature of intelligence. You can compare these two kinds of change in the development of memory. The fact that Vicky at age 7 will remember more out of an array of objects shown to her than she was able to remember at age 3 illustrates quantitative change. The fact that at 7 she is able to use memory strategies (like grouping the objects into categories to help her remember them), a skill she did not have at 3, shows qualitative change.

The field of child development itself developed as a scientific discipline as its goals evolved to include *description, explanation, prediction,* and *modification* of

10

behavior. Its original focus was on *describing* behavior, to determine age norms for growth and development. Today, developmentalists try to *explain* why certain behaviors occur. The next step is the *prediction* of behavior—a challenging and complex task.

What are the practical implications in the study of child development? There are many. By learning about the usual course of development, we can look at the different factors in a child's life and attempt to *predict* future behavior. If our predictions hint at future problems, we can try to *modify* development by offering training or treatment. For example, if a girl seems to be developing slowly, a professional may either reassure the child's parents that she is normal, or advise them how to help her overcome her deficiencies.

Students of child development draw on a wide range of disciplines, including psychology, sociology, anthropology, biology, education, and medicine. This book includes findings from research in all these fields.

THE WHOLE CHILD: ASPECTS OF DEVELOPMENT

As we follow changes in Vicky and Jason, we will see that these changes affect every facet of development. To simplify discussion, we talk separately in this book about *physical* development, *intellectual* development, and *personality-social-emotional* development. But we need to remember that these divisions are often arbitrary and rarely neat. They overlap and interact with each other throughout life, since development in one sphere affects development in the others.

Physical Development

Changes in height, weight, sensory capacity, and motor abilities, development of the brain, and health-related issues are all part of *physical development* and exert a major influence on both personality and intellect. For example, much of the infant Jason's knowledge about the world comes to him from his senses and his motor activity, and physical and mental development in infancy proceed in close harmony. Later, the physical and hormonal changes of puberty will dramatically affect the developing concept of the self.

physical development
Changes in body, brain, sensory capacity, and motor skills over time.

Intellectual (Cognitive) Development

As children grow older, more of their abilities can be characterized as *intellectual development.* The wide variety of mental abilities, such as learning, language, memory, reasoning, and thinking—in sum, our intellectual capabilities—change over time and are closely related to both motor and emotional aspects of being. Vicky's growing memory capacity, for example, underlies the development of *separation anxiety*, the fear that Ellen will not return once she has gone away. If Vicky did not have the ability to remember the past and anticipate the future, she could not be anxious about her mother's absence.

intellectual development
Changes in mental abilities, activities, or organization over time; also called cognitive development.

Personality-Social-Emotional Development

Our unique way of dealing with the world, the way we get along with other people, and our feelings—which make up our *personality-social-emotional development*—affect both the physical and the cognitive aspects of our functioning. Jason's anxiety when taking a test, for example, can result in poor performance and an underestimation of his intellectual competence.

personality-social-emotional development
Changes in a person's unique style of responding, feeling, and reacting.

This little boy's bright-eyed expression is typical of babies' and toddlers' alert response to people and objects in their world. Children become amazingly competent in the first 3 years of life.

PERIODS OF CHILDHOOD

For our discussion of childhood, we have divided it into the following five periods:

- Prenatal period—conception to birth
- Infancy and toddlerhood—birth to age 3
- Early childhood—ages 3 to 6
- Middle childhood—ages 6 to 12
- Adolescence—ages 12 to 18

Let us preview these stages.

Prenatal Stage

The prenatal stage is the period of greatest physical growth in the life span, when the human being goes from a single cell (a zygote) to—9 months later—a being made up of billions of cells. The basic body structure and organs are formed, making this a time of great vulnerability, especially during the first 3 months. Brain development in the womb also seems to make possible the beginnings of learning, as some exciting recent research suggests.

Infancy and Toddlerhood

The first part of the second stage, infancy, lasts for the first 1½ to 2 years of life. While newborn babies (neonates) are of course dependent on adults, they are amazingly competent. Infants can use all their senses right from birth and are capable of simple learning. And these skills improve rapidly. Infants form attachments to their parents, their brothers and sisters, and other caregivers, who in turn become attached to them.

During toddlerhood, which lasts from about 18 months to 3 years of age, children become highly skilled in language and motor abilities, and they become quite independent. Although children of this age usually spend most of their time with adults, they show a geat deal of interest in other children.

Early Childhood

During the years from 3 to 6, language becomes more important in children's lives. It lets them communicate better with playmates, as well as with adults. By this age, children are better able to ask for and get what they want, to take care of themselves, and to exercise self-control. Although children already reflect many influences of their culture, they still have much to learn. In their language, play, and drawing, they display an exciting breadth of imagination and inventiveness.

Middle Childhood

During the years from age 6 to age 12, children are in school. Since they are developing a greater and greater ability to think logically, they are now able to gain a great deal from formal education. Other children assume a major place in their lives, even though the family is still important.

During these years, children absorb many aspects of their particular culture, and although adults tend to consider these years the most typical ones of childhood, specific activities vary greatly from one culture to another. For example, an urban American child may learn how to operate a computer, while a child of the same age in rural France may learn to take produce to town and sell it at market, and while a third child, in east Africa, might learn how to treat injuries suffered by cattle as they are herded across the plains. All three of these children are pursuing a similar underlying purpose—preparing for adulthood.

Adolescence

The most important concern during the ages of about 12 to 18 is the search for identity, a concern that may echo throughout life. The many physical changes that signal the onset of adolescence influence young people's lives in many ways, and the cognitive changes that allow them to engage in abstract thought mean that their intellectual horizons can expand to include a world of possibilities. The teenage years see an increased involvement with peers amid efforts to separate from the parental nest. Although culture affects development in every stage, it is particularly influential in adolescence. Some societies see this period as a form of early adulthood, and many traditional societies celebrate puberty rites to mark a young person's "coming of age." In western societies, no one marker signals the end of adolescence.

INFLUENCES ON CHILDREN'S DEVELOPMENT

As we noted when we described Vicky and Jason in the Introduction, children are subjected to countless influences. First, as we will explain in Chapter 2, children are influenced by the genes that they inherit from their parents. That basic influence is then affected by a host of other kinds of influences that come under three categories: *normative age-graded influences, normative history-graded influences,* and *nonnormative life events* (Baltes, Reese, & Lipsitt, 1980)

Normative Age-Graded Influences

When we say that something is *normative,* we mean that it occurs in a similar way for most individuals in a given group. An *age-graded* influence is one closely related to chronological age. **Normative age-graded influences,** then, are influences on development that are highly similar for all people in a given age group. They include such biological events as puberty, as well as such cultural events as entry into formal education (which occurs at about age 6 in most societies today).

normative age-graded influence *Influence on development that is highly similar for all people in a given age group.*

Normative History-Graded Influences

Biological and environmental influences that are common to people of a particular generation, or cohort (those growing up at the same time and in the same place), are referred to as **normative history-graded influences.** These influences include the worldwide economic depression of the 1930s, the political turmoil in the United States during the 1960s and 1970s caused by the war in Vietnam, and the concern about acquired immune deficiency syndrome (AIDS) during the 1980s. These influences also encompass such cultural factors as the changing

normative history-graded influence *Biological or environmental influence on development that is common to people of a particular generation.*

(John Vachon/Library of Congress)

Normative history-graded influences, like the worldwide economic depression of the 1930s, can affect an entire cohort. Americans like these Missouri children who grew up in poverty were profoundly affected by the experience.

roles of women, the use of anesthesia during childbirth, the impact of the computer, and the kinds of social programs associated with the federal government's war on poverty during the 1960s—among them early childhood education programs like Head Start.

Nonnormative Life Events

nonnormative life event
Unusual event that may have a major effect on a person's life.

Nonnormative life events are unusual events that do not happen to most people. However, when they do occur, they can have a major impact on a person's life. They include the death of a parent when a child is young, a life-threatening illness or a handicapping disability, and the birth of a sibling with a congenital defect. They also, of course, include happy events like sudden wealth, the opportunity to live in a foreign country, or a particularly fortunate career opportunity. Whether such an event is positive or negative, it may cause more stress than a normative event because the person has not expected it, is not prepared for it, and may need special help adapting to it.

We often help create our own nonnormative life events, showing our ability to actively shape our own development. For example, a teenager may enter a writing competition and win a scholarship that opens up a new world of opportunity. Or a child who takes physical risks without considering the consequences may suffer a disabling accident. Furthermore, the way we respond to external forces can change the world around us, even as it changes us.

CRITICAL PERIODS IN DEVELOPMENT

If a woman undergoes irradiation, takes certain drugs, or contracts certain diseases at specific times during the first 3 months of pregnancy, her unborn baby may show specific effects. The amount and kind of damage to the fetus will vary according to the particular circumstance and its timing. Pregnant mice that receive x-rays 7 or 8 days after conception are likely to have pups with brain damage, whereas those irradiated 9½ days after conception are more likely to bear pups with spina bifida, a disease of the nervous system (L. B. Russell & Russell, 1952). Similar mechanisms operate in human beings.

A *critical period* in development is a specific time when a given event will have its greatest impact. The same event (such as irradiation) would not have as great an influence if it took place at a different time (another stage of pregnancy). This concept of critical periods has been incorporated into a number of theories regarding various aspects of human behavior, including language and the emotional attachment between babies and their mothers.

critical period Specific time during development when an event has its greatest impact.

Psychoanalysts, especially, have embraced this concept. As we shall see, Sigmund Freud maintained that certain experiences one has in infancy or early childhood can set one's personality for life, and Erik Erikson proposed eight stages in life, each of which constitutes a critical period for social and emotional development.

Some of the supporting evidence for critical periods of *physical* development is particularly strong, such as that involving fetal development. In other spheres of development, however, the concept of a critical period during which certain events can have irreversible consequences generally seems too limiting. Although children may be particularly sensitive to certain experiences at various times in their lives, later events can often reverse the effects of early ones. As we have already said, we believe that children are resilient. Love, care, and knowledge cannot solve all problems, but they accomplish more than cynics and fatalists could ever imagine.

A Child's World: Perspectives on Child Development

EARLY APPROACHES

People have long held differing ideas about what children are like and how they should be raised to become decent, socially useful adults. But for the past quarter century, the dominant view has been that until almost 400 years ago children had no place in history. According to the widely accepted view of the French historian Philippe Ariès (1962), not until the seventeenth century were children seen as qualitatively different from adults; before that, children were considered simply smaller, weaker, and less intelligent. Ariès based his opinion on various historical sources. Old paintings showed children dressed like their elders. Documents described children working long hours, leaving their parents at early ages for apprenticeships, and suffering brutality at the hands of adults. Statistics on high infant mortality rates led to the conclusion that parents, afraid that their children would die young, were reluctant to love them wholeheartedly.

More recent analyses, however, suggest a different picture. The psychologist David Elkind (1988) refers to a recognition of children's special nature in the Bible and in the works of the ancient Greeks and Romans. And after reexamining sources going back to the sixteenth century, exploring autobiographies, diaries, and literature from that time to the present, Linda A. Pollock (1983) makes a

This seventeenth-century painting by Georges de La Tour captures a tender moment between mother and baby, suggesting that—contrary to one widely held view—recognition and appreciation of children's special nature is not a recent phenomenon.

strong argument for the more sensible thesis that children have always been seen as different from adults, and that they have, in fact, been treated specially throughout history.

Diaries of both adults and children consistently show parents who loved their children and saw them as playful beings who needed guidance, care, and protection as they passed through developmental periods. Parent-child relationships were *not* formal and distant, there was little evidence of harsh discipline or widespread child abuse, and by and large, parents wanted their children, were concerned about such stages as weaning and teething, enjoyed their children's company, and suffered greatly when children fell ill or died. Like parents of today, parents of earlier days regarded child rearing as one of the most important and difficult challenges in life.

One reason for these differing interpretations lies in the sources used. Pollock, for example, found that autobiographers recalled stricter discipline than diarists, "a surprising result [that] highlights the need to use all available sources on the history of childhood since concentration on only one source will give a slightly distorted view" (1983, p. 266). This difference confirms the need to examine data carefully before drawing conclusions from any research study.

The first evidence of professional involvement in children's lives came with books of advice on child rearing. These began to appear during the sixteenth century; they were mostly written by physicians and relied on the pet theories and biases of their authors. Their lack of scientific truth shows up glaringly in advice given to mothers: not to nurse their babies soon after feeling angry, lest the milk prove fatal; to begin toilet-training infants at the age of 3 weeks; and to bind babies' arms for several months after birth to prevent thumb-sucking (Ryerson, 1961).

Then, during the eighteenth and nineteenth centuries, several important trends joined to form the basis for a new scientific study of child development:

- Scientists had unraveled the mysteries of conception and were arguing over the roles of heredity and environment (see Chapter 2). They had also discovered germs, and then immunization, which made it possible for many more children to survive infancy.
- The rise of Protestantism, which emphasized self-reliance and personal responsibility, made adults feel more responsible for the way children turned out, instead of accepting misfortune or misbehavior as fated.
- The passage of laws protecting children from long hours of work gave them more time to spend in school, and teachers needed to know more about their pupils.
- Parents and teachers wanted to identify and meet children's needs as the spirit of democracy filtered into both home and classroom.
- Finally, psychology, the new science of human behavior, led to interest in learning about influences on individual children.

By the end of the nineteenth century, all these trends had come together, and scientists were devising a variety of ways to study children. But this new discipline still had far to go. Adolescence, for example, was not recognized as a stage in human development until the twentieth century. Instead, immediately after puberty, young people entered an apprenticeship in the adult world. In 1904, G. Stanley Hall, a pioneer in the child study movement and the first psychologist to formulate a theory of adolescence, published his two-volume work *Adolescence* (G. S. Hall, 1904/1916). The book was popular, but it had little scientific basis. It served as a forum for Hall's theories, which did stimulate thinking about this period of life.

(Lewis Hine/International Museum of Photography at George Eastman House)

Child labor laws were designed to free children from the hard work that this boy had to perform in 1929. Long hours in fields or factories kept many children from going to school and from enjoying the kind of childhood most Americans now take for granted.

TODAY'S APPROACHES

The way we explain child development depends on the way we view the basic nature of human beings. Different thinkers have seen us through different lenses, and their ideas about our fundamental nature have given rise to different explanations, or theories, of why we behave as we do. A *theory* is set of interrelated statements about a phenomenon and an attempt to organize *data,* or information obtained through research, to explain why events occur.

Why do we need theories if we have facts? Theories give us frameworks to help us make sense of our data, the facts that we have obtained from scientific study. Theories take us beyond isolated observations; they allow us to make general statements about behavior. A good theory guides future research by serving as a rich source of testable hypotheses. *Hypotheses* are possible explanations; we test hypotheses with research. Sometimes research confirms our hypotheses, and we find support for our theories; but often we have to modify our theories as new facts emerge.

Theories can range in scope from simple hunches about why something happens to more complex interpretations or to elaborate explanations that try to integrate a great deal of information about a number of related events. Many theories are discussed in this book.

No one theory is universally accepted by developmentalists, nor does any one theory explain all facets of development. Different theorists look from different perspectives at the way people develop. These perspectives dictate the questions they ask, the research methods they use, and the way they interpret their data. Therefore, it is important to consider a researcher's perspective.

There are four major perspectives on human development: the *psychoanalytic,* the *mechanistic,* the *organismic,* and the *humanistic.* Each embraces its own theories, and each has its dedicated supporters and its equally impassioned critics. While some developmentalists align themselves strongly with a single theory, most thoughtful students of child development take an eclectic approach. That is, they find enough of value in each of the theories to explain parts of children's behavior over time, without taking any one of them as the entire explanation. In this brief overview, we highlight the most important aspect of each perspective and point out its strengths and weaknesses. We discuss the theories and the people associated with them more fully in pertinent places throughout the book.

Psychoanalytic Perspective

The *psychoanalytic perspective* concerns unconscious forces that motivate human behavior. Originated by Sigmund Freud, it has been expanded and taken in other directions by a number of other theorists, the most influential of whom is Erik H. Erikson.

Sigmund Freud: Psychosexual Theory Freud's view of personality (see Box 1-1) is what many people think of when they think of psychology—such as looking for meaning in dreams and in slips of the tongue. Freud's theory is complex. We now look briefly at some parts of it that relate to child development.

Id, ego, and superego Freud saw the human personality as made up of three elements: the id, the ego, and the superego.

---

theory Set of related statements about data; the goal of a theory is to integrate data, explain behavior, and predict behavior.

data Information obtained through research.

hypothesis Possible explanation for an observation; a hypothesis is used to predict the outcome of an experiment.

psychoanalytic perspective View of humanity concerned with the unconscious forces motivating behavior.

BOX 1-1 ■ PROFESSIONAL VOICES

PIONEER IN A CHILD'S WORLD:
SIGMUND FREUD (1856–1939)

Freud's life spanned the second half of the nineteenth century and most of the first half of the twentieth. Like all of us, Freud was in many ways a product of his upbringing and of the times in which he lived. As the eldest of eight children and (he believed) his mother's favorite, he set his sights high at an early age. He graduated from the medical school of the University of Vienna, planning to do scientific research. However, as a Jew he had limited opportunities, and as a husband and father he had pressing financial needs. Therefore, he went into the private practice of medicine, specializing in treating nervous disorders, at that time a new branch of medicine.

Freud tried to help his patients—mostly middle-aged, upper-middle-class Viennese women—through hypnosis. When this proved ineffective, he applied the "talking cure" of another physician and expanded and developed the technique into what we now know as *psychoanalysis*. As Freud listened to his patients talk about their experiences and their problems, he began to see some common threads: the lifelong influence of experiences in early childhood, the existence and importance of infantile sexuality, the significance of dreams, the way much of our lives is ruled by deeply rooted elements of which we are not consciously aware. On the basis of these and other observations, he formulated his theories, sometimes illustrating his points by writing up individual case histories.

Anna Freud, one of his six children, carried on her father's work, developing psychoanalytic techniques to use with children. Freud continued to modify his theories throughout his life, even toward the end, when he was in almost constant pain from cancer of the jaw. He fled from the Nazis in 1937 and died in London 2 years later.

Freud's notions shocked Victorian society—especially his claim that infants were sexual beings and that their powerful sexual urges establish lifelong personality patterns. However, the originality of his ideas, the force of his personality, and the persuasiveness of his writing won him many followers (a number of whom eventually left him to develop their own psychoanalytic theories) and a secure place in history.

Sources: C. Hall & Lindzey, 1978; E. Jones, 1961; P.H. Miller, 1983; *photo,* Bettmann Archive.

The *id,* which is present at birth, is the unconscious source of motives and desires; it operates on the "pleasure principle" and strives for immediate gratification of needs. At first, infants do not recognize that they are separate beings; only when gratification is delayed (as when they have to wait for food) do they begin to tell themselves apart from their surroundings. At this point, the ego develops.

id In Freud's theory, the unconscious source of motives and desires; it operates on the "pleasure principle."

The *ego,* which represents reason or common sense, develops during the first year of life. It operates on the "reality principle" and seeks an acceptable way to obtain gratification. Eventually it intervenes between the id and the superego to bring about an appropriate balance.

ego In Freud's theory, the representation of reason or common sense; it operates on the "reality principle."

The *superego,* which does not develop until age 4 or 5, represents the values of society, communicated by parents and other adults. Largely through the child's identification with the parent of the same sex, the superego incorporates socially approved "shoulds" and "should nots" into the child's own value system.

superego In Freud's theory, the representation of social values, communicated by parents and other adults.

Stages of psychosexual development In Freudian thought, children go through several different stages of *psychosexual development* in which gratification shifts from one body zone to another—from the mouth (the oral stage) to the anus (anal stage) and then to the genitals (genital stage). At each stage, the behavior that is the chief source of pleasure changes—from feeding to elimination and later to sexual stimulation. The order of the stages is always the same, but the level of a child's maturation determines when the shifts will take place.

psychosexual development In Freudian theory, the different stages of development in which gratification shifts from one body zone to another.

See Table 1-1, below, for a summary of Freud's stages. Each stage is discussed in the appropriate chapter.

If the children are gratified too little or too much at any of these stages, they may become fixated (stuck) at that stage. This is reflected in later behaviors. For example, a baby who is weaned too early—or is allowed to nurse for too long—may, according to Freud, become either dependent or suspicious as an adult. Freud believed that the way parents help children resolve the conflicts during these stages sets their personality for life, and that adult personality is determined by the age of 5 or 6 years.

TABLE 1-1

DEVELOPMENTAL STAGES ACCORDING TO VARIOUS THEORIES

PSYCHOSEXUAL STAGE (FREUD)	PSYCHOSOCIAL STAGE (ERIKSON)	COGNITIVE STAGE (PIAGET)
Oral (birth to 12–18 months). Baby's chief source of pleasure is mouth-oriented activities like sucking and eating.	*Basic trust versus mistrust (birth to 12–18 months).* Baby develops sense of whether world can be trusted. Virtue: hope.	*Sensorimotor (birth to 2 years).* Infant changes from a being who responds primarily through reflexes to one who can organize activities in relation to the environment.
Anal (12–18 months to 3 years). Child derives sensual gratification from withholding and expelling feces. Zone of gratification is anal region.	*Autonomy versus shame and doubt (12–18 months to 3 years).* Child develops a balance of independence over doubt and shame. Virtue: will.	*Preoperational (2 to 7 years).* Child develops a representational system and uses symbols such as words to represent people, places, and events.
Phallic (3 to 6 years). Time of the "family romance": Oedipus complex in boys and Electra complex in girls. Zone of gratification shifts to genital region.	*Initiative versus guilt (3 to 6 years).* Child develops initiative when trying out new things and is not overwhelmed by failure. Virtue: purpose.	
Latency (6 years to puberty). Time of relative calm between more turbulent stages.	*Industry versus inferiority (6 years to puberty).* Child must learn skills of the culture or face feelings of inferiority. Virtue: skill.	*Concrete operations (7 to 12 years).* Child can solve problems logically if they are focused on the here and now.
Genital (puberty through adulthood). Time of mature adult sexuality.	*Identity versus identity confusion (puberty to young adulthood).* Adolescent must determine own sense of self. Virtue: fidelity.	*Formal operations (12 years through adulthood).* Person can think in abstract terms and deal with hypothetical situations.
	Intimacy versus isolation (young adulthood). Person seeks to make commitments to others; if unsuccessful, may suffer from sense of isolation and self-absorption. Virtue: love.	
	Generativity versus stagnation (middle adulthood). Mature adult is concerned with establishing and guiding the next generation or else feels personal impoverishment. Virtue: care.	
	Integrity versus despair (old age). Elderly person achieves a sense of acceptance of own life, allowing the acceptance of death, or else falls into despair. Virtue: wisdom.	

Note: All ages are approximate.

TABLE 1-2

FREUDIAN DEFENSE MECHANISMS

MECHANISM	DESCRIPTION AND EXAMPLES
Regression	Return to behavior of an earlier age, during stressful times, to try to recapture remembered security. A girl who has just entered school may go back to sucking her thumb or wetting the bed. Or a high school student may react to his parents' recent separation by asking them to make decisions for him as they did when he was a child. When the crisis becomes less acute or the person is able to deal with it, the inappropriate behavior usually disappears.
Repression	Blocking from consciousness those feelings and experiences that arouse anxiety. Freud believed that people's inability to remember much about their early years is due to their having repressed disturbing sexual feelings toward their parents (see discussion of the Oedipus and Electra conflicts in Chapter 10).
Sublimation	Channeling of disturbing sexual or aggressive impulses into such "acceptable" activities as study, work, sports, and hobbies.
Projection	Attribution of unacceptable thoughts and motives to another person. For example, a little girl talks about how jealous of her the new baby is, when she herself is jealous of the new baby.
Reaction formation	Saying the opposite of what one really feels. Buddy says, "I don't want to play with Tony, because I don't like him," when the truth is that Buddy likes Tony a lot but is afraid that Tony does not want to play with him.

Defense mechanisms   Freud also described a number of *defense mechanisms*, ways in which people unconsciously distort reality to protect the ego against anxiety. Everyone uses defense mechanisms at times; only when they are so overused that they interfere with healthy emotional development are they pathological. Table 1-2 describes some common defense mechanisms.

defense mechanism
Unconscious distortion of reality to protect the ego against anxiety.

Erik H. Erikson: Psychosocial Theory—The Eight Crises
Erik H. Erikson modified Freud's theory, partly because of his own wide-ranging personal and professional experiences (see Box 1-2). While extending the Freudian concept of ego, Erikson stresses society's influence on the developing personality.

Erikson's theory of *psychosocial development* follows personality development through the life span, stressing societal and cultural influences on the ego at each of eight age periods (1950). Each stage of development revolves around a "crisis" in personality involving a different major conflict. Each crisis is a turning point for dealing with an issue that is particularly important at the time, even though it will remain an issue to some degree throughout life. The crises emerge according to a timetable based on the person's level of maturation. If the person adjusts to the demands of each crisis, the ego will develop toward the next crisis; if any crisis is not satisfactorily resolved, the person will continue to struggle with it, and it will interfere with healthy ego development.

Successful resolution of each of the eight crises (which were listed earlier, in Table 1-1, and are discussed later, in the appropriate chapters) requires a balance between a positive trait and a corresponding negative one. Although the positive quality should predominate, some degree of the negative is needed, too. The first crisis of infancy, for example, is *trust versus mistrust*. People need to trust the world and the people in it—but they also need to learn some mistrust so that they can protect themselves from danger. The successful outcome of each crisis includes the development of a particular "virtue." This first crisis results in the virtue of hope.

psychosocial development
Erikson's theory of personality development through the life span, stressing societal and cultural influences on the ego at eight stages.

BOX 1-2 ■ PROFESSIONAL VOICES

PIONEER IN A CHILD'S WORLD: ERIK H. ERIKSON (B. 1902)

Not only did Erik H. Erikson focus his life's work on the search for identity; in a way he created his own identity. Born in Germany of a Jewish mother who separated from her Danish husband before Erikson was born, he was adopted by his mother's second husband, a Dr. Homburger, whose name he took. Many years later he added the surname Erikson, making him the "son of Erik"—or his own child!

After he left school at the age of 18, Erikson wandered around Europe for 7 years, unsure of his career goal. After trying painting and wood carving, he sowed the seeds for his future at age 25 when he was hired to teach art and other subjects to children of Americans who had come to Vienna for training in psychoanalysis. He studied and was impressed by the emphasis in the Montessori method (an educational approach for young children) on the ways play and work can develop a child's initiative. He was immensely impressed by psychoanalysis and became a follower of Freud. After Erikson and his Canadian wife fled Vienna from the Nazis in 1933, he became the first child psychoanalyst in the city of Boston. He taught at Harvard and Yale medical schools and studied combat crises in American soldiers, child rearing among native Americans, social customs in India, and normal and disturbed children and adolescents in various settings. He kept finding echoes of his own search for identity—and kept finding ways in which society and culture influenced the development of personality.

Erikson expanded upon Freudian theory to emphasize the strong and often positive role that culture plays in personality development. He brought his wide experience to developing a theory that went well beyond Freud's, which had been based largely on a population of disturbed upper-middle-class female patients in early twentieth-century Vienna. Erikson also emphasized the importance of development throughout life, and as of this writing, he is focusing on how his theories can help us to understand old age.

Sources: C. Hall & Lindzey, 1978; P.H. Miller, 1983; *photo,* UPI/Bettmann Newsphotos.

Evaluation of Psychoanalytic Theory Freud's original and creative thinking made immense contributions to our understanding of children and has had a major impact on child-rearing practices in the western world. He made us aware of infantile sexuality (that people are sexual creatures from birth), the nature of our unconscious thoughts and emotions, our defense mechanisms, the significance of dreams, the importance of early parent-child relationships and the ambivalence in those relationships, and many other aspects of emotional functioning. He also originated psychoanalysis, an important influence on psychotherapy as practiced today.

Yet Freud's theory grew out of his own place in history and in society. For example, much of his theory seems to patronize or demean women, no doubt because of its roots in the social system of a Victorian-era European culture convinced of the superiority of the male. Also, the source of the data on which Freud based his theories about *normal* development was not a population of average children but a highly selective clientele of upper-middle-class neurotic adults in therapy. His concentration on the resolution of psychosexual conflict as the key to healthy development seems too narrow, and the subjective way in which he phrased his theories has made them difficult to test with research studies.

A strength of Erikson's theory is its emphasis on social and cultural influences on development, which takes it beyond Freud's narrow focus on biological and maturational factors. Also, Erikson's theory covers the entire life span, while Freud's stops at adolescence. Erikson, too, however, has been criticized for an antifemale bias, since he uses the male as the norm for healthy development. Furthermore, some of his concepts are also hard to assess objectively or to use as the basis for research.

Mechanistic Perspective: Learning Theories

The *mechanistic perspective* sees people as responders, rather than initiators—more or less as machines that react automatically to outside stimuli. It views human development primarily as a response to events, discounting purpose, will, and intelligence, as well as unconscious forces. According to this perspective, if we can identify all the significant influences in a person's environment, we can predict how that person will react.

Mechanistic theorists see change as quantitative. And they see development as continuous, allowing prediction of later behaviors from earlier ones. Research spurred by this view tries to identify and isolate the factors in the environment that make people behave in certain ways. It focuses on how experiences affect later behavior and tries to understand the effects of experience by breaking down complex stimuli and complex behaviors into simpler elements.

The mechanistic model includes two related theories: behaviorism and social-learning theory.

mechanistic perspective View of humanity which assumes that all change is a reaction to external events; purpose, will, and intelligence are ignored or given little weight.

Behaviorism   Unlike psychoanalytic theory, which digs for unconscious motives driving human behavior, *behaviorism* is interested only in behaviors that can be seen, measured, and recorded. Behaviorists look for immediate, observable factors that determine whether a particular behavior will continue to occur. Although they recognize that biology sets limits on what people do, they view the environment as much more influential in directing behavior.

Behaviorism—which is also known as *traditional learning theory*—holds that *learning* is what changes behavior and advances development. It maintains that human beings learn about the world the same way as other animals: by reacting to the aspects of their environment that they find pleasing, painful, or threatening.

Since behaviorists are interested only in quantitative change and since they believe that people of all ages learn the same way, they do not describe stages of development. Instead, they describe conditioning, the mechanism by which learning takes place. There are two basic kinds of conditioning: classical and operant.

behaviorism   School of psychology that emphasizes the study of observable behaviors and events and the role of the environment in causing behavior.

Classical conditioning   Eager to capture Vicky's memorable moments, Charles took pictures of her smiling, waving good-bye, crawling, "dancing," and showing off her other achievements. Whenever the flashbulb went off, Vicky blinked. One evening when Vicky was 11 months old, she saw Charles hold the camera up to his eye—and she blinked *before* the flash. She had learned to associate the camera with the bright light, and her blinking reflex operated even without the flash itself.

Vicky's blinking is an example of classical conditioning. While doing research on the salivating reflex of dogs, the Russian physiologist Ivan Pavlov (1849–1936) accidentally discovered that his dogs had learned to associate the sound of a bell with food. The dogs would salivate in response to the bell even before seeing food. Through experiments, Pavlov confirmed the power of *classical conditioning*, a kind of learning in which an animal or a person learns a response to a stimulus that does not originally bring that response, after the stimulus has repeatedly been associated with a stimulus that *does* bring the response.

classical conditioning Learning in which a previously neutral stimulus (conditioned stimulus) acquires the power to elicit a response (conditioned response) by association with an unconditioned stimulus that ordinarily elicits a particular response (unconditioned response).

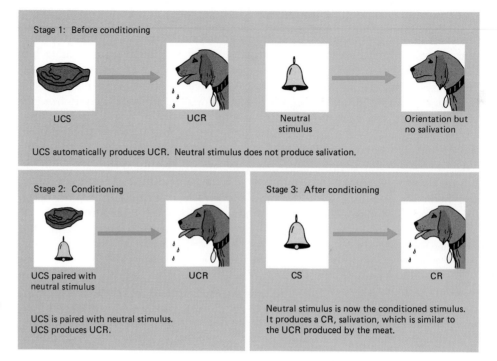

Stage 1: Before conditioning

UCS → UCR   Neutral stimulus → Orientation but no salivation

UCS automatically produces UCR. Neutral stimulus does not produce salivation.

Stage 2: Conditioning

UCS paired with neutral stimulus → UCR

UCS is paired with neutral stimulus.
UCS produces UCR.

Stage 3: After conditioning

CS → CR

Neutral stimulus is now the conditioned stimulus. It produces a CR, salivation, which is similar to the UCR produced by the meat.

FIGURE 1-1
Classical conditioning occurs in three stages. The neutral stimulus eventually produces a conditioned response.

Figure 1-1 shows the steps in classical conditioning:

1 *Before conditioning*: The dog salivates when food appears. The food is an *unconditioned stimulus (UCS)*, a stimulus that automatically elicits an unlearned, or unconditioned, response. Salivation is an *unconditioned response*, or *unconditioned reflex (UCR)*, an automatic, unlearned response to a particular stimulus. The sound of a bell is a *neutral stimulus*, one that does not ordinarily evoke a reflex response.

2 *During conditioning*: The experimenter repeatedly pairs the neutral stimulus (the bell) with the unconditioned stimulus (food). Every time the bell rings, food appears. The dog reflexively salivates in response to the food.

3 *After conditioning*: The dog salivates at the sound of the bell alone. The dog has learned to associate the bell with food and to respond in the same way to both stimuli. The bell has become a *conditioned stimulus (CS)*, an originally neutral stimulus that, after repeated pairings with an unconditioned stimulus (food), elicits a response (salivation) similar to that elicited by the unconditioned stimulus. The salivation has become a *conditioned response (CR)*, a response evoked by a conditioned stimulus (the bell).

The first behaviorist to apply stimulus-response theories of learning to the study of child development, John B. Watson (1878–1958), expressed his philosophy in these words:

> Give me a dozen healthy infants, well formed, and my own special world to bring them up in, and I'll guarantee to take any one at random and train him to become any type of specialist I might select—doctor, lawyer, artist, merchantchief, and yes, even beggar and thief, regardless of his talents, penchants, tendencies, abilities, vocations and race of his ancestors. (1958, p. 104)

unconditioned stimulus (UCS) *In classical conditioning, a stimulus that automatically elicits an unlearned response.*

unconditioned response (UCR) *In classical conditioning, an automatic, unlearned response to an unconditioned stimulus; also called an **unconditioned reflex**.*

neutral stimulus *Stimulus that does not ordinarily evoke a reflex response.*

conditioned stimulus (CS) *In classical conditioning, an originally neutral stimulus that, after repeated pairing with an unconditioned stimulus, provokes a conditioned response.*

conditioned response (CR) *In classical conditioning, a response to a conditioned stimulus; also known as **conditioned reflex**.*

While Watson never got his dozen infants, he did manage, through classical conditioning, to teach one baby, known as "Little Albert," to fear furry white objects (see Chapter 6).

Operant conditioning   As early as 3 days after birth, Jason will suck more on a nipple if it produces Julia's voice than he will if his sucking produces the voice of a strange woman. Through operant conditioning he has learned that something that he knows how to do (sucking) can produce something that he likes (a familiar voice).

This kind of learning occurs as the result of rewards and punishments and is widely used by parents, teachers, and animal trainers. B. F. Skinner (b. 1904), an American and the most prominent behaviorist, taught pigeons to respond to bars of different colors by giving them food when they happened to press the right bar. He then showed how the principle underlying the birds' responses could also be used to direct human behavior (Skinner, 1938). This principle is that an animal or a person will tend to repeat behavior that is followed by a satisfying experience and will not repeat behavior that is followed by an unsatisfactory experience. In other words, both people and animals seek to get rewards and avoid punishment.

Operant conditioning is a kind of learning in which a person or an animal continues to make a response because the response has been reinforced (rewarded) or stops making the response because it has been punished. A *reinforcement* is a stimulus that follows a behavior and *increases* the likelihood that the behavior will be repeated. *Punishment* is a stimulus that follows a behavior and *decreases* the likelihood that the behavior will be repeated. This kind of learning is also called *instrumental conditioning*, because the learner is instrumental in changing the environment in some way, by bringing about either reinforcement or punishment.

Figure 1-2 (page 26) shows the sequence in operant conditioning. A pigeon happens to press a red bar. This random or accidental response (AR) is reinforced (R) by food. The pigeon keeps pressing the red bar to get the food. The originally accidental response is now a deliberate response (DR).

Reinforcement is most effective when it is immediate. If a response is no longer reinforced—that is, if the pigeon presses the red bar and does not get food—then the bird will eventually stop pressing the bar or at least will not press it any more than it did in the first place. This process, whereby a response that is no longer reinforced stops or returns to its original (baseline) level, is called *extinction*.

Reinforcement can be either positive or negative. *Positive reinforcement* consists of giving a reward like food, gold stars, money, or praise. *Negative reinforcement* consists of taking away something that the person or animal does not like (known as an *aversive* event), like a bright light or a loud noise.

Negative reinforcement is sometimes confused with punishment, but they are different. Negative reinforcement *takes away* an aversive event to encourage repeating a behavior, while punishment *brings on* an aversive event (like spanking a child or giving an electric shock to an animal) to try to keep a behavior from being repeated. Whether or not a stimulus is reinforcing or punishing depends on the particular person involved. What is reinforcing for one person may be punishing for another.

Intermittent reinforcement (reinforcing a response on some occasions and not on others) produces more durable behaviors than reinforcement on every occasion. Because it takes longer to realize that reinforcement has ended, the behav-

(Archives of the History of American Psychology, University of Akron)

John B. Watson, an American psychologist who has been called the "father of modern behaviorism," believed that humans are highly trainable and tried to prove this by showing how people could be trained to respond to various stimuli.

operant conditioning Learning in which a response continues to be made because it has been reinforced; also called instrumental conditioning.

reinforcement Stimulus that follows a response and increases the likelihood that the response will be repeated.

punishment Stimulus that follows a behavior and decreases the likelihood that the behavior will be repeated.

extinction Process whereby a response that is no longer reinforced stops or returns to its original (baseline) level.

ior tends to persist. This is why parents who only occasionally give in to a child's temper tantrum strengthen that kind of behavior even more than if they gave in every time.

What if a person or animal does not exhibit any of the desired behavior? *Shaping* is a way to bring about new responses by reinforcing responses that are progressively like the desired one. For example, the parent of a boy who can talk but refuses to might first give him a little toy after he made any sound at all. Then the parent would give the toy only after the child said a word, and then only after he spoke a sentence.

Shaping may be used in programs of *behavior modification*, a form of operant conditioning that is used to eliminate undesirable behavior in children. This practical application of the principles of operant conditioning is used to teach a variety of behaviors, including toilet training (see Box 6-1 in Chapter 6) and obeying classroom rules. It is used most often for children with special needs, like retarded or emotionally disturbed youngsters, but its techniques are also effective in the day-to-day management of normal children.

Social-Learning Theory An outgrowth of behaviorism called *social-learning theory* focuses on children rather than animals. It maintains that children learn by observing and imitating models and that the learned behavior is then reinforced by a system of rewards and punishments. The leading social-learning theorist is Albert Bandura (b. 1925), a professor at Stanford University.

Social-learning theory is mechanistic in its emphasis on response to the environment. But it differs from behaviorism by regarding the learner as an active contributor to his or her learning. It breaks with behaviorism another way, too. Although social-learning theorists also emphasize rigorous laboratory experimentation, they believe that human behavior cannot be explained by theories based on animal research. People learn in a social context, and human learning is more complex than simple conditioning allows for.

According to this view, children's identification with, and subsequent reinforcement by, adults (usually their parents) explains how they learn a language, deal with aggression, develop a moral sense, and learn the behaviors their society holds appropriate for their gender.

Children actively advance their own learning. One way they do this is by choosing the models they want to imitate. The choice is influenced by characteristics of the model, the child, and the environment. A child may choose one parent over the other and other adults (like a teacher, a television personality, a sports figure, or a drug dealer) in addition to—or instead of—either parent. Children tend to imitate people of high status and people who reflect their own personality. Thus, a boy who already has aggressive tendencies will look to Rambo rather than to Mister Rogers.

Another way in which children act as agents of their own learning is in creating their environment. First, their personalities evoke certain responses from other people, which they then react to. Then, at a certain point, they become active in peopling their world with potential models. For example, Jason, an avid television watcher, models his behavior on the children in situation comedies, while Vicky, who is serious about her dancing, walks and talks like—even if she cannot pirouette like—her ballet teacher.

The specific behavior that children imitate depends on the behavior that is present and valued in their culture. If all the teachers in Jason's school are women, he will avoid modeling their behavior, thinking that it would not be

shaping *Bringing about a new response by reinforcing responses that are progressively like the desired one.*

FIGURE 1-2
Operant, or instrumental, conditioning.

AR (accidental response)

Pigeon presses bar

R (reinforcement)

Pigeon gets food

DR (deliberate response)

Pigeon keeps pressing bar

manly. But if he meets a male teacher he likes, he may change his mind. He can learn by observation and modify his behavior.

Social-learning theory also differs from behaviorism in acknowledging the influence of cognitive processes on learning. Children see behaviors, abstract the parts of the behavior that seem useful, and put the parts together in new and unique ways. Vicky, for example, may copy the toes-out walk of her dance teacher but model her actual dance steps after those of a slightly advanced student. The developing ability to use symbols (like words) to remember and to reorganize what they observe helps children to become more efficient learners.

Evaluation of Learning Theories   Both behaviorism and social-learning theory have helped to make the study of psychology more scientific. This comes from two major emphases—defining terms precisely and conducting rigorous laboratory experiments.

By stressing environmental influences, learning theories explain cultural differences in behavior very well. But they underplay the importance of hereditary and biological factors. Further, they are not really developmental, since they apply the same basic laws of learning to explain behavior at all ages—from infancy through adulthood—and are not concerned with differences between various stages of development.

Behaviorism has been especially useful in designing behavior modification programs and therapies that can help people learn new behaviors (like using the toilet) or give up old ones (like nail biting). But psychoanalysts charge that the theory's failure to consider the causes of symptoms is a basic flaw. Without knowing the underlying problems that cause undesirable behaviors, they say, eliminating one negative behavior (like stealing) by punishing it will only result in the substitution of another (like bed-wetting), leaving the basic problem unresolved. Furthermore, some people object to the ethics of one person's "playing God" by controlling another's behavior.

Social-learning theory's refinements on traditional learning theory include its recognition of the active role people play in their own learning and of the cognitive influences on behavior. Both these aspects are central to the organismic perspective.

Organismic Perspective

The *organismic perspective* has two major features. First is its view of people as actors, not reactors. The second is its emphasis on qualitative change, like changes in the way people of different ages think, rather than quantitative change, like increases in the number of words they use to think with.

As organisms with their own internal motivations and purposes, people set their development in motion through their own acts. Change proceeds from the inside out rather than from the outside in—from internal motivations rather than external influences. Since the whole of a human being's behavior is greater than the sum of its parts, it is impossible, say organicists, to break behavior down into separate elements to predict cause-and-effect relationships.

Organicists are more interested in process than in product. They are more concerned with *how* a person comes to believe certain things and act in certain ways, and less interested in the specifics of the person's thought or behavior. They are more interested in qualitative change—the leaps from one stage of development to another—than in quantitative change. They tend to describe

social-learning theory
Theory proposed by Bandura that behaviors are learned by observing and imitating models.

organismic perspective
View of humanity that sees people as active agents in their own development, focuses on qualitative changes, and sees development as discontinuous, or occurring in stages.

BOX 1-3 ■ PROFESSIONAL VOICES

PIONEER IN A CHILD'S WORLD: JEAN PIAGET (1896–1980)

Jean Piaget, who was born in Switzerland, was a serious little boy, interested in mechanics, birds, fossils, and seashells. He published his first scientific paper at the age of 10, on an albino sparrow he had seen in a park. At about this time he began to assist the director of a museum of natural history and thus learned about mollusks, a kind of shellfish, which he also wrote about. He had to turn down the offer of a curatorship of mollusks at another museum because he was still in school!

Piaget continued his scientific studies and wrote a thesis on mollusks for his doctorate. He then took up the study of psychoanalysis, psychology, and philosophy. While studying in Paris, he set out to standardize the tests that Alfred Binet had developed to assess the intelligence of French schoolchildren. But when Piaget became more interested in the children's wrong answers than in their right ones, since they offered so many clues to children's thought processes, he realized that he had found his field of research.

Continuing his interest in the way children's minds develop, Piaget became director of a Swiss institute for studying children and training teachers. The institute student whom he married eventually helped him study the day-by-day intellectual development of their three children. From his meticulous observations of his own and other children, Piaget built a comprehensive theory of cognitive development.

Up to the time of his death at age 84, Piaget continued to study and write; he wrote more than 40 books and more than 100 articles on child psychology, as well as works on biology, philosophy, and education. Much of his work was done with his longtime collaborator, Bärbel Inhelder, an experimental child psychologist who did her own research on how children and adolescents come to understand the laws of natural science.

Sources: C. Hall & Lindzey, 1978; P.H. Miller, 1983; Pulaski, 1971; *photo,* Ives deBraine/Black Star.

---

development as occurring in a set sequence of different stages. Each stage constitutes a qualitative change from one type of thought or behavior to another. Each stage builds on the stage before it and becomes the foundation for the one that comes next. And each stage has many facets. All people go through the same stages in the same order, even though the actual timing varies from one person to another, making any cutoff age only approximate.

Unlike mechanists, organicists do not try to determine how a child's responses are shaped by reinforcement from other people or by outside forces. They see life experiences not as the basic cause of development but as factors that can speed it up or slow it down. Nor do they focus, as psychoanalysts do, on underlying motivational forces of which the child is unaware. Instead, they look at the child as an actor and a doer—someone who actively constructs his or her world.

Jean Piaget: Cognitive-Stage Theory Jean Piaget (1896–1980), a Swiss scholar, was the most prominent advocate of the organismic view, and much of what we know about the way children think is due to his creative inquiry. He applied his broad knowledge of biology, philosophy, logic, and psychology to meticulous observations of children, and he constructed complex theories abut cognitive, or knowledge-acquiring, development (see Box 1-3).

Cognitive structures According to Piaget, the core of intelligent behavior is an inborn ability to adapt to the environment. Children build upon their sensory, motor, and reflex capacities to learn about and act upon their world. As children engage in thousands of day-to-day activities (seeing, hearing, feeling, touching, moving), they learn from their experiences and develop more complex cognitive structures. (Refer to Table 1-1 earlier in this chapter for a summary of Piaget's stages. The different stages are described fully in age-related discussions in Chapters 6, 9, 12, and 15.)

At each stage of development, a person has his or her own individual representation of the world. Within this representation lie a number of basic cognitive structures known as *schemas*. A **schema** is an organized pattern of behavior that a person uses to think about and act in a situation. In infancy, schemas are known by the behavior they involve—sucking, biting, shaking, and so forth. From the first days of life, infants have many schemas; as babies vary the schemas, they differentiate them. For example, babies develop different ways to suck at the breast, a bottle, and a thumb. As children develop intellectually, their schemas become patterns of thought, related to behaviors, and become progressively more complex, going from concrete thinking to abstractions.

Principles of cognitive development How does this cognitive growth occur? A two-step process of taking in new information about the world and changing one's ideas to include the new knowledge is accomplished by three interrelated principles known as *functional invariants*. They are inherited, they operate at all stages of development, and they affect all interactions with the environment. These principles are organization, adaptation, and equilibration.

Organization involves the integration of schemas into a higher-order system. For example, a baby's schemas of looking and grasping operate independently at first, but babies organize these two schemas, eventually integrating them into a higher-order schema in which they look at an object at the same time they hold it.

Cognitive growth results from a two-step *adaptation* process that includes taking in new information about the world and changing one's ideas to include it. *Adaptation* refers to the complementary processes of assimilation and accommodation. When Jason responds to a rubber nipple on a bottle as he does to his mother's breast, he is showing **assimilation**, using old schemas to deal with new objects and situations. When he uses somewhat different mouth movements to suck on a bottle after he has become used to nursing at the breast, he is showing **accommodation**, modifying old schemas to deal with new objects and situations.

Equilibration is the constant striving for *equilibrium*, a state of balance between the child and the outside world, and among the child's own cognitive structures. Assimilation and accommodation constantly work together to produce changes in the way children conceptualize and react to the world. Equilibrium is a necessary state that protects them from being overwhelmed by new experiences and new information and from overreaching in an attempt to accommodate to a rapidly changing environment.

Evaluation of Piaget's Organismic Theory Piaget was the forerunner of the "cognitive revolution" in psychology today, with its emphasis on internal cognitive processes, as opposed to learning theory's emphasis on outside influences and observable behaviors. Although American psychologists were slow at first to accept his beliefs, Piaget has inspired more research on cognitive development in childhood than any other theorist. (His collaborator, Bärbel Inhelder, for example, also performed her own research.) Among the important offshoots of Piaget's theory are Lawrence Kohlberg's cognitive-developmental approaches to gender identity and moral reasoning, which will be discussed in Chapters 10 and 12, respectively.

schema *In Piaget's terminology, the basic cognitive unit; a schema is generally named after the behavior involved.*

adaptation *In Piaget's terminology, the complementary processes of assimilation and accommodation.*

assimilation *In Piaget's terminology, the incorporation of a new object, experience, or concept into existing cognitive structures.*

accommodation *In Piaget's terminology, changes in existing cognitive structures to include new experiences.*

equilibration *Striving for cognitive balance.*

(Courtesy of Dr. Inhelder)

Bärbel Inhelder, a child psychologist, collaborated with Piaget for many years and also conducted her own research on how children and adolescents come to understand the laws of natural science.

Yet Piaget can be criticized. He speaks primarily of the "average" child's abilities without taking much notice either of individual differences or of the ways in which education and culture affect performance. He says little about emotional and personality development, except as they relate to cognitive growth. Many of his ideas emerged not from scientific research, but from highly personal observations of his own three children and from his own idiosyncratic way of interviewing children. Finally, he seems to have underestimated the abilities of young children.

Still, these reservations cannot diminish the great contribution of Piaget's theory to our understanding of intellectual development. Those personal observations that some critics question have yielded a wealth of surprising insights. Who, for example, would have thought that even very bright children do not realize that a ball of clay that has been rolled into a "worm" before their eyes still contains the same amount of clay—until they are about 5 or 6 years old? Or that an infant might think that a person no longer in sight may no longer exist? Piaget has shown us dramatically that children's minds are not just miniatures of adults' minds, but that children think differently, depending on their level of cognitive maturity.

Understanding how children think makes it easier for parents to teach them about money, about illness, about family crises. And it helps teachers to know how and when to introduce topics into the curriculum.

Humanistic Perspective

In 1962 a group of psychologists reacted against the mechanistic and what they considered the essentially negative beliefs underlying behaviorist and psychoanalytic theories. Maintaining that human nature is either neutral or good and that negative characteristics are the result of damage inflicted on the developing self, they founded the Association of Humanistic Psychology to put this belief into practice. The *humanistic perspective*, like organicism, views people as having the ability to take charge of their lives and to foster their own development. Furthermore, these theories emphasize people's ability to do this in healthy, positive ways through the distinctively human qualities of choice, creativity, and self-realization.

humanistic perspective
View of humanity that sees people as able to foster their own development in healthy, positive ways.

In this book we do not discuss the humanistic perspective, since it is not truly developmental and since it says little about the years before adolescence. It does not clearly distinguish stages of the life span, but makes a broad distinction only between the periods before adolescence and after adolescence. We mention it here, however, because it offers a currently influential view of the development of personality. Abraham Maslow was one important humanistic psychologist.

Abraham Maslow: Hierarchy of Needs   Abraham Maslow (1908–1970) identified a hierarchy of needs that motivate human behavior. According to Maslow (1954), these needs operate on a number of levels, from basic survival up to the acme of psychological fulfillment. People must meet their most elemental needs first before they can strive to meet those on the next level, and so forth, until they reach the highest order of needs. Starving people, for example, will take great risks to obtain food; once they know they will live, they can worry about personal safety; once safe, they consider their need for love, and so forth. As

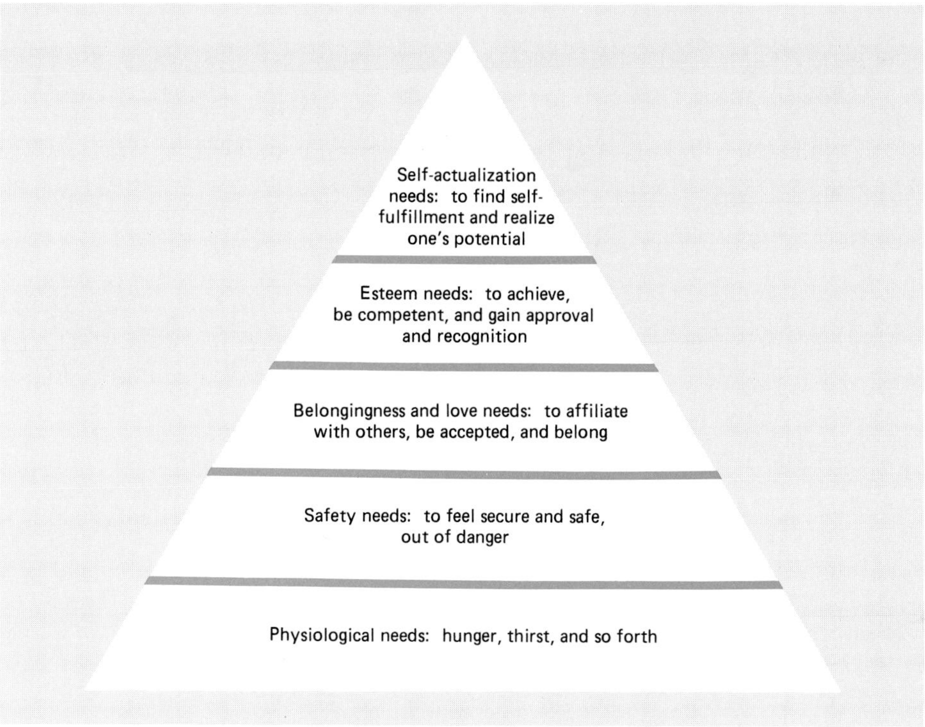

FIGURE 1-3
Maslow's hierarchy of needs. According to Maslow, human needs have different priorities. First comes survival (base of pyramid). Starving people will take great risks to obtain food; once they know they will not die of starvation, they start to worry about safety. Then needs for security must be met, at least in part, before people think about needs for love. As each level of needs is met, a person looks to the needs at the next higher step. This progression is not invariant, however; for example, self-sacrifice would be an exception. (*Source:* Maslow, 1954.)

each succeeding layer of needs is addressed, people look to the next higher level (see Figure 1-3). Maslow's ideal is the "self-actualized person," who fulfills the loftiest level, attained by possibly 1 percent of the population.

A self-actualized (or self-fulfilled) person displays high levels of all the following characteristics: perception of reality; acceptance of self, of others, and of nature; spontaneity; problem-solving ability; self-direction; detachment and the desire for privacy; freshness of appreciation and richness of emotional reaction; frequency of peak experiences; identification with other human beings; satisfying and changing relationships with other people; a democratic character structure; creativity; and a sense of values (Maslow, 1968). No one ever becomes completely self-actualized, but the person who is developing in a healthy way is always moving up to levels that are even more self-fulfilling.

Evaluation of Humanistic Theories   Humanistic theories have made a valuable contribution in promoting child-rearing approaches that respect every child's uniqueness. Humanism is an optimistic, positive model of humankind, as opposed to the more negative Freudian viewpoint. It goes deeper than behaviorism by considering internal factors like feelings, values, and hopes, as opposed to limiting itself to observable behavior. Its limitations as a scientific theory rest largely on its subjectiveness: since concepts are not clearly defined, they are difficult to communicate and to use as the basis for research. Furthermore, since humanistic theories do not focus on issues of different times of life, they do not provide insights into the process of development.

For a summary of the four major perspectives, see Table 1-3 (page 32).

TABLE 1-3

FOUR PERSPECTIVES ON CHILD DEVELOPMENT			
PERSPECTIVE	IMPORTANT THEORIES	BASIC BELIEF	TECHNIQUE USED
Psychoanalytic	Freud's psychosexual theory	Freud: Behavior is controlled by powerful unconscious urges.	Clinical observation
	Erikson's psychosocial theory	Erikson: Personality develops throughout life in a series of stages.	
Mechanistic	Behaviorism, or traditional learning theory (Pavlov, Skinner, Watson)	Behaviorism: People are responders; concern is with how the environment controls behavior.	Rigorous and scientific (experimental) procedures
	Social-learning theory (Bandura)	Social-learning theory: Children learn in a social context, by observing and imitating models; person is an active contributor to learning.	
Organismic	Piaget's cognitive-stage theory	There are qualitative changes in the way children think that develop in a series of four stages between infancy and adolescence. Person is an active initiator of development.	Flexible interviews; meticulous observation
Humanistic	Maslow's self-actualization theory	People have the ability to take charge of their lives and foster their own development.	Discussion of feelings

A Child's World: How We Discover It

scientific method *Means of inquiry that depends on observation to establish findings, uses further observations to test alternative explanations for the findings, and then uses new observers to demonstrate the continuing validity of the observations.*

Each of the four perspectives inspires its own questions and techniques for answering them. In our evaluation of these models, we discussed ways of testing them to see whether they merit the name of science. *Scientific method* incorporates these principles: careful observation and recording of data, development and testing of various hypotheses (explanations for the data), and public dissemination of findings to allow other observers to learn from, analyze, repeat, and build on the work. Only in this way can we reliably explain and predict human behavior. The more closely we stick to these principles, the more soundly based our information will be.

METHODS FOR STUDYING CHILD DEVELOPMENT

How do we know what children are like at various stages of development? Researchers use a variety of methods to observe children, either in daily life or in planned situations. Let us look first at the nonexperimental methods that have been used over the years, next at experimental techniques, and then at methods of collecting data.

Nonexperimental Methods

Nonexperimental methods include case studies, naturalistic observation, clinical studies, interviews, and correlational studies. See Table 1-4 for characteristics of these methods, as well as experimental techniques.

Case Studies   *Case studies* are studies of a single case, or individual life. Much of the support for Freudian theory comes from such studies, detailed descriptions of individual patients based on notes and interpretations by Freud and other psychoanalysts.

One type of case study is the baby biography. Our earliest information about infants' development comes from journals kept to record the progress of a

case studies   *Studies of a single case, or individual life.*

TABLE 1-4

CHARACTERISTICS OF MAJOR RESEARCH METHODS

TYPE	MAIN CHARACTERISTICS	ADVANTAGES	DISADVANTAGES
NONEXPERIMENTAL METHODS			
Case study	Study of single individual in depth	Provides detailed picture of one person's behavior and development.	May not generalize to others; may reflect observer bias.
Naturalistic observation	Observation of people in their normal setting with no attempt to manipulate behavior	Does not subject persons to unnatural settings (such as the laboratory) that may distort behavior. Is a source of research hypotheses.	Lack of control; inability to explain cause-and-effect relationships. Observer bias.
Clinical method	Combination of observation and individualized questioning developed by Piaget to study children	Flexibility allows researcher to follow up on interesting responses.	Quality of insights about development depends on the skillfulness of the researcher; difficult for other researchers to duplicate procedures because of individualized approach.
Interview	Participants asked about some aspect of their lives; ranges from highly structured to more flexible questioning	Goes beyond observation in getting information about a person's life, attitudes, or opinions.	Interviewee may not remember information accurately or may distort responses in a socially desirable way.
Correlational studies	Measure direction and magnitude of a relationship between variables	Allow predictions from one variable about another variable.	Do not determine cause-and-effect relationships.
EXPERIMENTAL METHODS			
Experiment	Controlled procedure in which an experimenter manipulates the independent variable to determine its effect on the dependent variable; may be conducted in the laboratory or field or make use of naturally occurring events	Establishes cause-and-effect relationships; highly controlled procedure that can be repeated by another investigator. Degree of control is strongest in the laboratory experiment and least in the natural experiment.	Findings, especially when derived from laboratory experiments, may not generalize to situations outside the laboratory.

single baby. The first known baby biography was begun in 1601, and the first to be published in English was by an American educator, Emma Willard, in 1835. In 1877, Charles Darwin published notes about his son and put forth the view that we could better understand the origins of our species by carefully studying infants and children. About 30 such studies were published over the next 30 years (Dennis, 1936). Piaget (1952b) based his highly original theories about the ways infants learn on his meticulous, day-by-day observations of his own three children.

Baby biographies and other case studies give us much useful, in-depth information about development. They allow us to glimpse a single child's personality as we could in no other way, as is shown by this excerpt from a very recent journal:

> Elizabeth [at 4½ years] loves riddles. Her favorite, which always evokes gales of laughter (from her), is ''What color was the Lone Ranger's white horse?'' (N. Gordon, personal communication, 1985)

But baby biographies and other case studies have several shortcomings from a scientific point of view. Often they only record behavior; they do not explain it. Even if they do, it is difficult, if not impossible, to test the explanations. Also, they may suffer from ''observer bias''; that is, the recorder (often a fond parent) emphasizes some aspects of development and gives short shrift to others. Furthermore, isolated biographies tell us a great deal about an individual child, but because of the uniqueness of each child, we cannot apply the information to children in general.

naturalistic observation
Study of people in a real-life setting with no attempt to manipulate behavior.

Naturalistic Observation In *naturalistic observation,* researchers look at children in such normal settings as home, school, or playground, making no effort to alter behavior or to change the environment. Some naturalistic studies yield *normative* information, or information about the average times at which behaviors occur among normal people. Researchers observe groups of children and record information about their development at different ages to establish average ages for the appearance of various skills and behaviors, or to derive measures of growth.

One type of naturalistic observation is *time sampling.* Researchers record the occurrence of a certain type of behavior—like aggression, babbling, or crying—during a given time period. One researcher studied the ways infants and their parents act with one another. He went into the homes of forty 15-month-old babies and looked around during two typical 2-hour periods on separate days. He did not give the parents any guidance or instructions but just watched what went on. He had drawn up a checklist of 15 behaviors of parents and 8 behaviors of infants, and he recorded the presence or absence of these behaviors during alternating 15-second observe-record periods during each 2-hour session. From his observations, he concluded that mothers and fathers are more alike than different in the ways they treat their babies, that parents pay slightly more attention to a child of their own sex, that parents do more with their babies when they are alone with them than when both parents are present, and that babies are more sociable when they are alone with one parent (Belsky, 1979).

Naturalistic studies are an important source of research hypotheses. However, they do not explain behavior or determine cause and effect. The study just described, for example, does not tell us *why* parents prefer to be with children of their own sex or whether being alone with one parent *causes* a baby to be more

Naturalistic studies—like this one, in which the psychologist David Elkind is observing kindergartners—allow children to be themselves. Researchers observe but do not participate and do not establish experimental conditions or controls.

sociable. Also, an observer's presence can alter behavior: babies may be more or less sociable around a stranger. For this reason, observers sometimes stay behind one-way mirrors (they can see the children, but the children cannot see them) or try to blend into the background.

Clinical Method   The *clinical method* combines observation with careful, individualized questioning. This is a flexible way of assessing thought that tailors the test situation to the person being questioned so that no two people are questioned in exactly the same fashion. This open-ended, individualized method is quite different from the standardized testing technique, which aims to make the testing situation as similar as possible for all subjects.

clinical method
Technique of observation in which questioning is flexible and the interviewer asks additional questions in response to particular answers.

Piaget developed this method to find out how children think. After asking children questions so that he could determine which questions they should be able to answer at various ages, he became more interested in their wrong answers than in their right ones, since he felt that the wrong answers held clues to the ways children reason. For example, Piaget demonstrates that Gui (aged 4 years, 4 months) believes that things in a row are more plentiful than the same number of things in a pile. The child, Gui, exchanges six pennies for six flowers.

Piaget asks, "What have we done?"
Gui answers, "We exchanged them," showing that he recognizes what has happened.
Piaget then asks a seemingly obvious question: "Then is there the same number of flowers and pennies?"
Gui gives the astonishing reply, "No."
Piaget probes further. "Are there more on one side?"
Gui is consistent and says, "Yes."
"Where?" asks Piaget.
Gui points at the row of pennies and says, "There."

The results of this observation and questioning are ambiguous, and so the exchange is made again. This time the flowers are set in a row and the pennies go into a pile. Again, Gui says that the number of flowers and the number of pennies are not the same.

Piaget asks, "Where are there more?"
"Here," says Gui, pointing to the row of flowers.
"And here?" Piaget asks, pointing to the pile of pennies.
"Less," says Gui, confident and consistent in his observation that things in piles are not as numerous as things in rows. (Piaget, 1952a)

The clinical method lets an experimenter follow up especially interesting responses, use language that a particular child understands, and even change to the language that a child is using spontaneously. Although the experimenter asks each child the same basic questions, the experimenter responds flexibly to each child's unique answers, letting the replies determine the next question. In this way the experimenter can probe for the underlying meaning behind what a child says.

This kind of clinical procedure elicits surprising answers that could hardly be discovered by any other strategy. But the method has its drawbacks: the interviewer needs imagination and perception to use it effectively. Furthermore, the flexibility of the questioning makes it difficult for other researchers to duplicate the results exactly. Because it can discover ideas that might otherwise never be found, the clinical method is important, but its findings can be accepted only after many researchers with differing viewpoints corroborate one another's observations.

Interview Method   In the *interview method,* researchers ask people to state their attitudes or opinions or to relate information about one or more aspects of their lives. By interviewing a large number of people, investigators get a broad picture—at least of what the interviewees say that they believe or do or have done. Interview studies focus on many topics—parent-child relationships, sexual activity, occupational goals, life in general. A problem with relying on interviews alone is that interviewees often do not remember accurately. Some people forget when and how certain events actually took place, and others distort their replies to make them more acceptable to the interviewers or to themselves.

Correlational Studies   Suppose you want to measure the relationship between two factors, such as the amount of violence children see on television and the amount of aggressive behavior during free play. Each of these factors is called a *variable,* because it varies among members of a group or can be varied for purposes of an experiment.

Correlational studies show the direction and magnitude of a relationship between variables. That is, are two variables related *positively* (so that they increase and decrease together) or *negatively* (so that as one increases, the other decreases)? We might see, for example, a *positive correlation* between televised violence and aggressiveness in children: the more they watch, the more they hit other children. Or we might see a *negative correlation:* the more they watch, the less they fight. Correlations are reported as numbers ranging from -1.0 (a perfect negative, or inverse, relationship) to $+1.0$ (a perfect positive, or direct, relationship). The higher the number (whether $+$ or $-$), the stronger the relationship (either positive or negative). A correlation of zero indicates that there is no relationship between the two variables. Correlations practically never reach either -1.0 or $+1.0$, but are somewhere between 0 and ± 1.

Correlations allow us to predict one variable on the basis of another. If, for example, there is a positive correlation between watching televised violence and fighting, we would predict that children who watch violent shows are more likely to get into fights. Obviously, the higher the correlation between two variables, the greater the ability to predict one from the other.

However, we cannot conclude that watching violence on television *causes* aggressive play or makes it less likely. We can conclude only that the two variables are related. It is possible that a third factor—perhaps an inborn predisposition toward aggressiveness—causes a child both to watch violent programs and to act aggressively. Before we can come to a conclusion about cause and effect, we need to design a controlled experiment.

Experimental Methods

An *experiment* is a strictly controlled procedure in which an investigator (the experimenter) manipulates variables to determine how one affects another. Scientific experiments must be conducted and reported in a way that allows another investigator to replicate (repeat) them to verify results and conclusions.

To examine the influence of watching television on the development of aggressive and prosocial behavior (helping behavior, like sharing), researchers

interview method
Research technique in which people are asked to state their attitudes, opinions, or histories.

correlational study
Study that assesses the direction and extent of a relationship between variables.

experiment   *Highly controlled, replicable (repeatable) procedure in which a researcher assesses the effect of manipulating variables; an experiment provides information about cause and effect.*

(Eric Roth/Picture Cube)

designed an experiment that compared three groups of children: a group of 3- to 5-year-olds who saw a prosocial program *(Mr. Rogers' Neighborhood)*, a similar group of preschoolers who saw aggressive cartoons *(Batman* and *Superman)*, and a third group who saw neutral films. They assessed the groups on measures of aggressive and prosocial behavior (like hitting or cooperating), and concluded that the kind of program did influence the children's behavior. Since the groups were similar before the programs began, the differences between them afterward were attributed to the programs they watched (Friedrich & Stein, 1973).

Variables and Groups In such an experiment, we call the viewing of the prosocial or aggressive program the *independent variable,* and the prosocial or aggressive behavior the *dependent variable.* The **independent variable,** then, is the one over which the experimenter has control. The **dependent variable** is the characteristic that is examined for changes that may occur as a result of changes in the independent variable (in other words, to determine whether and how it *depends* on the independent variable). In an experiment, we manipulate the independent variable to see the effect that changes in it have on the dependent variable.

To conduct an experiment, we need two types of groups of subjects: one or more experimental groups and one or more control groups. An **experimental group** consists of people who will be exposed to the experimental manipulation, or **treatment** (like being shown either prosocial or aggressive programs)—that is, the independent variable. After exposure, the effect of the treatment on the dependent variable is measured one or more times. The **control group** is composed of people who are similar to the experimental group but who have not received the treatment whose effects we want to measure. (In the experiment just described, the children viewing the neutral films were the control group.) They are sometimes called the *comparison group,* since we compare their behavior with that of the experimental subjects.

Sampling and Assignment Suppose we want to study the value of an enrichment program for children in day care. We offer the program to a group of

independent variable *In an experiment, the variable that is directly controlled and manipulated by the experimenter.*

dependent variable *In an experiment, the variable that may or may not change as a result of changes in the independent variable.*

experimental group *In an experiment, people who receive the treatment under study; changes in these people are compared with changes in a control group.*

treatment *In an experiment, a controlled form of manipulation; a treatment is the cause of any effects observed during the experiment.*

control group *In an experiment, people who are similar to people in the experimental group but do not receive the treatment whose effects are to be measured; the results obtained with this group are compared with the results obtained with the experimental group to assess cause and effect.*

children, and we find that their IQ scores rise. How can we be sure that the relationship between being in the program and having higher IQ scores will hold for other children, and not just the subjects in this experiment? And how can we rule out the impact of some unknown third factor that might account for the results (like the possibility that the children in the program are brighter than those not offered the program)? The key to answering both these questions is very careful selection and assignment of subjects, essential elements in any well-designed experiment.

Selecting a sample First, the **sample** (the people who serve as subjects in an experiment) must be typical of the **population,** the larger group that we want to study, such as, for example, all the high school graduates of 1990 or all urban children in day care in 1989. Since it is generally too costly and time-consuming to study the entire population, experimenters choose a subgroup, or sample, of this population. Only if the sample is typical are we able to *generalize* the experimental results, that is, apply them to the population as a whole.

The best way to ensure that a sample is typical is to choose a **random sample,** a sample for which each member of the population has an equal chance of being selected. Using this method for our study of the enrichment program, we might get our sample by putting the names of all the students in a preschool class into a hat, shaking it, and drawing out the number we want. Or we might choose every other name on a list.

Assigning subjects Once we have our sample, we need to assign subjects to either the experimental group or the control group. We can assign people randomly; that is, we can allow each participant an equal chance of being in either the experimental or the control group. If the sample is large enough, the two groups will be comparable in virtually every respect—age, sex, race, socioeconomic status, school attendance, IQ, and so forth. With two very similar groups, only one of which will receive the independent variable (the enrichment program), we will be able to draw conclusions about the effect of that variable.

Another way of dividing the sample is through **matching,** in which we try to identify any characteristics that might affect the results of the experiment—like age, sex, race, and socioeconomic status—and then make sure that the experimental group and the control group are alike on these characteristics. However, in matching the two groups on some factors, we will probably miss other factors, which may turn out to be just as important.

Types of Experiments There are three principal types of experiments: those conducted in the *laboratory;* those conducted in the *field,* a setting that is part of the subject's everyday life; and those that make use of *naturally occurring* experiences, like hospitalization.

Laboratory experiments Currently, much developmental research depends on **laboratory experiments.** The subject is brought into the laboratory and exposed to certain controlled conditions, and the subject's reaction to these conditions is recorded. It may be contrasted with the same person's behavior under various other conditions or with the behavior of people who are brought into the laboratory and subjected to a different set of conditions.

An example of the first type of experiment is the "strange situation" (Ainsworth & Bell, 1970), in which parents and children are brought into the labora-

sample *In an experiment, a group of people who are used to represent the total population.*

population *All the members of a group to be studied.*

random sample *Sampling technique in which the members of the control group and the experimental group are randomly selected from the larger population.*

matching *Sampling technique in which the members of the control group and the experimental group are selected by comparing and matching certain characteristics.*

laboratory experiment *Experiment performed in a psychological laboratory setting that is subject to the experimenter's control.*

tory together so that researchers can measure the strength of parent-child attachment. They look to see what happens when the mother leaves the child, when the father leaves the child, or when a stranger leaves the child. An example of the second type of laboratory experiment is one in which some children see a person behaving aggressively while other children do not; then both groups of children are measured on how aggressively they act themselves (Bandura, Ross, & Ross, 1961).

These experiments permit the greatest control over the situation and are the easiest studies to replicate (that is, they are easiest for other researchers to carry out in exactly the same way). But because of the artificiality of the situation, the subjects may not always act as they would outside the laboratory.

Field experiments   In *field experiments,* researchers introduce a change into a familiar setting, like the school or the home. The experiment described earlier, in which preschoolers saw prosocial or aggressive television programs (Friedrich & Stein, 1973) is a field experiment. It was conducted during regular school hours in the nursery school the children were attending.

field experiment
Experiment performed in a setting familiar to the subject, such as a day care center.

Natural experiments   **Natural experiments** compare people whom circumstances of life have accidentally divided into separate groups. They are not true experiments, since they do not attempt to modify behavior, but they provide a natural way to study the effects of different events. For example, finding and studying identical twins who were separated at birth and raised in different circumstances offers the chance to compare different environmental effects on identical genes. Since it is unethical to separate identical twins or otherwise manipulate people's lives merely to do interesting research, natural experiments are a good alternative: they provide a way of studying events that cannot be created artificially.

natural experiment
Comparison of a person or a group of people who were exposed to some naturally occurring event (such as hospitalization or malnutrition) with a person or a group of people who were not exposed to the event.

Comparing types of experiments   The three types of experiments—laboratory, field, and natural—differ in two major respects. One is the degree of control exerted by the experimenter. Laboratory experiments are the most rigidly controlled, and field experiments are under a considerable degree of control; but the only control exerted by researchers in natural experiments is the way they collect and use the data.

The other major difference between the three kinds of experiments is the degree to which the findings from a study can be *generalized,* or applied to a broad range of people. The degree of generalizability is in inverse proportion to the degree of control. Laboratory experiments, which are the most controlled, typically have the least generalizability. Because they are carried out in an artificial setting, the laboratory, we cannot always be sure that their findings will apply to real-life situations.

Experiments in general have several advantages over nonexperimental methods. Only experiments can establish cause-and-effect relationships. Furthermore, experiments are so highly regulated and carefully described that the study can be replicated. By repeating studies with different groups of subjects, the reliability of results can be checked.

On the other hand, many experiments look at only one or two facets of development at a time. By focusing so narrowly, they sometimes miss larger, more general variables in people's lives. Another problem with experiments is that we cannot necessarily generalize from the laboratory to real life. Experimental manipulation shows what *can* happen if certain conditions are present, for example, that children who watch violent television shows in the laboratory *can* become more aggressive in that setting. It does not tell us what actually *does* happen in the real world: *do* children who watch a lot of "shoot-'em-ups" hit their little brothers or sisters more than children who watch a different kind of show?

One route to greater understanding of child development may well be combining nonexperimental and experimental methods. Researchers can first observe people as they go about their everyday lives, determine whether correlations might exist, and then go on to design experimental studies of these apparent relationships.

Methods of Data Collection

Developmentalists use three chief methods to collect data; these are called *longitudinal, cross-sectional,* and *sequential studies*.

longitudinal study
Research that follows the same people over a period of time.

Longitudinal Studies   In a *longitudinal study,* we measure the same people more than once to see how they change with age. We may measure one specific characteristic, such as size of vocabulary, IQ, height, or aggressiveness. Or we may look at several aspects of development to find relationships among various factors. This approach provides a more accurate picture of the *process* of development, rather than its status at any given time.

A classic longitudinal study of gifted children (discussed in Chapter 12) was started by Terman: young schoolchildren with high IQs were followed through adulthood and into old age. The intellectual, scholastic, and vocational superiority of these subjects held up over time, and, looking at differences within the group itself, researchers identified factors aside from intelligence that seem to foster success in life (Sears & Barbee, 1978; Terman & Oden, 1959).

cross-sectional study
Research that assesses different people of different ages at the same time.

Cross-Sectional Studies   In a *cross-sectional study* we assess people of different ages at one time. This kind of study does not follow the same person or people over a period of time. It provides information about differences in behavior among people of different ages, rather than about changes with age in the same person.

One cross-sectional study examined 60 children in three separate age groups: ages 3 to 4, 7 to 8, and 11 to 12. To learn about children's concepts of where babies come from, the researchers used Piaget's clinical method (Bernstein & Cowen, 1977). They used four tasks to see whether children's understanding of the origin of babies develops according to Piagetian stages. By examining the concepts held by children of different ages, these researchers gave us a picture of the growth in children's understanding of pregnancy and birth.

Comparing Longitudinal and Cross-Sectional Studies   Longitudinal studies assess *changes* undergone by one or more persons at more than one time, and cross-sectional studies look at *differences* between groups of people. Each approach has strengths and weaknesses. Because of the different designs of the two methods, developmental trends derived from them are sometimes contradictory.

Longitudinal studies are more sensitive to behavioral change and stability. They are also more difficult to run. It is hard to keep track of a large group of subjects over a period of years, to keep records, and to keep the study unified despite turnover in research personnel. Then, there is a probable bias in the sample: people who volunteer tend to be of higher-than-average socioeconomic status and intelligence, and those who stay with the study over time tend to be more competent than those who drop out. There is also the effect of repeated testing. People may do better on subsequent administrations of certain tests simply because of the "practice effect." How might this affect test scores in a study like the Berkeley Growth Study, which tested most of its subjects at least 38 times over a period of 18 years (Bayley, 1949)?

The cross-sectional method has its drawbacks too. It masks differences among subjects by yielding average measures for various age groups, and thus it may give a misleading picture of changes in specific subjects over time. The major disadvantage of this method is that it cannot eliminate the effects of cohort, or generational, influences on people born at different times.

Sequential Strategies The *cross-sequential study* is one of several sequential strategies that have been designed to overcome the drawbacks of the longitudinal and cross-sectional methods. This method combines the other two: people in a cross-sectional sample are tested more than once, and the results are analyzed to determine the differences that show up over time for the different groups of subjects.

cross-sequential study Research that assesses the people in a cross-sectional study two or more times.

The cross-sequential approach is not the perfect solution either, because it is complicated and expensive. Furthermore, researchers need to be sensitive to issues in which cohort membership (the year in which subjects were born and their different life circumstances due to their place in history) is likely to have an effect. When this does not seem significant, the simpler longitudinal strategy may serve better than the more complex sequential one.

ETHICAL CONSIDERATIONS IN STUDYING CHILDREN

We have learned the dangers of some kinds of experimentation. In the thirteenth century, Frederick II wanted to find out whether there was a universal language that babies would speak if they did not hear the language of their own culture:

> So he bade foster mothers and nurses to suckle the children, to bathe and wash them, but in no way to prattle with them, or to speak to them, for he wanted to learn whether they would speak the Hebrew language, which was the oldest, or Greek, or Latin, or Arabic, or perhaps the language of their parents, of whom they had been born. But he labored in vain because the children all died. For they could not live without the petting and joyful faces and loving words of their foster mothers. (Ross & McLaughlin, 1949, p. 366)

Today we would not dream of depriving infants of the loving care they need. Because of what we now know about the possible long-term effects of children's early experiences, we would forgo many of the experiments that were carried out in the past.

The intellectual, emotional, and physical integrity of children deserves serious respect. At the same time, the quest for knowledge drives us to probe children's intellectual, emotional, and physical nature. Sometimes respect for subjects' integrity and the quest for knowledge conflict, raising thorny ethical questions. Then developmentalists turn to a risk-benefit analysis, asking questions like these: Are the potential benefits of the research great enough to justify posing some risk to the research subjects? Are the possible benefits more likely than the possible risks?

To help answer such questions, many research institutes have set up their own review boards to determine whether proposed projects meet ethical criteria. Two of the most prestigious bodies that have published guidelines are the federally supported National Commission for the Protection of Human Subjects of Biomedical and Behavioral Research and the American Psychological Association's Committee on Ethical Standards in Psychological Research.

Now let us see what some of these ethical issues are.

Rights of Participants

Right to Privacy A few years ago, a doctor made the front pages of newspapers nationwide when he recommended giving psychological tests to underprivileged children, with the aim of predicting which ones would someday become delinquent. These children could be watched and given extra social help to try to forestall their criminal tendencies. The doctor's proposal was attacked by many who felt that labeling children as potential delinquents would have damaging effects. The principle of the *self-fulfilling prophecy* might operate: these children might be treated differently and might actually *become* delinquent because of the predictions. This is one potentially harmful way that research can be used. Similar concerns have been voiced with regard to research subjects' scores on intelligence and other psychological tests. Such material has the potential for being used against a person.

One-way mirrors and hidden cameras and tape recorders enable psychologists to observe and record behavior without the subjects' knowing. Furthermore, much private information surfaces during personal interviews—information about income, education, child-rearing techniques, and parent-child relationships. What is the experimenter's obligation with regard to collecting and storing such information? The basic rule is that confidentiality should be respected, and no information collected from children for research should ever be used to their disadvantage.

Right to the Truth Some experiments depend on deceiving subjects. Children are told that they are trying out a new game, when they are actually being tested on their reactions to success or failure. Is it legitimate to deceive subjects about the real purpose of an experiment? If such deception is practiced, how can people's right to the truth and to their own integrity be protected? Does telling a subject the truth *after* an experiment undo the lie?

Right to Informed Consent Children are not always asked to give their consent to be part of scientific experiments, and even when they are, they may not be able to make mature judgments. We often have to rely on parents' regard for their children's well-being or on school personnel's judgment regarding their students. Since investigators do not have to justify their procedures to the children, how can we be sure that their judgment considers the best interests of the individual child, as well as the best interests of the study of children in general? How much do parents have to know about an experiment before the consent they give can be considered "informed"? Can laypeople *ever* give truly informed consent? When the true purpose of an experiment is withheld from a subject, can consent be considered informed? There are no easy answers to these questions, and responsible researchers continue to look for the best ways to resolve these issues.

The National Commission for the Protection of Human Subjects of Biomedical and Behavioral Research (1978) recommends that parents and investigators seek the assent of children aged 7 and over to take part in research and that children's objections should be overruled only if the research promises a direct benefit to them, such as the use of a new, still experimental drug.

Right to Self-Esteem   Researchers often try to discover when people acquire certain skills or become capable of certain types of reasoning. Sometimes they test children known to be too young to have developed the ability under study. Sometimes, in studies designed to identify age-related abilities, investigators pose progressively harder problems until a child is unable to answer. Built into the design of such studies is the certainty of failure. How will the experience of failure and the feelings connected with it affect children? Even if an experimenter takes special pains to see that a child experiences success by the end of an experimental session, does this make up for artificially induced failures? What are the long-term effects of such failures? Is the quest for scientific truth worth the possibility of damaging the self-concept of a single child?

Social Decisions

All these issues force researchers to make fundamental decisions. Researchers want to learn and to contribute to society. They need to ask how they can work in an ethical way to balance scientific independence with the rights of a democratic society. This balance is achieved on several levels: first by the individual researcher, then by professional peers, and ultimately by concerned laypeople. How does this process work?

First, investigators need to think carefully about the projects they design to see whether there is any risk to subjects or others; this is a matter of the integrity of individual researchers. They need to be sensitive to the ethics of research and to reflect that sensitivity in their designs.

Second, because an investigator (especially one who is strongly committed to a project) cannot anticipate all possible ethical issues, safeguards must be provided. Proposed research projects should be approved by juries of professional peers, according to standards that reflect concern for both the quest for knowledge and the rights of children and their families.

Last, individual citizens must be alert to the dual aims of expanding our knowledge and protecting our rights. In a democracy, ethical questions are too important to be reserved for the experts. Laypeople have interests in both promoting increased knowledge about children and protecting the rights of individual children. To further this interest, they may organize in groups to give their individual voices a collective force.

Thus, decisions about ethics in research emerge from a complex circle of individual researchers, professional peers, citizens, and groups of citizens. The optimal result would be a society in which research into child development does no harm and offers a genuine and lasting service for us all.

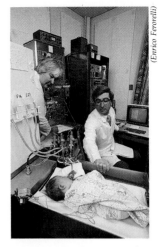

Babies—like this one, who is participating in an experiment on newborns' perception of pleasurable and annoying stimuli—cannot give consent as research subjects. Thus experimenters, parents, and other concerned adults must weigh the possible consequences of such projects before allowing children to take part.

A Word to Students

Our final word in this chapter is that this entire book is far from the final word. Researchers are still learning about children. Some research findings have put old ideas to rest forever. Others are still ambiguous and must be pursued vigorously. Some theories seem to make sense but are hard to test.

As you read this book, you will no doubt consider many issues that will raise questions of values in your mind. If you can pursue your questions through research and thought, you yourself, now just embarking on the study of child development, may in future years advance this study to the benefit of all.

Summary

1 The study of child development is the scientific study of the quantitative and qualitative ways children change over time. *Quantitative change* refers to changes in amount, such as those in height, weight, or vocabulary. *Qualitative change* refers to changes in kind, such as in the nature of intelligence or memory.

2 Although we can look separately at various aspects of development (that is, physical, intellectual, and personality-social-emotional development), we must remember that these do not occur in isolation. Each affects the other.

3 We discuss five periods: the prenatal period (conception to birth), infancy and toddlerhood (birth to age 3), early childhood (3 to 6), middle childhood (6 to 12), and adolescence (12 to 18). Although we can describe normative behavior for each period, individual differences must be taken into account.

4 Influences on development include both hereditary and environmental factors. Influences that affect large groups of people in a similar way are either normative age-graded or normative history-graded influences. Nonnormative life events are those that are unusual in their occurrence or timing and often have a major impact on people's lives.

5 The concept of a critical period, or a specific time when a given event will have its greatest impact, seems more applicable to physical development—perhaps especially prenatal development—than to psychological development.

6 The question whether children have throughout history been seen as qualitatively different from adults is controversial. Aries (1962) held that not until the seventeenth century were children seen as qualitatively different from adults. More recent analyses suggest that children have always been regarded as qualitatively different from adults.

7 The first evidence of professional interest in child development came with books of child-rearing advice in the sixteenth century.

8 A theory is a set of interrelated statements about a phenomenon and an attempt to organize data to explain why events occur. In this book we consider four different groups of theories about development: psychoanalytic, mechanistic, organismic, and humanistic.

9 Theories from the psychoanalytic perspective focus on the underlying forces that motivate behavior. Although they differ markedly in some of the specifics of their theories, Sigmund Freud and Erik Erikson take this perspective. Freud described a series of psychosexual stages in which gratification shifts from one body zone to another (from mouth, to anus, to genitals); the child's maturational level determines when the shift will occur. Erikson described eight stages of psychosocial development that occur between infancy and old age. Each stage involves the resolution of a

particular crisis, achieving a balance between extremes; the crises emerge according to a maturationally based timetable.

10   The mechanistic perspective holds that human beings are responders rather than initiators; it views change as quantitative. The focus is on observable behaviors. Behaviorists and social-learning theorists are of the mechanistic perspective. Behaviorists are interested in how behavior is shaped through conditioning. Social-learning theorists maintain that children learn by observing and imitating models. Social-learning theory incorporates some aspects of the organismic perspective; the child is considered to be an active contributor to learning.

11   The organismic perspective, represented by Jean Piaget, sees people as active contributors to their own development. Piaget described children's cognitive development as occurring through a series of four qualitatively different stages: sensorimotor (birth to 2 years), preoperational (2 to 7 years), concrete operations (7 to 12 years), and formal operations (12 years through adulthood).

12   The humanistic perspective views people as having the ability to take charge of their lives and foster their own development. Abraham Maslow is representative of this school of thought.

13   Scientific method incorporates careful observation and recording of data, development and testing of various hypotheses, and public dissemination of findings.

14   There are five major nonexperimental methods for studying children: case studies, naturalistic observation, clinical studies (clinical method), interviews, and correlational studies. Each approach has its strengths and weaknesses. No nonexperimental method can determine cause-and-effect relationships.

15   Experiments are the only method of assessing cause-and-effect relationships. The three principal types of experiments are laboratory experiments, field experiments, and natural experiments.

16   Developmentalists use three chief methods of data collection: longitudinal, cross-sectional, and sequential. In a longitudinal study, changes with age are determined by measuring the same people more than once. In a cross-sectional study, differences between age groups are revealed by measuring people of different ages. The cross-sequential strategy combines aspects of the cross-sectional and longitudinal approaches. Each of these methods has strengths and shortcomings.

17   The study of children must reflect certain ethical considerations. In a carefully designed study, the researcher must consider its effects on the participants as well as its potential benefits to the field of child development.

Key Terms

child development (page 10)
quantitative change (10)
qualitative change (10)
physical development (11)
intellectual development (11)
personality-social-emotional
   development (11)
normative age-graded influence (12)
normative history-graded influence (12)
nonnormative life event (14)
critical period (15)
theory (18)
data (18)
hypothesis (18)
psychoanalytic perspective (18)

id (19)
ego (19)
superego (19)
psychosexual development (19)
defense mechanism (21)
psychosocial development (21)
mechanistic perspective (23)
behaviorism (23)
classical conditioning (23)
unconditioned stimulus (UCS)
   (24)
unconditioned response
   (unconditioned reflex) (UCR) (24)
neutral stimulus (24)
conditioned stimulus (CS) (24)

conditioned response
   (conditioned reflex) (CR) (24)
operant conditioning (25)
reinforcement (25)
punishment (25)
extinction (25)
shaping (26)
social-learning theory (26–27)
organismic perspective (27)
schema (29)
adaptation (29)
assimilation (29)
accommodation (29)
equilibration (29)
humanistic perspective (30)
scientific method (32)
case studies (33)
naturalistic observation (34)
clinical method (35)

interview method (36)
correlational study (36)
experiment (36)
independent variable (37)
dependent variable (37)
experimental group (37)
treatment (37)
control group (37)
sample (38)
population (38)
random sample (38)
matching (38)
laboratory experiment (38)
field experiment (39)
natural experiment (39)
longitudinal study (40)
cross-sectional study (40)
cross-sequential study (41)

Suggested Readings

American Psychological Association. (1982). *Ethical principles in the conduct of research with human participants.* Washington, DC: Author. Ethical guidelines for psychological experimentation.

Bringuier, J. (1980). *Conversations with Jean Piaget.* Chicago: University of Chicago Press. Fourteen conversations with Piaget which give insight into both the man and his theory of cognitive development.

Erikson, E. H. (1963). *Childhood and society.* New York: Norton. A collection of writings by Erik Erikson, including "Eight Ages of Man," in which he outlines his theory of psychosocial development from infancy to old age.

Freud, S. (1930). *Civilization and its discontents* (J. Strachey, Trans.). New York: Norton. A classic statement of the author's tragic view of human nature. The work is more philosophical than psychological, but whether it is scientific or not, it is one of the landmarks of modern thought.

Kagan, J. (1984). *The nature of the child.* New York: Basic Books. A beautifully written and compelling argument against the idea that early experiences have irreversible effects. Professor Kagan believes that people have the ability to change throughout life and that later events transform early childhood experiences.

Kuhn, T. S. (1970). *The structure of scientific revolutions.* Chicago: University of Chicago Press. A provocative account of what science is and what scientists do.

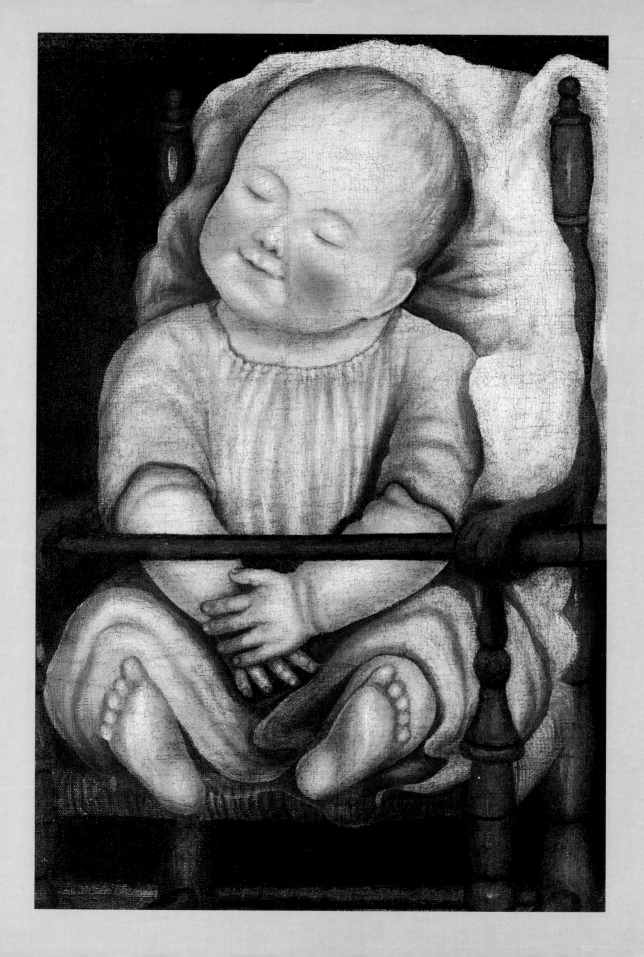

BEGINNINGS

By the time babies are born, they already have an impressive history, a history that began at the moment of conception. Thus our study of the child begins at this moment. Part of this early history is a hereditary endowment, determined when fertilization occurs. Another part is environmental, for the organism in the womb is affected by many events that occur during gestation. As Vicky and Jason grow from single cells into newborn babies, genes and experience affect their development, and so at birth they are already individuals, distinguishable not just by sex, but by size, temperament, appearance, and history.

In Chapters 2, 3, and 4 we trace the earliest development of a child. Chapter 2 presents the two great contributors to individual development—genes and the environment. In Chapter 3 we see the interaction of these two elements as the organism develops in the womb. Chapter 4 describes the birth of a child, ways of evaluating a newborn's immediate condition, and the normal abilities of a newborn. In science we never speak of miracles, but more precise words seem insufficient when we are faced with the marvel of a newborn—eyes bright, little fingers grasping a parent's thumb, and the whisper of a smile on tiny lips.

HEREDITY AND ENVIRONMENT

O f the cell, the wondrous seed
Becoming plant and animal and mind
Unerringly forever after its kind
In its omnipotence, in flower and weed
And beast and bird and fish, and many a breed
Of man and woman from all years behind
Building its future.

William Ellery Leonard, 1923

PREVIEW QUESTIONS

- How does human reproduction occur?
- Through what genetic mechanisms do people inherit various characteristics?
- How are birth defects transmitted?
- How can genetic counseling and prenatal diagnosis help parents who are worried about bearing a handicapped child?
- How do heredity and environment interact—and how can their effects be studied?

WHEN ELLEN AND CHARLES first thought about having a child, they tried to imagine what their baby might be like. Would it be a girl with dimples like Ellen's? Or might it be a boy who would laugh like Charles? And what sort of world could they provide for their child? What impact would their own economic and other stresses have on the child's life? Of course, all these questions were impossible to answer. At that time they had only a faint suspicion of the way one small child would forever alter their lives. Changes in parents' lives are especially dramatic after the birth of a first child, but every child brings new satisfactions (such as insights, achievements, and a transformed sense of purpose) and new stresses (like responsibilities, costs, and demands on time).

heredity Inborn factors inherited from parents that affect development.

environment Combination of outside influences such as family, community, and personal experience that affect development.

nature-versus-nurture controversy Dispute over the relative importance of hereditary and environmental factors in influencing human development; since both factors interact continuously, debate is widely seen as futile.

Throughout this book we will discuss many of the questions that parents wonder about. The science of child development is concerned with all the factors that influence human growth from conception to adulthood. What *are* these factors? And how important is each one? These are hard questions to answer, and in this chapter we will consider one of the greatest puzzles of them all—the importance of both hereditary and environmental influences on the developing person.

We begin by exploring what people think about when they consider having a child. The issues are deeply personal and emotional: What do I have to offer a child? What can a child offer me? Then we discuss the beginning of pregnancy—the moment when *heredity,* the inborn factors inherited from parents which affect development, is most powerful in controlling development. Yet, even at this stage, the *environment,* a combination of outside influences like family, community and personal experience, plays a role. Therefore we examine in detail the so-called *nature-versus-nurture controversy.* We look at how heredity (nature) and the environment (nurture) interact and how their relative effects are discovered and studied. This theme recurs throughout this book and is woven through almost all the accounts of Vicky's and Jason's development.

The chapter continues by examining the mechanisms and patterns of heredity. It then shows how new genetic knowledge helps prospective parents to understand the adventure they are embarking upon. With genetic counseling and new therapeutic techniques, couples can think more clearly and confidently about the prospect of becoming parents.

Choosing Parenthood

People often have mixed feelings about the joys and burdens of parenthood, but until recently what they thought hardly mattered. Parenthood was the nearly inevitable consequence of sexual intercourse. Today, with the availability of reliable birth control, parenthood is more likely to be a freely chosen option. Still, most people in their thirties have children, and most find parenting a major source of satisfaction (Veroff, Douvan, & Kulka, 1981).

One reason why people, like this mother in Nepal, have children is the complex, challenging, and gratifying intimacy that parenthood provides.

WHY PEOPLE HAVE CHILDREN

For centuries, having children has been considered the primary reason for marriage. In preindustrial societies, families needed to be large. The children helped with the family's work and would someday care for their aging parents. Parenthood—and especially motherhood—had a unique emotional significance. Only the woman who became a mother was considered truly fulfilled; only the woman who wanted children was thought normal.

Today, though, there are fewer economic and cultural reasons for parenthood. Overpopulation is a major world problem. Improved medical care makes the survival of children more likely. Social security and other government programs assume some care of the aged. Furthermore, it has become clear that children can have negative, as well as positive, effects on a marriage. Some couples should never have children, often because they are concentrating on career goals that they consider more fulfilling than parenthood.

What, then, makes a couple decide to bring children into their world? One team of researchers studied 199 married couples who ranged from having no children to having four children. The major motivations for parenthood were the desire for a close relationship with another human being and the wish to take part in educating and training a child. The major deterrents were the expenses of child rearing and the parents' perception that a child would interfere with their education and career goals (Campbell, Townes, & Beach, 1982).

Researchers who examined the well-being of women between the ages of 35 and 55 concluded that some reasons for or against parenthood are more sound than others (Baruch, Barnett, & Rivers, 1983). When women have children for the "wrong" reasons, like the following, they may be creating major problems for themselves and their families:

- *Children will give my life meaning.* This puts the heavy burden of a woman's self-worth on her children's shoulders.
- *I will be a good daughter if I have children.* A woman who has children to please her own parents may be miserable if she is not living the life she wants to

live. Furthermore, she is neither resolving her own identity needs nor providing her children with a healthy model.

- *I can't be a real woman without having a baby.* Women who do not have children have no more neurotic symptoms or problems with "feminine identification" than those who do.
- *A baby will patch up my marriage.* Since children bring conflict to even a good marriage, they can make a troubled one even worse.

How, then, should a woman—or man—make such an important decision? People thinking about having children should ask themselves whether they like being with children; whether the idea of being part of a family that includes children appeals to them; and whether they would feel comfortable juggling the demands of their careers with the demands of children. They might ask themselves whether they think they would be what some child-care professionals have called "good enough" parents (Bettelheim, 1987): not perfect, but giving enough of themselves to offer a promise of healthy development for their children.

Most of all, people should understand what a child *cannot* do for them. Children can add riches and variety to life, but they cannot guarantee their parents' happiness.

WHEN TO HAVE CHILDREN

Today, most people who can have children do. But they tend to have fewer children and to have them later in life, usually because they are spending their early years getting an education and establishing a career. (See Box 2-1.) More women these days are having their first child after the age of 30; their numbers have doubled over the past generation. These mothers are more like the women of their grandmothers' time than like their mothers, more of whom had a first child in their twenties (C. C. Rogers & O'Connell, 1984).

This pattern is not an accident: national surveys show that today's women believe in a later ideal age for a first birth. This is especially true of the women who are best-educated, most recently married, and most feminist (Pebly, 1981). Educational level at the time of marriage is the most important predictor of age at the first birth: the more schooling, the later the birth (Rindfuss & St. John, 1983).

THE NATURE OF THE CHOICE

Deciding to have a child is like deciding between one unknown route and another. You can guess at some of the more predictable landmarks, but you don't know what the actual journey will be like. First, you cannot foresee the world your child will inhabit. Second, you cannot predict your child's genetic makeup.

When Jason was born, Jess imagined that his son would be just like him. But Jason is growing up in a different world from the one his father knew as a child. For example, Jason has two working parents, whereas Jess's mother kept house. Furthermore, Jess and Julia are under considerable pressure to produce a "superbaby"; Jess's parents were content to have a normal child. Then, as Jason's personality develops—in ways that are partly a result of the genes he has inherited from both parents—and he turns out to be very different from Jess, father and son will each need to adjust to reality.

BOX 2-1 ■ THE EVERYDAY WORLD

WHEN TO HAVE CHILDREN

What's the best age to have children? There are certain advantages to having children early:

■ From a health standpoint, the best time for a woman to conceive is the decade between ages 20 and 30. Her body is mature, she is likely to have fewer medical problems with pregnancy and childbirth, and her chances of having a child with a birth defect are lower than in later years. Women who conceive after ages 35 and 40 are statistically more likely to suffer from high blood pressure, kidney disorders, and other medical problems; and they run a higher risk of bearing a child with a birth defect.

■ Both parents are likely to have more physical energy. They can cope better with getting up in the middle of the night, staying up all night with a sick baby, and keeping up with the heavy demands of a job and a family.

■ The parents will be younger with their children—more energetic and psychologically more in tune with them later as they become teenagers and then young adults.

■ The prospective parents will be giving themselves a cushion of time if they have trouble conceiving immediately. (Some older couples who do not conceive quickly hear the clock ticking away. The more trouble they have, the more anxious they get and this very anxiety may lead to further difficulty.)

■ Both parents will have had fewer years to engage in various activities that have been identified as risk factors for birth defects—like drinking and smoking. Furthermore, hypertension and related circulatory problems, glucose intolerance, and diabetes (which

complicate pregnancy) are not as likely to develop as they are in middle age.

■ The parents will not be as likely to have built up an unrealistically high set of expectations for their children as many couples do who have waited years to have a family.

On the other hand, there are also advantages to having children late:

■ The parents will have had a chance to think more about their goals—what they want in life, both from their family and from their careers.

■ The parents are more mature and can bring the benefits of their life experience to their role as parents.

■ The parents will be better established in their careers, and so they won't have to press so hard on the job at the very time when their children's needs are likely to be greatest.

■ The parents have already proved to themselves that they can make it on the job, and so they won't feel as if their children are keeping them from success; they can relax a little and enjoy them.

■ The parents are likely to have more money, which will make it easier to handle the expenses of children, buy timesaving and labor-saving services, and get more child care.

■ The parents will be in a stronger position to negotiate a favorable maternity or paternity leave, a part-time work schedule, an arrangement whereby they can do some work at home, or some other benefit. Knowing their value to an organization, an employer will be more likely to make concessions to hold on to them.

Source: Adapted from Olds, 1989.

The Beginning of Pregnancy

For all its uniqueness and unpredictability, a human life always begins in the same way: with the union of genetic material from one father and one mother. The beginning of life has always fascinated both scientists and laypeople, who struggled for centuries to find a plausible explanation.

During the 1600s and 1700s, for example, a debate raged between two schools of thought. "Ovists" believed that a female's ovaries contained tiny embryos that were activated by the male's sperm. "Homunculists" held an opposed view—that preformed embryos were contained in the head of the sperm and would begin to grow only after being deposited in the nurturing environment of the womb. (Figure 2-1 on page 56 shows a homunculus.)

Both these ideas, of course, were incorrect. A truer understanding of repro-

FIGURE 2-1
Left: Homunculus. Human sperm as imagined by a seventeenth-century scientist. The general shape is correct, since by then sperm had been seen through a microscope. But the head was thought to contain a preformed embryo; today, we know that the head contains genetic information. (*Source:* National Library of Medicine.)

duction began with fundamental discoveries by two scientists from the Netherlands: Regnier de Graaf, who first viewed some embryonic cells that had been removed from the reproductive tubes of a female rabbit; and Anton van Leeuwenhoek, who, in 1677, noticed live sperm in a drop of semen viewed under the newly invented microscope. By the middle of the eighteenth century the work of the German anatomist Caspar Friedrich Wolff had clearly demonstrated to the scientific world that both parents contribute equally to the beginning of a new life and that this new being is not preformed but grows from single cells, one male and one female. (Figure 2-2 shows the male and female sexual organs which together make up the human reproductive system.) Let us see how this momentous event takes place.

FERTILIZATION

About 14 days after the beginning of the menstrual period, fertilization can occur. This is the process by which a sperm cell (or, simply, a sperm) from a male unites with an ovum from a female to form a single new cell, called a *zygote.*

zygote *Single cell formed through fertilization.*

gamete *Sex cell.*

follicle *Small sac containing an ovum, or female gamete.*

The sex cells involved in fertilization, the ovum and the sperm, are known as *gametes.* A newborn girl has about 400,000 immature ova (plural of *ovum*) in her two ovaries, each one in its own small sac (also immature), called a *follicle.* The ovum, which is only about one-fourth the size of the period that ends this sentence, is the *largest* cell in the adult human body. Ovulation occurs about once every 28 days in a sexually mature female; that is, one mature follicle in

FIGURE 2-2
Human reproductive system. Cross-sections of the female and male pelvic regions, showing organs of reproduction.

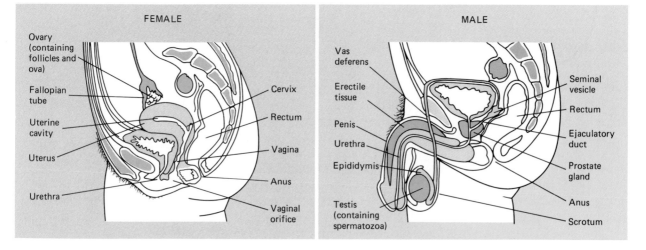

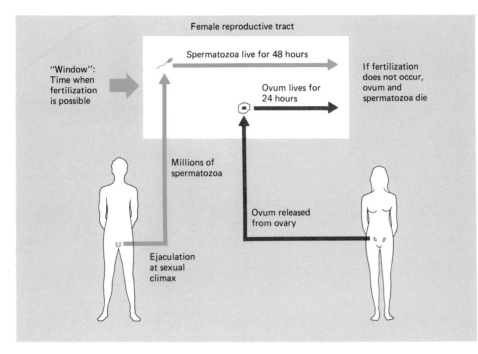

FIGURE 2-3
Fertilization. Spermatozoa can live for 48 hours in a woman's reproductive tract. If a live sperm is present during the 24-hour period after an ovum has been released, fertilization may occur. If it does not, both ovum and sperm die, and fertilization cannot occur until another ovum is released, usually about 28 days later.

either of the ovaries ruptures and expels an ovum. This ovum travels toward the *uterus* (the womb) through one of the two *fallopian tubes,* where fertilization normally occurs.

The tadpolelike sperm, which measures ¹⁄₆₀₀ inch from head to tail, is one of the *smallest* cells in the body. Spermatozoa (plural of *spermatozoon,* the formal word for a sperm) are much more active than ova, and there are many more of them. Sperm are produced in the testicles (testes) of a mature male at a rate of several hundred million a day and are ejected in the semen at sexual climax. An ejaculation carries about 500 million sperm; for fertilization to occur, at least 20 million sperm must enter a woman's body at one time. They enter the vagina and try to swim through the cervix (the opening to the uterus) and into the fallopian tubes, but only a tiny fraction make it this far. More than one sperm may penetrate the ovum, but only one can fertilize it.

From the time of ejaculation, sperm maintain their ability to fertilize an ovum for up to 48 hours. And ova can be fertilized for about 24 hours after release from the ovary. Thus there is a "window" of about 48 hours during each menstrual cycle when sexual intercourse can result in fertilization. Spermatozoa that reach a woman's reproductive tract up to 24 hours before or after an ovum is released from her ovary are capable of fertilizing that ovum. If fertilization does not occur, the ovum and any sperm cells in the woman's body die. The sperm are devoured by the woman's white blood cells, and the ovum passes through the uterus and exits through the vagina (see Figure 2-3). If sperm and ovum do meet, however, they endow the new life with a rich genetic legacy.

THE MECHANISMS OF HEREDITY

The sperm and the ovum—the sex cells, or gametes—each contain 23 *chromosomes,* rod-shaped particles that contain all the hereditary material passed from

uterus Organ of gestation where the fertilized ovum develops until ready for birth; the womb.

fallopian tube Either of two slender ducts connecting the ovaries to the uterus; a fallopian tube is normally the site of fertilization.

chromosome Rod-shaped particle found in every living cell; it carries the genes.

FIGURE 2-4

Genetic transmission: how the zygote receives genes. Genes—the basic units of inheritance—are carried on the chromosomes contributed by both male and female gametes (sex cells). (a) Body cells of women and men each contain 23 pairs of chromosomes; each chromosome consists of thousands of genes. (b) Each gamete (ovum and sperm) has only 23 chromosomes, because of a special kind of cell division, meiosis, in which the total number of chromosomes is halved. (c) At fertilization the 23 chromosomes from the sperm join the 23 from the ovum. The total number of chromosomes is 46, arranged in 23 pairs.

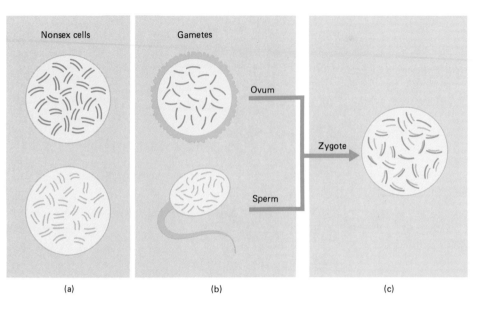

meiosis Type of cell division in which the gametes receive one of each pair of chromosomes.

mitosis Process by which a cell divides in half, over and over again.

gene Functional unit of heredity; genes determine the traits that are passed from one generation to the next.

DNA (deoxyribonucleic acid) Chemical carrying the instructions that tell all the cells in the body how to make the proteins which enable them to carry out their various functions.

parents to children. Every cell in the body except the sex cells has 46 chromosomes (23 pairs). But through the kind of cell division in which they are formed, called *meiosis,* the gametes receive only one of each pair. Then, when gametes fuse at conception, they form a zygote with 46 chromosomes (the normal number for a cell). Thus, the zygote receives half its total number of chromosomes from each parent, and therefore half the hereditary material for the new life is from the father and half is from the mother.

After the zygote is formed, it develops into an *embryo* through **mitosis,** the process by which the cells divide in half over and over again. Each division by mitosis creates duplicates of the original cell, each with all the original hereditary information. When development is normal, each cell in the developing embryo has 46 chromosomes. (See Figure 2-4.) Later in this chapter, we discuss disorders that can occur when there are too many or too few chromosomes.

Eventually, the new being will have billions of cells specializing in hundreds of functions. Every cell except the sex cells has the same hereditary information, and every one—again, except the sex cells—has 46 chromosomes. Each chromosome contains thousands of segments strung out on it lengthwise like beads. These segments are the **genes,** the most basic units of our inherited characteristics. Genes are made of the chemical **DNA (deoxyribonucleic acid).** DNA carries the biochemical instructions that tell all the cells in the body how to make the proteins that enable them to carry out the various functions in the human body. Various genes seem to be located according to their functions in definite positions on particular chromosomes. Each cell in the body contains an estimated 100,000 genes.

The genes transmitted on one specific pair of the 23 pairs of chromosomes in the zygote determine whether the new human being will be male or female, as we shall now explain.

DETERMINATION OF SEX

King Henry VIII divorced Catherine of Aragon because she bore him a daughter rather than a son. It is ironic that this basis for divorce has been valid in many societies, since it is now known that the father determines the child's sex.

As we have noted, at the moment of conception, every normal human being receives a total of 46 chromosomes—23 from the single sperm and 23 from the single ovum. These chromosomes from the father and the mother align themselves in pairs. Twenty-two pairs are autosomes, chromosomes that are not related to sexual expression.

The twenty-third pair, referred to as the *sex chromosomes*, determine the child's sex. The sex chromosome of every ovum from the mother is an X chromosome, whereas the sperm from the father may carry either an X or a Y chromosome. When an ovum (X) meets an X-carrying sperm, the zygote formed is XX, a female. When an ovum (X) is fertilized by a Y-carrying sperm, the resulting zygote is XY, a male.

Differences between the sexes begin to appear immediately. The first difference is that females have an XX and males have an XY chromosome pair. This chromosomal difference is present at conception, when the zygote is formed. Another basic difference, appearing soon after conception, is hormonal; it results in different body structures for males and females, beginning at about 6 weeks.

All human beings begin prenatal life with sexually undifferentiated body structures. Then, at about the sixth week, the male sex hormone testosterone begins to act on the bodies of those babies destined to be male. When testosterone is present, the external and internal genital structures develop in a male fashion. In the absence of testosterone, these structures develop into a female form.

A recent discovery of a single gene that seems to determine the sex of a fetus sheds some light on this process (Page et al., 1987). This gene, called *testes determining factor* (TDF), is located on the Y chromosome. It seems to act as a biological switch, telling other cells to produce testosterone, which will cause the fetus to develop male body parts. If TDF is absent because the sperm that came from the father contained an X chromosome, not a Y, the fetus will develop female body parts.

Another early difference between the sexes is in survival. On average, some 120 to 170 males are conceived for every 100 females. But since males are more likely to be miscarried or stillborn, only 106 are actually born for every 100 females (U.S. Department of Health and Human Services, USDHHS, 1982). More males die during the first few years and males remain more susceptible to many disorders throughout life, and so there are now only 95 males for every 100 females in the United States.

Furthermore, the male's physical development is slower, from early fetal life into adulthood. At 20 weeks after conception he is 2 weeks behind the female; at 40 weeks he is 4 weeks behind; and he continues to lag behind till maturity (Hutt, 1972).

Why are males more vulnerable? No one knows for sure, but hypotheses include the possibility that the X chromosome contains genes which protect females against life stresses, that the Y chromosome contains harmful genes, and that there are different mechanisms in the sexes for providing immunity to various infections and diseases.

MULTIPLE BIRTHS

By contrast with most of the animal kingdom, the human baby usually comes into the world alone. Exceptions—multiple births—occur through two mechanisms.

(Lenore Weber/Taurus Photos)

These monozygotic twins are identical in their physical traits—and are strikingly similar in those intellectual and personality characteristics that have a strong hereditary basis—since they have the same genetic heritage. They seem to like the same flavor of drink, too.

One mechanism produces fraternal twins, the most common type of multiple birth. In this case, the woman's body releases two ova within a short time of each other, both are fertilized, and two babies are thus conceived. These two infants will be known as *fraternal*, **dizygotic,** or *two-egg* twins. Since they are created by different ova and different sperm, they may be of the same sex or different sexes and are no more alike in genetic makeup than any other siblings.

The other twinning mechanism is the division in two of a single ovum after it has been fertilized by a single sperm. The babies that result from this cell division are called *identical*, **monozygotic,** or *one-egg* twins. They have exactly the same genetic heritage, and any differences that they exhibit later must be due to the influences of the environment (including the prenatal environment). They are, of course, always of the same sex.

Other multiple births—triplets, quadruplets, quintuplets, and so forth—result from either one of these processes or a combination of both.

How can parents tell whether newborn twins are identical or fraternal? If the babies are of different sexes, they are, of course, fraternal. If they are of the same sex, it may be hard to tell. To determine this, technicians can examine the placenta (the organ that conveys food and oxygen to the developing fetus and carries its body wastes away), compare physical characteristics like ear shape and head circumference, do detailed blood typings, or perform a trial tissue transplant from one baby to the other—if the transplant takes, the babies are identical.

Identical twins seem to be born through an accident of prenatal life. The incidence of identical twins is about the same in all ethnic groups.

Fraternal twins, on the other hand, are more common in some ethnic groups and under certain circumstances. In recent years, more have been born because of the increased use of fertility drugs, which spur ovulation and often cause the release of more than one egg. (These drugs have also caused a surge in births of three or more babies at a time.) In addition, fraternal twins are more likely to be born in third and later pregnancies, to older women, in families with a history of fraternal twins, and in families in certain ethnic groups (Vaughan, McKay, & Behrman, 1979). Fraternal twins are most common among black people, East Indians, and white northern Europeans; they are least common among Asians (see Table 2-1). The different rates may be due to inherited hormonal differences among women in the various groups, which make some more likely to release two ova at the same time.

dizygotic twins *Two people who are conceived by the mother and born at approximately the same time as a result of the fertilization of two ova; fraternal twins.*

monozygotic twins *Two people with identical genes, arising from the formation of one zygote that divided; identical twins.*

TABLE 2-1

INCIDENCE OF FRATERNAL TWINS (BIRTHS) IN VARIOUS ETHNIC GROUPS	
GROUP	INCIDENCE
Belgians	1 in 56 births
Black Americans	1 in 70 births
Italians	1 in 86 births
White Americans	1 in 86 births
Greeks	1 in 130 births
Japanese	1 in 150 births
Chinese	1 in 300 births

Note: These figures do not reflect the effects of fertility drugs.
Source: Vaughan, McKay, & Behrman, 1979.

Genetics

PATTERNS OF GENETIC TRANSMISSION

Can you curl your tongue the long way? You may never have thought about or tried it, but read on to see how this somewhat dubious ability is related to many other characteristics you have inherited from your ancestors. When you look in the mirror, besides seeing your tongue, you'll see some of the most obvious characteristics that have come to you through your genes—the color of your eyes, the shape of your nose, the length of your legs. The same hereditary processes also affect a wide range of characteristics that you cannot see, including your health, your intellect, and your personality.

Mendelian Laws

Gregor Mendel, an Austrian monk whose work was generally ignored during his lifetime, conducted experiments during the 1860s that unraveled much of the mystery of heredity, as it applies to all forms of life. Mendel selectively bred peas grown in the monastery garden and developed pure strains for a variety of *traits,* or hereditary characteristics, such as short or tall, green or yellow, wrinkled or smooth. (Purebred species always breed true: if you breed a green pea with a green pea, the offspring will always be green.) He then cross-bred these strains in a variety of ways. Finally, using statistical techniques that were novel for his day, he analyzed his findings.

trait   Hereditary characteristic, such as shortness and tallness.

Among Mendel's important discoveries, which were confirmed by later research, are the following.

Appearance of Traits   Traits appear in either of two alternative forms. Mendel noticed that a plant would not have both green and yellow seeds, or both wrinkled and smooth seeds, but would have one or the other. We now know that:

- Genes occur in pairs. Each member of a pair of genes is called an *allele.*
- Every living thing receives a pair of alleles for every trait.
- One allele for every trait comes from the mother, and the other comes from the father.
- Each gene occupies a particular fixed position on a particular chromosome.

allele   One of a pair of genes affecting a trait; the genes may be identical or different.

Law of Independent Segregation   Individual traits (like height, color, and texture of pea plants) are transmitted separately. Mendel called this the law of *independent segregation.*

independent segregation   Mendel's law that individual traits are transmitted separately.

- Individual traits do not blend into each other, but preserve their original nature as they are passed on from generation to generation.
- Traits are transmitted as separate units.

Law of Dominant Inheritance   When an animal or a plant inherits competing traits (like green and yellow seeds), the dominant allele will express one of those traits, through what Mendel called the law of *dominant inheritance.*

Law of Recessive Inheritance   The trait that is not expressed, the recessive trait, may show up in future generations, through the law of *recessive inheritance.*

FIGURE 2-5

Mendel's experiments with colors of pea seeds. Mendel's experiments with peas established the pattern of dominant inheritance. When plants are cross-bred, the dominant characteristic (yellow seeds) is expressed. When the offspring breed, dominant and recessive characteristics show up in a 3:1 ratio. Because of dominant inheritance, the same observable phenotype (in this case, yellow seeds) can result from two different genotypes (yellow-yellow and yellow-green). However, a phenotype expressing a recessive characteristic (such as green seeds) can have only one genotype (green-green).

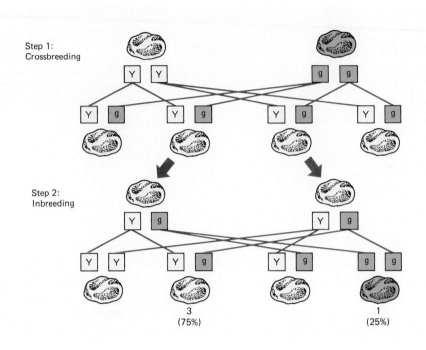

Step 1:
Crossbreeding

Step 2:
Inbreeding

3
(75%)

1
(25%)

Types of Inheritance

Though Mendel laid the foundation for much of what we now know about heredity, subsequent researchers have found that traits are passed on in more ways, and that heredity is more complex, than he believed. Let us look at the different ways that characteristics are inherited.

Dominant and Recessive Inheritance   When Mendel cross-bred purebred yellow peas with purebred peas, he saw that *all* of the "daughter" plants that resulted from this combination had yellow seeds. Then he cross-bred the daughters. This time, only 75 percent of the second generation's offspring had yellow seeds. The other 25 percent had green seeds (see Figure 2-5).

Mendel explained this phenomenon by his law of ***dominant inheritance:*** when an offspring receives genes for contradictory traits (like green and yellow coloring), only one of the traits—the *dominant* trait—will be expressed. As we noted, genes that govern different expressions of the same trait (like the color of seeds) are called *alleles*. Genes occur in pairs, and so a pea plant may have two alleles for yellow (YY), two for green (gg), or one for green and one for yellow (Yg). In these cases, yellow is the dominant allele, and is therefore represented by a capital letter (Y); the recessive allele for green is shown by a lowercase letter (g).

Homozygous and heterozygous alleles   In dominant inheritance, if the dominant allele is present in one of the gene locations, the characteristic expressed by that gene will always appear in the offspring. That is, a cross between a dominant yellow (Y) and a recessive green (g) will always yield a yellow pea. When both alleles are the same, the plant is ***homozygous*** for that trait; when they are different, the plant is ***heterozygous.***

dominant inheritance
Mendel's law that when an offspring receives genes for contradictory traits, only one of the traits—the dominant trait—will be expressed.

homozygous   *Possessing identical alleles for a trait.*

heterozygous   *Possessing different alleles for a trait.*

In a heterozygous cell, one allele is dominant—that is, the trait it carries is the one that will be expressed (Y)—and one is recessive, meaning that the trait (g) will not be expressed. *Recessive inheritance* occurs only if a person (or an animal or a plant) is homozygous for the recessive trait (has two alleles carrying it). A recessive trait (like red hair) may be passed along for several generations but not be expressed because it is always suppressed by a dominant allele (say, for dark hair). Then, if two people carrying the recessive trait mate and pass on their recessive alleles, the trait will be expressed. The taboo against close relatives' marrying stems from the fact that people who have common ancestors are more likely to carry the same recessive traits, and there is a greater chance that both will pass them on to their children. While an unexpected redhead in the family is often welcome, other results of recessive inheritance can be grave, as we shall see.

Phenotypes and genotypes   Observable traits (like eye color, skin color, and blood type) constitute an individual organism's *phenotype.* The underlying genetic pattern, which cannot be seen, is called the *genotype.* Organisms with identical phenotypes do not necessarily have the same genotype, since identical traits may come from several different genetic patterns. In Figure 2-5, for example, the three second-generation offspring that look yellow all have the same phenotype, but they have two different genotypes (YY and Yg). There are many more genotypes than will ever be expressed. According to one estimate, there are about 70 trillion potential human genotypes (Hetherington & Parke, 1979); the number of people in the world today, on the other hand, is only about 5 billion.

Genotypes can be modified by experience; thus, even if Jason has a genotype that would make him tall, he may end up being shorter than his genetic blueprint calls for if he suffers from illness or malnutrition.

Mendel demonstrated that, as shown in Figure 2-5, the allele for yellow seeds is dominant over the one for green seeds. The 3 to 1 ratio he found in the colors of the plants is the basic pattern of dominant inheritance. Although this pattern is the same for many traits throughout nature, it is not true for all traits and falls short in explaining the complicated genetics of human inheritance. In fact, practically the only normal human trait that is clearly inherited through simple dominant transmission is the ability to curl the tongue lengthwise. (If you can do it, at least one of your parents can, too.) Dominant and recessive inheritance are seen most clearly in the patterns of inherited defects and diseases, as we will explain shortly.

Other Forms of Inheritance   Hereditary traits can be passed on in other ways, too. Let us look at some of the other ways we inherit our thousands of characteristics.

Incomplete dominance   Sometimes a trait combines the attributes of both alleles; that is, the interaction between alleles does not always produce completely dominant effects. Some genes, like blood groupings, exist in three or more allelic states and are known as *multiple alleles.* Thus, someone who has alleles for two types of blood, A and B, can end up having blood type AB. Or in the case of cross-bred red and white snapdragons, neither color dominates: pink flowers result.

recessive inheritance *Expression of recessive trait, which occurs only if a person (or an animal or a plant) is homozygous for the trait (has two alleles carrying it).*

phenotype   *Observable characteristics of a person.*

genotype   *Pattern of alleles carried by a person.*

multiple alleles   *Genes that exist in three or more allelic states.*

sex-linked inheritance
Process by which certain recessive genes are transmitted differently to male and female children.

Sex-linked inheritance   In **sex-linked inheritance,** certain recessive traits are inherited differently by male and female children. The Y chromosome (which only males have) is the smallest of all chromosomes, and as far as anyone knows, it carries no important genes apart from the gene that determines sex. Therefore, sex-linked traits are those carried by genes on the X chromosome. Most of these sex-linked genes are recessive; therefore, if a female has received a dominant gene on the X chromosome from one parent and a recessive gene on the other X chromosome, she will not express the trait. She can still pass it on, however. And since genes on the X chromosome have no known alleles on the Y chromosome, any allele on a male's X chromosome will be expressed, whether or not it is recessive in the mother. The most common mode of transmission for sex-linked traits, then, is from mother to son. Red-green color blindness is commonly passed on in this way.

polygenic inheritance
Interaction of a number of different genes to produce certain traits.

Polygenic inheritance   Many traits seem to be inherited in a much more complicated way. Traits that result from the interaction of a number of different genes are said to be transmitted by **polygenic inheritance.** Human skin color is inherited this way, through the interaction of three or more separate sets of genes on three different chromosomes. These genes work together to produce different amounts of brown pigment in the skin, resulting in an infinite number of shades.

multifactorial inheritance
Interaction of both genetic and environmental factors to produce certain traits.

Multifactorial inheritance   Some other physical characteristics (like height) and mental and psychological characteristics (like intelligence, personality traits, and schizophrenia) are transmitted by **multifactorial inheritance,** which involves the interaction of genetic and environmental factors. As we pointed out earlier, if Jason experienced prolonged illness or malnutrition, he would be shorter than his genes would otherwise dictate. However, he would still be taller than another boy who experienced the same kind of deprivation but inherited "short" genes. Throughout this book, we will talk about how the environment interacts with genetic predispositions to affect various aspects of physical, intellectual, and personality development.

Transmission of Genetic Abnormalities

About 95 percent of all babies born in the United States are healthy and normal. Each year, however, more than 250,000 infants are born with physical or mental handicaps of varying degrees of severity (March of Dimes Birth Defects Foundation, 1983b). These babies account for about 5 percent of total births and for at least 20 percent of deaths in infancy (National Institutes of Health, NIH, 1979). Nearly half of the serious malformations involve the central nervous system. (See Table 2-2 on pages 66–67.)

While the overall picture is promising and birth disorders are rare, some disorders are devastating. Moreover, the distribution of disorders is uneven. Some people and families are more likely than others to be in the unfortunate 5 percent.

Many of us carry genes with potentially harmful effects. Most of the time, however, no harm results, since many genes are recessive and are expressed only when two people both pass the same recessive gene to the zygote. Let us see how some birth defects are transmitted genetically.

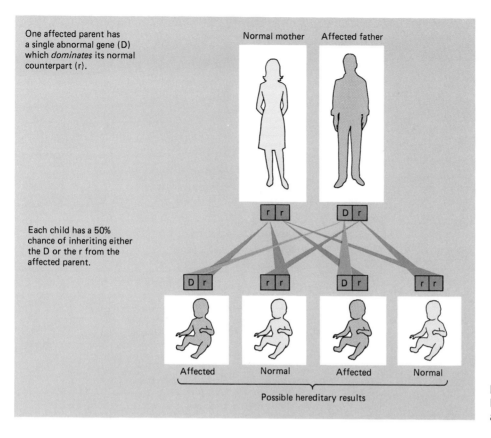

One affected parent has a single abnormal gene (D) which *dominates* its normal counterpart (r).

Normal mother   Affected father

Each child has a 50% chance of inheriting either the D or the r from the affected parent.

Affected   Normal   Affected   Normal

Possible hereditary results

FIGURE 2-6
Dominant inheritance of a birth defect.

Defects Transmitted by Dominant Inheritance Most of the time, normal genes are dominant over those carrying abnormal traits. But sometimes this situation is reversed and an abnormal trait is carried by a dominant gene.

When one parent, say, the father, has one normal gene (r = recessive) and one abnormal gene (D = dominant) and the other parent, the mother, has two normal genes (rr), each of the children will have a 50-50 chance of inheriting the abnormal gene from the father and of having the same defect he has (see Figure 2-6).

Every person who has this abnormal gene has the defect. The defect cannot be one that kills a person before the age of reproduction: if it did, the defect could not be passed on to the next generation. Among the more than 1800 disorders now known to be passed on in this way are achondroplasia (a type of dwarfism) and Huntington's disease (a progressive degeneration of the nervous system).

Defects Transmitted by Recessive Inheritance Many more defects are transmitted by recessive genes, passed along by parents who are healthy themselves. Such disorders are often killers early in life. Examples are sickle-cell anemia, a blood disorder seen more often among black people; and Tay-Sachs disease, a degenerative disease of the central nervous system that occurs mainly among Jews of eastern European ancestry.

TABLE 2-2

BIRTH DEFECTS

PROBLEM	EFFECTS
Alpha$_1$ antitrypsin deficiency	Enzyme deficiency that can lead to cirrhosis of the liver in early infancy and pulmonary emphysema and degenerative lung disease in middle age.
Alpha thalassemia	Severe anemia that reduces ability of the blood to carry oxygen. Nearly all affected infants are stillborn or die soon after birth.
Beta thalassemia (Cooley's anemia)	Severe anemia resulting in weakness, fatigue, and frequent illness. Usually fatal in adolescence or young adulthood.
Cystic fibrosis	Body makes too much mucus, which collects in the lungs and digestive tract. Children do not grow normally and usually do not live beyond age 20.
Down syndrome	Minor to severe mental retardation caused by an extra 21st chromosome.
Duchenne's muscular dystrophy	Fatal disease found only in males, marked by muscle weakness. Minor mental retardation is common. Respiratory failure and death usually occur in young adulthood.
Fragile X syndrome	Minor to severe mental retardation. Symptoms, which are more severe in males, include delayed speech and motor development, speech impairments, and hyperactivity. Considered one of the main causes of autism.
Hemophilia	Excessive bleeding affecting only males. In its most severe form, can lead to crippling arthritis in adulthood.
Neural tube defects Anencephaly Spina bifida	Absence of brain tissue. Infants are stillborn or die soon after birth. Incompletely closed spinal canal, resulting in muscle weakness or paralysis and loss of bladder and bowel control. Often accompanied by hydrocephalus, an accumulation of spinal fluid in the brain, which can lead to mental retardation.
Polycystic kidney disease	Infantile form: enlarged kidneys, leading to respiratory problems and congestive heart failure. Adult form: kidney pain, kidney stones, and hypertension resulting in chronic kidney failure. Symptoms usually begin around age 30.
Sex chromosome abnormality	Minor to severe developmental and learning disabilities, caused by missing X or extra X or Y chromosome.
Sickle-cell anemia	Deformed, fragile red blood cells that can clog the blood vessels, depriving the body of oxygen. Symptoms include severe pain, stunted growth, frequent infections, leg ulcers, gallstones, susceptibility to pneumonia, and stroke.
Tay-Sachs disease	Degenerative disease of the brain and nerve cells, resulting in death before the age of 5.

Source: Adapted from Tisdale, 1988, pp. 68-69.

carrier *In genetics, a person with an allele which is not expressed but can be passed on to future generations.*

As we have seen, recessive traits are expressed only if a child has received the same recessive gene from each parent. If only one parent—say, the father—has the abnormal recessive gene, he is considered a *carrier* for a defect; that is, he does not suffer from it, and none of his children will, either. However, each child has a 50-50 chance of being a carrier and of passing the recessive gene on to his or her children.

WHO IS AT RISK	TESTS AND THEIR ACCURACY	WHAT CAN BE DONE
1 in 1000 Caucasians	Amniocentesis, CVS (chorionic villus sampling). Accuracy varies, but can sometimes predict severity.	No treatment
Primarily families of Malaysian, African, and southeast Asian descent	Amniocentesis, CVS. Accuracy varies; more accurate if other family members tested for gene.	Frequent blood transfusions
Primarily families of Mediterranean descent	Amniocentesis, CVS; 95% accurate.	Frequent blood transfusions
1 in 2000 Caucasians	Amniocentesis, CVS. Accuracy varies; more accurate if other family members tested for gene.	Daily physical therapy to loosen mucus
1 in 350 women over age 35; 1 in 800, all women	Amniocentesis, CVS; nearly 100% accurate.	No treatment, although programs of intellectual stimulation are effective
1 in 7000 male births	Amniocentesis, CVS; 95% accurate.	No treatment
1 in 1200 male births; 1 in 2000 female births	Amniocentesis, CVS; 95% accurate.	No treatment
1 in 10,000 families with a history of hemophilia	Amniocentesis, CVS; 95% accurate	Frequent transfusions of blood with clotting factors
1 in 1000	Ultrasound, amniocentesis; 100% accurate.	No treatment
1 in 1000	Ultrasound, amniocentesis. Test works only if the spinal cord is leaking fluid into the uterus or is exposed and visible during ultrasound.	Surgery to close spinal canal prevents further injury; shunt placed in brain drains excess fluid and prevents mental retardation
1 in 1000	Infantile form: ultrasound; 100% accurate. Adult form: amniocentesis; 95% accurate.	Kidney transplants
1 in 500	Amniocentesis, CVS; nearly 100% accurate.	Hormonal treatments to trigger puberty
1 in 500 blacks	Amniocentesis, CVS; 95% accurate.	Painkillers, transfusions for anemia, antibiotics for infections
1 in 3000 eastern European Jews	Amniocentesis, CVS; 100% accurate.	No treatment

If both parents carry the abnormal recessive gene, their children each have a 50-50 chance of inheriting one dominant gene (D) and one recessive gene (r) and of being carriers themselves. And each child has 1 chance in 4 of inheriting the abnormal gene from each parent—and suffering the disorder. (See Figure 2-7 on page 68).

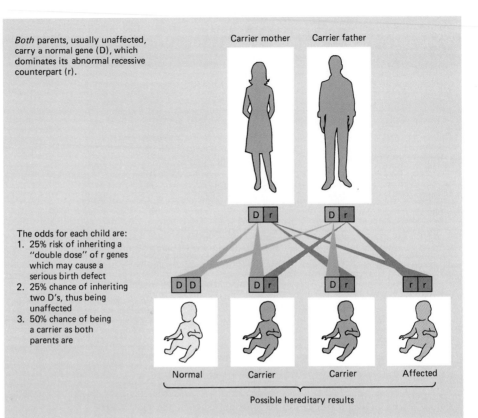

Both parents, usually unaffected, carry a normal gene (D), which dominates its abnormal recessive counterpart (r).

Carrier mother   Carrier father

The odds for each child are:
1. 25% risk of inheriting a "double dose" of r genes which may cause a serious birth defect
2. 25% chance of inheriting two D's, thus being unaffected
3. 50% chance of being a carrier as both parents are

Normal   Carrier   Carrier   Affected

Possible hereditary results

FIGURE 2-7
Recessive inheritance of a birth defect.

In the most common form, the female sex chromosome of an unaffected mother carries one abnormal gene and one normal one (X). The father has normal male X and Y chromosome complement.

Carrier mother   Normal father

The odds for each *male* child are 50/50:
1. 50% risk of inheriting the abnormal X and the disorder
2. 50% chance of inheriting normal X and Y chromosomes

For each *female* child, the odds are:
1. 50% risk of inheriting one abnormal X, to be a carrier like mother
2. 50% chance of inheriting no abnormal gene

Normal   Normal   Affected   Carrier

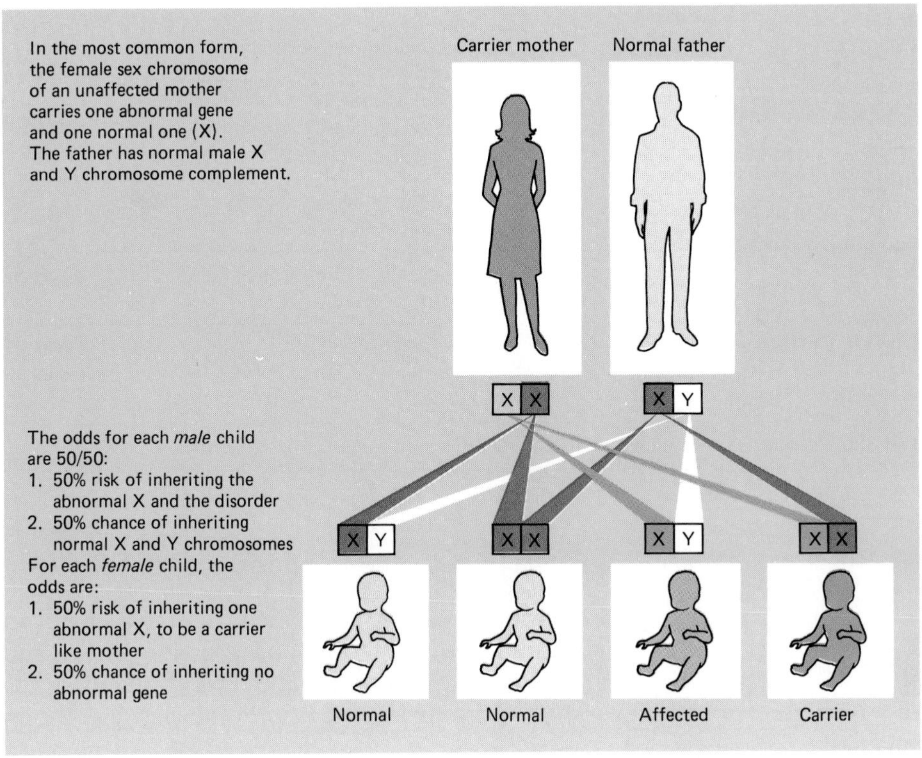

FIGURE 2-8
Sex-linked inheritance of a birth defect.

Defects Transmitted by Sex-Linked Inheritance   The blood-clotting disorder hemophilia used to be known as the "royal" disease, because it affected many members of the highly inbred ruling family of England. Hemophilia is a sex-linked condition carried by a recessive gene on the X chromosome. As we have seen, this kind of transmission will almost always affect the son of a woman who carries the abnormal gene.

Each son of a normal man and of a woman with one abnormal gene will have a 50 percent chance of inheriting the mother's harmful gene and the disorder, and a 50 percent chance of inheriting the mother's normal X chromosome and being unaffected. Daughters will have a 50 percent chance of being carriers. (See Figure 2-8). An affected father can never pass on such a gene to his sons, since he contributes a Y chromosome to them; but he can pass the gene on to his daughters, who then become carriers.

In rare instances, a female can inherit one of these sex-linked conditions. The daughter of a hemophiliac man and a woman who is a carrier for the disease has a 50 percent chance of inheriting the abnormal X chromosome from each of her parents. Should this happen, she will suffer from the disease. Females typically do not inherit this way, because the normal X chromosome will override the X chromosome with the defective gene. Males, however, do not have this protection.

Chromosomal Abnormalities

What Are Chromosomal Abnormalities?   Most of the time, chromosomal development proceeds normally, but in those exceptional cases when something does go wrong, serious abnormalities may occur. Some chromosomal defects are inherited, while others result from accidents that occur during the development of an individual organism. Accidental abnormalities are not likely to recur in the same family.

Some chromosomal disorders of varying degrees of severity are caused by either a missing or an extra sex chromosome. Relatively rare conditions—for example, Klinefelter's syndrome (or XXY syndrome), caused by an extra X chromosome in males—have a variety of effects. The most obvious are sexually related characteristics (underdevelopment, sterility, or the appearance of secondary sex characteristics of the other sex). The long-term outlook for children with these disorders generally does not include serious mental retardation but does include reading and general learning disabilities ("Long-Term Outlook," 1982). Unfortunately, this is not the case for children born with Down syndrome, the most common chromosomal disorder.

Down Syndrome   As opposed to the disorders mentioned above, which are caused by abnormalities of the sex chromosomes, *Down syndrome* results from an extra autosome. This condition used to be called *mongolism*, because affected persons have a downward-sloping skin fold at the inner corners of the eyes, somewhat resembling the eye structure typical of what used to be called the *Mongoloid race*, which includes many Asian groups. Other signs of this syndrome are a small head, a flat nose, and protruding tongue, a defective heart, defective eyes and ears, and mental and motor retardation.

This disorder, which is caused by an extra twenty-first chromosome or the translocation of part of the twenty-first chromosome onto another chromosome

Down syndrome   Disorder caused by an extra twenty-first chromosome; it is characterized by mental retardation and often heart defects and other physical abnormalities.

This lively little girl has Down syndrome. Although her intellectual potential is limited, loving care and patient teaching are likely to help her achieve much more than was once thought possible for such children.

(and is sometimes known as *trisomy-21),* occurs once in every 800 live births (Allore et al., 1988). Older parents are at greatest risk: the chances rise from 1 such birth in 2000 among 25-year-old mothers up to 1 in 40 for women over 45; the risk also rises with the age of the father, especially among men over 50 (Abroms & Bennett, 1981). (For years, the father's influence was underestimated as researchers concentrated on the mother's age, failing to consider the fact that the older a woman is, the older her husband is likely to be. Recent research has determined a definite relationship between Down syndrome and the father's age.)

In more than 90 percent of cases of Down syndrome, the defect is caused by a chromosomal accident, a mistake in chromosome distribution that occurs during development of either the ovum, the sperm, or the zygote. (Such an accident can happen, for example, in the development of one identical twin and not the other.) However, among mothers under age 35, who give birth to more than 90 percent of all infants and bear 65 to 80 percent of babies with Down syndrome, the disorder is more likely to have a hereditary cause (L. Holmes, 1978). A promising lead to its genetic basis is the recent discovery of a gene on chromosome 21. This gene expresses a brain protein that seems to lead to Down syndrome (Allore et al., 1988).

The birth of a child with Down syndrome is nearly always a trauma that can strain the parents' marriage and place an emotional burden on the entire family. However, the effect on marriages may be due more to the initial reaction—grief—than to the burden of care (Gath, 1985).

It is difficult to predict the eventual ability of any particular child—either intellectual capacity or the ability to get along in everyday life—when the syndrome is first detected. Pediatricians who try to forecast often rely on their clinical experience, without realizing that they tend to see primarily children with serious problems and seldom see those who are doing well. In surveys of families who have a child with Down syndrome, the positive aspects of living with these children become apparent. Most such families do well, and family members are often very attached to the child (Gath, 1985).

In recent years, many programs have been developed to help children with Down syndrome improve their skills. (See Resources on page R1.) One of the most comprehensive was established in 1971 at the experimental education unit at the Child Development and Mental Retardation Center of the University of Washington (Hayden & Haring, 1976). In this program, children between the ages of 2 weeks and 6 years and their parents work on a variety of exercises and activities to help the children develop motor, language, social, cognitive, and self-help skills.

Many children have shown remarkable early gains, making educators revise their expectations upward for children with Down syndrome, but long-term studies are needed to determine whether the children will maintain these gains over time.

The mortality rate for people with Down syndrome used to be very high early in life, but now they have a longer life expectancy because of the increased use of antibiotics to treat infections that used to be fatal. More than 70 percent live until at least age 30 (P.A. Baird & Sadovnick, 1987), and 25 percent until age 50 (D. Patterson, 1987).

GENETIC COUNSELING

The practical value of our growing understanding of genetics becomes apparent when we look at the personal tragedy that inherited disorders bring to individual lives.

Five years after their marriage, Bill and Mary Brown felt ready to start their family. Mary became pregnant, the couple turned their study into a nursery, and they eagerly looked forward to bringing the baby home. But their baby was born dead, a victim of anencephaly, a rare birth defect in which the skull is missing and some of the internal organs are malformed. Bill and Mary were heartbroken over the loss of the baby they had both wanted. More than that, they were afraid to try again, afraid that they might not be able to conceive a normal child. They still wanted a baby but feared that they could not face so much grief again.

Today, couples like the Browns can find help and advice through *genetic counseling.* In genetic counseling, couples try to determine the cause of a particular problem in a specific child, to establish patterns of inheritance, and to determine their chances of producing healthy children.

genetic counseling Clinical service that advises couples of their probable risk of having a child with a particular hereditary disorder.

A genetic counselor may be a pediatrician, an obstetrician, a family doctor, or a genetic specialist. He or she takes a thorough family history, including information relating to diseases and causes of death of siblings, parents, and other close blood relatives; any marriages between relatives; previous abortions or stillbirths; and other relevant factors. Then each parent and any children in the family receive a physical examination, since physical conditions often give clues to genetic abnormalities.

Laboratory investigations of blood, skin, urine, or fingerprints may also be performed. Chromosomes from body tissues may be analyzed and photographed, with the photographs cut out and arranged according to size and structure on a chart called a *karyotype.* This chart can demonstrate chromosomal abnormalities and can indicate whether a person who appears normal is likely to transmit genetic defects to his or her children (see Figure 2-9, page 72).

karyotype Photograph made through a microscope showing the chromosomes when they are separated and aligned for cell division; the chromosomes are displayed according to a standard array.

FIGURE 2-9
Karyotype. Chromosomes of a child with Down syndrome, showing three chromosomes instead of the usual two on number 21. (Since pair 23 consists of two X's, we know that this is the karyotype of a girl.) (*Source:* Vanderbilt University and March of Dimes.)

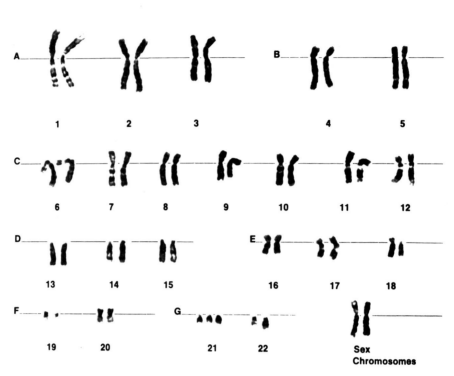

amniocentesis Prenatal diagnostic procedure for examining the chromosomes of a fetus; sample cells are withdrawn from the amniotic fluid, in which the fetus floats, and are examined for signs of birth defects.

chorionic villus sampling (CVS) Prenatal diagnostic procedure for obtaining sample villi from the membrane surrounding the embryo and then examining the embryo's chromosomes for birth defects.

alpha fetoprotein (AFP) Blood test used to indicate the possibility of a defect in the formation of the brain or spinal cord of a fetus.

ultrasound Medical procedure using high-frequency sound waves to detect the outlines of a fetus and determine whether the pregnancy is progressing normally.

fetoscopy Medical procedure permitting direct viewing of the fetus in the uterus.

On the basis of all these tests, the counselor determines the mathematical odds that a couple will have a child afflicted with inherited defects. If the couple feel that the risks are too high, one partner may choose to be sterilized, or the couple may consider adoption or an alternative type of conception (see the section "Alternative Ways to Conceive" in Chapter 3).

A genetic counselor does not give advice on whether to take risks. Rather, the counselor can only try to find out, and help a couple understand, the mathematical risk of a particular condition, explain the implications of that risk, and make the prospective parents aware of alternative courses of action.

In order to understand what a genetic counselor is saying, it is important to understand probabilities. Overall, as we saw when it was noted that defects occur in only about 5 percent of all births, the chances of having a healthy baby are good. To make these chances even better, prospective parents can take tests developed to identify carriers of genetic defects. If a husband and wife know that they both carry a recessive gene for a disorder, they may decide to conceive a baby and then order prenatal tests to find out whether the fetus does indeed have the condition. For example, simple blood tests can identify carriers of the blood disorders sickle-cell anemia (which affects an estimated 10 percent of American blacks) and thalassemia (which affects persons of Mediterranean origin), and carriers of the nervous system disorder Tay-Sachs disease (which affects about 4 percent of American Jews). Box 2-2 (pages 74–75) describes techniques of prenatal diagnosis—*amniocentesis, chorionic villus sampling (CVS), the alpha fetoprotein (AFP) test, ultrasound,* and *fetoscopy.*

Suppose that a genetic counselor determines that a husband and wife are both carriers of a harmful recessive allele. This means, just as with Mendel's green peas, that there is a 25 percent chance that they will have a child with the disorder. Some people think that a 25 percent risk of giving birth to children with a genetic disease means that if the first child is affected, the next three children will not be affected. But the saying "Chance has no memory" applies here. A 25 percent risk means that the odds are 1 in 4 that any given child born of the union will inherit the disease.

If a disorder is not particularly disabling or can be treated, a couple may take a chance. In other cases, through counseling, a couple may realize that the risk they fear so much is actually very slight or even nonexistent. In the future, geneticists hope to be able to do much more to help parents. Much help may come from current scientific progress in locating defective genes on chromosomes.

Investigators use complex instruments developed in the science of molecular biology to identify and locate specific genes. They then determine the proteins manufactured by these genes, and by detecting the presence or absence of proteins associated with particular disorders, they gain information that has many practical implications. Such knowledge can lead to new prenatal tests to predict birth defects; diagnostic tests to indicate whether children or adults have or are likely to develop a disorder; drugs to prevent or treat disease; and "gene therapy," the technology to repair abnormal genes. More than 1250 human genes have been mapped so far, some linked to various cancers, one to the emotional disorder known as *bipolar disorder* (manic depression). And the work continues.

Nature versus Nurture

It is clear from seeing how various traits, both normal and abnormal, are transmitted genetically that your life, like the life of every other human being, is greatly influenced by biology. At the same time, you have also been influenced by your surroundings and experiences. These two sets of influences have fueled a centuries-old "nature versus nurture" debate, which asks whether genetic factors or environmental factors are more important in determining how a person will behave, think, and view the world.

The most radical position in favor of the "nurture" (or environmental) side of the controversy was taken by the British philosopher John Locke (1632–1704). He argued that newborns are like a *tabula rasa,* or "clean slate," whose ultimate contents will depend on what experience "writes." According to Locke, nature contributes *nothing* to the process of development apart from providing a live body. In this book we talk about the evidence for powerful inborn components for many traits, and it is obvious that Locke's extreme position is not valid. His ideas, however, have had a profound effect on philosophy, politics, and psychology, and his metaphor of the blank slate has not been abandoned easily or lightly.

The opposite position—the "nature" side of the debate—holds that we are born with complete genetic instructions that determine our response to every situation. This view has never been accepted as widely as Locke's. The strongest argument for nature was made by the mathematician Wilhelm von Leibnitz (1646–1716), but his ideas proved too abstract for most people. Only after the

tabula rasa *Philosophical metaphor implying that at birth a baby is a blank slate with no inborn predispositions, a position espoused by John Locke.*

BOX 2-2 ■ THE EVERYDAY WORLD:

PRENATAL DIAGNOSIS OF BIRTH DEFECTS

An impressive array of new techniques can help couples who have reason to fear bearing a child with a birth defect. Tests performed prenatally can often reassure such couples that their babies will be normal. Even when the news is not good because the tests detect a disorder, the expectant parents are still helped. Some decide to terminate the problem pregnancy and to try again for a normal conception. Others, who choose to continue the pregnancy of a handicapped child, have time to adjust to, and plan for, the child's special needs. Some conditions can be diagnosed prenatally and successfully treated right from birth. The use of the techniques discussed below may have the happy result of decreasing the incidence of mental retardation and other congenital conditions.

AMNIOCENTESIS

Through the process of *amniocentesis,* a sample of the amniotic fluid (which contains fetal cells because the fetus floats in it while in the uterus) is withdrawn and analyzed to detect the presence of a variety of birth defects. Through this process, which is usually done between the sixteenth and eighteenth weeks of pregnancy, we can also find out a baby's sex, which may be crucial in the case of a sex-linked disorder like hemophilia.

Amniocentesis can be used to identify about 100 inborn errors of metabolism, and to diagnose spina bifida and anencephaly. For 97 percent of women at high risk, the procedure determines that the fetus is normal. One analysis of 3000 women who had amniocentesis indicates that it is "safe, highly reliable and extremely accurate" (Golbus et al., 1979, p. 157), but another study, of 4600 women, found a slightly higher risk of miscarriage among women who had the procedure (Tabor et al., 1986).

Amniocentesis is recommended for women over 35. It is also recommended for women when they and their partners are both known carriers of Tay-Sachs disease or sickle-cell anemia, and for women who have a family history of such conditions as Down syndrome, spina bifida, Rh disease (a potentially fatal complication of blood incompatibility between mother and fetus), or muscular dystrophy. Only 10 percent of such women now undergo the procedure; reasons include unavailability of the procedure in the community, lack of information, expense, and the slightly increased risk of miscarriage (F. Fuchs, 1980; NIH, 1979; Tabor et al., 1986).

CHORIONIC VILLUS SAMPLING

Chorionic villus sampling (CVS) consists of taking tissue from the end of one or more villi (hairlike projections of the chorion, the membrane around the embryo) and examining this tissue, which contains fetal cells, for the presence of various conditions. This procedure can be performed earlier than amniocentesis (typically between the ninth and twelfth weeks of pregnancy) and yields results faster (within about a week). When CVS is performed from the ninth to the eleventh week of pregnancy, the rate of miscarriage is equivalent to rates in comparable normal pregnancies (Hogge, Schonberg, & Golbus, 1986). The procedure is becoming more common around the world, and it appears to be about as safe for mother and fetus as amniocentesis (Goldsmith, 1988). Among its risks are the possibility of maternal cramping, fluid leakage, spotting, or bleeding (Goldsmith, 1988).

---

invention of the computer did the ordinary person have a clear example of the kind of complex programmed behavior described by Leibnitz. The strength of the claim that we are the way we are born depended chiefly on its commonsense appeal to the belief that genes must contribute something important to development. An enormous amount of animal behavior has been shown to be inborn; the "nature"of the argument holds that humans are not exempt from this principle.

Most modern-day theorists see this entire question as a picture of "nature *and* nurture": heredity and environment constantly interact. Vicky's intelligence, for example, may be determined partly by her genes, but the kind of home she grows up in, the degree to which she is encouraged to pursue intellectual interests, her physical health, the kind of education she receives, and her own decisions in life will all affect the eventual expression of her intelligence (see Box 2-3, page 76).

ALPHA FETOPROTEIN (AFP) TEST

Blood taken from the mother between the sixteenth and eighteenth weeks of pregnancy can be tested for the amount of alpha fetoprotein (AFP) it contains. High AFP levels may indicate the possibility of a defect in the formation of the brain or spinal cord in the fetus, like spina bifida or anencephaly. Low AFP levels have been found in women carrying a fetus with Down syndrome (Cuckle, Wald, & Lindenbaum, 1984; DiMaio, Baumgarten, Greenstein, Saal, & Mahoney, 1987). Ultrasound or amniocentesis, or both, may be performed to confirm or refute the presence of suspected conditions.

ULTRASOUND

Through ultrasound, high-frequency sound waves are directed into the abdomen of a pregnant woman to yield a *sonogram,* a picture of the uterus, fetus, and placenta. This technique provides the clearest images yet obtained of a fetus in the womb and has proved so popular with pregnant women that they sometimes bring their other children to the doctor's office for their first look at their sibling-to-be. Ultrasound provides a wealth of information with little or no discomfort to the mother as it projects images of a fetus's limbs and profile that are clear enough for an untrained observer to recognize.

While many doctors recommend ultrasound as a routine screening device in all pregnancies, the National Institutes of Health (NIH) (1984) warns of a possible risk (long-term effects are unknown) and points out that ultrasound's effectiveness in improving the management and outcome of a pregnancy has often been assumed rather than demonstrated.

Some of the questions ultrasound can answer are:

- How far along is the pregnancy?
- Is the fetus growing normally?
- Is more than one fetus in the womb?
- What position is the fetus in?
- Is the fetus male or female?
- Is the uterus normal?
- Has the fetus died? (NIH, 1984)
- Does the fetus have Down syndrome? (Benacerraf, Gelman, & Frigoletto, 1987)

UMBILICAL CORD ASSESSMENT

Through a new technique that involves threading a needle into tiny blood vessels of the umbilical cord under the guidance of ultrasound, doctors can take samples of fetal blood. This allows them to get a blood count, examine liver function, and assess various other body functions that neither amniocentesis nor CVS can measure. It can test, for example, for infection, anemia, certain metabolic disorders and immunodeficiencies, and heart failure, and it seems to offer promise for identifying other condition as well. The technique needs to be perfected, to resolve several problems that sometimes occur, including bleeding from the umbilical cord, early labor, and—most serious—infection (Chervenak, Isaacson, & Mahoney, 1986; Kolata, 1988b).

FETOSCOPY

In fetoscopy, doctors insert a tiny lens equipped with a light directly into the uterus, enabling them to see parts of the fetus and thus to see a suspected abnormality. Another use of the technique is to guide the insertion of a small needle to draw a fetal blood sample for the diagnosis of certain disorders. While fetoscopy is 98 percent accurate, it carries a greater risk to the fetus than amniocentesis.

In thinking about the nature-nurture controversy, the idea of a **reaction range** is useful. In any matter that is controlled by heredity, there is a range of possible responses, depending on the environment. Body size, for example, depends on biological processes, all of which are genetically regulated. Even so, a range of sizes is possible, depending on the nutrition of the growing child. In societies that undergo a sudden improvement in diet, an entire generation of people may tower over their parents. The better-fed children share their parents' genes, but have responded to their healthier world. Once diet is adequate for the entire society over more than one generation, children tend to grow to heights similar to their parents'.

Another important concept in the nature-nurture debate is **maturation,** the unfolding of genetically programmed patterns of behavior in a biologically determined, age-related sequence. Maturation is programmed by our genes, and environmental forces interfere with this hereditary timetable only when they

reaction range *In genetics, a potential variability in the expression of a hereditary trait, depending on environmental conditions.*

maturation *Triggering of expression of a trait as a function of biology rather than of the environment.*

BOX 2-3 ▪ PROFESSIONAL VOICES

SANDRA SCARR

Sandra Scarr is Commonwealth Professor of Psychology at the University of Virginia. The focus of her work is on the relation between hereditary factors and environmental input. Here she discusses some of her findings:

QUESTION: You are best known for your research examining the effects of heredity and environment on intelligence. In general, what conclusions have you reached?

SCARR: Overall, I think that for most children in industrialized countries, the majority of the differences in IQ test scores have to do with genetic variability. That assumes public schooling, reasonable nutrition, and adequate exposure to the culture being sampled, because IQ tests are samples of knowledge and skills that are valued by the majority culture.

Q: And that's why you believe that average IQ differences between whites and blacks are environmental, while the major differences among whites are heredity?

SCARR: That's right. If you have less than adequate exposure to those skills and knowledge, you can't learn them, and children reared in the black culture simply lack adequate exposure. When Richard Weinberg and I studied black and interracial children who were adopted by white families, we found that these children scored as high on IQ tests as adopted white children. . . .

Q: In the study you and Susan Grajeck did on siblings, you conclude that upper-middle-class brothers who attend the same school, whose parents take them to the same plays [and] sporting events and use similar child-rearing practices on them, are virtually no more similar in personality to each other than they are to working-class or farm boys, whose lives are totally different. That seems to say the environment has very little effect on personality.

SCARR: Our studies suggest that there's virtually no family environmental effect on personality. If there were, adopted children would grow up to resemble their adoptive parents and siblings in some way. They don't. Any personality similarities between siblings appear to be entirely genetic.

Source: Adapted from E. Hall, 1984, pp. 62–63; *photo,* Rhoda Baer.

take extreme forms, like long-term deprivation. The effect of such deprivation was seen in infants in an Iranian orphanage who received little attention and got no exercise. These babies sat up and walked quite late, compared with well-cared-for Iranian children (Dennis, 1960). Yet, even under these extreme conditions, maturation was only slowed, not stopped.

It is in the development of intellect and personality that the balance between nature and nurture appears most delicate. Consider your use of language, for example, a tool whose development we discuss throughout this book. The prominent behaviorist B. F. Skinner (1957) and other behaviorists long argued that language is entirely the product of environmental factors, but then a wealth of studies during the 1960s and 1970s suggested that language development depends largely on maturation.

Both muscular development and neurological development contribute to linguistic maturation. Newborn babies simply do not have the muscle control or shape of throat needed to speak words. At 6 months, however, they have developed well enough to babble. At that time, too, the brain has reached the level of development necessary for babbling. Thereafter, so strong is the tendency to vocalize that even children born without hearing will happily lie in a crib cooing and "saying" syllables. And yet clearly the environment has much to add to language development. The children of English-speaking parents do, after all, learn English. And a trained professional, on hearing the babbling of a deaf child, will quickly recognize that the child cannot hear. In complex situations like these, maturation lays the foundation, and the environment builds upon it.

| Hereditary defect causes mental retardation. Superior environment has no beneficial effect. | Hereditary defect or disease (such as deafness and long-term illness) interferes with normal life and may contribute to retarded development. | Inherited factors that have social implications (such as race, sex, and body build) may affect environment and limit opportunities for personal development. | Lower social class, poor education, or emotional deprivation may stunt intellectual development. | Birth injury or prenatal event causes physical problem that interferes with regular schooling and retards development. | Birth injury or prenatal insult is so massive that it causes mental retardation despite normal, healthy genetic endowment. |

FIGURE 2-10
Nature-nurture continuum, related to intellectual retardation. (*Source:* Adapted from Anastasi, 1958.)

HOW HEREDITY AND ENVIRONMENT INTERACT

The mixing of influences of nature and nurture can be shown as a continuum, as in Figure 2-10, which illustrates how these two forces in different degrees can cause intellectual retardation. Eye color and blood type are relatively simple inherited characteristics. But more complex traits such as health, intelligence, and personality are subject to an interplay between heredity and environment.

How much is inherited? How much is environmentally influenced? The answers to these questions really matter. For example, discovering that a trait like high intelligence can be influenced by environment inspires Ellen and Charles to talk to Vicky and read to her, and to offer her toys that will help her learn. On the other hand, learning that their son's activity level is mostly inherited helps Julia and Jess accept and work with Jason's temperament. Finding that a problem is hereditary does not mean that you cannot do anything about it. Special diets, medication, and other treatments of genetic problems have helped children with various inborn problems.

EFFECTS OF HEREDITY AND ENVIRONMENT

Ways to Study the Relative Effects of Heredity and Environment

To study how heredity and environment interact to create differences between people, a new interdisciplinary field of study has emerged, called *developmental behavioral genetics.* Methods of learning how people inherit various traits include:

developmental behavioral genetics Study of interactions of heredity and environment which create differences between people.

- ■ *Studies of twins.* When identical twins (who have the same genetic legacy) are more alike on a trait than fraternal twins (who are no more alike than any brother or sister), a hereditary basis for the trait seems indicated. Identical twins who have been raised in different homes are especially sought after, since their identical heredity can be contrasted with their different environments, but such people are hard to find. Even when they are found, their cultural environments often turn out to be quite similar.
- ■ *Adoption studies.* When adopted children are more like their biological parents and siblings, the influence of heredity shows up; when they resemble their adoptive families more, the influence of environment is clear.
- ■ *Consanguinity studies.* By doing consanguinity studies—that is, examining as many blood relatives as possible in a particular family—researchers can dis-

cover the degree to which they share certain characteristics and whether the closeness of the relationship affects the degree of similarity. This is also called the *pedigree method.*

■ *Selective breeding in animals.* If animals can be bred for certain characteristics (such as the ability to run mazes or the tendency to become obese), the trait is seen as at least partly hereditary. Such findings can sometimes be generalized to human beings, sometimes not.

Other lines of research concentrate on determining possible environmental causes for particular characteristics:

■ *Prenatal studies.* By investigating relationships between various conditions and the experiences of the patients' mothers during pregnancy, researchers can often pinpoint a specific cause for a specific condition. This sort of detective work in the 1960s led to the identification of an innocent-seeming sedative, thalidomide, as the agent that caused thousands of children to be born without arms or legs.

■ *Manipulating the environment.* Changing the diet, exercise, intellectual enrichment, or sensory stimulation in one group of animals or people and then comparing this group with a control group allows researchers to draw conclusions about the effects of such environmental differences. Manipulation of the heredity or the environment of human beings is, of course, limited by both ethical and practical considerations. For example, we cannot mate human beings as we do animals, and it would be morally abhorrent to separate identical twins, make adoption placements, institutionalize children, or prescribe questionable drugs for experimental purposes. Researchers therefore have to rely on animal studies or after-the-fact observations of events that have occurred naturally.

■ *Comparisons of actual histories.* By interviewing parents about their child-rearing practices (remembering to discount the effects of faulty and distorted memories!) and by identifying and comparing other life-history factors, researchers can sometimes determine environmental influences on specific characteristics.

Throughout our discussion of children and their development, we will refer to studies that have made use of one or more of these research techniques.

Characteristics Influenced by Heredity and Environment

Physical and Physiological Traits On September 3, 1980, Robert Shafran, who was 19 years old, enrolled as a freshman in a New York college. For 2 days, students he had never met before greeted him like an old friend and called him "Eddy." Finally, one showed him a snapshot of Eddy Galland, who had attended the same school the year before. Bobby Shafran said later, "What I saw was a photograph of myself." The story became even more startling when a third look-alike, David Kellman, turned up, and the three youths learned that they were identical triplets who had been separated at birth and adopted by different families (Battelle, 1981).

The many instances of mistaken identity among identical twins attest to their strong physical likeness. Identical twins also have a number of physiologi-

Separated at birth, these reunited monozygotic triplets—Bobby, Eddy, and David—show the powerful impact of heredity.

cal traits in common, supporting a belief that these characteristics are genetically determined. For example, identical twins are more similar than fraternal twins in their rates of breathing, perspiration, and pulse and in their blood pressure (Jost & Sontag, 1944).

When both identical and fraternal twins were measured on galvanic skin response (GSR), a measure of the rate of electrical changes of the skin, identical twins were more similar than fraternal twins (Lehtovaara, Saarinen, & Jarvinen, 1965). Identical twin sisters are likely to begin to menstruate within 2 months of each other; fraternal twin sisters show a mean difference of 1 year for the age of menarche (first menstruation) (Petri, 1934).

Another physical trait that females seem to inherit is the tendency to release more than one ovum at one time, as shown by the different frequencies of fraternal twins in various ethnic groups (refer back to Table 2-1) and in the fact that a woman who is a fraternal twin has a greater chance of having twins herself.

Height and weight can both be environmentally influenced, but they seem to be determined primarily by heredity, since identical twins reared together or apart are more similar in both respects than fraternal twins reared together. In our overweight society, it is especially interesting to note that obesity seems to have a very strong hereditary component; it is twice as likely that both identical twins will be overweight as that fraternal twins will be (Stunkard, Foch, & Hrubec, 1986). Visual, sensory, and perceptual functions are also highly influenced by heredity (Mittler, 1971).

Our days on earth may even be numbered by our genes. A recent adoption study (Sorensen, Nielsen, Andersen, & Teasdale, 1988) found that heredity seems to influence the cause of death and the age of death more than environment. Adopted children (born between 1924 and 1926) whose biological parents had died before age 50 had twice the risk of dying prematurely of people whose parents were alive at age 50. There was no significant correlation in age at death between adoptees and their adoptive parents. The practical significance of this finding is clear. If you have been to the doctor recently, you were probably asked for your family's medical history: knowing the particular diseases you may be at risk of may help you prevent them and live longer.

Intelligence Behavioral geneticists have probably studied intelligence more extensively than all other characteristics combined (Plomin, 1983). Until recently, it was believed that during infancy intelligence is determined mainly by heredity but that as a child grows older, the environment increases in importance and finally becomes the dominant factor. Various findings from research conducted during the 1980s have challenged this belief.

Research on training techniques for promoting intellectual development does support the classic environmental view. For example, when caregivers talk to and play with children in ways that help them make sense of their world, the children show enhanced intellectual development (Bradley & Caldwell, 1976; Elardo, Bradley, & Caldwell, 1975). Another line of study shows how the effects of an impoverished environment can be offset. Researchers have raised children's scores on intelligence tests by working with parents (Karnes, Teska, Hodgkins, & Badger, 1970) and directly with children (Blank & Soloman, 1968).

This kind of "applied" research consistently finds that changes in the environment do lead to improved scores on intelligence tests; however, more theoretical research raises a puzzle. Investigators who try to sort the hereditary and environmental factors in intelligence commonly rely on the twin, consanguinity, and adoption study techniques discussed earlier in this chapter. Their findings have also been consistent with one another, but not in the way expected.

One important study in Minnesota compared IQ scores of adopted children with those of their adoptive siblings and parents and with the educational levels of their biological mothers (whose IQs were not known). Young siblings scored similarly, whether related by blood or adoption, but adolescents' scores had a zero correlation with those of their adoptive siblings. Furthermore, the adolescents' IQs correlated more highly with their biological mothers' levels of schooling than with their adoptive parents' IQs. The researchers concluded that family environment is more important for younger children but that older children and adolescents find their own "niche" in life on the basis of innate abilities (Scarr & Weinberg, 1983).

Another project studied the IQs of adopted children, aged 3 to 10 years and over, in relation to the scores of their adoptive parents and their biological mothers. The resemblance in IQ scores between children and mothers they had been separated from since they were less than 1 week old was *twice* that found between the same children and the adoptive parents who had raised them from birth (Horn, 1983).

A third study followed 500 pairs of twins, both identical and fraternal, and their siblings from infancy to adolescence. Genetic influences became more important with age. Identical twins became increasingly similar in IQ, while fraternal twins dropped to a lower level of similarity, comparable to that between any two siblings. This study also found that individual children followed their own distinct patterns of "spurts" and "lags" in mental development. The home environment had some impact, but not to the same degree as hereditary factors (R. S. Wilson, 1983).

What are we to make of these findings? Taken at face value, they seem to justify the old saying, "Blood will tell." But then why do other experiments bear out the value of training? Clearly, there is room for more research, but perhaps we can spot a clue in what the Minnesota study says about finding one's niche.

Finding one's place in the world is not automatic. The richer one's environment, the more "niches" it has to offer. In an impoverished environment, there will be some niches and some people will fit into them; other people in such an environment will find no niches suited to their ability, while similarly endowed people in a richer environment find their place and flourish. Thus, perhaps we see once again a case where heredity provides the foundation and environment provides the structure.

Personality   We can define *personality* as a person's overall pattern of character, behavioral, temperamental, emotional, and mental traits. It is obvious that something so complicated cannot be ascribed to any one major influence, either hereditary or environmental. But when we separate specific aspects of personality, we can find many grounds for assuming that some individual factors are inherited, at least in part.

In 1956, two psychiatrists and a pediatrician (A. Thomas, Chess, & Birch, 1968) launched the New York Longitudinal Study to determine those aspects of personality which babies seem to be born with and which remain consistent through the years. By closely following 133 children from infancy through young adulthood and examining them in regard to several traits, the researchers concluded that temperament, or a person's basic behavioral style, appears to be inborn.

They looked at such characteristics as a baby's activity level; regularity in biological functioning (hunger, sleep, and bowel movements); readiness to accept new people and new situations; adaptability to changes in routine; sensitivity to noise, bright lights, and other sensory stimuli; general tendency toward cheerfulness or unhappiness; intensity of responses; distractibility; and degree of persistence.

This study found that babies vary enormously in all these characteristics, almost from birth, and that they tend to continue to behave according to their initial behavioral style. Many children, however, do change their behavioral style, apparently reacting to special experiences or to parental handling.

Another study, focusing on twins, has also found that many personality traits seem to be shaped more by our genes than by our experiences—but that experience can modify inborn disposition. Since 1979, researchers at the University of Minnesota have tested more than 350 pairs of identical twins (some raised together and some in different families) and have found that for a wide range of personality traits, more than half the variation from one person to another is due to heredity (Tellegen et al., in press). Each trait seems to be inherited through the combination of a number of genes.

Among the traits most strongly linked to heredity are leadership, obedience to authority, the tendency to get upset easily, and a cheerful, optimistic outlook on life (see Figure 2-11, page 82). These traits are not unalterably imprinted at birth, however. For example, if Jason is timid, his parents may not be able to make him fearless, but they can help him develop the confidence to take more risks by giving him opportunities to do so rather than sheltering him.

Findings from both these studies, then, lead to a similar conclusion: children are not blank slates. Parents do not have the power to cast a child's personality into any form they choose. They still exert a major influence, however. When parents respect and adapt to their children's individuality, they can help each child make the most of his or her unique personality and abilities.

Other researchers have found evidence for genetic influence on a wide

(Erika Stone, 1987)

Although some traits, like shyness or a tendency toward fussiness, seem to be hereditary, sensitive handling by parents who understand their children's temperaments can often help children to change the way they meet life's challenges.

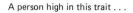

A person high in this trait . . .

Is masterful, a forceful leader who likes to be the center of attention

Follows rules and authority, endorses high moral standards and strict discipline

Feels vulnerable and sensitive and is given to worries and easily upset

Has a vivid imagination readily captured by rich experience; relinquishes sense of reality

Feels mistreated and used; feels that "the world is out to get me"

Has a cheerful disposition, feels confident and optimistic

Shuns the excitement of risk and danger, prefers the safe route even if it is tedious

Is physically aggressive and vindictive, has taste for violence and is "out to get the world"

Works hard, strives for mastery, and puts work and accomplishment ahead of other things

Is cautious and plodding, rational and sensible, likes carefully planned events

Prefers emotional intimacy and close ties, turns to others for comfort and help

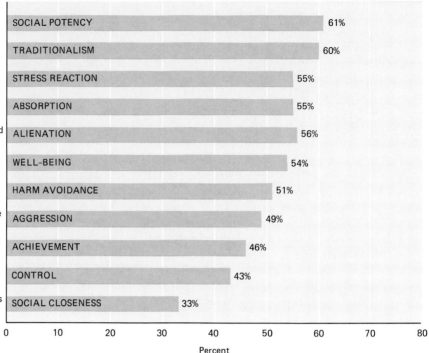

SOCIAL POTENCY — 61%
TRADITIONALISM — 60%
STRESS REACTION — 55%
ABSORPTION — 55%
ALIENATION — 56%
WELL-BEING — 54%
HARM AVOIDANCE — 51%
AGGRESSION — 49%
ACHIEVEMENT — 46%
CONTROL — 43%
SOCIAL CLOSENESS — 33%

Percent (0 10 20 30 40 50 60 70 80)

FIGURE 2-11
Roots of personality. Degree to which 11 personality traits are estimated to be inherited, on the basis of tests with twins. Traits were measured by the Multidimensional Personality Questionnaire, developed by Auke Tellegen at the University of Minnesota. (*Source:* Tellegen et al., in press.)

concordance Probability of agreement; used to measure the relative importance of hereditary and environmental factors in development.

range of personality traits, which suggests that there are genetic factors in such characteristics as shyness (see Box 2-4, opposite); extroversion or introversion, emotionality, and activity (Vandenberg, 1967); depression, anxiety, psycho- pathic behaviors, obsessions, and social introversion (Gottesman, 1962, 1963, 1965; Inouye 1965); neuroticism (Eysenck & Prell, 1951; E. Slater with Shields, 1953; P. Slater, 1958); and some fears (R. J. Rose & Ditto, 1983). Hyperactivity (see Chapter 12) and behavior traits like sleepwalking, bed-wetting, nail biting, and car sickness (Bakwin, 1970, 1971a, 1971b, 1971c, 1971d) also seem to have a genetic base. Studies of babies from different ethnic groups also indicate that some temperamental traits are inborn (see Box 2-5, page 84).

Mental Disorders with Probable Hereditary Factors One of the most profound and pressing questions in psychology concerns the source of mental disabilities. Over the centuries, many of these ailments have been diagnosed as possession by the devil, laziness, neurotic responses to family pressures, and disease. It is now widely agreed that many forms of mental disability do have a physical and genetic basis, although the environment can have a strong influence over their expression.

In searching for evidence that a disease is genetically based, one of the first clues sought is *concordance,* that is, a probability of agreement. If a relationship depends entirely on genetic factors, then identical twins (who share identical genes) will have a concordance rate of 100 percent. Thus, by knowing one twin's condition, we can predict with 100 percent certainty that the other twin will have the same condition. If the environment plays some role, the concordance might be 70 percent. If the environment plays a very large role, the concordance might

BOX 2-4 ■ THE RESEARCH WORLD

SHYNESS

At age 4, Jason went with his parents to a Christmas party given by Julia's employer. For the first half hour he did not say a word; for the next hour he clung to Julia's side as he stared wide-eyed at the other children, the strange adults, and the array of new toys. By the time he was feeling comfortable enough to venture away from Julia, it was time to go home.

Vicky was at the same party. She had barely burst into the room when she ran up to the Christmas tree, grabbed the first brightly wrapped package, and asked the man standing next to it (whom she had never seen before) if he could help her open it—hardly giving her parents a backward glance.

Classical psychoanalytic thought has held for years that such differences between children are likely to have been created by their early experiences—perhaps Jason is wary of the world because he has not learned to trust, while Vicky's experiences have been more positive. A major body of recent research, however, strongly suggests that shyness and boldness are inborn characteristics, which are related to various physiological functions and which tend to stay with people throughout life. These traits do not seem related to sex or socioeconomic class.

Jerome Kagan, a professor of psychology at Harvard University, has led much of this research, centering on a series of longitudinal studies of some 400 children from intact middle- and working-class white families who were followed for over 5 years, starting at just under 2 years of age (Garcia-Coll, Kagan, & Reznick, 1984; Kagan, Reznick, Clarke, Snidman, & Garcia-Coll, 1984; Kagan, Reznick, & Snidman, 1988; Reznick et al., 1986). The trait which Kagan and his colleagues call *inhibition to the unfamiliar* and translate as "shyness" appeared to a marked degree in about 10 percent of the children, first showing up at 21 months of age and persisting in most cases at 7½ years. The

opposite trait, "boldness," or comfort in strange situations, also was especially strong in about 10 percent of the children. Most of the children fell between these two extremes.

Both the genetic influence and the stability of the trait were most marked for the children at either extreme, whose personality characteristics were associated with a number of physiological signs that may provide clues to the heritability of such traits. When the children were asked to solve problems or learn new information, the heart rates of the very shy children were higher and less variable and the pupils of their eyes dilated more than was the case for middle-range and bolder children. The shy children seemed to feel more anxious in situations that the other youngsters did not find particularly stressful.

A genetic factor in shyness also showed up in a study that compared adopted children with those being raised by their own parents. Two-year-olds who had been adopted soon after birth closely resembled their biological mothers in terms of shyness. However, these babies also resembled their adoptive mothers, showing an environmental influence, as well (Daniels & Plomin, 1985). The parents of shy babies tended to have less active social lives, exposing neither themselves nor their babies to new social situations. This was true for the adoptive parents, and even more so for biological parents raising their own children.

Here again, then, is an intertwining of factors. While a *tendency* toward shyness may be inherited, some shy children become more outgoing and spontaneous, apparently in response to their parents' efforts to help them become more comfortable with new people and situations.

Parents can help their shy children by bringing other children into the home, by protecting them from as much stress as possible, and by teaching them coping skills for stressful situations. "Parents need to push their children—gently and not too much—into doing the things they fear" (Kagan, quoted in J. Asher, 1987).

be only 30 percent. Although concordance is not direct proof of a genetic relationship, a pattern of high concordance among identical twins, lower concordance among immediate relatives, still lower concordance among more distant relations, and nearly random concordance among nonrelatives argues powerfully that a hereditary factor is present. This analytical tool has been valuable in establishing the presence of genetic factors in the disorders described below.

Autism **Infantile autism** is a rare developmental disorder involving the inability to communicate with and respond to other people. The symptoms show up within the first 2½ years of life, sometimes as early as the fourth month, when a

infantile autism Rare developmental disorder involving the inability to communicate with and respond to other people.

BOX 2-5 ■ AROUND THE WORLD

TEMPERAMENT

Heredity seems to be particularly important in determining temperament (one's general mode of thinking, behaving, and responding to stimuli). Some people are more aggressive than others, some more adaptable, some more good-humored, some more nervous, some more speculative, and so forth. These differences often show up right from birth, as a visitor to a hospital nursery can see by observing how differently the newborns react to the same stimuli. Thus it is reasonable to talk about even newborns as individuals. Daniel Freedman, who has paid particular attention to the question of differences in temperament among newborns of different racial background, has come up with some interesting findings.

In western cultures, when children's noses are briefly pressed with a cloth, they show the "defensive reaction"; they immediately turn their heads away or swipe at the cloth. Chinese babies, however, do not put up a fight but simply open their mouths promptly to restore breathing.

Another typical behavior among newborns in western societies is the Moro reflex. To test for this reflex, the baby's body is lifted, and the head supported. The head support is then released, and the head is allowed to drop. Typical white American newborns reflexively extend both arms and legs, cry persistently, and move about in an agitated manner. Navajo babies, however, typically respond with a reflexive retraction of the limbs. The babies rarely cry, and they almost immediately stop any agitated motion.

Freedman's group also studied newborns' behavior in Australia, Bali, India, Italy, Kenya, Nigeria, and Sweden, and he reports that "in each place, it is fair to say, we observed some kind of uniqueness." It is hard to imagine that these reflexive differences have anything to do with environment or culture. Instead, investigations like this suggest that even the most fundamental-seeming reflexes are subject to genetic and ethnic variability. We must do much more research before declaring any particular inherited characteristic to be "normal" for all children.

Source: D. G. Freedman, 1979.

---

baby may lie in the crib, apathetic and oblivious to other people. He—boys are 3 times more likely than girls to be afflicted—does not cuddle, does not make eye contact with caregivers, and either treats adults as interchangeable or clings mechanically to one person. This child may never learn to speak (grossly deficient language development is an important symptom), but may be able to sing a wide repertory of songs.

Parents often think that an autistic child is deaf, brain-damaged, or mentally retarded. Many *are* retarded; only 30 percent have an IQ of 70 or more. They often perform well, however, on tasks requiring manipulative or visual-spatial skills, and may perform unusual feats of memory (like memorizing entire train schedules). Their behavior is often bizarre: they may scream when their place at the table is changed, insist on always carrying a particular rubber band, clap their hands constantly, or stare for hours at a moving object like an electric fan.

Although in the past clinicians thought that autism was caused by cold, unresponsive parents or other environmental factors, it is now recognized as a biological disorder of the nervous system that is frequently found in association with other physical syndromes such as epilepsy and mental retardation (*Diagnostic and Statistical Manual of Mental Disorders* (3d ed., rev.), DSM III-R, 1987). New research has revealed that the brains of autistic people are not fully developed and that the interference with development seems to occur either during early prenatal life or during the first or second year after birth (Courchesne, Yeung-Courchesne, Press, Hesselink, & Jernigan, 1988). Since concordance between identical twins is 96 percent, compared with 23 percent for fraternal twins, autism is probably inherited, perhaps through a recessive gene, and the impact of the environment is minimal (Ritvo et al., 1985).

Some autistic children have been helped in developing some social and language skills through operant conditioning techniques, as described in Chapter 1 (McDaniel, 1986). Overall, 1 in 6 make an adequate adjustment and are able to do some kind of work as adults, 1 in 6 make a fair adjustment, and the other two-thirds remain severely incapacitated for life (Geller, Ritvo, Freeman, & Yuwiler, 1982). Fortunately, the disorder is very rare (about 3 cases per 10,000 people).

Depression **Depression** is an emotional disorder characterized by feeble responses to a variety of stimuli, low initiative, and sullen or despondent attitudes. Depressed people are sad and often have trouble eating, sleeping, and concentrating. A 6-month survey of over 9000 adults suggests that depression affects about 6 percent of American adults, with women suffering from it more than men (J. K. Myers et al., 1984). It is hard to determine how common depression is among children, but it has been reported in infants, where it often takes the form of failure to thrive (McDaniel, 1986). (Childhood depression is discussed more extensively in Chapter 13.)

depression Emotional disturbance characterized by feeble responses to stimuli, low initiative, and sullen or despondent attitude.

Although depression has often been regarded as an overreaction to actual sorrow and stress, it does have a physical basis. Laboratory experiments have shown that the use of a chemical inhibitor to increase body levels of the chemical acetylcholine can induce temporary depression in well people and increase the depression of already depressed people. Also, depressive episodes are an occupational hazard for agricultural workers who are exposed for prolonged periods to insecticides containing similar chemical inhibitors. (Acetylcholine is a ***neurotransmitter,*** a chemical in the brain that transmits messages between nerve cells.) This evidence of a chemical influence has suggested to many researchers the probability of a reaction range, a genetically varied response to the same chemical stimulus. If such a response could be established, depression, or at least a tendency to depression, would prove to be a hereditary condition.

neurotransmitter Chemical that transmits signals between neurons (nerve cells).

There is, in fact, strong evidence that a predisposition to depression is often inherited. The cells of depressed patients and their similarly disturbed relatives do have a greater sensitivity to acetylcholine than the cells of people without a history of depression (Nadi, Nurnberger, & Gershon, 1984). And identical twins have a 70 percent concordance rate for depression, whereas fraternal twins, other siblings, and parents and their children have only about a 15 percent concordance rate (USDHHS, 1981).

Many of the classic elements of nature-nurture interaction appear when we analyze depression. Nature defines the biochemical relationship between body and behavior. The environment can change the probability of encountering a particular chemical, or having an experience that triggers a chemical reaction causing depression. Hereditary factors then establish a range of responses, making different people respond to the environment in different ways.

Schizophrenia **Schizophrenia** is a mental disorder marked by loss of contact with reality and by such symptoms as hallucinations, delusions, and other thought disorders. Although schizophrenia typically occurs among young adults, it can begin in childhood. The study by Myers et al. cited above, which measured the rate of depression, found that over a 6-month period about 1 percent of the American population suffers from schizophrenia (J. K. Myers et al., 1984). From many studies, evidence has emerged for a strong hereditary element in this disorder. The biological children of schizophrenic mothers are

schizophrenia Psychological disorder marked by a loss of contact with reality; symptoms include hallucinations and delusions.

BOX 2-6 ■ A CHILD'S WORLD AND YOU

WHAT DO YOU THINK?

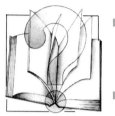

■ To prevent the transmission of hereditary disorders, should genetic counseling before marriage be made compulsory? Give reasons for your answer.

■ If amniocentesis uncovers the presence of a severe disease or defect in a fetus, do you think that a free therapeutic abortion should be made available to the pregnant woman? Why, or why not?

■ In choosing to become parents, people face a number of issues that were previously left to chance. What arguments do you see for and against the following choices? (1) Postponing parenthood until after age 30.

(2) Having a child before age 30 even if financial security does not yet seem assured.

■ In the continual debate over the role of heredity and environment, a number of theoretical positions have been adopted by people on opposing sides of various social issues. What do you think of the following arguments? (1) Some people and groups are genetically different from others. Our laws and institutions should take these differences into account. (2) The environment shapes so much of our lives and opportunities that people born into an impoverished environment should be given extra help so that they will have the same prospects as people born into a richer environment.

---

more likely to suffer from it themselves than people in the general population; identical twins are more likely to be concordant than fraternal twins; and the closer a person's biological relationship is to someone with schizophrenia, the more likely the person is to develop it (Gottesman & Shields, 1966; Heston, 1966; Kallman, 1953; Mittler, 1971).

Although there is strong evidence, then, for biological transmission of schizophrenia, we have to ask why not all identical twins are concordant for it. One answer may lie in tendencies and environmental situations. In other words, it may be that what is transmitted is not the illness itself, but the predisposition toward the illness. If certain environmental stresses occur in the life of someone who is genetically predisposed, that person may respond by becoming schizophrenic. At this time, however, we still do not know the precise stresses that act as the trigger.

Alcoholism Alcoholism, inability to control drinking even after it has caused major problems in one's life, used to be considered a moral failure. Today it is generally looked upon as a disease with both hereditary and environmental causes.

Researchers have found many genetic links to alcoholism (the following findings are all summarized in Schuckit, 1985, 1987). First, identical twins are more likely than fraternal twins to be concordant for the condition. Then, there is evidence from adoption studies. Biological children of alcoholics are 4 times more likely to become alcoholics themselves even when they are adopted soon after birth and raised by nonalcoholics. And children whose biological parents are nonalcoholics but who are brought up by alcoholics are *not* at unusual risk of alcoholism.

A particularly interesting series of experiments have focused on nonalcoholic preteen and teenage boys and young men who have alcoholic close relatives but who do not drink themselves. These subjects' physiological reactions to alcohol in the experiment can be observed without interference from any that would occur as the result of drinking. These youths *have* been found to be biologically different from control groups—youths without alcoholic relatives—in that the boys and men related to alcoholics show a less intense physical response to ethanol, the type of alcohol in alcoholic drinks. Such people, then, may not get the signal from their bodies to stop drinking that most people get when they have a certain amount of alcohol in their system. While they are not *fated* to become alcoholics, they are more vulnerable to the condition.

This work has many practical implications in a society in which alcohol is the most abused drug. Identifying people who are especially at risk of alcoholism may help them learn that they need to be very careful about drinking, and identifying physical markers associated with alcoholism may lead to more effective treatment.

The power of heredity is great—but so is the power of the environment, a force that begins to act even within the child's first world, the womb, as we shall see in Chapter 3.

Summary

1   Even though the economic and cultural pressures to have children have diminished, parenthood offers a unique opportunity for love and nurturing. Most couples do become parents, but compared with those of earlier generations, today's couples tend to have fewer children and to start having them later.

2   Human life begins with the union of an ovum and a sperm, which form a one-celled zygote. At conception, each normal human being receives 23 chromosomes from the mother and 23 from the father. These align into 23 pairs of chromosomes—22 pairs of autosomes and 1 pair of sex chromosomes. Chromosomes carry the genes that determine inherited characteristics.

3   The sex of the child depends on whether the father contributes an X or a Y chromosome at the time of fertilization. The mother always contributes an X chromosome. A Y chromosome from the father results in a male. An X chromosome from the father results in a female.

4   Although conception usually results in a single birth, multiple births can occur. When two ova are fertilized, fraternal (dizygotic) twins result; these are different in genetic makeup and may be of different sex. When a single fertilized ovum divides in two, identical (monozygotic) twins result. These have the same genetic makeup and therefore are always of the same sex. Larger multiple births result from one of these processes or a combination of the two.

5   Patterns of genetic transmission are dominant inheritance, recessive inheritance, incomplete dominance, sex-linked inheritance, polygenic inheritance, and multifactorial inheritance. Various human characteristics, and several diseases and birth defects, are transmitted through these patterns.

6   If an organism carries genes for contradictory traits, the trait expressed will not be random. Instead, one trait will generally be dominant, and that is the one that will be expressed. Observable traits constitute a person's *phenotype*, while the underlying genetic pattern is called the *genotype*.

7   Recessive traits can be expressed only if both parents contribute the same recessive gene at fertilization.

8   Sometimes a trait combines the attributes on both alleles and neither characteristic dominates. This is known as *incomplete dominance*.

9   Some recessive traits may be carried on an X chromosome. Since males have only one X chromosome, two recessive genes are not needed for the trait to be expressed in

them. Females, who carry two X chromosomes, need two recessive genes for a recessive sex-linked trait to be expressed. Thus, sex-linked inheritance is much more common among males than females.

10   Traits that result from the interaction of a number of genes are transmitted by *polygenic* inheritance.

11   *Multifactorial* inheritance involves the interaction of genetic and environmental forces.

12   Chromosomal abnormalities can result in birth defects. The most common is Down syndrome.

13   Through genetic counseling, expectant parents can receive information about the mathematical odds of having children who will be afflicted with certain birth defects.

14   Amniocentesis, chorionic villus sampling, alpha fetoprotein testing, ultrasound, umbilical cord assessment, and fetoscopy are procedures used to determine whether a fetus is developing normally or is afflicted with certain birth defects.

15   It is difficult to disentangle the relative contributions of heredity and environment to development. Today, developmentalists consider these factors to interact. Methods for studying their relative effects include selective breeding in animals, twin studies, adoption studies, consanguinity studies, prenatal studies, studies that manipulate the environment, and studies that compare histories.

16   Physical and physiological traits are strongly influenced by heredity. The influence of heredity on intelligence increases with age, although the environment is also important. Some aspects of personality, too, seem to be inherited. Temperamental characteristics such as shyness, and mental disorders such as autism, depression, schizophrenia, and alcoholism, are all influenced by heredity.

Key Terms

heredity (page 52)
environment (52)
nature-versus-nurture controversy (52)
zygote (56)
gamete (56)
follicle (56)
uterus (57)
fallopian tube (57)
chromosome (57)
meiosis (58)
mitosis (58)
gene (58)
DNA (deoxyribonucleic acid) (58)
dizygotic twins (60)
monozygotic twins (60)
traits (61)
allele (61)
independent segregation (61)
dominant inheritance (62)
homozygous (62)
heterozygous (62)
recessive inheritance (63)
phenotype (63)

genotype (63)
multiple alleles (63)
sex-linked inheritance (64)
polygenic inheritance (64)
multifactorial inheritance (64)
carrier (66)
Down syndrome (69)
genetic counseling (71)
karyotype (71)
amniocentesis (72)
chorionic villus sampling (CVS) (72)
alpha fetoprotein (AFP) (72)
ultrasound (72)
fetoscopy (72)
tabula rasa (73)
reaction range (75)
maturation (75)
developmental behavioral genetics (77)
concordance (82)
infantile autism (83)
depression (85)
neurotransmitter (85)
schizophrenia (85)

Suggested Readings

Apgar, V., & Beck, J. (1983). *Is my baby all right?* New York: Trident. An explanation, for the lay reader, of birth defects—what they are, how they are caused, how they may be prevented, and when to seek genetic counseling. The book includes many good illustrations.

Kitzinger, S. (1988). *Your baby, your way—Making pregnancy decisions & birth plans.* New York: Pantheon. A book written by a childbirth educator that offers a step-by-step guide for making decisions concerning childbirth.

Singer, S. (1985). *Human genetics* (2d ed.). New York: Freeman. A solid account of genetic principles and how they apply to people. Beginning with Mendel's principles, it considers genes, gene pools, genetic disorders, and counseling.

Tannenhaus, N. (1988). *Pre-conceptions.* Chicago: Contemporary Press. Up-to-date information on the effects of all aspects of one's lifestyle on an unborn child's health and development.

Watson, J. (1968). *The double helix: Being a personal account of the discovery of the structure of DNA.* New York: Atheneum. Classic, gossipy account of one of the great discoveries in genetic research. Watson pats himself on the back in an amusing and memorable set of portraits.

CHAPTER 3

PRENATAL DEVELOPMENT

I f I could have watched you grow
as a magical mother might,
if I could have seen through my magical transparent belly,
there would have been such ripening within. . . .

Anne Sexton, 1966

PREVIEW QUESTIONS

- How is a new life created?
- What happens during the three stages of prenatal development?
- What capabilities does the fetus have?
- How does a mother's lifestyle affect her fetus?
- What kinds of birth defects can be transmitted by mothers and by fathers?
- How can infertility be treated or overcome?

JASON'S LIFE BEGINS long before he gives his first lusty yell after leaving his mother's womb. If he were to be born in China rather than the United States, his birthday would be the supposed date of his conception rather than the date of his birth—and thus would appropriately recognize the importance of his 9 months in the womb.

Julia recognizes the importance of those months. From the time she realizes that a new life is growing within her, she makes dozens of decisions that change her own life—about smoking, drinking, eating, every activity in her life. In short, almost every choice she makes in pregnancy is influenced by the presence of this child, whose arrival, she knows, will alter her life even more. Julia's awareness is all to the good, because the months before Jason sees the light of day are vital for his future well-being.

In this chapter, we see what happens during the time when a baby is still inside the mother's body—how it grows, how its parents feel about its expected arrival, and how the rest of its life is influenced by this first environment. We also consider how a pregnancy can end before term, and how a pregnancy may begin in ways which would have been impossible only a few years ago.

The Experience of Pregnancy

The birth of a baby—especially a firstborn—changes the life of everyone in the family. Jason's arrival is a milestone in Jess and Julia's lives, as it changes their personal identity, their emotional outlook, and their relationships with each other, with their own parents, and with the rest of the world. Even before a baby is born, lasting transformations begin to take place. First, the woman's physiological changes of pregnancy (see Table 3-1) are more dramatic than any she experiences at any other time of life (Abrams & Viederman, 1988). Then, the psychological effects for both expectant parents are profound.

TABLE 3-1

SIGNS OF PREGNANCY

SIGN	WHEN IT APPEARS	OTHER POSSIBLE CAUSES
POSSIBLE SIGNS		
Amenorrhea (absence of menstruation)	Usually throughout pregnancy	Travel, fatigue, stress, fear of pregnancy, hormonal problems or illness, extreme weight gain or loss
Morning sickness (any time)	2–7 weeks after conception	Food poisoning, tension, infection, a variety of diseases
Frequent urination	Usually 6–12 weeks after conception	Urinary tract infection, diuretics, tension
Tingling, tender, swollen breasts	As early as a few days after conception	Birth control pills, menstruation
Changes in color of vaginal and cervical tissue as blood flow increases to area*	First trimester	Menstruation
Darkening of areola around nipple and elevation of tiny glands around nipple	First trimester	Hormonal imbalance
Blue and pink lines under skin on breast and later on abdomen	First trimester	Hormonal imbalance
Food cravings	First trimester	Poor diet, imagination
Darkening of line from navel to pubis	Fourth or fifth month	Hormonal imbalance
PROBABLE SIGNS		
Softening of uterus and cervix*	2–8 weeks after conception	Delayed menstrual period
Enlarging of uterus and cervix*	8–12 weeks	Tumor
Intermittent painless contractions	Early in pregnancy, increasing in frequency	Bowel contractions
Fetal movements	First noted at 14–20 weeks of pregnancy	Gas, bowel contractions
POSITIVE SIGNS		
Visualization of fetus through ultrasound*	4–6 weeks after conception	None
Fetal heartbeat*	At 10–20 weeks[†]	None
Fetal movements felt through abdomen*	After 16 weeks	None

*Signs of pregnancy looked for in a medical examination.
[†]Depending on device used.
Source: A. Eisenberg, Murkoff, & Hathaway, 1984, pp. 19–21.

Parents typically face four tasks:

- Development of an emotional attachment to the fetus
- Acceptance of a relationship with the fetus
- Resolution of their relationship with their same-sex parents
- Resolution of dependency issues (Valentine, 1982)

Emotional attachment to the fetus takes time. At first, as the medical signs (Table 3-1) begin to confirm Julia's pregnancy, she and Jess are excited, nervous, joyful, and uncertain, all at once. But the baby is still months away, and Julia and Jess base their first reactions on their fantasies and anxieties about parenthood. Yet even before they have a baby to hold, they, like most parents, already feel attached to their developing child.

Still, they are ambivalent: they realize how much this baby will change their lives, and they wonder, "Can I afford this? Won't this tie me down? Am I ready to be a parent?" As with most parents-to-be, positive feelings outweigh negative ones. Julia feels the intimate physical presence of the fetus, of course; and Jess is among those expectant fathers who experience physical symptoms of pregnancy like nausea, backaches, headaches, weight gain, and intensified oral cravings (Colman & Colman, 1971; Liebenberg, 1969). Such symptoms seem to help these fathers participate in the pregnancy.

By the eighth month, Julia and Jess are aware of the fetus's sleep-wake cycles and temperament, feel attached to the fetus, and have a mental portrait of the fetus, imagining what it looks like and what its sex is (Stainton, 1985). Julia sometimes has nightmares that her baby will be born with a birth defect; when she awakens, she tells herself that the odds of having a normal, healthy baby are in her favor—and she pushes the worrisome thoughts away. By the end of the pregnancy, both parents' emotional attachment to the coming baby appears to be well established (even though they may have guessed the sex wrong).

As Julia and Jess accept their relationship with the child they will have, they try to recognize that their child will be an individual, not just an extension of themselves. They also acknowledge their willingness to take responsibility for raising and caring for the child. This awareness of the job of parenthood enables them to accomplish a vital task in their own development—resolving their relationship with their own parents. This begins as the expectant parents realize that they are about to take on the very roles they once resented and rebelled against. With the birth of a first child, the new mother steps into the role her own mother once assumed, and the new father takes on the role his father held. Typically, both prospective parents gain a new appreciation of the challenges of parenthood and of their own parents.

Finally, expectant parents work on the resolution of their own dependency issues. Ideally, in marriage, husband and wife help each other through difficult periods, but during pregnancy, when both partners go through great changes, neither can support the other as much as each would like. They often find themselves thinking along traditional lines: Julia is anxious about her ability to be a good parent and Jess worries about financial responsibilities. Each one has to become more independent and has to change identity from that of a child who is taken care of to that of a parent who gives care.

Some of these issues are most prominent before the birth of the first child; others are important in each successive pregnancy. With each new baby, the parents' responsibility is greater, their anxiety about the baby's and the mother's health is just as sharp, and they now have a new worry—how the older children will be affected by the new arrival.

Many couples find help by attending classes for prospective parents. Such classes can provide far more than physical instruction for the delivery itself; the best of them also offer help in making the necessary psychological adjustments.

Before Jason's parents and Vicky's can beam and grin at their new babies and their new status as parents, a complex and rapid development is going on inside the womb. Let us see what is happening.

Prenatal Development

THE THREE STAGES OF PRENATAL DEVELOPMENT

The average length of pregnancy, or *gestation*, is 266 days. After fertilization and throughout the prenatal (gestational) period, an immensely complicated genetic program begins to direct the development of billions of specialized cells. The single fertilized cell quickly divides, grows, and divides again. The three stages of prenatal development—*germinal, embryonic,* and *fetal*—are all marked by a rapid increase in the number of cells making up the new being, which becomes increasingly complex. (Figure 3-1, below, shows the early development of the ovum and embryo; and a month-by-month description of prenatal development is given in Table 3-2, on pages 96–97.)

gestation Period of time from conception to birth; normal full-term gestation is 266 days.

Germinal Stage (Fertilization to 2 Weeks)

During the *germinal stage,* the organism divides, becomes more complex, and implants itself in the wall of the uterus. Attachment to the uterus marks the end of the germinal stage and occurs about 2 weeks after conception.

Within 36 hours after fertilization, the single-celled zygote that will be the child Vicky enters a period of rapid cell division (mitosis). Seventy-two hours after fertilization, it has divided into 32 cells; a day later it has about 70 cells. This division continues until the original single cell has developed into the 800 billion or more specialized cells that make up the person who will be born and known as Vicky.

While the fertilized ovum is dividing, it is also making its way down the fallopian tube to the uterus, which it reaches in 3 or 4 days. By the time it gets there, its form has changed into a fluid-filled sphere called a *blastocyst*, which then floats freely in the uterus for a day or two. Some cells around the edge of

germinal stage First 2 weeks of development of a conceptus, beginning at fertilization, characterized by rapid cell division and increasing complexity, and ending when the conceptus attaches to the wall of the uterus.

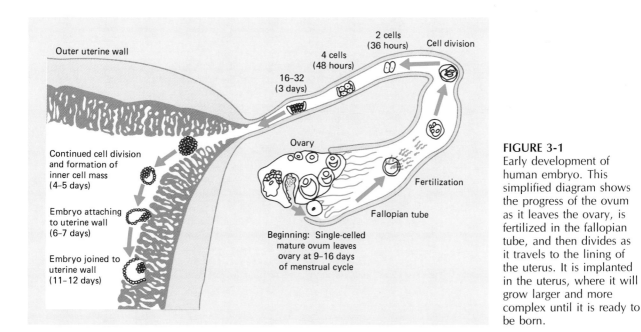

FIGURE 3-1
Early development of human embryo. This simplified diagram shows the progress of the ovum as it leaves the ovary, is fertilized in the fallopian tube, and then divides as it travels to the lining of the uterus. It is implanted in the uterus, where it will grow larger and more complex until it is ready to be born.

TABLE 3-2

	MONTH	DESCRIPTION
	First month	During the first month, growth is more rapid than at any other time during prenatal or postnatal life: the embryo reaches a size 10,000 times greater than the zygote. By the end of the first month it measures from ¼ to ½ inch in length. Blood flows through its veins and arteries, which are very small. It has a minuscule heart, beating 65 times a minute. It already has the beginnings of brain, kidneys, liver, and digestive tract. The umbilical cord, its lifeline to the mother, is working. By looking very closely through a microscope, it is possible to see swellings on the head that will eventually become eyes, ears, mouth, and nose. Sex cannot yet be determined.
	Second month	By the end of the second month, the embryo looks like a well-proportioned, small-scale baby. It is less than 1 inch long and weighs only $\frac{1}{13}$ ounce. Its head is half its total body length. Facial parts are clearly developed, with tongue and teeth buds. The arms have hands, fingers, and thumbs, and the legs have knees, ankles, and toes. It has a thin covering of skin and can make handprints and footprints. The first bone cells appear at about 8 weeks. Brain impulses coordinate the function of the organ system. Sex organs are developing; the heartbeat is steady. The stomach produces digestive juices; the liver, blood cells. The kidneys remove uric acid from the blood. The skin is now sensitive enough to react to tactile stimulation. If an aborted 8-week-old embryo is stroked, it reacts by flexing its trunk, extending its head, and moving back its arms.
	Third month	By the end of the third month, the developing person (now called a *fetus*) weighs 1 ounce and measures about 3 inches in length. It has fingernails, toenails, eyelids (still closed), vocal cords, lips, and a prominent nose. Its head is still large—about one-third its total length—and its forehead is high. Sex can be easily determined. The organ systems are functioning, and so the fetus may now breathe, swallow amniotic fluid into the lungs and expel it, and occasionally urinate. Its ribs and vertebrae have turned to cartilage. The fetus can now make a variety of specialized responses: it can move its legs, feet, thumbs, and head; its mouth can open and close and swallow. If its eyelids are touched, it squints; if its palm is touched, it makes a partial fist; if its lip is touched, it will suck; and if the sole of the foot is stroked, the toes will fan out. These reflex behaviors will be present at birth but will disappear during the first months of life.
	Fourth month	The body is catching up to the head, which is now only one-fourth the total body length, the same proportion it will be at birth. The fetus now measures 8 to 10 inches and weighs about 6 ounces. The umbilical cord is as long as the fetus and will continue to grow with it. The placenta is now fully developed. The mother may be able to feel the fetus kicking, a movement known as *quickening*, which some societies and religious groups consider the beginning of human life. The reflex activities that appeared in the third month are now brisker because of increased muscular development.
	Fifth month	The fetus, now weighing about 12 ounces to 1 pound and measuring about 1 foot, begins to show signs of an individual personality. It has definite sleep-wake patterns, has a favorite position in the uterus (called its *lie*), and becomes more active—kicking, stretching, squirming, and even hiccuping. By putting an ear to the mother's abdomen, it is possible to hear the fetal heartbeat. The sweat and sebaceous glands are functioning. The respiratory system is not yet adequate to sustain life outside the womb; a baby born at this time does not usually survive. Coarse hair has begun to grow for eyebrows and eyelashes, fine hair is on the head, and a woolly hair called *lanugo* covers the body.

TABLE 3-2

CONTINUED

MONTH	DESCRIPTION	
Sixth month	The rate of fetal growth has slowed down a little—by the end of the sixth month the fetus is about 14 inches long and weighs 1¼ pounds. It now has fat pads under the skin; the eyes are complete, opening and closing and looking in all directions; and it is able to hear. It can maintain regular breathing for 24 hours; it cries, and it can make a fist with a strong grip. A fetus born during the sixth month still has only a slight chance of survival, because the breathing apparatus has still not matured. Some fetuses of this age do survive outside the womb, however.	
Seventh month	By the end of the seventh month, the fetus, 16 inches long and weighing 3 to 5 pounds, now has fully developed reflex patterns. It cries, breathes, and swallows, and may suck its thumb. The lanugo may disappear at about this time, or it may remain until shortly after birth. Head hair may continue to grow. The chances that a fetus weighing at least 3½ pounds will survive are good, provided it receives intensive medical attention. It will probably need to be kept in an isolette until a weight of 5 pounds is attained.	
Eighth month	The 8-month-old fetus is 18 to 20 inches long and weighs between 5 and 7 pounds. Its living quarters are becoming cramped, and so its movements are curtailed. During this month and the next, a layer of fat is developing over the fetus's entire body, which enables it to adjust to varying temperatures outside the womb.	
Ninth month	About a week before birth, the fetus stops growing, having reached an average weight of about 7½ pounds and a length of about 20 inches, with boys tending to be a little longer and heavier than girls. Fat pads continue to form, the organ systems are operating more efficiently, the heart rate increases, and more wastes are expelled through the umbilical cord. The reddish color of the skin is fading. At birth, the fetus will have been in the womb for approximately 266 days, although gestational age is usually estimated at 280 days, since most doctors date the pregnancy from the mother's last menstrual period.	

Sources for photos: © Petit Format/Nestle/Science Source/Photo Researchers (1 month, 2 months, 7 months, and 8–9 months); © Lennart Nilsson, *A Child Is Born,* English trans. © 1966, 1977 by Dell Publishing Co. Inc. (3 months); © J. S. Allen/Daily Telegraph/International Stock (4 months); James Stevenson/Photo Researchers (5 months).

the blastocyst cluster on one side to form the *embryonic disk,* a thickened cell mass from which the baby will develop. This mass is already differentiating into two layers. The upper layer, the *ectoderm,* will eventually become the outer layer of Vicky's skin and her nails, hair, teeth, sensory organs, and nervous system, including the brain and spinal cord. The lower layer, the *endoderm,* will develop into her digestive system, liver, pancreas, salivary glands, and respiratory system. Later, a middle layer, the *mesoderm,* will develop and differentiate into her inner layer of skin and her muscles, skeleton, and excretory and circulatory systems.

During the germinal stage, other parts of the blastocyst develop into the organs that will nurture and protect the unborn child: the *placenta,* the *umbilical cord,* and the *amniotic sac.* The placenta, an unusual multipurpose organ, is connected to the embryo by the umbilical cord, through which it delivers oxygen and nourishment to the fetus and removes its body wastes. The placenta also helps combat internal infection and gives the unborn child immunity to various diseases. It produces the hormones that support pregnancy, prepare the mother's breasts for lactation, and eventually stimulate the uterine contractions that will expel the baby from her body. The amniotic sac is a fluid-filled membrane that encases the developing baby, protecting it and giving it room to move.

The *trophoblast,* the outer cell layer of the blastocyst, produces very small, threadlike structures that penetrate the lining of the uterine wall and enable the blastocyst to cling there until it is implanted. Upon implantation, the blastocyst has about 150 cells; when this cell mass is fully implanted in the uterus, it is an *embryo.*

Embryonic Stage (2 to 8–12 Weeks)

embryonic stage Second stage of pregnancy (2 to 8–12 weeks), characterized by differentiation of body parts and systems and ending when the bone cells begin to appear.

critical period Specific time during development when an event has its greatest impact.

trimester First, second, or third 3-month period of pregnancy.

spontaneous abortion Natural expulsion from the uterus of a conceptus that cannot survive outside the womb; also called miscarriage.

The Embryonic Stage as a Critical Period During the *embryonic stage,* Vicky's organs and major body systems—respiratory, digestive, and nervous—develop. Because growth and development now proceed rapidly, this is a critical period when the embryo is most vulnerable to influences of the prenatal environment. A *critical period* is a specific time during development when an animal or a person needs to have appropriate experiences to bring about normal adult functioning. Almost all developmental birth defects (cleft palate, incomplete or missing limbs, blindness, deafness) occur during the first *trimester* (3-month period) of pregnancy. The most severely defective embryos usually do not survive beyond this time and are aborted spontaneously (Garn, 1966).

Spontaneous Abortion in the Embryonic Stage Since normal development depends on many precisely controlled events, it is inevitable that something will go seriously wrong in some pregnancies. When this happens, a common result is a naturally occurring end to the pregnancy. A *miscarriage,* technically referred to as a *spontaneous abortion,* is the expulsion from the uterus of an embryo or fetus that could not survive outside the womb. Three out of four miscarriages occur within the first trimester (Garn, 1966; J. F. Miller et al., 1980). About one-third (31 percent) of all conceptions end in miscarriage (Wilcox et al., 1988).

In ancient times, people believed that a woman could be frightened into miscarrying by a clap of thunder or jostled into it if her chariot hit a rut in the street. But today we realize that the unborn child is well protected against almost all jolts and cannot be shaken loose any more easily than a good unripe apple can be shaken from the tree (Guttmacher, 1973). Most miscarriages result from abnormal pregnancies.

Chromosomal abnormalities may be present in about half of all spontaneous abortions (Ash, Vennart, & Carter, 1977). Other possible causes include a defective ovum or sperm, an unfavorable location for implantation, a breakdown in supplies of oxygen or nourishment caused by abnormal development of the umbilical cord, and some physiological abnormality of the mother. Some 30 percent of spontaneous abortions may be caused by a symptomless herpes virus in the uterus; although the mother seems healthy, the virus apparently crosses the placenta and harms the embryo (Goldsmith, 1985).

Women who have previously had babies with such neural-tube defects as spina bifida (a defect in the closure of the vertebral canal) or anencephaly (a condition in which a major part of the brain is missing) are more likely to abort.

This may be because of the presence of transferrin C3, a gene that occurs in about 17 percent of white couples, seems linked to recurrent miscarriages, and may be implicated in neural-tube defects (Weitkamp & Schacter, 1985).

A promising new treatment to help women who repeatedly miscarry is based on the belief that such women have a defect of the immune system: they lack a type of antibody that normally masks the cells of the trophoblast so that the mother's body does not see them as foreign (that is, not part of her body). A new experimental therapy which immunizes women with foreign white blood cells to induce their bodies to make the blocking antibodies has enabled 75 to 80 percent of repeated aborters to carry babies to term, but since a small minority of babies (one-third of 1 percent) born through this technique have had medical problems possibly linked to the technique, it is still controversial (Kolata, 1988a).

While the risk to the mother in a spontaneous abortion is small, an infection, a hemorrhage, or an embolism (obstruction of a blood vessel) can sometimes complicate a miscarriage. The risk of complications is greatest for women over 29, as well as for women who have less access to health care, such as single women and members of minority groups. The risk is also greater for women who miscarry in the second trimester (Berman, MacKay, Grimes, & Binkin, 1985).

Fetal Stage (8–12 Weeks to Birth)

Happily, Vicky's gestation proceeds normally. With the appearance of the first bone cells at about 8 weeks, the embryo begins to become a *fetus;* by 12 weeks Vicky is fully in the *fetal stage.* During the long period until birth, the finishing touches are put on her various body parts, and her body changes in form and grows about 20 times in length.

fetus Conceptus between 8 to 12 weeks and birth.

fetal stage Final stage of pregnancy (8–12 weeks to birth), characterized by increased detail of body parts and greatly enlarged body size.

The appearance of the first bone cells at about 8 weeks is considered a sign of the beginning of the fetal stage. However, since organs in some systems continue to form beyond 8 weeks, the embryonic period is sometimes designated as lasting the first 12 weeks. The fetal stage is distinguished by rapid growth and increased complexity of function.

As a fetus, Vicky is far from a passive passenger in Ellen's womb. She kicks, turns, flexes her body, somersaults, squints, swallows, makes a fist, hiccups, and sucks her thumb. She responds to both sound and vibrations, showing that she can hear and feel.

Even inside the womb, Vicky is a unique human being. Women who bear more than one child often notice differences in the amount of activity from one to another. One mother of a child who later turned out to be hyperactive said, "I knew while Curt was still in the womb that he was going to be a pistol! He bounced around so much inside me that I would automatically put my hand over my abdomen to keep him from popping out!" (M. A. Stewart & Olds, 1973, p. 253). Similarly, many mothers claim that their offspring were as placid before birth as they are afterwards.

Furthermore, fetuses move in different ways. Jason likes to kick with his feet or punch with his hands, Vicky tends to squirm slowly, and some other babies make sharp, spasmodic movements. Differences in kind or amount of fetal activity seem to predict how active, restless, or resistant to handling a baby will be during the first year (Sontag, 1966). Some of these patterns seem to persist into adulthood, supporting the notion of inborn temperament.

By the last months of pregnancy, Julia impatiently awaits her baby's birth,

We have good scientific evidence that fetuses can hear, but we do not know whether early exposure will make them appreciate classical music.

for reasons both negative and positive. She feels big and awkward, has trouble finding a comfortable position for sleeping, tires easily—and is longing to return to her normal shape and size. But she is also eager to see and hold this new person who has been such an intimate part of her.

PRENATAL ABILITIES AND ACTIVITIES

Fetal Hearing

"Which sense is the first to develop?" asks a popular trivia game. But until we have scientific evidence that a fetus prefers, say, the smell of lilacs over the smell of rotten eggs, anyone playing this game should challenge the answer card, which says, "smell." Babies only hours old do show that they can smell (as we shall see in Chapter 5), but a considerable body of research has found that fetuses show other senses: they respond to being touched (refer back to Table 3-2), and they can hear.

When Julia was 7 months pregnant, she went to a fireworks display. At each burst, she felt the fetus within rock about and these agitated movements did not stop until the flares and Roman candles did. Stories like this are common; most parents are convinced that a child does hear before birth—and they seem to be right. Over the past 50 years, scientific experiments have demonstrated that fetuses respond to bells and vibrations and can discriminate between different tones (Bernard & Sontag, 1947; Sontag & Richards, 1938; Sontag & Wallace, 1934, 1936).

A recent experiment on fetal hearing used ultrasound to observe eye blinks in 236 fetuses between 16 and 32 weeks of gestation (Birnholz & Benacerraf, 1983). When investigators held a battery-powered noise source firmly on the mother's abdomen directly above the fetus's ear, 24-week-old fetuses began to blink at the sounds. By 28 weeks (the start of the third trimester), such responses were consistent in all but eight fetuses. After birth, two of the eight fetuses in the group who had not shown any such blink response turned out to be deaf. Since none of the children who had blinked to the sounds in utero (in the uterus) was deaf after birth, this procedure may serve as a prenatal test for deafness.

Fetal Learning

Vicky and Jason not only can hear inside the womb; they also seem able to remember and discriminate what they have heard. The fact that newborns prefer their own mothers' voices to those of other women, and female voices to male voices, suggests that babies may develop preferences for the kinds of sounds they hear before birth (DeCasper & Spence, 1986).

Researchers testing this hypothesis asked pregnant women to tape-record three different readings—one from the book *The Cat in the Hat*, by Dr. Seuss, one called *The Dog in the Fog* (the last 28 paragraphs of *The Cat in the Hat*, with major nouns changed), and a third from the story *The King, the Mice, and the Cheese* (DeCasper & Spence, 1986). During the last 6 weeks of pregnancy, the women recited just one of the readings (the "target" story) an average of 67 times.

On the third day after birth, babies who had heard one of the readings prenatally sucked more (on nipples that activated recordings of these stories) to hear the recording of the story they had heard in the womb, showing that they

BOX 3-1 ■ AROUND THE WORLD

CULTURE AND TECHNOLOGY

What happens when state-of-the-art technology is applied in the service of ancient cultural mores? One problematic meeting of high technology and centuries-old attitudes can be seen in the use of amniocentesis in India. This diagnostic procedure for examining fetal chromosomes involves withdrawing cells from the amniotic fluid in which the fetus floats. The procedure was developed to detect the presence of certain birth defects; it always discloses the sex of the fetus, which may be pertinent for determining the risk of sex-linked disorders.

In the United States today, amniocentesis is commonly performed on pregnant women over age 35 to detect disorders in the fetus. The woman is usually asked whether she wants to know her baby's sex ahead of time—and often the answer is no. Over the past few years in India, however, thousands of women have undergone amniocentesis solely to determine the sex of their unborn children. And tens of thousands of abortions have followed the news that the fetus is female.

One woman pregnant with a fifth daughter burst into tears, crying that her husband was going to throw her out of the house if she did not produce a son (Weisman, 1988). In India, it is sons who typically support aging parents; daugh-ters usually live with their in-laws after marriage. Further-more, a bride is expected to have a dowry, which may be as much as $10,000, equivalent to a family's yearly in-come. It is no wonder that families with daughters and no sons are often terrified of bankruptcy and are willing to heed advertisements to clinics that say, "Better to spend 500 rupees now than 50,000 rupees later" (p. A9).

As the result of protests in India by feminist groups and health officials, a law was recently passed to permit amnio-centesis only for the purpose of determining genetic dis-orders. It requires that the woman be at least 35 years old or have a medical or family history that indicates risk, and it prescribes prison sentences and fines for doctors and pa-tients involved with illegal amniocentesis. Even though the law does not provide for strict enforcement its very exis-tence seems to have reduced testing for sex determination— or at least to have driven it underground.

One obstetrician, however, responded to the shocked comments of some foreign physicians by saying, "You can-not pass judgment on what is happening in our country— taking your norms and applying them to us. Others may regard it as a barbaric practice . . . but nobody can have a 100 percent purist view in this world. The law has been changed, but what have we done to change social atti-tudes?" (Weisman, 1988, p. A9)

recognized their own target story. On the other hand, babies in a control group, who had not heard a reading before birth, responded equally to all three record-ings. This seems to show that babies can learn even before birth.

The Prenatal Environment

During her pregnancy, Ellen finds it increasingly easy to think of the fetus as a person, especially after she has chosen the baby's name—Victoria. As a first-time mother over age 35 she has had amniocentesis, and she is happy to learn that her baby will be a girl. (For a different perspective on sex determination by amniocentesis, see Box 3-1.) With this new attitude, Ellen begins thinking even more seriously about how to take care of her child-to-be. From her reading she learns that a mother's nutrition, drug intake, and perhaps even moods alter the environment of the developing fetus and affect its growth. She stops smoking, gives up her daily glass of wine, and eats better. Such changes are all to the good. A fetus is a tough and resilient organism capable of withstanding many shocks and stresses, but providing the best prenatal environment possible gives the best start in life.

Most of what we know about prenatal hazards we have learned either from animal research or from studies in which mothers reported, after childbirth, what they had eaten while they were pregnant, what drugs they had taken, how much radiation they had been exposed to, what illnesses they had had, and so forth. Both these methods have limitations: it is not always accurate to apply findings from animals to human beings, and mothers do not always remember what they did during pregnancy. Because of ethical considerations, it is impossible to set up the kind of controlled experiments that might provide more definitive answers, but even with such limitations, we have a great deal of knowledge about prenatal influences.

teratogenic *Capable of causing birth defects.*

Particular factors in the prenatal environment affect different fetuses differently. Some environmental factors are ***teratogenic***—a term which means "producing birth defects"—in some cases but have little or no effect in others. We do not know why this is so, but research seems to indicate that the timing of an environmental insult, its intensity, and its interaction with other factors are important.

What are some prenatal influences?

MATERNAL FACTORS

Nutrition

It is a mistake to use the cliché "eating for two" as an excuse to double the amount of food a pregnant woman eats, but it is certainly true that the mother is eating for the fetus's health as well as her own. Although the genetic information directs the fetus's growth, the mother has to supply the nutrients that make growth possible. If an essential nutrient is missing for the diet or if a toxic substance is added, the results can be serious and lasting.

Importance of Good Nutrition in Pregnancy Babies develop best when their mothers eat well. Women who gain in the recommended range (between 26 and 35 pounds) are less likely to miscarry, or to bear stillborn or low-birthweight babies. Most women, however, gain less than they should during pregnancy—partly because obstetricians used to recommend gaining less and partly because of societal pressures to look thin. Gaining too little is actually riskier than gaining too much (National Center for Health Statistics, 1986). Women at greatest risk of gaining too little are those who smoke, are underweight or overweight before pregnancy, are under age 20 or over age 35, have only a grade school education, already have three or more children, or are poor, black, or unwed.

Other recent research has established the importance of eating breakfast during pregnancy, since pregnant women who skip breakfast show changes in the levels of various substances in the bloodstream that are not shown by nonpregnant women (Metzger, Ravnikar, Vileisis, & Freinkel, 1982).

A well-balanced diet for anyone includes daily intake of foods from the seven different food groups: dairy products, meat and meat alternatives, fruits, and vegetables containing vitamin A, fruits and vegetables with vitamin C, other fruits and vegetables, breads and cereals, and fats and oils. When pregnant, women need an extra 300 to 500 calories daily and 30 more grams of protein (Winick, 1981). Pregnant teenagers, ill or undernourished women, women who took birth control pills till shortly before pregnancy, and women who are under considerable stress need extra nutrients (J.E. Brown, 1983).

Malnutrition *Malnutrition and fetal development* Mothers who eat well—both before and during pregnancy—have fewer complications during pregnancy and childbirth and bear healthier babies, while mothers whose diet is inadequate are more likely to bear premature or low-birthweight infants or to have babies who are born dead or die soon after birth (Burke, Beal, Kirkwood, & Stuart, 1943; Read, Habicht, Lechtig, & Klein, 1973).

Malnutrition also affects the developing brain. Researchers examined the brains of fetuses obtained from therapeutic abortions (those done to protect the mother's health or to prevent the birth of a child with defects) performed on malnourished women; they also examined the brains of infants who died accidentally or of severe malnutrition in the first year of life. They found that the number of cells in the human brain increases in a linear fashion until birth, and then more slowly until 6 months of age. After that, there is no increase in the number of brain cells; there is only an increase in weight. Since the brains of malnourished infants contain as few as 60 percent of the normal number, these infants seem to have suffered malnutrition in utero (Winick, Brasel, & Rosso, 1972).

A fetus develops best when the mother eats well. Pregnant women need extra calories and extra protein and should gain 26 to 35 pounds. It is possible to get all the essential nutrients without gaining too much.

Overcoming the effects of malnutrition Different kinds of help can aid the offspring of malnourished women. When extra food was given to malnourished pregnant women, their babies showed increased birthweight, improved visual alertness, and higher activity levels than the babies of mothers in control groups who did not receive dietary supplements (Read et al., 1973; Vuori et al., 1979). In addition, better-nourished mothers breastfeed longer, conferring an advantage upon their infants, as we will see in Chapter 5 (Read et al., 1973).

A malnourished fetus may also benefit from help after birth. In one study of mothers and babies from poor socioeconomic circumstances, researchers randomly assigned some infants who showed signs of poor development to an intellectually enriching program at a day care center before 3 months of age, while others remained at home with their mothers. Three years later the children took intelligence tests, and the babies who had been in the enrichment program tested higher (Zeskind & Ramey, 1981).

Since fetal nutrition affects both the long-term physical and the long-term intellectual development of the child, proper care of the fetus is important both to the infant's parents and to society as a whole. This is a special concern for babies from low-income families, in which other kinds of deprivation can aggravate the effects of poor nutrition. More effective prenatal care can help reduce the need for extensive postnatal attention.

Drug Intake

At one time, the placenta was thought to protect the developing baby for injurious elements in the mother's body. We now know that virtually everything the mother takes in makes its way in some form and to some degree to the new life in her uterus. Drugs may cross the placenta, just as oxygen, carbon dioxide, and water do, and they have the strongest effects if taken early in pregnancy. As we have seen, the embryo develops most rapidly in its first few months and is especially vulnerable to disease and accident during this period.

Drugs known to be harmful are the antibiotics streptomycin and tetracycline; the sulfonamides; vitamins A, B6, C, D, and K in excessive amounts; certain barbiturates, opiates, and other central nervous system depressants; and several hormones, including progestin, androgens, and synthetic estrogens such as diethylstilbestrol (DES). Accutane, a drug frequently prescribed for severe acne, has been linked to a variety of birth defects, including facial malformation, missing or misplaced ears, mental retardation, and heart defects (Lott, Bocian, Pribram, & Leitner, 1984). The U.S. Food and Drug Administration has taken unusual new measures, ordering this drug's manufacturer to place a photograph of a deformed infant in the warning label given to patients and asking doctors to have patients sign a consent form indicating that they are taking measures to avoid pregnancy (Altman, 1988b).

Even ordinary aspirin can cause trouble. When a woman takes aspirin within 5 days before delivery, there is an increased tendency toward bleeding in both mother and infant (Stuart, Gross, Elrad, & Graeber, 1982). While this bleeding is not serious for normal full-term babies, it can be harmful to low-birth-weight infants. For safety's sake, then, aspirin should be added to the list of drugs to be avoided throughout pregnancy. In fact, the Committee on Drugs of the American Academy of Pediatrics (1982) recommends that *no* medication be prescribed for a pregnant or breastfeeding woman unless it is absolutely essential for her health or that of her child.

Birth Control Pills   The children of women who take oral contraceptives early in pregnancy may suffer birth defects. The most likely problem is a slightly higher incidence of certain cardiovascular defects. Women who smoke more than a pack of cigarettes a day and also take oral contraceptives are more likely to have babies with birth defects (Bracken, Holford, White, & Kelsy, 1978).

Diethylstilbestrol (DES)   The effects of taking a drug during pregnancy do not always show up immediately. In the late 1940s and early 1950s the synthetic hormone diethylstilbestrol was widely prescribed (ineffectually, as it turned out) to prevent miscarriage. Years later, when the daughters of women who had taken DES during pregnancy reached puberty, and young adulthood, some developed a rare form of vaginal cancer. At first, doctors were afraid that as many as 1 in 250 "DES daughters" would develop this cancer (Herbst, Kurman, Scully, & Poskanzer, 1971) or show microscopic abnormalities of the vaginal tract (A. Sherman et al., 1974). A recent estimate is that 1 in 1000 DES daughters will contract genital cancer by the mid-thirties (Melnick, Cole, Anderson, & Herbst, 1987).

A number of other problems linked to DES have emerged. DES daughters have more trouble bearing their own children, with higher risks of miscarriage or premature delivery (A. Barnes et al., 1980) , and DES sons show a higher rate of infertility and reproductive abnormalities (Stenchever et al., 1981). In light of all these problems, it is advisable for all children of women who took DES during pregnancy to get regular checkups.

Caffeine   How is a fetus affected by caffeine ingested by the mother in coffee, cola drinks, chocolate, or tea? Can this cause trouble? In animal studies, force-feeding very high doses of caffeine to pregnant rats has not been found to have any ill effects on the baby (S. Linn et al., 1982). Because questions do remain, however, the U.S. Food and Drug Administration recommends that pregnant women avoid or use sparingly any foods, drinks, or drugs with caffeine.

Nicotine   Ellen was wise to stop smoking, since cigarettes contain nicotine, a potent drug. Aside from affecting the body systems of the smoker, nicotine has a variety of harmful effects on a fetus. The clearest finding is the tendency of pregnant smokers to bear smaller babies. On the average, a woman who smokes is twice as likely as a nonsmoker to deliver a baby whose weight is low for gestational age (Landesman-Dwyer & Emanuel, 1979; Sexton & Hebel, 1984). However, a woman who stops smoking by her fourth month of pregnancy is like a nonsmoker in her risk of delivering a low-birthweight baby (Sexton & Hebel, 1984).

Doctors at the Centers for Disease Control have identified a "fetal tobacco syndrome" of slow fetal growth caused by mothers' smoking five or more cigarettes daily, and they say that smoking during pregnancy is the most important cause of retarded growth in the developed world (Nieburg, Marks, McLaren, & Remington, 1985). Smoking by expectant mothers is linked to other complications, too—bleeding during pregnancy, miscarriage, stillbirth, and death of a baby soon after birth (U.S. Department of Health, Education, and Welfare, 1980).

Smoking also has long-term effects on children's health. A newly discovered danger is that children whose mothers smoked 10 or more cigarettes a day during pregnancy have a risk 50 percent higher than normal of developing childhood cancer (Stjernfeldt, Berglund, Lindsten, & Ludvigsson, 1986). The increased risk may turn out to be even higher, since the first large group of people whose mothers smoked during pregnancy are just reaching the age when most cancers occur (D.H. Rubin, Krasilnikoff, Leventhal, Weile, & Berget, 1986).

Also disturbing is the mounting evidence that smoking during pregnancy can affect children's cognitive and psychological development. Children aged 4 to 11 whose mothers smoked during pregnancy show poor attention span, hyperactivity, and problems with reading, spelling, mathematics, perceptual motor skills, linguistic skills, and social adjustment. They score lower on IQ tests and are more likely to be diagnosed as having minimal brain dysfunction (Landesman-Dwyer & Emanuel, 1979; Naeye & Peters, 1984; Streissguth et al., 1984). Since many of the mothers kept smoking after the birth, the children may also be suffering from the effects of passive smoking.

Alcohol   Although it is difficult to give up addictive or compulsive habits like smoking and drinking during pregnancy, many women can and do. According to one national survey, 30 percent of women who drank at all before becoming pregnant stopped during pregnancy. Still, 40 percent of pregnant women drink, compared with the 25 percent who smoke (Prager et al., 1983). And the effects of drinking on fetal development can be devastating.

Each year more than 40,000 American babies are born with alcohol-related birth defects. About 1 in 750 newborns suffer from *fetal alcohol syndrome (FAS),* a combination of facial and body abnormalities, central nervous system disorders, and mental, motor, and growth retardation. Fetal alcohol syndrome is one of the three leading causes of mental retardation, and, unlike the other two—Down syndrome and neural-tube defects—a cause that is completely preventable.

The full cluster of FAS symptoms includes, in infancy, poor sucking response, brain-wave abnormalities, and sleep disturbances; and, later in childhood, the same kinds of problems that show up in the children of smokers— short attention span, restlessness, irritability, hyperactivity, learning disabilities,

(American Cancer Society)

Nicotine has several harmful effects on a fetus. The most clearly established is the risk of low birthweight—but if a woman stops smoking by the fourth month of pregnancy, her baby is likely to be of normal weight.

fetal alcohol syndrome (FAS)   *Combination of mental, motor, and developmental abnormalities affecting the offspring of some women who drink heavily during pregnancy.*

and motor problems. Only about 1 in 10 alcohol-affected children show all these symptoms; most have just one or a few, and the link to the mother's drinking may not always be obvious (N.L. Golden, Sokol, Kuhnert, & Bottoms, 1982; K.L. Jones, Smith, Ulleland, & Streissguth; Wright et al., 1973; Ioffe, Childiaeva, & Chernick, 1984; National Institute on Alcohol Abuse and Alcoholism, NIAAA, 1986; Shaywitz, Cohen, & Shaywitz, 1980; Streissguth et al., 1984). Mothers who both drink *and* smoke while pregnant have a higher chance of bearing low-birth-weight babies who will show early learning problems (J. Martin, Martin, Lund, & Streissguth, 1977; Wright et al., 1983).

While alcoholic women are most likely to bear babies with FAS, even moderate social drinking may affect the fetus. Two recent studies of about 32,000 women assessed different outcomes. One found that women who took one or more alcoholic drinks a day, especially during early pregnancy, were more likely to have growth-retarded babies, but that women who had less than one drink a day were not putting their babies at risk (Mills, Graubard, Harley, Rhoads, & Berendes, 1984). The other study found that even women who had up to two drinks a day were no more likely than nondrinkers to have babies with congenital malformations (Mills & Graubard, 1987).

The authors of these studies, however, as well as other experts, caution that there is no known "safe" level of drinking for pregnant women. Therefore, pregnant women should limit themselves to no more than an occasional drink—or should stop drinking completely from the time they plan to conceive until they stop breastfeeding (March of Dimes Birth Defects Foundation, 1983a; NIAAA, 1986). (See Box 3–2.)

Marijuana   Until recently, researchers said that there was no clear relation between smoking marijuana and fetal development. However, fetal malformations have been produced experimentally in animals, and as long ago as 1972 the National Institute of Mental Health recommended that women of childbearing age not use marijuana, since its potential for producing birth defects was unknown.

Evidence has also mounted associating birth defects with a general lifestyle that includes heavy use of marijuana. One study found that pregnant women who used marijuana were 5 times more likely than nonusers to deliver infants with features compatible with FAS, but it was difficult to isolate the role of marijuana from other factors in the users' lives (Hingson et al., 1982).

One Canadian study used a statistical technique for determining the effects of marijuana. Researchers surveyed 583 volunteers; they interviewed them once during each trimester and examined their babies after birth. The women were grouped into four categories, ranging from nonusers (by far the largest group) to heavy users, who smoked more than five marijuana cigarettes per week. A relationship was found between marijuana and abnormalities of the nervous system, although no long-term damage has yet been proved (Fried, 1982). A later analysis of the survey data showed earlier deliveries among heavy users, averaging about 1 week earlier deliveries (Fried, Watkinson, & Willan, 1984). In themselves, such deliveries are not a serious risk, but when other factors like use of alcohol and tobacco are also involved, each source of small potential harm can contribute to a more serious consequence. For example, the earlier delivery associated with marijuana use might combine with the lower birthweight associated with tobacco, converting two small risks into one larger risk—a baby smaller than normal who is born earlier than normal.

BOX 3-2 ▪ THE EVERYDAY WORLD

ALCOHOL AND PREGNANCY

WHAT YOU SHOULD KNOW

▪ *Heavy drinking—and possibly even moderate drinking—can cause birth defects.* The most severe is fetal alcohol syndrome (FAS), a cluster of birth defects that includes facial and body abnormalities, central nervous system disorders, and mental, motor, and growth retardation. (For specifics, see text.)

▪ *You can prevent alcohol-related birth defects.* If you do not drink during your pregnancy, your baby will be free of all alcohol-related birth defects, including FAS.

WHAT YOU SHOULD DO

▪ *Stop drinking when you first begin to think about becoming pregnant.* You may not know you are pregnant until a month or two after you have conceived. Your fetus is especially vulnerable during the early stages of prenatal development, when its organs are forming.

▪ *If you have been drinking during pregnancy, stop now.* It is probably not too late to prevent harm to your baby if you stop drinking now for the rest of your pregnancy.

▪ *Avoid "party drinking."* Some research has suggested that binge drinking—five or more drinks at one time—can harm the developing baby.

▪ *Do not smoke, do not take drugs, and do eat a well-balanced diet.* Alcohol-related birth defects are more likely to occur if, in addition to drinking, you smoke, use prescription or street drugs, or are poorly nourished.

▪ *If you breastfeed your baby, use alcohol very sparingly or not at all.* Alcohol can be transmitted to your baby through your milk, and large amounts can depress the baby's nervous system.

HOW YOU CAN GET HELP

▪ *Ask your health care practitioner.* Your doctor or midwife can probably answer your questions and give you information about drinking and its effects on you and your baby.

▪ *Get help for a drinking problem.* If you think you have a drinking problem, you probably do. You owe it to your baby, as well as yourself, to get help. Check the yellow pages of your local telephone directory under "Alcoholism Information and Treatment Centers." Some of these, like Alcoholics Anonymous and some hospital and community programs, are free. Also see Resources, on page R1 of this book.

Source: Adapted from National Clearinghouse for Alcohol Information, undated.

Opiates Women addicted to such drugs as morphine, heroin, and codeine are likely to bear premature babies who have become addicted to the drugs while in the womb. The babies can often be cured of the addiction by administering other drugs in gradually decreasing amounts, but the consequences of prenatal addiction may linger at least until the age of 6.

At birth, addicted infants are restless and irritable and often suffer from tremors, convulsions, fever, vomiting, and breathing difficulties; they are twice as likely to die soon after birth as nonaddicted babies (Cobrinick, Hood, & Chused, 1959; Henly & Fitch, 1966; Ostrea & Chavez, 1979). When these babies are older, they cry more and are less alert and less responsive to stimuli (Householder, Hatcher, Burns, & Chasnoff, 1982; Strauss, Lessen-Firestone, Starr, & Ostrea, 1975). And in early childhood—from age 3 to age 6—they weigh less, are shorter, are less well adjusted socially, have a short attention span, show disturbed sleep patterns, and do poorly on tests of perception and learning (Householder et al., 1982; G. Wilson, McCreary, Kean, & Baxter, 1979). Children exposed to heroin prenatally often differ from other children in one more way: They have less early contact with their natural mothers, a factor that may also influence their development.

There have been few long-term follow-up studies on children of addicted mothers, and the ones we have tend to be inconclusive. One of the problems with locating the source of these children's problems is that few of the mothers

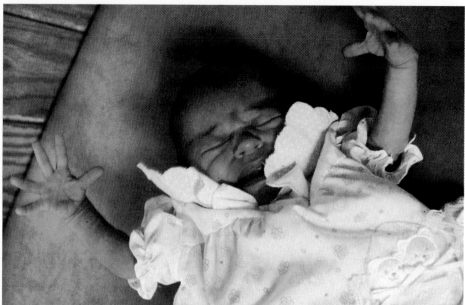

Babies whose mothers used cocaine during pregnancy begin life with massive problems. Many are preterm and small, many have neurological problems, and many—like this one-month-old baby girl—cry for long periods of time and cannot be comforted.

abuse only one drug, and so it is hard to isolate the effect of any single one. It is also difficult to separate the physiological and the psychological effects of the drugs on both parent and child. It seems clear, though, that such children are at risk and that more needs to be done to see how they can be helped.

Cocaine   Recently, the effects of cocaine have begun to be studied, and the first indications are that cocaine can influence both the outcome of a pregnancy and the health of the baby. Women who use cocaine seem to have a higher rate of spontaneous abortion; and their babies have a greater risk of developing neurological problems—they do not interact as well as other babies, nor do they respond as appropriately to environmental stimuli (Chasnoff, Burns, Schnoll, & Burns, 1985). In addition, such babies tend to be shorter and lighter and to have smaller heads than babies of drug-free mothers. Also, more malformed and stillborn babies are born to cocaine abusers (Bingol, Fuchs, Diaz, Stone, & Gromisch, 1987), and use of cocaine by the mother has also been linked to sudden infant death syndrome (see Chapter 5) (Chasnoff, Hunt, Kletter, & Kaplan, 1986). The dangers of using cocaine during pregnancy are clearly alarming.

Other Maternal Factors

Illness   A number of illnesses contracted during pregnancy can have serious effects on the developing fetus, depending partly on *when* the mother gets sick. When rubella (German measles) is contracted before the eleventh week of gestation, it is almost certain to cause deafness and heart defects in the baby. But between 13 and 16 weeks of pregnancy, the chances of such consequences are only about 1 in 3, and after 16 weeks they are almost nonexistent (E. Miller, Cradock-Watson, & Pollock, 1982).

Fortunately, such defects are rarer these days, since most children are inoculated against rubella, lowering the odds that a pregnant woman will contract the disease. Furthermore, a nonpregnant woman can find out through a blood test whether she is immune to the disease. If not, she can be immunized—but only until 3 months before becoming pregnant, since the vaccine itself could injure a fetus (Behrman & Vaughan, 1983). Diabetes, tuberculosis, and syphilis can also cause problems in fetal development, and both gonorrhea and genital herpes can have harmful effects on the baby at the time of delivery.

A mild infection called *toxoplasmosis* is contracted by about 1 in every 4 Americans (National Foundation/March of Dimes, 1972). It usually produces either no symptoms or symptoms like those of the common cold, but when contracted by a pregnant woman, it can cause brain damage or blindness in the baby or even death of the baby. A pregnant woman should avoid the most common sources of infection—she should not eat raw or very rare meat, should not get a new cat or handle the cats of friends, and should not dig in the garden if there is any possibility that cat feces are buried in the area. If she already has a cat, she should have a veterinarian check it for the disease, she should not feed it raw meat, and she should not empty the litter box herself.

With the increase in the number of reported cases of genital herpes simplex virus (HSV) since the mid-1960s, its incidence has also increased among new-borns, who can acquire the disease from the mother or the father either at or soon after birth (Sullivan-Bolyai, Hull, Wison, and Corey, 1983). HSV has grave consequences for newborns, possibly causing blindness, other abnormalities, and even death.

Acquired immune deficiency syndrome (AIDS) may be contracted by a fetus if the mother has the disease or even has the virus in her blood. The danger arises because the contents of the mother's blood are shared with the fetus through the placenta, and blood is a carrier of the virus that causes AIDS. Abnormalities detected in infants and young children born with AIDS include growth failure and such head and face abnormalities as small heads; big eyes; protruding lips; short, flat noses and flat nose bridges; slanting eyes; and prominent, boxlike foreheads (Iosub, Bamji, Stone, Gromisch, & Wasserman, 1987; Marion, Wiznia, Hutcheon, & Rubinstein, 1986). (See Figure 3-2.)

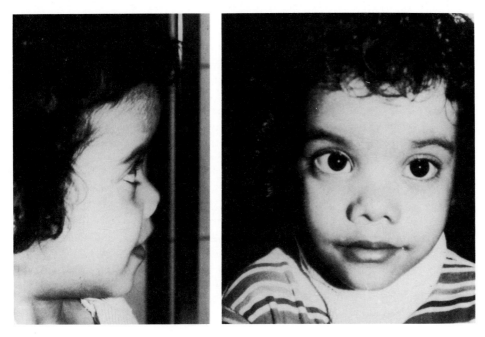

FIGURE 3-2
Transmission of AIDS from mother to child. This 3-year-old girl, born to a mother with AIDS, has suffered retarded growth and incomplete brain development; she has a flat nose; slanted, large eyes; and a prominent, boxlike forehead. (*Source:* Marion, Wiznia, Hutcheon, & Rubinstein, 1986, p. 639; courtesy of Dr. Robert Marion, Montefiore Medical Center.)

Incompatibility of Blood Type   Heredity can interact with the prenatal environment to cause incompatibility of blood type between mother and baby, most commonly due to the *Rh factor.* When a fetus's blood contains this protein substance (is Rh-positive) but its mother's blood does not (is Rh-negative), antibodies in the mother's blood may attack the fetus and bring about miscarriage or stillbirth, jaundice, anemia, heart defects, mental retardation, or death soon after birth. Usually, the first Rh-positive baby of an Rh-negative mother is not affected, but with each succeeding pregnancy the risk becomes greater. A vaccine can now be given to an Rh-negative mother which, when administered within 3 days of childbirth or abortion, will prevent her body from making antibodies that will attack future Rh-positive fetuses. Babies already affected by Rh disease can be treated with repeated blood transfusions, sometimes even before birth.

Rh factor   Protein substance found in the blood of most people; when it is present in the blood of a fetus but not in the blood of the mother, death of the fetus can result.

Emotional States   Does a mother's emotional state affect her fetus? The belief that it can has a long history, going back to the Bible, the ancient Greeks, and the Middle Ages in Europe. Some writers thought that a pregnant woman who was frightened by a dog might have a baby with doglike features; others thought that there might be long-term effects but were not sure what form they would take.

However, a recent survey of the literature over the past 25 years about the effects on offspring of stress in the mother found little evidence that a mother's anxiety during pregnancy has any effect on the baby's delivery or health status after birth (Istvan, 1986). Even the most dramatic studies, which have concerned stress in pregnant rats rather than humans, have found that behavioral effects produced during the fetal stage can be altered by changing the environment of the offspring after birth (Spezzano, 1981).

Still, stress can interfere with a woman's ability to nurture her baby once it is born, and therefore a pregnant woman who is undergoing exceptional stress should be provided with special counseling and help.

Environmental Hazards   In recent years we have become more conscious of the dangers to the fetus of extremes of heat and humidity and of chemicals, radiation, and other hazards of modern industrial life.

Industrial chemicals   Babies of mothers who, during pregnancy, ate fish contaminated with polychlorinated biphenyls (PCBs)—chemicals widely used in industry before they were banned in 1976—showed weak reflexes and jerky, unbalanced movements and weighed less at birth and had smaller heads than babies of mothers who had not eaten the fish (J.L. Jacobson, Jacobson, Fein, Schwartz, & Dowler, 1984). Furthermore, some effects show up later. A number of such prenatally exposed babies who seemed normal at birth showed poor visual-recognition memory at 7 months of age when they were asked to distinguish between paired sets of babies' and women's faces (S.W. Jacobson, Fein, Jacobson, Schwartz, & Dowler, 1985). The nursing babies in this study did not seem to be affected by the PCB levels in their mothers' breast milk; whatever effect there was had apparently occurred before birth. Although it is possible that these effects are only temporary, women of childbearing age should play safe by avoiding PCBs, either by not eating fatty fish from such areas as Lake Michigan or by broiling the fish or cutting off the fatty parts, where the PCBs accumulate.

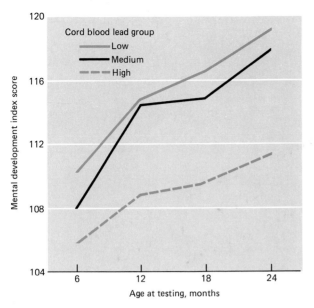

FIGURE 3-3
Prenatal lead contamination inhibits early mental development. When babies were tested at 6, 12, 18, and 24 months, those who had had high levels of lead in umbilical-cord blood, tested more poorly later on the Bayley Scales of Infant Development. (*Source:* Adapted from Bellinger, Leviton, Waternaux, Needleman, & Rabinowitz, 1987, p. 1041).

Lead contamination   Another environmental pollutant that seems to affect children's early mental development is lead. Some children are exposed to lead prenatally, usually because their mothers are living in rooms where old lead-based paint is flaking off the walls. Children in whom lead had shown up in blood taken from the umbilical cord, even at levels that had been thought safe, showed a slower-than-expected level of mental development by the age of 2, as measured on the Bayley Scales of Infant Development (Bellinger, Leviton, Waternaux, Needleman, & Rabinowitz, 1987). The higher a baby's lead level, the worse the score (see Figure 3-3). The babies' scores were not related to their blood lead levels *after* birth, however, indicating that prenatal exposure is more influential.

Radiation   We have known for more than 50 years that radiation can cause gene **mutations,** changes that lead a gene to produce some new, often harmful trait (D. P. Murphy, 1929). The first 2 weeks of pregnancy, when a woman often does not even realize that she is pregnant, seem to be the worst time to be exposed to low doses of radiation (University of Texas Health Science Center at Dallas, 1983). A study of twins born over a 40-year period (1930 to 1969) found that those who developed cancer in childhood were twice as likely to have been exposed prenatally to x-rays as children who did not develop cancer. Often the x-rays had been used specifically to diagnose the presence of twins, a technique now replaced by ultrasound (Harvey, Boice, Honeyman, & Flannery, 1985). In planning medical x-rays, women and their doctors need to take into account a potential or actual pregnancy and determine whether the need for a radiological examination is great enough to justify the risk.

mutation   *Change in a gene that leads to the production of a new, often harmful trait.*

Video display terminals   Women who use video display terminals (VDTs) for more than 20 hours per week during the first trimester were found to have a miscarriage rate twice that of women doing other office work. Birth defects were also slightly higher in the VDT users' offspring. This may be due to low levels of

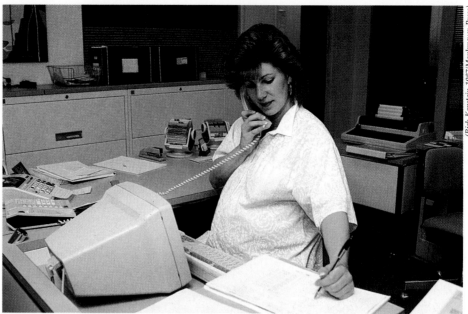

(Rick Kopstein 1987/Monkmeyer Press)

The environment can present hazards to babies in utero. For example, if this woman worked at her video display terminal for more than 20 hours a week during her first trimester, she might be at risk of miscarriage or of bearing a child with a birth defect.

electromagnetic radiation from VDTs, but it may also be due to such other factors as job-related stress (Goldhaber et al. in Altman, 1988a).

Exercise   Fortunately, not all things an expectant mother does or is exposed to are harmful to a fetus. Moderate physical activity (including jogging, swimming, cycling, or playing tennis) during pregnancy does not seem to endanger the fetuses of healthy women (Carpenter et al., 1988). A study involving 45 women in midpregnancy who pedaled exercise bicycles found that only when the women were pushed to the point of exhaustion did their fetuses show any decline in heart rate. And even in these cases, this decline was short-lived and occurred only after the exercise was stopped; all the fetuses showed normal heart response within half an hour after the exercise session. Moreover, all the babies, except two who had unrelated complications, were fine at birth. The doctors who led this experiment recommend that pregnant women continue to exercise moderately—not pushing themselves to the limit and not raising their heart rate above 150—and that they taper off their workouts rather than stop abruptly.

BIRTH DEFECTS TRANSMITTED BY THE FATHER

We have already seen how the genes of both mother and father and maternal and environmental factors can cause birth defects. In recent years, researchers have looked more closely at the male's role in transmitting defects.

Exposure to lead, marijuana and tobacco smoke, large amounts of alcohol and radiation, DES, and certain pesticides may result in the production of sperm that are abnormal in number, shape, and motility and may also produce genetic abnormalities in the sperm (J. E. Brody, 1981; R. Lester & Van Thiel, 1977). One recent study found a higher incidence of nervous system tumors in children whose fathers were exposed to electromagnetic fields through their work (M. R.

Spitz & Johnson, 1985). The highest rates in this study were among the children of electrical and electronics workers; other studies have implicated a number of paternal occupations in producing nervous system tumors in offspring. These jobs include auto mechanic, service station attendant, machinist, miner, painter, dyer, printer, machine repairer, steelworker or construction worker, carpenter, paper or pulp mill worker, and aircraft industry worker (M. R. Spitz & Johnson, 1985).

A harmful influence in the mother's environment is nicotine in the cloud from a father's smoking. One recent study showed that babies of fathers who smoked were lighter at birth by about 4 ounces per pack of cigarettes smoked per day by the father (or the equivalent in cigar or pipe smoking) (D. H. Rubin et al., 1986). And another found that children of men who smoked were twice as likely as children of men who did not to contract cancer in adulthood (Sandler, Everson, Wilcox, & Browder, 1985).

Mutations occur more frequently as a man ages and may be responsible for some disorders. Advanced age of the father is associated with increases in several rare conditions, including a type of dwarfism, Marfan's syndrome (deformities of the head and limbs), and fibrodysplasia ossificans progressiva (bone malformations). In studies on each of these conditions, the mean age of the father was in the late thirties (G. Evans, 1976). Advanced age of the father also seems to be a factor, as we have seen, in about 1 out of 4 cases of Down syndrome (Abroms & Bennett, 1979).

MEDICAL THERAPY WITHIN THE WOMB

The womb is no longer just a place for nurturing and protecting a healthy fetus. With the development of sophisticated techniques, it has become a "mini-hospital" where certain conditions can be corrected. Although most disorders are best treated after birth, there are a few that can be corrected prenatally (Harrison, Golbus, Filly, Nakayama, & Delorimier, 1982). Fetuses can swallow and absorb medicines, nutrients, vitamins, and hormones that are injected into the amniotic fluid.

A recently developed technique allows doctors to treat babies through the umbilical cord. Blood transfusions given in this way, which may be vital to save the lives of Rh-positive babies, can be administered beginning as early as the eighteenth week of pregnancy and continuing every 2 weeks until birth, and drugs that might not pass through the placenta can be injected directly through the cord (Kolata, 1988b).

Experimental work with sheep and other animals shows promise for performing various types of surgery on fetuses to correct several conditions, including hernia and hydrocephalus. In fact, a catheter was implanted in the bladder of a human fetus with a urinary tract obstruction (Harrison et al., 1982). However, the advantages of prenatal therapy, which include rapid postoperative healing and the possible prevention of irreversible damage, need to be weighed against surgical risks to mother and fetus.

The availability of such powerful therapeutic techniques even in the womb provides another dramatic illustration of the importance of this time of life. In fact, advances in knowledge about prenatal life and in technology of treating the unborn have given rise to an ethical debate, which is explored in Box 3-3, on page 114.

BOX 3-3 ▪ THE RESEARCH WORLD

WHAT CONSTITUTES FETAL ABUSE?

Suit is brought against the mother on behalf of a 5-year-old for prenatal injuries suffered in a car accident; on behalf of another child, the mother is sued for discoloration of the baby teeth caused by the mother's having taken the antibiotic tetracycline when she was 7 months pregnant (Fleisher, 1987).

A New Jersey court charges that parents neglected their unborn child by refusing consent for a potentially lifesaving prenatal blood transfusion, a Michigan child-protection agency asks for custody of an unborn child of a couple who had physically and sexually abused another child, and a Maryland court orders a drug-addicted pregnant woman whose previous child was born addicted to enroll in a rehabilitation program and be tested weekly (Landwirth, 1987).

A pregnant woman diagnosed with terminal cancer is ordered by a judge to have her baby by cesarean delivery, even though her own doctor warns that the operation may shorten her life and cannot save that of the fetus, which is not yet viable. The surgery is performed, and both mother and baby die—the baby almost immediately, the mother within 2 days (Paltrow, 1988).

In all these cases, the issue is the conflict between a fetus's right to be born healthy and a pregnant woman's right to privacy and bodily autonomy. It is hard to argue against protecting a fetus, since we have access to sophisticated techniques for prenatal diagnosis and treatment and know much about the potentially damaging effects of much maternal behavior (like drug and alcohol abuse and malnutrition). It is extremely tempting to place legal constraints on a pregnant woman who seems to be disregarding the practices that will ensure her baby's health. But what about her personal freedom?

Can society force a woman against her will to submit to procedures that pose a risk to her, like surgery or intrauterine transfusions? Medical, legal, and social critics are deeply concerned about this issue, and the overwhelming attitude expressed by people writing about it is that the state should intervene only in limited circumstances. These procedures are intrusive. Legal coercion could jeopardize the doctor-patient relationship; it could also open the door to go further into pregnant women's lives, by demanding prenatal screening, fetal surgery, and restrictions on women's diet, work, and athletic and sexual activity (Kolder, Gallagher, & Parsons, 1987).

Circumstances warranting intervention might be limited to the following: a high likelihood of serious fetal disease, a high level of diagnostic accuracy, strong scientific evidence that the proposed treatment will be effective, danger that deferring treatment until after birth will cause serious damage, minimal risk to the mother and modest interference with her privacy, and unsuccessful persistent efforts at educating her and obtaining her informed consent (Landwirth, 1987). Many procedures have been ordered by courts in situations not meeting these criteria, and as a result have been performed on the basis of "dubious legal grounds" (Kolder et al., 1987).

Instead of concentrating on such coercive measures, society might well protect fetuses better by providing easy access to prenatal care for all women, no matter what their racial or ethnic background or income level, and by enhancing their status. If failure to follow medical advice can result in forced surgery or confinement or in criminal charges, some women may avoid doctors altogether, thus depriving their fetuses of prenatal care. If so, more mothers and babies would be harmed than helped (Annas, 1987).

A NOTE ON PRENATAL HAZARDS

It is important to consider the many ways development can go awry and how best to avoid problems (see Box 3-4, opposite page). But we need to remember that normal fetal development is overwhelmingly the rule. Both Ellen and Julia feel good during pregnancy, both physically and emotionally—and Vicky and Jason, like most children, develop normally. Pregnancy is a time of excitement, planning, and thinking. Today's techniques for monitoring fetal development and our increased knowledge of ways to improve the child's prenatal world make pregnancy much less a cause for concern than it was in earlier days. (And even in former times, most pregnancies ended with the delivery of a healthy baby.)

BOX 3-4 ■ THE EVERYDAY WORLD

REDUCING RISKS DURING PREGNANCY

Women can help ensure the best prenatal environment for their child by following these guidelines:

- *Get good medical care.* Even a low-risk pregnancy can become high-risk if prenatal care is lacking or poor. See a qualified practitioner regularly, beginning as soon as you suspect you are pregnant. If you are in a high-risk category, use an obstetrician who has experience with your particular condition. Participate actively in your medical care by asking questions and reporting symptoms.
- *Eat well.* Eat a well-balanced diet to increase your odds of having a successful pregnancy and a healthy baby, and to prevent various disorders of pregnancy.
- *Be fit.* If you didn't begin pregnancy with a well-toned exercised body, start to get fit now. Regular exercise prevents constipation and improves respiration, circulation, muscle tone, and skin elasticity, all of which contribute to a more comfortable pregnancy and an easier, safer delivery.
- *Gain weight sensibly.* Gain weight gradually, steadily, and moderately to help prevent a variety of complications, including diabetes, hypertension, varicose veins, hemorrhoids, and a difficult delivery due to an overly large fetus.

- *Don't smoke.* Stop smoking as early in pregnancy as possible to reduce risks to yourself and the baby, including low birthweight.
- *Don't drink alcohol.* Drink very rarely or not at all, to reduce the risk of birth defects, particularly of fetal alcohol syndrome, which results from high alcohol intake.
- *Don't take drugs.* Avoid taking any drugs that are not absolutely essential and prescribed by your doctor when you are pregnant or breastfeeding.
- *Prevent infections or treat them promptly.* Try to prevent all infections—from common colds and flu to urinary tract and vaginal infections and the increasingly common venereal diseases—whenever possible. When contracted, however, infection should be treated promptly by a physician who knows you are pregnant.
- *Don't try to be "Superwoman."* Resist the temptation to overachieve and overdo. Getting enough rest during pregnancy is far more important then getting everything done, especially in high-risk pregnancies. If your doctor recommends that you begin your maternity leave earlier than you've planned, take the advice. Some studies suggest a higher incidence of premature delivery among women who work up until term, particularly if their job entails physical labor or long periods of standing.

Source: Adapted from A. Eisenberg et al., 1984.

Other Ways to Parenthood

Donna has dreamed of having children from the time she was a little girl playing with dolls. But her life took unexpected turns. She pursued a career and did not meet a man she wanted to marry until her late twenties. "Even though I was 31 when I got married," she says now, "no doctor ever told me, 'If you want to have children, you'd better start trying now, because the older you are, the less fertile you are.'" She didn't find this out until 6 years later, when she and her husband decided to start their family.

Donna did not conceive the first month, as she had expected—nor the second, nor the month after that, and so on, until it seemed she had been trying forever to have a baby. Finally, she and her husband—depressed and angry with themselves, each other, and everyone they knew who had children—went to a fertility clinic.

Reproduction is a biological function, but raising a family is a social act. Since human beings seldom abandon their desires simply because they run into obstacles, it is no surprise to find that couples who want children eagerly embrace ways that bypass ordinary biological processes.

INFERTILITY

infertility *Inability to conceive after 1 year of trying to have a baby.*

The most common reason why people look for alternative methods is that they are unable to conceive. Rates of **infertility** (inability to conceive after 1 year of trying to have a baby) have tripled over the past 25 years: some 10 to 15 percent of couples who want a baby cannot conceive one (Francoeur, 1985; National Center for Health Statistics, 1984a). The increase seems to be due to several factors—the growing number of couples who delay starting a family until the woman is in her thirties (often not realizing that fertility declines with age), an increase in sexually transmitted infections, and the side effects of some contraceptives, such as birth control pills and intrauterine devices (Cramer et al., 1985; Daling et al., 1985). There is also an association between infertility and cigarette smoking by women: women who smoke heavily are less fertile than lighter smokers (D. D. Baird & Wilcox, 1985).

The reasons for infertility may lie with either the man or the woman. Sometimes surgery can correct the problem, and sometimes hormones can raise the sperm count or enhance ovulation (Loucopoulous, Ferin, & VandeWiele, 1984). In fact, some fertility drugs cause superovulation, producing two, three or more babies at a time. In about 13 percent of cases, however, both the man and the woman seem perfectly normal but are not able to have a child (J. A. Collins, Wrixon, Janes, & Wilson, 1983).

Infertility sometimes burdens a marriage with psychological problems, since people who have assumed that they will be able to reproduce often have trouble accepting the fact that they cannot do what seems to come naturally and easily to others. Women become more upset than men (37 percent of infertile women showed psychological disturbance in one study, compared with 1 percent of men; McEwan, Costello, & Taylor, 1987), possibly because they see reproduction as central to their identity more than men do. The couple's sexual relationship often suffers as sex becomes a matter of "making babies, not love" (Liebmann-Smith, personal communication; Porter & Christopher, 1984).

Many infertile couples do eventually conceive, some without any treatment at all. In one study of 1145 infertile couples, pregnancy occurred in 41 percent of those who received treatment—and also in 35 percent of those who did not (J. A. Collins et al., 1983). The outcome was related to the reason for the infertility: with or without treatment, couples whose infertility had no known cause or was attributed to cervical factors were most likely to conceive (96 percent), and women with ovulatory problems were least likely to get pregnant—but even among these, 44 percent did go on to bear babies.

ALTERNATIVE WAYS TO CONCEIVE

Artificial Insemination

artificial insemination *Nonsexual introduction of sperm into a woman's body with the intent to cause pregnancy.*

The oldest medical technique to help infertile couples conceive is **artificial insemination,** in which a woman receives injections of her husband's sperm directly into her cervix. Artificial insemination by a donor (AID) uses the sperm of an anonymous donor, whose physical characteristics and ethnic background may resemble the husband's. If the woman conceives, the pregnancy proceeds like any other; many couples who have a family in this way never tell anyone how the children were conceived, including the children themselves.

In Vitro Fertilization

Front-page stories around the world heralded the birth of Louise Brown, the "test-tube baby," who was born in 1978. More than 3000 such babies have been born in the United States, and follow-up studies have found them developing normally (Seibel, 1988). Conception outside the body, a procedure known as *in vitro fertilization,* begins with the extraction of an ovum from the mother. The ovum matures in a dish placed in an incubator and is then fertilized with a few drops of the father's sperm. After the zygote divides into four cells, the doctor implants the embryo in the mother's uterus, where it grows normally. This procedure is sometimes performed when a woman's fallopian tubes are blocked or absent, preventing the ovum and sperm from meeting, or when conditions of her uterus or ovaries prevent the release of ova. The cost in most centers is about $6000.

Donor Eggs

The same kind of procedure can be performed with the use of ova contributed by another woman. This technique, known as *donor eggs,* is the female equivalent of AID. So far, this has been performed in two different ways. In one, an ovum is taken from the body of a fertile woman and is allowed to mature and be fertilized, and the embryo is then implanted in the uterus of another woman (Lutjen et al., 1984). The other technique involves fertilizing the donor's ovum through artificial insemination while it is still in the donor's body, flushing the embryo out of the uterus 5 days later, and inserting the embryo into the uterus of the recipient (Bustillo et al., 1984).

Surrogate Motherhood

Surrogate motherhood, which takes the donor-eggs method one step further, raises many emotional, legal, and ethical issues. After a woman—the surrogate mother—is impregnated by the prospective father (usually artificially), she carries the baby to term. The child is then given to the father and his wife to raise. The surrogate mother experiences the entire pregnancy, with its risks and emotions. Since she is paid a fee—commonly $5000 to $15,000—plus all medical expenses, some people consider the process a form of child buying. At present, surrogate motherhood is in a legally uncertain position, partly as a result of the controversial "Baby M" case, in which the surrogate mother changed her mind and wanted to keep the baby (Hanley, 1988a, 1988b; Shipp, 1988). The surrogate mother was not awarded custody of the little girl, but she has been granted visiting rights.

ADOPTION

Adoption, a system found in all cultures throughout history, is the oldest solution to infertility. It is also often sought by families who do not want to bear their own children or who already have children and seek to enlarge their families by taking children who need a home.

Since 1970, adoption has undergone many changes in the United States. Because of the availability of legal abortion for unwanted pregnancy and because

(IVF Australia)

Thousands of babies—like Matthew Martinez, shown here with his mother—have been born through in vitro fertilization, a type of conception outside the body that has been in use since 1978. Studies indicate that these babies develop normally.

in vitro fertilization
Conception outside the body.

adoption *Taking a child into one's family through legal means and accepting the child as one's own.*

This unmarried schoolteacher's adoption of emotionally and physically handicapped boys illustrates the lifting of restrictions on adoptive parents in recent years and the greater scope in finding homes for children.

more unmarried mothers keep their babies these days, adoption agencies have far fewer babies available than they had 20 years ago. As a result, more adoptive parents than ever before make their arrangements independently or adopt children from other countries.

Adoption is widely accepted in the United States. However, there is still some prejudice against it. This prejudice appears as "a notion that no surrogate parent, regardless of how emotionally mature or psychologically aware, can totally compensate for the loss to the child of its biological mother" (Marquis & Detweiler, 1985, p. 1054). Such a view has been reinforced by some research, but the studies which support that idea typically drew their samples of adopted children from people who were already seeking some form of mental health service.

On the other hand, in a study of a sample selected from adopted children placed by one adoption agency in New Jersey, researchers found that although there was a measurable difference between the attitudes of adopted and non-adopted children, the positive differences were all on the adopted children's side. Contrary to expectation, they were more confident, viewed the world more positively, felt better able to control their lives, and saw their adoptive parents as more nurturing than the nonadopted children saw their parents (Marquis & Detweiler, 1985).

No matter how children are conceived, no matter whether they are raised by biological or adoptive parents, the birth itself and the few weeks afterward are among the most dramatic periods in anyone's life—as we will see next, in Chapter 4.

BOX 3-5 ■ A CHILD'S WORLD AND YOU

WHAT DO YOU THINK?

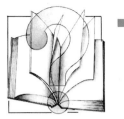

■ Hundreds of people are now alive who suffered gross abnormalities of development because their mothers took the tranquilizer thalidomide during pregnancy. The families of many of these young people sued the pharmaceutical company that manufactured the drug. Does the company have a moral or legal obligation to provide financial assistance to the disabled people?

■ During pregnancy, prospective parents usually have a number of emotional issues to resolve. Which concerns seem most likely to affect you?
—Accepting the idea that your child will be an individual with his or her own interests, which may not be compatible with your own
—Resolving your relationship with your own parents
—The effect the new baby will have on your marriage

■ Much of the debate about induced abortion concerns the nature of the organism growing in the woman's body. As a college student, you have presumably considered this important social issue already. Has anything in this chapter challenged your opinion on the matter? Has anything reinforced it?

■ Infertile couples can find help in different ways. Medical procedures like in vitro fertilization can result in a child whose genes come from the parents. Surrogate motherhood or artificial insemination can lead to the birth of a baby who contains the genes of at least one parent. Adoption gives the parents a child who is not related to them genetically but who needs a home. Which of these solutions seem more attractive to you?

Summary

1 Expectant parents typically face four psychological tasks: development of an emotional attachment to the fetus, acceptance of a relationship with the fetus, resolution of the relationship with the same-sex parent, and resolution of dependency issues.

2 Prenatal development occurs in three stages. The germinal stage (fertilization to 2 weeks) is characterized by rapid cell division and increased complexity of the organism. The embryonic stage (2 to 8–12 weeks) is marked by rapid growth and differentiation of major body systems and organs. The fetal stage (8–12 weeks to birth) begins with the appearance of the first bone cells and is characterized by rapid growth and change in body form.

3 About one-third of all conceptions end in spontaneous abortion (miscarriage). Three out of four miscarriages occur in the first trimester of pregnancy.

4 There are individual differences among fetuses in activity level. Fetuses appear to be able to hear and learn.

5 The developing organism can be greatly affected by its prenatal environment. Some environmental factors are teratogenic; that is, they are able to produce birth defects.

6 Important prenatal influences include the mother's nutrition, the mother's intake of drugs (including caffeine, nicotine, and alcohol as well as illicit drugs), illness of the mother, incompatibility of blood type between mother and fetus, stress of the mother, and factors in the external environment. Paternal factors have also been related to birth defects in offspring. Despite these risk factors, normal fetal development is the rule.

7 Scientific advances have allowed certain medical conditions to be treated while the fetus is in the womb.

8 An important ethical debate today considers the conflict between a fetus's right to be born healthy and a mother's right to privacy and bodily autonomy.

9 Some 10 to 15 percent of couples who want to have a baby are infertile (unable to conceive after one year of trying). Artificial insemination, in vitro fertilization, donor eggs, and surrogate motherhood represent new ways for infertile couples to attain parenthood. Adoption is the oldest solution to infertility and also provides a home to a child who otherwise would not have one.

Key Terms

gestation (page 95)
germinal stage (95)
embryonic stage (98)
critical period (98)
trimester (98)
spontaneous abortion (98)
fetus (99)
fetal stage (99)

teratogenic (102)
fetal alcohol syndrome (FAS) (105)
Rh factor (110)
mutation (111)
infertility (116)
artificial insemination (116)
in vitro fertilization (117)
adoption (117)

Suggested Readings

Bolles, E. B. (1984). *The Penguin adoption handbook.* New York: Penguin. A complete survey of adoption methods and practices in the United States, written as a practical guide to successful adoption. The book discusses agency, independent, and international adoptions and how to accomplish them.

Eisenberg, A., Murkoff, H. E., & Hathaway, S. E. (1984). *What to expect when you're expecting.* New York: Workman. An excellent, comprehensive description of pregnancy, month to month, that incorporates the most up-to-date research on care for both mother and baby.

Frank, D., & Vogel, M. (1988). *The baby makers.* New York: Carroll & Graf. An exploration of the various new technologies for parenthood, describing the techniques and examining the moral and ethical issues. Many anecdotes offer a clear picture of the people who choose these methods in the desire to have biological children.

Hess, M. A., & Hunt, A. E. (1982). *Pickles & ice cream.* New York: McGraw-Hill (paperback ed., 1984, New York: Dell). A thorough exploration of nutrition for pregnant women. It is replete with charts and tables and is written for expectant mothers.

Krauss, M., & Castle, S. (1988). *Your newborn baby.* New York: Warner. An excellent source for new parents. Using guidelines set by the American Academy of Pediatrics, this book contains both medical and practical advice ranging from how to diaper a baby to when to call a doctor.

Lesko, M., & Lesko, W. (1984). *The maternity sourcebook: 230 basic decisions for pregnancy, birth, and baby care.* New York: Warner. A comprehensive listing of facts and pros and cons concerning every major decision that must be made about pregnancy and the first year of life. The book includes lists of helpful organizations and further readings.

Nilsson, L., Ingelman-Sundberg, A., & Wirsen, C. (1966). *A child is born: The drama of life before birth.* New York: Delacorte. A clear description of fetal development, including beautiful photos of a live fetus inside the womb.

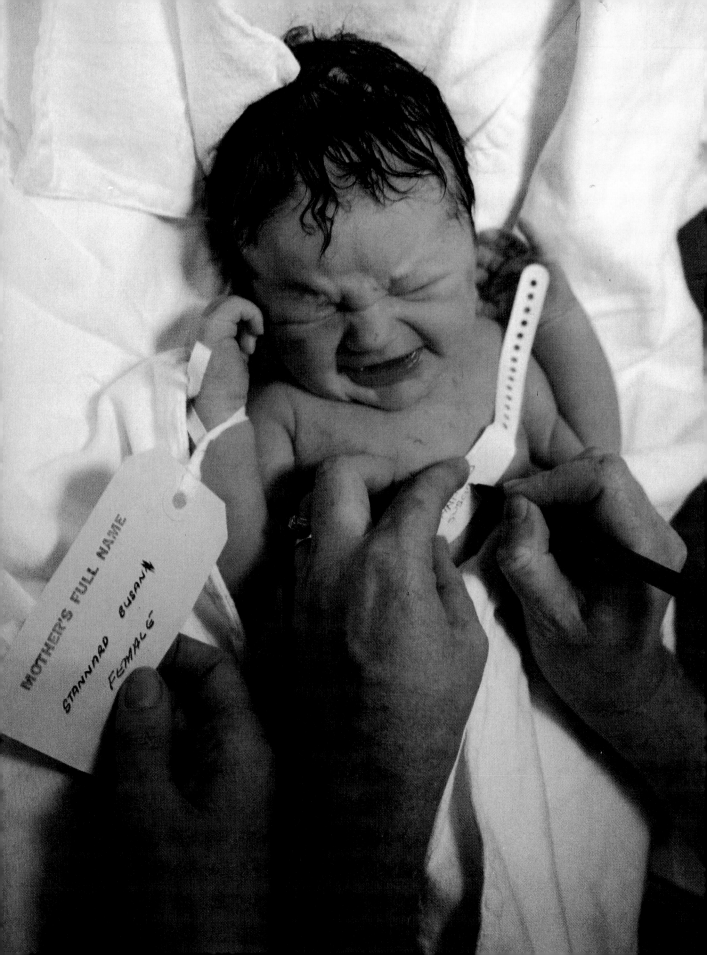

BIRTH AND THE NEWBORN BABY

The experiences of the first three years of life are almost entirely lost to us, and when we attempt to enter into a small child's world, we come as foreigners who have forgotten the landscape and no longer speak the native tongue.

Selma Fraiberg, *The Magic Years*, 1959

PREVIEW QUESTIONS

■ What happens during the three stages of childbirth, and how do different methods of childbirth affect the baby?
■ How does the stress of childbirth affect babies, for good or ill?
■ How do complications at birth affect babies, and what can be done to prevent and treat low birthweight?
■ What can newborn infants do, and how can we tell whether they are developing normally?
■ How can adults comfort crying babies?

VICKY'S CRIES announced her arrival in the outside world before her legs had fully emerged from her mother's body. When the doctor held her up before Ellen and Charles, they were enthralled. Vicky was already gazing about the room, looking at the flurry of activity, and listening to a buzz of excited voices. The world was pouring into her senses, and, like a new immigrant in an unknown land, Vicky was taking it all in.

After a difficult journey, Vicky was faced with more than learning the language and customs of her new home. A baby has to start to breathe, eat, adapt to the climate, and respond to confusing surroundings. This is a mighty challenge for a creature who weighs but a few pounds and whose organ systems are still not fully mature. Fortunately, as you'll see, infants are remarkably capable when they come into the world, with body systems and senses already working.

In this chapter we continue to look at the foundations of a child's development. We explore the phases, methods, joys, and complications of the birth process. Then we talk about the newborn, who for the first 4 weeks of life is known technically as a *neonate.* What is this newcomer like? How can a new baby's status be assessed quickly so that parents can rejoice, knowing that all is well—or, more rarely, so that any necessary special attention can be given? We also discuss the body systems that are vital for babies' independent survival, now that they are no longer attached to the mother through the umbilical cord. Finally, we discuss the *states* of infants (their sleep-wake cycles) and what they mean in everyday life.

neonate Newborn in the first 4 weeks of life.

The Birth Process

gestation Period of time from conception to birth; normal full-term gestation is 266 days.

Ellen woke up feeling some new sensations in her belly, heavy with child. According to her doctor, the baby was not due for another 2 weeks, at the end of the estimated normal full-term *gestation* of 266 days. But she believed that she was feeling the birth contractions which she had heard and read so much about.

About every 10 or 15 minutes she felt a mild tightening of her uterus, lasting for 15 to 25 seconds. These contractions were stronger and more regular than similar contractions she had occasionally felt over the past few months. As the intervals between them became shorter, the sensation intensified. She remembered reading a comparison to "the rising, breaking, and falling of waves on the shore" (Boston Women's Health Book Collective, 1976, p. 271). These contractions did remind her of waves she had seen when a storm was building out at sea; they kept swelling, breaking faster and harder.

One of the first mysteries in human life is precisely what mechanism triggers the contractions of the uterus to expel a fetus. One possibility rests on the discovery that urine from a human fetus, put in a laboratory dish, stimulates the action of *prostaglandins* (hormones that carry out a number of functions in the body and may initiate birth). It is possible that a specific substance released into the urine of the fetus and then into the amniotic fluid causes labor to begin (Strickland, Saeed, Casey, & Mitchell, 1983). Another clue is suggested by the fact that the 24-hour fast undergone in observance of the Jewish holy day Yom Kippur is often followed in pregnant women by early labor; perhaps the uterus contracts in response to a lessened flow of blood in the body during a fast, and perhaps blood flow also decreases just before labor begins (Kaplan, Eidelman, & Aboulafia, 1983). Changes in the size of the fetus and the uterus also seem significant, since twins are usually born about 3 weeks early and other multiple births even earlier. Finally, it is possible that the placenta is genetically programmed to begin the birth process.

BIRTH AND BIOLOGY: THE PHASES OF CHILDBIRTH

Childbirth, or labor, takes place in three overlapping phases (see Figure 4-1, page 126). The *first stage* is the longest, lasting an average 12 to 24 hours for a woman having her first child, like Ellen. In this stage, uterine contractions cause the cervix, the opening of the uterus, to widen until it becomes large enough for the baby's head to pass through. At first, the contractions tend to be fairly mild. Toward the end of this stage, they become more severe and more uncomfortable, even though the mother's pituitary gland (the body's "master gland," which controls the activity of all other glands) secretes a painkiller, beta endorphin (chemically similar to heroin), which eases the pain (Gintzler, 1980). Women who have been prepared for childbirth through special classes learn breathing techniques that help them overcome the discomfort of these stronger contractions.

Much of the pain of labor is caused by the stretching of the lower part of the uterus, especially the cervix. If a women's cervix dilates quickly, she will feel little or no pain. But if her cervix is rigid and is forcibly dilated by the contractions of her uterus, the contractions will be painful (Timiras, 1972).

The *second stage* typically lasts about 1½ hours. It beings when the baby's head begins to move through the cervix and the vaginal canal, and it ends when the baby emerges completely from the mother's body. During the second stage, the mother who is prepared knows that she must bear down hard with her abdominal muscles at each contraction, helping the baby to leave her body. At the end of this stage, the baby is born but is still attached by the umbilical cord to the placenta, which is inside the mother's body.

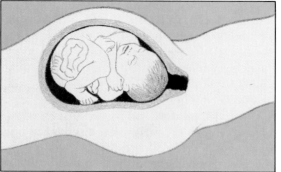

(a) First stage

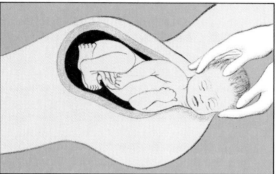

(b) Second stage

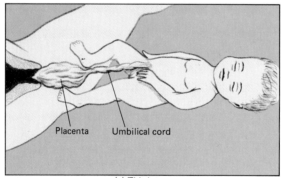

Placenta   Umbilical cord

(c) Third stage

FIGURE 4-1
Birth of a baby. (a) During the first stage of labor, stronger and stronger contractions dilate the cervix, the opening of the mother's womb. (b) During the second stage, the baby's head moves down the birth canal and emerges from the vagina. (c) During the brief third stage, the placenta and umbilical cord are expelled from the womb. Then, the cord is cut. (*Source:* Adapted from Lagercrantz & Slotkin, 1986.)

During the *third stage*, which lasts only a few minutes, the umbilical cord and the placenta are expelled.

BIRTH AND SOCIETY: HELPING THE MOTHER AND BABY

The basic biology of childbirth, of course, does not change, but the ways that society helps mothers and babies are always changing.

Childbearing Positions

Women have given birth to their babies sitting on birth stools, kneeling while bracing themselves with their hands, crouching, and standing. Women did not begin to recline for childbirth until 1738, when th obstetrician to the queen of

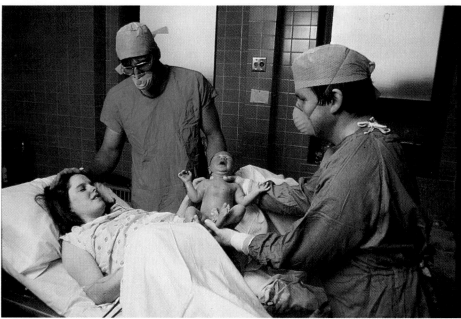

(S.I.U. Science Source/Photo Researchers)

"Labor" is an apt term. Birth is hard work for both mother and baby—work that yields a rich reward. The work will continue for years as the parents learn to care for their child and the child learns how to make a life in the world.

France suggested that it would be easier for the doctor if the woman delivered lying on her back. This position, now the most common, is criticized by some because on rare occasions it can obstruct a large vein drawing blood into the fetus's heart (Timiras, 1972).

A motorized version of the old-fashioned birth stool is now in use at many hospitals in the United States. It is said to be more comfortable, easier, and faster, because the vertical position is the way the natural expulsive forces work. It can shorten the second stage of labor by half, especially for women giving birth for the first time (Brozan, 1981).

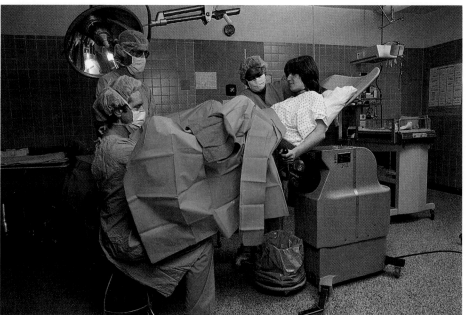

(© 1984 John Troha/Black Star)

A motorized version of the old-fashioned birth stool is now in use at many hospitals. Because the mother's position allows gravity to assist in the birth, the second stage of labor may be shortened by half.

CHAPTER 4 ■ BIRTH AND THE NEWBORN BABY   **127**

Medical Monitoring

Electronic fetal monitoring is the use of machines that monitor the baby's heart-beat during labor and delivery. This procedure provides valuable information (especially in detecting a lack of oxygen) in high-risk deliveries, including deliveries of premature and low-birthweight babies, and fetuses who seem to be in distress.

But monitoring has a number of drawbacks. First, it has a high "false positive" rate—that is, monitors often suggest that babies are in trouble when they are not. Acting on monitor warnings, doctors often deliver these babies by the riskier cesarean method (a surgical birth procedure) rather than vaginally. But research has shown that: (1) monitored babies do not do any better, (2) monitoring has not lessened the incidence of cerebral palsy, and (3) advances in infants' survival are generally attributable not to monitoring but to better neonatal care (Levano et al., 1986; Lewin, 1988). Furthermore, many women find the procedure uncomfortable, since it makes moving around during labor more difficult. And finally, the technology is extremely costly—in terms of the machines themselves and the more expensive cesarean deliveries they often lead to.

Why, then, are monitors used so much? One reason is that they replace the nurses who would otherwise have to check on babies periodically—and we are suffering from a nationwide nursing shortage. Also, in an age when doctors are often sued for not having done everything possible to deliver a healthy baby, the use of a monitor often seems prudent. Thus, while current recommendations are *against* routine fetal monitoring (E.A. Friedman, 1986; Levano et al., 1986), monitors are likely to remain in wide use.

Methods of Childbirth

Charles was able to spend the night in the hospital with Ellen, to be in the delivery room during Vicky's birth, and to cut the umbilical cord. Both expectant parents had taken a 6-week course given by the hospital, and if they had had other children, the children could have taken a special course for "expectant siblings" and could also have been in the delivery room during the birth. Ellen was happy to use the hospital's childbirth beds, which provided options for a number of different positions; to have her baby in her room with her; and to take a class in, and to get help with, breastfeeding immediately after birth.

Historically, the primary concern in delivering a baby has been to find a method that is comfortable for the mother and safe for both mother and baby. More recently, as safety has been assured in most births, obstetric workers have focused on making the experience more pleasant for the mother and the baby, and on allowing the father and other family members to feel that they are part of it. Such new efforts reflect a growing sensitivity to the emotional needs of all family members.

Medicated Delivery   Biblical scholars still debate whether God's injunction to Eve, "In travail shalt thou bring forth children," implied labor or sorrow. Whichever it was, most societies have evolved techniques to hasten delivery, make the mother's work easier, and lessen her discomfort. Some type of pain relief during labor and delivery is taken for granted among most western middle-class women. One study found that a *medicated delivery,* a delivery in which the mother is given anesthesia, was used in 95 percent of all deliveries performed in 18 teaching hospitals (Brackbill & Broman, 1979).

Some women receive general anesthesia, which renders them completely unconscious; others get a regional anesthetic (such as a spinal or caudal block), which blocks the nerve pathways that carry the sensation of pain to the brain; still others receive analgesics—painkillers—which also help them relax.

All these drugs pass through the placenta and enter the blood supply and tissues of the fetus, and some critics attribute the relatively high rate of infant mortality in the United States to the routine use of obstetric medication (Haire, 1972; personal communication, 1986).

Regional, or local, anesthetics seem to have fewer harmful effects on babies. Still, one study found that infants whose mothers received the drug bupivacaine by spinal block were not as alert and responsive as babies whose mothers received little or no medication. The effects of the drug were strongest on the first day, when the babies of women who received it showed poorer motor and physiological responses. By the fifth day, the differences were less dramatic but still favored the babies whose mothers had not received the drug (A.D. Murray, Dolby, Nation, & Thomas, 1981).

By 1 month, the babies in the two groups were not acting differently—but their mothers had different feelings about them. The mothers who had received bupivacaine seemed to view their infants less favorably and to find them harder to care for. This may well have been because there is no such thing in human beings as a "maternal instinct." Much of a woman's motherly feeling comes about because of the positive responses she receives from her baby. An infant who nurses eagerly and acts alert sets up positive feelings in her mother. If the first encounters between mother and baby do not draw a strong reaction from the baby, the effects of the mother's early impressions of her baby may remain even after the effects of the drug have worn off. (It is also possible that mothers who choose unmedicated deliveries are different from other mothers in their attitudes toward parenting and that their attitudes affect the way they act with their babies.)

Other research suggests that the physical effects of medication given during childbirth may persist through the first year of life—and possibly longer. A study of 3500 healthy full-term babies found that those whose mothers had received no obstetric medication showed the most progress in sitting, standing, and moving around; those whose mothers had received regional anesthetics showed less progress; and babies of mothers who had received general anesthetics showed the least (Brackbill & Broman, 1979).

The Committee on Drugs of the American Academy of Pediatrics (1978) recommends avoiding drugs or drug dosages known to produce significant changes in a baby's behavior and administering the minimum effective dose for women who do need relief from pain. Because the woman is the only person who can gauge the degree of her pain and is the one who is most personally concerned about the well-being of her child, she should have a strong voice, along with her doctor, in making decisions about obstetric medication.

It may be easier for women to make these decisions if the criticisms of one team of researchers prove to be sound (Kraemer, Korner, Anders, Jacklin, & Dimiceli, 1985). These investigators compared babies born to medicated and nonmedicated mothers on strength and tactile sensitivity, activity and irritability, and sleep. *No* evidence of *any* drug effect showed up in this study, or in

(Erika Stone, 1987)

In classes for expectant parents, the mother learns breathing and muscular exercises to make labor easier, and the father learns how to assist her through labor and delivery.

other well-designed studies. Kraemer and her colleagues (1985) charge that the research done in this area is poorly designed and misleading, and that it may have, on the one hand, kept appropriate drugs from some mothers, making them suffer unnecessary pain and discomfort, and, on the other hand, caused guilt in others who did take drugs. These authors also recommend more study, paying special attention to other factors that may help to explain correlations between medication and a poor outcome. Influences like birth order, maternal age and health, socioeconomic status, length and difficulty of labor, and condition and position of the fetus, which may have led to the medication in the first place, may actually be the causes of many poor outcomes—not the medication itself.

Natural and Prepared Childbirth In 1914, a British physician, Dr. Grantly Dick-Read, claimed that pain in childbirth was not inevitable but was caused largely by fear. To eliminate such fear, he developed the concept of *natural childbirth,* which involves educating women in the physiology of reproduction and delivery and training them in breathing, relaxation, and physical fitness. By mid-century, Dr. Fernand Lamaze was using the psychoprophylactic, or *prepared childbirth,* method of obstetrics. This method substituted new breathing and muscular responses to the sensations of uterine contractions for the old responses of fear and pain.

The Lamaze method, which has become very popular in the United States, has five elements:

1 *Instruction in the anatomy and physiology of childbirth* to reduce fear.
2 *Training in respiration techniques* (like rapid breathing and panting) to ease pain through controlled breathing. Many people in western societies consider such methods an aspect of eastern mysticism, and therefore somewhat dubious, but they do work (V.A. Harris, Katkin, Lick, & Haberfield, 1976).
3 *Use of a labor "coach"* (usually the husband or a friend) to help with relaxation. The coach's voice becomes a conditioned stimulus, helping the woman to relax or tense her muscles as appropriate.
4 *Cognitive restructuring,* which trains the woman to concentrate on sensations other than the birth contractions.
5 *Social support.* Having the coach attend classes with the mother, help in the exercises, and participate in the delivery increases the expectant mother's sense of worth and reduces her fear of loneliness (Wideman & Singer, 1984). The participation of fathers has proved especially popular. In 1945, one small hospital in Texas began allowing fathers into the delivery room; by 1983, 99 percent of hospitals surveyed allowed fathers to be present, often during cesarean deliveries as well as vaginal deliveries (May & Perrin, 1985; Wideman & Singer, 1984).

Gentle Birth The controversial technique of *gentle birth* (sometimes called the *Leboyer method,* after its developer) involves delivering babies in dimly lit, quiet rooms. No forceps are used, and the umbilical cord is not clamped immediately. No anesthesia, or only a local anesthetic, is used. The baby is bathed in warm water and calmly placed on the mother's belly right after birth. Leboyer (1975) maintains that such practices eliminate much birth trauma and result in happier mothers and babies.

Critics charge that the dim lighting may cause doctors to miss signs of dis-

natural childbirth *Method of childbirth developed by Dr. Grantly Dick-Read that seeks to prevent pain by eliminating the mother's fear of childbirth.*

prepared childbirth *Method of childbirth developed by Dr. Fernand Lamaze that uses instruction, breathing exercises, and social support to eliminate fear and pain.*

gentle birth *Delivering babies in dimly lit, quiet rooms, without forceps and with only local anesthesia or none; sometimes called the Leboyer method.*

tress and that the baby is exposed to infection from the water or the mother's body (Cohn, 1975). And the advantages of this method have not been substantiated by research. A 1986 study found that babies delivered by "gentle birth" were no different temperamentally during the first year of life from conventionally delivered babies or were only slightly easier (Maziade, Boudreault, Cote, & Thivierge, 1986). A 1980 study that compared the health and behavior of "gentle birth" babies with conventionally delivered babies found no differences up to 8 months of age except the Leboyer mothers' feeling 8 months after birth that the method had influenced their child's behavior (N. Nelson et al., 1980).

It seems, then, that gentle birth provides no advantages for health or personality development. But it poses no inevitable dangers. Its greatest benefit may be mothers' positive perception of their babies.

Cesarean Delivery *Cesarean delivery* is a surgical procedure to remove the baby from the uterus. The operation is commonly performed when labor is not progressing as quickly as it should, often because the baby is in the **breech position** (from which legs or buttocks would emerge before the head) or in the **transverse position** (lying crosswise in the uterus). It is also done when the baby's head is too big to pass through the mother's pelvis, the baby seems to be in trouble, or the mother is bleeding vaginally. Also, if the mother has had a cesarean delivery before, her delivery will probably be by cesarean; only 5 percent who have had cesareans have vaginal deliveries afterward. (Figure 4-2 shows rates on cesarean deliveries in several industrialized countries.)

cesarean delivery Surgical removal of the baby from the uterus.

breech position Misalignment of a fetus in the uterus causing the feet or buttocks to emerge before the head.

transverse position Misalignment of a fetus that causes it to lie crosswise in the uterus.

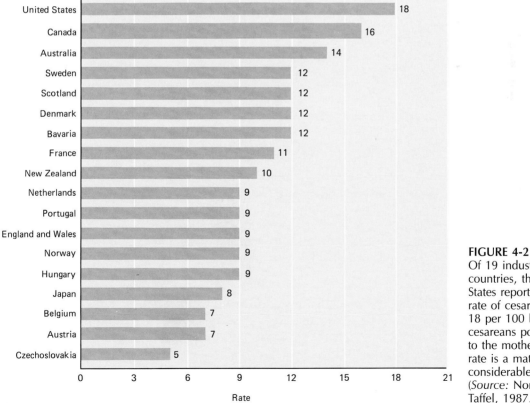

FIGURE 4-2
Of 19 industrialized countries, the United States reported the highest rate of cesarean deliveries: 18 per 100 births. Since cesareans pose more risk to the mother, this rising rate is a matter of considerable concern. (*Source:* Norton, Placek, & Taffel, 1987.)

BOX 4-1 ■ THE RESEARCH WORLD

THE STRESS OF BEING BORN

Not all stress is bad. Hans Selye, M.D., a major figure in stress research until his death in 1982, maintained that some stress is essential to life—in fact, that "complete freedom from stress is death" (1980, p. 128). Recent discoveries about the release of "stress hormones" both prenatally and during normal birth seem to confirm this viewpoint that stress is not only unavoidable but vital.

Human beings become introduced to stress very early, possibly within the womb and certainly during the struggle of a typical birth. First, the head is squeezed and subjected to pressure as the baby pushes through the narrow birth canal. Then, as contractions of the uterus compress the placenta and umbilical cord, they cause more pressure on the head, plus intermittent oxygen deprivation. Last, the newborn baby is forcibly expelled from the warm shelter of the womb to the bright lights of the outside world, "where some large creature holds it upside down and in many cases slaps it on the buttocks" (Lagercrantz & Slotkin, 1986, p. 100).

Yet most babies come through this struggle very well. They are helped by the release of two stress hormones—adrenaline and noradrenaline, which are in the class of catecholamines. (Catecholamines exert an important influence on nervous system functioning.) These stress hormones are secreted in extra quantities throughout life—in lower animals as well as human beings—in any dangerous situation, helping the threatened organism prepare for "fight or flight." They are released early in prenatal life, but at birth their levels soar, to rise above those seen in an adult having a heart attack. The first major task of these hormones may be to help the fetus make the necessary transition to life outside the womb.

How does this happen? The surge of these hormones at birth clears the lungs of excess liquid and produces a substance that keeps the lungs open and makes breathing possible. The hormones also mobilize fuel to nourish cells and send a rich supply of blood to the heart and brain. All this activity helps the baby to survive such hardships as lack of food or low levels of oxygen in the first hours of life. Furthermore, by making the baby alert and ready to interact with its mother, these hormones may even promote the mother-infant bond.

Babies born by emergency cesarean surgery, after the onset of labor, show levels of catecholamines that are almost as high as infants born vaginally. But babies born through elective cesarean deliveries *before labor has begun* do not experience this surge of hormones, which seems to be triggered by contractions of the mother's uterus. Many of these babies have trouble breathing, possibly because smaller amounts of stress hormones are released during birth. These findings support concerns about the overuse of elective cesareans, which may be bringing many babies into the world at a disadvantage.

Ironically, the normal release of catecholamines may lead to unnecessary cesarean deliveries. These hormones sometimes cause an irregular heartbeat in the fetus; this is picked up by electronic fetal monitoring and seen as cause for a cesarean delivery. To determine whether a baby is truly in trouble, biochemical analysis of blood samples from the fetus's scalp should accompany the electronic data.

The benefits of a cesarean birth need to be weighed against its risks. It does boast a superior safety record for delivery of breech babies. Its disadvantages include a higher risk of infection and a longer hospital stay and recovery from childbirth for the mother, greater expense, and the psychological and physical impact that go along with any surgery (Sachs et al., 1983). Furthermore, although cesarean deliveries have saved the lives of some mothers and babies who could not have survived vaginal deliveries, a review of 65,647 births in four hospitals in Brooklyn found that in most birthweight categories, delivering babies by cesarean did not improve the outcome (deRegt, Minkoff, Feldman, & Schwarz, 1986). Another drawback to this type of birth is the absence of an experience that some observers believe important to healthy development (see Box 4-1).

Critics of current American childbirth practices claim that too many unnecessary cesareans are performed in the United States. Of 19 industrialized countries surveyed in 1981, the United States reported the highest rate of cesarean deliveries—18 per 100 births (Norton, Placek, & Taffel, 1987; refer back to Figure 4-2). More recent surveys show an even higher rate, of 23 percent, or almost 1 in 4 (Placek, 1986). Why has this rate soared over the past two decades?

The Brooklyn study found that private physicians performed more cesareans than hospital residents did, probably for a variety of reasons, including private doctors' concerns about being sued if a baby is born with problems, scheduling pressures, and less familiarity with new techniques to judge fetal distress (deRegt et al., 1986). Cesarean rates might decrease if doctors received in-service education on the newer techniques and in legal medicine, if they were subjected to peer review of diagnosis and management, and if a second opinion were required before operating.

Alternative Settings for Childbirth Ellen, giving birth for the first time in her mid-thirties, wanted as much medical and technological support as she could muster, and so, like 99 percent of women in the United States (Wegman, 1987), she had her baby in a hospital. Like most of these women, she was assisted by an *obstetrician,* a physician who specializes in delivering babies.

Julia, on the other hand, felt that a hospital would be too big and impersonal, and so she followed the example of a small but growing number of women with a good medical history and an uncomplicated pregnancy who give birth at home or in small, homelike birth centers, or maternity centers. Like many of these women, Julia was attended by a certified *nurse-midwife,* someone who holds a degree in nursing and has been specially trained to assist at births. In 1985, midwives attended more births than they had in the previous year (in hospitals, 3 percent of births among blacks and 2 percent among whites; and more for out-of-hospital births—15 percent among blacks and 47 percent among whites; Wegman, 1987).

obstetrician *Physician who specializes in delivering babies.*

nurse-midwife *Certified nurse who has been specially trained to assist at births.*

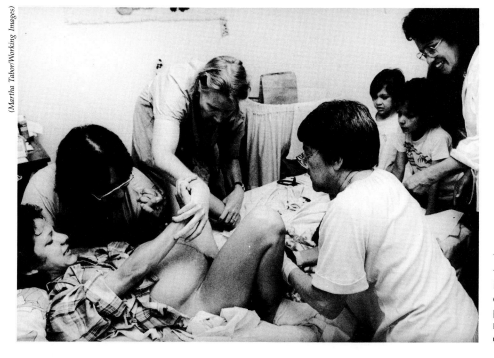

(Martha Tabor/Working Images)

Some couples, like these Texans, choose to have their babies delivered at home, with the assistance of a nurse-midwife in the presence of other family members. The experience can be exhilarating.

BOX 4-2 ■ A CHILD'S WORLD AND YOU

WHAT DO YOU THINK?

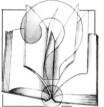

The birth process is affected by changing tastes and customs. Which of the following choices do you prefer?

THIS?

■ Having a normal delivery overseen by a doctor in a hospital

■ Arranging for a cesarean delivery at the first sign of a potentially difficult birth

■ Having the father absent during delivery

■ Having the mother unconscious during delivery

■ Having the baby stay in a nursery

■ Keeping the mother in bed for a few days after delivery

OR THIS?

■ Having a normal delivery overseen by a midwife in a clinic or at home

■ Having a nonsurgical delivery unless it is absolutely impossible

■ Letting the father be present during delivery

■ Having the mother conscious during delivery

■ Allowing the baby to stay with the mother

■ Letting the mother get back on her feet almost immediately after delivery

---

If a pregnancy is of low risk and the birth is uncomplicated, virtually any arrangement can work well. But since there may be a sudden emergency during any childbirth, it is vital to have backup plans in case of trouble. A good birth center will have a contract with an ambulance service, an agreement with a nearby hospital, and on-premises emergency equipment for resuscitation and for administration of oxygen. Provisions for a home birth should include arrangements for emergency transportation to a hospital no more than 10 minutes away.

While many hospitals *are* big and impersonal, with rigid rules that seem designed for the smooth functioning of the institution rather than the benefit of patients, others are designed more for the comfort of patients. As hospitals compete more for fewer maternity cases (since the birth rate has dropped in recent years), they respond more to patients' desires. Many, like the hospital where Vicky was born, have rooming-in policies so that babies can stay in the mother's room for much or all of the day, and they attend to numerous other aspects of family-centered maternity care.

Freestanding maternity centers, or birth centers, are a compromise between the comfort of home and the security of a well-equipped facility. They are usually staffed principally by nurse-midwives, with one or more physicians and nurse-assistants; they are designed for low-risk, uncomplicated births; and they offer prenatal care, birth in a homelike setting, and discharge the same day.

What are the psychological implications of the new ways of giving birth? First, techniques that minimize drugs may give the baby a better start in life. Second, the active participation of both parents reinforces close family attachments. Last, women's insistence on assuming a major role in childbirth has contributed to an important movement in family health—the idea that people should take more responsibility for their own health rather than sit back passively and rely on doctors. Of course, there are many ways to have a baby, and many psychologically and physically healthy people have been born in very traditional hospital settings. In view of what is known about the importance of feeling in control of one's life, the availability of alternative means of childbirth seems like a healthy trend; the crucial element is *choice* (see Box 4-2).

PARENTS' REACTIONS TO CHILDBIRTH

Exultation, relief, pride, wonder—all these are typical reactions to the birth of a child. Still, some women never forget the pain and anxiety of the experience. What variables in the birth process are most likely to make it a happy or an unhappy memory for the mother? According to research, speed and ease of delivery are more important than pain or its relief.

Long labor and the use of forceps are most likely to be associated with dissatisfaction with a vaginal birth. Women who receive the most pain relievers are the ones with the longest deliveries—and the ones most likely to express dissatisfaction with the process. Women who undergo emergency cesarean delivery are more likely to express dissatisfaction than women who have either an elective cesarean or a vaginal delivery.

Not much research has been done into the father's experience of childbirth, and the little that has been done has been heavily influenced by the movement for prepared childbirth. Fathers who are present at the birth of a child often see the event as a "peak emotional experience" (May & Perrin, 1985), but there is no good evidence that attendance at the birth makes a man a better father. One extensive review of the father's role found that "fathers typically become engrossed in their newborn infants regardless of their birth attendance experience" (Palkovitz, 1985, p. 396). Attachment, an emotional commitment of loyalty and

Parents in the delivery room with a newborn usually feel excited, proud, and relieved. A fast, easy delivery is more important than the degree of pain the mother feels in making her memory of birth a happy one.

BOX 4-3 ■ THE EVERYDAY WORLD

THE TRANSITION TO PARENTHOOD

When people become parents, their day-to-day lives change more abruptly and to a much greater extent than when they marry. A few decades ago, researchers showed the birth or adoption of a first child to be a major upheaval in both parents' lives and in their marriage (Dyer, 1963; LeMasters, 1957). But more recent research has shown the event as a time of transition that is sometimes difficult but, by and large, positive (Hobbs & Cole, 1976; Hobbs & Wimbish, 1977).

Marriages do undergo stress after a baby is born, and this stress affects couples differently, depending on such factors as their expectations from parenthood, the sex and number of children, and the parents' age. But usually, the birth of a baby does not make a good marriage go bad or make a bad one better.

What does happen? Among 139 middle- and working-class couples married an average of 4 years and getting along smoothly, husbands and wives said that after their first child was born, their marriages were not quite as good as they had been. During the first month of the baby's life, they enjoyed a "honeymoon" with the baby. But during the next 2 months, their satisfaction plummeted as both parents—but especially the mothers (who, even in these "liberated" times, usually assume most of the responsibility for child care)—were plunged into sleepless nights and exhausting days.

The new parents saw their marriages less as romances and friendships—and more as partnerships. They became less affectionate with each other, did not talk as much, and engaged in fewer leisure activities together. Most of the change took place in the first 6 months. As fathers did more for their babies 3 to 9 months after birth, the wives were happier in their marriage, and by 9 months, husbands and wives viewed their marriages alike (Belsky, Lang, & Rovine, 1985; Belsky, Spanier, & Rovine, 1983). Still, the couples who had the best marriages before their babies were born had the happiest marriages afterward.

No one ever really knows beforehand what it is like to take care of a baby. But some people have a better idea than others of what to expect. The new parents who were prepared for the negative aspects of parenthood, along with its joys, felt less stress than those who had idealized it (Belsky, 1985).

Boys seem to strain a marriage more than girls, according to a study of 210 mothers in Georgia. While the mothers of girls were just as happy in their marriages as childless women, mothers of boys—especially those with two boys (an infant and a preschooler)—were unhappier than both other groups (Abbott & Brody, 1985). This may be because parents often find boys' temperament and behavior harder to manage and thus parents of boys argue more often about the best thing to do.

Parents of adults sometimes repeat an old saying: "Little children, little problems—big children, big problems." Researchers, too, conclude that the ongoing work of parenthood is even harder than the initial transition (B.C. Miller & Myers-Walls, 1983). Still, most parents feel good about being parents, and as one national survey of 2102 parents showed, 90 percent would choose it again (General Mills, Inc., 1977).

Anyone reading the scientific literature on parenting is likely to get a skewed view, since most research focuses not on the joys and satisfactions of rearing children, but on the stresses and dissatisfactions. This may be a reaction to rose-colored views of both bringing children into the world and bringing them up. In our attempt to see parenthood more realistically, however, we should remember its important role in the parents' own development.

One of the best things about parenthood is that it is never boring. Just as parents are adjusting to the needs of caring for an infant, the baby turns into an adventuresome toddler who needs to be watched vigilantly; just when parents have made the leap to this stage, the toddler becomes a preschooler. The changes continue, offering the chance for creative personal growth as parents are called upon to form new attitudes and behaviors, to relive their own childhood experiences and work out unresolved issues, and to respond to their children's unique personalities.

love between the father and the child, is unlikely to depend on a father's presence at the child's delivery.

Jess, however, would reply that studies of the long-term utility of the experience are beside the point. Like many men, he wants to be with his wife and his children at times of great emotion, both the triumphant moments and the difficult ones. "It was the most thrilling experience of my life," he tells everyone who will listen, and no research data could ever persuade him that he might just as well have gone bowling.

Both mother and father go through a great deal of development as they respond not only to the birth, but to the entire experience of parenthood. (See Box 4-3, opposite.)

COMPLICATIONS OF CHILDBIRTH

While the great majority of births result in normal, healthy babies, a small minority of babies are born very small, suffer birth trauma or other complications, or are born dead.

Low Birthweight

Nearly 7 percent of all newborns are *low-birthweight babies;* that is, they weigh less than 5½ pounds (2500 grams) at birth (Wegman, 1987). Depending on their size and hardiness and on the care they receive, low-birthweight infants are at varying degrees of risk.

All very small infants used to be assumed premature, that is, born before the full term of normal pregnancy. Now, though, doctors classify these babies into one or both of two categories:

- *Preterm (premature babies)* are babies born before the thirty-seventh gestational week as dated from the first day of the mother's last menstrual period (40 weeks is normal gestation). These babies typically weigh less than 5½ pounds and account for 60 percent of low-birthweight babies (U.S. Public Health Service, undated).
- *Small-for-date babies* are those weighing less than 90 percent of all babies of the same gestational age, whether or not they are born preterm; they have suffered from slowed fetal growth (R. Robinson, 1972). Such babies are also described as *small-for-gestational age*.

Since the distinction between preterm infants and small-for-date infants has evolved only within the past few decades, it has not been considered in most studies of the effects of "prematurity." Therefore, in many cases we do not know whether studies of low-birthweight babies yield information about babies who were born early or about babies who were small for their gestational age.

The risks to both types of low-birthweight babies are similar, but premature babies are more likely to die in infancy than small-for-date babies (Behrman, 1985). Babies born after 36 weeks of gestation generally have few problems; but under 36 weeks, the shorter the gestation period, the more problems infants are likely to have, because they are born before their body systems are fully developed. Babies who weigh less than 3 pounds at birth are especially at risk, accounting for about two-thirds of the babies who die in the first month of life (U.S. Department of Health and Human Services, USDHHS, 1980a). Today, however, dramatic medical advances have made it possible for many babies born at or before the twenty-sixth week of gestation and weighing less than 2 pounds to survive and do well (Buckwald, Zorn, & Egan, 1984).

Let us first consider why low birthweight is such a serious problem. Then we will describe women at risk and ways of preventing and treating low birthweight.

low-birthweight baby
General term used for both preterm and small-for-date babies; formerly called premature babies.

preterm (premature) baby
Baby born less than 37 weeks after the mother's last menstrual period.

small-for-date baby *Baby whose birthweight is less than that of 90 percent of all babies born at the same gestational age.*

This low-birthweight baby, spending the first days of life in a germ-free, temperature-controlled isolette, has a better chance for a healthy life than ever before. Recent dramatic advances enable even babies weighing less than 2 pounds at birth to survive.

Consequences of Low Birthweight   The most pressing fear for very small babies is that they will die in infancy. Babies weight 5½ pounds or less are 40 times more likely to die during the first 4 weeks of life than babies over this weight; very low-birthweight babies weighing 3⅓ pounds (1500 grams) or less are in much greater peril; their risk is 200 times normal (Behrman, 1985; S.S. Brown, 1985). Still, there is heartening progress in helping these babies. Today, 90 percent of babies weighing from 2 to 3 pounds survive; in the early 1960s, more than half died.

Low-birthweight babies have to struggle for life. Because they have less fat to insulate them and to generate heat, they have more trouble maintaining normal body temperature. Because their immune system is not fully developed, they are more vulnerable to infection. Their lungs may not be strong enough to sustain breathing. Their reflexes are not mature enough to perform basic functions; many cannot suck and have to be fed through a stomach tube (this is known as *gavage* feeding).

Low-birthweight babies have a higher incidence of low blood sugar, jaundice, and bleeding in the brain than babies of normal size (March of Dimes Birth Defects Foundation, undated). A common disorder among them is respiratory distress syndrome (also called *hyaline membrane disease*); because they lack an essential lung-coating substance, they breathe irregularly. They may even stop breathing completely, and thus succumb to this condition (as they may to some of the other conditions).

In the past, even when low-birthweight babies survived the dangerous early days, they were left with various disabling conditions. More recent research, however, gives cause for more optimism, such as a study of 351 very low-birthweight babies born in the Australian state of Victoria. Of these children, who had weighed from 1 to 2 pounds at birth (500 to 999 grams), 75 percent died. However, 72 percent of the survivors had no handicaps at all at age 5, and only 19 percent had severe disabilities (Kitchen et al., 1987). A number of the children who had been diagnosed at age 2 as having cerebral palsy had outgrown their condition by age 5, suggesting that age 2 is too early to evaluate future health.

Women at Risk of Having Low-Birthweight Babies   A number of different types of factors make some women more likely than others to bear low-birthweight infants (see Table 4-1). These include:

- *Demographic and socioeconomic factors*, like age, race, income, education, and marital status
- *Medical risks predating pregnancy*, like diabetes, abnormalities of the uterus, multiple miscarriages, and previous low-birthweight babies
- *Conditions of the current pregnancy*, like weight gain of less than 14 pounds, presence of twins, and infections such as rubella
- *Lifestyle factors*, like smoking, malnutrition, drug abuse, and poor prenatal care

Many of these factors may be interrelated. For example, teenagers' higher risk probably stems more from poor nutrition and inadequate prenatal care than from age. And socioeconomic status cuts across almost all risk factors. Poor women who smoke are more likely to have low-birthweight babies than affluent women who smoke, probably because such factors as poor nutrition and poor

TABLE 4-1

PRINCIPAL MATERNAL RISK FACTORS FOR DELIVERING UNDERWEIGHT INFANTS	
CATEGORY	RISKS
Demographic and socioeconomic factors	Age (under 17 or over 34) Race (black) Poverty Unmarried Low level of education
Medical risks predating current pregnancy	No children or more than four Low weight for height Genital or urinary abnormalities or past surgery Diseases such as diabetes or chronic hypertension Lack of immunity to certain infections, such as rubella Poor obstetric history, including previous low-birthweight infant and multiple miscarriages Genetic factors in the mother (such as low weight at her own birth)
Conditions of current pregnancy	Multiple pregnancy (twins or more) Poor weight gain (less than 14 pounds) Less than 6 months since previous pregnancy Low blood pressure Hypertension or toxemia Certain infections, such as rubella and urinary infections Bleeding in the first or second trimester Placental problems Anemia or abnormal blood count Fetal abnormalities Incompetent cervix Spontaneous premature rupture of membranes
Lifestyle factors	Smoking Poor nutritional status Abuse of alcohol and other substances Exposure to DES and other toxins, including those in the workplace High altitude
Risks involving health care	Absent or inadequate prenatal care Premature delivery by cesarean section or induced labor

Source: Adapted from S.S. Brown, 1985.

prenatal care compound the effects of smoking. The high rate for black women reflects greater poverty and a greater tendency to become a teenage mother. Even when these factors are controlled for, however, black women are more likely than white women to bear low-birthweight babies (S.S. Brown, 1985).

Preventing Low Birthweight   Even before pregnancy, women can cut down their chances of having a low-birthweight baby—by eating well, not smoking or using drugs, drinking little or not at all, and getting good medical care. During the pregnancy, medical care and lifestyle factors are also crucial. The American College of Obstetricians and Gynecologists recommends 13 to 15 medical checkups during the course of a normal pregnancy, beginning with one visit early in the first trimester.

The most effective way to reduce the number of low-birthweight babies is widespread prenatal care. Low birthweight is less a medical problem than a social one; it can often be prevented with enough effort, and this effort can pay off for society. More than $1.5 billion is spent every year on neonatal intensive care, most for low-birthweight babies, and research has shown that for every dollar spent on prenatal care, more than $3 is saved on care for low-birthweight infants (S.S. Brown, 1985). (See Box 4-4 for a description of services offered by the governments of some other countries.)

Treating Low-Birthweight Babies   In the past few years we have seen impressive advances in the care of newborn babies, so that today babies small enough to fit into an adult's palm can live and thrive.

isolette Crib which permits full temperature regulation under antiseptic conditions; formerly called an incubator.

Isolettes   Small babies are usually cared for in an antiseptic bed called an *isolette* and are fed through stomach tubes. The isolettes are heated, because these babies lack the fat that enables them to generate heat and maintain normal body temperature. Babies with special problems receive special care: jaundiced infants are placed under lights or given medication, anemic ones get iron supplements, and babies with low blood sugar receive glucose intravenously.

Until recently, most hospitals had a "hands off" policy, in the belief that small preterm babies were so delicate that they should be disturbed as little as possible. But life in an isolette lacks the stimulation of life in the womb, where the fetus senses sounds and motion, and the sensory impoverishment of the isolette is now believed to cause problems for both babies and parents.

Stimulation   Human babies, including the smallest, seem to need human touch. Low-birthweight babies whose bodies are stroked and whose arms and legs are gently flexed on a regular basis gain more weight than babies who do not receive this kind of stimulation, are awake more, are more active, show more mature behaviors, and leave the hospital earlier (T.M. Field, 1986; Schanberg & Field, 1987). These effects seem to last at least through the first 8 to 12 months of life, and the stroking seems to be especially important.

Even a simple step like giving low-birthweight babies pacifiers to suck on during their tubal feedings can bring results. Infants develop the sucking reflex faster, gain weight better, switch to mouth feeding earlier, and leave the hospital sooner (Bernbaum, Pereira, Watkins, & Peckham, 1983).

One group of 124 low-birthweight babies received a longer, more broad-based treatment program (Resnick, Eyler, Nelson, Eitzman, & Bucciarelli, 1987). In the hospital, these babies slept on insulated water mattresses, received gentle massage, and were given movement exercises. They also saw pictures of faces, mobiles, and color patterns, and listened to tapes of classical music, a human heartbeat, and their parents' voices. During the babies' first 2 years, child development experts visited their parents at home twice a month, showed them some 400 exercises designed to enhance the babies' physical and mental development, taught them how to recognize and respond to their babies' cues, and talked with them about their children.

What were the results? The babies showed significantly higher mental and physical developmental scores at 1 and 2 years of age than a control group who

(© Joseph Nettis 1986/Photo Researchers)

The tiniest babies thrive on human touch. This nurse's holding and stroking of a low-birthweight baby will help the baby grow and be more alert.

BOX 4-4 ■ AROUND THE WORLD

MATERNITY CARE IN WESTERN EUROPE

Why do more babies die at or soon after birth in the United States than in many western European countries? Why has the United States fallen lower in the world rankings over the past several decades? The answer may well lie in the kind of health care typically received by mothers in the United States and in countries that have lower infant mortality rates. Let's look at some of these differences.

Suppose you are a woman in one of ten western European countries that have established high standards of maternity care and universal health services and social support (Belgium, Denmark, West Germany, France, Ireland, Netherlands, Norway, Spain, Switzerland, and Great Britain). Although the specific services you received would vary depending on which country you lived in, in any of the countries you would receive either free or very low-cost prenatal and postnatal care, including a paid maternity leave from work (ranging from 9 to 40 weeks).

You would be highly motivated to seek prenatal care early, because only after your pregnancy was confirmed and officially registered would you begin receiving such benefits as transportation privileges and preferential hospital booking for delivery. You would probably go first to a general practitioner, who would coordinate your care with a midwife and an obstetrician. The midwife would give you most of your prenatal care and attend the birth—unless your pregnancy was considered high-risk, in which case a doctor would assist you.

The number of your prenatal visits might vary—from 4 if you were Swiss to 12 if you were Dutch, British, or Norwegian. If you missed an appointment or had a complicated pregnancy, your midwife would visit you at home, and in some countries you would receive one such visit routinely. If you lived in Norway, you would be reimbursed for up to 10 days' travel and living expenses, so that you could be near a hospital at the time of delivery.

After the baby was born, you would probably receive at least one home visit to get counseling about infant care, family planning, and your own health. If you were a single mother, you would get extra help; if you were an employed mother or the mother of a large family, you would have priority for day care and public housing. You would receive a monthly family allowance for each child, usually until adulthood or completion of education. And you would receive a financial bonus at the time of delivery (unless you were Danish), to help pay for the cost of supplies and equipment for the new baby. If you were French, this bonus would hinge on the number of prenatal visits you made, and if you were Swiss it would be larger if you breastfed.

In the Netherlands you could pay a token fee for a trained helper who would stay with you for up to 8 hours a day for 10 days, helping you shop, cook, and take care of the new baby and your other children. In West Germany either you or your husband could take paid child-care leave, and unpaid leave might last for 3 years.

The bottom line is that as a pregnant woman in Europe, you would never need to ask how or where you would receive care or who would pay for it. As a pregnant woman in the United States, you would face a very different situation. You would not get the benefits of uniform national standards for maternity care and thus you would not be assured of consistent, high-quality care. Furthermore, you could not count on universal financial coverage.

In 1985 it cost an average of $3100 for a normal delivery and $4800 for a cesarean birth, and 25 percent of American women of prime childbearing age are not protected by either public or private health insurance. Almost half of practicing obstetricians refuse to see Medicaid patients. It is not surprising, then, that rates of prenatal care are so low in the United States.

In 1985, 21 percent of white mothers and 38 percent of black mothers did not receive prenatal care in the first trimester, and 5 percent of white mothers and 10 percent of black mothers had none at all, or "too little, too late" (Wegman, 1986, p. 820). The rates for delayed prenatal care or none at all increased in 29 states and the District of Columbia, and only 11 states reported any improvement (Wegman, 1986). The lowest rates apply to the women most at risk of bearing low-birthweight babies—teenage and black women, and women with little education (S.S. Brown, 1985; Ingram, Makuc, & Kleinman, 1986).

This bleak picture might change if local and national government linked prenatal care with comprehensive social and financial benefits. The need is for a wide range of educational, social, and medical services (including outreach workers to identify women in need and to help with transportation, baby-sitting, and housing problems).

Sources: Behrman, 1985; S.S. Brown, 1985; C.A. Miller, 1987; Wegman, 1986.

received traditional care and who showed the developmental delays typically seen among low-birthweight babies. This family-centered program cost about $3600 per child, representing a fairly low-cost investment in each child's life, assuming that its effects hold up over the years. Follow-ups are planned to see whether this does happen—and which aspects of the program are most important.

Improving the parent-child relationship   Parents of low-birthweight babies are often reluctant to become attached to the baby right away, for fear that the baby will die (Jeffcoate, Humphrey, & Lloyd, 1979). They also tend to view their babies negatively.

self-fulfilling prophecy
Prediction of behavior that biases people to act as though the prophecy were already true.

Such parents may be setting up a *self-fulfilling prophecy,* a process by which one's expectation of another person influences one's behavior toward that person so that the other person responds by fulfilling the expectation. One study clearly shows how this can work. Researchers brought 27 mothers together with unfamiliar infants; all the babies were actually full-term, but the mothers were told that some were premature. The mothers touched the "premature" babies less, gave them more "immature" toys to play with, rated them less cute, and liked them less. Later, when college students saw videotapes of these interactions, they were able to tell which babies had been labeled "premature" (Stern & Hildebrandt, 1986). This seems to show that there is a stereotype of premature babies.

It is important, then, not to overstate long-term risks or discourage a parent's wish to be with and love the new child. One study showed how frequent visits to the isolette can help the parent-child relationship. Even though mothers who see their babies more have more negative perceptions of how the babies are doing at the time, they have more positive expectations for the future. Parents who visit often seem to be more realistic about their babies, and their babies recover faster, leave the hospital sooner, and seem to have a better chance for survival (Zeskind & Iacino, 1984).

Counseling for parents of low-birthweight babies is important. Those who receive it seem to care for their children better afterward, unless the mothers are so overwhelmed by other life stresses that they can barely get through each day (J. Brown et al., 1980; Minde et al., 1980). In such cases, intervention and support from professional agencies are especially important.

Postmaturity

Instead of coming too early, some babies do not show any signs of readiness for birth for weeks after they are expected. As many as 7 percent of women have not gone into labor 2 weeks after the due date. At this point, which is 42 weeks after the mother's last menstrual period, a baby is considered *postmature.* Sometimes as many as 5 weeks go by.

Postmature babies tend to be long and thin, because they have kept growing in the womb but have had an insufficient food supply at the end. This may be because the placenta has aged and become less efficient; if so, its delivery of oxygen may also be reduced. The babies' greater size also complicates labor: the mother has to deliver a baby the size of a normal 1-month-old.

Since postmature fetuses are at higher risk of brain damage or even death, doctors faced with a gestation of more than 42 weeks sometimes induce labor with drugs and sometimes perform cesarean deliveries. These courses carry their own risks; for example, if the due date has been miscalculated, a baby who is actually premature may be delivered. To help in this difficult decision, doctors monitor the baby's status with ultrasound. This lets them see whether the heart rate speeds up when the fetus moves; if not, the baby may be short of oxygen. Another test involves examining the volume of amniotic fluid; a low level may mean insufficient food. To help provide answers in these problematic cases, the National Institute of Child Health and Human Development has launched a study of 2800 women whose babies are late; within the next decade, then, we should have some idea of the best course to follow for late babies.

Birth Trauma

For a small minority of babies, the passage through the birth canal is a perilous journey that may leave lasting marks in the form of injury. In a study of 15,435 births over a period of 6 years at an outstanding medical school, where the level of care was of very high quality (A. Rubin, 1977), 1 infant in every 133 (fewer than 1 percent) suffered some type of *birth trauma,* an injury sustained at the time of birth. Birth injuries were the second most common cause of neonatal death (the most common cause was suffocation because lungs failed to expand).

birth trauma   Injury sustained by an infant at birth.

Brain injury is a particularly serious form of birth trauma. *Anoxia*—oxygen deprivation—at birth, mechanical birth injury, and neonatal diseases or infections leave some children with permanent brain injury, resulting in mental retardation or behavior problems.

anoxia   Oxygen deprivation.

A favorable environment can often overcome birth trauma. A longitudinal study of almost 900 children born on the island of Kauai, Hawaii, found that the homes children grew up in seem to exert more influence than their birth experiences (E. Werner et al., 1968). At age 10, most of the children who had had difficult births, had been sick when born, or had been of low birthweight were doing well. They were no more likely to earn poor grades or to have language, perceptual, or emotional problems than other children—unless they had been affected so severely that they had to be institutionalized. The same happy result was evident when these children reached age 18: only when children who had had problems around the time of birth grew up in a poor environment were they likely to suffer impaired physical and psychological development (E. Werner, 1985).

On the other hand, most of the children with language, perceptual, or emotional problems had suffered no stress at birth but had grown up in poor homes where they received little intellectual stimulation or emotional support. They may be said to have suffered "environmental trauma."

Thus, the long-term outlook for children is good when their environment is stable and enriching. Children are resilient, and, given good day-to-day surroundings, they can often bounce back from even very alarming transitory events.

Stillbirth

Delivery of a dead child, a *stillbirth,* is a tragic union of opposites—birth and death. Sometimes the death is diagnosed days or weeks before delivery *(as fetal death in utero)*; in other cases it is discovered during labor or delivery. Fortu-

stillbirth   Delivery of a dead infant.

fetal death in utero   Death of a fetus while in the uterus.

nately, less than 1 in 100 babies are stillborn (DeFrain, 1986). When parents do have a stillbirth, they should be encouraged to grieve for the child they have lost. Typically, such grieving has four phases:

1 *Shock and numbness characterized by disbelief.* The parents need to experience the reality of what has happened and may benefit from seeing and holding the dead infant, as well as from obtaining an autopsy report and having a funeral.
2 *Yearning and searching for the child.* Some parents try to "find" the lost child by immediately beginning another pregnancy; but this seems only to bury and complicate their grief rather than help resolve it. First, they need to experience the intensity of their grief.
3 *Disorganization.* The period up to 6 months to a year after the stillbirth is usually a time of depression, apathy, and self-devaluation. Programs that provide counseling and support seem helpful.
4 *Reorientation.* In this final stage of grief, the parents begin to resume their roles in society. They do not forget their stillborn child, and commonly they remember or commemorate the anniversary, but the focus of their thoughts returns to life and the living (Kirkley-Best & Kellner, 1982).

The Newborn

WHO IS THE NEWBORN?

neonatal period *First 4 weeks after birth.*

Who is this newcomer to the world? What does Vicky look like? What can Jason do? How can we tell whether a new baby is normal and able to withstand the stresses of the world outside the warm protection of the womb?

The first 4 weeks of life mark the **neonatal period,** a time of transition from intrauterine life—when the fetus is supported entirely by its mother—to an independent existence. This transition generally takes longer for low-birth-weight babies, since they enter the world with less fully developed body systems.

An average newborn, or *neonate,* is about 20 inches long and weighs about 7½ pounds. At birth, 95 percent of full-term babies weigh between 5½ and 10 pounds and measure between 18 and 22 inches in length (Behrman & Vaughan, 1983). Birth size is related to such factors as race, sex, parents' size, and mother's nutrition and health. Boys tend to be slightly longer and heavier than girls, and a firstborn child is likely to weigh less at birth than later-born siblings. Size at birth is related to size during childhood (Vuillamy, 1973).

The baby has distinctive features—a large head, big eyes set low, a small nose and retreating chin (which make nursing easier), and fat cheeks. Ethologists (scientists who study animal behavior) disagree whether such features automatically trigger affection in adults, or whether our experience with babies makes us look upon such features so fondly that we transfer our feelings toward other animals (see Figure 4-3).

In their first few days, neonates lose as much as 10 percent of body weight, primarily because of a loss of fluids. On about the fifth day, they begin to gain, and usually they are back to birthweight by the tenth to the fourteenth day. Light full-term infants lose less weight than heavy ones, and firstborns lose less than later-borns (Timiras, 1972).

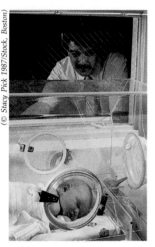

(© Stacy Pick 1987/Stock, Boston)

A father looking at his newborn baby is full of questions. Who is this newcomer? What can the baby do? What will this new member of the family be like?

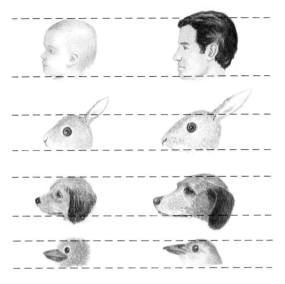

FIGURE 4-3
People are drawn to animals with babyish features: big eyes, bulging foreheads, and retreating chins (as shown in row at left). Such features may be a biological adaptation that encourages survival, since animals with small eyes and long snouts (as shown in row at right) do not call forth the same kind of affection. (*Source:* Lorenz, 1971.)

The neonate's head is one-fourth of the body length and may be long and misshapen because of the "molding" that has eased its passage through the mother's pelvis. This temporary molding is possible because the baby's skull bones are not yet fused; they will not be completely joined for 18 months. The places on the head where the bones have not yet grown together—the soft spots, or *fontanels*—are covered by a tough membrane. Since the cartilage in the baby's nose is also malleable, the trip through the birth canal leaves the nose looking squashed for a few days.

Newborns are quite pale—even babies who later will be very dark-skinned. They have a pinkish cast because their skin is so thin that it barely covers the capillaries through which blood flows. Some neonates are very hairy, since some of the **lanugo,** or fuzzy prenatal body hair, has not yet dropped off; it will fall off in a few days. All new babies are covered with **vernix caseosa** (Latin, "cheesy varnish"), an oily protection against infection that dries over a few days' time.

During the Middle Ages, special healing powers were attributed to "witch's milk," a secretion that sometimes issues from the swollen breasts of newborn boys and girls. Like the blood-tinged vaginal discharge of some baby girls, this results from high levels of the hormone estrogen, which is secreted by the placenta just before birth.

lanugo Fine, soft prenatal hair; present on some neonates at birth, but soon lost.
vernix caseosa Oily substance on a neonate's body that dries within a few days after birth.

HOW DOES THE NEWBORN FUNCTION?

The Newborn's Body Systems

Jason's need to survive on his own puts a host of new demands on his body systems, all of which prove up to the task. Before birth, his blood circulation, breathing, ingestion of nutrients, elimination of waste, and temperature regulation were all accomplished through his mother's body. After birth, he must carry out all these functions himself, and like most newborns, he does this so well that nobody even remarks on the feat. Never again will Jason undergo so thorough a change in his life support (see Table 4-2, page 146).

TABLE 4-2

A COMPARISON OF PRENATAL AND POSTNATAL LIFE		
CHARACTERISTIC	PRENATAL LIFE	POSTNATAL LIFE
Environment	Amniotic fluid	Air
Temperature	Relatively constant	Fluctuates with atmosphere
Stimulation	Minimal	All senses stimulated by various stimuli
Nutrition	Dependent on mother's blood	Dependent on external food and functioning of digestive system
Oxygen supply	Passed from maternal bloodstream via placenta	Passed from neonate's lungs to pulmonary blood vessels
Metabolic elimination	Passed into maternal bloodstream via placenta	Discharged by skin, kidneys, lungs, and gastrointestinal tract

Source: Timiras, (1972), p. 174.

Circulatory System   Before Jason's birth, Jason and Julia had independent circulatory systems and separate heartbeats; but the fetus's blood was cleansed through the umbilical cord, which carried "used" blood to the placenta and clean blood back. After his birth, Jason's own system must take over to circulate blood through his body. A neonate's heartbeat is still fast and irregular, and blood pressure does not stabilize until about the tenth day after birth.

Respiratory System   The umbilical cord also brings oxygen to the fetus and carries back carbon dioxide. As a newborn, Jason needs much more oxygen and must now get it all alone. Most babies start to breathe as soon as they are exposed to the air; one who is not breathing within 2 minutes after birth may be in trouble. If breathing has not begun within 5 minutes, the baby may, to a greater or lesser degree, suffer permanent brain injury caused by a lack of oxygen, or anoxia.

Gastrointestinal System   In the uterus, Jason also relied on the umbilical cord to bring food from his mother and to carry his body wastes away. At birth, he has a strong sucking reflex to take in milk, and he also has the gastrointestinal secretions to digest it. During the first few days after birth, he secretes *meconium,* which is a stringy, greenish-black waste matter formed in the fetal intestinal tract. When Jason's bowels and bladder are full, his sphincter muscles open automatically, and it will be many months before he will be able to control these muscles.

meconium   *Fetal waste matter.*

Three or four days after birth, about half of all babies develop *neonatal jaundice:* their skin and eyeballs are yellow. This kind of jaundice is caused by immaturity of the liver; it usually is not serious and has no long-term effects, and it occurs most often in premature babies. It is usually treated by putting the baby under fluorescent lights or, in severe cases, by administering drugs (Kappas, Drummond, Manola, Petmezaki, & Valaes, 1988).

neonatal jaundice
Yellowing of the skin and eyeballs that is common among newborns and seldom serious.

Temperature Regulation The layers of fat that developed during the last 2 months of fetal life enable Jason, as a healthy full-term infant, to keep his body temperature constant, despite changes in air temperature. He also maintains his body temperature by increasing his activity when air temperature drops.

Medical and Behavioral Screening: Is the Baby Healthy?

Because the first few weeks, days, and even minutes after birth are important for future development, Vicky and Jason are monitored immediately after birth to see whether they have any problems requiring special care. Doctors and psychologists use a variety of tests to measure physical and behavioral development.

Immediate Medical Assessment: Apgar Scale One minute after delivery—and then again 5 minutes after delivery—Vicky and Jason are checked according to the *Apgar scale* (see Table 4-3). Its name commemorates its developer, Dr. Virginia Apgar (1953), and also helps us remember its five subtests: *a*ppearance (color), *p*ulse (heart rate), *g*rimace (reflex irritability), *a*ctivity (muscle tone), and *r*espiration (breathing).

Apgar scale Standard measurement of a newborn's condition that assesses appearance, pulse, grimace, activity, and respiration.

The infant receives a rating of 0, 1, or 2 on each measure, for a maximum score of 10. Ninety percent of normal infants score 7 or better. A score below 7 means that the body needs help to establish breathing. A score below 4 means that the baby is in danger and needs immediate lifesaving treatment. If resuscitation is successful, bringing the baby's score to 4 or over, no long-term damage is likely to result. But scores from 0 to 3 at 10, 15, and 20 minutes after birth may signal the danger of cerebral palsy or other neurological (central nervous system) problems (American Academy of Pediatrics Committee on Fetus and Newborn, 1986).

A low Apgar score does not always indicate lack of oxygen. Babies' failure to respond well may result because the mother was sedated or anesthetized during birth; because they were born with certain conditions of the heart, the lungs, or the central nervous system; or—as in the case of low-birthweight babies—because their bodies are immature.

TABLE 4-3

APGAR SCALE			
SIGN*	0	1	2
Appearance (color)	Blue, pale	Body pink, extremities blue	Entirely pink
Pulse (heart rate)	Absent	Slow (below 100)	Rapid (over 100)
Grimace (reflex irritability)	No response	Grimace	Coughing, sneezing, crying
Activity (muscle tone)	Limp	Weak, inactive	Strong, active
Respiration (breathing)	Absent	Irregular, slow	Good, crying

*Each sign is rated in terms of absence or presence from 0 to 2; highest overall score is 10.
Source: Adapted from Apgar, 1953.

Screening Newborns for Medical Conditions   Children born with the genetic disorder *phenylketonuria (PKU)*, if left untreated, will suffer irreparable damage to the developing central nervous system and become mentally retarded. This defect leaves its victims unable to metabolize a vital enzyme. Brain damage results—unless the infants receive a special diet beginning in the first 3 to 6 weeks of life. With this diet they develop normally.

Children born with the blood disorder sickle-cell anemia (among African Americans, this disorder affects 1 in 400 newborns) are susceptible to infection and at risk of early death. Preventive oral doses of penicillin can cut the infection rate in these children by 85 percent and reduce fatalities (National Institutes of Health, NIH, 1987).

To discover the presence of these and other correctable defects, researchers have developed a number of screening tests that can be administered immediately after birth. But routine screening of all newborn babies is expensive. Is it cost-effective for a society with ever-rising medical costs, especially for such rare conditions as PKU (1 case in 14,000 births), hypothyroidism (a condition affecting 1 baby in 4250, which results from deficient production of thyroid hormone and causes retarded physical and mental development), or other, even rarer, disorders? Yes, it is, since the cost of detecting one case of a rare disease is often less than the cost of caring for a mentally retarded child over a lifetime. Therefore, almost all states require routine screening for PKU, and about half screen for one or more other conditions for which reliable, simple, and cost-effective screening techniques and effective remedies are available.

Brazelton Neonatal Behavioral Assessment Scale *Measure of a newborn's behavioral ability that assesses interactive behaviors, motor skills, self-control, and response to stress.*

Assessing Responses: Brazelton Scale   The *Brazelton Neonatal Behavioral Assessment Scale* measures the way newborn babies respond to their environment (Brazelton, 1973). It assesses four dimensions of infants' behavior:

1   *Interactive behaviors* that affect the way the baby adapts in the home (such as alertness and cuddliness)
2   *Motor behaviors* (reflexes, muscle tone, and hand-mouth activity)
3   *Control of physiological state* (such as a baby's ability to quiet down after being upset)
4   *Response to stress* (the startle reaction)

The test takes about 30 minutes, and scores are based on a baby's best performance, rather than an average. Testers try to get babies to do their best, sometimes repeating an item and sometimes asking the mother to alert her baby. The Brazelton test may be better at predicting a baby's future development than the Apgar scale or traditional neurological testing (Behrman & Vaughan, 1983).

The States of Infants

state *Periodic variation in an infant's cycle of wakefulness, sleep, and activity.*

Like all babies, Jason was born with an internal "clock," which regulates the timing of his cycles of eating and sleeping, and perhaps even his moods. These cycles, which govern the various *states* of infancy, seem to be inborn (see Table 4-4). Although the different states are common to all neonates, their patterns are different from one baby to another. Jason sleeps 20 hours a day, while Vicky's pattern is at the other extreme—she sleeps only 11 hours. The average amount of sleep is 16 hours a day, but there is great variation around it (Parmelee, Wenner, & Schulz, 1964).

TABLE 4-4

STATE	EYES	BREATHING	MOVEMENTS	RESPONSIVENESS
Regular sleep	Closed	Regular	None, except for sudden, generalized startles	Unable to be aroused by mild stimuli.
Irregular sleep	Closed	Irregular	Muscles twitch, but no major movements	Sounds or light bring smiles or grimaces in sleep.
Drowsiness	Open or closed	Irregular	Somewhat active	May smile, startle, suck, or have erections in response to stimuli.
Alert inactivity	Open		Quiet; may move head, limbs, and trunk while looking around	An interesting environment (with people or things to watch) may initiate or maintain this state.
Waking activity and crying	Open		Much activity	External stimuli (such as hunger, cold, pain, being restrained, or being put down) bring about more activity, perhaps starting with soft whimpering and gentle movements and turning into a rhythmic crescendo of crying or kicking, or perhaps beginning and enduring as uncoordinated thrashing and spasmodic screeching.

Source: Adapted from information in Wolff, 1966, and Prechtl & Beintema, 1964.

Sleep dominates the neonatal period. "She's asleep" and "Don't wake him up" are heard often near the nursery. But the cliché "sleeping like a baby" is off the mark. Neonates (unlike adults) do not sleep for long periods. They wake up every 2 or 3 hours, so that their day consists of stretches of sleep and shorter periods of consciousness. To the relief of parents, this pattern soon changes. At around 3 months, babies grow more wakeful in late afternoon and early evening, and they start to sleep through the night. By 6 months, more than half their sleep takes place at night.

Newborns have about six to eight sleep periods, which alternate between quiet and active sleep. Active sleep—probably the equivalent of rapid-eye-movement (REM) sleep, which in adults is associated with dreaming—appears rhythmically in cycles of about 1 hour and accounts for 50 to 80 percent of a newborn's total sleep time. Over the first 6 months, the amount of this active sleep diminishes and accounts for only 30 percent of sleep time, and the length of the cycle becomes more consistent (Coons & Guilleminault, 1982). The amount of REM sleep continues to decrease steadily throughout life.

As babies become more awake, alert, and active, they develop according to their own unique patterns. And these early patterns can have far-reaching effects. Parents, for example, respond very differently to a placid baby and an excitable one, to one they can quiet and one who is inconsolable, to a baby who is awake and alert and to one who seems uninterested in people and places. The parents' attitudes and behaviors in turn influence the children, and so babies affect their own lives in basic, important ways.

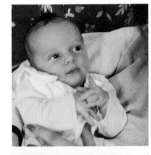

(Michael R. Elia)

Right: In infancy, life is one state after another. Richard, like other babies, goes from alert interest to drowsiness and then to sleep, according to his own internal "clock."

BOX 4-5 ■ THE EVERYDAY WORLD

COMFORTING A CRYING BABY

All babies cry sometimes. This is their only way to signal that they are hungry, uncomfortable, lonely, or unhappy for some other reason. And since few sounds are as distressing as a baby's cry, parents usually rush to feed or pick up a crying infant. Sometimes the baby shows that the problem has been solved by quieting down and either falling asleep or gazing about in alert contentment.

At other times, though, communication is not so clear and the caregiver cannot figure out what the baby wants. The baby keeps crying. It is worth trying to find ways to help, since babies whose cries bring relief seem to become more self-confident, seeing that they can affect their own lives. By the end of the first year, babies whose cries have brought tender, soothing care cry less and communicate more in other ways, while babies of punitive or ignoring caregivers cry more (Ainsworth & Bell, 1977; Bell & Ainsworth, 1972).

Thus, parents do not have to be afraid of spoiling their babies by going to them when they cry. Infants cannot be spoiled by being picked up and held; the holding itself may be what they are crying for.

In Chapter 7, we discuss several kinds of crying and what they may mean—particularly, whether some may indicate illness. But for healthy babies who just seem unhappy, some of the measures below often prove helpful (Eiger & Olds, 1987):

■ Hold the baby in your arms. Babies may miss the rhythms present in the womb, where they felt the mother's heartbeat and breathing at all times.

■ Sit with the baby in a comfortable rocking chair.

■ If you are nervous and upset, ask someone else to hold the baby for a while, since babies sometimes respond to their caregivers' moods.

■ Hold the baby to your chest vertically. Hold the baby's head over your shoulder, and walk around.

■ Change the diaper. Some babies are uncomfortable with wet or soiled diapers, although most don't seem to mind.

■ Try switching positions, perhaps letting the baby lie over your shoulder, with his or her stomach resting on top of your shoulder.

■ Pat or rub the baby's back.

■ Burp the baby. A bubble of air may be causing discomfort.

■ Change the baby's position in the crib—to lying on the back, stomach, or side, or with the head where the feet have been.

■ Wrap the baby snugly in a small blanket; some infants feel more secure when firmly swaddled from neck to toes, with arms held close to the sides.

■ Make the baby warmer or cooler, either putting on or taking off clothing or changing the temperature in the room.

■ Lay the baby on his or her stomach on your chest, to feel your heartbeat and breathing.

■ Give the baby a massage.

■ Give the baby a warm bath.

■ Put the baby in a baby pack next to your chest and walk around. While you're holding a baby in this way, you can get some of your work done at the same time.

■ Sing or talk to the baby.

■ Provide a continuous or rhythmic sound, like music from the radio, a simulated heartbeat, or background noise from a whirring fan, a vacuum cleaner, or another appliance.

■ Lay the baby across your knees and move them up and down.

■ Put the baby in a windup swing seat or cradle.

■ Put springs on the crib legs that turn it into a rocker. At first you can gently rock the baby in it; older babies can do this themselves.

■ Take the baby out of the house—for a ride in a stroller or car seat—at any hour of the day or night. In bad weather, some parents walk around in an enclosed mall, and the distraction helps them, as well as the baby.

■ Lay the baby on top of a folded towel on a washing machine or dryer that has been running for a few minutes. Some babies like the warmth and the motion. Of course, do not leave the baby, even for a moment.

■ If someone other than the mother is taking care of the baby, it sometimes helps if the caregiver puts on a garment that the mother has recently worn (such as a robe or a sweater), so that the baby can sense the familiar smell.

■ "Dance" with the baby to music from the radio or stereo.

■ Let the baby cry for a short time. Time the amount the baby cries before going to sleep. You may be relieved to find that although it may seem like hours, it is really only a few minutes. Some babies seem to need a few minutes of crying before falling asleep.

Parents spend a great deal of time and energy trying to change their babies' states. Sometimes they try to ease a waking baby back to sleep; at other times, they want to feed an infant too sleepy to nurse. Most of their efforts seem to focus on quieting a crying baby. While crying is usually more distressing than serious, it is particularly important to quiet low-birthweight babies, because quiet babies maintain their weight better. Steady stimulation is the time-proven way to soothe crying babies—letting them hear a rhythmic sound or suck on a pacifier, rocking them, walking them, or wrapping them snugly (see Box 4-5).

Babies behave uniquely right from birth. Vicky sticks her tongue out repetitively; Jason makes rhythmic sucking movements; Nancy does neither. Some infant boys have frequent erections; others never do. Some babies smile often; others rarely. New babies differ in their activity levels, too, and the differences may hold important clues about later functioning. In one study, children whose movements had been measured during the first days of life were checked again at 4 and 8 years of age. The most vigorous newborns continued to be very active as 4- and 8-year-olds, while the least active infants were less active children. The active youngsters showed another trait: they approached and welcomed new situations rather than avoiding them (Korner et al., 1985).

Although as neonates Vicky and Jason sleep most of the time and utter no language but a cry, their families find them fascinating company. The gripping reflex of tiny fingers, the wide-eyed gaze, the innocent, flat features, and the little, well-formed bodies are hard to resist. By the end of the neonatal period, babies have charmed an appreciative audience and been the subject of scores of photos. These pictures chronicle the remarkable and rapid development during these weeks in all facets of their lives—physical, intellectual, and social.

Summary

1 Normal full-term gestation is 266 days after conception. The birth process occurs in three stages: (1) dilation of the cervix, (2) descent and emergence of the baby, and (3) expulsion of the placenta and umbilical cord.

2 Although lying on the back is the most common position for childbirth, women may also give birth kneeling, crouching, standing, or sitting on a birth stool. Electronic fetal monitoring is the use of machines that monitor fetal heartbeat during labor and delivery.

3 Whether obstetrical medication causes harm to the baby, and how much, is controversial. Some research suggests that physical effects of medication may persist through at least the first year of life, but critics question the methodology and conclusions of many studies.

4 Natural and prepared childbirth can offer both physical and psychological benefits. "Gentle birth" is a childbirth technique designed to minimize the trauma of birth.

5 In recent years, the rate of cesarean deliveries has risen to over 20 percent in the United States. However, in most birthweight categories, delivery by cesarean has not improved the outcome for the infant. In addition, the stress involved in the normal birth process seems to help the fetus make the transition to life outside the uterus.

6 Delivery at home or in birth centers is a feasible alternative for some women with normal low-risk pregnancies.

7 Prolonged labor, use of forceps, and cesarean (rather than vaginal) delivery are most likely to be associated with mothers' dissatisfaction with the birth experience. Most fathers become attached to their newborns, whether or not they attend the birth.

8 The transition to parenthood is often stressful. Mothers of sons seem to be most affected.

9 Nearly 7 percent of all American babies are of low birthweight. They can be either preterm (premature) or small for date or both. Low birthweight is associated with infant mortality and sickness, although a supportive postnatal environment can often improve the outcome. A number of demographic factors, medical conditions (both preexisting and connected with the pregnancy), and lifestyle factors are associated with the likelihood of having a low-birthweight baby. The most effective way to reduce the number of low-birthweight babies is to provide widespread prenatal care, as done in many western European countries.

10 Postmature babies are those born after a gestation of more than 42 weeks. They sometimes suffer from inadequate delivery of nourishment and oxygen.

11 A small minority of babies suffer birth trauma, or injury sustained at the time of birth. This may result in mental retardation or behavior problems, although a supportive postnatal environment can often result in a more favorable outcome.

12 Stillbirth occurs in less than 1 percent of pregnancies. Grieving for the dead child helps parents deal with their loss.

13 The neonatal period, the first 4 weeks of life, is a time of transition from life inside the womb to life outside it.

14 At birth, the neonate's circulatory, respiratory, gastrointestinal, and temperature-regulation systems become independent of the mother's.

15 At 1 minute and 5 minutes after birth, the neonate is assessed medically using the Apgar scale, which measures five factors (appearance, pulse, grimace, activity, and respiration) that indicate how well the newborn is adjusting to extrauterine life. The newborn may also be screened for one or more medical conditions. The Brazelton Neonatal Behavioral Assessment Scale may be used to assess the way a newborn is responding to the environment and to predict future development.

16 Newborns alternate between states of sleep, wakefulness, and activity, with sleep taking up the major (but a diminishing) amount of their time. There is considerable individual difference in patterns, and a baby's state patterns are clues to later functioning.

Key Terms

neonate (page 124)
gestation (124)
electronic fetal monitoring (128)
medicated delivery (128)
natural childbirth (130)
prepared childbirth (130)
gentle birth (130)
cesarean delivery (131)
breech position (131)
transverse position (131)
obstetrician (133)
nurse-midwife (133)
low-birthweight baby (137)
preterm (premature) baby (137)
small-for-date baby (137)
isolette (140)

self-fulfilling prophecy (142)
birth trauma (143)
anoxia (143)
stillbirth (143)
fetal death in utero (143)
neonatal period (144)
lanugo (145)
vernix caseosa (145)
meconium (146)
neonatal jaundice (146)
Apgar scale (147)
Phenylketonuria (PKU) (148)
Brazelton Neonatal Behavioral
  Assessment Scale (148)
state (148)

Suggested Readings

DeFrain, J., Montens, L., Stork, J., & Stork, W. (1986). *Stillborn: An invisible death.* Lexington, MA: Heath. A sensitive study of the effects of a stillbirth on a family, based on data from 300 questionnaires and 25 in-depth interviews. The book recounts the reactions of parents, family, and friends to this experience and gives suggestions for coping.

Gansberg, J.M., & Mostel, A.P. (1984). *The second nine months.* New York: Pocket Books. A reassuring, compassionate guide for new mothers based on interviews with mothers of young babies. The book covers common physical and emotional concerns, including typical experiences in the hospital and such at-home postpartum issues as coping with fatigue, the husband-wife relationship, going back to work, and the impact of a second child.

Goldberg, S., & Divitto, B.A. (1983). *Born too soon: Preterm birth and early development.* San Francisco: Freeman. A sympathetic book about the problems and special experiences of a preterm infant, focusing on the first 3 years of life.

Leach, P. (1983). *Babyhood* (2d ed.). New York: Knopf. A comprehensive look at infancy, and particularly the neonatal period. Although written for the layperson, the text covers the whole field of study about babies.

Maurer, D., & Maurer, C. (1988). *The world of the newborn.* New York: Basic Books. A fascinating book by a psychologist and a science writer that explores a newborn baby's world—what it looks like, feels like, tastes like, and sounds like. The authors cite and explain both classic and recent research and offer nuggets of advice to parents.

Worth, C. (1988). *The birth of a father.* New York: McGraw-Hill. A supportive book that answers new fathers' questions about their new world, using interviews with fathers taken during the first year of parenthood.

INFANCY AND TODDLERHOOD

T*he abilities of infants and toddlers have been greatly underestimated throughout history. Until recently, psychologists did relatively little research on the period from birth to age 3; although it is a time when foundations are laid, the "bricks" have perhaps seemed too ordinary to require study.*

Jason at 15 months walks along a sidewalk with his parents and accidentally kicks a can. The can goes flying, and Jason does a double take. He begins deliberately kicking the can along the sidewalk, delighted by his discovery of a way to affect the world. This process of development from the total dependence of the newborn to the self-aware independence of the 3-year-old is the theme of Chapters 5, 6, and 7.

These chapters, like others throughout this book, consider three types of development: physical, intellectual, and personality. Reality, of course, is never compartmentalized so neatly. Each aspect of development connects to the other two and supports their development. Jason's intellectual growth is a natural accompaniment of his physical and emotional growth; Vicky's emotional development is influenced by her mental development. We see children most clearly when we see how these attributes combine in one child.

CHAPTER 5

PHYSICAL DEVELOPMENT IN INFANCY AND TODDLERHOOD

T here he lay upon his back
The yearling creature, warm and moist with life
To the bottom of his dimples,—to the ends
Of the lovely tumbled curls about his face.

Elizabeth Barrett Browning, *Aurora Leigh*, 1857

PREVIEW QUESTIONS

- What principles govern physical development, and how does the environment affect it?
- How does early brain growth affect development—and how does the environment affect brain growth?
- What are the primitive reflexes, and what is their significance?
- How should babies be nourished?
- How do the senses function in infancy?
- What milestones in motor development mark the first 3 years?

WHAT IS GOING ON in Jason's home? Jess and Julia are checking every corner of their apartment—moving breakables to high places, covering all the electrical outlets, and jamming each book so tightly into the shelf that even *they* can hardly pull it out—much less Jason, which is the whole idea. The impetus for all this "child-proofing" is Jason's newest ability: crawling. This stage in his physical development affects the way he influences his environment and also the way he reacts to it, intellectually and emotionally as well as physically.

Jason's physical growth and developing coordination are intertwined with his intellectual and social development throughout infancy and toddlerhood. We examine this early development in this chapter (and in Chapters 6 and 7) as we explore the first 3 years of life.

Infancy lasts for about the first 1½ years and ends when the child, now walking, begins to string two words together; toddlerhood is the final 18 months of the first 3 years. During toddlerhood, children become more and more verbal, independent, and able to move about in their world.

In this chapter, we discuss physical development—especially growth and how adults can assist it. We also consider such issues of physical development as methods of feeding, nutrition, and obesity. Next, we look at the sensory capacities of children of this age and see that at first their perception does not match that of adults. They are also less adept at motor skills than adults, and they need to develop coordinated movement, a progression we follow. Finally, we discuss two sober topics: infant mortality and sudden infant death syndrome.

How Physical Development Takes Place

Vicky learns by doing. Her hand knows how to tug, how to lift, how to find her mouth—long before she can understand or say the names of the things she knows. And when she does begin to speak, she speaks with her body as well as her mouth. "Up," she says and thrusts her arms up high. By touching and picking up her food or her clothes, by playing with toes she learns about the world.

At first, Vicky probably has no ideas about either the world or herself. Is there a difference between the two? She apparently has no notion. With experience she begins to tell her body apart from other things. She recognizes Charles's face and smiles in pleasure; she sees a strange man and knows that he is unfamiliar. She learns that she can drop a toy but that her thumb is always there for sucking. She finds out, when she splashes water all over the bathroom and hurls sand at other children, that she can affect other objects (and other people).

It is impossible to understand babies and toddlers without knowing about their physical development. Only with physical maturation—the unfolding of biologically predetermined patterns of behavior—do such fundamental activities as walking, carrying, talking, and controlling elimination become possible. For example, only after her muscles and legs are sturdy enough can Vicky explore her room. As she becomes more mobile—crawling, and eventually starting to walk— people react differently to her, and she begins to hear admonitions like "No, don't go there" and "Don't touch." She also encounters loving assistance as her parents pick her up after a fall, comfort her, and encourage her to stand on her feet again. Thus, physical changes are an intimate part of the psychological development of an infant or toddler.

Normal physical development follows an apparently predetermined course, even though the times when individual babies perform specific activities vary widely. There is no "right" age when a child should reach a certain height or weight or should be performing specific activities. But even though the range of normal development is broad, almost all children progress in a definite order from certain activities to others. Even though one baby is able to sit up at 6 months of age and another is not able to sit up until 11 months, both babies can hold up the chin before they can raise the chest, both sit with support before they sit alone, and both stand before they walk. Basically, children learn simple movements before they learn complicated ones.

TWO PRINCIPLES OF PHYSICAL DEVELOPMENT

Before babies learn how to walk, they can do things with their hands. And before they can use their hands skillfully, they can move their arms with purpose. These aspects of development illustrate two complementary principles of physical development, both in growth and in motor development.

The *cephalocaudal principle* (from Latin and Greek roots, meaning "head to tail") dictates that development will proceed from the head to the lower parts of the body. Thus, an embryo's head, brain, and eyes develop ahead of the lower parts and are disproportionately large until the other parts catch up. The head of a 2-month-old embryo is half the length of the entire body, and the head of a newborn infant is one-fourth the size of the rest of the body. The brain of a 1-year-old baby is 70 percent of its full adult weight; the rest of the body, by contrast, is only about 10 to 20 percent of adult weight. Furthermore, infants learn to use the upper parts of the body before the lower parts. Babies see objects before they can control the trunk, and they learn to do many things with their hands long before their legs are very useful.

According to the *proximodistal principle* (from Latin, "near to far"), devel-

cephalocaudal principle
Principle that development proceeds in a "head-to-tail" direction: the upper body parts develop before the lower parts.

proximodistal principle
Principle that development proceeds in a near-to-far manner: the parts of the body near its center (spinal cord) develop before the extremities.

(Laima Druskis © 1988/Stock, Boston)

In accordance with the cephalocaudal principle, infants can use their hands adeptly before their legs are very useful, as this baby reaching for a toy demonstrates.

opment proceeds from the central part of the body to the outer parts. The head and trunk of the embryo develop before the limbs, and the arms and legs before the fingers and toes. Babies first develop the ability to use their upper arms and upper legs (which are closest to the central axis), then their forearms and forelegs, then their hands and feet, and finally their fingers and toes.

Both these principles govern development before and after birth.

PHYSICAL DEVELOPMENT OF THE TWO SEXES

During the first 2 years of life, boys and girls are equally active and show no differences in their sensitivity to touch and very little difference in strength (although boys *may* be slightly stronger). They show more similarities than differences in reaching maturational milestones (such as sitting up, teething, and walking). Recently, researchers have looked for differences in the brains of males and females, such as differences in the number of brain cells, size of brain structures, or organization of the brain. Such efforts have led to research which tries to explain why girls start to talk and read earlier and why more boys have problems in learning to read. But analysis of the brains of babies who died at birth or soon afterward has yielded no evidence of any marked sex difference that would affect newborns' readiness for language acquisition (Maccoby, 1980).

Growth

GROWTH OF THE BODY

Physical growth is faster during the first 3 years than it will ever be again. At 5 months, the average baby's birthweight has doubled to a weight of about 15 pounds; by 1 year, the birthweight has tripled, and the baby now weighs about 22 pounds. This rapid rate tapers off during the second year, when about 5 to 6

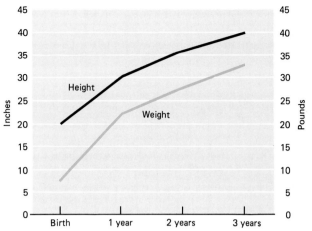

FIGURE 5-1
Growth in height and weight during infancy and toddlerhood. Growth in both height and weight is most rapid during the first few months of life and then tapers off somewhat by the third birthday.

pounds are gained, so that birthweight is quadrupled by the second birthday. During the third year, the gain is even less, about 4 to 5 pounds.

Height increases by about 10 to 12 inches during the first year (making the typical 1-year-old about 30 inches tall), by about 5 inches during the second year (so that the average 2-year-old is about 3 feet tall), and by about 3 to 4 inches during the third year (see Figure 5-1).

As a young child grows in size, body shape changes too. The rest of the body catches up with the head, which becomes proportionately smaller until full adult height is reached, as shown in Figure 5-2. Most children become leaner in the first 3 years; the 3-year-old is slender, compared with the chubby, potbellied 1-year-old.

In most babies the first tooth erupts sometime between the ages of 5 and 9 months, and by 1 year babies usually have 6 to 8 teeth; by age 2½, they have 20 (Behrman & Vaughan, 1983).

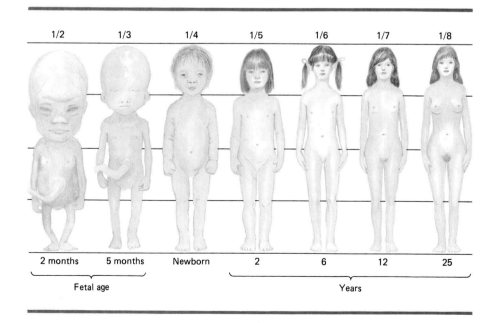

FIGURE 5-2
Changes in the proportions of the human body during growth. The most striking change is that the head becomes smaller in proportion to the rest of the body: the fractions indicate head size as a proportion of total body length at different ages. More subtle is the stability of the trunk proportions (from neck to crotch). Thus the increasing leg proportion is almost exactly the reverse of the decreasing head proportion.

The genes that Jason inherits have the biggest influence on his body type—whether he will be tall or short, thin or stocky, or somewhere in between (Mittler, 1971). However, height and weight are also affected by such environmental factors as nutrition, living conditions, and general health.

Well-fed, well-cared-for children grow taller and heavier than children who are less well nourished and nurtured; they also mature sexually and attain maximum height earlier, and their teeth erupt sooner. The differences usually begin showing up by the first year and remain consistent throughout life (American Academy of Pediatrics, 1973). Today, children are growing taller and achieving maturity sooner than they did a century ago, probably because of better nutrition, improved sanitation, and the decrease in child labor. Better medical care, especially the use of immunization and antibiotic drugs, also plays a part, since heart disease, kidney disease, and some infectious illnesses can have grave effects on growth. Children who are ill for a long time may never achieve their genetically programmed stature, because they may never be able to make up for the growth time lost while they were sick.

Boys are slightly longer and heavier than girls at birth and remain larger through adulthood, except for a brief time during puberty when girls' growth spurts make them overtake boys. The bones of black children harden earlier than those of white children, and the permanent teeth appear sooner; also, black children mature earlier and tend to be larger than white children (American Academy of Pediatrics, 1973).

GROWTH OF THE BRAIN

The human brain grows fastest while the baby is still in the womb and in the first few months of life. In the developing fetus, an average of 250,000 brain cells per minute are formed through cell division (mitosis); thus most of the 100 billion cells in the human brain are already present at birth (Cowan, 1979; see Figure 5-3, opposite).

The Nervous System

The brain, the spinal cord (a bundle of nerves running down the backbone), and a network of nerves reaching every part of the body constitute the *nervous system*. This complex communication system sends sensory messages from all parts of the body to the brain and carries motor commands back from the brain.

cerebral cortex Upper layer of the brain.

Just before and just after birth there is a spurt in the growth of brain cells. The newly formed cells sort themselves out by function, migrating to their proper position either in the upper layer of the brain, called the **cerebral cortex,** or in the lower layer, called the *subcortex,* or the subcortical levels. In a newborn, the subcortical structures, which regulate such basic biological functions as breathing and digestion, are the most fully developed; cells in the cerebral cortex (or, simply, the cortex), which is responsible for thinking and problem solving, are not yet well connected. Connections between cells in the cortex increase markedly as the baby matures, making possible higher-level motor and intellectual functioning.

The rate of formation of new cells drops within 2 months after birth (Lipsitt, 1986). Newly formed cells that do not function well or have migrated to the wrong part of the brain die out. This pruning of excess cells helps to create an efficient nervous system. In addition, the nerve fibers become encased in *myelin,*

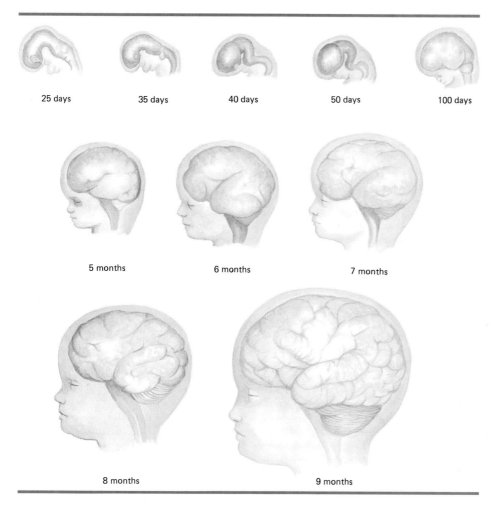

FIGURE 5-3
Fetal brain development from 25 days of gestation through birth. As the brain develops, the front part expands greatly to form the cerebrum (the large, convoluted upper mass). Specific areas of the cerebral cortex (the gray outer covering of the brain) are devoted to particular functions, such as sensory and motor activities; but large areas are "uncommitted" and thus are free for higher intellectual activities, such as thinking, remembering, and problem solving. The subcortex (the brain stem and other structures below the cortical layer) handles reflex behavior and other lower-level functions. The newborn's brain contains most of the cells it will eventually have, but it is only about 25 percent of its adult weight. A rapid increase in cortical connections during the first 2 years of life results in a dramatic weight gain (to four-fifths of adult weight) and in the capacity for thought. (*Source:* Restak, 1984).

25 days

35 days

40 days

50 days

100 days

5 months

6 months

7 months

8 months

9 months

a white, fatty substance that speeds the transmission of messages between nerve cells within the brain as well as to and from the brain and the nervous system.

The brain is only 25 percent of its adult weight at birth; it reaches about 70 percent of its eventual weight by the end of the first year (as noted earlier) and 80 percent by the end of the second year. It continues to grow more slowly, until by age 12 it is virtually full size (Behrman & Vaughan, 1983). This neurological growth permits a corresponding growth in motor and intellectual activities.

How the Environment Influences Brain Development

Until the middle of the twentieth century, scientists believed that the brain grew in an unchangeable, genetically determined pattern. We now know that the brain can be "molded" by experience, especially during early life, when it grows most quickly. The technical term for this is *plasticity*. We can measure plasticity by studying differences in the number of nerve cells, in the connections between them, and in their chemistry.

Early experiences may have lasting effects, for better or worse, on the capacity of the central nervous system to learn and to store information (Greenough, Black, & Wallace, 1987; Wittrock, 1980). Chronic malnutrition of a fetus and fetal

FIGURE 5-4
Kitten wearing training goggles, one lens with horizontal stripes and the other with vertical stripes. The eye that sees only horizontal stripes will be blind to vertical lines when the animal matures, and the eye that sees only vertical stripes will be blind to horizontal lines.

critical period *Specific time during development when an event has its greatest impact.*

alcohol syndrome, for example, can both result in brain damage (see Chapter 3), and undernourishment in the critical period just after birth can have the same effect. (A ***critical period*** is a specific time during development when a person or an animal needs to have appropriate experiences to bring about normal functioning.)

Actual physical changes can occur in response to early experience. Young cats that have been fitted with goggles (like those shown in Figure 5-4) which allow them to see only vertical lines will in maturity be unable to see horizontal lines and will bump into horizontal boards in front of them (H.V. Hirsch & Spinelli, 1970). If the goggles let them see only horizontal lines, they will be effectively blind to vertical columns. This seems to be due to modifications in the cortical layers early in life as the result of experience—that is, the kinds of lines they are used to seeing. Apparently, most of the neurons (nerve cells) in the visual cortex, the part of the cerebral cortex that controls vision, are programmed to respond to lines only in the direction that the cats have been permitted to see. This does not happen when the same procedure is carried out with adult cats, suggesting that crucial cells in the visual cortex develop early in life.

On the other hand, animal experiments have shown that an enriched environment can enhance brain growth and functioning. Enrichment can be physical (providing toys) or social (having other animals to interact with). In a series of experiments starting in the late 1950s, rats and other animals were raised in cages enriched with a variety of stimulating apparatus (like wheels to run on, rocks to climb and stand on, and levers to manipulate) and compared with littermates raised in "standard" cages or in isolation. The "enriched" animals turned out to have heavier brains with thicker cortical layers, more cells in the visual cortex, greater complexity of these cells, more connective cells, and higher levels of neurochemical activity (making it easier to form connections between brain cells) (Rosenzweig, 1984; Rosenzweig & Bennett, 1976). Furthermore, the brain's plasticity seems to continue, to a lesser degree, throughout most of life; the researchers found similar differences in brain function when older animals were exposed to differing environments. The changes were similar in form to the changes in the brains of younger animals, though smaller in degree.

These findings have sparked successful efforts to stimulate the physical and mental development of children with Down syndrome, to keep aging people mentally alert, and to help victims of brain damage recover function. The findings also help explain why, as we saw in Chapter 4, some infants with birth complications develop normally.

Reflex Behaviors

reflex behavior *Involuntary reaction to stimulation.*

When Vicky blinks at a bright light, she is acting through a ***reflex behavior***, an automatic, involuntary response to external stimulation. Human beings have an arsenal of reflexes, some of which seem to offer protection, even extending to survival itself.

The so-called *primitive reflexes*, or newborn reflexes, are present at birth or shortly after, and many can be elicited even before birth (see Table 5-1). In a neurologically healthy baby, these reflexes drop out (disappear) at different times during the first year (for example, the Moro reflex drops out at about 3 months; the rooting reflex—by which a baby roots around for a nipple—at 9 months; and the Babinski reflex, at 6 to 9 months). The brief appearance of these primitive reflexes reflects the subcortical control of an infant's nervous system,

TABLE 5-1

HUMAN PRIMITIVE REFLEXES

REFLEX	STIMULATION	BEHAVIOR
Rooting	Baby's cheek is stroked with finger or nipple.	Baby's head turns; mouth opens; sucking movements begin.
Darwinian (grasping)	Palm of baby's hand is stroked.	Baby makes strong fist; can be raised to standing position if both fists are closed around a stick.
Swimming	Baby is put into water face down.	Baby makes well-coordinated swimming movements.
Tonic neck	Baby is laid down on back.	Baby turns head to one side, assumes "fencer" position, extends arms and legs on preferred side, flexes opposite limbs.
Moro (startle)	Baby is dropped or hears loud noise.	Baby extends legs, arms, and fingers; arches back: draws back head.
Babinski	Sole of baby's foot is stroked.	Baby's toes fan out; foot twists in.
Walking	Baby is held under arms, with bare feet touching flat surface.	Baby makes steplike motions that look like well-coordinated walking.
Placing	Backs of baby's feet are drawn against edge of flat surface.	Baby withdraws foot.

Rooting reflex.

Darwinian reflex.

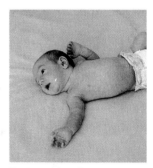

Tonic neck reflex.

Moro reflex.

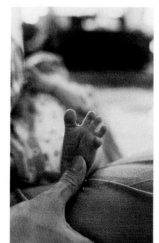

Babinski reflex.

Walking reflex.

Sources for photos: Kathryn Abbe (rooting); Elizabeth Crews (Moro, Babinski, and walking); Lew Merrim/Monkmeyer Press (Darwinian); Laura Dwight/Black Star (tonic neck).

since the maturation of the cerebral cortex inhibits their expression. Those reflexes that are clearly protective—like yawning, coughing, gagging, sneezing, shivering, and blinking—remain and grow stronger and continue to help us to survive. These, of course, are not primitive reflexes.

Primitive reflexes are normal in newborns. But over the first few months it is normal for them to drop out, as a sign of neurological development, as the infant's nervous system shifts from subcortical to cortical control. Although some of the primitive reflexes are needed for early survival (like rooting to get food), others may be part of our evolutionary legacy (like grasping, which infant monkeys do to hold on to the hair on their mothers' bodies). Whatever their significance, the presence or absence of primitive reflexes at appropriate ages is an important sign of normal—or abnormal—development.

The primitive reflexes are controlled by the subcortex; their disappearance is evidence that the cortex is developing, resulting in the shift from reflex to voluntary behavior. Since there is a timetable for the development and dropping out of primitive reflexes, a baby's neurological development can be evaluated by seeing which reflexes are present or absent. One of the first tests after a baby's birth is for normal reflexes. The primitive reflexes appear and drop out later in preterm infants than in full-term infants. However, reflexes vary somewhat according to culture; see Box 2-5 in Chapter 2.)

NUTRITION IN INFANCY

For as long as doctors, psychologists, psychotherapists, and other professionals have been advising parents on the best way to raise children, they have based their recommendations on a combination of research findings, impressions gained from their professional and personal lives, and what may be considered wisdom in one person and superstition in another. Even the experts do not always know what is best for children. This is true about feeding babies, as well as about other aspects of caring for them.

Most babies in industrialized countries (as opposed to those third world countries where poor sanitary conditions, inadequate medical care, and other problems contribute to health problems for all ages) seem to grow normally and to stay healthy under a variety of different feeding practices. But one group of prominent pediatricians pointed out that "little is known about long-term consequences of infant feeding practices" (Fomon, Filer, Anderson, & Ziegler, 1979, p. 52). Still, as these same doctors state, "infants must be fed and decisions must be made about how this should be done" (p. 52). Let us see what they and other experts recommend. Some ways to tell whether a baby is well nourished are listed in Table 5-2.

Breastfeeding

After a 50-year decline in popularity, breastfeeding, the natural means of feeding infants, is returning to favor, especially among women who are older, better-educated, and from higher-income groups, and (in particular) among mothers who have attended childbirth classes (Kurinij, Shiono, & Rhoads, 1988). Between 1971 and 1981, the rate for in-hospital breastfeeding in the United States more than doubled (from 1 out of 4 mothers to more than half), and the rate of 5- to 6-month-old babies being breastfed more than quintupled (from 1 in 20 to more than 1 in 4). While these increases are occurring across

TABLE 5-2

HOW TO TELL WHETHER A BABY IS WELL NOURISHED*

ADEQUATE (GOOD)	LESS THAN ADEQUATE (POOR)
General appearance of vitality, well-being, and alertness	Strained expression; dull and listless; apathetic
Bright, clear eyes; smiling, happy expression; no dark circles under eyes	Sad-looking; dark circles under eyes; little smiling; prone to tears
Recovers quickly from fatigue; endurance during activity	Chronic fatigue; tires easily; takes excessive time to bounce back from physical activity; lack of endurance
Full of energy; vigorous	Lack of energy; weakness
Smooth, glossy hair	Dry, brittle, easily "pluckable" hair
Good appetite; curious and eager to try new foods	Poor appetite; unwilling to try new foods; may have many food dislikes
Good posture; stands erect; well-developed muscles	Poor posture; slumping; muscles weak and underdeveloped
Skin is firm and resilient and "feels alive"; subcutaneous fat layers	Skin is dry; has little or no tone; little or no subcutaneous fat
Interested in environment; curious; responsive	Irritable, nervous, slow to react; indifferent, passive, unresponsive; unable to cope with stimuli
Good growth; adequate weight and height for age	Stunted growth; thin and small for age; overweight for height
Attentive; eager to learn and experiment	Shortened attention span; reduced capacity to concentrate

*While it is not easy to evaluate marginal inadequate nutrition, some of the characteristics listed here may be helpful.
Source: Adapted from Alford & Boyle, 1982, p. 56.

socioeconomic and educational levels (Martinez & Krieger, 1985), breastfeeding is still less popular than bottle-feeding among younger, poorer, and minority-group women. It is especially ironic that many poor women do not breastfeed, since breast milk is more economical than commercially prepared formula.

White mothers are more inclined to nurse their babies than Mexican American or African American mothers, even after economic factors are taken into account; and African Americans tend to stop breastfeeding earlier, possibly because they are more likely to be employed than white mothers (Fetterly & Graubard, 1984; Kurinij et al., 1988; Rassin et al., 1984).

Even in a society where technological advances have provided excellent infant formulas that approximate breast milk, the American Academy of Pediatrics (1982) states that the best food for every newborn infant is breast milk, unless the mother or the child has some physical condition that makes nursing impossible.

Breast milk has been described as the "ultimate health food" (Eiger & Olds, 1987), because of the benefits it offers to babies. Breastfed children are protected in varying degrees against a number of illnesses, including diarrhea, respiratory infections, pneumonia, and bronchitis (Fallot, Boyd, & Oski, 1980; Forman et al., 1984; Jelliffe & Jelliffe, 1983). The specific mouth movements breastfed babies make seem to result in straighter teeth (Labbok & Hendershot, 1987). Low-birth-weight infants get special benefits: they digest and absorb the fat in breast milk better than that in cow's milk formula (Alemi, Hamosh, Scanlon, Salzman-Mann, & Hamosh, 1981), and the milk of mothers of premature babies has a different composition from that of mothers of full-term infants and is thus specially constituted to meet these infants' special needs (Bitman, Wood, Hamosh, Hamosh, & Mehta, 1983; Gross, Geller, & Tomarelli, 1981). Besides its nutri-

Breast milk can be called the "ultimate health food" because it offers so many benefits to babies. These mothers are also reaping physical and emotional advantages.

tional advantages, breastfeeding may also strengthen the mother-infant bond (see Chapter 7). However, a mother's health, emotional state, and attitude toward breastfeeding affect her ability to nurse.

The American Academy of Pediatrics (1978a, 1982) recommends that schoolchildren, expectant parents, doctors, and nurses be educated about nutrition and, specifically, breastfeeding; that "demand" feeding schedules (feeding whenever the baby is hungry) rather than rigid 3- to 4-hour feeding times be set up in the hospital and at home; and that day nurseries be set up near workplaces so that working women may nurse their infants.

Although breastfeeding is generally preferable, it is certainly not the only way to nourish a baby. A very small proportion of women are physically unable to nurse, and others have strong feelings against nursing or are prevented by factors such as work and travel. Breastfeeding can also pose its own problems—as physicians noted in the case of a 2-week-old baby girl who became intoxicated after being breastfed a few hours after her mother had used cocaine (Chasnoff, Lewis, & Squires, 1987). To avoid toxic reactions like this, nursing mothers often observe the same care as pregnant women in what they eat and drink and which drugs they take.

Bottle-Feeding

The reasons why some women decide not to breastfeed are varied. Rarely, a woman cannot nurse her baby—when she has such a serious infectious illness that she should avoid close contact with her baby, when the baby is too ill to nurse, or when the mother must take some kind of medication that would not be safe for the baby. Fortunately, such cases are unusual. Virtually every healthy woman can breastfeed her baby.

Why do some women decide to feed by bottle? The question has no single or simple answer. Women say that they do not want to breastfeed because they are modest, because they do not want to be tied down, because they have to go back to work and do not want to start something they cannot finish, because they are afraid that they will not know whether the baby is getting enough to eat, because their husbands want to help feed the baby, or because breastfeeding just seems too complicated (Eiger & Olds, 1987).

Modern formulas closely approximate breast milk (although they are not identical) and contain supplements of vitamins and minerals that breast milk does not have. Many babies thrive on formula, which, like breast milk, is all that a baby will need during the first 5 or 6 months, and mothers and fathers who bottle-feed their babies can give them many of the emotional benefits of breast-feeding by holding their children close during feedings.

Babies fed with formula and raised with love can grow up healthy and well adjusted. Long-term studies that have compared breastfed and bottle-fed children have found no significant differences (M. H. Schmitt, 1970). The quality of the relationship between parents and children is more important than the feeding method:

> A baby raised in a loving home can grow up to be healthy and psychologically secure no matter how he or she receives nourishment. While nursing is usually a beautiful, happy experience for both mother and child, the woman who nurses grudgingly, tight-lipped and stiff-armed, because she feels she *should*, will probably do more harm to her baby by communicating her feelings of resentment and unhappiness than she would if she were a relaxed, loving, bottle-feeding mother. (Eiger & Olds, 1987, pp. 33–34)

One common early dental problem, however, arises from the widespread practice of letting a baby take a bottle of milk, juice, or other liquid containing sugar to bed. In "nursing-bottle mouth," the sugar in the liquid causes tooth decay in a pattern that corresponds to the area where it comes out of the bottle. Dentists recommend that children who nurse for a long time between meals or while sleeping be given only water in their bottles. Other ways to prevent nursing-bottle mouth include teaching a baby to drink from a cup before the first birthday, offering juice only from a cup, and not giving milk in a bottle to a baby as a "sleeping pill" (American Academy of Pediatrics, 1978b).

Solid Foods and Cow's Milk

Up until 6 months of age, babies should be given breast milk or formula (American Academy of Pediatrics, Committee on Nutrition, 1986), since some infants fed plain cow's milk in the early months of life have been found to suffer from iron deficiency (Sadowitz & Oski, 1983). After 6 months, they can switch to homogenized vitamin D–fortified whole milk; they should not be drinking skim milk—at least not until after age 2.

At about 4 to 6 months, babies should be starting to eat solid foods. Their nutritional needs coincide with their muscular development; therefore, this is a good time to begin spoon-feeding. When babies can sit with support and control the head and neck muscles, they can let their caregivers know when they have had enough to eat. They show that they want food by opening the mouth (like a baby bird in the nest) and leaning forward in the high chair, and they show when they are full by leaning back and turning away.

At about this age, then, babies should begin eating a balanced diet of cereal,

Babies do not need solid food until they are at least 4 months old—and they do not eat neatly until much later. This 6½-month-old boy can sit with support, has good control of head and neck muscles, and can indicate when he has eaten as much cereal as he wants.

vegetables, fruits, and other foods, and by 1 year they should be eating foods from each of the major food groups—the foods just mentioned, plus meats, fish, or other sources of protein (American Academy of Pediatrics Committee on Nutrition, 1986).

In the mistaken belief that early feeding of solid foods will help babies sleep through the night or will foster healthy growth, some parents are feeding their babies solids at 2 months. This practice is condemned by pediatric nutritionists as unnecessary and an interference with the intake of breast milk or formula, which is better for babies at this age (Fomon et al., 1979).

Is Obesity a Problem in Infancy?

Seven babies on Long Island were fed a diet that sounds like the kind of healthy regimen everyone should be on—skim milk rather than whole milk, no animal fat or sugar, and restricted snacking. But their well-intentioned parents were starving these babies, who were not getting enough calories for proper growth (Pugliese, Weyman-Daum, Moses, & Lifschitz, 1987).

In the United States, obesity is the chief nutritional problem of children. It occurs when people—children or adults—consume more calories than they expend as energy in bodily processes and physical activity: the excess calories are stored as fat. Why this imbalance develops in some people is not known, though various theories have been proposed, some based on physical factors, some on psychological factors, and some on cultural factors. At present, there is considerable interest in the role of metabolism; and some recent research suggests that a tendency toward overweight is inherited (Stunkard et al., 1986).

Some nutritionists have suggested that people may become obese in later life as a result of overfeeding in infancy (Jelliffe & Jelliffe, 1974; Mayer, 1973). This belief rests on research on rats, which has shown that feeding rat pups too many calories makes them develop too many fat cells, which persist through life (J. Hirsch, 1972). Recent research, however, has cast doubt on the long-term effects of fatness in human infants. One study found almost no relationship between measures of obesity before age 6 and the same measures at age 16. Only after age 6 was there a correlation: children who were fat at age 6 or later were more likely to be fat adults. This researcher concluded: "The medical significance of infantile obesity may have been exaggerated" (Roche, 1981, p. 38).

Because there is no evidence that fatness hurts babies and since children have strong growth needs, the Committee on Nutrition of the American Academy of Pediatrics (1986) warns against putting young children on any kind of special diet without a strong demonstration that restrictions are needed. However, parents concerned about healthy weight levels for their children might well adopt a more active lifestyle for the entire family. The parents as well as the children are likely to reap many benefits.

Early Sensory Capacities

In 1890, the psychologist William James said: "The baby, assailed by eyes, ears, nose, skin, and entrails at once, feels that all is one great blooming, buzzing confusion." We now know that this is far from true: babies are able to make some sense of their perceptions. In this section, we discuss sight, hearing, taste, smell, and touch and note how babies can discriminate in these areas.

SIGHT

The eyes of newborns differ from those of adults; they are smaller, the retinal structures are incomplete, and the optic nerve is underdeveloped. But at birth, babies blink at bright lights, shift their gaze to follow a moving light, and can follow a moving target like a beam of light with their eyes (Behrman & Vaughan, 1983).

Peripheral vision, which is very narrow at birth, more than doubles between 2 weeks and 10 weeks of age (Tronick, 1972). A baby's eyesight, which is at first relatively poor, becomes much more acute during the first year, and by age 3 it seems to be within the adult range (Behrman & Vaughan, 1983). These first 3 years of life seem to represent a critical period for the development of binocular vision (using both eyes to focus on objects, allowing the perception of depth and distance). If children whose two eyes are not aligned properly do not have corrective surgery by age 3, they do not develop binocular sight as well as those who have their visual problem repaired early (Bertenthal & Campos, 1987).

Infants can perceive color very early. By about 2 months they can tell red and green; by about 3 months they can see blue (Haith, 1986); and 4-month-old babies can distinguish among red, green, blue, and yellow, and—like adults—they prefer red and blue (Bornstein, Kessen, & Weiskopf, 1976; Teller & Bornstein, 1987).

Depth Perception

A classic contribution to the study of infants' perception, and to the nature-nurture controversy (see Chapter 2), made use of a *visual cliff* (Walk & Gibson, 1961). Some observers of children believe that children are born with no knowledge of space and come to know about height, depth, and distance only through experience. To test this thesis, researchers placed babies on a glass tabletop, over a checkerboard pattern. The glass formed a continuous surface, but to an adult's eye it appeared that one side of the checkerboard pattern was a flat ledge and the other a vertical drop—that is, there was an illusion of depth. Would infants see the same illusion and feel themselves in danger?

The exact answer to this question is still being argued. There is no doubt that infants do see a *difference* between the "ledge" and the "drop." Six-month-old babies crawl freely on the ledge, but they avoid the drop, even when they see their mothers on the "far side." An experiment with even younger infants, aged 2 and 3 months, showed that when they are placed face down over the visual cliff, the heart slows down, probably in response to the illusion of depth (Campos, Langer, & Krowitz, 1970).

These findings suggest that depth perception is either innate or learned very early. However, the ability to *perceive* depth (as shown by a slowed heart rate, which indicates interest) does not indicate a *fear* of heights (a faster heart rate would indicate fear). The sense of danger does not develop until later and is related to children's ability to get around by themselves (see Box 5-2 later in this chapter). Vicky, for instance, will avoid a visual cliff at 6 months; not until 8 months will she refuse to cross it, even if her mother calls to her. Apparently some mix of innate abilities and learned responses is reflected in studies of a visual cliff. As usual, when researchers attempt to sort out nature and nurture, they end up seeing how closely the two interact.

visual cliff Apparatus for testing depth perception.

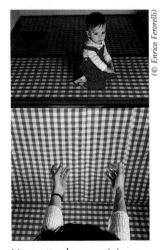

No matter how enticing a mother's arms are, this baby is staying away from them. Even at this age, a baby can perceive depth and wants to avoid falling off the "visual cliff."

Visual Preferences

The ability to distinguish one sight from another is essential to human survival and to much intelligent behavior. New research shows that the ability to view things selectively begins at birth.

How do we know what babies prefer to look at? Usually we can tell by finding out how much time they look at certain patterns. When Jason spends a longer time looking at one item than another, we conclude that he can tell the difference between the two and for some reason likes one of them better. For an extensive series of experiments to study what infants can see and what they like to look at, the researcher Robert Fantz designed a special apparatus containing a chamber in which, say, Jason can lie and look at a specific visual stimulus chosen by the experimenter. While Jason is lying in this chamber, an observer can peek through a small hole in the ceiling of the chamber and see a reflection of the visual stimulus over the pupil of Jason's eye. As soon as this reflection is seen on one or both of Jason's eyes, the observer starts to time Jason's visual fixation (how long he keeps looking at the stimulus), stopping only when Jason closes his eyes or turns away.

Using Fantz's "visual preference" methodology, researchers have found that infants less than 2 days old show definite preferences. Babies prefer curved lines to straight, complex patterns to simple, three-dimensional objects to two-dimensional objects, pictures of faces to pictures of other things, and new sights to familiar ones (Fantz, 1963, 1964, 1965; Fantz, Fagen, & Miranda, 1975; Fantz & Nevis, 1967).

In another type of study, 1- and 2-month-olds were shown three different faces: the mother's, a strange woman's, and a strange man's (Maurer and Salapatek, 1976). All the adults remained still and showed no expression. Age differences showed up in the babies' responses. The 1-month-olds tended to look away from these faces, particularly the mother's. This may have been because these expressionless faces seemed incongruous. The fact that the babies looked away more from the mother's face indicates that by the age of 1 month, babies can recognize their mothers. Photographs of the babies' eyes showed that the 1-month-olds' eyes focused on the borders of the faces, suggesting that their recognition was probably based on the mother's chin or hairline.

The 2-month-olds gazed longer at the faces, especially at the eyes. (Other studies have shown that by this age babies look longer at a face if the eyes are open and that they smile at it only if they can see both eyes.) The 2-month-olds may have looked longer at these expressionless faces because they had become more familiar with faces wearing a variety of expressions, so that the expressionless faces were novel.

Other studies show that infants respond to *part* of what they see rather than to *all* of it. Young infants (4 to 6 weeks old) tend to look at smaller areas of a visual stimulus than older infants (10 to 12 weeks old); that is, they focus on one small part of it (Leahy, 1976). And newborns look at a single feature of a geometric figure rather than at the whole figure (Salapatek & Kessen, 1966).

Visual preferences indicate that a newborn's world is not chaotic. Certain inborn mechanisms, which predispose children as early as a few hours after birth to gaze at other human beings, help them become social beings. While the complexity of the human face is probably what makes it so interesting to babies, the tendency to look long and hard at a face may help infants develop an interest in people.

Neonatal "pattern vision"—which is related to visual preferences—may be used to predict future development. Thirty-three newborns thought to be at high risk of developing neurological and intellectual handicaps were tested on their ability to tell one pattern from another. On the basis of their performance, they were designated "normal," "suspect," or "abnormal." A few days later, the babies' reflexes and neuromuscular maturation were examined. Then, at age 3 or 4 years, 19 of them were tested on the Stanford-Binet Intelligence Scale. The ratings on the neonatal visual pattern test predicted the children's IQ scores better than the ratings on the neurological tests (Miranda, Hack, Fantz, Fanaroff, & Klaus, 1977).

HEARING

Hearing is good in the womb just before birth, but immediately after birth it may be impaired because of fluid that fills the inner ear as a result of the birth process. A day or two after birth, when the fluid disappears, hearing becomes efficient again.

In Chapter 3, we saw that a fetus responds to sounds and that newborns show some signs of having learned sounds while still in the womb. Sounds continue to be important during infancy. Infants in a crib cannot see much, but they can hear a steady flow of sounds. Newborns are well equipped to hear these sounds, since the inner ear and middle ear reach adult size and shape even before birth (Aslin, Pisoni, & Jusczyk, 1983). The world of the infant may buzz and sing more than it blooms and smiles. Some milestones of hearing ability are shown in Table 5-3. Children who deviate markedly from these descriptions should receive special hearing tests.

Infants' hearing is often studied through the phenomenon of *habituation*, a simple type of learning in which a baby becomes used to a stimulus and stops responding to it. A baby who hears a new sound pays attention to it; after repeated presentations of the sound, the baby stops responding. Other studies of infants' hearing use *discriminative sucking*; when a baby sucks more to hear one sound than another, we assume that the baby can hear the difference between the two sounds.

In an experiment similar to the one described in Chapter 3, infants less than 3 days old showed through discriminative sucking that they could tell the moth-

habituation Simple type of learning in which familiarity with a stimulus reduces, slows, or even stops a response.

TABLE 5-3

MILESTONES OF HEARING	
AGE (MONTHS)	CONDITION
3	Is startled by loud sounds; is soothed by mother's voice; turns in general direction of sound source.
6	Responds to mother's voice; turns head and eyes toward sound but may not find source on first attempt.
10	Looks directly, promptly, and predictably to sound source.
12	Begins to show voluntary control over response to sounds; may or may not pay attention to a sound. Thus, a hearing loss becomes harder to distinguish from lack of concentration.

Source: Bolles, 1982, p. 200.

er's voice from a stranger's and that the mother's voice seemed to have a special importance. (DeCasper & Fifer, 1980). By sucking on a nipple, a baby was able to turn on a recording of his or her mother reading a story; at certain times, though, the apparatus turned on a recording of another woman reading a story. As young as they were, these babies sucked about 24 percent more when it was their mother's voice on the recording. Apparently, since they knew this voice, they were more interested in hearing it. This early preference for the mother's voice may be an important mechanism for bonding between mother and baby and, as suggested in Chapter 3, may be based on recognition of the mother's voice heard while the fetus is still in the womb.

In an experiment drawing on habituation, infants showed that 3 days after birth, they could already distinguish between new speech sounds and those they had already heard (L.R. Brody, Zelazo, & Chaika, 1984). The babies in the experiment steadily stopped responding to familiar words, but when they heard new words, they paid more attention.

In another experiment, 1-month-old babies showed that they could discriminate between two sounds as close as "bah" and "pah" (Eimas, Siqueland, Jusczyk, & Vigorito, 1971). The babies could suck on special nipples to turn on a recording. At first they sucked vigorously to hear the "bah" sound, but after they got used to that, their sucking slowed down. When the "pah" sound replaced the "bah" sound, they started to suck strongly again, showing that they could tell this minor difference in sound.

This early sensitivity to sounds may provide a way to estimate infants' intelligence. Most attempts to predict later IQ scores have proved disappointing (see Chapter 6), but a recent study found a highly significant correlation between ability to discriminate between sounds at 4 months of age and IQ score at 5 years. Thus, auditory sensitivity to changes in the environment may be one of the earliest indicators of cognitive functioning (O'Connor, Cohen, & Parmelee, 1984). In Chapter 6 we will look further at the relationship between childhood IQ and early sensory abilities (specifically, the ability to process sensory information efficiently).

SMELL

Newborns can tell distinctive odors apart, and they seem to show by their expression that they like the way vanilla and strawberries smell but they do not like the smell of rotten eggs or fish (Steiner, 1979). They can also tell where odors are coming from. When an ammonium compound is dabbed on one side of the nose, babies from 16 hours to 5 days old will turn the nose to the other side (Rieser, Yonas, & Wilkner, 1976).

The nose knows. Three-day-old infants, like this one, act more peaceful when they smell pieces of gauze that their mothers have worn than when they smell cloth worn by other women. And blindfolded mothers can identify by smell shirts their own babies have worn from shirts worn by other babies.

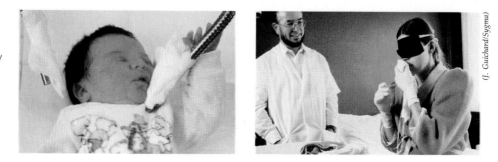

(J. Guichard/Sygma)

Smell is a powerful means of communication among human beings, beginning soon after birth. A 6-day-old infant will turn the head more often to a pad that his or her nursing mother has worn in her bra than toward a pad worn by another nursing mother, but a 2-day-old infant will not, suggesting that babies need a few days' experience to learn what their mothers smell like (Macfarlane, 1975).

TASTE

Most people's preference for lemonade over lemons demonstrates a specieswide inborn sweet tooth. Newborns can tell different tastes apart, and they seem to prefer sweet tastes to sour or bitter ones. The sweeter the fluid, the harder they suck and the more they drink (Haith, 1986). Also, when either pure water or a sweet sugar solution is placed on a baby's tongue, the baby moves the tongue to the side. The higher the concentration of sugar, the stronger the response (Weiffenback & Thach, 1975). Newborns reject bad-tasting food, an ability that probably serves as a survival mechanism.

TOUCH—AND PAIN

Touch seems to be the earliest sense to develop, and for the first several months of life, it is the most mature sensory system. When you stroke a hungry newborn's cheek near the mouth, the baby will respond by trying to find and connect with a nipple. Early signs of this rooting reflex show up in 2-month-old fetuses. By 32 weeks of gestation, all body parts are sensitive to touch (Haith, 1986), and infants' sensitivity to touch—and particularly to pain—increases during the first 5 days of life.

Historically, when an 8-day-old Jewish boy was circumcised by a ritual practitioner, the baby was given a piece of wine-soaked cloth to suck on to dull the pain. In recent years, however, physicians have shied away from giving newborn babies anesthesia during surgery because of their persistent belief that neonates cannot feel pain and because of the known side effects of many pain relievers. Parents have suffered as their infants have cried out in apparent pain from various procedures, wondering whether there might be long-term psychological effects of early painful experiences.

Recent reports state unequivocally that even on the first day of life babies can and do feel pain. Preterm and full-term newborns undergoing circumcision and such procedures as heel lancing (to obtain blood samples) cry more, have higher heart rates and blood pressure, and sweat more during and after the procedures. They also react to pain through body movements, like pulling a leg away from a pinprick, grimacing, and crying (Anand & Hickey, 1987). It seems, then, that the nervous system of a newborn is more highly developed than we used to think.

These findings have had important practical consequences, such as the following:

■ *Changes in some neonatal surgical procedures.* A newer mechanical method of heel lancing, for example, seems less painful than the manual method.
■ *Reconsideration of some procedures.* Routine, nonritual circumcision, a procedure that surgically removes the foreskin of the penis and was at one time performed on almost 90 percent of newborn boys in the United States, is

now done on only about 60 percent (Lindsey, 1988; National Center for Health Statistics, 1987). Although the American Academy of Pediatrics (1989) has concluded that there are medical benefits associated with circumcision, it should be performed only on healthy infants.

- *Administration of safe levels of pain medication to newborns.* The American Academy of Pediatrics Committees on Fetus and Newborn and on Drugs (1987), pointing to the availability of new, relatively safe pain relievers, recommend their use in most surgery on infants and urge that the decision whether to use them be based on medical criteria rather than age. In one study, infants given the local anesthetic lidocaine during circumcision cried 23 percent of the time, whereas babies given a placebo cried 68 percent of the time and those in a control group, 71 percent; the anesthetized babies also showed lower levels of cortisol, a chemical that signals the presence of stress (Stang, Snellman, Condon, & Kastenbaum, 1988). As one physician writes, the evidence is now "so overwhelming that physicians can no longer act as if infants were indifferent to pain" (Fletcher, 1987).

Motor Development of Infants and Toddlers

Vicky's activity began long before she saw the light of day—and has never stopped. In the womb, she moved around, kicked, turned somersaults, and sucked her thumb. In her new postnatal life, she lifts her head, looks around, kicks her legs, and flails her arms. All these first movements are simple, representing a very generalized kind of activity, with little conscious control. These early motor activities are under the control of the subcortex, but by about the fourth month of life they begin to give way to more deliberate movements directed by the cortex.

There is a definite order for the acquisition of motor skills, showing progress in the ability to move deliberately and accurately. Vicky's skills proceed from the simple to the complex (and they follow the cephalocaudal and proximodistal principles described earlier in this chapter). First, for example, Vicky picks up relatively large objects (large, at least, for her) with her whole hand; then she graduates to using neat little pincer motions with thumb and forefinger to pick up very small objects (which all too often she carries automatically to her mouth). After she has gained control over separate movements of her arms, hands, legs, and feet, she will be able to put these movements together to manage walking.

The ability to walk and the precision grip (in which the thumb and index finger meet at the tips to form a circle) are two of the most distinctively human motor capabilities. Neither is present at birth.

Vicky's growing control over her different body parts reflects the growing role of the cortex, allowing her to do more specific tasks. As soon as she learns one new skill, she keeps practicing it and getting better at it. This becomes tiresome for Ellen and Charles when their child's new skill involves dropping small objects from her high chair—and then crying for them, so that she can drop them again—but this repetition is an important part of Vicky's learning. Each newly mastered ability prepares her to tackle the next skill in the sequence. The more she can do, the more she can explore; the more she can explore, the more she can learn—and the more she can do.

BOX 5-1 ■ PROFESSIONAL VOICES

MARY S. CALDERONE

Capacities evident in early infancy include sexuality, according to Mary S. Calderone, M.D., a pioneer in sex education.

CALDERONE: The child begins to function in the uterus. The heart is functioning, the circulation, the neuromuscular system—everything. The only system "on hold" is the reproductive system [which is capable of creating a new life]. Not the sexual system [which responds to sexual stimulation]. The sexual system functions in the uterus and continues its function after birth. We now have proof of this, in ultrasound pictures that show an erection in a 29-week-old fetus. Prenatal penile erection seems to be cyclical on a pretty regular basis, just as it will be throughout the rest of that person's life. While we don't have direct observation of the baby girl before birth, clitoral erection and vaginal lubrication are evident from birth onward, to continue cyclically throughout her life.

Sometime in the first 6 months after birth, the baby discovers his penis or her vulva and finds that it is pleasurable to touch. This discovery is part of the natural evolution of the child, and parents need to treat it by socializing the child. We don't try to stop children from urinating and defecating—we just teach when and where to do it. Parents can do the same thing with self-pleasuring.

You cannot socialize a 6-month-old baby, of course. You can stand back and smile and let the baby have its fun for a few minutes, and then put the diaper on. And then, sometime between a year and 18 months, you can pick the baby up when it is pleasuring itself and you can say, "That feels so good. Now you must learn that this is also very private." Talking and smiling that way, you bring the baby on the bed. It may not work the first time, but if you do it consistently it will work. The baby will reach the age of 2 knowing that it's appropriate to go into its own room for privacy. It's a long, slow process, but then so is every other thing in the evolution of a child. So it should not be any more subject to panic or interference than any other learning process. It should fit into the child's growth pattern, the way we teach children other things, like table manners.

You have to begin by communicating the right information early in children's lives. Information alone is not the answer, though. Knowledge is important, and wisdom is the most important of all. We've been very brutal in discouraging children's enjoyment of their own bodies. No wonder we have sexual problems!

Even if parents haven't started out this way, they can change. They can say to their child, "You know, there are an awful lot of things about your sexuality that I haven't shared with you. It's very important. My mother and father were not good about that—they were embarrassed, so they passed their embarrassment on to me, but I don't have to be embarrassed with you, I realize that. So I am going to get a lot of books and you can ask questions about them. One of the things I want to say to you is that if you've ever gotten the idea from me that it isn't a good idea to touch yourself for pleasure, I was wrong. As long as you have a sense of privacy, and don't put any foreign objects into any parts of your body, it's OK to touch yourself anywhere you want to."

Source: Interview by S.W. Olds, New York, July 20, 1983; *photo:* ©1975 Karsh-Ottowa.

MILESTONES OF MOTOR DEVELOPMENT

Babies do not have to be taught basic motor skills like crawling, walking, and grasping. They just need room to move and freedom from interference. As soon as the central nervous system, muscles, and bones are mature enough, babies keep surprising the adults around them with their new abilities.

Motor development is marked by a series of milestones, that is, achievements that show how far along development has come. The *Denver Developmental Screening Test* was designed to spot children who are not developing normally (Frankenburg, Dodds, Fandal, Kazuk, & Cohrs, 1975), but it can also be used to chart normal progress between the ages of 1 month and 6 years. The test assesses four kinds of skills: *gross motor* (like rolling over or catching a ball), *fine motor* (grasping a rattle or copying a square), *personal and social* (smiling spontaneously or dressing oneself), and *language* (laughing or knowing the definitions of words).

Denver Developmental Screening Test Screening test given to children (1 month to 6 years old) to identify abnormal development; it assesses personal-social, fine motor–adaptive, language, and gross motor behavior.

Heads up! For the first 2 or 3 months, babies keep lifting their heads higher and higher—especially when they have an interesting toy or person to look at.

The test provides norms for the ages at which 25 percent, 50 percent, 75 percent, and 90 percent of children pass in each skill (see Table 5-4 for some milestones). A child who fails to pass an item at an age when 90 percent of children ordinarily pass is considered developmentally delayed. A child with two or more delays in two or more categories may need special attention. A short, 3- to 4-item version of the test (rather than the usual 20 to 25 items) takes only 3 to 5 minutes instead of the 15 to 20 minutes generally required; a child who fails any of the 3 to 4 items should be given the full-length test (Frankenburg, Fandal, Sciarillo, & Burgess, 1981).

As we describe Jason and Vicky, our "average" children, their motor development represents the 50 percent norms on the Denver Developmental Screening Test. We have to remember, however, that there is no average child. Normal progress covers a wide range; about half of all babies master the following skills before the ages given and about half afterward.

Head Control

At birth, Jason can turn his head from side to side while lying on his back and, when lying on his chest, can lift his head enough to turn it. First he masters lifting his head while on his stomach, then he holds his head erect while being held, and then he lifts his head while on his back. For his first 2 or 3 months, he keeps lifting his head higher, and by 4 months of age he can keep it erect while being held or supported in a sitting position.

Hand Control

At about 3½ months, Vicky can grasp an object of moderate size (like a teething ring), although she still has trouble holding anything much smaller. Then she begins to grasp the ring with one hand and transfer it to the other, and then to hold a smaller teether (but not pick it up). At about 7 months, Vicky's hands are coordinated enough that she can pick up a pea from her high-chair tray, using a pincerlike motion. (Jason, however, does not do this before 11 months.) After

TABLE 5-4

MILESTONES OF MOTOR DEVELOPMENT			
SKILL	25 PERCENT	50 PERCENT	90 PERCENT
Rolling over	2 months	3 months	5 months
Grasping rattle	2½ months	3½ months	4½ months
Sitting without support	5 months	5½ months	8 months
Standing while holding on	5 months	6 months	10 months
Grasping with thumb and finger	7½ months	8½ months	10½ months
Standing alone well	10 months	11½ months	14 months
Walking well	11 months	12 months	14½ months
Building tower of two cubes	12 months	14 months	20 months
Walking up steps	14 months	17 months	22 months
Jumping in place	20½ months	22 months	36 months
Copying circle	26 months	33 months	39 months

Note: Table shows approximate ages when 25 percent, 50 percent, and 90 percent of children can perform each skill.
Source: Adapted from Frankenburg, 1978.

that, her hand control becomes more and more precise. At 14 months she can build a tower of two cubes; by 2 years she can hold and drink from a cup, and her hand preference is quite well established; and about 3 months before her third birthday, she can copy a circle fairly well.

Locomotion

At the age of 3 months, after a quarter year as a prisoner of gravity, Jason begins to roll over purposefully, first from his stomach to his back and later from back to stomach. Before this time, however, when he lay on his stomach and rested on his hands with his head up, he sometimes rolled over accidentally. This is why Jess and Julia never left him alone on a surface where he might roll off.

Babies learn to sit either by raising themselves from a lying position or by plopping from a standing position. The average baby can sit without support between 5 and 6 months and can assume a sitting position without any help 2 months later.

Beginning at about 6 months, babies start to get around in a variety of ways under their own steam. They wriggle on their bellies and pull their bodies along with their arms, dragging their feet behind. They sometimes scoot along in a sitting position, pushing forward with their arms and legs. They bear-walk, with their hands and feet touching the ground. And they crawl on their hands and knees with their trunks above and parallel to the floor. Most babies are getting around quite well on their own by 9 to 10 months, an achievement that has important effects on psychological development (see Box 5-2, page 180).

With a helping hand or the support of a piece of furniture, Jason can pull himself to a standing position just before he is 6 months old, but he only rarely achieves an erect posture. At about 10 months, after some 4 months of practice pulling himself up on anything he can (and learning in the process that not

(© John Coletti/Stock, Boston)

Parents almost always show great excitement when their babies first learn to walk. The mother of this 1-year-old will soon realize how she needs to "baby-proof" her home from now on.

BOX 5-2 ■ THE RESEARCH WORLD

THE FAR-REACHING EFFECTS OF CRAWLING

Have you ever driven for the first time to a place where you had previously gone only as a passenger? If so, when you had to find your own way, you very probably saw landmarks you had never noticed, were aware of turns you had never felt, and—after getting there under your own steam—felt much more familiar with the entire route. The same kind of thing seems to happen to babies after they begin to get around on their own, after always having been carried or wheeled. In fact, the emergence of "self-produced locomotion" seems to be a turning point in the second half of the first year of life, influencing many aspects of physical, intellectual, and emotional development.

Sometime between 7 and 9 months of age, babies show vast changes. They show by their behavior that they are starting to understand concepts like "near" and "far"; they imitate more complex kinds of behavior; they show new fears—of strangers, heights, and unfamiliar objects; and on the other hand, they show a new sense of security around their parents or other caregivers. Since changes like these involve so many different psychological functions, affect processes that are so different from each other, and occur over such a short time span, some observers tie them all in with a major reorganization of brain function. This neurological development may be set in motion by one basic skill that emerges at this time—a baby's ability to crawl, which makes it possible to get around without depending on anyone else (Bertenthal & Campos, 1987; Bertenthal, Campos, & Barrett, 1984). (The occasional baby who skips the crawling stage but begins to walk upright very early would, presumably, go through the same kinds of changes.)

How does crawling exert such a powerful influence on babies' lives? Basically, it gives them a new view of the world. When Jason was carried, he paid little attention to his surroundings. But when he began to crawl, he became very sensitive to where objects were, how big they were in relation to each other. He started to pay attention to what objects look like—and indeed, studies have shown that babies who are already crawling are able to tell apart similar forms that differ in color, size, and which way they are situated in space (Campos, Bertenthal, & Benson, 1980). In other research (discussed in Chapter 6), babies were more successful in finding a toy that was hidden in a box when they crawled around the box than when they were carried around it (Benson & Uzgiris, 1985).

Moving around on their own also helps babies learn to judge distances and to perceive depth. Depth perception seems to be due less to maturation and age than to babies' experience in getting around by themselves—on all fours, in infant walkers, or walking upright. Perceiving depth does not imply fear of high places, however. When babies first become aware of depth, their heartbeat slows down; it is only sometime later that the heart rate speeds up, indicating fear. When babies start to move around by themselves, they put themselves in danger of falling, and so, to keep them from getting hurt, their caregivers usually hover over them, remove them from dangerous locations, or cry out and jump up when the babies are about to get into trouble. Babies are sensitive to these actions and emotions—and learn to be afraid of places from which they might fall.

The ability to move from one place to another also has social implications. For one thing, crawling babies seem to be better able to differentiate themselves from the rest of the world; as Jason moves about in space, he sees that the people and objects around him look different depending on how near or far they are. For another, being able to get around means that children can produce various effects on their world. They are no longer kept "prisoner" in a particular location. A baby who wants to be close to his or her mother and far away from a strange dog can now move toward the one and away from the other. This is an important step in developing mastery over the world, which enhances self-confidence and self-esteem.

Jason's new abilities get him into new situations, and he learns to look for clues to whether an ambiguous situation is secure or dangerous, showing growth in a skill known as *social referencing*. Crawling babies look at—or socially reference—their mothers more than babies who have not yet begun to crawl, apparently to try to pick up emotional signals from their mothers' faces or gestures, which in turn influence the babies' behavior (Garland, 1982). Social referencing is discussed further in Chapter 7.

We see, then, how a single milestone of physical development, learning to crawl, may have far-reaching effects in helping babies see their world and themselves in a new way.

everything will support his weight), he can let go and stand alone. About 2 weeks before his first birthday, he is standing well by himself.

All these developments are milestones along the path to the most important motor achievement of infancy: walking. Vicky's first walking is done with support, holding on to Charles's hand or the couch or table. When there is nothing and no one to hold on to, she reverts to the security of crawling. A few days after she can stand unaided, she takes her first step, throws herself off balance, lets her well-padded seat hit the floor—and then stands up and tries again. Soon she is taking two steps at a time, then more; and soon after her first birthday she is walking well. She is now a bona fide toddler.

During his second year, Jason is fascinated by climbing stairs, one at a time (he could crawl up before this—and fall down long before, and so his parents installed a baby gate and exercised constant vigilance). At first, he puts one foot after the other on the same step before going on to the next higher step, but later he alternates feet. Going down comes later. By age 3 he can balance briefly on one foot, and he is learning how to hop.

REPETITIVE PROCESSES IN MOTOR DEVELOPMENT

As children grow older, they become progressively better at all sorts of tasks. T. G. R. Bower (1976), however, has pointed out a few specific instances in which children display a particular ability at a very early age, after which they seem to lose it until regaining it at a later time. Walking is an example. At the age of 4 to 8 weeks, Vicky will make steplike motions that look like well-coordinated walking if she is held under her arms, with her bare feet touching a flat surface; this is known as the *walking reflex*. After 8 weeks, though, she loses this reflex and will not walk at all for about a year.

The same thing seems to happen with regard to reaching out for objects that are seen or heard. In the first few weeks of life, Jason will reach out, but at about the age of 4 weeks, eye-hand coordination—that is, the ability to reach out and grasp objects that one can see—disappears, not to reappear till the age of 20 weeks. And at the age of 5 or 6 months, ear-hand coordination—that is, the ability to reach out and grasp objects that can be heard but not seen—disappears.

T. G. R. Bower believes that the various phases of development are related and that the early appearance of some of these abilities is important in a child's use of them later on. He also believes that the reason such abilities disappear is that they are not exercised. To test this hypothesis, he provided practice for some infants in some abilities. The results were mixed. Babies who were given practice in eye-hand coordination in their first 4 weeks showed an earlier reappearance of the ability later on, and indeed, some of the babies never lost the ability to reach. However, the babies who practiced ear-hand coordination the most seemed to lose the ability quicker and to regain it later than the babies who did not practice (T. G. R. Bower, 1976).

Experiments like these raise ethical questions about providing artificial practice, especially since normal development seems to be retarded in some cases. Furthermore, we do not know the long-term effects of artificially induced precocious development. The concepts are intriguing, but their practical effects are questionable.

BOX 5-3 ■ AROUND THE WORLD

HOW UNIVERSAL IS "NORMAL" DEVELOPMENT?

The milestones Vicky and Jason pass in their motor development would seem so basic that babies in all cultures could be expected to pass them in the same sequence and at about the same time. But babies in different societies develop along somewhat different patterns. What is normal and typical for children in one culture may not be so in another.

This holds true even for such basic behaviors as reflexes, as we saw in Box 2-5 in Chapter 2 (D. G. Freedman, 1979). In addition, black African babies tend to be more advanced than white infants in gross motor skills like standing and walking, and Asian infants are apt to show slower development in these areas. Some of these differences may be related to temperament. Asian babies, for example, tend to be more docile, a trait which may explain why they show a calmer response when a cloth is pressed to the nose (as described in Box 2-5)—and which may also make them less likely to explore and move away from their parents (Kaplan & Dove, 1987).

Child-rearing practices and cultural norms also seem to play a part. A cross-sectional study of 288 normal full-term babies from the Yucatán peninsula in Mexico found that at 3 months of age these babies were ahead of American babies in motor skills. By 11 months, however, the Mexican babies were so far behind American babies that an American baby at the typical level of a Mexican baby might be considered neurologically impaired (Solomons, 1978).

The differences again might reflect child-rearing practices. The Mexican babies were slow by American norms, but were not considered retarded under the standards of their own culture. The Mexican babies' delayed skills in moving about may be related to several conditions in their lives: as infants, they are swaddled, and so their freedom of movement is restricted; as older children, they continue to be restrained by being carried more, by sleeping in hammocks (which become net "cages," compared with the open space of a firm-mattressed crib), and by not being put on the ground to play (partly because of tropical insects and partly because of local beliefs about the dangers of cold floors). By the same token, Mexican babies may be more advanced in manipulative skills, because, not having toys to play with, they discover and play with their fingers earlier than American babies.

The difficulty of coming up with environmental explanations for differences like these, however, is highlighted by the finding that Navajo babies—who are also swaddled for most of the day—begin to walk at about the same age as other American babies (Chisholm, 1983).

We also see cultural differences in childrens' performance on tasks like those in the Denver Developmental Screening Test, such as playing pat-a-cake, picking up raisins, and dressing themselves at a certain age. In one study (V. Miller, Onotera, & Deinard, 1984), southeast Asian children did not do these things, but that did not indicate abnormally slow development. In their culture, children do not play pat-a-cake, raisins look like a medicine they are told to avoid, and they are not expected to dress themselves until a later age than western children. We must be cautious, then, in applying the norms derived from one culture to children who are brought up differently.

Other research has also pointed to environmental causes for differences in gross motor skills. Children of the Ache in eastern Paraguay, for example, do not learn to walk until 18 to 20 months of age—about 9 months later than American babies (Kaplan & Dove, 1987). This delay may stem from early child-rearing practices. Ache mothers inhibit their children from exploring in the forest by pulling their babies back to their laps when the babies begin to crawl away. These mothers supervise their babies very closely, not only because of the hazards of nomadic life, but also because their primary responsibility is child rearing rather than subsistence labor. It is possible that children whose mothers spend less time with them become independent sooner because their caretakers are less vigilant. This may apply to American babies now, when day care is prevalent and when children seem to be developing more quickly.

Even when motor development is slowed, children often catch up, given a favorable environment. We see this with the Ache children, who in their early years show the slowest motor development reported for any human group, but who typically catch up later on. Ache 8- to 10-year-olds climb tall trees, chop branches, and play in ways that enhance their motor skills. Development, then, may be viewed "as a series of immediate adjustments to current conditions as well as a cumulative process in which succeeding stages build upon earlier ones" (Kaplan & Dove, 1987, p. 197).

Short-term experiments suggest that it is hard to speed up motor development (whether this would be desirable is yet another question), but these illustrations show how certain child-rearing practices may advance or retard it. We see that there is no universal standard of what is best for children and that cultures encourage their children to develop along somewhat different lines. Before we adopt or condemn another culture's child-rearing practices, we have to ask, "What is best for *our* children at this time and in this place?"

ENVIRONMENTAL INFLUENCES ON MOTOR DEVELOPMENT

Human beings appear to be genetically programmed to perform many different activities such as sitting, standing, and walking. All these skills unfold in a regular, largely predetermined pattern, and children have to reach a certain level of physiological maturity before they can exercise them.

The environment also plays a role, influencing children's development through specific child-rearing practices. (See Box 5-3.) However, motor development does not appear to be affected by sex, place of residence, or parents' education (Bayley, 1965). When children are well nourished, receive good health care, have physical freedom, and are given the opportunity to practice motor skills, their motor development is likely to be normal (Clarke-Stewart, 1977). But an environment that is grossly deficient in any of these areas may retard development significantly, as can be seen in the following classic study of orphans in institutions in Iran.

How Environment Can Retard Development

In two Iranian orphanages, the children were hardly ever handled by the overworked attendants. The younger babies spent practically all their time lying on the backs in the crib. They drank from propped bottles. They were never put in a sitting position or placed stomach down. They had no toys and were not taken out of bed until they could sit, without help (often not till 2 years of age, much later than the average American child). And once a sitting child was put on the floor, there was no child-sized furniture or play equipment. These children were retarded in their motor development because of the deficient environment, which initially kept them from moving around and provided little stimulation.

The children in a third orphanage were fed in the arms of trained attendants, were placed on the stomach and were propped up so that they could sit and had many toys. These children showed normal levels of motor development.

When the children in the first two orphanages did start to get about, they moved around in a sitting position, pushing their bodies forward with their arms and feet, rather than creeping on their hands and knees. Since they had never been placed on their stomachs, they had had no opportunity to practice raising the head or pulling the arms and legs beneath the body—the movements needed for creeping. Also, since they had never been propped in a sitting position, they had not practiced raising the head and shoulders to learn how to sit at the usual age. However, their retardation appeared to be temporary. Older children in one of the two "poor" institutions, who presumably had also been retarded as toddlers, worked and played normally (Dennis, 1960).

Such severe levels of environmental deprivation are fortunately rare. But the environment does play a part in motor development, and the more deficient it is, the greater its effect can be.

Can Motor Development Be Speeded Up?

Although (as we saw in Box 5-3) pervasive cultural practices can affect the rate of motor development, in limited experiments it has not been possible to train children to walk, climb stairs, or control the bladder and bowels earlier than usual.

In a classic experiment, Gesell (1929) examined one set of identical twins to study the effects of training babies to perform a number of motor activities. He trained twin T, but not twin C, in climbing stairs, building with blocks, and hand coordination. As the twins got older, twin C became just as expert as twin T. Gesell concluded that "the powerful influence of maturation on infant behavior patterns is made clear." Even though this study was conducted more than 50 years ago on only two infants, its conclusion still seems to stand. Children perform certain activities only when they are ready, despite the efforts of parents and psychologists.

Toilet training, for example, is often begun long before babies can control the necessary muscles. When a child is successful at a very early age, it is usually because the *parent* is trained to recognize the child's readiness and can get the child to the potty in time. Before children can control elimination, they have to learn a great deal. Initially, elimination is involuntary: when an infant's bladder or bowels are full, the appropriate muscles open automatically. To control these muscles, children have to know that there is a proper time and place to allow them to open. They have to become familiar with the feelings that indicate the need to eliminate and they have to learn to tighten the muscles until they are on the potty, and only then to loosen them.

In another classic study, McGraw (1940) measured the effects of very early training on twins. She put one twin on the toilet every hour of every day from 2 months of age, but did not put the other twin on until 23 months. The first twin began to show some control at 20 months, and by about 23 months he had achieved almost perfect success. The other twin quickly caught up. It seems

clear, then, that for some abilities—like the control of elimination—experience or training counts for little if the child is not mature enough to benefit from it.

Over the past few years, however, some parents have put their babies in infant walkers, partly to amuse the babies but partly to encourage them to walk earlier. As Box 5-4 shows, these appliances do not help babies walk earlier, and they do pose serious risks.

Death in Infancy

One of the most tragic losses is the death of a child. Even though the parents of a baby who has died have not had the chance to get to know their child well, they are usually deeply grieved. Parents may say that their arms "ache to hold their baby," and they are often overwhelmed by depression (National SIDS Clearinghouse, undated).

INFANT MORTALITY

We have made great strides over the years in protecting the lives of newborn babies. Today in the United States the *infant mortality rate*—the proportion of babies who die within the first year of life—is the lowest in the country's history. In 1985 there were fewer than 11 deaths for every 1000 live births, a 63.7 percent improvement over the 29.2 per 1000 in 1950 (National Center for Health Statistics, 1987). However, while infant mortality rates among both whites and blacks have declined, the rate for blacks (at 18.2) continues to be about twice that for whites (Wegman, 1987). The gap becomes more pronounced after the first month of life, possibly because socioeconomic factors become more influential—and because more black than white families are at low socioeconomic levels. Furthermore, it comes as a shock to realize that in terms of infant mortality, the United States ranks only nineteenth among 25 countries with a population of more than 2.5 million (Wegman, 1987). (See Figure 5-5, page 186.)

Besides the important health problem represented by these babies' deaths (which represent the largest number of deaths in any single year of life up to age 65), infant mortality is the tip of an iceberg—a sign of children's health problems in general (American Academy of Pediatrics Task Force on Infant Mortality, 1986). By analyzing the unhappy picture of infant mortality, we can better understand the health needs of children, and indeed of the entire population. We can, for example, learn about factors affecting pregnancy and birth as well as babies.

The term *neonatal mortality* refers to death in the first 4 weeks; *postneonatal mortality* refers to death in the rest of the first year. *Neonatal* mortality, which accounts for 70 percent of deaths in the first year, has two major causes. One is congenital defects (defects present at birth); this is the only cause of infant mortality that does not affect blacks more than whites (Wegman, 1987). The other major cause, which accounts for 70 percent of neonatal deaths, is low birthweight (discussed in Chapter 4). This affects black babies more than twice as often as white babies: 12.4 percent of black babies, compared with 5.6 percent of white babies, weigh less than 5½ pounds at birth (Wegman, 1987). The considerable decline in neonatal mortality since the late 1960s is due to medical advances in keeping very small babies alive and in treating sick newborns.

infant mortality rate
Proportion of babies who die within the first year of life.

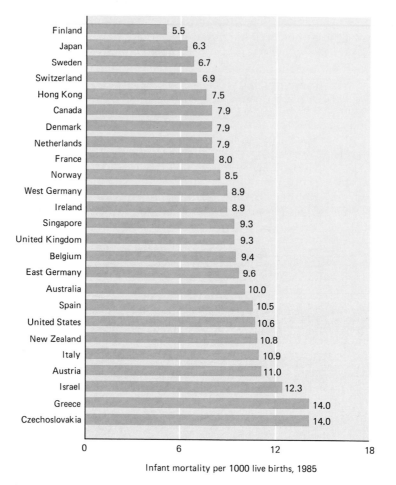

FIGURE 5-5
Infant mortality rate (deaths before 1 year per 1000 live births) is one indication of a nation's health status. The United States is nineteenth among 25 industrialized nations with populations of 2.5 million or more. *Note:* Some data are provisional; rate for Spain is for 1983. (*Source:* Wegman, 1987.)

The overall decline in infant mortality during the first half of the twentieth century reflected improvements in the *postneonatal* mortality rate, which resulted largely from better nutrition and sanitation. Some postneonatal deaths are due to complications of low birthweight and congenital defects, but most are caused by infection, injury, and sudden infant death syndrome (SIDS, discussed in the next section). Since some of these conditions can be treated, the babies who die of them are usually from poor families that have little or no access to medical care.

This is especially poignant in the case of Native American babies, since there is a low rate of neonatal death among Native Americans. Their babies leave the hospital healthy but during the first year of life die at twice the rate of white babies. The causes are often preventable accidents and treatable conditions like pneumonia and gastroenteritis (Honigfeld & Kaplan, 1987).

Our present rates of infant death are chilling to any concerned person. The American Academy of Pediatrics Task Force on Infant Mortality (1986) asks several questions. First, why—in a wealthy country like the United States—is infant mortality not declining at a faster rate, and why is there an apparent increase in postneonatal mortality? Second, why is there such a large disparity

BOX 5-5 ■ THE EVERYDAY WORLD

PUTTING RESEARCH TO WORK

If you are a parent, or are about to become a parent, or if you have occasion to care for infants or toddlers, you can put into practice some of the most important findings to emerge from recent research into child development. The following recommendations are just a sampling:*

- *Respond to babies' signals.* This is probably the single most important thing that caregivers can do. Meeting an infant's needs—whether it's for food, cuddling, or comforting—establishes a sense of trust that the world is a friendly place. Answering cries or requests for help gives a baby a sense of having a measure of control over his or her life, an important awareness for emotional and intellectual development. Adults often worry about spoiling children by reacting too quickly to meet their needs, but the children who have the most problems in life are those whose needs go unmet. As one old saying goes, "Baby a baby when he's a baby, and you won't have to baby him the rest of his life" (Chapters 6 and 7).

- *Provide interesting things for babies to look at and do.* By first watching a mobile hanging over a crib and then handling brightly colored toys and simple household objects, babies learn about shapes, sizes, and textures. Playing helps them develop their senses and motor skills. And handling objects helps them distinguish between themselves and things that are not themselves (Chapters 5 and 6).

- *Talk to babies and read to them.* By hearing and being able to respond to speech directed especially to them, babies learn how to express themselves. You'll be most effective if you pitch your voice high and speak slowly, use short words and simple sentences, leave off word endings (saying "go" instead of "going," for example), ask questions, repeat words and phrases, and talk about things in the baby's world. You'll probably do most of these things intuitively as you talk in "baby talk," or "motherese" (Chapter 6).

- *Give babies freedom to explore.* It's better to "baby-proof" an environment (by taking away breakables, small things that can be swallowed, and sharp objects that can injure and by jamming books into a bookcase so tightly that a baby can't pull them out) than it is to confine a baby in a playpen. Babies need to have opportunities to crawl and eventually walk, and they need opportunities to exercise their large muscles. They also need to learn about their environment in order to feel in control of it. And they need the freedom to go off on their own in order to develop a sense of independence (Chapters 5, 6, and 7).

*For research findings, see the chapter or chapters referenced at the end of each entry.

---

between black and white babies? And, third, what effects do budget cuts in health care have on babies?

The knowledge and the technology needed to diagnose and treat high-risk pregnancies and to help vulnerable infants are at our fingertips. It has been clearly shown that babies' survival rate improves with good prenatal and postnatal care for mothers and babies. Education and availability of contraceptives can also help, by enabling women to space their pregnancies better and thus reduce the number of high-risk births. Unfortunately, much of this know-how has not benefited poor and minority-group mothers and babies.

Babies from disadvantaged groups weigh on average ½ pound less at birth than middle-class babies. Yet, as one pediatric nutritionist has pointed out, "Pound for pound, the poor baby does as well as the rich baby; black babies do as well as white babies" (Winick, 1981, p. 80). Therefore, a major advance in saving the lives of babies would be to raise the average birthweight by even half a pound. This can be done if society and government are committed to make good prenatal care and general health care available and affordable to all prospective mothers.

SUDDEN INFANT DEATH SYNDROME (SIDS)

One kind of death among infants follows a typical, tragic sequence: a baby goes to sleep normally at the usual time, but a parent later finds the baby dead. *Sudden infant death syndrome (SIDS)*, the sudden and unexpected death of an apparently healthy infant, is a medical condition that takes the lives of some 7000 babies a year, or 2 out of every 1000 born. In 1985 it accounted for 12 percent of all infant mortality, affecting black babies more than white babies (Wegman, 1987). It is the leading cause of death among infants aged 1 month to 1 year and is most likely to strike babies between 2 and 6 months old (Arnon, Midura, Damus, Wood, & Chin, 1978; Hunt & Brouillette, 1987).

Despite the fact that SIDS, also known as *crib death*, has been observed since biblical times and was as common in the eighteenth and nineteenth centuries as it is today, we know very little about it. It is as mystifying as it is sad: the death is not caused by suffocation, vomiting, or choking, it is not due to a contagious condition, and there is no known way to predict or prevent it. It is most common in winter.

According to some observers, one reason for the mystery surrounding SIDS is that it is being overdiagnosed—that some deaths from other causes, including accidents, are attributed to SIDS (Bass, Kravath, & Glass, 1986; Hunt & Brouillette, 1987).

SIDS is particularly confusing and dismaying to parents because they do not know what has caused it and because it is so sudden. One woman described it as follows:

> This is the most painful time I have ever had to accept. It is hard to be a mother one day and not the next. The first months my arms actually ached to hold her again. I kept thinking I could hear her in bed playing, but it was just the furnace kicking on. (DeFrain, Taylor, & Ernst, 1982, p. 19)

A bereaved family as a whole also suffers greatly, seeing SIDS as the most severe family crisis it has ever experienced (DeFrain & Ernst, 1978; DeFrain et al., 1982). Parents feel guilty and under criticism from society, and siblings react with such emotional problems as nightmares and difficulty in school. It usually takes almost 18 months for a family to regain happiness. Recovery often seems impossible to the parents, but it does eventually come about. One mother recalled:

> So many people tell you when your child dies that things will someday be okay. At that time you seriously doubt that you can ever feel happy and normal again. But it does happen; and it is a blessing and a relief that it does. (DeFrain et al., 1982, p. 69)

A number of risk factors do seem to be important in SIDS. Babies most likely to succumb are black males whose birthweight was low. Their mothers tend to be young, unmarried, and poor; to have received little or no prenatal care; to have been ill during pregnancy; to smoke, abuse drugs, or both; and to have had another baby less than a year before the baby that has died of SIDS. Their fathers are also likely to be young (Babson & Clarke, 1983; Kleinberg, 1984; Shannon & Kelly, 1982a, 1982b; Valdes-Dapena, 1980; Wegman, 1987). Apparently, whatever these babies' problems are, they are worsened by living in a poor environment. Yet poverty is not the whole story. The picture is similar to that of birth

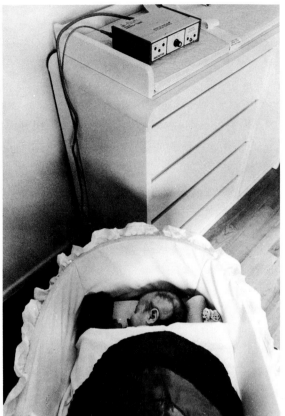

Monitoring machines have been developed in an attempt to prevent sudden infant death syndrome, but they are expensive, hard to operate, and anxiety-producing—and apparently they have not saved babies' lives.

trauma: infants in advantaged families sometimes succumb, but poverty worsens the odds.

A recent review of the literature concluded that the most compelling explanation seems to be an abnormality in the way the brain regulates breathing and heart rate (Hunt & Brouillette, 1987), since many SIDS babies had abnormal breathing patterns and some respiratory tract infection. *Apnea*—a temporary cessation of breathing—was once considered a possible cause; and although very few SIDS babies now seem to have any history of apnea, it may be related to this hypothesized brain abnormality.

So far, none of the research has suggested how SIDS might be prevented. Studies of babies with respiratory problems have not, so far, been sensitive enough to identify babies at risk. Monitoring devices have been developed that sound an alarm during a period of apnea, but they are expensive and hard to operate, they cause the parents considerable anxiety and stress, and there is no evidence that they have helped at all to prevent SIDS deaths (Hunt & Brouillette, 1987; Wasserman, 1984).

Fortunately, most infants do not succumb to SIDS or any other problem and will go on to grow up normally, making the great advances in cognitive and social-personality development which are typical of the first 3 years and which will be the subject of Chapters 6 and 7.

apnea *Temporary cessation of breathing.*

Summary

1 Normal physical growth and motor development proceed in a largely predetermined sequence. Two complementary principles are the cephalocaudal principle (development proceeds from the head to the lower body parts) and the proximodistal principle (development proceeds from the center of the body to the outer parts).

2 A child's body grows most rapidly during the first year of life. Growth proceeds at a rapid but diminishing rate for the next 2 years.

3 Growth is influenced by heredity, sex, and race as well as environmental factors such as nutrition and health care.

4 The newborn baby's brain is 25 percent of its eventual adult weight at birth and reaches 80 percent of its adult weight by the end of the second year. The environment can influence brain development positively or negatively, depending on the type of experience.

5 "Primitive reflexes" disappear as involuntary (subcortical) control of behavior gives way to cortical control. The timetable for their dropping out reflects whether neurological development is proceeding normally.

6 Breastfeeding offers physiological benefits to the infant and may facilitate the formation of the mother-infant bond. In promoting healthy development, however, the quality of the relationship between parents and infant is more important than the feeding method.

7 At about 4 to 6 months, babies should begin to eat solid foods. Obesity in infancy does not necessarily predict obesity later in life.

8 Sensory capacities, all of which operate to some extent at birth, develop rapidly in the first few months of life. Very young infants show pronounced ability to discriminate among stimuli.

9 Early motor development occurs when an infant is maturationally ready to engage in certain activities. Locomotion (as by crawling) influences many aspects of physical, intellectual, and emotional development.

10 Environmental factors may influence the expression of specific motor behaviors. Children raised in isolated, impoverished conditions may show motor retardation, but environmental influences have to be significant to accelerate or retard motor development markedly. Cross-cultural differences may lead to differences in patterns of motor behavior. However, short-term experiments aimed at speeding up specific types of motor development—such as climbing stairs and toilet training—generally have had little effect.

11 Although the infant mortality rate in the United States has improved, it is still disturbingly high, especially among blacks. It is related to poor prenatal care, which often contributes to low birthweight.

12 Sudden infant death syndrome (SIDS) is the leading cause of death in infants between 1 month and 1 year of age, affecting some 7000 infants each year in the United States. The cause of SIDS has not been determined, but the most likely explanation now appears to be an abnormality in the way the brain regulates breathing and heart rate.

Key Terms

cephalocaudal principle (page 159)
proximodistal principle (159)
cerebral cortex (162)
critical period (164)
reflex behavior (164)
visual cliff (171)
habituation (173)

Denver Developmental Screening Test
  (177)
infant mortality rate (185)
sudden infant death syndrome (SIDS)
  (188)
apnea (189)

Suggested Readings

Adebonojo, F., & Sherman, W., with Jones, L.C. (1985). *How baby grows: A parent's guide to nutrition.* New York: Arbor. An up-to-date study of feeding of infants during the first year. The book includes clear discussions of topics like breastfeeding and obesity in infancy.

Bower, T.G.R. (1977). *The perceptual world of the child.* Cambridge, MA: Harvard University Press. A fascinating discussion of the sensory and perceptual abilities of infants.

Chess, S., & Thomas, A. (1987). *Know your child—An authoritative guide for today's parents.* New York: Basic Books. A handbook which answers the common questions parents and caregivers ask concerning children's development from infancy through adolescence. The authors stress the importance of acknowledging individual differences when making parenting choices.

DeFrain, J., Taylor, J., & Ernst, L. (1982). *Coping with sudden infant death.* Lexington, MA: Heath. An investigation of the experiences and special problems of families who have lost a child through sudden infant death syndrome.

Eiger, M.S., & Olds, S.W. (1987). *Complete book of breastfeeding* (rev. ed.). New York: Workman. A comprehensive guide that pays particular attention to how breastfeeding benefits mother and baby and how it fits into family life. The book includes beautiful photographs and is up to date.

Hotchner, T. (1988). *Childbirth & marriage—The transition to parenthood.* New York: Avon. A resource book for parents that not only covers child care but also addresses such issues as how to combine a rewarding marriage with raising happy, healthy children.

Spock, B., & Rothenberg, M. (1985). *Dr. Spock's baby and child care* (40th anniversary ed.). New York: Pocket Books. An extensively revised version of the classic work on child care, which covers such issues as the role of the father in childbirth and child rearing, vegetarian diets, day care, children's fear of nuclear war, and other current topics.

CHAPTER 6

INTELLECTUAL DEVELOPMENT IN INFANCY AND TODDLERHOOD

I wish I could travel by the road that crosses baby's mind, and out beyond all bounds;
Where messengers run errands for no cause between the kingdoms of kings of no history;
Where Reason makes kites of her laws and flies them, and Truth sets Fact free from its fetters.

Rabindranath Tagore, 1913

PREVIEW QUESTIONS

- How do infants learn?
- How do the psychometric, Piagetian, and information-processing approaches address and measure infants' intelligence?
- How do babies and toddlers learn to speak and understand language?
- What are some milestones of language development in the first 3 years?
- How do toddlers display competence, how can their parents help them acquire it, and how can society help parents?

"'ICKY! 'ICKY!" 18-month-old Vicky shouts excitedly as she waves her hand at photos of herself. She has just discovered the photos—mounted in her parents' bedroom just one day earlier—and she recognizes herself, captured in color in the course of her everyday activities. Her recognition of herself in these pictures, her awareness of her own name, and her ability to pronounce a close approximation of it are all signs of her continuing cognitive development. The intellect that showed itself at birth has been advancing, giving her more tools for understanding her world and functioning in it.

If newborn infants could speak, they would protest that their intelligence has been underestimated for centuries. This underestimation persisted almost to the present through a coincidence of two major social movements toward the end of the nineteenth century. Psychologists, on the one hand, were beginning to propose theories of human development, while doctors, on the other, were establishing a routine under which babies were born in hospitals and were exposed to sedative drugs and isolated from their mothers. Thus, observations of newborns were strongly biased. Furthermore, psychologists' first tests to study infants' intelligence were based on the tests they were using for adults or animals, none of which were suited to human infants. Fortunately, all this has changed over the past few decades, which have seen more research on infants' abilities than took place during all previous history (Lipsitt, 1982; Rovee-Collier & Lipsitt, 1982).

We now know that the normal, healthy human baby is remarkably competent. Infants enter the world with all their senses working, with the ability to learn, and with a capacity for using language. Beginning at birth, humans take an active part in affecting their environment as well as reacting to it.

In this chapter, we marvel at babies' progress in their first 3 years. We see how they learn. We examine three different approaches to the study of intelligence, and we see how we can learn about babies' intelligence by watching them at play. We look at what may be the one intellectual power that most sets humans apart from the lower animals—the ability to learn and use language—and we see how young children manage this complicated task. Finally, we see how babies respond to intellectual stimulation, what parents can do to stimulate them, and how society can help parents provide stimulation.

Early Learning

Do infants *learn* how to suck on a nipple? Usually, they do not; they are born with a reflex for getting food. As we saw in an experiment described in Chapter 5, however, as early as 3 days after birth, a baby will suck more on a nipple if doing so produces the mother's voice than if it produces the voice of a strange woman (DeCasper & Fifer, 1980). The baby has, then, learned two separate things. One is an intellectual skill: distinguishing between the mother's voice and someone else's. The other is a behavioral skill: the baby has discovered that something he or she knows how to do (sucking) can produce something pleasant or desirable (a familiar voice).

Learning is a relatively permanent change in behavior that occurs as a result of experience. This experience can take the form of study, instruction, observation, exploration, experimentation, or practice. Babies learn from what they see, hear, smell, taste, and touch. As we saw in Chapter 5, newborns come into the world with an array of sensory abilities and a repertoire of adaptive behaviors (like the sucking reflex). These reflexes can ensure survival as long as a concerned adult is around. But they do not permit much more than survival.

learning Relatively permanent change in behavior that results from experience.

Jason must rely on his active brain to learn the details of his environment. He begins sizing up matters right away, using his intellect to distinguish between experiences, and then using his small repertoire of behavioral abilities as the building blocks of learning. From early on, to understand Jason it is critical to understand how he learns.

LEARNING AND MATURATION

The first sounds that Vicky makes are not learned, although later sounds, which have meaning for her, are. Vicky's first vocal activity is crying, a feat no more complex than blowing steam out of a valve. The "goo" sounds she makes next are still simple, but to make them she has to do some manipulation of the back of her mouth. A month or two later she babbles, using her tongue in different ways to shape her sounds. By her first birthday, Vicky speaks a few short words formed from simple sounds. She can speak them well, showing subtle and voluntary control of her body.

Mastering speech is not merely a question of learning; it is also a function of maturation. Even if Vicky was born with the soul of a poet, she will not be able to speak like one until her vocal cords and her tongue are mature enough to let her form sounds, and until her brain and nervous system are mature enough to let her understand that such sounds have meanings and to let her remember both the meanings and the sounds.

maturation Unfolding of patterns of behavior in a biologically determined age-related sequence.

Thus, we see the importance of **maturation,** the unfolding of patterns of behavior in a biologically determined age-related sequence. These changes are programmed by the genes. In other words, before Vicky can master new abilities, she has to be biologically ready. Maturation is also important for such motor skills as crawling, walking, and toilet training, and for a host of other physical abilities and for many cognitive abilities. Maturation, then, does not rely on learning, but it is a necessary condition for learning to take place.

The connection between maturation and learning can be seen in the development of crawling. As we saw earlier, in Chapter 5, young babies placed on a "visual cliff" show that they perceive depth, but they do not become afraid of the "drop" until they have begun to get around on their own (Bertenthal & Campos, 1987). Perhaps they have fallen off something—or perhaps when they were on a high surface they heard their caretakers cry out in fear. In any case, their experience has allowed them to learn that the edge of a "cliff" is something to be afraid of. Thus, a skill that has come about through maturation (crawling) apparently contributes to a baby's ability to learn about and interpret the environment. On the other hand, we saw in Chapter 5 that the environment can sometimes influence maturation and, by extension, also influence learning—as in the experiment in which cats were fitted with training goggles.

TYPES OF LEARNING

Babies learn in a number of ways—through the more or less simple processes of habituation, classical conditioning, and operant conditioning, and by building up more complex behaviors, sometimes by combining more than one mode of learning.

Habituation

The most primitive kind of learning is *habituation,* the process of getting used to a sound, a sight, or some other stimulus, which results in reduced response,

habituation Simple type of learning in which familiarity with a stimulus reduces, slows, or even stops a response.

(© James Kilkelly)

Can this baby tell the difference between Raggedy Ann and Raggedy Andy? The researcher may find out by seeing whether the baby has habituated (gotten used to) one face. Stopping sucking on the nipple when a new face appears shows that the baby recognizes the difference.

suggesting loss of interest. It meets the definition of *learning*, since it involves a change in behavior based on experience.

The significance of habituation is that it helps people (and animals) conserve energy and maintain alertness, by allowing them to pay attention only to important aspects of their environment, like those offering food or threatening danger. Some lowered or reduced responses, however, result not from habituation but from other causes; these include sensory adaptation (for example, becoming unaware of the feel of your clothing), maturation, illness, aging, or drug use (Lipsitt, 1986).

Researchers study habituation in infants by repeatedly presenting a stimulus (like a picture or music). Typically, the baby initially shows interest in one of several ways, such as turning toward the stimulus, looking at it, or interrupting an activity, like sucking on a nipple. Researchers can also measure habituation by monitoring babies' eye movements, heart rate, brain activity, and other physical responses. After the same sight or sound has been presented again and again, it loses its novelty and the baby loses interest, showing habituation. A new sight or sound, however, will get the baby's attention.

FIGURE 6-1
Visual recognition in infancy. The more two pictures or patterns differ, the less time a baby needs to distinguish them. A 5-month-old baby may need only 4 seconds to distinguish two very different patterns (top pair) but may need 17 seconds to distinguish faces. (*Source:* Fagen, 1982.)

Habituation studies show how well babies can see and hear, how much they can remember, and what their neurological status is. Researchers have found, for example, that 3-day-old infants can tell the difference between new speech sounds and those they have already heard (L.R. Brody, Zelazo, & Chaika, 1984), that babies less than a week old can tell visual patterns apart (J.S. Werner & Siqueland, 1978), and that babies become better at differentiating patterns by 5 months of age (Fantz et al., 1975). The greater the difference between the patterns, the less time a baby needs to tell them apart (Fagen, 1982; see Figure 6-1).

The capacity to habituate increases within the first 10 weeks of life. Its presence or absence, as well as the speed with which it occurs, can yield information about a baby's present and future development. As we shall discuss later, the speed of habituation in early infancy (an indication of how efficiently an infant processes information) seems to predict later intelligence. Newborns who habituate poorly are likely to show slow intellectual development later on, and those who do not habituate at all are likely to have learning problems in the future (Lipsitt, 1986).

Classical Conditioning

In Chapter 1 we saw how Vicky, after her father had taken many pictures of her, eventually blinked *before* the flashbulb on his camera went off. This is an example of *classical conditioning,* which was described in Chapter 1 in connection with Pavlov's experiments with dogs. In classical conditioning, a person or an animal learns to respond automatically to a stimulus that is originally neutral (does not provoke the response). Such conditioning occurs after repeated pairings of the neutral stimulus with a stimulus that automatically elicits a response.

In Vicky's case, the flash was an *unconditioned stimulus (UCS);* it automatically caused her to blink. The blinking after the flash was an *unconditioned response (UCR);* it came of its own accord. The camera was originally a *neutral stimulus;* it did not elicit blinking. After the two stimuli—camera and flash—were paired repeatedly, the camera became a *conditioned stimulus (CS);* that is, it was neutral before the conditioning, but after repeated pairing with the flash it

classical conditioning
Learning in which a previously neutral stimulus (conditioned stimulus) acquires the power to elicit a response (conditioned response) by association with an unconditioned stimulus that ordinarily elicits a particular response (unconditioned response).

elicited blinking. Vicky's blinking at the camera alone was a ***conditioned response (CR):*** a learned response that arose only after repeated association of the camera with the flash.

The classic example of such conditioning in humans was the conditioning of fear in a baby known as "Little Albert" (J.B. Watson & Rayner, 1920). When "Little Albert" was 9 months old, he loved furry animals. When he was 11 months old, he was brought into a laboratory, and just as he was about to grasp a white rat, a loud noise (a hammer striking against a steel bar just behind his head) frightened him, and he began to cry (showing a UCR). After repeated pairings of the rat (originally a neutral stimulus) with the loud noise (a UCS), the rat became a conditioned stimulus (CS). Eventually, as soon as "Little Albert" saw the rat, he whimpered in fear; his crying became a conditioned response (CR). He also became afraid of rabbits, dogs, a Santa Claus mask, and other furry white objects. That is, his fear response generalized to other stimuli.

John B. Watson and Rosalie Rayner's conditioning of "Little Albert" raises at least two controversial issues. First, of course, is the moral question. Under today's ethical standards, this experiment would never be permitted. According to the principles set out in Chapter 1, it would be unethical to create fear in a baby's mind in the name of science. Second, critics of the conclusions charge that this experiment was not pure classical conditioning. Rather, because the loud noise might be considered a form of punishment, the experiment may include aspects of operant conditioning (B. Harris, 1979), a type of learning that will be discussed next. However, this study does suggest that emotional responses can be conditioned.

The ethical and procedural issues raised by the experiment with "Little Albert" are by no means the only twentieth-century controversy about research on classical conditioning. According to Lipsitt and Werner (1981), a number of studies supposedly of classical conditioning have not met two important criteria. These two criteria for the occurrence of classical conditioning are (1) that the learned response must occur *only* in response to the conditioned stimulus and (2) that the response has to be the result of learning and not simply a response that comes as the natural result of reaching a certain age (that is, of maturation).

Another controversy revolves around the question, "When is the earliest time that human beings can learn?" Although some critics maintain that newborns cannot be classically conditioned (Sameroff, 1971; Stamps, 1977), more recent research suggests that there *are* ways to classically condition newborns. Newborns have been classically conditioned to suck when they hear a buzzer or a tone, to show the Babkin reflex (turning the head and opening the mouth) when their arms are moved (instead of the unconditioned stimulus, pressure on the palm of the hand), to dilate and constrict the pupils of the eye, to blink, and to show a change in heart rate (Rovee-Collier & Lipsitt, 1982).

Operant Conditioning

A baby's sucking to produce the sound of the mother's voice is an example of ***operant*** (or ***instrumental***) ***conditioning.*** In operant conditioning, a baby learns to make a certain response in order to produce a particular effect. The behavior of sucking is being reinforced, or rewarded; this reinforcement encourages the baby to repeat the behavior. Operant conditioning differs from classical conditioning in that the learner influences the environment. Operant conditioning can be used to learn voluntary behaviors (as opposed to involuntary behaviors like salivation).

Because babies can learn through operant conditioning, researchers can learn about their sensory abilities and preferences. In one study, 2-day-old infants were rewarded with music as long as they sucked on a dry nipple. The babies would keep sucking as long as the music played, but would stop when their sucking turned the music off (Butterfield & Siperstein, 1972). The researchers concluded that babies find music reinforcing and that they can learn to do certain things in order to keep music playing. Studies like this, which change what babies do by reinforcing certain kinds of behavior, show that neonates can learn by operant conditioning, *if* the conditioning encourages them to perform some kind of behavior they already know (like sucking or turning the head), rather than something they would not ordinarily do.

Complex Learning

Classical and operant conditioning can occur separately or in combination to produce increasingly complex learning. In one series of studies involving 1- to 20-week-old infants, babies received milk if they turned the head left at the sound of a bell. This was operant conditioning: the milk reinforced the response of turning the head to the left. The babies who did not learn to turn the head through operant conditioning were then classically conditioned. When the bell sounded, the left corner of the mouth was touched, and the baby turned the head and received the milk. (The touch was the unconditioned stimulus and turning the head the unconditioned response; the bell was the conditioned stimulus, and turning the head to the bell became the conditioned response.)

By the age of 4 to 6 weeks, all the babies had learned to turn the head when hearing the bell. Then the babies learned to differentiate the bell from a buzzer. When the bell rang they were fed on the left; when the buzzer rasped they were fed on the right. At about 3 months of age, the babies had learned to turn to the side that brought food. By 4 months, they even learned to reverse their responses to bell and buzzer—an impressively complex response (Papousek, 1959, 1960a, 1960b, 1961).

Other researchers found that babies only 2 to 4 days old, with less than an hour's training, could learn to differentiate between a buzzer and a tone and could reverse their responses when the two sounds were switched (Siqueland & Lipsitt, 1966).

Babies learn in other ways besides habituation and conditioning. For example, social learning, which is based on observing and imitating models, is discussed later in this book. Children learn many complicated abilities through a mix of different kinds of learning and natural growth, or maturation. An example is discussed in Box 6-1 (page 200).

INFANTS' MEMORY

If Vicky had not remembered the bright light associated with Charles's camera, she would not have blinked at the camera alone. If Jason could not remember that sucking on a nipple could produce his mother's voice, he would not continue to suck on a nipple that produced no food. Even the primitive process of

BOX 6-1 ■ THE EVERYDAY WORLD

TOILET TRAINING

One of the most difficult jobs a parent faces is teaching a child how to use the toilet. Toilet training does not have to bring tears, shouting, and unhappiness, however. Two psychologists who devised a program using a combination of learning principles to teach retarded people how to use the toilet applied the same principles to a program for normal children (Azrin & Foxx, 1981). If you were using Azrin and Foxx's method to toilet-train Jason, you would take the following basic steps:

1   Wait till Jason is about 20 months of age and then test him for bladder control (does he stay dry for 2 or 3 hours at a time?), physical readiness (can he dress and undress himself?), and readiness to take instructions. If he doesn't seem ready, wait a few weeks and test him again. Maturation is essential.

2   Before you begin training, encourage Jason to dress himself as much as he can, allow him to watch family members using the toilet, and teach him to follow instructions. Teach him the words to describe both his body functions and the use of the toilet. Imitation (learning based on observing models) is important (see the description of social learning in Chapter 1).

3   Accumulate a variety of items to use as reinforcers (balloons, toys, or small snacks). You'll also be using praise, hugs, smiles, and applause. Knowing your child, you'll know which reinforcers will be most effective. (The use of food as a reinforcer is controversial; some nutritionists believe that associating food with approval can lead to overeating.)

4   Get a potty that's easy for Jason to empty. The more responsibility he takes, the quicker he'll learn.

5   Buy a doll that drinks from a bottle, wets, and can wear "training pants." It will provide another form of learning by imitation, as well as learning by teaching.

6   Dress Jason in training pants and show him how to put them on and take them off. Part of being a "big boy" is dressing and undressing himself.

7   Have Jason teach his doll to use the potty. Encourage him to praise the doll enthusiastically and to offer it a prize (which Jason himself will get, once he agrees to do the same). This is the beginning of "shaping" Jason's behavior.

8   Teach Jason to check his pants for dryness and reward him with a prize and praise when he tells you that he's dry. This is another step in shaping.

9   Teach him to walk to the potty, lower his pants, sit down, stay there quietly for several minutes, and then stand up and raise his pants—more shaping.

10   Praise and reassure him to encourage him to relax while on the potty. Anxiety and tension often interfere with learning; feeling relaxed enhances it.

11   Develop a way to detect urination on the potty as soon as it starts, and praise Jason immediately. This emphasizes the pairing of the biological mechanism of relaxing the relevant muscles with being on the potty, an important element of classical conditioning. It also strengthens the association between the action and the rewards, an important element of operant conditioning.

12   Deal with accidents by encouraging him to use the potty right afterward, making him aware of his wet pants, and having him take them off and put them into the laundry hamper himself. While the major emphasis throughout this program is on reward and encouragement, Azrin and Foxx also suggest that accidents can be met with a mild form of punishment, showing disapproval in words and body language.

habituation requires that babies remember what they have already seen or heard; otherwise they would not respond differently to new stimuli. Since very young infants *can* learn, it is clear that very soon after birth the human memory is working to some extent and that its efficiency improves rapidly (Lipsitt, 1986).

Many learning experiments are most significant for what they reveal about the beginnings of memory. When mothers of 2- to 4-week-old infants repeated a single word 60 times a day for 13 days and their babies were tested up to a day and a half later, the babies responded more (by moving their eyes) to the "target" word than to other words, including their own name (Ungerer, Brody, & Zelazo, 1978).

Other research has shown that infants less than 2 months old can remember past events, especially if those events gave them pleasure. Researchers studying

6-week-old babies tied a ribbon to each baby's left leg and also attached the ribbon to a bright mobile hung above the crib. The babies quickly learned that kicking would activate the mobile. Then the mobile was taken away. When the mobiles were hung again, 2 to 4 weeks later, ribbons were not attached to the babies' legs—but the babies still kicked when they saw the mobiles, especially with the left leg, showing that they remembered the pleasure that a little kicking could bring (Rovee-Collier & Fagen, 1976, 1981; M.W. Sullivan, 1982).

When new mobiles—differently colored or differently shaped—were hung, the babies kicked less in response to them than to the old, familiar ones (Fagen, 1984). And babies who were trained with different mobiles on different days learned to expect a different mobile each time (Fagen, Morrongiello, Rovee-Collier, & Gekoski, 1984). Their ability to mentally incorporate the idea of change was shown by their responding more to a new mobile than to the old. Findings like these "suggest that infants are 'built' to organize and find structure in what must otherwise appear to be a random and chaotic world" (p. 942). This ability to organize the world is closely tied in with the development of intelligence.

Three Approaches to Studying Intellectual Development

One-year-old Vicky loves to play games with Charles. One day he put some Cheerios into his hand, closed it, and put his hand on the tray of Vicky's high chair. Vicky immediately pulled Charles's fingers open to reach for the Cheerios, but as soon as she released his fingers, they closed over the Cheerios. After two more tries, she began holding his fingers open with one hand while she picked up the Cheerios with her other. One day, when she was holding a toy in one hand, she opened Charles's fingers with her free hand and then held them open with her chin. She flashed a roguish smile as she scooped up the Cheerios with her hand.

Like most parents, Charles was delighted by his child's ingenuity, but it never occurred to him to wonder how Vicky was able to think up such an original solution to a problem. Psychologists do wonder about this. They ask why children are so intelligent, why some seem more intelligent than others, and whether intelligence early in life can predict later functioning. Why do they ask such questions? First, of course, an overwhelming scientific curiosity about human beings and how they function fuels much research. Then, there are practical reasons: if a baby is not developing normally, finding out early in life may allow parents, educators, and other professionals to provide special help that will enable the child to do better later on in life.

Intelligence is complex—hard to analyze, difficult to describe, and seemingly impossible to account for fully. It is not surprising that those who study it often disagree about how to assess it—and even what it is. Generally, investigators of intelligence have taken one of three approaches:

■ The **psychometric approach** looks at intelligence in terms of *quantity*, or *how much* intelligence a person has. Psychometricians (people who take this approach) assess intelligence using tests; the higher the test score, the more intelligent the person is considered to be.

psychometric approach
Study of intellectual development based on attempts to measure the quantity of intelligence.

- The *Piagetian approach* looks at the *qualitative* changes in intellectual functioning, or *what* people can do. Researchers following this approach describe how the nature of intelligence changes in stages from infancy through adolescence.
- The *information-processing approach* analyzes the *processes* underlying intelligent behavior, or *how* people do what they do. It examines processes like perception, memory, and problem solving.

It may well be necessary to use all three approaches to understand intelligence. No single approach can provide enough information to understand the nature of intelligence, but a combination of approaches may open a window to understanding (Siegler & Richards, 1982). Before we describe the three approaches individually, we will explain what we mean in this book when we use the term *intelligence*.

WHAT IS INTELLIGENCE?

While there are almost as many definitions of intelligence as there are researchers in the field, most of them focus on two forms of behavior:

1 *Goal-oriented* behavior is conscious and deliberate rather than accidental.
2 *Adaptive behavior* is directed to solving specific problems—understanding that there is a problem, defining it, and then solving it.

When we use the term *intelligence* in this book, we define it as an interaction between inherited ability and environmental experience which results in a person's ability to acquire, retain, and use knowledge; to understand both concrete and abstract concepts; to understand the relationships between objects, events, and ideas and to apply this understanding; and to use all this in solving the problems of everyday life. It is the ability to adapt behavior in pursuit of a goal.

We will describe how the three different approaches to studying intelligence differ in the particular problems they consider and the ways they measure successful problem solving.

PSYCHOMETRIC APPROACH

Intelligence Tests

At the beginning of the twentieth century, the schools in Paris were overcrowded, and administrators wanted to remove children who could not benefit from an academic education. They asked the psychologist Alfred Binet to devise a test to identify those pupils. The test that Binet developed with his colleague Théodore Simon has been modified since then, and the American version—known formally as the *Stanford-Binet Intelligence Scale,* and informally as the *IQ test*—exemplifies the psychometric approach to studying intelligence. Binet's test led the way for a wide variety of tests that try to assign intelligence a numerical score.

Although Binet focused on finding children who were least likely to benefit from an education, today intelligence testing is also used to identify very bright children who can benefit from an enriched program.

(Culver Pictures)

The French psychologist Alfred Binet (1857–1911) devised a test that exemplifies the psychometric view of intelligence.

How Are Intelligence Tests Developed? People using the psychometric approach try (1) to identify the different factors that make up intelligence, (2) to develop ways to measure these factors, and (3) to predict a person's future intelligence and achievements (like school performance). They are interested in how people are different in the factors that constitute "intelligence," and they use complex statistical techniques to measure the differences.

Standardization Test developers make up questions or tasks which they think will show levels of intellectual functioning. They then give these questions to a **standardization sample,** that is, a large and representative group of test takers whose scores are used as **norms,** or performance averages. The scores of later test takers are measured against these standardized norms. A standardized test is given, using the same procedures for all test takers.

Validity Test developers are concerned with a test's **validity**—the degree to which it measures what it is designed to measure. They compare its results with other measures and look for correlations. One way to assess the validity of an intelligence test is to look at the relationship of scores on IQ tests with school performance. The Stanford-Binet Intelligence Scale, for example, is especially good at predicting success in verbal courses like English, not so good with mathematics, and virtually useless with creativity.

Reliability Test-retest **reliability** refers to constancy of scores when a person is tested more than once.* IQ tests for infants and young children are so unreliable that some people consider it impossible to measure intelligence at an early age— an issue we address in the next section. However, these tests are quite reliable for children after age 5, and for adults, especially if the two tests are repeated after only a fairly short time. However, a person's IQ is by no means fixed at birth, as we shall see.

Calculating IQ Scores The Stanford-Binet yields a score in terms of **mental age (MA).** This corresponds to the average age of children in the standardized sample (normal children between the ages of 3 and 13) who passed about the same number of test items as the test taker. A child who passed items that were passed by 80 to 90 percent of the normal 3-year-olds in the standardization sample would be considered to have a mental age of 3.

The **intelligence quotient (IQ)** translates mental age into a number that can be used for people in all age groups. The traditional way of computing IQ was to take the ratio of a person's mental age (MA) to his or her actual, chronological age (CA) and multiply it by 100. The equation looks like this:

$$IQ = \frac{MA}{CA} \times 100$$

According to this calculation, when mental age is the same as chronological age, the test taker has an IQ of 100, which is average, or normal; when mental age is greater than chronological age, the IQ is over 100; and when mental age is less than chronological age, the IQ is under 100.

*There are other kinds of reliability, but these need not concern us here.

standardization sample *Large, representative group of people used in developing a statistical standard against which other people will be compared.*

norm *Average performance, with which a person's score on a test is compared*

validity *Extent to which a test measures what it is designed to measure.*

reliability (test-retest reliability) *Constancy of scores when a person is tested more than once.*

mental age (MA) *Assessment of a person's intellectual ability, determined by administering an intelligence test and matching the test taker's score with the average age of those who have scored similarly.*

intelligence quotient (IQ) *Score calculated by dividing a person's mental age by his or her chronological age and multiplying the result by 100.*

Thus:

■ A 10-year-old (CA = 10) who scores a mental age of 10 (MA = 10) has an IQ of 100.
■ A 10-year-old (CA = 10) who scores a mental age of 8 (MA = 8) has an IQ of 80.
■ A 10-year-old (CA = 10) who scores a mental age of 12 (MA = 12) has an IQ of 120.

This traditional calculation does not take into account the fact that an IQ figured this way would not mean the same thing at different ages, because at some ages there is more variability among people than at others. To resolve this problem, the method of arriving at scores, standardized for all ages, has become somewhat more complex. However, the scores themselves are not very different from what they would be in the traditional system. The great majority of people (two-thirds) score between 85 and 115, with a few people scoring considerably higher (2 percent above 130) and a few scoring considerably lower (2 percent below 70).

Can Infants' and Toddlers' Intelligence Be Measured? Although we know that infants are intelligent and that they seem to show different levels of ability, measuring such differences is not easy. Defining and measuring intelligence in adults is hard enough; in infants, it is even harder. Babies can't talk. You can't ask them questions, and they can't tell you in words what they know and how they think. The most obvious way to test their intelligence is to watch what they do. Experimenters often coax them to act, but if the babies do not do what an experimenter is looking for, it is hard to know whether they are unable or uninterested.

It is no wonder, then, that infants' test scores are so unreliable: that is, for a normal child there is almost no correlation between intelligence scores in infancy and in childhood. In fact, we would be better able to predict Jason's future IQ from his parents' IQ scores or educational level than from his own test score. Not until after Jason's second birthday would his own score add anything to such a prediction (Kopp & McCall, 1982). Only as he gets closer to his fifth birthday will the relationship between his present score and his future scores become stronger (Bornstein & Sigman, 1986).

One reason for this lack of reliability in early intelligence tests is that tests for children in different age groups are quite different. Older children typically take IQ tests that contain more verbal items; tests for infants and toddlers typically measure primarily motor ability. Thus, tests for infants and children measure different, and largely unrelated, kinds of intelligence (Bornstein & Sigman, 1986). Even if we considered only motor ability, the tests for different age groups measure different kinds of motor skills. For example, a child may be good at large-muscle activities at an early age and at 1 year may score high on a task that consists of building a tower with large blocks. At the age of 7, however, the same child may not do so well when asked to use his or her manipulative skills to copy a design made from small colored blocks.

It is somewhat easier to predict the future IQ of handicapped infants, or of infants thought to be at risk of developing a handicap as a result of prematurity or some other cause. But even for these infants, correlations between scores in infancy and later childhood tend to be low, partly because a supportive environment can make a fundamental difference in overcoming initial difficulties.

Standardized intelligence measures are particularly inappropriate for young children with motor disabilities, because the tests focus on motor development.

Later in this chapter, in the discussion of information processing, we will talk about new tests of infants' attention, which are different from traditional intelligence tests, and which hold promise in predicting childhood IQ for both normal and handicapped children.

Is Intelligence Fixed?   Intelligence tests are often thought to measure aptitude—that is, native intelligence, a quality that people are born with and retain virtually unchanged through life. But nothing could be farther from the truth. First, intelligence tests invariably measure achievement—what children have learned at home or in the community and how well they can demonstrate what they have learned. Furthermore, an increase in IQ scores often occurs (Kopp & McCall, 1982), and because of infants' special capacity for adaptive change, this is not surprising. In one longitudinal study, 1 in 7 children changed by 40 or more IQ points from age 2½ to age 17, and the average child showed a change during these years of 28½ points (R.B. McCall, Appelbaum, & Hogarty, 1973). Most often the change was an increase, but in some cases IQ scores were lower at later testing. It is important to remember that a child's intellectual fate is by no means settled in the early years. Binet himself did not regard intelligence as fixed, and he urged that students who did poorly on his test be given special training to increase their intelligence (Kamin, 1981).

A supportive environment can help a child with problems learn special ways to cope. Human beings seem to have what some observers have called a "strong self-righting tendency" (Kopp & McCall, 1982). Given a favorable environment, infants will generally develop normally, as long as they have not suffered severe damage. Sometime between 18 and 24 months this self-righting tendency seems to diminish, as children begin to acquire skills in which there will eventually be great variation in proficiency. Children will vary greatly, for example, in their ability to read and write, and the differences will tend to persist over time. It is a challenge to society to find ways to diminish the gap between children in such skills and to ensure that as many children as possible will get the benefit of a favorable environment that now gives many youngsters a head start in life.

Developmental Tests

What Are Developmental Tests?   Julia's next-door neighbor, Jan, has a son, Johnny, who is Jason's age, but Johnny does everything later than Jason. Worried that Johnny may not be developing normally, Jan takes him to the pediatrician, who recommends testing Johnny on a development scale. It is for situations like this, as well as for research purposes, that developmental scales for infants have been created. Jan will either be reassured that Johnny's progress is within normal limits, or be advised that he needs some kind of special help.

To design developmental tests, researchers observe a large number of babies. They see what most infants can do at particular ages and then develop a standardized scale, assigning a developmental age for each specific activity. The DQ (development quotient) is computed in much the same way as the IQ, by deriving the score from a test in which tasks are set up in order of increasing difficulty. Each task is given a numerical value, and the final score is the child's mental age. One widely used test is the Bayley Scales of Infant Development.

(Bancroft Library, University of California, Berkeley)

Nancy Bayley of the University of California at Berkeley developed a test to assess the developmental status of babies from 2 months to 2½ years.

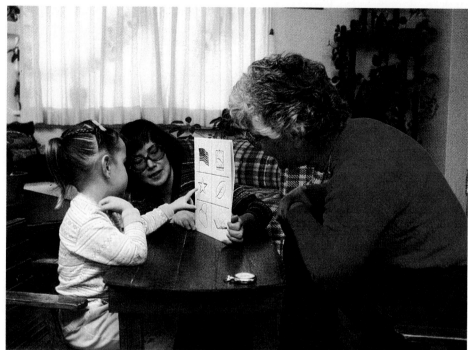

By assessing this toddler on the Bayley Scales, testers can detect sensory and neurological problems, emotional disturbances, or environmental problems.

Bayley Scales
Standardized test of infants' intelligence.

Bayley Scales   The *Bayley Scales* (Bayley, 1933; revised 1969) are used to assess the developmental status of babies from 2 months to 2½ years. This test has three parts:

1 *Mental scale* measures such abilities as perception, memory, learning, and verbal communication. Test items include turning the head to follow an object, imitating simple actions, and repeating words.
2 *Motor scale* measures such gross motor skills as standing and walking, and such fine motor skills as grasping a piece of paper and drinking from a cup.
3 *"Infant behavior record"* is a history of what the baby has done, and when.

The Bayley Scales are particularly useful for assessing a baby's current abilities, rather than predicting intelligence later in childhood. They can help to detect sensory and neurological problems, emotional disturbances, and problems in a child's environment (Anastasi, 1976).

PIAGETIAN APPROACH

Piaget's Theory

Jean Piaget (1896–1980), the Swiss theoretician we introduced in Chapter 1, took a totally different approach from the psychometricians to the issue of children's intelligence. He was concerned with *cognitive development,* the growth in children's thought processes that lets them acquire knowledge about the world.

cognitive development
Changes in mental powers and qualities that permit understanding.

Piaget's approach began as a deliberate rebellion against the concept of measurement itself. He had worked in France to help standardize the early IQ tests, and he concluded that such tests miss much that is unique and interesting in children's thought processes. Instead, he chose to describe these processes.

(It is ironic that today Piaget's own work is the basis for several standardized measures of development.)

Rather than use psychological experiments as the foundation for his work, Piaget based his theory on careful observation of his own three children; he then applied his findings to the development of children in general. He did not judge the children's behavior, but instead tried to understand exactly what he saw. Eventually he constructed a coherent model to account for the way children think and act, and in the process he explains many behaviors that had seemed random or incomprehensible.

Fundamental to Piaget's theory is the idea that children develop through stages and that their experience and interpretation of the world will depend on the stage they are in. Let us see what happens in Piaget's first stage, the sensorimotor stage of infancy.

Piaget's Sensorimotor Stage (Birth to about 2 Years)

For the first 2 years after birth, according to Piaget, infants experience the world almost solely through their senses and motor activity. Thus, this span of time constitutes the *sensorimotor stage,* a period when babies change from creatures who respond primarily through reflexes and random behaviors to goal-directed beings who organize their activities in relation to the people and things around them, generalize behavior to a variety of situations, and coordinate old and new behaviors.

sensorimotor stage In Piaget's theory, the first stage in human cognitive development (birth to about age 2), during which infants acquire knowledge through sensory experience and motor activity.

We see how this happens with sucking. Even before birth, Vicky's sucking reflex could be activated by whatever came close to her mouth. Then, at a very early age, she would deliberately bring her thumb or fingers to her mouth to suck on them. By 6 months of age, she could see an object, decide that she would like to suck on it, close her fingers around it, and bring it to her mouth. This sequence of development requires coordination of several previously reflexive behaviors: looking, reaching, grasping, bringing to the mouth, and sucking (Siegler & Richards, 1982).

Cognitive Concepts of the Sensorimotor Stage During the sensorimotor stage, infants lay the groundwork for several concepts that will be invaluable throughout life for functioning in the world—and also for forming bonds with other people.

Object permanence One day just before her first birthday, Charles watched Vicky move her head sideways, to and fro, like a Balinese dancer. He eventually realized that she was changing her angle of view so that a little clown doll popped in and out of sight. When she moved her head to the left, the corner of a living-room chair hid the doll from view. When she pulled her head back to the right, she saw the clown again. Vicky was playing with—testing the truth of— object permanence.

Object permanence is the concept that even when objects or other people can no longer be seen, they still exist. Without an awareness of object permanence, children would be more anxious about change. For example, if Jason thinks that his mother may have disappeared forever when she leaves the room, he is likely to be distressed. But when he knows that Julia still exists even if she is out of his sight, he can endure her absence more calmly. Object permanence also enables children to realize that objects and other people are separate from

object permanence In Piaget's theory, awareness that a person or thing continues to exist when out of sight.

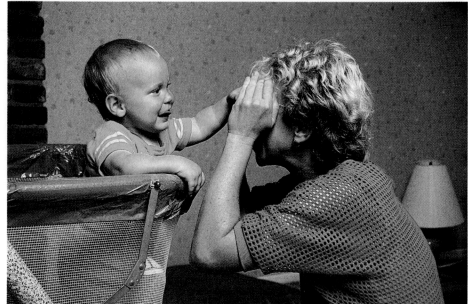

A baby's delight in playing peekaboo is based on object permanence—the knowledge that a familiar face is still there even when the baby cannot see it. Object permanence develops gradually over the first 18 months of life.

themselves. It is essential to the understanding of such concepts as time, space, and the multiplicity of objects in the world.

Causality   Another important concept of the sensorimotor stage is *causality*, the recognition that certain events cause other events. At about 10 months of age, Vicky begins to play with switches and buttons, and delights in making lights, the radio, or the television go on and off, again and again. Her favorite toys are those she can do something with—the toys she can whirl around, make noise with, or drop. By her actions she shows that she realizes that she is causing certain events.

In one study, babies saw films of physically impossible events (like a ball moving toward a second ball, which then moves before the first ball touches it). Babies under 10 months of age were not surprised, but older babies were, showing that they realized that the cause was missing (Michotte, cited in Siegler & Richards, 1982).

Representational abilities   Although infants are beginning to develop object permanence and a sense of causality, they cannot fully grasp these concepts, because they have limited **representational ability,** or capacity to represent objects and actions in memory, largely through the use of symbols like words, numbers, and mental pictures. The ability to act out and imagine things and events appears as children are about to enter the next cognitive stage, the preoperational stage, which occurs in early childhood and is discussed in Chapter 9.

We now look at the six substages of the sensorimotor stage and see the immense cognitive growth babies achieve even before they can talk.

representational ability *Capacity to represent objects and actions in memory, largely through the use of symbols.*

scheme *Organized pattern of behavior.*

Substages of the Sensorimotor Stage   The six substages of the sensorimotor stage (see Table 6-1) flow easily from one to another as a baby's **schemes** (organized patterns of behavior, described in Chapter 1) become more sophisticated. From the few reflexes that Jason is born with, he progresses to various random behaviors—kicking, moving, blowing bubbles, gurgling, and so forth. When these behaviors are pleasurable, he repeats them, creating a cycle Piaget calls a ***circular reaction,*** in which repetition feeds on itself, so that it is hard to tell the cause of the activity from its effect. (See Figure 6-2, which accompanies the discussion of substage 2, below.) As a result of his continuous development through the six stages, Jason will experience many things as a toddler that are beyond the scope of a neonate.

circular reaction *In Piaget's theory, a simple behavior that is repeated often.*

As we discuss each substage, we will trace what Piaget considered the single most important achievement of the sensorimotor stage—object permanence.

Substage 1: Use of reflexes (birth to 1 month) Babies come into the world with an array of *reflexes*, automatic responses to external stimulation. During the first month of life they exercise these reflexes, practice them, and gain some control over them. Then they start to show them even when the stimulus that ordinarily elicits the reflex is not present. For example, Vicky as a newborn sucks reflexively when her lips are touched. During the first month, she begins to suck even when she is not touched, and she sucks at times when she is not hungry. This shows that she has become an energetic initiator of activity, not just a passive

TABLE 6-1

SIX SUBSTAGES OF PIAGET'S SENSORIMOTOR STAGE OF COGNITIVE DEVELOPMENT	
SUBSTAGE	DESCRIPTION
Substage 1 (birth to 1 month): Use of reflexes	Infants exercise their inborn reflexes and gain some control over them. They do not coordinate information from their senses. They do not grasp an object they are looking at. They have not developed object permanence.
Substage 2 (1 to 4 months): Primary circular reactions	Infants repeat pleasurable behaviors that first occur by chance (such as sucking). Activities focus on infant's body rather than the effects of the behavior on the environment. Infants make first acquired adaptations; that is, they suck different objects differently. They begin to coordinate sensory information. They have still not developed object permanence.
Substage 3 (4 to 8 months): Secondary circular reactions	Infants become more interested in the environment and repeat actions that bring interesting results and prolong interesting experiences. Actions are intentional but not initially goal-directed. Infants show partial object permanence. They will search for a partially hidden object.
Substage 4 (8 to 12 months): Coordination of secondary schemes	Behavior is more deliberate and purposeful as infants coordinate previously learned schemes (such as looking at and grasping a rattle) and use previously learned behaviors to attain their goals (such as crawling across the room to get a desired toy). They can anticipate events. Object permanence is developing, although infants will search for an object in its first hiding place, even if they saw it being moved.
Substage 5 (12 to 18 months): Tertiary circular reactions	Infants show curiosity as they purposefully vary their actions to see results. They actively explore their world to determine how an object, event, or situation is novel. They try out new activities and use trial and error in solving problems. Infants will follow a series of object displacements, but since they cannot imagine movement they do not see, they will not search for an object where they have not observed it being hidden.
Substage 6 (18 to 24 months): Mental combinations	Since toddlers have developed a primitive symbol system (such as language) to represent events, they are no longer confined to trial and error to solve problems. Their symbol system allows toddlers to begin to think about events and anticipate their consequences without always resorting to action. Toddlers begin to demonstrate insight. Object permanence is fully developed.

Note: Infants show enormous cognitive growth during Piaget's sensorimotor stage, as they learn about the world through their senses and their motor activities. Note their progress in problem solving, object permanence, and the coordination of sensory information.

responder to stimulation. With experience, her inborn schemes (for sucking and other behaviors) are modified and expanded.

Object permanence is completely lacking in the newborn. The presence or absence of any object appears random and unpredictable.

Substage 2: Primary circular reactions—The first acquired adaptations (1 to 4 months)   Jason's sucking his thumb as he lies in the crib exemplifies a *primary circular reaction:* a simple repetitive act, *centered on the baby's own body,* to reproduce a pleasant sensation first achieved by chance. (See Figure 6-2). One day, Jason puts his thumb into his mouth, exercises his inborn sucking reflex, and likes the feeling. This happens several times. After a while he makes deliberate efforts to put his thumb into his mouth, keep it there, and keep sucking. During this substage, Jason makes his first *acquired adaptations:* changes in behaviors to accommodate new situations. Thus Jason sucks his thumb differently from the bottle nipple or from Julia's breast. He now has a reorganized scheme for sucking.

Jason is now starting to coordinate different kinds of sensory information, like vision and hearing. He looks at, listens to, and touches his mother. When he hears her voice, he turns toward the sound and eventually discovers that it comes from Julia's mouth. His world begins to make sense.

Object permanence is still absent. Jason can follow a moving object with his eyes, but he does not look for objects—or people—when they disappear. However, a hint that he will soon achieve object permanence can be seen in the fact that, after an object disappears, he continues to stare briefly at the spot where he last saw it.

Substage 3: Secondary circular reactions (4 to 8 months)   The third substage, *secondary circular reactions,* is the beginning of intentional action. It coincides with a new interest in reaching out to manipulate objects in the environment. In substage 2, Vicky repeated primary circular reactions for their own sake; now she performs them to see results *beyond her own body.* She enjoys shaking a rattle to hear the noise it makes, and she babbles—not just for fun but to get a response. She discovers tricks to prolong interesting experiences; for example, she finds that making a soft sound when a friendly face appears can make the face stay longer. Her behavior is not fully goal-directed; before she can pursue a goal, she has to come upon it accidentally. (Refer again to Figure 6-2.)

Object permanence is just beginning. Vicky looks for (or cries for) an object if she can see any part of it; if it is completely hidden, she acts as if it no longer existed.

Substage 4: Coordination of secondary schemes and their application to new situations (8 to 12 months)   Behavior now becomes more purposeful. After months of interesting and varied experiences, Jason has adapted and elaborated on the schemes he was born with. He solves new problems by generalizing from past experience and calling upon responses he has previously mastered. He makes up his mind what he wants and goes after it, figuring out ways to overcome obstacles (as we saw Vicky do with the Cheerios). Now that he can crawl around on his own, he can more easily go after things he wants—and he may cry with frustration if he cannot reach them or if they are taken away from him.

Object permanence develops further. At 9 to 10 months, Jason looks for an object behind a screen if he has seen it being hidden there. But even if he sees it

primary circular reaction *Simple repetitive act, centered on the baby's own body, to reproduce a pleasant sensation first achieved by chance.*

acquired adaptation *Change in behavior to accommodate a new situation.*

secondary circular reaction *Repetition of an action to see results outside the body.*

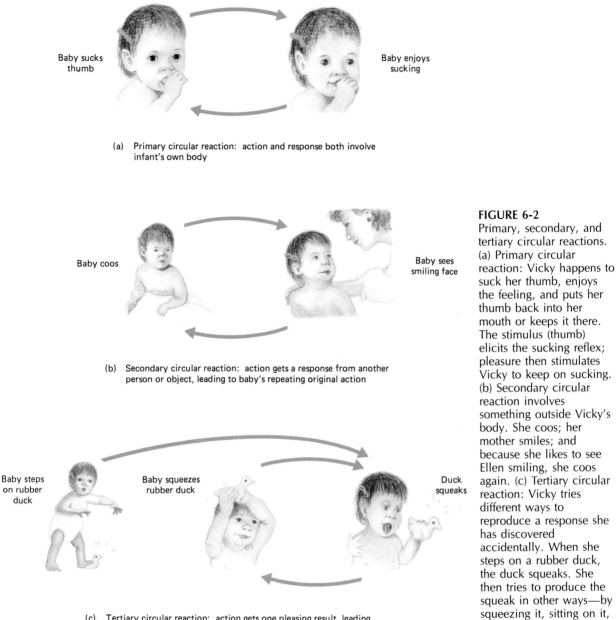

(a) Primary circular reaction: action and response both involve infant's own body

(b) Secondary circular reaction: action gets a response from another person or object, leading to baby's repeating original action

(c) Tertiary circular reaction: action gets one pleasing result, leading baby to perform similar actions to get similar results

Baby sucks thumb

Baby enjoys sucking

Baby coos

Baby sees smiling face

Baby steps on rubber duck

Baby squeezes rubber duck

Duck squeaks

FIGURE 6-2
Primary, secondary, and tertiary circular reactions. (a) Primary circular reaction: Vicky happens to suck her thumb, enjoys the feeling, and puts her thumb back into her mouth or keeps it there. The stimulus (thumb) elicits the sucking reflex; pleasure then stimulates Vicky to keep on sucking. (b) Secondary circular reaction involves something outside Vicky's body. She coos; her mother smiles; and because she likes to see Ellen smiling, she coos again. (c) Tertiary circular reaction: Vicky tries different ways to reproduce a response she has discovered accidentally. When she steps on a rubber duck, the duck squeaks. She then tries to produce the squeak in other ways—by squeezing it, sitting on it, etc.

being moved from one hiding place to another, he looks for it in the first hiding place.

Substage 5: Tertiary circular reactions (12 to 18 months)   Substage 5 is the last cognitive substage that does not include mental representations of external events, or what we mean by the word *thought*. It is the first stage that includes actively trying out new activities rather than repeating the old ones. Through **tertiary circular reactions,** babies deliberately vary their actions to see what will happen. Since they like novelty, they experiment to find out what is new about an object, event, or situation. For example, Vicky steps on her rubber duck and

tertiary circular reaction
Deliberate varying of actions to see what will happen.

This baby girl seems to be using the steering wheel more for support than anything else, but in a few months she will probably be twirling it around, pretending to drive. At that point she will be showing a major cognitive achievement, deferred imitation.

deferred imitation
Ability to observe an action and repeat it after a passage of time.

hears it squeak. Then she tries pressing it, and after that works, she sits on it. (Refer back to Figure 6-2.)

For the first time, Vicky shows originality, by finding new solutions to problems; and she shows curiosity by conceptualizing new problems. She tries out new behavior patterns to reach some goal, and she learns by trial and error. By varying her actions, she looks for the most effective way of attaining a goal. When Vicky, for example, wanted to take the Cheerios from her father's hand, she tried prying his fingers open with one hand, then using both hands, and then using her chin as an additional tool. As she varied her actions and caused new results, she performed completely new acts arising out of her intelligence.

In substage 5, object permanence continues to develop. Babies look in the last place they saw something being hidden rather than the first, as in substage 4. In other words, Vicky can now watch Charles first hide an object behind a screen and then move it under a pillow. She will now search for it under the pillow, the last place she saw it being hidden. Still, she cannot imagine movement that she has not seen. If Charles were to put a toy in his hand, put his hand behind a pillow, leave the toy there, and bring out his closed hand, Vicky would look for the toy in his hand. It would not occur to her that the toy might be behind the pillow, because she did not see him put it there. This achievement will not occur until substage 6.

Substage 6: Beginning of thought—Mental combinations (18 to 24 months) By the age of 18 months, the toddler begins to become capable of thinking before doing. Jason has a representational system that lets him think about his actions before he takes them—at least to a limited extent. He now has some understanding of cause and effect, as well as other relationships between objects and events. He can picture events in his mind and follow them through to some degree. This stage represents a breakthrough, since he no longer has to go through the laborious process of trial and error to solve new problems. He can now try out solutions in his mind and discard the ones that he is sure will not work. He can also imitate actions, even after whatever or whomever he is copying is no longer in front of him. This ability, known as *deferred imitation,* also lets him pretend—to "shave" like his father or "drive" like his mother.

Object permanence is fully developed. Jason can see an object being moved from one place to another, look for it in the last hiding place, and even search for objects that he has not witnessed being hidden.

Research Based on the Sensorimotor Stage Since Piaget first proposed his theories of cognitive development in the 1920s and 1930s, they have moved in and out of favor in the educational, psychological, and scientific communities. While Piaget's theories are highly regarded as a basically sound way to chart children's intellectual growth, researchers testing them have questioned some of his claims. So far, the sequences he outlined have held up fairly well, but follow-up studies have raised questions about the timing of various concepts. Also, abilities that appear, disappear, and then reappear sometime later are a phenomenon not addressed by Piaget.

Some researchers observing infants from 4 weeks to about 2 years of age have confirmed Piaget's unvarying order for the progression of sensorimotor stages (Uzgiris, 1972). Other investigators gave tasks in object permanence to children aged 5 to 32 months (like finding partially and completely hidden objects, finding objects that had been moved and hidden several times, and finding objects hidden under three layers of cloth). These babies proceeded through the steps leading to the concept of object permanence in the order outlined by Piaget (Kramer, Hill, & Cohen, 1975).

Researchers have developed tests based on Piaget's theories in order to measure intellectual development in children who have not begun to speak. Standardized tests of sensorimotor development, like the Infant Psychological Development Scales (IPDS) created by Uzgiris and Hunt (1975), combine the psychometric and Piagetian approaches. In one study, 23 babies were tested on the IPDS every 3 months between 1 and 2 years of age, and at 31 months they were given the Stanford-Binet Intelligence Scale. A positive relationship showed up between scores on the Stanford-Binet and scores on each of the eight sub-scales of the IPDS. The age of attaining object permanence was the strongest predictor of later scores on intelligence tests (Wachs, 1975). This seems to be a useful way to predict childhood intelligence from infants' abilities, a goal, as we have seen, that has been hard to achieve.

Piaget's thesis that children are active participants in their own learning, and that much of what they know comes about as the result of their own activity, has been supported in new research examining the impact of children's ability to get around on their own (discussed in Box 5-2 in Chapter 5). In one study, twenty-six 10-month-olds crawled around a box in which a toy had been hidden and at other times were carried around the box by their parents (Benson & Uzgiris, 1985). The babies were more successful in finding the toy after they had crawled around the hiding area on their own than when they were carried.

Piaget's Timing:
When Do Children Actually Attain Various Abilities?

A number of researchers studying cognitive concepts first described by Piaget have found them in children at earlier ages than he proposed. It seems likely that Piaget underestimated children's abilities because of the way he tested them; revelation of the earlier flowering of many abilities is probably the result of many innovative testing techniques used in recent years. We will briefly describe some of the newer findings.

Achievement of Object Permanence   Piaget maintained that babies do not look for an object that they cannot see any part of—even if it was hidden right in front of their eyes—until they are about 9 months old; before that, if it is completely hidden, they act as if it does not exist. But new studies using different methods suggest that Piaget may have underestimated infants' grasp of object permanence because of the way he tested them (Baillargeon, 1987).

The new research underscores the point that the way an experiment is conducted can affect the results. Young infants may fail to *search* for hidden objects because they are not yet able to perform sequences of actions—like moving a cushion to look for something hidden behind it. This does not necessarily mean they do not know that the objects are there. The phenomenon may be like toddlers' ability to understand speech before they are able to form words themselves.

Invisible Imitation   Piaget said that *invisible imitation*—imitation using parts of the body that babies cannot see for themselves, like the mouth—begins at about 9 months. It follows a period of *visible imitation*—imitation using the hands and feet, for example, which babies *can* see.

invisible imitation
Imitation of an action with a part of the body that cannot be seen by oneself, such as imitation of facial expressions.

visible imitation
Imitation of an action with a part of the body, such as the hands or feet, that can be seen by oneself.

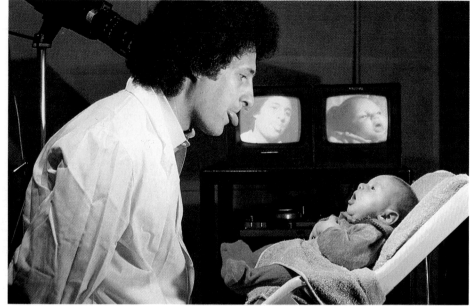

Is this baby expressing contempt for the researcher? No; infants as young as 2 weeks old will stick out their tongues after adults do. Some researchers maintain that this is invisible imitation; but others, who found that only the youngest babies did this, suggest that the tongue movement may be a primitive reflex.

In newer studies, 2- to 3-week-old babies imitated adults by sticking the tongue out, opening the mouth, and making the lips protrude—all actions, of course, that they could not see (Meltzoff & Moore, 1977). Even younger infants—newborns less than 72 hours old (including one who had been born only 42 minutes earlier!)—imitated an adult's opening the mouth and sticking out the tongue (Meltzoff & Moore, 1983). Another group of newborns, whose average age was 36 hours, imitated three different expressions—a smile, a pout, and the wide-open mouth and eyes that usually denote surprise (T. M. Field, Woodson, Greenberg, & Cohen, 1982). The researchers who conducted these studies have concluded that the capacity to imitate is present at birth and does not need to be learned, and that newborn infants can, at some level, understand that body changes they can see in other people are the same kinds of changes they can produce themselves.

Other researchers, however, have studied infants aged 2 to 21 weeks and failed to find invisible imitation (Abravanel & Sigafoos, 1984; Hayes & Watson, 1981). Only the youngest infants stuck out the tongue, and not completely. It is possible, then, that sticking the tongue out is a reflexive action that disappears in older infants or that the previous presence of a pacifier in a baby's mouth may cause mouth movements that seem like imitation. Meltzoff and Moore (1983) suggest that procedures used by other researchers may have masked the imitative capacities of infants. More research seems to be called for to resolve this controversy and firmly establish the age when such imitation first occurs.

Deferred Imitation Piaget said that *deferred imitation*—the ability to imitate an action that has been seen some time before—does not begin until the age of at least 18 months. This ability shows that a baby has a long-term memory for an event, and thus that the baby has a mental representation for it, a "picture" in the mind.

Newer research has found deferred imitation in infants aged 14 months (Meltzoff, 1985) and even 9 months (Meltzoff, 1988). In separate studies involving infants of the two ages, adults performed specific actions (such as pulling apart a two-piece wooden toy or shaking a plastic rattle) in front of the babies; the babies then went home, and they returned to the lab 24 hours later. Upon seeing the same toys, a greater proportion among babies who had seen the adults' actions repeated them than among a control group of babies who had been in the lab the day before and had merely seen the toys. (The researchers took precautions to ensure that the actions could not occur accidentally.)

The actions the babies imitated were simple, and the research samples were small, but these studies still show that at least some babies as young as 9 months old can remember several kinds of actions over a 24-hour period well enough to copy them. Older babies were more likely to reproduce the actions, perhaps showing a superior ability to receive and encode information in memory. Future research may establish how far deferred imitation extends in early infancy—whether it extends to more complex behaviors.

Understanding of Number Concepts   According to Piaget, children do not begin to understand the concept of counting until the preoperational stage, which begins at about age 2, when they begin to use symbols such as words and numbers. But newer research suggests that an understanding of number begins earlier. In one study, 7-month-old babies heard two or three drumbeats while at the same time they saw slides of either two or three common household objects (like a key, a pillow, or a water glass). Most of the infants looked longer at the displays that matched the number of beats they heard (that is, a photo of two objects accompanied by two drumbeats rather than three drumbeats), suggesting that these babies had at least a primitive sense of number (Starkey, Spelke, & Gelman, 1983).

Achievement of Conservation   One of the first to question Piaget's timetables, T. G. R. Bower (1976), suggested that certain abilities show up earlier than Piaget proposed and then disappear, to be relearned later. Piaget said, for example, that children under 9 years old do not understand the principle of *weight conservation*—that an object weighs the same if nothing is added to it or taken away from it, even though its appearance may change. Bower, however, found that 18-month-old babies who picked up a piece of clay that was molded first into one shape, and then into a different shape, moved their arms in a way that showed that they knew the weight remained the same—though 2 years later, the same children no longer acted as if they understood the principle. Children seem to reacquire this concept at the age of 7 or 8, lose it again, and not have a stable grasp of it until they are 9 or 10 (T. G. R. Bower, 1976).

weight conservation
Understanding that an object weighs the same if nothing is added to it or taken away from it, even though its appearance may change.

Even as Piaget's theories are modified in response to the work of other psychologists, his far-reaching contributions to developmental psychology will continue to hold a prominent place in the history of science. He was a pioneer in taking children seriously. And if it had not been for his creative, prolific work, the experiments that questioned his hypotheses might not have been conceived, let alone carried out.

INFORMATION-PROCESSING APPROACH

At 2 months, Jason begins to make sucking motions and wave his arms excitedly as Julia comes near him. Anyone can see that he recognizes her and that the sight and sound of her fill him with a joy he is bursting to express. But just how does recognition take place? What is going on in Jason's head? Neither Piaget nor the psychometric school has a good answer.

For explanations of how intelligence works, we turn to the relatively new and increasingly important information-processing approach. This approach does not make assumptions from analyzing test performance (as psychometricians do) or from observing behavior (as Piagetians do). Instead, the information-processing approach focuses on direct study of the mental capacities and processes that support thought—what actually happens when people receive information, and how they integrate and use it. In other words, what do people do with information from the time they perceive it until the time they use it? This approach sees people as manipulators of symbols; it looks at the processes by which they use these symbols, focusing on areas like perception, memory, and problem solving.

The information-processing approach is similar to the psychometric approach in its focus on individual differences, but dissimilar in the way it examines these differences. Instead of finding differences from the answers people give to test questions, researchers try to describe the actual processes that people go through in coming up with their answers.

Information Processing in Infancy

Because the scores infants have made on intelligence tests have had so little relationship to their intelligence scores later in life, psychologists long believed that intellectual functioning in infancy is different in kind from that in childhood and adulthood. With the recent explosion of information-processing research, it appears that mental development is continuous from birth into childhood (Bornstein & Sigman, 1986). This conclusion follows revolutionary discoveries which show that even very young babies can process information they receive through the senses (see Chapter 5).

Information Processing as a Predictor of Intelligence   Very young infants demonstrate *visual-recognition memory* (the ability to remember and recognize something they have seen) and *auditory-recognition memory* (the same ability for sounds). During the first week of life, even infants born 5 weeks early can look at pictures or patterns for 5 minutes and then tell the difference between fairly different patterns, like checkerboards that vary in size, hue, brightness, and number of pattern elements (J. S. Werner & Siqueland, 1978). Patterns with more subtle differences are a greater challenge, of course: babies need to be 3, 4, or 5 months old to tell them apart (Fantz et al., 1975). By 5 months of age, babies may remember a pattern for as long as 2 weeks (Fagen, 1973). And as we saw in Chapter 5, three-day-old babies can tell new speech sounds apart from sounds they have heard before (L. R. Brody et al., 1984). If babies can differentiate new sights or sounds from old ones, they must be able to remember the old.

Babies—like adults—apparently acquire such differentiation by forming mental images, or representations, of stimuli. Otherwise, they would not be able to compare one with another. How fast do they form these images and refer to them? By answering this question, researchers determine how efficient babies are at processing information. To measure how well infants can process information, researchers keep track of how long it takes babies to habituate to familiar stimuli and how long it takes experimenters to recover their attention for new

visual-recognition memory Remembrance of a visual stimulus.

auditory-recognition memory Ability to remember and recognize sounds.

ones, and how long babies pay attention to paired stimuli (Bornstein, 1985a; Bornstein & Sigman, 1986).

Some babies process information more efficiently than others, and the differences in efficiency are the very area in which information-processing testing is most promising for its ability to predict variations in intelligence later in childhood. We can predict childhood intelligence better from infants' habituation scores than from traditional tests of infant development (Bornstein & Sigman, 1986).

Such predictive ability may be especially important for preterm infants, who are at risk of developing a number of cognitive problems, which often are not discovered until the children go to school (S. A. Rose & Wallace, 1985). At 6 months of age, preterm babies in one study were tested for *novelty preference*—how long they spent looking at pictures of new faces and patterns, compared with familiar ones. The babies who had spent the most time looking at the new sights were likely to do the best on cognitive tests taken when they were 2 and 6 years old. The babies' preference for new things to look at turned out to be an even better predictor of childhood IQ than parents' educational levels, which have consistently proved superior to any other intelligence tests for infants.

Of course, there is still much that we have to learn. Why, for example, should attention in infancy be a better predictor of vocabulary at ages 4 and 7 than of recognition memory or problem-solving ability (Bornstein, 1985b; Bornstein & Sigman, 1986)? What environmental influences operate to affect variability of intelligence not attributable to early measures of attention and recovery? With the surge of research in this field, more answers should soon be forthcoming.

Influences on Information Processing and Cognitive Development What accounts for early differences in the ability to discriminate and remember stimuli? So far, we have few answers to this question, but researchers are addressing it.

The socioeconomic status of infants' families seems unrelated to individual differences in early information processing. However, both infants' attention and recovery scores and parents' educational levels are related to later intelligence (S. A. Rose & Wallace, 1985).

A study of full-term babies found that certain kinds of interaction with parents seemed to enhance the cognitive development of babies who were already good information processors (Bornstein, 1985b). Fourteen babies from middle- to upper-class families took habituation tests at 4 months of age. Observers visited these babies at home when they were 4 months old and when they were 1 year old, and recorded how much the babies' mothers prompted their attention by handing them toys, pointing something out, or naming objects. The babies who habituated fastest at 4 months *and* whose parents took an active role at the same age had larger vocabularies at 1 year, and at age 4 they scored higher on preschool intelligence tests. However, the mothers' behavior when their babies were 1 year old did not seem to have the same kind of effect on their children's intelligence at age 4.

These findings give rise to a number of conclusions. First, attentiveness is one of many areas in which parents and children seem to influence each other. It is very likely that the most attentive babies stimulate their mothers to encourage their attentiveness, and that mothers' encouragement in turn stimulates the babies to do and learn even more. Second, such teaching may have longer-lasting value early in the first year than later on, helping to explain why babies from

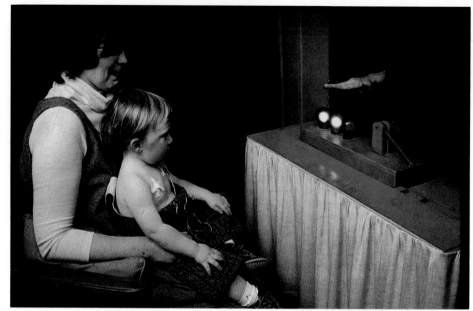

This 2-year-old is taking part in a new kind of intelligence test, especially effective with developmentally disabled babies. Electrodes attached to the child's chest measure changes in heart rate, which speeds up when events violate expectations. Here, light bulbs glow and darken in response to a wand. Testers estimate children's intelligence on the basis of how long it takes them to learn what to expect. This child was thought to be a slow learner, but the test indicated normal intelligence.

disadvantaged homes who are adopted into advantaged homes do better if they are placed before they are 6 months old (Scarr & Weinberg, 1983).

Using Information-Processing Tests to Measure Disabled Children's Intelligence
A major reason why psychometric tests of intelligence in infancy predict later intelligence poorly is their heavy emphasis on motor skills. This emphasis makes them especially prone to underestimate the intelligence of children with motor disabilities. Because of these problems and because they believe that a sensorimotor definition of early intelligence is too restrictive, some psychologists have turned to information processing as the basis for a new kind of intelligence test (Kearsley, 1981; Zelazo, 1981).

In taking one of the new tests, a child—say, a boy, aged 3 months to 3 years—sits on his mother's lap in a room set up like a puppet theater. Through wires attached to his chest (which do not cause any discomfort), the child is hooked up to an instrument that records changes in his heartbeat, while hidden observers watch and record any facial and physical changes. Over a 45-minute period, the child sees or hears five episodes that are designed to set up expectations and then to surprise him by not completing the expected pattern. In one of the dramas, a toy car rolls down a ramp and knocks over a doll. A hand sets the doll back upright and rolls the car back up the ramp. The same action occurs six times. The seventh time, the doll does not fall down when it is hit by the car. This happens twice more, and then the original sequence is presented a few more times.

Children react to these events in a number of ways: they may stare at the stage, point, clap, wave, twist, or turn to their mothers. At two points—the first time the doll does not fall down and the first time it falls down again—the child's heart is likely to speed up; the child may frown the first time the doll does not fall and may smile the next time it does. By reactions like these, children show whether they have learned to expect the doll to fall, how they react when their expectation is not met, and whether they can tell that the action has gone back to the original scenario when the doll falls again. In this way, children show whether they have formed a memory for these events.

While each child's reactions are somewhat different, of course, the researchers have charted the ways children typically react and have developed standards for different age levels, paying special attention to the speed with which a child reacts to the episodes. At 5½ months, infants are likely to make sounds when they recognize the familiar pattern of the doll falling. One-year-olds tend to stare and search. A typical 20-month-old smiles, vocalizes, and points. Not until about 30 months of age do most children respond to the change when the doll does not fall, whereas 3-year-olds react almost immediately to both situations. Zelazo (1981) concludes that the test measures the child's "increasing speed of information processing over the first three years of life" (p. 244). Thus, it provides a way to assess intellectual development quite apart from motor development.

One advantage of this test—for normal children as well as disabled children—is that it eliminates the worry about whether a child understands, likes, or is willing to cooperate with the examiner. The test is so interesting that the child pays close attention.

The information-processing approach itself is still quite new. With further research, we may learn more about the precise mechanisms that enable very young children to move from one developmental stage to the next and to show an increasing ability to use their intelligence.

Play as a Measure of Intelligence

At 10 months, Vicky "dances" (bounces up and down on her feet while holding on to anything handy) when she hears music—or even when Ellen lifts the cover on the stereo. At 1 year, Vicky gets a treat—the opportunity to open the bottom drawer of the kitchen cabinet. For 45 minutes, she quietly takes out measuring cups, a potato masher, cake decorators, and other utensils, examining each item, putting some back, and then taking them out again. At 14 months, she lets Charles know when she wants to "sing" and play the finger-play song "Itsy Bitsy Spider" by putting her right index finger on her left thumb and making the gestures that go with the words.

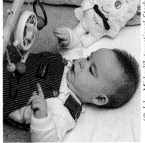

(© John Michael/International Stock)

Children's play is a prime example of the interrelationship of physical, intellectual, and emotional development. The kind of play that Vicky engages in is determined by what her body can do, by what her mind can grasp, and by the way she feels. By looking at the way she is playing, we can learn a great deal about her level of development and her processing of information.

Zelazo and Kearsley (1980) suggest that an important cognitive change begins at about 11½ months, when babies show that they can generate ideas. This change shows up in the way they play. These researchers analyzed the play of 64 babies between 9½ and 15½ months of age in 15-minute free-play situations on the floor of a playroom within reach of such toys as a telephone, dolls, blocks, a truck and garage, a tea set, and a baseball set.

The babies played differently at each age. The youngest fingered and banged the toys and put them in their mouths. Babies aged 13½ months used two or more toys together, though in ways that may not have made sense in

The serious expression on Megan's face shows that her exploration of what she can do with this crib toy is more than a way of passing time. Play is babies' work—and it is a useful way for observers to judge a baby's level of cognitive and physical development.

terms of the toys' design (like banging a teapot lid on a saucer). The oldest babies used the toys in a more adult way, babbling into a telephone and putting a doll into a chair or a truck into a garage.

Motor development probably does not account for these differences, since it is no harder to put a telephone receiver to the ear than in the mouth. The oldest babies' way of playing was probably due to their ability to put into action a growing knowledge of the world.

Looking at children's play may be a useful additional way to assess their cognitive development, especially when children have behavior problems and refuse to cooperate with ordinary testing procedures. Most early play, however, is highly physical, and so it should not be the only measure of a child's intellectual level. This (as we have seen) is especially true of children with motor handicaps.

Language

HOW CHILDREN ACQUIRE LANGUAGE

At 4½ months Jason chuckles out loud. He also says "ngoo-ooo" and "ngaah." At 7 months he makes more sounds, most sounding like "da" or "ga." At 9 months he looks up at his neighbor Jan and says, "Hi." At 14 months he points to everything, asking, "Whatzis?" or saying "da" for "I want that." At 17 months he points to the right places when asked, "Where is your nose? Where is your tongue? Where is your belly button?" By 21 months he says, or tries to say, at least 50 words, and understands many more. He can now tell you, more or less, what he does or does not want, in his own language. His first two-word sentence is "Bye-bye, Daddy," and his first three-word sentence is "Choo-choo bye-bye dada" ("The train went away and now it's all gone").

language Communication system that uses words and grammar.

Aside from being a source of amusement, delight, and pride to his parents, Jason's *language* development is a crucial element in his cognitive growth. Once he knows the words for things, he can use them as symbols for objects, and he can communicate his needs, feelings, and opinions to exert a growing amount of control over his life. Despite all the complexities involved in understanding and speaking a language, children become proficient at it quite early in life. (See Table 6-2 for a list of language milestones.)

Psychologists devote a great deal of effort today to studying the way early language develops, constantly coming up with new findings—some expected, some surprising—about this universal human phenomenon. While the essential process remains a mystery, we do know some facts about it. For example, children's level of maturation and their living environment are both important in learning language. And as we shall see, human beings seem to be born with a predisposition for learning language.

Findings like these have come about through a variety of methods for studying language development in infancy. Studies of habituation, based on heart rate or sucking behavior, tell us when babies can distinguish one sound from another. A procedure in which electrodes fastened to a baby's scalp measure the brain responses elicited by sounds, and any differences in these responses, also measures a baby's ability to differentiate between sounds. Researchers also tape and videotape children, and they rely on records kept by trained observers during set intervals. Thus we have been able to learn a great

TABLE 6-2

LANGUAGE MILESTONES IN INFANCY AND TODDLERHOOD

AGE IN MONTHS	LANGUAGE DEVELOPMENT
0.25	Makes some response to sound
1.25	Smiles in response to stimulation
1.6	Coos; makes long vowel sounds
4	Turns toward speaker; says "ah-goo"; makes razzing sound
6	Cooing changes to babbling, with introduction of consonants
8	Says "dada" and "mama" but does not use them as names
9	Plays gesture games like peekaboo; understands word *no*
11	Uses *dada* and *mama* as names; responds to one-step command and gesture indicating activity
12	Says gibberish "sentences" without real words; says first word; imitates sounds
13	Says third word
14	Responds to one-step command without gesture
15	Says four to six words
17	Says gibberish sentence with some real words; points to body parts; says 7 to 20 words
18	Patterns of sounds sound like speech
19	Says two-word combinations
21	Says two-word "sentences"; has 50-word vocabulary
24	Uses pronouns (*I, me, you*) indiscriminately; two-word phrases are most common; more interested in talking; no more babbling
30	Uses pronouns appropriately; learns new words almost every day; most utterances have three words; excellent comprehension; many mistakes in grammar
36	Vocabulary of 250 to 1000 words (about 80 percent intelligible); uses plurals; uses all pronouns appropriately; grammar close to informal adult speech; fewer mistakes in syntax

Sources: Adapted from Capute, Shapiro, & Palmer, 1987; Lenneberg, 1969.

deal about babies' ability to communicate even before they can say a single word.

Prelinguistic Speech

Before Jason looked up at Jan and said "Hi"—his first recognizable word (which typically occurs between 9 and 17 months)—his vocal development went through an established pattern called *prelinguistic speech.* His first sound, of course, was crying, which became a means of communication as different patterns, intensities, and pitches signaled hunger, sleepiness, anger, or pain. At about 6 weeks of age, babies *coo* when they are happy (making squeals, gurgles, and vowel sounds like "ahhh"). Beginning at about 4 to 6 months, babies *babble*, repeating a number of simple sounds (usually combinations of consonants and vowels like "ma-ma-ma-me-mo").

During their second 6 months, babies *accidentally imitate* sounds heard, and then imitate themselves making these sounds. At about 9 or 10 months they *deliberately* imitate sounds, even when they do not understand them.

Once babies have a basic repertoire of sounds, they string them together in ways that sound like language but do not seem to have any meaning (Eisenson, Auer, & Irwin, 1963; Lenneberg, 1967). Although this prelinguistic speech does not represent specific concepts and therefore does not have any semantic importance, it can be used to express a broad range of emotions. Starting at about 2 months, when they coo to express contentment, babies steadily increase their

prelinguistic speech
Communicative use of sounds by infants without using words or grammar.

BOX 6-2 ■ THE RESEARCH WORLD

SYMBOLIC GESTURING

Charles is puzzled as Vicky stands by the doorway waving her hands up and down with small, quick motions, until he realizes that she is telling him to turn on the light. Outside, on a blustery day, Vicky picks up a piece of paper and waves it sideways to tell Ellen that the wind is blowing. Vicky's use of gestures to represent objects, events, desires, and conditions is known as *symbolic gesturing* and is a common stage of communication that overlaps with the beginning of children's use of words.

Babies—especially firstborn girls—use a wide range of gestures to mean different things (see Table 6-3). Typically, children start to use them at about 14 months to make requests, at about 15 months to describe attributes (like "hot"), and about 2 weeks later to "name" objects. These gestures fulfill children's need to communicate before they know or can say words; they usually appear before children attain a vocabulary of 25 words; they drop out when chil-

dren learn the word for the idea they have been expressing in gestures; and the children who speak the earliest are most likely to use them.

In one study of thirty-eight 17-month-olds, 87 percent of the babies used at least one such gesture, and the average baby used four (Acredolo & Goodwyn, 1988). More than half of the children developed gestures as a result of routines with their parents; several bounced the torso to mean "horse," stemming from bouncing on an adult's knee. While children make up most of these gestures themselves, their parents' role is important. It takes two to communicate, and if parents do not interpret and respond to the gestures, children are likely to drop them and try to get adults' attention in other ways—like grabbing or making sounds.

These gestures are closely related to cognitive development, showing that even before children can talk, they understand that objects and concepts have names and that they can use symbols to refer to the things and happenings in their everyday lives.

---

range of emotional intonation. Long before children can express ideas in words, parents are in touch with their infants' feelings through the sounds the babies make (Tonkova-Yompol'skaya, 1973). Babies also communicate through the use of gestures, as described in Box 6-2 and Table 6-3.

Linguistic Speech

linguistic speech Spoken use of language; besides words and grammar, it relies on pronunciation, intonation, and rhythm to convey meaning.

holophrase Single word that conveys a complete thought; the typical speech form of children aged 12 to 18 months.

The First Word Vicky, an "average" baby, said "dada," her first word, on her first birthday, thus initiating **linguistic speech.** (Since there is no such thing as an average baby, some babies utter the first word 2 or 3 months earlier than 1 year, and some afterward.) When the first word is not *mama* or *dada,* it may be a single syllable that has a variety of meanings, depending on what is going on at the moment. Thus "da" may mean "I want that," "I want to go out," "Where's Daddy?" and so forth. A single word like this, which seems to express a complete thought, is called a **holophrase.**

When K. Nelson (1973, 1981) studied the first 50 words spoken by a group of 1- and 2-year-olds, she found that the most common words were *names* of things, in either the general sense (*oof-oof* for any dog) or the specific (*Bo* for one particular dog). Others were *action* words (*bye-bye*), *modifiers* (*hot*), and words that express *feelings* or *relationships* (the ever-popular *no*), and a few *grammatical* words (*for*). The second year of life is also important for the growth of language comprehension. Children understand more and more of what is said to them, even though they may not use the same words themselves (K. Nelson, 1973, 1981).

Typically, by 15 months of age a child of either sex has spoken 10 different words or names (K. Nelson, 1973), and vocabulary continues to grow through-

TABLE 6-3

SYMBOLIC GESTURES SHOWN BY 17-MONTH-OLDS		
CATEGORY	EXAMPLE	AGE FIRST USED
Naming attribute	"Flower": child sniffs "Dog": child pants "Airplane": child holds out arms	13.47 months
Making request	"Go out": child makes knob-turning gesture without touching doorknob "Nurse": child pats mother's chest "Food": child smacks lips	12.88 months
Naming event	"Hot": child blows or waves hand "Many": child waves hand back and forth "Big": child raises arms	12.40 months
Naming object	"I don't know": child opens palms	14.12 months
Replying	"Baseball game": child claps	13 months

Source: Adapted from Acredolo & Goodwyn, 1988, p. 454.

out the single-word stage (which usually lasts till about 18 months). There is also an increasing reliance on words. More and more occasions inspire the child to speak a word or a name. A flair for the music of language grows as the sounds and rhythms of children's speech become more elaborate. Even if much of the child's speech is still babbling (and many children over the age of 1 year babble steadily), it sounds quite expressive.

During the one-word period, there seems to be a very close relationship between cognitive and linguistic achievements, according to a study by Gopnik and Meltzoff (1986). Within a few weeks of learning complex tasks related to object permanence, babies tend to acquire words connoting disappearance (like *gone*), and after they learn how to solve problems (using a stick to obtain an object or putting a necklace into a bottle), they are likely to use words associated with success or failure (like *there, did it,* and *uh-oh*). The babies in the study learned how to solve the tasks between 15 and 22 months of age, and they used the associated words by 2 years. The cognitive-linguistic link was very specific; solving the object permanence task did not lead to the use of words for success and failure, and vice versa, suggesting that children are motivated to learn words that are important to them at the time (Gopnik & Meltzoff, 1986).

The First Sentence At 18 months, Vicky first spoke two words to express one idea. "Shoe fall," she said, looking up from her stroller at Charles, who was pushing her along. Charles paused, saw Vicky's sandal on the sidewalk, and picked it up. Vicky had spoken her first sentence, using two words to express a single thought, clearly a practical one. The appearance of sentences marks the start of structured speech. Even in their early sentences, toddlers usually put the words in the order adults would.

The age at which children begin combining words varies. Generally, they do this before the second birthday. Although prelinguistic speech is fairly closely tied to chronological age, linguistic speech is not. Roger Brown (1973a, 1973b), of Harvard University, who has done a great deal of work on this phase of language acquisition, maintains that knowing a child's age tells us very little about his or her language development.

(© Erika Stone)

This toddler is clearly communicating something—perhaps saying "spot" while pointing to the horse's white patch. The most common first words are names of things, either general ("horse") or specific (this horse's name).

Stages of Linguistic Speech Jason's language development goes through five stages, says Brown, based on **mean length of utterance (MLU)**. MLU is the average length of utterances in **morphemes**, the smallest units of speech that have meaning. (Thus, *skate* and *s* and *ed* are all single morphemes, while the words *skates* and *skated* each consist of two morphemes.)

Calculating MLU is a useful way to note a child's progress in speaking. According to Brown's scheme, children are in stage 1 when they first begin to combine morphemes and words, making their MLU over 1.0, and they are in stage 2 when it is 2.0. At this time they actually utter as many as seven morphemes, even though the mean, or average, is only 2. With each increase of 0.5 in MLU, children advance to the next stage, up to stage 5. Different children attain different levels of MLU at different ages. Vicky, for example, may have an MLU of 3 at age 2, while Jason does not achieve this until he turns 3.

Stage 1 is primitive speech, in which tense and case endings, articles, and prepositions are missing (as in "No," "More ball," "Hit ball," "Big ball," "Book table," "Go," and "Mommy sock"). When the MLU is 1.5, the child may string two basic relations together ("Adam hit" and "Hit ball") to get a more complicated relation ("Adam hit ball").

In *stage 2,* children acquire functional morphemes, including articles (*a, the*), prepositions (*in, on*), plurals, verb endings, and forms of the verb *to be* (*am, are, is*). Children start to use these forms gradually, sometimes over several years. In his intensive study of three children, Brown (1973a) noted that the variation in rate of development even among such a small sample was great, but that the *order* in which the children acquired the different constructions was almost constant.

As children leave stage 2, their speech becomes longer and more complex. Speech in *stage 3* is called **telegraphic speech.** It omits many parts of speech, but still conveys meaning (as in "Put dolly table"). The next two stages develop later in childhood. Grammar used in *stage 4* is close to that of adults, although children often cannot use the subjunctive ("If I were a bird, I could fly") or ask tag questions ("That's a zebra, isn't it?"). By *stage 5*, which occurs by late childhood, children are fully competent in grammar, although they continue to enlarge their vocabulary and improve their style.

Some Characteristics of Early Speech When Vicky was 14 months old, she jumped in excitement at the sight of a gray-haired man on the television screen and shouted, "Gampa!" At 15 months, Jason saw a cow and squealed, "Oof-oof!" Both were doing something common in early speech—overgeneralizing. Vicky thought that because her grandfather had gray hair, all gray-haired men could be called Grandpa; Jason thought that because a dog has four legs and a tail, any animal with four legs and a tail is a dog.

Children's speech is not just a simplified version of adults' speech. Whether a child is speaking German, Russian, Finnish, Samoan, or English, the speech has a special character common to children's speech around the world (Slobin, 1971). The words children speak come from the language around them, but the sentences of toddlers around the world are structured more like the sentences of other toddlers than like the sentences, even the short sentences, of adults. The speech of small children around the world is filled with phrases that translate exactly into the English phrases *more high, bye-bye dirty,* or *no down.*

Characteristics of early speech include the following:

- Children *simplify,* saying just enough to get their meaning across (as in "No drink," meaning, "I don't want to drink any more milk").
- They *overregularize rules,* applying them rigidly without using exceptions—saying "mouses" and "goed," even though they may have said "mice" and "went" earlier. This apparent regression is really a sign of progress, showing that children are now learning the rules of grammar. They no longer simply imitate what other people say, but they apply rules, like the rule that adding an *s* creates a plural. To Jason, therefore, Mickey and Minnie are "mouses." He will soon learn the exceptions to grammatical rules—and will lose some of that charm of early, creative speech.
- They *understand grammatical relations that they cannot express.* At stage 1, Vicky may understand that a dog is chasing a cat, but she cannot string together enough words to explain the complete action. She says, "Puppy chase," instead of "Puppy chase kitty."

THEORIES OF LANGUAGE ACQUISITION

Both maturation and environment are important in the development of language, but different linguists assign greater importance to one or the other of these factors. *Learning theory* is based on a strong belief in the power of the environment, while *nativism* advocates belief in an inborn capacity for learning language.

learning theory Theory that most behavior is learned from experience.

nativism Theory that behavior is inborn; nativist linguistics holds that speech arises from an inborn capacity.

Learning Theory

Behaviorists maintain that we learn language the same way we learn everything else—through reinforcement. Parents reinforce children for making sounds like adults' speech, and so children make more of these sounds, generalizing and abstracting as they go along.

Supporting this view is the fact that children reared at home, who presumably get more attention and more reinforcement than those who grow up in institutions, do babble more (Brodbeck & Irwin, 1946). Arguing against it is the fact that parents rarely bother to correct the grammar of their young children, realizing that they will outgrow their incorrect usages (R. Brown, Cazden, & Bellugi, 1969).

Social-learning theorists maintain that children learn to speak by hearing their parents, imitating them, and being reinforced for this behavior. This explains why children in English-speaking countries speak English rather than French or Swahili. But it does not explain the novel things that children say—like Vicky's description of walking on her heels as "tip-heeling" or Jason's saying he "goed" to the store.

Nativism

According to *nativism,* the view held by Noam Chomsky (1972) and his followers, human beings have an inborn capacity for acquiring language and learn to talk as naturally as they learn to walk. Several facts support this viewpoint. First, all normal children learn their native language, no matter how complex, mastering the basics in the same age-related sequence. Second, human beings, the only animals to master a spoken language, are the only species whose brain is larger on one side (the left) than the other. It seems that an innate mechanism for language is localized in the left hemisphere of the human brain.

Finally, a large body of research has found that very young babies respond to language in surprisingly sophisticated ways. Newborns move their bodies in the same rhythm as the adult speech they hear (Condon & Sander, 1974) and can tell the mother's voice from a stranger's (DeCasper & Fifer, 1980). Infants less than 5 months old can even lip-read. When babies aged 18 to 20 weeks were shown two filmed speakers, they looked longer at one whose mouth movements matched the sounds being made than at the other, whose mouth mimed a different sound (Kuhl & Meltzoff, 1982). This early ability of babies to relate speech in two ways—what they hear and what they see—may encourage them to pay attention to their caregivers, affecting both emotional and cognitive development. Furthermore, some of these babies imitated the sounds and the patterns of speech they heard, suggesting that listening *and* looking may help babies learn to speak.

Because of findings like these—which show that infants the world over pick up fine distinctions between speech sounds, respond to speech in a social way almost from birth, and show a variety of apparently inborn linguistic skills—it seems that babies are born with perceptual mechanisms tuned to the properties of speech (Eimas, 1985). They are born with the ability to distinguish all speech sounds, but then tailor their perception to the sounds they hear around them. This would explain why 1-year-olds from English-speaking families cannot differentiate speech sounds in Hindi which they were able to tell apart at 8 months of age (Werker & Tees, cited in Eimas, 1985).

Noam Chomsky (1972) proposes that the human brain is specifically constructed to learn language through an inborn ability called the *language acquisition device (LAD).* The LAD lets children analyze the language they hear and extract the rules of grammar that allow them to create brand-new sentences that no one has ever spoken before. The LAD programs the brain to extract these rules; all that is needed is the basic experiences to activate them.

While the evidence for some biologically programmed ability to learn language is persuasive, LAD does not, by itself, explain the development of speech. Some learning has to take place if children are to use English grammar rather than Japanese grammar. Furthermore, individual children differ considerably in their fluency. Finally, the nativists have not addressed issues related to the meaning of the words children use or to the social settings in which they use them.

Again, the answer to linguistic development seems to be a combination of viewpoints—that children do enter the world with an inborn capacity to acquire a language, which is then activated by learning. (For insight into children's creativity with language, see Box 6-3.)

INFLUENCES ON LANGUAGE ACQUISITION

It is obvious to anyone who spends much time around children that they vary greatly in the age at which they begin to speak, and also in their ability both to comprehend what others are saying and to express themselves. The differences seem to be partly hereditary, partly acquired.

language acquisition device (LAD) In nativist linguistics, the inborn ability to learn a language.

BOX 6-3 ■ AROUND THE WORLD

LANGUAGES CREATED BY CHILDREN

What happens to language if children have no access to the culture of their parents? Since Columbus discovered the new world, many children have found themselves in this predicament. Slaves and indentured servants transported to new lands were often put to work among strangers, where they could not preserve their old ways and could not gain access to the reigning culture. Five hundred years later, descendants of these captive people still speak so-called *creole* languages, which arose among the people themselves. These new languages include Creole in Haiti and Gullah, spoken by blacks on the sea islands of Georgia. One of the world's newest languages, Hawaiian English Creole, truly sprang from the mouths of babes (Bickerton, 1981).

Hawaiian Creole is so new that some of its creators are still alive. By interviewing aged immigrants and their children, the English linguist Derek Bickerton reconstructed the language's history. After 1890 and the annexation of the islands by the United States, pidgin English was widely used by traders in Hawaii. During the same period, many indentured servants were brought to Hawaii from China, the Philippines, Japan, Korea, Portugal, and Puerto Rico. At first these newcomers communicated through pidgin English, but in 1905 a common tongue, Hawaiian Creole, began to appear. Many words in the new language seem to come from English, although they are pronounced differ-

ently; but much of the grammar is radically different from English grammar. For instance, the sentence "I come stay for hanahana rice field" has its own verb form (*come stay* for *had come*), uses *for* instead of *to* in the infinitive, and includes a word unknown in English (*hanahana* for *work*).

Where did this language come from? When Bickerton studied the history of Hawaiian Creole, 50 or more years after its appearance, the surviving immigrants from those early years still had not mastered the new language. To that day they still spoke some form of the pidgin English they used at the time of their arrival. It seems that the language was created by the children of the immigrants as they talked among themselves.

The evidence for this conclusion is strong. First, Hawaiian Creole is spoken only by people born in Hawaii, and so it could not have been imported from somewhere else. Second, we can see signs of the language's developmental history in the speech of its creators. Although the language arose quickly, it did not appear instantaneously. People who were born before a feature appeared do not include that feature in their speech even now. Thus, by listening to a Hawaiian's grammar, it is possible to tell what stage of development the language was in when he or she was born. Third, if the parents did not know the language and if the white masters were barely even aware of it, who else could have created it but the children themselves? It seems that children have much greater language gifts than they have been given credit for.

Genetic Influences

A recent study comparing adopted 1-year-olds and a control group being reared by their biological parents suggests that part of the variation in the ability to communicate may originate in the genes (Hardy-Brown & Plomin, 1985). The babies' language skills were assessed on the basis of how often they made speech sounds and what kinds of sounds they were (true words, babbling, and other attempts to communicate that used sounds but not real words), the frequency and levels of gesturing, and other aspects of communication. The parents raising the children took cognitive tests, and researchers noted information about the socioeconomic status and education of adoptive parents, of the biological mothers of adopted children, and of the biological parents in the control group.

Since moderate correlations were found between babies' language use and control biological parents' cognitive scores, but not adoptive parents' scores, there appears to be some genetic influence. However, the researchers also discovered environmental relationships: the mothers (both adoptive and control) of the most advanced babies were most likely to imitate their babies' sounds, perhaps encouraging them to make more sounds. Of course, it is possible that the more advanced babies were motivating the parents to imitate them more by their own precocity in language, but other research has shown that such feedback from parents does encourage language development (C. E. Snow, 1977).

Influence of Adults

While heredity, then, seems to play some role in language capacity, it does not account for all the variations among children. Other research has found that many of the differences in children's speech that show up by age 2 can be traced to differences in the children's homes (K. Nelson, 1981). Most of these differences, of course, relate to the adults in those homes.

The overwhelming impression received from research on children's speech is that small children need to have a communicative adult partner if they are to learn to speak. They need someone who can speak to them, give them a chance to speak, and then respond to what they say. This shows up from a very early age.

Three-month-olds whose mothers talk to them while breastfeeding make more sounds than babies whose mothers are silent (M. K. Rosenthal, 1982). And among 2-year-olds in day care centers in Bermuda, children in centers where caregivers talk to them often (especially to give or ask for information rather than to control their behavior) are more advanced in language development than children who do not have such conversations (McCartney, 1984).

We also see the importance of adult speakers in the retardation of speech in children with normal hearing who grow up in homes with deaf parents who communicate with them through sign language. No matter how fluent the children are in signing (and mastery of sign language does show ability to learn a language) and no matter how much television they watch, they do not become fluent in *spoken* language unless adults actually speak to them. This may not happen until they go to school (Moskowitz, 1978). Simply hearing speech is not enough: young Dutch children who watched German television every day, for example, did not learn German (C. E. Snow et al., 1976). To learn how to speak, then, children need both to speak and to be spoken to.

"Motherese"

motherese Simplified, slow, repetitive, high-pitched speech used by most adults and slightly older children when speaking with an infant.

If you are in the presence of a small child, you're likely to find yourself pitching your voice high, using short words and sentences, speaking slowly, asking questions, and repeating your words. You're speaking *motherese,* also known as *child-directed speech.* You don't have to be a mother to speak motherese: most adults—and even slightly older children—do it intuitively. At one time, most linguists believed that motherese was important in helping children learn to speak. Recently, however, some have questioned its value. Let's look at this debate.

Those who consider motherese important believe that it serves several functions (C. E. Snow, 1972). Emotionally, it helps adults develop a relationship with children. Socially, it teaches children how to carry on a conversation—how to introduce a topic, comment and expand on an idea, and take turns talking. Linguistically, it teaches children how to use new words, structure phrases, and put ideas into language.

In one study, women—both mothers and nonmothers—were found to speak differently to 2-year-olds and 10-year-olds (C. E. Snow, 1972). The children's input was essential, as shown by the fact that when the women were asked to make tapes to unseen children of the same two ages, they did not modify their speech as much. This may explain why adults do not begin using motherese until babies show some understanding of what the adults are saying. To start the flow of motherese, children need to show by their expressions, their actions, and their own speech how closely they are following the conversation. Since motherese is usually confined to simple, down-to-earth topics (C. E. Snow, 1977), children use their own knowledge of familiar things to help them work out the meanings of the words they hear.

The idea that motherese is valuable seems to be supported by a recent study of twins. It has been known for more than 50 years that twins usually speak later than single-born children; research sheds some light on the reasons. After observing 6 pairs of twins and 12 firstborn singleton children at the ages of 15 and 21 months, researchers found substantial differences in mother-child interactions, mostly due to the practical pressures on harried mothers of twin infants (Tomasello, Mannle, & Kruger, 1986).

"Motherese"—a simplified form of language used for speaking to babies and toddlers—seems to come naturally, not only to parents and grandparents, but also to slightly older children.

Mothers of twins speak to and interact with their babies about as much as mothers of singletons, but since they have to divide their attention between two babies, each one often gets less. Compared with mothers of singletons, mothers of twins do not speak to each child as often, pay less attention to each one, and have shorter conversations. When they do speak to their babies, more of what they say involves directing a child to do something rather than chattier comments and questions. They imitate more, and they elaborate less on topics the children bring up. Other research has found that directive speech is not as effective as questioning in encouraging children's fluency (K. Nelson, 1981). Thus, while twins have each other to talk to—and often develop a private language between themselves—their interaction is not as influential as the kind that they would have with an adult.

Another researcher found modest support for the value of motherese in a study of language functioning in 2½-year-olds, but still concluded that "the differences among mothers that predicted rate of language growth in their children were not differences in the use of motherese per se" (Hoff-Ginsberg, 1985, p. 384). What are these differences? One seems to be a mother's goals in talking to a child—whether, for example, she prods her child to speak in ways just beyond the range of the child's current competence, which may motivate the child to move up to the next level of language skill (Hoff-Ginsberg, 1986).

Investigators who question the value of motherese contend that children speak sooner and better if they hear and can respond to more complex speech from adults. The children, then, can select from this speech the parts that they are interested in and are able to deal with. In fact, these researchers say, children discover the rules of language faster when they hear complex sentences that use the rules more often and in more ways (Gleitman, Newport, & Gleitman, 1984).

What are we to conclude about this controversy? It seems that however parents speak, the important element is their interest in and close interaction with their babies. The more they talk with their children, the sooner the babies can pick up the nuances of speech and correct wrong assumptions. Ultimately, as one review of the research literature concluded, "No child has been observed to speak a human language without having had a communicative partner from whom to learn" (Hoff-Ginsberg & Shatz, 1982, p. 22). (See Box 6-4, page 23.)

BOX 6-4 ▪ THE EVERYDAY WORLD

TALKING WITH BABIES AND TODDLERS

For many parents, it is natural to talk to their babies, greeting them when they first awaken, cooing at them while changing their diapers, chatting during their bath. This beginning communication expands over the years, especially as babies assume a more active role—first imitating, then responding, and then initiating.

Talking, reading, and singing to babies are not only among the joys of child-rearing; they also help children's cognitive and emotional development. This is how babies learn the language; learn that they are valued, special people; and learn how to get along with other people.

Here are some suggestions for talking with a baby at different stages of language development:

▪ *Babbling stage.* When a baby babbles, repeat the syllables. Make a game of it, and soon the baby will repeat your sound. Aside from being fun, this kind of game gives a baby the idea that a conversation consists of taking turns, an idea babies seem to grasp at about 7½ or 8 months of age. A round of stimulating chitchat like "dee, dee, dee; dah, dah, dah" helps babies to experience the social aspect of speech.

▪ *First words.* By the time babies speak their first words, at about 1 year, parents can help them learn even more by repeating these first words and pronouncing them correctly. If you can't understand what the baby is saying, smile in approval and say something yourself. Babies can understand many more words than they can utter, and they can learn the names for the objects in their world. For example, Julia points to Jason's doll and says, "Please give me Kermit." If Jason doesn't respond, she reaches over, picks up the doll, and says,

"Kermit." Jason's ability to understand grows as he learns to discover through language what another person is thinking.

▪ *Multiword speech.* You can help a toddler who has begun to string words together to make sentences by expanding on what the child says. For example, if Vicky says "Mommy sock," Ellen replies, "Yes, that is Mommy's sock." Even though expansion may not speed up the acquisition of grammar, it has a strong social use.

▪ *Reading to young children.* Encourage your child's participation in reading-aloud sessions by asking challenging open-ended questions rather than those calling for a yes or a no. Thus, Jess asks Jason, "What is the cat doing?" instead of "Is the cat asleep?" Start with simple questions ("Where is the ball?") and then pose more challenging ones ("What color is the ball?" "Who is playing with the ball?" "What is happening to the boy in the corner?"). Then expand on the child's answers, correct wrong ones, give alternative possibilities, and bestow praise. A study comparing methods like these with standard reading aloud practices found that 21- to 35-month-old children participating in this kind of reading session scored 6 months higher than control children in vocabulary and expressive language skills (Whitehurst et al., 1988).

Above all, talking and reading with a child should be fun. Not every conversation should be a lesson or a test. And the baby should be able to decline to play occasionally, because sometimes a small child just doesn't feel like talking. Most children who begin talking fairly late catch up eventually (Albert Einstein did not speak until he was 3 years old)—and many make up for lost time by talking nonstop to anyone who will listen!

Competence

WHAT IS COMPETENCE?

A child's competence is rarely such a life-and-death issue as it was for a 17-month-old girl who survived untended for 2 to 3 weeks after her parents had been shot dead, apparently by eating potato chips and drinking water from a toilet (Associated Press, 1987). But since the ability to function well from day to day obviously has many other implications, Burton L. White and his colleagues wanted to find out why some children get along in life much better than others. In 1965, they began the Harvard Preschool Project to test and observe some 400 preschoolers and rate them on their competence in both cognitive and social skills (B. L. White, 1971; B. L. White, Kaban & Attanucci, 1979).

The most competent children—the researchers called them A's—showed such *social skills* as getting and holding the attention of adults in acceptable ways, using adults as resources, and showing both affection and hostility. They got along well with other children, were proud of their accomplishments, and wanted to act in grown-up ways. Among their *cognitive skills* were using language well, showing a range of intellectual abilities, planning and carrying out complicated activities, and "dual focusing" (paying attention to a task while being aware of what else was going on). Children classified as B's were less accomplished in these skills; and children classified as C's were very deficient. Follow-up studies 2 years later showed a notable stability in the classifications.

WHAT INFLUENCES COMPETENCE?

To find out how the A and C children became the way they were, the researchers identified A's and C's who had younger siblings, and they looked at the ways the A and C mothers acted with their younger children. (The researchers focused on mothers, feeling that few fathers spent enough time with children of this age to be influential, a conclusion they might not draw today, as will be seen in Chapter 7.) As it turned out, there were sizable differences in mothering after children were about 8 months old. At this age, children start to understand language, and so the way parents talk to them is important. They also begin to crawl; some parents react with pleasure, and some with annoyance. And since they become attached to the person they spend the most time with, this person's personality becomes more important.

The major differences revolved around three aspects of child rearing—the ability to "design" a child's world, to serve as a "consultant" for a child, and to provide a good balance between freedom and restraint. Mothers from all socio-economic levels fell into both groups, with some welfare mothers raising A children and some middle-class women raising C's.

The A mothers designed a safe physical environment full of interesting things to see and touch (common household objects as often as expensive toys). They tended to be "on call" with their babies, without devoting their entire lives to them. A number had part-time jobs, and those who did stay home generally spent less than 10 percent of their time interacting with their infants. They went about their own routine but made themselves available for a few seconds or minutes when needed to answer a question, label an object, help a toddler climb stairs, or share in an exciting discovery. These women generally had a positive attitude toward life, enjoyed being with young children, and gave of themselves generously. They were energetic, patient, tolerant of messiness, and relatively casual about minor risks. They were firm and consistent, setting reasonable limits while showing love and respect. When they wanted to change their babies' behavior, they distracted infants under 1 year of age, and used a combination of distraction, physical removal, and firm words with older children.

The C mothers were a diverse group. Some were overwhelmed by life, ran chaotic homes, and were too absorbed by daily struggles to spend much time with their children. Others spent too much time: hovering, being overprotective, pushing their babies to learn, and making them dependent. Some were physically present but rarely made real contact, apparently because they did not

BOX 6-5 ■ THE EVERYDAY WORLD

HOW PARENTS CAN HELP CHILDREN BE MORE COMPETENT

The findings from the Harvard Pre-school Project can be useful to any parents of young children and can be translated into the following guidelines:

■ The best time for enhancing your child's competence is from the age of 6 to 8 months up until about 2 years, but it is never too late.

■ Encourage your children to have close social relationships with important people in their lives (parents or others), especially from the first few months after their first birthday.

■ Do not worry if you are not with your child full time. Instead, make the most of the time you do spend with your child, and provide the best parent substitutes you can find.

■ Give your children help when they need it rather than pressing it on them too soon, ignoring them, or seeing them as a burden to be dealt with as quickly as possible.

■ Stay fairly close to your young children, but do not hover so much that you discourage them from developing attention-seeking skills.

■ Talk to them about whatever they are interested in at the moment instead of trying to redirect their attention to something else.

■ Speak to them. They will not pick up language from listening to the radio or television, or overhearing adults' conversation. They need interaction with adults.

■ Give them physical freedom to explore. Do not confine them regularly in a playpen, crib, jump seat, or small room.

Source: Adapted from B. L. White, 1971; B. L. White, Kaban, & Attanucci, 1979.

---

really enjoy the company of babies and toddlers. These mothers provided for their children materially but confined them in cribs or playpens.

Once the team had identified guidelines for successful parenting (see Box 6-5), they undertook a pilot training study with 11 carefully chosen families. The researchers helped the parents, who were considered to have "average child-rearing ability," to help their children develop curiosity, attachment, social skills and language skills, and what they called "the roots of intelligence." They wanted to make the parents more aware of the course of development in these areas and to help them adopt practices that seemed to enhance competence in children.

What were the results of this study? The children's progress more closely resembled that of the original A children than that of C children, but these children did not, by and large, do as well as the A's. Thus, in this extremely complex business, professionals again have some of the answers, but clearly not all. No one knows how to write a "cookbook" for perfect child rearing.

One important element, for example, which the researchers did not investigate in depth was the children's own contribution to their mothers' child-rearing styles. Children call forth responses from the people around them, and they in turn react to those responses. Children are actors, reactors, and interactors. It is quite possible, then, that the children of the A mothers showed the kind of personality characteristics that made their mothers *want* to respond as they did. Perhaps they showed more curiosity, more independence, and more interest in what their mothers said and did than the C children did. Researchers are now finding a great deal of evidence of the ways in which children influence their world. In Chapter 7, we will look more at these bidirectional influences, from children to those around them and from the important people in a child's world to the child, as we explore early social and emotional development.

When Families Need Help

Under the influence of what Keniston (1977) called the "myth of the self-sufficient family," the belief has arisen that the ideal nuclear family in the United States brings up its children with no help from other forces in society and that "for a family to need help—or at least to admit it publicly—is to confess failure" (p. 12). Yet families at every socioeconomic level have always received help from others—from members of the extended family, from governmental institutions such as schools and hospitals, from friends and neighbors, and from paid servants and service organizations.

Today, with the vast changes that have taken place in society, families turn more than ever to outside forces for help with various kinds of problems, including their children's intellectual development. Parents, Keniston says, have had to become executives who choose and coordinate the experts, the technology, and the institutions that help bring up their children. At the same time, with the proliferation of research on child development and the abundance of (often conflicting) advice from experts, parents have taken more and more seriously their role in helping their children meet the demands of today's complex society.

As a result, parents sign up for prenatal classes that will enhance their experience of childbirth and aid them in caring for their new babies; for courses in parental effectiveness that will help them help their children weather the storms of growing up; and for innumerable lectures and workshops in schools, churches, and the community. For a variety of reasons, this push toward parental education has been largely a middle-class phenomenon. Yet when low-income parents have been offered programs that hold promise of helping their children improve their verbal, academic, and general coping skills, they have often embraced them eagerly. When middle-class professionals run these programs, they need to be extremely careful to avoid imposing middle-class values in an arbitrary way, and they need to be sensitive to the parents' feelings about themselves and their children.

A successful program that seems to have embodied this philosophy concentrated on developing children's intellectual abilities—not by making a frontal attack on parents, but by educating them and giving them a wide range of support services (Andrews et al., 1982). From 1970 to 1975, federally sponsored Child Development Centers operated in three cities—Birmingham, Alabama; Houston, Texas; and New Orleans, Louisiana. The mothers of children aged 3 months to 3 years received information and training in child development and child rearing, home management, nutrition, health, and other topics, plus health services for the family and referrals to community resources. The children attended nursery programs. In recognition of cultural differences in parenting practices (participants included low-income white, African American, and Mexican American mothers), the centers encouraged parents to make decisions involving their children and hired staff members of the parents' ethnic and cultural backgrounds.

The results were dramatic. Children in the program did better at age 3 on the Stanford-Binet than a control group, and they maintained their gains a year later. Their mothers gave them more instruction, information, and praise; asked them more questions and encouraged them to think and talk; offered more appropriate play materials and more flexible routines; and were more sensitive, accepting, and emotionally responsive and less interfering and critical than control mothers.

BOX 6-6 ■ A CHILD'S WORLD AND YOU

WHAT DO YOU THINK?

■ Charles Dickens spoke of "the blank of my infancy." What are your earliest memories? Can you recall anything from before the age of 3?

■ Watson and Rayner's experiments with "Little Albert" remain controversial. Where would you draw the line between society's need to learn and an infant's rights?

■ "Intervention programs" use professional people to teach parents new ways of behaving with their children. Are such programs valid?

■ Do you think that intelligence is more affected by environment or heredity?

■ Was your intelligence ever tested during your first 3 years? If so, why?

■ The study of competence reminds us that intellectual development has immediate consequences as well as being important over the long term. What do you think might be the immediate value of each of the following?

    Infants' memory
    Babbling
    Object permanence

Unfortunately, this project was dropped because the federal government ended its funding, and so it is not known how these children did after they entered school. But this study and similar studies indicate that professionals can work successfully with parents to help them help their children—and themselves. One mother in a similar program has said that when she first entered as a 17-year-old unwed mother and high school dropout, "I was only taking care of [the baby's] physical needs. I never even thought that I was his first teacher. I was a child myself. In [the program], I learned that I needed to read to my child and I began labeling everything" ("Teach a child's first teacher," 1988).

Programs like these also contribute to children's emotional development. As we will see in Chapter 7, the sense of self that comes from feeling competent and the give-and-take that comes from being with other children are both important elements of social and personality development.

Summary

1   Learning is a relatively permanent change in behavior that occurs as a result of experience. Maturation produces changes in cognitive abilities and enables learning to take place.

2   Very young infants are capable of several types of simple learning, including habituation (reduced response to a stimulus that has become familiar), classical conditioning (learning a conditioned response to a stimulus that is originally neutral), and operant conditioning (learning a response to produce a particular effect). Complex learning can be achieved through various learning modes separately or in combination.

3   Infants show some memory ability virtually from birth, and this ability improves rapidly.

4   Intelligence involves both adaptive and goal-oriented behavior. Three major ap-

proaches for studying intelligence are the psychometric, Piagetian, and information-processing approaches.

5 The psychometric approach seeks to determine and measure quantitatively the factors that make up intelligence. Psychometric tests for infants emphasize motor ability. These tests are generally poor predictors of intelligence later in childhood and in adulthood.

6 The Piagetian approach is concerned with the qualitatively changing nature of cognitive development, or the way people acquire and use knowledge about the world. During the sensorimotor stage, children develop from primarily reflexive infants to toddlers capable of symbolic thought. A major development of the sensorimotor stage is object permanence, the realization that an object or person continues to exist even when out of sight. Much recent research suggests that infants develop sensorimotor behaviors earlier than Piaget's theory holds.

7 The information-processing approach is concerned with the processes underlying intelligent behavior, that is, how people manipulate symbols and what they do with the information they perceive. Assessment of how efficiently an infant processes information appears to be promising as a predictor of later intelligence.

8 The development of language is a crucial aspect of cognitive growth.

9 Prelinguistic speech, which precedes the first words, includes crying, cooing, babbling, and imitation. Babies also communicate through the use of gestures. During the second year of life, the typical toddler begins to speak the language; the second year is also important for growth of language comprehension.

10 Early speech is characterized by simplicity, overgeneralizing concepts, and over-regularizing rules. Calculating mean length of utterance (MLU) is a useful way to assess children's progress in speaking.

11 Two major theories of language acquisition are learning theory (which emphasizes the role of reinforcement and imitation) and nativism (which maintains that people have an inborn capacity to acquire language).

12 Individual differences in language acquisition are influenced by both genetic and environmental factors. Communication with an adult partner is essential if a child is to learn to speak. It is not clear whether hearing simple, direct, repetitive language ("motherese") is important to infants' language development.

13 Parents' child-rearing styles (especially during the first 2 years) affect children's intellectual, social, and emotional competence. Parents of the most competent children are skilled at "designing" a child's environment, are available as "consultants" to a child, and use appropriate control. Programs for parents can help them improve their children's intellectual functioning.

Key Terms

learning (page 195)
maturation (195)
habituation (196)
classical conditioning (197)
unconditioned stimulus (UCS)
 (197–198)
unconditioned response (UCR)
 (197–198)
neutral stimulus (197–198)
conditioned stimulus (CS) (197–198)
conditioned response (CR) (198)
operant (or instrumental)
 conditioning (198)
psychometric approach (201)
Piagetian approach (202)
information-processing approach (202)
intelligence (202)
standardization sample (203)
norm (203)
validity (203)
reliability (203)
mental age (MA) (203)
intelligence quotient (IQ) (203)
Bayley Scales (206)
cognitive development (206)
sensorimotor stage (207)

object permanence (207)
representational ability (208)
scheme (208)
circular reaction (209)
primary circular reaction (210)
acquired adaptation (210)
secondary circular reaction (210)
tertiary circular reaction (211)
deferred imitation (212)
invisible imitation (213)
visible imitation (213)
weight conservation (215)
visual-recognition memory (216)
auditory-recognition memory (216)
language (220)
prelinguistic speech (221)
linguistic speech (222)
holophrase (222)
mean length of utterance (MLU) (224)
morpheme (224)
telegraphic speech (224)
learning theory (225)
nativism (225)
language acquisition device (LAD)
 (226)
motherese (228)

Suggested Readings

Brown, R. (1973). *A first language: The early stages.* Cambridge, MA: Harvard University Press. A classic book that describes the grammatical development of three toddlers—Adam, Eve, and Sarah.

Ginsburg, H., & Opper, S. (1979). *Piaget's theory of intellectual development* (2d ed.). Englewood Cliffs, NJ: Prentice-Hall. A clear, readable discussion of Piaget's concepts that includes outlines of Piaget's basic ideas, his early research and theory, his use of logic as a model for adolescents' thinking, and a discussion of implications of his work.

Green, B. (1984). *Good morning, Merry Sunshine.* New York: Atheneum. An intimate, funny account by a father of the first year of his daughter's life. It is a diary of the baby's progress and of the father's feelings about fatherhood.

Piaget, J. (1952). *The origins of intelligence in children.* New York: International Universities Press. Piaget's now classic presentation of the six substages of sensorimotor development. The book contains numerous examples of his observations of his own children.

White, B. L. (1985). *The first three years of life* (rev. ed.). Englewood Cliffs, NJ: Prentice-Hall. A presentation for lay readers of White's findings on children's competence. It is a thorough treatment of cognitive changes during infancy and toddlerhood.

CHAPTER 7

PERSONALITY AND SOCIAL DEVELOPMENT IN INFANCY AND TODDLERHOOD

B ut what am I?
An infant crying in the night:
An infant crying for the light:
And with no language but a cry.

Alfred, Lord Tennyson, *In Memoriam*, 1850

PREVIEW QUESTIONS

- How did Sigmund Freud and Erik Erikson explain the development of personality in infancy?
- What emotions do babies have, and how do they show them?
- How do temperament and gender affect personality?
- How does the family influence personality development?
- How does mothers' employment affect babies?
- What differences in sociability do babies show?
- How do babies learn how to control their behavior?

JASON, at the age of 2 years and 2 months, makes it clear that he has finished dinner. From his high chair, he throws down, in rapid succession, spoon, plate, food, and bib. He makes something else clear, too—that he knows he should not be doing this. When Julia speaks sharply to him about raining peas, potatoes, and plastic on the floor, he lowers his eyes and pulls his fingers along the side of his stomach, stroking and patting himself in a gesture that seems to mean, "I know I did something you didn't like—but love me, anyway."

Jason, in the midst of the "terrible twos," is showing one of the most important aspects of early psychosocial development. Beyond the tears and the tantrums, the "no's" and the noise, toddlers' emphatic expressions of what they want to do—as opposed to what adults want them to do—signal the shift from the dependence of infancy to the independence of childhood. That shift is a major theme of this chapter. Another theme is parents' impact on their children—and children's impact on their parents.

We will also consider two important theories of early personality development: Sigmund Freud's and Erik Erikson's.

We also look at the development and measurement of emotions in infancy: what emotions babies have, and how they express them.

We go on to consider how babies are like one another and how they differ because of temperament, birth order, and early experiences.

We also look at various influences on personality and social development: at relationships between babies and their mothers and fathers, as well as their other caretakers, their siblings, and other babies; and at situations in which parent-child relationships are disrupted by separation.

The last sections of the chapter discuss the development of sociability and of self-control and self-regulation. By examining all these issues, we will be asking some basic questions about the roots of *personality*. (See Table 7-1 for highlights of social and personality development discussed in this chapter.)

personality Person's unique way of behaving, feeling, and reacting.

240

TABLE 7-1

HIGHLIGHTS OF INFANTS' AND TODDLERS' PERSONALITY AND SOCIAL DEVELOPMENT, BIRTH TO 36 MONTHS	
APPROXIMATE AGE IN MONTHS	**CHARACTERISTICS**
0–1	Infants are relatively unresponsive, rarely reacting to outside stimulation.
1–3	Infants are open to stimulation. They begin to show interest and curiosity, and they smile readily at people.
3–6	Babies can anticipate what is to happen and experience disappointment when it does not. They show this by becoming angry or acting wary. They smile, coo, and laugh often. This is a time of social awakening and early reciprocal exchanges between the baby and the caregiver.
7–9	Babies play "social games" and try to get responses from people. They "talk" to, touch, and cajole other babies to get them to respond. They express more differentiated emotions, showing joy, fear, anger, and surprise.
9–12	Babies are intensely preoccupied with their principal caregiver, may become afraid of strangers, and act subdued in new situations. By 1 year, they communicate emotions more clearly, showing moods, ambivalence, and gradations of feeling.
12–18	Babies explore their environment, using the people they are most attached to as a secure base. As they master the environment, they become more confident and more eager to assert themselves.
18–36	Toddlers sometimes become anxious because they now realize how much they are separating from their caregiver. They work out their awareness of their limitations in fantasy, in play, and by identifying with adults.

Source: Adapted from Sroufe, 1979.

Early Personality Development: Two Theories

What accounts for the development of personality—a person's unique way of looking at, acting upon, and reacting to other people and events? A number of theories have been proposed. Among the most important models of early personality development are those of the psychoanalytic theorists Sigmund Freud and Erik H. Erikson (both introduced in Chapter 1). Although subsequent research has not always upheld these theories, they have had a great influence on the way we think about and act toward children today.

SIGMUND FREUD: PSYCHOSEXUAL THEORY

Freud came to believe that the key to the formation of personality lay in the conflicts between children's early biological urges and the requirements of society, as expressed by their parents. He described these conflicts in terms of a series of psychosexual stages (see Table 1-1 in Chapter 1), two of which occur during the first 3 years. These are the oral stage (birth to 12–18 months) and the anal stage (12–18 months to 3 years).

According to Freud, babies are "all mouth." In this oral stage, a baby gets pleasure from feeding—and even from gnawing on a wooden truck.

Oral Stage (Birth to 12–18 Months)*

oral stage In Freud's theory, the psychosexual stage of infancy (birth to 12–18 months), characterized by gratification in the area around the mouth; feeding is the most common gratifying situation.

id In Freud's theory, the unconscious source of motives and desires; it operates on the "pleasure principle."

pleasure principle In Freud's theory, the attempt to gratify needs immediately; the operating principle of the id.

ego In Freud's theory, the representation of reason or common sense; it operates on the "reality principle."

reality principle In Freud's theory, the search for acceptable and realistic ways to obtain gratification; the operating principle of the ego.

anal stage In Freud's theory, the psychosexual stage of toddlerhood (12–18 to 36 months), in which the child receives pleasure through anal stimulation; toilet training is the most important gratifying situation.

Babies in the *oral stage* are "all mouth." At this stage, feeding is the main source of pleasure, as it stimulates the mouth, lips, and tongue. This stimulation can also come from fingers, pacifiers, and anything else babies can put into the mouth. Infants first get gratification from sucking and swallowing, and then, after their teeth erupt, from biting and chewing.

Newborns are governed by that part of the personality present at birth, which Freud termed the *id;* the id contains instinctual urges and operates on the *pleasure principle*, striving for immediate gratification. The *ego,* which develops later, operates on the *reality principle*—finding acceptable and realistic ways to obtain gratification. The ego helps babies deal with life's inevitable delays in giving them what they want.

Freud maintained that babies who receive too little or too much gratification during any stage of psychosexual development can become *fixated*, or stuck, in that stage; they will then continue trying to resolve that stage throughout life. Thus, people whose oral needs are not met may become nail biters or develop "bitingly" critical personalities. Those who receive so much satisfaction at the oral stage that they do not want to move on to the next stage may become compulsive eaters or smokers, or gullible "swallowers" of whatever they hear.

Because a baby in the oral stage is completely dependent on the mother, Freud believed that inappropriate mothering at this time can lead to a dependent personality. At times of stress, such a person will yearn to go back to the cradle or the womb to be taken care of.

Anal Stage (12–18 Months to 3 Years)

During the *anal stage,* the chief zone of gratification shifts from the mouth to the anus and rectum. Toddlers find moving their bowels pleasurable, and the way toilet training is handled determines the resolution of this stage. This is the first time children themselves are expected to delay gratification by regulating an instinctual need.

The "anal" personality, according to Freud, is shaped by the mother's attitude and by toilet-training practices. If these are too rigid and severe, the child may withhold feces, become constipated, and eventually turn into a person who is pedantic, obsessively precise, and tied to schedules and routines. Or a child who regards feces as a gift to the parents may grow up to be a hoarder of possessions or may identify love with the bestowal of material objects.

ERIK H. ERIKSON: PSYCHOSOCIAL THEORY

Erikson's main concern is the growth of the self and the ways society, rather than biology, shapes its development. In each of his eight stages (see Table 1-1 in Chapter 1), a crisis occurs that influences ego development. Each crisis can have either a good or a bad resolution, depending on the person's ability to strike a healthy balance of opposite qualities. Unsatisfactory resolution of a crisis can interfere with the progress of the next stage. Erikson's first two crises occur at about the same ages as Freud's oral and anal stages.

*All ages are approximate.

Crisis 1: Basic Trust versus Basic Mistrust (Birth to 12–18 Months)

From Erikson's first crisis, **basic trust versus basic mistrust,** babies develop a sense of how reliable the people and objects in their world are. They need to develop the right balance between trust (which allows them to form intimate relationships) and mistrust (which enables them to protect themselves). If the scales are weighted on the side of trust—which Erikson favors—children develop what he calls the virtue of *hope:* the belief that they can fulfill their needs and obtain their desires. If mistrust predominates, children will view the world as unfriendly and unpredictable and will have trouble forming close relationships.

Erikson emphasizes the feeding situation as the setting in which the mother establishes the right mix of trust and mistrust. Unlike Freud, who was interested in oral gratification—the act of feeding itself—Erikson is interested in the mother-infant interactions having to do with feeding. Does the mother respond quickly enough? Can the baby count on being fed when he or she is hungry and therefore trust the mother as a representative of the world? Trust enables an infant to let the mother out of sight, "because she has become an inner certainty as well as an outer predictability" (Erikson, 1950, p. 247).

basic trust versus basic mistrust In Erikson's theory, the first critical alternative of psychosocial development, in which infants (birth to 18 months) develop a sense of how reliable people in their world are.

Crisis 2: Autonomy versus Shame and Doubt (18 Months to 3 Years)

In the crisis of **autonomy versus shame and doubt,** children need to strike the right balance between **autonomy,** or self-control, and external control. Children need to learn what they can do, what is safe to do, what they should do—and what kind of guidance they still need from their parents. The virtue of *will* emerges from this stage: children learn to make their own choices and decisions, to exercise self-restraint, and to follow their own interests.

Maturation plays an important role as children use their developing muscles to do things for themselves—to walk, to feed and dress themselves, and to exert

autonomy versus shame and doubt In Erikson's theory, the second critical alternative of psychosocial development (18 months to 3 years), in which the child achieves a balance between self-determination and control by others.

autonomy Self-control.

(© George Goodwin/Monkmeyer Press)

According to Erikson, toddlers need to develop autonomy. During this stage, parents need to ignore messy faces, bibs, tables, and floors, and let children learn how to master such basic tasks as feeding themselves.

This toddler seems to be negotiating Freud's anal stage happily—and also seems to consider his toilet training as Erikson does, as a major achievement in learning control and self-determination.

self-control. The "agreement to agree" with the mother, which characterized the earlier atmosphere of mutual trust, must now be violated as children increasingly substitute their own judgment for that of adults.

To achieve autonomy, children need an appropriate amount of control and guidance from adults. Too much or not enough may make them compulsive about controlling themselves. Fear of losing self-control may inhibit their self-expression and cause them to doubt themselves, be ashamed, and suffer a loss of self-esteem.

Toilet training is an important achievement in learning control and self-determination. So is language: as children learn to express their wishes, they become more powerful and more independent. Meanwhile, parents provide a safe harbor from which the child can set out and discover the world, and to which the child can keep coming back for support.

The "terrible twos" are a normal manifestation of this need for autonomy. The change from a dependent and mostly docile infant to a strong-willed and sometimes terrible-tempered 2-year-old is normal. Toddlers have to test new notions: that they are individuals, that they have a measure of control over their world, and that they have increasing powers. No longer content to let someone else decide what they should be doing at any given time, they try out their own ideas and find their own preferences. Their favorite way of testing seems to be to shout "No!" at every opportunity; this behavior is often known as *negativism*. (See Box 7-1.)

TACKLING THE "TERRIBLE TWOS"

"No! I don't want to go home! I want to stay here and play!" Vicky, at the age of 3, shouts, running away from Charles as soon as she sees him walking over to the sandbox. Getting Vicky to do anything her parents suggest has become harder and harder since she began exhibiting *negativism*, but this is a perfectly normal behavior for her stage of development. Almost all children show it to some degree; it usually begins before 2 years of age, tends to peak at about 3½ to 4, and declines by age 6. Many children playfully tease their parents to show their control—but do not really mean what they say and will eventually comply with requests.

Children's expressions of self-will not only are normal, but are probably an essential step in becoming independent. The following techniques for parents are designed to minimize conflict and maximize a child's sense of competence (Haswell, Hock, & Wenar, 1981):

■ *Be flexible.* Cultivate sensitivity to your child's natural rhythms and special likes and dislikes. The most flexible parents tend to have the least resistant children.

■ *Don't interrupt an activity unless absolutely necessary,* since this usually arouses the most intense resistance. Try to wait until the child's attention has shifted to something else.

■ *If you must interrupt, give warning:* "In 10 minutes we have to leave the playground." This gives the child time to prepare and either finish an activity or think about when and how to resume it next time.

■ *Suggest rather than command,* and smile or hug when you make your request instead of criticizing or threatening.

■ *Wait a few moments before repeating your request* if the child does not comply immediately.

■ *Give the child a choice*—even a limited one—to allow the child some control. ("Would you like to have your bath now, or in 5 minutes?" or "Do you want to take your last turn on the slide or the seesaw?")

■ *Be consistent* in enforcing necessary requests.

■ *Use "time out"* to end conflicts. In a nonpunitive way, remove either the child or yourself from the situation. Very often, when parents stop paying attention to a resistant child, the resistance diminishes or even disappears.

EVALUATING THE THEORIES

Both these theories have contributed useful insights into the way children develop, and Erikson's model is especially helpful in describing the shift from the dependency of infancy to the autonomy of toddlerhood. Both Erikson's theory and Freud's, however, have serious shortcomings.

First, they place the major responsibility for the way children turn out on what their mothers do or fail to do, paying little attention to the child's own contribution or the impact of other people and circumstances in the child's life. Mothers are certainly influential in their children's development, but there are other important influences, including other family members, people outside the family (like other children), the school, the community, and the child's own characteristics (Chess & Thomas, 1982).

Second, both these theories emphasize the lifelong effects of early experiences, even though long-term research has shown that such effects are often overshadowed by the effects of later experiences, either favorable or unfavorable. There is no single all-important factor or age period.

Finally, these theories are difficult to test objectively. It is hard to define concepts like *oral personality* or *basic trust* precisely enough for scientific testing. Thus, although there have been many attempts to prove (or disprove) each theory, very little conclusive evidence exists for the theories. Still, Freud and Erikson have given us new ways to think about personality factors that persist throughout life, like the sense of self, the ability to form attachments to other people, and emotions.

Factors in Personality Development

EMOTIONS: THE BASIS OF PERSONALITY AND SOCIAL DEVELOPMENT

Lying in her crib, watching a colorful mobile overhead as a small bubble rises between her lips, Vicky seems the picture of contentment. But is she? How does she feel? And how do her *emotions*—subjective reactions to the environment which are accompanied by physiological responses and which are generally experienced as pleasant or unpleasant—affect the way she thinks and acts?

emotion *Psychological response to a situation; although the response can lead to altered behavior, the primary characteristic is a change in subjective feeling rather than in objective action.*

Studying Babies' Emotions

At first, recognizing infants' emotions seems nearly impossible. It is hard to determine what an infant is feeling—and why. Recently, however, researchers have developed creative methods for studying babies, and we have been able to explore the psyche of infants in more depth than ever before, making some fascinating discoveries.

Early researchers believed that infants were born with only one emotion—an undifferentiated excitement that came to be called *distress* (Bridges, 1932)—or perhaps a total of three: love, rage, and fear (J. B. Watson, 1919). Now, however, innovative studies conducted by Carroll Izard and his colleagues (1982) suggest that babies have a fairly wide range of emotions in the first few months of life, at least judging by their facial expressions.

TABLE 7-2

ARRIVAL TIMES OF INFANTS' EMOTIONAL EXPRESSIONS

EXPRESSION OF FUNDAMENTAL EMOTIONS	APPROXIMATE TIME OF EMERGENCE
Interest	Present at birth
Neonatal smile (a "half smile" that appears spontaneously for no apparent reason)	
Startle response*	
Distress* (in response to pain)	
Disgust (in response to unpleasant taste or smell)	
Social smile	4–6 weeks
Anger	3–4 months
Surprise	
Sadness	
Fear	5–7 months
Shame, shyness, self-awareness	6–8 months
Contempt	2d year of life
Guilt	

*The neonatal smile, the startle response, and distress in response to pain are precursors of the social smile and the emotions of surprise and sadness, which appear later. There is no evidence that they are related to inner feelings when they are seen in the first few weeks of life. The most recent research suggests that infants have a wide range of emotion, even in the early months of life, and that specific feelings appear in a typical sequence.
Source: Adapted from Trotter, 1983.

In Izard's research, the facial expressions of 5-, 7-, and 9-month-olds were recorded on videotape as the babies played games with the mother, were surprised by a jack-in-the box, were given shots from a doctor, and were approached by a stranger. When college students and health professionals were asked to identify the babies' expressions from the tapes, they identified expressions of joy, sadness, interest, and fear, and to a lesser degree anger, surprise, and disgust (Izard et al., 1980). When observers were trained with Izard's Facial Expression Scoring Manual, a guide to classifying emotional expressions (1971, 1977), they were even more accurate.

Did these babies actually have the feelings they were credited with? Although it is hard to be sure, they did show a range of expressions that were very similar to adults' expressions of these emotions, and so these expressions very likely mirrored similar feelings in the babies. (See Table 7-2 for a list of emotions and the ages when they appear.)

How Babies' Emotions Develop: The Sense of Self

Jason cried as soon as he was born and smiled a few weeks later, but he did not laugh until he was 4 months old. Jason was following a normal timetable. His emotional development depends on many factors, some of them inborn and visible at birth, and others appearing only after some time. This timing may spring from a biological "clock" governed by the maturing brain, which triggers specific feelings at different ages (see Table 7-2). This chronology may have value for survival: expressions of pain from helpless 2-month-olds may bring the help they need, whereas anger expressed by the same babies in the same situation 7 months later may mobilize them to do something to help themselves—to push away an offender, for example (Trotter, 1983).

Experience also affects emotional development. Abused infants show fear several months earlier than other babies, suggesting that they may have developed a capacity for fear through their unfortunate experience (Gaensbauer & Hiatt, 1984). And differences in the facial expressions that parents show to baby boys and baby girls (mothers typically show a wider range of emotions to their daughters than to their sons) may provide a clue to the finding that at all ages studied, girls are better than boys at understanding emotional expression (Malatesta, cited in Trotter, 1983).

Soon after birth, babies show interest, distress, and disgust. Within the next few months, they move beyond these primary emotions to express joy, anger, surprise, sadness, shyness, and fear. But more complex emotions that depend on the sense of self—like empathy, jealousy, shame, guilt, and pride—come later, some not until the second year. At that time, most babies develop *self-awareness*—the ability to recognize their own actions, intentions, states, and competence, and to understand that they are separate from other people and things. With this realization, they can think about, and judge, their own actions (Kopp, 1982; Lewis, cited in Trotter, 1983).

self-awareness Ability to recognize one's own actions, intentions, states, and abilities.

At about 8 months of age, most babies develop a fear of strangers (discussed later in this chapter). When the psychologist Michael Lewis saw that his 8-month-old daughter did not show this fear if the stranger was another child, he concluded that she realized the other child was like her. This inspired him to investigate the beginnings of self-awareness (Trotter, 1987).

Lewis and his colleagues found that self-awareness was present by 18 months of age, the same age as the emergence of *self-recognition*, as indicated by babies' ability to recognize their own image. To test for self-recognition, observers counted the number of times babies aged 6 to 24 months touched their noses. Then, the researchers dabbed rouge on the babies' noses, put the babies in front of a mirror, and noted whether they touched their noses more often. The big increase in nose touching that occurred among 18-month-olds indicated that babies of this age know their noses are normally not red and thus suggests that this is the age when babies recognize themselves (M. Lewis & Brooks, 1974).

self-recognition Ability to recognize one's own image.

The achievement of self-awareness represents a great leap toward children's understanding of—and relating to—other people. Once they have a sense of themselves, they can recognize their own preference to be with other people like them—like same-sex playmates, or other children rather than adults. They can put themselves in another person's place—and thus develop the feeling of empathy. They can think about their own feelings. When they recognize that no one else (not even their parents) can know their thoughts, they develop the ability to lie. (Parents who are busy teaching honesty may find it hard to look upon a child's lying as a positive step!) Thus, learning about the self (often a lifelong task) begins early, affects and is affected by relationships with other people, and underlies social competence, peer relationships, and gender identity (Brooks-Gunn & Lewis, 1984).

Jerome Kagan (1982a) has suggested an almost exclusively biological explanation for self-awareness, attributing it to maturation of the central nervous system. Thus, its emergence would require only time, a normal brain, and experience with a world containing objects. Challenging an environmental point of view, Kagan says, "Perhaps there is no self prior to the second year, as there is no frog in the tadpole" (1982a, p. 376).

How Do Babies Express Their Emotions?

It is easy to tell when the newborn Vicky is unhappy. She emits a piercing cry in an ever-rising crescendo; she flails her arms and legs; and she stiffens her body until it is completely rigid. It is harder to tell when she is happy. During her first month, she quiets at the sound of a human voice or when she is picked up, and she smiles when her hands are moved together to play pat-a-cake. With every passing day, she responds more to people—smiling, cooing, reaching out, and eventually going to them.

These early signals hold clues to her feelings. They are important steps in Vicky's development. When Vicky wants or needs something, she cries; when she wants to reach out to Ellen or Charles, she often breaks into an engaging smile or a chortle. And when her messages bring a response, her sense of connection with other people grows. Her sense of personal power is also enhanced as she sees that cries bring help and comfort, and that her smiles and laughter elicit smiles and laughter in return.

Over time, the meaning of Vicky's emotional signals changes. At birth, her cry signals physical discomfort; later on it is more likely to express psychological distress. Her early smile often comes spontaneously as an expression of internal well-being; smiles after a few months of age are more often social signals, in which Vicky shows her pleasure in other people.

crying Innate nonlinguistic form of communication that in newborns and infants expresses a need for attention or a strong emotion; basic infants' cries include the rhythmic cry of need, the angry cry, the cry of pain, and the cry of frustration.

Crying As the most powerful way—and sometimes the only way—that babies can signal the outside world when they need something, *crying* is a vital means of communication. From the first week of life, infants cry when they feel hunger, cold, or pain and when they are undressed or awakened. Over the next few weeks, they also cry when their feedings are interrupted, when stimulated while in a fussy state, and when left alone in a room.

Patterns of crying There are four patterns of crying:

1 Basic *hunger cry*, a rhythmic cry not always associated with hunger
2 *Angry cry*, a variation of the rhythmic cry in which a baby forces excess air through the vocal cords
3 *Pain cry*, a sudden onset of loud crying without preliminary moaning, or an initial long cry followed by an extended period of holding the breath
4 *Cry of frustration*, starting with two or three long-drawn-out cries without long periods of holding the breath (Wolff, 1969).

A team of investigators recorded the cries of babies undergoing routine medical procedures (like the taking of blood samples) and minor surgery (like circumcision) and found that babies in distress cry louder, longer, and more irregularly than hungry babies. Also, distressed babies are more likely to gag and to interrupt their crying (Oswald & Peltzman, 1974).

Responding to crying   Parents often wonder how to respond to crying. If they respond whenever a baby cries, do they risk creating a spoiled child who whines and fusses when frustrated? If they ignore crying, will the baby feel abandoned?

Babies whose cries of distress bring relief seem to gain confidence in their power to affect their world. By the end of the first year, babies whose mothers have regularly responded to their crying with tender, soothing care cry less (Ainsworth & Bell, 1977; Bell & Ainsworth, 1972). By now they are communicating more in other ways—with babbling, gestures, and facial expressions—than babies of more punitive or ignoring mothers, who cry more. Thus, while parents need not leap to a baby's side at every whimper, it seems better to err in the direction of responding more than responding less—and not worry about spoiling a baby. (See Box 4-5 in Chapter 4.)

Crying as a diagnostic tool   Babies' cries may help parents and doctors to tell when infants are sick or at risk of not developing normally. Charts of sound waves show that many newborns cry at a very high pitch for the first day or two in response to the trauma of birth, but screeching like this that lasts into the first month may signal nervous system problems. One study showed that the cries of newborn preterm and full-term babies could be used to predict how they would score on developmental tests at 18 months of age and at 5 years (B. M. Lester, 1987). Thus, analysis of crying shows promise in picking up early signs of trouble.

Parents are very sensitive to differences in babies' crying. When 28 mothers listened to a tape recording of the first 10 seconds of cries by 2-day-old infants who had been snapped on the soles of the feet with a rubber band, the mothers were especially distressed by the more high-pitched cries. When the cries included an up-and-down warbling, the mothers thought that the babies sounded sick (Zeskind & Marshall, 1988). Some parents respond to this kind of cry with extra care, but others find it so upsetting that they neglect or abuse the baby. Thus, again we see how babies and parents interact to influence the child's future development.

This baby won't be "spoiled" by being picked up; babies whose cries of distress bring relief seem to gain confidence in their power to affect their world, and they end up crying less.

Smiling   Vicky's winning smile is one of the ways she makes people—especially her parents—fall in love with her. Her smile sets in motion a cycle of trust and affection: it is the rare adult who does not smile back and the infant smiles even more.

Smiling develops in stages. The earliest faint smile appears soon after birth and is a reflex; it was once explained as being due to gas, but we now know that it occurs spontaneously as a result of central nervous system activity. It frequently appears as the infant is falling asleep (Sroufe & Waters, 1976).

In the second week after birth, Vicky often smiles drowsily after feeding, possibly responding to Ellen's sounds. After the second week, she is more likely to smile when she is alert but inactive; and at about 1 month, her smiles become more frequent and more social. The first social smiles are brief. Whereas the early reflex smile uses only the lower facial muscles, the social smile also involves the eye muscles. Babies of this age smile when their hands are clapped together (Kreutzer & Charlesworth, 1973) and when they hear a familiar voice. During the second month, babies can recognize different people, and they smile more at people they know. At about 3 months, their smiles are broader and longer-lasting.

smiling   *Innate form of communication that begins as a reflex and soon expresses pleasure, trust, and contentment.*

(© John Michael/International Stock)

Aside from cheering up anyone in the area, this baby's laughter may be giving us clues to cognitive, as well as emotional, development.

Some infants smile much more than others (Tautermannova, 1973), a difference that can have important consequences. A happy, cheerful baby who rewards the parents' caretaking efforts with smiles and gurgles is likely to form a more positive relationship than one who smiles less.

Laughing   During his fourth month, Jason starts to laugh out loud at being kissed on his stomach, hearing certain sounds, and seeing Jess and Julia do unusual things. Some researchers suggest that babies' laughter is related to fear, since sometimes they show both fear and laughter in reaction to the same thing—like an object looming toward them (Sroufe & Wunsch, 1972).

As Jason grows older, he laughs more often and at more things. At the age of 4 to 6 months, he giggles in response to sound and touch, but by 7 to 9 months, he throws his head back and laughs just as much in more complex situations—when Julia covers her face with a mask or Jess plays peekaboo with him. The change reflects increasing cognitive development. By laughing at the unexpected, Jason shows that he knows what to expect. Laughter also helps him discharge tension. At 2 years of age, an edge of hysteria tinges his laughter at a pop-up dinosaur in a book before he turns the page, saying, "I don't like dat." By using laughter at difficult times, he shows competence. We see, then, a relationship between emotional and cognitive development.

DIFFERENCES IN PERSONALITY

Jason is a cheerful baby who greets each day and most people with a smile, and the only sign that he is awake during the night is the tinkle of a musical toy as he plays happily in his crib. His neighbor, Johnny, opens his mouth to cry before he opens his eyes to face the day; and he throws at least one tantrum a day.

Even in the womb, Vicky and Jason began to show unique personalities. They already had different activity levels and favorite positions in utero. After birth, differences between them became more apparent.

What accounts for these differences? Part of the answer seems to lie in the way babies are treated. Infants of depressed, unresponsive mothers sometimes become sad themselves, showing this by crying, ignoring people, or sleeping an unusual amount (see Box 7-2, page 252). And babies whose parents reject, neglect, or abuse them often show signs of emotional disturbance (Rutter, 1974; L. Yarrow, 1961).

However, infants' emotional responses often follow patterns that persist through the years, suggesting that basic mood is inborn. At 2 months, for example, both Jason and Johnny received shots: Jason whimpered a little when he got his, but Johnny screamed in rage. At 19 months, Johnny yanked a shovel out of Jason's hand and threw sand in his face; when Johnny took Jason's toys, Jason usually found something else to play with. Babies as young as 8 weeks of age already show signs of emotional differences that form an important part of the personality (Izard, Hembree, et al., cited in Trotter, 1987). Such differences in mood have been identified as one aspect of inborn temperament.

We now look at differences in emotional makeup and temperament. We then look at differences between the sexes, which also seem to result from both biological and social influences.

Temperamental Differences

Besides her cheerful disposition, Vicky is an easy baby to take care of because she eats, sleeps, and eliminates at regular times and adapts quickly to new situations. On the other hand, Johnny sleeps and eats little and irregularly, laughs and cries loudly, and has to be convinced that new people and new

(Drawing by Chas. Addams; © 1984 The New Yorker Magazine, Inc.)

Although many aspects of temperament seem to be inborn and largely hereditary, people's behavioral styles can and do change over the years, often in reaction to special experiences or to parents' handling.

BOX 7-2 ■ THE RESEARCH WORLD

HOW A MOTHER'S DEPRESSION AFFECTS HER BABY

Jason smiles at Julia; she interprets this as an invitation to play, and kisses his stomach, sending him into gales of giggles. But the next day when she begins to kiss his stomach, he looks at her glassy-eyed and turns his head away. Julia interprets this as "I want to be quiet now," and so she tucks him into a carrier and lets him rest quietly against her body.

This process, called the *mutual regulation model* (Tronick & Gianino, 1986), illustrates the ways a baby has to regulate internal emotional states, the kinds of signals baby and mother send to each other, and the kind of interaction that occurs when a mother "reads" her baby's behaviors accurately and responds appropriately. Of course, mothers do not always get the babies' messages; when the babies do not get the results they want, they may be upset at first, but they usually keep on sending signals so that they can "repair" the interaction. Normally, interaction moves back and forth between poorly regulated and well-regulated states, and babies learn from these shifts how to send their signals and what to do when their initial signals do not bring what they want.

When mothers are consistently unresponsive, however—as depressed mothers often are—babies tend to stop sending signals and try to comfort themselves by such behaviors as sucking or rocking. The babies will try for a while to repair the interaction, but with repeated failure will fall back on their own resources. If this defensive reaction becomes habitual, it can create major problems for the babies, who feel powerless to elicit responses from other people and who feel that their mothers are unreliable and the world is an untrustworthy place. The babies themselves then become sad—not as a reflection of the mother's depression but as the result of impaired interaction.

This cycle may explain why children of depressed mothers are at risk of a variety of emotional and cognitive disturbances. Unfortunately, some 12 to 20 percent of American mothers with children under 5 are estimated to suffer from depression, an emotional state characterized by sadness and such other symptoms as difficulty in eating, sleeping, and concentrating (W. T. Garrison & Earls, 1986). Factors that increase the risk of depression include poverty, poor education, dissatisfaction with marriage or living conditions, being a single mother or an immigrant, having a temperamentally difficult or handicapped child, and not having family and friends to turn to for social support (W. T. Garrison & Earls, 1986; Zuckerman & Beardslee, 1987). About 20 percent of new mothers suffer from postpartum depression, which lasts 6 to 8 weeks after birth (Zuckerman & Beardslee, 1987).

Depressed mothers tend to be anxious and punitive toward their children, and to feel as if their lives are out of control (T. Field et al., 1985). Their children are more likely to have low birthweight and to be drowsy as infants, show tension by squirming and arching their backs, and cry a lot. As toddlers, they tend to be especially emotional and to engage in a low level of symbolic play; and later on they tend to grow poorly, to have a high rate of accidents, and to present a variety of behavior problems, many of which last into adolescence (T. Field et al., 1985; Zuckerman & Beardslee, 1987).

Most depressed mothers know that their feelings affect their children, and they often feel guilty about feeling depressed. Many, however, can be helped if they can identify the causes of their problems and then seek social services, counseling, or psychotherapy. Their infants may benefit from being cared for part of the time by someone else, and their older children may need more extensive help, depending on the nature and severity of their problems.

---

experiences are not threatening before he will have anything to do with them. And Jason is mild in his responses, both positive and negative: he does not like most new situations, but if allowed to proceed at his own slow pace, he eventually becomes interested and involved.

temperament *Person's style of approaching other people and situations.*

Each of these babies is showing aspects of *temperament*—one's characteristic style of approaching and reacting to people and situations. Temperament can be considered the *how* of behavior, rather than the *what* (abilities) or the *why* (motivation). Vicky and Johnny may be equally adept at dressing, but Vicky will do it more quickly, will be more willing to put on a new shirt, and will be less distracted if, say, the cat jumps onto the bed.

Aspects of Temperament   The New York Longitudinal Study (NYLS)—which we introduced in Chapter 2—followed 133 subjects from infancy into young adulthood. In many of them, though some aspects of temperament changed considerably, often as a result of life changes, nine aspects showed up soon after birth and remained relatively stable into adulthood (A. Thomas & Chess, 1984; A. Thomas et al., 1968):

1 *Activity level*—how much and how often a person moves
2 *Rhythmicity*, or *regularity*—predictability of biological functions (like appetite, sleep, and elimination)
3 *Approach-withdrawal*—how readily a person accepts new people and situations
4 *Adaptability*—how readily a person accepts transitions, like switching to a new activity
5 *Sensory threshold*—sensitivity to physical stimuli (like noise, light, and touch)
6 *Quality of mood*—whether a person's usual state is cheerful and pleasant or gloomy and unfriendly
7 *Intensity*—how strong a person's responses are (loudness of laughter, force of temper)
8 *Distractibility*—whether a person changes behavior easily or quickly in response to external stimuli
9 *Attention span–persistence*—how long a person pursues an activity; how long attention lasts in the face of obstacles

Stella Chess.

Alexander Thomas. This husband-wife team traced temperamental traits from infancy to young adulthood.

Three Temperamental Patterns   Almost two-thirds of the children studied fitted into one of three categories identified by these researchers (see Table 7-3, page 254). Forty percent of the children in the NYLS sample were, like Vicky, *easy children,* who are generally happy, rhythmic in their biological functioning, and accepting of new experiences. Ten percent of the children in the sample were, like Johnny, *difficult children,* who are more irritable and harder to please, irregular in biological rhythms, and more intense in expressing emotion. *Slow-to-warm-up children,* like Jason, made up 15 percent of the sample. They tend to react mildly and need time to adapt to new people and situations (A. Thomas & Chess, 1977).

Not all children, of course, fit neatly into one of these three groups, and even those who do fit often have some traits more characteristic of another category. For example, a child may sleep and eat well but be afraid of new people; or be very persistent but become easily irritated by scratchy clothes, showing a low sensory threshold. Such variations are normal (A. Thomas & Chess, 1984).

Influences on Temperament   Judging from this and other research, it seems that the temperamental differences between Vicky and Jason are inborn and largely hereditary (A. Thomas & Chess, 1977; 1984). Other research has found that individual differences in basic temperament do not seem to be determined by parents' attitudes (A. Thomas & Chess, 1984) or by gender, birth order, or social class (Persson-Blennow & McNeil, 1981).

Some people's behavioral styles do change over the years, however, apparently in reaction to special experiences or to parents' handling. One "difficult" girl in the NYLS who was having a hard time in childhood suddenly showed musical and dramatic talent at about age 10, leading her parents to see her in a new way and to respond differently to her; and by age 22 she was a well-adjusted young woman. Another "difficult" child was doing well with her par-

easy child   *Child with a generally happy temperament, regular biological rhythms, and a readiness to accept new experiences.*

difficult child   *Child who has an irritable temperament, irregular biological rhythms, and intense responses to situations.*

slow-to-warm-up child   *Child whose temperament is generally mild and who is hesitant about accepting new experiences.*

TABLE 7-3

THREE TEMPERAMENTAL PATTERNS

EASY CHILD	DIFFICULT CHILD	SLOW-TO-WARM-UP CHILD
Has moods of mild to moderate intensity, usually positive	Displays intense and frequently negative moods	Has mildly intense reactions, both positive and negative
Responds well to novelty and change	Responds poorly to novelty and change	Responds slowly to novelty and change
Quickly develops regular sleep and feeding schedules	Sleeps and eats irregularly	Sleeps and eats more regularly than difficult child; less regularly than easy child
Takes to new foods easily	Accepts new foods slowly	
Smiles at strangers	Is suspicious of strangers	Shows mildly negative initial response to new stimuli (like a first encounter with a bath; a new food, person, or place; entering school or another new situation)
Adapts easily to new situations	Adapts slowly to new situations	
Accepts most frustrations with little fuss	Reacts to frustration with tantrums	
Adapts quickly to new routines and rules of new games	Adjusts slowly to new routines	
	Cries often and loudly; also laughs loudly	Gradually develops liking for new stimuli after repeated, unpressured exposures

Source: Adapted from A. Thomas & Chess, 1984.

ents' quiet way of setting firm limits—until, when she was 13, her father died and her mother felt overwhelmed and could not cope with the child's needs; the girl developed a severe behavior disorder. An "easy" child got into trouble at age 14 after experimenting with drugs; he gave up drugs a year later when he began following an Indian guru; then, several years later, he broke with the mystic, and in his early twenties he was doing well (A. Thomas & Chess, 1984).

One analysis based on NYLS data found that the way mothers feel about their role—whether they are happy or unhappy about being employed or being at home full time—seems to affect children's adjustment. Mothers who were dissatisfied with their roles when their children were 3 years old were more likely to reject the children, and at age 4 the children were more likely to show a difficult temperament (Lerner & Galambos, 1985). Parents can also help children adapt their behavior so as to function better.

How Temperament Affects Children's Adjustment: "Goodness of Fit" According to the NYLS, Johnny, as a difficult child, is more likely to develop some sort of behavior problem than either Vicky or Jason. About 1 out of 3 of the children in the sample did develop such problems at some time. Most were mild problems that showed up between ages 3 and 5 and cleared up by adolescence, but some remained or grew worse by adulthood.

No temperamental type, however, was immune to such problems. Even easy children had them, when their lives held too much stress. One form of stress is being expected to act in ways that are contrary to basic temperament. If a highly active child is confined in a small apartment and expected to sit still for long periods, if a slow-to-warm-up child is pushed to adjust to many new people and situations, or if a persistent child is constantly taken away from absorbing projects, trouble may result. The key to healthy adjustment is "goodness of fit" between children and the demands made upon them. This, of course, carries an important message for parents.

The notion of inborn temperament relieves parents of a lot of emotional baggage. When they recognize that a child behaves in a certain way not out of willfulness, laziness, or stupidity but because of inborn temperament, they are less likely to feel guilty, anxious, or hostile, or to act rigid or impatient. They can focus on helping the child use his or her temperament as a strength rather than an impediment. In this way they can change "poorness of fit" to "goodness of fit" and thus make a major, positive contribution to their children's development.

One of the most important things parents can do is to accept their children's basic temperament instead of trying to cast them into a mold of the parents' design. For example, the parents of a "rhythmic" baby girl can use a "demand" feeding schedule, in which the baby sets the pace; the parents of an irregular baby boy can help him by setting a flexible schedule based on both his needs and theirs. The parents of a slow-to-warm-up child need to learn to give the child time to adjust to new situations; they also need to ask other people, like relatives and nursery school teachers, to do the same.

Parents can also help their children make the most of the temperament they are born with—by quietly setting firm, consistent limits for an active, intense child; by preparing a nonadaptable child for transitions ("In 5 minutes it will be time to put away your toys"); and by stimulating an easygoing, docile child. Parents are not omnipotent, but they can do a great deal to help children navigate the passage through life.

Gender Differences

Are personality differences between Vicky and Jason due to her femaleness and his maleness? As we saw in Chapter 5, there are few physiological differences between baby boys and baby girls. Research has been done on infants' activity levels, their responses to things they see as opposed to those they hear, how irritable they are, and how interested they are in exploring their surroundings instead of staying close to a parent. A number of studies have found some differences between the sexes, but the problem is that these findings have rarely held up when the studies are repeated by the same or other investigators. After a careful review of the literature, Birns (1976) concludes that sex differences cannot be described clearly until after age 2.

Other studies have focused on the ways adults act toward infants. These findings are much clearer: there is a tendency for a newborn baby identified as a female to be treated differently from one identified as a male, and for her behavior to be interpreted differently. When strangers think that a crying baby is a boy, they are likely to see "him" as crying from anger; when they think that the baby is a girl, they assume that "she" is afraid (Condry & Condry, 1974). Parents' reactions toward their babies are affected by the parents' own sex and the age and personality of the infant, but there do seem to be some consistent findings. Boys get more attention in infancy, but the attention baby girls get is designed to make them smile more and be more sociable (Birns, 1976).

Adults' different treatment of girls and boys is demonstrated in a study in which twenty-four 14-month-old children, 12 boys and 12 girls, were introduced to adults who did not know them. Some of the children were introduced as the sex they actually were, and some as the other sex. When the adults were asked to play with the children, they were more likely to encourage the "boys" in active play and more likely to choose a ball than a doll to play with. The adults tended to talk more to the ''girls'' and to pick a doll or a bottle to play with. Interestingly, though, the children did not show sex differences themselves; the boys and girls played in very similar ways. What did differ was the way they were treated by the adults (H. Frisch, 1977).

Thus, although some differences may not be present at birth, environmental shaping of personality does occur very early in life. The sex of an infant seems to be more important than behavioral and physiological differences in bringing about parents' behaviors.

THE FAMILY AND PERSONALITY DEVELOPMENT

The families that Vicky and Jason grow up in are probably the largest single influence on their development. Were their births planned and welcomed? How old were their parents? How well do the personalities of parents and child mesh? Are the parents healthy? Are they wealthy or poor? How many people live at home? Influence travels in the other direction, too. Children also affect their parents in untold ways, transforming parents' day-to-day moods, priorities and plans for the future—even a marriage itself.

Family life for both Vicky and Jason is quite different from what it would have been a century ago, and family life is likely to change even more in the future. A child growing up today is likely to have only one sibling, a mother who works outside the home, and a father who is more involved in his children's lives than his own father was; and to receive a considerable amount of daily care from nonrelatives, first in a caregiver's home or a day care center and then at a preschool. Today's children have a 40 percent chance of spending part of their childhood with only one parent, probably the mother and probably because of divorce (Bane, 1980; Masnick & Bane, 1980).

socialization *Learning of behaviors deemed appropriate by one's culture.*

These changes have revolutionized the study of *socialization*—how children learn the behaviors their culture considers appropriate. In the past, most research focused on mothers and their children, but now researchers are studying the bonds between children and their fathers, their brothers and sisters, their grandparents, and other caregivers.

Another fascinating trend in research is the focus on the entire family. How does Ellen and Charles's marital relationship affect the relationship that each spouse has with Vicky? Do Julia and Jess act differently with Jason when either one is alone with him from the way they act when all are together? Questions like these have yielded provocative findings. For example, when both parents are present and talking to each other, they pay less attention to the child. In some families, the spouses' closeness to each other may detract their ability to be close to their children; in others, the parenting experience strengthens the marriage tie (Belsky, 1979). By looking at the family as a unit, we get a fuller picture of the web of relationships among family members.

The Mother's Role

Until recently, most developmentalists seemed to agree with Napoleon, who said, ''My opinion is that the future good or bad conduct of a child entirely depends upon the mother.'' Although we now recognize that mothers are not the only important people in babies' lives, they are still central characters in the drama of development.

The Mother-Infant Bond To find out how and when the special intimacy between mothers and their babies forms, some researchers have looked at animals. Newly hatched chicks will follow the first moving object they see, whether or not it is a member of their own species, and they become increasingly attached to it. Usually this first attachment is to the mother; but if the natural course of events is disturbed, other (often bizarre) attachments can occur. The ethologist Konrad Lorenz (1957), who studied animal behavior, waddled, honked, and flapped his arms—and got newborn ducklings to "love him like a mother." Lorenz called this behavior *imprinting:* an instinctual form of learning in which, after a single encounter, an animal learns to recognize and trust a single individual. Imprinting is said to take place automatically and irreversibly during a brief critical period in the animal's early life.

Among goats and cows, certain rituals occur right after birth. If these rituals are prevented or interrupted, mother and offspring will not recognize each other. The results for the baby animal are devastating—physical withering and death, or abnormal development (Blauvelt, 1955; A. U. Moore, 1960; Scott, 1958). These findings raise questions for human beings.

Is there a critical period for forming the mother-infant bond? In 1976, two researchers said that the first hours after birth are crucial, that if mother and newborn are separated then, the **mother-infant bond**—the mother's feeling of close, caring connection with her newborn—may not develop normally (Klaus & Kennell, 1976). They reached this conclusion by comparing mothers and babies who had "extended contact" right after birth with mothers and babies who followed the usual hospital routine and were kept apart for long periods. Klaus and Kennell reported differences in bonding that persisted over the first few years of life.

This research inspired many hospitals to establish rooming-in policies that let mothers and babies remain together from birth throughout the hospital stay. Although developmentalists have not criticized these humane and welcome changes, follow-up research has not confirmed the existence of a critical time for bonding (Chess & Thomas, 1982; Lamb, 1982a, 1982b; Rutter, 1979b). While some mothers in some circumstances seemed to achieve closer bonding with their babies after early extended contact, no long-term effects were demonstrated. In 1982, Klaus and Kennell modified their original position, and in 1983 the researcher and psychiatrist Stella Chess wrote, "By now the whole 'critical period concept' has been generally discredited in human development theory" (p. 975).

This finding has relieved adoptive parents, and parents who have had to be separated from their infants after birth, of much unnecessary worry and guilt. Concern with bonding is still a vital issue, however, and some developmentalists urge research on groups at risk of problems in bonding (such as poor, young, or single mothers or fathers) to find out what factors other than early contact affect parent-child bonds (Lamb et al., 1983).

Happily, the human organism is resilient, and many babies overcome traumatic early experiences. As Chess (1983) has written, "The emotionally traumatized child is not doomed, the parents' early mistakes are not irrevocable, and our preventive and therapeutic intervention can make a difference at all age-periods" (p. 976).

What do babies need from their mothers? In one famous study, rhesus monkeys were separated from their mothers 6 to 12 hours after birth and were raised

(Thomas McAvoy/*LIFE Magazine* © Time Inc.)

Newly hatched chicks will follow and become attached to the first moving object they see. The ethologist Konrad Lorenz, who got newborn ducklings to "love him like a mother," called this behavior *imprinting*.

imprinting Instinctive form of learning in which, after a single encounter, an animal recognizes and trusts one particular individual.

mother-infant bond Mother's feeling of attachment to her child.

(Harlow Primate Laboratory/University of Wisconsin)

In a series of classic experiments, Harry Harlow and Margaret Harlow showed that food is not the most important way to a baby's heart. When infant rhesus monkeys could choose whether to go to a wire surrogate "mother" or to a terrycloth "mother," they spent more time clinging to the cloth mother, even if they were being fed by bottles connected to the wire mother.

in a laboratory. The infant monkeys were put into cages with one of two kinds of surrogate "mothers"—either a plain cylindrical wire-mesh form or a wire-mesh form covered with terry cloth. Some monkeys were fed from bottles connected to the wire "mothers"; others were fed from bottles connected to the cloth "mothers."

When the monkeys were allowed to spend time with either kind of "mother," they all spent more time clinging to the cloth surrogates—even those that were being fed by the wire ones. In an unfamiliar room, the babies "raised" by cloth surrogates showed more interest in exploring than those "raised" by wire surrogates, even when the surrogates were there. The monkeys apparently remembered the cloth surrogates better, too. After a year's separation, the "cloth-raised" monkeys eagerly ran to embrace the terry-cloth forms, whereas the "wire-raised" monkeys showed no interest in the wire forms (Harlow & Zimmerman, 1959). None of the monkeys in either group grew up normally, however (Harlow & Harlow, 1962); for example, none of them were able to mother their own offspring (Suomi & Harlow, 1972).

It is hardly surprising that a dummy mother would not provide the same kind of stimulation and opportunity for development as a live mother. These experiments show that (contrary to the Freudian emphasis on satisfying biological needs) feeding is not the most important thing mothers do for their babies. Mothering includes the comfort of close bodily contact and, in monkeys, the satisfaction of an innate need to cling. Surely, human infants also have needs that must be satisfied, or at least acted upon, if they are to grow up normally. A major task of psychology is to find out what those needs are.

Going beyond such one-way concepts as imprinting and the mother-infant bond, research over the past few decades has shifted its focus to the two-way process of *attachment* between babies and the important people in their lives.

Attachment: A Reciprocal Connection   When Julia is near, Jason looks at her, smiles at her, talks to her, and crawls after her. When she leaves, he cries; when she comes back, he squeals with joy. When he is frightened or unhappy, he clings to her. Jason has formed his first attachment to another person.

Attachment is an active, affectionate, reciprocal relationship between two people. In unscientific circles we might call it *love*. The interaction between the two people continues to strengthen their bond. It may be, says Ainsworth (1979), that "an essential part of the ground plan of the human species [is] for an infant to become attached to a mother figure" (p. 932)—who does not have to be the biological mother, but may be anyone who acts as the primary caregiver.

Carrying a baby close to the parent's body, as this Thai mother does, helps the baby become attached.

Studying attachment   The most common way to study attachment is by the eight-episode *strange situation* devised by Ainsworth, which calls forth behaviors involving closeness between an adult and a child (Ainsworth, Blehar, Waters, & Wall, 1978):

1   Mother and baby enter an unfamiliar room.
2   Mother sits down, and the baby is free to explore.
3   Unfamiliar adult enters.
4   Baby is left alone with the stranger.
5   Mother comes back, and the stranger leaves the room.
6   Mother leaves the baby alone in the room.
7   Stranger comes back instead of the mother.
8   Finally, stranger goes out as the mother returns. She encourages the baby to explore and play again and gives comfort if the baby seems to need it.

Almost all the research on attachment is based on this situation, and so the conclusions may be questionable. The strange situation is not only strange but artificial. It sets up a series of 3-minute staged episodes, asks mothers not to initiate interaction, and exposes children to repeated comings and goings and expects the children to pay attention to them. Attachment cuts across a wider range of behaviors; if it is to be measured sensitively, a more complex method may be needed. As Field says, "To understand attachment one must observe how the mother and infant interact and what they provide each other during natural, nonstressful situations" (T. Field, 1987, p. 858). Furthermore, as we will see, the strange situation may be an especially poor way to study attachment in children who are used to routine separation from the mother and to the presence of other caregivers (L. W. Hoffman, 1989).

Patterns of attachment between mother and child   Still, strange-situation research has yielded a number of findings that help us understand attachment. When Ainsworth and her colleagues observed 1-year-olds in the strange situation and also at home, they found three main patterns of attachment: *secure attachment* (the most common category, into which 66 percent of the babies fell), and two forms of anxious attachment—*avoidant attachment* (20 percent of the babies) and *ambivalent attachment* (12 percent).

Securely attached babies use their mothers as a base from which to explore. They are able to separate readily from the mother to take stock of their surroundings, so long as they can go back to her from time to time for reassurance. They are usually cooperative and relatively free from anger.

attachment   *Active, affectionate, reciprocal relationship between two people; their interaction reinforces and strengthens the bond. The term often refers to an infant's relationship with parents.*

strange situation   *Experimental procedure used to assess the attachment between a mother and her infant.*

secure attachment   *Attachment style in which an infant separates readily from the primary caregiver and actively seeks out the caregiver when he or she returns.*

(Jean-Claude Lejeune/Stock, Boston)

Securely attached children, as this toddler seems to be, can confidently explore the world away from their parents.

Securely attached 18-month-olds get around better on their own than anxiously attached toddlers (Cassidy, 1986). They are better at crossing open spaces; reaching for, playing with, and holding on to toys; and keeping themselves from tripping and falling. Perhaps, knowing that the mother is available, they do not have to focus energy and attention on keeping track of her—and can apply themselves to their environment.

Avoidant babies rarely cry when the mother leaves, and they avoid her upon her return. They fail to reach out in time of need and tend to be very angry. They do not like being held, but they like being put down even less.

Ambivalent (*resistant*) babies become anxious even before the mother leaves. They are extremely upset when she does go out, and they show their ambivalence when she comes back by seeking contact with her while at the same time resisting it by kicking or squirming. These babies explore less and are harder to comfort (Egeland & Farber, 1984).

A fourth pattern, *disorganized-disoriented*, has recently been identified (Main & Solomon, 1986). Babies with this pattern of attachment often show contradictory behaviors, greeting the mother brightly when she returns but then turning away, or approaching without looking at her. They seem confused and afraid and may represent the least secure pattern (O'Connor, Sigman, & Brill, 1987).

How is attachment established? To establish an attachment pattern, says Ainsworth, the baby builds up a "working model" of what to expect from the mother, and as long as the mother continues to act in basically the same way, the model holds up. If, say, Ellen changes the way she acts with Vicky—not just on one or two occasions, but consistently—Vicky can revise the model, and the nature of the attachment may well change. A baby's own personality—the tendency to cuddle, to cry, or to adapt to new situations—exerts an influence, too. The quality of attachment is influenced by what both mother and baby do and how they respond to each other.

What does the mother do? Ellen is affectionate, attentive, and responsive to Vicky's behavior, and secure attachment develops. The amount of positive interaction between the two is more important than the amount of time they spend together (Clarke-Stewart, 1977).

In the study by Ainsworth and colleagues (1978), several sharp differences in the quality of mothering appeared, and these were related to the patterns of attachment found in babies. The mothers of the securely attached babies were the most sensitive to their babies throughout the first year of life. They truly observed "demand" feeding, not only taking their cues from their babies to feed them, but also responding to the babies' signals to stop feeding or to speed up or slow the feeding (Ainsworth, 1979).

Furthermore, these mothers tended to hold their babies closer than the mothers in either of the other two groups. The value of body contact was confirmed by a study of 49 low-income mothers and infants in New York (Cunningham, Anisfeld, Casper, & Nozyce, 1987). Babies whose mothers had carried them on their bodies in soft baby carriers rather than in infant seats in the first months of life were more securely attached at 13 months of age.

The mothers of the avoidant babies were the angriest of all three groups of mothers. But they had difficulty expressing their feelings and shied away from close physical contact with their babies. Babies who were subjected to such physical distancing and rebuffs became angry in turn.

In a study of low-income, mostly single mothers (Egeland & Farber, 1984), the mothers of securely attached infants were responsive and skilled in caretaking, had positive feelings about themselves, "and, consequently, had more to give their infants" (p. 768). Mothers of avoidant babies were tense, irritable, and lacking in confidence and seemed uninterested in caring for their babies. By contrast, mothers of resistant babies were well-meaning but less capable; they tended to score lower on intelligence tests and to understand less how to meet their babies' needs. Such mothers could probably be helped by education and counseling.

The use of alcohol may affect a mother's ability to take care of and relate to her baby. In one study, the majority of babies of mothers who drank lightly or abstained were securely attached, while babies of moderate to heavy drinkers were more likely to be insecurely attached—most often in the disorganized-disoriented pattern (O'Connor et al., 1987).

"Mother love" is not automatic, nor is love enough to guarantee nurturance and a sound mother-child attachment. Many factors can affect the way a woman acts toward her baby, such as her reasons for having the baby, her experience and competence in child care, her emotional state and view of her own life, her relationship with the baby's father, her interest in work and other activities, her living circumstances, and the presence of other relatives in her home, like a supportive or intrusive grandmother (Egeland & Farber, 1984).

What does the baby do? Far from being a passive recipient of child rearing, Jason influences the people who take care of him. Virtually any activity on a baby's part that leads to a response from an adult is an attachment behavior: sucking, crying, smiling, clinging, choking, hiccuping, moving the body, changing the rhythm of breathing, sneezing, burping, and looking into the caregiver's eyes (Bowlby, 1958; M. P. M. Richards, 1971; Robson, 1967).

As early as the eighth week, Jason initiated some of these behaviors more toward his mother than toward anyone else. His overtures were successful when Julia responded warmly by showing delight and making frequent physical contact, while giving him freedom to explore (Ainsworth, 1969). Thus babies gain a sense of the consequence of their own actions—a feeling of power and confidence in their ability to bring about results.

An infant's early characteristics may be a strong predictor of attachment. Many resistant babies, for example, have had problems as neonates—about half, in one study (Ainsworth et al., 1978). Many showed developmental lags that may have made them harder to care for. However, no infant is doomed to be anxiously attached; one study, for example, found that prematurity is not associated with impaired attachment (Macey, Harmon, & Easterbrooks, 1987). "As in any relationship, the partner's responses are critical" (Egeland & Farber, 1984, p. 769). It is the interaction between mother and infant that determines the quality of attachment.

Changes in attachment Although attachment patterns normally remain set, they may be altered by outside events (Ainsworth, 1982). In one study, almost half of a group of 43 middle-class babies changed attachment pattern between the ages of 1 year and 19 months (R. A. Thompson, Lamb, & Estes, 1982). The changes were associated with changes in family and caregiving circumstances, including mothers' taking jobs outside the home and providing other kinds of care for their children. Changes that affected the babies' everyday lives "forced a renegotiation . . . of the mother-infant relationship" (p. 148). The changes were not all in one direction: some of the babies became less securely attached, but most of the babies who changed attachment pattern became more securely attached.

What made the difference? Although a mother's caretaking skills are important in forming the initial attachment, her emotional expressions—the joy she shows in feeding or bathing her baby—may help the attachment pattern evolve, especially during the second year of life. Some initially resistant infants of young, immature mothers become more secure as their mothers gain experience, skill, and more positive attitudes (Egeland & Farber, 1984).

What are the long-term effects of attachment? Common sense might make us think that infants who are very closely attached to their mothers will grow into children who are very dependent on adults, but research says that this is not so. Paradoxically, the stronger a child's attachment to the nurturing adult, the easier it is for the child to leave that adult. Children who are secure in their attachment do not need to stay close to the mother. Their freedom to explore enables them to try new things, attack problems in new ways, and have more positive attitudes toward the unfamiliar.

These effects may persist for at least 5 years after birth. When securely attached 18-month-olds were followed up at age 2, they turned out to be more enthusiastic, persistent, cooperative, and, in general, effective than children who had been insecurely attached babies (Matas, Arend, & Sroufe, 1978). At age 3, securely attached children get more positive responses from their playmates than anxiously attached children (J. L. Jacobson & Wille, 1986). At age 3½, securely attached children are described as "peer leaders, socially involved, attracting the attention of others, curious, and actively engaged in their surroundings" (Waters, Wippman, & Sroufe, 1979). At the age of 4 or 5 years, they are more curious and more competent (Arend, Gove, & Sroufe, 1979).

One study of 4- and 5-year-olds found that those who had been *securely* attached at 12 and 18 months were most likely to be independent, seeking help from their nursery school teachers only when they needed it. The children who had been *anxiously* attached earlier, however, were now more likely to be so dependent on their teachers that their need for contact, approval, and attention interfered with their ability to form relationships with other children and to learn how to do things appropriate for their age (Sroufe, Fox, & Pancake, 1983).

Conclusions about long-term effects of attachment are controversial, however. A recent review of the literature concluded that the association between attachment in infancy and development in childhood is weak and inconclusive (Lamb, 1987). What is seen in older children may very well stem from parent-child interaction after infancy. In many cases, of course, interaction patterns are set early and remain fairly consistent over the years, and it is hard to tell at what time they are most influential. We will probably learn more about attachment as researchers use other measures besides the strange situation and as they integrate new attachment patterns into their research designs.

Effects of other caregivers on mother-child attachment A decade ago, most babies whose mothers went to work were taken care of at home (Hofferth, 1979). Today, about 55 percent of such infants (including some as young as 3 weeks) receive care outside the home. This is especially significant, since 1987 was a turning point—the first year when more mothers of babies under 1 year old were out working than home with their infants (U. S. Bureau of the Census, 1988; see Figure 7-1). (We will discuss this again in Chapter 13.) Although babies are placed in various settings, including licensed and unlicensed day care centers and family or group day care homes, most of these infants spend weekdays in the homes of relatives or friends (Gamble & Zigler, 1986; U. S. Bureau of the Census, 1987; Young & Zigler, 1986).

Observers of these trends have raised questions about the effects of such care on babies' attachment to the mother. The effects may depend on many factors, including the mother's satisfaction with her marriage; whether she works full time or part time and why she works; the baby's age, sex, and temperament; and the kind and quality of care the baby gets.

The first year of life seems the most critical. When babies from stable families receive high-quality care, most studies report optimistic findings (L. W. Hoffman, 1989). On the other hand, when infants receive unstable or poor-

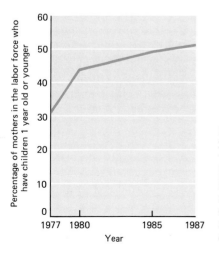

FIGURE 7-1
Since 1987, more mothers of babies under 1 year old have been in the work force. This has meant that many of these babies have been cared for by people besides the mother. Most studies report that good, stable care does not interfere with mother-child attachment, but that poor, unstable care does. (*Source: New York Times*, 1987.)

quality day care, they are more likely to avoid their mothers and to have emotional and social problems later on. These effects are worse when there is a poor fit between the mother's personality and the baby's, when the family is under great stress, and when the mother is not responsive to the baby (Gamble & Zigler, 1986; Young & Zigler, 1986).

Some recent controversial research suggests that extensive substitute care during the first year may be detrimental for some children, especially boys. When 67 children whose mothers had been at home during the first year were compared with 82 children who had been taken care of by someone else for 10 or more hours a week, beginning before the age of 9 months and continuing through the first year, some differences appeared (Belsky & Rovine, 1988). Most (57 percent) of the babies receiving 20 or more hours of care per week still formed a secure attachment to the mother, but some of the babies—most of them boys—who received this much substitute care were insecurely attached to their mothers, unless they were cared for by their fathers. Baby boys who received more than 35 hours a week of substitute care tended to be insecurely attached to their fathers as well, and the most vulnerable had been "difficult babies" at 3 months of age and had mothers who were not satisfied with their marriage, were insensitive to other people, and had strong career motivation. Other research has found that working mothers who are warm, accepting, and available when they are home still have securely attached 18-month-old sons (Benn, 1986). It seems, then, that we cannot make a blanket statement about day care without taking into account specific characteristics of the people, the kind of care, and the situation.

In a review of recent studies of parent-infant attachment, Lois W. Hoffman (1989) concluded that if there is a relationship between a mother's employment during her baby's first year and the baby's attachment security, it is weak, since most studies find that most babies of mothers employed full time are securely attached. It is possible that a mother's working outside the home during the first few months of the baby's life is a stress which can interfere with attachment when combined with other stresses but in itself does not make a difference. Another possibility is that babies who *seem* insecurely attached in the strange situation are really showing independence. Because they are used to the mother's comings and goings, they are not anxious but are doing what works for them on a day-to-day basis: showing an "avoidant" pattern in an appropriate way.

The time when the mother first goes out to work seems to matter. One study found that 18-month-old boys whose mothers started work when the boys were 6 to 12 months old were more likely to be insecurely attached than boys whose mothers went to work earlier (Benn, 1986). If a mother has a choice about going back to work, it is probably best to go when the baby is under 6 months old, between 12 and 18 months old, or more than 2½ years old. These seem to be ages when, for a variety of reasons, children react better to changes in situation (Olds, 1989).

The mother-child attachment is important, but it is not babies' only significant tie. The mother may be the only one who can suckle an infant, but fathers, grandparents, siblings, friends, and babysitters can also comfort and play with infants and give them a sense of security. (See Box 7-3.) Fathers are especially important in a child's world.

BOX 7-3 ■ PROFESSIONAL VOICES

MARGARET MEAD

MEAD: The best kind of care for babies is an individual person who pays attention to them. It does not have to be the mother. Ideally it ought to be more than one person—about six people. The worst thing is just having the mother boxed up with the baby 24 hours a day, which nobody ever meant to have happen in the whole history of the human race.

The essential thing with an infant and a child who's just learning to talk and to understand the world is somebody who remembers what happened yesterday. The minute you have a large institution, you have a big turnover in personnel. So one day something happens, and the person who comes in the next day doesn't know about it. Or the child comes to the center with a favorite little rag that he carries around, and the next person puts it in the laundry and it's never seen again. There's simply no guaranteeable continuity in the things that matter most in giving a child a sense of security.

Family-based care is better. The woman who takes three or four children—who wants to take them and enjoys it—is there every day; she knows what happened yesterday. You have a baby who's just discovered—or thinks he's discovered—that "boo-boo" means bedroom slippers. A great discovery! He says "boo-boo"; he gets his bedroom slippers. Next day he says "boo-boo," and nothing happens. And this begins a life of distrust and uncertainty.

I agree with Erikson. Trust in the infant and the little child under 2 is the important thing.

Community-based care is the thing we want. We want Grandmother in the community, too. Somebody's grandmother. We need to build the community so she can live there—provide one-room flats, which are not a lot of work, not a lot of steps, within an easy walk to the store. The isolated mother, especially the single parent, who sits home with a baby without friends or neighbors—this is probably the most disastrous situation. And this is happening in suburbs everywhere. When you build the one-class, one-income suburb, with one age group, you don't have any old people. Everybody's the same age, with the same problems.

We should be providing safe day care—if necessary 12 hours a day—for the mothers who have no other recourse. If they have to work, they should work under a welfare program that will treat them as individuals, not just dependents. Then we should be absolutely certain there's no baby tied to a bedpost, there's no baby left for hours with no one there. Day care should be subsidized by the government. It ought to be available like other community services such as light, fire department, ambulance, and hospital. This would ensure the care of well children as well as sick ones.

Source: From an interview with S. W. Olds, December 20, 1977, New York City; *photo:* Wide World.

The Father's Role

Charles, who plays a large role in Vicky's life, is one of a new generation of fathers. Television commercials now show fathers diapering and bathing their children; stores sell strollers with long, man-sized handles; and airports install diaper-changing tables in men's rest rooms. Psychologists are devoting more attention to the father's role in children's lives, a role that generally used to be ignored or minimized. The findings from their research underscore the importance of sensitive, responsive fathering. Bonds and attachments form between fathers and children during the first year of life, and fathers go on to exert a strong influence on children's social, emotional, and cognitive development.

When Do Infants Form Attachments to Their Fathers? Many fathers form close attachments to their babies soon after birth. Proud new fathers are often preoccupied with newborns, a phenomenon called *engrossment* (M. Greenberg & Morris, 1974). Babies contribute to this bond by doing the things all normal babies do—opening their eyes, grasping their fathers' fingers, and moving in their fathers' arms.

Fathers and children often form close bonds during the first year of life. This father is likely to go on to exert a strong influence on his child's social, emotional, and cognitive development.

Babies develop attachments to their fathers at about the same time as to their mothers. In one study, babies 1 year old or older protested about equally when separated from their fathers and from their mothers, while babies 9 months old or younger did not protest when separated from either parent (Kotelchuck, 1973). When both parents were present, just over half were more likely to go to their mothers, but almost half showed as much or more attachment to their fathers.

Another study found that while babies prefer either the mother or the father to a stranger, they usually prefer their mothers to their fathers, especially when they are upset (Lamb, 1981). This is probably because mothers typically care for babies more than fathers do. It will be interesting to see whether the nature of father-infant attachment changes in families in which the father is the primary caregiver.

How Do Fathers Act with Babies?   The earliest studies on father-infant interactions tried to find out how much time fathers spent with their babies, but more recent research has emphasized what fathers *do* with them. Despite a long-held belief that women are biologically predisposed to respond more sensitively to babies' cues, research suggests that there may be "no biologically based sex differences in responsiveness to infants" (Lamb, 1981, p. 463). Fathers speak "motherese" (see Chapter 6); they adjust the feeding pace to the baby's cues; and when they see crying or smiling infants on a television monitor they show the same kinds of physiological responses (like changes in heart rate and blood pressure) as mothers (Lamb, 1981).

Still, fathers are typically not as responsive as mothers. Societal expectations have led them to take a less active role in child rearing, and the crucial factor that determines how sensitive an adult will be to a baby's cues seems to be the amount of care that the adult gives a baby (Zelazo, Kotelchuck, Barber & David, 1977).

In our culture, fathers *care for* their babies less than they *play with* them (Clarke-Stewart, 1978; Easterbrooks & Goldberg, 1984; Kotelchuck, 1975; Rendina & Dickerscheid, 1976). And whatever they do, they tend to do differently. Playing with children, fathers toss infants up in the air and wrestle with toddlers; mothers typically play gentler games and sing and read to their children (Lamb, 1977; Parke & Tinsley, 1981).

What Influences Fathers' Involvement with Their Infants?   The degree to which a father cares for and plays with his baby depends on his own background, his marriage, and the attitudes of society. The single most important influence may be his wife's feelings, which have probably been influenced by her relationship with her own father (Radin, 1981b). The mother seems to serve as the "gate-keeper" of her husband's involvement with the baby, both in her direct actions and in the way she talks about the father when he is not home (Yogman, 1984).

Many other forces can also have an impact. If the mother is sick or the baby is premature, the father may assume a larger role in child care to help his wife. On the other hand, if he is sick or has job problems, he is likely to do less.

One factor that has assumed more importance in recent years is mothers' employment. Working mothers stimulate their babies more than at-home mothers, play with their babies more than their husbands do, and still typically spend more time taking care of their babies than the fathers (Pedersen, Cain, & Zaslow, 1982). But one study found that fathers who were their babies' primary caretakers behaved more like mothers than like "typical" fathers (T. M. Field, 1978). It seems likely, then, that society's differing expectations for fathers and mothers strongly influence how they act with their children.

What Is the Significance of the Father-Infant Relationship?   The differences between Ellen and Charles, both biological and social, make each one's role in the family unique—and each one's contribution special. For example, the physical way in which fathers typically play with babies offers excitement and a challenge to overcome fears. During the first 2 years, Vicky smiles at and "talks" to Charles more, probably because he is more of a novelty than Ellen (Lamb, 1981).

In one study, a group of toddlers—two-thirds of whose mothers were employed outside the home—showed the benefits of the father's involvement in caring for them and playing with them, especially when the father's attitudes toward the child were sensitive and positive. The father's behavior had a particularly strong influence on competence in problem solving, and although the mother's behavior had more impact on attachment, the father's involvement helped to make boys' attachment to the mother more secure (Easterbrooks & Goldberg, 1984).

Fathers—along with mothers—also seem to play an important part in helping toddlers become more independent. In an experiment on the interaction of forty-four 2-year-old boys and girls with their fathers and their mothers (who were the primary caregivers), parents were to get their toddlers to put away toys and refrain from touching a tape recorder. Since both parents were quite similar in the ways they dealt with their children, the researchers concluded that fathers do not play the part of disciplinarian in the family, but act in far less stereotyped ways (Yogman, Cooley, & Kindlon, 1988).

As was noted earlier in this chapter, adults behave differently toward babies they think are boys and babies they think are girls. Fathers behave *more* differently toward girls and boys than mothers do, even during a baby's first year (M. E. Snow, Jacklin, & Maccoby, 1983). By the second year, the difference intensifies; fathers talk to and spend more time with their sons than their daughters (Lamb, 1981). For these reasons, fathers more than mothers seem to promote the development of gender identity and *gender-typing*—the process by

gender-typing   *Process by which a person learns a gender role.*

which children learn behavior that their culture considers appropriate for their sex (P. Bronstein, 1988).

Some research also suggests that fathers may influence their sons' cognitive development more than mothers. The more attention a father pays to his baby son, the brighter, more alert, more inquisitive, and happier that baby is likely to be at 5 or 6 months (Pedersen, Rubenstein, & Yarrow, 1973). Baby boys raised without fathers are cognitively behind those raised in two-parent families, even when the mother does not seem to behave differently (Pedersen, Rubenstein, & Yarrow, 1979). This may be further evidence of the father's importance in cognitive development (Radin, 1988)—or it may reveal economic or social disadvantages of growing up in a single-parent family.

The very fact that a child's two parents have two different personalities—no matter what their personalities are like—influences development in unknown ways. We do not know how Jason is affected by learning that the same kind of action will produce different reactions from his mother and father. It seems clear, though, that anyone who plays a large part in a baby's day-to-day life will have an important influence.

Brothers and Sisters—or No Siblings

If you have brothers or sisters, your relationships with them are likely to be the longest-lasting you'll ever have. This is especially true today, when few people spend their whole life in one place among the same group of neighbors. Bonds between siblings are unique; they begin in infancy and persist into old age. Siblings are the people who share your roots and who probably deal with you more objectively than your parents and more candidly than virtually anyone else you'll ever know. Not surprisingly, siblings are a major influence on one's life. Not having siblings also influences a person's life. An only child has experiences that are often very different from that of a child with brothers and sisters (see Chapter 10 for a discussion of the only child).

Birth Order The earliest interest in siblings revolved around the order in which children arrived in the family. The most clear-cut findings about birth-order effects concern the high achievement of firstborn and only children, who are more likely to score higher on IQ tests, to do better in school in general, to be National Merit scholars, to go to college, to earn a Ph.D., and to appear in *Who's Who* (Belmont & Marolla, 1973; Helmreich, 1968; Sutton-Smith, 1982). Middle children, on the other hand, tend to achieve less (Bayer, 1967).

Why should these differences exist? One theory is based on factors related to birth order, such as the number of children in the family and the spacing between them (Zajonc, 1976, 1983). In this model, a person's intelligence is affected by the average intelligence level in the family. The term *intelligence* here refers not to IQ, but to general knowledge and achievement. Thus, an adult with an IQ of 100 is considered more intelligent than a 5-year-old with an IQ of 160. By this standard, the more children there are in a family, the more people of lower intelligence there are to bring the average down. Moreover, if siblings are very close together, they hinder one another. According to this theory, firstborn children, only children, and children spaced far from their closest siblings probably do best because their parents spend more time with them, talk to them more, play with them more, and expect more from them.

In a study testing this model, researchers compared 176 adopted children with 143 children being raised by their biological parents in 101 middle- to upper-middle-class families (Grotevant, Scarr, & Weinberg, 1977).

The IQs of the children who were not adopted were closer to their parents' IQs than those of the adopted children were to the IQs of their adoptive parents. The researchers concluded that while Zajonc's generalizations apply to large groups of people and can be used to predict population trends, they do not apply to individual families because they do not take into account a particular child's genetic endowment and specific environmental influences. Genetic variance seemed more important than the combination of birth order, family size, and spacing of children.

However, this conclusion does not explain the higher-than-average achievements of firstborn and only children. Mendel's laws of heredity are not altered by birth order, and thus it is hard to believe that firstborn children consistently receive a better genetic endowment than later-borns.

Early Sibling Relationships   The birth of a younger sibling radically changes an older child's life. The mother, for example, is likely to play less with the older child, be less sensitive to the older child's interests, give more orders, have more confrontations, and initiate fewer conversations and games (Dunn & Kendrick, 1982). However, the extent of these changes often depends on the older child's personality. Some children take the initiative themselves—coming up to the mother to start a conversation or asking her to play a game—while other children respond by withdrawing. The "initiators" may have less of a problem with sibling rivalry, because they have found a way to salvage their closeness with the mother; the withdrawers, losing more, resent the usurper more.

The interaction between siblings is complex, swathed in layers of contradictory emotions. Babies begin interacting with their older siblings to a significant degree after the first 6 months, and 1-year-olds spend almost as much time with their siblings as with their mothers and far more time than with their fathers (Dunn & Kendrick, 1982; Lawson & Ingleby, 1974). In many societies around the world, including the United States, older siblings assume some responsibility for taking care of babies (Dunn, 1985).

What is the ideal spacing between siblings? Psychologists disagree. One believes that the hostility and aggression of a child who is only 1 year older than a sibling will be harmful to the baby's development (B. L. White, 1975). Another contends that close age spacing will encourage closeness and companionship and will help children learn how to deal with peer competition from a very early age (R. Gardner, 1973). And a third points out that children under 5 years old are more likely than older children to be upset by the birth of a sibling (Dunn, 1985).

What do young siblings do when they are together? In one study, researchers observed 34 pairs of same-sex siblings in middle-class families. The younger ones averaged 20 months; their brothers and sisters were 1 to 4 years older. All the siblings affected each other. The older siblings more often initiated both positive and negative behaviors, while the younger ones imitated more. Older boys were more aggressive; older girls were more likely to share, cooperate, and hug. Among children with different-sex siblings, however, a follow-up study found no sex-based difference in aggression (Abramovitch, Corter & Pepler, 1980.) The researchers described interaction between siblings as "rich and varied, clearly not based predominantly on rivalry" (Abramovitch, Corter, & Lando, 1979, p. 1003).

Babies and toddlers become closely attached to their older brothers and sisters, especially when, as with these Thai children, the older siblings assume a large measure of care for the younger ones.

Young children commonly develop feelings of attachment to their older brothers and sisters, as one 1-year-old showed by referring to her 4- and 6-year-old sisters as "my choo-jun" ("my children"). Infants get upset when their siblings go away, greet them when they come back, prefer them as playmates, and go to them for security when a stranger enters the room. Younger siblings take great joy in imitating older ones (Dunn, 1983; R. B. Stewart, 1983).

Children under the age of 3 also hug and kiss their little sisters and brothers and try to help and comfort them when they are upset. They also tease and annoy them, and by the second year the younger siblings are teasing and annoying the older ones. Often the relationship is out of balance, with one sibling (more often the younger) acting friendly and the other one being hostile and aggressive. When this happens, we see how siblings create very different environments for one another (Dunn & Kendrick, 1982; Pepler, Corter, & Abramovitch, 1982).

The environment that siblings create for each other affects not only their future relationship but each one's personality development as well (Dunn, 1983). For example, when little girls imitate their big brothers, they may take on some characteristics commonly thought of as masculine, and vice versa. And 4-year-olds who have close relationships with their siblings are better able to understand another person's viewpoint than 4-year-olds who do not (Light, 1973), but it is not clear which comes first. (See Box 7-4.)

BOX 7-4 ■ THE EVERYDAY WORLD

HELPING CHILDREN ADJUST TO A NEW BABY

Jason, now almost 3, cannot believe that the new baby has come to stay. After his mother has been busy for as long as he can bear, he goes up to her and says, "Baby bye-bye." "It all comes down to love and hate, doesn't it?" a mother remarked while discussing the ambivalence of her firstborn toward a younger child (Dunn, 1985, p. 11).

Children react in a variety of ways to the arrival of a new baby. Some regress to earlier behaviors like sucking their thumb, wetting their pants, asking to nurse at breast or bottle, or using baby talk. Others become silent and refuse to talk or play. Some, like Jason, openly suggest getting rid of the baby—by returning it to the hospital or, more directly, flushing it down the toilet. And some take pride in being the "big ones," who can dress themselves, use the potty, eat with the grown-ups, and help take care of the baby.

Sibling rivalry, of course, goes back to Cain and Abel. Alfred Adler (1928), one of Freud's early disciples, explained it by maintaining that the "dethroning" of the first child was bound to produce feelings of competition. Affection between siblings is also an old story, and while sibling rivalry is often present, so are genuine affection and caring behavior (Dunn, 1985).

Research on sibling relationships has uncovered the following:

■ The more confrontational the relationship between the mother and the firstborn before the birth of the sibling, the more upset the older child is likely to be.

■ If the mother becomes fatigued or depressed after the birth of the new baby, the firstborn is more likely to become withdrawn.

■ Fortunately, most behavioral problems with older siblings disappear by the time the younger one reaches 8 months of age (Dunn, 1985).

■ Children adjust better to the birth of a new baby if their fathers devote extra time and attention to them to make up for the mother's sudden involvement with the new baby (Lamb, 1978).

While there is hardly any research on encouragement of positive attitudes, popular wisdom—influenced by the writings of the pediatrician Benjamin Spock (1976; Spock & Rothenberg, 1985) and others—is that parents should prepare the older child ahead of time for the birth of the new baby and make many changes in the first child's life well beforehand (like moving into another bedroom, giving up the crib for a big bed, or going to nursery school) to minimize any feeling of being displaced. Parents should accept as normal the child's anxiety and jealousy—while being careful to protect the new baby. They should also talk to the older child, emphasizing the individuality of each person in the family and encouraging the older child to play with and help the baby.

Stranger Anxiety and Separation Anxiety

At 8 months, Vicky suddenly seems like a different baby. She used to be friendly, smiling at strangers and cooing whenever someone—anyone—was around. But now she grows quiet and suspiciously eyes a strange face. It used to be easy to leave her with a babysitter. But now Vicky howls when Ellen or Charles is out of sight.

Vicky is showing two new anxieties—*stranger anxiety,* a wariness of unknown people; and *separation anxiety,* distress when a familiar caregiver leaves. These are usually normal, though not universal, and there are a number of hypotheses about their development and significance.

Cognitive Factors   There may be a cognitive explanation for stranger anxiety and separation anxiety. Jerome Kagan (1979) suggests that the baby's improved memory can explain the development of both emotional events. Children can now recall people and things they cannot see. Thus Vicky becomes attached to Charles because, even in his absence, she remembers the warmth and good feelings she experiences when he is with her. She cries when he leaves the room because she remembers what it was like when he was there—but cannot yet

stranger anxiety
Wariness of strange people and places often shown by infants in the second half of the first year.

separation anxiety
Distress shown by an infant when a familiar caregiver leaves.

"Please, Jason. Don't you want to grow up to be an autonomous person?"

Jason may not want to stay with his baby-sitter for two reasons: he feels "separation anxiety" as his parents leave and "stranger anxiety" toward the unfamiliar teenager. His reaction is normal and not an omen of a lifetime of dependence.

predict what it will be like when he is *not* there. She is at a stage of cognitive development when she tries to anticipate her future—but is not yet able to.

This interpretation helps to explain why it is rare for babies in many different cultures to show distress upon being left with an unfamiliar person or in an unfamiliar place before the age of 7 months; why the likelihood of their being disturbed rises to a peak at 13 to 15 months; and why separation anxiety declines after that, becoming quite rare by age 3.

Attachment occurs and separation anxiety emerges between 8 and 12 months of age—about the time when babies develop object permanence (see Chapter 6). Thus, circumstances which threaten a baby's confidence that the mother still exists seem to increase separation anxiety. Babies who are playing happily will begin to cry if the mother leaves the room and shuts the door (Ainsworth & Bell, 1970), but not if she leaves without shutting the door (J. N. Anderson, 1972; Corter, 1976; Corter, Rheingold, & Eckerman, 1972).

Attachment-Related Factors   It has been observed that the more securely attached babies are, the less separation anxiety they show; perhaps they have learned to trust their parents to return (Ainsworth, 1982; J. L. Jacobson & Wille, 1984). On the other hand, securely attached infants tend to be warier of strangers than other babies are. Why is this? It may simply be a matter of temperament (see below). Or it may be that if babies are given enough time to get used to a new person while their mothers are present, secure infants will play with a stranger as readily as they might explore any new experience. But if a stranger tries to pick them up while the mother is out of sight or before they have had a chance to settle down after her return, they may stiffen and scream. It is the less securely attached infant who will readily go to a stranger while in distress from being left alone (Sroufe, 1977). Many avoidant babies would rather be picked up by a stranger than by their mothers (Harmon, Suwalsky, & Klein, 1979).

Other Factors   Circumstances, as we have just seen, affect a child's reaction. Sometimes babies react against being disturbed: 40 percent of a group of 1-year-olds reacted negatively when picked up by a stranger, but so did 25 percent when picked up by their mothers (R. P. Klein & Durfee, 1975). Children also rarely like to be taken by surprise and are more likely to protest against a stranger who swoops down on them unexpectedly. Babies are more likely to accept a stranger's approach if their parents are present—and if their parents talk to them positively about the unknown person (Feinman & Lewis, 1983). And they are more likely to welcome a strange child than a strange adult (Brooks & Lewis, 1976; M. Lewis & Brooks, 1974).

Temperament is another factor; some current research suggests that it may be the major factor. Easy children are usually only mildly upset by strangers, if at all, and recover quickly; difficult and slow-to-warm-up children become more disturbed and remain upset longer (A. Thomas & Chess, 1977). Still another factor is past experience: babies raised around many adults show less stranger anxiety than those who know just a few (Schaffer & Emerson, 1964; Spiro, 1958).

Social Referencing

How Babies Use Adults as Resources   If you have ever cast a sidelong glance at a formal dinner table to see which fork the person next to you was using, you have read another person's nonverbal signals to get information on how to act. Babies learn how to do this at a very early age.

In the phenomenon known as *social referencing,* one person forms an understanding of an ambiguous situation by seeking out another person's perception of it. Since babies are confronted by many situations they do not understand and do not know how to respond to, the ability to "read" the emotional and cognitive reactions of important people in their lives is valuable. Babies develop social referencing sometime after 6 months of age, when they begin to judge the possible consequences of events, imitate complex behaviors, and distinguish among and react to various emotional expressions. They show such referencing by the way they look at their caregivers when they encounter a new person or toy (Feinman & Lewis, 1983).

social referencing
Understanding an ambiguous situation by seeking out another person's perception of it.

Whom Do Babies Reference?   How do infants learn which strangers they can trust and which they cannot? At first, they base their opinions on their mothers' (or other caregivers') reactions. In one study, the mothers of 10-month-old babies who were approached by an unfamiliar young woman spoke to their babies either positively or neutrally about the woman, or spoke to the woman herself positively or neutrally, or remained silent (Feinman & Lewis, 1983). When the mothers spoke positively to the babies about the stranger, the babies—especially those with an easy temperament—were friendlier to her than in any of the other situations, and were more likely to lean toward her from the high chair and offer her a toy.

Most of the research on social referencing has focused on mothers, but babies also look for emotional and informational cues from their fathers (Dickstein & Parke, 1988) and from other friendly adults (Klinnert, Emde, Butterfield, & Campos, 1986).

Social Referencing and the Visual Cliff   A study using the visual cliff (described in Chapter 5) found that when the "drop" looked very shallow or very deep, 1-year-olds did not look toward their mothers; they were able to judge for themselves whether they would cross over or not. But when the "drop" was to a depth that the babies were uncertain about, they paused at the "edge," looked down, and then looked up to their mothers' faces. Meanwhile, the mother posed one of several expressions—fear, anger, interest, happiness, or sadness. The particular emotion influenced the babies' actions: most of those whose mothers showed joy or interest crossed the "drop"; very few whose mothers looked angry or afraid crossed over; and an intermediate number of those whose mothers looked sad crossed (Sorce, Emde, Campos, & Klinnert, 1985). Apparently, social referencing to facial expressions is done most often in puzzling situations.

Disturbances in Family Relationships: Separation from Parents

The attachments that children form with their parents exert a major influence on the children's physical, intellectual, personality, and social development. When these attachments are disrupted because a child is separated from the parents or has a painful relationship with them, the consequences can be grave.

What happens to infants who are deprived of their parents early in life? This depends on why child and parent are apart, what kind of care the child gets from other people, how old the child is, and what the child's family relationships are like both before and after the separation.

Institutionalization   When orphanages were the most common way of taking care of children whose parents were dead or unable to care for them, many of the babies in orphanages died in the first year (R. A. Spitz, 1945). Children who were institutionalized for long periods often showed a drop in intellectual functioning and also suffered from major psychiatric problems. The devastating effect of institutionalizing healthy children for long periods of time is termed *hospitalism* (as opposed to *hospitalization*, which refers to the hospital care of an ill child).

In a classic study, René Spitz (1945, 1946) compared 134 institutionalized babies under age 1 with 34 home-reared children. Those who were being raised in one institution (known as "Nursery") were well developed and normal, like the home-reared babies. But those in a second institution ("Founding Home") were below average in height and weight, were highly susceptible to disease, and showed a drop in developmental quotient (from 124 to 75 after 1 year, and then down to 45 by the end of the second year). The nature of these differences was especially surprising, since the babies in "Nursery" were the offspring of delinquent girls, many of whom were emotionally disturbed or retarded, while those in "Foundling Home" came from a variety of backgrounds, many quite favorable.

The most significant difference between the homes was the amount of personal attention the babies got. In "Nursery," all received full-time care from their own mothers or from individual full-time substitutes. In "Foundling Home," eight children shared one nurse.

Spitz's studies pointed out the urgency of providing foster care that would approach "good mothering" as closely as possible. His work hastened the trend toward placement in foster homes and much earlier adoption (Stone, Smith, & Murphy, 1973). Even though other studies have confirmed Spitz's findings—that children do not suffer impairment of general intelligence in well-run institutions where they have a variety of stimulating experiences, including a great deal of conversation (Rutter, 1979)—institutional care is still a form of social deprivation.

Children who live in institutions—even good ones—during the first 2 years of life are likely to have trouble making friends and forming close relationships, a problem that children placed in foster homes are less likely to have (Rutter, 1979b). The major problem, apparently, is not separation from the parents and not the presence of several caregivers, but frequent changes in caregivers, which prevents the formation of a close attachment to a specific person.

The decline in responsiveness in institutionalized infants may appear because babies are not stimulated enough or are reacting to the unfamiliar people and place. However, babies who get more attention and stimulation from a "substitute mother" (Clarke-Stewart, 1977) can make dramatic gains, especially in vocalization. Six-month-old babies who were "mothered" by a psychologist all day, 5 days a week for 2 months, were much more likely to smile and babble than babies getting the usual institutional care (Rheingold, 1956).

In a classic study of enrichment that yielded striking long-term results, 13 apparently retarded 2-year-olds were moved from an orphanage to an institution for mentally retarded young adults. The adult patients doted on them and spent much time playing with, talking to, and training "their" children. When the children grew up, all 13 functioned in the community, married, and had normal children of their own. Four attended college. By contrast, a control group of 12 youngsters who had stayed in the orphanage until later placement had a much lower average IQ, and 4 remained in institutions (Skeels, 1966; Skeels & Dye, 1939). Thus, we see that individual attention from warm, affectionate people can compensate considerably for the absence of a close mother-child relationship.

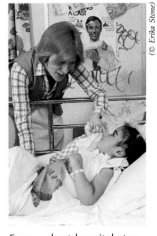

Even a short hospital stay can upset small children, but familiar faces and familiar routines can help children overcome the stress of the unfamiliar situation.

Hospitalization   Even short-term hospital stays can be disturbing to small children, of course. In another classic analysis, John Bowlby (1960) found that hospitalized 15- to 30-month-old infants go through three fairly well-defined stages of separation anxiety:

1   *Protest:* Babies actively try to get the mother back by crying, shaking the crib, and throwing themselves about; they continually expect the mother to return.
2   *Despair:* Babies move less actively, cry monotonously or intermittently, and become withdrawn and inactive; because they are so quiet, it is often assumed that they have accepted the situation positively.
3   *Detachment:* Babies accept care from a succession of nurses and are willing to

eat, play with toys, smile, and be sociable; but when their mothers visit, they remain apathetic and even turn away. Children between 6 months and 4 years old are most likely to react this way, but not all children show this degree of disturbance (Rutter, 1979b).

When a child needs to be hospitalized, steps can be taken to reduce stress. Many hospitals now allow parents to stay with the child, even sleeping overnight. Daily visiting by other family members, limiting the number of caregivers, and maintaining familiar routines help allay the strangeness of the situation (Rutter, 1979b).

Arranging "happy separations" ahead of time can take some of the sting out of a hospital stay, too. Children who are used to being left with grandparents or sitters or who have stayed overnight at a friend's house are less likely to be upset by having to go to the hospital (Stacey, Dearden, Pill, & Robinson, 1970).

Other Temporary Separations   As we have seen, even temporary replacement of both a child's primary caretakers and the child's familiar environment can produce severe emotional disturbance, at least on a short-term basis. But young children can be separated from their parents for long periods of time with few long-term ill effects (Rutter, 1971).

Children who are separated from one parent for at least 4 consecutive weeks are no more likely to develop a psychiatric or behavioral disorder than children who have never been separated (Rutter, 1971). It does not matter how old a child is at the time of separation or which parent is absent.

Children who are separated from *both* parents are more likely to be disturbed, but it is not only the *fact* of separation that matters but the *reason* for it. When the separation results from family discord or deviance, children are 4 times more likely to show antisocial behavior than when the separation is due to vacation or physical illness. Children separated from both parents are more likely to become disturbed when the parents' marriage is rated very poor than when it is rated good or fair. Some separation experience seems beneficial, since "children used to brief separations of a happy kind are less distressed by *unhappy* separations such as hospital admission" (Rutter, 1971, p. 237).

One of the most damaging family disturbances comes about when parents and children are *not* separated. If parents neglect or abuse their children, the children's physical, intellectual, and emotional development suffers. Since such mistreatment is largely physical, we will discuss it in Chapter 8.

Development of Sociability

CHANGES IN SOCIABILITY

Although the family is the center of a baby's social world, infants and (to an even greater degree) toddlers also show interest in people outside the home, especially people their own size. Since more babies now spend time in day care settings where they come into contact with other babies, psychologists have become more interested in studying the way infants and toddlers react to each other.

As early as 18 hours after birth, infants who have been lying quietly in a hospital nursery will start to cry when they hear the cries of another baby (G. B. Martin & Clark, 1982; Sagi & Hoffman, 1976; Simner, 1971). Newborns cry only in response to the cries of other infants, either live or tape-recorded—not to the tape-recorded sound of their own crying and not to cries of chimpanzees or older children (G. B. Martin & Clark, 1982).

Babies' interest in other children rises and falls, depending on developmental priorities. During the first few months of life, babies are very interested in other babies and respond to them in about the same way they respond to their own mothers: they look, smile, and coo (T. M. Field, 1978). From the age of 6 months till about the end of the first year, they increasingly smile at, touch, and babble to another baby, especially when they are not distracted by the presence of either adults or toys (Hay, Pedersen, & Nash, 1982). At about 1 year, however, when their priorities seem to be learning to walk and to manipulate objects, they pay more attention to toys and less to other people (T. M. Field & Roopnarine, 1982).

In the second year, babies again become more sociable, and they now have a deeper understanding of their relationships. A 10-month-old is just as likely to hold out a toy to another baby when the other child's back is turned, but a child over 1 year old knows when such an offer has the best chance of being accepted and how to respond to another child's overtures (Eckerman & Stein, 1982).

INDIVIDUAL DIFFERENCES IN SOCIABILITY

Some people, of course, are more sociable than others, starting from an early age. Among a group of five 8- to 10-month-old babies in a day care center, R. V. Lee (1973) was able to identify a most popular and a least popular child. The baby whom the others approached most consistently was nonassertive but reciprocated the attention the others paid her. The baby who was avoided most consistently was described as "almost asocial." He acted very differently to other children, depending on whether or not he had initiated the contact with them.

What makes some babies friendlier than others? Some aspects of sociability, such as readiness to accept new people, adaptability to change, and a baby's usual mood, appear to be inherited and fairly stable traits of temperament, as we have seen.

Babies are also influenced by the attitudes of the people around them. Sociable infants tend to have sociable mothers, according to a study of 40 middle-class 1-year-olds and their mothers. The sociable babies also scored higher on intelligence tests, suggesting that babies who feel comfortable with a strange tester may perform better than those who are uncomfortable with new people (M. Stevenson & Lamb, 1979).

Children who spend time from infancy with other babies seem to become sociable at earlier ages than those who spend most of their time at home. Babies in day care interact more with other children—both positively and negatively—and are, in general, more socially competent. As children leave infancy and toddlerhood, they explore more and more the world beyond the home, and social skills become more and more important.

Development of Self-Control and Self-Regulation

As Jason, at the age of 1 year, is about to poke his finger into an electrical outlet, Jess shouts, "No!" and Jason pulls his hand back. The next time he goes near an outlet, he starts to point his finger, and then hesitates and says, "No." He has stopped himself from doing something he remembers he is not supposed to do. This episode demonstrates the beginning of *self-regulation*—control of behavior to conform with social expectations.

self-regulation   Control of behavior in order to conform with social expectations.

The growth of self-regulation parallels that of cognitive awareness. Jason is continually absorbing information about the kinds of behavior approved by his parents, the most important people in his life and the ones whose approval he wants more than anything else in the world. As he processes, stores, and acts upon this information, a gradual shift from external to internal control takes place.

PHASES LEADING TO SELF-REGULATION

Children seem to go through the following phases in the development of self-regulation (Kopp, 1982):

- *Phase 1: Neurophysiological modulation (birth to 2–3 months)*. Infants learn to use such inborn behaviors as sucking to soothe themselves. But since they have limited control over arousal, they need help to quiet or divert them when they are overstimulated.
- *Phase 2: Sensorimotor modulation (2–3 to 9–12 months)*. Babies become more aware that their actions can affect their world, but they still act only when their attention is captured, not from conscious intent.
- *Phase 3: Control (9–12 months and over)*. Babies are now walking and can plan their movements more, and they pay more attention to the effects of their actions. They begin to recognize demands from caregivers and to respond to them, either by complying or defying. Either way, they are showing conscious control. Their learning is still limited to a specific situation, however, and so Jason may stay away from the outlet only for a little while and only when Jess is around—and he may keep poking his finger into other dangerous places.
- *Phase 4: Self-control and progression to self-regulation (18–24 months and over)*. Children can now think and remember better and thus connect what they do with what they have been told to do. At 2, for example, Jason knows the rules about what and how to eat (even though he does not always follow them) and how to dress for sleep or play. He now stays away from all electrical outlets and is cautious around everything resembling one. He sometimes puts away his toys without being reminded.

Self-control, then, is children's ability to adjust what they do to fit what they know is socially acceptable. However, when they want *very* badly to do something, they easily forget the rules—and thus will run into the street after a ball or take a forbidden cookie. Not until they are about 3 can they develop *self-regulation*, which involves greater flexibility, conscious thought, and the ability to wait for gratification.

BOX 7-5 ■ A CHILD'S WORLD AND YOU

WHAT DO YOU THINK?

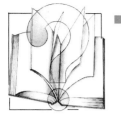

■ The theories of Freud and Erikson have much in common, but Freud's emphasizes the interaction of the ego and biology and Erikson's stresses the interaction of the ego and society. Which approach do you find most persuasive? Are your reasons based on general principles and logic, or on specific experiences?

■ Emotions are powerfully felt, but ambiguously expressed. It is hard to prove that an infant or a toddler does or does not feel a particular emotion. Do you think that parents are wise to assume that their children's emotional repertoire is rich, or that they should follow the theorists who say that very young children have only a few emotions? Which assumption about children's emotions do you think psychologists should begin with?

■ "Despite the women's liberation movement and changes in child care, a mother will always be more important to young children than a father." Do you agree or disagree?

HELPING BABIES DEVELOP SELF-CONTROL AND SELF-REGULATION

Some babies advance through the stages toward self-regulation more quickly than others, depending on their energy level, maturation, language ability, experiences, and urge to explore and the way their caregivers act.

To help babies advance, caregivers should follow guidelines like the following, which research has found effective (Kopp, 1982; Power & Chapieski, 1986):

■ Remind the child repeatedly of what you expect.
■ Suggest alternative activities.
■ Avoid physical punishment (it does not work and may even lead a toddler to do more damage).
■ Fill the environment with unbreakable objects that are safe to explore.
■ Link commands with pleasurable activities ("It's time to stop playing, so that you can go to the store with me").
■ Expect less self-control during times of stress (like illness, divorce, the birth of a new baby, or a move to a new home).

Self-regulation is only one of the skills that children develop and use in the years from 3 to 6, as we shall see in Chapters 8, 9, and 10, where we describe development in early childhood.

Summary

1. Two important theories of personality development are the psychosexual theory of Sigmund Freud (which stresses biological and maturational factors) and the psychosocial theory of Erik Erikson (which emphasizes cultural influences).

2. According to Freud, an infant (a child from birth to the age of 12–18 months) is in the oral stage and receives pleasure and gratification through oral stimulation. A toddler (aged 12–18 months to 3 years) is in the anal stage and receives pleasurable stimulation from moving the bowels. During infancy the personality is governed by the id, which operates on the pleasure principle, striving for immediate gratification. When

gratification is delayed, the ego develops; it operates on the reality principle, striving to find acceptable ways to obtain gratification. Freud maintains that events during these periods influence adult personality.

3   According to Erikson, an infant experiences the first in a series of eight crises that influence personality development throughout life. The first crisis is finding the appropriate balance between a sense of basic trust and mistrust about the world. The virtue of this stage is hope. Like the Freudian oral stage, the resolution of this crisis is influenced greatly by events surrounding the feeding situation and by the quality of the mother-infant relationship. Between the ages of 1½ and 3 years, the child faces the second crisis: autonomy versus shame and doubt. The virtue of this stage is will. Erikson emphasizes the importance of parents in helping a child resolve this crisis.

4   There is some controversy over what emotions infants have and when they appear. Emotional expression and self-awareness appear to be tied to maturation of the brain, although experiences also affect the timing of their arrival. Babies communicate their feelings through crying, smiling, and laughing, and it is likely that they do so through a variety of facial expressions, as well. Crying, smiling, and laughing reveal much about the progress of development.

5   Individual differences in personality result in part from temperament, sex, and family relationships.

6   The New York Longitudinal Study (NYLS) has identified nine fairly stable aspects of temperament—a person's characteristic style of approaching and reacting to people and situations—which appear to be inborn. Most children can be classified as "easy," "difficult," or "slow to warm up." Temperament can be influenced by environmental factors. A child's temperament has implications for psychological well-being and for parenting practices.

7   Significant physiological and behavioral differences between the sexes typically do not appear until after infancy. However, parents treat their sons and daughters differently from birth, resulting in some personality differences.

8   Mother-infant attachment has received considerable theoretical and research attention. Patterns of attachment (secure, avoidant, ambivalent, and disorganized-disoriented), as determined by using the strange-situation test, may have long-term implications for the child's development. Research suggesting that the first few hours and days of life constitute a critical period for forming the mother-infant bond has been questioned.

9   The impact of nonmaternal care on mother-infant attachment patterns is controversial. The effect seems to be influenced by the amount of time the infant spends away from the mother, the infant's sex, age and temperament, the mother's attitudes, and the quality of substitute care.

10   Fathers and babies typically become attached early in the baby's life. The nature of infants' and toddlers' experiences with their mothers and fathers appears to differ, and both kinds of experiences are valuable.

11   The most clear-cut findings about birth order is that firstborn and only children, as a group, have higher achievement levels than later-born children.

12   Siblings interact with and influence each other both positively and negatively from an early age. Parents' actions and attitudes can help reduce a sibling rivalry.

13   Stranger anxiety (wariness of strangers) and separation anxiety (distress upon departure of the caregiver) are normal phenomena that usually arise during the second half of the first year of life. There is considerable individual difference in the expression of both these reactions.

14   Babies seek out information about what to do in an ambiguous situation through what is known as *social referencing*.

15   Studies of parental deprivation conducted among orphans in institutions point to the

need for regular caregivers and a stimulating environment. Attempts at enriching institutional environments have dramatically benefited children's emotional and intellectual development. Effects of short-term deprivation, such as hospitalization, depend on particular circumstances.

16 Infants and toddlers are social creatures whose interest in each other fluctuates with their developmental priorities. Individual differences in babies' sociability tend to remain stable over time.

17 During the first 3 years and beyond, children move gradually toward self-control and, eventually, self-regulation (control of behavior to conform with social expectations). This development is largely dependent on cognitive self-awareness, awareness of social standards, and the ability to apply this knowledge to new situations. By understanding individual variations in this process, parents can help children develop more positive behavior.

Key Terms

personality (page 240–241)
oral stage (242)
id (242)
pleasure principle (242)
ego (242)
reality principle (242)
anal stage (242)
basic trust versus basic mistrust (243)
autonomy versus shame and doubt (243)
autonomy (243)
emotion (245)
self-awareness (247)
self-recognition (247)
crying (248)
smiling (249)
temperament (252)

easy child (253)
difficult child (253)
slow-to-warm-up child (253)
socialization (256)
imprinting (257)
mother-infant bond (257)
attachment (259)
strange situation (259)
secure attachment (259)
avoidant attachment (260)
ambivalent attachment (260)
gender-typing (267)
stranger anxiety (271)
separation anxiety (271)
social referencing (273)
self-regulation (278)

Suggested Readings

Bank, S. P., & Kahn, M. D. (1982). *The sibling bond.* New York: Basic Books. A fascinating book, full of examples from the lives of celebrities and ordinary people, that explores many aspects of sibling relations. The authors, both clinical psychologists, draw on research and clinical evidence to examine such issues as attachment theory, the development of self, and the emergence of sexual identity.

Dunn, J. (1985). *Sisters and brothers.* Cambridge MA: Harvard University Press. A beautiful little volume summarizing what is known about sibling relationships.

Fraiberg, S. H. (1959). *The magic years.* New York: Scribner. A classic by a psychoanalyst who describes in warm, insightful terms how children mature from birth to age 6.

Klaus, M., & Kennell, J. H. (1982). *Parent-infant bonding* (2d ed.). St. Louis: Mosby. A discussion emphasizing the role of early experience in the formation of the parent-infant bond.

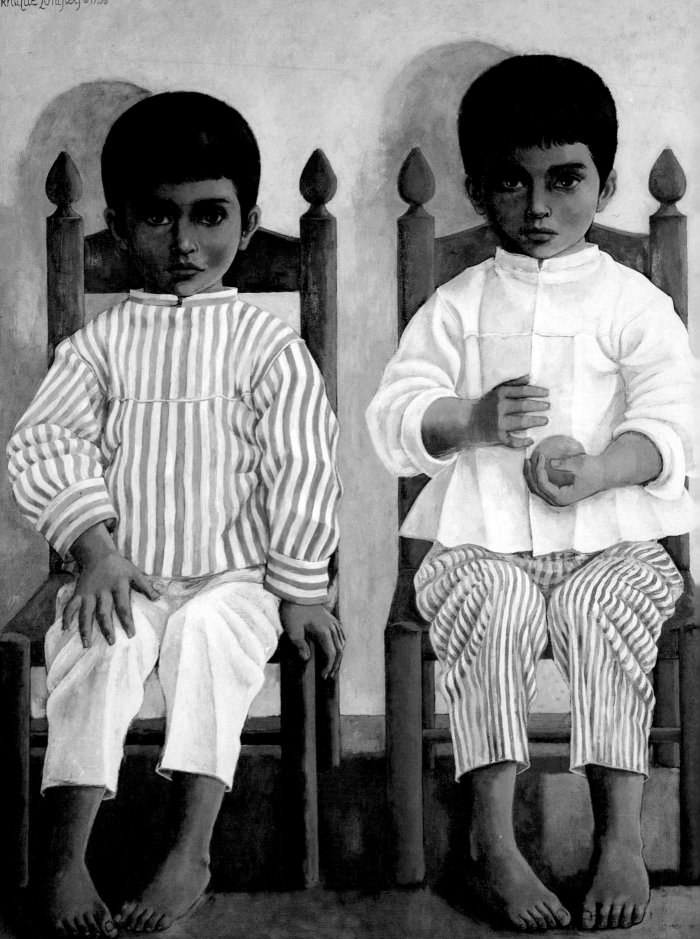

EARLY CHILDHOOD

Change continues in early childhood—ages 3 to 6—but not so rapidly as in infancy and toddlerhood. Even though revolutionary developments no longer appear daily or weekly, they still characterize the three major aspects of development.

During this period Vicky and Jason both become more adept physically, more competent intellectually, and more complex socially. For example, Jason's language ability improves dramatically as he masters both the rules of English syntax and the secrets of conversation. He can explain himself to others and can deliberately learn from what they have to say. Vicky increasingly thinks of herself as a member of groups—she is part of a family and learns from others in the family how to behave; she is a girl and she busily learns how females should act; she is a child and she learns childhood games and lore from her peers.

In Chapters 8, 9, and 10 we see children's tendency to become more like the rest of society. Physically, the child takes on more and more adult proportions. Intellectually, he or she begins to use symbols and can sometimes have strikingly adult insights. Emotionally, children begin to identify with others and show a social conscience as well. Thus, by the end of this period the adults who love Jason can look at him and say, "He is one of us," with a depth of meaning that was impossible when he first emerged from toddlerhood.

PHYSICAL DEVELOPMENT IN EARLY CHILDHOOD

"I love you,"
said a great mother.
"I love you for what you are
knowing so well what you are.
And I love you more yet, child,
deeper yet than ever, child,
for what you are going to be,
knowing so well you are going far,
knowing your great works are ahead,
ahead and beyond,
yonder and far over yet."

Carl Sandburg, *The People, Yes*, 1936

PREVIEW QUESTIONS

■ How do children grow and change between the ages of 3 and 6?
■ How healthy are the years of early childhood, and how can society make them even healthier?
■ What are the normal sleep needs of young children, and what are the most common sleep problems?
■ How does children's artwork show the maturation of the brain?
■ How prevalent are child abuse and neglect, and how do they affect children?

IT IS THE DAY BEFORE Vicky's third birthday. "Pretty soon," she tells Ellen, "I'll be big enough to sleep without sucking my thumb. And maybe tomorrow I'll be big enough to wear pajamas like Daddy's."

The big day dawns. Vicky leaps out of bed and runs to the mirror. She stands there, first on one foot and then on the other, scrutinizing herself; then she runs to her parents' room. "Mommy! Daddy!" she squeals into sleepy ears. "I'm 3!" But then a note of disappointment creeps into her voice: "But I don't look different."

In comparison with a year ago, Vicky is very different indeed. She is bigger, and she is capable of bigger things. In her next 3 years of life there will be still greater changes.

Vicky grows more slowly now than in her first 3 years, but she makes much progress in coordination and muscle development between age 3 and age 6 and can do many more things. During this period, known as *early childhood*, children are sturdier, having come through the more dangerous stage of infancy to enter a healthier time of life, as we will see when we look at health in these years. Since proper growth and health depend on good nutrition, we will examine nutritional needs as well.

We will also look at sleep patterns of young children, since these are the years when sleep problems often develop.

We will consider motor development during this period, including children's growing artistic abilities.

Finally, we will see the tragic results of physical maltreatment of children, and we will explore ways of preventing abuse and neglect.

Physical Growth and Change

APPEARANCE, HEIGHT, AND WEIGHT

During the years from 3 to 6, children lose their roundness and take on a more slender, athletic appearance. The potbelly typical of a 3-year-old slims down as the trunk, arms, and legs get longer. The head is still relatively large, but the other parts of the body are catching up, and bodily proportions are steadily becoming more like those of adults.

Although a 3-year-old does not grow as quickly as an infant or a toddler, Vicky is 4 inches taller than she was a year ago. The pencil mark on the wall that shows her height at 3 years is now almost 38 inches from the floor, and so the yardstick cannot reach the top of her head anymore. Boys at age 3 are slightly taller and heavier than girls, with more muscle per pound of body weight. Girls, on the other hand, have more fatty tissue. Over the next few years, both Vicky and Jason will continue to grow a steady 2 to 3 inches per year and gain 4 to 6 pounds annually, until they reach the growth spurt of puberty. Vicky will then shoot up ahead of her male classmates—until, a year or two later, they begin to overtake her in height. (See Table 8-1.)

STRUCTURAL AND SYSTEMIC CHANGES

Important developments take place inside children's bodies, too. Their muscular and skeletal growth progresses, and they become stronger. Cartilage turns to bone at a faster rate, and bones become harder, giving the child a firmer shape and protecting internal organs. These changes allow children to develop many new large-muscle and small-muscle motor skills. Other changes help children stay healthy. Stamina increases, because the respiratory and circulatory systems develop greater capacity; and children's developing immune system protects them from infection.

TABLE 8-1

PHYSICAL GROWTH, AGES 3 TO 6 (50TH PERCENTILE)				
	HEIGHT, INCHES		WEIGHT, POUNDS	
AGE	BOYS	GIRLS	BOYS	GIRLS
3	38	37¼	32¼	31¼
3½	39¼	39¼	34¼	34
4	40¼	40½	36½	36¼
4½	42	42	38½	38½
5	43¼	43	41½	41
5½	45	44½	45½	44
6	46	46	48	47

Source: Lowrey, 1978.

BOX 8-1 ■ THE EVERYDAY WORLD

ENCOURAGING HEALTHY EATING HABITS

Vicky refuses to eat almost anything but peanut butter and jelly sandwiches. Jason seems to live on bananas. They make snowmen out of mashed potatoes or lakes out of applesauce—and their food remains uneaten on the plate.

What is a parent to do? First—don't worry, since a diminished appetite in early childhood is normal. Then—look at the child. A child who is energetic, with good muscle tone, bright eyes, glossy hair, and an ability to spring back quickly from fatigue is unlikely to be suffering from inadequate nutrition, no matter how traumatic mealtimes are (E. R. Williams & Caliendo, 1984). The following suggestions can make mealtimes more pleasant, children healthier, and the home atmosphere happier.

■ Keep a record of what your child actually eats. The child may in fact be eating enough, so that there is no cause for concern.

■ Serve simple, easily identifiable foods. Preschoolers like to know what they are eating and often balk at mixed dishes like casseroles.

■ Serve finger foods as often as possible.

■ Introduce only one new food at a time, along with a familiar one that the child likes.

■ Offer small servings, especially of new or previously disliked foods. It is better to give seconds than to set out what to a small child may look overwhelming.

■ After a reasonable time, remove the food and do not serve any more until the next meal. A healthy child will not suffer from missing a meal, and some children need to learn that certain times are appropriate for eating and others are not.

■ Give the child a choice—whether to have rye or whole wheat bread; whether to have a peach or an apple; whether to have yogurt or milk. No one food is essential; there is always a substitute that can provide the same nutrients.

■ Encourage your child to help prepare food by making sandwiches, cutting up vegetables, or mixing and spooning out cookie dough.

■ Allow for a quiet period before a meal to prevent the fatigue or overexcitement that often causes eating problems.

■ Have nutritious snack foods handy and allow the child to select favorites from among them.

■ Turn typically childish behavior to advantage. Serve food in appealing dishes; dress it up with garnishes or little toys; make a "party" out of an ordinary meal.

■ Don't fight "rituals," in which a child eats foods one at a time, in a certain order.

■ Make mealtimes pleasant with conversation on interesting topics, keeping any talk about eating itself to a minimum.

■ Provide a good example yourself by eating healthy, well-balanced meals.

■ To prevent choking, avoid giving children under 5 hard candies, nuts, grapes, and hot dogs; cut their food into small pieces; encourage them to chew vigorously; do not allow them to eat while talking, running, jumping, or lying down, or to toss or pour food directly into the mouth (Univ. of California, Berkeley Wellness Letter, 1988).

NUTRITION

Ellen looks at the tiny amount of food Vicky eats these days and wonders where she is getting all her energy—surely not from those bird-sized portions. But this change in Vicky's appetite is normal. As children's growth rate slows, they need fewer calories per pound of body weight. Thus, preschoolers eat less in proportion to their size than infants, which often makes parents worry that their children are not eating enough.

Actually, the nutritional demands of early childhood are satisfied quite easily. For example, protein can be supplied by two glasses of milk and one serving of meat or an alternative (like fish, cheese, or eggs) every day; vitamin A can be supplied by eating modest amounts of carrots, spinach, egg yolk, or whole milk (among other foods); and vitamin C can be supplied by citrus fruits, tomatoes, and leafy dark-green vegetables (E. R. Williams & Caliendo, 1984).

Too many children do not get these and other essential nutrients because their families are seduced by television commercials for foods heavy in sugar and fat. If Vicky's diet includes much sugared cereal, chocolate cake, and other low-nutrient snacks and fast foods, she will not have enough appetite for the foods she needs. Therefore even her snacks should be nutritious. (See Box 8-1.)

Health

Although Vicky comes home from nursery school with an occasional runny nose, the years of early childhood are basically healthy. In the past, early childhood was a dangerous period, but because of widespread vaccination, many of the major diseases that used to fell young children are now relatively rare. Today, accidents are more of a threat.

HEALTH PROBLEMS

Minor Illnesses

Young children suffer fairly frequent coughs, sniffles, and stomachaches, which typically last from 2 days to 2 weeks but are seldom serious enough to see a doctor about. Between the ages of 3 and 5, they average about seven to eight colds and other respiratory illnesses a year, which will drop to fewer than six in middle childhood (Denny & Clyde, 1983). (For a surprising viewpoint on such minor illnesses, see Box 8-2, page 290.)

Respiratory problems, though less common during these years than in infancy, are still prevalent, because children's lungs are still not fully developed. By middle childhood, the maturation of the respiratory and immune systems will protect them more efficiently.

Major Illnesses

After the doctor gave him a vaccination, Jason proudly told Jess, "I didn't even cry." Modern immunization practices have largely wiped out such contagious diseases as measles, rubella (German measles), mumps, whooping cough, diphtheria, and poliomyelitis. More than 90 percent of kindergartners and first-graders are immunized against major childhood illness (U.S. Department of Health and Human Services, USDHHS, 1982).

The incidence of all these diseases has dropped since 1950, and diphtheria and polio have virtually disappeared in recent years (USDHHS, 1982). The vaccine-preventable diseases do still exist, however, and can still be dangerous. Between 1971 and 1977, immunizations declined, apparently because parents thought that the diseases had disappeared; and in 1977, forty percent of children under age 15 were unprotected against at least one childhood disease for which a safe and effective vaccine was available (Bumpers, 1984). As a result, a number of diseases regained some strength. Between 1968 and 1971, the number of cases of measles more than tripled, until alarmed health officials sponsored a publicity campaign and the disease again declined until once again parents relaxed, and the incidence rose again in 1977.

Apparently, we have developed a new disease cycle: "alarm-action" and "relaxation-inaction." The rising disease rate in 1977 provoked renewed alarm

Although preschoolers eat less in proportion to their size than infants do, they can fulfill their nutritional needs quite easily—and even enjoy the process. Since they eat so little, it is important for their snacks, as well as their regular meals, to be nutritious.

BOX 8-2 ■ THE RESEARCH WORLD

BENEFITS OF CHILDHOOD ILLNESS

Vicky's cheeks are flushed, her normally bright eyes are glazed, her eyelids are drooping, and she has the wan and pathetic look of a sick child. Although Ellen and Charles hate to see their little girl looking so miserable, the minor illnesses of childhood may help Vicky build up immunity to more serious illness. Their distress is also eased by thinking of some of the cognitive and emotional benefits of common childhood illnesses (Parmelee, 1986).

For one thing, Vicky becomes more aware of her physical self as she experiences bodily changes: first the aches and pains, the muscular weakness, the low energy, and the depressed mood of illness—and then, after recovery, her usual sense of well-being. She learns about the variety of physical sensations she can feel, and she also learns how to cope when she does not feel well, enhancing her sense of competence.

Also, when Vicky sees her parents, her playmates, her brother, and other people in her world going through similar bouts with illness, she has a better understanding of their feelings. Because she remembers how she felt, she learns *empathy*, the ability to put herself in another person's place. And she can help to comfort and care for someone else.

Vicky's illness also helps her progress in her understanding of language. She may have confused two meanings of the word *bad*—the way she feels physically when her throat hurts, and her emotional state when she has done something wrong—and so she may think she is sick ("feels bad") because she wet her pants (was a "bad" girl). Her illness gives her parents a chance to talk to her, clarify meanings, and reassure her: "I know you feel bad because you're sick, but you'll soon be well." It also points up the value of avoiding the word *bad* to apply to a child's behavior or to the child as a person.

and action, leading to a new federal program to promote education and provide money for vaccination. Again the disease rate among children declined, until 1981, when the budget of the Childhood Immunization Initiative program was cut by one-third and the rate began to climb again (Bumpers, 1984). (See Box 8-3, opposite.)

Fortunately, death rates from illness have come down in recent years. Since 1950, deaths from influenza and pneumonia have dropped by 84 percent, although respiratory diseases are still the major cause of death among infants and children worldwide. Deaths from cancer have dropped by 48 percent, primarily because of advances in the treatment of leukemia, lymphoma, and Hodgkin's disease, forms of cancer that often strike children (USDHHS, 1982). The 5-year survival rate for cancer has risen dramatically among children under 15 diagnosed between 1977 and 1983, compared with children under 15 diagnosed between 1967 and 1973. Survival rates for children diagnosed with leukemia increased from 15 percent to 61 percent; for those with brain tumors, from 45 to 54 percent; and for those with Hodgkin's disease, from 78 percent to 88 percent (American Cancer Society, 1988).

Accidents

In the United States, accidents are now the leading cause of death in childhood. At the top of the tragic list are deaths due to automobile accidents. Today, all 50 states and the District of Columbia have laws requiring young children to be restrained in cars, either in specially designed seats or by standard seat belts. Such laws are important: children *not* in restraints are 11 times more likely to die in a car accident than children who are restrained (Decker, Dewey, Hutcheson, & Schaffner, 1984).

BOX 8-3 ■ AROUND THE WORLD

IMMUNIZING CHILDREN

At Kano Airport in Nigeria, a small boy, his legs withered by polio, moved crablike through the crowd, holding out his hand. "All for the lack of a few drops of vaccine," a bystander noted as he dropped a coin into the boy's hand (Brooke, 1988). Despite medical advances in prevention and treatment which have dramatically increased survival from childhood diseases, preventable diseases continue to threaten the world's population. Children are the prime victims.

The contagious diseases of childhood are largely the same the world over; fortunately, they have been largely checked by aggressive treatment. Rates of immunization in third world countries have been rising—from 5 percent of children in 1974 to 50 percent in 1987 (K. S. Warren, 1988). Smallpox has been eliminated. But although measles, polio, tetanus, tuberculosis, whooping cough, and diphtheria are in retreat, too many children are still stricken with them.

The United Nations has targeted 1990 for vaccinating 80 percent of all third world children against these six diseases, using new, powerful, specific vaccines and new technology that can keep vaccines cold in tropical temperatures. The crucial element in attaining this goal, however, is the social commitment to getting vaccines to the population of developing countries.

China, which is approaching 85 percent coverage, has done it through its health care system; India, with the greatest number of nonimmunized children, is focusing on strengthening its primary care system (Warren, 1988). Nigeria has mobilized hundreds of thousands of local volunteers (Brooke, 1988). National wealth is not the issue: the extremely poor African country of Tanzania has an infant mortality rate for vaccine-preventable disease that is less than half the rate of Africa's richest country (South Africa), simply because Tanzania has made vaccination a high priority (UNICEF, 1984).

By the year 2000, the number of cases of vaccine-preventable childhood diseases may be halved, as a result of higher rates of immunization. Work is now progressing on vaccines to combat the bacteria and viruses that cause the diarrhea and respiratory illness that are the biggest killers of children in the developing world, and concerted efforts are under way to expand immunization services to all the world's infants and pregnant women ("Immunizing the World's Children," 1986).

Besides saving millions of lives and millions of dollars in health care, universal immunization is expected to have another result—greater acceptance of family planning. As parents become confident that children will survive, they tend to have fewer (Brooke, 1988). Thus immunization can help to solve another major health problem in developing countries—too many people and too few resources.

Legislation, however, does not ensure that children will *use* seat belts. Many children do not like them, and parents often give in. A recent Australian study, however, found that children whose preschool teachers use songs, cartoons, and other aids to stress the importance of seat belts will, in fact, insist not only that they be buckled in, but that their parents use belts as well. Educating children brought better results than threatening parents with police checks and fines (Bowman, Sanson-Fisher, & Webb, 1987).

Most other accidents occur in and around the home: children drown in bathtubs and pools (as well as lakes, rivers, and oceans); are burned in fires and explosions; drink poisonous substances; choke on loose parts of toys; shoot each other playing with loaded guns; fall from heights; get caught in mechanical contrivances; and suffocate in unexpected traps like abandoned refrigerators.

Children are naturally venturesome and unaware of danger. Their innocence puts a large burden on parents and other caretakers, who must tread a delicate line between not protecting children and smothering them. The greatest burden, though, should be on society at large. Federal laws have already been passed requiring "child-proof" caps on medicine bottles, and minimum spacing between bars on cribs to prevent babies from getting caught and strangling.

One ironic development followed the passage of a national law requiring children's sleepwear to be made flame-retardant. Further research suggested

(© S. Sweezy/Stock, Boston)

Since children are naturally venturesome and naive, parents and other adults have to be sure they take precautions to avoid accidents, as this little girl is doing by wearing a life preserver.

that the chemicals originally used in fireproofing the sleepwear might be carcinogenic, posing a different hazard. Thus, concerned citizens must be eternally vigilant to protect children.

The Environment and Health Problems

Vaccination helps children stay healthy. Vigilance helps keep them safe. What other factors affect children's health? Heredity is one. Some people seem to inherit the predisposition of particular medical conditions, showing high cholesterol levels, for example, at a very early age. The medical history taken during health checkups can bring out any family tendencies and suggest special care that parents can give (like paying special attention to diet or running specific tests on a regular basis). However, many elements in the outside world influence children as much as or more than their genetic heritage.

Exposure to Other Children   Children freely pass germs back and forth through close contact and their generally lackadaisical sanitary practices. This helps to explain why children in large families are sick more often than those in small families (Loda, 1980), and why children in day care centers often come home with colds and other infections. In one study, children in group care (in groups of 2 to 6) and children in day care (in groups of 7 or more) were more likely than children raised at home to have respiratory infections, more than 60 days of illness, and more than 4 severe illnesses over the course of a year. There is a definite correlation: those in day care were sick most; those at home, least (Wald, Dashevsky, Byers, Guerra, & Taylor, 1988).

The spread of disease can be minimized if caregivers take the following steps (American Academy of Pediatrics, 1986c):

■   Teaching children to wash their hands thoroughly with soap after using the toilet or blowing their nose, before brushing their teeth, and before and after eating

- Washing their own hands after diapering children or taking them to the toilet, and before handling food
- Preparing food well away from toilet and diapering areas
- Cleaning toilet and diapering areas after every use
- Separating infants, children in diapers, and toilet-trained children
- Not letting children share teething rings, pacifiers, washcloths, towels, brushes, and combs
- Rinsing all toys and surfaces in infants' and toddlers' areas with a sanitizing solution
- Allowing only machine-washable stuffed animals, washing them often, and not letting children share them
- Checking for and reporting infectious diseases
- Maintaining a written policy for the management of sick children

Such practices can cut the rate of illness by more than half (Marwick & Simmons, 1984). In fact, children in *high-quality* day care are healthier than children being raised at home, thanks to early detection and treatment of illness (American Academy of Pediatrics, 1986c). Some observers believe that early day care experience can help children's health in the long run: by developing infections early in life, children may build immunities that they retain later on, but this premise needs to be confirmed by long-term studies.

Stress *Stressful life events* From what we know about the relationship between body and mind, it is likely that stress increases a child's susceptibility both to illness and to injury. This supposition has, in fact, been supported by research. Children up to age 4 who experienced such stressful life events as

TABLE 8-2

STRESS AND HEALTH
STRESSFUL EVENTS THAT CAN AFFECT CHILDREN'S HEALTH

Moving to a different house
Father's changing job
Mother's starting new job
Serious or prolonged disagreement between parents and their own parents or in-laws
Death of close friend or relative of child or parents
Increased financial problems of parents related to mortgage or business
Father's unemployment
Serious financial problems of parents
Serious or prolonged argument between parents or with a former spouse
Divorce or legal separation of parents
Reconciliation of parents after divorce or legal separation
Parents' sexual problems
Assault of mother by father
Serious illness or accident suffered by either parent
Serious illness or accident suffered by sibling
Serious illness among other family members
Mother's pregnancy
Court case involving mother or father

Source: Adapted from Beautrais, Fergusson, & Shannon, 1982.

those listed in Table 8-2 (page 293) were more likely to suffer respiratory illness, stomach and intestinal problems, and accidental injury. Children from families experiencing 12 or more such events were more than twice as likely to see a doctor and 6 times as likely to have to go into the hospital as children from families experiencing fewer than 4 such events (Beautrais, Fergusson, & Shannon, 1982).

In families experiencing many stressful events, parents may be so distraught that they neglect basic safety and sanitary procedures. They may forget to put away knives and poisonous cleaning supplies, fasten a safety gate, or see that children wash their hands.

Emotional stress: Suicide   It is painful and difficult to imagine that young children can become so unhappy that they will try—sometimes successfully—to take their own lives. But recent research strongly suggests that some childhood "accidents" may actually be suicide attempts. In one study, 16 children, aged 2½ to 5, who had suffered serious accidents were compared with 16 children having serious behavioral problems. The children diagnosed as suicidal showed more aggression directed toward themselves, had more morbid ideas, ran away more, and were less responsive to pain and injury. This study strongly suggests that small children can indeed feel so compelled to escape from their situation and so alienated from the people they know that they can deliberately take an overdose of medicine, run out into traffic, or leap from a great height (P. A. Rosenthal & Rosenthal, 1984).

The psychiatrists who conducted this study recommend asking preschoolers about the circumstances of their accidents to try to uncover any underlying psychological reason. They conclude: "We think we are probably dealing with a phenomenon . . . that might well parallel the history of the recognition of child abuse when multiple injuries were observed in similar 'accident' cases" (P. A. Rosenthal & Rosenthal, 1984, p. 524).

Poverty and Hunger   Poverty is a major contributor to children's health problems. According to research, income is the prime factor associated with poor health (J. L. Brown, 1987). Some 20 percent of all people in the United States do not have enough money to maintain an adequate standard of living. The children do not grow properly, because they do not eat properly. They do not receive the immunizations they should, and they do not get sound medical and dental care. They live in crowded, unsanitary housing, with parents who are too busy keeping body and soul together to provide adequate supervision. Poverty is unhealthy, and not only for the poor: all of society suffers when hunger and disease flourish.

In 1987, according to the World Food Council, as many as 730 million men, women, and children around the world were hungry. The ranks of the hungry—people chronically deprived of the nutrients needed for an active, healthy life—were growing by 8 million a year. Even in the affluent United States, 1 in 5 people in 1985 were poor (had less than $11,000 annual income for a family of four). Eight percent of the population—12 million children and 8 million adults—were hungry, and the problem seems to be growing worse (J. L. Brown, 1987). Minorities are especially at risk: about 43 percent of black children and 40 percent of Hispanic children are poor, compared with fewer than 16 percent of white children.

The problems of poor children begin long before birth. Poor mothers often

Poverty is unhealthy. Poor children often do not eat properly, do not receive necessary immunizations, and do not get sound medical and dental care. Even in the affluent United States, the number of poor children is rising—a fact that poses a major challenge to our society.

do not eat well themselves and do not get adequate prenatal care. They are at high risk of having low-birthweight babies and babies who are born dead or who die soon after birth. The children themselves are at risk of a variety of health problems, including lead poisoning, ear infections and hearing loss, vision problems, iron-deficiency anemia and other malnutrition-related problems, behavioral and psychological difficulties (like learning disabilities), and such possibly stress-related disorders as asthma, headaches, insomnia, and irritable bowel (J. L. Brown, 1987; Egbuono & Starfield, 1982).

During the late 1960s the federal "war on poverty" included several very effective food programs: free breakfast and lunch for schoolchildren, nutritional help for pregnant women, and food stamps for the family. In 1981, however, the government made drastic cuts in these programs, and by 1983 hunger was once more a serious national problem (J. L. Brown, 1987).

DENTAL HEALTH

When Vicky bursts into laughter, she throws her head back and opens her mouth wide, showing off her teeth. By age 3, all a child's primary, or deciduous, teeth are in place. Vicky can now chew whatever she wants. Fortunately, she has stopped sucking her thumb: the permanent teeth, which begin to appear at about age 6, are developing during early childhood and will be affected if thumb-sucking does not stop before the age of 6.

The foundation for future dental health is set in these early years. Even though the first "baby teeth" will fall out by age 6, they are important for jaw development, and the habits established now are important for lifelong dental health.

The improvement in children's dental health over recent years stems from such preventive measures as fluoridation (in drinking water, vitamins, and toothpaste, or by direct application to the teeth) and regular brushing.

Preventive Care

The most effective way to prevent cavities is to see that children receive fluoride from birth through age 14 to 16, either in drinking water, in vitamin pills, in toothpaste, or by direct application to the teeth. The widespread use of fluoride and high levels of dental care have dramatically reduced the incidence of tooth decay in children over the past 15 years (Herrmann & Roberts, 1987).

Other preventive measures include daily cleaning by the parent (with a small toothbrush, a washcloth, or cotton gauze) as soon as the first teeth erupt. By age 2, a little toothpaste can be used, and as soon as children can handle a toothbrush, they should begin to use it, with an adult's supervision and help. Not until age 5 to 8 can most children do a good enough job of removing the bacterial plaque that forms the basis for decay. Children should keep sweet foods to a minimum, especially sticky ones and especially between meals, and they should brush their teeth right after eating. By age 1 they should begin to see a dentist (Herrmann & Roberts, 1987).

Thumb-Sucking

Many children are thumb-suckers or finger-suckers, but since most give it up before or during early childhood, no harm is done. Aside from giving a baby a pacifier to help satisfy sucking needs, parents can usually safely ignore the habit in children under 3 or 4 years of age. If children stop sucking before age 6, their teeth are not likely to be permanently affected (Herrmann & Roberts, 1987).

Prolonged sucking seems to be more a habit than the result of emotional disturbance, and it responds better to treatment designed to break the habit, like a dental appliance, than to psychological counseling, which has little or no effect. Children over 4 who are still thumb-suckers are sometimes fitted with a dental appliance that corrects any existing malformation of the teeth and also discourages sucking. Success rates with these appliances have been high—about 80 percent (Haryett, Hansen, & Davidson, 1970).

Sleep: Patterns and Problems

"Daddy, leave the light on!" Jason calls after Jess has tiptoed out of the room in the mistaken belief that Jason has finally fallen asleep. Jess turns the light back on. Silence reigns for about 5 minutes, and then Jess hears, "I want a drink of water," "What's that noise outside my window?" "I'm cold," "I'm hot." Jason is showing a typical change in bedtime behavior.

Sleep patterns change throughout life, and early childhood has its own distinct rhythms (see Figure 8-1). Young children no longer wake up every 2 to

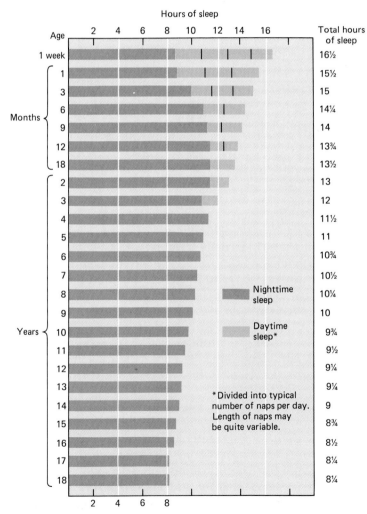

FIGURE 8-1
Typical sleep requirements in childhood. Children go from sleeping about equal amounts day and night to getting all their sleep in one long, extended nighttime period. While the pattern of steadily decreasing hours of sleep holds true generally, individual children may need more or fewer hours than shown here. (*Source:* Ferber, 1985.)

3 hours around the clock, but tend to sleep through the night and take one daytime nap; and they experience more deep sleep than they will later in life (Webb & Bonnet, 1979).

NORMAL SLEEP BEHAVIOR

Preschoolers go to sleep differently from infants and toddlers. The bedtime rituals of 109 children, aged 1 through 5, were found to show definite patterns. Older children were more likely to want to prolong the routine. After they were already in bed, supposedly tucked in and ready to fall asleep, they tended to call for their parents.

It is hard for children aged 3 to 6 to let go of a stimulating world full of people, to be by themselves in bed. Also, they take longer than younger children to fall asleep, and they are more likely to do something about that. While children under 2 will play quietly by themselves or with a sibling before falling asleep, children 3 years old and older are more likely to want a light left on in the room and to sleep with a favorite toy or blanket (Beltramini & Hertzig, 1983).

Parents sometimes worry about a child's inability to fall asleep without taking a favorite tattered blanket, a stuffed animal, or some other cuddly object to bed. At the same time that Jason's parents smile to see him clutching his favorite bear, they worry that he is too dependent on "Teddy" and wonder about the long-term effects. Psychologists call such items *transitional objects,* because they help a child make the transition from dependent baby to independent child. There appears to be no basis for worry. In one study, 11-year-olds who at age 4 had slept with cuddly objects were now gregarious, sociable with adults, and likely to be self-confident; they still enjoyed playing by themselves and were not likely to be worriers. At age 16 the ones who had insisted on taking a cuddly object to bed were just as well adjusted as those who had not (Newson, Newson, & Mahalski, 1982).

Taking a favorite blanket, a stuffed animal, or some other cuddly object to bed is normal. Many children depend on such transitional objects to help them fall asleep, but they eventually outgrow this need.

transitional object
Object—commonly a soft, cuddly one—used repeatedly by a child as a bedtime companion.

PROBLEMS WITH SLEEP

Sometimes, of course, troubles having to do with sleep are more serious. They may be merely annoying for parent or child, or they may indicate a deep-seated emotional problem. Any sleep problem that persists over a period of time needs to be examined closely.

Bedtime Struggles

Many children—from 20 to 30 percent, according to one study—engage in prolonged bedtime struggles (lasting more than 1 hour) and wake their parents frequently at night. When researchers looked at 96 children between 6 months and 4 years of age, they found five experiences that distinguish children with these problems from children without them (Lozoff, Wolf, & Davis, 1985). One is sleeping in the same bed with parents, which may simply mean that it is more tempting and easier to wake people when they are in the same bed than when they are in the next room.

The other four conditions, however, may signal the presence of family stress. The children's families were more likely to have experienced an accident or illness; or the children were more likely to have mothers who were depressed, were ambivalent toward the child, or had recently changed schedule to be away for most of the day.

Night Terrors and Nightmares

Night terrors and nightmares, which are very different, both begin to appear in early childhood; about 1 in 4 children between the ages of 3 and 8 suffer from one or the other (Hartmann, 1981). Boys are more likely than girls to experience night terrors, but there is no sex difference for experiencing nightmares (Parkes, 1986).

night terror Common sleep disorder of childhood in which a child suddenly awakens from a deep sleep in a state of panic.

In a *night terror,* the sleeper appears to awaken abruptly from a deep sleep in a state of panic. Children who experience night terrors may scream and sit up in bed, breathing quickly and staring. Yet they are not really awake, they quiet down quickly, and the next morning they do not remember anything. These episodes alarm parents more than they do children, and they are rarely a serious problem. They usually go away by themselves, do not signal underlying emotional problems, and may simply be an effect of very deep sleep. If they are severe and long-lasting, and occur once a week or more, causing conflict between child and parents, a short course of therapy with an antihistamine or antidepressant drug may be undertaken (McDaniel, 1986).

nightmare Frightening dream, occurring toward morning and often vividly recalled.

Whereas night terrors usually occur within an hour of falling asleep, *nightmares* come toward morning and are often vividly recalled (Hartmann, 1981). An occasional bad dream is not cause for alarm, especially in children under 6, who are most likely to be troubled by bad dreams. Persistent nightmares, however, especially nightmares that make a child fearful and anxious during waking hours, may be a signal that the child is under too much stress. Repetitive themes often point to a specific problem which a person cannot solve when awake and which rises to the surface during sleep.

Sleepwalking and Sleeptalking

Walking and talking during sleep are both fairly common and harmless.

Sleepwalking children typically sit up abruptly, with their eyes open. They get out of bed and move about so clumsily that they need to be protected from hurting themselves, by gates at the top of stairs and in front of windows; but nothing else needs to be done, since most children outgrow the tendency. Some 15 percent of all children between the ages of 5 and 12 sleepwalk at least once; and some 1 to 6 percent do it regularly (Anders, Caraskadon, & Dement, 1980). The behavior seems at least partly hereditary; 20 percent of sleepwalkers have other night roamers in the family (Parkes, 1986).

Sleeptalking is also purposeless and does not require any corrective action. It is usually difficult, if not impossible, to understand what children talking in their sleep are saying; and contrary to popular belief, it is next to impossible to engage them in conversation.

Nighttime Fears

Fear of the dark and fears at bedtime can be treated. A group of children 6 to 13½ years old who had had severe and chronic fears for an average of 5 years were treated by a 3-week self-control training program that they attended with their parents. They learned how to relax, how to substitute pleasant thoughts for frightening ones, and how to talk to themselves to cope with stressful situations. Of 34 children followed up 2½ to 3 years after treatment, 31 had maintained significant improvement (Graziano & Mooney, 1982). A number of children and parents felt that the children's ability to deal with their night fears helped them become more confident in facing problems in general. Thus, again, we see the beneficial effect of control over one's life.

Bed-Wetting

Most children stay dry, day and night, by the age of 3 to 5 years, but **enuresis,** repeated urination during the day or night in clothing or in bed, is the most common chronic condition seen by the typical pediatrician (Starfield, 1978). The condition is most common at night, and is thus considered a sleep problem; diagnosis of the problem hinges on at least 2 occurrences per month after age 5. About 7 percent of 5-year-old boys wet the bed, compared with 3 percent of girls; and at age 10 it is 3 percent of boys and 2 percent of girls (DSM III-R, 1987). Most outgrow the habit without any special help; and by age 18, only 1 percent of males and virtually no females have the problem. Fewer than 1 percent of bed-wetters have any true physical disorder; heredity and rate of development may be factors.

enuresis   Bed-wetting.

Enuresis runs in families. About 75 percent of bed-wetters have a close relative who also wet the bed, and identical twins are more concordant for the condition than fraternal twins (DSM III-R, 1987). In fact, a recent study of more than 1000 children in New Zealand found that family history is the strongest predictor of childhood bed-wetting (Fergusson, Horwood, & Shannon, 1986). Among these children, psychosocial factors like social and economic background or stressful life events like divorce and change of residence had little or no effect on whether children wet the bed. Instead, factors related to biology—in addition to family history—seemed to be crucial. Children who were small at birth, slept more at ages 1 and 2, and developed slowly in infancy and toddlerhood were slower to attain bladder control, and boys were slightly slower in controlling the bladder than girls. The only environmental influence that was significant was age of toilet training; when this did not begin until after 18 months, it took the child longer to attain bladder control.

The only emotional factor in bed-wetting seems to be a tendency for it to recur among children who have already had the problem, especially at times of upset over such events as birth of a new baby or entering school (DSM III-R, 1987).

Children and their parents should be reassured that the problem is common and not serious, and that the child is not to blame and should not be punished. In general, parents need not do anything unless children themselves see the bed-wetting as a problem. The most effective treatments include rewarding children for staying dry; waking children when they begin to urinate by using electric devices that ring bells or buzzers; administering antidepressant drugs (as a last resort, no more than 6 months after the last occurrence, and then tapering off, McDaniel, 1986), and teaching children to practice controlling the sphincter muscles (Chapman, 1974).

During early childhood, children make great strides in motor development.

"We're a great team, Sash—you with your small and large motor skills, me with my spatial awareness and hand-eye coördination."

Motor Development

MOTOR SKILLS

At 3 years of age, Vicky loves jumping on a wet spot in the carpet—she likes the sound and the squishy feel. Jason is happiest when he can climb things: ladders, steps, the slide at the playground. Vicky and Jason like to do everything themselves; although they will accept a helping hand when they need one, they need help less and less.

Children aged 3 to 6 make great strides in large-muscle skills. At 3, Jason can walk in a straight line. At 4, he can walk in a circle that has been chalked on a playground. And at 5, he manages to run in adult style, hard and fast. Meanwhile, Vicky's throwing ability is developing. At 3, she can throw without losing her balance, although her aim, form, and distance are still not much to boast about. At 4, she can play ringtoss when the peg is nearly 5 feet away. And at 5, she begins shifting her weight, stepping forward and getting her weight behind the throw.

These increasingly complex motor behaviors are possible because the sensory and motor areas of the cortex are better developed, permitting better coordination between what children feel, what they want to do, and what they can do. In addition, their bones are stronger, their muscles are more powerful, and their lung power is greater. The motor skills of early childhood have advanced well beyond the reflexes of infancy to establish the foundation of later proficiency in sports, dance, and other lifelong leisure activities. (See Table 8-3 for a summary of the development of motor skills.)

TABLE 8-3

LARGE-MUSCLE MOTOR SKILLS IN EARLY CHILDHOOD		
3-YEAR-OLDS	4-YEAR-OLDS	5-YEAR-OLDS
Cannot turn or stop suddenly or quickly	Have more effective control of stopping, starting, and turning	Start, turn, and stop effectively in games
Jump a distance of 15 to 24 inches	Jump a distance of 24 to 33 inches	Can make a running jump of 28 to 36 inches
Ascend a stairway unaided, alternating the feet	Descend a long stairway alternating the feet, if supported	Descend a long stairway unaided, alternating the feet
Can hop, using largely an irregular series of jumps with some variations added	Hop 4 to 6 steps on one foot	Easily hop a distance of 16 feet

Source: Corbin, 1973.

Boys are slightly stronger than girls and have slightly more muscle even at this age (Garai & Scheinfeld, 1968), and they are better at throwing a ball, jumping, and going up and down ladders (McCaskill & Wellman, 1938). But girls outshine boys at several other tasks involving limb coordination. Five-year-old girls, for example, are better than boys at doing jumping jacks, foot tapping, balancing on one foot, hopping, and catching a ball (Cratty, 1979). And girls tend to excel at small-muscle coordination. These differences may be a result of different skeletal makeup, but they may simply reflect societal attitudes that encourage different types of activities for boys and girls.

Three-year-olds have made significant gains in eye-hand and small-muscle coordination. Vicky can take a crayon and a big sheet of newsprint and draw a circle. She can pour her own milk into her cereal bowl, and she can button and unbutton her clothes well enough to dress herself and use the toilet. At 4, Jason can cut along a line with scissors, draw a person, make designs and crude letters, and fold paper into a double triangle. At 5, children can string beads well, control a pencil, and copy a square, and they will show a preference for using one hand over the over. About 1 in 10 children are left-handed, and more of these are boys than girls.

ARTISTIC DEVELOPMENT

"I like my drawings myself," Jason says. "I draw them for myself." At 4, he draws one car or truck after another. When Julia encourages him to draw a person, he does—and then carefully draws wheels under the feet. Julia and Jess encourage Jason's drawing and enjoy his pleasure in doing it, but they attach little importance to his artistic output. In this respect they are similar to many earlier professional observers of child development. Today, however, we look at children's early artistic creations with new eyes, thanks largely to the efforts of one scholar.

Rhoda Kellogg (1970) has examined more than 1 million drawings by children, half under age 6, concentrating on "self-taught" art rather than pictures in coloring books, stencils, and other exercises provided by adults. Since she has found that drawings by young children are similar in different cultures and countries, she concludes that early drawing reflects maturation of the brain. Let us see how this development unfolds (see Figure 8-2, page 302).

(© Erika Stone 1988)

Drawings of early childhood are similar in different cultures and countries. As they progress from scribbles through shapes, designs, and pictures, they reflect maturation of the brain.

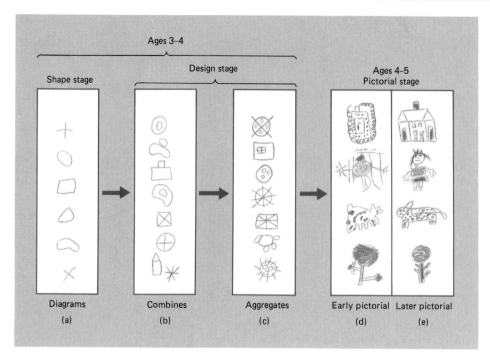

FIGURE 8-2
Artistic development in early childhood. There is a great difference between the very simple shapes shown in (a) and the detailed drawings in (e). While acknowledging children's growing facility in drawing, adults need to encourage their creativity. (*Source:* Kellogg, 1970.)

Ages 3–4

Shape stage

Design stage

Ages 4–5
Pictorial stage

Diagrams
(a)

Combines
(b)

Aggregates
(c)

Early pictorial   Later pictorial
(d)   (e)

scribble   Early form of drawing (appearing by age 2) in which the chief distinctions are the nature and placement of the line.

shape stage   Period in artistic development (at about age 3) when children begin drawing basic shapes—circles, squares, triangles, crosses, X's, and odd forms.

design stage   Period in artistic development (commonly at age 3) in which children combine basic shapes into more complex patterns.

pictorial stage   Period of artistic development (between ages 4 and 5) in which drawing becomes less abstract and more representational.

Two-year-olds are able to *scribble.* Although adults tend to dismiss scribbling as random and meaningless, Kellogg has identified 20 basic scribbles such as vertical and zigzag lines. At 2, Jason's hand control is not yet fine, but neither is it random, and at this first stage of drawing he is concerned chiefly with the *placement* of his scribbles. Kellogg has identified 17 patterns of placement of scribbles on paper, which appear by age 2.

By age 3, the *shape stage* appears. Now Jason can draw diagrams in six basic shapes—circles, squares or rectangles, triangles, crosses, X's, and odd forms. Once they reach this stage, children quickly move on to the *design stage,* where they mix two basic shapes into a complex pattern. These designs are abstract rather than representational. Most adults, including parents and teachers, dismiss the drawings of early childhood because they are not pictures *of* anything. But Kellogg argues: "Adults who coach children to draw real-life objects are not really being helpful; they may even be causing harm. The child's purpose is not that of drawing what he sees around him; rather, he is probably a very experienced master of self-taught art, concerned primarily with the production of esthetic combinations that are often the envy of adult artists" (1970, p. 35).

The *pictorial stage* begins between ages 4 and 5. Early drawings at this stage tend to suggest things from real life; later drawings are better defined. Although most adults tend to see the later drawings as a sign of progress, Kellogg points out that the switch from abstract design to representation marks a fundamental change in the purpose of children's drawing. They move away from a concern with form and design, primary elements in art. Usually after the first years of school, children who once happily drew with crayons abandon all interest in art, often because of the "guidance" of adults who encourage them to portray reality. Thus, we have a sad irony. As children develop better control of their hands, they lose interest in putting their growing skills to use (Kellogg, 1970).

Kellogg quotes the great artist Pablo Picasso: "Adults should not teach children to draw but should learn from them" (1970, p. 36). In other words, we should sustain children's early creativity by letting them draw what they like without imposing our own suggestions or standards. They may well surprise us. "What the great artist struggles to achieve, the child creates naturally" (1970, p. 39).

Child Abuse and Neglect

While most parents try to do the best they can for their children, some not only fail to foster their children's special abilities, but cannot or will not meet their most basic needs. Neglected children starve because their parents do not feed them; they freeze when they are left without clothing in frigid temperatures; and, left alone, they perish in fires. Emotionally neglected children fail to grow properly. Other children are actively abused: they are kicked, beaten, burned, thrown against walls and radiators, strangled, suffocated, sexually molested, and even buried alive. They are humiliated and terrorized by the people who are supposed to nurture them.

Maltreatment of children can assume a number of guises. *Child abuse* involves physical injury. The pattern has been identified as the *battered child syndrome* (Kempe, Silverman, Steele, Droegmueller, & Silver, 1962). *Sexual abuse* refers to any kind of sexual contact between a child and an older person. *Neglect* is the withholding of adequate care, usually physical care such as food, clothing, and supervision. However, emotional neglect also occurs, resulting in a syndrome called *nonorganic failure to thrive,* in which a baby fails to grow and gain weight at home despite adequate nutrition but improves rapidly when

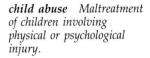

child abuse *Maltreatment of children involving physical or psychological injury.*

battered child syndrome *Syndrome of child abuse and neglect first identified in 1962.*

sexual abuse *Sexual contact between a child and an older person.*

neglect *Withholding of adequate care, usually referring to such physical care as food, clothing, and supervision.*

nonorganic failure to thrive *Emotional neglect resulting in a baby's failure to grow and gain weight at home despite adequate nutrition.*

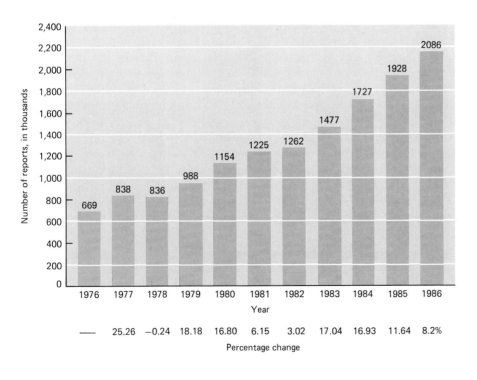

FIGURE 8-3
Reports of child abuse and neglect. Between 1976 and 1986, reports have more than tripled, from 669,000 reported cases in 1976 to nearly 2.2 million cases in 1986. This may represent a greater willingness to report mistreatment, or it may indicate that mistreatment is increasing, or both. (*Source:* American Humane Society, 1987.)

(Illinois Department of Children and Family Services)

Care enough to call

TOLL FREE / 24 HOURS

1-800-25ABUSE

TO REPORT CHILD ABUSE AND NEGLECT

ILLINOIS DEPARTMENT OF CHILDREN AND FAMILY SERVICES

Too many children not only do not receive the care they should—some are physically or emotionally neglected and some are actually harmed physically or induced into sexual contact with an older person. Since such maltreatment can have devastating long-term consequences, virtually every community in the nation provides for anonymous reporting of suspected child abuse or neglect.

moved to a hospital and given emotional support. (Psychological abuse will be discussed more fully in Chapter 13.)

Even though mistreatment of children is more widely recognized today than ever before, it still goes on. In 1986, nearly 2.2 million children in the United States were reported to be victims of abuse and neglect (see Figure 8-3). One in 7 of these cases involved sexual abuse. There has been a rise in reported cases of abuse—including sexual abuse—which may represent an actual increase in mistreatment, or better reporting, or a combination of both.

CAUSES OF ABUSE AND NEGLECT

Why do adults hurt or neglect children? Researchers suggest various causes on different levels, including characteristics of the abuser or neglecter, the victim, the family, the community, and the larger culture (Belsky, 1980).

Abusers and Neglecters

Despite highly publicized reports of sexual abuse in day care centers, more than 90 percent of all child abuse occurs at home (Child Welfare League of America, 1986). In the past, the mother was usually the abusive parent, but recent analyses suggest that men are committing more child abuse, especially sexual abuse and serious and fatal injury (Bergman, Larsen, & Mueller, 1986; Browne & Finkelhor, 1986). While over 90 percent of abusers are not psychotic and do not have criminal personalities, many are lonely, unhappy, depressed, angry, and under great stress; or they have health problems that impair their ability to raise children. The power they exert over their children through abuse may be a misplaced effort to gain control over their own lives (B. D. Schmitt & Kempe, 1983; Wolfe, 1985). They are likely to have been mistreated in their own childhood and to have felt rejected by their parents.

Abusers often hate themselves for what they do and yet feel powerless to stop. Often deprived of good parenting themselves, they do not know how to be good parents to their own children. They do not know how to make a baby stop crying, for example, and will sometimes lose all control when they cannot get their children to behave as they want. Furthermore, they often expect their children to take care of them and become furious when this does not happen. They are often grossly ignorant of normal child development, expecting their children to be toilet-trained or to stay clean and neat at an unrealistically early age. They have more confrontations with their children than nonabusive parents and are less effective in resolving problems (J. R. Reid, Patterson, & Loeber, 1982; Wolfe, 1985). Research has shown that abusive parents have trouble reading babies' emotional expressions; thus they may not be ignoring the babies' needs, but misinterpreting them. A parent may try to feed a child who is actually crying in pain, and then be frustrated when the baby spits the food back (Kropp & Haynes, 1987).

Neglectful parents, on the other hand, are likely to be personally irresponsible and apathetic, and to ignore their children (Wolfe, 1985). Mothers of infants who fail to thrive tend to have been poorly nurtured themselves and to have had stressful relationships with the babies' fathers. These mothers tend to have more complications during pregnancy and childbirth than other mothers, gaining less weight, delivering earlier, and bearing smaller babies; they also have more trouble feeding their infants (Altemeir, O'Connor, Sherrod, & Vietze, 1985). They do not hug or talk to their babies; are apparently unable to organize a safe, warm home environment; and seem to resent their babies (P. H. Casey, Bradley, & Wortham, 1984).

Victims

Abused children tend to need or demand more from their parents than other children, because of their personalities or other factors. They are more likely to have been preterm or low-birthweight babies; to be hyperactive, mentally retarded, or physically handicapped; or to show various behavioral abnormalities (J. R. Reid et al., 1982). They cry more and show more negative behavior than other children—almost 50 percent more, in one study (Tsai & Wagner, 1979). Babies who fail to thrive because of emotional neglect have often had medical problems at or soon after birth (Altemeir et al., 1985). The victims of sexual abuse seem to have a greater-than-average need for affection, which may make them easy prey to child molesters (Tsai & Wagner, 1979).

Families

Abusive parents are more likely to have marital problems than other couples and to fight physically with each other. They have more children and have them closer together, and their households are more disorganized. They experience more stressful events than other families (Reid et al., 1982). The arrival of a new man in the home—a stepfather or the mother's boyfriend—may trigger abuse by the man.

Abusive parents tend to cut themselves off from neighbors, family, and friends; consequently, there is no one to turn to in times of stress and no one to see what is happening within the family. Neglectful parents are isolated within the family, tending to be emotionally withdrawn from spouse and children (Wolfe, 1985).

Communities

The outside world can create a climate for violence inside the family. Unemployment, job dissatisfaction, and chronic financial hardship are all closely correlated with child and spouse abuse (Wolfe, 1985). Men who are unhappy in their jobs or unemployed are more likely than other men to maltreat their wives and children (Gil, 1971; McKinley, 1964).

Cultures

A culture may set the stage for violence by fostering certain attitudes in its citizens. Two cultural factors that seem to lead to child abuse are violent crime and physical punishment of children. Murder is 10 times more common in the United States than in Great Britain, and assault is 5 times greater in the United States than in Canada. More than 9 out of 10 American parents spank their children, almost 9 out of 10 Americans feel that children need strong discipline, and half of American adults approve of teachers' hitting students for "a good reason" like being noisy in class, destroying school property, or hitting someone else (Stark & McEvoy 1970). It is possible that the higher rate of child abuse in the United States is related to these facts. In countries where violent crime is infrequent, and in countries where parents rarely spank children, child abuse is rare.

LONG-TERM EFFECTS OF ABUSE AND NEGLECT

Both abuse and neglect often have grave long-term consequences. Teenagers who failed to thrive in infancy are likely to have a variety of physical, intellectual, and emotional problems, apparently due to the emotional neglect they suffered (Oates, Peacock, & Forrest, 1985). Adults who were sexually abused as children are often fearful, anxious, depressed, angry, hostile, or aggressive. They frequently suffer from low self-esteem, are unable to trust people, and feel isolated and stigmatized. Not surprisingly, they tend to be sexually maladjusted themselves. They often engage in self-destructive behavior like drug abuse, or antisocial behavior like crime and they are likely to be raped or sexually assaulted as adults.

Abuse is most traumatic if a nonabusive parent is unsupportive on hearing of it, if the child is removed from the home, and if the child has suffered from more than one type of abuse (Browne & Finkelhor, 1986; Bryer, Nelson, Miller, & Krol, 1987; Burgess, Hartman, & McCormack, 1987).

Many abused and neglected babies are surprisingly resilient, especially if there is a supportive grandparent or other family member to whom the baby can form an attachment (Egeland & Sroufe, 1981). Two-thirds of abused children go on to take good care of their own children, and only one-third perpetuate the cycle of abuse (Kaufman & Zigler, 1987). Those who become good parents are likely to have had more people caring for them to whom they could turn for help, are more likely to have a good marriage or love relationship in adulthood, and are more openly angry about and better able to describe their own experience of abuse. Furthermore, they are more likely to have been abused by only one parent and to have had a loving, supportive relationship with one parent or a foster parent.

Growing up to become an abuser is far from an inevitable result of being abused as a child. The expectation that the one always causes the other seems to have led to self-fulfilling prophecies in some cases; in other cases, parents who have broken the cycle feel like "walking time bombs," ready to explode into violence against their own children (Kaufman & Zigler, 1987).

HELPING FAMILIES IN TROUBLE OR AT RISK

There are two major kinds of help for families in which abuse is occurring or likely to occur—preventing abuse or neglect, and stopping abuse that has already occurred and repairing its effects.

Prevention

Neglectful and abusive parents feel overwhelmed by the demands of parenting, especially of caring for children with special needs. Helping parents under stress may involve community educational and support programs, subsidized day care, volunteer homemakers, and temporary "respite homes" or "relief parents" to take the children when the parents feel too burdened (Wolfe, 1985). Within the past 10 years, such programs have emerged in many communities.

Some of the most popular elements in these programs include training young parents thought to be at risk, giving them pointers in managing their children's behavior (including the use of social rewards like smiles and praise for good behavior and time-out procedures for misbehavior), teaching parents activities to help their children develop language and social skills, giving both expectant and new mothers information about their babies' health, recruiting help from relatives and friends, and involving local social service agencies.

Help for the Abused and Their Families

Sometimes a child must be separated from abusive parents, but if at all possible it is better to keep the child in the family and stop the abuse. One of the most effective ways to do this is to treat abusers as criminal offenders: people who are arrested for family violence are less likely to continue the maltreatment (L. W. Sherman & Berk, 1984). Other valuable services for abused children and adults include shelters, education, and therapy. One effective program teaches parents child management skills while providing therapy to help them deal with stress (G. R. Patterson, Chamberlain, & Reid, 1982).

The first step in helping victims of sexual abuse is recognizing the signs. These include any extreme change of behavior, such as loss of appetite: sleep disturbance or nightmares; regression to bed-wetting, thumb-sucking, or frequent crying; torn or stained underclothes; vaginal or rectal bleeding or discharge; vaginal or throat infection; painful, itching, or swollen genitals; unusual interest in or knowledge of sexual matters; and fear or dislike of being left in a certain place or with a certain person (USDHHS, 1984).

Young children need to be told that their bodies belong to them and that they can say no to anyone who might try to touch them or kiss them against their will, even if it is someone they love and trust. They also need to know that

(Janet Fries/Time Magazine)

This adult volunteer uses dolls to help young children realize that they have control over their bodies and need not let anyone—even friends or family members—touch them. Such programs for preventing sexual abuse need to walk a fine line between alerting children to danger and frightening them.

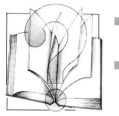
they are never to blame for what an adult does, and that they can talk to their parents about anything without fear of punishment. Furthermore, they need to be reassured that most adults want to help and take care of children, not hurt them.

One program helped 3- to 5-year-olds in preschool who had been abused or neglected and were now severely withdrawn. A teacher's aide and other children (average age 4 years) were trained to suggest or direct play activities and to give or receive objects during play, with the aim of encouraging the maltreated children to play with them. The actions of the 4-year-old initiators did help the withdrawn children become more sociable—more effectively, in fact, than the adults' efforts (Fantuzzo et al., 1988).

This kind of program shows the very practical impact that child development research can have on the lives of children. It also underscores once more the close relationship among physical, intellectual, and social development in early childhood.

Summary

1 Children continue to grow quickly between the ages of 3 and 6, but more slowly than during infancy and toddlerhood. Boys are, on average, slightly taller and heavier than girls. The muscular, skeletal, nervous, respiratory, circulatory, and immune systems are maturing.

2 Proper growth and health depend on nutrition. Children between 3 and 6 eat less than before; a balanced diet of essential nutrients is important.

3 Minor illnesses such as colds and other respiratory illnesses are common during early childhood and may have cognitive and emotional benefits.

4 Because of the availability of vaccinations, major contagious illnesses are rare among children in developed countries.

5 Accidents are the leading cause of death in childhood; most occur in automobiles or at home.

6 Factors such as exposure to other children, family stress, and poverty and hunger increase children's risk of illness or injury. A small number of childhood "accidents" may actually be suicide attempts.

7 All the primary teeth have erupted by age 3. Preventive measures such as use of fluoride and early dental care have dramatically reduced the incidence of tooth decay in children. Sucking of fingers or thumb before age 6 is unlikely to cause permanent problems.

8 Sleep patterns change during early childhood, as they do throughout life. Young children tend to sleep through the night, take one daytime nap, and sleep more deeply than later in life.

9 It is normal for children to develop bedtime rituals to delay going to sleep. However, prolonged bedtime struggles and persistent nightmares may indicate emotional disturbances that need attention.

10 Night terrors, nightmares, sleepwalking, sleeptalking, and nighttime fears may appear in early childhood.

11 Enuresis (bed-wetting) is the most common chronic condition seen by pediatricians. It appears to have a genetic basis and is influenced by biological factors.

12 Motor development advances rapidly in early childhood. Children make great strides in large- and small-muscle and eye-hand coordination. There are some sex differences in motor abilities that may reflect skeletal differences or societal expectations or both.

13 "Self-taught" art appears to reflect brain development. It progresses from scribbling to the shape stage, design stage, and pictorial stage.

14 Abuse and neglect of children is receiving more widespread attention than it used to. In 1986, nearly 2.2 million American children were reported as abused and neglected. Characteristics of the victim and abuser, the family, the community, and the larger culture all contribute to child abuse and neglect. Abuse and neglect can have grave long-term effects; however, some prevention and intervention programs seem to be effective.

Key Terms

transitional object (page 297)
night terror (298)
nightmare (298)
enuresis (299)
scribble (302)
shape stage (302)
design stage (302)

pictorial stage (302)
child abuse (303)
battered child syndrome (303)
sexual abuse (303)
neglect (303)
nonorganic failure to thrive (303)

Suggested Readings

Crewdson, J. (1988). *By silence betrayed*. Boston: Little Brown. An eye-opening and sometimes painful account of sexual abuse in America, exploring many aspects from victims to child-protection workers.

Hardyment, C. (1983). *Dream babies: Three centuries of good advice on child care*. New York: St. Martin's. An intriguing and cheerful account of child-rearing advice through the ages that can reassure parents and entertain parents and nonparents.

Moss, S. J. (1977). *Your child's teeth: A parent's guide to making and keeping them perfect*. Boston: Houghton Mifflin. A clear and useful guidebook for parents which discusses all aspects of dental health, from the prenatal period through adolescence, emphasizing prevention of dental problems.

INTELLECTUAL DEVELOPMENT IN EARLY CHILDHOOD

T he next stage is up to five years of age. During this period, it is not a good idea to try and teach them anything or make them do tasks that would interfere with their development.

Aristotle, *Politics*, c. 345 B.C.

PREVIEW QUESTIONS

- How do the three major approaches to intellectual development look at the advances of early childhood?
- How do young children think and remember?
- What research shows that young children are more competent than psychologists once believed?
- What factors influence intellectual achievement in early childhood?
- How do the three major group experiences of early childhood—day care, preschool, and kindergarten—affect children's intellectual development?
- How does language develop in early childhood?

JASON, at 3½, calls his aunt "Grandma," and as soon as he realizes his mistake, he laughs and tells everyone what he has said. After saying good night to visiting relatives, he says, "Goodnight, Jason!" and bursts into more laughter. He is so proud of this joke that he repeats it to be sure everybody gets it.

These jokes may not make him a professional comic, but they are a clear signal of his cognitive development. He knows when something he says or does is incongruous—and he knows that this is a basis of humor. The more he learns, the funnier he finds life.

Jason's growing facility with language and ideas is helping him form his own view of the world—in ways that often surprise adults. Between the ages of 3 and 6, Jason becomes more competent in cognition, intelligence, language, and learning. He learns to use symbols in thought and action, and he is able to handle such concepts as age, time, and space more efficiently.

Children's intellectual skills blossom rapidly during these years, and in this chapter we examine them. We first examine children's accomplishments in terms of the three major approaches to cognitive development: the important work of Piaget; the focus on memory of the information-processing approach; and the attention that psychometric studies pay to performance in standardized intelligence testing.

We also explore such influences on intellectual development as family, school, and television. Finally, we look at young children's increasing linguistic fluency and their social use of language.

Approaches to Intellectual Development

PIAGETIAN APPROACH: THE PREOPERATIONAL STAGE

During her preschool years, Vicky is in Piaget's second major stage of cognitive development—the *preoperational stage.* At this stage, children are able to think in symbols but are limited by their inability to use logic.

Like most children in western cultures, Vicky entered this stage at about age 2, as she came out of the sensorimotor stage of infancy—Piaget's first stage of cognitive development, when infants acquire knowledge through the senses and through motor activities. By the final (sixth) sensorimotor substage, toddlers begin to be capable of thought, as they work with ideas and solve problems by mental representation. But not until the preoperational stage can children go beyond the information they can take in through the senses and through motor activities. They can now think—that is, use mental representations for objects, people, or events that are not physically present. And when they reach Piaget's third stage, *concrete operations,* at about age 6 or 7, they will be able to apply logic to the use of these mental representations.

preoperational stage In Piaget's theory, the second major period of cognitive development (approximately age 2 to age 7), in which children are able to think in symbols but are limited by their inability to use logic.

Characteristics of the Preoperational Stage

The Symbolic Function "I want an ice cream cone!" Vicky, aged 4, says, trudging indoors from the hot, dusty backyard. She has not seen anything that might have triggered this desire—no open freezer door, no television commercial, no one else eating ice cream. In order to think about something, she no longer needs this kind of sensory cue. She remembers ice cream (she has a mental representation which includes its refreshing coldness and its delicious taste), and she purposefully seeks it out. This absence of sensory or motor cues characterizes the *symbolic function*—the ability to use mental representations to which, consciously or unconsciously, the child has attached meaning. In other words, through the symbolic function the child can make one thing represent (stand for) something else.

symbolic function Ability, described by Piaget, to use mental representation, shown in language, symbolic play, and deferred imitation.

Symbols and signs If there are no sensory cues, Piaget thought, there must be mental cues. Mental representations can be either symbols or signs. *Symbols* are personal (idiosyncratic) mental representations of a sensory experience. Vicky's symbol of an ice cream cone, for example, includes the remembered sensations of coldness, flavor, texture, and look. A *sign* is more abstract: it can be a word or a numeral, and it need not have a sensory connotation. Signs are socially agreed-upon (conventional), not personal, representations. Not surprisingly, children first think almost entirely in symbols. It is the sensory representation of ice cream that makes Vicky want an ice cream cone, not the words. As she matures, she uses signs more, making it easier for her to communicate (and to ask for ice cream).

symbol In Piaget's terminology, a personal mental representation of a sensory experience.

sign In Piaget's terminology, a conventional mental representation—such as a word—of a concept.

signifier Term used by Piaget for symbols and signs.

Piaget called both symbols and signs *signifiers,* and whatever they represent to a particular child he called *significates.* Signifiers have meaning to a child because of experience with the real objects or events they represent. Thus, an ice cream cone signifies one thing to Vicky, but to a child who has never tasted one it may mean nothing more than a picture of a cone-shaped object.

significate Term used by Piaget for the real-world object or event represented by a signifier.

This budding musician playing "panjo" is engaging in symbolic play, that is, making one object (a frying pan) stand for something else (a banjo). It's hard to tell how advanced his musical development is—but in terms of cognitive development he is in Piaget's preoperational stage.

deferred imitation
Ability to observe an action and imitate it after a passage of time.

symbolic play *Play in which an object stands for something else.*

language *Communication system that uses words and grammar.*

Manifestations of the symbolic function   Children display the symbolic function in three ways: by deferred imitation, symbolic play, and language.

Deferred imitation is imitation of an action the child has seen after some time has passed and the child can no longer see it. Jason, aged 3, sees Jess shaving. When he goes to preschool for the day, he heads for the housekeeping corner and begins to "shave." Piaget explains this by saying that Jason sees shaving, then forms and stores a mental symbol of it, and later—when he can no longer see it—calls up the symbol and is able to copy the behavior.

In ***symbolic play,*** children make an object stand for something else. Jason, for example, uses a flat block as the "razor." Piaget's daughter Jacqueline found a cloth with fringed edges that reminded her of her pillow, lay down on it as she would with her pillow, but laughed unreservedly, showing that she knew that this piece of cloth was not the pillow (Ginsburg & Opper, 1979).

Language is the most obvious manifestation of the symbolic function. Preoperational children use language to stand for absent things or events, investing words with a symbolic character, as Vicky did when she said "ice cream cone" for something that was not present. We will discuss language in detail later in this chapter.

Development of the symbolic function   A fascinating experiment suggests that some aspects of the symbolic function (the ability to use mental representations) are in place by the age of 2½, but that it is not fully developed until age 3 (DeLoache, 1987). In one part of the experiment, the experimenter pointed to various hiding places shown in a photograph of a room and asked children to find a toy hidden in the real room. At 2½ years of age, children were able to find the toy in the real room, using the picture as a guide. This showed that they already recognized the photograph as a representation or symbol of the room.

However, another part of the experiment was more complex. A child watched the experimenter hiding a very small model of a toy dog in a scale model of a real room (say, behind a model couch); the child then had to find a large toy dog in the real room (behind the real couch). Children 2½ years old were not able to find the big toy dog, but 3-year-olds were. Apparently, the older children realized that the scale model was not only a thing itself—a dollhouse-sized room—but also a symbol of something else, the real room. The younger children could not think of the model in two ways at once, as a real thing and as a representation of something else. Apparently, then, understanding that symbolic objects can have dual roles is a crucial developmental step.

Achievements of Preoperational Thought   The appearance of symbols allows children to use memories and to think in new and creative ways. Their thinking is not strictly logical, but is what Flavell (1977) calls "a partial logic or semilogic" (p. 72). Let us see how a child at the semilogical level of cognitive development thinks.

Understanding of identities   Jason now understands that certain things stay the same even though they may change in form, size, or appearance. For example, the day Pumpkin, his cat, was nowhere to be found, Jason suggested, "Maybe Pumpkin put on a bear suit and went to someone else's house to be their pet bear." But when his baby-sitter asked him if that was really possible, Jason said that he knew Pumpkin would still be Pumpkin, even in disguise.

Jason also knows that even though he has grown and changed since he was a baby, he is still Jason. In the early part of the preoperational stage, however, he may still have thought that he could change certain unchangeable aspects of his identity. For example, at times he may have believed that if he did "girlish" things, such as wearing girls' clothes, and that if he *wanted* to turn into a girl, he could (DeVries, 1969).

Understanding of functions   A child in the preoperational stage now understands, in a general way, basic relationships between two events. For example, Vicky knows that when she pulls the curtain cord, the curtain will open; when she flicks the light switch, the light will go on; and when she puts a videocassette into the VCR, she can watch a movie. According to Piaget, she does not fully grasp the fact that one event causes the other, but she knows they are related.

This developing grasp of identities and functions is often taken for granted, but it is an important achievement of early childhood. The ability to recognize that certain things stay themselves even though they change in some ways, and that certain events will regularly bring about other events, makes the world more predictable and orderly. It allows children to make better sense of life (Flavell, 1977).

Limitations of Preoperational Thought   In some ways, of course, preoperational thought is still rudimentary, compared with what children are capable of at the next level, concrete operations (the stage of middle childhood, which will be examined in Chapter 12). Let us look at some ways in which, according to Piaget, Jason and Vicky are still immature.

Egocentrism   Vicky, at age 3, loves the scented pictures of flowers in her new picture book. When Charles asks her to smell the flowers, she holds the picture up to her nose and sniffs. But when he asks her if *he* can smell the flowers, she holds the book so that the page containing the flower still faces her—and the cover is facing Charles. Her thinking is egocentric; she is focused on herself and does not realize that Charles has a different perspective from hers.

   Egocentrism is the inability to see things from another person's point of view. A classic experiment known as the *mountain task* illustrates the limitations of egocentric thought (Piaget & Inhelder, 1967; see Figure 9-1). A child faces a table on which there are three large mounds. The experimenter places a doll in a series of locations around the table and asks the child to choose a photo showing what the "mountains" look like to the doll. Children usually cannot identify the right pictures until they are 7 or older; before that, they describe the mountains

egocentrism   As used by Piaget, a child's inability to consider another person's point of view.

FIGURE 9-1
Piaget's "mountain task." A preoperational child is unable to describe the "mountain" from the doll's point of view—an indication of egocentrism.

as they see them themselves. Piaget concluded from this that children younger than 7 cannot imagine what another person is thinking (Piaget & Inhelder, 1967).

In the Piagetian framework, egocentrism does not mean *selfishness* and implies no moral judgment. It is simply an intellectual limitation that prevents children from imagining another person's point of view and experience. It is egocentric thinking which makes Jason think that you cannot see him when he covers his eyes. And it is egocentric thinking which makes him unable to understand why Julia would rather sit and read than play a game with him. If he feels a certain way, he cannot imagine anyone else's feeling differently.

centrate In Piaget's terminology, to think about one aspect of a situation while neglecting others.

decenter In Piaget's terminology, to think simultaneously about several aspects of a situation.

Centration Children in the preoperational stage tend to **centrate**: they focus on one aspect of a situation and neglect others. As a result, their reasoning is often illogical. They cannot **decenter**, or think about several aspects of a situation at once.

For example, in a reproduction of one of Piaget's most famous experiments, Jason is shown two identical glasses, each one short and wide and each holding the same amount of water. When asked which contains more water, he responds, correctly, "They're both the same." Then, Jason helps the experimenter pour the water from one of the short, wide glasses into a tall, thin glass and is asked, "Now, do they both have the same amount of water, or does one glass have more water?" Jason says that the tall glass holds more water. (Vicky, on the other hand, said that the short glass had more.)

When asked why, Jason says, "This one is bigger *this* way," pointing to the height. (Vicky said, "This one is bigger *that* way," indicating width.) Children of this age cannot consider height and width at the same time: they center (focus) on one dimension only. They are not yet able to think logically, because their thought is still tied to their perception: if one glass *looks* taller or wider, they think it must be larger. They do not yet understand that greater height may be negated by less width, or vice versa.

conservation Piaget's term for awareness that two stimuli which are equal (in length, weight, or amount, for example) remain equal in the face of perceptual alteration, so long as nothing has been added to or taken away from either stimulus.

Piaget designed this experiment to test the development of **conservation,** the awareness that two things that are equal in amount remain equal if their shape is altered as long as nothing is added or taken away. He found that children do not fully understand this principle until the stage of concrete operations, sometime after age 6 or 7 (see Chapter 12 for a fuller discussion of conservation, and see Box 9-1 for another example of centration).

Irreversibility Children in the preoperational stage are also limited by *irreversibility:* for example, they do not understand that pouring from one glass to another can go both ways. If Jason could imagine restoring the original state of the water by pouring it back into the glass it came from, he would realize that the amount of water in both glasses is the same. He does not realize this; therefore, his thought is illogical.

Focus on states rather than transformations Preoperational thought is something like a filmstrip: one static frame after another. Children focus on successive states and are not able to understand transformations from one state to another. We see this in experiments with conservation. We also see it when we ask children to identify the successive movements of a bar that falls from an upright to a horizontal position, as when a pencil drops after one has tried to balance it on end (Flavell, 1963). Children in the preoperational stage find it very difficult to

BOX 9-1 ■ THE RESEARCH WORLD

CAN CHILDREN TELL WHAT *IS* REAL FROM WHAT *LOOKS* REAL?

Charles brought home a surprise from a novelty store—a grayish, irregular-shaped sponge made to look exactly like a rock. When he showed it to Vicky and asked her what it was, she said, "A rock." He let her hold it and squeeze it, and then asked her, "What is this *really* and *truly*? Is it *really* and *truly* a rock, or is it *really* and *truly* a sponge?" Vicky puzzled a moment, and then said, "A rock." Although she was familiar with both sponges and rocks and with the way they feel, her failure to identify the sponge was typical for a 3-year-old. Vicky could just as easily have erred in the other direction. If Charles had asked her, "When you look at this with your eyes right now, does it look like a rock or does it look like a sponge?" she might well have said, "A sponge" (Flavell, 1986).

Children aged 3 to 6 have great trouble telling the difference between what things appear to be and what they really are. By 6 or 7 years, however, Vicky will clearly understand the distinction between appearance (the sponge *looks like* a rock) and reality (the object really *is* a sponge). This will be an important achievement, since the relation between what is and what seems to be figures in many everyday situations and can have serious implications. It is hard to imagine a society in which normal people do not learn to tell the difference.

John H. Flavell and his colleagues have been posing a variety of appearance-reality tasks before young children to find out at what age they begin to tell the difference. They show children a red car and ask them what color it is, then cover the car with a filter that makes it look black and again ask the children what color the car really is. With such tasks, they have found that most 3-year-olds have trouble telling the difference between the way things are and the way they look. Not until children are 6 or 7 do most of them get almost all the answers right.

The most common mistake is giving the same answer twice—saying that something *is* what it *looks like* (that it *is* a rock and it *looks like* a rock) or saying that it *looks like*

what it *is* (when it does not). The children generally cannot answer, say, that Charles's novelty *is* a sponge but *looks like* a rock. This pattern suggests that children have trouble understanding that a person can have two different mental representations of an object or event. Vicky cannot understand that Charles knows that something appears to be a rock but really is a sponge, or that yesterday he pretended the sponge was a rock to fool Ellen but today he will give it to Vicky to play with in her bath, showing that he knows it is a sponge. Nor can she understand that two different people can have two different mental representations of the same thing; this understanding will come as she becomes less egocentric.

Aware that researchers have often underestimated children's cognitive abilities by posing tasks that are too hard for them for other reasons, Flavell and his colleagues have made the tasks easier (Flavell, Green, Wahl, & Flavell, 1987). In one, for example, they use special sunglasses to change the color of milk (which even very young children know is white). They have an experimenter put on a Halloween mask in front of the children and then ask who he or she really is. They have simplified their language to help the children understand the tasks better. Still, the children have made the same mistakes, confusing appearance and reality.

They have also tried training the children. Training works for some other cognitive tasks, but it does not help the children learn to distinguish appearance and reality. Finally, they have conducted cross-cultural tests with Chinese 3- to 5-year-olds from a preschool in Peking (Beijing) and found remarkably similar responses (Flavell, Zhang, Zou, Dong, & Qui, 1983).

The conclusion, then, is that the difficulty in distinguishing between appearance and reality is universal in young children. Not until children are old enough to realize that the same object or event can be represented in different ways by the same person and by different people can they tell appearance from reality. Understanding the development of this achievement is important because it "is part of the larger development of our conscious knowledge about our own and other minds" (Flavell, 1986, p. 419).

---

reconstruct the various positions occupied by a quickly falling bar. They focus on the first and final states, but not on the transformations in between. The failure to understand how things are transformed from one state to another is one more limitation of preoperational thinking.

Transductive reasoning   Logical reasoning is of two basic types: deduction and induction.

Deduction goes from the general to the particular: "All people are mammals. I am a person. Therefore, I am a mammal."

deduction *Reasoning that shows a particular conclusion to be implied by a general premise.*

induction *Reasoning which asserts that a general rule can be made on the basis of one or more particular examples.*

transduction *In Piaget's terminology, a child's method of thinking about two or more experiences without relying on abstract logic.*

Induction goes from the particular to the general: "Investigation has shown that the red blood cells of horses, porpoises, tree shrews, people, and other mammals lack nuclei. Therefore, we can probably assume that the red blood cells of all mammals lack nuclei."

In preoperational thought, children reason along neither of these lines. Instead, Jason goes from one particular to another particular and perhaps to another without taking the general into account. This kind of reasoning is called **transduction.** It involves no abstract logic, and when it is used to form general principles, it often leads to error, especially when a child uses it in unfamiliar situations. For example, transductive reasoning may ascribe a cause-and-effect relationship to two unrelated events. ("I had mean thoughts about my sister. My sister got sick. Therefore, I made my sister sick.") In transductive reasoning, Jason sees a relationship between "mean thoughts" and his sister's illness where none actually exists. Jason mistakenly assumes that the occurrence of two events at about the same time means that one has caused the other. However, even if the two events were related, one would not necessarily be the cause of the other. Jason's having had a mean thought about his sister at about the same time his sister got sick is just a coincidence.

(Transduction plays a part when children feel responsible for parents divorcing. Another reason for a child's feeling responsible is egocentrism: children assume that all events center on them.)

Evaluating Piaget's Theory: Did Piaget Underestimate Children's Abilities?

With regard to cognitive development during early childhood, no theorist has been more influential than Piaget. Yet recent research suggests that the thought processes of early childhood are more advanced than Piaget's original theory allowed. Ironically, Piaget may have underestimated children's thought processes because he overestimated their language abilities. When children gave wrong answers to various questions, he assumed that this was due to an error in their basic thinking processes. Now, in some cases, it seems that they may not understand the problem.

In many of the classic tasks, children misinterpreted questions and may have given answers to questions the experimenter was not asking (Donaldson, 1979). One psychologist looked up some stories Piaget had asked children to retell, and she had trouble remembering them herself. When she rewrote them to simplify them and to clarify cause-and-effect connections, first-graders had no trouble retelling them correctly (Mandler, cited in Pines, 1983). The nature of the task or situation in an experiment is crucial to its findings.

By designing experiments that use things with which children are already familiar and by asking questions in language they understand, researchers have found that children are more cognitively advanced than Piaget thought. Let us look at some newer experiments.

Can Young Children Understand Cause and Effect? "He's crying because he doesn't want to put his pajamas on. He wants to be naked," said a 27-month-old girl, watching (and listening to) her twin brother crying loudly as he was being changed for bed. This statement—so commonplace that it probably would have gone unnoticed if the twins' aunt had not been a developmental psychologist—shows that even at this early age children understand that some things cause

FIGURE 9-2
Examples of sequences to test understanding of causality. A child is asked to look at pictures like those at the left, to pick the one in the row at the right that would show what happened, and to tell a story about what happened.

Story A

Choices for A

other things. The use of the words *because* and *so*, which children use in spontaneous speech before they can answer adults' "why" questions, suggests that children understand causality very early.

In an experiment that supported this, 3- and 4-year-olds were asked to look at pictures like those at the left in Figure 9-2, and then to choose the picture on the right that would tell "what happened" (Gelman, Bullock, & Meck, 1980). The children showed an understanding of causality, telling stories—for example, "First you have dry glasses, and then water gets on the glasses, and you end up with wet glasses."

How Egocentric Are Young Children? Young children are also not as egocentric as Piaget thought. We can see this in an experimental task similar to Piaget's mountain task in some respects—but crucially different in others. In this new task, a child is seated in front of a square board, with dividers that separate it into four sectors. A toy "police officer" is put at the edge of the board. Then a doll is put into one of the sectors, and every time the doll is put into a different place, the child is asked whether the police officer can see the doll. Another police officer is then brought into the action, and the child is told to hide the doll from both police officers. When 30 children between the ages of 3½ and 5 were given this task, they gave the correct answer or did the right thing 90 percent of the time (Hughes, 1975).

Why were these children able to take another person's point of view—in this case, the police officer's—when children doing the mountain task were not? The answer is that this task involves thinking in more familiar and less abstract ways. Most children do not look at mountains and do not think about what other people might see when looking at a mountain. But even 3-year-olds know about dolls and police officers and hiding.

An incident at Vicky's fourth birthday party also casts doubt on Piaget's concept of young children's egocentrism. When she opened the present Jason gave her, she found a bag of marbles. "I already have some marbles," she said, and then added quickly, "but it's okay; I need some more." Vicky surely added this remark because she could imagine how Jason might feel if he thought that she did not like his gift. When children are in settings that are familiar and important to them, they are likely to show *empathy*, the ability to put themselves in another person's place.

This understanding also shows up in the many instances of altruistic behavior displayed by young children. (*Altruistic behavior*, action that benefits another rather than oneself, is discussed in Chapter 10.) Even babies reach out to people in distress. Between the ages of 10 and 12 months, babies often cry when they see another child crying; by 13 or 14 months, they pat or hug a crying child; and

(© Miro Vintoniv/Stock, Boston)

As this 5-year-old stacks alphabet blocks by size, he demonstrates that he can arrange objects by at least one attribute. He can probably do it by several attributes, according to recent research.

by 18 months, they offer specific kinds of help like holding out a new toy to replace a broken one or giving a bandage to someone with a cut finger (M. R. Yarrow, 1978).

It is true that young children are often egocentric in their speech, speaking without knowing or caring whether the person they are talking to is interested or even listening. But the crucial question here is whether children speak in egocentric ways because they cannot take another person's viewpoint or whether, at times, they just do not care about it. (We all know adults who sometimes speak egocentrically, too.) Research suggests that they sometimes do not care, since they do "tailor" their speech in certain situations. For example, even children as young as 4 years old speak "motherese" to 2-year-olds (Shatz & Gelman, 1973), and young children can be very effective communicators when performing tasks they understand.

How Well Can Young Children Classify? Researchers today also differ with Piaget on children's ability to classify. Let us consider this issue.

Piaget's stages of classification Piaget identified three stages of classification (Inhelder & Piaget, 1964).

- *Stage 1 (2½ to 5 years)*: Children group items to form a design or figure (like a house); or they group them according to criteria that keep changing (like adding a blue square to a red square because both are squares and then adding a red triangle to the group because it is red, like the red squares).
- *Stage 2 (5 to 7 or 8 years)*: Children group by similarity but may switch criteria during a task, sorting some groups on the basis of color and others on the basis of shape or size. They often subclassify—for example, first putting all the red items into one group and then grouping all the red squares, triangles, circles, and so forth.
- *Stage 3 (7 to 8 years)*: At the stage of concrete operations, children are truly classifying: they *start out* with an overall plan to group items according to two criteria (like color and shape), showing that they understand the relationships between classes and subclasses.

Recent research Other researchers, however, have found that many 4-year-olds can classify by two criteria (Denney, 1972). And recent research suggests that some aspects of classification behavior appear early in the second year of life (Gopnik & Meltzoff, 1987).

Researchers brought 12 children (average age, 15½ months) into the laboratory and set before them three different sets of eight objects, four of one kind and four of another. The sets included (1) four flat yellow rectangles and four bright-colored plastic figures of people, (2) four clear pillboxes and four balls of red Play-Doh, and (3) four Raggedy Andy dolls and four red cars. The children were told to "play with these things" or "fix them all up." These problems, posed at 3-week intervals and continuing until every child had passed a series of cognitive tests, revealed an unvarying sequence in acquiring classification ability.

- *Level 1—Single-category grouping (average age, 16.04 months)*: The child moves four objects of one kind and groups them together.

- *Level 2—Serial touching (average age 16.39 months):* The child first touches four items from one group and then four from the other group.
- *Level 3—Two-category grouping (average age, 17.24 months):* The child moves all eight objects and either sorts them into two distinct groups or establishes one-to-one correspondence (like putting each of the four dolls on top of a red car).

At about 18 months, children typically go through a "naming explosion": they suddenly acquire many new words to label objects. Their interest in naming things seems to show that they now realize that objects belong to different categories. It is not surprising that they develop two-category classification at about the same time as they feverishly try to name objects.

They seem "to want to divide the world into 'natural kinds,' both in word and in deed" (Gopnik & Meltzoff, 1987, p. 1530).

Can Cognitive Abilities Be Accelerated? A number of programs have been designed specifically to teach various cognitive abilities. Can these programs help children acquire such abilities at an earlier age than they otherwise would? The results seem to show that training works when a child is already on the verge of grasping the concept being taught and that some kinds of training work better than others.

In one study, 4-year-olds learned conservation (the awareness that two things that are equal in amount remain equal if their shape is altered as long as nothing is added or taken away) and retained it up to 5 months later. Three-year-olds could not grasp conservation as well and tended to lose whatever understanding they did not gain (D. Field, 1981). Furthermore, the kind of training made a difference.

In the experiment, a child was shown various sets of items such as checkers, candies, jacks, sticks, and rods. The child was asked to pick the two rows that had the same number of items or to show which two objects were the same length. Then the objects were moved or changed, and the child was asked whether they were the same.

The child was then given one of three verbal rules explaining *why* they were the same:

1. *Identity,* or equivalence of the materials: "No matter where you put them, the number of candies is just the same."
2. *Reversibility,* or the possibility of returning the items to their original arrangement: "Look, we just have to put the sticks back together to see that they're the same length."
3. *Compensation,* or showing that a change in one dimension is balanced by a change in the other: "Yes, this stick does go farther in this direction, but at the other end the other stick is going farther, and so they balance each other."

These different kinds of training had different effects. The children who learned the "identity" rule made the most progress in understanding conservation, and those who learned about reversibility also advanced—although the children who were taught compensation benefited little. But why did these 4-year-olds improve at all with training? The researcher has suggested that training benefits children whose intellectual structures are well enough developed to handle this kind of thinking, by giving them a strategy for integrating it into their thought processes; the strategy works because it is useful in everyday life (D. Field, 1981).

Such experiments suggest that "preoperational" children are more competent than Piaget supposed. They do, of course, have a number of cognitive limitations, compared with children at the next stage of development, which Piaget called *concrete operations*. However, when "preoperational" children are faced with tasks that are compatible with what they already understand and are explained in familiar language, these children show more competence than they do on traditional Piagetian cognitive tasks, such as the mountain task. Our new appreciation of all the things that young children *can* do owes a great deal to new research techniques, which enable us to tap more of children's impressive intellectual abilities.

Follow-up research has, as we have seen, supported the concept of the symbolic function. The information-processing approach, a second way to explain intellectual development in early childhood, discusses learning in terms of memory rather than symbols.

INFORMATION-PROCESSING APPROACH: DEVELOPMENT OF MEMORY IN EARLY CHILDHOOD

Jason was 4 when he first became aware of memory. "Do you know that whenever you say 'Hi' to somebody, it spins around in your head and you keep hearing it?" he asked excitedly. Until then, Jason had not realized how much he actually held in his head—even though he had been able to sing many television commercials as soon as he learned how to say the words. Children remember a great deal from a very early age.

Until the mid-1960s, little information was available about memory in children under the age of 5. Since then, interest in the development of children's memory has surged (Ornstein, 1978). There are still few theories about memory in early childhood, but we do have a picture of the "remembering" child. Jason, for instance, is a processor of information who bases his actions on the information he receives and remembers. He is limited at this age, however, in both the amount of information he possesses (small, compared with what he will have later in life) and the ability to transfer information from long-term memory into a form he can use (N. Myers & Perlmutter, 1978).

Recognition and Recall

In general, in early childhood *recognition* is good, *recall* is poor, and both improve between the ages of 2 and 5 (N. Myers & Perlmutter, 1978). Children's recognition has improved considerably since infancy.

We know this mostly from laboratory experiments that test children by means of "memory games." Testing sessions, which generally last less than half an hour, usually involve children's ability to recognize or recall a series of small toys or pictures seen a short time before (N. Myers & Perlmutter, 1978).

Recognition is measured by showing a child a number of objects, putting them away, and then showing them again, along with other items the child has

recognition *Type of memory that enables a person to correctly identify a stimulus as something previously known; compare recall.*

(Suzanne Haldane)

"Remember when we went to the beach?" It is easier for this little boy to recognize a scene he saw before than it would be for him to answer the question, "Where did we go last summer?" Recognition is easier than recall for adults, too.

not yet seen. The child is then asked which items he or she has not yet seen. The child is then asked which items he or she has seen before and which are new. *Recall* is tested by showing a child a number of objects, putting the objects away, and then asking the child to name all the objects.

At all ages, people can recognize better than they can recall. Two-year-olds average about 80 percent of nine items on recognition tasks but recall on average just over 20 percent. Four-year-olds average about 90 percent correct on recognition tasks but recall best the item presented last in order. The older children remember significantly more items in the other eight positions than the younger children (N. Myers & Perlmutter, 1978).

recall *Ability to reproduce material from memory; compare recognition.*

Autobiographical Memory

Instead of asking, as Freud did, what happens to block early memories, Katherine Nelson (1989) has asked, "What happens during the early childhood years that makes enduring memories possible?" (p. 5). By reading diaries kept by mothers about the kinds of things their children remember, by tape-recording bedtime "self-talk" of one child from 21 months until age 3, by interviewing children, and from other studies of early memories, Nelson drew a number of conclusions:

- *Autobiographical memory*—that is, memory of specific events in one's own life—begins for most people sometime in early childhood, rarely before 3 years of age. It then increases slowly between ages 5 and 8, and memories from then on are often remembered for 20, 40, or more years.
- Memory in early childhood is rarely deliberate. Young children typically do not try to commit facts to memory but instead remember events that have made a particular impression.
- Most early memories are transitory. A 2½-year-old who looks at pictures of

autobiographical memory *Memory of specific events in one's own life.*

his birthday party 6 months before and recalls that a guest broke his new toy bus will probably not remember the incident later in life.

- Children as young as 3 years old remember events better when they are unique and novel, and may recall many details from a trip to the zoo or an unusual museum for up to a year or longer (Fivush, Hudson, & Nelson, 1983). They also remember ordinary events connected with recurring experiences (having lunch, going to the beach, or attending a series of workshops), but one instance tends to blur into another.

Autobiographical memory is fascinating to study, since it rarely has a practical purpose but is valued for its own sake "as a kind of personal and social treasure, a continuing reservoir of knowledge about [the] self and others" (Nelson, 1989, p. 9). This kind of memory is uniquely human, the basis for song, story, epic, and myth in all cultures.

Influences on Children's Memory

At all ages, as we noted above, people cannot recall as well as they can recognize. It is especially hard for young children to recall because they have less general knowledge, are familiar with fewer items, know fewer words to identify what they do remember, and do not yet have strategies for remembering (like repeating a list of items they want to remember). All these factors seem to influence memory. The improvements that occur between ages 2 and 5 seem to be related to an increase in general knowledge, since children under 5 do not show any signs that they make any special effort to remember (N. Myers & Perlmutter, 1978).

General Knowledge Young children recall items better when these items are related to each other—a fact which indicates the importance of general knowledge. When 3- and 4-year-olds saw pairs of pictures, they did much better recalling pairs that were related in some way than recalling pairs of unrelated pictures (Staub, 1973). In addition, children remembered pictures in which one member of the pair was a part of the other (like a tire and a car) better than those in which one item was the usual habitat of the other (like a fish and a lake), and they remembered to a lesser degree those in which the two items belonged to the same category (like a hat and a sock). It seems that the more children know about the world and the things in it, the better their tools will be for remembering.

Social Interactions How people talk with a child about an event influences how the child will remember it. In one field experiment, ten 3-year-olds and their mothers visited a natural history museum (Tessler, cited in Nelson, 1989). Half the mothers talked naturally with their children as they walked through the museum. The other half, as requested, did not initiate discussions but responded to their children's comments. All conversations were tape-recorded. A week later the researchers interviewed mothers and children separately and asked 30 questions about objects seen the week before.

The results were dramatic. The children remembered only those objects they had talked about with their mothers, and the children in the natural-conservation group remembered better. Furthermore, the mothers' style of talking to the children had an effect. Four of the mothers used a narrative style, reminiscing about shared experiences ("Remember when we went to Vermont and saw Cousin Bill?"), and six mothers adopted a more practical style, using memory for a specific purpose like solving a problem ("Where does this puzzle piece go? You remember we did that one yesterday"). The children of the "narrators" averaged 13 correct answers, compared with fewer than 5 for the children of "practical" mothers. Thus it seems that adults' style of talking about events influences how well children remember them.

PSYCHOMETRIC APPROACH: MEASURING INTELLIGENCE IN EARLY CHILDHOOD

Vicky, now 4, is sitting in a room with a man she has never seen before. He places a toy automobile, a toy dog, and a shoe on the table in front of her and asks her to name each object. Then he says, "Shut your eyes tight now so that you can't see them." He puts a screen between her and the objects and then covers the dog. Removing the screen, he asks Vicky, "Which one did I hide?" Vicky exclaims, "The doggie!" and gets credit for her correct answer.

Since children can now communicate with words, sit at a table, and manipulate test objects, they can respond to tasks like this on intelligence tests. Since these tests are more verbal than the tests of infancy (see Chapter 6), they are more reliable and more valid for predicting school performance. By the age of 5, there is a high correlation between present and future intelligence scores (Bornstein & Sigman, 1986; Honzik, Macfarlane, & Allen, 1948).

Two of the most important tests in early childhood, the Stanford-Binet and the Wechsler Preschool and Primary Scale of Intelligence (WPPSI), are both administered to one child at a time.

Stanford-Binet Intelligence Scale

The *Stanford-Binet Intelligence Scale* takes 30 to 40 minutes. The child is asked to give the meanings of words, to string beads, to build with blocks, to identify the missing parts of a picture, to trace mazes, and to show an understanding of numbers. The IQ yielded by the Stanford-Binet is supposed to be a measure of practical judgment in real-life situations, memory, and spatial relations.

Stanford-Binet Intelligence Scale Individual intelligence test that includes verbal, nonverbal, quantitative, and memory items.

In 1985, to address various criticisms of the Stanford-Binet, its publisher issued a fourth edition, the first new edition since 1960. This new edition is revised in a number of important ways. Instead of a heavy loading of verbal items, the new scale balances verbal and nonverbal, quantitative, and memory items.

Furthermore, whereas the third edition yielded an IQ as a single overall measure of intelligence, the fourth edition assesses both patterns and levels of cognitive development. It is still possible to assign an IQ, but the new emphasis is on "developed abilities," and on differences from one cognitive ability to another for an individual test taker.

The standardization sample was revamped, so that it is now well balanced geographically, over the United States; ethnically, in proportion to ethnic groups' presence in the population; and by gender, representing both sexes equally. The norms for the test were corrected to offer a socioeconomic balance and to include handicapped children.

Wechsler Preschool and Primary Scale of Intelligence (WPPSI)

The *Wechsler Preschool and Primary Scale of Intelligence (WPPSI)* is used with children aged 4 to 6½, takes about an hour, and is sometimes given in two separate sessions, since children of this age are distracted easily and soon tire. Its 11 subtests are grouped into two separate scales: verbal and performance. The WPPSI yields a verbal IQ, a performance IQ, and a full-scale IQ. The verbal subtests test children's information base, vocabulary, arithmetic, comprehension, and ability to see similarities in different items; the performance scale asks them to complete pictures, follow mazes, code pictures of animals with different-colored cylinders representing their houses, and copy geometric and block designs. An eleventh subtest, which asks the child to repeat a sentence after the examiner says it, can be used as an alternative for one of the verbal tests.

Factors in Intellectual Development

When Jason was 6 months old, his parents enrolled him in a book club and began reading to him at bedtime—a routine he now cherishes. Seeing his books as another kind of toy, Jason sometimes looked at the pictures by himself. Once, when he was 18 months old, Julia put a picture book into his stroller, and enjoyed the double takes as passersby saw Jason sucking his thumb and "reading." Parents and the attitudes they project are among many factors that affect children's cognitive development. Other important influences are the child's own personality and day care and schooling. We now consider these , beginning with personality.

HOW DOES PERSONALITY INFLUENCE INTELLECTUAL DEVELOPMENT?

Intellectual functioning is closely related to emotional functioning and temperament. An active child who is assertive and curious and takes initiative is likely to do well on IQ tests. Children's social and emotional functioning in preschool appears to influence their performance in the first and second grades.

A group of 323 three-year-olds attending public day care centers in New York City were rated on their social and emotional functioning—how well they got along with teachers and other children and adapted to daily routines—and were then followed up in the first and second grades. When their test scores and their teachers' academic ratings of them were compared with their preschool social and emotional ratings, a strong relationship appeared (Kohn & Rosman, 1973). Kohn and Rosman say that the findings "suggest that the child who is curious, alert, and assertive will learn from [the] environment and . . . the child who is passive, apathetic, and withdrawn will . . . learn less about [it] because of diminished contact; he may even actively avoid contact" (p. 450).

HOW DO PARENTS INFLUENCE INTELLECTUAL DEVELOPMENT?

Do parents of bright children do something special? Are they different from parents of other children? On the basis of the results of many studies (Clarke-Stewart, 1977), we can form a picture of the parents of young children who score high on intelligence tests and whose IQ *increases* in early childhood. Although most of these studies have concentrated on the mother's role, the findings apply to fathers and other caregivers as well.

These parents are sensitive, warm, and loving. They are very accepting of their children's behavior, encouraging them to explore and to express themselves. When they want to change their children's behavior, they reason with them or appeal to their feelings rather than enforce rigid rules. They use relatively sophisticated language and teaching strategies, and they encourage their children's independence, creativity, and growth by reading to them, teaching them to do things, and playing with them. The children respond by expressing curiosity, being creative, exploring new situations, and doing well in school.

The Home Environment

A measure that assesses the impact of the home surroundings in infancy and early childhood on a child's later intellectual growth is the *Home Observation for Measurement of the Environment (HOME)*. This aptly named scale looks at the number of books in the home, at the presence of challenging toys that encourage the development of concepts, and at the mother's involvement in her child's play. It also evaluates the way mother and child talk to each other, and gives a high mark for a mother's friendly, nonpunitive attitude toward her child. Scores on all these factors are fairly reliable in predicting children's IQ; when combined with the mother's level of education, they are even more accurate.

Researchers compared HOME scores for low-income 2-year-olds with the children's Stanford-Binet scores 2 years later. They found that the single most important factor in predicting high intelligence was the mother's ability to create and structure an environment that fostered learning (Stevens & Bakeman, 1985). This result supports the findings of the Harvard Preschool Project regarding the characteristics of the A mothers (see Chapter 6). Again, although the research studied mothers, other people, too, can offer children the same kinds of benefits. Fathers and other caregivers can also provide books and toys that encourage conceptual thinking and language development, can talk with and read regularly to children, can pay attention to and get involved in their play, and can use punishment sparingly.

The Father's Role

Researchers have been paying more attention to fathers' impact on children's intellectual development. Norma Radin (1981b) has reviewed the literature on the father's role, and unless otherwise noted, all material in this section is drawn from her review.

Fathers influence their children's intellectual development in many ways. The way they feel and act toward their children, the attitudes they have picked up from their own parents and communities, their own abilities and intellectual interests, and the quality of their marriages all play a part. A father's involvement can be helpful or harmful: when he is strict, dogmatic, and authoritarian, for example, his children are likely to do poorly in school.

Fathers seem to exert more influence over sons than daughters, probably because boys are more likely to identify with their fathers and vice versa (see the discussion of identification in Chapter 10). As Jason takes on Jess's attitudes, values, roles, gestures, and emotional reactions, he also picks up Jess's problem-

Parents and the attitudes they project are among many factors that affect children's cognitive development. The reading that this mother does with her children will enrich their knowledge and stimulate their imagination —especially if she makes special efforts to ask them open-ended questions.

solving strategies, Jess's styles of thinking, and the very words Jess utters. Boys are especially likely to copy fathers who are nurturant, approve of them, and are seen as strong but do not use their strength to dominate and intimidate.

It is harder to draw neat conclusions about the complex effect that fathers have on daughters. Vicky, whose father is interested in her intellectual development and also encourages her independence, is likely to do well.

What happens when there is no father in the home? The literature about the effects of the father's absence is contradictory and confusing, partly because research techniques vary from study to study and partly because of our changing society. It does seem, though, that a father's absence has a negative effect on children's cognitive development, an effect most marked in ethnic groups that view the father unequivocally as the head of the household. Boys who lose their fathers before the age of 5 do more poorly in mathematics (Shinn, 1978), as do girls who lose their fathers before age 9 (Radin, 1981a).

This finding may not continue to hold up, however, now that single-parent families are common. As this lifestyle becomes more prevalent, some of its disadvantages—like social stigma, lack of male models, and lack of support systems—may diminish over time.

If the mother has trouble reacting to the father's death or absence and if his loss brings financial hardship, the child's development is likely to suffer. But the child will be less affected by the father's absence if the mother copes well, has enough money, and compensates by what she does herself and by enlisting relatives, friends, or community representatives to provide a male presence in her child's life. Each family situation needs to be assessed individually.

DAY CARE AND SCHOOLING IN EARLY CHILDHOOD

Children's experiences in day care, preschool, and kindergarten are an important influence on their cognitive development. In this section, we examine each of these—and a related factor, educational television.

day care *Program designed to care for young children outside the home.*

preschool *Program designed to provide educational experiences for young children.*

Day care involves the physical care and supervision of young children, usually for the entire day, while their parents are at school or at work. *Preschool* (also known as *nursery school*) has existed since early in the twentieth century to provide educational experiences for young children and to meet their developmental needs; typically, sessions last only a few morning or afternoon hours. Today, many preschools and day care centers have virtually identical programs and facilities; preschools have lengthened their hours and expanded their services to meet the needs of working parents, and day care centers are focusing more on children's developmental needs. What a program is called matters less than what it actually does.

kindergarten *Traditional introduction to school for 5-year-olds, an optional year of transition between the relative freedom of home or preschool and the structure of formal schooling.*

Kindergarten is the traditional introduction to school for 5-year-olds, an optional year of transition between the relative freedom of home or preschool and the structure of formal schooling. Historically, it has been offered on a half-day basis, but today some communities are offering full-day kindergarten. Historically, also, its curriculum has been geared to introducing children to letters, numbers, and other basic tools for learning, but over the past 20 years many kindergarten programs have become much more academic, teaching children skills that used to be reserved for first grade.

Pointing to the success of preschools for disadvantaged children, some educators advocate compulsory public schooling for 4- or 5-year-olds; others, however, worry about the effects of pressuring children into intellectual activities prematurely. Let us look at the trends in more detail.

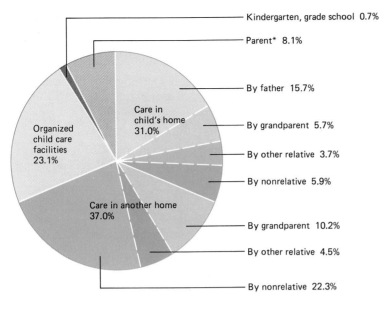

Kindergarten, grade school 0.7%

Parent* 8.1%

By father 15.7%

Care in child's home 31.0%

By grandparent 5.7%

Organized child care facilities 23.1%

By other relative 3.7%

By nonrelative 5.9%

Care in another home 37.0%

By grandparent 10.2%

By other relative 4.5%

By nonrelative 22.3%

*Includes mothers working at home or away from home.

FIGURE 9-3
Primary child care arrangements used by working mothers for children under 5 years old. *Note:* Figures from winter 1984–1985 have been rounded. (*Source:* U.S. Bureau of the Census, 1987.)

Day Care

The United States is experiencing a crisis in day care, as the traditional "Dick and Jane" family, with a breadwinner father and homemaker mother, becomes rare. Today, more than two-thirds of all mothers of children under the age of 18 are working outside the home. Among the reasons are such societal changes as an increase in the number of single-parent families, more employment opportunities for women, and an economy in which two incomes are often needed to maintain a desired standard of living.

The biggest increase in the number of working mothers in recent years has been among those with children under age 6: more than half of these mothers work outside the home, and this figure is expected to increase to two-thirds by 1995 (American Academy of Pediatrics, 1986a). There are now 10 million children under 6, at least half of whom need some form of day care. Sixty percent of children under 5 whose mothers work are cared for outside the home, many in unlicensed, unsupervised settings (see Figure 9-3). The demand for good, affordable care is so great that parents who cannot afford the high cost of private care often have to wait up to 2 years to get their children into subsidized programs (American Academy of Pediatrics, 1986c).

What Is Good Day Care?   The best day care is characterized by small groups of children. A high ratio of staff members to children is also important; but when groups are too large, adding more adults to the staff does not help. The caregiving adults should be competent and knowledgeable about child development, but they need not have many years of formal education or a college degree. What is important is specialized training in a child-related field (Abt Associates, 1978).

The best caregivers are sensitive to the needs of small children—stimulating, responsive, affectionate, and firm but not restrictive—and they stay

BOX 9-2 ■ THE EVERYDAY WORLD

HOW TO CHOOSE A DAY CARE CENTER

Because children's physical, intellectual, and emotional development is shaped by everyday experiences, the quality of substitute care is vital. To make the best choice, parents should visit a center, stay at least 2 hours, and follow guidelines for choosing a center that is safe, sanitary, and psychologically sound (American Academy of Pediatrics, 1986c; Olds, 1989).

CAREGIVERS

- Do caregivers greet the children and say good-bye?
- How do caregivers handle crying, fighting, or sleepiness; transitions between activities; and mealtimes?
- Do caregivers hug and touch the children and take them on their laps?
- Do they set limits firmly and kindly?
- Do they plan and conduct interesting activities and stimulating conversations with the children?
- Is there a busy hum of voices—or constant crying, quarreling, scolding, or unnatural silence?
- Are there enough adults to manage all the children?
- Are caregivers close enough to each other to prevent anyone's acting inappropriately to children?

CHILDREN

- Are the children involved and interested in what they're doing?
- Are they happy to come to school and content to go home?
- Are they friendly to visitors without seeking undue attention from them?
- Do they get along fairly well with one another?
- Are they cheerful most of the time?
- Can they play alone or in small groups without close supervision?
- Can they wait their turn when necessary?
- Do they have to spend too much time waiting for toilets, toys, or equipment?
- Are children in diapers kept clean?

POLICIES

- Are there sensible goals for development?
- Is there one adult to seven 3-, 4-, and 5-year-olds and one adult to four infants under age 2?

- Is each group no larger than 18 children?
- Is there an absence of racial, ethnic, and sex-role stereotypes?
- Are unannounced visits by parents welcome?
- Are there written plans for meals and emergencies, including injured or sick children?
- Is there an easily reached medical consultant?
- Is television limited?

PHYSICAL SETTING

- Does the center meet all safety codes—with marked exits, covered electrical outlets, and toys and equipment in good repair?
- Are floors, furniture, kitchen, and toilets clean?
- Does each child have a special place for his or her own things?
- Are there separate areas for playing, feeding, resting, and diapering?
- Does the building smell good—or is there an odor of mildew, decay, or poor plumbing?
- Are inside or outside areas crowded?

TOYS AND EQUIPMENT

- For large-muscle development: large balls, riding toys, a climbing apparatus, balance beams, large blocks.
- For small-muscle development: beads to string, wooden puzzles, toys to nest or stack, small blocks.
- For dramatic play: dress-up clothes, dolls, tools, child-size furniture.
- For the arts: materials to paint, draw, cut, paste, and sculpture; musical instruments.
- For quiet moments: books; records; stuffed animals.

PARENTS' CONCERNS

- Are other parents happy with the center?
- Do you feel welcome as a visitor?
- Does the center welcome your ideas and suggestions?
- If it is a community-run program, are you encouraged to participate in decisions about policy, finances, or programs?
- Do the staff members care about your whole family?
- Could you turn to the center as a resource in times of special need?

with the same children over a long period of time. Children who experience such care thrive physically, and become more capable intellectually and more secure emotionally (Belsky, 1984). (See Box 9-2 for suggestions on finding a good day care program.)

What Are the Benefits of Good Day Care?   Most of what we know about day care comes from studies of high-quality, well-funded university-based centers. Children in this kind of program tend to do as well as or better than children raised at home—physically, cognitively, and emotionally. And children from low-income families or families undergoing stress benefit most from good day care. They are less likely to show a decline in IQ scores when they go to school than children from similar backgrounds who have not had the educational experiences provided by good day care (American Academy of Pediatrics, 1986c; Belsky, 1984; Bronfenbrenner, Belsky, & Steinberg, 1977; Clarke-Stewart, 1987).

Children's language development can be greatly affected by day care, according to one of the few studies comparing care at different levels of quality—a study of 166 children from nine different day care centers in Bermuda, where 84 percent of 2-year-olds spend most of the workweek in day care. When caregivers speak often to children—especially to give or ask for information rather than to control behavior—and encourage children to initiate conversations with them, the children do better on tests of language development than children who do not have conversations with adults (McCartney, 1984).

A follow-up study of these children (Phillips, McCartney, & Scarr, 1987) found that the ones who talked often with their caregivers were also more sociable and considerate. In fact, the quality and amount of verbal stimulation seemed even more important for the children's social development than their family background. Again we see the intertwining of different aspects of development and the connection between cognitive influences and personality.

Other studies have confirmed these findings: the most important aspects of day care are matters of quality. Children do best in settings where they have access to educational toys and materials, are cared for by adults who teach them and accept them (are neither too controlling nor merely custodial), and have a balance between structured activities and freedom to explore on their own (Clarke-Stewart, 1987).

All this must be seen in perspective, however. Most of the research has focused on high-quality group care centers, but most children in the United States are cared for in their own or other people's homes by relatives, neighbors, or baby-sitters—and much of this day care is barely adequate. Until we know more about typical American day care, we cannot draw firm conclusions about benefits of day care. (We do have considerable information about growing up in the care of people other than parents on Israeli kibbutzim; some findings are described in Box 9-3, page 332.)

Preschool

Preschools have flourished in the United States since 1919, and despite a lower birthrate over the past 20 years, enrollment in preschools has soared: they now serve some 2.5 million children (see Table 9-1, page 333). This growth has stemmed largely from the greater role of the public schools, which now operate one-third of preschool programs.

(Miro Vintoniv/Stock, Boston)

This preschooler's concentration on the task at hand is typical. In preschool, children learn new skills and improve old ones, and grow in many ways—physically, intellectually, socially, and emotionally.

BOX 9-3 ■ AROUND THE WORLD

MULTIPLE PARENTING ON THE KIBBUTZ

At a time when many American children receive care from people beside their parents, interest has been renewed in Israeli children who have grown up in settlements known as *kibbutzim* (the plural of *kibbutz*), where children are raised more by nurses and teachers than by parents.

The first kibbutzim were agricultural communities, but many of the newer ones are based on manufacturing. Members of a kibbutz (kibbutzniks) share equally in the settlement's work, decision making, and resources. They eat in a common dining hall; and in a classically organized kibbutz, soon after birth infants are removed from their mothers' care to sleep in a common nursery. For the rest of their childhood they will share bedrooms, meals, and playtime with age-mates of both sexes. Although the children know who their parents are and see them every day, the parents have a lesser role than parents in American families or in the traditional families of the kibbutzniks' ancestors.

This radical departure from traditional family life was deliberate. The initial idea behind the kibbutzim was to create socialist systems in which "people would be less selfish, more secure, and more generous," with the aim of changing people psychologically (Beit-Hallahmi & Rabin, 1977, p. 533). Group child rearing was adopted to combat individualism, teach the collective values of the kibbutz, and free mothers for other duties.

While the economic success of the kibbutz has been shown, its social success is harder to judge. No special "kibbutz personality" has emerged, but by and large, kibbutzniks have turned out to be well-adjusted, productive people in spite of—or perhaps because of—multiple mothering (Beit-Hallahmi & Rabin, 1977). Thus, even extreme forms of nonparental care need not lead to emotional deprivation.

More recent work points to differences between children reared on kibbutzim and children reared at home. A study of the moral reasoning of kibbutzniks found that at every age and stage of development they tend to think more than American children in terms of obligations to others. As young adults, kibbutzniks are much more concerned than middle-class Americans with preserving and maintaining social solidarity (Snarey, Reimer, & Kohlberg, 1985).

An unexpected development on the kibbutz has been a growing emphasis on family. In 1954, Spiro said that the kibbutz proved that the family was not a universal necessity; but since then the role of the family in child rearing has increased notably. Today, very few kibbutzim follow the traditional organization of placing children in separate facilities before they reach age 6. In the most innovative ones, children sleep in the same quarters as their parents until they reach age 12, only then going to a common sleeping area. There are many disputes about these changes and the reasons for them, but none of the explanations involve complaints about the way children were turning out.

How Good Preschools Foster Development   There goes Vicky, aged 4, scooting around in a wheelchair since breaking her leg in a sledding accident 3 weeks ago. Is she staying home to recuperate? No, she is already back at school making paper place mats, painting pictures, and building with blocks. Vicky attends a good preschool and does not want to miss anything.

A good preschool helps children grow in many ways—physically, intellectually, socially, and emotionally. It helps them learn about themselves and develop a sense of self. Their autonomy flourishes as they explore a world outside the home and choose from among many activities. Since these activities are tailored to their interests and abilities, they experience many successes. And with each success, their confidence grows and their self-image prospers.

As Vicky plays with other children, she has many chances to cooperate in pursuing goals and to understand other people's perspectives and feelings, thus becoming less egocentric. And when cooperation turns into conflict, she learns how to deal with frustration, anger, and hurt feelings. Preschool is particularly valuable in helping children from one- or two-child families (what most families are today) learn how to get along with other people.

The teachers in a good preschool try to advance cognitive development in many ways. They provide a variety of experiences to let children learn by doing. They stimulate the senses through art, music, and tactile materials such as clay,

TABLE 9-1

EARLY SCHOOL ENROLLMENT AS A PERCENTAGE OF ALL CHILDREN IN EACH AGE GROUP		
	3 AND 4 YEARS OLD (%)	5 AND 6 YEARS OLD (%)
1970	20.5	89.5
1980	36.7	95.7
1984	36.3	94.5

Source: National Center for Education Statistics, 1986.

water, and wood. They encourage observation, curiosity, creativity, and proficiency in language. They encourage children to solve social, practical, and intellectual problems. And they encourage children to talk.

Over the past decade, pressures have built to provide more formal education in preschool. The rising demand for day care, an appreciation of the "head start" obtained by disadvantaged children in compensatory preschool programs, the numbers of teachers put out of work by declining school enrollments, and the growing desire among parents to give their children an early start up the educational ladder have combined to bring the three R's into nursery school. Many educators and psychologists, however, maintain that the only children who benefit from early schooling are those from disadvantaged families who can thus catch up to their more privileged peers—and that most middle-class children are better served by a relaxed preschool experience (Elkind, 1988).

One study compared children who had been enrolled in a heavily academic preschool with children who had been enrolled in several traditional preschools. In the early grades, the children from the academic preschool did better, but 10 years later the boys from the traditional preschools did better in reading and math than the boys from the academic preschool. The girls from the academic school did better in reading, but they did not do better in math (L.B. Miller & Bizzell, 1983). Although children may learn more in the short term, there may be something in the early academic emphasis that affects their interest or ability to learn in the long run.

The preschool's most important contribution may well be the feeling that children receive from it: that school is fun, that learning is satisfying, and that they are competent in a school setting. (See Box 9-4, page 334.)

The Montessori Method   Although it was originally designed to teach retarded and poor Italian children, the method developed by the Italian physician Maria Montessori has become extremely popular in the United States, especially among normal children of people who can afford private schooling.

The Montessori curriculum is child-centered. It is based on an arrangement of surroundings, equipment, and materials carefully planned to help children realize their full potential. Learning is seen as something that children do for themselves; the teachers are a resource, providing emotional support and intellectual help. Teachers observe the children closely and determine when they are ready to advance to the next phase of the program, which has motor, sensory, and language components.

Montessori children are grouped by age and follow a carefully planned, graduated sequence of learning from the simple to the complex. The method

BOX 9-4 ■ PROFESSIONAL VOICES

DAVID ELKIND

David Elkind, Ph.D., who is a professor of child study at Tufts University, has written several books about the problems of growing up in the United States today. Dr. Elkind's primary concern is the tendency of our society to push children academically, socially, and emotionally.

ELKIND: Today's parents, like parents in the past, want to do what is best for their children. But they are victims of social pressure, of media oversell, and of faddish educational practices. All these forces conspire to victimize their children, too.

A huge pressure on parents is their belief that what they do determines whether a child makes it or not. They feel, "I've got to give them the right parenting, provide the right schooling, put them in the right activities, do everything right." They don't stop to think of the other influences on children—their inherited abilities and characteristics, their level of maturation, the influences from society at large. And so parents are anxious as they try to offer their children the best of everything.

I tell parents, "It's certainly true that you play a large role, but genetics plays a role and maturation plays a role. The most important thing that you can do for your children is to create a safe environment that is also intellectually stimulating. If you're interested in reading with your children, talking to them, walking with them, going to museums—that sort of thing is much more critical than pushing them into learning reading or other skills at the age of 3."

Parents often have to be away from home longer than they would like. And there isn't enough good, affordable child care. But instead of acknowledging that certain arrangements are something neither parents nor children would choose, and helping children make the best of them, too many parents and professionals are now making a virtue out of a necessity. They're saying that being alone after school is good because it teaches children independence, or that an academically demanding full-day program is important for a 4-year-old.

Little children are feeling pressures all over the country—we're a global village, and with television and other mass media, we all get the same message no matter where we're living. So what began as an upper-class phenomenon filtered down. . . . And now parents who have

very little spare cash or time are buying their kids computer games and pushing for academic achievement. There's one encouraging sign, though. Now the tide seems to be turning as a lot of upper-middle-class parents hold their kids back, keeping them out of kindergarten till age 6.

These parents know about the age effect—that the youngest children in a kindergarten class do more poorly than the oldest children. This has been consistently documented and is among the most solid data we have in educational psychology. This says to me that these children are being confronted with a curriculum which is too difficult and frustrates them. Clearly, the kindergarten curriculum is geared to the oldest children.

School systems recognize this problem and try to deal with it. But they're still trying to squeeze children into ready-made molds rather than saying, "How do we change our molds?" Professionals want to contribute to social responsibility, but we're people, too, and we tend to get carried away and exaggerate our case. I do, too, to a certain extent, but I feel I need to counter the move in the other direction, since the other case has been made so strongly. I've been very consistent over the past 25 years. But I believe what Erikson said: "To be heard in society, you have to take a strong position and shout it loudly." And that's what I'm doing.

And what I'm shouting for is flexibility, relaxation, letting kids be kids. Children are very variable at this age—you can't limit that, so you might as well adapt to it, and the best way to adapt is to provide a program that is sufficiently flexible to accommodate children at different developmental levels. Put your 5- and 6-year-olds together in school, so that you won't be expecting every child to be doing the same thing, and so that the older ones can help the younger ones. Give parents the option of a half-day or full-day kindergarten. Working parents will know their kids are in a good, safe environment, and at-home parents can be assured that afternoon activities are usually quiet, nonacademic ones—reading stories, watching television, listening to music—so half-day kindergartners who may not be ready for a long school day won't be at an academic disadvantage. Parents know their own children and their own schedules and know which would be better for their family. And we professionals have to trust that knowledge.

Source: Interview with S. W. Olds, November 6, 1987; *photo:* © Thomas Victor.

aims to foster moral development, too, as it emphasizes cooperation, self-control, order, responsibility, patience, and the common good.

Compensatory Preschools For more than 50 years, educators have recognized that children from a deprived socioeconomic background often enter school with a considerable handicap. Some have never seen a crayon or scissors or been out of their neighborhood. Their parents, struggling to survive, may have little time to talk or read to them, answer their questions, and take them to interesting places. Not before the 1960s, though, have large-scale programs been developed to help these children compensate for experiences that they have missed out on and to prepare them for school.

Project Head Start The best-known compensatory preschool program in the United States is ***Project Head Start,*** launched in 1965 as part of the federal government's war on poverty. The program has provided services to 10.5 million children and their families—but still it reaches fewer than 1 in 6 of the nation's eligible 3- and 4-year-olds.

Project Head Start
Compensatory preschool educational program begun in 1965.

During 1987, Head Start enrolled 446,523 children, 12.7 percent of whom had some kind of disability. Thirty-nine percent were African American, 32 percent white, 22 percent Hispanic, 4 percent Native American, and 3 percent Asian (U.S. Department of Health and Human Services, USDHHS, 1988).

Goals of Head Start programs: The founders of the program felt that providing health care, intellectual enrichment, and a supportive environment to the children of low-income families could improve their everyday effectiveness in dealing with the present and preparing for the future. The program still aims to do this, and specifically to bring about the following, for both children and families:

1 Improved health and physical abilities
2 Spontaneity, curiosity, and self-discipline
3 Enhanced ability to understand concepts and to communicate with others
4 Self-confidence
5 Better personal relationships
6 Enhanced sense of dignity and self worth (USDHHS, 1987)

Components of Head Start programs: To achieve its aims, Head Start provides a range of services to children and their families:

- *Education.* Indoor and outdoor play, concepts of words and numbers, and a variety of experiences (presented in the child's native language)
- *Health.* Comprehensive physical and mental health services, including medical and dental examinations, vision and hearing tests, identification of problems, immunization, and any necessary treatment; services and counseling for handicapped children; at least one hot meal and snack every day meeting at least one-third of the day's nutritional needs, nutrition education for parents, and assistance with food stamps; and mental health training for staff and parents
- *Involvement of parents.* Participation in program planning, operating activities, and educational programs, either as volunteers or paid staff
- *Social services.* Helping families determine their needs and helping them meet those needs with referrals, information, emergency assistance, and crisis intervention (USDHHS, 1986)

Benefits of compensatory programs   *Short-term benefits:* Head Start can make a major difference in children's lives, according to a review of more than 1500 reports (R.C. Collins & Deloria, 1983). Head Start children are more likely than non–Head Start children of similar backgrounds to be of average height and weight, to do better on tests of motor control and physical development, and to have fewer absences from school. They have shown gains in intellectual functioning and language, with the neediest children benefiting the most. These effects have been limited, however: children in Head Start programs have not equaled average middle-class children either in school performance or on standardized tests, and some of their gains in IQ have not held up over time. Children suffering from some disabilities—speech and learning disabilities and emotional disturbances—have improved in intellectual functioning and language, but retarded and physically handicapped youngsters have not.

The effects of Head Start on social and emotional development are less clear-cut, possibly because of difficulties in measuring them. Youngsters in Head Start programs are generally comparable with children in the general population in social development, however; they tend to be more sociable and assertive, to seek attention more, and to be more aggressive than other children.

One team of researchers compared children with 1 year of Head Start, children with 1 year of another preschool, and children with no preschool experience. On nearly every cognitive and lifestyle measure, the Head Start children started out at a considerable disadvantage. By the end of the year, they had improved more than the children in the other two groups, with the biggest gains shown by black children of below-average initial ability. It would be unrealistic to expect the Head Start experience to completely make up for these children's initial cognitive disadvantages—and in fact it did not—but the gains the children did make are a strong argument for enhancing the program and extending it (V. E. Lee, Brooks-Gunn, & Schnur, 1988).

The effects of the program go beyond the children themselves. Parents have become actively involved: two parents volunteer to serve for every three children enrolled. A major benefit for families is the increased sense of control that parents gain over their own lives, bringing more self-confidence and satisfaction with life—and often an improvement in their own educational or financial status (R. C. Collins & Deloria, 1983).

The most successful programs have had the best teachers, the most involvement of parents, the smallest groups, and the most comprehensive services.

Long-term benefits: Some of the benefits of compensatory education are long-lasting and pay back society's investment. Although increases in IQ have been temporary, other positive effects of Head Start have held up through high school. Students who have been in Head Start are less likely to be held back and more likely to stay in school and to be in regular (not special) classes than other needy children who have not participated (L. B. Miller & Bizzell, 1983).

One major study followed two groups of poor black children from early childhood through age 19. About half had intensive preschool education when they were 3 and 4 years old; the others did not get any formal schooling until kindergarten or first grade (Clement, Schweinhart, Barnett, Epstein, & Weikart, 1984). Young adults who had had preschool education were much more likely to have graduated from high school, to have enrolled in college or a vocational training program, and to have a job. They did better on tests of competence and were less likely to have required special education for slow learners or to have been arrested; and the young women were less likely to have become pregnant.

As a 1-year, 5-day-week, 2½-hour-a-day program, Head Start cost about $4000 per child in 1981 dollars; in 1984, the benefits realized from the program came to 7 times the cost. People who had been in Head Start programs were likely to earn more money over a lifetime and to cost society less for special education, welfare, and criminal proceedings. Thus, such programs can end up saving money for society, as well as helping individuals lead more fulfilling lives.

In trying to determine the most important elements of the program, the same researchers conducted another study (Schweinhart, Weikart, & Larner, 1986). This time they compared children from poor families who had attended three different types of preschools. One stressed social and emotional development and child-initiated activities; one was a teacher-directed program with a heavy emphasis on learning numbers, letters, and words; and the third fell in between. All three groups did better in elementary school than children who had not gone to preschool, and the children from the academic program did the best work in school. But the children in this group had the most behavior problems, and by the time they were 15 years old, they had largely lost interest in school and were showing such serious social and emotional problems as vandalism and delinquency.

A final word on preschools: We need to tread carefully, it seems, in developing programs for young children. If children are deprived of opportunities to explore the world in their own way, there may be a heavy price to pay later on. Too much academic stress too soon may be detrimental to children from both advantaged and disadvantaged backgrounds.

Kindergarten

In many ways, kindergarten is an extension of preschool, but there are differences. Kindergarten is usually located in a neighborhood public school, and thus marks the beginning of "real" school. Kindergarten teachers usually have to be certified by the state; preschool teachers sometimes do not. There is usually a fair amount of emphasis on preparing children for the first grade by teaching them letters and numbers—although with the gradual raising of educational expectations for various age groups, this is now happening in preschool, and kindergarten is more like first grade. Instead of learning basic number concepts from setting a snack table and dividing crackers, today's kindergartners tend to learn their numbers by poring over workbooks and counting and matching pictures of chickens and eggs. And many kindergartners now spend a full day in class rather than the traditional half day.

Advocates of full-day kindergarten stress its longer blocks of uninterrupted time for unhurried experiences and educational activities, its greater opportunity for pupil-teacher and parent-teacher contact because a teacher is responsible for one rather than two classes, and the higher energy levels of teachers and children resulting from a structured morning and a more relaxed afternoon. Opponents point to the fact that some 5-year-olds cannot handle a 6-hour day and a long separation from their parents, and to the danger of overemphasizing academic skills and sedentary activities.

Some educators and psychologists express alarm over "treating kindergarten like a miniature elementary school with a heavy cognitive-academic orientation" (Zigler, 1987, p. 258). Furthermore, they caution against sending children

Some major educational controversies center on children like these kindergartners in North Carolina. Should they be in school all day or just half a day? Should they be learning how to read or just get ready for reading?

to kindergarten too early, pointing to studies showing the "age effect"—that the youngest children in a class do more poorly than the oldest (Sweetland & DeSimone, 1987). One alternative solution is a half-day kindergarten program taught by licensed, qualified teachers, followed by a half day of care given by certified child-care workers to those children who need day care (Zigler, 1987). This provides some academic preparation, and all-day supervision for those who need it.

Educational Television

At 3, Vicky not only enjoys watching *Sesame Street*—she likes it so much that she has learned how to switch on the set and insert a videocassette into the VCR. When she is not watching, she carries around her *Sesame Street* cassette as tenderly as Jason carries his teddy bear.

Television programs are an important influence on the intellectual development of children today. In fact, some researchers believe that American children are developing cognitive concepts earlier now because of such programs (Denney, 1972). The best-known and most far-reaching attempt to teach "over the tube" is the show *Sesame Street*. The program was specifically designed to teach such cognitive skills as using letters and numbers, solving problems, reasoning, and understanding the physical and social environment. How well has it succeeded? Although most of the research on this and other educational programs was conducted in the 1970s, its conclusions still seem valid.

Frequent viewers of *Sesame Street* often tend to improve more on the skills taught than children who watch seldom or never, according to a review of several studies (A. Stein and Friedrich, 1975). Furthermore, this learning often carries over to a wide range of verbal skills that are not specifically taught. Although improvements were noted in all groups of children tested, there were some variations. Younger children (3-year-olds) make more gains than 5-year-olds. Disadvantaged youngsters who are frequent watchers gain as much as advantaged children who watch often; but when viewing is infrequent, advantaged children gain more than disadvantaged ones. Apparently, a little viewing builds on other sources of learning, which advantaged children have access to but disadvantaged children do not. Thus, even though watching *Sesame Street* does not close the gap in achievement between advantaged and disadvantaged children, it may help prevent that gap from widening.

At first, some educators were afraid that the fast pace and slapstick approach on *Sesame Street* would make school seem boring by comparison; but as it has turned out, frequent viewers like school more and do better than children who rarely watch (Bogatz & Ball, 1971). Other critics have expressed concern that the program's fast pace would discourage children from developing a long enough attention span for work requiring a sustained effort. However, children do not seem to become impulsive when they see impulsive or fast-moving models.

Another area of concern has been attitudinal. When *Sesame Street* first rose to popularity, it was characterized by physical aggression (slapstick sequences), verbal aggression (name-calling), and gender stereotypes (showing fewer females than males and portraying females as passive). Criticisms of these aspects

GUIDING CHILDREN'S TELEVISION VIEWING

As a typical preschooler, Jason is now watching 3 to 5 hours of television every day. By the time he graduates from high school, he will have spent more time in front of the TV set than in the classroom (American Academy of Pediatrics, 1986b). Television has many far-reaching effects: it influences children's attitudes about hurting or helping other people, gender roles, alcohol and other drugs, and sexuality and relationships. It can teach positive messages—or negative ones. To help children reap the benefits and avoid the dangers of this electronic teacher, parents, teachers, and other adults can follow these guidelines suggested by the American Academy of Pediatrics (1986b) and Action for Children's Television (undated):

■ *Plan your child's viewing in advance.* Approach TV the way you would a movie by deciding with your child which show to watch, turning the set on for that program, and turning it off when the program is over.

■ *Set limits.* Restrict your child's viewing to 1 or 2 hours a day at certain set times, taking into account the child's favorite programs.

■ *Do not use television as a reward or punishment,* although you may want to reserve viewing time until after the child has carried out responsibilities like homework and chores.

■ *Watch with your child.* This way you will know what

your child is seeing and you will be able to use TV to express your own values and feelings about complex issues and to explain confusing scenes.

■ *Talk to your child* about such topics as love, work, war, family life, sex, drugs, and crime. You can open up conversations about the difference between make-believe and real life, about ways characters could solve problems without violence, and about violence and how it hurts.

■ *Set a good example.* Examine your own viewing habits and change them if necessary to help your children develop good habits.

■ *Provide alternatives.* Encourage and participate in both indoor and outdoor activities like games, sports, hobbies, reading, and household duties. Use television as a baby-sitter as little as possible.

■ *Resist commercials.* Help your child become a smart consumer by teaching how to recognize a sales pitch and how to tell when a product on a TV show is presented as an advertisement. Talk about foods that can cause cavities and about toys that may break too soon.

■ *Supplement television with new technologies.* If you have a video recorder, tape desirable shows or rent movies or special tapes made for children. If you have cable, ask about devices to lock out inappropriate channels.

■ *Recognize your power* in channeling the power of television so that it will enhance your child's life.

(Sybil Shackman/Monkmeyer Press)

Critics of children's television worry that too much viewing will discourage children from activities requiring a sustained effort, like coloring and figuring out how many fingers add up to 4.

of the show have brought about a number of changes, especially with regard to gender stereotyping.

The influence of television on children's attitudes toward gender roles and violence seems considerable, and child development professionals have expressed great concern about the need for adults to help young children reap the educational and other benefits of television, with a minimum of negative influence (see Box 9-5, page 339).

Language in Early Childhood

At 3½, Jason talks constantly and has a comment for everything. He creates his own language as he describes how Daddy "hatches" wood (chops it with a hatchet) or asks Mommy to "piece" his food (cut it into little pieces). This new language sounds more and more like English. When he was a toddler, you could have translated one of his short sentences word for word into French and the translation would have sounded exactly like something a Parisian child might say. Now, however, Jason is thinking in English and using English grammar and style. Now a translator would have to pay attention to differences in syntax as well as vocabulary.

WORDS, SENTENCES, AND GRAMMAR

"How did the first animal get born?" "Where did the first tree come from?" "Why is the sky blue?" Vicky is so busy asking questions that she rarely waits for answers.

At 3 years, Vicky can give and follow simple commands and name familiar things like animals, body parts, and important people. She uses plurals and the past tense, and uses *I*, *you*, and *me* correctly. Between the ages of 4 and 5, her sentences average four to five words, and she can now deal with prepositions like *over*, *under*, *in*, *on*, and *behind*. She uses verbs more than nouns.

Between the ages of 5 and 6, Vicky begins to use sentences of six to eight words. She can define simple words, and she knows some opposites. In her everyday speech she uses more conjunctions, prepositions, and articles. Her speech is fairly grammatical, but she still neglects the exceptions to rules ("I've already thinken of some ideas—or is it, 'I thunk'?"). Between 6 and 7 years of age, her speech becomes quite sophisticated. She now speaks in compound, complex, and grammatically correct sentences, and she uses all parts of speech.

While young children speak fluently and understandably, their speech is still full of expressions that parents consider cute and linguists see as clues to how people learn a language. Young children, for example, *overgeneralize* linguistic rules; that is, they ignore exceptions to rules. At age 3, Vicky correctly said, "Mommy held the milk," but at 4 she says "Jason holded my toy." Paradoxically, this is a sign of linguistic progress. At 3, Vicky spoke correctly because she quoted what she had heard others say. Now, at 4, she has discovered a general rule—"use *-ed* for the past tense"—and she follows it *whenever* she needs a past tense. Usually this practice leads to correct speech, but in the case of an irregular verb like *hold* it results in an error. Thus, her apparent decline in grammar is really a case of taking one step backward in order to take two steps forward. Further progress will come when Vicky notices that certain words are exceptions to a general rule.

PRIVATE SPEECH

As Jason, 4, picks up Julia's art book, he says quietly to himself, "Now I can use this—I washed my hands and so they're clean and I can hold this book." As he jumps onto his bed, he says—also to himself—"Take off my shoes. . . . Now they're off. Now I can jump."

Private speech—talking aloud to oneself with no intent to communicate with anyone else—is normal and common in early and middle childhood, accounting for 20 to 60 percent of what children say. The youngest children playfully repeat rhythmic sounds in a pattern like infants' babbling ("Minga-minga-minga," Vicky at 3 sings as she plays with her blocks); slightly older children "think out loud" in speech related to their actions; and the oldest children mutter in barely audible tones (See Table 9-2.)

private speech Talking aloud to oneself with no intent to communicate with anyone else.

TABLE 9-2

TYPES OF PRIVATE SPEECH

TYPE	CHILD'S ACTIVITY	EXAMPLES
Wordplay, repetition	Repeating words and sounds, often in playful, rhythmic recitation	Peter wanders around the room, repeating in a singsong manner, "Put the mushroom on your head, put the mushroom in your pocket, put the mushroom on your nose."
Solitary fantasy play and speech addressed to nonhuman objects	Talking to objects, playing roles, producing sound effects for objects	John says, "Ka-powee ka-powee," aiming his finger like a gun. Nancy says in a high-pitched voice while playing in the doll corner, "I'll be better after the doctor gives me a shot. Ow!" she remarks as she pokes herself with her finger (a pretend needle).
Emotional release and expression	Expressing emotions or feelings directed inward rather than to a listener	Paula is given a new box of crayons and says to no one in particular, "Wow! Neat!" Rachel is sitting at her desk with an anxious expression on her face, repeating to herself, "My mom's sick, my mom's sick."
Egocentric communication	Communicating with another person, but expressing the information so incompletely or peculiarly that it can't be understood	David and Mark are seated next to one another on the rug. David says to Mark, "It broke," without explaining what or when. Susan says to Ann at the art table, "Where are the paste-ons?" Ann says, "What paste-ons?" Susan shrugs and walks off.
Describing or guiding one's own activity	Narrating one's actions, thinking out loud	Omar sits down at the art table and says to himself, "I want to draw something. Let's see. I need a big piece of paper. I want to draw my cat." Working in her arithmetic workbook, Cathy says to no one in particular, "Six." Then, counting on her fingers she continues, "Seven, eight, nine, ten. It's ten, it's ten. The answer's ten."
Reading aloud, sounding out words	Reading aloud or sounding out words while reading	While reading a book, Tom begins to sound out a difficult word. "Sher-lock Holm-lock," he says slowly and quietly. Then he tries again. "Sher-lock Holm-lock, Sherlock Holme," he says, leaving off the final *s* in his most successful attempt.
Inaudible muttering	Speaking so quietly that the words cannot be understood by an observer	Tony mumbles inaudibly to himself as he works a math problem.

Source: Adapted from Berk & Garvin, 1984.

What is the function of such speech? Psychologists disagree. The behaviorist John Watson saw it as inappropriate activity that parents get their children to stop. Piaget defined it as egocentric speech reflecting the young child's inability to recognize another person's viewpoint. He believed that young children talk while they do things because they do not yet know the difference between words and what the words stand for.

Instead of looking on such speech negatively as irrelevant or immature, Vygotsky (1962) saw it as positive—a special form of communication with oneself. Like Piaget, he believed that private speech helps children integrate language with thought and helps them control their actions. Unlike Piaget, he believed that private speech increases during the early school years, as children use it to guide and master their actions, and then fades away as they become able to think silently.

A number of studies support this interpretation. Among nearly 150 middle-class children aged 4 to 10, private speech was found to rise and fall with age; and the most sociable and popular children used it the most, apparently confirming Vygotsky's view that private speech is stimulated by social experience (Berk, 1986; Kohlberg, Yaeger, & Hjertholm, 1968). The brightest children used it earliest—for them it peaked at about age 4, compared with age 5 to 7 for average children; by age 9 it had practically disappeared for all these children.

The impact of culture can be seen in the different pattern of private speech among low-income 5- to 10-year-olds in the mountains of Kentucky. In the Appalachian subculture, communication—especially between men and boys—depends more on gestures than words. "Talk is women's work," say men, admonishing their sons to be quiet. This may explain why private speech persists for a longer time: 25 percent of the children (especially boys) still used it at age 10. The children used private speech most when they were trying to solve difficult problems and when no adults were around (Berk & Garvin, 1984).

Understanding the significance of private speech has practical implications, especially when children go to school (Berk, 1986):

- Talking aloud or muttering should not be considered misbehavior.
- A teacher who hears it should be alert to the possibility that children may be struggling with a problem they are having trouble solving and may welcome adult help.
- Instead of insisting that children be quiet, teachers can set aside special corners where they can talk (and thus learn) without disturbing the other students.
- Children should be encouraged to play with others to develop the internal thought that will eventually displace the thinking out loud.

SOCIAL SPEECH

As a toddler, Jason often seemed to be speaking to himself. He hardly seemed to care whether someone else heard or understood him. After his third birthday, however, he changes. His pronunciation improves quickly, and strangers find it easier to understand what he says. He wants people to listen, and if they look away, he sometimes moves to face them. He wants to be understood, and if people cannot understand what he says, he tries to explain himself more clearly. The function of his speech is changing as quickly as its form. (See Table 9-3.)

(© George Godwin/Monkmeyer Press)

From a very early age, children communicate through social speech. They take other people's needs into account and use words to establish and maintain social contacts. Whatever these little girls are talking about seems engrossing.

TABLE 9-3

DEVELOPMENT OF SOCIAL SPEECH

AGE	CHARACTERISTICS OF SPEECH

2½	Beginnings of conversation:
	    Speech is increasingly relevant to others' remarks.
	    Need for clarity is being recognized.

3	Breakthrough in attention to communication:
	    Child seeks ways to clarify and correct misunderstandings.
	    Pronunciation and grammar sharply improve.
	    Speech with children the same age expands dramatically.
	    Use of language as instrument of control increases.

4	Knowledge of fundamentals of conversation:
	    Child is able to shift speech according to listener's knowledge.
	    Literal definitions are no longer a sure guide to meaning.
	    Collaborative suggestions have become common.
	    Disputes can be resolved with words.

5	Good control of elements of conversation.

Source: E. B. Bolles, 1982, p. 93.

Social speech is intended to be understood by someone other than the speaker. It takes into account the needs of other people and is adapted to the other person's speech patterns and behavior (Garvey & Hogan, 1973). It may involve an exchange of information, with or without questions and answers; criticism; or commands, requests, and threats (Piaget, 1955).

Whereas Piaget characterized most preschool speech as egocentric, recent research shows that children's speech is quite social from a very early age and that it may indeed make sense to regard children as *sociocentric* right from birth (Garvey & Hogan, 1973). When 3- to 5-year-olds were asked to communicate their choice of a toy, they behaved very differently with a person who *could* see them and a person who was blindfolded and could *not* see them. They were likely to point to the toy for the listener who could see them but to describe it to the blindfolded listener (Maratsos, 1973). Four-year-olds speak "motherese" to 2-year-olds (Shatz & Gelman, 1973). Even 2-year-olds use a great deal of social speech: they point out or show objects to one another or to adults, and most of the time (79 percent, in one study) they get feedback showing that they have captured their listeners' attention (Wellman & Lempers, 1977).

The nature of a task also makes a difference. One research project found that youngsters as old as 14 were not able to describe various unusual, abstract designs clearly enough to let other children know which ones they were talking about, probably showing that the task was just too hard, even for ninth-graders (Krauss & Glucksberg, 1977). On the other hand, when younger children were given a similar task—to describe a variety of pictures ranging from simple, familiar objects (like monkeys and people) to abstract designs—even 4½-year-olds described the pictures of familiar objects well (Dickson, 1979).

The reason children often do not tailor their speech to the requirements of a specific situation is not so much that they do not recognize a need for doing this as that they do not know how. We see something similar among adult tourists in a foreign country who ask a question in their own language, receive an uncomprehending stare, and then repeat the question—louder. Frustrated, they ignore

social speech Speech intended to be understood by a listener.

BOX 9-6 ■ A CHILD'S WORLD AND YOU

WHAT DO YOU THINK?

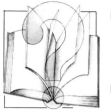

- Since young children are considered egocentric, is it a waste of time to try to get them to understand another person's point of view?
- Should parents and nursery schools try to give children a head start by teaching reading, arithmetic, and such Piagetian concepts as classification and conservation?
- "Intelligence testing of children does more harm than good." Do you agree or disagree? Why?

- Why do you think children use private speech?
- "Refusing to fund preschool programs for the disadvantaged is like adding to the national debt. We will have to pay more in the future because of what we do now." Discuss.
- Many studies show that middle-class children are more fluent in language than lower-class children. Does society therefore have a moral obligation to establish programs that will teach lower-class parents how to improve their children's language abilities?

the obvious truth that raising the volume of the voice is not a substitute for translating the words. Similarly, a child who does not have certain basic knowledge cannot communicate. It is important to remember that the method used in research often determines the conclusions (Krauss & Glucksberg, 1977).

Summary

1   According to Piaget, from approximately 2 to 7 years of age children are in the preoperational stage of cognitive development. The symbolic function—as shown in deferred imitation, symbolic play, and language—enables children to mentally represent and reflect upon people, objects, and events through the use of symbols (idiosyncratic mental representations) and signs (conventional representations).

2   Children in the preoperational stage can understand basic functional relationships and the concept of identity. However, preoperational thought has a number of limitations. Children in this stage tend to be egocentric. They are unable to decenter, they do not understand reversibility, transformations, and conservation, and they reason transductively. They also do not understand the distinction between appearance and reality.

3   Piaget may have underestimated some of the abilities of "preoperational" children. Experiments using situations familiar to young children suggest that these children are better able to understand causal relationships, are less egocentric, and have a better grasp of classification than Piaget described. Researchers have been able to teach young children conservation when they are already on the verge of grasping it.

4   Recognition memory is better than recall during early childhood, as throughout life. Autobiographical memory (memory for specific events in one's life) typically begins in early childhood. Children's memory is influenced by their general knowledge and social interaction.

5   Psychometric tests of intelligence for young children include the Stanford-Binet Intelligence Scale and the Wechsler Preschool and Primary Scale of Intelligence. Since these tests contain more verbal items than the tests of infancy, they are better at predicting later intelligence and school performance. Intelligence test scores and achievement are influenced by the child's personality as well as parent-child interaction.

6   High-quality day care, where children are cared for in small groups by sensitive adults who are trained in a child-related field, can enhance children's physical, intellectual, social, and emotional development.

7 Preschool programs are of many types. A good preschool fosters children's cognitive, social-emotional, and physical development.

8 Evaluations of compensatory programs such as Project Head Start indicate that such programs can have short-term and long-term benefits. However, it is important not to put too much academic pressure on 3- and 4-year-olds.

9 Kindergarten prepares children for formal schooling. The academic content of kindergarten has increased in recent years.

10 Children who view educational television, most notably *Sesame Street*, show enhanced cognitive skills.

11 Speech and grammar become fairly sophisticated during early childhood. Speech is of two types: private and social. Private speech is not intended to communicate to a listener but appears to help children gain control over their actions. Social speech is intended to communicate with others. Piaget characterized most preschool speech as egocentric, but recent research shows that children's speech is quite social.

Key Terms

preoperational stage (page 313)
symbolic function (313)
symbol (313)
sign (313)
signifier (313)
significates (313)
deferred imitation (314)
symbolic play (314)
language (314)
egocentrism (315)
centrate (316)
decenter (316)
conservation (316)
deduction (317)

induction (318)
transduction (318)
recognition (322)
recall (323)
autobiographical memory (323)
Stanford-Binet Intelligence Scale (325)
Wechsler Preschool and Primary Scale
   of Intelligence (WPPSI) (326)
day care (328)
preschool (328)
kindergarten (328)
Project Head Start (335)
private speech (341)
social speech (343)

Suggested Readings

Action for Children's Television. (1983). *Fighting TV stereotypes: An ACT Handbook.* Newtonville, MA: Author. A pamphlet discussing harmful stereotyping on television and offering suggestions for change. It contains specific guidelines for improving messages televised to children.

Iwamura, S.G. (1980). *The verbal games of pre-school children.* New York: St. Martin's. A study of children's speech as they travel to and from nursery school; an unusually good source for a sense of what preschool children actually say.

Piaget, J., & Inhelder, B. (1969). *The psychology of the child.* New York: Basic Books. Piaget's own summary of his theory of cognitive development. Piaget and his long-time collaborator, Bärbel Inhelder, trace stages of cognitive development.

Scarr, S. (1984). *Mother care/other care.* New York: Basic Books. An optimistic report on child-care alternatives that reflects Scarr's belief that children can thrive under a variety of arrangements. The book is designed to assist parents in making appropriate childcare decisions and is of particular value for mothers who work.

Schorr, L. & Schorr, D. (1988). *Within our reach—Breaking the cycle of disadvantage.* New York: Doubleday. An optimistic book describing how the cycle of disadvantage can be turned around by large-scale social programs for children.

CHAPTER 10

PERSONALITY AND SOCIAL DEVELOPMENT IN EARLY CHILDHOOD

W hat folly it is that daughters are always supposed to be
In love with Papa. It wasn't the case with me
I couldn't take to him at all
But he took to me.
What a sad case to befall
A child of three.

Stevie Smith, "Papa Love Baby," 1972

PREVIEW QUESTIONS

- How did Freud and Erikson explain personality development in early childhood?
- How do boys and girls come to identify with adults?
- How do children develop gender identity and adopt "boyish" or "girlish" behaviors?
- How do personality factors such as fearfulness, aggression, and altruistic behavior develop?
- What is the significance of play in early childhood?
- How do parents influence children's personality development?
- How do children's relationships with other children, like siblings and friends, influence their development?

VICKY, at age 5, is full of opinions and eager to voice them in no uncertain terms: "I don't want to go to David's party, because he's too sloppy. Sometimes at school his pants slide down, and he doesn't feel it and doesn't pull them up, and I don't like to look. Besides, his nose drizzles down and he doesn't blow it." Jason also knows his own mind—but is less apt to sit in judgment. "Sure, I want to go to David's party. He's nice. He lets me play with He-Man."

During these years, Vicky's and Jason's personalities emerge in sharper focus. They reflect not only differences in temperament that were present at birth, but the results of different experiences—and of maturing abilities. Characteristic ways of relating to other people are becoming more pronounced, and Vicky and Jason are developing many aspects of the personalities that will stay with them throughout life.

In this chapter, we discuss several aspects of personality development in early childhood. First, we see how Sigmund Freud and Erik Erikson analyze the changes occurring in early childhood. We then discuss some building blocks of personality. One of the most important is identification, which influences children's recognition of their own gender and also affects the degree to which they will be altruistic, aggressive, or fearful. We also explore the most pressing activity of these years, one that brings together social, physical, and cognitive abilities. This is the "business" of early childhood—known as *play*.

In these years, as always, personality affects and is affected by a child's social network, including relations with parents, brothers and sisters, and playmates. We close the chapter by considering these influences.

Perspectives on Personality in Early Childhood: Psychosexual and Psychosocial Theory

SIGMUND FREUD: THE PHALLIC (EARLY GENITAL) STAGE

"Granny, do you have breasts like Mommy?" Jason, 5, asks, barely taking a breath before he continues. "Do little girls have them? When did you get yours? What do little girls have? I have nipples. Do little girls have nipples?"

Bodily differences between girls and boys and adults and children fascinate young children. They want to find out where babies come from and to learn about the adult sex act. "Dirty" jokes fill their conversation, although more of these still seem to be centered on the bathroom than the bedroom. Freud explains this interest by saying that the site of biological gratification has shifted from the the mouth and the anus to the genital area. He called early childhood the *phallic stage* (from the word *phallus*, meaning the penis), and he proposed that at this stage boys are influenced by sexual attachment to the mother, and girls to the father.

phallic stage Stage of the preschool child in Freud's theory of psychosexual development, in which gratification is centered on the genital area.

The Oedipus Complex

"I love you, Mommy," Jason says, bestowing kisses on Julia. "When I grow up, I'm going to marry you." "I'm already married," Julia smiles. Not sure what to do about the solid presence of Jess, Jason thinks a moment, and then says, "I don't care—I'm going to marry you, anyway." Jason's behavior is an example of what Freud called the *Oedipus complex*. This attachment of a boy to his mother is paralleled by the *Electra complex*, a girl's attachment to her father (discussed below). Both situations give rise to considerable anxiety, which, Freud believed, must be dealt with. In resolving these conflicts, Freud held, children come to identify with the parent of the same sex, fostering the development of their identity as male or female.

Oedipus complex In Freud's theory, the process—involving sexual feelings for the mother, fear of the father, and repression of these emotions—by which a boy comes to identify with his father.

Freud based the term *Oedipus complex* on an ancient Greek myth. At Oedipus's birth, according to this myth, a soothsayer prophesied that the baby would grow up to kill his father and marry his mother. Oedipus's father, the king, ordered him killed; but instead, Oedipus was left in a faraway field, and found and raised by a shepherd. Oedipus grew up, not knowing his origins—and did kill a man, not realizing that it was his own father, and then married the widowed queen, never imagining that she was his mother. Upon learning the truth, he put out his eyes and went into exile. Freud gave the name of this tragic hero to his concept that every little boy falls in love with his mother and has murderous thoughts about his father.

Electra complex In Freud's theory, the process—involving sexual feelings for the father, fear of the mother, and repression of these emotions—by which a girl comes to identify with her mother.

According to Freudian theory, a 3- to 6-year-old boy's love for his mother is profuse and has decidedly sexual overtones, thus putting the boy in competition with his father. Unconsciously, the little boy wants to take his father's place, but he recognizes his father's power. The child is caught between conflicting feelings—on one side, genuine affection for his father, and on the other, hostility, rivalry, and fear of what his father might do to him. Noticing that little girls do not have a penis, a boy imagines that something has happened to them, and his anxiety over his feelings for his mother and father makes him worry that he will be castrated by his father. This is *castration anxiety*. Fearful, he represses his sexual feelings for his mother and his hostility toward his father, stops trying to rival his father, and begins to identify with him.

castration anxiety Part of the Oedipus complex in Freud's theory: a boy's fear of castration by the father, which leads to repression of sexual feelings for the mother and identification with the father.

Freud would say that this little girl is expressing the Electra complex: desiring her father and fearing her mother, she will eventually achieve the relationship with her father indirectly by identifying with her mother.

penis envy *Idea in Freud's theory that a young girl envies the male's penis and wishes that she had a penis herself.*

superego *In Freud's theory, the representation of social values, communicated by parents and other adults.*

The Electra Complex

Another Greek myth tells of a king murdered by his unfaithful wife and her lover and of Electra, the king's daughter, who with her brother kills the mother to avenge their father's death. The Electra complex is a little girl's desire for her father and fear of her mother. Since this situation makes the girl anxious, she eventually achieves the desired relationship with her father *indirectly* by identifying with her mother.

Penis Envy

At the age of 3, Vicky saw a boy's penis for the first time. While two little boys in her play group urinated behind a fence, Vicky watched, fascinated. That evening she told Charles about the "little sticks on their bodies that Nate and Joshua squirted water with." Some years later, Ellen asked Vicky, "Were you upset when you realized that a boy has a penis and you don't?" Now a sophisticated 11-year-old, Vicky answered, "To tell you the truth, I thought they were kind of funny-looking."

Freud would have dismissed Vicky's comment as a cover-up of her true feelings. He believed that a major motivating force in the female is **penis envy**, a little girl's desire for that very visible organ which she does not have. According to Freud, a little girl cannot win. If she succumbs to penis envy, she will unconsciously keep hoping to get a penis for herself and become a man; if she denies her envy, that denial can cause neurosis in adulthood. Either way, she feels inferior and is likely to become jealous and turn against her mother, whom she blames for her lack of a penis. Eventually, a normal girl turns her desire for a penis into a desire for a child and is most fully satisfied by the birth of a son, whose arrival indirectly grants her desire for a penis.

Development of the Superego

With successful resolution of the Oedipus or Electra complex at about age 5 or 6, children develop the **superego**—the aspect of personality that represents the values and ideals held by parents and other social mentors. The development of the superego comes about through *introjection*, the process by which a child identifies with the parent of the same sex and integrates that parent's moral standards.

The superego has two aspects: (1) the *ego-ideal* (the "shoulds": behavior that we aspire to, are rewarded for, and feel proud of), and (2) the *conscience* (the "should nots": behavior that we are punished for and feel guilty and ashamed about). The superego strives for perfection. It tries to prevent the id from acting on its impulses, particularly when they are sexual or aggressive. The ego, then, has to mediate between the two, to find gratification for the id while accommodating the moral demands of the superego.

Through the superego, which operates unconsciously, children incorporate concepts of right and wrong so that they can control their behavior themselves, rather than rely on control by other people, mainly their parents. Freud believed that girls cannot become as moral as boys, because, since they do not fear castration, they do not develop as strong a superego.

In early childhood, the superego is rigid. The daughter of parents who value cleanliness, for example, may want to change her clothes six times a day in order to please them. Or a little boy may be tormented with guilt after fighting with a friend, even though his parents do not disapprove of harmless tussling. With maturity, the superego becomes more realistic and flexible, allowing people to function according to higher principles while also considering their self-interest.

ERIK ERIKSON: CRISIS 3—INITIATIVE VERSUS GUILT

Erikson accepts Freud's concept of the superego and its Oedipal origins, but he continues to believe that social issues are more important than sexual issues in affecting a person's life. Erikson's third crisis is **initiative versus guilt**, the conflict between the sense of purpose, which allows a child to plan and carry out activities, and the moral reservations the child may have about such plans. For example, Jason may want to eat a candy bar but may also know that he is not usually allowed to have sweets.

intitiative versus guilt Third of Erikson's psychosocial crises, in which the child must balance the desire to pursue goals with the moral reservations that prevent carrying them out; successful resolution leads to the virtue of purpose.

This crisis marks a split between the part of the personality that remains a *child*, full of exuberance and a desire to try new things and test new powers, and the part that is becoming an *adult*, constantly examining the propriety of motives and actions. Children who learn how to regulate these conflicting goals develop the *virtue of purpose*, the courage to envision and pursue goals, without being inhibited by guilt or fear of punishment (Erikson, 1964).

If this crisis is not fully resolved, children may develop into adults who suffer from psychosomatic illnesses, inhibition, or impotence; who overcompensate by showing off; or who become self-righteous and intolerant, concerned more with prohibiting impulses (their own and people's) than with enjoying spontaneity.

Parents can help their children strike a healthy balance between a developing sense of initiative that may lead them to overdo new things and a tendency to become repressed and guilty. They can do this by giving children opportunities to do things on their own while protecting them with guidance and firm limits, so that they can turn out to be people who are responsible—and enjoy life.

EVALUATING THE PSYCHOSEXUAL AND PSYCHOSOCIAL THEORIES

A major problem with Freud's and Erikson's theories is that they are based not on scientifically controlled research, but on personal and clinical experience. Neither theory lends itself to confirmation by follow-up research, although some studies have upheld certain aspects of both.

Freudian Theory

Although Freud gave new depth to our perception of personality development in childhood, many of his ideas have been sharply criticized. Many parents can see moments in their children's development that might be considered Oedipal, but Freud's concepts of penis envy and castration anxiety have not been backed up scientifically (Matlin, 1987). Furthermore, his "phallocentric" belief that the male is the norm and the ideal by which both sexes are to be judged is a narrow view, and one that is particularly offensive to women. According to Karen Horney (1939), a psychoanalyst who began as a disciple of Freud, any envy that females do have of males is envy not of the penis itself, but of the greater social power males possess. Horney also maintained that boys are as likely to experience *womb envy*—envy of a woman's ability to conceive and bear children—as girls are to experience penis envy.

Freud's bold and imaginative ideas inspired new ways of thinking about personality and childhood, but today his theories are generally considered inadequate for explaining the way personality develops.

Eriksonian Theory

Erikson, too, has been criticized for taking the male as the normal standard for development, ignoring or minimizing different cultural influences on the two sexes. The strength of his theory, however, is its broad scope, taking in the entire life span, and the provocative ways it suggests to think about development throughout life. Furthermore, in recent years Erikson has modified some aspects of his beliefs in keeping with his philosophy that social influences are indeed important.

Important Personality Developments in Early Childhood

As Vicky, aged 5, and her favorite baby-sitter walk to a new playground, Vicky confides, "I like to hold your hand. I'm a big girl now, so I don't have to hold it, but I like to—it feels good. I like you." Once there, Vicky holds her temper when a toddler tumbles onto the sand castle she has worked on for 20 minutes, but loses it when a little boy grabs her pail. She is brave enough to run after him, but her courage leaves her when the sitter suggests that she climb to the top of the tallest slide. Vicky is dealing with important issues—identification and affection, altruism and aggression, fears and fun.

EMOTIONS AND ATTITUDES

Identification

Jason sometimes goes to the library with his grandfather. One afternoon, the librarian teasingly asks, "Can you read?" and hands him an open volume of Shakespeare. Jason is momentarily taken aback by this book without pictures, but then in perfect imitation of his grandfather he pats all his pockets and says, "I must have left my glasses home."

Jason's action illustrates an important personality development. Through the process of *identification*, a child adopts the characteristics, beliefs, attitudes, values, and behaviors of another person or a group. As we have seen, the psychoanalytic perspective explains this as the result of the resolution of the Oedipus or Electra conflict.

Social-learning theorists, on the other hand, see identification as the conse-

identification Process by which a person acquires the characteristics of another person or a group; one of the most important personality developments of early childhood.

(© Erika Stone)

"There, there, baby!" As this little girl "feeds" her doll the same way her mother feeds the baby—even adopting the same posture as her mother—she demonstrates identification, one of the most important personality developments of early childhood.

quence of observing and imitating a model. Typically, one model is a parent, but children can also model themselves after other people, like a grandparent, an older brother or sister, a teacher, a baby-sitter, a baseball player, or a TV personality. Children usually pick up characteristics from several different models, whom they choose on the basis of how much power a person seems to have and how nurturant, or caring, the person is (Bandura & Huston, 1961).

Jerome Kagan (1958, 1971) describes four interrelated processes that establish and strengthen identification:

1 Children want to be like the model. For example, they feel that if they are like a famous athlete, they will be able to do what the athlete can do.
2 Children believe that they are like the model. They feel that they look like the model, tell jokes like the model, walk like the model. Identification with a parent or another relative is often buttressed by the comments of other people ("You have your father's eyes").
3 Children experience emotions like those the model is feeling. For example, when Vicky saw Ellen cry after Ellen's brother's death, Vicky felt sad and cried too, not for an uncle she barely knew but because her mother's sadness made her feel sad.
4 Children act like the model. In play and in everyday conversation, they often adopt the mannerisms, voice inflections, and phrasing of the model. Parents are often startled to hear their own words and tone of voice come out of a child's mouth.

Through identification, then, children come to believe that they have the same characteristics as a model. Thus, when they identify with a nurturant and competent model, children are pleased and proud. When the model is inadequate, they may feel unhappy and insecure.

Sexual Identity

Vicky, aged 5, is playing house with Jason. "I'm the mother," she says, proving it by cooking, cleaning, and taking care of the "babies," while Jason puts on a hat and "goes to work." Since he has no clear idea of how to pretend to be at work, he soon returns "home," sits at the table, and says, "I'm hungry." This vignette shows some of the values small children absorb from society, which exerts great influence on gender roles and the behavior of males and females. Before we consider these matters, let us distinguish between sex and gender differences, gender roles, and gender-typing.

sex difference Actual biological difference between the sexes.

gender difference Psychological difference between the sexes.

gender roles Behaviors and attitudes that a culture deems appropriate for males and females.

gender-typing Process by which a person learns a gender role.

Sex Differences, Gender Roles, and Gender-Typing *Sex differences* are actual biological differences between the sexes; *gender differences* are psychological differences between the sexes; *gender roles* are behaviors and attitudes that a culture deems appropriate for males and females; and *gender-typing* is the process by which a person learns a gender role.

Sex and gender differences How do Vicky and Jason differ from each other? They are anatomically dissimilar, of course, with distinct internal and external sexual organs. But how many of their other differences, in size, strength, physical and intellectual abilities, and personality, are due to Vicky's being a girl and Jason's being a boy? According to research, very few are. While some statistical differences exist between large groups of boys and large groups of girls, there is so much overlap that we cannot predict whether a particular boy or a particular girl will be, for instance, faster, stronger, smarter, more confident, or more of a leader.

In their analysis of more than 2000 studies on gender differences, Maccoby and Jacklin (1974) found only a few characteristics on which the sexes were markedly different. Three cognitive differences that they found do not develop until after age 10 or 11—verbal ability, mathematical ability, and spatial ability. Many studies have found that girls show superior verbal ability and boys show better mathematical and spatial ability. However, within these cognitive areas, there are differences in specific skills (Deaux, 1985). For example, although boys do better on algebra problems, girls do just as well in arithmetic and geometry (B. J. Becker, 1983; Marshall, 1984). And more recent research indicates that the differences are very small indeed. In fact, a recent analysis found that gender differences in verbal abilities were so small as to be virtually meaningless (Hyde & Linn, 1988).

Maccoby (1980) summarized some other differences in girls' and boys' behavior. Boys play more boisterously; they roughhouse more, they fight more, and they are more apt to try to establish dominance over other children. Girls more often set up rules for play (like taking turns) to avoid conflict. Boys resist and challenge their parents more than girls, who are more likely to have a comfortable, cooperative relationship with parents. And boys are more careful to avoid "sissy" behavior than girls are to avoid "tomboyishness."

A number of studies have found that girls are more likely to respond to and help babies and younger children, and are more likely to be *empathic*, that is, to have such an intimate understanding of other people's feelings that when others are happy they are happy, and when others are sad they are sad (Maccoby, 1980). However, recent research has found that this difference does not appear until about age 4 or 5; until then, boys and girls show equal interest in babies.

And even after that age, boys know just as much about babies and their care as girls and respond as enthusiastically as girls to adult encouragement to take an interest in and help care for a baby (Berman & Goodman, 1984).

Thus while some differences—usually small and based on overall group behavior—do appear, they are not necessarily inborn, and they can be changed with the help of interested adults. Both boys and girls become attached to their parents; by and large, neither sex is more helpful than the other; and some girls love rough play, while some boys hate it. As Maccoby points out, "Men and women, boys and girls, are more alike than they are different" (1980, p. 223).

Gender roles and gender typing   Vicky's stereotyped play as the housewife-mother and Jason's as the working father would not be so surprising if both children's mothers did not work outside the home and if both their fathers did not share in the housework. These children have absorbed the gender roles of their culture, in which women are expected to be nurturant, compliant, and dependent and men are supposed to be dominant, aggressive, active, independent, and competitive. Children acquire these gender-role stereotypes early, and the brighter they are, the faster they pick them up.

Children become increasingly gender-typed in early childhood. When asked whether it was okay for a little boy to play with dolls, Jack, aged 4, said, "Yes, . . . because it's up to him. (If his sister gets to play with dolls, he should be able to, too) because him and she want to play with dolls." Michael, almost 6, however, said, "He should only play with things that boys play with. He should stop playing with the girls' dolls and start playing with the G.I. Joe. Because he's just going to get people teasing him" (Damon, 1977, pp. 249, 255).

Strong gender-typing in early childhood may help children develop *gender identity*, awareness of one's own sex and the sex of others. It is possible that children can be more flexible in their thinking about attitudes and behaviors only after they are sure that they are male or female and will always be, even if they change clothes, haircut, or playmates. We will discuss theoretical explanations for gender identity after we examine some of the factors responsible for sex differences and some consequences of these differences.

gender identity
Awareness of one's own sex and the sex of others.

Origins of Differences   The differences between Vicky's and Jason's roles in play illustrate a profound problem in understanding early childhood development. Inevitably, in any attempt to explain gender differences, the nature-nurture controversy arises. Some people insist that all differences are biological: men are men, women are women. Most psychologists, however, believe that the general environment, culture, and parents are at least as influential as biology. Let us look at all these influences.

Biological influences   Despite the chromosomal difference between male and female zygotes at fertilization, male and female embryos remain identical in appearance until about 5 or 6 weeks after conception. At about the sixth week of gestation, *androgens* (male sex hormones, including *testosterone*), appear in embryos destined to be male, apparently on instructions from the testes-determining factor (TDF), a gene on the Y chromosome (Page et al., 1987). These hormones initiate the formation of male body structures, including the sex organs. Female body structures do not form until about 11 or 12 weeks (Hoyenga & Hoyenga, 1979; Money & Ehrhardt, 1972).

Hormones circulating before or at about the time of birth seem to cause sex

androgens   *General term for the male sex hormones.*

testosterone   *Male sex hormone.*

differences in animals. Testosterone has been linked to aggressive behavior in mice, guinea pigs, rats, and primates; and prolactin can cause maternal behavior in virgin or male animals (Bronson & Desjardins, 1969; Gray, Lean, & Keynes, 1969; R. M. Rose, Gordon & Bernstein, 1972). Animals are not people, of course. Human behavior is influenced far more by learning than is the behavior of any animal. Thus, we need to be very careful about drawing conclusions about human beings on the basis of animal studies.

One line of biological investigation has studied babies who are born with ambiguous sexual organs and whose sex cannot be readily determined at birth. In a classic study, Ehrhardt and Money (1967) assessed the development of 10 girls, aged 3 to 14, whose mothers had taken certain hormones during pregnancy. Nine of the girls had been born with abnormal external sexual organs. After surgery, these girls looked normal and were capable of normal female reproduction, and they were raised as girls from birth. But they were considered "tomboys," liked to play with trucks and guns, and competed with boys in active sports. Something that occurs in fetal masculinization may affect the part of the central nervous system that controls energy-expending behavior—or these girls' parents may have been influenced by their daughters' genital masculinity at birth, or the girls' own awareness of their endocrine problems may have led to their tomboyish behavior. Furthermore, tomboyishness is common, and since there was no control group, it is not clear how different from the norm these girls were, or even whether they were different at all.

In another study, young men who suffered from a disorder that causes low production of male hormones at puberty did much worse than normal men on spatial-relations tasks—identifying geometric forms camouflaged by distracting lines, and building geometric designs with blocks. The researchers, who were neurologists, concluded that androgens seem responsible for the development of spatial abilities (Hier & Crowley, 1982). However, gender differences in spatial-relations tasks do not show up in all cultures. They seem to be especially large in cultures that expect them, like American and European culture. People try harder when they expect to succeed: if women do not expect to do well on spatial tasks, they will be more anxious, will expect to fail, and will give up more easily; if men who see themselves as not fully masculine feel that spatial-relations tasks are for "real men," they will react the same way (Kagan, 1982b).

Another line of research points to different brain structures in males and females, and some studies seem to show that the two hemispheres of the brain are more specialized in men, while in women they share more functions.

A classic study points more to nurture than to nature. Ten people aged 13 to 30 looked like females but were chromosomally males, had testes instead of ovaries, and were unable to bear children, since they could not ovulate. Their condition appeared to have been inherited; the particular mechanism may have been an inability to utilize androgens prenatally. They all looked like normal girls, had been brought up as females, and were typically "female" in behavior and outlook. All 10 considered marriage and raising a family to be very important, and all had dreams and fantasies about bringing up children. Eight had played primarily with dolls and other "girls'" toys, and seven of them had played house in childhood and had always played the mother. Since there was no ambiguity in their psychological gender roles, the study strongly shows how the environment influences gender-typing (Money, Ehrhardt, & Masica, 1968).

In all these studies, the samples were quite small; thus the findings are inconclusive. Furthermore, since variations among people of the same sex are always larger than the average differences between men and women, biology fails to explain large differences in behavior between the sexes.

Cultural influences   In Afghan refugee camps in Pakistan, when a boy is born, the event is celebrated with feasts and rifle shots. A girl's birth goes unnoticed. In these camps, where food is in short supply, women and girls must wait to eat until the men and boys have had their fill (Reeves, 1984). It is easy to see how, in such a society, personality would be strongly influenced by gender. But even in the United States, boys and girls, and men and women, are treated and valued differently.

Do societal forces accentuate biological differences between the sexes, or does the culture itself create gender differences? This question is hard to answer. We do know that in almost all societies, some roles are considered appropriate for males and others for females. Gender roles vary from culture to culture, but in most societies men are more aggressive, competitive, and powerful than women, and the pattern is hard to change.

Yet attitudes and roles *are* changing. Today in the United States, women are moving into untraditional occupations and are gaining power in business, government, and the family. Egalitarian attitudes are becoming more prevalent, especially among younger and better-educated people and people with higher incomes (Deaux, 1985). And both men and women are exploring aspects of their personalities that have been suppressed by gender stereotypes.

Influence of parents   *How do parents treat boys and girls?* Parents, too, of course, are influenced by the culture they have grown up in and so will treat sons and daughters differently. The differences in their treatment of sons and daughters are even more pronounced in early childhood than in infancy.

Parents tend to socialize boys more intensely than girls—to punish them more, but also to praise and encourage them more. Parents are more likely to pressure boys to act "like real boys" and avoid acting "like girls" than they are to pressure girls to avoid "masculine" behavior and act in "feminine" ways. Girls have had much more freedom in the clothes they wear, the games they play, and the people they play with (Maccoby & Jacklin, 1974).

Why do many adults seem to show more interest in boys? Even in this supposedly enlightened age, many parents seem to think that boys are more important and that it therefore matters more how they turn out. It is also possible, however, that boys' greater resistance to parents' guidance demands more attention. No matter what the cause of this different treatment, its result is the accentuation of personality differences between males and females. This attitude seems to be changing as adult roles in society change. For example, preschool children (especially girls) of women who work outside the home tend to show less stereotyping (Huston, 1983).

Young children also get messages about "sex-appropriate" behavior from differences in the way their mothers and fathers act. Fathers, more than mothers, engage in active, physical play and encourage children's performance on tasks. They also dominate conversations more, telling their children what to do and interrupting them more often (P. Bronstein, 1988). Thus, children see two different styles of behavior—and in the process of identification are likely to adopt the style of the same-sex parent. Changing parents' attitudes is often hard, but it can be done. (See Box 10-1, page 358.)

BOX 10-1 ■ THE EVERYDAY WORLD

RAISING CHILDREN WITHOUT GENDER-ROLE STEREOTYPES

Parents who want to raise their children to feel good about themselves, no matter which sex they belong to—and to feel empowered by their gender, rather than limited by it—cannot simply ignore cultural stereotypes. They need to "inoculate" children against stereotypes, according to the psychologist Sandra Bem (1983, 1985), a pioneer in gender-role research. The following guidelines are based on her recommendations:

■ Present models of men and women who are competent in many aspects of life by taking turns making dinner, bathing the children, making household repairs, and driving the car—and by arranging for children to see adults in nontraditional occupations.

■ Dress both boys and girls in both pink and blue or in such gender-neutral colors as red, orange, and green.

■ Buy a full range of toys—dolls (to help children pretend to be parents) and trucks, as well as blocks, paints, tricycles, and balls—so that children of both sexes can develop diverse skills.

■ Find both male and female playmates for every child.

■ Compliment children in nonsexist ways. Tell a little girl how strong she is becoming and a little boy how caring he is.

■ Seek out nonsexist materials or create them by modifying whatever materials are available—change the sex of a book's main character, delete or alter stereotyped descriptions, and use pronouns carefully ("What is this little piggy doing? Why, he or she seems to be building a bridge").

■ Teach children anatomical definitions of sex: "If you have a penis and testicles, you're a boy, no matter what you wear or do. If you have a vagina, you're a girl."

■ Comment on classic books or contemporary TV shows, helping children to enjoy the works while recognizing stereotyped attitudes. ("Isn't it interesting that the person who wrote this story seems to think that girls always need to be rescued?")

The father's role: Fathers seem particularly important in gender-role development. For one thing, they care much more about gender-typing than mothers do. Mothers are often accepting when their daughters play with trucks and their sons with dolls, but this kind of cross-sex play tends to upset men, especially in regard to their sons. Men are more accepting of a very active and temperamentally "difficult" son than of a daughter with the same traits; but they spank their sons more than their daughters (Biller, 1981). Furthermore, fathers are more social with, more approving of, and more affectionate toward their preschool-age daughters but are more controlling and directive with their sons, and more concerned with their sons' cognitive achievements than with their daughters' (P. Bronstein, 1988).

These differences in father's treatment of children have long-range implications (P. Bronstein, 1988). By reserving their gentleness for their daughters, they may be restricting their sons' social and emotional development. By controlling their sons more, they imply that boys are expected to be aggressive and out of control—and are not expected to be cooperative and empathic. And in their greater concern with boys' cognitive development, they are telling girls that they are not expected to shine intellectually.

Fathers can help their sons and daughters feel comfortable with their gender without limiting their potential for either success in a career or nurturance. Heterosexual adults who function well at work and in their sexual relationships are most likely to have had warm relationships with fathers who were competent, strong, secure in their own masculinity, and nurturant toward their children. A son of such a father identifies with him, and a daughter will be able to carry over her good feelings from her relationship with him to relationships with other males. Conversely, the children of a punitive, rejecting father or a passive, ineffectual father are less likely to feel secure in their gender (Biller, 1981).

Mothers, too, contribute to gender-typing of their children, but research on children from one-parent families (which are usually headed by the mother) underscores how strong the father's influence is. Such children tend to be less stereotyped than children from families with both parents present (Katz, 1987). Why should this be so? First, a single mother has to serve as both mother and father, doing everything herself, and thus provides a more androgynous model. Second, the father—the parent who seems to be more concerned with and more active in gender-typing—is not around to exert his influence.

Influence of television By the time Vicky and Jason graduate from high school, they will have watched more than 25,000 hours of television, including 356,000 commercials (Action for Children's Television, undated), and they will have absorbed highly gender-stereotyped attitudes from it. Television, in fact, has more stereotypes than real life.

For example, there are about twice as many males as females on both commercial and public TV both in the United States and Canada, and the males are usually more powerful, dominant, and authoritative than the females (Calvert & Huston, 1987). Typically, men on television have been more aggressive, more active, and more competent than women, who have been portrayed as submissive, inactive, and interested mainly in either keeping house or becoming more beautiful (Mamay & Simpson, 1981; Sternglanz & Serbin, 1974; D. M. Zuckerman & Zuckerman, 1985).

Television producers have become more sensitive to the damaging effects of gender stereotypes and have made some changes. But while women are now portrayed differently, and are more likely to be working out of the home and using their brains for activities other than housework or child care—and while men are sometimes shown caring for children or doing the marketing—a high level of gender-stereotyping still prevails (Calvert & Huston, 1987).

According to social-learning theory, children who watch a great deal of television will imitate the models they see and become more gender-typed themselves, and research has borne this out (Frueh & McGhee, 1975).

Can the media help abolish stereotypes? The answer seems to be "Yes, but . . . " By and large, children come to the TV set with preformed attitudes, and they watch and process information selectively. Boys, for example, turn on more cartoons and adventure programs than girls, and both sexes remember TV sequences that confirm the stereotypes they already hold better than they remember nonstereotypical sequences (Calvert & Huston, 1987). However, if a great effort is made to present strong counterstereotyping, children's attitudes can change.

In one study, girls who saw commercials showing women as pharmacists or butchers became more interested in such nontraditional occupations (O'Bryant & Corder-Boltz, 1978). And young children who watched a series of nontraditional episodes, like one showing a father and son having fun cooking together, had less stereotyped views than children who had not seen the series (Johnston & Ettema, 1982). Such success suggests that if a serious effort were made, the media could help teach children to focus on possibilities—their own and others—rather than limitations.

Effects of Gender Prejudice Children absorb stereotypes very early. Both Vicky and Jason already believe that he is supposed to be braver and more daring than she is, and that her tears are expected while his are shameful. Such ideas frame children's views of themselves and their future. Even today, in supposedly liberated times, children as young as 3 describe an unknown baby differently, depending on whether the baby is introduced as a girl or a boy. They are more likely to say that a boy is "big" and a girl "little"; that a boy is "mad" and a girl "scared"; that a boy is "strong" and a girl "weak" (Haugh, Hoffman, & Cowan, 1980).

The wholesale acceptance of gender restrictions has far-reaching implications. Such restrictions often lead people to deny natural inclinations and abilities that seem "unmasculine" or "unfeminine" and force themselves into ill-fitting molds in their careers or social life. They often have the effect of inhibiting someone from doing anything at all in a situation where he or she is not sure what is "right." Stereotypes can restrict people in even the simplest, most ordinary behaviors, preventing men from preparing a baby's bottle or winding yarn and women from nailing boards together or attaching artificial bait to fishing hooks, even if they could earn more money from "cross-gender" activities than from gender-typed work (Bem, 1976).

androgynous Having characteristics considered typical of males and other characteristics considered typical of females.

Convinced that gender-role stereotyping constricts both men and women, preventing people of either sex from achieving their potential, Sandra Bem (1974, 1976) has developed a new concept of psychological well-being. She maintains that the healthiest personality includes a balanced combination of the most positive characteristics normally thought of as appropriate for one sex or the other. Bem calls this personality *androgynous*; an androgynous person might be assertive, dominant, and self-reliant ("masculine" traits), as well as compassionate, sympathetic, and understanding ("feminine" traits).

Today, conscious of the constricting effects of gender stereotypes, many people and institutions are making strong efforts to overcome old ideas, like the once strongly held psychoanalytic view that children's healthy sexual identification depends on strict differentiation between male and female roles. Preschools, for example, are recruiting male teachers to show children that men, too, can enjoy being with, teaching, and caring for children. The "doll corner" is now the "family corner," and it is stocked with tools as well as dishes. The emphasis in school, in the media, and in the family is less on what *boys* can do or what *girls* can do and more on what *children* can do.

Acquiring Gender Roles: Theoretical Explanations Children are not born knowing what sex they are and understanding gender roles. How, then, do they learn that they are male or female, that this is a basic element of their identity which (in the normal course of events) will never change, and that certain kinds of behaviors are expected of them? We will examine four theories that explain the development of sexual identity in different ways: psychoanalytic, social-learning, cognitive-developmental, and gender-schema theory.

Psychoanalytic theory As we saw, Freud explained gender-typing as an indirect result of anatomy and the identification by the child with the parent of the same sex. Children emerge from the phallic period with a strong sense of their maleness or femaleness, and the way they resolve the crisis of the Oedipus or Electra complex determines their degree of adjustment to their gender.

Psychoanalytic theory is hard to test scientifically, and what research has been undertaken does not support it (Stangor & Ruble, 1987). For example, both boys and girls are more similar to their mothers than their fathers, and other people besides parents influence children's development. For these reasons, this theory is not popular with research psychologists.

Social-learning theory   Jason sees that he looks more like Jess than like Julia; he imitates Jess (especially when he sees him as nurturant, competent, and powerful); and he is then rewarded (perhaps by praise or gifts of "boys'" toys) for acting "like a boy" and punished (perhaps by ridicule or scorn) for "girlish" behavior. This is the underlying view of *social-learning theory*, which applies the same laws of learning to gender roles as to other aspects of development. In doing so, it implies that gender-typing is learned by imitating models, and that it can be modified if the models change their behavior.

While it seems to make sense, this theory, too, has been hard to prove. First of all, children do imitate adults, but they do not necessarily imitate the parent of the same sex, as you know if you have ever seen a little girl put on her father's hat, or a little boy his mother's shoes. Often they do not imitate the gender-role behaviors of a parent. When children are tested on masculinity or femininity, they are no more like their own parents than like a random group of parents, and those who do test as similar to their own parents score no closer to the parent of the same sex than to the other parent (Hetherington, 1965; Mussen & Rutherford, 1963).

Furthermore, Maccoby and Jacklin (1974) found that in many ways parents treat their sons and daughters similarly; they discourage fighting and encourage helping behavior for both boys and girls, for example. Of course, parents may treat boys and girls more differently than the literature shows, since most of the studies have dealt with mothers' treatment of their children, and most have focused on children aged 5 and younger. Since fathers gender-type more than mothers, and parents differentiate more between older boys and girls, any analysis that does not take these factors into account is bound to be skewed (Block, 1978). It is also possible that parents transmit gender-role standards in such subtle ways that the research methods now in use cannot measure them.

Cognitive-developmental theory   Vicky learns that she is called a *girl*, learns the kinds of things girls are supposed to do, does them, and feels secure in her gender identity. According to Kohlberg (1966), all this comes about as a natural corollary of cognitive development. Such learning begins quite early, by about age 2. By 3 years of age, most children have a firm idea of the sex they belong to (their gender identity) and will object strenuously if anyone teases them by telling a girl, "You're a boy," or vice versa. This knowledge of gender identity motivates children to act as they believe they are supposed to.

Jason, at age 3, told Julia, "When I grow up, I want to be a mother just like you so I can play tennis and drive a car." Vicky, also at age 3, said, "Snoopy is a boy, but when he grows up he'll be a girl and he'll have little baby puppies." Neither of these children has acquired the concept of **gender constancy**, an awareness that one will always remain of a given sex. Gender constancy is usually acquired between ages 5 and 7.

gender constancy
Awareness that one will always be male or female.

In one study of gender constancy, experimenters showed pictures to economically disadvantaged 4- to 7-year-olds. First the children saw a drawing of a nude girl, including genitalia, and were told, "This is Janie." The experimenters then flipped pages to cover most of the drawing, and showed Janie in various styles of dress and different hairstyles. Then they asked whether Janie could be a boy if she really wanted to, if she played with trucks and did things that boys do, if she put on boys' clothes, or if she had her hair cut short.

Although the experimenters used a gender-typed name and kept the pronoun *she* constant, only about 24 percent of the children thought that Janie remained a girl when she changed her activities, clothing, and hairstyle. The most cognitively advanced of these 24 percent explained their answers, saying, "She was born a girl" and "Cause she ain't got no magic; can't change without an operation" (Emmerich, Goldman, Kirsh, & Sharabany, 1976, p. 75).

There are ambiguities in this experiment, since changing the sex of a drawing is not the same as changing the sex of a person. The children may not have believed that a real little girl could become a boy merely by putting on a boy's clothes. But other studies have also found that young children do not fully understand gender constancy.

A major appeal of cognitive-developmental theory is its concept of the child as the primary agent of his or her own gender socialization. Furthermore, the linkage of cognitive development with gender concepts has held up under testing, even though the timing is often different from Kohlberg's chronology. Even 2-year-olds can classify pictures as "boys" or "girls," or "mommies" or "daddies." By 2½ years, children can tell which pictures look most like them and can say whether they will be fathers or mothers when they grow up (S. K. Thompson, 1975). And children under 3 often show gender-typed attitudes.

However, as children get older, they have a better grasp of gender constancy (Emmerich et al., 1977), which reflects their growing mastery of conservation, the ability to recognize that things in general remain the same despite superficial alterations.

Cognitive-developmental theory also has shortcomings. Kohlberg assumes that gender-typing is an inevitable result of cognitive development, does not look for other influential forces, and does not explain why sex is more important than other factors (like race or religion) in children's self-concept. For this we have to turn to Bem's gender-schema theory.

gender-schema theory
Theory that children socialize themselves in their gender roles by developing a concept of what it means to be male or female.

Gender-schema theory **Gender-schema theory** is a "cognitive-social" approach, with elements of both cognitive-developmental theory and social-learning theory. It revolves around the concept of a gender schema (Bem, 1983, 1985). A schema (a term originated by Piaget; the plural form is *schemata*) is a mentally organized pattern of behavior that helps a child sort out information. Bem maintains that children socialize themselves in their gender roles. First, they develop a concept of what it means to be male or female by organizing information around the schema of gender. They pick up this schema because they see that society classifies people more by gender than by anything else: males and females wear different clothes, play with different toys, use separate bathrooms, and line up separately in school.

As children see what boys and girls are supposed to be and do—the culture's gender schema—they adapt their own attitudes and behavior. From the full range of human attributes, they pick and choose the ones in their society's gender schema that fit them. In the United States, for example, boys learn that it is important to be strong and aggressive, while girls learn that it is important to be nurturant. Children then look at themselves: if they act in "gender-appropriate" ways, their self-esteem rises; if not, they feel inadequate.

This theory assumes that since gender-typing is learned, it can be modified and that stereotypes can be eliminated if children do one or more of the following:

- Discard all schemata, distinguishing the sexes only by anatomical and reproductive differences. (Young children usually fail to do this, basing their decision about a person's sex on other external signals like clothing or hairstyle.)
- Learn the *individual-differences schema*, that there is great variation within groups. For example, some girls do not like to play baseball, but others do—and some boys do not.
- Learn the *cultural-relativism schema*, the understanding that people in different cultures and at different historical times hold different beliefs and customs about what is appropriate for males and females.
- Learn the *sexism schema*, the conviction that gender-stereotyped roles are not only different but wrong, no matter how common they are.

Whatever may have happened to make this child cry, being held close by her father is likely to make her feel better. As our society's gender attitudes loosen up, men are freer to show their nurturing side.

We are living through a real-life test of gender-schema theory, which elegantly combines aspects of social-learning and cognitive developmental theory. In many countries around the world today, the gender schema is undergoing change. Both official and informal standards for gender-appropriate behavior have changed considerably over the past several decades, with mixed results.

As far back as 1910, for example, the founders of the Israeli kibbutzim (communal farming or manufacturing settlements) tried to eliminate special roles for men and women by changing family structure and by allocating chores without regard to gender. However, many of their ideas were short-lived. Today, work on the kibbutz generally follows traditional gender lines, with men tending to do skilled work and women to cook, laundry, and care for children (Tiger & Shepher, 1975).

In the United States today, some changes in gender schemata have taken hold. More women today enter—and succeed in—professions that were once almost exclusively pursued by men, and more men assume an active role in child care and household tasks; there is greater acceptance of assertiveness in women and nurturance in men. A clear view of the changes in people's *thinking* about gender roles emerges from comparing movies, books, or popular magazines of today with those of 30 years ago; men's and women's behavior in the old pictures usually seems quaintly outdated. However, in many respects customary gender-based patterns of behavior persist. For example, women are still responsible for most child care and household work, and men are still, by and large, more career-oriented. Change in ingrained attitudes about basic aspects of human existence is slow.

None of these theories fully explains why boys and girls turn out differently in some respects while retaining many characteristics in common. As with other developmental phenomena, it is probable that each theory contributes something to our understanding.

Fearfulness

Jason does not like monsters and spooky things. At Halloween he refuses to open the front door because he does not want anyone in a mask in his home. He knows—or says he knows—that the people underneath the costumes are little children, but still he finds the transformations wrought by costume and mask frightening. Fortunately, Julia and Jess are wise enough to accept his fears without ridiculing him or trying to pressure him to overcome them.

What Do Children Fear, and Why?   Children between the ages of 2 and 4 harbor the greatest number of new fears. Almost all are afraid of animals, especially dogs; the next most common fears are of thunder, storms, and doctors. By age 6 fear of the dark is most common, but this and other fears tend to disappear as children grow older and feel more powerful (DuPont, 1983).

Why do children become so fearful at this age? For one thing, they become aware of just how small and powerless they are. For another, they cannot always tell fantasy from reality. In one study, almost 75 percent of kindergartners expressed fear of ghosts and monsters, while only 50 percent of second-graders and 5 percent of sixth-graders did (Bauer, 1976). Sometimes small children's imaginations go wild, and they worry about being attacked by a lion, being in the dark, being abandoned, or falling from high places (Jersild & Holmes, 1935).

As children grow older, bigger, and more competent, some of the things that once seemed very menacing become less so—but children may then develop new fears. Four- to six-year-olds are sometimes afraid of people or animals that look "ugly"; and 10- to 12-year-olds, who are more realistic and better able to recognize cause and effect, are more afraid of bodily injury and physical danger (Bauer, 1976). Some children have had frightening experiences or heard of frightening things that have happened to others. The more children know and have experienced, the more they understand that there are genuine reasons to be afraid (see Table 10-1).

Girls tend to be more fearful than boys, and poor children are more fearful than children from better-off families, possibly because both girls and poorer children both feel more powerless. Parents may encourage girls to be more dependent and may discourage boys' fears more (Bauer, 1976; Croake, 1973;

TABLE 10-1

CHILDHOOD FEARS	
AGE	FEARS
0–6 months	Loss of support, loud noises
7–12 months	Strangers; heights; sudden, unexpected, and looming objects
1 year	Separation from parent, toilet, injury, strangers
2 years	A multitude of stimuli, including loud noises (vacuum cleaners, sirens and alarms, trucks, and thunder), animals, dark rooms, separation from parent, large objects or machines, changes in personal environment, strange peers
3 years	Masks, dark, animals, separation from parent
4 years	Separation from parent, animals, dark, noises (including noises at night)
5 years	Animals, "bad" people, dark, separation from parent, bodily harm
6 years	Supernatural beings (e.g., ghosts, witches, Darth Vader), bodily injury, thunder and lightning, dark, sleeping or staying alone, separation from parent
7–8 years	Supernatural beings, dark, media events (e.g., news reports on the threat of nuclear war or child kidnapping), staying alone, bodily injury
9–12 years	Tests and examinations in school, school performances, bodily injury, physical appearance, thunder and lightning, death, dark
Teens	Social performance, sexuality

Source: Adapted from Morris & Kralochwill, 1983.

DuPont, 1983; Jersild & Holmes, 1935). And poor children's fears may reflect the reality of their life.

Fear is influenced by society. Over the past 50 years, children's fears have changed. School-age American children used to be most afraid of the supernatural, a later generation worried about communists; and now a major fear in childhood is of nuclear war (Croake, 1973; Schwebel, 1982; Yudkin, 1984). The change results probably at least in part from the influence of television, which brings war and politics into the living room. Television and movies themselves are often frightening; some children have nightmares after every "cops and robbers" show. The shows themselves may not make children fearful, but they provide images which give shape to fears.

Phobias Most childhood fears are normal and even healthy. They may be passing fears representing a developmental stage, as described above. Or they may be self-protective appraisals of such real dangers as fast cars, strange dogs, and strangers who offer rides.

Some children, however, develop *phobias,* irrational, involuntary fears that are inappropriate to the situation and interfere with normal activities. Phobias occasionally grow out of specific events (a menacing dog, a car accident), but more often they arise from some inner anxiety. Children whose parents have phobias are more likely to develop phobias themselves. Fortunately, most childhood phobias disappear before adulthood; most adult phobias appear between ages 17 and 40 (DuPont, 1983).

phobia Irrational, involuntary fear that is inappropriate to the situation and interferes with normal activities.

Preventing and Treating Fears Parents can help prevent children's fears by instilling a sense of trust and normal caution, without being too protective, and by overcoming their own unrealistic fears. They can help a child who is already fearful by reassurance and by encouraging open expression of feelings. They should avoid ridicule ("Don't be such a baby!"), coercion ("Pat the nice doggie—it won't hurt you"), logical persuasion ("The closest bear is 20 miles away, locked in a zoo!"), ignoring the fear, or allowing the child to continue avoiding the feared object or event. None of these approaches seems to work (DuPont, 1983).

Children overcome fears best by their own activities—by finding practical methods to deal with what they fear and by gradually experiencing the situations they are afraid of. In one study involving *systematic desensitization—* gradual exposure to a feared object—experimenters helped first- through third-graders overcome fear of snakes by providing gradually closer, more frequent contact. After an average of two 15-minute sessions, 39 out of 45 children held snakes in their laps for 15 seconds, compared with only 5 of 22 children in a control group (C. M. Murphy & Bootzin, 1973).

systematic desensitization Gradual exposure to a feared object for the purpose of overcoming the fear.

Modeling—observing fearlessness in others—is also useful. In another study, nursery school children who were afraid of dogs took part in eight brief sessions in which they saw an unafraid child playing happily with a dog. Later, two-thirds of the fearful children were able to climb into a playpen with the dog (Bandura, Grusec, & Menlove, 1976).

Fearful children do best if they continue to practice these techniques. If the techniques are not helpful, or if the phobia recurs, the child may be referred to a phobia clinic.

(© Erika Stone)

What parents do and say is a major influence on whether children will be likely to help other people, strangers as well as family members.

prosocial behavior
Altruistic behavior; selflessness.

BEHAVIORS

Prosocial Behavior

One day when Vicky, at 4, was picnicking with her family, she saw a ragged man going through a garbage can. Holding up her tuna fish sandwich (her favorite food) to Ellen, she asked, "Can I give this to him?"

What Is Prosocial Behavior?   This was not the only time Vicky showed altruistic behavior, or *prosocial behavior*—action taken at some cost or risk to benefit another person, with no expectation of reward. Why do some people reach out generously and compassionately to others? What makes some children sensitive to other people at a very early age?

Influences on Prosocial Behavior   Over the past several decades, researchers have examined the origins of caring behavior (Mussen & Eisenberg-Berg, 1977). Socioeconomic status, for example, is *not* a factor: parents' income and social standing make no difference in how a youngster will behave toward others.

In most studies, no sex differences have turned up, either, although some research has found more generosity, helpfulness, and consideration in girls than boys. This may be because nurturance is generally considered a feminine trait, and so girls are more often encouraged to help others; it may also be related to the fact that girls are physically punished by their parents less than boys, receive more affection from their parents, and are given more explanations of the consequences of their actions.

Age is a factor in altruism. Although 18-month-olds will show sympathy toward someone who is hurt or unhappy and may try to help, it is not clear whether they understand what the other person is feeling or are just upset by how the person is acting. Not until about age 4 do children display a significant amount of altruism. The level increases steadily until the age of 13, apparently as children become more able to put themselves in another person's place.

Altruistic children tend to be advanced in mental reasoning and able to take the role of others; they are also relatively active and self-confident. How do they become this way? The results of many studies point to the home. The family is important as a model, as a source of explicit standards, and as a guide in adopting other models.

Encouraging Prosocial Behavior   *What parents do*   One very important way that parents can encourage altruism is to love and respect children. One reason for the generosity of altruistic children seems to be their own security in their parents' love and affection. Preschoolers who were securely attached as infants are more likely than insecurely attached children to respond to other children's distress. Not surprisingly, they have more friends, and their teachers consider them more socially competent (Sroufe, 1983).

The parents of prosocial children also set an example. In Vicky's home, for as long as she can remember, two elderly neighbors have come to the house for holiday celebrations. Vicky knows that if it were not for her parents' friendship, the neighbors would be alone. When Charles clears the snow from his driveway, he clears the neighbors' driveway as well.

Parents of prosocial children commonly teach the children that their actions have consequences, and they encourage the children to empathize with others.

When Jason was 4, he took some candy from a store. Julia did not punish or lecture him, but instead talked to him about how the store's owner would be hurt because Jason had not paid for the candy. Then she took Jason back to the store to return the candy. When such incidents take place, the parents of prosocial children often ask, for example, "How do you think Mr. Jones feels?" or "How would you feel if you were Mary?"

These parents usually hold their children to high standards. The children are taught explicitly that they are expected to be honest and helpful. They have some responsibility in the home and are expected to meet it.

The parents also point out other models, and steer their children toward stories and television programs—like *Mister Rogers' Neighborhood*—that depict cooperation, sharing, and understanding the feelings of others; they discourage viewing aggressive cartoons. And many studies do show that prosocial television programs can encourage children to be more sympathetic, generous, and helpful (Mussen & Eisenberg-Berg, 1977; National Institute of Mental Health, NIMH, 1982; D. M. Zuckerman & Zuckerman, 1985).

A recent study identified 406 Europeans who, during the 1930s and 1940s, had risked their lives to rescue Jews in Nazi-occupied countries, and then compared these rescuers with people who had lived in the same countries at the same time but did not help Jews. The researchers found a number of factors more likely to be present in the childhood homes of the rescuers than the homes of the control group (Oliner & Oliner, 1988). Rescuers' parents had emphasized strong ethical principles—compassion and caring for others and a sense of fairness, extending beyond friends and loved ones to include all people. They put less emphasis on such values as obedience, economic competence, and the importance of self. In addition, the rescuers reported closer early family relationships, especially with their parents, who disciplined them more by reasoning, explanations, persuasion, advice, and suggestions of ways to right a wrong than by physical punishment. Furthermore, the parents often behaved altruistically themselves, giving the children models to copy.

Cultural values   In today's complex society, it is more important than ever to encourage people's concern for one another. Cultures that value this can—and do—encourage it. The founders of the Israeli kibbutzim aimed to create a society of less selfish, more generous citizens; a measure of their success is that at every age and stage of development, children reared on a kibbutz tend to think more about obligations to others than do children raised at home (Snarey et al., 1985). As research in this area continues, we look to it for answers in our continuing quest for a richer quality of life.

Aggression

As Vicky was playing in the sandbox at the park, a little boy came up to her, threw sand in her face, snatched away her shovel, and told her, "I'm a pirate and I live under the slide and I'm going to hurt you."

This "playground pirate" exemplifies two types of aggression—instrumental and hostile. While all aggression carries some element of hostility, instrumental aggression generally has some goal other than injuring another person. In this case, the goal was Vicky's shovel. Hostile aggression is behavior intended to cause pain—in this instance, throwing sand and threatening violence.

Babies display neither instrumental nor hostile aggression. Even a toddler who roughly grabs a toy from another child is interested only in the toy, not in hurting or dominating the other child. Anyone with much experience with children past the age of 2½ or 3, however, has seen enough hitting, punching, kicking, biting, and throwing to be convinced that the age of aggression has arrived. Over the next 3 years or so, aggression normally shifts from action to talk (Maccoby, 1980). Let us see how this happens—and why it sometimes fails to happen.

The Rise and Decline of Aggression In the early stages of aggression, children focus on a desired object and make threatening gestures toward the person holding it. Between the ages of 2½ and 5, children's aggression centers on struggles over playthings and the control of space. Aggression surfaces mostly during social play, and the children who fight most are the very ones who are most sociable and competent. This may mean that the ability to show aggression is a necessary step in human beings' social development.

dominance hierarchy
System of social ranking, recognized by all the members of a group, in which some members have power over all other members, some have power over certain other members and are subordinate to others, and some are subordinate to all other members.

The establishment of a ***dominance hierarchy***—a recognized pecking order of leaders and followers—reduces the number of bloody noses. Children do not fight, because they can predict the outcome. In addition, as children become physically stronger and more able to inflict harm, they turn to their growing language skills as a safer alternative. The tools of aggression shift from blows to insults, as the issues change from wanting a toy to establishing status.

After age 6 or 7, most children become less aggressive as they become less egocentric and more empathic. They can now put themselves in someone else's place, can understand why the other person may be acting in a certain way, and can develop more positive ways of dealing with that person. They also have more positive social skills—they can communicate better and can cooperate in achieving joint goals.

Some children, however, do not learn how to control aggression. Instead, destructive tendencies appear to rule their lives. And even for an ordinary child who seems to be progressing normally, aggression can get dangerously out of hand. Because of these problems, researchers have sought to discover what causes and what sustains aggression.

Triggers of Aggression Although the male hormone testosterone may well underlie the tendency toward aggressive behavior and explain why males are more likely to be aggressive than females, social-learning theorists point to other contributing factors. These include reinforcement for aggressive behavior, frustration, and imitation of aggressive models, in real life or on television.

Reinforcement Children's clearest reward, of course, is getting what they want. But sometimes scolding or spanking can reinforce aggressive behavior, since some children seem to prefer negative attention to none at all. Preschool teachers have decreased the amount of aggression exhibited by 3- and 4-year-old boys by ignoring aggressive behavior and rewarding cooperative attitudes (P. Brown & Elliott, 1965). However, it is not always safe to ignore aggression. Indeed, permitting it by not interfering can communicate approval.

Some parents actively reward and encourage aggression toward other children, while discouraging it toward themselves: the children learn not to hit their parents, but they become aggressive toward other children (Bandura, 1960).

Frustration Frustration—often brought about by punishment, insults, and fears—does not necessarily lead to aggression, but a frustrated child is more likely to act aggressively than a contented one (Bandura et al., 1961).

Imitation In one classic study, children were exposed to different models or to no model (Bandura et al., 1961). Albert Bandura and his colleagues divided seventy-two 3- to 6-year-olds into three groups. One by one, each of the children in the first group went into a playroom. An adult model (male for half the children, female for the other half) quietly played in a corner with some toys. The model for the second group began to assemble Tinker Toys, but after a minute they spent the rest of the 10-minute session punching, throwing, and kicking a 5-foot-tall inflated doll. The children in the third group saw no model.

After the sessions, all the children were shown toys but not allowed to play with them—a mild form of frustration. Then the children were taken into another playroom. The children who had seen the aggressive model were much more aggressive than those in the other groups, saying and doing many of the same things they had seen the model do. Both boys and girls were more strongly influenced by an aggressive male model than an agressive female, apparently because they considered aggression appropriate only for males (in line with the gender schema they had learned). The children who had been with the quiet model were less aggressive than the children who had not seen any model. We see, then, how adult models can influence children's behavior in more than one direction.

Televised violence Even children who do not see aggressive models in real life see hundreds of them on television. Ironically, children's programs are 6 times as violent as programs aimed at adults (Signorielli, Gross, & Morgan, 1982). And research suggests that children are influenced even more by seeing filmed violence than by seeing real people act aggressively (Bandura et al., 1963).

A large body of research since the 1950s shows that children who see televised violence act more aggressively themselves. This effect is true across all geographic and socioeconomic levels, for children of both sexes, and for normal children as well as children with emotional problems (NIMH, 1982). Television encourages aggressive behavior in two ways: children imitate what they see, and they absorb the message that aggression is appropriate behavior.

Children who see both heroes and villains on television accomplishing their aims through violence and lawbreaking are more willing to break rules themselves. Furthermore, they may become less sensitive to real-life aggression; for example, they may fail to protect a child from a bully. And they may be less likely to think of cooperating to resolve differences. These results may occur because children remember aggressive acts that they see much more vividly than they remember any negative outcome for the aggressor. The fact that "bad guys" are punished does not seem to outweigh the effects of the violence they have committed (Liebert & Poulos, 1976).

Watching violence seems to make children more willing to hurt people. In one study of 136 boys and girls aged 5 to 9, an experimental group watched a 3½-minute segment from a popular television series, which included a chase, two fistfights, two shootings, and a knifing. A control group watched 3½ minutes of athletic competition. Afterward, the children were asked to play a "game" that involved pushing either a "help" button (to help an unseen child win a game) or a "hurt" button (to make a handle touched by that child so hot

Children often imitate what they see on television, including acts of violence. They may also absorb the idea that aggression is appropriate behavior.

that it would hurt). Of course, the unseen child did not exist, the only child in the experiment was the one pushing the buttons. The effects were dramatic: children who had watched the violent programming were more willing to hurt the unseen child and more willing to inflict more severe pain than those who had watched the sports program (Liebert, 1972).

Certain kinds of programs are most likely to promote aggressive behavior. The programs most closely tied to aggression are detective shows, frenetic situation comedies, and game shows "where there's all that yelling and jumping around," according to Jerome L. Singer (quoted in Locke, 1979).

Some of the effects of televised violence seem to endure for years (D. M. Zuckerman & Zuckerman, 1985). Among 427 young men and women whose viewing habits had been studied when they were third-graders, the single best predictor of aggressiveness at age 19 was the amount of violence on the television programs that they had watched at age 8 (Eron, 1980, 1982). Third-graders may be at a critical period of development in which they are particularly susceptible to the effects of televised violence. Aggressive children watch more television in general, identify more strongly with aggressive characters on television, and are more likely to believe that aggression on television reflects real life. However, television may not *cause* aggressiveness as much as *reinforce* a tendency toward it.

The American Psychological Association (1985), in a policy resolution, has called for a joint effort by parents and broadcasters to reduce the number of aggressive models shown on television. Along with favoring parents' monitoring of children's watching, the resolution urges broadcasters to take more responsibility for limiting violence in children's programming, and it advocates research into ways to ameliorate the effects of televised violence.

Meanwhile, television becomes more and more violent. War cartoons broadcast across the nation went up from 1½ hours a week in 1982 to 48 hours a week in 1987. The average American child saw 250 episodes over a year, and contributed to the 700 percent increase in sales of war toys during those years. In one small Canadian community that had been without television, both verbal and physical aggression increased after its introduction (T. M. Williams, 1978). And 40 studies of about 4500 children in seven countries show the effects of cartoon violence and violent play: increases in fighting, kicking, choking, loss of temper, cruelty to animals, and disrespect for others—and decreases in sharing, imagination, and school performance (National Coalition on Television Violence, undated).

Reducing Aggression   Parents who want to discourage children's aggressive behavior can take steps to counteract the effects of violent television. For one thing, they can monitor their children's watching—limiting total time and selecting appropriate programs. The parents of the most aggressive children often do *not* monitor their children's watching (Locke, 1979).

Parents' general child-rearing practices also exert a major influence (we discuss these in greater detail later in the chapter). The least aggressive children have parents who deal with misbehavior by reasoning with them, making them feel guilty, or withdrawing approval and affection. All these techniques are likely to produce children who have a strong conscience and suffer from guilt feelings. On the other hand, children who are disciplined by spanking, threats, or withdrawal of privileges are more likely to be aggressive. (Of course, it is possible that parents are more likely to spank aggressive children.) Parents' tendency to use the former methods with girls and the latter with boys may accentuate girls' inclination to feel guilty and boys' to be aggressive (R. R. Sears, Maccoby, & Levin, 1957).

Punishment—especially physical punishment—may backfire, because hitting children provides a double incentive for violence. In addition to suffering frustration, pain, and humiliation, they see an adult with whom they identify acting aggressively. Parents who spank provide a "living example of the use of aggression at the very moment they are trying to teach the child not to be aggressive" (R. R. Sears et al., 1957, p. 226). Parents, then, need to think about the results they want to achieve—and what methods can bring them about.

Play

Vicky wakes up to see her clothes laid out for her. Just for fun, she tries putting her overalls on backward, her socks on her hands, her shoes on opposite feet. When she comes to breakfast, she pretends that the bits of cereal floating in her bowl are fish, and she "fishes," spoonful by spoonful.

Throughout the long, busy morning, she plays. She puts on Ellen's old hat, picks up Ellen's discarded briefcase, and is the "mother" going to work. Next, she becomes the "doctor." "There, there, dolly, this'll hurt a little, but then you won't get sick," she says soothingly as she administers a "shot" to her doll. She runs outside to splash in the puddles, comes in for an imaginary telephone conversation, turns a wooden block into a truck and makes the appropriate sound effects, and on and on. Vicky's day is one round of play after another.

An adult might be tempted to smile indulgently at Vicky, envy her, and dismiss her activities as pleasant but trivial. Such a judgment would be grievously in error—play, which is characteristic of all young mammals, is the "work" of the young.

Through play, children grow. They learn how to use their muscles; they coordinate what they see with what they do; and they gain mastery over their bodies. They find out what the world is like and what they are like. They acquire new skills and learn when to use them. They imitate various adult roles. They cope with complex and conflicting emotions by reenacting real-life situations.

Preschoolers engage in many types of play. They gratify the senses by playing with water, sand, and mud. They master a new skill like riding a tricycle. They pretend to be things or other people. By the end of the preschool years, they delight in formal games that have routines and rules. Children progress first from playing alone to playing alongside other children but not with them, and from there to cooperative play, when they interact with others.

Concepts of Play   Play, with its multiple functions, can be considered from different perspectives. Children have different styles of playing, and they play at different things. On entering a kindergarten class, an observer might see Vicky happily playing with a friend while Jason is absorbed in building a block tower. What can we learn about individual children by observing how they play?

social play Play in which children interact with other children.

cognitive play Play that reflects the level of the child's intellectual development.

In trying to answer this question, researchers have approached play in two broadly different ways—as a social phenomenon and as an aspect of cognition. Considering play as a social activity, researchers evaluate children's social competence on the basis of how they play. *Social play* is play in which children interact with other children; it can be looked upon as a measure of children's socialization. Parten's (1932) classic research was particularly important in developing this concept. A second approach looks at *cognitive play,* a kind of play that shows the level of a child's cognitive development and also enhances such development. Piaget (1951) and Smilansky (1968) did particularly important work using this approach.

Studies of Play   During the 1920s, Mildred B. Parten (1932) observed thirty-four 2- to 5-year-olds during free-play periods at nursery school. She distinguished six types of play ranging from the most nonsocial to the most social (see Table 10-2), determined the proportion of time devoted to each type, and charted the children's activities. She found that as children get older, their play tends to become more social and cooperative.

More recent research, however, suggests somewhat different conclusions. In a similar study done 40 years after Parten's, forty-four 3- and 4-year-olds who were observed during recess at nursery school played much less socially than the children in Parten's group (K. E. Barnes, 1971). Why did they? The change might have reflected a different environment: because these children watched television and played less with other children, they may have become more passive; their elaborate toys may have encouraged solitary play more than simple toys of the past, and, having fewer siblings, they may have had less experience playing with other children.

Another possible explanation may be differences in the groups' social class. Preschoolers from families lower on the socioeconomic scale engage in more parallel play; middle-class children play in more associative and cooperative ways. In one study focusing on social class differences, socioeconomically less advantaged children engaged in more nonsocial play than middle-class children (K. Rubin, Maioni, & Hornung, 1976).

Broad studies like Parten's have helped distinguish between types of play. But when we look at individual children, we find different mixes, with some children engaged in a large amount of nonsocial play (unoccupied behavior, onlooker behavior, and solitary independent play). Other children are more

TABLE 10-2

TYPE	DESCRIPTION
Unoccupied behavior	The child apparently is not playing, but occupies himself with watching anything that happens to be of momentary interest. When there is nothing exciting taking place, he plays with his own body, gets on and off chairs, just stands around, follows the teacher, or sits in one spot glancing around the room (p. 249).
Onlooker behavior	The child spends most of his time watching the other children play. He often talks to the children whom he is observing, asks questions, or gives suggestions, but does not overtly enter into the play himself. This type differs from the unoccupied in that the onlooker is definitely observing particular groups of children rather than anything that happens to be exciting. The child stands or sits within speaking distance of the group so that he can see and hear everything that takes place (p. 249).
Solitary independent play	The child plays alone and independently with toys that are different from those used by the children within speaking distance and makes no effort to get close to other children. He pursues his own activity without reference to what others are doing (p. 250).
Parallel activity	The child plays independently, but the activity he chooses naturally brings him among the other children. He plays with toys that are like those which the children around him are using, but he plays with the toy as he sees fit, and does not try to influence or modify the activity of the children near him. He plays *beside* rather than *with* the other children. There is no attempt to control the coming or going of children in the group (p. 250).
Associative play	The child plays with other children. The conversation concerns the common activity; there is a borrowing and loaning of play material; following one another with trains or wagons; mild attempts to control which children may or may not play in the group. All the members engage in similar if not identical activity; there is no division of labor, and no organization of the activity of several individuals around any material goal or product. The children do not subordinate their individual interests to that of the group; instead each child acts as he wishes. By his conversation with the other children one can tell that his interest is primarily in his associations, not in his activity. Occasionally, two or three children engage in no activity of any duration, but are merely doing whatever happens to draw the attention of any of them (p. 251).
Cooperative or organized supplementary play	The child plays in a group that is organized for the purpose of making some material product, or of striving to attain some competitive goal, or of dramatizing situations of adult and group life, or of playing formal games. There is a marked sense of belonging or of not belonging to the group. The control of the group situation is in the hands of one or two of the members who direct the activity of the others. The goal as well as the method of attaining it necessitates a division of labor, taking of different roles by the various group members and the organization of activity so that the efforts of one child are supplemented by those of another (p. 251).

Source: Parten, 1932, pp. 249–251.

given to social play (parallel activity, associative play, and cooperative or organized supplementary play). Parten believed that solitary independent play is less mature than group forms of play, and some other observers have suggested that young children who play by themselves may be at risk of developing a number of social, mental health, and educational problems. Recent research, however, has found that a considerable amount of nonsocial play consists of constructive or educational activities and contributes to a child's cognitive, physical, and social development.

In one analysis of children in six kindergartens, about one-third of the solitary play that took place consisted of such goal-directed activities as building with blocks and artwork; about one-fourth consisted of large-muscle play; about 15 percent was educational; and only about 10 percent involved just looking at the other children (N. Moore, Evertson, & Brophy, 1974). Solitary play, the researchers concluded, shows independence and maturity, not poor social adjustment.

Another study assessed the relationship between various kinds of nonsocial

"Let's make a castle!" Associative play, like the kind these girls are engaging in, has traditionally been considered at a higher level of development than solitary independent play, but recent research has given nonsocial play equally high marks in certain situations.

play in 4-year-olds and measures of their cognitive and social competence, such as role-taking and problem-solving tests, teachers' ratings of social competence, and popularity with other children. It found that some kinds of nonsocial play are associated with a high level of competence. For example, parallel constructive play (activities like playing with blocks and working on puzzles near another child) is most common among children who are good problem solvers, are popular with other children, and are seen by their teachers as socially skilled (K. Rubin, 1982).

Not all nonsocial play, then, is immature. Children need some time alone to concentrate on tasks and problems, and some well-adjusted children simply enjoy nonsocial activities more than group activities. We need to look at what children actually do when they play, not just whether they are playing alone or with someone else.

"Pretend" Play   A 13-month-old girl pushes an imaginary spoon into the mouth of her very real father. A 2-year-old boy talks to a doll as if he were addressing a baby. A 3-year-old boy makes the sound "vroom-vroom" as he runs around the room with a toy airplane. And a 5-year-old girl puts on her mother's riding helmet as she straddles a chair, pretending to ride a horse.

All these children are engaged in what is called *pretend play*, *fantasy play*, *dramatic play*, or *imaginative play*. At one time, professionals' major interest in such play was its supposed role in helping children express their emotional concerns, but interest now focuses more on the role of such play in cognitive and general personality development (see Table 10-3).

Piaget (1962) noted that pretend play emerges during the second year of life, when *sensorimotor play* is on the wane; increases over the next 3 to 4 years; and then declines as children become more interested in playing *games with rules*. He maintained that children's ability to pretend to do or be something rests on their ability to use and remember symbols—to retain in their minds pictures of things

In his pretend play, this little boy may be assuming the role of father, doctor, dentist, or explorer finding a member of a strange tribe. Giving boys dolls to play with helps them stretch their imagination and try out a range of roles.

TABLE 10-3

TYPES OF COGNITIVE PLAY

TYPE	DESCRIPTION
Functional play (sensorimotor play)	Any simple, repetitive muscle movement with or without objects, such as rolling a ball or pulling a pull toy
Constructive play	Manipulation of objects to construct or "create" something
Dramatic play (pretend play)	Substitution of an imaginary situation to satisfy the child's personal wishes and needs; pretending to be someone or something (doctor, nurse, Superman), beginning with fairly simple activities but going on to develop more elaborate plots
Games with rules	Any activity with rules, structure, and a goal (such as winning), like tag, hopscotch, marbles; acceptance of prearranged rules and adjustment to them

Source: Piaget, 1951; Smilansky, 1968.

they have seen or heard of—and that its emergence marks the beginning of the preoperational stage (Chapter 9).

Among preschoolers, about 10 to 17 percent of play is pretend play; among kindergartners, the proportion rises to about 33 percent (K. Rubin et al., 1976; K. Rubin, Watson, & Jambor, 1978). The kind of play, as well as its amount, changes during these years from solitary pretending to *sociodramatic play* involving other children. Thus, at age 3 Jason climbs inside a big box by himself and pretends to be a train conductor; by age 6 he will want to have passengers on his train with whom he can enact minidramas. During the years from 3 to 6, children become more involved with one another's roles (Iwanaga, 1973).

About 15 to 30 percent of children between the ages of 3 and 10 create imaginary companions, with whom they talk and play. This is a perfectly normal manifestation of childhood most often seen in bright, creative firstborn and only children (Manosevitz, Prentice, & Wilson, 1973).

Through pretending, children learn how to understand another person's point of view, develop skills in solving social problems, and become more creative. Certain parenting practices seem to encourage the flowering of fantasy play (Fein, 1981). Parents of children who are the most imaginative in their play get along well with each other, expose their children to interesting experiences, engage them in conversation, and do not spank them. Television, on the other hand, seems to stifle children's imagination, possibly because heavy viewers get into the habit of passively absorbing images rather than generating their own.

Influences on Personality Development

Why does Nicole hit and bite when she cannot finish a jigsaw puzzle? What makes David sit patiently with the same puzzle for hours, until he solves it? Why does Michele walk away from it after a minute's effort? In short, what makes children's personalities turn out the way they do?

To answer this fundamental question, developmental psychologists look closely at the most important people in most children's lives, their parents.

Parents are not all-powerful, of course, and they seem to have only limited ability to change children's basic inborn personality traits. But they do exert a major influence on the way children express those traits. After we examine how parents leave their stamp on children's social and personality development, we will look at how brothers and sisters influence each other, and at the impact of being an only child. Finally, we will consider relationships with other children.

HOW DOES THE FAMILY AFFECT PERSONALITY DEVELOPMENT?

Child-Rearing Practices

How are parents raising their children today? Some parents repeat the child-rearing patterns they are most familiar with, those their own parents followed. Others adopt practices that are very different from their parents'. As in any generation, different styles of parenting exist at the same time.

Baumrind's Studies: Parents' Styles and Children's Competence   Diana Baumrind set out to discover relationships between different styles of child rearing and children's social competence. After lengthy interviews, standardized testing, and home studies of 103 preschool children from 95 families, she identified three categories of parenting styles—authoritarian, permissive, and authoritative—and described typical behavior patterns of children raised according to each style (Baumrind, 1971; Baumrind & Black, 1967).

authoritarian parents In Baumrind's terminology, parents whose primary child-rearing values are based on control and obedience.

Three Styles of Parenting   *Authoritarian parents* try to control their children's behavior and attitudes and make them conform to a set and usually absolute standard of conduct. They value unquestioning obedience and punish their children forcefully for acting contrary to the parents' standards. They are more detached, more controlling, and less warm than other parents, and their children tend to be more discontented, withdrawn, and distrustful.

permissive parents In Baumrind's terminology, parents whose primary child-rearing values are self-expression and self-regulation.

Permissive parents make few demands, allowing their children to regulate their own activities as much as possible. They consider themselves resources, but not standard-bearers or ideal models. They explain to their children the reasons underlying the few family rules that do exist, consult with them about policy decisions, and hardly ever punish them. They are noncontrolling, nondemanding, and relatively warm, and their children as preschoolers tend to be immature—the least self-controlled and the least exploratory.

authoritative parents In Baumrind's terminology, parents whose primary child-rearing values blend respect for the child's individuality with a desire to instill social values in the child.

Authoritative parents try to direct their children's activities rationally, with attention to the issues rather than the children's fear of punishment or loss of love. They exert firm control when necessary, but they explain the reasoning behind a stand and encourage verbal give-and-take. They have confidence in their ability to guide their children, and they respect their children's interests, opinions, and unique personalities. They are loving, consistent, demanding, and respectful of their children's independent decisions, but they are firm in maintaining standards and willing to impose limited punishment. They combine control with encouragement. Their children apparently feel secure in knowing that they are loved and also in knowing what is expected of them; and as preschoolers, these children are the most self-reliant, self-controlled, self-assertive, exploratory, and content.

(Drawing by Koren; © 1988 The New Yorker Magazine, Inc.)

"Sam, neither your father nor I consider your response appropriate."

Do Sam's parents seem authoritarian, authoritative, or permissive? Children seem to respond in distinct ways to each of these three styles of parenting.

Why Authoritative Parenting Seems Best   Children from authoritarian homes are so strictly controlled, by either punishment or guilt, that they often cannot make a conscious choice about the merit of a particular behavior; they are too concerned about what their parents will do. Those from permissive homes receive so little guidance that they often become uncertain and anxious about whether they are doing the right thing.

But in authoritative homes, children know when they are meeting expectations, learn how to judge those expectations, and are able to decide when the pursuit of some goal is worth risking their parents' displeasure or other unpleasant consequences. Children whose parents expect them to perform well, to fulfill commitments, and to participate actively in family duties as well as family fun learn how to formulate goals. They also experience the satisfaction that comes from meeting responsibilities and achieving success. The essential factor appears to be the parents' reasonable expectations and realistic standards.

Evaluating Baumrind's Work   Baumrind's work has raised important issues about the effects of parenting practices, but some questions remain. For one thing, she does not consider any innate differences between children, assuming that all differences in social competence are related to what parents do. Nor does she consider children's influence on parents. It is possible, for example, that "easy" children will induce their parents to be authoritative, while "difficult" children may drive their parents to authoritarianism. As Sandra Scarr has said, "A smiley, cheerful baby gets a lot more social interaction than one who is

Parent-child influence goes both ways. A child like Stefan, who is basically cheerful, grows up in a different social world from one whose usual mood is anger or sadness.

crabby or passive; he or she grows up in a different social world. This evocative influence probably remains fairly steady throughout life'' (quoted in E. Hall, 1984, p. 63).

Furthermore, even if parents *usually* act toward their children in a certain way, they do not respond to *all* situations in that way. Being human, they are subject to different moods. And they react differently to different kinds of behavior.

In one study, for example, 178 adults were asked how they would respond to a 3-year-old's interrupting a telephone conversation, to a tired child's misbehaving in a supermarket, and to four other situations (Carter & Welch, 1981). Adults whose responses were usually authoritative or permissive sometimes became authoritarian, which suggests that it is often easy to know the "right" way to act with children but hard to put such knowledge into action. The researchers also found that single people were more likely than married people to be authoritative and that the most experienced parents—those with two or more children—were most likely to be authoritarian, but were also more likely to be sensitive to their children's needs as opposed to their own (accepting, for example, a child's right not to share a favorite toy with the child of the parents' friends).

Rewards and Punishment Almost all parents sometimes offer rewards to their children to get them to do something desired, and punish them to get them to stop some *un*desirable behavior. Many parents are less comfortable with rewards—seeing them as bribes—than with punishment, but the weight of research shows that children learn more by being rewarded for good behavior than by being punished for bad behavior.

Using rewards: Behavior modification Rewarding children for certain behaviors is an old approach, now often referred to by a new term—*behavior modification*. It is a form of operant, or instrumental, learning (see Chapter 6). *External rewards* may be social—a smile, a word of praise, a hug, or a special privilege. Or they may take a more tangible form such as candy, money, toys, or gold stars. Whatever the prize, the child must want it and must get it fairly consistently after showing the desired behavior. Eventually, the behavior should provide its own *internal reward*, a sense of pleasure and accomplishment.

Julia and Jess generously bestow praise, affection, and attention on Jason when he behaves well. As a result, he is motivated to continue to behave well. Some parents, however, tend to ignore children when they behave well and pay more attention to them when they start acting up. Most children prefer affectionate attention to disapproval. Some, however, would rather get disapproval than be ignored. When children deliberately misbehave to get attention, they and their parents can be caught in a destructive cycle: the parents try to halt a behavior with punishment and the children increase the behavior to get more attention.

Using punishment: When does punishment work? Over the long term, rewarding good behavior is better than punishing wrong behavior, but there are times when the short term must be considered. For example, children must learn quickly not to run out into traffic and not to bash each other over the head with heavy toys. Sometimes, too, undesirable behavior is so deep-seated that rewarding an alternative, desirable behavior just does not work.

When is punishment effective? After reviewing many reports of laboratory and field experiments and interviews with parents, Parke (1977) summarized the conclusions about the most effective ways to control children's behavior with punishment. Let us look at these.

Timing: Earlier is better than later. The less time elapses between a behavior and its punishment, the more effective the punishment will be. If *no* time elapses, that is even better. For example, when children are punished as they *begin* to approach an object they have been told to stay away from, they will go to it less often than if they are not punished until after they have actually touched it. In practical terms, of course, it is not always possible to punish children as they are about to misbehave; however, parents and teachers may be able to act quickly when a child is about to *repeat* misbehavior. And they can act immediately afterward rather than postponing punishment "until your father gets home" (a practice that has, fortunately, diminished over the years).

Explaining: Punishment is more effective when accompanied by an explanation. Children will be less likely to play with a forbidden object if they are told, "That vase is fragile and may break" than if they are punished without an explanation. School-age children will respond to a statement designed to elicit sympathy ("I'll be sad if you do this"), although this approach is relatively ineffective with a 3- or 4-year-old. A short, simple explanation is generally more effective than a long, involved one.

Consistency: The more consistently a child is punished, the more effective the punishment will be. When the same behavior brings punishment only some of the time, it is likely to continue longer than if unpunished all the time. This is not surprising, since, as we saw in Chapter 6, intermittent reinforcement produces the most durable responses. It is better to ignore undesirable behavior all the time than to punish it one day, be amused by it (thus rewarding it) the next day, and ignore it the third day.

The person who punishes: The better the relationship between the punishing adult and the child, the more effective the punishment. Punishment is two-edged: it both presents something negative and withholds something positive. Therefore, the more positive the element being withheld, the more effective the punishment. When the relationship between the child and the punishing person is close, affectionate, and nurturant, the child is losing more than he or she would in a less rewarding relationship.

The child's role: To a large degree, children determine the extent of their own punishment. Those who are defiant or who ignore an adult after they have misbehaved tend to be punished most severely; those who express remorse and try to make up for what they have done often escape punishment altogether. Sometimes, in fact, they are mildly rewarded. "Children can play a role in sparing the rod!" (Parke, 1977, p. 217).

Side effects of punishment. Although punishment can be effective in controlling behavior in the short run, it can also have some unwanted side effects over time. Physical punishment is the most clearly dangerous kind, since—aside from the possibility of injury to a child—its use presents the parent as a model of aggression and teaches the child to be aggressive. Continued use of punishment may make a child avoid the punitive adult, thus undermining that person's ability to influence the child's behavior in the future. Furthermore, a child who is punished regularly may get a feeling of helplessness—a sense that punishment is inescapable—and may become either passive or aggressive toward the punishing parent.

To sum up: Punishment is not always harmful. It is most likely to hurt a child's development when it is inconsistent or administered in an atmosphere of hostility. When used with care, it can be both effective and helpful, as Baumrind (1971) found. Authoritative parents, the most effective of her three types, did use punishment at times, with good results.

Long-Term Effects of Child-Rearing Practices   In the long run, how important are the specific ways parents deal with a variety of child-rearing issues in their children's first 5 years? One team of researchers has concluded, "Not very." In a major follow-up study of 78 adults, aged 31, whose mothers had been interviewed 20 years earlier about their child-rearing techniques (R. R. Sears et al., 1957), researchers found that specific parenting practices in the first 5 years are less important than the overall way parents feel about their children (McClelland, Constantian, Regalado, & Stone, 1978).

The way these adults had turned out seemed to bear little or no relation to the length of time they had been breastfed, whether they had had early or late bedtimes, and a number of other matters. The most important influence in these people's lives—dwarfing all others—was how much their parents had really loved them and had shown their affection and enjoyment.

The most beloved children grew up to be the most prosocial—the most tolerant of other people, the most understanding, and the most likely to show active concern for others. (These standards for psychosocial maturity were based on both Erikson's and Kohlberg's theories.) The least mature adults had grown up in homes where they were considered a nuisance and an interference in adults' lives. Their parents had been intolerant of noise, mess, and roughhousing and had reacted unkindly to the children's aggressiveness toward them, to normal childhood sex play, and to expressions of dependency.

The children of easygoing, loving parents often seemed to show less moral behavior as they were growing up than the children of stricter parents. Some amount of misbehavior may be a necessary step in moving away from wholesale adoption of parents' values toward developing one's own value system. The researchers conclude:

> Parents also need faith—faith that loving and believing in their children will promote maturity in the long run, even though some of their offsprings' behavior seems outrageous in the short run as they learn to make their own decisions. There are no shortcuts to perfection. Children have to explore some detours if they are to reach the heights. The best we parents can do to help is to love them, and not stand in the way of their groping attempts to grow up or force them at all times to conform to adult-centered codes of moral behavior. (McClelland et al., 1978, p. 114)

Brothers and Sisters

Vicky, now 6, has enjoyed playing with her brother Bobby, now 2½ years old, since he was an infant. At first, she would arrange her dolls around him as he sat in his infant seat, using him as another doll as she played mommy. Now the two of them gallop around the house together, pretending to be horses; they play kickball and other games; and she sometimes talks him into playing daddy. Realizing that Bobby cannot yet follow rules, Vicky makes allowances for him, sometimes stopping during play to say to Ellen, "Isn't he cute?"

How Do Siblings Interact in Early Childhood? As we pointed out in Chapter 7, sibling rivalry is not a dominant pattern between brothers and sisters early in life. While a certain degree of rivalry does exist, so do affection, interest, companionship—and influence. In one study, systematic observation of young pairs of siblings (same-sex and mixed-sex pairs) showed that siblings separated by as little as 1 year and as much as 4 years consistently interact a great deal, and do so in many different ways as they move through early childhood (Abramovitch, Corter, Pepler, & Stanhope, 1986; Abramovitch, Pepler, & Corter, 1982). At the first observation, the younger siblings were about 1½ years old, and the elder siblings ranged from 3 to 4½. It was clear that the children played important roles in each other's lives. Not surprisingly, the elder siblings initiated more behavior, both friendly (sharing a toy, smiling, hugging, or starting a game) and less benign (hitting, fighting over a toy, teasing, or tattling). The younger siblings initiated behavior some of the time, more often in a friendly way; apparently, children learn from an early age not to pick a fight with someone bigger and stronger! Also unsurprising was the tendency for younger children to imitate elder siblings, whether in something educational like using scissors, or in something less useful, like blowing cake crumbs out of the mouth.

While a certain degree of sibling rivalry does exist in early childhood, this picture shows that affection, interest, and companionship are present, too.

At the first follow-up 18 months later, when the younger children were 3 years old and the elder siblings were 4½ to 6, the children were more equal partners. The same basic patterns remained, however, no matter what the age difference between siblings. Young siblings got along better when the mother was not with them, suggesting that a great deal of squabbling between siblings is a bid for parents' attention.

The third observation took place 2 years later, when the younger siblings were 5 years old and the elder siblings were 6½ to 8. By this time, the elder siblings were again more dominant—both more aggressive and more prosocial. The sibling pairs were now less physical and more verbal with each other. They tended to express aggression through commands, insults, threats, tattling, and teasing—and to show affection with compliments and comfort rather than hugs and kisses. In closely spaced pairs, elder siblings were more altruistic. Siblings of the same sex tended to be a little closer and to play together more amicably than boy-girl pairs.

The elder siblings continued to initiate activities that the younger ones went along with. These included all kinds of play and rules for play. There was less imitation now, but what there was usually involved younger siblings' copying elder siblings. Over the years, most of these siblings' behavior with each other was play-oriented and prosocial, not primarily competitive or negative.

What Do Sibling Relationships Imply about the Future? Sibling relationships set the stage for other relationships in children's lives. If children's relationships with brothers and sisters are marked by easy trust and companionship, they may carry this pattern over to their dealings with playmates, classmates, and eventually the friends and lovers of adulthood. If early relationships with siblings have an aggressive cast, this, too, may influence later social relations.

Being an only child also has implications for future development, which we discuss in Boxes 10-2 and 10-3 (pages 382–383). Box 10-2 summarizes research findings about children without brothers or sisters, and Box 10-3 considers the situation in China, which has a national policy of encouraging one-child families.

BOX 10-2 ■ THE RESEARCH WORLD

IN DEFENSE OF THE ONLY CHILD

At the turn of the century, the psychologist G. Stanley Hall said that "being an only child is a disease in itself" (cited in Fenton, 1928, p. 547). The only child has had a bad reputation over the years—but the latest news is that it has been undeserved. Only children have traditionally been thought of as spoiled, selfish, lonely, and maladjusted; however, research does not bear this out. After performing statistical analysis on 115 research reports, Toni Falbo and Denise Polit (1986) concluded that only children compare very well with children who have siblings, and are very much like firstborn children and children in small (two-child) families.

Overall, compared with all children who have siblings, only children are superior in intelligence, achievement, character, and quality of relationships with parents, and they are just as sociable and well adjusted. They are more intelligent and achieve more than later-born children in medium-sized families (three to four children) and large families (five or more children). They rate higher on character than people from medium-sized and large families, and have better relationships with their parents than children in large families do.

Falbo and Polit (1986) suggest that parents of only children, firstborn, and two children have certain characteristics in common. For one thing, they tend to be anxious about parenting. They are inexperienced, do not know what to expect from their children, and do not know what to do for them. As a result, they are apt to respond quickly to a crying child—and this response makes the child feel more in control of life. They also have unrealistically high expectations for their children—which make the children want to achieve more to live up to those expectations.

Another common thread is the amount of attention these parents give to their children. First-time or second-time parents have more time to spend with each child and do spend more individual time and more "quality time" with them. As a result, the children become more verbal and act more maturely. These parents are also likely to have more money, so that they can provide more outside activities for their children, as well as better health care.

If these explanations are correct, it is ironic that the very event which reduces anxiety for parents and helps them relax—the birth of a third child—also lowers the level of their parenting. However, since fewer parents in developed countries are having a third child these days (in the United States, 1 couple in 10 has only one child), society may reap the benefits of a citizenry advantaged by membership in small families.

This may seem to contradict the conclusion being drawn by psychologists in China, who are disturbed by tendencies seen in only children there (discussed in Box 10-3). But the situations are so different in the United States and China that no accurate comparison can be made at this point.

RELATIONSHIPS WITH OTHER CHILDREN

At 3, Vicky has found a friend. She and Nancy, the little girl who lives next door, have worn a path through their backyards. They ask for each other as soon as they wake up in the morning, and neither is happier than when she is in the other's company. In the years from 3 to 6, many children form their first true friendships, relationships that may last beyond brief play periods to become an important element in their lives.

Early Friendships

Through friendships and more casual interactions, young children learn how to get along with others. They learn the importance of *being* a friend in order to *have* a friend. They learn how to solve problems (especially those centering on relationships) and how to put themselves in another person's place, and they see models of other kinds of behavior. They also learn values (including moral attitudes and gender-role norms), and they can practice adult roles.

Young children, like people of all ages, define a friend as "someone you like." As Furman (1982) has said, "Affection is the 'glue' which binds the rela-

BOX 10-3 ■ AROUND THE WORLD

A NATION OF ONLY CHILDREN

A group of Chinese kindergartners are learning a new skill—how to fold paper to make toys. When the toys do not come out right, some of the children try again on their own or watch their classmates and copy what they do. Other children become bored and impatient and ask someone else to do it for them, or else they give up, bursting into tears (Jiao, Ji, & Jing, 1986). The children in the second category tend to come from one-child families—a fact that worries citizens in the People's Republic of China, which in 1979 adopted an official policy of limiting families to one child each (Huang, 1982).

The government is intensely serious about this aim, since China's exploding population has had severe effects: not enough places in classrooms for all its children, not enough jobs for adults, not even enough food for everyone. To lower the birthrate, family-planning workers oversee factory workshops and agricultural brigades, and special birth control departments exist in every inhabited area. Furthermore, the policy goes beyond using propaganda campaigns and rewards (housing, money, child care, and school priorities) to induce voluntary compliance. There have been millions of involuntary abortions, sterilizations, and vasectomies, and people who have children without permission are fined and denied job promotions and bonuses, although recent reports indicate some easing of controls.

As a result, the nursery schools, kindergartens, and early elementary grades of China are already filled with children who have no brothers or sisters. This situation marks a great change in Chinese society, in which newly-wed couples were traditionally congratulated with the wish, "May you have a hundred sons and a thousand grandsons." No culture in human history has ever been composed entirely of only children. And now that the Chinese are seeing the possibility of achieving their population goal, some critics are asking whether they are sowing the seeds of their own destruction.

Kindergarten teachers complain that only children, raised by overindulgent parents, are spoiled brats who show an unusually large number of behavioral problems and are fussy about what they eat and wear, careless with property, and selfish and ill-tempered. In an effort to test the truth of these comments, psychologists asked urban and rural schoolchildren, aged 4 to 6 and 9 to 10 years, to rate their classmates on seven characteristics—independence and self-reliance, persistence, willingness to control their own behavior, tendency to become frustrated, cooperation, popularity with other children, and egocentrism. When the ratings of children from one-child families were compared with those of children with siblings, the results were disturbing: only children were seen as more egocentric and less persistent, cooperative, and well liked (Jiao et al., 1986). They were more likely to refuse help to another child or to give help grudgingly; less likely to share their toys or to enjoy playing or working with other children; less modest; less helpful in group activities; and more irresponsible. It is no wonder that children liked them less than they liked children with siblings.

In a second study, however, teachers in Peking (Beijing) rated only children quite favorably, finding them gentle, shy, obedient, considerate, respectful of elders, and eager to join in collective activities. They also found them academically superior, especially in language ability. Are these children perhaps Jekyll-and-Hyde characters who are angels around adults but demons around other children? If so, they may not be model members of society, particularly a society that emphasizes individual sacrifice for the sake of collective development.

China's population policy also has wider implications which are of considerable concern. If it succeeds, eventually most Chinese will lack not only siblings but also aunts and uncles, nephews and nieces, and cousins. How this would affect individuals, families, and the social fabric is at present incalculable.

---

tionship together" (p. 328). The voluntary nature of friendships makes them more fragile than the more permanent ties with siblings, parents, and other relatives. These early friendships are, like later ones, one-on-one relationships. We may play with a group, but we are friends with the individuals within it.

How do young children choose friends? They usually become friendly with other children who like to do the same kinds of things, and so friends usually have similar energy and activity levels and are of the same age and sex (Gamer, Thomas, & Kendall, 1975). When Vicky is 6, she plays happily for hours with Nancy. But when Jason comes to play, they have trouble deciding on things to

BOX 10-4 ■ THE EVERYDAY WORLD

HELPING CHILDREN MAKE FRIENDS

Few sights are more pathetic than a child who is all alone because "nobody wants to play with me." Having friends is important to a child's self-esteem, as well as to other aspects of personality development. Research suggests the following ways in which adults can help unpopular children improve their relationships with peers (Roopnarine & Honig, 1985):

■ Praise children generously and reward them in other ways for cooperative behavior.

■ Keep the number of rules to a minimum, make them clear, and explain the reasons for them.

■ Set a good example by being warm and nurturant and sharing with both children and adults. Work toward building the child's self-esteem.

■ Encourage children to participate in small groups of two or three rather than in larger groups.

■ Read to children from books about lonely or shy animals and children who learn to make friends.

■ Play with them, using dolls, puppets, and role-playing, to show social skills.

■ Find or start a play group for children who do not have the opportunity to play with other children; only by being with others can a child learn the kind of give-and-take that is necessary for getting along with peers.

do. They seem to need suggestions from an adult, and Vicky often says, "He doesn't want to do what I want to do."

One investigation of the conceptions of friendship held by 4- to 7-year-olds confirms and adds to these findings (Furman & Bierman, 1983). After interviewing the children, the investigators showed them pictures and asked them which activities shown would make children friends, and which were the important features of friendship in the pictures.

The most important features of friendship were *common activities* (doing things together), *affection* (liking and caring for each other), *support* (sharing and helping), and, to a lesser degree, *propinquity* (living nearby or going to the same school). The older children rated affection and support higher than the younger children and rated *physical characteristics* (appearance and size) lower.

Why is one child sought out as a playmate or friend when another is not? Children who have friends talk more to other children and take turns directing and following. They smile often, share their toys, and offer help. On the other hand, children who are disruptive or aggressive tend to be rejected by their age-mates, and those who are shy or withdrawn are ignored (Roopnarine & Honig, 1985). Friendless children either fight with others or stand on the side-lines and watch them (Roopnarine & Field, 1984).

In one study, 65 kindergartners were shown pictures illustrating story situations related to making and keeping friends and were asked what the child in the picture should do. Unpopular children were more likely to be aggressive (12 percent suggested that the child should beat up a child who grabs toys, compared with only 2 percent of popular children). They were also less resourceful, giving only vague suggestions or looking for help from an authority rather than coping independently with situations. While both groups were assertive, the popular children were more cooperative and more effective (Asher, Renshaw, Geraci, & Dor, 1979).

It is encouraging to note, however, that the two groups were not greatly different: about two-thirds of the responses by popular children were also given by the unpopular children. This suggests that unpopular children can be taught the kinds of responses that will help them make friends. (See Box 10-4.)

BOX 10-5 ■ A CHILD'S WORLD AND YOU

WHAT DO YOU THINK?

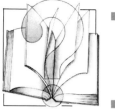

■ "Males are innately more aggressive, and females more nurturing. While these traits can be altered to some degree, the basic tendencies will remain." Do you agree or disagree? Why?

■ Where would you place yourself on the continuum between the following extremes? Explain.

FAMILY A
Thinks that girls should wear only ruffly dresses and that boys should never wash dishes or cry
FAMILY Z
Treats sons and daughters exactly alike, without making any references to the children's sex

■ Is it possible to have a female personality in a male body?

■ One way in which small children confront fears is to play at such potentially frightening activities as dressing up on Halloween, going on scary rides at amusement parks, and listening to ghost stories. Do you approve or disapprove? Why?

■ Hostile aggression is widely condemned, but instrumental aggression has many defenders. Is it wise to teach a child never to be aggressive?

■ During early childhood, children develop a conscience. What do you think is the best basis for a conscience: obedience to clear rules, self-control according to general principles, or self-expression? Why?

Family Ties and Popularity

As we noted earlier, young children's relationships with brothers and sisters often carry over to relationships with other children. However, patterns established with siblings are not always repeated with friends. For example, a child who is dominated by an elder sibling can easily step into a dominant role with a playmate when appropriate; and by and large, children are more prosocial and playful with playmates than with siblings (Abramovitch et al., 1986).

Young children's relationships with their parents also affect the way they get along with other children. Preschoolers who were securely attached as infants tend to have more friends and to be considered more socially competent by their teachers than children who were insecurely attached (Sroufe, 1983).

Parents of rejected or isolated children often have distinct profiles. The mothers do not have confidence in their parenting, rarely praise their children, and do not encourage them to be independent; the fathers pay little attention to their children, do not like being disturbed by them, and consider child rearing women's work (Peery, Jensen, & Adams, cited in Roopnarine & Honig, 1985). The parents of popular children, on the other hand, have warm, positive relationships with their children, discipline them with reasoning rather than punishment, and are more likely to be authoritative than authoritarian (Baumrind, 1977; Roopnarine & Honig, 1985).

Furthermore, children seem to pick up social behaviors from their parents: one study of first-graders found that agreeable mothers have agreeable children, mothers who talk about their feelings to other adults have children who focus on their own feelings, and disagreeable mothers have disagreeable children (Putallaz, 1987). Parents are powerful models in peer relationships as in many other aspects of behavior, a fact that clearly emerges from the ways young children play. In their play—which, as we have seen, is an important part of personality development in early childhood—children often show how closely they have been watching and listening to their parents.

Summary

1 According to Freud, children between about 3 and 6 years of age are in the phallic stage of psychosexual development and receive pleasure from genital stimulation. Their sexuality is not like the mature adult's. Freud's concept of the Oedipus complex in males and the Electra complex in females is meant to explain a child's feelings toward the parent of the other sex. Because of the anxiety the child feels, he or she eventually represses sexual urges toward the parent of the other sex and identifies with the same-sex parent. The superego (made up of the ego-ideal and the conscience) develops when either complex is resolved.

2 Erikson maintains that the chief developmental crisis of early childhood is initiative versus guilt. Successful resolution of this conflict results in the virtue of purpose and enables the child to plan and carry out activities. Parents can help children achieve a healthy balance by encouraging them to do things on their own while still providing guidance.

3 Identification is the adoption of the characteristics, beliefs, attitudes, values, and behaviors of another person or of a group. There are several theoretical interpretations of identification. In psychoanalytic theory, the child identifies with the same-sex parent at the resolution of the Oedipus or Electra complex. According to social-learning theory, identification occurs when the child observes and imitates one or more models.

4 Sex differences are physical differences between males and females. Gender differences are psychological differences between the sexes that may or may not be based on biology. Gender roles are the behaviors and attitudes that a culture deems appropriate for males and females. Gender-typing is the learning of culturally determined gender roles.

5 In general, the sexes are more similar than different. Gender differences are few, and their extent and significance are minimal. Explanations for the differences that do exist focus on biological or environmental origins.

6 Even though gender differences are minor, society holds strong ideas about appropriate behaviors for the sexes, and children learn these expectations at an early age. Because gender-role stereotyping can restrict the development of both sexes, androgynous child rearing, which encourages children to express both "male" and "female" characteristics, is being fostered by many people and institutions.

7 Four theories about gender-role acquisition are the psychoanalytic, social-learning, cognitive-developmental, and gender-schema theories. According to psychoanalytic theory, children emerge from the Oedipus complex or Electra complex having identified with the parent of the same sex. The social-learning perspective holds that chil-

dren observe models of the same sex and are rewarded for imitating them. Cognitive-developmental theory maintains that gender identity is related to cognitive development. Gender-schema theory combines aspects of cognitive-developmental and social-learning theory. It holds that children fit their self-concept to the gender schema of their culture, a socially organized pattern of behavior for males and females. According to this theory, the gender schema of a culture or an individual can be changed.

8 During early childhood, children show many fears of both real and imaginary objects and events. Sometimes these fears develop into phobias, which are irrational, involuntary, and inappropriate to the situation. Systematic desensitization and modeling can help children overcome fears and phobias.

9 Whether children show prosocial or aggressive behavior is influenced by the way their parents treat them as well as by other factors, including what they learn from the media, the values of their culture, and whether they observe aggressive or prosocial models.

10 Play is both a social and a cognitive activity. Changes in the type of play children engage in reflect their development. Through play, children exercise their physical abilities, grow cognitively, and learn to interact with other children.

11 Baumrind has identified three types of child-rearing styles: authoritarian, permissive, and authoritative. Each is related to certain behavior patterns in children. The authoritative style is associated with the most positive outcomes.

12 Parents influence children's behavior partly through rewards and punishments. Rewards are generally more effective than punishments. Punishments are most effective when they are immediate, accompanied by an explanation, consistent, and carried out by a person who has a good relationship with the child. The child's behavior also affects the extent of punishment. Physical punishment, in particular, can have a number of damaging effects.

13 Parents' love is the most important influence on the social maturity that their children will exhibit as adults.

14 Relationships with siblings and peers seem to affect patterns of relationships later in life. As siblings move through early childhood, most of their interactions are positive. As they mature, their interaction is less often physical and more often verbal. Older siblings tend to be dominant and are both more aggressive and more prosocial.

15 Only children in the United States tend to exhibit positive characteristics, but being an only child in China is associated with a number of negative traits.

16 Children who are aggressive or withdrawn tend to be less popular with playmates than children who act friendly. The types of attachments they have had in infancy, as well as their parents' attitudes, disciplinary techniques, and child-rearing styles, affect the ease with which young children find playmates and friends.

Key Terms

phallic stage (page 349)
Oedipus complex (349)
Electra complex (349)
castration anxiety (349)
penis envy (350)
superego (350)
initiative versus guilt (351)
identification (352)
sex difference (354)
gender difference (354)
gender roles (354)
gender-typing (354)
gender identity (355)
androgens (355)

testosterone (355)
androgynous (360)
gender constancy (361)
gender-schema theory (362)
phobia (365)
systematic desensitization (365)
prosocial behavior (366)
dominance hierarchy (368)
social play (372)
cognitive play (372)
authoritarian parents (376)
permissive parents (376)
authoritative parents (376)

Suggested Readings

Bettelheim, B. (1988). *A good enough parent: A book on childrearing.* New York: Random House. A commonsense book on child rearing which helps parents see each child as unique in developmental style.

Garvey, C. (1977). *Play.* Cambridge, MA: Harvard University Press. A look at the development of play, from the infant's game of peekaboo to play with objects, language, and social materials—and finally, play with rules.

Ginott, H.G. (1965). *Between parent and child.* New York: Avon. An approach to parenting emphasizing communication, with many case histories.

Gordon, T. (1970). *P.E.T.: Parent effectiveness training.* New York: New American Library. A program of training for parenting, based on the ''active listening'' method.

Oliner, S.P., & Oliner, P.M. (1988). *The altruistic personality: Rescuers of Jews in Nazi Europe.* New York: Free Press. By comparing rescuers (who risked their lives for no personal gain) with bystanders during the Holocaust, the authors, both sociologists (one of whom was rescued himself), found a number of factors in childhood that encouraged rescuers' altruistic behavior. The book is full of compelling accounts of the heroism of ''ordinary'' people.

Pogrebin, L.C. (1980). *Growing up free: Raising your child in the 80's.* New York: Bantam. An extensively researched and extremely readable account of the ways society locks children into stereotyped gender roles, with many suggestions for parents who want to liberate both themselves and their children.

MIDDLE CHILDHOOD

The years of middle childhood, from about age 6 to age 12, are often called the *school years*, since the school experience is the central one of this time of life. It is in school that both Vicky and Jason find friends, games, and ideas, and a complex society. In Chapters 11, 12, and 13 we look at the physical, intellectual, and personality development of these school years and at Vicky's and Jason's increasing socialization.

Chapter 11, on physical development, discusses children's steady growth and improving motor abilities. During these years children acquire many of the physical skills needed to participate in the games of our society. Chapter 12, which is about intellectual development, presents the child's new ability to think logically and creatively about the here and now. This is the period when many children first realize which aspects of our complex society most interest them and in which areas they are more competent. Chapter 13, on personality development, discusses a stage that traditionally has been considered calm and idyllic. This stage never was as peaceful as some believed, and many modern social features like divorce and prejudice take their toll, but usually children emerge from the period with a healthy sense of self-esteem.

PHYSICAL DEVELOPMENT IN MIDDLE CHILDHOOD

The boy is growing
as fast as he can, elongated
wrists dangling, lean meat
showing between the shirt and the belt
If there were a rack to stretch himself, he would
strap his slight body to it.
If there were a machine to enter,
skip the next ten years and be
sixteen immediately, this boy would
do it.

Sharon Olds, "Size and Sheer Will,"
The Dead and the Living, 1983

PREVIEW QUESTIONS

- What factors influence height and weight in middle childhood?
- What are the causes and implications of childhood obesity? How is it treated?
- What are the principal health problems in middle childhood?
- How does children's understanding of health and illness develop in middle childhood?
- How can adults make middle childhood healthier and safer?
- What motor skills do most children have at this age?

HIGHER AND HIGHER pencil marks on the wall of Jason's room show his growth over the years. His height is a source of pride—and worry—as he measures his new abilities (like reaching the highest shelf in the refrigerator) and as he measures himself against his classmates (and finds too many of them taller than he is). By the time he is 12, he can look Julia squarely in the eye, and she can fit into his blue jeans. Soon, though, after his adolescent growth spurt (discussed in Chapter 14), he will be taller than his mother.

Vicky, too, has been growing slowly and steadily during her first 6 years at school. At first her pace is about the same as Jason's, but later it becomes slightly faster. At 12 she is half a head taller than Jason, and a little heavier. The facial proportions of both children have also changed. In accordance with the cephalocaudal principle of development (see Chapter 5), during the early years the upper parts of the head grow faster than the lower parts. Now, in middle childhood, the lower half of the face catches up, and the forehead is not so high anymore. The facial features become more prominent and more distinctly individual.

Both Vicky and Jason are in robust health, and they take for granted their increasing physical power and coordination. Middle childhood is among the healthiest stages in the life span, despite the prevalence of colds and sore throats. Fortunately, debilitating diseases are rare.

In this chapter we examine physical growth, including predictions of height in adulthood and certain abnormal growth patterns. Normal growth depends on proper nutrition and good health, and so we also discuss health and illness, and we look at an increasingly common problem, childhood obesity.

As we explore health concerns, we examine two subjects that overlap discussions in other chapters. One is Type A behavior, which has been linked to heart disease later in life, and illustrates the relationship between physical changes and personality. The other is children's understanding of health and illness, which links physical and cognitive issues. Both involve a mixture of physical, personality, and intellectual development and thus remind us that despite the distinction often made between mind and body, the two are hard to separate.

We also consider safety concerns. As children develop, they do more, and their risk of accidents increases; we look at some ways to lower this risk.

The final portion of the chapter considers motor development. At age 6, children are bundles of poorly focused energy. They run a lot, for example, but not efficiently or smoothly. At 12 they run less, but more productively. In addition to motor skills, we look at one of the more mysterious features of motor development, *handedness*—the tendency to use one hand rather than the other.

We begin by considering the fundamentals of growth during this period.

School-age children are taller and thinner than they were as preschoolers. Girls retain somewhat more fatty tissue than boys, a physical characteristic that will persist through adulthood. And black children tend to be slightly taller than white children.

Growth during the School Years

HEIGHT AND WEIGHT

If we were to walk by a typical elementary school just after the three o'clock bell, we would see a virtual explosion of children of all shapes and sizes. Tall ones, short ones, fat ones, and skinny ones would be bursting out of the school doors into the freedom of the open air.

We would see that these 6- to 12-year-olds look very different from children a few years younger. They are much taller, and most are fairly wiry, although the rate of obesity has increased in the past few decades. Girls retain somewhat more fatty tissue than boys, a physical characteristic that will persist through adulthood. And black children tend to be slightly taller than white children (American Academy of Pediatrics, 1973).

During middle childhood, children grow about 2 or 3 inches each year and gain about 5 to 7 pounds. Late in this stage, usually between the ages of 10 and 12, girls begin their growth spurt, and suddenly are looking down at the boys in their class. (See Table 11-1 for a summary of data for the various groups.) Changes in height and weight are not completely parallel in boys and girls. By the time girls are 9, they have caught up with boys in height after a slight dip, but they fall steadily behind in weight until they overtake boys—at age 10 for nonwhite girls and at age 11 for white girls.

Variations in Growth

The figures we have just noted, of course, are averages. Individual children vary widely—so widely that "if a child who was of exactly average height at his

TABLE 11-1

	HEIGHT, INCHES				WEIGHT, POUNDS			
AGE	WHITE MALES	NONWHITE MALES	WHITE FEMALES	NONWHITE FEMALES	WHITE MALES	NONWHITE MALES	WHITE FEMALES	NONWHITE FEMALES
6	46	47	46	47	48	49	47	46
7	49	49	49	49	53	55	52	51
8	51	52	50	51	61	61	57	58
9	53	53	53	53	66	66	63	65
10	55	55	57	57	73	72	70	78
11	57	58	58	59	81	80	87	90
12	59	60	60	61	91	93	95	99

PHYSICAL GROWTH, AGE 6 TO AGE 12 (50TH PERCENTILE)

Source: Adapted from Rauh, Schumsky, & Witt, 1967, pp. 515–530.

seventh birthday grew not at all for two years, he would still be just within the normal limits of height attained at age nine" (Tanner, 1973, p. 35).

Figures also vary for different groups. Table 11-1 shows that nonwhite boys and girls tend to be a bit bigger than white children of the same age and sex. There is also a difference between richer and poorer children. Children from more affluent homes tend to be larger and more mature than children from poorer homes. This difference arises from differences in nutrition. Later in this chapter we will discuss malnutrition, which usually hinders growth. Over-nourished, or fat, children mature earliest of all, and heavy girls experience **menarche,** or the first menstruation, earlier than more slender girls.

menarche   Girl's first menstruation.

Ethnic differences also affect children's average size. One study of 8-year-old children in several parts of the world found a range of about 9 inches between the mean heights of the shortest children (mostly from southeast Asia, Oceania, and South America) and the tallest (mostly from northern and central Europe, eastern Australia, and the United States) (Meredith, 1969). Although genetic differences probably account for some of this diversity, environmental influences also play a part. The tallest children come from parts of the world "where nutritious food is abundant and where . . . infectious diseases are well controlled or largely eliminated" (Meredith, 1969).

Implicit in this wide range of average sizes is a warning. When judging health or screening for abnormalities, observers often rely on measures of a child's physical growth and development. However, in the face of evidence that children from different ethnic groups develop differently, it would be useful to establish separate growth standards for different populations (Goldstein & Tanner, 1980). In the United States especially, where many different subcultures live side by side, judgments of what is normal need to be made cautiously.

Predicting Height

Since the time Jason was a toddler, he has seemed to show the physical agility, grace, and sense of rhythm that—to Julia—suggest a career in dance. Just after his eighth birthday, she enrolls him in dancing class, where his teachers are impressed with his ability and enthusiasm. But the decision to set him on this path, with all the special training it entails, depends partly on how tall he will be as an adult. If he is too tall or too short, no important dance company will accept him. But Jason is only 8. How can anyone predict his adult height?

This question illustrates one practical reason for trying to predict height. The computer has made methods of analysis more sophisticated, but still we can predict height in adulthood with an accuracy of only plus or minus 2 inches. If we predict that Jason will grow to be 5 feet 10 inches tall, he may be as much as 2 inches taller (6 feet) or 2 inches shorter (5 feet 8 inches). The chief difficulty in accurate prediction is the uncertainty about the growth spurt in adolescence. It can make short people tall; but if it is small, it can disappoint short people who expect to become much taller (Tanner, 1973).

Abnormal Growth

Children whose growth is below normal are often significantly shorter than their classmates, even at age 6 or 7. There are many different types of growth disorders. One of the most important arises from the body's failure to produce enough growth hormone. This is sometimes treated by giving children injections of human growth hormone, but that therapy is expensive and carries a risk of infection. Recently, biochemists have developed a technique for inserting the genetic code for human growth hormone into bacteria, cloning the bacteria, and then allowing the bacteria to make the growth hormone. This method costs less and results in a purer hormone (Angier, 1982).

Would some ambitious parents try to use the hormone to turn a child of normal height into an especially tall adult? This might be dangerous, since we have no clear idea what the long-term effects on health are likely to be for a person who is genetically designed to be 5 feet 10 inches tall but has been artificially "stretched" to 6 feet 3 inches. Yet even the fact that we can worry about such things is a startling sign of how much power biochemistry has given us.

Because the use of growth hormone is so new, and because there are so many uncertainties about its safety and long-term effects, the American Academy of Pediatrics (1983) has recommended that growth hormone be used *only* for children who are naturally deficient in it. Further, since many of the handicaps associated with being short are due not to short stature itself but to a person's feelings about it, growth hormone should be given only to children whose prospects for emotional improvement outweigh the problems of long-term hormone therapy.

NUTRITION AND GROWTH

During the middle years, average body weight doubles, and children's play demands great expenditures of energy. To support this steady growth and constant exertion, children need plenty of food. In these years, children usually eat a greater amount of food—and eat it fast. On average, they need, every day, 2400 calories; their daily food intake should contain 34 grams of protein, plus high levels of complex carbohydrates, found in potatoes and cereal grains. Simple carbohydrates, found in sweets, should be kept to a minimum (E. R. Williams & Caliendo, 1984).

We have already seen that poor nutrition causes slowed growth, and that malnourished children are shorter than well-fed children. It takes some energy and protein just to stay alive, and more energy and protein to grow. When a child does not take in enough food to sustain life and promote growth, growth is sacrificed in order to maintain the body. Good nutrition is also essential for normal mental, physical, and social activities.

To carry on their normal mental, physical, and social activities, these children need to be well nourished. They should get many of their daily 2400 calories in complex carbohydrates (found in potatoes and cereal grains) and should eat a minimum of sweets.

Malnutrition

Do malnourished children suffer socially as well as physically? Chronic malnutrition is a problem even in the prosperous United States, and it is even more serious in many other parts of the world. An especially valuable longitudinal study in Guatemala has helped identify many long-term effects of early malnutrition. Researchers studied 138 schoolchildren aged 6 to 8, in three farming villages. At younger ages, these children had all received dietary supplements. The supplements, however, had differed. Some children received a mix of proteins, essential vitamins, and sources of extra calories, while other received sources of extra calories and vitamins, but not proteins. Children who as infants had not received protein supplements tended to be passive, or dependent on adults, and more anxious; the children who had received protein supplements were happier and livelier and got along better with other children (Barrett, Radke-Yarrow, & Klein, 1982).

This finding supports the conclusion that poor nutrition leads to less activity. The way this happens is complex. The study found that a child's diet from birth to age 2 is a good predictor of social behavior from age 6 to age 8. Why is there such a long-term effect? It may arise from a complex feedback system. Mothers of malnourished infants may respond to them less frequently and less sensitively because the infants do not have the energy to engage their mothers' attention and induce the mother to do things with them. As the babies develop poor social skills and become generally unresponsive, other people, too, become less and less interested in interacting with them (B. M. Lester, 1979).

This process gains momentum if, as often happens, the mother is also malnourished. She, too, lacks the energy and ability to engage the attention of other people and to get them to have much to do with her. Mother and child, then, become caught in a cycle of passive unsociability (Rosetti-Ferreira, 1978).

Studies like the long-term research in Guatemala show how the different domains of development—in this case, physical growth and personality—are related. A particularly powerful example of the intertwining of physical and social effects can be seen in "overnutrition," the excess of calories that leads to obesity.

Obesity

At the age of 6, Vicky looks into every mirror she passes, and she often refuses a favorite food because she is afraid of getting fat. Like most girls her age, she is of normal weight. However, her attitude is typical: preoccupation with weight is becoming increasingly common among young children. According to a recent study, children develop a dislike of obesity between the ages of 6 and 9—largely, it seems, because American society equates thinness with beauty (W. Feldman, Feldman, & Goodman, 1988). It is paradoxical, then, that there are more fat children in the United States than ever before. And because of societal attitudes, these children are likely to suffer psychologically, as well as physically.

What is Obesity, and How Common Is It? In one 6-year study of nearly 2600 mostly white middle-class children under age 12 who were enrolled in a prepaid health maintenance plan, about 4 percent of the total and 5½ percent of 8- to 11-year-olds were considered obese (Starfield et al., 1984). One way to determine *obesity* is to measure the thickness of skin from the upper arm pinched between two fingers: a child whose skin fold is in the 85th percentile (thicker than that of 85 percent of children of the same age and sex in 1963 to 1970) would be considered obese; a child in the 95th percentile would be diagnosed as superobese.

obesity Overweight condition marked by a skin-fold measurement in the 85th percentile (thicker than the skin fold of 85 percent of children of the same age and sex).

Both obesity and superobesity have increased among school-age children and adolescents. From 1963 to 1980, obesity became 54 percent more common among school-age children and 39 percent more common among adolescents, and superobesity soared by 98 percent and 64 percent, respectively (Figure 11-1 shows the increase in obesity among schoolchildren since 1965). Among younger children, boys showed the greatest increase; among adolescents, the greatest increase was for girls. Rates vary geographically, too, with more obesity occurring in the northeast and midwest than in the west (Gortmaker, Dietz, Sobol, & Wehler, 1987).

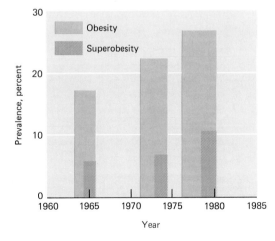

FIGURE 11-1
Estimated trends in obesity and superobesity in children 6 to 11 years old in the United States. The increase in childhood obesity has serious implications for both physical and mental health. (*Source:* Adapted from Gortmaker, Dietz, Sobol, & Wehler, 1987.)

(© Bob Daemmrich/Stock, Boston)

Children, like adults, become overweight when they take in more calories than they expend. The basic approach for preventing or treating obesity involves more physical exercise, like this tug of war, and less food.

What Causes Obesity?   As we noted in Chapter 5, people become overweight when they consume more calories than they expend. And the amount of excess calories need not be large: children who eat as little as 50 extra calories a day will put on 5 extra pounds a year (Kolata, 1986). But when two people eat the same amount of calories, why does only one get fat? And what makes some people eat more than they need? Although the precise cause of childhood obesity is not known, there are a number of theories:

■ One possibility is *genetic predisposition.* A study of 540 adopted adults found a very strong correlation in weight between these people and their biological parents, but virtually none with their adoptive parents (Stunkard et al., 1986).

■ *Environment* is also influential, since children tend to eat the same kinds of foods and develop the same kinds of habits as the people around them. Obesity is more common among lower socioeconomic groups, especially among women (Kolata, 1986).

■ There is also a correlation (negative) between *activity level* and weight. But are heavier children less active because they are fat, or do they become fat because they are less active? So far, there is no answer (Kolata, 1986); but informed opinion tends toward the second conclusion.

■ Evidently, *television* is also a factor. According to two studies—one of nearly 700 six- to eleven-year-olds and one of 6500 adolescents—every hour a day spent watching television results in a 2 percent increase in the prevalence of obesity. Children who watch television a great deal tend to eat more snacks (especially the high-calorie snacks they see in commercials) and are less active than other children (Dietz & Gortmaker, 1985).

Treating Childhood Obesity   A compelling reason for treating childhood obesity is that fat children usually become fat adults. Both their self-esteem and their health are likely to suffer: they will be considered unattractive, and they will be at risk of high blood pressure, certain orthopedic problems, and diabetes. But the current treatment for children is so recent that we cannot say much about its effectiveness.

The basic approach today involves a restricted diet, more exercise, and behavior modification. Behavioral therapies, which help children change their eating and exercise habits, have been more effective than no treatment at all (L. H. Epstein & Wing, 1987). Because these approaches focus on changing a child's behavior (eating fewer meals per day, eating more slowly, exercising more), they are more effective when they involve parents. Parents, for example, can be trained to avoid using sweets as a reward for good behavior and to stop buying tempting high-calorie foods. Parents can also lose weight themselves, but whether they do or not does not seem to matter to children, as long as they support the children's efforts.

There is some controversy about the significance of exercise, though almost all weight-loss programs include it. "Lifestyle" exercise programs, which include a wide choice of daily activities that can be done from childhood into adulthood, seem to be more effective than aerobic programs based on a limited set of high-intensity, repetitive exercises (L. H. Epstein & Wing, 1987).

Health and Safety

Vicky, aged 10, is home in bed with a cold, her second of the year. She sneezes, snoozes, watches daytime TV, and enjoys her break from the school routine. She is lucky: apart from her two colds, she has had no other illnesses this year. During middle childhood, germs pass so freely among children at school or during play that many youngsters have six or seven respiratory infections a year (Behrman & Vaughan, 1983). Even children who do get a lot of colds, however, are healthier than their counterparts early in this century. As we pointed out in Chapter 8, vaccines for many childhood illnesses have made the elementary school years an extremely healthy time of life for most children.

There are potential problems, of course. In addition to obesity, which has just been discussed, there are minor medical conditions, problems with vision and teeth, such psychological disorders as stuttering and tics, high blood pressure, and Type A behavior. In this section, we discuss these; we also talk about improving children's fitness, and about children's understanding of health and illness (an example of the intertwining of physical and cognitive aspects of development), and about accidental injuries.

HEALTH CONCERNS

Minor Medical Conditions

Children's minor medical problems run the gamut from colds and sore throats to warts and earaches. A typical child may experience five to seven different types of problems over a 6-year period (Starfield et al., 1984). Most illnesses run a brief course, but children who have a particular condition once are likely to have it again. Over a 6-year period, more than 90 percent of basically healthy children are likely to suffer from severe medical conditions, like a viral infection, strep throat, bronchitis, or eczema. Only 1 in 9, however, have such persistent prob-

BOX 11-1 ■ THE RESEARCH WORLD

CHILDREN'S UNDERSTANDING OF HEALTH AND ILLNESS

Being sick is a frightening experience at any age. For children, who do not fully understand what is happening, it can be especially distressing and confusing. (When Vicky overheard the doctor refer to *edema*—an accumulation of fluid, which causes swelling—she thought that her problem was "a demon.") Two separate studies found nearly identical stages of development for children's understanding of their own diseases (Brewster, 1982; Perrin & Gerrity, 1981).

At the beginning of middle childhood, children are in Piaget's preoperational stage (see Chapter 9) and are incapable of abstract logic. During this period children tend to believe that illness is magically produced by human actions, often their own. Magical explanations can last well into childhood. One 12-year-old with leukemia said, "I know that my doctor told me that my illness is caused by too many white cells, but I still wonder if it was caused by something I did" (Brewster, 1982, p. 361). It would be hard for parents or professionals who overheard this remark to keep from rushing in and saying, "There, there, of course it wasn't anything you did." But this reaction may not be as supportive as one might think. Egocentric explanations for illness can serve as an important defense against feelings of helplessness. Children may feel that if something they did made them ill, then perhaps they can do something else to get better. One investigator warns, "It is never wise to break down defenses until one is sure that more desirable concepts will take their place" (Brewster, 1982, p. 362).

As children grow beyond the preoperational stage, their explanations for disease change. They enter a stage in which all diseases are explained—hardly less magically—by germs. "Watch out for germs" is the motto of children of this age, who believe that germs cause disease automatically. The only "prevention" is a variety of superstitious behaviors to ward off germs.

Last, as children approach adolescence, they enter a third stage when they see that there can be multiple causes of disease, that contact with the dreaded germs does not automatically lead to illness, and that people can do much to keep healthy.

---

lems as migraine headaches or nearsightedness. Upper-respiratory illnesses, sore throats and strep throats, and ear infections decrease with age; but as children approach puberty, they suffer more from acne, headaches, and passing emotional problems. As children's physical health concerns change with age, so does their understanding of health and illness, as shown in Box 11-1.

Vision and Visual Problems

Jason, like most youngsters in middle childhood, has much keener vision now than he did earlier, because his visual apparatus is more developed. Children under 6 years of age tend to be farsighted, since their eyes have not matured and are shaped differently from those of adults. By the age of 6, their vision is more acute, and since the eyes work together better, they can focus better.

Still, some children have problems with vision. By the age of six, 10 percent have defective near vision and 7 percent have poor distant vision (20/40 or less, meaning that in order to see something that they should be able to see at 40 feet, they have to be 20 feet from it). By 11 years of age, 17 percent have poor distant vision. Yet many of these children have either no eyeglasses or inadequate glasses (U.S. Department of Health, Education, and Welfare, USDHEW, 1976).

Dental Health and Dental Problems

Most of the adult teeth arrive during middle childhood. The "tooth fairy" first appeared when Vicky was about 6, replacing the tooth under her pillow with a dollar. Her primary teeth will continue to fall out, to be replaced by permanent teeth at a rate of about four teeth per year for the next 5 years. The first molars erupt at about age 6; at about Vicky's thirteenth birthday, her second molars will come in; and in her early twenties she will have her third molars—the wisdom teeth (Behrman & Vaughan, 1983).

Given the importance of sound teeth for nutrition, general health, and appearance, a major health concern in the United States up until very recently was the high rate of dental problems among children. Now, however, the picture is much brighter (see Figure 11-2). A government survey of about 40,000 children aged 5 to 17 found that half of American children have no cavities or other tooth decay (Herrmann & Roberts, 1987).

This turnaround seems to be due to the widespread use of fluoride in drinking water, toothpaste, and mouthwash, to the use of fluoridated water in food preparation, and to better dental care. Two-thirds of the decay in children's teeth is on the rough, chewing surfaces; much of this can be prevented with the use of adhesive sealants, plastic films that harden after being painted onto teeth.

Improvements in dental care can be seen in the fact that today 82 percent of damaged tooth surfaces have been repaired, compared with only 76 percent in 1980. In the 1940s, there was probably 5 times as much tooth decay in children as there is today, and it was rare for a child not to have any cavities at all.

Some children, however, resist dental care because they are afraid of the dentist. Young children are usually cooperative at the dentist's office, and with repeated visits they become even more cooperative and less anxious. But in middle childhood youngsters become more fearful. Is this because children have had more experience with dentists and have learned to fear them? There is little evidence to support this hypothesis. A more likely cause is children's modeling of their parents' behavior. They see that their parents are nervous about going to the dentist, and the children grow anxious themselves. Fears can be reduced if a child sees another person fearlessly doing something the child is afraid of and also if the child is repeatedly and gradually exposed to the fear-producing stimulus (as we saw in Chapter 10). If parents go to the dentist without showing

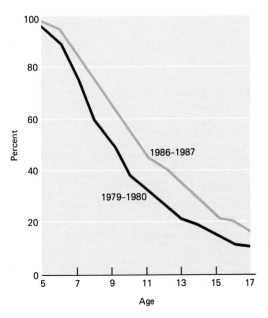

FIGURE 11-2
Percentage of children with no cavities or other decay problems at ages 5 through 17. The improvement in children's dental health seems to have resulted from use of fluoride and from better dental care. (*Source:* Leary, 1988a.)

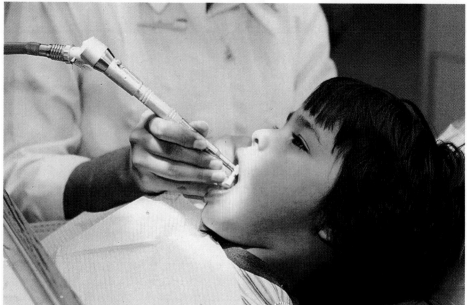

Some children, unlike this apparently calm girl, are afraid of the dentist. Since regular dental care is important for the growth of healthy teeth, parents can help their children by modeling sensible behavior—going to the dentist without showing anxiety.

anxiety, and if they take their children along on their own visits, the children are likely to overcome their fears (Winer, 1982).

Stuttering

stuttering *Involuntary repetition or prolongation of syllables.*

Stuttering, involuntary frequent repetition or prolongation of sounds and syllables, is an embarrassing disorder that interferes with social functioning. As stutterers become frustrated and anxious about ordinary conversation, their self-esteem tends to plummet. The condition runs in families and is 3 times more common in boys than in girls. In 98 percent of cases, it begins before age 10, and it is more prevalent among younger children than older ones. Some 10 percent of schoolchildren stutter; of these, 80 percent stop stuttering before age 16—60 percent on their own and 20 percent in response to treatment. But about 1 percent continue to stutter in adulthood (*Diagnostic and Statistical Manual of Mental Disorders,* 3d ed., rev., DSM III-R, 1987).

Theories about causes include physical explanations like faulty training in articulation and breathing; problems with brain functioning, including defective feedback about one's own speech; and emotional explanations like deep-seated conflicts and being pressured by parents to speak properly (Barker, 1979; Pines, 1977).

Treatment is varied: it includes psychotherapy and counseling, speech therapy, and drugs. The most effective training methods teach stutterers to unlearn the patterns of motor responses they have developed. They learn to speak slowly and deliberately; to breathe slowly and deeply, using abdominal muscles rather than those of the upper chest; and to start up their voices gently, not in the abrupt and almost explosive way in which many stutterers begin to speak. Computers to monitor the voice, and videotape machines, are among the technological aids that help stutterers.

Tics

About 5 to 24 percent of schoolchildren—more boys than girls—develop *tics*, repetitive, involuntary muscular movements. They blink their eyes, hunch their shoulders, twist their neck, bob their head, lick their lips, grimace, grunt, snort, and utter guttural or nasal sounds. Tics usually appear first between the ages of 4 and 10. Some are transient, lasting less than a year, but others last longer. They usually go away before adolescence, but they sometimes reappear at times of stress (DSM III-R, 1987).

tic Involuntary, repetitive muscular movement; also called stereotyped movement disorder.

Emotionally caused tics may arise from stresses in the child's past or current relationships and may serve as a release for emotional turmoil. One very passive and inhibited 8-year-old boy, for example, had several different tics. After a year of weekly psychotherapy sessions, he became more assertive and gradually lost about 95 percent of them (Chapman, 1974). Treatment should include relief of the emotional conflicts underlying these tics.

Not all tics are emotionally caused, however. Some, like *Tourette's syndrome*, seem to have a neurological basis. This disorder is characterized by a variety of muscular and vocal tics, often including outbursts of obscenities. This malady is rare, with a lifetime prevalence of 1 person in 2000 people in the population. It can appear as early as 1 year of age, but the median age of onset is 7 years, and almost all sufferers develop the syndrome before age 14. The disorder seems to be physiological in origin, possibly the result of a chemical imbalance in the brain, and seems to be transmitted as an autosomal dominant disorder (see Chapter 2). Dramatic relief often comes from a drug that blocks the effects of a brain chemical.

Children who suffer from Tourette's syndrome often lose one tic only to replace it with another. In this regard, they are unlike children who suffer from transient tics of childhood, which tend to disappear without being replaced (DSM III-R, 1987).

High Blood Pressure

High blood pressure, or hypertension, in both children and adults, is often associated with obesity (Gortmaker et al., 1987). Although hypertension in children is not a major public health problem, and although we do not know what its role is in causing heart disease, we do know that hypertension in adulthood has roots going back to childhood. The American Academy of Pediatrics Task Force on Blood Pressure Control in Children (1987) therefore recommends measuring blood pressure once a year from age 3 through adolescence.

If a child's blood pressure is above the 95th percentile for age and sex after three measurements, treatment should begin. Taking off excess weight, reducing salt intake, and increasing aerobic exercise are usually beneficial, but some children are also given drugs to avoid heart damage.

Type A Behavior

A major factor in developing coronary heart disease in adulthood may be the kind of personality that has become known as *Type A.* Some physicians maintain that Type A adults, who are aggressive, impatient, and competitive, are more

Type A Personality type which includes traits such as aggressiveness, impatience, anger, hostility, and competitiveness and when present in adults is correlated with coronary disease.

likely to suffer a heart attack than *Type B* adults, who are more easygoing and more relaxed (M. Friedman & Rosenman, 1974). Even though this theory is highly controversial, a considerable amount of recent research has focused on personality traits in children that seem to predict the development of Type A behavior later in life.

As early as 3 years of age some children show the kinds of behavior that seem to foreshadow the Type A pattern. They are more aggressive to Bobo dolls (big rubber dolls used in psychological laboratories to test children's aggressiveness) with less encouragement from the experimenter, and they are more likely to interrupt the experimenter, squirm, sigh, click the tongue, and show other signs of impatience and restlessness. Furthermore, they try harder to excel at tasks that have no clear criteria for performance, they tend to measure their own performance against that of children who have done better, and they set higher standards for themselves. Finally, they talk louder, eat and walk faster, and are, in general, more competitive (Corrigan & Moskowitz, 1983; Matthews & Angulo, 1980; Matthews & Volkin, 1981; T. M. Wolf, Sklov, Wenzl, Hunter, & Berenson, 1982).

To see whether Type A behavior is stable from childhood through adulthood, one researcher drew on the records of the New York Longitudinal Study (described in Chapters 2 and 7). Steinberg (1986b) followed subjects who had been characterized as Type A in first and second grade (on the basis of interviews with teachers), in adolescence (on the basis of interviews with the subjects themselves), and in young adulthood (again on the basis of interviews with the subjects). Analysis of these records yielded a new description of Type A behavior and the conclusion that Type A children do not necessarily grow up to be Type A adults.

Type A behavior, says Steinberg, has two dimensions. The *prosocial* dimension is marked by striving to achieve, competitiveness, perseverance, and self-motivation; the *antisocial* dimension is characterized by impatience, quickness to anger, and low tolerance for frustration. The relationship between these two dimensions shifts with age. Young schoolchildren who have the prosocial dimension usually have the antisocial dimension, too, and vice versa; in adolescence the presence of one dimension is unrelated to the other; and young adults who have one are *less* likely to have the other.

The various Type A behaviors do not remain consistent from childhood into adolescence or adulthood. However, people who are classified as Type A in adolescence are likely to become Type A adults. The most stable behavior is striving for achievement among males.

One relationship that did hold up from childhood to adulthood was childhood temperament and adult behavior. Children who had a low sensory threshold, a generally negative mood, high approach, and low adaptability (see Chapter 7) were more likely to become Type A adults.

Thus we can identify Type A children, though we cannot predict their future. This identification may also have implications for their health in childhood: changing their behavior may improve their health. (We may also be able to prevent some heart problems in adulthood by identifying adolescents who are at risk and helping them to adopt healthful behaviors.)

Box 11-2, on the opposite page, describes some other ways of improving children's health.

BOX 11-2 ■ THE EVERYDAY WORLD

IMPROVING CHILDREN'S HEALTH

Today's schoolchildren are not as healthy as youngsters were during the mid-1960s. Children are fatter today, and their heart and lung fitness is generally inferior to that of a typical middle-aged jogger.

Why are children in such poor physical condition? For one reason, only half of all elementary school children take physical education classes as often as twice a week, fewer than half stay active during cold weather, and most are not spending enough time learning such lifetime fitness skills as running, swimming, bicycling, and walking. Also, many are spending too much time in front of a television set (Dietz & Gortmaker, 1985). And most physical activities, in school and out of school, are team and competitive sports and games. These do not promote fitness, will usually be dropped once the young person is no longer in school, and are generally engaged in by the fittest and most athletic youngsters, not by those who most need help.

One study found that 98 percent of the 7- to 12-year-olds in a typical midwestern working-class community had at least one major risk factor for developing heart disease later in life. Their level of body fat averaged 2 to 5 percent above the national average (which is itself too high), 41 percent had high levels of cholesterol, and 28 percent had higher-than-normal blood pressure (Kuntzleman, 1984).

Children can improve their physical health, however, by changing their everyday behavior. One program of education and behavior modification has been teaching 24,000 children in Michigan how to analyze the foods they eat; how to measure their own blood pressure, heart rate, and body fat; and how to withstand peer and advertising pressure to smoke and to eat junk food. It also encourages them to take part in physically demanding games. When researchers looked at the effects of the program on 360 second-, fifth-, and seventh-graders, they found heartening results: the children in the program had significantly improved the time in which they could run a mile; they had lowered their cholesterol level, their blood pressure, and their body fat; and the number of children without any risk factors for developing coronary disease had risen by 55 percent (Fitness Finders, 1984).

This program is in line with recent recommendations by the American Academy of Pediatrics, which urges schools to provide a sound physical education program with a variety of competitive and recreational sports for all children, emphasizing activities that can be part of a lifetime fitness regimen, such as tennis, bowling, running, swimming, golf, and skating (American Academy of Pediatrics, Committee on Pediatric Aspects of Physical Fitness, Recreation, and Sports, 1981).

SAFETY CONCERNS: ACCIDENTAL INJURIES

Almost 22 million children are injured in the United States each year, and injury is the leading cause of disability and death in children over 1 year of age (Sheps & Evans, 1987). As more becomes known about childhood injuries, efforts at preventing them should be more successful. We have already looked at the problem of intentionally inflicted injuries in our discussion of child abuse (in Chapter 8). After examining the family and school settings in which accidental injuries occur, we will offer some suggestions about safety.

Which Children Are Most Likely to Be Hurt?

At age 3, Jason cracked his collarbone after he fell off the top bunk bed where he was playing with a friend; at 6, he broke his leg in a skating accident; and at 10 he broke his arm falling off the jungle gym at school. Some children have more accidents than others, either because of physical reasons like poor coordination (not Jason's problem) or because of personality factors, like the tendency to take risks or daydream.

Boys, on the average, have more accidents than girls, probably because they take more physical risks (Ginsburg & Miller, 1982). And injuries increase from age 5 to age 14, possibly because children become involved in more physical activities (Schor, 1987). (See Figure 11-3, page 408.)

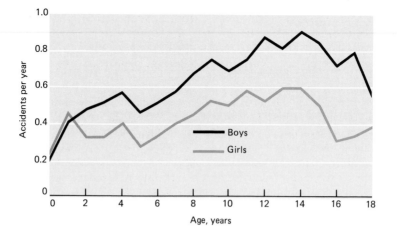

FIGURE 11-3
Average annual rates of injury by age and sex of children. Boys typically have a higher yearly accident rate than girls, except at age 1. Rates are especially high for both sexes in late middle childhood and early adolescence. (*Source:* Schor, 1987.)

The family also affects children's safety. A longitudinal study of 693 families that sought medical care over a 6-year period found that a small number of families accounted for a disproportionately large number of injuries: after adjustment for family size, 10 percent of the families accounted for almost 25 percent of injuries (Schor, 1987). Only children have fewer injuries than children with siblings, suggesting that parents of more than one child are not able to be as vigilant as parents of one child. But the family has a wider influence, since injuries tended to run in patterns by family; an accident-prone child was likely to come from an accident-prone family. Families with high injury rates may be undergoing stress that they cannot cope with; as a result, they may not be as careful in making the home safe or in watching over their children. High injury rates, therefore, may point to family problems in other areas.

How Are Children Most Likely to Be Hurt?

Most childhood accidents occur in automobiles or in the home (see Chapter 8), but between 10 and 20 percent take place in and around school. In an analysis of injuries at school over a 2-year period in Vancouver, Canada, researchers found that elementary school children were most likely to be injured from falls in the playground, while secondary school students suffered more injuries in sports areas. This suggests a greater need for controlling students' behaviors on the playground and in sports activities (Sheps & Evans, 1987).

For all ages studied, children were most likely to suffer head injuries. Every year more than 500,000 children in the United States are injured in this way; 140,000 of these head injuries are fatal and more than 70,000 result in brain damage that can permanently affect physical, intellectual, and emotional functioning (New Medico Head Injury System, 1987).

Parents, teachers, and coaches can help prevent injuries—particularly head injuries—by taking precautions like the following:

- *In or near cars.* Infants and toddlers should always be well anchored in a sturdy car seat while in a car, children over age 5 should wear snug-fitting seat belts, and children should be taught to look both ways when crossing streets and to cross only at corners.
- *On the playground.* Children should play on soft surfaces like sand, grass, or

cedar chips. They should be taught to walk around swings and give them a wide berth; to slide down sliding boards feet first, sitting up—never head first; to use both hands on a jungle gym and never climb wet bars; and to sit facing one another on the seesaw, to grip it with both hands, never to stand on it, and never to jump off.

■ *In other activities.* Children should wear approved helmets or other protective headgear for cycling, football, roller skating, skateboarding, horseback riding, hockey, speed sledding, or tobogganing. Cycling helmets should carry Snell or ANSI stickers, showing they have met standards for crash protection. Children should be taught how to fall properly; never to skate at night or wear skates on steps; to ride with the traffic, not to wear headphones, and not to carry anything in their arms while cycling; not to swing hockey sticks, baseball bats, or other sports equipment; and to be sure all sports equipment is in good shape.

Motor Development

MOTOR SKILLS IN MIDDLE CHILDHOOD

If we were to follow a group of children on their way home from school, we would see some of them running or skipping, and some leaping up onto narrow ledges and walking along, balancing till they jump off, trying to break records—but occasionally breaking a bone instead. Some of these youngsters will reach home (or, often, a baby-sitter's house), get a snack, and dash outside again. There they will jump rope, play ball, skate, cycle, sled, throw snowballs, or splash in the swimming hole, depending on the season, the community, and the

TABLE 11-2

MOTOR DEVELOPMENT IN MIDDLE CHILDHOOD	
AGE	SELECTED BEHAVIORS
6	Girls are superior in movement accuracy; boys are superior in forceful, less complex acts. Skipping is possible. Can throw with proper weight shift and step.
7	One-footed balancing without looking becomes possible. Can walk 2-inch-wide balance beams. Can hop and jump accurately into small squares. Can execute accurate jumping-jack exercise.
8	Have 12-pound pressure on grip strength. Number of games participated in by both sexes is greatest at this age. Can engage in alternate rhythmic hopping in a 2-2, 2-3, or 3-3 pattern. Girls can throw a small ball 40 feet.
9	Boys can run 16½ feet per second. Boys can throw a small ball 70 feet.
10	Can judge and intercept pathways of small balls thrown from a distance. Girls can run 17 feet per second.
11	Standing broad jump of 5 feet is possible for boys; 6 inches less for girls.
12	Standing high jump of 3 feet is possible.

Source: Adapted from Cratty, 1979, p. 222.

Children's motor abilities improve with age, and as they practice their new skills—alone or with friends, on the playing field or at home—they improve their physical and mental health.

child. They keep getting stronger, faster, and better coordinated—and they derive great pleasure from testing their bodies and learning new skills.

Many children these days, however, go inside after school, not to emerge for the rest of the day. Instead of practicing new skills that stretch their bodies, they will stay indoors watching television or playing quietly.

Studies of 7- to 12-year-olds done more than 20 years ago, when children seem to have been more physically active, suggest that children's motor abilities improve with age. (Examples of motor abilities are shown in Table 11-2.) These studies also show that boys tend to run faster, jump higher, throw farther, and display more strength than girls (Espenschade, 1960; Gavotos, 1959). After age 13, the differences between the sexes become even greater; boys improve in motor abilities while girls stay the same or decline (Espenschade, 1960).

Today, however, the assessment of girls' abilities is changing. It now seems clear that much of the difference between boys' and girls' motor abilities has been due to different expectations and different rates of participation. When researchers study prepubescent boys and girls who take part in similar activities, they find that their abilities are quite similar (E. G. Hall & Lee, 1984).

Such findings confirm statements by pediatricians that there is no reason to separate prepubertal boys and girls for physical activities. After puberty, however, the picture is very different: girls should not be playing heavy collision sports with boys, because their lighter, smaller frame makes them too subject to injury (American Academy of Pediatrics, Committee on Pediatric Aspects of Physical Fitness, Recreation and Sports, 1981). Postpubescent girls still need to be physically active, however, for general fitness and for the benefit that weight-bearing exercise offers in preventing osteoporosis, a thinning of the bones that occurs mostly among elderly women. It is dismaying, therefore, that 75 percent of 15- to 18-year-old girls do not participate in sports (Eskenazi, 1988).

HANDEDNESS

Vicky uses her right hand to draw. Jason, now on a Little League baseball team, pitches with his left arm. The preference for using one hand more than the other is called **handedness.** Although the concept seems simple, determination of a person's handedness may be difficult, since not everybody prefers one hand for every task. Vicky, for example, will reach for another crayon with her left hand.

Around the world and over the ages, many cultures have considered right-handedness ''better'' than left-handedness (see Box 11-3). What are the facts?

handedness Preference for using one hand rather than the other; determination may be difficult, because not everyone prefers one hand for every task.

PREJUDICE AGAINST ''LEFTIES''

In Japan, many parents try to force their children to use the right hand, even going to such extremes as binding the left hand with tape (''Lefty Liberation,'' 1974). In many Islamic societies, the left hand is used for private washing; using it for writing, for eating, or for serving food (among other things) is considered offensive. Even in the United States, many middle-aged adults who showed an early preference for the left hand remember being forced to learn how to write with the right hand.

Traces of the idea that left-handedness is abnormal or evil can be found in words like *sinister* (suggesting something evil), from the Latin word meaning ''on the left''; and *gauche* (meaning ''awkward''), from the French word for ''left.'' And the favorable connotations of right-handedness live on in *dexterity* and *adroitness* (both meaning ''skillful-

ness'')—the first from the Latin word and the second from the French word for ''right.'' The word *right* itself has favorable connotations: ''correct,'' ''moral,'' ''fitting,'' and ''proper.''

No culture has encouraged left-handedness and, though none has completely abolished it, some societies have apparently succeeded in reducing its incidence. In ''extremely permissive'' societies, 10.4 percent of the population is left-handed (about the proportion in the United States); in ''permissive'' societies, the proportion drops to 5.9 percent; in ''harsh, restrictive'' societies it is only 1.8 percent (Hardyck & Petrinovich, 1977).

However, since scientific evidence so far does not provide any reason for favoring ''righties,'' prejudice against the left-handed is on the wane in western industrial countries. Other parts of the world may soon follow on the right (oops, we mean the *correct*) path to equal rights (oops, we mean equal *treatment*) for the left-handed.

Left-handed people, like this boy, are likely to be better than right-handed people at spatial tasks and to recover more quickly from brain damage. However, they are also more likely to have allergies and reading and behavior problems. For the most part, neither left- nor right-handedness is clearly superior.

Both "lefties" and "righties" have some advantages and disadvantages. Left-handed people suffer more from allergies and migraine headaches, and are more prone to dyslexia (a reading disability) and attention-deficit disorder (a behavior disorder), both of which are discussed in Chapter 12; to stuttering; and to alcoholism (Geschwind & Galaburda, 1985). But lefties are likely to be better at spatial tasks and to recover more quickly from brain damage (Hardyck & Petrinovich, 1977).

Benjamin Franklin, Michelangelo, Leonardo da Vinci, and Pablo Picasso were all left-handed. All these men (males are more likely than females to favor the left hand) had highly developed spatial imagination, a quality that may be stronger in left-handed people. This may explain the high proportion of left-handed architects. And left-handed people may actually be more likely to have special intellectual gifts. A study of over 100,000 twelve- and thirteen-year-olds identified nearly 300 who scored extremely high on the Scholastic Aptitude Test (SAT). Twenty percent of this top-scoring group were left-handed, twice the rate of left-handedness in the general population (B. Bower, 1985). Any serious attempt to explain left-handedness as a symptom of underlying trouble must also explain these successes.

None of the many environmental, anatomic, and genetic theories about the causes of handedness has been able to settle the matter. A growing consensus favors the anatomic theories, especially those concerned with the anatomy of the brain. The hypothesis seems logical: the brain regulates motor behavior; left-handedness is a feature of motor behavior; therefore, the brain regulates left-handedness. To some extent this syllogism must be true, but we still do not know how much regulation depends on qualities in the brain itself and how much depends on other factors. We do know that in cases of severe injury to the brain, left-handed people tend to recover the damaged brain functions more quickly than right-handed people. We also know, however, that about 10 percent of identical twins have different dominant hands, showing that innate brain organization cannot be the entire story and that other factors, perhaps position in the womb, may also explain handedness (Lykken, cited in "Questions, Science Times," 1988).

Researchers generally agree that there is a relationship between the brain's general organization—especially whether the left or right side is dominant—and handedness, but the relationship is not precise and does not permit any easy generalization about the thinking of left-handed and right-handed people. We can conclude neither that left-handedness arises from abnormal brain organization nor that it arises from superior brain organization.

One team of researchers who surveyed the literature on handedness reported that the idea of a cognitive deficit associated with left-handedness has persisted, as they put it, "through generations of research workers. There is usually just enough of a relationship to suggest a possible link and never enough of one to establish firmly a solid correlation" (Hardyck & Petrinovich, 1977, p. 394).

It is always prudent to doubt any suggestion of mysterious virtues in the majority and vague peculiarities among a minority. Until there is more research, it seems evident that knowing which hand you hold your pencil in or pitch a ball with tells little about your physical or intellectual ability. More soundly based conclusions about intellectual ability in middle childhood will be discussed in Chapter 12.

BOX 11-4 ■ A CHILD'S WORLD AND YOU

WHAT DO YOU THINK?

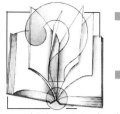

■ Because height is very important to many people, should parents be free to give their children growth hormone?

■ Malnutrition early in life has long-term effects on physical and social development. How do you think society should express its concern about this phenomenon?

■ Although Type A behavior is dangerous to a person's health, many people admire those with hard-driving, Type A personalities and consider them the "doers" of society. Is it in society's interest to discourage Type A behavior?

■ Many people who consider themselves right-handed or left-handed are surprised, when they think about it, to realize that their preference is ambiguous. Do you consistently use the same hand to perform the following tasks: deal cards, unscrew a jar lid, shovel, sweep, thread a needle, write, strike a match, throw a ball, hammer, brush your teeth, swing a racket, and use scissors?

Summary

1 Physical development is less rapid in middle childhood than in the earlier years. Boys are slightly larger than girls at the beginning of this period, but girls undergo the growth spurt of adolescence at an earlier age and thus tend to be larger than boys at the end of the period. Wide differences in height and weight exist between individuals and between groups.

2 The best predictions of a child's height as an adult are accurate only to within plus or minus 2 inches. Growth can be stimulated with growth hormones, but these should be used only in cases of natural growth-hormone deficiency.

3 Proper nutrition is essential for normal growth and health. Malnutrition can diminish activity and sociability. On average, children need 2400 calories a day.

4 Obesity among children is an increasingly common problem. It seems to have both genetic and environmental roots. Behavioral therapies—especially when they involve parents—are the most successful in treating obesity.

5 Respiratory problems and other common health problems of middle childhood tend to be frequent and of short duration, and medical conditions often recur. Children's understanding of illness is related to their cognitive level.

6 Vision improves during middle childhood, although a minority of children have vision problems.

7 Tooth decay rates have declined over the past few decades, mainly because of use of fluoride and improved dental care.

8 Stuttering and tics are both fairly common in middle childhood and are more prevalent among boys.

9 High blood pressure (hypertension) is often associated with obesity; blood pressure should be measured yearly from the age of 3.

10 Type A behavior has been associated with heart disease. Although children can be classified as Type A, the relationship between this behavior in childhood and heart problems in adulthood is controversial.

11 Although children today are healthier than children at the turn of the century, they are less healthy and less fit than children in the mid-1960s. This disturbing trend seems to be occurring because children are less physically active today. With education and behavior modification, children can learn habits to improve their health, including physical exercise.

12 Accidents are the leading cause of disability and death in children over 1 year of age. Boys, and children from certain families, tend to have more accidents. Most accidents occur in automobiles, at home, or in and around school.

13 Because of improved motor development, boys and girls in middle childhood can engage in a wider range of motor activities than preschoolers. Studies done several decades ago suggest that boys excel in motor skills, but recent research indicates similar abilities for boys and girls. There is no safety-related reason to separate prepubertal boys and girls for physical activities.

14 Left-handedness occurs in about 10 percent of people in the United States. Both advantages and disadvantages are associated with left-handedness.

Key Terms

menarche (page 396)
obesity (399)
stuttering (404)
tic (405)

Type A (405)
Type B (406)
handedness (411)

Suggested Readings

Berbrich, R., & Parker, A. (1988). *The available pediatrician—Every parent's guide to common childhood illnesses*. New York: Pantheon. A valuable guide for parents to the common illnesses of childhood.

Brett, D. (1988). *Annie stories—A special kind of storytelling*. New York: Workman. A unique book by a clinical psychologist for children under 10. It shows how to fit a child's own experience into stories used to help explain life events.

Fincher, J. (1980). *Lefties*. New York: Perigree. A comprehensive study of handedness that explores theories explaining left- or right-handedness, examines societal customs and their implications for left-handed people, delves into historical attitudes toward left-handedness, and identifies a slew of famous "lefties."

Pomeranz, V. E., & Schultz, D. (1978). *The mothers' and fathers' medical encyclopedia*. New York: New American Library. A source of up-to-date information about all aspects of children's health, including the prevention and treatment of ills that affect young people from the cradle to college.

CHAPTER 12

INTELLECTUAL DEVELOPMENT IN MIDDLE CHILDHOOD

C hildhood is a world of miracle and wonder: as if creation rose, bathed in light, out of darkness, utterly new and fresh and astonishing. The end of childhood is when things cease to astonish us. When the world seems familiar, when one has got used to existence, one has become an adult.

Eugene Ionesco, *Fragments of a Journal,* 1976

PREVIEW QUESTIONS

- How is the thinking of schoolchildren different from that of preschoolers?
- How is the development of moral reasoning related to cognitive development?
- What advances in memory and language occur during middle childhood?
- How is intelligence measured in middle childhood, and why is IQ testing controversial?
- What role does school play in children's lives?
- How can gifted and talented children's abilities be best nurtured?

PROUDLY CARRYING his shiny new pencil case, Jason walks into his first-grade classroom. A veteran of both preschool and kindergarten, he is not anxious. On the contrary, like most first-graders, he finds the idea of school exhilarating, and the first day of "regular" school is a milestone and a sign that he has entered a distinctly new stage of development.

By age 11, Vicky trots off to school without a second thought. Learning is what she does. She reads, thinks, talks, and imagines things in ways that were well beyond her only a few years before.

In this chapter we examine the changes that occur in children during the first 6 years of elementary school. We consider intellectual development according to the three approaches introduced in Chapter 6. First, we discuss the Piagetian approach to cognitive development; second, the information-processing approach; third, the psychometric approach. Then we look at an important aspect of schoolchildren's intellectual development: language. We consider not only grammar and communication, but also children's humor, which (like all humor) has a strong verbal component. In the final portion of the chapter, we discuss the role of school in a child's life.

Approaches to Intellectual Development

In this section, we consider three approaches to studying intellectual development: the Piagetian approach (showing advances in children's thinking in the stage of concrete operations), the information-processing approach (emphasizing the development of memory), and the psychometric approach (discussing the controversy over the use of intelligence tests).

PIAGETIAN APPROACH: THE STAGE OF CONCRETE OPERATIONS (ABOUT 7 TO 11 YEARS)

As Vicky enters middle childhood, she also enters a new stage of cognitive development: *concrete operations.* Her thinking is now marked by the ability to apply logical principles to actual situations. Children in this stage are more logical and less egocentric than children in the previous, preoperational stage of early childhood.

Now that Vicky has reached the stage of concrete operations, she can apply logical principles to concrete (actual) situations. She uses internal mental operations (thinking) to solve problems set in the here and now. This means that she can perform many tasks at a much higher level than she could at the previous stage. For example, she is better at doing the following:

■ Classifying objects—grouping them in similar categories
■ Seriating—arranging items (like different-size sticks) in a series according to a particular dimension (like length, from shortest to longest)
■ Dealing with numbers
■ Understanding concepts of time and space
■ Distinguishing between reality and fantasy
■ Understanding the principle of conservation

However, children in this stage are still limited to actual, present situations: they cannot yet think in abstract or hypothetical terms, about what *could* be rather than what *is.* The ability to think abstractly, which characterizes Piaget's highest level of cognitive development, does not occur until adolescence.

Conservation

One of the best-known aspects of Piaget's work is his study of *conservation,* the ability to recognize that the quantity or amount of something remains the same even if the matter is rearranged, as long as nothing is added or taken away. (This concept was introduced in Chapter 9, in our discussion of preoperational thinking.) Piaget and other researchers have tested children's grasp of conservation with regard to a variety of attributes, such as number, substance, length, area, weight, and volume. As you can see in Box 12-1 (page 420), Piaget was surprised when he discovered that children had to learn conservation.

Testing Conservation   The characteristics of concrete operational thinking show up dramatically if we compare two children—one in the preoperational stage (Peter) and one in the concrete operations stage (Connie)—on a task of conservation. We can see how Connie, in the concrete operations stage, shows her grasp of logical principles in assessing the conservation of substance.

In this task, an experimenter shows a child two identical clay balls and asks the child whether the amount of clay in both balls is the same. The child agrees that it is. The experimenter then changes one of the balls into a different shape— say, a long, thin sausage shape, and then asks the child again if the two objects contain the same amount of clay or if one contains more. Peter, the preoperational child, is deceived by appearances: he says that the long, thin roll contains more clay because it *looks* longer. Connie, the concrete operational child, realizes that in this case appearance does not matter. She understands that a transforma-

concrete operations
Piaget's third stage of cognitive development, during which children develop the ability to think logically about the here and now, but not about abstractions.

conservation   *Piaget's term for awareness that two stimuli which are equal (in length, weight, or amount, for example) remain equal in the face of perceptual alteration, so long as nothing has been added to or taken away from either stimulus.*

(Mimi Forsyth/Monkmeyer Press)

Does this girl seem to have developed what Piaget called *conservation*— the realization that even if liquid is poured into a differently shaped container, the amount remains the same?

BOX 12-1 ▪ PROFESSIONAL VOICES

JEAN PIAGET

PIAGET: It's just that no adult ever had the idea of asking children about conservation. It was so obvious that if you change the shape of an object, the quantity will be conserved. Why ask a child? The novelty lay in asking the question.

I first discovered the problem of conservation when I worked with young epileptics from 10 to 15. I wanted to find some empirical way of distinguishing them from normal children. I went around with four coins and four beads, and I would put the coins and beads in one-to-one correspondence and then hide one of the coins. If the three re- maining coins were then stretched out into a longer line, the epileptic children said they had more coins than beads. No conservation at all.

I thought I had discovered a method to distinguish normal from abnormal children. Then I went on to work with normal children and discovered that all children lack conservation.

Question: Isn't it fortunate that you checked?

PIAGET: A biologist would have to verify; a philosopher would not have checked.

Source: E. Hall, 1970, pp. 27–28; *photo:* Yves deBraine/Black Star.

---

tion like this one changes only how a thing is perceived, and she correctly answers that the ball and the "sausage" contain the same amount of clay.

When children are asked about the reasoning behind their answers, they reveal their thinking processes and show whether they understand the principles underlying the task. Connie, for example, understands the principle of *identity:* she knows that the clay is still the same clay, even though it has a different shape. She understands the principle of *reversibility:* that she could reverse the transformation (change the sausage back into a ball) and restore the original shape. Preoperational children do not understand either of these principles. Finally, Connie can *decenter:* she can focus on more than one relevant dimension (in this case, on length and width). Peter, the preoperational child, centers on one dimension to the exclusion of the other.

Development of Different Types of Conservation   The ability to solve conservation problems varies with age and with the particular attribute involved. Typically, children can solve tasks involving conservation of *substance* (like the one just described) by about age 7. In tasks involving conservation of *weight*—where they are asked, say, whether the ball and the sausage weigh the same—children typically do not give correct answers until about age 9 or 10. And in tasks involving conservation of *volume*—where children must judge whether the sausage and the ball displace an equal amount of liquid when placed in a glass of water— correct answers are rarely given before age 12. In solving these problems, children can apply internal mental operations—that is, they can work the problems out "in their heads." They do not have to measure or weigh the objects.

horizontal decalage   In Piaget's terminology, the development of different types of conservation at different ages; thus a child can conserve substance before weight, and substance and weight before volume.

Piaget called the development of different types of conservation at different ages *horizontal decalage.* The phenomenon is fascinating because—since the principle in each task is exactly the same—the time lags illustrate how concrete children's thinking is at this stage. Their reasoning is so closely tied to a particular situation that they cannot readily apply the same basic internal mental operations to different situations.

Effects of Experience on Conservation   Piaget stressed the maturational aspects of conservation. He believed that children will show the ability to conserve when they are mature enough neurologically and that it is only minimally affected by experience. However, factors other than maturation also affect conservation. Children who learn conservation skills earliest tend to get high grades and to have high IQs, high verbal ability, and nondominating mothers (Almy, Chittenden, & Miller, 1966; Goldschmid & Bentler, 1968). Children from different countries—such as Switzerland, the United States, and Great Britain—typically achieve conservation at different ages, and so this ability also seems to be affected by cultural factors.

Schooling seems to be especially important. One researcher conducted tests of conservation to compare African children who lived and went to school in a city with children who lived and went to school in the bush (rural areas), and with children who lived in the bush but had never gone to school. She found wide differences in ability to conserve. Rural children who had gone to school conserved earlier than rural children who had not gone to school. And the urban children—who had all gone to school—conserved slightly earlier than the rural children who had gone to school. By age 11 or 12, virtually all the children who had gone to school could conserve liquid quantity, compared with only half the children who had not (Greenfield, 1966).

Obviously, something the children were learning in school was helping them understand the principles of conservation. This study, then, indicates that maturation alone cannot account for the development of conservation.

Moral Development: Three Theories

Why should we be discussing morality in a chapter about intellectual development? It is true that moral thinking is an outgrowth of personality, emotional attitudes, and cultural influences, and that psychoanalytic and social-learning theories draw on all these factors to explain moral development. However, the most influential concept today is that moral values develop along with cognitive growth.

The golden rule, "Do unto others as you would have them do unto you," provides a justification for linking moral development to cognitive growth. This moral principle requires us to step into someone else's shoes—to imagine how another person would feel. But it has already been shown that small children are quite egocentric. The golden rule is difficult for them to follow, not because they are evil, but because they have a hard time imagining how anyone else feels.

Jean Piaget and Lawrence Kohlberg, two of the most influential theorists of the development of moral reasoning, maintain that children cannot make sound moral judgments until they achieve a high enough level of cognitive maturity to look at things as another person might see them. Robert Selman carries this view further, holding that moral development is linked to "role-taking."

Piaget: Constraint and Cooperation   Piaget believed that moral reasoning develops in two major stages, which coincide roughly with the preoperational and concrete operational stages of cognitive development.

In the first stage, the ***morality of constraint,*** also called *heteronomous morality*, the young child thinks rigidly about moral concepts. Because Vicky, when she is in this stage, is still quite egocentric, she cannot imagine more than one way of looking at a moral issue. She believes that rules cannot be changed, that behavior is either right or wrong, and that any offense deserves severe punishment (unless, of course, she herself is the offender!).

morality of constraint
In Piaget's theory, the first stage of moral reasoning, in which a child thinks rigidly about moral concepts; also called heteronomous morality.

morality of cooperation
In Piaget's theory, the second stage of moral reasoning, in which a child has moral flexibility; also called autonomous morality.

The second stage, the ***morality of cooperation,*** also called *autonomous morality,* is characterized by moral flexibility. As Vicky matures and interacts more with other people, she thinks less egocentrically. She comes into contact with an increasingly wide range of viewpoints, many of which contradict what she has learned at home. She concludes, then, that there is not one unchangeable, absolute moral standard, but that people (including herself) can formulate their own codes of right and wrong. At this point she can make more subtle judgments of behavior, considering the intent behind it and using punishment judiciously. She is now on the way to formulating her own moral code.

Let us look at one example of Piaget's approach. To see how children at different levels of morality think about behavior, Piaget (1932) would tell them a story about two little boys, Augustus and Julian, which went something like this: "One day Augustus noticed that his father's inkpot was empty and decided to help his father by filling it. But while he was opening the bottle, he spilled the ink and made a large stain on the tablecloth. The other boy, Julian, played with his father's inkpot one day and spilled some, making a small stain on the tablecloth." Then Piaget would ask, "Which boy was naughtier, and why?"

Children under about age 7, still in the stage of constraint, usually consider Augustus naughtier, since he made the bigger stain. But older children, in the stage of cooperation, recognize that Augustus meant well and made the large stain by accident, whereas Julian made a small stain while doing something he should not have been doing. Immature moral judgments center only on the degree of offense; more mature judgments consider intent.

Table 12-1 shows how children in the two stages differ on a number of moral concepts studied by Piaget, such as rules, intention, and punishment.

TABLE 12-1

PIAGET'S TWO STAGES OF MORAL DEVELOPMENT		
	STAGE I	STAGE II
MORAL CONCEPTS	Morality of constraint.	Morality of cooperation.
POINT OF VIEW	Child views an act as either totally right or totally wrong, and thinks everyone sees it the same way. Children cannot put themselves in place of others.	Children can put themselves in place of others. They are not absolutist in judgments but see that more than one point of view is possible.
INTENTION	Child judges acts in terms of actual physical consequences, not the motivation behind them.	Child judges acts by intentions, not consequences.
RULES	Child obeys rules because they are sacred and unalterable.	Child recognizes that rules are made by people and can be changed by people. Children consider themselves just as capable of changing rules as anyone else.
RESPECT FOR AUTHORITY	Unilateral respect leads to feeling of obligation to conform to adult standards and obey adult rules.	Mutual respect for authority and peers allows children to value their own opinions and abilities and to judge other people realistically.
PUNISHMENT	Child favors severe punishment. Child feels that punishment itself defines the wrongness of an act; an act is bad if it will elicit punishment.	Child favors milder punishment that compensates the victim and helps the culprit recognize why an act is wrong, thus leading to reform.
CONCEPT OF JUSTICE	Child confuses moral law with physical law and believes that any physical accident or misfortune that occurs after a misdeed is a punishment willed by God or some other supernatural force.	Child does not confuse natural misfortune with punishment.

Source: Adapted partly from M. Hoffman, 1970; Kohlberg, in M. Hoffman & Hoffman, 1964.

TABLE 12-2

STAGE	APPROXIMATE AGES	DEVELOPMENT
0	4–6	Child thinks that his or her own point of view is the only one possible.
1	6–8	Child realizes that others may interpret a situation in a way different from his or her own.
2	8–10	Child has reciprocal awareness, realizing that others have a different point of view and that others are aware that he or she has a particular point of view. Child understands the importance of letting others know that their requests have not been ignored or forgotten.
3	10–12	Child can imagine a third person's perspective, taking into account several different points of view.
4	Adolescence	Person realizes that communication and mutual role-taking do not always resolve disputes over rival values.

Source: Selman, 1973.

Selman: Role-Taking In examining the progression from egocentric to moral thinking, Selman (1973) looked at *role-taking*—that is, assuming another person's point of view. Since morality involves consideration of other people's welfare, it is reasonable to suppose that increased ability to imagine how another person might think and feel should be related to the ability to make moral judgments. And in fact, research has demonstrated that the two are related.

Selman divided the development of role-taking into the following five stages, numbered 0 to 4 (see Table 12-2 for a summary):

role-taking In Selman's terminology, assuming another person's point of view.

■ *Stage 0* (about ages 4 to 6): Children are egocentric, think that their own point of view is the only one possible, and judge accordingly. Suppose that we tell Vicky this story and ask for her opinion: "A little girl has promised her father not to climb trees but then sees a kitten trapped up in a tree. What should the little girl do?" At stage 0, Vicky sees no problem. Since she likes kittens, she assumes that everyone else will automatically favor climbing the tree to save the kitten.

■ *Stage 1* (about ages 6 to 8): Children realize that other people may interpret a situation differently. Vicky now says, "If the father doesn't know why she climbed the tree, he will be angry. But if he knows why she did it, he will be glad." She now realizes the importance of intention—and also that the father's viewpoint may be different from the little girl's.

■ *Stage 2* (8 to 10 years): Children develop reciprocal awareness. Not only does Vicky know that other people have their own points of view (stage 1); she now realizes that others know that *she* has a particular point of view. Vicky now knows that besides telling her father about the kitten, the little girl should also let him know that she did not forget her promise not to climb trees.

■ *Stage 3* (10 to 12 years): Children can imagine a third person's perspective, taking several different points of view into account.

■ *Stage 4* (adolescence or later): People realize that mutual role-taking does not always resolve disputes. Some rival values simply cannot be communicated away.

Selman's theory was inspired by both Piaget and Kohlberg. In the following section, we examine Kohlberg's very influential theory of the development of moral reasoning. As you read this discussion, you can note how advances in role-taking ability are related to advances in moral thinking.

Kohlberg: Levels of Moral Reasoning *Kohlberg's moral dilemmas* Lawrence Kohlberg devised a series of moral dilemmas to assess a person's level of moral reasoning. The most famous of these is the following story:

> A woman was near death from cancer. A druggist had discovered a drug that could save her. The druggist was charging $2000 for a small dose of the drug—10 times what it cost him to make. The sick woman's husband, Heinz, borrowed as much as he could, but he could get together only about $1000. He told the druggist that his wife was dying, and asked him to sell it cheaper or let him pay later. But the druggist said, "No. I discovered the drug and I'm going to make money from it." Heinz, desperate, broke into the man's store to steal the drug for his wife. Should Heinz have done that? Why or why not? (Kohlberg, 1969)

For over 20 years, Kohlberg periodically queried a group of 75 boys who had ranged in age from 10 to 16 years at the start of the study. Kohlberg told them hypothetical stories that posed moral dilemmas of the kind Heinz faced, and asked the boys how they would solve them. At the center of each dilemma was a concept of justice—a question of behavior and how it was to be judged in relation to one or more of 25 basic moral issues like the value of human life, motives for actions, individual rights, and respect for moral authority.

After telling the stories, Kohlberg and his colleagues asked the boys questions designed to show how they had arrived at their decisions. Kohlberg was less interested in the answers themselves than in the *reasoning* that led to them.

Kohlberg's levels and stages From the responses he received, Kohlberg concluded that one's level of moral reasoning is related to one's cognitive level. The reasoning behind the boys' answers convinced Kohlberg that many people actively work out moral judgments on their own, rather than merely "internalizing" the standards of parents, teachers, or peers. On the basis of the different thought processes revealed in the answers, Kohlberg described three levels of moral reasoning:

preconventional morality *Kohlberg's first level of moral reasoning, in which the emphasis is on external control, obedience to the rules and standards of others, and the desire to avoid punishment.*

morality of conventional role conformity *Second level in Kohlberg's theory of moral reasoning, in which children want to please other people and have internalized the standards of authority figures.*

morality of autonomous moral principles *Third level of Kohlberg's theory of moral reasoning, in which people follow internally held moral principles and decide between conflicting moral standards.*

- *Level I: **preconventional morality** (ages 4 to 10 years).* The emphasis in this level is on external control. Children observe the standards of others either to avoid punishment or to obtain rewards.
- *Level II: **morality of conventional role conformity** (ages 10 to 13).* Children now want to please other people. They still observe the standards of others, but they have internalized these standards to some extent. Now they want to be considered "good" by people whose opinions are important to them. They are now able to take the roles of authority figures well enough to decide whether an action is good by their standards.
- *Level III: **morality of autonomous moral principles** (age 13 or later, if ever).* This level marks the attainment of true morality. For the first time, the person acknowledges the possibility of conflict between two socially accepted standards and tries to decide between them. The control of conduct is now internal, both in standards observed and in reasoning about right and wrong.

Each of these three levels is divided into two stages. Table 12-3 describes each of the six stages, with examples of typical reasoning at each stage.

Kohlberg's early stages correspond to Piaget's, but his advanced stages go further, into adulthood. Kohlberg's stages are also related to Selman's stages: the better a person is at role-taking, the more complicated Heinz's dilemma becomes.

TABLE 12-3

KOHLBERG'S SIX STAGES OF MORAL REASONING

LEVELS	STAGES OF REASONING	TYPICAL ANSWERS TO HEINZ'S DILEMMA
Level 1: Preconventional (ages 4 to 10) Emphasis in this level is on external control. The standards are those of others, and they are observed either to avoid punishment or to reap rewards.	**Stage 1:** *Orientation toward punishment and obedience.* "What will happen to me?" Children obey the rules of others to avoid punishment. They ignore the motives of an act and focus on its physical form (such as the size of a lie) or its consequences (for example the amount of physical damage).	*Pro:* "He should steal the drug. It isn't really bad to take it. It isn't as if he hadn't asked to pay for it first. The drug he'd take is worth only $200: he's not really taking a $2000 drug." *Con:* "He shouldn't steal the drug. It's a big crime. He didn't get permission; he used force and broke and entered. He did a lot of damage, stealing a very expensive drug and breaking up the store, too."
	Stage 2: *Instrumental purpose and exchange.* "You scratch my back, I'll scratch yours." Children conform to rules out of self-interest and consideration for what others can do for them in return. They look at an act in terms of the human needs it meets and differentiate this value from the act's physical form and consequences.	*Pro:* "It's all right to steal the drug, because his wife needs it and he wants her to live. It isn't that he wants to steal, but that's what he has to do to get the drug to save her." *Con:* "He shouldn't steal it. The druggist isn't wrong or bad; he just wants to make a profit. That's what you're in business for—to make money."
Level II: Morality of conventional role conformity (ages 10 to 13) Children now want to please other people. They still observe the standards of others, but they have internalized these standards to some extent. Now they want to be considered "good" by those persons whose opinions are important to them. They are now able to take the roles of authority figures well enough to decide whether an action is good by their standards.	**Stage 3:** *Maintaining mutual relations, approval of others, the golden rule.* "Am I a good boy or girl?" Children want to please and help others, can judge the intentions of others, and develop their own ideas of what a good person is. They evaluate an act according to the motive behind it or the person performing it, and they take circumstances into account.	*Pro:* "He should steal the drug. He is only doing something that is natural for a good husband to do. You can't blame him for doing something out of love for his wife. You'd blame him if he didn't love his wife enough to save her." *Con:* "He shouldn't steal. If his wife dies, he can't be blamed. It isn't because he's heartless or that he doesn't love her enough to do everything that he legally can. The druggist is the selfish or heartless one."
	Stage 4: *Social system and conscience.* "What if everybody did it?" People are concerned with doing their duty, showing respect for higher authority, and maintaining the social order. They consider an act always wrong, regardless of motive or circumstances, if it violates a rule and harms others.	*Pro:* "You should steal it. If you did nothing you'd be letting your wife die. It's your responsibility if she dies. You have to take it with the idea of paying the druggist." *Con:* "It is a natural thing for Heinz to want so save his wife, but it's still always wrong to steal. He still knows that he's stealing and taking a valuable drug from the man who made it."

(Continued)

TABLE 12-3

LEVELS	STAGES OF REASONING	TYPICAL ANSWERS TO HEINZ'S DILEMMA
Level III: Morality of autonomous moral principles (age 13, or not until young adulthood, or never) This level marks the attainment of true morality. For the first time, the person acknowledges the possibility of conflict between two socially accepted standards and tries to decide between them. The control of conduct is now internal, both in the standards observed and in the reasoning about right and wrong. Stages 5 and 6 may be alternative methods of the highest level of moral reasoning.	**Stage 5:** *Morality of contract, of individual rights, and of democratically accepted law.* People think in rational terms, valuing the will of the majority and the welfare of society. They generally see these values best supported by adherence to the law. While they recognize that there are times when human need and the law conflict, they believe that it is better for society in the long run if they obey the law.	*Pro:* "The law wasn't set up for these circumstances. Taking the drug in this situation isn't really right, but its' justified." *Con:* "You can't completely blame someone for stealing, but extreme circumstances don't really justify taking the law into your own hands. You can't have people stealing whenever they are desperate. The end may be good, but the ends don't justify the means."
	Stage 6: *Morality of universal ethical principles.* People do what they as individuals think right, regardless of legal restrictions or the opinions of others. They act in accordance with internalized standards, knowing that they would condemn themselves if they did not.	*Pro:* "This is a situation that forces him to choose between stealing and letting his wife die. In a situation where the choice must be made, it is morally right to steal. He has to act in terms of the principle of preserving and respecting life." *Con:* "Heinz is faced with the decision of whether to consider the other people who need the drug just as badly as his wife. Heinz ought to act not according to his particular feelings toward his wife, but considering the value of all the lives involved."

Source: Adapted from Kohlberg, 1969, 1976.

When Vicky is at Selman's stage 3 of role-taking development, for example, she says that if Heinz were caught, a judge would listen to his explanation, see that he was right, and let him go. But in Selman's stage 4, Vicky realizes that no matter how good the explanation seems to Heinz, the judge cannot excuse the theft, because he must uphold the law.

Evaluating Kohlberg's theory. Kohlberg's theory has generated much research, confirming some aspects but leaving others in question. In his own 20-year study of American boys (aged 10, 13, and 16 at the first testing), the boys progressed through the stages in sequence and none skipped a stage. Furthermore, moral judgments correlated positively with the boys' age, education, IQ, and socioeconomic status (Colby, Kohlberg, Gibbs, & Lieberman, 1983).

Cross-cultural validity: Cross-cultural studies confirm this sequence—up to a point. Although older subjects from countries other than the United States do tend to score at higher stages than younger subjects, people from nonwestern cultures rarely give answers that would place them above stage 4 (C.P. Edwards, 1977; Nisan & Kohlberg, 1982; Snarey, 1985). It is possible that these cultures do not foster higher development—but it is also likely that Kohlberg's definition of morality as a system of justice is not as appropriate for nonwestern as for western societies, and that his procedures may not identify higher levels of reasoning in some cultures (Snarey, 1985). (See Box 15-1 in Chapter 15.) Just as a culture helps people define intelligent behavior, it also sets the standards for what constitutes moral behavior.

Validity for females: Furthermore, critics have also questioned the appropriateness of Kohlberg's definition of morality for American girls and women. Although some studies of moral reasoning in adulthood have shown that men tend to score higher than women on Kohlberg's tasks, other researchers have claimed that this apparent difference is due to the men's higher educational and occupational status rather than to gender itself (Walker, 1984, 1987).

Leaving the scoring controversy aside, critics like Carol Gilligan (1982) maintain that women *define* morality differently from men and base their moral decisions on different factors. Women, she says, see morality not in abstract terms of justice and fairness, but in specific terms of selfishness versus responsibility, as an obligation to exercise care and avoid hurting other people.

The role of experience: Research has found that moral judgments are strongly influenced by education and even by simply telling children the "right" answers to questions involving moral reasoning (Carroll & Rest, 1982; Lickona, 1973). Such findings call into question the traditional cognitive-developmental position that children actively work out their moral systems through self-discovery.

Testing procedures and the meaning of results: Problems have also emerged concerning the testing procedure and the meaning of subjects' responses. To overcome the time and labor requirements of presenting the standard tasks (like the story of Heinz) individually and having them scored by trained judges, the Defining Issues Test (DIT) was developed (Rest, 1975). This presents a subject with six moral dilemmas and then, for each dilemma, asks for responses to 12 statements about the issues involved. The DIT can be administered to a group and scored objectively, and it still correlates moderately well with scores on the traditional tasks.

But the link between a moral judgment about a hypothetical dilemma and actual moral behavior is not well established. Knowing a person's performance on a test assessing moral judgment does not predict how that person would actually behave (Kupfersmid & Wonderly, 1980).

While Kohlberg's stages, then, do seem to apply to American males, they are limited in their applicability to women and to people in nonwestern cultures. Questions about testing methods and about the connection between moral judgments and moral behavior raise serious doubts about some aspects of the theory. Nevertheless, Kohlberg's influential theory has enriched our thinking about the way moral development occurs, has supported the association between cognitive maturity and moral maturity, and has stimulated a great deal of research on moral development.

INFORMATION-PROCESSING APPROACH: DEVELOPMENT OF MEMORY IN MIDDLE CHILDHOOD

When police showed 12 photographs to a 3-year-old girl who had been kidnapped and sexually abused, she gasped at one and identified the man as her abductor. He was arrested and confessed to the crime (Goodman, 1984). In this case, a very young child seemed to be an accurate witness, but in other instances children's testimony has turned out to be unreliable, mixing fact with imagination or blurring details. The accuracy of children's memory has been controversial since the turn of the century. Recent research shows that very young children can sometimes recall details better than adults, but that at other times their memory is poorer. They have the most trouble remembering events they do not understand, apparently because they cannot organize such events in their minds. As cognitive development advances, so does memory.

In this section we look at three aspects of memory: capacity, strategies for remembering, and metamemory.

Memory Capacity

According to one theory, there are three different types of memory: sensory memory, short-term memory, and long-term memory (Atkinson & Shiffrin, 1968, 1971). *Sensory memory* is a fleeting awareness of images, which lasts about 1 second. *Short-term memory* is working memory, the active repository of information one is currently using. *Long-term memory* is a storehouse of memories. Ability to retrieve information from long-term memory depends on how well it was perceived, organized, and stored in the first place.

The capacity of short-term memory increases rapidly in middle childhood. One classic paper states that short-term memory is limited to 7 pieces ("chunks") of information, plus or minus 2: this means that there is a range of 5 to 9 items which people can hold in short-term memory, with 7 being average (G. A. Miller, 1956). We can assess short-term memory by asking children to recall a series of digits (to hear and try to recite, for example, "8-3-7-5-1-4-9". At age 5 to 6, children can typically remember only two digits; by adolescence, they can remember six digits.

Young children's relatively poor short-term memory may help to explain why they have trouble solving certain kinds of problems—like conservation. They may not be able to hold all the relevant pieces of information in working memory (Siegler & Richards, 1982). They may, for example, forget that the two balls of clay were equal in the first place, and so by the time they are asked about the ball and the "sausage," they can judge only on appearance.

Strategies for Remembering

Jason, at age 5, has just learned how to use the telephone to call his grandmother. "What's Grandma's number?" he asks his mother, and as he runs into the other room to use the telephone, he says the number out loud, again and again. He is using the strategy of rehearsal, one of the most common techniques to improve memory.

During middle childhood, children discover that they can take deliberate actions to help them remember things. As children get older, they develop better strategies and tailor them to specific things they need to remember. Some children discover these techniques on their own, but they can be taught to use them earlier than they otherwise would. Let us take a look at some of the most common strategies: rehearsal, categorization, elaboration, and external aids.

Rehearsal *Rehearsal,* or conscious repetition, is an important strategy for keeping something in short-term memory. Classic research suggests that children do not usually rehearse spontaneously until after first grade (Flavell, Beach, &

sensory memory Awareness of images and sensations that disappears quickly unless it is transferred into short-term memory.

short-term memory Working memory, which has a limited capacity; the content fades rapidly unless it is stored or actively preserved through rehearsal. Compare long-term memory.

long-term memory Stored memories; the capacity seems unlimited and the duration of a memory may be permanent. Compare short-term memory.

rehearsal Strategy to keep an item in short-term memory through conscious repetition.

Chinsky, 1966). When an experimenter pointed to several pictures that children knew they would be asked to recall, first-graders just sat, waited till they were asked for the information, and then tried to recall the pictures in the order in which they had seen them. Second- and fifth-graders moved their lips and muttered almost inaudibly between the time they saw the pictures and the time they were asked to recall them. Not surprisingly, the older children remembered the material better. When the experimenters asked first-graders to name the pictures out loud when they first saw them (a form of rehearsal), the children remembered the pictures better, and also the order in which they had been presented. A later study showed that young children who were taught to rehearse before they did it spontaneously applied rehearsal to a situation in which they were taught but did not *generalize* the learning; that is, they did not carry it over to new situations (Keeney, Cannizzo, & Flavell, 1967).

More recent research, however, shows that Jason is not that unusual in using rehearsal at the age of 5 and that children as young as 3 can use it effectively. Although 6-year-olds are more likely to rehearse, 3-year-old rehearsers can remember a grocery list as well as 6-year-olds (Paris & Weissberg-Benchell, cited in Chance & Fischman, 1987). Rehearsal—at whatever age it is used—is important for improving short-term memory.

Categorization   It is much easier to remember material if we use *categorization,* that is, if we mentally organize it into related groupings. Adults tend to categorize automatically. Children younger than 10 or 11 do *not* ordinarily categorize, but they can be taught to do it, or they may do it in imitation of older children or adults (Chance & Fischman, 1987). If they are shown randomly arranged pictures of, say, animals, furniture, vehicles, and clothing, they do not mentally sort the items into categories. If shown how to do so, they recall the pictures as well as older children, but they do not apply this strategy to other situations.

categorization   Process of organizing material in one's mind into related groupings to aid in remembering.

Elaboration   Through the strategy of *elaboration,* we link items we want to remember by creating a story about them or a visual image of them. Thus, to remember to buy lemons, ketchup, and napkins, we might imagine a ketchup bottle balanced on a lemon, with a pile of napkins handy to wipe up spilled ketchup. Older children are more likely than younger children to do this spontaneously, and they remember better when they make up the elaboration themselves. Younger children remember better when someone else makes up the elaboration for them (Paris & Lindauer, 1976; Reese, 1977).

elaboration   Linking items to be remembered by creating a story about them or a visual image of them.

External Aids   The memory strategies probably used most by both children and adults involve external aids. You write down a telephone number, you make a list, you tie a string around your finger, you ask someone to remind you, you set a timer, or you put a library book by the front door, where you cannot miss it when you go out. Even kindergartners recognize the value of such *external aids,* and as children mature, they make increasing use of them (Kreutzer, Leonard, & Flavell, 1975).

Metamemory

The general understanding of the processes of memory is called *metamemory.* Recent research has shown that children's understanding of memory processes develops during middle childhood.

metamemory   Knowledge of the process of memory.

In one important study, researchers interviewed children from kindergarten through fifth grade and found steady progress in understanding memory (Kreutzer et al., 1975). At the beginning of middle childhood (kindergarten and first grade), children already understand what it means to learn, remember, and forget, and they have a few ideas about each process. They understand that longer study time improves learning and that the passage of time leads to forgetting. They also know that external aids like writing down a phone number and asking another person to remind them of something can help them remember. Perhaps the most sophisticated thing they know about memory, because it combines a knowledge of learning with a knowledge of forgetting, is that relearning something is easier than learning it for the first time.

The older children in the study (third- and fifth-graders) had a better understanding of memory than the younger ones. They were generally aware that some people remember more than others and that some things are easier to remember than others. Because of their greater knowledge, they could plan better to remember something. For example, they were more likely to think of putting their skates by their schoolbooks if they wanted to remember to take their skates to school the next day. Other research has shown that by sixth grade, children consider categorization a more effective memory device then rehearsal (Justice, 1985).

PSYCHOMETRIC APPROACH: MEASURING INTELLIGENCE IN MIDDLE CHILDHOOD

Vicky's school gives group intelligence tests every few years, partly to assess its students' ability and partly to judge how well it is preparing them. After the fourth grade, Vicky wanted to change schools and took a test individually—to help the new school decide whether to admit her and also to see whether she would benefit from an enriched program or whether she needed any special help.

The use of intelligence tests is controversial. They have both pros and cons. On the positive side, these tests have been standardized, and therefore there is extensive information about their norms, validity, and reliability. IQ scores are good predictors of achievement in schools, especially for highly verbal children, and they help identify youngsters who are especially bright or who need special help.

On the other hand, there are problems with using intelligence tests, besides those that we have already pointed out regarding tests for infants and handicapped children.

The psychologist Robert Sternberg (1985a, 1987) believes that intelligence is more than what IQ tests measure. He and other critics point out that these tests do not assess skills directly, but instead infer ability from how children score. This leads to problems of cultural bias and to underestimation of the intellectual abilities of members of minority groups. Furthermore, while the tests do predict academic performance well, critics charge that they miss other aspects of intelligence, which are at least as important, especially outside of school. These other aspects of intelligent behavior include "street smarts" (common sense and shrewdness in everyday life), social skills (getting along with other people), skills in music and art, and self-knowledge (H. Gardner, 1985; Sternberg, 1987).

Let us look at the tests themselves and at some of the issues surrounding them.

Psychometric Intelligence Tests for Schoolchildren

Schoolchildren can be tested either individually or in groups. The most widely used individual test is the *Wechsler Intelligence Scale for Children (WISC-R).** This measures verbal and performance abilities, yielding separate scores for each, as well as a total score. Separating the subtest scores pinpoints a child's strengths and also makes the diagnosis of specific deficits easier. For example, if a child does significantly better on the verbal tests (such as understanding a written passage and knowing vocabulary words) than on the performance tests (such as figuring out mazes and copying a block design), the child may have problems with perceptual or motor development. If the child does much better on the performance tests than on the verbal tests, there may be a problem with language development.

Another important individual test is the Stanford-Binet Intelligence Scale, described in Chapter 9.

A popular group test is the *Otis-Lennon School Ability Test,* which has several levels covering children from kindergarten to twelfth grade. Children are usually tested in groups of 10 to 15 and are asked to classify items, to show an understanding of verbal and numerical concepts, to display general information, and to follow directions. (See Figure 12-1, page 432, for a sample of items in this test.)

This girl is taking one of the most widely used tests of intelligence for children, WISC-R, which yields separate scores for verbal and performance abilities.

Implications of Intelligence Tests

Cross-Cultural Testing *Culture-free and culture-fair tests* As early as 1910, researchers recognized the difficulty of designing intelligence tests for people in diverse cultural groups. Ever since, they have tried to design tests that can measure innate (inborn) intelligence without introducing cultural bias. They have designed tests that do not require language: testers use gestures, pantomime, and demonstrations for tasks like tracing mazes, finding absurdities in pictures, putting the right shapes in the right holes, and completing pictures. But they have not been able to eliminate all cultural content.

For example, conventions of art affect the way a test taker views a picture. When Jason is asked to identify the missing detail in a picture of a face with no mouth, he immediately says, "the mouth." But a group of Asian immigrant children in Israel said that the *body* was missing. The art they were used to would not present a head as a complete picture. Therefore, they thought that the absence of a body was more important than the omission of "a mere detail like the mouth" (Anastasi, 1988, p. 360).

Apparently, it is impossible to design a *culture-free* test—one that would have no culture-linked content. Instead, test developers have tried to produce *culture-fair* tests, that is, tests dealing with experiences common to people in various cultures. But critics charge that these tests are not really culture-fair, because it is almost impossible to screen for culturally determined values and attitudes, which reflect what people in a culture consider intelligent behavior. For example, in the United States, parents at lower socioeconomic levels encourage children to learn by rote, while middle- and upper-class parents try to teach children to reason. Cultural differences also affect cognitive processing. For in-

Wechsler Intelligence Scale for Children (WISC-R) *Individual intelligence test for children that includes verbal and performance subtests.*

Otis-Lennon School Ability Test *Group intelligence test for children.*

---

*The R in WISC-R stands for "revised."

Part I. *Classification*: Mark the picture that does not belong with the other three, the one that is different.

(Pictorial)

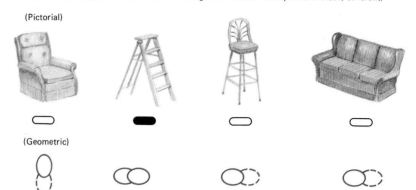

⊂⊃   ⬛   ⊂⊃   ⊂⊃

(Geometric)

⊂⊃   ⬛   ⊂⊃   ⊂⊃

Part II. *Verbal conceptualization*: Mark the picture that shows a flame.

⊂⊃   ⊂⊃   ⬛   ⊂⊃

Quantitative reasoning: Mark the picture that shows the same number of dots as there are parts in the circle.

    •• •••   •••• •••••

⊂⊃   ⊂⊃   ⊂⊃   ⊂⊃   ⬛

General information: Mark the picture of the thing we talk into.

⬛   ⊂⊃   ⊂⊃   ⊂⊃

Following directions: Mark the picture that shows a glass inside a square with a cross on top.

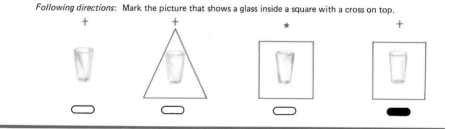

⊂⊃   ⊂⊃   ⊂⊃   ⬛

FIGURE 12-1
Items illustrative of Otis-Lennon School Ability Test (Primary I and Primary II Levels), a paper-and-pencil test administered to groups of children. (*Source:* Psychological Corporation. *See* Otis & Lennon, 1967.)

stance, western cultures consider it more intelligent to categorize things by what they *are* (as by putting *bird* and *fish* in the category *animal*); but the Kpelle tribe in Nigeria sorts things by what they *do* (as by grouping *fish* with *swim*) (Sternberg, quoted in Quinby, 1985; Sternberg, 1985a; Sternberg, 1986).

Also, the content of a test—the tasks it poses—calls for skills that the test developer values; but people from other cultural groups may not value the same abilities. This may help to explain the fact that discrepancies between the scores of black and white children are at least as great on performance and other non-verbal tests as on verbal tests (Anastasi, 1988; Sternberg, 1985a). These nonlanguage tests, too, must be heavily affected by cultural factors and values. But since such factors are largely invisible in these tests, they are hard to allow for.

Other cultural attitudes affect the testing situation itself. Does a society value competition or cooperation? A child from a culture that emphasizes sociability and cooperation will be handicapped taking a test alone. Does a society value speed or deliberation? A child from a society that emphasizes slow, deliberate, painstaking work is handicapped in a timed test (Anastasi, 1988).

Rapport with the examiner and familiarity with the surroundings are also important. African American and Hispanic children, disabled children, and children from low socioeconomic levels often earn higher scores when people they know (like their own teachers) give tests in places they know (like their own classrooms) than when they take tests in unfamiliar rooms with unknown examiners. These children also do better when they are tested more than once on the same type of test and when the test is based on work they have been studying (D. Fuchs & L.S. Fuchs, 1986; L.S. Fuchs & D. Fuchs, 1986).

But perhaps we should ask ourselves: Even if we could devise a test that had no relevance to culture, what would we be measuring? Doesn't intelligence have something to do with how well a person perceives and adapts to the culture? Isn't culture so pervasive that it is bound to affect every aspect of a person's intellectual functioning? Such questions have more to do with social issues than with science.

We might ask why schools should use tests that ignore cultural bias, when, to succeed, the children will have to function in a particular culture. On the other hand, shouldn't tests take a minority culture into account? And shouldn't society as a whole make room for that culture? These issues affect the way we apply our knowledge of child development. Two phenomena apparently influenced by culture are the high achievement levels of Asian children, which we consider in Box 12-2 (page 434); and the disparity in intelligence test scores between black and white American children, which we consider below.

Intelligence testing of black children   Black Americans tend to score about 15 points lower on IQ tests than white Americans (E.B. Brody & Brody, 1976). There is considerable overlap; some blacks score higher than most whites. Still, the difference exists, and what it means is highly controversial. There are two basic ways of interpreting it. Most modern educators maintain that it reflects typical differences in environment between the two groups—in education, in cultural traditions, and in other circumstances that affect self-esteem and motivation, as well as academic performance itself (Kamin, 1974). The other view— that such disparities reflect hereditary differences and that blacks are innately inferior intellectually (Jensen, 1969)—overlooks much evidence showing the importance of the environment. Let us see why the first position seems more solidly based.

BOX 12-2 ■ AROUND THE WORLD

HOW CAN ASIAN CHILDREN ACHIEVE SO MUCH?

Of the 14 New York City finalists in the 1988 national Westinghouse science awards competition, 11 were Asian (Graubard, 1988). In the San Diego area, Asian high school students have higher grade-point averages than other students. According to a United States Department of Education study, Asian students take more advanced high school courses and graduate with more credits than their peers (Brand, 1987). How are young Asian Americans able to make such a strong showing by almost every educational measure? A number of researchers have looked at this question and have come up with the following answers.

GENERAL COGNITIVE ABILITY

In a cross-cultural study of American, Japanese, and Chinese children, an international research team designed a test to assess children's cognitive abilities on the basis of common experiences (H.W. Stevenson et al., 1985). Test items, given in all three languages, included verbal tasks (repeating lists of words and numbers, following spoken directions, answering questions about stories and everyday facts, and defining words) and nonverbal tasks (learning a code, completing a square, matching shapes, and recalling rhythms). Urban first- and fifth-graders in all three countries also took specially designed reading and math tests.

Judged by this study, Asian students do not start out with any overall cognitive superiority. In fact, American first-graders outperformed the others on many tasks, possibly because they were more used to answering adults' questions (Chinese children are expected to be "seen but not heard") and had had more cultural experiences, like going to museums, zoos, and movies (which Asian children do not have until they go to school). In another study, American children did better at ages 4 to 6 years on "informal" mathematics (judging when one thing is more or less than another and counting), but by age 7 or 8, Korean children had surpassed them (Song & Ginsburg, 1987).

The Japanese and Chinese children performed better on math tests, and the Chinese children did best in reading; but by the fifth grade the children from all three cultures performed very similarly on the tests of cognition. It seems, then, that Asian children do not start out with any cognitive advantage, and that their superiority is due to cultural and educational differences.

ASIAN CULTURAL STANDARDS

According to a United States government–sponsored study of Japanese schools (McKinney, 1987) and a study comparing Korean and American children (Song & Ginsburg, 1987), many educational differences between east and west stem from major cultural differences. In Japan, for example, a child's entrance into school is a greater occasion

for celebration than graduation from high school; first-graders receive such expensive gifts as desks, chairs, and leather backpacks. Both Japanese and Korean parents spend a great deal of time helping children with schoolwork, and Japanese children who fall behind receive private tutoring or go to *jukus*, private remedial and enrichment schools.

EDUCATIONAL DIFFERENCES

Another major explanation for Asian students' mathematical and scientific superiority lies in academic practices. Classroom observation in China, Japan, and the United States (Stigler, Lee, & Stevenson, 1987) and in Korea and the United States (Song & Ginsburg, 1987) shows large cross-cultural differences in classroom routine. Asian teachers spend more time teaching the class as a whole, while American teachers focus more on small groups. Japanese and Chinese teachers, for example, spend more than three-quarters of their time with the entire class, whereas American teachers spend less than half. American children spend more time working alone (often at problems they do not understand) or in small groups (with other children who do not understand the work), rather than listening to the teacher teach. Although the American approach seems to offer more individual attention, each child ends up with less total instruction.

Finally, Asian children spend more time in school each year, more time in classes each day, and more time being taught mathematics—partly because the curriculum is centrally set rather than left to individual teachers. Furthermore, although Asian teachers generally do not have as much education as their American counterparts, they are more knowledgeable in their own subjects. To raise American students' proficiency in math and science, it would be necessary not only to provide more hours of education, possibly by lengthening the school day and school year, but also to help American teachers improve their own proficiency and motivate them to teach these subjects.

A major question, however, is what happens to students when they leave school. Although 90 percent of Japanese students graduate from high school, compared with 76 percent of American students, only 29 percent go on to college, compared with 58 percent in the United States (Simons, 1987). Furthermore, we need to ask what kinds of adults the students become. Many Japanese parents, students, and lawyers argue that regimentation stifles individuality, and are raising legal challenges to many long-established practices (Chira, 1988). Ultimately, in designing an educational system, a society's leaders have to ask what kinds of citizens they want to produce, since, as we have seen, culture shapes attitudes and encourages some kinds of behaviors rather than others. It is apparently culture rather than inborn ability that has helped Asian students achieve so much in school.

For one thing, differences between black children and white children do not appear in infancy. Not until children are about 2 or 3 years old do blacks lag behind whites in intelligence test scores (M. Golden, Birns, & Bridger, 1973). Some research suggests, in fact, that black babies are precocious on tests of infants' intelligence (Bayley, 1965; Geber, 1962; Geber & Dean, 1957). The difference that shows up later may reflect the switch from predominantly motor to predominantly verbal tests—and verbal ability is highly influenced by environmental factors. After the first 2 or 3 years of life, the environment seems to make more of a difference.

We can also see the important influence of the environment when we compare people from different socioeconomic levels. The same pattern that holds for American white and black test takers (an average difference of 15 points) also holds for American middle-class and deprived rural and mountain children and for English middle-class and low-income canal-boat and Gypsy children (Pettigrew, 1964). Furthermore, black children who live in northern cities score higher than those in the rural south (Baughman, 1971), and middle-class blacks score better than poor blacks (Loehlin, Lindzey, & Spuhler, 1975).

Considering the major effect of the environment, then, psychologists and educators need to develop tests that take environmental factors into account. One test already in use in some states is the *System of Multicultural Pluralistic Assessment (SOMPA)*. This is a battery of measures for 5- to 11-year-olds including a medical exam, a Wechsler IQ test, and an interview with the parent or parents. The interview yields information about the environment (how many people live in the home, their educational level, and so forth) and the child's level of social competence (how many classmates the child knows by name, whether the child prepares his or her own lunch, and so forth).

System of Multicultural Pluralistic Assessment (SOMPA) Battery of measures designed to take environmental factors into account in assessing intelligence.

Thus, for instance, a 9-year-old girl who scored only 68 on the WISC-R test might be eligible for placement in a class for the mentally retarded. But if we learn that she is living in a poor urban ghetto and compare her with other children from a similar background, we realize that her IQ score of 68 is only 9 points below the mean for her group. If, in addition, her adaptive-behavior scores show that she is unusually capable of taking care of herself and getting along in her community, her estimated learning potential, or "adjusted IQ," will be 89. This adjusted score indicates that she belongs in a regular class which will take her background into account (Rice, 1979).

Changes in Performance on Intelligence Tests Intelligence is not fixed and unchangeable. Test performance in general has improved over the years, probably in response to such changes in recent decades as higher average levels of education, increasing literacy, new kinds of educational experiences (like television and computers), and other broad social factors. In addition, a person's score often improves with repeated testing, showing the effects of practice (Anastasi, 1988).

A child's development itself can enhance performance on intelligence tests. As children mature, learn from experience and schooling, and use their minds, their intelligence scores frequently rise. How motivated a test taker is and what his or her personality is like can also contribute to a rise—or fall—in intelligence test scores. Furthermore, recent research suggests that children can be taught how to think more effectively (Sternberg, 1984, 1985a, 1985b). (See Box 12-3, page 436.) Adults can also help children develop talents and creativity, as we see later in this chapter when we discuss various kinds of giftedness.

BOX 12-3 ■ THE EVERYDAY WORLD

TEACHING CHILDREN TO THINK

Teachers often complain that it is easier to teach children bald facts to feed back on tests than it is to teach them to think for themselves. *Can* children be taught to think? Research says yes.

Thinking arises at least partly from experience. Therefore, for children to learn to think—to evaluate a situation, focus on its most important aspects, decide what to do, and do it—they need experience. The following suggestions for parents and teachers come from cognitive studies (Marzano & Hutchins, 1987; Maxwell, 1987):

■ Teach thinking skills in the context of everyday activities at home or at school. This can begin very early. As suggested in Box 6-5, asking toddlers open-ended questions (beginning with *what, why,* and *how*) while reading to them encourages them to improve their verbal skills; it also helps them learn to think. The same kind of approach helps older children.

■ Ask children to "match" information, to compare new data with what they already know. In this way they learn to identify links between words or concepts (what two items have in common or how they differ). Schoolchildren can categorize a country, for example, as European or African, democratic or totalitarian. Such categorization can help them remember facts better, too, as we pointed out in our discussion of memory earlier in this chapter.

■ Demonstrate "critical thinking." Teach children to ask four questions about anything they hear or read: (1) Is it unusual? (2) Is it common knowledge ("the sky is sometimes blue")? (3) If it is not common knowledge, what is the proof? (4) If there is proof, is it reliable? If not, they should learn not to accept the statement.

■ Show children how to approach a problem: (1) To understand it, they need to identify what they know, what they don't know, and what has to be done. (2) They can then design a plan to solve it, (3) carry out the plan, and (4) evaluate the plan (decide whether it has worked).

■ Use "guided imagery" (imagining an event or experience). Sensory images help store information in long-term memory, and the more senses are involved, the better. Thus, children studying the Sahara Desert might be asked to "see" it, "touch" the sand, "hear" the wind, and "feel" hot and thirsty. This approach uses the memory strategy of elaboration, which was described in the discussion of memory in this chapter.

■ Teach children to go beyond what they have learned. Children studying the American Revolution might be asked, "How do you think the soldiers felt at Valley Forge? What do you suppose they wore? Imagine you were there, and write a letter to your family."

■ Inspire invention. Ask children to create new information or products, like a gadget to help in some household chore.

■ Suggest creative projects, like writing a poem or drawing a picture. Encourage children to produce a first version—and then to polish or revise it.

■ Teach children some helpful procedures, like reading a map, performing arithmetic operations, and using a microscope; and show some examples of their use.

■ Encourage children to set goals within a time frame, and to write down the goals so that they can check their progress.

■ Help them learn to find the most important points in what they read, see, or hear.

■ Encourage children to write, since the process of putting thoughts on paper forces the writer to organize them. Projects that children can enjoy, as well as learn from, include keeping a journal, presenting an argument to parents (for an increase in allowance or a special purchase or privilege), and writing a letter to a business or famous person.

Development of Language in Middle Childhood

Popular wisdom holds that by the time they enter first grade, all normal children have learned a language. In one sense this is true: as a first-grader, Vicky talks her parents' ears off, pronounces words clearly, and can converse easily about many things. But there are still many words she does not know and many subtleties of language she does not appreciate. Her language abilities continue to grow during middle childhood. Children are now better able to understand and interpret communications—and to make themselves understood.

GRAMMAR: THE STRUCTURE OF LANGUAGE

Let us imagine that you are home on a winter day; you look out the window at a snow-covered driveway, and you ask your father how you are going to get the family car out of the garage. Your father would probably just tell you where to find the snow shovel; but for the purposes of this discussion, let's assume that he says something like, "John promised Mary to shovel the driveway" or "John told Mary to shovel the driveway." Depending on which answer you receive, you know whether to expect John or Mary to appear, shovel in hand. But many children under 5 or 6 years of age do not understand the difference between these two sentences and think that they *both* mean that Mary is to do the shoveling (C. S. Chomsky, 1969). Their confusion is understandable, since almost all English verbs that might replace *told* in the second sentence (such as *ordered*, *wanted*, *persuaded*, *advised*, *allowed*, and *expected*) would put the shovel in Mary's hand.

Most 6-year-olds have not yet learned how to deal with grammatical constructions in which a word is used the way *promise* is used in the first sentence, even though they know what a promise is and are able to use and understand the word correctly in other sentences. By the age of 8, most children can interpret the first sentence correctly. They know the concept attached to the word *promise*, and they know how the word can be used.

The above example shows us that even though 6-year-olds use complex grammar and a vocabulary of several thousand words, they still have to master many of the fine points of language. During the early school years, they rarely use the passive voice, verb tenses that include the auxiliary *have*, and conditional (*if . . . then*) sentences.

Up to and possibly after the age of 9, children develop an increasingly complex understanding of **syntax**, the way words are organized into phrases and sentences (C. S. Chomsky, 1969). When testing forty 5- to 10-year-old children's understanding of various syntactic structures, Carol S. Chomsky found considerable variation in the ages of children who understood them and children who did not (see Table 12-4).

syntax *Way in which words are organized into phrases and sentences.*

TABLE 12-4

ACQUISITION OF COMPLEX SYNTACTIC STRUCTURES		
STRUCTURE	DIFFICULT CONCEPT	AGE OF ACQUISITION
John is easy to see.	Who is doing the seeing?	5.6 to 9 years.*
John promised Bill to go.	Who is going?	5.6 to 9 years.*
John asked Bill what to do.	Who is doing it?	Some 10-year-olds have still not learned this.
He knew that John was going to win the race.	Does the "he" refer to John?	5.6 years.

*All children 9 and over know this.
Source: C.S. Chomsky, 1969.

LANGUAGE AND COMMUNICATION

When the dentist gave 6-year-old Jason a fluoride treatment, she told him not to eat for half an hour. Jason interpreted this to mean that he was not to *swallow* for half an hour. Soon after leaving the examining room, he started to drool and looked very upset, and he was greatly relieved when the dentist noticed this and told him that, yes, he could swallow his saliva.

metacommunication
Knowledge of communication processes.

Even though Jason had arrived at a rather sophisticated level of linguistic ability, he was still having problems with communication, like many children of his age. Of course, adults, too, often misinterpret what people say—often resulting in major misunderstandings, both cognitive and emotional. But children's failures in interpreting messages often stem from ignorance of *metacommunication*, that is, knowledge of the processes of communication. This knowledge grows throughout middle childhood.

To study children's ability to transmit and understand spoken information, researchers have designed a variety of ingenious experiments. In one, kindergartners and second-graders were asked to construct block buildings exactly like those built by another child and to do this on the basis of the first child's audiotaped instructions—without seeing the buildings themselves. The instructions were often incomplete, ambiguous, or contradictory. The "builders" were then asked whether they thought that their buildings looked like the models they were copying and whether they thought that the instructions were good or bad.

The older children were more likely to notice when instructions were inadequate and to pause or look puzzled. They were more likely to know when they did not understand something and to see the implications of unclear communication—that their buildings might not look exactly like the models because they had not received good enough instructions. The younger children sometimes knew that the instructions were not clear, but they did not seem to realize that they might therefore not be able to do their job well. Even the older children (who, after all, were only 8 years old or so) did not show a thorough understanding of communication (Flavell, Speer, Green, & August, 1981).

Findings like these have important implications for parents, teachers, and others who work with children. Young children often do not understand what they see, hear, or read, but they are also often not aware of not understanding. They may be so used to not understanding things in the world around them that it does not seem unusual to them. Much of the time, then, they just go along, nodding, trying to follow unclear directions, and not asking questions. Adults need to realize that they cannot take children's understanding for granted. For the sake of children's safety, well-being, and academic advancement, we have to learn to be aware whether children do, in fact, know what we want them to know.

CHILDREN'S HUMOR

At 6 years of age, Jason likes to tell made-up "jokes" like this: "Do you know why the fat lady sat in the chair? Because she was too fat to sit in two chairs!" He then has a fit of giggles. By age 8 he is telling jokes which show his ability to play with words and which alleviate his anxieties, like this one: "'Mom, Sis is really spoiled!' 'She is *not*.' 'Oh, no? You should see what the steamroller did to her!'"

Jason continues to make puns, use wrong words and deliberate mispronunciations, and tell riddles, not only to express his feelings, but also to show his factual knowledge, his mastery of language, and his ability in symbolic, logical, and abstract reasoning. His appreciation of humor and his ability to create it himself grow as his cognitive abilities develop (McGhee & Chapman, cited in Masten, 1986).

In one study, a multiethnic sample of children in grades 5 through 8 looked at "Ziggy" cartoons and were asked to grade them on funniness, to explain what made them funny, and to make up captions or titles ("What could the bird be saying to Ziggy that would be funny here?"). The children were also tested for competence.

The most competent children had the best sense of humor—they were most capable of understanding and appreciating humor and creating their own, and these abilities seemed to grow sharper with age. Furthermore, these children were seen more positively in school. Their teachers considered them more attentive, cooperative, responsive, and productive; and they were popular with their classmates, who saw them as happy, gregarious leaders with good ideas for things to do (Masten, 1986). It seems likely that general cognitive abilities underlie both successful adaptation in the classroom and the development of humor. (A sense of humor also affects the way people handle the emotional situations in their lives and the way they get along with others—issues dealt with in Chapter 13.)

These girls' ability to "get" a joke depends largely on their intellectual development. As they recognize more subtle incongruities, their appreciation of humor becomes more sophisticated. A sense of humor is also, of course, a strong social asset.

The Child in School

Jason, along with the other children in his second-grade class, is in the auditorium, listening to a guest speaker, the author of a book about the brain. After her talk, the speaker asks the 200 or so assembled children whether they have any questions. Shyly, Jason raises his hand and asks, "Do headaches come from the brain?"

Ten years later, Jason remembers that day with pain. "The woman laughed at me. The way she smiled and her tone of voice made me feel that I had asked the dumbest question in the world. I was really embarrassed. And I think that's one of the things that happened to me when I was little that made me the way I am today. I *hate* to ask questions in class!"

School assumes a central place in Jason's life. His experience in school affects and is affected by every aspect of his development—intellectual, physical, social, and emotional. But child-care professionals and educators often disagree on the ways school can best enhance children's development, as we can see in the swings in educational theory over the past several decades.

RECENT TRENDS IN EDUCATION

The three R's are back in style. Basic academic subjects like reading, writing, and arithmetic were the backbone of American schools during the 1920s and 1930s. Then the reform movement of the 1940s and 1950s, reacting against regimentation, introduced methods that tried to build on students' interests. In 1957, when the Soviet Union launched *Sputnik,* the first satellite, Americans put a new emphasis on science and math in fear that American students were not as well prepared in science as Russian children. During the political turbulence of the late 1960s, such curricula seemed less relevant than children's ability to think for themselves and direct the course of their own education. Experiments like

How children learn about the human circulatory system (as these youngsters are doing) has changed over the past few decades as educational theories have changed. Today's students are expected to be more actively involved than children used to be.

"open classrooms" came into being, with children in the same room engaged in a variety of different activities and with teachers acting more as "facilitators" and overseers than as transmitters of knowledge. High school students chose more of their courses on their own; as a result, fewer studied foreign languages or signed up for difficult science courses (Ravitch, 1983).

In the mid-1970s, high school students' scores on the Scholastic Aptitude Test (SAT) dropped, and American educators became concerned that schools were not giving students enough grounding in basic academic skills which would help them think better. Since then, the byword has been "back to basics." One result is that high school and college students have shown a renewed interest in foreign languages—with the biggest increases in enrollment in Japanese, Chinese, and Russian courses (Maeroff, 1984).

These changes illustrate an underlying faith that the future rests on the way children turn out and that education influences children's development. That faith can also be seen in parents' concern about their children's education. Most parents want their children to do well in school, and a large body of research shows that they can help their children. (See Box 12-4.)

TEACHERS

Teachers' Influence

During the early school years, a teacher becomes a parent substitute, an imparter of values, and a contributor to a child's self-esteem. The importance of the teacher in these years was dramatically brought out by one study that linked a number of people's successes in adulthood to their having been in the first-grade classroom of a very special teacher. The study was originally launched to track changes in IQ among children from a poor inner-city neighborhood. By chance, however, it discovered an amazingly enduring relationship between having been in "Miss A's" first-grade classroom and a number of happy events. Many

BOX 12-4 ■ THE RESEARCH WORLD

HOW PARENTS INFLUENCE CHILDREN'S ACHIEVEMENT IN SCHOOL

An 11-year-old student in New York City beams as he shows his mother how to run a computer program, in a parent-child class at the boy's school. Other parents are exploring the possibility of such classes in other schools. The Pepsa program (Parents Involved in Education Planning for Students' Achievement), unique to this district, serves a low-income, minority-group population (Wells, 1988a, 1988b). But it seems to be the wave of the future as research shows the importance of parents' participation in the academic success of children from all socioeconomic levels.

WHAT PARENTS OF ACHIEVING CHILDREN DO

A recent review of the literature on the relationship between the family and schools shows the importance of an active family role in a number of school-related areas (Hess & Holloway, 1984). How do parents of achieving children help their children do well in school? Five major areas of involvement seem important:

- *Parents talk to their children.* The parents of achieving children spend time with them, read to them and listen to the children read, ask them for information (even when the parents already know the answer), and encourage them to speak correctly and take part in family conversation.
- *Parents have high expectations for their children.* These parents have high hopes. They encourage children to master developmental tasks early and do them completely and correctly, expect their children to do well in school and then in careers, and put pressure on them to achieve.
- *Parents have warm relationships with their children.* They are close to their children, nurture them, praise them when they do well, and rarely restrict or punish them.
- *Parents use the authoritative style of child rearing.* They are firm but reasonable, expecting children to remember—and follow—everyday routines, chores, and schedules. They tend to be neither permissive nor authoritarian. (See Chapter 10 for descriptions of these three styles.)
- *Parents believe in their children.* Their belief that their children can do well boosts the children's self-esteem, motivation, expectations for themselves, and performance.

HOW PARENTS HELP CHILDREN ACHIEVE

Such parents help children assume an active role in organizing their environment. The parents provide the raw materials of experience and help the child learn to solve prob-

lems, thus helping the child learn and apply educationally useful skills (Hess & Holloway, 1984). Parents are most effective when their goals for the child are consistent with the school's; when they, the child's teachers, and other important people take these goals seriously; and when they and others can counter contradictory values, like those from television and peers.

SUGGESTIONS FOR HELPING CHILDREN READ BETTER

By determining what such parents do with their children, researchers have correlated certain activities with children's reading achievement (Hess & Holloway, 1984). The following suggestions for parents are based on these research findings:

- Show your children that you value literacy by reading and by talking about books and ideas.
- Respond to your children's interests by answering questions about written words in everyday settings (stop signs, signs on stores, signs on rest rooms).
- Take your children to the library. Encourage them to feel at home in the children's room and to select their own books.
- Read—and reread—their favorite books to them. Ask them questions that require more than a yes-no answer. Ask them to identify objects in pictures. Refer to the books in conversation.
- When they are able, ask them to read to you. (Before children can read, they often memorize stories and welcome "reading" to you from memory.) Your interest means a lot.
- Buy them books—storybooks, picture dictionaries, alphabet books, and early readers.
- Provide writing materials, like paper, pencils, and blackboards.
- Talk to children about everyday events, things or people you see on the street, or their favorite television programs. Expand on or clarify what they say.
- Play games that involve repetition of language patterns, like filling in words of familiar poems.
- Break tasks into manageable pieces and help children when they run into trouble (like pronouncing a new word).
- Encourage children and praise them—but learning has to remain fun. Too much pressure leads to tears and learning blocks. Do not try to teach children to read at an early age; this is not correlated with early reading and can push children beyond their abilities.
- Above all, believe in the children—and show your confidence. They can do much more when they believe they can do it.

(Menuez/Stock, Boston)

Teachers exert a great deal of influence over their students. If this teacher believes that these girls are capable of high achievement, they will probably do better in school than if she has less faith in them—an illustration of the self-fulfilling prophecy.

more of Miss A's former students showed impressive increases in IQ over the years than children who had been in other first-grade classrooms in the same school. Even more remarkable, however, was the relationship between having been a student of Miss A and such measures of adult success as occupational status, type of housing, and personal appearance (posture, dress, and grooming). When graduates of the school were interviewed by researchers who did not know which students had had which first-grade teacher, the graduates who had been in Miss A's class scored better on all these measures (Pederson, Faucher, & Eaton, 1978).

What did Miss A do that was so special? She showed confidence in the children's ability and encouraged them to work hard to justify that confidence. She gave extra time to those who needed it, staying after school with them. And she cared. She was affectionate, she shared her own lunch with children who had forgotten theirs, and she remembered former students by name, even 20 years later. What miracles schools could accomplish with more Miss A's!

Teachers' Expectations: The Self-Fulfilling Prophecy

How does the opinion Vicky's teacher holds of her affect Vicky's performance in school? According to an impressive body of research, teachers' expectations carry a great deal of weight. The principle of the *self-fulfilling prophecy* is that students live up to (or down to) the expectations that other people have of them.

self-fulfilling prophecy
Prediction of behavior that biases people to act as though the prophecy were already true.

In the famous "Oak School" experiment, some teachers were told at the beginning of the term that some of their students had shown unusual potential for intellectual growth. Actually, the children identified as potential "bloomers" had been chosen at random. Yet several months later, many of them—especially first- and second-graders—showed unusual gains in IQ. And the teachers seemed to like the "bloomers" better. They do not appear to have spent more time with them than with the other children or to have treated them differently in any obvious ways. Subtler influences may have been at work, such as the teachers' tone of voice, facial expressions, touch, and posture (R. Rosenthal & Jacobson, 1968).

This research has been criticized for methodological shortcomings. Nevertheless, work by many other researchers using a variety of methods has established the same basic principle—that teachers' expectations "can and do function as self-fulfilling prophecies, although not always or automatically" (Brophy & Good, 1974, p. 32). A recent study has shown that even first-graders are aware that teachers treat high and low achievers differently. In first grade, this awareness does not seem to affect the children's opinions of themselves very much, but by fifth grade the effect is marked (Weinstein, Marshall, Sharp, & Botkin, 1987).

SCHOOLCHILDREN WITH SPECIAL NEEDS

Children with Disabilities

Education for handicapped children has come a long way since the beginning of this century, when the family of Helen Keller, who was deaf and blind, had to travel to distant cities to find help for her. Let us look at three of the most common educational disabilities—and then at the way children with disabilities are educated in American schools.

Mentally Retarded, Learning-Disabled, and Hyperactive Children *Mental retardation* Most mentally retarded children can benefit from schooling, at least up to sixth-grade level. ***Mental retardation*** is defined as below-average intellectual functioning together with a deficiency in adaptive behavior appropriate to current age—and the appearance of such characteristics before age 18 (*Diagnostic*

mental retardation
Below-average intellectual functioning.

TABLE 12-5

LEVELS OF MENTAL RETARDATION	
LEVEL	DESCRIPTION
Mildly retarded	About 85 percent of the retarded population. Mildly retarded people can acquire skills up to about the sixth-grade level, hold low-level paid jobs in adulthood, and live in the community. Although they can usually function on their own, they may need guidance and help at times of unusual stress.
Moderately retarded	About 10 percent of the retarded population. Moderately retarded people can learn academic subjects to the second-grade level, can learn occupational and social skills, and in adulthood may work in sheltered workshops or in regular jobs with close supervision. They can do a fair amount for themselves, but usually live in supervised group homes.
Severely retarded	About 3 to 4 percent of the retarded population. Severely retarded people may learn to talk during the school years, can be trained in personal hygiene, and can sometimes learn to recognize such "survival" words as *men, women,* and *stop.* They typically live in group homes or with their families.
Profoundly retarded	About 1 to 2 percent of the retarded population. Profoundly retarded people have minimal sensorimotor functioning, but may respond to some training in getting around, in self-care, and in communicating, especially if they have a one-to-one relationship with a caregiver. They live in group homes, in intermediate-care facilities, with their families, or in institutions.

and *Statistical Manual of Mental Disorders*, 3d ed., rev., DSM III-R, 1987). Low-level intellectual functioning in this case is detected by IQ tests; the adaptive behaviors include everyday skills: communication and social skills, and skills in practical matters such as self-care. A supportive and stimulating early environment, and continued guidance and help, promise a reasonably good outcome for many mentally retarded children, including many born with Down syndrome (see Chapter 2).

The mentally retarded account for about 1 percent of the population, with about 1.5 males affected for every female. The retarded are generally classified in four categories, based on severity—mildly, moderately, severely, and profoundly retarded (see Table 12-5 on the preceding page).

In about 30 to 40 percent of cases, the cause of mental retardation is unknown. The known causes of retardation include problems in embryonic development (30 percent), environmental influences and mental disorders (15 to 20 percent), problems in pregnancy and childbirth (10 percent), hereditary factors (5 percent), and physical disorders acquired in childhood (5 percent; DSM III-R, 1987).

Learning disabilities   Nelson Rockefeller, the former governor of New York and vice president of the United States, had so much trouble reading that he ad-libbed his speeches instead of using a script. Thomas Edison was considered slow as a child and never did learn how to spell or write grammatically. General George Patton read poorly and got through West Point by memorizing entire lectures (Schulman, 1986). All these people suffered from *dyslexia*—inability or difficulty in learning to read, one of the most common learning disabilities. Dyslexic children often confuse up and down and left and right; they may read *saw* for *was* and have trouble with arithmetic as well as reading.

dyslexia *Inability or difficulty in learning to read.*

Learning disabilities (LDs) are disorders that interfere with some specific aspect of school achievement. These problems affect an estimated 5 to 10 percent of the population—a somewhat higher proportion of boys and children from low socioeconomic groups (Interagency Committee on Learning Disabilities, 1987). Since success in school is important for self-esteem, learning disabilities can have devastating effects on the psyche as well as the report card.

learning disabilities (LDs) *Disorders that interfere with specific aspects of learning and school achievement.*

Learning-disabled children have at least normal intelligence, vision, and hearing (Feagans, 1983). But they have trouble processing what comes through their senses. As one child said, "I know it in my head, but I can't get it into my hand."

Dozens of individual disorders affect one or more aspects of learning. Arlene, like Rockefeller, has trouble reading. Barbara has problems processing what she hears: she cannot grasp what the teacher says. Charles has poor small-muscle coordination: he cannot color inside the lines or draw and write clearly. Derek's clumsiness in large-muscle movements is painfully apparent in the schoolyard when he tries to run, climb, or play ball. Ellen has speech problems: she began to speak very late and her speech is still so unclear that she is embarrassed to speak out in class and to read aloud.

The cause of most of these disabilities is unknown. They may be related to behavioral problems; learning-disabled children tend to be less task-oriented, more easily distracted, and less able to concentrate than other children. There may be a failure of cognitive processing; these children are less organized as learners and less likely to use memory strategies (Feagans, 1983). Or the cause may be physiological; some studies have found differences in the brains of people with learning disabilities (Blakeslee, 1984). And learning disorders tend to run in families; reading disabilities, for example, seem to be at least partly inherited (DeFries, Fulker, & LaBuda, 1987).

The outlook is poorest for learning-disabled children whose birthweight was very low, who suffered other birth trauma or malnutrition in infancy, who have a "difficult" temperament, or who come from poor, chaotic families. The outlook is best for those whose problem is discovered and responded to early (Levine, 1987). Among the most successful courses of action are behavior modification techniques to help concentration, techniques for improving basic skills and using cognitive strategies, help in organizing life outside school as well as in school, and encouragement of progress in both academic and nonacademic areas.

Children do not outgrow learning disabilities; some 5 to 10 million adults suffer from them (Schulman, 1987). But if children or adults take tests to establish their strengths and weaknesses, learn skills to help them use their strengths to compensate for their weaknesses, and get psychological help for such problems as poor self-esteem (often caused by school problems), they can often lead satisfying, productive lives. Some go on to college and professional careers and—while never cured of their disabilities—learn how to compensate for them.

Hyperactivity One behavior disorder that often accompanies learning disorders is hyperactivity. The story is all too familiar to many parents and teachers. Johnny cannot sit still, cannot finish a simple task, cannot keep a friend, and is always in trouble. His teacher says, "I can't do a thing with him." His family doctor says, "Don't worry; he'll grow out of it." And his next-door neighbor says, "He's a spoiled brat."

The syndrome that Johnny is probably suffering from, formally known as ***attention-deficit hyperactivity disorder (ADHD)*** (DSM III-R, 1987), is marked by inattention, impulsivity, low tolerance of frustration, temper tantrums, and a great deal of activity at the wrong time and the wrong place, like the classroom. These traits appear to some degree in all children; but in about 3 percent of school-age children (6 to 9 times more boys than girls), they are so pervasive that they interfere with the child's functioning in school and daily life. These children are considered hyperactive. The disorder shows up before age 4 in about half the cases, but often it is not recognized until the child starts school.

attention-deficit hyperactivity disorder (ADHD) *Syndrome characterized by inattention, impulsivity, and considerable activity at inappropriate times and places.*

A combination of genetic, neurological, biochemical, and environmental factors probably causes this kind of behavior (Hadley, 1984). In fact, there are so many possible causes of hyperactivity that it is difficult to know the origin of any particular case. It often runs in families, suggesting a hereditary factor (DSM III-R, 1987).

Whatever the cause, parents and teachers can often help hyperactive children do better at home and in school. First, they have to understand and accept the child's basic temperament. Then they can teach the child how to break up work into small, manageable segments; they can incorporate physical activity into the daily classroom schedule; and they can offer alternative ways for the child to demonstrate what he or she has learned, such as individual conferences or tape-recorded reports, instead of written reports (M.A. Stewart & Olds, 1973).

ADHD is sometimes treated with psychoactive (mood-altering) drugs, most often stimulants, prescribed to help children focus on the task at hand and reduce problem behaviors. In the short run, the drugs often help, but at the end of a few years, children who have been treated with drugs do not do any better on academic achievement tests than children who have not (McDaniel, 1986). Furthermore, drugs do not help all hyperactive children, and the long-range effects of drugs on these children—whom many believe to be basically normal—is not known. It is best, then, to consider drugs only as a last resort. If they are used, they work best combined with behavior modification programs that teach social skills and control of impulsive behavior (McDaniel, 1986; M.A. Stewart & Olds, 1973).

One treatment that has received much attention is a diet free of artificial food colorings and flavorings. However, an additive-free diet seems to help only a small number of hyperactive children, and the National Institutes of Health do not recommend it as a treatment in all cases (Hadley, 1984). Recent research suggests that hyperactive children may benefit from eating protein-rich breakfasts, but such findings are only preliminary (Conners, 1988).

Many hyperactive children grow up to function normally as adults, and only a few have significant psychiatric or antisocial disorders (Mannuzza, Klein, Bonagura, Konig, & Shenker, 1988).

Educating Children with Disabilities   In 1975, Congress passed the Education for All Handicapped Children Act (Public Law 94-142), which ensures appropriate public education for all handicapped children. This law provides for evaluation of each child's needs and design of an appropriate program, for involvement of parents in deciding about children's education, and for allocation of necessary funds. Of the children affected by the law, 8 out of 10 are mentally retarded, learning-disabled, or speech-impaired.

mainstreaming Integration of handicapped and nonhandicapped children in the same classroom.

This law requires *mainstreaming*, integration of handicapped with nonhandicapped youngsters, as much as possible. Under mainstreaming, handicapped children are in regular classes with nonhandicapped youngsters for all or part of the day, instead of being segregated in special classes. This approach helps handicapped people learn to get along in a society in which most people do not share their impediments, and helps nonhandicapped people get to know

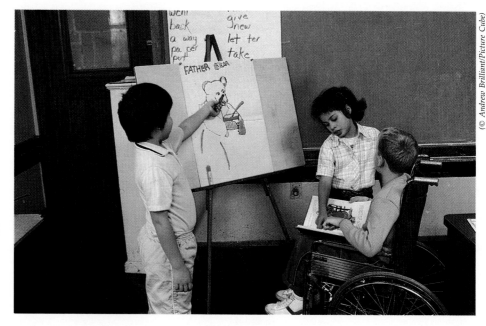

Children with disabilities seem to do best in schools that combine mainstreaming with special classes. This boy in a wheelchair might be in a regular academic class but receive special physical training while his classmates go to gym.

and understand handicapped people. However, critics of this policy maintain that handicapped children can be taught better and more humanely in small classes by specially trained teachers.

Retarded children do about the same academically in mainstreamed classes as in special classes (Gruen, Korte, & Baum, 1974). However, they are not accepted socially by their normal classmates; mainstreaming does not seem to diminish the stigma of being retarded (Taylor, Asher, & Williams, 1987).

Mainstreaming requires innovative teaching techniques that meet the needs of all students, and not all teachers can rise to the challenge. Many, however, have effectively taught classes of both handicapped and nonhandicapped students, drawing on teachers' aides, individual tutors, and computers (D. Thomas, 1985). The best solution seems to be a combination of mainstreaming and special classes. A retarded child, for example, might be able to take physical education or shop in a regular class, but receive academic instruction in a class with slow learners. Or a child with cerebral palsy might be in a regular academic class but receive special physical training while classmates go to gym.

Gifted, Creative, and Talented Children

Giftedness   Stephen A. Baccus began to study law at age 14 and graduated from law school at age 16. At the time of this writing he is 19—and cannot take the New York State bar examination until he turns 21, even though he is already a partner in a law firm in Florida. He did win one legal victory, however. In ruling as unconstitutional the state law that those who take the bar exam must have begun legal study after age 18, a judge said, "The prospective Mozarts of the legal profession deserve better" (Howe, 1988, p. 31).

The obstacles in the path of this former child prodigy are a sign that giftedness can be a mixed blessing. This young lawyer's problems are apparently due more to factors outside himself, but many promising children—more than half, according to one report—achieve below their tested potential (National Commission on Excellence in Education, 1983). Why is this so? One reason is that schools often do not meet their needs for intellectual stimulation.

About 2.5 million children—some 3 to 5 percent of the school population—are estimated to be gifted, but fewer than 1 million receive special attention. The number of mentally retarded children in the population is about the same, but more funds are allocated for their education (Horowitz & O'Brien, 1986). This is ironic when we consider the potential value to society of people with special gifts. In considering the gifted among us, we need to define our terms—and then look at the best way to nurture special abilities.

Defining and identifying giftedness   Like intelligence, giftedness is hard to define and is defined differently by different people. The traditional definition and the one most often used to select children for special programs has been quite narrow—an IQ score of 130 or higher (Horowitz & O'Brien, 1986). But this definition makes it difficult to identify creative children (whose unusual answers often lower their test scores), gifted children from minority groups (whose abilities may not be well developed, even though the potential is there), and children with aptitudes in only single areas.

We favor a broader definition of *giftedness,* including—but not limited to—one or more of the following: superior general intellect, superiority in a single

giftedness   One or more of the following: superior general intellect, superiority in a single domain (like mathematics or science), artistic talent, leadership ability, or creative thinking.

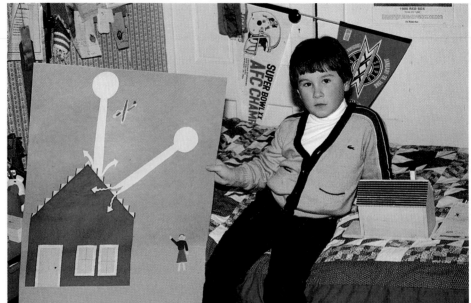

Christopher, 7, shown here with the model of a solar house that he designed, is a gifted child. In line with Gardner's theories of multiple intelligences, Christopher's logical reasoning ability far outdistances some of his other capacities.

domain (like mathematics or science), artistic talent (like painting, writing, or acting), leadership ability, or creative thinking (the ability to look at problems in a new way).

Two new ways of looking at giftedness stem from new theories of intelligence. According to Sternberg (1985a; Davidson & Sternberg, 1984), gifted children process information very efficiently, especially on novel tasks requiring insight. And according to Gardner's controversial theory of multiple intelligences (1985), people can be gifted in one or more of at least seven separate "intelligences," each relatively independent of the others. Some of these "intelligences"—like the musical, the bodily-kinesthetic (moving precisely, as in dance), the interpersonal (understanding others), and the intrapersonal (knowing oneself)—are not tapped by traditional intelligence tests. Others are, including the linguistic (reading and writing), the logical-mathematical (using numbers and solving logical problems), and the spatial (finding one's way around an environment).

The lives of gifted children In the 1920s, Lewis Terman, the professor who brought the Binet test to the United States, located more than 1500 children with IQs of 140 or higher. He tested them for intelligence, school achievement, character, personality, and interests. They were examined medically, their physical measurements were taken, and their parents and teachers were interviewed. The data that emerged demolished the popular stereotype of the bright child as a puny, pasty-faced bookworm. On the contrary, these gifted children were superior in all areas. They tended to be taller, healthier, and better coordinated than the average child. They were also better adjusted and more popular with other children (Wallach & Kogan, 1965).

Researchers at Stanford University have followed the progress of these subjects for more than 6 decades up to the present time. They have found that the subjects' intellectual, scholastic, and vocational superiority has held up over the years. They were 10 times more likely than an unselected group to have graduated from college and 3 times more likely to have been elected to honorary societies like Phi Beta Kappa. By midlife, they were highly represented in listings like *Who's Who* and *American Men of Science* (which also lists women). Almost 90 percent of the men* were in the two highest occupational categories: the professions and higher echelons of business (Terman & Oden, 1959).

The lives of these people seemed to show that intelligence tests can spot children with promise, and that intellectually gifted children do tend to fulfill their promise. However, before we draw a sweeping conclusion, we should note that there were some methodological problems with Terman's study. A major problem is that the sample was not representative of the population of the United States at large. All the subjects were Californians, most came from relatively advantaged homes, Jewish children were overrepresented, and African American and Asian American children were underrepresented.

More recent studies have found that intellectually gifted children have fairly mature and sophisticated attitudes about social relationships and are mature in their moral reasoning. However, they do not always behave according to their attitudes; even though they are gifted, they are still children. On the whole, though, they show average or superior adjustment in their self-concept, the way they handle their lives, and the way they get along with others (Janos & Robinson, 1985).

Two groups of gifted children, however, tend to have social and emotional problems—those with IQs over 180 and those who have high IQs but do not do well in school. The problems of both groups of children seem to stem in part from unsatisfactory schooling—inflexibility, overemphasis on grades, lack of challenge, and unsupportive teachers (Janos & Robinson, 1985). And many very bright children hide their intelligence in an attempt to fit in with their classmates (R.D. Feldman, 1982). Whereas the parents of most children identified as gifted in the United States are well educated and well off, get along well with each other, and are supportive of their children, the homes of underachieving gifted children are less harmonious (Janos & Robinson, 1985).

Educating gifted children Two major approaches to meeting the educational needs of gifted children are skipping grades and enrichment. *Skipping* simply accelerates children's education, moving them through the curriculum quickly. *Enrichment* broadens and deepens their knowledge by providing additional activities like individual research projects and special experiences.

Terman's study inspired the movement to enrich gifted children's education and also suggested that skipping grades is not harmful to bright children (Rafferty, 1984). Other studies, too, indicate that children who have taken part in accelerated programs for the mathematically gifted have not had social or emotional problems (Fox & Washington, 1985). But advocates of enrichment believe that putting gifted children in classes with older students is likely to expose them to psychosocial pressures they are not ready for.

As we find with most issues in child development, individual children have their own unique needs, and the best educational programs are tailored to specific children and specific situations. All children benefit from being encouraged in their areas of interest and ability, and many respond with surprising achievements.

*Because of different societal attitudes toward careers for men and women, the sexes were evaluated separately. Both sexes made a good showing.

Creativity *Defining and identifying creativity* Despite their academic achievements and generally successful lives, the unusually bright people studied by Terman did not show signs of unusual creativity—for example, the group did not produce a great musician, an exceptional painter, or a Nobel laureate. Other studies, too, have found only modest correlations between creativity and intelligence in children and adults (Anastasi & Schaefer, 1971; Getzels & Jackson, 1963; McKinnon, 1968).

This is not surprising when you think about the essence of creativity. *Creativity* is the ability to see things in a new light, to see problems that others may fail to recognize, and then to come up with new, unusual, and effective solutions. Standard intelligence tests measure *convergent thinking*—the ability to come up with a single correct answer. By definition, however, creativity involves *divergent thinking*—the ability to come up with new and unusual answers (Guilford, 1967).

Test developers have tried to use their own creativity to design instruments for testing divergent thinking and identifying creative children. The *Torrance Tests of Creative Thinking,* for example, consist of three parts. In "Thinking Creatively with Words," children are asked to think of ways to improve a toy to make it more fun to play with, and to list unusual uses for and ask unusual questions about common objects. "Thinking Creatively with Pictures" asks children to draw pictures that start from a colored curved shape, a few lines, or pairs of short parallel lines. And "Thinking Creatively with Sounds and Words" uses recordings of words (like *crunch* and *pop*) whose sound suggests their meaning, and asks children to write down what the sounds suggest.

Another popular test of creativity is illustrated in Figure 12-2.

creativity *Ability to see things in a new light, to see problems that others may fail to recognize, and to come up with new, unusual, and effective solutions.*

convergent thinking *Thinking aimed at finding the one "right" answer to a problem.*

divergent thinking *Creative thinking; the ability to discover new, unusual answers to a problem.*

Torrance Tests of Creative Thinking *Test battery developed for use with schoolchildren that measures creativity with words, pictures, and sounds and words.*

FIGURE 12-2
Tests of creativity. It has proven very difficult to develop tests to measure creativity. Part of the reason may be that creative people express their creativity best in situations other than tests. Another reason has to do with the subjectivity of scoring these tests. (*Source:* Adapted from Wallach & Kogan, 1967.)

QUESTIONS	COMMON ANSWER	CREATIVE ANSWER
How many things could these drawings be?		
	Table with things on top.	Foot and toes.
	Three people sitting around a table.	Three mice eating a piece of cheese.
	Flower.	Lollipop bursting into pieces.
	Two igloos.	Two haystacks on a flying carpet.
What do meat and milk have in common?	Both come from animals.	Both are government-inspected.
How many ways could you use a newspaper?	Make paper hats.	Rip it up if you're angry.

BOX 12-5 ■ THE EVERYDAY WORLD

FOSTERING CREATIVITY

The following suggestions to parents for fostering creativity in children are based on research findings (Amabile, 1983; B. Miller & Gerard, 1979).

■ Provide a stimulating environment, tailored as much as possible to a child's special interests and aptitudes, and including lessons or classes and necessary materials. For children who do not show a single special interest, offer a variety of experiences and materials.

■ Teach by focusing on a child's strengths rather than criticizing weaknesses.

■ Tolerate and even encourage nonconforming, unpredictable behavior and help your children avoid or withstand peer pressure. It is easier to do this if you feel secure about your own social station, are uninhibited and unconventional, and do not care what other people think.

■ Set an example by pursuing absorbing occupations or intellectual or artistic hobbies.

■ Deemphasize traditional gender roles and expose children to cultural diversity and to other creative people. All this opens up children's thinking and allows them to recognize new possibilities for expressing their creativity.

■ Respect your children and show confidence in their ability to do well. Give them both freedom and responsibilities. Give children warm support, but enough space to breathe and think for themselves.

■ Do not exert rigid control over children. The most consistent and best-supported finding to emerge from the literature is that on the part of parents vigilance, authoritarianism, dominance, and restrictiveness inhibit the development of creativity. Children who are constantly directed and molded apparently lose the confidence and spontaneity that are essential for the creative spirit.

As of now, tests of creativity are more important for research than for educational or vocational counseling. One problem is that scoring depends heavily on speed—and creative people do not always respond rapidly. Another problem is that although the tests are *reliable* (they yield consistent results), so far there is little or no evidence that they are *valid*—that they identify children who show creativity in nontest situations (Anastasi, 1988).

Fostering creativity Both parents and teachers can encourage creativity. Up till now, however, most schools have discouraged it. Very young children are imaginative in their stories, drawings, and play; but too often when they enter school, their creativity is stifled by teachers who tell them not to color outside the lines, not to make clouds blue and grass red, and to focus on doing things the "right" way (H. Gardner, 1985). On the other hand, schoolchildren are more creative—and better behaved—when their teachers are open to unconventional questions ("Do rocks grow?"), welcome and praise original ideas, and do not grade everything the children do (Torrance, cited in Chance & Fischman, 1987).

Parents, too, can encourage their children to be more creative. Research has found that families of highly creative children help them in specific ways, described in Box 12-5.

Talent: Recognizing and Encouraging Talented Children If Johann Sebastian Bach had not recognized and fostered his children's talents, the world would be poorer. The elements of artistic success seem to be inborn talent, encouragement of that talent, and the artist's own drive to excel (H. Gardner, 1979). A study conducted in Chicago has confirmed and amplified this conclusion. It investigated 120 high achievers who, before the age of 35, had become internationally known pianists, sculptors, athletes, mathematicians, and neurologists (Bloom, 1985).

(Archiv für Kunst und Geschichte/Photo Researchers)

Johann Sebastian Bach plays at the keyboard as his children sing and perform on other musical instruments. Thanks to the children's own talent and to the encouragement they received, several of them became proficient and composed music that is still performed today.

First, a child's talent has to be recognized. Most of the high achievers in the Chicago study became intensely involved in their field before age 12, and many became involved before 10 years of age. Commonly, a parent or another relative who was talented in the same area recognized and encouraged the child's talent at an early age. The mother of one leading ballerina reported that she herself had wanted to be a dancer and that in the delivery room, when she first saw her newborn daughter's long feet, "I knew what I had" (Franceschi, personal communication, 1985).

Second, talent must be nurtured. The teachers who developed the talent of the high achievers in the Chicago study were special themselves. Often, the child's first teacher emphasized joy and playfulness, making talented children first fall in love with their field. Then, when the children discovered how demanding it was, they wanted to master its discipline. Teachers who give rigorous training should take a "longitudinal" approach, getting to know children well, staying with them over several years, and emphasizing long-term goals and each child's individual progress over time. The typical classroom teacher, on the other hand, takes a "cross-sectional" approach, being responsible for children for only 1 school year and judging them by comparing them with their classmates.

The people in this study received periodic emotional "highs" when they were young from regular participation in such public events as recitals and contests that provided a series of short-term goals and served as benchmarks of progress. When they performed well, the praise and rewards inspired them to continue to work, and when they did poorly, they were motivated to try to do better the next time. (At one time, schooling was full of events like spelling bees, debates, and competitions in writing, scientific, and mathematical projects; today such events are rare.)

BOX 12-6 ■ A CHILD'S WORLD AND YOU

WHAT DO YOU THINK?

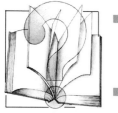

■ Which sort of thinking do you believe benefits society more—convergent or divergent? Does your answer result from divergent thinking?

■ Do you believe that creativity and intelligence are closely linked, loosely linked, or not linked at all?

■ Should schools actively seek out the most creative students and give them special training?

■ Creative children often devote many hours a week to learning the techniques of their field. Do you think that it would be better for them to lead more normal lives?

■ Do you think that mainstreaming imposes too many obstacles for disabled children and that they would be better off in special classes or special schools?

■ Can you think of an example in your own life of a self-fulfilling prophecy?

■ Which approach do you think is better for helping gifted children—enrichment or acceleration?

Finally, the growing child must want to excel. The joys and rewards of the labor must seem like full payment for its rigors. When the people in this study were growing up, their talent continued to assume the most important role in their lives. As adolescents, they often devoted 15 to 25 hours a week to their activity, and they chose their friends from among others with the same interest (Bloom, 1985).

Summary

1   From about age 7 to age 11, children are in the Piagetian stage of concrete operations and can use mental operations to solve problems. Children at this stage are less egocentric than before and are more proficient at tasks requiring logical reasoning, such as conservation. But their reasoning is largely limited to the here and now.

2   Moral development is influenced by the child's maturational level, social role-taking skills, and interactions with other children and adults. According to Piaget, Kohlberg, and Selman, moral development coincides with cognitive development.

3   According to Piaget, moral development occurs in two stages. The first, morality of constraint, is characterized by moral rigidity. The second, morality of cooperation, is characterized by moral flexibility.

4   Selman's theory links moral development with the ability to take roles.

5   Kohlberg extended Piaget's view to include six stages of moral reasoning organized on three levels: preconventional morality, morality of conventional role conformity, and morality of autonomous moral principles.

6   Memory improves greatly during middle childhood because children's short-term memory capacity increases rapidly and because children become more adept at using mnemonic strategies such as rehearsal, categorization, elaboration, and external aids. Metamemory (the understanding of how memory works) also improves.

7   The intelligence of school-age children is assessed by group tests (such as the Otis-Lennon School Ability Test) and individual tests (such as the WISC-R). While IQ tests are good predictors of school success, critics claim that intelligence tests miss other important aspects of intelligent behavior.

8   Developers of intelligence tests have tried to devise "culture-fair" tests, tests that focus on experiences common across cultures. None of these attempts have been completely successful.

9 Differences in performance on intelligence tests between cultural and ethnic groups appear to result from differences in typical environment rather than any inborn differences between groups.

10 Children develop understanding of increasingly complex syntax during middle childhood. Although the ability to communicate improves, even older children may not have a complete awareness of the processes of communication. Children's humor grows as cognitive and linguistic abilities develop.

11 Teachers influence children's success in school and thus their self-esteem. Self-fulfilling prophecies often limit the achievement of poor and minority children. Parents' involvement enhances learning.

12 Mental retardation is below-average intellectual functioning, a deficiency in adaptive behavior appropriate to current age, and the appearance of these characteristics before age 18. Both biological and environmental factors are related to mental retardation.

13 Learning disabilities are disorders that interfere with specific aspects of school achievement. The causes are unclear. Many learning-disabled children can lead productive lives if they get early individual attention.

14 Under the law in the United States, every handicapped child is entitled to an appropriate education at public expense. Children must be mainstreamed (placed in regular classes) as much as possible.

15 The traditional definition of giftedness is having an IQ score of 130 or higher, although this narrow definition misses some gifted children. The validity of tests of creativity is questionable.

16 Although Terman's study found that gifted children tend to be successful as adults, some fail to live up to their potential, possibly because schools do not meet their needs.

17 The development of gifts, talents, and creativity depends greatly on nurturance. The child's drive is also important. Special school programs stress enrichment or acceleration. Each meets the needs of some students.

Key Terms

concrete operations (page 419)
conservation (419)
horizontal decalage (420)
morality of constraint (421)
morality of cooperation (422)
role-taking (423)
preconventional morality (424)
morality of conventional role conformity (424)
morality of autonomous moral principles (424)
sensory memory (428)
short-term memory (428)
long-term memory (428)
rehearsal (428)
categorization (428)
elaboration (428)
metamemory (428)
Wechsler Intelligence Scale for Children (WISC-R) (431)

Otis-Lennon School Ability Test (431)
System of Multicultural Pluralistic Assessment (SOMPA) (435)
syntax (437)
metacommunication (438)
self-fulfilling prophecy (442)
mental retardation (443)
dyslexia (444)
learning disabilities (LDs) (444)
attention-deficit hyperactivity disorder (ADHD) (445)
mainstreaming (446)
giftedness (447)
creativity (450)
convergent thinking (450)
divergent thinking (450)
Torrance Tests of Creative Thinking (450)

Suggested Readings

Bloom, B.S. (1985). *Developing talent in young people.* New York: Ballantine. An absorbing report of a project in which researchers interviewed 120 accomplished young pianists, sculptors, swimmers, tennis champions, mathematicians, and research neurologists and their parents, teachers, and coaches. The book emphasizes the importance of parents' and teachers' active development of young people's abilities.

Coles, R. (1986). *The moral life of children.* Boston: Atlantic Monthly. A prominent child psychiatrist offers his rebuttal to the Kohlbergian theory that moral development rests on cognitive development and that schoolchildren are too young to live profoundly moral lives. The special strength of the book is its many moving quotations of children discussing morality in their own experience.

Eysenck, H.J., & Kamin, L. (1981). *The intelligence controversy.* New York: Wiley. A lively debate on whether intelligence is the result of heredity or environment, by prominent advocates of the two points of view, complete with attacks, counterattacks, and rebuttals.

Goertzel, V., & Goertzel, M.G. (1978). *Cradles of eminence.* Boston: Little, Brown. An absorbing study of the childhood of some 400 prominent persons that seeks to relate factors of early life to eventual success. It brings together biography, autobiography, and professional literature about gifted children and adults.

Simon, S.B., & Olds, S.W. (1977). *Helping your child learn right from wrong.* New York: McGraw-Hill. A self-help manual for parents for establishing moral values and emotional self-awareness in children. The authors explain why values themselves cannot be taught but how parents can teach children a process for arriving at their own values.

CHAPTER 13

PERSONALITY AND SOCIAL DEVELOPMENT IN MIDDLE CHILDHOOD

Have you ever felt like nobody?
Just a tiny speck of air.
When everyone's around you,
And you are just not there.

Karen Crawford, age 9

PREVIEW QUESTIONS

■ How do Freud and Erikson explain the personality changes of middle childhood?
■ How do children develop a self-concept?
■ How do schoolchildren view friendship, and what role does it play in their lives?
■ What is the impact on children of parents' jobs, divorce, and remarriage?
■ What are some common childhood emotional disturbances, and how are they treated?
■ What enables "resilient" children to withstand stress?

WHEN VICKY WAS 9½, she went to a 2-week sleep-away camp for the first time. The brief notes and cards she sent home during the first week were cheerful and businesslike. Then, 10 days after camp began, she wrote this letter:

> Dear Mommy,
>
> I'm very homesick. My counselors expect me to have my sneakers on in 1 second. And if I don't have them on in 10 seconds, they start yelling at me. If we aren't at a certain place at a certain time, they start yelling—even if we're 2 minutes late! If we go canoeing and we're late for the next period, they blame it all on us! I miss you terribly! I just want to come home now! The girls in my cabin are all 10, and they aren't very nice at all. I don't want to stay here anymore. I want to be home with you! I miss you and Daddy and everybody else. Please write to me soon.
>
> Love, Vicky

After shedding a few maternal tears, Ellen comforted herself with the thought that Vicky would be home with her family the next day. More important, though, Ellen realized that although a child's loneliness is hard on a mother, parents cannot protect their children from all unhappiness. Nor should they. Children need to learn to overcome the low moments in life, and they have to become independent, fully functioning human beings. (The following summer, in fact, Vicky eagerly went to another sleep-away camp, a place she returned to for two more summers; in later years she considered these summers high points of her life.)

In this chapter, we trace the rich and varied lives of school-age children as their world expands, and we look at the social and personality growth that accompanies their cognitive growth. We explore the way youngsters develop a more realistic concept of themselves and of surviving and succeeding in their culture. We examine the shift in their relationships as they become more independent of parents and more involved with other people, particularly other children. And we see how, through interaction with peers, they make discoveries about their own attitudes, values, and skills. Still, the family remains a vital influence, and we explore how the lives of children of this age have been profoundly affected by such new family patterns as dual employment, divorce, and remarriage.

Although most children are healthy, both physically and emotionally, some suffer emotional disorders of one sort or another; we look at some of these problems and see how some seem to result from stress and others from biological malfunction. And we look at resilient children, who emerge from the stresses of childhood healthier and stronger.

We begin our discussion by considering the self-concept, which is central to personality and social development during the middle childhood years.

The Self-Concept

DEVELOPING A SELF-CONCEPT

"Who in the world am I? Ah, *that's* the great puzzle," said Alice in Wonderland, after her size had abruptly changed—again. Solving Alice's "puzzle" entails a lifelong process of getting to know the developing self.

The *self-concept* is our sense of self. The *basis* of our self-concept is our knowledge of what we have been and done; its *function* is to guide us in deciding what to be and do in the future. The self-concept, then, helps us to understand ourselves and also to control or regulate our behavior (Markus & Nurius, 1984). Let us see how children develop both self-knowledge and self-regulation.

Beginnings: Self-Recognition and Self-Definition

The sense of self grows slowly. It begins in infancy, with *self-awareness:* Vicky gradually realizes that she is a being separate from other people and things, with the ability to reflect on herself and her actions. At about 18 months, she has her first moment of *self-recognition* when she recognizes herself in the mirror.

The next step is *self-definition.* This comes when Vicky identifies the characteristics she considers important to describe herself. At age 3, Vicky thinks of herself mostly in terms of externals—her ponytailed hair, her neat house, her activities in preschool. Not until about age 6 or 7 does Vicky begin to define herself in psychological terms. She now develops a concept of who she is (the *real self*) and also of who she would like to be (the *ideal self*). By the time she achieves this growth in self-understanding, Vicky has made significant progress in a related area: her behavior is regulated less by her parents and more by herself (see Chapter 7 for a discussion of self-regulation). The ideal self incorporates many of the "shoulds" and "oughts" Vicky has learned and helps her control her impulses for the sake of being considered a "good" girl (Maccoby, 1980).

self-concept Sense of self, which guides one in deciding what to do in the future.

self-awareness Realization, beginning in infancy, of separateness from other people, eventually allowing reflection on one's own actions in relation to social standards.

self-recognition Ability to recognize one's own image.

self-definition Physical and psychological characteristics one considers important to describe oneself.

real self Person's concept of what he or she is like; compare *ideal self.*

ideal self Person's concept of what he or she wishes to be like; compare *real self.*

Coordination of Self-Regulation and Social Regulation

The sense of self might seem like the most personal thing in the world. But most theoreticians and researchers see self-concept as a *social* phenomenon, "the meeting ground of the individual and society" (Markus & Nurius, 1984, p. 147). In middle childhood, Jason looks around himself, sees what his society expects, and blends its expectations with the picture he already has of himself—and his self-concept evolves.

Now, in middle childhood, Jason can do more things than he could as a preschooler. And in fact he does more things and is involved with more people. He is also handed more responsibilities: to do his homework, to rake leaves, to wash dishes, to obey rules at home and school, and sometimes to help care for his younger sister. Jason begins to regulate his behavior not only to get what he needs and wants (as he did earlier), but also to meet other people's needs and wants.

As Jason internalizes society's behavioral standards and values, he coordinates personal and social demands, and he now does things voluntarily (like homework and sharing) that he would have needed prodding to do at an earlier age.

As they strive to become functioning members of society, children must fulfill several important tasks toward the development of self-concept (Markus & Nurius, 1984). They must (among other things) do the following:

- *Expand their self-understanding* to reflect other people's perceptions, needs, and expectations. They have to learn what it means to be a friend, a teammate, or a member of a dramatic cast.
- *Learn more about how society works*—about complex relationships, roles, and rules. Jason comes to realize, for example, that his mother had a mother herself, and that his track coach can be nice at one moment and mean at another.
- *Develop behavioral standards* that are both personally satisfying and accepted in society. This is sometimes difficult for children, since they belong to *two* societies—that of the peer group and that of adults—which sometimes have conflicting standards.
- *Manage their own behavior.* As children take responsibility for their own actions, they must *believe* that they can follow both personal and social standards, and they must develop the ability to *do* it.

Self-Esteem

Self-Esteem in Middle Childhood Middle childhood is an important time for the development of **self-esteem,** a positive self-image or self-evaluation. Children compare their real selves and their ideal selves and judge themselves by how well they measure up to the social standards and expectations they have taken into their self-concept and by how well they perform. Children's opinions of themselves have tremendous impact on their personality development. Indeed, a favorable self-image may be the key to success and happiness throughout life. Let us look at two typical examples.

Jason likes himself. Confident of his own abilities, he approaches life with an open attitude that unlocks many doors. He can take criticism without going to pieces; and when he feels strongly about something he wants to say or do, he

self-esteem *Favorable self-evaluation or self-image.*

is willing to risk making other people angry. This makes him able to challenge parents, teachers, and others in authority. Unburdened by self-doubt, he feels that he can cope with obstacles, and he solves problems in original, innovative ways. Because he believes that he *can* succeed in the goals he sets for himself, he generally *does* succeed. His success enhances his self-respect and makes it easier for him to respect and love others. They, in turn, admire, respect, and enjoy him.

On the other hand, Peter, who does not feel good about himself, is hampered wherever he turns. Convinced that he cannot succeed, he does not try very hard, and his lack of effort almost always ensures failure, resulting in a spiral of lack of confidence and lack of success. He often worries about whether he is doing the right thing—and often, in fact, he is not. He breaks things and hurts people's feelings, even though he tries so hard to please others that he often strikes people as "wimpy." He is plagued by one unexplained pain after another. Because of his self-doubt, he is not much fun to be with, and so he has trouble making and keeping friends—which, of course, drives his opinion of himself even lower.

These two portraits are composites drawn from an important study on self-esteem in children. Coopersmith (1967) administered a questionnaire to hundreds of fifth- and sixth-graders of both sexes. The boys and girls in the initial sample did not differ, on the average; but for intensive interviewing and observation, Coopersmith chose 85 boys and no girls, to eliminate gender as a possible factor. Although the final sample was limited to middle-class white boys within only a 2-year age span, the findings may apply more widely.

Coopersmith concluded that people base their self-image on four criteria:

1 *Significance*—the extent to which they feel loved and approved by those who are important to them
2 *Competence*—ability to perform tasks they consider important
3 *Virtue*—attainment of moral and ethical standards
4 *Power*—the extent to which they influence their own and others' lives

Although people may draw favorable pictures of themselves if they rate high on some of these measures and low on others, they are more likely to rate themselves high if they rate high on all four criteria.

Not surprisingly, the boys in the study who had high self-esteem were more popular and did better in school than those with low self-esteem, who were more likely to be loners, bed-wetters, or poor students. No relationship showed up between self-esteem and height, weight, or physical attractiveness. But family influences did make a difference. Boys who were firstborn or only children, those who had warm parents, and those with dominant mothers were likely to have high self-esteem.

Parenting Styles and Self-Esteem By and large, the parents of the boys with a good self-image were authoritative (see Chapter 10). These parents loved and accepted their sons and made strong demands for academic performance and good behavior. Within clearly defined and firmly enforced limits, they showed respect and allowed individual expression. In disciplining their sons, they relied more on rewards than on punishment. Furthermore, the parents themselves had high self-esteem and led active, rewarding lives.

Parents who are both democratic and strict help their children in several

Self-image has a major impact on personality development. This little girl is likely to feel good about herself if she considers herself both competent and "good," if she feels a measure of control over her life, and if she feels that the important people in her life love and approve of her.

ways, according to Coopersmith. By establishing clear, consistent rules, they let children know what behavior is expected of them. Knowing what to expect helps children gain internal control; as they function within rule systems, they learn to consider the demands of the outside world. And children of demanding parents know that their parents believe in their ability to meet demands—and care enough to insist that they do.

It seems obvious that parents' treatment of children affects the children's feelings about themselves, but there is another way to look at the relationship between parenting and children's self-esteem. Children with high self-esteem may have characteristics that encourage their parents to be loving, firm, and democratic. Children who are self-confident, cooperative, and competent are easy to bring up. Thus, we again see the bidirectionality of influence between parents and children—how they continually affect each other (Maccoby, 1980).

THEORETICAL PERSPECTIVES ON THE SELF-CONCEPT IN MIDDLE CHILDHOOD

Each of the major theories of personality we discuss in this book offers a perspective on why and how the self-concept develops in middle childhood.

Sigmund Freud: The Latency Period

latency period In Freud's terminology, a period of relative sexual calm that occurs during middle childhood after the Oedipus complex has been resolved.

Freud—whose central concern was the development of the self—termed middle childhood the *latency period* of psychosexual development, a period of relative sexual calm between the turbulence of early childhood and the storminess of adolescence. By this time, he said, youngsters have resolved the Oedipal conflict, adopted gender roles, and developed a superego to keep the id in check. Freed from dominance of the id, children can become socialized rapidly, develop skills, and learn about themselves and society. Thus the self-concept can evolve.

Although middle childhood clearly *is* a time of rapid socialization, Freud's idea that it is a period of asexuality, or lack of interest in sex, has been largely discredited. Instead, many contemporary researchers believe that children of this age hide their interest in sex because they have learned that adults disapprove of it, but that they still engage in sex play, masturbate, and ask questions about sex (Calderone & Johnson, 1981).

Erik Erikson: Crisis 4—Industry versus Inferiority

industry versus inferiority In Erikson's theory, the fourth crisis that children face; they must learn the skills of their culture or risk developing feelings of inferiority.

Erikson, too, sees middle childhood as a time of relative emotional calm, when children can attend to their schooling and learn the skills their culture requires. The characteristic crisis of this period is that of *industry versus inferiority,* and the issue to be resolved is a child's capacity for productive work. Children in all cultures have to learn the skills they need to survive; the specifics depend on what is important in a society. For example, Arapesh boys in New Guinea, no longer content merely to play, learn to make bows and arrows and to lay traps for rats; Arapesh girls learn to plant, weed, and harvest. Inuit children of Alaska learn to hunt and fish. Children in industrialized countries learn to count, read, and use computers.

These efforts at mastery can help children form a positive self-concept. The "virtue" that develops with successful resolution of this crisis is *competence,* a

Middle childhood is a time for learning the skills that one's culture considers important. In rural Haiti, children learn how to load a donkey's baskets and lead it to market. In the United States, children learn to count, read, and use computers.

view of the self as able to master skills and complete tasks. As children compare their own abilities with those of their peers, they construct a sense of who they are. If they feel inadequate by comparison, they may return to "the more isolated, less tool-conscious familial rivalry of the oedipal time" (Erikson, 1950, p. 260). If, on the other hand, they become *too* industrious, they may neglect their relationships with other people and become "workaholic" adults.

Social-Learning Theory

Social-learning theorists believe that school-age children's keen self-awareness and observation make them more receptive to the influence of people they admire or people they perceive as powerful and rewarding. Whereas the younger child responds mostly to material reinforcers, in middle childhood social reinforcers—the approval or disapproval of parents, teachers, and peers—become more powerful shapers of self-concept and behavior.

Cognitive-Developmental Theory

Because school-age children are less egocentric than younger children (according to Piaget), they can see themselves better from other people's viewpoints and are more sensitive to what others think of them. Their increasing ability to decenter enables them to take more than one view of the self. Instead of thinking of himself as "always nice," Jason can recognize that "Today I'm generous, but yesterday I was mean." This change allows greater complexity in moral reasoning and enables him to consider social as well as personal needs.

The information-processing approach (one branch of cognitive theory) views the self-concept as a **self-schema** (plural, *self-schemata*), or set of "knowledge structures," which organizes and guides the processing of information about the self (Markus & Nurius, 1984, p. 158). Children build, test, and modify their self-schemata (hypotheses about themselves) on the basis of their social

self-schema *According to the information-processing approach, a set of "knowledge structures" which guide and organize the processing of information about the self and help children decide how to act.*

experiences. Self-schemata help children use the results of their past behavior to make quick judgments for acting in the present and to define the possible self of the future. Strong and lasting self-schemata ("I am popular," "I am a good student," "I am a fast runner") may take shape during middle childhood as the many physical, intellectual, and social skills that children develop allow them to see themselves as valuable members of society (Markus, 1980).

Aspects of Personality Development in Middle Childhood

EVERYDAY LIFE

"You're it!" "No, *you're* it!" For thousands of years, impromptu games of tag, catch, jacks, marbles, and "let's pretend" have served the time-honored mandate of childhood: to learn through play. Through games like these, children are in physical contact with others, gain confidence in their ability to do a variety of things, and practice using their imagination and getting along with others. Play offers socially acceptable ways to compete, to blow off energy, and to act aggressively.

Today, however, we are seeing new social patterns, as technology changes the tools and habits of leisure. Television has turned many children into "couch potatoes." Computer games demand few social skills. Children are engaging in more organized sports, which replace children's rules with adult rules, and in which adult referees settle disputes so that children need not find ways to resolve matters among themselves.

In other ways, too, the society of childhood mirrors changes in the larger society. Children of today's changing families act, think, and live differently from children born a generation or two ago. Many children live with only one parent. Some go to day care after school instead of coming home to a waiting parent; others care for themselves and for younger brothers or sisters. Some children spend a great deal of time without supervision; some have heavily organized schedules of activities.

How Do Children Spend Their Time?

Studies of the time children spend on various activities sketch a virtual portrait of elementary school children. American children spend about two-thirds of their time on sleeping, eating, school, personal care, housework, and attendance at church or synagogue—leaving about 55 hours a week for leisure (Institute for Social Research, 1985; see Table 13-1).

What do children *choose* to do? Mainly, they like to play (alone or with other children) and watch television. These two activities take up from 50 to 70 percent of their free time. Younger children (ages 6 to 8) spend more time playing. But somewhat older children (9 to 11 years old) have been seduced by television which now consumes an average of 2½ to 4 hours a day, according to various studies (W.A. Collins, 1984; Institute for Social Research, 1985).

Even though many school-age youngsters spend much of their leisure time on sports, clubs, church groups, scouting, camps, private lessons, and other organized activities (W.A. Collins, 1984), children watch more television during

TABLE 13-1

HOW SCHOOL-AGE CHILDREN SPEND THEIR TIME; CHILDREN'S TOP 10 ACTIVITIES (AVERAGE HOURS AND MINUTES PER DAY)				
	WEEKDAY		WEEKEND	
ACTIVITY	AGES 6–8	AGES 9–11	AGES 6–8	AGES 9–11
Sleeping	9:55	9:08	10:41	9:56
School	4:52	5:15	—	—
Television	1:39	2:26	2:16	3:05
Playing	1:51	1:05	3:00	1:32
Eating	1:21	1:13	1:20	1:18
Personal care	0:49	0:40	0:45	0:44
Household work	0:15	0:18	0:27	0:51
Sports	0:24	0:21	0:30	0:42
Church	0:09	0:09	0:56	0:53
Visiting someone	0:15	0:10	0:08	0:13

Source: Institute for Social Research, 1985.

the elementary school years than during any other period of childhood. Eleven- and twelve-year-old boys watch most, particularly action and adventure shows; and disadvantaged children are 3 times as likely to be heavy viewers as other children (W.A. Collins, 1984; Institute for Social Research, 1985; Medrich, Roizen, Rubin, & Buckley, 1982). It is not surprising that children who read every day watch less television. But even children who read almost every day at age 9 are less likely to read by age 13 (National Assessment of Educational Progress, 1982).

With Whom Do Children Spend Their Time?

When Jason was 10, Julia and Jess drove 300 miles to visit him at summer camp. When they arrived, he waved, said, "Hi, Mom; hi, Dad," and then went back to playing softball.

School-age children spend relatively little time with their parents (Medrich et al., 1982); the peer group takes up more time. Just counting minutes and hours can be misleading, however. Qualitative measures reveal that in middle childhood, just as in earlier years, relationships with parents are still the most important ones in children's lives.

In one recent study, for example, researchers gave questionnaires about relationships to 199 fifth- and sixth-graders, most of them middle-class (Furman & Buhrmester, 1985). The way the children rated the important people in their lives revealed that different relationships serve different purposes. The children rated relationships with parents most important. They looked to their parents for affection; guidance; lasting, dependable bonds; and affirmation of competence or value as a person. They rated mothers higher than fathers as companions, and were generally more satisfied with their relationships with their mothers than those with their fathers.

After parents, the most important people in the children's lives were grandparents, because grandparents are often warm and supportive, offering affection and enhancement of worth. Although the children looked for and got guidance from teachers, they were least satisfied with relationships with teachers.

Children turned most often to friends for companionship, and to friends

After their parents, the most important people in many children's lives are their grandparents. A warm and supportive grandfather, who is also handy at fixing a bike, can boost self-esteem—and is fun to be with.

and mothers for intimacy. Although the children also looked to siblings (especially those of the same sex and close in age) for companionship and intimacy and to older siblings for guidance, sibling relationships generally involved the most conflict.

Some gender differences showed up. Girls were closer to their mothers than their fathers; for boys, there was no difference. Also, girls relied on best friends more than boys did, and their friendships were more intimate, affectionate, and worth-enhancing. Since these three qualities seem to be more characteristic of older children's friendships, school-age girls' closest friendships may be more mature than boys'. Other research has also shown that girls value *depth* of relationships, while boys value *number* of relationships (Furman, 1982).

Now, let us look more closely at this diverse and nurturing social world to see the importance of the peer group and the family.

THE CHILD IN THE PEER GROUP

Babies are aware of one another, and preschoolers begin to make friends; but not until middle childhood does the peer group come into its own.

Functions and Influence of the Peer Group

In our highly mobile, age-segregated society, the peer group is a particularly strong influence, for both good and ill, as the following discussion shows.

Positive Effects It is among other children that youngsters develop a self-concept and build self-esteem. They form opinions of themselves by seeing themselves as others see them. They have a basis of comparison—a realistic gauge of their own abilities and skills. Only within a large group of their peers can children get a sense of how smart, how athletic, and how personable they are.

The peer group also helps children choose values to live by. Testing their opinions, feelings, and attitudes against those of other children helps them sift through the values they previously accepted unquestioningly from parents and decide which to keep, which to discard. And the peer group offers emotional security. Sometimes another child can provide comfort that an adult cannot. It is reassuring to find out that a friend also harbors "wicked" thoughts that would offend an adult. Finally, the peer group helps children learn how to adjust their needs and desires to those of others—when to yield and when to stand firm.

On the positive side, then, the peer group counterbalances parents' influence, opens new perspectives, and frees children to make independent judgments.

Negative Effects: Conformity On the other hand, the peer group may hold out some undesirable values at this age of emerging self-regulation, and some children (especially if they have low status in the group) may be too weak to resist. Children are most susceptible to pressure to conform during middle childhood (Costanzo & Shaw, 1966).

One classic study on conformity tested children's reactions to group pressure to give answers contrary to what they saw with their own eyes. First, ninety 7- to 13-year-olds took a written test asking them to compare the lengths of lines on 12 cards and indicate which line was shorter or longer. Next, the subjects

(© 1984 Roger V. Dollarhide/Monkmeyer Press)

Only among peers—like this group of summer campers shown with their counselors—can children get a sense of how smart, how athletic, and how personable they are.

repeated the test orally. But this time each subject sat in a room with eight "confederates." The "confederates" were the eight brightest children in the actual subject's class, and they had been told to give wrong answers to 7 of the 12 cards. The actual subject—the ninth child—was caught unaware by the wrong answers and was torn between describing what he or she actually saw and going along with the group. Only 43 percent of the 7- to 10-year-old subjects and 54 percent of the 10- to 13-year-old subjects answered the seven questions correctly, even though almost all these youngsters had given the correct answers on the written test (Berenda, 1950).

In talking about the experiment afterward, children indicated that even though they were anxious about the task, they still conformed. One 11-year-old girl said:

> I had a funny feeling inside. You know you are right and they are wrong and you agree with them. And you still feel you are right and you say nothing about it. . . . I just gave their answers. If I had the test alone, I wouldn't give the answers I gave. (Berenda, 1950, p. 232)

The effects of conformity can, of course, be more serious than giving wrong answers on a test. Peer influence is strongest when issues are ambiguous; since we live in a world with many ambiguous issues that call for careful judgment, peer-group influences can have major consequences. And although peer groups do many constructive things together—playing games, scouting, and the like—it is usually in the company of peers that children shoplift, begin to smoke and drink, sneak into movies, and perform other antisocial acts. Sixth-graders who are rated more "peer-oriented" report engaging in more of this kind of antisocial behavior than "parent-oriented" children (J. C. Condry, Siman, & Bronfenbrenner, 1968). On the other hand, youngsters who are headed for real trouble with the law tend to be those who do *not* get along with peers. These children are often immature and lack social skills (Hartup, 1984).

For children as well as adults, some degree of conformity to group standards is a healthy mechanism of adaptation. It is unhealthy only when it becomes destructive or makes people act against their better judgment.

Who Is in the Peer Group?

How Do Peer Groups Generally Form?   Peer groups form naturally among children who live in the same neighborhood or go to school together (Hartup, 1984). Children who play together are usually within a year or two of the same age, though an occasional neighborhood play group will form that includes small children along with older ones. Too wide an age range brings problems with differences in size, interests, and ability levels.

In the elementary school years, peer groups are usually all girls or all boys, for at least two reasons: children of the same sex have common interests, and girls are generally more mature than boys.

How Can Interracial Peer Groups Be Encouraged? *Integration*   Children seek out peers who are like themselves in race and socioeconomic status. Children in segregated neighborhoods may have no other option. However, racial segregation in peer groups (as in adult society) often results from *prejudice*—negative attitudes toward certain groups, which can corrode the self-esteem of members of these groups. Studies conducted from the 1960s to the mid-1970s found anti-black bias among both white and black children in northern and southern American cities, from preschool through the early school years (Morland, 1966; J Williams, Best, & Boswell, 1975).

prejudice Negative attitudes toward certain groups.

Court-ordered school integration, which began in the mid-1950s, has brought more acceptance of different races, even though children still tend to choose friends of the same race. One study of midwestern black and white third- and sixth-graders who had been in integrated classrooms from kindergarten on found that although the youngsters (particularly the older black children) preferred members of their own race, they rated classmates of the other race quite positively (Singleton & Asher, 1979). Integration from the beginning of school may have contributed to these children's acceptance of each other; being together only in the upper grades does not necessarily foster interracial friendships. Singleton and Asher recommend the institution of programs to improve such relations; some programs have been quite effective.

School-based programs   In one study aimed at reducing racial prejudice, researchers tested four different techniques on a sample of white second- and fifth-graders (Katz & Zalk, 1978). The children in the experimental groups were exposed to one of these conditions:

1 *Increased positive racial contact* (children in the study worked in interracial groups on an interesting puzzle and all the children were praised)
2 *Vicarious interracial contact* (subjects heard a story about a sympathetic, resourceful black child)
3 *Reinforcement of the color black* (subjects were given prizes every time they chose a picture of a black animal instead of a white one)
4 *Encouragement to look beyond skin color to find individual differences* (subjects were shown pictures of a black woman with various hairdos and facial expressions; each different-appearing face had a name)

(Erik Anderson/Stock, Boston)

Although children usually choose friends from their own racial group, some school programs have succeeded in breaking down barriers of ignorance and prejudice that often prevent children of different races from working and playing together.

Two weeks after the experiment, the children who had been exposed to any of these conditions showed less prejudice than children in control groups who had received no special treatment. These differences held up 4 to 6 months later, especially for children who had learned to tell the "different" black faces apart and those who had heard the stories about black children. The younger children showed more gains, suggesting that bias can be changed more easily earlier in life.

Another successful program is the *jigsaw* technique. Teachers assign different parts of a project to different children of various ethnic and racial backgrounds. The children soon learn that they can do their assignments more easily if they consult, teach, and listen to each other. They end up liking school better, liking each other better, and liking themselves better (Aronson & Bridgeman, 1979; Aronson, Stephan, Sikes, Blaney, & Snapp, 1978; Geffner, 1978).

Schools provide many other opportunities to rout prejudice. For example, many have recruited and trained minority-group teachers and have emphasized the cultural contributions of minorities.

Friendship

Jason and his best friend play ball together and are in the same scout troop. Vicky met her best friend at school; they eat lunch together, play together during recess, talk on the phone after school, and visit each other's home on the weekends. Having a true friend is a milestone in development. Mutual affection enables children to express intimacy, to bask in a sense of self-worth, and to learn what being human is all about (Furman, 1982; H. S. Sullivan, 1953).

Children may spend much of their free time in groups, but only as individuals do they form friendships. Children's ideas about friendship change enormously during the elementary school years. In middle childhood, a friend is someone a child feels comfortable with, likes to do things with, and can share

Girls tend to develop just one or two close friendships, while boys have more, but less intimate, friendships. These girls are probably in Selman's reciprocal or mutual stage of friendship.

feelings and secrets with. Friendship makes children more sensitive and loving, more able to give and receive respect. Children cannot be true friends or have true friends until they achieve the cognitive maturity to consider other people's viewpoints and needs, as well as their own.

Robert Selman has traced changing forms of friendship through five overlapping stages, on the basis of interviews with more than 250 people between ages 3 and 45 (Selman & Selman, 1979). Although stage 1 includes ages at the beginning of middle childhood, most school-age children are in either stage 2 or stage 3. Selman's five stages are as follows, and all ages are approximate:

■ *Stage 0: Momentary playmateship (ages 3 to 7).* This is the *undifferentiated* level of friendship, when children are egocentric and have trouble considering another person's point of view; they tend to think only about what they want from a relationship. As a result, most very young children define their friends in terms of how close they live ("She's my friend—she lives on my street") and value them for their material or physical attributes ("He's my friend. He has a giant Superman doll and a real swing set").

■ *Stage 1: One-way assistance (ages 4 to 9).* At this *unilateral* level, a "good friend" does what the child wants the friend to do ("She's not my friend anymore, because she wouldn't go with me when I wanted her to" or "He is my friend because he always says yes when I want to borrow his eraser").

■ *Stage 2: Two-way fair-weather cooperation (ages 6 to 12).* This *reciprocal* level overlaps stage 1. It involves give-and-take, but it still serves many separate self-interests, rather than the common interests of the two friends ("We are friends; we do things for each other" or "A friend is someone who plays with you when you don't have anybody else to play with").

■ *Stage 3: Intimate, mutually shared relationships (ages 9 to 15).* At this *mutual* level, children view a friendship as having a life of its own. It is an ongoing, systematic, committed relationship that incorporates more than doing things for each other. The friends become possessive and demand exclusivity ("It takes a long time to make a close friend, so you really feel bad if you find out that your friend is trying to make other friends too"). Girls tend to develop just one or two close friendships; boys have more, less intimate friendships.

■ *Stage 4: Autonomous interdependence (beginning at age 12).* In this *interdependent* stage, children respect friends' need for both dependency and autonomy ("A good friendship is a real commitment, a risk you have to take; you have to be able to support and trust and give, but you have to be able to let go too").

Friendship is very important to the developing child; thus the plight of unpopular children is especially poignant. We next consider popularity and unpopularity.

Popularity

We all want other people to like us. What our peers think of us matters terribly, affecting our present happiness and often our success and well-being for many years.

Why are some children sought out while others are ignored or rebuffed? Why do some children have many friends while others have none? What are popular and unpopular children like? What can be done to help children who are neglected or rejected by their peers? Let us look at these issues.

The Popular Child Popular children share a number of characteristics. They tend to be cooperative and to help other children (Coie & Kupersmidt, 1983; Gottman, Gonso, & Rasmussen, 1975; K. H. Rubin, Daniels-Beirness, & Hayvren, 1982). They are likely to have a good sense of humor (Masten, 1986) and to be physically attractive (R. Lerner & Lerner, 1977). They are healthy and vigorous, well poised, capable of initiative, adaptable, dependable, affectionate, and considerate; and they are original thinkers (Bonney, 1946). They think well of themselves, radiating self-confidence without being overbearing or seeming conceited (Reese, 1961).

Popular children show mature dependence on other children: they ask for help when they need it, and for approval when they think that they deserve it; but they do not cling or make infantile plays for affection (Hartup, 1970). They are not goody-goodies, but they make other people feel good about being with them (Feinberg, Smith, & Schmidt, 1958; Tuddenham, 1951).

The Unpopular Child One of life's saddest figures is the child who is chosen last for every team, is on the fringes of every group, walks home alone after school, is not invited to birthday parties, and sobs in despair. "Nobody wants to play with me."

Why are some children unpopular? Children can be unpopular for many reasons. Some of the causes are in their power to change; others are not. Some unpopular youngsters walk around with a chip on the shoulder, expressing unprovoked aggression and hostility (Dodge, 1983). Others are withdrawn (K. H. Rubin et al., 1982). Unpopular children may act silly and infantile, showing off in immature ways; or they may be anxious and uncertain, so pathetic in their lack of confidence that they repel other children, who find them no fun to

Unpopular children can become better liked if they learn social skills, like carrying on a conversation in which they share information about themselves and show interest in others.

be with. Extremely fat or unattractive children, children who act strange in any way, and retarded or slow-learning youngsters also tend to be outcasts.

How can unpopular children be helped? Popularity in childhood is not a frivolous issue. Aside from the sadness, sense of rejection, and poor self-esteem that unpopular children feel, they are also deprived of a basic developmental experience: the positive interaction with other youngsters that helps them grow as individuals.

Unpopularity during the preschool years is not necessarily cause for concern; but by middle childhood, peer relationships are strong predictors of later adjustment. Children who have trouble getting along with peers are more likely to have psychological problems, to drop out of school, and to become delinquent (Hartup, 1984; Lamb, 1987; Parker & Asher, 1987). (It is not clear, though, whether unpopularity during middle childhood *causes* later disturbances or merely *reflects* developmental problems that show up in more serious form later on.)

Since relationships with other children are vital to children's happiness and healthy emotional development, adults sometimes try to help unpopular children make friends. Children who are simply *neglected* or overlooked by their classmates or other peers may do better in a different class or a new school, or if they join a new club or go to a new camp. But children who are actively *rejected* by their peers usually cannot be helped simply by being moved into a new group or situation; and it is these children who are most at risk of emotional and behavioral problems in adolescence and adulthood. They need to learn how to make other children like them.

In one study, fifth- and sixth-graders received training in social skills. They learned how to carry on a conversation: how to share information about themselves, how to show interest in others by asking questions and how to give help, suggestions, invitations, and advice. When they had a chance to practice their new skills in a group project with other children of their acquaintance, they became better liked by the others than they had been and interacted more with them (Bierman & Furman, 1984).

The children who received the training showed more general and lasting improvement over a 6-week period (according to measures of conversational skills, rates of interaction, acceptance by peers, and self-perception) than a control group who received no training, children who received the training but then did not participate in the peer-group project, and children who took part in the group project but were not taught any skills. We see, then, that unpopular children not only need to be taught social skills but also have to be in situations in which they can use them and in which their peers can see the changes in them. Otherwise, their acquaintances may hold on to their former opinions and not give them a chance to show their new skills.

THE CHILD IN THE FAMILY

"I'm home!" shouts Vicky as she throws open the door, cheeks glowing from the cold, and snow cascading from hat, mittens, and boots. She tries—honestly—to take off all her dripping clothes before she reaches the new rug, but because she is ready to burst with the news of the day, she cannot always remember such trivia.

School-age children today spend more time away from home than ever before. School, friends, games, and entertainments all keep them apart from the family. Yet home is still the most important part of their world, and the people who live there matter most (Furman & Buhrmester, 1985). Let us see how relationships with parents and siblings develop during middle childhood and how societal changes are affecting family life.

Parents and Children: Relationships and Issues

Not surprisingly, Vicky's and Jason's outside obligations and interests increase at a time when they are more self-sufficient and require less physical care and supervision than they used to. Parents spend less than half as much time caring for 5- to 12-year-olds—teaching them, reading and talking to them, and playing with them—as they spend caring for preschoolers (C. R. Hill & Stafford, 1980). Still, parents are very much on the job.

As children's lives change, so do the issues between them and their parents (Maccoby, 1984). One important new area of concern is school. Parents worry about a child's schoolwork and wonder how involved they should be. They may have to deal with a child who complains about the teacher, pretends to be sick to avoid going to school, or plays hooky.

Another issue is friends. Parents usually want to know where their children are and whom they are with when they are not in school. Some parents even tell children whom they may and may not play with. Parents and children often disagree over what household chores children should do, whether they should be paid for doing them, and how much allowance they should get. (Of course, many of these issues are nonexistent in some nonwestern societies, where children over the age of 6 must work to help the family survive.)

The profound changes in children's lives and in the issues that arise with parents bring changes in the ways parents handle discipline and control. Yet, as we will see, most parents do *not* change their basic approach to their job as their children mature.

Discipline   All parents struggle continually to make the right decisions in bringing up their children. They want to raise human beings who think well of themselves and will fulfill their potential. In this struggle, they have to develop effective methods of *discipline.* Although many people think of *discipline* as a synonym for "punishment," the word itself is from the Latin for "knowledge" or "instruction" and is principally defined this way in the dictionary. Parents have different ways of teaching children character, self-control, and moral behavior. And most parents use different methods with school-age children and younger children (Maccoby, 1984; G.C. Roberts, Block, & Block, 1984).

discipline Teaching children character, self-control, and moral behavior.

For example, Jess and Julia rely more on praising Jason for what he does right than on punishing him for what he does wrong. When they do feel that punishment is called for, they usually deprive him of some privilege, like watching his favorite television show. Most of their discipline consists of reasoning. They appeal to his self-esteem ("What happened to the helpful boy who was here yesterday?"), sense of humor ("If you go one more day without a bath, we won't have to look to know when you're coming!"), moral values ("A big, strong boy like you shouldn't sit on the train and let an old person stand"), or appreciation ("Aren't you glad that you have a father who cares enough to remind you to wear boots so that you won't catch a cold?"). Above all, Jason's parents let him know that he is responsible for what happens to him and has to bear the consequences of his behavior. ("No wonder you missed the school bus today—you stayed up too late last night reading in bed! Now you'll have to walk to school.")

This approach to discipline becomes typical as children gain cognitive awareness. School-age children are less likely to knuckle under to sheer power. They are more likely to defer to parents' wishes because they recognize that their parents are fair, that they contribute to the whole family's well-being, and that they often "know better" because of their wider experience. On the other hand, parents often defer to children's growing judgment and take a strong stand only on issues they consider important. For example, parents of schoolchildren tend to relax the imposition of their own taste in clothing except for special occasions, recognizing that children use clothing to express personality and assert independence (Schiro, 1988).

Yet a parent's underlying philosophy seems to remain fairly consistent over time, especially with regard to control over a child, enjoyment of the child, and emotional investment in the child. In one longitudinal study, parents of 3-year-old boys and girls from a wide range of backgrounds filled out long questionnaires—and answered the same questions again when the children were 12 years old (G.C. Roberts et al., 1984). The questions related to independence, control, handling aggression and sex, early training, emphasis on health and achievement, expression of feelings, protectiveness, supervision, and punishment. Over the 9-year period, the mothers' answers correlated on three-fourths of the items and the fathers' on more than half. The parents' basic values and approach to child rearing seemed to remain constant (most of them emphasized rational guidance and praise), although they did change in some ways appropriate to the children's development.

Control and Coregulation   At some point, control of a child's behavior shifts from the parents to the child. During the preschool years, a child's gradual acquisition of self-control and self-regulation reduces the need for constant scrutiny. (But not until adolescence or even later can most young people decide how late to stay out, who their friends should be, and how to spend their money.)

coregulation Transitional stage in the control of behavior in which parents exercise general supervision and children exercise moment-to-moment self-regulation.

Middle childhood is a transitional stage of *coregulation,* in which parent and child share power; "parents continue to exercise general supervisory control, while children begin to exercise moment-to-moment self-regulation" (Maccoby, 1984, p. 191). Coregulation reflects the child's developing self-concept. As children of this age begin to coordinate their own wishes with societal demands, they are more likely to anticipate how their parents or other people will react to what they do, or to accept a reminder from their parents that others will think better of them if they behave differently.

Coregulation is a cooperative process; it succeeds only if parents and children communicate clearly. If children do not let their parents know where they are, what they are doing, and what their problems are—or if parents become preoccupied with their own activities and do not take an interest in their children's—the parents will not be able to judge when to step in (Maccoby, 1984).

To make this transitional phase work, parents need to influence their children when the children are with them and to monitor their behavior when they are not (by phone or through a baby-sitter). Most important is the need for children to learn to monitor their *own* behavior—to adopt acceptable standards, avoid undue risks, and recognize when they need support or guidance from parents (Maccoby, 1984).

No matter what their social class or ethnic group, most parents give their children the all-important gifts of warmth, love, and acceptance.

Variations in Parenting Of course, parents do not treat all their children the same, and a parent may treat the same child differently from one day to the next. Part of this stems from children's differences in personality and behavior, and part from variations in the parents' attitude. Then, different parents vary in the kinds of behavior they allow, their goals for and demands on children, their way of disciplining and motivating children, and the control they exercise.

Research shows some ethnic differences, but we must be careful in interpreting these, because they often turn out to be linked to educational level or prevalence of single-parent families. For example, African American parents appear to be stricter and more punitive than white parents, and Hispanic families tend to stress traditional values like respect for authority (Maccoby, 1984).

Social class differences also show up. Perhaps because they typically have more time available and are freer of financial worries, and perhaps because they have generally had more education, middle-class parents are more likely than working-class parents to pay attention to children and spend time with them; to use complex language with them; to be permissive about their activities and about sexual issues; to tolerate anger; to value happiness, curiosity, and creativity above obedience and respect; to listen to children's views and give children a voice in family decisions; and to demand more maturity, achievement, and independence. Middle-class parents are likely to try to motivate a child rather than give direct orders, and to reason and explain rather than punish (Maccoby, 1984).

No matter what social class or ethnic group they come from, though, most parents give their children warmth, love, and acceptance—the most important requirements for a successful transition to adolescence.

How Parents' Work Affects Children

Since so much of an adult's time, effort, and ego goes into an occupation, a number of researchers have explored how the nature of parents' work affects the family. It is particularly interesting to look at this issue today, since this is a time of transition in American society; the view in the 1990s is very different from that of the 1950s. For example, researchers have studied how the values expressed in adults' roles are passed on to children. In traditional societies, where women stay close to home and men work away from home (in nonindustrial societies, the men might go out to hunt), children are socialized for such adult roles. In such a society Vicky would be encouraged to develop traits consistent with mothering, while Jason would be steered toward risk taking and independence. The United States was largely a traditional society 40 years ago, but now that male and female occupations are converging, children are socialized differently— even those who belong to families that do not follow the currently dominant pattern of two working parents. Let us look at some of the ways parents' work can affect children.*

Mothers' Work   Most of the research on the way mothers' work affects children has focused not on what kind of work mothers do or what demands it makes on them, but on whether they work at all for pay. And much of this research was conducted in, or refers to, a time when working mothers were the exception rather than the rule. Today the working mother is typical: almost 7 out of 10 married women with children under 18, and 8 out of 10 single mothers, are in the work force. About 25 million children have mothers who work outside the home for at least part of the day. Indeed, with more than half of all new mothers going to work soon after giving birth, a growing number of children have never known a time when their mothers were *not* working.

How does outside employment of mothers affect children? The answer depends on many variables, including whether a working mother is married or single, whether she works full time or part time, how she feels about her work and herself, what the family's economic circumstances are, and what arrangements are made for child care. Fifty years of research do not show an overall ill effect of working in and of itself, although some problems are indirectly related to a mother's work, some having to do with substitute child care and some with the mother's task overload, for example. Still, many researchers today emphasize the positive effects of a mother's employment on the entire family.

The mother's psychological state   Since working women often feel more competent, more economically secure, and more in charge of their lives, they tend to have higher self-esteem than homemakers, whose work is generally undervalued in American society. And in general, the more satisfied a woman is with her life, the more effective she is as a parent. This effect cuts across socioeconomic levels, but may be especially significant at lower levels, particularly for single mothers who have had little education.

Working mothers and family interactions   The husband of a working mother can relax more, knowing that he is not solely responsible for the family's financial support. And he can spend more time with his children, since he is less likely to hold a second job.

In working-mother families, the division of labor between parents is some-

---

*This section on the impact of parents' work on children is indebted to Lois Wladis Hoffman (1984), who conceptualized and researched many of the issues. Statements not otherwise referenced in the discussion are based on her analysis.

what less traditional. Even though the typical working mother still has more responsibility for housework and child care, her husband is likely to be somewhat more involved than his counterpart in a homemaker-mother family. He is most involved when the mother has a full-time job, when there is more than one child, when the children are quite young, and when the mother earns at least something close to what he earns (L. W. Hoffman, 1986). Some studies have found that fathers in two-earner families seem to spend very little extra time on child care—only a few minutes a day, and usually only with children under age 3 (Maccoby, 1984). But this conclusion may be misleading, since working-mother families tend to have fewer children and older children and so there are fewer child-care tasks to perform. The father who is involved with his children shows them a nurturing side—shows love, tries to help them with their worries and problems, makes them feel better when they are upset, and gives them continuing care and attention (Carlson, 1984). Thus they see a side of personality that has traditionally been less visible in men.

Working mothers and children's values Daughters of working women and sons of fathers who participate in child care have fewer stereotypes about gender roles than children in "traditional" families (Carlson, 1984). However, this effect seems to depend more on the mother's attitude toward the father's participation in home duties than on how much he actually does (Baruch & Barnett, 1986).

How children react to mothers' working *Infants, toddlers, and preschoolers:* A substantial body of research suggests that no ill effects on babies' or preschoolers' social, emotional, and cognitive development can be traced to mothers' employment (Benn, 1986; Zimmerman & Bernstein, 1983).

But some studies have found that middle-class boys have lower IQs and poorer academic achievement later on if their mothers have worked full time during the boys' preschool years (Bronfenbrenner, Alvarez, & Henderson, 1984; D. Gold & Andres, 1978b; D. Gold, Andres, & Glorieux, 1979). Also, some research suggests that baby boys whose mothers work full time and who, therefore, receive extensive care from other people may become insecurely attached to *both* parents and may have later adjustment problems—unless they are cared for by their fathers (Belsky & Rovine, 1988). The risk is greater for babies who are temperamentally "difficult," who receive poor-quality day care, whose mothers are emotionally distant or insensitive, or whose parents are having marital problems (Belsky & Rovine, 1988; Gamble & Zigler, 1986; Young & Zigler, 1986). It is clear, then, that we have to look at parents' employment in the overall picture of family life.

School-age children: School-age children of employed mothers seem to have two advantages over children of homemakers: they tend to live in more structured homes, with clear-cut rules giving them more household responsibilities; and they are encouraged to be more independent. Encouragement of independence seems to be especially good for girls, helping them to become more competent, to achieve more in school, and to have higher self-esteem; but it may put pressure on some boys (Bronfenbrenner & Crouter, 1982).

The findings for boys are less clear-cut and more varied by social class. For example, boys in both single-parent and two-parent lower-income families seem to benefit when their mothers work; these boys achieve more in school. They are probably benefiting from the family's higher income. Research indicates that

Children whose parents work outside the home become more independent and more self-confident when they know that they are trusted to handle a variety of tasks, like taking a telephone message safely and accurately.

sons of middle-class working mothers have done less well in school than sons of middle-class homemakers (Heyns & Catsambis, 1986). However, the data for this study were collected in the 1960s and 1970s when opportunities for women and options for child care were not as broad as they are today. As society adjusts to the fact that now the working mother is *typical,* there should be fewer negative effects on boys.

Both working mothers and their school-age children complain that they have too little time together (General Mills, Inc., 1977). And many mothers are concerned about the difficulties of supervising their children, especially when the children care for themselves part of the day (see Box 13-1). Problems like these are not, of course, as severe for women who work part time or have flexible hours (Maccoby, 1984).

Adolescents: Both adolescents and their parents can benefit from mothers' employment. In one study, 7 out of 10 teenagers said that their mothers' working had either positive effects or no effects on them (General Mills, Inc., 1981). Teenagers want to be independent—to make their own decisions. Mothers who are at home are more likely to continue to direct adolescents' activities, and when their well-meaning advice or questions are rejected, they often feel rebuffed.

The working mother avoids some of this conflict. She also gains in self-esteem on the job; at home, by contrast, her mothering abilities are needed less—and tested more—at this stage of her children's lives. It is not surprising, then, that working mothers of adolescents seem to feel better about themselves—about their competence, attractiveness, and self-fulfillment—than nonworking mothers of teenagers. Their adolescent children are better adjusted socially, feel better about themselves, have more of a sense of belonging, and get along better than other teenagers with family and with friends at school (D. Gold & Andres, 1978a). Daughters of working women make a particularly strong showing. They "are more outgoing, independent, active, [and] highly motivated, score higher on a variety of indices of academic achievement, and appear better adjusted on social and personality measures" (L. W. Hoffman, 1979, p. 864).

There is a negative side, though: adolescent children of working mothers tend to spend less time on homework and reading and more time watching television (Milne, Myers, Rosenthal, & Ginsburg, 1986); and, with less supervision, they may be more subject to peer pressure leading to behavior problems (see Chapter 16).

What are we to conclude from all these findings on working mothers? The major point is that the dual-income family does not follow any single pattern. We have to look at all the different factors involved. Probably the most influential factor is the parents' attitudes, which seem more significant than whether or not a mother works. "Where the pattern itself produces difficulties, they seem often to stem mainly from the slow pace with which society has adapted to this new family form" (Hoffman, 1989, p. 290). When good child care is available and affordable, when men assume a larger role in the home, and when employers support workers' family roles, the benefits should be felt in millions of American families.

Fathers' Work   Since men have historically worked outside the home whether or not they are fathers, most of the research on how men's work affects families

BOX 13-1 ■ THE EVERYDAY WORLD

WHEN SCHOOL-AGE CHILDREN CARE FOR THEMSELVES

When Jason, 11, comes home from school, he unlocks the door to his house, throws down his books, and feeds his cat before sitting down for a snack. Then he calls Jess (who can be reached at work more easily than Julia) to check in and tell him whether he'll be staying home, going outside to play, or going to a friend's home. Depending on what needs to be done, he may fold clean laundry, set the table, or start dinner. If he wants to watch a special television show at night, he may do his homework in the afternoon.

Jason is among some 2 million "self-care children," school-age children who regularly care for themselves at home without adult supervision because both parents or a single custodial parent works outside the home (C. Cole & Rodman, 1987). Although most self-care takes place after school, some children spend some time alone in the morning or evening, too.

The earlier term *latchkey children* took on negative connotations because there was an image of these children as lonely and neglected. This image now seems to be changing; but there is still very little solid information about the impact of self-care on a child's development. What research exists is contradictory. Some studies report no differences between supervised and self-care children in self-esteem, adjustment at school, or social adjustment; others have found higher levels of fear and more problems at school among self-care children (C. Cole & Rodman, 1987; Rodman & Cole, 1987).

How can parents tell when children are ready for self-care, and how can they make the situation as comfortable as possible? Following are some guidelines (C. Cole & Rodman, 1987; Olds, 1989).

Before children take care of themselves, they should be able to do the following:

■ Control their bodies well enough to keep from injuring themselves
■ Keep track of keys, and handle doors well enough to avoid locking themselves in or out
■ Safely operate necessary household equipment
■ Stay alone without being afraid or lonely
■ Be flexible and resourceful enough to handle the unexpected
■ Be responsible enough to follow important rules
■ Understand and remember spoken and written instructions
■ Read and write well enough to take telephone messages and use a pay phone in an emergency
■ Know what to say and do about visitors and callers (not to tell people they do not know that they are alone, and not to open the door to anyone but family and close friends)
■ Know how to get help in an emergency (how to call police and firefighters, which friends and neighbors to call, what other resources to call on)

Parents and guardians can help self-care children by doing the following:

■ Staying in contact by telephone (preferably by setting up a regular time for check-in calls)
■ Telling children what to do and how to reach parents or another responsible adult in an emergency
■ Setting up a comfortable structure for children's self-care time
■ Instituting safety procedures

Alone at Home: Self-Care for Children of Working Parents, by H. Swan and V. Huston (Prentice-Hall, 1985), is a training manual for 9- to 14-year-olds, giving useful guidance for dealing with difficult situations.

---

has focused on the nature of the work itself. But there are some findings about wider ramifications of fathers' work, which can also apply to women.

The father's psychological state   Some men (like some women) have jobs that do not fully satisfy their psychological needs. This situation can have positive effects: a man whose work is not exciting may throw himself enthusiastically into family life, and through his children gain a sense of accomplishment, fun, intellectual stimulation, moral values, and self-esteem. But it can, of course, have negative effects: for example, some men who have little autonomy at work take out their frustration by being hostile and severe with their children (McKinley, 1964).

Work that does satisfy a father's needs can also have negative effects in addition to its obvious benefits. A father's work may fulfill his needs to such an extent that he will not invest much of himself in his family (Veroff et al., 1981).

The dominant mood of a father's work may also affect his home life—whether it is a feeling of satisfaction or the kind of tension that often follows police officers home (Nordlicht, 1979).

Fathers' work and children's values   Since people come to cherish the values that help them at work, researchers have explored the extent to which they pass these values on to their children. There is some evidence that middle-class fathers, whose work involves personal judgment in dealing with ideas, symbols, and other people, do value self-direction and independence in their children; whereas working-class men who are more closely supervised in their work, which tends to be more concrete in nature, encourage their children to be obedient and conforming (Pearlin & Kohn, 1966). College students tend to choose occupations that involve experiences and rewards similar to those of their father's jobs, reflecting the communication of job-related values (Mortimer, 1975; 1976).

Other factors   How does a father's work schedule affect his paternal role? According to wives' reports, there seems to be little if any relationship between how many hours a father works and how much interest he takes in his children (Clark & Gecas, 1977).

Unemployment, however, is an important factor. When a father loses his job, his tension may lead to child abuse (Justice & Duncan, 1977). In general, a father's *not* having a job is considered damaging to his children—though a mother's *having* a job has been considered disruptive for her family (Bronfenbrenner & Couter, 1982).

We see, then, that the work lives of both mothers and fathers affect children in many different ways. But—as we stress so often in this book—any single influence like parents employment must always be considered in context with other aspects of a child's world.

Children of Divorce

Children suffer when their parents split up. The children, as much as or more than the parents, may feel pain, confusion, anger, hate, bitter disappointment, a sense of failure, and self-doubt. For many, this family disruption is the central event of childhood, with effects that persist into adult life.

More than 1 million children under the age of 18 are involved in divorces each year. This figure, which has held fairly steady during the 1980s, is double what it was 20 years ago (Wegman, 1986).

No matter how unhappy a marriage has been, its breakup usually comes as a shock to the children. During the process of adjustment, the children of divorcing parents often feel afraid of the future, guilty about their own (usually imaginary) role in causing the divorce, hurt at the rejection they feel from the parent who moves out, and angry at both parents. They may become depressed, hostile, disruptive, irritable, lonely, sad, accident-prone, or even suicidal; they may suffer from fatigue, insomnia, skin disorders, loss of appetite, or inability to concentrate; and they may lose interest in schoolwork and in social life.

How Do Children React to Divorce at Different Ages? Although no two children react in exactly the same way, certain patterns emerge for children of different ages, and these patterns reflect their levels of cognitive and emotional development (Neal, 1983; Wallerstein & Kelly, 1980). The reactions described below generally diminish in the first year or so (Hetherington, 1986; Kelly, 1987).

Preschoolers (2½ to 6 years) often show signs of great stress. Those from 2½ to 3½ whine, cry, cling, have sleep problems, and wet the bed. Four-year-olds whine and cry, and hit other children. Five- and six-year-olds are more anxious and more aggressive; they crave physical contact. Because young children are egocentric, they may feel that they have caused the divorce—that the parent who has left has done so because of something bad the child has done. Preschool children are likely to have two kinds of fantasies: terrifying ones in which they are abandoned, and soothing ones in which their parents reunite. In one study of children of divorced parents, all the preschoolers who played house put the mother and father dolls in bed together, hugging each other (Wallerstein, 1983).

Children of elementary school age (6 to 12 years) may also be very frightened. When they first hear the news, they may run to a neighbor in a state of panic or be overcome by severe vomiting spells. They often become bitter toward, and angry with, one or both parents, especially the parent they blame for causing the divorce. They may act out their anger by stealing or lying, or they may take it out on themselves with headaches and stomachaches.

Although they are often aware of conflicts between their parents, younger schoolchildren still feel responsible for having caused a divorce (perhaps thinking that they have caused a fight between the parents), and they also feel responsible for making their parents feel better. Older schoolchildren have a better understanding of parents' inner feelings and of the conflict that arises when two people's attitudes and expectations conflict. Older schoolchildren often believe that their parents are separating because they have changed or because their relationship has changed, but the same children also believe that such changes can be reversed if the parents try hard enough.

Young adolescents (13 to 15 years) feel anger, depression, guilt, and despair. They may worry about money or become very active sexually. They may begin to compete with the parent of the same sex or buckle under the strain of being the "man" or "woman" of the household. They tend to believe that their parents have divorced because their relationship has gone bad on account of personality problems or irreconcilable differences.

Parents and counselors who want to help a child adjust to divorce need to be aware of what the child believes and is capable of grasping.

What "Tasks" Face Children of Divorce? Children face special challenges and burdens brought on by parents' divorcing in addition to the usual tasks of emotional development. In a longitudinal study of 60 divorcing couples in California whose children ranged in age from 3 to 18 at the time of the separation, six special tasks emerged as crucial to children's emotional development (Wallerstein, 1983; Wallerstein & Kelly, 1980):

1 *Acknowledging the reality of the marital rupture.* Small children often do not understand what has happened, and many children of various ages initially deny the separation. Others may be overwhelmed by fantasies of abandon-

ment, or retreat into fantasies of reconciliation. Most children, however, do face the fact of the divorce by the end of the first year of separation.

2 *Disengaging from parental conflict and distress and resuming customary pursuits.* At first, children are often so worried that they cannot concentrate in school, play with other children, or take part in their usual activities. They need to put some distance between themselves and their distraught parents and go back to living their own lives. Fortunately, most children are able to do this by the end of the first 1 to 1½ years after the separation.

3 *Resolving loss.* Absorbing the losses caused by divorce may be the single most difficult task for children. They need to adjust to the loss of the parent they are not living with, the loss of the security of feeling loved and cared for by both parents, the loss of familiar daily routines and family traditions, and often the loss of a whole way of life. Some children take years to deal with these losses, and some never do, carrying a sense of being rejected, unworthy, and unlovable into adulthood.

4 *Resolving anger and self-blame.* Children realize that divorce, unlike death, is voluntary, and they often remain angry for years at the parent (or parents) who could do such a terrible thing to them. When and if they do reach the stage of forgiving both their parents and themselves, they feel more powerful and more in control of their lives.

5 *Accepting the permanence of the divorce.* Many children hold on for years to the fantasy that their parents will be reunited, even after both have remarried. Many youngsters accept the situation only after achieving psychological separation from their parents in adolescence or early adulthood.

6 *Achieving realistic hope regarding relationships.* Many youngsters who have adjusted well in other ways come through a divorce feeling afraid to take a chance on intimate relationships themselves, for fear that they will fail as their parents did. They may become cynical, depressed, or simply doubtful of the possibility of finding lasting love.

Many children do, of course, succeed at most or all of these tasks and are able to come through the painful experience of divorce with the ego basically intact. Children's ability to do this seems to be related partly to their own resilience (see the discussion of resilient children later in this chapter) and partly to the way their parents handle issues related to the separation (see Box 13-2) and the challenge of raising children alone.

What Are the Long-Term Effects of Divorce on Children? Several longitudinal studies have followed up children of divorcing parents and found that a substantial number of these children adjust well, but that others have a number of problems at least 10 years later.

Among thirty-eight 16- to 18-year-olds whose parents had divorced 10 years earlier, three-quarters of the girls and about half of the boys were doing fairly well. Most were in school full time, working part time, law-abiding, and living at home—three-quarters with their mothers (those who were with their fathers had moved during adolescence). The girls were getting along well with their mothers and were more likely to be dating and involved in sexual relationships, while the boys were far more likely to be lonely and emotionally constricted and to hold back in relationships with girls.

In one way or another, the divorce had left its mark on most of these young people. They were burdened by feelings of sadness, unmet needs, and a sense

BOX 13-2 ■ THE EVERYDAY WORLD

HELPING CHILDREN ADJUST TO DIVORCE

The following guidelines for parents are based on the advice of numerous experts on family relations:

■ *All the children should be told at the same time about the divorce, in language suited to their age.* Some 80 percent of preschoolers are given no explanation because their parents think that they're too young to understand (Wallerstein & Kelly, 1980). Even very young children do understand, however, that a change is taking place, and they need to be told, often in different words, what's happening. Both parents should be present so that the children can see that both parents are still deeply involved with their lives and will continue to be available to them.

■ *Children should be told only as much as they need to know.* It may be tempting for parents to discuss openly what they see as the cause of the divorce—an affair, alcoholism, compulsive gambling, or sexual incompatibility, for example. Yet this may confuse and wound children far more than it helps them. It puts a heavy burden on them to judge the parent who is "in the wrong." At a time when they need as much emotional support as possible, they may lose faith in one parent, and maybe both.

■ *Children need to know that they did not cause the divorce.* Young children tend to see the whole world as revolving around them and often assume that something they did or thought drove their parents to divorce. The ensuing guilt can torture a child.

■ *Parents must emphasize the finality of their decision.* The fantasy of parents' reunion is almost universal. As long as children dream of this, they can't make progress in accepting reality. Once they give up believing that they have the power to reunite their parents, they can pay attention to lessening the pain of the rupture.

■ *Arrangements for the children's care should be carefully explained.* Although children may not express their fear of abandonment, they need reassurance that they will continue to be cared for. Parents need to explain custody arrangements in detail.

■ *Children should be reassured of both parents' continuing love.* They need to know that there is no such thing as divorce between parent and child and that even the parent who does not have custody will continue to love and care for them.

■ *Children should be encouraged to express feelings of fear, sadness, and anger.* When they can express these emotions openly, they can begin to understand and deal with them. Parents can help by admitting their own sadness, anger, and confusion. They can also seek out a discussion group for children of divorced parents.

■ *Limits should be set on children's behavior.* The single parent should maintain firm, friendly discipline. Children need to know that someone stronger loves them enough to stop them from losing control.

■ *Parents should enlist the help of other adults—teachers, scout leaders, or relatives and friends.* A person outside the immediate family can often show a caring concern that helps a child through this crisis.

■ *Battling parents should declare a truce around the children.* Divorced parents don't have to be friends, but it's a great help to their children if they can cooperate on child-rearing issues.

■ *Children should not be used as weapons.* Children suffer when they're forced to transmit angry messages or relay information, when they're asked to choose sides, or when family visits turn into battles. Parents who use children this way are sacrificing their children's welfare for their own immediate satisfaction.

■ *Parents must recognize that there is a real conflict between their needs and their children's needs.* Parents need to be out with other adults, but children need their parents' company. Adults have to be sensitive to this problem and work out solutions that will meet the needs of both generations.

■ *Children's lives should be changed as little as possible.* Any change is stressful, and so the fewer adjustments children have to make, the more energy they have to cope with the major change. If possible, the parent who has custody should postpone taking a job for the first time or moving to a new house. If changes must be made, parents need to realize that children need extra understanding.

■ *Parents should use whatever resources they can find for themselves and their children.* This includes helpful books, discussion groups, and community programs.

Source: Adapted from Olds, 1989.

of powerlessness. They missed their fathers (whom they tended to idealize), were anxious about their own love relationships and chances for successful marriage, and were afraid of being betrayed, hurt, and abandoned (Wallerstein, 1987).

What Factors Influence Children's Adjustment to Divorce? A review of the literature on long-term adjustment to divorce found that children—especially boys—who live with divorced mothers have more social, academic, and behavioral problems than children in intact homes (Kelly, 1987). However, a number of factors, like the following, seem to influence how well children adjust.

Parenting styles and parents' attitudes Children of authoritative parents (see Chapter 10) usually show fewer behavior problems than children of authoritarian or permissive parents (Hetherington, 1986). They do better in school and have fewer problems getting along with other children (Guidubaldi & Perry, 1985). These effects are especially significant for boys.

In a study of families in which the parents had divorced 6 years earlier, Hetherington (1986) found that custodial mothers who did not remarry had more emotional problems and were less satisfied with their lives than remarried or nondivorced mothers. The unmarried mothers were still in intense, ambivalent, conflicted relationships with sons, who tended to show behavior problems and spend less time at home with adults. However, the mothers had good relationships with daughters, who tended to be fairly well adjusted.

Children of custodial parents with psychiatric problems have adjustment problems themselves, and the children of parents who still fight often and intensely after the divorce have more personality and behavior problems (Kelly, 1987).

Remarriage of the mother Both boys and girls go through a period of adjustment after their mothers remarry. Mothers are happier, better adjusted, and more satisfied with life after remarriage, and their sons do better with a stepfather. However, daughters of remarried mothers often have more problems both with their own adjustment and in getting along with their families than do daughters of divorced women who have not remarried or of nondivorced mothers. Typically, however, these girls do adjust eventually (Hetherington, 1986).

Relationship with the father Among 16- to 18-year-old boys whose parents had divorced 10 years earlier, the quality of the relationship with the father was important in the boys' adjustment. When fathers were erratic and rejecting, the boys felt hurt, trapped, and humiliated. They often took out these feelings in anger against their mothers (Wallerstein, 1987).

Parents' accessibility The best custody arrangement for children of divorced parents usually seems to be with the parent of the same sex, but predictable and frequent contact with the other parent is important, too. The typical practice of limited visitation for fathers leaves children deprived, especially boys. Children who have reliable, frequent contact with the noncustodial parent (most often the father) are usually better adjusted; this association is especially strong for boys (Kelly, 1987). But joint custody—shared custody by both parents—does not seem to improve a child's situation in an amicable divorce and may worsen it in a bitter divorce (Kline, Tschann, Johnston, & Wallerstein, 1988).

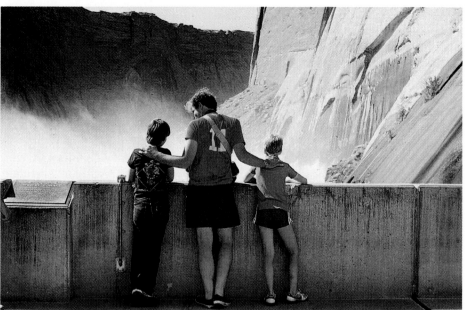

For optimal adjustment, children of divorced parents—especially boys—need reliable, frequent contact with both parents.

Adolescents who do not get along with their mothers and are able to make their home with their fathers often have adjustment problems at the time of the divorce, but show psychological growth in the long run. When the parent a young person turns to is responsive, this parent can protect and help the child; but if the parent is unresponsive, "bitter, even tragic disappointment" often results (Wallerstein, 1987, p. 211).

Although divorce is a wrenching experience for everyone in the family, the resilience of the human spirit allows many children to come through the painful times with an increased sensitivity and compassion that serve them well in adulthood.

One-Parent Families

An important consequence of a high divorce rate is the large number of children being raised by single parents. One-parent families may be created by the death of one parent or a mother's never marrying, but they most commonly result from divorce, separation, or desertion. Nearly 1 in 4 American children (almost 15 million) live in homes with only one parent. This includes 18 percent of white children, 30 percent of Hispanic children, and 53 percent of African American children (U.S. Bureau of the Census, 1988b). The number of single-parent families almost tripled between 1960 and 1986, but the rate of increase has slowed.

In 90 percent of families where parents have divorced or separated, the mother is the custodial parent, but the number of fathers caring for children increased by almost 300 percent between 1970 and 1984, when there were more than 600,000 such men (U.S. Bureau of the Census, 1985). Children who live with their fathers tend to be of school age or older and are more often boys (Hanson, 1988). The fathers generally are better educated, are better paid, and have more prestigious occupations than the average father; most in the general community are white, but many in the armed forces are nonwhite (Hanson, 1988).

Most of these men rely more on child-care resources in the community (preschools and day care centers, after-school care, and friends and family) or on self-care than on hired housekeepers, and they generally bemoan the lack of high-quality, low-cost child care. The fathers who do best were actively involved in child care and household tasks before divorce, sought extra counseling and education before or after the divorce, and purposefully worked toward a good relationship with their children. Most are happy with their decision to be the custodial parent and feel that they are the better choice (Hanson, 1988).

What Stresses Does the One-Parent Family Place on Children?   Children growing up with one parent do not have two adults who can share child-rearing responsibilities, take them to out-of-school activities, serve as gender-role models, and demonstrate the interplay of personalities. Also, the family's income is likely to be at or near the poverty level, with negative effects on children's health, well-being, and achievement in school. The average income of families headed by women is less than half that of families with two parents (U.S. Bureau of the Census, 1984).

If the parent is divorced, the strains of the divorce can affect parenting. For several years following the separation, the parent may be preoccupied with personal concerns and be less attentive and responsive to the child. Housekeeping and routines such as bedtime and bath time may be neglected (Hetherington, Cox, & Cox, 1979). These effects often wear off in time, especially if the custodial parent forms a relationship with a new partner. But school-age children may continue to feel torn between their two parents if the parents are hostile toward each other (Maccoby, 1984).

How Does the One-Parent Family Affect Schooling?   One study of 18,000 elementary school and high school students in 14 states found that students from one-parent homes achieved less in school, liked school less, had more problems with peers, and were more likely to need disciplinary action than students with two parents. However, a follow-up analysis and interviews with parents showed once again that family income is an important factor. Lower income affected achievement more strongly than the number of parents at home—an important finding, since one-parent households tend to have lower incomes (Zakariya, 1982). According to another study (Milne et al., 1986), negative effects on elementary school children living with one parent are almost entirely dependent on other factors—and particularly on income. It is possible, then, that what looks like a "single-parent" effect is in many cases a "low-income" effect. Other factors that were found to influence a child's achievement were the parent's expectations for the child and the number of books in the home (Milne et al., 1986).

Teachers can help the children of single parents. A study in Maryland found that when first-, third-, and fifth-grade teachers made systematic efforts to get single parents as well as couples to help children at home, single parents helped as much and as effectively as married parents (J. L. Epstein, 1984). Schools have begun to look at other ways to cooperate with single parents (most of whom are working mothers), including evening, breakfast, or weekend meetings, conferences, and programs; baby-sitters for younger children during school events; late-afternoon transportation for students after sports or band practice; and sending notices and report cards to the noncustodial parent (who may also want to be involved).

What Are the Long-Term Effects of the One-Parent Family?   Do youngsters with only one parent get into more trouble than children with two parents? Some recent studies indicate that they do, and that they may also be at greater risk of marital and parenting problems themselves (Rutter, 1979a). It seems that children benefit from rich family relationships—and also that as children grow older and more independent, single parents need more help in guiding them.

Yet the one-parent home is not necessarily pathological, and the two-parent family is not always healthy. Other research has concluded that in general, children are better adjusted when they have had a good relationship with one parent than when they have grown up in a two-parent home characterized by discord and discontent (Rutter, 1983); and that an inaccessible, rejecting, or hostile parent is more damaging than an absent one (Hetherington, 1980).

Stepfamilies

The word *stepparent* conjures up vivid storybook images of wicked and cruel interlopers in the family. Such images often sabotage real-life stepparents' efforts to forge close, warm relationships with a spouse's children. Yet many make the effort, and many do succeed. With today's high rate of divorce and remarriage, families made up of "yours, mine, and ours" are common. Four out of five divorced adults remarry within 3 years; and by 1990, one out of every three or four children will have lived for some time in a stepfamily (Glick, 1980; 1984).

The stepfamily—also called the *blended* or *reconstituted* family—is different from the "natural" family. It has a larger supporting cast, with all the relatives of four adults (the married pair, plus both ex-spouses). And it has many stresses to deal with. Because of losses to death or divorce, children and adults alike may be afraid to trust and love. Children's loyalties to absent or dead parents may interfere with forming ties to the stepparent, especially when the children go back and forth between two households. Disparities in life cycles often arise, if, for instance, a father of adolescents marries a woman who has never had a child (Visher & Visher, 1983).

The most common stepfamily consists of a mother, her children, and a stepfather. One study of such families (Santrock, Sitterle, & Warshak, 1988) found that remarried mothers were just as involved with their children as mothers in intact marriages. They were highly involved, nurturant, and available to their children, even though many were working. Apparently, a woman's greater satisfaction with life carries over to relationships with her children.

Most of the children were doing well and had positive feelings about their stepfathers, who had been in the role an average of 3 years. These men were somewhat involved with the care and supervision of the children, but were relatively distant from them. Their detachment seemed to be deliberate, prompted by what they saw as the children's needs. Nearly one-fourth of the men said that they had tried to assume a parental role too fast and that this had caused problems in their relationships with the children. Other research has found that a man has the best chance of gaining acceptance with a stepson if he makes friends with the boy first, supports the mother's parenting, and later moves into an authoritative role (Hetherington, 1986). Unfortunately, this does not work so well with a stepdaughter, who is less likely to accept a stepfather as a parent. Boys benefit from having a stepfather; stepdaughters seem to have more behavioral problems than daughters of nondivorced mothers or divorced mothers who do not remarry (Kelly, 1987).

Although American children do less active caretaking of younger siblings than do children in many other countries, scenes like this one are not uncommon. The most harmonious sibling relationships tend to be those with older sisters.

A comparison group of stepmothers were much more involved with their stepchildren, taking them to and from school and other activities, providing emotional support and comfort, and disciplining them (Santrock et al., 1988). Still, most stepchildren's most enduring ties tend to be with the custodial biological parent, and "the positive nature of the relationship between the remarried parent and the child [is] a key ingredient in helping the child through the disruption and disequilibrium, as the family [moves] from the status of intact to divorced to becoming a stepfamily" (Santrock et al., 1988, p. 161).

Sibling Relationships

"I fight more with my little brother than I do with my friends," reports Vicky at 8 years of age. "But when I fight with Bobby, we always make up." Vicky recognizes the special nature of her relationship with Bobby. She can see that their tie is deeper and more lasting than ordinary friendship, which may founder on a quarrel or just fade away. She is also aware that her relationship with her brother is ambivalent, marked by special affection as well as intense competition and resentment.

Siblings influence each other in many ways, both *directly*, through the way they interact with each other; and *indirectly*, through their impact on each other's relationship with the parents. One of the important direct influences is the way brothers and sisters help each other develop a self-concept. When Vicky compares herself with Bobby and sees how different they are despite the bonds between them, she forms a stronger sense of herself as an individual.

Sibling relations are also a laboratory for resolving conflicts. Although brothers and sisters often quarrel, the ties of blood and physical closeness impel them to make up, since they cannot avoid seeing each other every day. They learn at an early age that the expression of anger does not mean the end of a relationship. Since siblings' quarrels often have to do with uneven power bases, younger siblings in particular may become quite skillful at sensing other people's needs, negotiating for what they want, and compromising. Elder children like Vicky tend to be bossy; they are more likely to attack, interfere with, ignore, or bribe their siblings. Second-borns like Bobby plead, reason, and cajole—or sometimes take the older sibling's things (Cicirelli, 1976a).

Vicky's relationship with Bobby is helped by the fact that she is a girl and he is a boy. Children are more likely to squabble with same-sex siblings and to be conciliatory with siblings of the other sex; two brothers quarrel more than any other combination (Cicirelli, 1976a). When girls want their younger siblings to do something, they are more likely to reason with them or make them feel obligated, whereas older brothers tend to attack (Cicirelli, 1976b).

Siblings learn how to deal with dependency in relationships by experiencing their dependency on each other. Although children in American society take care of their younger brothers and sisters less than is common in many other countries, a good deal of caretaking does take place. Working parents often depend on an older child to mind the younger ones until the parents come home, and older children often help younger siblings with homework. This help is most likely to be effective (and accepted) when it comes from a sibling—especially a sister—who is at least 4 years older.

Girls talk more to younger siblings than boys do: they give more explanations and feedback, and they are more likely to use the *deductive* method (explaining, describing, demonstrating, and illustrating), while boys more often use the *inductive* approach (giving examples and letting the learner abstract the concept) (Cicirelli, 1976a). Some of the differences in the way boys and girls behave toward younger siblings may be due to gender-typing—the fact that certain kinds of behavior are encouraged more for one sex than the other. It may also have roots in girls' tendency to identify more with their mothers. And it may relate to boys' greater emotional vulnerability, which may cause them to be more jealous and act more hostile to a younger "usurper."

One form of indirect influence shows up in the way parents divide their time among their children. For example, because girls seem to be more effective in handling younger siblings, mothers tend to talk more, explain more, and give more feedback to children with older brothers than to children with older sisters (Cicirelli, 1976a).

Emotional Disturbances in Childhood

Unfortunately, emotional disturbances in childhood are not uncommon. Between 5 and 15 percent of American children—some 3 to 9 million children—are estimated to have some kind of mental health problem that should be treated. However, 2 out of 3 seriously disturbed children and adolescents do not get the help they need (Knitzer, 1984; U.S. Department of Health and Human Services, USDHHS, 1980c). We discussed tics, stuttering, and hyperactivity in Chapters 11 and 12; now we examine some other childhood emotional problems.

THREE TYPES OF EMOTIONAL DISTURBANCES

Acting-Out Behavior

Children's emotional difficulties often surface in their behavior. They show by what they do that they need help. They fight, they lie, they steal, they destroy property, and they break rules laid down by parents, schools, and other authorities. These are common forms of *acting-out behavior*—misbehavior that is an outward expression of emotional turmoil.

Of course, almost all children engage in make-believe or lie occasionally to avoid punishment. But when children past the age of 6 or 7 continue telling tall tales, they are often signaling a sense of insecurity. They may need to make up glamorous stories about themselves to gain attention and esteem; or, when lying becomes habitual or transparent, they may be showing hostility toward their parents (Chapman, 1974).

Similarly, occasional minor stealing is common among children. Although it needs to be dealt with, it is not necessarily a sign that anything is seriously wrong. But when children repeatedly steal from their parents or steal so openly from others that they are easily caught, they are again often showing hostility toward their parents and their parents' standards. In some cases, the stolen items appear to be "symbolic tokens of parental love, power, or authority" (Chapman, 1974, p. 158) of which the child feels deprived.

Any chronic antisocial behavior needs to be regarded as a possible symptom of deep-seated emotional upset. In Chapter 16, we discuss some extreme forms of misbehavior, those that get young people into trouble with the law.

acting-out behavior
Misbehavior (for example, lying or stealing) spurred by emotional difficulties.

Anxiety Disorders

Various anxiety disorders may begin in childhood. They include separation anxiety disorder and school phobia (*Diagnostic and Statistical Manual of Mental Disorders*, 3d ed., rev., DSM III-R, 1987).

Separation Anxiety Disorder Jimmy wakes up complaining of nausea. Yesterday morning he had a headache, the day before it was a stomachache, and last week he vomited three mornings in a row. Yet as soon as his mother gives him permission to stay home from day camp, his symptoms disappear, and he spends the rest of the day happily playing in his room.

separation anxiety disorder Condition involving excessive anxiety for at least 2 weeks, concerning separation from people to whom a child is attached.

Jimmy is suffering from *separation anxiety disorder,* a condition involving excessive anxiety for at least 2 weeks, concerning separation from people to whom the child is attached. The child may refuse to visit or sleep at a friend's home, go on errands, or attend camp or school; may "cling" to a parent and shadow him or her around the house; and may have such physical complaints as stomachaches, headaches, nausea, and vomiting before or during separation. The condition affects boys and girls equally and may begin in early childhood and persist through the college years. Children with the disorder tend to come from close-knit, caring families and tend to develop the anxiety after a life stress like the death of a pet, an illness, or a move to a new neighborhood.

school phobia Unrealistic fear of school, probably reflecting separation anxiety.

School Phobia *School phobia*—unrealistic fear that keeps children away from school—may be a form of separation anxiety disorder. It seems to have more to do with a fear of leaving the parent than a fear of school itself. Virtually no research has been done on the school situation of school-phobic youngsters, and so we know very little about their perception of school or how they get along there. If there *is* a problem at school—a sarcastic teacher, a bully in the schoolyard, or overly difficult work—the child's fears may be *realistic*; it may be the environment that needs changing, not the child.

What *do* we know about school-phobic children? Research on school phobia has found that they are not truants; their parents usually know when they are absent. They tend to have average or higher-than-average intelligence and to be average or better-than-average students. Their ages are evenly distributed from 5 to 15, and they are equally likely to be boys or girls. Although they come from a variety of backgrounds, their parents tend to be professionals. Their parents are also more likely than a control group to be depressed, to suffer from anxiety disorders themselves, and to report disturbed family functioning (G. A. Bernstein & Garfinkel, 1988).

Not all school phobias are the same. *Neurotic school phobia*, which largely affects children from kindergarten through fourth grade, comes on suddenly; the child continues to function well in other areas. *Characterological school phobia*, seen in early adolescence, comes on more gradually; the child is more deeply disturbed, and the outlook for the future is less hopeful.

The most important element in the treatment of a school-phobic child is an early return to school. The longer school-phobic children are out of school, the harder it is to get them back. They are often timid and inhibited away from home, but willful, stubborn, and demanding with their parents. Most experts recommend getting the child back to school first, and then taking whatever other steps may be called for, such as therapy for the child, for one or both parents, and possibly for the entire family. Getting the child back into school breaks the phobic cycle by restoring the child to a more normal environment and reducing the extreme interdependence between mother and child. It also keeps the child from falling farther behind in schoolwork, which can aggravate the problem.

The return to school may be accomplished gradually. First, the parents may drive the child to school and just sit in the car. Then they may get out and walk around the outside of the building with the child. Next, a parent may go with the child to the principal's office, and finally have the child go to school alone—first, possibly, for an hour a day, then several hours, and eventually for an entire day. An approach like this requires working closely with school officials. Children can usually be returned to school without too much difficulty once treatment is begun. The few studies that have followed up school-phobic children years later are unclear, though, in determining how well treatment has helped overall adjustment (D. Gordon & Young, 1976).

Childhood Depression

"Nobody likes me" is a common complaint in middle childhood, when children tend to be popularity-conscious. But when these words were addressed to a school principal by an 8-year-old boy in Florida whose classmates had accused him of stealing from the teacher's purse, it was a danger signal. The boy vowed that he would never return to school—and he never did. Two days later, he hanged himself by a belt from the top rail of his bunk bed ("Doctors rule out," 1984).

Fortunately, depressed children rarely go to such lengths, though suicide among young people is on the increase. How can we tell the difference between a harmless period of the "blues" (which we all experience at times) and a major *affective disorder*—that is, a disorder of mood? The basic symptoms of an affective disorder are similar from childhood through adulthood, but some features are age-specific (DSM III-R, 1987).

Friendlessness is only one sign of *childhood depression.* This disorder is also characterized by inability to have fun or to concentrate, and by an absence of normal emotional reactions. Depressed children are frequently tired, extremely active, or inactive. They walk very little, cry a great deal, have trouble concentrating, sleep too much or too little, lose their appetite, start doing poorly in school, look unhappy, complain of physical ailments, feel overwhelmingly guilty, suffer severe separation anxiety (which may take the form of school phobia), or think often about death or suicide (Malmquist, 1983; Poznanski 1982). Any four or five of these symptoms may support a diagnosis of depression, especially when they represent a marked change from the child's usual pattern. Parents do not always recognize "minor" problems like sleep disturbances, loss of appetite, and irritability as signs of depression, but children themselves are often able to describe how they feel (Children's Hospital of Pittsburgh, 1987a).

No one is sure of the exact cause of depression in children or adults. There is some evidence for a biochemical predisposition, which may be triggered by specific experiences. Depressed school-age children are likely to lack social and academic competence, but it is not clear whether incompetence causes depression or vice versa (Blechman, McEnroe, Carella, & Audette, 1986). The parents of depressed children are more likely to be depressed themselves, suggesting a possible genetic factor, a reflection of general stress in ill families, or the result of poor parenting practices by disturbed parents (Weissman et al., 1987).

affective disorder
Disorder of mood, such as depression.

childhood depression
Affective disorder characterized by inability to have fun or to concentrate, and by an absence of normal emotional reactions.

Moderate to severe depression is fairly easy to spot; milder forms are harder to diagnose. The presence of any of the above symptoms should therefore be followed closely; if they persist, the child should be given psychological help.

TREATMENT TECHNIQUES

The choice of a specific treatment for a disorder depends on many factors: the nature of the problem, the child's personality, the family's financial resources and willingness to participate, availability of treatment in the community, and, very often, the orientation of the professional first consulted.

Psychological Therapies

psychotherapy *Treatment technique in which a therapist generally helps patients gain insight into their personalities and relationships and helps them interpret their feelings and behaviors.*

Individual Psychotherapy *Psychotherapy* is a treatment technique in which a therapist helps people gain insights into their personality and relationships, and helps them interpret their feelings and behaviors. In individual psychotherapy, the therapist sees a child one on one. This may be helpful at a time of great stress in the child's life, like the death of a parent, even if the child has not shown any symptoms of disturbance. Occasional therapy sessions may be indicated for a child who has shown signs of anxiety, worry, or behavior that may point to an emotional problem.

To help children understand and cope with their feelings, a therapist interprets what the child says and does—both in the therapy sessions, and in everyday life as reported at the sessions. In doing so, the therapist needs to show acceptance of the child's feelings—and the child's right to them.

Child psychotherapy is usually much more effective when combined with counseling for the parents, who often feel guilty about having "caused" the child's problem and inadequate because they cannot deal with it on their own. A professional can help them focus on ways to cope most effectively.

family therapy *Treatment technique in which the whole family is treated together and is viewed as the client.*

Family Therapy In *family therapy,* the entire family is the client. The therapist sees the whole family together, observes the way family members interact, and points out their patterns of functioning—both the growth-producing and the inhibiting or destructive patterns.

Sometimes the child whose problem brings the family into therapy is, ironically, the healthiest member and is responding to a sick situation. This was true in the case of a 10-year-old girl who threatened her parents with a kitchen knife after they told her that her dog had died when, in fact, they had taken him to the Society for the Prevention of Cruelty to Animals. Therapy revealed an atmosphere of hostility and dishonesty that permeated all the family's relationships, avoidance by all members of coming to grips with their problems, and, ultimately, a basic conflict between husband and wife that had set the stage for the girl's problems and those of her 16-year-old brother, who was getting into trouble at school. Through therapy the parents were able to confront their own differences and begin to resolve them—the first step toward solving the children's problems as well.

behavior therapy *Treatment approach using principles of learning theory to alter behavior; also called behavior modification.*

Behavior Therapy *Behavior therapy,* also called *behavior modification,* uses principles of learning theory to alter behavior—to eliminate undesirable behaviors like bed-wetting and temper tantrums, or to develop desirable behaviors like being on time and doing household chores. A behavior therapist does not look for underlying reasons for behavior and does not try to offer a child insight into his or her situation, but aims to change the behavior itself. For example, the therapist may use operant conditioning to encourage a desired behavior, such as putting dirty clothes into the hamper. Every time the child does so, he or she gets a reward, like words of praise or a token that can be exchanged for toys.

This approach is effective in dealing with specific fears and behavior problems. When a child's problems are more deep-seated, though, behavior therapy needs to be supplemented by psychotherapy for the child, the parents, or both.

Evaluating Psychological Therapies A review of 75 well-designed studies of the use of various types of psychological therapy with children concluded that these therapies generally help (R. J. Casey & Berman, 1985). Children who received treatment scored better on a variety of measures (including self-concept, adjustment, personality, social skills, achievement in school, cognitive functioning, and resolution of fears and anxieties) than children who received none. However, children gained less in self-esteem and adjustment than adults in therapy usually do.

Treatment for such specific problems as phobias, impulsiveness, hyperactivity, and bed-wetting brought more improvement than therapy aimed at better social adjustment. No particular form of therapy (play or nonplay, individual or group, "child-only" or treatment of children and parents) seemed best.

While parents, therapists, and researchers saw definite gains in treated children, teachers and peers tended not to notice much improvement. First impressions may be hard to overcome—which suggests that parents may want to point out a child's improvement to the teacher and help the child make new friends who do not know what the child was like before treatment.

Drug Therapy

Over the past 3 decades, the number of available prescription drugs has increased dramatically. With the proliferation of new drugs has come the use of *drug therapy*—the administration of drugs to treat emotional disorders. Today, antidepressants are commonly prescribed for bed-wetters, stimulants for hyperactive children, and a range of other medications for children with other psychological problems.

drug therapy
Administration of drugs to treat emotional disorders.

Giving pills to children in order to change their behavior is a radical step, especially since many medicines have undesirable side effects. In some cases, drugs relieve only behavioral symptoms and do not get at underlying causes. Drugs do have a place in the treatment of some emotional disturbances of childhood, but their use should not eliminate psychotherapy for troubled children.

Stress and Resilience

SOURCES OF STRESS

Stressful events are part of every childhood. Illness, the birth of a sibling, frustration, and parents' temporary absence are common sources of stress. Other stresses are not routine, but are nevertheless all too likely to occur in a child's world. Divorce or death of parents, hospitalization, and the day-in, day-out

BOX 13-3 ■ AROUND THE WORLD

WHAT CHILDREN ARE AFRAID OF

Over the past several years, adults have become increasingly concerned about the number of dangers facing children and have worried about children's own fears of personal or global catastrophe. Children do have anxieties about homelessness, AIDS, drug abuse, criminal attack, and nuclear war, but many childhood fears are about things much closer to youngsters' daily lives. According to recent research in six countries—Australia, Canada, Egypt, Japan, the Philippines, and the United States—children from many different cultures are remarkably alike in what they are afraid of (Yamamoto, Soliman, Parsons, & Davies, 1987).

When third- through ninth-grade children were asked to rank a list of 20 events in order of how upsetting they would be, the primary fear among children in each country was the same: fear of losing a parent (showing the great importance parents still have). Close in importance to this,

however, were events that would embarrass children—being kept back in school, wetting their pants in public, or being sent to the principal. Surprisingly, children of every country rated the birth of a new sibling least upsetting of all (perhaps showing that at this age children are so busy outside the home that they are less affected by a new arrival—or that at age 8 and older, few were dealing with the birth of a new baby at home). Boys and girls rated the events about the same; by and large, so did children of different ages.

For many children, school is a source of insecurity—partly because it is very important in their lives and partly because many belittling practices (like accusing children of lying, or ridiculing them in class) flourish there. Adults can do a great deal to stem many of these fears by respecting children, encouraging them to talk about their worries, and not expecting fears to simply disappear.

Most childhood fears are normal, and overcoming them helps children grow, achieve identity, and master their world.

---

psychological maltreatment Action or failure to act that damages children's behavioral, cognitive, emotional, or physical functioning; emotional abuse.

grind of poverty affect many children. Other children survive wars and earthquakes. The increase in the number of homeless families in the United States has brought severe psychological difficulties to many children (Bassuk & Rubin, 1987). Violent events like kidnappings and playground sniper attacks make children realize that their world is not always safe and that parents cannot always protect them. This realization is stressful to children in the short run and may affect them in the long run as well (Garmezy, 1983; Pynoos et al., 1987). Children's fears reflect their awareness of many modern stresses, as seen in Box 13-3.

Sometimes—for example, when children are subjected to physical abuse or *psychological maltreatment*—the parents themselves are a source of stress (see Box 13-4). In other cases, society imposes pressures, like forcing children to grow up too soon. Some children, however, are able to overcome enormous stress in their lives, as we note in the discussion of resilient children below.

THE "HURRIED CHILD"

Children today have a special set of pressures to cope with. Because families move more than they used to, children are more likely to change schools and friends and less likely to know many adults well. They know more than children of previous generations about technology, sex, and violence; and when they live in single-parent homes or have to cope with parents' work schedules, they are likely to shoulder adult responsibilities.

The child psychologist David Elkind has called today's child the "hurried child" (1981, 1988). Like some other thoughtful observers, he is concerned that the pressures of life today are making children grow up too soon and are making

BOX 13-4 ■ THE RESEARCH WORLD

PSYCHOLOGICAL MALTREATMENT

The physical pain of abuse may heal quickly, but the psychological scars may never go away. Lasting scars may also result when parents regularly ridicule children or coldly turn away from a child's pleas for affection and attention.

Physicians, legislators, and mental health professionals are becoming increasingly concerned about *psychological maltreatment,* which has been broadly (and vaguely) defined as action (or failure to act) that damages children's behavioral, cognitive, emotional, or physical functioning (Hart & Brassard, 1987). Abusive parents may reject, terrorize, isolate, exploit, degrade, or corrupt children and be emotionally unresponsive to them (Hart & Brassard, 1987; Rosenberg, 1987). As a result, children may fail to reach their full potential as adults (Garrison, 1987). The impact of maltreatment is unpredictable; many maltreated children grow up to lead healthy, productive lives (Hart & Brassard, 1987; Rosenberg, 1987). (Such children are considered "resilient," and we talk about them later in this chapter.) Many others, however, suffer for years as the result of psychological abuse.

Psychological maltreatment, of course, is an element in the more than 2 million cases of child abuse and neglect. But it also occurs without physical abuse. It has been linked to children's lying, stealing, low self-esteem, emotional maladjustment, dependency, underachievement, depression, failure to thrive, aggression, homicide, and suicide, as well as to psychological distress in later life; and it may also play a part in learning disorders (Hart & Brassard, 1987).

Psychological maltreatment occurs both in families and in institutions, such as schools, hospitals, day care centers, and juvenile justice programs. School has come a long way since lessons were "taught to the tune of a hick'ry stick," with a dunce cap as a "reward"; but some schools still attempt to instill discipline through fear, intimidation, and degradation (Hart & Brassard, 1987).

Institutional maltreatment is easier to stop than maltreatment by *parents.* In most states, children may be taken from abusive parents; however, the courts are often reluctant to take this step except in extreme cases, especially when it is unclear that institutional care will be better (Melton & Davidson, 1987).

The best way to prevent such behavior is intervention before birth. Social service agencies can teach high-risk parents about child development, offer them support services, and train them to be more sensitive to babies' needs. To eliminate psychological maltreatment, society needs to question its values and make the needs of children a clear priority.

---

their shortened childhood too stressful. Today's children are pressured to succeed in school, to compete in sports, and to meet parents' emotional needs. Children are exposed to many adult problems on television and in real life before they have mastered the problems of childhood. Yet children are not small adults. They feel and think like children, and they need the years of childhood for healthy development.

COPING WITH STRESS: THE RESILIENT CHILD

The effects of stress are unpredictable, because people are unpredictable. Children's reactions to stressful events may depend on such factors as the event itself (children respond differently to a parent's death and to divorce), the child's age (preschoolers and adolescents react differently), and the child's sex (boys are more vulnerable than girls) (Rutter, 1984). Yet of two children of the same age and sex who are exposed to the same stressful experience, one may crumble while the other remains whole and healthy. Why is this so?

Resilient children are those who bounce back from circumstances that would blight the emotional development of most children. They are the children of the ghetto who go on to distinguish themselves in the professions. They are the neglected or abused children who go on to form intimate relationships, be good parents to their own children, and lead fulfilling lives. In spite of the bad

resilient children
Children who bounce back from unfortunate circumstances that would have a highly negative impact on the emotional development of most children.

BOX 13-5 ■ PROFESSIONAL VOICES

MICHAEL RUTTER

Michael Rutter is a British psychiatrist whose current field of interest is the "invulnerable child," that is, a child who can bounce back from even the harshest blows that life can offer. Besides conducting research, he has a clinical practice. Most of Rutter's patients are children.

QUESTION: What are the most important things parents can do to make their children resilient?

RUTTER: Good gracious! There's no simple, straightforward answer to that. I think that the sort of qualities we want a child to have are, first, a sense of self-esteem and efficacy—a feeling of your own worth, as well as a feeling that you can deal with things, that you can control what happens to you. One of the striking features of problem families is that they feel at the mercy of fate, which is always doing them an ill turn. So one important quality is a feeling that you are in fact master of your own destiny. Second, you need good relationships and security in those relationships. It's clear that throughout life, from infancy to old age, the support of these relationships is very important. Third, children need to become adaptable, to learn to cope with changing circumstances. To give a concrete example, one study I know of looked at how the stress of hospital admission affected young children and found that the ones who had previously had happy separation experiences— who had stayed overnight with friends, had been looked after by their grannies, or had had good baby-sitters—did better. Fourth, children need some experience with what is now talked about as social problem solving. It's a trendy thing at the moment, but it has a reality.

Q: I hadn't heard much about that. What is it?

RUTTER: Well, there are a number of programs in the United States, particularly, which help parents teach their children how to deal with social problems. This often means getting the child to think of alternative solutions. Suppose another child takes your toy—what do you do? Hit him? Go crying to your mother? See if you can share it? The idea is to get children to think of a range of solutions and show them the implications of each. But there is a danger that this may become just an intellectual exercise, and one of the real needs is to make it useful in real life.

Q: Are parents the best people to do this?

RUTTER: Yes, Not the only people, though. Schools play a very important role too. Children learn problem solving mostly from seeing how their parents deal with things. I mean, what do their parents do when they're frustrated, when they've had a bad day at work, or when somebody is unpleasant to them on their way home? Do they shout and swear and take it out on those around them, or do they find a way to make the situation more positive? It's more important for parents to show children what to do in everyday life than to tell them. . . .

Q: But what if parents give a bad example? Is it possible to teach, "Do as I say, not as I do"?

RUTTER: I think that's an uphill struggle. But it is important to recognize that children have multiple models. There's not just one parent, there are two—or nowadays, three, four, or six. There are older brothers and sisters. There are friends of the family, and there is school. School is thought of as a setting for pedagogy, but it is also a social organization and provides an opportunity for social learning. Teachers experience plenty of stress, and how they deal with it gives important messages to children.

Source: Pines, 1984; *photo:* Chris Steele-Perkins/Magnum.

cards they have been dealt, these children are winners. They are creative, resourceful, independent, and enjoyable to be with. What is special about them?

Several studies have identified "protective factors" that may operate to reduce the effects of such stressors as kidnapping or poor parenting (Anthony & Koupernik, 1974; Garmezy, 1983; Rutter, 1984). Several of these factors may also protect children who have been psychologically abused (Rosenberg, 1987).

Are some children born with stress-proof personalities? Or must children *develop* resilience in response to environmental factors? There has been little research on hereditary factors in handling stress or on the effect of differences in temperament, which seem to be partly hereditary (Rutter, 1983). (For suggestions on helping children become resilient, see Box 13-5.) Factors like the following seem to contribute to children's resilience.

- *Personality.* Resilient children tend to be adaptable enough to cope with changing circumstances. They are usually positive thinkers, friendly, sensitive to other people, and independent. They feel competent and have high self-esteem. Intelligence, too, may be a factor: good students seem to cope better (Rutter, 1984).
- *Family.* Resilient children are likely to have good relationships with parents who are emotionally supportive of them and each other, or, failing that, to have a close relationship with at least one parent. If they lack even this, they are likely to be close to at least one relative or other adult who shows interest in them and obviously cares for them, and whom they trust. Resilient abused children are likely to have been abused by only one parent rather than both and to have had a loving, supportive relationship with one parent or a foster parent when growing up (Kaufman & Zigler, 1987).
- *Learning experiences.* Resilient children are likely to have had experience solving social problems. They have seen parents, older siblings, or others dealing with frustration and making the best of a bad situation. They have faced challenges themselves, worked out solutions, and learned that they can exert some control over their lives.
- *Reduced risk.* Children who have been exposed to only one of a number of factors strongly related to psychiatric disorder (such as discord between the parents, low social status, overcrowding at home, a disturbed mother, a criminal father, and experience in foster care or an institution) are often able to overcome the stress; but when two or more of these factors are present, children's risk of developing an emotional disturbance increases fourfold or more (Rutter, quoted in Pines, 1979). When children are not besieged on all sides, they can often cope with adverse circumstances.
- *Compensating experiences.* A supportive school environment and successful experiences in sports, in music, or with other children or interested adults can help make up for a dismal home life. In adulthood, a good marriage can compensate for poor relationships earlier in life.

All this research, of course, does not mean that what happens in a child's life does not matter. In general, children with an unfavorable background have more problems in adjustment than children with a favorable background. What is heartening about these findings is the recognition that childhood experiences do not necessarily determine the outcome of a person's life (Kagan, 1984), that many people do have the strength to rise above the most difficult circumstances, and that we are constantly rewriting the stories of our lives as long as we live.

BOX 13-6 ■ A CHILD'S WORLD AND YOU

WHAT DO YOU THINK?

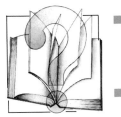

- Since children's peers are so influential, should parents restrict their friendships to children the parents approve of? Give reasons for your answer.
- Should schools actively seek to reduce racial prejudice?

- Do you think that parents who want a divorce should stay married until all their children have grown up?
- Should a mother whose finances permit a choice stay home and take care of the children instead of going to work?
- When was the first time you remember being treated in a special way, either positive or negative, because of your race, religion, or ethnic background?

Summary

1 Self-concept is the sense of self. It is based on one's knowledge of what one has done; it guides future behavior. Self-concept develops greatly in middle childhood. Children begin to define themselves in psychological and social terms and to compare the real self with an ideal self. As children internalize social values and become aware of the views of others, they coordinate personal and social demands and values.

2 Self-esteem, or a favorable evaluation of oneself, is important to success and happiness. Four factors that contribute to self-esteem are a sense of significance, competence, virtue, and power. Parents of children with high self-esteem tend to have authoritative parenting styles.

3 Freud saw middle childhood as a latency period of sexuality, or period of relative sexual calm. The development of the superego at the end of early childhood keeps the id under control, allowing children to become socialized rapidly and to develop skills. The extent of sexual latency has come into question.

4 Erikson's fourth crisis, which occurs during middle childhood, is industry versus inferiority. The "virtue" of this period is competence, a view of the self as able to master and complete tasks.

5 Social-learning theorists point to the influence of parents, teachers, and peers as models who become powerful shapers of self-concept.

6 Piaget's cognitive-developmental approach holds that the decline of egocentrism and the ability to decenter make children more sensitive to what others think of them and more able to see themselves from different viewpoints.

7 According to the information-processing approach, children build, test, and modify self-schemata (hypotheses or knowledge structures about the self) on the basis of experience. Many lasting self-schemata develop during middle childhood.

8 Schoolchildren today spend more of their leisure time watching television and less time playing than children in the past. As children move through elementary school, they do less reading for pleasure. Many children are involved in sports and other organized activities.

9 The peer group assumes particular importance during middle childhood. However, relationships with parents continue to be the most important relationships in children's lives.

10 The peer group is an important testing ground for self-concept and self-esteem. School-age youngsters are most susceptible to pressure to conform, which may encourage antisocial behavior. Most children select peers who are like them in age, sex, and socioeconomic status. Racial prejudice among schoolchildren appears to be diminishing as a result of school integration.

11 The basis of friendship changes during middle childhood. Children choose friends they feel comfortable with, and they see friendships as involving give-and-take.

12 Popularity influences self-esteem, and vice versa. Children who think well of themselves are more popular than those with low self-esteem. Children who are not only ignored by their peers but rejected by them are at risk of emotional and behavioral problems. Training in social skills can help such children be accepted by their peers.

13 Although school-age children require less direct supervision than younger children, it is still important for parents to monitor their children's activities. Disciplinary methods evolve with the child's cognitive development, but there appears to be an underlying consistency in parents' child-rearing attitudes. There appear to be some social class differences in parenting styles.

14 Children grow up in a variety of family situations besides the traditional nuclear family. These include families in which mothers work outside the home (now a majority of families), families with divorced parents, stepfamilies, and one-parent families. In some families, children regularly care for themselves for significant periods of time. There are age differences in reaction to family situations. The way parents handle a situation influences how children will adjust to it.

15 Siblings exert a powerful influence on each other, either directly (through their interaction) or indirectly (through their impact on each other's relationship with parents).

16 Emotional disturbances during childhood are not uncommon. These include acting-out behavior, anxiety disorders (including separation anxiety disorder and school phobia), and childhood depression. Treatment techniques include individual psychotherapy, family therapy, behavior therapy, and drug therapy. Psychological therapies are generally effective. Drug therapy is effective in certain situations; when used it should be accompanied by psychotherapy.

17 Normal childhood stresses take many forms and can affect healthy emotional development. As a result of the pressures of modern life, many children are experiencing a shortened and stressful childhood.

18 Psychological maltreatment of children is widespread among both families and institutions. It can result in damage to children's behavioral, cognitive, emotional, or physical functioning and may prevent them from fulfilling their potential.

19 Some children are more resilient than others; they are better able to withstand stress. Factors related to personality, family, experience, and degree of risk are associated with the ability to bounce back from unfortunate circumstances.

Key Terms

self-concept (page 459)
self-awareness (459)
self-recognition (459)
self-definition (459)
real self (459)
ideal self (459)
self-esteem (460)
latency period (462)
industry versus inferiority (462)
self-schema (463)
prejudice (468)
discipline (473)

coregulation (474)
acting-out behavior (489)
separation anxiety disorder (490)
school phobia (490)
affective disorder (491)
childhood depression (491)
psychotherapy (492)
family therapy (492)
behavior therapy (492)
drug therapy (493)
psychological maltreatment (494)
resilient children (495)

Suggested Readings

Coopersmith, S. (1967).   *The antecedents of self-esteem.* San Francisco: Freeman. A report of a study of 85 boys, 10 to 12 years of age, which correlated self-esteem with parents' attitudes and child-rearing practices, and with the boys' functioning.

Elkind, D. (1988).   *The hurried child (rev. ed.).* New York: Addison-Wesley. This book, by a well-known psychologist, examines how parents can raise healthy children who enjoy childhood, despite a social trend toward pressure to grow up fast.

Olds, S.W. (1989).   *The working parents' survival guide.* Rocklin, CA: Prima. A manual for mothers and fathers which draws on up-to-date research on concerns of working parents and their children. It offers practical solutions for a variety of problems.

Pogrebin, L.C. (1983).   *Family politics.* New York: McGraw-Hill. A lively, profamily book by a feminist who compares traditional and present-day families, identifies the strengths and weaknesses of various kinds of families, and urges changes.

Stewart, M.A., & Olds, S.W. (1973).   *Raising a hyperactive child.* New York: Harper & Row. A book for the lay reader that defines the characteristics of hyperactivity, explores possible causes, and offers practical suggestions to parents and teachers concerning day-to-day living with hyperactive children.

ADOLESCENCE

Vicky and Jason, sweltering under their caps and gowns, are in their high school auditorium. As they listen to the graduation day speeches and sing school songs, they think about this turning point in their lives. From now on they will be moving in different circles, as they leave behind the world of children and enter the world of adults.

The last few years leading to this moment were sometimes stormy, sometimes sublime. How could they be anything else when they were so filled with changes? In Chapter 14, 15, and 16 we will examine those changes.

The physical changes are enormous. Jason and Vicky haven't just grown taller and heavier. They have matured, taking on the bodies of adults. Intellectually, too, they have blossomed. Both can now think abstractly and hypothetically; they can aspire to ideas as well as to competence. Their personalities have matured also. They have not settled everything, but they have a clearer sense of their own identities, of who they are and who they wish to become. On the threshold of adulthood, Vicky and Jason are becoming mature individuals.

PHYSICAL DEVELOPMENT IN ADOLESCENCE

Thirteen's anomalous—not that, not this:
Not folded bud, or wave that laps a shore,
Or moth proverbial from the chrysalis.
Is the one age defeats the metaphor.
Is not a town, like childhood, strongly walled
But easily surrounded; is no city.
Nor, quitted once, can it be quite recalled—
Not even with pity.

Phyllis McGinley, "A Certain Age," 1956

PREVIEW QUESTIONS

- What physical changes occur during adolescence?
- How does early or late sexual maturation affect an adolescent psychologically?
- What are the most common health problems of adolescence?
- Which drugs are most used—and abused—by adolescents? What are the ramifications of such use?
- Which sexually transmitted diseases are adolescents at risk of?

VICKY, WHO IS NOW 13, cannot pass a mirror without gazing into it, and she never feels the same way twice about what she sees. Every week she seems to have a different body, and this both intrigues and perplexes her. "Am I too fat? Why is my nose so big? Will I ever be pretty?" she wonders. Vicky has entered adolescence, and her body is changing as it becomes capable of a new function—sexual reproduction.

At a slightly later age, Jason, too, undergoes great physical changes, although the ability to father a child puts less radical demands on his body than the ability to give birth puts on Vicky's. Jason likes the changes he sees. With peach fuzz on his cheeks and a new, deeper voice (nobody mistakes him for his mother on the phone anymore), Jason feels that he is leaving childhood behind. By the end of adolescence Jason has the body of a grown man, and Vicky the body of a grown woman. Both look quite different from the way they did when they entered their teens.

adolescence
Developmental transition period between childhood and adulthood.

Adolescence is a developmental transition between childhood and adulthood. In this chapter we begin to explore it by examining the many physical changes that take place.

First, we look at the timing and the psychological impact of the changes. We then discuss some health issues associated with this time of life—the importance of good nutrition, common eating disorders, use and abuse of drugs, and sexually transmitted diseases that adolescents are most at risk of. We also examine two especially tragic problems affecting growing numbers of adolescents—

abuse and neglect, and teenage suicide. These topics are painful to read about, but since they affect many young people today, anyone interested in adolescence needs to know about them. Fortunately, as we shall see, most young people come through adolescence in good physical and mental health.

Adolescence: A Developmental Transition

It is easier to determine when adolescence begins than when it has ended. The biological changes that signal the end of childhood produce rapid growth in height and weight, changes in body proportions, and the attainment of *sexual maturity*—the ability to reproduce. Adolescence is generally considered to begin with the onset of *puberty,* the process that leads to sexual maturity (puberty may also be described as *adolescent maturation*).* But the end of adolescence has to do with social and emotional factors rather than physiological change. It has been said that adolescence "begins in biology and ends in culture" (Conger & Peterson, 1984, p. 92).

Before the twentieth century, children entered the adult world when they matured physically or when they began a vocational apprenticeship. Today, however, the entry into adulthood is not so clear-cut. One reason is that puberty occurs earlier than it used to (see the discussion of the secular trend later in this chapter), so that there is a lapse of time between puberty and adulthood. A second reason is that our complex society requires a longer period of education, which postpones adulthood. A third reason is that there are no really definitive markers to establish adulthood. Many traditional cultures do mark the arrival of adulthood with a "coming-of-age" rite. The ritual may be held at a certain age, such as the bar mitzvah and bas mitzvah observances that welcome 13-year-old Jewish boys and girls into adult society. Or it can be tied to a specific event like a girl's first menstruation; the Apaches' 4-day ritual of sunrise-to-sunset chanting is an example (see Box 14-1, page 506). But the start of adulthood in modern industrial societies tends to be ambiguous.

Vicky thinks she's an adult when she gets her driver's license, Jason when he casts his first vote. Jess says, "I'll know Jason's an adult when he stops calling home collect!" American young people consider themselves adult at various ages, depending on which marker they use. For example, they can draw on a variety of legal definitions of adulthood: at age 18, people may marry without their parents permission; at 17, they may enlist in the armed forces; at 18 to 21 (depending on the state), they may enter into binding contracts. People can also use sociological definitions, and call themselves adults when they are self-supporting, or have chosen a career, married, or founded a family. There are also psychological definitions. Intellectual maturity is generally considered to coincide with the capacity for abstract thought (see Chapter 15); emotional maturity depends on such achievements as discovering one's identity, becoming independent of one's parents, developing a system of values, and forming mature relationships of friendship and love (see Chapter 16). Some people, of course, never leave adolescence, no matter what their chronological age.

The bar mitzvah, the Jewish ritual that this 13-year-old boy is celebrating, is one of the few formal coming-of-age rites that are still celebrated in western cultures.

puberty Process that leads to sexual maturity and the ability to reproduce.

---

*The term *puberty* is sometimes used to mean the end point—that is, sexual maturity—and *pubescence* to mean the process by which sexual maturity is reached; but our usage conforms to that of most psychologists today.

BOX 14-1 ■ AROUND THE WORLD

FEMALE CIRCUMCISION

Many traditional societies have coming-of-age rituals that signal membership in the adult community. These ceremonies often include putting an enduring mark on the body—tattooing or scarring the face, removing the foreskin from the penis, sharpening the teeth, and so forth. One custom widely practiced in some parts of Africa, the middle east, and southeast Asia is *clitoridectomy,* the removal of a portion of the clitoris. The operation is performed on girls of varying ages from infancy to puberty.

The purposes of this procedure include preserving virginity, reducing the sex drive, maintaining cleanliness, and enhancing beauty. The consequences are often less benign, including—besides the loss of sexual fulfillment—infection from unsterilized instruments and serious loss of blood, which, not infrequently, lead to death.

The operation has been extremely controversial for years. In the countries where it is practiced, government officials, physicians, and women's groups have tried to end it, but because most women in the tribes that practice it believe in the procedure and are often the ones who carry it out, it still goes on.

Some 50 years ago, before Jomo Kenyatta became the first president of Kenya, he published a book explaining and defending the customs of his tribe, the Kikuyu (or Gikuyu), including clitoridectomy. Although his successors outlawed the practice, it is still performed on some Kikuyu girls. In a later book, Kenyatta (1965) described the ceremony:

> A woman specialist, known as *moruithia,* who has studied this form of surgery from childhood, dashes out of the crowd, dressed in a very peculiar way, with her face painted with white and black ochre. This disguise tends to make her look rather terrifying, with her rhythmic movement accompanied by rattles tied to her legs. She takes out from her pocket the operating Gikuyu razor, and in quick movements, and with the dexterity of a Harley Street surgeon, proceeds to operate upon the girls. With a stroke she cuts off the tip of the clitoris. As no other part of the girl's sexual organ is interfered with, this completes the girl's operation. (p. 140)

In some areas, attitudes do seem to be changing. A survey of 150 female third-year high school students in the Sudan found that even though about 96 percent had had some form of circumcision performed on them, more than 70 percent were strongly opposed to the same operation for their sisters and other young girls. These girl's attitudes may have been influenced by the campaign to do away with female circumcision being led by a growing number of women throughout Africa.

Sources: Kenyatta, 1965; Pugh, 1983.

THE TIMING OF PUBERTY

A picture of any eighth- or ninth-grade class will present startling contrasts: flat-chested little girls next to full-bosomed, full-grown young women, and scrawny little boys looking up at broad-shouldered, mustached young men. This variance is normal. There is about a 6- to 7-year range for puberty in both boys and girls.

During puberty, the reproductive functions mature, the sex organs (see Table 14-1) enlarge, and the secondary sex characteristics appear (see Table 14-2).

TABLE 14-1

PRIMARY SEX CHARACTERISTICS: SEX ORGANS	
FEMALE	MALE
Ovaries	Testes
Fallopian tubes	Penis
Uterus	Scrotum
Vagina	Seminal vesicles
	Prostate gland

TABLE 14-2

SECONDARY SEX CHARACTERISTICS	
GIRLS	BOYS
Breasts	Pubic hair
Pubic hair	Axillary (underarm) hair
Axillary (underarm) hair	Facial hair
Increased width and depth of pelvis	Changes in voice
Changes in voice	Changes in skin
Changes in skin	Broadening of shoulders

This process lasts for about 2 years. It is the time of life when the greatest sexual differentiation since the early prenatal stage takes place. These changes affect adolescents' lives in many ways, including how they get along with their families, which we discuss in Chapter 16. Box 14-2 discusses some effects of the ability to reproduce.

The *average* age for the beginning of puberty in girls is 10 years (with full sexual maturity at 12); however, normal girls may show the first signs as early as the age of 7 or as late as age 14 (with maturity from age 9 to age 16). The average age for boys' entry into puberty is 12 (maturity at age 14), but there is a normal range from age 9 to age 16 (maturity from age 11 to age 18) (Chumlea, 1982).

The physical changes of adolescence unfold in a sequence that is much more consistent than their actual timing, although even the order in which they appear varies somewhat from one person to another (for example, growth of pubic

---

BOX 14-2 ■ PROFESSIONAL VOICES

SOL GORDON

Sex for teenagers is a health hazard. Teenagers are too young, too vulnerable, too available for exploitation. They don't know that the first experiences of sex are usually grim. Almost no girl has an orgasm. The guy gets his orgasm three days later when he tells his friends about it.

I also know that half of all young people are going to have intercourse whether we like it or not, and whether they like it or not. So we're going to have to say to them, "Listen, if you're not going to listen to us, at least use birth control." And I'm tired of all this research that says all these girls get pregnant because of an unresolved Oedipus complex; or because they can't understand moral development; or because they have all this peer pressure; or because they want to get pregnant. I know why teenage girls get pregnant. It is because they have sexual intercourse.

We're not helping them when we try just explaining to them why they're having sex. We had better start giving some messages in advance of pregnancy, such as the fact that almost 90 percent of teenage boys who make a teenage girl pregnant abandon her. This includes those who marry to cover the pregnancy.

We also have to say that sex is never a test of love. Boys say "If you really loved me, you'd have sex with me." I wrote this little book entitled *You Would If You Loved Me.* It's a book of lines that boys use to seduce girls. I have received hundreds of letters from teenage girls, most surprisingly the same. They start, "Dr. Gordon, you don't know me. I'm 14 years old, and you saved my life. . . . Last week this guy came across with a line, and you know what I said to him? 'Hey, that's a line.'"

I talk about teenage girls because only they get pregnant. In the sexist society we live in, where boys are programmed to have sex, . . . we have to protect the girls. We have to tell them that if boys are going to play games, then girls have to be good at it too. Until such time as boys and girls don't play such games with each other, we're going to have to teach young people to be assertive.

Source: S. Gordon, 1982; *photo:* Sol Gordon.

TABLE 14-3

USUAL SEQUENCE OF PHYSIOLOGICAL CHANGES IN ADOLESCENCE	
GIRLS' CHARACTERISTICS	**AGE OF FIRST APPEARANCE**
Growth of breasts	8–13
Growth of pubic hair	8–14
Body growth	9.5–14.5 (average peak, 12)
Menarche	10–16.5 (average, 12.5)
Underarm hair	About 2 years after pubic hair
Increased output of oil- and sweat-producing glands (which may lead to acne)	About the same time as underarm hair
BOYS' CHARACTERISTICS	**AGE OF FIRST APPEARANCE**
Growth of testes, scrotal sac	10–13.5
Growth of pubic hair	10–15
Body growth	10.5–16 (average peak, 14)
Growth of penis, prostate gland, seminal vesicles	11–14.5 (average, 12.5)
Change in voice	About the same time as growth of penis
First ejaculation of semen	About 1 year after beginning of growth of penis
Facial and underarm hair	About 2 years after appearance of pubic hair
Increased output of oil- and sweat-producing glands (which may lead to acne)	About the same time as underarm hair

hair precedes breast development in about one-third of all girls). The usual sequences are shown in Table 14-3.

No one fully understands why puberty begins when it does or precisely what mechanism triggers it. We know only that at some biologically determined time—a time apparently regulated by the interaction of genes, individual health, and environment—the pituitary gland sends a message to a young person's sex glands. Upon receipt of that message, a girl's ovaries sharply step up their production of *estrogen,* and a boy's testes increase the manufacture of androgens, especially testosterone. These hormones stimulate sexual maturation.

Hormones are also closely associated with emotions, specifically, with aggressive feelings in boys and with both aggression and depression in girls (Brooks-Gunn, 1988). Since early adolescence is a time of great hormonal change, some researchers attribute the general rise of emotionality and moodiness at this time to hormones. However, we need to remember that social influences are also present, and sometimes predominate. For example, even though there is a well-established relationship between production of the hormone testosterone and sexuality, adolescents begin sexual behavior in accord with the norms of their social group (Brooks-Gunn, 1988).

The onset of puberty may be influenced by heredity, perhaps by inborn differences in hormone production. This is suggested by findings that body size in infancy seems to correlate with the timing of puberty. Among 78 healthy, well-nourished 14-year-old boys, the ones who were more advanced in sexual development had been heavier and more muscular at 6 months of age (Mills, Shiono, Shapiro, Crawford, & Rhoads, 1986).

THE SECULAR TREND

On the basis of historical sources, developmentalists have identified a *secular trend*—a lowering of the age at which Americans reach adult height and sexual

estrogen Female sex hormone.

secular trend Trend noted by observing several generations; in child development, a trend toward earlier attainment of adult height and sexual maturity, which began a century ago and appears to have ended in the United States.

maturity. It began about 100 years ago, probably as a reflection of higher living standards in most segments of our population, but it now seems to have ended, at least in the United States (Schmeck, 1976). This secular trend has also occurred in western Europe and Japan, but it has not been seen at all in some other countries (Chumlea, 1982). The leveling off of the trend suggests that some of the elements of maturity—such as the age at which girls begin to menstruate—have reached a genetically determined limit and that factors such as better nutrition are unlikely to bring it any lower.

The most obvious explanation for the secular trend, as we have just suggested, seems to be a higher standard of living. Children who are healthier, better nourished, and better cared for mature earlier and grow bigger. Evidence of this is the fact that menarche comes later in less developed countries than in more industrialized cultures. In New Guinea, for example, where nutrition is poor, girls do not begin to menstruate until sometime between 15.4 and 18.4 years of age (Eveleth & Tanner, 1976).

Puberty: The Physical Changes of Adolescence

WHAT PHYSICAL CHANGES TAKE PLACE DURING ADOLESCENCE?

Adolescent maturation, or puberty, has several aspects. These are the physical changes of adolescence, which we will describe in turn:

- Growth spurt
- Menarche—the beginning of menstruation for girls
- Primary sex characteristics—changes in the organs directly related to reproduction
- Secondary sex characteristics—physiological signs of sexual maturity that do not directly involve the reproductive organs

We will also note when most young people in the United States experience these changes; later, we will go on to consider their psychological effects.

Adolescent Growth Spurt

An early sign of maturation is the ***adolescent growth spurt***—a sharp increase in height and weight that generally begins in girls between the ages of 9½ and 14½ (usually at about age 10) and in boys between the ages of 10½ and 16 (usually at about age 12 or 13). It typically lasts about 2 years. Soon after the growth spurt ends, the young person reaches sexual maturity. Growth in height is virtually complete by age 18 (Behrman & Vaughan, 1983).

Before the growth spurt, boys are typically only about 2 percent taller than girls; during the years from age 11 to age 13, girls are taller, heavier, and stronger; after the growth spurt, boys are again larger, now by about 8 percent. The growth spurt in males is more intense, and its later appearance allows for an extra period of growth, since growth goes on at a faster rate before puberty than afterward.

Boys and girls grow differently during adolescence. Jason becomes larger

adolescent growth spurt
Sharp increase in height and weight that precedes sexual maturity.

(© Bob Daemmrich/Stock, Boston)

During the years from 11 to 13, girls are on the average taller, heavier, and stronger than boys, who achieve their adolescent growth spurt later than girls do—as these choristers in junior high demonstrate. If our society did not have such a rigid belief that males should be taller than females, this temporary state would be less embarrassing for the boys.

overall; his shoulders will be wider, his legs longer relative to his trunk, and his forearms longer relative to both his upper arms and his height (Tanner, 1964). Vicky's pelvis widens to make childbearing possible; and layers of fat develop under her skin, giving her a more rounded appearance.

In both sexes the adolescent growth spurt affects practically all skeletal and muscular dimensions. Even the eye grows faster, causing an increase in near-sightedness during this period. The lower jaw usually becomes longer and thicker, both jaw and nose project more, and the incisors of both jaws become more upright.

These changes are greater in boys than in girls and follow their own time-tables, so that parts of the body may be out of proportion for a while. The result is the familiar teenage awkwardness or gawkiness that accompanies unbalanced, accelerated growth. Balance is almost always restored eventually, but meanwhile, just when the ability to charm members of the opposite sex seems of the utmost importance, the typical adolescent has a most uncharming clumsiness. Adolescents apparently do not like to be told that this is "just a phase"; but Jason, for one, secretly welcomes the reassurance that his clumsiness is a matter of being at an awkward age rather than of having an awkward personality.

Primary Sex Characteristics

primary sex characteristics Organs directly related to reproduction, which enlarge and mature in early adolescence (compare *secondary sex characteristics*).

The *primary sex characteristics* are the organs that are necessary for reproduction. In the female, the body structures involved are the ovaries, uterus, and vagina; in the male they are the testes, penis, prostate gland, and seminal vesicles (refer to Table 14-1). During puberty, these organs enlarge and mature.

The principal sign of sexual maturity in girls is menstruation, which will be discussed shortly. In boys, the first sign of puberty is the growth of the testes and scrotum, and the principal sign of sexual maturity is the presence of sperm in the urine (a boy is fertile as soon as viable sperm are present). Like menstruation, the timing of the appearance of sperm is highly variable. It is difficult to determine when sperm first appear, but one longitudinal study found that only 2 percent of 11- to 12-year-old boys had sperm present in the urine, compared with 24 percent of 15-year-old boys (Richardson & Short, 1978).

A pubescent boy often wakes to find a wet spot or a hardened, dried spot in the bed, letting him know that while he was asleep he had a *nocturnal emission*, an involuntary ejaculation of semen that is commonly referred to as a *wet dream*. Most adolescents who are neither having sexual intercourse nor masturbating regularly have these perfectly normal emissions, which may or may not occur in connection with an erotic dream.

Secondary Sex Characteristics

The ***secondary sex characteristics*** are physiological signs of sexual maturity that do not directly involve the reproductive organs. They include such characteristics as the breasts of females and the broad shoulders of males. Other secondary sex characteristics involve changes in the voice, texture of skin, and pubic, facial, axillary (armpit), and body hair characteristic of an adult male or female (see Table 14-2).

The first sign of puberty in girls is usually the budding of the breasts: the nipples enlarge and protrude; the areolae, which are the pigmented areas surrounding the nipples, enlarge; and the breasts assume first a conical and then a rounded shape. The breasts are usually fully developed before menstruation begins. Much to their distress, some adolescent boys experience temporary breast enlargement; this is normal and may last from 12 to 18 months.

Various forms of hair growth also signal maturity. Pubic hair, which is at first straight and silky and eventually becomes coarse, dark, and curly, appears in different patterns in males and females. Axillary hair grows in the armpits. Adolescent boys are usually happy to see hair on the face and chest; but girls are

secondary sex characteristics
*Physiological signs of sexual maturation (such as breast development and growth of body hair) that do not involve the sex organs (compare **primary sex characteristics**).*

Adolescent boys usually welcome the need to shave, since facial hair is one of the secondary sex characteristics that signal sexual maturity.

(Culver)

When Anne Frank wrote her now-famous diary, she probably never dreamed that her intimate thoughts about her sexual maturation would be read by people all over the world. One of the most poignant aspects of her tragic death is the universality of so many of the feelings that she expressed so well.

menarche *Girl's first menstruation.*

usually dismayed at the appearance of even a slight amount of facial hair or hair around the nipples, although this is a normal phenomenon.

The skin of both boys and girls becomes coarser and oilier. The increased activity of the sebaceous glands (which secrete a fatty substance) gives rise to the outbreaks of pimples and blackheads that are the bane of many teenagers' lives. Acne is more troublesome in boys than girls and seems to be related to increased amounts of the male hormone testosterone.

The voices of both boys and girls deepen, partly in response to the growth of the larynx and partly—especially in boys—in response to the production of male hormones.

Menarche: The Beginning of Menstruation

I think what is happening to me is so wonderful, and not only what can be seen on my body, but all that is taking place inside. I never discuss myself or any of these things with anybody: that is why I have to talk to myself about them. . . . Each time I have a period—and that has only been three times—I have the feeling that in spite of all the pain, unpleasantness, and nastiness, I have a sweet secret, and that is why, although it is nothing but a nuisance to me in a way, I always long for the time that I shall feel that secret within me again. (Anne Frank, 1952, pp. 115–116)

These words, in Anne Frank's diary, typify the ambivalence of many girls to the onset of menstruation, the monthly shedding of tissue from the lining of the womb. *Menarche,* the first menstruation, is the most dramatic sign of a girl's sexual maturity. The early menstrual periods usually do not include ovulation, and many girls are not able to conceive for 12 to 18 months after menarche. Since ovulation and conception do sometimes occur in the early months, however, girls who have begun to menstruate should assume that if they have sexual intercourse, they can become pregnant.

Timing of Menarche   We have already noted the secular trend, or the lowering of the age at which boys and girls reach adult height and become sexually mature. Over the past century, girls have experienced menarche at a younger age; however, the average age at the first menstruation has remained stable since the 1940s (Zacharias, Rand, & Wurtman, 1976). Climate has little or no effect: Eskimo and Nigerian (west African) girls have similar menarcheal ages. However, city girls, girls from small families, mildly obese girls, and girls born early in the year mature earlier than country girls, girls from large families, girls of normal weight, extremely obese girls, and girls born at the end of the year (Zacharias &Wurtman, 1969). Some of these factors seem to be related to economic situation and nutrition.

Genetics also seems to play a part. On average, identical twin sisters differ by only 2.8 months in the timing of menarche, whereas fraternal twins differ by a year, nontwin sisters by 12.9 months, and unrelated women by 18.6 months (Hiernaux, 1968).

Effects of Exercise on Menstruation   One line of research has looked at the relationship between exercise and menstruation. Serious athletes, dancers, and swimmers often begin to menstruate quite late, sometimes not till after age 18 (R. E. Frisch, Wyshak, & Vincent, 1980). This may be due to the stress of training or to diminished blood circulation. Reduction in body fat also seems to play a part, since the effect is greater when young women lose weight (Bullen, Skrinar, von Mering, Turnbull, & McArthur, 1985). However, most female athletes do not experience menstrual irregularity, and those who do usually become regular when training stops and can then go on to normal childbearing (Bullen et al., 1985; Shangold, 1978).

WHAT IS THE PSYCHOLOGICAL IMPACT OF PHYSICAL CHANGES?

Adolescence is probably the most embarrassing part of the life span. Teenagers are acutely self-conscious and sure that everyone is watching them, and their bodies are constantly betraying them. Jason's voice often squeaks when he is trying to seem mature, and his penis becomes obviously erect at the most embarrassing times. Vicky hides her budding breasts under bulky clothing and worries about getting menstrual blood on her clothes.

But adolescence also offers new possibilities, which young people approach in different ways. It is not surprising that the dramatic physical changes of adolescence have many psychological ramifications. Especially keen are psychological reactions to the onset of menstruation, to changes in physical appearance, and to early or late maturation. (This last is discussed in Box 14-3, page 514.)

Feelings about Menarche and Menstruation

A girl's psychological reaction to menarche depends on many things. Among the most important are the ways her culture, her subculture, and her family view this event.

Many girls learn about menstruation from their mothers, but even today a sizable number of girls are not prepared ahead of time. This is regrettable, since girls who are prepared for menarche have a more positive attitude toward menstruation and experience less distress (Koff, Rierdan, & Sheingold, 1982; Ruble & Brooks-Gunn, 1982). Girls who begin to menstruate earlier than most of their classmates find it most disruptive (Ruble & Brooks-Gunn, 1982), possibly because they are less well prepared or simply because they feel out of step. Again, we see how the timing of an event can affect the way a person responds to the event itself.

Unfortunately, most American women remember menarche negatively, and girls who have already begun to menstruate have a more negative attitude toward menstruation than those who have not. One reason for this may be that menstruation is a forbidden subject in our society, even within many families. Thus there are no meaningful rituals to celebrate menarche (Grief & Ulman, 1982). Moreover, American culture treats menstruation as a hygienic crisis, emphasizing women's need to stay clean and sweet-smelling rather than instilling pride in womanhood (Whisnant & Zegans, 1975).

Menstruation is much more than a physical event. It "is a concrete symbol of a shift from girl to woman" (Ruble & Brooks-Gunn, 1982, p. 1557). Girls who have begun to menstruate are more conscious of their femaleness than premarcheal girls of the same age. They are more interested in boy-girl relations and in adorning their bodies; and when they draw female figures, they show more explicit breasts. In addition, they seem more mature in certain personality characteristics (Grief & Ulman, 1982).

BOX 14-3 ■ THE RESEARCH WORLD

PSYCHOLOGICAL EFFECTS OF EARLY AND LATE MATURATION

A paradox of adolescence is a young person's yearning to find an individual identity—to assert a self different from anyone else in the world—and at the same time wanting to be exactly like other adolescents. Anything that obviously sets an adolescent apart from the crowd is unsettling.

This is seen in adolescents who experience puberty much earlier or much later than most of their friends. The timing of puberty has significant psychological effects, and early and late maturity can create different kinds of problems. Neither situation is necessarily troublesome, however—or advantageous.

EARLY AND LATE MATURATION IN BOYS

Some research has shown early-maturing boys to be more poised, more relaxed, more good-natured, less affected, more popular with peers, more likely to be school leaders, and less impulsive than late maturers; but other studies have found them to be more worried about being liked, more cautious, and more bound by rules and routines. Late maturers have been variously found to feel more inadequate, rejected, and dominated; to be more dependent, aggressive, and insecure; to rebel more against their parents; and to think less of themselves (Mussen & Jones, 1957; Peskin, 1967, 1973; Siegel, 1982). Although some studies have shown that early maturers retain a head start in intellectual performance into late adolescence and adulthood (Gross & Duke, 1980; Tanner, 1978), many differences seem to disappear by adulthood (M. C. Jones, 1957).

We see pluses and minuses in both situations. By and large, early maturers seem to be at an advantage. They have an edge in sports and in dating, since they are stronger, and have a more favorable body image (Blyth et al., 1981). But they sometimes have problems living up to others' expectations—particularly, they should act as mature as they look. Furthermore, they may have too little time to prepare for the changes of adolescence. Late maturers may feel and act more childish, but they may benefit from the longer period of childhood, when they do not have to deal with the new and different demands of adolescence; and they may become more flexible as they adapt to the problems of being

smaller and more childish-looking than their peers (Livson & Peskin, 1980).

EARLY AND LATE MATURATION IN GIRLS

Advantages and disadvantages show up for girls too, but are less clear-cut. Early-maturing girls have been found to be less sociable, expressive, and poised, to be more introverted and shy, and to react more negatively to menarche (M. C. Jones, 1958; Livson & Peskin, 1980; Ruble & Brooks-Gunn, 1982). They have a poorer body image and lower self-esteem than later-maturing girls (Simmons, Blyth, Van Cleave, & Bush, 1979). Early maturers may feel less attractive (Crockett & Peterson, 1987) because the curviness that comes with puberty clashes with cultural standards of beauty that emphasize thinness. It is also possible that they are reacting to other people's concern about their sexuality. Parents and teachers, for example, may treat girls who have physically mature bodies more strictly and more disapprovingly than they treat less developed girls.

The effects of timing of puberty are most likely to be negative when adolescents are very different from their peers, maturing either much earlier or much later. Earlier maturers may also feel dismayed when they do not see the changes as advantageous (Simmons, Blyth, & McKinney, 1983); for example, Vicky's best friend, the star of the school gymnastics team, feared that her budding breasts might interfere with her agility on the bars.

Some of the problems of early-maturing girls may stem from feeling conspicuous: they are bigger than most boys and more bosomy than other girls. But the process of working through these problems may give them valuable experience for dealing with problems later in life. Some researchers have, in fact, found that early-maturing girls make a better adjustment in adulthood (M. C. Jones & Mussen, 1958; Livson & Peskin, 1980).

Finally, it is difficult to generalize about the effect of timing of puberty, because it depends—at least in part—on how the individual adolescent and the people in his or her world interpret it. In all cases, the adults in an adolescent's world need to be sensitive to the impact of change so that they can help the young person experience this period of the life span as positively as possible.

Most modern girls take menstruation in stride. One survey of more than 600 fifth- to twelfth-graders found that girls do not find their first menstruation painful and do not find menstruation restricting. They trade stories about symptoms and seem fairly relaxed, although they recognize that a significant change has occurred in their lives (Ruble & Brooks-Gunn, 1982).

What can be done to make menstruation a more positive experience? Ellen and Charles helped Vicky see this event as a special sign of maturity. First, they explained menstruation—in concrete, personal terms that she could understand—as soon as her breasts and pubic hair began to develop. They reassured her that she could engage in all her normal activities, including sports, during her menstrual period—and that she could take baths. They encouraged her to ask questions, and they maintained an open, matter-of-fact attitude with Vicky and with her brother as well. Ellen gave Vicky practical suggestions for coping with discomfort and profuse bleeding, and Charles marked her womanhood by taking her out to a celebratory lunch.

Feelings about Physical Appearance

Most young teenagers are more concerned about their physical appearance than about any other aspect of themselves, and many are dissatisfied with their reflection in the mirror (Siegel, 1982). Boys want to be tall and broad-shouldered; girls want to be slim though bosomy. Anything that causes boys to think they look feminine (like lacking muscles or a beard) or girls to think they look masculine (like having a large-boned frame or facial hair) makes them miserable. Teenagers of both sexes worry about weight, complexion, and facial features—a nose that is too large, a chin that is too small, cheeks that are too fat. Vicky, however, is unhappier about her looks than Jason is, probably because the culture places greater emphasis on women's physical attributes than on men's (Clifford, 1971; Siegel, 1982).

Most young teenagers are more concerned about their physical appearance than about any other aspect of themselves, and many are dissatisfied with what they see in the mirror—especially if they are maturing much sooner or later than most of their friends.

Adults often dismiss adolescents' feelings about their looks, but those feelings can have long-lasting repercussions. First of all, the way adolescents look *is* important for their social life, which in turn is important for their self-esteem. It is sad but true that appearance affects how others react to us: for example, physically attractive people are generally thought to have attractive personalities (Dion, Berscheid, & Walster, 1972). Second, adults who considered themselves attractive during their teenage years have higher self-esteem and are happier than those who did not. Not until midlife do these differences generally disappear (Berscheid, Walster, & Bohrnstedt, 1973). Also, the pursuit of physical attractiveness often propels adolescents into eating disorders (discussed in the next section). We see, then, that the physical aspects of adolescence exert a major influence on psychological well-being.

Health Issues in Adolescence

Both Vicky and Jason enjoy robust health. Although illness is rare among adolescents, they constitute the only age group in the United States that has not experienced an improvement in health status in the past 30 years. While teenagers suffer from fewer communicable diseases, they have health problems that result from personality, poverty, and lifestyle. Adolescents' increasing tendency to take risks is reflected in their high rates of death from accidents, homicide, and suicide. Teenagers' concerns about health tend to revolve around stress and nervousness (Blum, 1987).

In this section, we discuss such major health problems as eating disorders, drug abuse, physical and sexual abuse, and suicide; in Chapter 16, we will examine teenage pregnancy.

NUTRITION

Adolescents' Nutritional Needs

The adolescent growth spurt entails an eating spurt, as Jess and Julia can testify. They laugh about Jason's "hollow leg" as he shovels in stacks of sandwiches and downs quarts of milk, pausing only to ask for more. He needs more calories than Vicky does. The average girl needs about 2200 calories per day, while the average boy needs about 2800. Protein is important in sustaining growth, and teenagers (like everyone else) should avoid "junk foods" like french fries, soft drinks, ice cream, and snack chips and dips, which are high in cholesterol and calories and low in nutrients.

The most common mineral deficiencies of adolescents are of calcium, zinc, and iron. Adolescents' need for calcium, which supports bone growth, is best met by drinking enough milk. Girls are especially prone to calcium deficiency, a problem that may have serious consequences later in life—1 in 4 postmenopausal women develop osteoporosis (thinning of the bones). Iron-deficiency anemia is common among American adolescents, because their diet tends to be iron-poor. Teenagers need a steady source of iron-fortified breads, dried fruits, and leafy green vegetables. Foods containing zinc—like meats, eggs, seafood, and whole-grain cereal products—belong in the diet, since even a mild zinc deficiency can delay sexual maturity (E. R. Williams & Caliendo, 1984).

Eating Disorders

obesity *Overweight condition marked by a skin-fold measurement in the 85th percentile.*

Obesity *Obesity* (see Chapters 5 and 11) is the most common eating disorder in the United States, affecting some 15 percent of adolescents. Obese teenagers tend to become obese adults, subject to a variety of health risks (Maloney & Klykylo, 1983). And even during adolescence, obesity is a health problem, associated with degenerative disorders of the circulatory system, an increased likelihood of heart disease, and other conditions. It is a matter for serious concern, therefore, that obesity has been on the rise among adolescents. Between 1963 and 1980, there was a 39 percent increase in obesity and a 64 percent increase in superobesity (Gortmaker et al., 1987; see Figure 14-1).

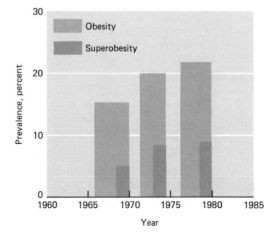

FIGURE 14-1
Estimated trends in obesity and superobesity in adolescents 12 to 17 years old in the United States. Even in these years, obesity is associated with a number of health problems. (*Source:* Adapted from Gortmaker, Dietz, Sobol, & Wehler, 1987.)

As we noted in Chapter 5, overweight or obesity develops when people consume more calories than they expend (or "burn up"), but it is not clear why some people eat more than their bodies need. Obese adolescents—along with obese adults and children—are often regarded as lacking "willpower." In most cases, this is probably an oversimplification; various risk factors having nothing to do with willpower seem to make some people more likely than others to become obese. These factors include genetic regulation of metabolism (obesity often runs in families), developmental history (inability to recognize body clues about hunger and satiety, or the development of an abnormally larger number of fat cells during childhood), physical activity (recall the study discussed in Chapter 11 correlating excess weight with watching television), emotional stress, and brain damage.

Fortunately, programs using behavior modification to help adolescents make changes in diet and exercise have had some success in treating obesity (see the discussion in Chapter 11).

Anorexia Nervosa and Bulimia Nervosa   On the other side of the coin are two disorders characterized by abnormal behavior which apparently arises from a determination *not* to become obese: anorexia nervosa and bulimia nervosa. Both tend to reflect problems in society as well as in families and individuals, since they stem in large part from today's idea of female beauty—with its stringent standards in general, and its unrealistic glorification of slenderness in particular. This cultural factor interacts with family and personal factors to make many adolescent girls and young women obsessed with their weight. By the end of high school, more than half have dieted "seriously"; some never stop (J. D. Brown, Childers, & Waszak, 1988), and some adopt bizarre eating habits.

Anorexia nervosa   Someone suggests to an adolescent girl that she could stand to lose a few pounds. She loses them—and then continues to diet obsessively, until she has lost at least 25 percent of her original body weight. She stops menstruating; thick, soft hair spreads over her body; and she becomes intensely overactive. She may eventually die. This is a typical scenario for ***anorexia nervosa,*** a disorder characterized by self-starvation. It may affect people of both sexes from age 8 to the thirties or even older, but the typical patient is a bright, well-behaved, appealing white female between puberty and the early twenties, from an apparently stable, well-educated, well-off family. It is estimated to affect from 0.5 to 1 percent of 12- to 18-year-old girls; only about 6 percent of anorexics are adolescent boys (*Diagnostic and Statistical Manual of Mental Disorders*, 3d ed., rev., DSM III-R, 1987; Dove, undated).

anorexia nervosa   Eating disorder, seen mostly in young women, characterized by self-starvation.

Anorexics are preoccupied with food—cooking it, talking about it, and urging others to eat—but they eat very little themselves. They have a grossly distorted body image and cannot see how shockingly thin they are. To an anorexic girl, the skeleton in the mirror appears svelte and beautiful—or even fat. Anorexics tend to be good students and "model" children, but are often socially withdrawn, depressed, and obsessive perfectionists.

The cause of anorexia is unknown. Many observers consider it a reaction to extreme societal pressure to be slender. They point out that the current standard of attractiveness on television and in movies and magazines is thinner for women than for men and is the slimmest it has been since the 1920s, the time of the last epidemic of similar eating disorders (Silverstein, Perdue, Peterson, et al., 1986; Silverstein, Peterson, & Perdue, 1986).

Before this girl received therapy for anorexia nervosa, she had a grossly distorted body image. When she looked like the girl in the picture she is holding, she could not see how shockingly thin she was.

Others see anorexia as a psychological disturbance related to a fear of growing up, a fear of sexuality, or extreme family malfunction. The families of anorexic girls are often overdependent and too involved in each others' lives, and apparently some anorexics feel that their weight is the only part of their lives they can control. Depressive symptoms are often a part of the disorder, and a Canadian study that followed anorexics (some of whom were also bulimic—see the next section) between 5 and 14 years after treatment found that they were likely to suffer from depression or anxiety disorders later in life (Toner, Garfinkel, & Garner, 1986).

Still others suggest that anorexia may be a physical disorder caused by deficiency of a crucial chemical in the brain or by a disturbance of the hypothalamus. It seems likely that the syndrome is due to a combination of factors.

Early warning signs of anorexia include very strict dieting, continually lowering weight goals, dieting in isolation, dissatisfaction even after losing weight, and interruption of regular menstruation. As soon as symptoms like these are present, treatment should be sought.

Bulimia nervosa An eating disorder closely related to anorexia, which also affects mostly adolescent girls and young women, is **bulimia nervosa.** A bulimic regularly (at least twice a week) goes on huge eating binges (consuming up to 5000 calories in a single sitting, often in secret) and then purges herself by self-induced vomiting, strict dieting or fasting, vigorous exercise, or use of laxatives or diuretics (DSM III-R, 1987). Though they do not become abnormally thin, bulimics are obsessed with their weight and body shape; and they are overwhelmed with shame, self-contempt, and depression over their abnormal eating habits. They also suffer extensive tooth decay (caused by repeated vomiting of stomach acid), gastric irritation, and loss of hair. There is some overlap between

bulimia nervosa *Eating disorder in which a person regularly eats huge quantities of food (binges) and then purges the body by taking laxatives or inducing vomiting.*

anorexia and bulimia; some anorexics have bulimic episodes, and some bulimics lose weight. But the two are separate disorders.

The cause of bulimia is also unknown. The two major theories are that it stems from an electrophysiological disturbance in the brain (based on the high number of abnormalities in brain-wave tracings of bulimic patients) and that it results from a depressive disorder (McDaniel, 1986). Another theory provides a psychoanalytic explanation: that bulimics use food to satisfy a hunger for the love and attention they did not receive from their parents. There is some basis for this explanation; one sample of bulimics, for instance, reported that they felt abused, neglected, and deprived of nurturing from their parents (Humphrey, 1986).

Treating anorexia and bulimia The immediate goal of treatment for an anorexic is to her to eat, to gain weight—and to live. She is likely to be put in the hospital, where she may be given a 24-hour nurse, drugs to encourage eating and inhibit vomiting, and behavior therapy, which rewards eating by granting such privileges as getting out of bed and leaving the room.

Both anorexics and bulimics are also treated by other therapies, which help them gain insight into the feelings underlying their disorders. These may include cognitive therapy (giving information and changing attitudes), individual or group psychotherapy, and family therapy, or some combination of these approaches. Recently, antidepressant drugs have been used with some success to treat both disorders (Hudson, Pope & Jonas, 1983; McDaniel, 1986; Pope, Hudson, Jonas & Yurgelun-Todd, 1983). Since both anorexic and bulimic patients are at risk of depression, and bulimics are at risk of suicide, the discovery that antidepressant drugs can help is heartening.

Treatment is generally more effective for patients whose illness begins before age 18 and lasts less than 3 years before they seek treatment (Russell, Szmukler, Dare, & Eisler, 1987). Patients with anorexia seem to need long-term support even after they have stopped starving themselves. One study found that, some 27 months after completion of treatment, most of 63 females had continued to gain weight, had resumed menstruating, and were functioning in school or at work. Still, they continued to have problems with body image. Even though they averaged 8 percent below ideal weight, most thought of themselves as overweight and as having excessive appetites, and many felt depressed and lonely (Nussbaum, Shenker, Baird & Saravay, 1985).

USE AND ABUSE OF DRUGS

Trends and Patterns of Drug Abuse

Throughout history, humankind has sought to relieve with drugs the ills that flesh and spirit are heir to. People have relied on drugs to alleviate unhappiness as well as physical ailments, and to give their lives a lift. The ancient Greeks drank alcohol; marijuana was used in China and India long before the birth of Christ; and cocaine, obtained by chewing coca leaves, was a staple among the sixteenth-century Incas. American Indians used to be so addicted to tobacco that they would not undertake a journey without bringing along a supply, and many nineteenth-century American women drank freely and gave their babies syrups heavily laced with opium (Brecher, 1972).

Why, then, are we so concerned about drugs today? A major reason is that many people are using drugs at a very young age. And while certain drugs may not be harmful in moderation, adolescents are not known for being moderate. They often turn to drugs as short-cut answers, endangering their physical and psychological health but leaving their problems unsolved.

Drug abuse by young people is less common now than it was at its peak during the 1960s. Surveys of high school students and young adults conducted by the National Institute on Drug Abuse (NIDA) show that use of most drugs has been dropping steadily from 1979 to 1987 (Johnston, O'Malley, & Bachman, 1988). Still, many young people continue to use legal drugs like alcohol and nicotine and illegal ones like marijuana, LSD, amphetamines, barbiturates, heroin, and cocaine; and use of illicit drugs in the United States is the highest in the industrialized world. In NIDA's 1987 survey of some 16,000 high school seniors and 10,000 graduates in their twenties (see Table 14-4), 57 percent said that they had used illicit drugs at some time in their lives, and over one-third had tried an illicit drug other than marijuana.

Use of marijuana, hashish, stimulants, and sedatives is continuing to decline, however. The most encouraging finding is the decline in use of cocaine among high school seniors and young adults, after 7 years of peak levels. Use of crack—a particularly dangerous smokable form of cocaine—seems to have leveled off and may even be declining, after a rapid increase between 1983 and 1986. But, about 1 in every 6 or 7 high school seniors has tried cocaine, and 1 in 18 has tried crack (see Figure 14-2).

Furthermore, cigarette smoking (which is estimated to take the lives of more people than all other drugs combined) and use of alcohol, the number one problem drug in the United States, remain distressingly common. Little change was found in usage of LSD, heroin, and other opiates; and the use of inhalants has continued to increase. The NIDA survey did not reach high school dropouts

TABLE 14-4

COMPARATIVE DRUG USE			
DRUG	LIFETIME	PAST YEAR	PAST MONTH
Alcohol	92.2%	85.7%	66.4%
Cigarettes	67.2	Not available	29.4
Marijuana and hashish	50.2	36.3	21.0
Inhalants	18.6	8.1	3.5
Amyl and butyl nitrites	4.7	2.6	1.3
Hallucinogens	10.6	6.7	2.8
LSD	8.4	5.2	1.8
PCP	3.0	1.3	0.6
Cocaine	15.2	10.3	4.3
"Crack"	5.6	4.0	1.5
Other cocaine	14.0	9.8	4.1
Heroin	1.2	0.5	0.2
Other opiates	9.2	5.3	1.8
Stimulants	21.6	12.2	5.2
Sedatives	8.7	4.1	.7
Barbiturates	7.0	3.6	1.4
Methaqualone	4.0	1.5	0.6
Tranquilizers	10.9	5.5	2.0

Note: This table shows the percent of 16,300 high school seniors in 1987 who reported having used specific drugs at any time during their lives, during the previous year, and during the previous month.
Source: Adapted from Johnston, O'Malley, & Bachman, 1988.

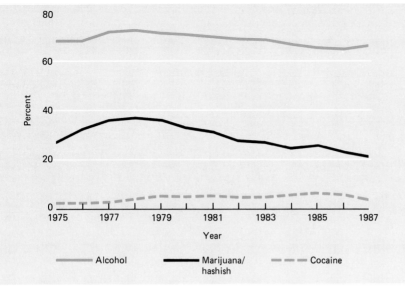

FIGURE 14-2
Use of drugs and alcohol
among high school
seniors. Percentages of
students who used the
drug at least once in the
previous 30 days, based
on a survey of about
17,000 high school seniors
around the United States.
(*Source:* Leary, 1988b;
University of Michigan
News and Information
Services, 1988.)

(about 15 percent of the age group studied), who may well have higher levels of use.

Patterns of drug abuse among adolescents generally follow those among adults, and just as adults take barbiturates and stimulants to alleviate unhappiness, depression, and day-to-day pressures, so do young people. Although pharmaceutical companies and drug-oriented adolescents alike extol the use of drugs in virtually every human situation, there are grave dangers. First, chemical solutions obscure the nature of real problems facing young people and can keep them from acting to solve these problems. Furthermore, drugs may cast a long shadow into the future.

Among more than 1000 adults in their mid-twenties, those who had begun using a certain drug in their teens tended to continue using it. Those who used marijuana or other illicit drugs were in poorer physical health than nonusers, had more unstable job and marital histories, and were more likely to have been delinquent. Cigarette smokers tended to be depressed and to have lung problems, breathing difficulties, and symptoms with no physical cause (Kandel, Davies, Karus, & Yamaguchi, 1986).

Let us look at the three drugs used most frequently by adolescents: alcohol, tobacco, and marijuana.

Alcohol

Many of the same people who are deeply worried about illegal use of marijuana by young people are brought up short when reminded that alcohol, too, is a powerful mind-altering drug which is also illegal for most high school students and many college students (even though it is usually easy to get)—and is a much more serious problem nationwide. Alcohol is the drug most often abused by children and adolescents (American Academy of Pediatrics Committee on Adolescence, 1987a).

Nearly all high school seniors (92 percent) in the NIDA survey had drunk alcoholic beverages in the previous year, two-thirds (66 percent) had had a drink in the past month, and nearly 4 in 10 (37.5 percent) had engaged in binge drink-

To prevent deaths among young Americans caused by alcohol-related motor vehicle accidents, educational campaigns now stress the importance of naming a "designated driver," one person in a group who agrees not to drink on a specific night.

ing (defined as having five or more drinks in a row) over the previous 2 weeks. (This last figure, however, was down from 39 percent in 1984 and 41 percent in 1979.) Boys are more than twice as likely as girls to drink every day or to drink a large amount in one sitting, and young people who do not plan to go to college drink more than the college-bound. Most young people have their first drink before they get to high school (Johnston et al., 1988).

Most teenagers start to drink because it seems a grown-up thing to do, and they continue for the same reasons as adults—to add a glow to social occasions, to be accepted by peers, to reduce anxiety, and to escape from problems. Most drink moderately and infrequently and have no problems with alcohol, but some young people, like some adults, cannot handle it. The most troubling finding of the NIAAA survey was the high proportion of young problem drinkers. More than 3 out of 10 had been drunk at least four times in the past year or had gotten into trouble—with friends, school authorities, or the police—because of drinking at least twice in the past year. The danger of driving after drinking is well known: the leading cause of death among 15- to 24-year-old Americans is alcohol-related motor vehicle accidents (American Academy of Pediatrics Committee on Adolescence, 1987a).

Tobacco

A young person sneaking a cigarette behind a barn used to be a humorous image among adults. But indulgence toward young people's use of tobacco has turned to concern, with new awareness that "cigarette smoking is the chief single avoidable cause of death in our society" (Brandt, 1982). The publication in 1964 of the U.S. Surgeon General's report made it clear that relationships exist between smoking and lung cancer, heart disease, emphysema, and other illnesses.

Many adolescents got the message: from 1977 to 1984, daily cigarette smoking went down from 29 percent to less than 20 percent, and in 1987 it held at 18.7 percent. Teenagers now express concern about the effects of smoking on health, and teenage smokers feel the disapproval of their peers. Still, 2 out of 3 high school seniors have tried cigarettes, and in the NIDA survey almost 30 percent had smoked in the previous month (Johnston et al., 1988).

The traditional male-female ratio has been reversed: more adolescent girls than boys now smoke. This has serious implications for later life. Women now have a death rate from lung cancer almost equal to that of men, although about 2½ times as many men develop the disease (American Cancer Society, 1985). Women who take oral contraceptives are at a higher risk of stroke or heart disease if they smoke, and women who smoke during pregnancy are at risk of birth complications (American Academy of Pediatrics Committee on Adolescence, 1987b).

Why do teenagers start to smoke? Most drift into it, often smoking a first cigarette sometime between the ages of 10 and 12. Although few enjoy it, many force themselves to have another, and they keep smoking until they become physically dependent on nicotine at about 15 years of age (McAlister, Perry, & Maccoby, 1979; National Institute of Child Health and Human Development, 1978).

Young people are most likely to smoke when their friends and families do. If one parent smokes, a child is twice as likely to smoke as when neither parent smokes. If both parents smoke or if one parent and an older brother or sister smoke, the chances are 4 to 1 that a youngster will follow suit. And if a child's best friend smokes, the chances soar to 9 out of 10 that the child will also (National Institute of Child Health and Human Development, 1978).

Teenagers who smoke are likely to be more rebellious, to want to be older, to achieve less well at school, and to go out less for sports than those who do not smoke (McAlister et al., 1979). They are also likely to be late maturers; they try to look older by smoking (Clausen, 1978). It is ironic that adolescents, who often rebel against adult values, see smoking as an adult activity and yet take it up eagerly. Thus they copy the very persons they are rebelling against.

Since peer pressure seems to be an important factor in inducing people to smoke, peer pressure *not* to smoke may be the best preventive mechanism (Johnston, Bachman, & O'Malley, 1982; McAlister et al., 1979).

Marijuana

Marijuana has been used all over the world for centuries, but only within the past 3 decades has it become popular among the American middle class. It is now the most widely used illicit drug in the United States, even though consumption by high school seniors and young adults has declined since 1979 (from 60.4 percent to 50.2 percent) (Johnston et al., 1988).

Adolescents start to smoke marijuana for many of the same reasons they begin to drink alcohol. They are curious, they want to do what their friends do, and they want to feel more adult. Another appeal of marijuana has been that its use is a rebellion against parents' values, but this attraction may be slipping, since today's teenagers are much more likely to have parents who have smoked marijuana themselves.

Heavy use of marijuana can lead to heart and lung problems, contribute to traffic accidents, and impede memory and learning. It may also lessen motivation, interfere with schoolwork, and cause family problems. Among 49 teenage boys (average age about 16), those who drank alcoholic beverages and also smoked marijuana more than twice a week were more likely than drinkers who did not use marijuana to have poor eating habits and signs of poor health such as respiratory infections and general fatigue. Heavy marijuana users who did not drink showed some, but not all, of these symptoms (Farrow, Rees, & Worthington-Roberts, 1987).

The Committee on Drugs of the American Academy of Pediatrics says, however, that although *heavy* use of marijuana poses a number of risks, there is little evidence that a person who smokes it only rarely will be harmed (American Academy of Pediatrics Committee on Drugs, 1980).

SEXUALLY TRANSMITTED DISEASES

What Are STDs?

sexually transmitted disease (STD) Disease spread by sexual contact; also called venereal disease.

Sexually transmitted diseases (STDs), also referred to as *venereal diseases,* are diseases spread by sexual contact. In the past 20 years, rates of STDs have soared for all age groups, but particularly among adolescents. Of the 8 to 12 million cases of STDs each year in the United States, 3 out of 4 occur among 15- to 24-year-olds (U.S. Department of Health and Human Services, USDHHS, 1980c).

Table 14-5 (pages 525 and 526) lists the most common STDs, with their incidence, causes, major symptoms, treatment, and consequences. Let us now look at them in somewhat more detail.

The most prevalent of these diseases is chlamydia, which causes infections of the urinary tract, the rectum, and the cervix and can lead, in women, to pelvic inflammatory disease (PID), a serious abdominal infection. Other STDs, in order of decreasing incidence, are gonorrhea, genital (venereal) warts, herpes simplex, syphilis, and acquired immune deficiency syndrome (AIDS).

Genital herpes simplex is a chronic, recurring, often painful disease caused by a virus (a different strain of which also causes cold sores on the face). Although no hard figures on its incidence are available, it is highly contagious, with about 500,000 new cases reported every year. The condition is more troublesome than dangerous, but it can be fatal to a newborn whose mother has an outbreak of genital herpes at the time of the delivery, and persons with a deficiency of the immune system. It has also been associated with increased incidence of cervical cancer. There is no cure, but the antiviral drug acyclovir can prevent active outbreaks.

AIDS is a failure of the immune system that leaves affected persons vulnerable to a variety of fatal diseases. The virus that causes it is transmitted through bodily fluids (mainly blood and semen) and stays in the body for life, even though the person carrying it may not show any signs of illness. Symptoms may not appear until 6 months to 7 or more years after infection. Most victims in this country are homosexual and bisexual men, especially those who have had many sexual partners; drug abusers who share contaminated hypodermic needles; people who have received transfusions of infected blood or blood products; and infants who have been infected in the womb or during birth. More than 90 percent of AIDS patients diagnosed in 1981 have since died of it (Blue Cross and Blue Shield Association, BCBSA, 1988).

Some 1.5 million Americans are estimated to be carriers; one-third of these may develop AIDS or a related condition (BCBSA, 1988). The disease has continued to spread over the past decade. The number of cases is predicted to be

TABLE 14-5

DISEASE	NEW CASES IN 1986	CASES (%) MALE/FEMALE	CAUSE	SYMPTOMS: MALE	SYMPTOMS: FEMALE	TREATMENT	CONSEQUENCES IF UNTREATED
Chlamydia	4.6 million	60/40	Bacterial infection	Pain during urination, discharge from penis.*	Vaginal discharge, abdominal discomfort.†	Tetracycline or erythromycin.	Can cause pelvic inflammatory disease or eventual sterility.
Gonorrhea	1.8 million	60/40	Bacterial infection	Discharge from penis, pain during urination.*	Discomfort when urinating, vaginal discharge, abnormal menses.†	Penicillin or other antibiotics.	Can cause pelvic inflammatory disease or eventual sterility; can also cause arthritis, dermatitis, and meningitis.
Genital warts	1.0 million	40/60	Viral infection	Painless growths that usually appear on penis, but may also appear on urethra or in rectal area.*	Small, painless growths on genitalia and anus; may also occur inside the vagina without external symptoms.*	Removal of warts	May be associated with cervical cancer; in pregnancy, warts enlarge and may obstruct birth canal.
Herpes	500,000	40/60	Viral infection	Painful blisters anywhere on the genitalia, usually on the penis.*	Painful blisters on the genitalia, sometimes with fever and aching muscles; women with sores on cervix may be unaware of outbreaks.*	No known cure, but controlled with antiviral drug acyclovir.	Increased risk of cervical cancer.
Syphilis	90,000	70/30	Bacterial infection	In first stage, reddish-brown sores on the mouth or genitalia or both, which may disappear, though the bacteria remain; in the second, more infectious stage, a widespread skin rash.*	Same as in men.	Penicillin or other antibiotics.	Paralysis convulsions, brain damage, and sometimes death.

(Continued)

TABLE 14-5

CONTINUED

DISEASE	NEW CASES IN 1986	CASES (%) MALE/FEMALE	CAUSE	SYMPTOMS: MALE	SYMPTOMS: FEMALE	TREATMENT	CONSEQUENCES IF UNTREATED
AIDS (acquired immune deficiency syndrome)	40,000	93/7	Viral infection	Extreme fatigue, fever, swollen lymph nodes, weight loss, diarrhea, night sweats, susceptibility to other diseases.*	Same as in men.	No known cure, but experimental drug AZT extends life.	Death usually due to other diseases such as cancer.

*May be asymptomatic.
†Often asymptomatic.
Source: Adapted from Centers for Disease Control, 1986; Morbidity and Mortality Weekly Report, 1987.

270,000 in 1991 (Morbidity & Mortality Weekly Report, MMWR, 1986). Education has reduced its spread in the homosexual community; blood screening has reduced the risk of contraction by transfusion; and current efforts are focused on halting it among drug users. As of now, it is incurable.

Box 14-4 (on the opposite page) offers some practical suggestions for preventing STDs and for seeking treatment.

Implications for Adolescents

The reasons for the high rates of sexually transmitted diseases among young people are many: increased sexual activity, especially among teenage girls; use of oral contraceptives—which do not protect against STDs—instead of condoms, which do; a mistaken belief that STDs can be cured easily; adolescents' reluctance to accept that unpleasant things that happen to *other* people can also happen to them; and young people's willingness to take risks because they want sexual intercourse more than they fear disease.

Young girls may be even more susceptible than mature women to STD-caused infections of the upper genital tract, which can lead to serious, even dangerous, complications. Teenagers are more likely than adults to put off getting medical care, they are less likely to follow through with treatment, and STDs are more likely to be misdiagnosed in teenagers than in adults (Center for Disease Control, 1983).

Most teenagers know the basic facts—that STDs are transmitted through sexual contact, that they are serious, and that anyone can get them (R. C. Sorenson, 1973), even though, as we would have noted, they tend to think that "anyone" means "anyone except *me*." But teenagers are often reluctant to seek help because they are afraid that their parents will find out, and they are ashamed and embarrassed to inform their sexual partners when they do contract an STD. Most educational campaigns aimed at eradicating this group of diseases focus on early diagnosis and treatment. Not until at least equal prominence is given to prevention and the moral obligation to avoid spreading them will headway be made in stopping this epidemic.

BOX 14-4 ■ THE EVERYDAY WORLD

PREVENTING SEXUALLY TRANSMITTED DISEASES

People who are sexually active can do a great deal to protect themselves against sexually transmitted diseases. The following guidelines will minimize the possibility of contracting an STD. They will also maximize the chances of getting adequate treatment if an STD is contracted.

■ Have regular medical checkups. All sexually active persons should request tests specifically aimed at detecting the presence of STDs.
■ Know your partner. The more discriminating you are, the less likely you are to be exposed to STDs. Partners with whom you develop a serious and caring relationship are more likely to inform you of any medical problems they have.
■ Avoid having sexual intercourse with many partners, promiscuous persons, and known drug abusers.
■ Avoid any sexual activity involving exchange of bodily fluids. Use a latex condom during intercourse.
■ Avoid exposing any cut or break in the skin to anyone else's blood, body fluids, or secretions.
■ Avoid anal intercourse.
■ Do not have any sexual contact if you suspect that you or your partner may be infected. Abstinence is the most reliable preventive measure.
■ Use a vaginal contraceptive foam, cream, or jelly; it will kill many germs and help prevent certain STDs.
■ Just before and just after sexual contact, wash the genital and rectal areas with soap and water; males should urinate after washing.

■ Practice good routine hygiene: frequent thorough hand washing and daily fingernail brushing.
■ Learn the symptoms of STDs: vaginal or penile discharge; inflammation, itching, or pain in the genital or anal area; burning during urination; pain during intercourse; sores, blisters, bumps, or rashes in the genital area, on the body, or in the mouth; pain in the lower abdomen or the testicles; discharge from or itching of eyes; and fever or swollen glands.
■ Learn the symptoms of AIDS: night sweats, swollen glands, tiredness, fever, loss of appetite and weight, diarrhea, and "flu" that does not go away. If these symptoms last more than 2 weeks, a doctor should be consulted. (Some AIDS victims, however, show no symptoms for months or years after infection.)
■ Inspect your partner for symptoms.
■ If you develop any symptoms yourself, see a doctor.
■ If you contract any STD, notify all recent sexual partners immediately so that they can obtain treatment and avoid passing the infection back to you or on to someone else; inform your doctor and dentist so that they can take precautions to avoid transmission; and do not donate blood, plasma, sperm, body organs, or other body tissue.

For more information, write to the American Foundation for the Prevention of Venereal Disease, 799 Broadway, Suite 638, New York, NY 10003. Or call the U.S. Public Heath Service AIDS hot line (1-800-342-AIDS) or the AIDS hot line for adolescents (1-800-234-TEEN).

Sources: American Foundation for the Prevention of Venereal Disease, 1986; Blue Cross & Blue Shield Association, 1988; Upjohn, 1984.

ABUSE AND NEGLECT DURING ADOLESCENCE

A frail 12-year-old boy arrives at the hospital emergency room with a fractured wrist. After relating an implausible version of the "accident" that caused it, he finally breaks down and confides to the resident physician that his father did it during the most recent of his frequent beatings. A 15-year-old girl tells the counselor at an abortion clinic that she is pregnant by her own father, who has been forcing her to have sexual relations with him for the past 4 years.

The extent of abuse and neglect suffered by adolescents is vastly underestimated, according to the U.S. Department of Health and Human Services (1980c). The number of children abused and neglected declines only slightly from age 2 through age 16. No matter how brutal or unloving a home is, most teenagers cannot fight back or run away, because they are still dependent on their families.

Adolescent girls are more likely to be abused and neglected than boys (at earlier ages, boys are more likely to be victimized). Sexual abuse rises in adolescence, accounting for 7 percent of all cases of abuse among 12- to 17-year-olds, compared with 4 percent among children of all ages. Almost 3 out of 4 cases of reported sexual abuse involve victims between the ages of 9 and 17.

Physical abuse of teenagers accounts for between 16 and 30 percent of all physical abuse (Blum, 1987). It typically occurs in situations where an adult, enraged by a teenager's disobedience, whips the youngster or inflicts facial injuries such as bruises, a black eye, or a split lip. (Abused younger children tend to suffer whiplash injuries, fractures, burns, and internal trauma.) Neglect is more common than abuse: 70 percent of all cases of abuse and neglect among adolescents fall into this category.

Treatment of abuse and neglect should, ideally, take place within the context of the teenager's family, school, and community, but this is easier said than done. To help abused and neglected adolescents, the federal government is currently mounting a major campaign to educate teachers, police officers, and health professionals.

DEATH IN ADOLESCENCE

Death Rates and Causes of Death

When adolescents die, violence is usually the cause. In 1980, eighty percent of all deaths of adolescents were due to accidents, homicide, and suicide. This fact reflects the general good health and vigor of young people; but it also reflects adolescents' lifestyle—risk taking and carelessness, fueled by the myth of invulnerability ("It can't happen to me").

Teenage boys account for 4 out of 5 accidental injuries, and the rate of violent injury for 18- to 19-year-olds is almost 2½ times greater than that for 12- to 15-year-olds (Blum, 1987). The death rate is 3 times higher for teenage boys than for girls, and 20 percent higher for blacks than for whites. The prime causes of death differ for the races: automobile accidents are the leading cause for young whites; homicide is the leading cause for young blacks. Among both black and white teenagers the third leading cause of death is suicide (USDHHS, 1982).

Suicide

Trends and Patterns of Suicide Early in 1986, an "epidemic" of suicides and suicide attempts swept through a high school in Nebraska, leaving three dead. Similar waves of suicides have occurred in other schools. Between 1960 and 1980, the suicide rate among 15- to 19-year-olds tripled (American Academy of Pediatrics Committee on Adolescence, 1988). In 1984, about 6000 teenagers were reported to have killed themselves, which would be an average of more than 15 per day. The number of suicides, moreover, is probably *under*reported, since many "accidental" deaths are actually suicides. There may be 50 to 200 unsuccessful attempts at suicide for every successful one.

Girls attempt suicide about 3 times more often than boys, but boys succeed more often. White males have the highest suicide rate, followed by black males, white females, and black females (American Academy of Pediatrics, Committee on Adolescence, 1980, 1988). The "success" rate among males seems to reflect their use of ropes and guns, girls favor slower-acting pills.

Some professionals who study children believe that suicide rates among

After three students at Bryan High School committed suicide within 5 days, Nebraskans began calling it "Suicide High." Guidance counselors like this one try to alleviate classmates' anxiety and to prevent more young people from taking their own lives.

teenagers have risen because today's adolescents are under much more stress than their counterparts in the past (Elkind, 1984). Many young people who attempt suicide, however, do not want to die. Their attempts are a desperate cry for attention and an appeal for help in changing their lives. Through impulsiveness or miscalculation, they often die before help can reach them.

Who Is at Risk? Although there is no sure way to identify young people who will try to kill themselves, those who do are likely to have a history including one or more of the following (American Academy of Pediatrics Committee on Adolescence, 1988; Crumley, 1979; P. Cantor, 1977; Deykin, Alpert, & McNamara, 1985; Salk, Lipsitt, Sturner, Reilly, & Levat, 1985; Rohn, Sarles, Kenny, Reynolds, & Heald, 1977).

- Previous suicide attempt
- Family disruption, with father absent
- Psychiatric disorders in family, especially suicidal behaviors and depression (possibly biochemically based, since low levels of a metabolite, 5-HIAA, have been found in the cerebrospinal fluid of depressed persons attempting suicide—Asberg, Traskman, & Thoren, 1976)
- Chronic or debilitating physical or psychiatric illness
- Living in a group home or correctional facility
- Such current stresses as conflicts or poor communication with parents, breakup of a love relationship, school problems, drug abuse, social isolation, and physical ailments
- Being abused or neglected
- Problems prenatally or at time of birth, such as mother's chronic illness, lack of prenatal care, or respiratory distress for more than 1 hour at birth
- Minimal brain dysfunction
- Poor impulse control and impulsive behavior
- Low tolerance of frustration and stress

BOX 14-5 ■ THE EVERYDAY WORLD

PREVENTING SUICIDE

How can you help prevent suicide? After someone commits suicide, friends and family are usually overwhelmed, not only with grief but also with guilt. They ask themselves, "Why didn't I know? Why didn't I do something?" Very often, people intent on killing themselves keep their plans secret; but at other times signs appear well in advance. In fact, an attempt at suicide is sometimes a call for help, and some people die because they are more successful than they intend to be. People who want to help prevent suicide need to learn the warning signs and the kinds of actions that are often effective. Let's see what these are.

WARNING SIGNS OF SUICIDE
- Withdrawal from family or friends
- Talking about death, the hereafter, or suicide
- Giving away prized possessions
- Drug or alcohol abuse
- Personality changes like anger, boredom, and apathy
- Unusual neglect of appearance
- Difficulty concentrating at work on in school
- Staying away from work, school, or other usual activities
- Complaints of physical problems when nothing is organically wrong
- Changes in sleeping or eating habits—eating or sleeping much more or much less than usual

WHAT A CONCERNED PERSON CAN DO
- Talk to the person about his or her suicidal thoughts. Bringing up the subject will not put ideas into the mind of someone who has not already thought of suicide, and it will bring feelings out into the open.

- Tell others who are in a position to do something—the person's parents or spouse, other family members, a close friend, a therapist, or a counselor. It is better to break a confidence than to let someone die.
- Do as much as possible to relieve the real-life pressures that seem so intolerable, whether that means calling a rejecting boyfriend or girlfriend, lending money, or interceding with an employer.
- Show the person that he or she has other options besides death, even though none of them may be ideal. One therapist talked nonjudgmentally to a suicidal pregnant teenager, raising the possibility of a number of alternatives, including abortion, adoption, keeping the baby, telling her parents, telling the baby's father, and committing suicide. She was able to rank the options in order of preference, and suicide no longer headed the list. She and the therapist were now "'haggling' about life" (Shneidman, 1985). This therapist says that it is important to remind the patient "that life is often the best choice among lousy alternatives" and that functioning well may mean choosing "the least lousy alternative that is practically attainable" (p. 325).
- Consider the impact of choice of method. Suicide rates declined in England and Wales between 1960 and 1975, apparently because natural gas—which had been a popular method—was no longer in use. In the United States and in Australia, the number of suicides in which the method was barbiturates declined in proportion to the number of prescriptions written for barbiturates. Since the number of suicides involving guns has risen in recent years, gun control legislation would probably decrease such deaths. Many suicides are impulsive, and if a convenient means is not at hand, the depressed person may not go any farther or may at least defer action long enough to get help.

In 1986, two researchers suggested that some teenagers in New York City had taken their own lives after seeing fictional dramas about suicide (M. S. Gould & Shaffer, 1986). But two later researchers (Phillips & Paight, 1987) compared the number of teenage suicides in California, Pennsylvania, and the New York City area for 2 weeks *after* the broadcast of each of three movies about suicide and 2 weeks *before* the broadcasts and found no increase afterward. They concluded that fictionalized suicide on television does not induce actual suicide among young people.

This does not, however, disprove the finding of another study that suicide does increase following extensive reporting of *real* suicides (Phillips & Carstensen, 1986). The reason for the difference may be that people contemplating suicide identify more with real people than with fictional characters, or the greater

BOX 14-6 ■ A CHILD'S WORLD AND YOU

WHAT DO YOU THINK?

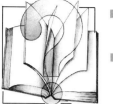

■ How would *you* define the end of adolescence and entry into adulthood?

■ Do you believe that western adolescents today miss something by not having a specific rite of passage from childhood? If so, what kind of observance do you think would be appropriate?

■ What do you think are the implications of attaining sexual maturity years before the customary age of marriage, and attaining physical maturity years before attaining physical independence from the family?

■ How do you think adolescents can be helped to change risky behaviors, like the use of drugs and careless sexual activity? How can adults educate and motivate young people, without engaging in scare tactics?

repetition in the reporting of a real case as compared with a single presentation of a fictional drama. Given the alarming rise in suicide among young people, more research is needed. Meanwhile, the family and friends of an adolescent who may be contemplating suicide can often help; Box 14-5 offers some suggestions.

Fortunately, suicide among adolescents remains rare. Most young people emerge from the teenage years with a mature body and a zest for life. While their bodies have been developing, their intellect has continued to develop too, as we see in Chapter 15.

Summary

1 Adolescence is a period of transition between childhood and adulthood. It begins with the onset of puberty, a period of rapid physical growth and physiological changes leading to sexual maturity. Puberty lasts about 2 years and ends when a person is able to reproduce.

2 The end of adolescence is not clear-cut in western societies, since no single sign indicates that adulthood has been reached. In some nonwestern cultures, adulthood is regarded as beginning at puberty and is signified by puberty rites, which take a variety of forms.

3 The term *secular trend* refers to a trend that can be observed over several generations. A secular trend toward earlier attainment of adult height and sexual maturity began about 100 years ago, probably because of improvements in living standards; it seems to have ended in the United States.

4 Both sexes undergo an adolescent growth spurt: sharp growth in height and weight, and advances in muscular and skeletal development.

5 The primary sex characteristics are the organs directly related to reproduction in the female and the male. These organs enlarge and mature during puberty.

6 The secondary sex characteristics—signs of sexual maturity other than the reproductive organs—include the breasts in females and the broad shoulders of males, and the body hair, skin, and voice typical of adult men or women.

7 Menarche (first menstruation), the principal sign of sexual maturity in girls, occurs at an average age of 12½ in the United States. Timing of menarche varies between cultures and is related to both genetic and environmental factors. In boys, the presence of sperm in the urine is the principal sign of sexual maturity. Adolescent boys may experience nocturnal emissions.

8 The rapid physical changes of adolescence affect self-concept and personality. Early or late maturation also may have an effect, though neither is clearly advantageous or disadvantageous. Girls adjust better to menarche if they are prepared for it.

9 The many physical changes of adolescence require a good, balanced diet. Calcium, iron-rich foods, and sources of zinc are necessary to sustain growth and bring on sexual maturity.

10 Obesity among adolescents has increased over the past several decades. It has both genetic and environmental causes. It is most successfully treated by a restricted diet, increased exercise, and behavior modification.

11 Anorexia nervosa is a disorder characterized by self-starvation. A person with bulimia nervosa regularly goes on eating binges and then deliberately induces vomiting. Both of these conditions are more common among females. The causes are unknown. Treatment can include hospitalization, psychotherapy, and sometimes the use of antidepressant drugs.

12 Drug abuse by adolescents was less common in the late 1980s than during the 1960s and 1970s. Still, many young people continue to use legal and illegal drugs. Alcohol abuse is the number one drug problem in the United States. Cigarette smoking has declined among adolescents overall. More adolescent girls than boys now smoke. Marijuana is the most widely used illicit drug.

13 Sexually transmitted diseases (STDs) are diseases transmitted by sexual contact. The most prevalent is chlamydia; it is followed by gonorrhea, genital warts, herpes simplex, syphilis, and acquired immune deficiency syndrome (AIDS). Sexually active people can do a great deal to protect themselves against STDs.

14 The extent of abuse and neglect among adolescents has been underestimated; abuse declines only slightly from age 2 through age 16. Almost 75 percent of reported sexual abuse cases involve victims between 9 and 17 years old.

15 The three leading causes of death among adolescents are accidents, homicide, and suicide.

Key Terms

adolescence (page 504)
puberty (505)
estrogen (508)
secular trend (508)
adolescent growth spurt (509)
primary sex characteristics (510)

secondary sex characteristics (511)
menarche (512)
obesity (516)
anorexia nervosa (517)
bulimia nervosa (518)
sexually transmitted disease (STD) (524)

Suggested Readings

Boston Women's Health Book Collective. (1984). *The new our bodies, ourselves.* New York: Simon & Schuster. An absorbing discussion of a variety of topics concerning women and their bodies.

Brumberg, J. J. (1988). *Fasting girls: The emergence of anorexia nervosa as a modern disease.* Cambridge, MA: Harvard University Press. This historical analysis of anorexia, written by a developmentalist with a special interest in women's studies, traces the disorder back to medieval times, and attributes its rise in modern times to pressures on young women. The author suggests ways to stem the epidemic, such as emphasizing attributes in women other than physical appearance.

Kolehmainen, J., & Handwerk, S. (1988). *Teen suicide.* Minneapolis: Lerner. An easy to read handbook about teenage suicide. It offers advice on coping with grief, and when to intervene; and it describes eight warning signs of suicide.

INTELLECTUAL DEVELOPMENT IN ADOLESCENCE

I should place [the prime of a man's life] at between fifteen and sixteen. It is then, it always seems to me, that his vitality is at its highest; he has greatest sense of the ludicrous and least sense of dignity. After that time, decay begins to set in.

Evelyn Waugh, aged 16, in a school debate, 1920

PREVIEW QUESTIONS

- How does cognitive development in adolescence enable teenagers to consider a range of possibilities?
- What egocentric attitudes influence adolescents' thought?
- How does adolescents' advanced cognitive development affect moral reasoning?
- How does high school affect adolescents' development?
- What factors influence high school students' thoughts about a career?
- Is part-time work helpful or harmful for most high school students?

JASON, AT AGE 14, is plagued by doubts. He used to have clear opinions about practically everything—opinions that almost always mirrored his parents' thoughts about religion, politics, moral standards, and values. These days, though, the ideas he was so sure of are no longer as compelling. His parents' beliefs do not seem as valid, nor do they seem to answer the questions that keep cropping up. Much seems possible; much is unclear. Where does the truth lie?

In this chapter, we examine adolescents' intellectual development. We first examine Jean Piaget's contribution to our understanding of cognitive development—the concept of formal operations, which underlies Jason's discovery that life holds many possibilities beyond his personal experience. We also explore areas of intellectual development not covered by Piaget's theory. Then we look at the egocentrism of adolescents' thought, and at adolescents' moral development as analyzed by Kohlberg and Gilligan. The final part of the chapter explores practical aspects of intellectual growth—issues of school and work.

Aspects of Intellectual Development

Adolescents look different from schoolchildren, and they think differently, too. Primarily, what sets adolescents' thinking on a higher level than children's is the concept "What if . . . ?" Adolescents can think in terms of what *might* be true, rather than just in terms of what they see *is* true. Since they can imagine possibilities, they are capable of hypothetical reasoning. But they often seesaw between childish and adult thought, because they are limited by forms of egocentric thinking that appear in adolescence. This sign of cognitive immaturity affects their everyday life in many ways—including how they think about moral issues. We look now at these aspects of cognitive growth in adolescence.

COGNITION

Cognitive Maturity: Piaget's Stage of Formal Operations

The dominant explanation for the nature of the changes in the way teenagers think has been Jean Piaget's. According to Piaget, adolescents enter the highest level of cognitive development; he called this level, which is marked by the capacity for abstract thought, *formal operations.*

The Nature of Formal Operations The attainment of formal operations gives adolescents a new way to manipulate—or operate on—information. In the earlier stage of concrete operations, children can think logically only about the concrete, the here and now. Adolescents are no longer limited in that way: they can now deal with abstractions, they can test hypotheses, and they can see infinite possibilities.

formal operations In Piaget's terminology, the final stage of cognitive development, characterized by the ability to think abstractly.

This advance opens many new doors. It enables teenagers to analyze political and philosophical doctrines, and sometimes to construct their own elaborate theories for reforming society. It even enables them to recognize that in some situations there are no definite answers. The ability to think abstractly has emotional ramifications, too. "Whereas earlier the adolescent could love his mother or hate a peer, now he can love freedom or hate exploitation. The adolescent has developed a new mode of life: the possible and the ideal captivate both mind and feeling" (Ginsburg & Opper, 1979, p. 201).

Much of childhood appears to be a struggle to come to grips with the world as it is. Adolescents become aware of the world as it could be.

Seeing new possibilities We can glimpse the nature of formal operations in different reactions to a story told by Peel (1967):

> Only brave pilots are allowed to fly over high mountains. A fighter pilot flying over the Alps collided with an aerial cable-way, and cut a main cable causing some cars to fall to the glacier below. Several people were killed.

Adolescents can now ask, "What if . . . ?" Since they can imagine an infinite variety of possibilities, they can look at the various components in a scientific experiment, as these high school science students are doing.

A child still at the concrete operational level said, "I think that the pilot was not very good at flying. He would have been better off if he went on fighting." Only one answer came to mind—that the pilot was inept and not doing his real job, fighting.

By contrast, an adolescent who had reached the level of *formal operations* paid no attention to the designation "fighter pilot" and found a variety of possible explanations for what had happened: "He was either not informed of the mountain railway on his route, or he was flying too low; also, his flying compass may have been affected by something before or after takeoff, thus setting him off course and causing the collision with the cable" (Peel, 1967). We see in this response a new flexibility of thinking.

The pendulum problem   Let us look at Jason's cognitive development through his progress in dealing with a classic Piagetian problem in formal reasoning, the *pendulum problem*. We can trace his stage-to-stage development by comparing typical responses that children make to the following problem in the preoperational, the concrete operations, and the formal operations stages. (This description of age-related differences in the approach to the pendulum problem is adapted from Ginsburg & Opper, 1979.)

Here is the task. Jason is shown a pendulum—an object hanging from a string. He is shown how he can change the length of the string, the weight of the object, the height from which the object is released, and the amount of force he uses to push it. Then he is asked to figure out which factor or combination of factors determines how fast the pendulum swings.

When Jason first saw the pendulum, he was not yet 7 years old and was in the preoperational stage. At this age, he was not able to formulate a plan for attacking the problem. He tried one thing after another in hit-or-miss fashion. First he put a light weight on a long pendulum and pushed it, then he tried swinging a short pendulum with a heavy weight, and then he removed the weight entirely. Not only was his method random, but he could not understand or report what had actually happened. He was convinced that the force of his pushes made the pendulum go faster, and even though this was not so, he reported it as observed fact.

The next time Jason was faced with the pendulum, he was 11 years old and in the stage of concrete operations. This time, he did look at some possible solutions, and he even hit on a partially correct answer. But he failed to try out every possible solution systematically. He varied the length of the string, and he varied the weight of the object, and he thought that both length and weight affected the speed of the swing. But because he varied both length and weight at the same time, he could not determine which factor was critical, or whether both were.

Not until Jason was confronted with the pendulum again, when he was 15, did he go at the problem systematically. He now realized that any one of the four factors, or some combination of them, might affect the speed. He carefully designed an experiment to test all possible hypotheses, varying only one factor at a time while holding the rest constant. By doing this, he was able to determine that only one factor—the length of the string—determines how fast the pendulum swings.

Jason's solution of the pendulum problem showed that he had arrived at the stage of *formal operations,* a cognitive level usually attained at about the age of 12. Jason could now think in terms of what might be true and not just in terms of what he saw in a concrete situation. Since he could imagine a variety of possible solutions, he was, for the first time, capable of *hypothetical-deductive* reasoning. At this stage, once he developed a hypothesis, he could then construct a scientific experiment to test the hypothesis. He considered all the possible relationships that might exist and went through them one by one, to eliminate the false and arrive at the true. We can see here (as in the story told by Peel) that adolescent thought has a *flexibility* that is not possible in the concrete operations stage.

This systematic process of reasoning operates for all sorts of problems. People in the formal operations stage are better equipped to integrate what they have learned in the past with their problems of the present and their planning for the future. They are able to apply these thought processes to the problems and issues of day-to-day living and also to the construction of elaborate political and philosophical theories. Of course, people who are capable of formal thought do not always use it, even when a situation calls for it. But at least they have attained a high *optimal* level of cognitive competence.

What Brings About Cognitive Maturity?   Inner and outer changes in the lives of adolescents combine to bring about cognitive maturity, according to Piaget: the brain has matured and the social environment is widening, giving more opportunities for experimentation. Interaction between the two kinds of changes is essential: even if young people's neurological development is sufficient to allow them to reach the stage of formal reasoning, they may never attain it if they are not encouraged culturally and educationally.

In fact, perhaps one-third to one-half of American adults appear never to reach this stage (Kohlberg & Gilligan, 1971). Studies of how well people of various ages do on formal operations tasks suggest that many adults have not attained formal operations (at least as measured by the pendulum problem and similar tasks). In one cross-sectional study, for example, 265 persons were asked to solve the pendulum problem; the percentages of people who succeeded were:

- Ages 10 to 15: 45 percent
- Ages 16 to 20: 53 percent
- Ages 21 to 30: 65 percent
- Ages 45 to 50: 57 percent*

This suggests that even by late adolescence or adulthood not everyone is capable of abstract thought. Studies assessing conservation of volume, considered a sign of formal thought, also found that not all adolescent subjects had achieved it (Papalia, 1972).

Assessing Cognitive Development: Limitations of Piaget's Theory   What do knowing and thinking mean? How do we define the highest reaches of cognitive development? Using measures like the pendulum problem and conservation of volume implies that cognition can be defined in terms of mathematical and scientific thinking. This is a rather narrow view, which "conveys a view of the individual as living in a timeless world of abstract rules" (Gilligan, 1987, p. 67).

The Piagetian view, then, does not consider the importance of other aspects of intelligence. It does not allow for practical intelligence—the ability to handle

---

* Although fewer 45- to 50-year-olds solved the problem than 21- to 30-year-olds, we cannot conclude that ability has declined. Cross-sectional studies let us see differences only between age groups, not changes with age. We would need to conduct longitudinal studies for that.

"real world" problems—or for the wisdom that helps people cope with an often chaotic world. Nor would it tend to foster "nonscientific" subjects such as history, languages, writing, and the arts. In fact, as more psychologists have defined cognition in Piaget's terms, more educators have emphasized scientific subjects and taken less interest in the humanities. Piaget's definition of cognitive maturity is important; but we need to remember that formal reasoning is not the only—or even the most prominent—aspect of mature thinking.

Egocentrism in Adolescents' Thought

Jason has trouble these days making up his mind about the simplest thing. Vicky, on the other hand, makes hers up too quickly—and her impulsiveness has gotten her into trouble more than once. Both are critical of their parents, whom they find incapable of doing anything right. If Jess and Julia and Ellen and Charles can look at their children's often puzzling, sometimes maddening behavior in the framework described by the psychologist David Elkind (1984), they may be able to understand the behavior itself and the thought processes underlying it. Let us look at some egocentric behaviors and attitudes of adolescents.

Finding Fault with Authority Figures   Young people have a new ability to imagine an ideal world. They realize that the people they once worshiped fall far short of their ideal, and they feel compelled to say so—often. Parents who do not take this criticism personally, but rather look at it as a stage in teenagers' cognitive and social development, will be able to answer such comments matter-of-factly (and even humorously), indicating that nothing—and nobody (not even a teenager!)—is perfect.

Argumentativeness   Adolescents want to practice their new ability to see the many nuances in an issue, and they often do this by arguing. If Jess encourages and takes part in arguments about principles, while carefully avoiding discussing personality, he can help Jason stretch his reasoning ability without getting embroiled in family feuding.

Self-Consciousness   Jason, hearing Julia whispering on the phone, "knows" that she is talking about him. Vicky, passing a couple of boys laughing raucously, "knows" that they are ridiculing her. The extreme self-consciousness of young adolescents has a great deal to do with the *imaginary audience,* a conceptualized observer who is as concerned with their thoughts and behavior as they are themselves.

imaginary audience
Observer who exists only in the mind of an adolescent and is as concerned with the adolescent's thoughts and behaviors as the adolescent is.

Adolescents can put themselves into the mind of someone else—can think about another person's thinking. Since they have trouble distinguishing what is interesting to them from what is interesting to others, however, they assume that everyone else is thinking about the same thing they are—themselves. A study that supported the existence of the imaginary audience in early adolescence assessed how students in the fourth, sixth, eighth, and twelfth grades would react in such situations as finding a grease spot on their clothes at the beginning of the most exciting dress-up party of the year and being asked to get up in front of the class to talk. The eighth-graders—especially the girls—turned out to be more self-conscious than the older and younger students and less willing to speak to an audience (Elkind & Bowen, 1979).

The imaginary audience stays with us to a certain degree in adulthood. Who

(Jeffrey W. Myers 1988/Stock, Boston)

The telephone is often a battleground for parents and teenagers. Even when a parent's point of view is valid, an adolescent's egocentrism often leads to argumentativeness and criticism.

among us, for example, has not agonized over what to wear to an event, thinking that others present would care—and then realized that most people were too busy thinking about the impression *they* were making to notice our carefully chosen outfit! Because this kind of self-consciousness is especially agonizing in adolescence, however, Elkind emphasizes that adults should avoid any public criticism or ridicule of young teenagers.

Self-Centeredness   Elkind uses the term *personal fable* for the conviction that we are special, that our experience is unique, and that we are not subject to the natural rules that govern the rest of the world. This is an important aspect of teenage egocentrism that is particularly evident in early adolescence, accounting for a great deal of self-destructive behavior by teenagers who think that they are magically protected from harm. A girl thinks that *she* cannot become pregnant; a boy thinks that *he* cannot be killed on the highway; teenagers who experiment with drugs think that *they* cannot get hooked. "These things happen only to other people, not to me," is the unconscious assumption that helps explain much risk taking in adolescence. Young people have to maintain a sense of being special while realizing that they are not exempt from the natural order of things.

personal fable
Conviction, typical in adolescence, that one is special, unique, and not subject to the rules that govern the rest of the world.

Indecisiveness   Teenagers have trouble making up their minds even about simple things because they are suddenly aware how many choices there are in life. Should Vicky go to the mall with her girlfriend on a Saturday—or to a movie with her mother, or to the library to look up something for a paper that is due next week? She may ponder the consequences of each choice for hours, even though how she decides will probably not change her life substantially.

Apparent Hypocrisy   Young adolescents often do not recognize the difference between expressing an ideal and actually working toward it. Thus Vicky marches against pollution while littering along the way, and Jason becomes aggressive as he protests for peace. Part of growing up involves the realization that "thinking does not make it so," that values have to be acted upon to bring about change.

The more adolescents talk about their personal theories and listen to those of other people, the sooner they arrive at a mature level of thinking (Looft, 1971). As adolescents mature in their thought processes, they are better able to think about their own identities, to form adult relationships, and to determine how and where they fit into society.

MORAL DEVELOPMENT

Kohlberg's Theory

Neither Vicky nor Jason can have a moral code based on ideals before developing a mind that is capable of imagining ideals. Moral reasoning is in part a function of cognitive development. Moral development continues during adolescence as young people acquire the capacity to think abstractly and to understand universal moral principles. According to Kohlberg, whose three-level theory was introduced in Chapter 12, advanced cognitive development does not *guarantee* advanced moral development, but it must *exist* for moral development to take place.

Kohlberg's Levels of Morality   Children's thinking about morality generally fits into Kohlberg's first two stages, both at level I. At this level, morality is considered in terms of obedience to avoid punishment or acting out of self-interest (refer back to Table 12-3). Some delinquent adolescents—as well as many other adolescents and adults—are also at level I; they think in terms of self-interest and satisfaction of their own needs, which is characteristic of stage 2.

Most adolescents, however—like most adults—are at Kohlberg's conventional level of moral development: level II, which contains stages 3 and 4. They have internalized the standards of others, and they conform to social conventions, support the status quo, and think in terms of doing the right thing to please others or to obey the law. As we listen to "law and order" political speeches, we realize how many adults function at stage 4.

Only a small number of people, in fact, appear to attain level III, postconventional morality. At level III, which may be attained in adolescence or adulthood, people can look at two socially accepted standards and choose the one that seems right to them. But even people who have achieved a high level of cognitive development do not always reach a comparably high level of moral development. This is because other factors besides cognition affect moral reasoning. Thus, a certain level of cognitive development is *necessary* but not *sufficient* for a comparable level of moral development.

How Do Adolescents at Different Levels React to Kohlberg's Dilemmas?   The different reactions of adolescents to Kohlberg's moral dilemmas illustrate differences in the way they think. In Kohlberg's theory, as we have seen, it is the reasoning underlying a person's response to a moral dilemma, not the answer itself, which indicates the person's stage of development. Let us see how young people at all three levels respond to questions about the value of human life (Kohlberg, 1968).

Preconventional level Stage 1: When Tommy, aged 10, is asked, "Is it better to save the life of one important person or a lot of unimportant people?" he says, "All the people that aren't important because one man just has one house, maybe a lot of furniture, but a whole bunch of people have an awful lot of furniture . . . "

He seems to be confusing the value of people with the value of their property, and since many people have more property than just *one* person, he believes it is better to save their lives.

Stage 2: When he is 13, Tommy is asked about "mercy killing": should a doctor kill a fatally ill woman who requests death because of pain? He answers, "Maybe it would be good to put her out of her pain; she'd be better off that way. But the husband wouldn't want it; it's not like an animal. If a pet dies you can get along without it—it isn't something you really need. Well, you can get a new wife, but it's not really the same."

He thinks of the woman's value in terms of what she can do for her husband.

Conventional level Stage 3: At 16, Tommy answers the question about mercy killing by saying, "It might be best for her, but her husband—it's a human life—not like an animal; it just doesn't have the same relationship that a human being does to a family . . . "

He identifies with the husband's distinctively human empathy and love, but he still does not realize that the woman's life would have value even if her husband did not love her or even if she had no husband.

Stage 4: Another boy, Richard, aged 16, answers by saying, "I don't know. In one way, it's murder; it's not a right or privilege of man to decide who shall live and who should die. God put life into everybody on earth, and you're taking away something from that person that came directly from God, and you're destroying something that is very sacred; it's in a way part of God, and it's almost destroying a part of God when you kill a person."

He sees life as sacred because it was created by God, an authority.

Postconventional level Stage 5: At 20, Richard says: "There are more and more people in the medical profession who think it is a hardship on everyone, the person, the family, when you know they are going to die. When a person is kept alive by an artificial lung or kidney it's more like being a vegetable than being a human. If it's her own choice, I think there are certain rights and privileges that go along with being a human being."

He now sees the value of life relative to other values: equal and universal human rights, concern for the quality of life, and concern for practical consequences.

Stage 6: When he is 24, Richard answers, "A human life takes precedence over any other moral or legal value, whoever it is. A human life has inherent value whether or not it is valued by a particular individual."

Richard now sees the value of human life as absolute, not as derived from or dependent on social or divine authority.

Cultural Aspects of Moral Development

Kohlberg maintains that moral thinking is universal, transcending cultural boundaries. Other research, however, suggests that culture exerts a major influ-

BOX 15-1 ▪ AROUND THE WORLD

A CHINESE PERSPECTIVE ON MORAL DEVELOPMENT

Kohlberg's dilemma of "Heinz," who could not afford a drug for his sick wife (see Chapter 12), was revised for use in Taiwan so that it described a shopkeeper who would not give a man food for his sick wife. This story would seem unbelievable to Chinese villagers—who in real life would be more likely to hear a shopkeeper say, "You have to let people have things whether they have money or not" (Wolf, 1968, p. 21). In Kohlberg's research, his subjects had to make either-or decisions, based on their individual value systems; but in the Chinese system of morality, people faced with such dilemmas would discuss them openly, would be guided by community standards, and would try to find a solution that pleased as many parties as possible (Dien, 1982).

From the Chinese perspective, human beings are seen as being born with moral tendencies, and their moral development rests on intuitive and spontaneous feelings supported by society, rather than on the kind of analytical thinking, individual choice, and personal responsibility inherent in Kohlberg's theory. Kohlberg's philosophy is oriented toward abstract principles of justice; the Chinese ethos leans toward conciliation and harmony. The Chinese system also differs from real-life morality in western cultures. In the west, good people may expect to be harshly punished if they are driven by circumstances to break a law. The Chinese are unaccustomed to universally applied laws; they prefer to abide by the decisions of a wise judge.

How, then, can Kohlberg's theory, which is rooted in western values and reflecting western ideals, measure moral development in an eastern society that has developed along very different lines? Some critics say that it cannot and that an alternative view of moral development is required, a view that measures morality by the ability to make a judgment on the basis of norms of reciprocity, rules of exchange, available resources, and complex relationships (Dien, 1982).

This viewpoint echoes the forceful protests made by Carol Gilligan (1982, 1987)—who has studied moral development in American women—that Kohlberg's stages esteem male-oriented values of justice and fairness rather than female-oriented moral imperatives of compassion and responsibility for the welfare of others.

These issues are important because of their implications for the education of our high school students. Adolescence is a time of idealism, a time of searching for answers, a time when people are receptive to moral education. If our schools and our leaders stress the value of justice and rights, as stressed by Kohlberg, rather than an alternative value of care and responsibility, we may be raising a generation of citizens who see morality as a black-and-white issue and who see attempts to resolve conflicts in a caring way as "utopian, outdated, impractical," or even as part of the "outworn philosophy of hippies" (Gilligan, 1987, p. 75).

In the interest of national and global harmony, perhaps we should rethink our concept of morality.

---

ence on moral reasoning (see Box 15-1, above, for an example of the Chinese perspective).

Research also suggests that it is possible to help young people move to higher levels of moral reasoning. The most effective way seems to be to give adolescents ample opportunities to talk about, interpret, and enact moral dilemmas and to expose them to people at a level of moral thinking slightly higher than their own present level.

Kohlberg and Gilligan (1971) assert that progress to postconventional moral thinking depends on appreciation of the relative nature of moral standards. Adolescents need to understand that every society evolves its own definition of right and wrong and that the values of one culture may seem shocking to another. (Refer back to Box 14-1 on page 506, describing the controversial practice of female circumcision.) Many young people discover arguments about morality when they enter the wider world of high school or college and encounter people whose values, culture, and ethnic background are different from their own.

High School

THE HIGH SCHOOL EXPERIENCE

High school is the central organizing experience in most adolescents' lives. It offers them opportunities to learn new information, master new skills, and sharpen old ones; to examine career choices; to participate in sports; and to get together with friends. It widens their intellectual and social horizons as it combines encounters with peers and encounters with a variety of adults. It is also an important life transition, from the security of the simpler world of childhood to a large-scale organizational environment. (For a discussion of the impact of this transition, see Box 15-2, page 546.)

The social, vocational, and athletic functions of high school are important, but the primary focus of high school continues to be on basic academic subjects. During the 1970s, scores on standardized tests fell, most dramatically in vocabulary and reading. A graduating senior in 1980 whose score was in the 50th percentile in vocabulary and reading would have been in only the 41st percentile in 1972. This represents a decline. One analysis has attributed the decline to "a decreased academic emphasis on the educational process" (Rock, Ekstrom, Goertz, Hilton, & Pollack, 1985). However, another reason for it seems to be the broader base of students going to high school. The National Commission on Excellence in Education (1983) found that the average high school or college *graduate* today is not as well educated as the average graduate of previous generations, when fewer people finished high school or college. However, the average *citizen* today is better educated than the average citizen of the past.

In response to concern over falling academic performance, the past decade has seen a greater emphasis on basic academic subjects. More students have been studying foreign languages (Maeroff, 1984), but some observers still believe that American high school students do not study as much science and mathematics as they should (National Center for Education Statistics, NCES, 1984).

Today, more than three-fourths of Americans 25 years old and older (76.5 percent) have earned high school diplomas, and nearly 1 in 5 (19.9 percent) have completed 4 years of college—a greater proportion than ever before (U.S. Bureau of the Census, 1988a). The increase stems from many causes—general expansion of educational opportunity, encouragement of minority-group students, and expanded financial aid programs that have helped many students from low-income families pursue higher education.

The high school experience reaches far beyond the classroom. It is the central organizing experience of most teenagers' lives, intellectually, socially, and—for sports-oriented adolescents—physically, too.

FAMILY INFLUENCES ON ACHIEVEMENT IN HIGH SCHOOL

Influence of Parents

Vicky and Jason are fortunate. They both come from families that value education and value children. Both sets of parents are involved with their children and their schooling, even though all four parents work outside the home and often have trouble finding time to do everything.

By and large, Ellen and Charles and Julia and Jess keep track of their children's whereabouts (even now that, as adolescents, Vicky and Jason are more

BOX 15-2 ▪ THE RESEARCH WORLD

THE TRANSITION TO JUNIOR HIGH OR HIGH SCHOOL

At the end of sixth grade, Jason experienced an important American rite of passage. He graduated from the small (500-student) elementary school he had gone to since kindergarten and entered a junior high school with 3 times as many students. Instead of staying with one teacher and the same children for the entire school day, he is now in a less personal setting in which teachers, classrooms, and classmates change constantly throughout the day. In 3 more years he will move again, this time to an even larger high school.

Vicky is following a different, less usual pattern. Since her elementary school runs from kindergarten to eighth grade, she will stay in a familiar setting with familiar people for a longer time, and then have only one transition to make, when, in ninth grade, she enters high school.

Which of these patterns is better? What benefits and drawbacks are associated with each? These questions have been the focus of research, which has found a number of stresses associated with Jason's more typical sequence. One 5-year longitudinal study followed 594 white students in the Milwaukee public schools from sixth through tenth grade, comparing those in the 6-3-3 pattern as in Jason's school with students in the 8-4 pattern found in Vicky's school (Blyth, Simmons, & Carlton-Ford, 1983). Researchers measured students' psychological adjustment by looking at their self-esteem and their perception of the "anonymity" of the school, that is, the degree to which they felt known by other people. Social adjustment was assessed by how much a student took part in extracurricular activities. And academic progress was judged according to grade-point average (GPA) and performance on achievement tests.

This study found that students who went to junior high school in seventh grade had more problems than those who did not leave elementary school until ninth grade, and that girls were especially vulnerable. Both boys and girls in the 6-3-3 pattern saw their grade-point averages drop, took less part in extracurricular activities, and saw their schools as more anonymous. Furthermore, the girls experienced a drop in self-esteem, persisting into tenth grade. Apparently, then, the timing of this initial transition to a more complex, impersonal school makes a difference, with older students finding it easier to make the switch.

The reason for girls' greater vulnerability may emerge from the findings of another study, which measured young adolescents' reactions when several life transitions occur at about the same time (Simmons, Burgeson, & Carlton-Ford, 1987). At the end of sixth grade, many students are likely to be experiencing the normative physical changes of early adolescence, and some may be beginning to date. A smaller number may be experiencing such changes as a move to a new house or school or the breakup of their parents' marriage. When Simmons and her colleagues looked at adjustment to school transition in relation to the number of other changes in a young person's life, they found that the more life changes are taking place, the more likely it is that both both sexes' GPA and extracurricular participation will decrease and that girls' self-esteem will drop.

We may have here the clue to girls' vulnerability: girls usually enter puberty sooner than boys and usually begin to date earlier than boys, making it more likely that they will experience "life-change overload." Furthermore, with the greater emphasis in early adolescence on girls' looks and popularity, they may miss the security of being with old friends. Other research, too, has shown that girls react more negatively than boys to stress in adolescence—though males are more vulnerable in childhood.

Total comfort and stability, of course, are not only impossible to achieve at any age, but also undesirable. Throughout life, we grow and develop as we learn to cope with challenges. We do this best, however, if we can deal with one change at a time, rather than several at once. If changes comes abruptly, or early, or in bunches, it helps if there is some "arena of comfort" in life, some area that is secure and familiar and nurturing (Simmons et al., 1987). When multiple changes are unavoidable, then, the adults in a young adolescent's life can help by being sensitive to the young person's need for extra emotional and social support. They can make a major transition like that to a new school setting less stressful.

independent) and of how they are doing in school (even now that Vicky and Jason rarely seek their help or advice with schoolwork). They try to attend as many parent-teacher meetings as possible. And they make time to talk to their children almost every day—at the dinner table when schedules allow, or at some other time if the parents' work or the children's track workouts or music lessons mean that the family cannot be together at dinner. Overall, the relationship between the generations is caring and interested, even though there are conflicts from time to time. When conflicts do arise, these parents resolve them in the same authoritative way they have always used (see Chapter 10).

Parents' Interest   This kind of attention from parents pays off in good grades, according to a survey of more than 30,000 high school seniors in more than 1000 schools (NCES, 1985). As Table 15-1 shows, the students with the highest grades have the most involved parents. The father's importance is especially note-worthy. Fathers seem to vary more than mothers in the degree to which they stay on top of children's schoolwork, and the more involved a father is, the better his children fare. The father's importance is also seen in the fact that children who live with both parents earned better grades.

These findings do not prove that parents' interest improves students' grades. The cause-and-effect relationship may, in fact, work the other way: young people who do well in school may stir parents' interest, encouraging their involvement. It seems more likely, however, that parents stimulate their children to do well by showing interest and concern, and that the students' achievements, in turn, stimulate their parents, so that the effect reinforces itself. Also, the parents of teenage students who do well are interested in more than their children's homework and grades. These parents make time to talk to their children, to know what they are doing, and to be available. They take the children seriously both in and out of school, and the children reward that interest.

Relationships with Parents   Another study showed that adolescents who get along well with their parents and whose parents are reasonably well adjusted get higher grades and behave better in school (Forehand, Long, Brody, & Fauber, 1986). Researchers looked at grade-point averages and teachers' behavior ratings of 46 boys and girls whose age averaged 13½, assessed parents' marital conflict and depression, and asked both parents and children to recall disagreements about such issues as cleaning the bedroom, homework, television, and drugs.

TABLE 15-1

PARENTS' INVOLVEMENT AND HIGH SCHOOL STUDENTS' GRADES

SURVEY ITEM	SELF-REPORTED GRADES			
	MOSTLY A'S	MOSTLY B'S	MOSTLY C'S	MOSTLY D'S
Mother keeps close track of how well child does in school.	92%	89%	84%	80%
Father keeps close track of how well child does in school.	85%	79%	69%	64%
Parents almost always know child's whereabouts.	88%	81%	72%	61%
Child talks with mother or father almost every day.	75%	67%	59%	45%
Parents attend PTA meetings at least once in a while.	25%	22%	20%	15%
Child lives in household with both parents.	80%	71%	64%	60%

Note: This table, based on a survey of more than 30,000 high school seniors, shows the percentage of students with various grade averages who gave positive answers to each survey item. In each instance, the higher the grades were, the more likely the parents were to be involved with the child.
Source: National Center for Education Statistics, NCES, 1985.

Parenting styles can influence how well adolescents do in school. Children of authoritative parents—who admit that teenagers sometimes know more than their elders, who talk about politics, and who welcome teenagers' participation in family decisions—tend to do better.

The teenagers who had the most conflict with a parent had the most behavior problems in school. Those whose mothers were depressed also tended to act up, but a father's depression did not have the same effect. Conflict with the father did have more impact than conflict with the mother. Frequent disagreement with the mother did not affect school performance, but students who got along poorly with their fathers had lower grades than those who got along better. Surprisingly, parents' marital relationship did not affect children's grades or behavior.

Why should conflict with the father be more upsetting than conflict with the mother? It is possible that teenagers and mothers clash so often over routine matters that young people do not take it seriously, but that conflicts with fathers are over more important issues or simply have more impact because they are less frequent. Causation may run in the other direction, too: when students do poorly in school, fathers may become more involved, and as they try to oversee students' work or behavior, more conflicts may erupt. In either case, both these studies underscore the importance of the father's involvement in the lives of adolescent children, an involvement that has been ignored in much developmental research.

Parenting Styles What do the authoritative, authoritarian, and permissive child-rearing patterns described by Baumrind (1971—see Chapter 10) involve when children are half-grown? More than 7000 high school students in the San Francisco Bay area filled out questionnaires showing how they perceived their parents' attitudes and behaviors (Dornbusch et al., 1987). An index for the survey showed that the three styles include the following:

- *Authoritative parents* tell adolescent children to look at both sides of issues, they admit that their children sometimes know more, they talk about politics, and they welcome teenagers' participation in family decisions. Students who get good grades receive praise and freedom; poor grades bring encouragement to try harder, offers of help, and loss of freedom.
- *Authoritarian parents* tell adolescents not to argue with adults, hold that parents are always right and should not be questioned, and say that young people will "know better when they are grown up." Good grades elicit admonitions to do even better, and poor grades upset parents and lead to reduction of allowances and "grounding."
- *Permissive parents* do not care about their teenage children's grades, make no rules about watching television, do not attend school programs, and neither help with nor check their children's homework. (The term *permissive* can apply either to parents who are neglectful and uncaring or to parents who are caring and concerned but believe that children should be responsible for their own lives.)

Analysis of students' grades and questionnaires showed a strong relationship between authoritative parenting and high achievement in school. Students who got low grades were more likely to have authoritarian or permissive parents or parents who were inconsistent in style. Inconsistency was associated with the lowest grades, possibly because children who do not know what to expect from their parents become anxious and less able to concentrate on their work. These relationships were stronger for white students than in Hispanic, African American, and Asian families, all of which tended to be more authoritarian. (Thus, the survey did not explain the success of Asian students in American schools.) This study suggests a reason for the lower school achievement that a number of studies have found in students in single-parent homes: single parents tend to be more permissive. Thus the style of parenting seems to make the difference, not the single-parent status itself.

Effects of Socioeconomic Status

So many educators consider socioeconomic status a factor in achievement in school that it is often cited as more or less self-evident. However, a statistical analysis of 101 studies found that socioeconomic status as typically defined (by income, education, and occupation of parents) is only weakly correlated with school performance (K. R. White, 1982). Furthermore, the correlation decreases as students get older, partly because students have experiences in school that they have not had at home and partly because many poor students have dropped out. (Socioeconomic status is associated with the dropout rate, as we point out in the next section.) It is also lower in more recent studies, suggesting that television, preschool, and other community resources have served as equalizing influences, and that compensatory education programs are having an effect.

The major influence on school achievement—across socioeconomic boundaries—is the atmosphere in the home. Do parents value education? Do they read to young children and take them to the library? Do they talk to their children? What goals do parents have for their children and how do they help them attain those goals? Do they show interest in their schoolwork and expect them to go to college? Is the family stable?

Whether a family is rich or poor, it is the answers to questions like these that seem to make a difference in how children do in school. "Even though family background does have a strong relationship to achievement, it may be *how* parents rear their children . . . and not the parents' occupation, income, or education that really makes the difference" (K. R. White, 1982, p. 471).

DROPPING OUT OF SCHOOL

Students who decide to leave school before receiving a diploma reduce the opportunities that the future will hold. Dropping out of high school does not guarantee poverty, but dropouts do have to scramble harder to start a career—if they ever have one. Many employers require a high school diploma, and many jobs require skills that are based on a solid education.

Who Drops Out?

More than 500,000 students (about 15 percent) who were sophomores in 1980 left high school before graduation and had not returned by 1982. Almost one-half left school in the eleventh grade, almost one-third in the senior year, and about one-fourth in the tenth grade. Boys are more likely to drop out than girls. Among racial and ethnic groups, Asian-Americans have the lowest dropout rate (4.8 percent), followed by whites (12.2 percent), African Americans (16.8 percent), Hispanics, (18.7 percent), and Native Americans (22.7 percent). When socioeconomic status is held constant, however, the difference among whites, blacks, and Hispanics narrows or even vanishes. In fact, at equal socioeconomic levels, blacks' attainment is higher than whites' (Center for Educational Statistics, 1987). Thus while socioeconomic status does not seem to affect performance when students are actually in school, it does make a difference in whether they stay there long enough to graduate.

Why Do They Drop Out?

The reasons dropouts give for their decision are not surprising, although they do not tell the whole story. When asked 2 years later why they had dropped out, one group of males pointed to poor grades (36 percent), not liking school (25 percent), being expelled or suspended (13 percent), or having to support the family (26 percent). Girls attributed dropping out to marriage or plans to marry (31 percent), feeling that "school is not for me" (31 percent), poor grades (30 percent), pregnancy (23 percent), and a job (11 percent) (NCES, 1983.)*

It is hard to determine the precise reasons for dropping out. More than half of the girls said that they had left because of pregnancy or marriage; however, they may have become pregnant or gotten married because they were not doing well or were not interested in school. And if the girls' reasons were true, why were they? The boys' explanations tell us just as little about their underlying reasons. Some researchers have attributed dropping out to such factors as lack of motivation and self-esteem, little encouragement of education by parents, low expectations by teachers, and disciplinary problems at home and at school (Rule, 1981).

The students who are the most likely to drop out of school tend to share a number of background characteristics. Those whose parents are poorly educated and in low-level jobs and who are in large, single-parent families are 3 to 5 times more likely to drop out than are children in more privileged circumstances (NCES, 1987). Other factors associated with dropping out include having repeated a grade in elementary school, working more than 15 hours a week while in high school, being married, having a child, and such signs of antisocial behavior as suspension, probation, or trouble with the law (Center for Educational Satistics, 1987).

What Happens to Dropouts?

Dropouts have trouble getting jobs; the work they do get is in low-level, poor-paying occupations; and they are more likely to lose their jobs. In 1982, 27 percent of male high school dropouts and 31 percent of female high school dropouts were looking for work; 32 percent of the young women were not looking for work because they were full-time homemakers. Of those who were working, only about 14 percent of the young men and 3 percent of the young women had jobs that required technical skills. Typical jobs were waiting on tables, manual labor, factory work, clerking in stores, baby-sitting, clerical work, and farm work. More than half the dropouts regretted leaving school very soon after they did so, and a small percentage took part in educational programs (Center for Educational Statistics, 1987).

*The figures total more than 100 percent because some respondents gave more than one reason for dropping out.

Can Dropping Out Be Prevented?

Society suffers, too, when many young people do not finish school. Dropouts are more likely to end up on welfare, to be unemployed, and to become involved with drugs, crime, and delinquency. In addition, the loss of taxable income burdens the public treasury (Center for Educational Statistics, 1987). In recognition of both societal and personal problems caused by dropping out, both public and private organizations have developed a variety of programs aimed at encouraging young people to stay in school. Some, of course, have had more success than others.

One particularly successful federally funded program, Upward Bound, was established in 1964 and by 1988 had seen 80 percent of its graduates go on to 4-year colleges (Wells, 1988a). Applicants—students from low-income families whose parents and siblings did not go to college—are selected on the basis of school records, teachers' recommendations, a personal interview, and an assessment of applicants' and parents' commitment to the program. This program emphasizes high expectations, provides a rigorous college preparatory curriculum, and offers tutoring and peer counseling. Upward Bound also offers workshops and counseling sessions on such topics as drug abuse, self-esteem, study skills, preparing for the Scholastic Aptitude Test (SAT), applying to college, and career planning. Although the program is expensive to administer, the recognized need has continued to attract Congressional support. The problem, however, is that there are not enough programs like this. According to one estimate, there are about 24,000 eligible students in the area served by the Columbia University Upward Bound program. Only 200 can be served (Wells, 1988a).

Upward Bound's insistence on parents' commitment reflects the importance of encouragement by parents. Most low-income parents want their children to be well educated and well employed, but they often do not know how to help. To assist such parents, the National Committee for Citizens in Education has established a dropout prevention center with a toll-free hot line (1-800-NETWORK). Callers get advice on helping students who face suspension, expulsion, reduction of grades, or withholding of credit because of absence. Such punishments cause students to fall farther behind, increase frustration, and make dropping out more likely.

The success of programs like Upward Bound shows that it is possible to prevent dropping out. With commitment by government, educators, and parents, millions of young people could be helped to have a brighter future.

Developing a Career

"Is there life after high school? Where will all this education lead to? What kind of work will I do after school? Do I need still more education?" These are the questions that concern adolescents as they think about the future.

STAGES IN VOCATIONAL PLANNING

When she was 6, Vicky told everyone that she was going to be an astronaut. Reminded of that ambition when she was 12, she laughed. Math and science were not her best subjects, and she knew she could never make it into the space

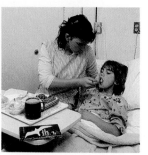

Volunteer work is one way to preview the rewards and frustrations of a particular career. If this teenage "candy-striper" finds hospital work rewarding, she may pursue a career as a nurse or a doctor.

program. At 15 she did some volunteer work at a hospital and began thinking about psychiatry as a career. Now, as a high school senior, she is applying to colleges. She has decided against medical school, and instead she is writing to colleges with a 5-year program leading to a master's degree in social work.

Jason's ambitions are less sharply focused. At 6 he wanted to be a baseball player. At 12, playing baseball still sounded good, but so did becoming a dancer. As the time to apply to college draws closer, he bounces from one interest to another—baseball, choreography, law, geology, and anthropology—and hates to have to drop any of them.

Vicky's development has followed three classic stages in career planning: the fantasy period, the tentative period, and the realistic period (Ginzberg et al., 1951). During the *fantasy* period of her elementary school years, Vicky's choices were active and exciting rather than realistic, and her decisions were emotional rather than practical. In the *tentative* period, at about the time of puberty, she began to make a somewhat more realistic effort to match her interests with her abilities and values. By the end of high school, she is in the *realistic* period and plans for the right education to meet her career requirements.

Jason, however, has not yet reached the realistic period. He is not alone: in one study, more than 6000 high school seniors in Texas were asked to name their top three career choices and to report on their educational plans. They were also asked about their preferred vocational styles: working alone versus working with others, working inside versus outdoors, and working with people, things, or ideas. At a time in their lives when they had to make crucial choices about education and work, these students knew little about occupations. Not surprisingly, they tended to know more about their first career choice and increasingly less about the next two. But even of those who felt that they had a good understanding of their first career choice, only about half planned to get the appropriate amount of education. Some seemed bent on schooling that would leave them overeducated, and others were not planning on getting enough training. Furthermore, most of the students did not seem to be making good matches between their career choices and their interests (Grotevant & Durrett, 1980).

INFLUENCES ON VOCATIONAL PLANNING

How do young people choose their career goals? Many factors enter in, including individual ability and personality; education; socioeconomic, racial, and ethnic background; societal values; and particular life experiences. One experience that is often thought to help adolescents plan their life's work is part-time work. However, work during the high school years may be virtually useless for career planning, and harmful for present school achievement besides (see Box 15-3). Let us look at such important influences on career planning as parents' ambitions for, and encouragement of, their children—and at gender.

How Do Parents Affect Vocational Plans?

Parents' encouragement and financial support are important influences on aspiration as well as achievement. If parents do not encourage children to pursue higher education and are not willing to help them through college, it is harder for the children. Some students, of course, do work their way through school, take out loans, or win scholarships. But in general, parents' encouragement is a better predictor of high ambition than social class.

BOX 15-3 ■ THE EVERYDAY WORLD

IS WORK GOOD FOR TEENAGERS?

When Vicky announced that she had taken an after-school and weekend job as a waitress in a local restaurant, Ellen and Charles applauded her initiative and her industry. They thought that her job would help her learn how to handle money responsibly and develop good work habits. But Vicky's high school counselor was less enthusiastic about it. Let's see why.

A greater proportion of teenage students are working today than at any other time in the past few decades—about one-half of all high school juniors and seniors and almost one-third of ninth- and tenth-graders (S. Cole, 1980). Some work because their families need the income; others, because they want the independence that comes from earning their own money.

This trend fits in well with the traditional American belief in moral benefits of working, but research has found that teenagers who work are no more independent in making financial or other decisions affecting their lives than classmates who do not (Greenberger & Steinberg, 1986). Most students who work part time do not learn the kinds of skills that will be useful later in life (Hamilton & Crouter, 1980), and those who work during high school are not likely to earn more money afterward than if they do not hold jobs (Greenberger & Steinberg, 1986).

Moreover, work seems to undermine performance in high school, especially for teenagers who put in more than about 15 or 20 hours of work per week. Grades, involvement in school, and attendance decline. In fact, working more than 15 hours a week is related to dropping out of school (National Center for Education Statistics, NCES, 1987). Thus, experience gained by working is offset by reduced experience in school.

There are other, hidden costs. Some teenage workers spend their earnings on alcohol or drugs, develop a cynical attitude toward working, and steal from their employers. Working teenagers tend to spend less time with their families and feel less close to them. Furthermore, they have little contact with adults on the job, and they are usually placed in gender-stereotyped jobs (Greenberger & Steinberg, 1986).

Some of working teenagers' undesirable tendencies may not be caused by working itself, but by the factors that motivate teenagers to take jobs. Some adolescents may want to work because they are uninterested in school and alienated from their families, or because they want to have money for drink and drugs. Working does not seem to help such young people manage their lives better. Part of the reason is probably the menial, dead-end nature of the jobs usually available to teenagers.

There are, of course, some advantages to part-time work. Some adolescent workers do learn how to manage both money and time, how to find a job, and how to get along with a variety of people. Some discover that the world of work is demanding and difficult, and that they need to complete their education to get a better, higher-paying job. In sum, though, work experience during school seems less important than a solid academic foundation. To prepare themselves for careers, adolescents should work hard in school rather than school themselves through work.

When 2622 sixth-, eighth-, tenth-, and twelfth-grade black and white students from all social strata were asked to describe their own expectations for their education and their fathers' and mothers' expectations for them, more than half the students agreed with the perceived goals of both parents. A greater level of agreement existed between students and mothers than between students and fathers, possibly because women have traditionally spent more time with their children (T. E. Smith, 1981).

What about the parents' own careers? How weighty is their influence? A review of the literature found that a man's occupation influences his son's career choices but not his daughter's (Conger & Peterson, 1984). Werts (1966, 1968), for example, in a study of fathers and sons, found that 43.6 percent of doctors' sons chose to enter medicine, that 27.7 percent of attorneys' sons opted for law, and that the sons of physical and social scientists were similarly influenced in their career choices. Newer research indicates that college-educated daughters of working mothers have higher career aspirations and achieve more in their careers than daughters of homemakers (L. W. Hoffman, 1979).

Is this career counselor influenced by the student's sex in advising him about possible career choices? Even though there is little or no difference between boys and girls in mathematical or verbal ability, many counselors still steer young people into gender-typed careers.

How Does Gender Affect Vocational Plans?

A woman who entered engineering school at Ohio State University in 1945 was one of six females in her class. Some 35 years later, women made up about 30 percent of the entering class (R. D. Feldman, 1982). Similar increases have been seen in the number of women studying law, medicine, and other traditionally male occupations. Women who pursue nontraditional careers are likely to be the eldest child in the family and to have well-educated parents (Matlin, 1987).

Even though there is much more flexibility in career goals today, gender often influences choice of a career. For example, there is little or no difference between boys and girls in mathematical or verbal ability (Hyde & Linn, 1988; Maccoby & Jacklin, 1974), but many career counselors still steer young people into gender-typed careers (Matlin, 1987).

As we noted earlier, researchers have found that differences do exist in specific skills within cognitive areas (Deaux, 1985). For example, although boys do better on algebra problems, girls do just as well in arithmetic and geometry (Becker, 1983; Marshall, 1984). Boys do better on some measures of spatial skills (such as visualizing what an object would look like from a different angle), but girls do just as well on measures that require a more analytic strategy and that are more closely related to mathematical and scientific reasoning (M. C. Linn & Petersen, 1985).

Males and females do about the same on vocabulary, analogies, reading comprehension, and essay writing. Earlier studies showed females to be slightly better on general verbal abilities and anagrams, but recent analysis has found that gender differences in verbal ability have virtually disappeared. Males achieved better scores in the 1985 Scholastic Aptitude Tests, possibly reflecting the increasingly technical content of the material in recent years or the fact that

BOX 15-4 ■ A CHILD'S WORLD AND YOU

WHAT DO YOU THINK?

Although most people eventually abandon adolescent idealism in favor of a more realistic viewpoint, not all do. Should they? On the scale below, where would you place yourself between the extremes?

VALUES SCALE

1	2	3	4	5	6	7	8	9	10

Scorning all authority figures because they must have "feet of clay"

Defending and insisting upon acting on every passing whim, while denouncing the opinions and tastes of others

Honoring all authority figures because of their position

Never challenging another's viewpoint, even when it goes against one's deepest beliefs and values

VALUES SCALE

1	2	3	4	5	6	7	8	9	10

Never making up one's mind

Refusing to tolerate any challenges to social policies because the policies are well-intentioned and would work if people only behaved themselves

Never having any doubts

Refusing to support any social programs to help people because inevitably they will fall short and assist a few scoundrels as well

---

more females took the test and that many females were disadvantaged compared with the males (Hyde & Linn, 1988).

Studies published before 1973 show larger gender differences than more recent research; thus it seems that many differences may have declined as a result of increased flexibility in gender roles. Or perhaps researchers today are more likely than they used to be to publish when they have found *no* significant gender differences.

In any case, the small differences in males' and females' abilities have no real psychological or educational implications. Particularly, there is no basis for steering males and females toward different careers. Even if differences do exist, there is much overlap: some girls are better at math and science than some boys, and some boys are better writers and speakers than some girls. Young people of both sexes, then, should be encouraged to pursue careers that fit their interests and abilities, regardless of gender.

The adolescent's search for identity is closely tied to vocational ambitions. The question "Who shall I be?" is very close to "What shall I do?" The choice of a career is crucial: when people feel that they are doing something worth doing and doing it well, they feel good about themselves. On the contrary, if they feel that their work does not matter to others or that they are not very good at it, they can feel very insecure in their emotional well-being. A major issue in adolescence is the continuing effort to define the self, to mold an identity, and to emerge with self-knowledge and self-esteem. We discuss this effort in Chapter 16.

Summary

1   Many adolescents attain Piaget's stage of formal operations, which is characterized by the ability to think abstractly. People in the stage of formal operations can engage in hypothetical-deductive reasoning, as demonstrated by performance on the pendulum task, for example. People in the formal operations stage can think in terms of possibilities, deal flexibly with problems, and test hypotheses. Since experience plays an important part in the attainment of this stage, not all people become capable of formal operations.

2   The attainment of formal operations is reflected in a number of "egocentric" behaviors characteristic of adolescence, including finding fault with authority figures, argumentativeness, self-consciousness, self-centeredness, indecisiveness, and apparent hypocrisy.

3   Most adolescents are at Kohlberg's conventional level (level II). Their moral judgments conform to social conventions, they support the status quo, and they think in terms of doing the "right" thing to please others or to obey the law. Some adolescents, however, are at the preconventional stage, and others are at the postconventional stage.

4   Cultural factors play a part in the attainment of the more advanced levels of moral judgment. Kohlberg's dilemmas appear not to be appropriate for use in every culture.

5   High school is the central organizing experience—intellectually and otherwise—in the lives of most adolescents. Efforts are being made to improve the quality of education in American high schools.

6   Home atmosphere, parents' involvement, family relationships, and parenting style appear to make more of a difference than a family's socioeconomic status in students' achievement in high school.

7   Although most adolescents in the United States graduate from high school, some 500,000 students who were sophomores in 1980 dropped out before graduating. Programs such as Upward Bound aim to encourage young people to stay in school.

8   Vocational choice is influenced by several factors, including gender and parents' attitude.

9   More teenagers today work part time after school than in the past few decades. Work seems to have little benefit for a teenager's educational, social, or occupational development. Its negative effect on schoolwork is greatest when the teenager works more than 15 or 20 hours a week.

Key Terms

formal operations (page 537)
imaginary audience (540)

personal fable (541)

Suggested Readings

Elkind, D. (1984). *All grown up and no place to go.* Reading, MA: Addison-Wesley. A thought-provoking book about the difficulties involved in being a teenager and raising teenagers today. Elkind argues that today's teenagers are unprepared for the adult challenges they have to face at an early age, resulting in many problem behaviors. The chapter relating thinking abilities at the formal operations stage to behaviors such as self-centeredness, self-consciousness, and argumentativeness is outstanding.

Inhelder, B., & Piaget, J. (1958). *The growth of logical thinking from childhood to adolescence.* Boston: Little, Brown. A classic account of Piaget's research, written with his longtime collaborator Barbel Inhelder. This book traces cognitive development through its four stages.

Schields, C. (1988). *The college guide for parents.* New York: College Board. An excellent guide for parents of adolescents getting ready to go to college. It contains information about a wide variety of topics—from financial aid to making a successful transition from home to college.

PERSONALITY AND SOCIAL DEVELOPMENT IN ADOLESCENCE

T his face in the mirror
stares at me
demanding *Who are you? What will you become?*
And taunting, *You don't even know.*
Chastened, I cringe and agree
and then
because I'm still young,
I stick out my tongue.

Eve Merriam, "Conversation with Myself," 1964

PREVIEW QUESTIONS

- Is "storm and stress" an inevitable part of adolescence?
- Do adolescent boys and girls seek identity in similar ways?
- How do teenagers' relationships with parents and peers help them achieve their own identity?
- What are the prevailing sexual practices and attitudes among adolescents today?
- What are some causes and consequences of teenage pregnancy and delinquency?
- What are some strengths of adolescents?

"THE TROUBLE IS," said 16-year-old Vicky to her mother after an intense argument, "that I don't know who I am. You know who you are. You're Ellen Smith Miller. You're a teacher. You're a wife. You're a mother. But who am I? You expect me to be just like you, to think just the way you do, and to do whatever you would do if you were me. But you're *not* me. I don't know who *is* me. I wish I could be myself with you, but I always feel under all this pressure not to talk about the things I think or do that I know you wouldn't approve of.

"Then when I do decide to open up a little bit of myself to you, it never seems to be a good time. I guess it's my fault. I don't pick the right times— whenever I want to talk, you always seem to be busy with something else and not to have enough time to listen to me. But if we can't talk to each other, we'll never understand each other." And Vicky leaves unspoken and barely thought, "And I'll never find out who I really am."

Vicky's plaint expresses what is probably the most important task of adolescence—the search for identity, the quest to find out "who I really am." Teenagers need to develop their own values and to be sure that they are not just parroting the ideas of their parents. They have to find out what they can do and to be proud of their accomplishments. They want to develop close relationships with both boys and girls their own age and to be liked and loved and respected for who they are and what they stand for. "The adolescent searches for his or her self-identity in many mirrors" (R.C. Sorensen, 1973, p. 37).

560

Adolescents pursue this search in many different ways. Vicky's high school years have been troubled by a recurring disquiet over the many changes she faces. She knows that she is no longer a child—but that she is not yet an adult. As she looks at her mother, who seems to fit all her roles so easily—teacher, mother, wife, friend—Vicky cannot imagine herself filling any of these roles comfortably and well. And she is not sure that she even wants to. Her biggest problem these days is that she does not know what she wants.

Jason's adolescence is quieter, less troubling to both him and his parents. Yes, one night he came home reeking of cheap wine, and yes, he sometimes offends his parents with his language and the loud rock music he plays. By and large, though, Jason's parents are proud of their son, and they trust him to do the right thing. He accepts their confidence in him, and—within what he considers responsible limits—he does what he pleases. This works out well, since what he wants to do often fits in with what his parents want him to do—achieve in school, socialize with friends they like, and go out for sports. Still, he, too, has doubts, anxieties, questions about the future.

In this chapter we continue our discussion of changes that adolescents face, focusing on social and personality development. We begin, as before, with several theoretical perspectives—those of G. Stanley Hall, Margaret Mead, Sigmund Freud, Anna Freud, and Erik Erikson.

We then consider the broad concept of the search for identity—a search for, or an attempt to create, some personal stability and certainty amid many changes and questions. The question, "Who am I?" may be broken down into subquestions, like "What do I really believe?" "What kinds of relationships do I have?" and "Who am I, sexually?"

After considering some important research on adolescents' identity, we discuss three crucial aspects of identity: relationships with parents, relationships with peers, and sexual identity. The final sections of the chapter cover two serious problems of adolescence—pregnancy and juvenile delinquency—and some of the strengths of adolescents.

Theoretical Perspectives on Adolescents' Personality Development

There are many different theories of the significance of adolescence and its effects on the young person. Here are some of the most important historical and contemporary views.

G. STANLEY HALL: "STORM AND STRESS"

The first psychologist to formulate a theory of adolescence, G. Stanley Hall (1916/1904), proposed that the major physical changes of adolescence cause major psychological changes. He believed that young people's efforts to adjust to their changing bodies usher in a period of *Sturm und Drang*, or **storm and stress**, from which adolescents can emerge morally stronger.

storm and stress *In Hall's terminology, the idea that adolescence is necessarily a time of strong and variable emotions; from the German Sturm und Drang.*

Hall's view of adolescence has been accepted by many observers of young people and hotly contested by others. The dominant opinion today is that storm and stress is not inevitable for most adolescents. Hall is important, however, for drawing attention to adolescence as a unique, special period of the life span.

MARGARET MEAD: THE CULTURAL FACTOR

Margaret Mead, an anthropologist who studied adolescence in Samoa (1928) and New Guinea (1953), pointed to the importance of cultural factors in development. She concluded that when a culture provides a serene and gradual transition from childhood to adulthood, as Samoa does, there is no storm and stress, but an easy acceptance of the adult role.

Mead wrote:

> The adolescent girl in Samoa differed from her sister who had not reached puberty in one chief respect, that in the older girl certain bodily changes were present which were absent in the younger girl. There were no other great differences to set off the group passing through adolescence from the group which would become adolescent in two years or the group which had become adolescent two years before. (1928, p. 196)

According to Mead, adolescence is relatively free of stress in a society that permits children to see adults' sexual activity, to watch the birth of a baby, to regard death as natural, to do important work, to exhibit assertive and even dominant behavior, to engage in sex play, and to know precisely what their adult roles will involve. In societies like our own, however, children are considered very different from adults, who have completely different expectations for them and shelter them from much of adult life and responsibilities. As a result, the shift from childhood to adulthood is discontinuous and much more stressful. Mead also held that cultural attitudes toward the phsyical changes of adolescence affect the nature of the transition.

Mead's work in Samoa has been criticized by D. Freeman (1983), who charges that her research was hasty and her findings biased and erroneous. Freeman holds that adolescence in Samoa is indeed tumultuous and stressful and that delinquency shows up more often in adolescence than at any other time of life in Samoa just as in a number of western countries. But others have defended Mead's work (L.D. Holmes, 1987); and in any case, coming nearly 60 years after Mead's fieldwork (which took place in 1925), these charges have had little impact. Today, storm and stress is no longer considered inevitable, even for children growing up in the United States, as we shall see.

SIGMUND FREUD: THE GENITAL STAGE

Like Hall, Sigmund Freud also saw conflict resulting from the biological changes of adolescence. According to Freud's (1953/1935) psychosexual theory of development, this conflict prepares the way for the *genital stage* of mature adult sexuality.

The physiological changes of puberty reawaken the *libido,* the basic energy that fuels the sex drive. The sexual urges of the phallic stage, which were repressed during the latency period of middle childhood, now assert themselves again. But now those urges are directed in socially approved channels— heterosexual relations with people outside the family.

Before adolescents can achieve mature sexuality, they have to free themselves from dependency on their parents, which persists because of unresolved sexual feelings toward the parent of the other sex. Through the defense mechanism of *reaction formation*—expressing the opposite of what one really feels—

Margaret Mead, shown here when she was in Samoa studying adolescence, believed that young girls felt comfortable confiding in her because she was only in her early twenties herself—not much older than her subjects.

genital stage In Freud's terminology, the psychosexual stage of mature sexuality; it occurs during adolescence.

libido In Freud's terminology, the basic energy that fuels the sexual drive.

reaction formation Defense mechanism characterized by replacement of an anxiety-producing feeling with the expression of its opposite.

adolescents replace sexual longing with hostility. Thus, Freud also saw storm and stress as an inevitable part of adolescence.

Freud also maintained that as young adolescents are freeing themselves from sexual dependency on the other-sex parent, they typically go through a homosexual stage, which may show up in hero worship of an adult or in a close friendship with a young person of the same sex. This phase is the forerunner of mature attachments with persons of the other sex.

Infantile forms of sexuality have no aim other than pleasure; but according to Freud the changes of puberty make reproduction an important component of sexuality and thus require certain transitions. The need to masturbate becomes more urgent in early adolescence, preparing the young person for eventual sexual release with a partner; after this is achieved, masturbation diminishes. Girls, Freud believed, need to progress from immature clitoral orgasm (obtained in masturbation) to mature vaginal orgasm (achieved in sexual intercourse) (S. Freud, 1953/1935, 1959/1925).

Research has challenged several aspects of Freud's theory. Masturbation, for example, does not decline with age and sexual activity. Older adolescents (16 to 19 years of age) and nonvirgins are actually more likely to masturbate than 13- to 15-year-olds and virgins (R.C. Sorensen, 1973). In addition, Freud's contention that the only mature form of orgasm is vaginal has been questioned, since clitoral orgasm is apparently characteristic of the sexual response of many normal, well-adjusted adult women (Masters & Johnson, 1966).

ANNA FREUD: EGO DEFENSES OF ADOLESCENCE

Anna Freud (1946), Sigmund Freud's daughter, who also became a psychoanalyst, considered the adolescent years more important for the formation of personality than her father had (Sigmund Freud emphasized the impact of early experience). She believed that the glandular changes which produce physiological changes also affect psychological functioning. The reawakened libido—sexual urge—threatens the id-ego balance that was maintained during the latency years, when the ego kept the id under control. The resultant conflicts cause anxiety, which in turn calls forth ego defense mechanisms. Anna Freud expanded Sigmund Freud's concept of defense mechanisms, to include intellectualization and asceticism.

Intellectualization—engaging in abstract thought to avoid unpleasant emotions—may be seen in the tendency of many adolescents to have all-night discussions of such topics as religion, politics, philosophy, and the meaning of life. Other investigators relate these to adolescents' search for identity or to their increased capacity for abstract thought. But Anna Freud considered such discussions a defense. She believed that young people are not trying to solve real problems through such intellectual speculations, but are instead using words and ideas to respond to basic instinctual needs created by their changing bodies.

She also saw a defense in *asceticism*, or self-denial. Because adolescents are afraid of losing control over their impulses, some take a self-denying approach to life, with the result that they overcontrol themselves. For example, an ascetic adolescent may wear drab, shapeless clothing and renounce many simple pleasures. Later in life, Anna Freud said, as people gain confidence in their ability to control their dangerous impulses, they tend to relax and to be less strict with themselves.

intellectualization In the terminology of Anna Freud, a defense mechanism characterized by participating in abstract intellectual discussions to avoid unpleasant, anxiety-producing feelings.

asceticism In Anna Freud's terminology, a defense mechanism characterized by self-denial in response to the fear of loss of control over one's impulses.

(Barton Silberman/NYT Pictures)

Anna Freud believed that the glandular changes which produce physiological changes in adolescence also affect psychological functioning, and result in the use of defense mechanisms, such as intellectualization and asceticism.

ERIK ERIKSON: CRISIS 5—IDENTITY VERSUS IDENTITY CONFUSION

identity versus identity confusion In Erikson's theory, the fifth crisis of psychosocial development, in which an adolescent must determine his or her own sense of self (identity), including the role he or she will play in society.

According to Erikson (1968), the chief task of adolescence is to resolve the conflict of *identity versus identity confusion*—to become a unique adult with an important role in life. To form an identity, the ego organizes the person's abilities, needs, and desires and helps to adapt them to the demands of society. The search for identity comes into focus during adolescence and persists throughout life, though it is more insistent at some times than at others.

On the basis of his own life (see Chapter 1) and his research with adolescents in several societies, Erikson concluded that a crucial aspect of the search for identity is deciding on a career. In the previous stage, that of *industry versus inferiority*, a child acquires the skills needed for success in the culture. Adolescents need to find ways to use these skills. Rapid physical growth and new genital maturity alert young people to their impending adulthood, and they begin to wonder about their roles in adult society.

Erikson sees the prime danger of this stage as identity confusion, or role confusion, which can express itself in a young person's taking an excessively long time to reach adulthood. (He himself did not resolve his own identity crisis until his mid-twenties.) A certain amount of identity confusion is normal, however, and accounts for the chaotic nature of much of adolescents' behavior, as well as their painful self-consciousness about their looks.

According to Erikson, teenagers' cliquishness and intolerance of differences are defenses against identity confusion. Adolescents may also express confusion by regressing into childishness to avoid resolving conflicts or by committing themselves impulsively to poorly thought-out courses of action. During the *psychosocial moratorium* (Erikson, 1950, p. 262)—the "time-out" period that adolescence and youth provide—many young people search for commitments to which they can be faithful. One adolescent may work for world peace, another may become a vegetarian, another may embark upon creative work in music or

According to Erikson, this flutist's musical talent and interest can help her resolve the conflict of identity versus identity confusion. If she does not plan a career in music, she will need to decide on an alternative, thus fulfilling a major task in the search for identity.

© Erika Stone 1985

art. Very often such youthful commitments will shape a person's life for many years to come. These commitments are both ideological and personal, and the extent to which young people can be true to them determines their ability to resolve the crisis of this stage.

The fundamental "virtue" that arises from this identity crisis is the *virtue of fidelity*. It involves a sense of belonging to a loved one, or to friends and companions. It also involves identifying with a set of values, an ideology, a religion, a movement, or an ethnic group. Self-identification emerges because the individual has selected the values and people he or she chooses to be loyal to, rather than simply accepting them from parents.

Fidelity now represents a more extensively developed sense of trust than it did in childhood. In infancy, it was important to trust in others, especially one's parents; now it is important to be trustworthy oneself. In addition, adolescents transfer their trust from their parents to other people who can help guide them through life. These may be mentors or loved ones.

Love, in fact, is an avenue to identity in Erikson's scheme. By becoming intimate with another person and sharing thoughts and feelings, the adolescent offers up his or her own tentative identity, sees it reflected in the loved one, and is better able to clarify the self.

Adolescents' intimacies differ from mature intimacy, which involves commitment and sacrifice. According to Erikson, for males intimacy cannot take place until after a stable identity is achieved; but a female puts her identity aside as she prepares to define herself through the man she will marry. Women, then, achieve identity and intimacy at the same time. Erikson's theory takes the male as the norm (as Freud did) and considers women's development a deviation from the norm. This point of view has been the basis for important criticisms of Erikson's theory.

Some recent research, most notably that done by James Marcia and his colleagues, explores the differences between males' and females' identity development, and expands and clarifies Erikson's theory of identity formation. We examine this research in the following section.

The Search for Identity

The search for identity is a lifelong voyage, launched in adolescence. As Erikson (1950) emphasizes, this effort to make sense of the self and the world is not "a kind of maturational malaise." It is, instead, a healthy, vital process that contributes to the ego strength of the adult. The conflicts in this struggle spur personal growth and development.

RESEARCH ON IDENTITY

Vicky and Jason, and many of their friends, are about to graduate from high school. Vicky, as we have seen, has looked at her interests and her talents and is planning to become a social worker. She has narrowed down her college choices and has applied to three schools—one that she is fairly sure of getting into, one "safe" school where she is quite sure of admission, and one very selective school. She knows that her experiences in college will either confirm her interest in social work or lead her in some other direction, and she is open to both possibilities.

One friend of Vicky's, Martha, knows exactly what she is going to do with her life. Martha's mother, the union leader at a plastics factory, has arranged for Martha to enter an apprenticeship program at the factory, and Martha has never considered doing anything else.

Jason still has no idea of what he wants to do, but he is not worried. He expects to go to college, take courses that sound interesting, and make up his mind when he is ready.

Jason's closest friend, Michael, is agonizing over the direction his future will take. He is torn between mathematics and music: he has shown talent for both but cannot decide which he prefers.

All four of these high school seniors are wrestling with issues of identity formation. What accounts for the differences in the way they are going about it—and in the eventual results?

Identity Statuses: Crisis and Commitment

A substantial amount of research on adolescents' identity has expanded Erikson's theory to identify several identity statuses and to correlate these statuses with other aspects of personality. The most prominent researcher in this area is the psychologist James E. Marcia, who defines identity as "an internal, self-constructed, dynamic organization of drives, abilities, beliefs, and individual history" (1980, p. 159).

Marcia identified four different statuses according to the presence or absence of crisis and commitment, the two elements that Erikson maintained were crucial to forming identity (see Table 16-1, below). He then related these identity statuses to a number of personality characteristics, including anxiety, self-esteem, moral reasoning, and patterns of behaving with other people. The categories are not permanent, and they change as people continue to develop (Marcia, 1979).

crisis Period of conscious decision making related to identity formation.

commitment Personal investment in an occupation or a system of beliefs.

Marcia defines *crisis* as a period of conscious decision making, and *commitment* as a personal investment in an occupation or a system of beliefs (ideology). To evaluate identity status, Marcia (1966) developed a 30-minute semistructured interview (see Table 16-2, on the opposite page).

TABLE 16-1

IDENTITY STATUSES		
	CRISIS	
COMMITMENT	PRESENT	ABSENT
PRESENT	Identity achievement	Foreclosure
ABSENT OR VAGUE	Moratorium Identity confusion	Identity confusion

Note: Marcia classifies young people into four identity statuses, depending on whether they have undergone a crisis about their position on occupation and ideology and whether they have made a commitment in these areas. Those who have undergone a crisis leading to commitment are in the state of *identity achievement* (upper left box in table). Those who have gone through a crisis but have not made a commitment or have made only a vague commitment are in *moratorium* (lower left box). Those who have made a commitment without going through a crisis are in *foreclosure* (upper right). And those who have made no commitment, whether or not they have undergone crisis, are in *identity confusion* (lower left and lower right).
Source: Marcia, 1980.

TABLE 16-2

IDENTITY-STATUS INTERVIEW	
SAMPLE QUESTIONS	TYPICAL ANSWERS FOR THE FOUR STATUSES
About occupational commitment: "How willing do you think you'd be to give up going into ___ if something better came along?"	*Identity achievement.* "Well, I might, but I doubt it. I can't see what 'something better' would be for me." *Foreclosure.* "Not very willing. It's what I've always wanted to do. The folks are happy with it and so am I." *Identity confusion.* "Oh sure. If something better came along, I'd change just like that." *Moratorium.* "I guess that if I knew for sure, I could answer that better. It would have to be something in the general area—something related. . . . "
About ideological commitment: "Have you ever had any doubts about your religious beliefs?"	*Identity achievement.* "Yes, I even started wondering whether there is a God. I've pretty much resolved that now, though. The way it seems to me is . . . " *Foreclosure.* "No, not really; our family is pretty much in agreement on these things." *Identity confusion.* "Oh, I don't know. I guess so. Everyone goes through some sort of stage like that. But it really doesn't bother me much. I figure that one religion is about as good as another!" *Moratorium.* "Yes, I guess I'm going through that now. I just don't see how there can be a God and still so much evil in the world or . . . "

Source: Adapted from Marcia, 1966.

On the basis of their answers, people are classified as being in one of the following four categories:

1 *Identity achievement (crisis leading to commitment).* Vicky is in this category. She has devoted much thought to important issues in her life (the crisis period), she has made choices, and she now expresses strong commitment to those choices. As an identity achiever, she has *flexible strength:* she is thoughtful but not so introspective that she is paralyzed. She has a sense of humor, functions well under stress, is capable of intimate relationships, and holds to her standards while being open to new ideas.

2 *Foreclosure (commitment with no crisis).* Martha is in this category because she has made commitments but, instead of questioning them and exploring other possible choices (going through the crisis period), has accepted other people's plans for her life. Her strength, as a person in foreclosure, is a *rigid strength:* she is happy and self-assured, sometimes even smug and self-satisfied. She has very close family ties, believes in law and order, likes to follow a strong leader (such as her mother), and becomes dogmatic when her opinions are questioned.

3 *Identity confusion (no commitment, crisis uncertain).* In a carefree way, Jason has considered various options, but so far has actively avoided commitment. Some others in this category are drifters without goals; they tend to be superficial or unhappy, and they are often lonely because they have also not made commitments to people.

4 *Moratorium (crisis, no commitment).* Michael, still in crisis, is struggling with a decision, seems to be heading for commitment, and will probably achieve identity. He is lively, talkative—and in conflict. He is close to his mother—and competitive and anxious. He is also wrestling with issues of intimacy: he wants a close relationship but has not yet achieved one.

Gender Differences in Identity Formation

Sigmund Freud's statement "Biology is destiny" has become infamous. It implies that the different patterns of development seen in males and females in almost all cultures are an inevitable result of anatomical differences. Today, however, psychologists are more likely to subscribe to the idea that "socialization is destiny." In other words, the prevailing modern belief is that most differences between males and females arise from societal attitudes and practices. Whatever the reasons, there are differences between the sexes in the struggle to define identity. Even early theorists like Freud and Erikson saw different paths in males' and females' identity development, but only in recent years have researchers explored the female's quest for identity.

Carol Gilligan (1982) has studied women in several contexts and has concluded that women define themselves less in terms of achieving a separate identity than in terms of relationships with other people. They judge themselves on their responsibilities and on their ability to care for others as well as themselves. They achieve identity more through cooperation than through competition.

Marcia (1979) modified his original interviews to explore issues of female identity. One change was the addition of questions about attitudes toward premarital intercourse, views on women's role, and concerns related to lifestyle. His findings were surprising: the men in moratorium (those who were in crisis but had not yet made commitments) most closely resembled men who had achieved identity. But the women who most closely resembled the men in the identity-achievement category were in foreclosure; that is, they had made a commitment but had not undergone a personal crisis.

Marcia points out that society pressures women to carry on social values from one generation to the next. Because of this role, *stability* of identity is extremely important for them. Therefore, he suggests that for women foreclosure of identity is just as adaptive as a struggle to achieve identity.

Marcia also maintains that women do not wait to develop the capacity for intimacy until after they have achieved identity, as in Erikson's male-based pattern. He believes that identity and intimacy develop together for women. This seems to build on other research indicating that intimacy is more important for girls than for boys, even in grade school friendships (Cooke, 1979). Part of the difference in males' and females' patterns may be due to different treatment of the sexes by parents, since several studies have found different child-rearing patterns to be associated with different identity statuses (Marcia, 1980).

PERSONAL RELATIONSHIPS IN ADOLESCENCE

A major element in becoming a separate person is the need to become independent of parents. We will consider how this need affects parent-child relationships in adolescence, and then look at the people to whom adolescents turn—their peers.

Relationships with Parents

Myth says that parents and teenagers do not like each other and do not get along with each other. The fact is that, despite conflicts, most adolescents feel close to and positive about their parents, have similar values on major issues, and value their parents' approval (J.P. Hill, 1987). As we discuss conflicts, it is important to keep this in mind.

(© Drawing by Ziegler; © 1985 The New Yorker Magazine, Inc.)

"While we're at supper, Billy, you'd make Daddy and Mommy very happy if you'd remove your hat, your sunglasses, and your earring."

"Billy's" hat, sunglasses, and earring symbolize his shedding the identity of his parents' "little boy" and establishing his own separate identity. Most arguments between parents and teenagers are about such mundane matters as personal appearance, and most are resolved with little trouble.

Conflict with Parents *The roots of conflict* Young people feel a constant tension between their need to break away from their parents and their dependency on the parents. They have to give up the identity of "the Smiths' little boy" or "the Millers' little girl" and establish their own private identity, while at the same time keeping their ties with parents and family (Siegel, 1982).

Adolescents' ambivalent feelings are often matched by parents' own ambivalence. Torn between wanting their children to be independent and wanting to keep them dependent, parents often find it hard to let go. As a result, parents may give teenage children "double messages," saying one thing but communicating just the opposite by actions. Conflict is more likely to surface between adolescents and their mothers than their fathers (Steinberg, 1981; 1987a). This may be partly because mothers have been more closely involved with their children and find it harder to give up their involvement.

Still, the emotions attending this transitional time do not necessarily lead to *adolescent rebellion*, a break with the values of both parents and society. In fact, a number of studies of American teenagers have found little turmoil or chaos (Brooks-Gunn, 1988). Research is fairly consistent in reporting conflict only in 15 to 25 percent of families, and these are often families that had problems *before* their children approached adolescence (J.P. Hill, 1987).

In his classic studies of midwestern boys, Offer (1969) found a high level of bickering over relatively unimportant issues between 12- and 14-year-olds and their parents, but he found little "turmoil" or "chaos." In a follow-up study of these same boys 8 years later, Offer and Offer (1974) found that most of them were happy, had a realistic self-image, and were reasonably well-adjusted. Less than one-fifth had experienced a tumultuous adolescence.

adolescent rebellion
Break with parental and societal values undergone by some but not all adolescents.

CHAPTER 16 ■ PERSONALITY AND SOCIAL DEVELOPMENT IN ADOLESCENCE **569**

The nature of conflict Conflict between adolescents and parents is described neatly by the subtitle of one report: "All Families Some of the Time and Some Families Most of the Time" (Montemayor, 1983). This is a survey of 50 years of literature on relations between adolescents and their parents. It concludes that the usual conflict is normal and healthy and has taken very similar form over the past half century.

By and large, parents and teenagers do not clash over economic, religious, social, and political values. Instead, most arguments are about mundane matters like schoolwork, chores, friends and dating, curfews, and personal appearance (see Table 16-3). Most of these disagreements are resolved with less trouble than is often believed. Such quarrels may reflect some deep quest for independence (as is often speculated), or they may just be a continuation of parents' efforts to teach children to conform to social rules. "This [socializing] task inescapably produces a certain amount of tension. . . . At this point it is simply not clear whether parent-adolescent conflict has a 'deeper meaning' than this" (Montemayor, 1983, p. 91).

Discord generally increases during early adolescence, stabilizes during middle adolescence, and then decreases after the young person is about 18 years of age. The increased conflict in early adolescence may be related more to puberty than to chronological age, and some intriguing new research suggests that the relationship may be bidirectional (see Box 16-1). The calmer climate in late adolescence may reflect entry into adulthood—or the tendency of 18-year-olds to move away from home.

It seems, then, that for most teenagers the concept of "storm and stress" is extreme. Conflict is part of every relationship, and since the transitions of ado-

TABLE 16-3

THREE MOST COMMON CAUSES OF ARGUMENTS WITH PARENTS ACCORDING TO ADOLESCENTS (SELECTED STUDIES, 1929–1982)		
STUDY	SAMPLE	CAUSES OF ARGUMENTS
Lynd & Lynd (1929)	348 males, 382 females: grades 10–12	1 Time I get in at night. 2 Number of times I go out during school nights. 3 Grades at school.
Punke (1943)	989 males, 1721 females: high school students	1 Social life and friends. 2 Work and spending money. 3 Clothes.
Remmers (1957)	15,000 males and females: high school students	1 I'm afraid to tell parents when I've done wrong. 2 Parents are too strict about my going out at night. 3 Parents are too strict about the family car.
Johnstone (1975)	1261 males and females: ages 13–20	1 Studying. 2 Use of spare time. 3 School.
Rosenthal (1982)	630 males and females: ages 13–16	1 Drinking or smoking. 2 Time and frequency of going out. 3 Doing jobs around the house.

Source: Condensed from Montemayor, 1983.

BOX 16-1 ■ THE RESEARCH WORLD

HOW PUBERTY AND PARENT-CHILD RELATIONSHIPS MAY INFLUENCE EACH OTHER

 Throughout the discussions of development in this text, many ways have been pointed out in which physical, intellectual, and personality development interlock, one influencing another. Sometimes the influences are predictable; at other times they are surprising. Some fascinating new research in the "surprising" category suggests not only that puberty influences how adolescents and their parents get along—but that the reverse may also be true, that parent-child relationships may speed up or retard puberty.

Laurence Steinberg (1988) conducted a two-phase study of 157 firstborns, aged 10 to 15, investigating pubertal status, timing of puberty, and parent-child relationships. First in 1985 and then 1 year later, researchers went to the adolescents' homes to assess pubertal status, defined on the basis of visible secondary sex characteristics, including facial shape, facial hair, body proportions, and chest and hip development.

At both times, the young people and their parents filled out questionnaires designed to measure the adolescents' autonomy, and the degree of conflict or closeness in the family. *Autonomy* was judged on the extent to which children no longer idealized their parents but saw them as real people, on the adolescents' sense that they were separate individuals, and on the degree to which the adolescents no longer felt dependent on their parents. *Conflict* was measured by the intensity of discussions about such everyday matters as curfews, clothing, and chores—and *closeness* by the frequency of calm discussions free of any anger.

PUBERTY SEEMS TO TRIGGER PARENT-CHILD CONFLICT

One unsurprising finding was that as young people developed physically, they bickered and squabbled more with their parents. Both boys and girls who had entered puberty were somewhat more likely to have more arguments with their mothers and to be less close to their fathers. Pubertal status was more important than chronological age, since the rise in conflict started earlier with earlier maturers and later with later maturers (refer back to Box 14-3). However, other factors were important, too, confirming that puberty does not inevitably bring on "storm and stress."

The effect that does occur may be related to evolution, Steinberg says. Adolescent monkeys and apes, for example, commonly leave their parents soon after puberty. Among some species only the female leaves; among others, both sexes go to found new family groups. This has its human parallels, too. At one time, it was usual for adolescents to leave home for apprenticeships in trade; and even now some cultures send young adolescents to live in other households. Today in the United States, of course, sexually mature adolescents may spend 7 or 8 years in their parents' homes. From an evolutionary point of view, then, it is not surprising that the early years of adolescence bring more conflict than any other time in childhood (except for the "terrible twos"). The good news, though, is that arguments "rarely undo close emotional bonds or lead adolescents and their parents to reject one another" (Steinberg, 1987c, p. 38).

PARENT-CHILD CONFLICT MAY TRIGGER PUBERTY IN GIRLS

The more surprising finding from this study is just the reverse of the above, at least for girls. According to the adolescents' reports, girls who argue more with their mothers mature physically somewhat faster than girls who have calmer relationships. The parents' reports were less clear-cut: according to them, close mother-child ties tended to slow girls' physical maturation, but arguments with either parent also tended to slow maturation. There was no comparable effect for boys.

What mechanism might account for such an influence? It is possible that a very close mother-daughter tie at a time when a girl is striving for independence might be stressful, and that stress might in turn affect the hormonal secretions that govern puberty. It is also possible that an angry woman gives off chemicals which are somehow sensed by her daughter's body, initiating hormonal messages. One of the mysteries of the female reproductive system is its sensitivity to environmental factors. Women in the same household or college dormitory, for example, often develop the same menstrual cycle. And among certain species of monkeys, pubertal females do not ovulate, mature sexually, or become fertile as long as they live with their mothers.

EVALUATING THESE FINDINGS

While these findings are intriguing, Steinberg himself has some reservations about them. First, they are more clear-cut when they are based on adolescents' reports of family relationships than when they are based on parents' reports. Second, even though physical maturation preceded higher levels of parent-child conflict and higher levels of conflict preceded physical signs of puberty, it is possible that both maturation and squabbling are caused by some unknown third factor. Still, the correlations that show up are provocative, and it will be interesting to see whether they hold up under further research. If they do, we may see a day when parents who want to keep their adolescent children at home go out of their way to keep peace in the family, and those who want to nudge them out of the nest do so with a few well-placed arguments. But maybe this is what parents already do.

BOX 16-2 ■ THE EVERYDAY WORLD

KEEPING COMMUNICATION OPEN BETWEEN PARENTS AND ADOLESCENTS

Are there "secrets" of good communication? While adolescence can be a trying period for both the people who are going through it and the people who are living with it, the home need not become a battleground if both parents and young people make special efforts to understand each other. The following guidelines may help.

WHAT PARENTS CAN DO

- Give your undivided attention when your children want to talk. Don't read, watch television, or busy yourself with other tasks.
- Listen calmly and concentrate on hearing and understanding your children's point of view.
- Speak to your children as courteously and pleasantly as you would to a stranger. Your tone of voice can set the tone of a conversation.
- Understand your children's feelings even if you don't always approve of their behavior. Try not to make judgments.
- Keep the door open on any subject. Be an "askable" parent.
- Avoid belittling and humiliating your children and laughing at what may seem to you to be naive or foolish questions and statements.
- Encourage your children to "test" new ideas in conversation by not judging their ideas and opinions, but instead by listening and then offering your own views as plainly and honestly as possible. Love and mutual respect can coexist with differing points of view.
- Help your children build self-confidence by encouraging their participation in activities of their choice (not yours).
- Make an effort to commend your children frequently and appropriately. Too often we take the good things for granted and focus on the bad, but everyone needs to be appreciated.
- Encourage your children to participate in family decision making and to work out family concerns together with you.
- Understand that your children need to challenge your opinions and your ways of doing things to achieve the separation from you that's essential for their own adult identity.

WHAT ADOLESCENTS CAN DO

- Avoid looking at your parents as the enemy. Chances are that they love you and have your best interests in mind, even if you don't necessarily agree with their way of showing that.
- Try to understand that your parents are human beings, with their own insecurities, needs, and feelings.
- Listen to your parents with an open mind and try to see situations from their point of view.
- Share your feelings with your parents so that they can understand you better.
- Live up to your responsibilities at home and in school so that your parents will be more inclined to grant you the kind of independence you want and need.
- Bolster your criticisms of family, school, and government with suggestions for practical improvements.
- Be as courteous and considerate to your own parents as you would be to the parents of your friends.

Source: Adapted from National Institute of Mental Health, NIMH, 1981.

lescence challenge the established parent-child interaction, it is not surprising that contention arises. Usually, however, parents and children resolve their disagreements to everybody's satisfaction, and parents continue to exercise considerable influence on their teenagers' basic values. When conflicts are severe and cannot be resolved easily, adolescents are at risk of serious problems. In such cases, intervention and counseling can often help families cope (see Box 16-2 for suggestions on communication between parents and adolescents).

What Adolescents Need from Their Parents Many arguments between teenagers and their parents are about "how much" and "how soon." How much freedom does Vicky have to schedule her activities? How soon can Jason take the family car for the weekend? Answers to questions like these are matters of judgment that require flexible thinking from parents—and more egalitarian relations with their children than existed when the children were younger.

Parents of adolescents have to walk a fine line between not granting their children sufficient independence and not protecting them from immature lapses in judgment. If separation or emotional independence from the family (or other significant adults) comes too early, it can spell trouble for a teenager. This trouble can take the form of alienation, susceptibility to negative peer influences, and participation in such physically or socially unhealthy behaviors as drug abuse or premature sexual activity (Steinberg & Silverberg, 1986; Steinberg, 1987a).

Still, parents should not try to keep their children from taking *any* risks. Positive exploration that involves trying a new activity, making new friends, learning a difficult skill, taking on a new challenge, or resisting peer pressure (thus taking the risk of alienating old friends) poses challenges that help people grow (Damon, 1984).

The kind of parenting that seems to provide the right balance is, again, authoritative parenting (see Chapter 15). This offers warmth and acceptance; assertiveness regarding rules, norms, and values; and a willingness to listen, explain, and negotiate (J.P. Hill, 1987). One reason it works so well with teenagers is that it takes their cognitive growth into account. By explaining the reasons behind a stance, parents acknowledge that adolescents are often able to evaluate situations on a very sophisticated level (Baumrind, 1968).

When Adolescents Care for Themselves Because many mothers are working and because adolescents are often considered too old for day care or baby-sitters, many young people are responsible for themselves for at least part of the day. Lack of supervision does not in itself leave preteens and young teenagers especially vulnerable to peer pressure. Differences do show up, however, depending on the nature of self-care, parents' involvement with the self-care, and parenting styles.

Steinberg (1986a) administered questionnaires to 865 10- to 15-year-olds in Madison, Wisconsin, asking them what they would do in a number of hypothetical situations involving antisocial behavior (like stealing, vandalism, or cheating on a test) if a "best friend" suggested one course when they really thought something else was right. Students who stayed home alone after school (where they could be in telephone contact with their parents, could follow an agreed-upon schedule of homework and chores, and were in a familiar environment that reminded them of family values) were no more influenced by their friends than were young people who were at home with adults or older siblings. The further removed youngsters were from even the possibility of adult supervision, the more they were affected by peers. Thus, those who spent time unsupervised at a friend's house were more influenced than those who stayed home alone, and those who just "hung out" with a group were most influenced. Yet even in this last group, students whose parents knew where they were turned out to be only slightly more susceptible to peer influence than those who were actually with adults. Furthermore, young people whose parents were authoritative found it easier to resist peer pressure, apparently because they had internalized their parents' standards—that is, taken these standards as their own.

Although this study emphasizes the importance of considering differences among "self-care" adolescents, we need more research before we can draw general conclusions. For one thing, since most of the subjects were suburban, the findings might not apply to young people in the country or in big cities, especially inner-city neighborhoods. For another, it is not clear whether adult supervision lessens susceptibility to peer pressure or whether adolescents who are more peer-oriented resist adult supervision. And finally, these subjects were responding to hypothetical situations; their responses may have been very different from their behavior in real instances. Another study of young people from the same schools, however, found that responses to hypothetical situations were related to youngsters' reports of actual misconduct (B. B. Brown, Clasen, & Eicher, 1986). Thus, this approach may hold the promise of predicting actual behavior.

Adolescents with Single Parents   An adolescent who does not live with his or her biological father runs a greater risk of giving in to peer pressure and getting into trouble, and this risk is not alleviated by the mother's remarriage.

One nationwide study of 6710 twelve- to seventeen-year-olds found that, across socioeconomic levels, teenagers living with only their mother were more likely than those living with both parents to be truant, to run away from home, to smoke, to have discipline problems in school, or to get into trouble with the police (Dornbusch et al., 1985). But the presence of another adult in the home— like a grandparent or a friend of the mother, but *not* a stepfather—lowers the risk almost to the level found in two-parent families, especially for boys. This suggests that some of the problems in single-parent homes may be due to the many pressures on the mother and that nontraditional family groupings can help relieve this pressure and thus help keep adolescents out of trouble.

Another study, in which Steinberg (1987b) analyzed the answers of the 865 subjects in the research described in the previous section, brought a similar conclusion. Young people who do not live with their biological father are susceptible to peer pressure for antisocial behavior, even if they live with a stepfather. Young people living with both natural parents were less likely to be influenced by their friends than those in either single-parent homes or stepfamilies. Only among the oldest children was the presence of a stepfather even slightly helpful in lowering susceptibility to peer pressure.

Since single and remarried mothers are less likely to be authoritative parents (Dornbusch, Ritter, Leiderman, Roberts, & Fraleigh, 1987), their teenagers' problems may stem from their parenting style rather than from the absence of the father. In any case, it seems clear that such families are more likely to encounter difficulties during the children's adolescence.

Relationships with Peers

As we enter the cafeteria of Vicky and Jason's high school, we see a roomful of adolescents eating, doing homework, talking, flirting, and just horsing around. The large room is divided into several "turfs," with boundaries that are unmarked but recognized by all the students. At one table are students from all socioeconomic backgrounds who work to achieve recognition within the "system"—the leaders in student government, the athletes, the honor students. At another table are alienated teenagers from middle-class or upper-middle-class families; they seem to be marking time until they can legally leave school, and they spend much of their spare time using drugs. In another area of the room are a group of boys and girls, mostly from working-class homes, who speak in "tough and cool" language and may have had brushes with the law. Ethnic and racial groups tend to stick together at lunchtime, even though students mingle freely in classes, on the playing fields, and in some other extracurricular activities.

Adolescents, like these students in a high school cafeteria, spend more than half their waking hours with other teenagers and only about 5 percent of their time with a parent. Before young people become truly independent, they go from being dependent on parents to being dependent on peers.

How Adolescents Spend Their Time—and with Whom What do teenagers do on a typical day? With whom do they do it? Where do they do it? And how do they feel about what they are doing? To answer these questions, for 1 week 75 high school students in a Chicago suburb carried beepers that rang at random once in every 2 (waking) hours. Each student was asked to report what he or she was doing when the beeper sounded—and where, and with whom. The average subject received and responded to 69 percent of the beeper signals, yielding a

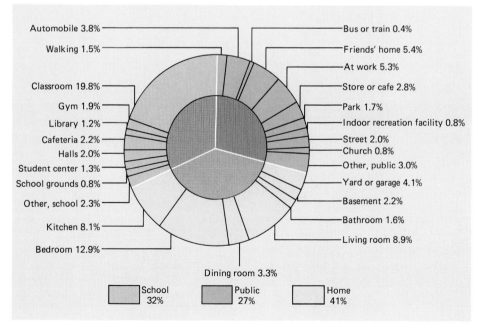

FIGURE 16-1
Where adolescents spend their time. Percentage of self-reports in each location by 2734 high school students. Here and in Figures 16-2 and 16-3, 1 percentage point is equivalent to about 1 hour per week spent in the given location or activity. (*Source:* Csikszentmihalyi & Larson, 1984, p. 59.)

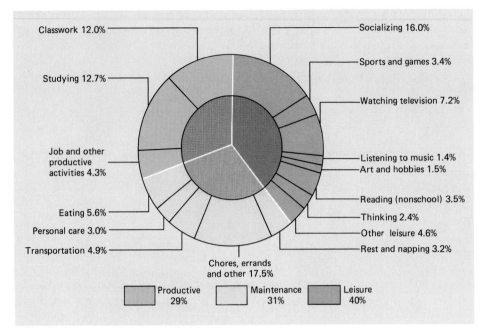

FIGURE 16-2
What adolescents spend their time doing. (*Source:* Csikszentmihalyi & Larson, 1984, p. 63.)

Classwork 12.0%
Socializing 16.0%
Sports and games 3.4%
Watching television 7.2%
Studying 12.7%
Job and other productive activities 4.3%
Listening to music 1.4%
Art and hobbies 1.5%
Reading (nonschool) 3.5%
Thinking 2.4%
Other leisure 4.6%
Eating 5.6%
Personal care 3.0%
Rest and napping 3.2%
Transportation 4.9%
Chores, errands and other 17.5%

Productive 29%　Maintenance 31%　Leisure 40%

total of 4489 self-reports, from which researchers described what it is like to be a teenager today (Csikszentmihalyi & Larson, 1984).

The results (see Figures 16-1, 16-2, and 16-3) showed the importance of peers. The adolescents studied spent more than half their waking hours with other teenagers—friends (29 percent of the time) and classmates (23 percent)—and only about 5 percent of their time with one or both parents. They were happiest when with friends; being with the family ranked second, next came being alone, and last, being with classmates. Teenagers have more fun with friends—joking, gossiping, and goofing around—than at home, where activities tend to be more serious and more humdrum.

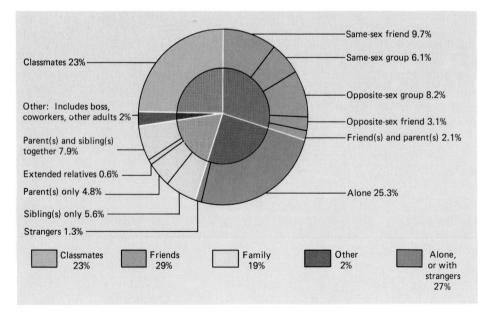

FIGURE 16-3
Whom adolescents spend their time with. (*Source:* Adapted from Csikszentmihalyi & Larson, 1984, p. 71.)

Classmates 23%
Same-sex friend 9.7%
Same-sex group 6.1%
Opposite-sex group 8.2%
Opposite-sex friend 3.1%
Friend(s) and parent(s) 2.1%
Other: Includes boss, coworkers, other adults 2%
Parent(s) and sibling(s) together 7.9%
Extended relatives 0.6%
Parent(s) only 4.8%
Alone 25.3%
Sibling(s) only 5.6%
Strangers 1.3%

Classmates 23%　Friends 29%　Family 19%　Other 2%　Alone, or with strangers 27%

Parents "versus" Peers   There is no one peer group for all teenagers. Which group Vicky is drawn to depends partly on her socioeconomic status (since most adolescent cliques are class-bound), partly on the values she has picked up at home, and partly on her personality.

Once Vicky has become part of a group, she influences its other members and they influence her. Though she considers herself a nonconformist, she will hew closely to the habits of her group. If the other girls in her crowd wear faded, torn jeans and black running shoes, Vicky will not come to school in a plaid skirt and saddle shoes. If her friends spend their evenings at a drive-in restaurant, she will not—by choice—spend hers in the library. The teenagers in Vicky's circle will influence not only the way she dresses and wears her hair but also her social activities, the music she listens to, her sexual behavior, her use or avoidance of drugs, and her pursuit or disdain of academic achievement—the basic patterns of her life.

Research has confirmed this shift from dependency on parents to dependency on peers, before young people become truly independent (Steinberg & Silverberg, 1986). Still, "peer power" is not everything in adolescence, and most teenagers still have positive ties with their parents (J.P. Hill, 1980, 1987). Parents count more than they realize, especially with regard to important issues and basic values. Two separate studies, done 15 years apart, asked teenagers whether they would rely more on parents or peers in choosing solutions to various common problems. Whether parents or peers carried more weight depended on the situation. On questions of how to dress, how to resolve school-related problems, and how to deal with other day-to-day concerns, peers' opinions were more influential. But on long-range issues like which job to take or how to resolve a moral conflict, the students in the first study (all girls) leaned more toward their parents' opinions (Brittain, 1963). In the second study, the particular situation that a boy or girl was considering also influenced whether he or she would pay more attention to parents or peers (Emmerick, 1978). (When parents and peers hold similar values, as they often do, there is no real conflict between them.)

We have already seen (in Chapter 15) how important parents are to their children's performance and achievement in school. The stronger the parents' interest is in their adolescents' lives, the more likely the teenagers are to get high marks in school.

The community has a major impact on whether an adolescent will pay more attention to adults or to other young people. A study of several hundred teenagers in several communities in New York State—a poor inner-city neighborhood with many minority-group residents, an upper-middle-class suburb, and a rural community—found that we cannot draw sweeping conclusions about teenagers, as if they were all alike (Ianni, 1983).

Unfortunately, there has been very little good research on African American, Hispanic, Native American, and Asian American adolescents, or on teenage children of single-parent, dual-income, and remarried families (J.P. Hill, 1987). The need for such research is suggested by the findings from the New York study. Urban teenagers faced with conflicting standards of family, school, and social agencies were likely to reject all these values and create their own, often in a street gang. Suburban and rural teenagers, however, were more likely to exhibit values very close to those held by the important adults in their lives—they might question adults' values, but they wanted consistent rules and standards that they could evaluate (Ianni, 1983).

Friendships are likely to be closer and more intense in adolescence than at any other time in the life span. When young people begin to separate from their parents, they look to their close friends for intimacy. This is especially true for girls, who confide more in their friends and count more on their emotional support than boys do.

Friendships in Adolescence "What *do* you talk about for so long?" Ellen asks, laughing. Vicky has been on the phone for over an hour talking with Martha, whom she left only 45 minutes before picking up the phone.

Friendships are likely to be closer and more intense in adolescence than at any other time in the life span (Berndt, 1982). One explanation for this rests on cognitive development. Adolescents are better able to express their thoughts and feelings and share them with friends; they are also better able to consider another person's point of view, and so they can better understand their friends' thoughts and feelings.

In addition, the intimacy and trust in close friendships fill the void created when young people begin to separate from their parents. Sharing confidences is a vital part of friendship in adolescence, especially among girls. Throughout life, girls and women tend to be more intimate with their friends, telling them more and counting more on their emotional support; boys and men have more friends but are rarely as close to any of them as girls and women are to their good friends.

However, those girls who look to their friends to make up for a lack of intimacy at home are likely to be disappointed. In a survey of 134 sixteen- to eighteen-year-old girls, those who had the closest friendships with other girls also had affectionate ties with their mothers, saw their mothers as democratic (nonauthoritarian), and wanted to be like them (M. Gold & Yanof, 1985). It is likely that, as Erikson has proposed, these girls had developed enough trust and autonomy through their relationships with their mothers to become intimate with others. Friendships of girls who had poor relationships with their mothers were likely to be less affectionate and to be dominated by one girl or the other instead of being pure give-and-take.

How do adolescents choose their friends? They tend to find friends who are already like them; then, they and their friends influence each other to become even more alike (Berndt, 1982). Similarity is more important to friendship in adolescence than later in life, probably because teenagers are struggling to differentiate themselves from their parents and, as a result, need support from people who are like them in certain important ways (Weiss & Lowenthal, 1975). Among the most important are attitudes with regard to two central areas in their lives: school and teenage culture. This is not surprising, since it is easy to imagine the arguments that would take place between a conscientious student and a friend who cuts classes, or between one who goes out to bars on Saturday nights and another who goes to choir practice. Friends usually like the same music, dress alike, do the same things after school, and have similar patterns of drinking and use of drugs.

ACHIEVING SEXUAL IDENTITY

Moving from close friendships with people of the same sex to romantic involvements with people of the other sex is one of the most profound changes in an adolescent's identity. Seeing oneself as a sexual being, coming to terms with one's sexual stirrings, and developing an intimate, romantic relationship are important aspects of achieving sexual identity.

An adolescent's self-image and relationships with peers and parents are bound up with sexuality. Sexual activity—casual kissing, necking and petting, genital contact—fulfills a number of adolescents' important needs, only one of which is physical pleasure. Teenagers become sexually active to enhance intimacy, to search for new experience, to prove their maturity, to be in tune with the peer group, to find relief from pressures, and to investigate the mysteries of love.

Studying Adolescents' Sexuality

A pair of researchers studying young people's sexual practices arrived at Vicky and Jason's high school to interview a sample of students. During his interview Jason denied ever masturbating even though, in fact, he does masturbate frequently. He told the interviewer that during the past month he had touched his girlfriend's breasts and genital area. He had not.

Vicky was also selected to take part in the research, but her parents were among several who refused to grant permission for their children's participation. In Vicky's place, the researchers interviewed Martha, whose parents gave their consent. At least some of Martha's answers must have differed from the ones that Vicky would have given, thus changing the results to some degree. But the significant point is not so much in the supposed differences between the two girls' answers as in the fact that the sample itself introduced bias: the final sample was limited to students whose parents permitted them to participate. These adolescents may have been different in some ways from the children of parents who refused permission.

Before we talk about what adolescents are saying and doing sexually these days, we need to think about the difficulties of doing sexual research, especially when it involves young people. Virtually every sex research project—from Kinsey's original surveys, undertaken in the 1940s, and on to the present day—has suffered from criticism that is not accurate because people who voluntarily take part are more sexually active, interested, and liberal, and are not representative of the population at large. Furthermore, critics charge that there is no way to corroborate what people say about their sex lives, and that some may lie to conceal their sexual activities while others exaggerate.

When the subjects are young people being asked by older people about behaviors that have "traditionally been regarded as inappropriate and immoral, if not illegal and sinful" (Dreyer, 1982, p. 564), the problems multiply. Then, too (as we have just seen), parents' consent is often needed for the participation of legal minors, and parents who grant this permission may not be a cross section of the population.

All these objections have some validity. Still, such surveys have merit: even if findings cannot be generalized to the population as a whole, within the groups that participate trends can be seen over time, and these reveal something about changing sexual mores. It is important to bear in mind, however, that attitudes may be changing more than behavior. Although teenagers today seem to be more sexually active than teenagers a generation or two ago, it is possible that they are not acting much differently but are simply more willing to talk about their sexual activities.

Sexual Attitudes and Behavior

masturbation
Sexual self-stimulation.

Masturbation *Masturbation,* or sexual self-stimulation, is the first sexual experience for most young people and is almost universal. Yet, because most adults in our society are more anxious in talking about this than any other aspect of sexuality (E.J. Roberts, Kline, & Gagnon, 1978), there has been very little research on it.

The research we do have shows an increase since the early 1960s in the number of adolescents who masturbate (Dreyer, 1982). In the early 1970s, for example, 50 percent of boys and 30 percent of girls under 15 years of age said that they masturbated; in the late 1970s, the figures had increased to 70 percent of boys and 45 percent of girls. Apparently, a significant change did take place, even though we do not know whether more boys and girls actually masturbated or whether they were simply more willing to say they did.

One recent survey found that teenagers continue to regard masturbation as shameful; fewer than one-third said that they felt no guilt when they masturbated (Coles & Stokes, 1985). This suggests that opinion has changed more radically among sex educators than among teenagers. Educators today stress that masturbation is normal and healthy, that it cannot result in physical harm, that it helps people learn how to give and receive sexual pleasure, and that it provides a way to gratify sexual desire without entering into a relationship for which the person is not emotionally ready (Olds, 1985; Reiss, 1986; Sarrel & Sarrel, 1984).

sexual orientation
Whether a person is heterosexual or homosexual.

heterosexual *Sexually interested in members of the other sex.*

homosexual *Sexually interested in members of the same sex.*

Sexual Preference: Heterosexuality and Homosexuality It is in adolescence that a person's *sexual orientation* is usually expressed, whether that person will be *heterosexual* (as most people are), that is, sexually interested in members of the other sex; or *homosexual,* sexually interested in persons of the same sex.

Homosexuality Many young people, more of them boys than girls, have one or more homosexual experiences, usually before age 15 (Dreyer, 1982). Few, however, go on to make this a regular pattern. In one study of adolescents, only 3 percent of the boys and 2 percent of the girls had ongoing homosexual relationships, even though about 15 percent of the boys and 10 percent of the girls had had such a contact during adolescence. Despite the fact that homosexuality is more visible today than it used to be, with more people openly declaring their sexual interest in people of the same sex, research indicates that homosexual behavior has been stable or has declined over the past 30 years (Chilman, 1980). Its incidence appears to be similar in a number of cultures (Hyde, 1986).

A number of hypotheses have been advanced to explain homosexuality. The oldest is that it represents a kind of mental illness. But in a classic study, Hooker (1957) could find no evidence to support this contention. Her conclusions and those of other researchers—along with political lobbying and changes in attitudes—eventually led the American Psychiatric Association to stop classifying homosexuality as a "mental disorder." The latest edition of the *Diagnostic and Statistical Manual* classifies as a disorder only "persistent and marked distress about one's sexual orientation" (*Diagnostic and Statistical Manual of Mental Disorders*, 3d ed., rev., DSM III-R, 1987, p. 296).

Other theories include a genetic factor, hormonal imbalance, a family with a dominating mother and a weak father (thought by some to cause male homosexuality), and chance learning (developing a homosexual orientation as a result of being seduced by someone of the same sex). So far, no scientific support has been found for family constellation and chance learning, and only tentative evidence for a genetic factor or hormonal imbalance. One study did find a biological difference between heterosexual and homosexual men, a different hormone response pattern to estrogen stimulation. However, the homosexual men in this study scored extremely high on an index of homosexual orientation, and so the findings may not apply to all homosexuals (Gladue, Green, & Hellman, 1984).

Another hypothesis is that there are probably several different reasons why a person becomes heterosexual or homosexual, and that interaction among various hormonal and environmental events is crucial. This broad hypothesis seems to have garnered the most support (A.P. Bell, Weinberg, & Hammersmith, 1981; Durden-Smith & DeSimone, 1982; Masters & Johnson, 1979).

Heterosexuality   The early 1920s through the late 1970s witnessed a sexual *evolution* (rather than a *revolution,* though this term is often used)—both in what people do sexually and in how they feel about their behaviors. There has been a steady trend toward acceptance of more sexual activity in more situations. One major change has been the approval of premarital sex in a loving relationship. Another is a decline in, although not an end to, the double standard: the assumption that males should have more sexual freedom than females. The sexual evolution may have reached a plateau or may even be reversing itself; but meanwhile, like the rest of the population, today's teenagers are more sexually active and liberal than the generation before them. This is especially true of girls.

In 1969, most studies showed that fewer than half of college students approved of sex before marriage (Mussen, Conger & Kagan, 1969); by 1979, 90 percent of college men and 83 percent of college women approved (Mahoney, 1983). And in 1986, well over half of a nationwide sample of 1000 white, black, and Hispanic teenagers reported having had intercourse by age 17. At 12 years, 4 percent have had intercourse; at 14 years, 20 percent have; and nonvirgins accounted for 57 percent of 17-year-olds (61 percent of boys and 53 percent of girls—Louis Harris & Associates, 1986).

Over the past 50 years, attitudes toward sexuality have changed to include approval of premarital sex in a loving relationship and a decline of the double standard by which males are freer sexually than females. Most teenagers are not promiscuous; if they are sexually active, it is usually within a monogamous relationship.

A girl is likely to have her first sexual intercourse with a steady boyfriend; a boy is likely to have his with someone he knows casually. A girl's first partner is usually 3 years older than she is; a boy's first partner tends to be about a year older (Dreyer, 1982; Zelnik, Kantner, & Ford, 1981; Zelnik & Shah, 1983).

Attitudes versus behavior: There is often a discrepancy between what people of any age *say* about sex and what they *do.* In the 1986 Harris poll, teenagers gave a median age of 18 as the "right age" to start having intercourse, even though nearly half of the 16-year-olds and most 17-year-olds were no longer virgins. In another study, of 3500 junior high and high school students, 83 percent of sexually active young people gave a "best age" for first intercourse older than the age at which they had experienced it themselves, and 88 percent of young mothers give an older best age for first birth than was true for them. Many adolescents, then, hold "values and attitudes consistent with responsible sexual conduct, but not all of them are able to translate these attitudes into personal behavior" (Zabin, Hirsch, Smith, & Hardy, 1984, p. 185). The researchers concluded that helping teenagers put their responsible values into practice may be more effective than trying to change the behavior of adolescents whose attitudes are less responsible.

Early sexual activity: A dramatic change in our society is the lowering of the age of first intercourse reported by adolescents. Even though most adolescents are not promiscuous and have a sexual relationship with only one person at a time, the fact that they begin sexual activity earlier means that they will, over their teenage years, have more sexual partners than their parents had.

Why do they start so early? Many feel under pressure to engage in sexual activity even when they are not ready for it. When asked in the Harris poll why many teenagers do not wait for sex until they are older, 73 percent of the girls and 50 percent of boys cited social pressure as the main reason, and about 1 in 4 of both sexes said that they themselves had been pressured to do more sexually than they wanted to. Both boys and girls also cited curiosity as a motivation for early sexual activity; but more boys than girls mentioned sexual feelings and desires. Where did love fit in? Only 6 percent of boys and 11 percent of girls gave love as a reason.

Although only 3 percent of these teenagers said they had been influenced toward sexual activity by the media, many professionals who deal with young people think that the real percentage is higher. Today's teenagers watch television for an average of 24 hours a week and listen to the radio for 21 hours; they are exposed to "more than 9000 sexual references, innuendos, and behaviors each year" (American Academy of Pediatrics Committee on Adolescence, 1986, p. 535). The frequency of sexual references on television has risen dramatically over the past decade, and movies, videocassettes, and records send out even more sexual images.

Furthermore, the media present a distorted view of sex. On television, as opposed to real life, unmarried couples have intercourse 4 to 8 times more often than married couples; contraceptives are almost never used, but women seldom become pregnant; and only prostitutes or homosexuals contract sexually transmitted diseases. Not surprisingly, then, adolescents who get their information about sex from television tend to believe that premarital and extramarital intercourse with several partners and without protection against pregnancy or disease is desirable. This may change as television producers, in response to the AIDS epidemic and to pressure from public interest groups, incorporate birth control and other evidence of responsible sexual behavior into popular shows. Signs of this new approach have already shown up on both daytime and prime-time shows (J.D. Brown et al., 1988).

A major reason for concern about early sexual activity is the greater risk of pregnancy (see the next section) and of sexually transmitted diseases (see Chapter 14). Most adolescents do not plan for their first intercourse: 85 percent of nonvirgins had not asked anyone about preventing either pregnancy or infection (American Academy of Pediatrics Committee on Adolescence, 1986).

Still, while teenagers are becoming sexually active earlier, few take sex casually. Teenagers tend to enter into sexual relationships that have meaning for them, and they are usually faithful to those bonds (Hass, 1979). Most adolescents, like most adults, value sex more for its emotional context than for its physical content. Those who can go to their parents or other adults with questions about sex may have a better chance of avoiding some of the common problems associated with burgeoning sexual activity—and of achieving a mature sexual identity.

Communicating with Parents about Sex

Many conflicts between parents and teenagers are about sex. Vicky's parents dislike her boyfriend, do not want him with her when no adults are home, and do not want her to stay out late with him. Perhaps they are protective of their daughter because they are somewhat uncomfortable with their own sexuality and thus are extremely unsure how to handle Vicky's.

Parents' values *are* more liberal now than they used to be. Today's parents are less likely to punish or cast out a pregnant daughter than to help her. Today's parents may worry about whether their daughter's boyfriend should share her bedroom when she brings him home from college for a weekend; parents 20 years ago would not have admitted knowing that a daughter was sexually involved with a boyfriend (and she would not have told them).

An extensive survey of teenagers' views on and experience with sex found that the guidance parents give is overwhelmingly positive. Only 3 percent of the teenagers recalled their parents' telling them that sex was not normal and healthy. Yet communication about sex remains a problem in many families. Parents often think that they have said more than their children have actually heard. One girl, already a mother at age 15, reported, "[My mother said] she'd told me to come to her when it was time for me to have sex and she'd get me some birth control, but she must have said it *very* softly" (Coles & Stokes, 1985, p. 37).

Almost one-third (31 percent) of all American teenagers and 28 percent of teenagers who are sexually active have never talked to their parents about sex, and close to half (42 percent) are nervous or afraid to bring it up. Almost two-thirds (64 percent) have never discussed birth control at home (Louis Harris & Associates, 1986). This is important, because teenagers who *have* talked to their parents about sex in general and birth control in particular are more likely to use it consistently than those who have not. As we see in the next section, ignorance increases the risk of pregnancy.

Adolescents' ambivalence makes it hard for their parents to talk to them about sex. Although teenagers say that they would like to be open and frank with their parents about sexual behavior, they often resent being questioned, and they tend to consider their sexual activities nobody else's business. But when parents ignore obvious signs of sexual activity, young people sometimes become puzzled and angry. Said one 16-year-old girl, anticipating parenthood:

> I'm not going to pretend that I don't know what's happening. If my daughter comes in at five in the morning, her skirt backwards and wearing some guy's sweater, I'm not going to ask her, "Did you have a nice time at the movies?" . . . I don't plan to fail! (R.C. Sorensen, 1973, p. 61)

Problems of Adolescence

Although most people weather adolescence well, many serious problems with long-term consequences arise during these years. We have already discussed eating disorders, sexually transmitted diseases, dropping out of school, abuse of alcohol and other drugs, and emotional disturbances. Two other problems that may affect the rest of a young person's life are unplanned pregnancy and juvenile delinquency. These problems are not "normal" or "typical." The danger in assuming that turmoil is a normal, necessary part of adolescence is that parents and other adults may fail to recognize when a young person is in trouble and thus fail to give help.

PREGNANCY

Trends in Teenage Pregnancy

The teenage pregnancy rate in the United States is one of the highest in the world—nearly 10 percent for girls aged 15 to 19—and still climbing (see Box 16-3). Although birthrates for older teenagers and nonwhite teenagers have fallen since 1970—largely because about 60 percent of their pregnancies end in legal abortion (E.F. Jones et al., 1985)—the birthrate for all unmarried teenagers

BOX 16-3 ■ AROUND THE WORLD

WHY DO SO MANY AMERICAN TEENAGERS BECOME PREGNANT?

In the Netherlands the pregnancy rate for girls aged 15 to 19 is 14 per 1000. In the United States it is 96 per 1000. The abortion rate for the same group in the Netherlands is about 8 per 1000, while in the United States it is over 60 per 1000. Are Dutch girls less sexually active than girls in this country? No. The two countries have similar rates of early sexual intercourse. Swedish girls are much more advanced sexually than American girls, but Sweden's pregnancy rate is also well below that of the United States: 35 pregnancies per 1000 fifteen- to nineteen-year-olds, with about 27 abortions per 1000.

Some Americans assume that our failure to keep pregnancy rates down, compared with the success of European countries, is due to the fact that the United States has an unusually large poor population, especially a large population of poor blacks. It is true that the industrial nations of Europe have no comparable level of urban impoverishment. However, the rates of pregnancy and abortion among white American teenagers are still far above the rates in European countries. (Our rate is also double that of Canada.) Many Americans believe that federal welfare programs, especially Aid to Families with Dependent Children, encourage early and frequent pregnancy, but other industrial countries are even more generous in their support of poor mothers. Yet their pregnancy rates among teenagers are much lower. Unemployment among American teenagers is also popularly cited as a reason for the high pregnancy rate, but unemployment among teenagers is a serious problem in the other countries too.

There are differences between the United States and these other countries that might explain our higher pregnancy rate among adolescents. One is the confidentiality of service to teenagers. In Sweden it is forbidden to inform parents that their teenage children have sought contraceptives, and in the Netherlands such information is kept from parents if teenagers request this. Another difference concerns price. Contraceptives are provided free of charge to adolescents in Britain, France, and Sweden. In the Netherlands contraceptives are provided free by family doctors or for a small charge by clinics.

Europe's industrial countries also provide extensive sex education. Sweden's compulsory curriculum includes sex education at all grade levels. Dutch schools have no special sex education programs, but the mass media and private groups provide extensive information about contraceptive techniques, and surveys show that nearly all Dutch teenagers are well informed about birth control.

The primary policy ambitions behind the various countries' decisions to encourage the use of contraceptives include a wish to prevent teenage girls from becoming pregnant and an eagerness to keep the abortion rate among teenagers from rising. This second concern has proved particularly important in persuading conservative groups to support the policy.

The programs that support the successes of European countries have all been proposed and debated in the United States. They generally fail to be implemented because of a concern that such programs might seem to endorse sexual activity among teenagers. The irony is that, as a result, we are the only industrial nation with an increasing pregnancy rate among teenagers.

Source: E. F. Jones et al., 1985.

---

has gone up. Moreover, the proportion of illegitimate births among teenagers is rising: in 1982, 39 percent of babies born to white teenagers and 90 percent of those born to black teenagers were born out of wedlock (Brooks-Gunn & Furstenberg, 1986; National Center for Health Statistics, 1984b).

More than 9 out of 10 teenagers who carry their babies to term choose, at least at first, to keep them rather than give them up for adoption or place them in foster care. Once these mothers discover how demanding caring for a baby is, they may leave the infant unattended for increasingly long periods. Their children often enter the state's foster care system, and years may pass before a child's permanent status is settled (Alan Guttmacher Institute, 1981).

There are fewer "shotgun" weddings among teenagers than there used to be. This is just as well, since teenage parents are 2 to 3 times as likely to split up as people who marry later in life or who become parents in their twenties (McCarthy & Menken, 1979). Many girls raise their children themselves, whether or not they marry; some turn their children over to their own mothers.

Teenage pregnancy has serious consequences for mothers, for their children, and for the young fathers as well.

Consequences of Teenage Pregnancy

The consequences of parenthood in adolescence are enormous for the mothers and fathers, their babies, and society at large. Teenage girls are more likely to have certain complications of pregnancy, including anemia, prolonged labor, and toxemia (McKenry, Walters, & Johnson, 1979). Young women are twice as likely as older women to bear low-birthweight and premature babies, 2 to 3 times more likely to have babies who die in the first year, and 2.4 times more likely to bear children with neurological defects (McKenry et al., 1979).

A major reason for the health problems of teenage mothers and their children is social, not medical. Many teenage mothers are poor, do not eat properly, and receive poor prenatal care or none (S.S. Brown, 1985). In two large-scale studies done in university hospitals, one in this country and one in Denmark, teenagers' pregnancies turned out better than those of women in any other age group, leading the researchers to conclude that "if early, regular, and high quality medical care is made available to pregnant teenagers, the likelihood is that pregnancies and deliveries in this age group will not entail any higher medical risk than those of women in their twenties" (Mednick, Baker, & Sutton-Smith, 1979, p. 17). (Refer back to Box 4-4 in Chapter 4 for a discussion of prenatal care in the United States and several European countries.)

Even with the best care, however, and the best physical outcome, the fate of teenage parents and their children is often unhappy. Eighty percent of pregnant girls aged 17 and under, and 90 percent of those aged 15 and under, never finish high school. As a result, they often become unemployable and go on welfare, beginning or continuing a cycle of dependency that saps their motivation in work and in their personal lives (Furstenberg, 1976; Jaslow, 1982). Unmarried pregnant girls attempt suicide more often than other girls of their age (McKenry et al., 1979).

The young father's life is also affected, of course. For one thing, a boy who becomes a father before the age of 18 is only two-fifths as likely to graduate from high school as a boy who postpones parenthood until a later age (Card & Wise, 1978).

The children of teenage parents are more likely than other children to have low IQ scores and to do poorly in school, and their problems increase as they get older (Baldwin & Cain, 1980). In the preschool years, they are often overactive, willful, and aggressive. In elementary school, they tend to be inattentive and easily distracted, and they give up easily. And in high school, they are often low achievers, at high risk of becoming delinquents or teenage parents themselves (Baldwin & Cain, 1980; Brooks-Gunn & Furstenberg, 1986). Sons of teenage parents typically have more problems in the early years; daughters have more problems in high school.

Understanding Teenage Pregnancy

Why Do Teenagers Become Pregnant?   Why, in an age of improved methods of contraception, do so many young girls become pregnant? Usually this is because they use no method of contraception at all. Two-thirds of sexually active teenagers do not always use birth control, and 27 percent never use it. Why don't they? The most common reason given is that they do not expect to have intercourse and therefore do not prepare for it (Louis Harris & Associates, 1986).

However, when researchers phrase their questions differently, another set of reasons emerges. Very often when people are asked not about themselves, but about *other* people, they project their own motivations and behaviors onto others and say things about other people that they may be reluctant to admit about themselves. When the Harris pollsters asked why *other* teenagers—not the respondents themselves—do not use contraceptives, they heard a different story. Nearly 40 percent said that young people prefer not to use birth control, do not think about it, do not care, enjoy sex more without it, or want to get pregnant. They also cite lack of knowledge about or access to contraceptives (25 percent), embarrassment about seeking contraceptives or fear that their parents will find out that they are sexually active (24 percent), and the belief that pregnancy "won't happen to me" (14 percent) (Louis Harris & Associates, 1986).

This last reason is an example of the personal fable, explained in Chapter 15. About 1 in 3 girls believe that a girl who does not want a baby will not have one. (R.C. Sorensen, 1973).

Some girls are reluctant to interfere with the spontaneity of the sex act by appearing too well prepared. Some feel that using contraception is too much trouble, or they forget to take adequate measures. Some feel that it is the man's responsibility. Since abortion is legal and accessible, some feel that they can use this alternative afterward.

The saying "I'm not that kind of girl" sums up many girls' reasons for not using birth control (Cassell, 1984). These girls feel that sexual intercourse is wrong, and so they avoid the appearance, even to themselves, of planning for it. They save their self-respect by considering themselves swept away by love and unable to help themselves. Unpremeditated sex is acceptable; carefully planned sex is for "bad" girls.

The guiltier a girl feels about premarital sex, the less likely she is to use an effective method of contraception (Herold & Goodwin, 1981). A girl who feels guilty is embarrassed to go to a birth control clinic and have an internal physical examination. She is less likely than a girl who does not feel guilty to read on her own about birth control, and she is more likely to think that oral contraceptives are hard to obtain.

Who Is Likely to Become Pregnant?   Young mothers do not differ much from their classmates in their sexual practices, a fact which suggests that they have not engaged in sex because they wanted to have a baby at this age, but have instead become pregnant by accident (Furstenberg, 1976).

Social factors affect both premarital sexual activity and the use of contraceptives. Black and Hispanic girls, girls who live with a single parent, and girls whose parents are relatively uneducated tend to be more sexually active, to use no birth control, or to use less effective methods than "the pill" or the diaphragm. On the other hand, girls who earn high grades, have career ambitions, or are involved in sports or other extracurricular activities *are* likely to use birth control carefully (Ford, Zelnik, & Kantner, 1979; Louis Harris & Associates, 1986).

Age, sexual knowledge, and experience are all major factors. The younger a girl is at first intercourse, the longer she waits before seeking help with contraception and the more likely she is to become pregnant (Tanfer & Horn, 1985). The less she knows about sex, the less likely she is to protect herself (Louis Harris & Associates, 1986). And the newer she is to sexual activity, the more vulnerable she is. The first few months after beginning sexual activity are the riskiest. Half of first premarital pregnancies occur in the first 6 months, and 1 out of 5 occur in the first month (Zabin, Kantner, & Zelnik, 1979). Teenagers seldom seek advice about contraceptives until they have been sexually active for a year or more. Only 41 percent use contraceptives the first time (Louis Harris & Associates, 1986).

What is known about the boy's role? Studies done in the 1970s found that boys were less likely to assume responsibility for preventing pregnancy than boys in previous generations. In one survey, more than 60 percent of boys who had had intercourse during the preceding month said that they never used a condom (R. C. Sorensen, 1973)—once the most commonly used contraceptive among young people. Some boys are afraid that if they bring up the possibility of pregnancy, the girl will change her mind about having sexual intercourse. Education directed toward adolescent boys, emphasizing their responsibility in preventing conception, is one way to stem the tide of pregnancy among teenagers, especially since so many boys express a belief in nonexploitative relationships (Scales, 1977). The increased emphasis on using condoms to prevent the spread of AIDS should help prevent pregnancy, too.

Preventing Teenage Pregnancy

Since teenagers who are knowledgeable about sex are more likely to use birth control, parents and schools should offer education about both facts and feelings regarding sex and parenthood. Many people fear that if teenagers know about sex, they will want to put their knowledge into practice, but community- or school-based sex education has not been found to result in more sexual activity by adolescents (Eisen & Zellman, 1987). Since the media are a powerful influence on adolescents' behavior, radio and television executives can initiate campaigns to present sexual situations responsibly and to permit advertisements for contraceptives. Since adolescents who have high aspirations for the future are also less likely to become pregnant, it is important to motivate young people in other areas of their lives and to raise their self-esteem. Programs that have focused on this approach rather than on the mechanics of contraception have achieved some success (Carrera, 1986), as we describe in Box 16-4.

Helping Pregnant Teenagers

Any pregnant woman needs to be reassured about her ability to bear and care for a child and about her continued attractiveness. She needs to express her anxieties and to receive sympathy. The unmarried teenager is especially vulnerable. Whatever she decides to do about the pregnancy, she has conflicting feelings. Just when she needs the most emotional support, she often gets the least. Her boyfriend may be frightened by the responsibility and turn away from her. Her family may be angry with her. She may be isolated from her friends if she does not attend school. To alleviate these pressures, the pregnant teenager should be able to discuss her problems with an interested, sympathetic, and knowledgeable counselor.

Programs that help pregnant girls stay in school can teach them both job skills and parenting skills and thus help them continue the quest for identity (Buie, 1987). A number of high schools operate day care centers for the children of unmarried students in order to help the young women continue their schooling. They also offer courses in parenting for mothers and occasionally for fathers (Purnick, 1984).

A study by T. M. Field and colleagues demonstrated the value of training

BOX 16-4 ■ THE EVERYDAY WORLD

HOW CAN TEENAGE PREGNANCY BE PREVENTED?

Because pregnancy in adolescence can be devastating to mother, father, and baby, it's up to parents, educators, and government officials to do everything within their power to help teenagers avoid becoming children who bear children. The following guidelines are based on findings from research studies and recommendations by those who work with adolescents:

■ Parents should discuss sex with children from an early age, instilling healthy, positive attitudes and being "askable," so that their children will feel free to go to them with questions. Children whose parents do discuss sex with them are likely to delay sexual activity until an appropriate time (Jaslow, 1982).

■ Schools, churches, and the media should offer realistic sex education, including information about risks and consequences of pregnancy in adolescence, different kinds of methods of contraception, and places where teenagers can obtain family planning services (Alan Guttmacher Institute, 1981).

■ Counseling programs that include peers should be instituted to encourage sexually active teenage girls to use contraceptives, since research has indicated that they are more responsive to girls close to their own age than they are to nurses who act as counselors (Jay, DuRant, Shoffitt, Linder, & Litt, 1984).

■ Community programs encouraging teenagers to delay sexual activity should be instituted. Such programs can help young people stand up against peer pressure urging them to be more sexually active than they want to be, can teach them ways to say no gracefully, and can offer guidance in problem solving (Howard, 1983).

■ Adolescents' use of birth control services should be kept confidential. Young teenagers cite this as the single most important consideration in choosing a birth control clinic (Zabin & Clark, 1981). Many young people say that they would not go to a clinic that insisted on notifying their parents or obtaining consent from parents (Jaslow, 1982).

■ Specific messages that need to be communicated to young people include the following (S. Gordon & Everly, 1985):

If someone says to you, "If you really love me, you'll have sex with me," it's always a line.

Sex is never a test of love.

It's not romantic to have sex without using a means of birth control—it's stupid.

"No" is a perfectly good oral contraceptive.

It is perfectly normal not to have sex.

Machismo is hurting and exploiting people to make a boy feel more secure.

More than 85 percent of boys who impregnate teenage girls will eventually abandon them.

Girls who feel that they don't amount to anything unless some guy loves them won't amount to much even after they are loved—if they get that far.

The most important components of a relationship are love, respect, caring, having a sense of humor, and honest communication without violating private thoughts and experiences.

---

young people to be parents. Eighty low-income teenage mothers received training either through a biweekly visit to their homes (by a graduate student and a teenage aide) or through paid job training as teachers' aides in the infants' nursery of a medical school. The infants in both parent-training groups did better than babies in a control group. They weighed more, had more advanced motor skills, and interacted better with their mothers. The mothers who worked as teachers' aides and their children showed the most gains: The mothers had fewer additional pregnancies, more of them returned to work or school, and their babies made the best progress (T. M. Field, Widmayer, Greenberg, & Stoller, 1982).

Although the mother feels the major impact of teenage parenthood, the father's life is often affected as well. A boy who feels emotionally committed to a girl he has impregnated has decisions to make. He may pay for an abortion. Or he may marry the girl, a move that will affect his educational and career plans. The father also needs someone to talk to, to help him sort out his feelings so that he and the mother can make the best decision for themselves and the child.

JUVENILE DELINQUENCY

There are two kinds of juvenile delinquents. One is the **status offender.** This is a young person who has been truant, has run away from home, has been sexually active, has not abided by parents' rules, or has done something else that is ordinarily not considered criminal—except when done by a minor. If Mark Twain's Huckleberry Finn were alive and active today, he would fit perfectly into this category.

The second kind of juvenile delinquent is one who has done something that is considered a crime no matter who commits it—like robbery, rape, or murder. If the young person is under the age of 16 or 18 (depending on the state), he or she is usually treated differently from an adult criminal. The court proceedings will probably not be public, the offender is likely to be tried and sentenced by a judge rather than a jury, and the sentence is usually more lenient. However, for some particularly violent crimes, minors may be tried as adults.

Statistics

Between 1985 and 1986, arrests of people under age 18 rose by 3 percent (U.S. Department of Justice, Federal Bureau of Investigation, FBI, 1987). People in this age group are responsible for a disproportionately high share of certain kinds of crimes. Although persons under age 18 constitute only about one-fourth of the total population, they account for about one-third of all crimes against property, including robbery, larceny, automobile theft and other kinds of theft, and arson (U.S. Department of Justice, FBI, 1987).

(Mike Kagan/Monkmeyer Press)

People under age 18 account for about one-third of crimes against property, including thefts such as shoplifting.

Boys are much more likely than girls to get into trouble with the law: for years, 4 or 5 boys were arrested for every girl. More recently the ratio has dropped to 3.5 to 1; but crime rates among girls are similar to rates among boys only for such status offenses as running away from home, incorrigibility, and engaging in sexual intercourse. Boys commit more of virtually all other offenses, especially violent offenses, and account for more than 90 percent of juveniles in correctional institutions (U.S. Department of Justice, 1988). The increase among girls of such behaviors as drug abuse and running away from home apparently leads to the kinds of activities that support them, like shoplifting, robbery, larceny, and prostitution (U.S. Department of Justice, FBI, 1987).

Who Are Juvenile Delinquents?

Personal Characteristics of Delinquents   What makes one child get into trouble, when another who lives on the same street or even in the same household remains law-abiding? Not surprisingly, children who get into trouble early in life are more likely to get into deeper trouble later on, although, as we will note later, there is some tendency for people to "outgrow" early misbehavior. Stealing, lying, truancy, and poor educational achievement are often predictors of future delinquency (Loeber & Dishion, 1983). Delinquents have been found to have a slightly lower average IQ (an IQ of 92) than the average for the general population (100), with the biggest deficits in verbal skills (Quay, 1987).

One study of 55 delinquents who had been patients at the Illinois State Psychiatric Institute concluded that delinquency is not a class phenomenon, but rather a result of emotional turmoil that affects young people from all levels of society. Delinquents from affluent families are likely to be taken to psychiatrists; delinquents from poor families are booked by the police (Offer, Ostrov, & Marohn, 1972).

In some cases, delinquency has been related to backgrounds of physical and sexual abuse and to neurological and psychiatric problems (Lewis et al., 1988). Relating problems such as these to delinquency may make it possible to treat some youthful offenders with medications such as anticonvulsants and antidepressants.

The Delinquent's Family   Several family characteristics are associated with juvenile delinquency. In a 1987 study of 18,226 boys and girls under 18 in long-term, state-operated correction institutes, more than half reported that a family member had also been imprisoned at least once, and nearly 3 out of 4 had not grown up with both parents (U.S. Department of Justice, 1988). Of course, these figures apply to young people who were actually caught, arrested, and convicted, and may thus describe young people who get caught up in the criminal justice system rather than young people whose families have the resources to keep them out of it.

Other research has found that antisocial behavior in adolescents is closely related to parents' inability to keep track of their children's activities and to discipline them. One team of researchers concluded: "It seems that parents of delinquents are indifferent trackers of their sons' whereabouts, the kind of companions they keep, or the type of activities in which they engage" (G. R. Patterson & Stouthamer-Loeber, 1984, p. 1305). These investigators also found that parents of delinquent children are less likely to punish rule breaking with anything more severe than a lecture or threat. An extensive analysis of studies of juvenile delinquency also reported that the strongest predictor of delinquency is the family's supervision and discipline of the children. Especially interesting was the finding that the poorest predictor is socioeconomic status (Loeber & Dishion, 1983).

These findings support the discussion earlier in this chapter about adolescent rebellion. Much of the tension often considered a sign of rebellion may arise over the conflict between adolescents' desire for prompt gratification and parents' desire to socialize their children. When parents cannot or will not fill their role as socializers, their children may become a problem for society.

Dealing with Delinquency

How can we help young people lead productive, law-abiding lives? And how can we protect society? So far, the answers to both these questions are unclear. Can we turn young offenders away from a life of crime by sentences that consider their youth, bolstered by social solutions such as probation and counseling? Or would we have less crime if we treated young offenders as we treat adults, basing sentences on the seriousness of the crime rather than the age of the offender?

One study suggests that how young offenders are treated is less important in most cases than just letting them grow up, and that—except for a relatively small group of "hard-core" offenders—it is almost impossible to predict which young people will commit crimes as adults (L. W. Shannon, 1982). This study was a longitudinal analysis of police and court records, plus interviews with more than 6000 adults, in Racine, Wisconsin.

More than 90 percent of the men in this study and 65 to 70 percent of the women had engaged in some misbehavior in adolescence (though not all of them had been caught), but only 5 to 8 percent of these had been booked for felonies as adults. Why had most of these people apparently become law-abiding? Fewer than 8 percent said that they were afraid of getting caught. Most said that they had realized that what seemed like fun in adolescence was no longer appropriate in adulthood.

It seems, then, that maturity does bring valuable reappraisals of attitudes and behavior for most people and that society must continue to explore ways to help those who cannot climb out of the morass of delinquency and alienation on their own.

Personality Strengths of Adolescents

Fortunately, the great majority of adolescents do not become pregnant or get into trouble with the law. Let us conclude our exploration of development, from conception through adolescence, with a look at some of the positive aspects of adolescents' lives.

Normal adolescence for young people like Jason and Vicky is exciting. All things seem possible. They are on the threshold of love and life's work and participation in the broader society. And they are getting to know the most interesting people in the world: themselves. Yet few adolescents recognize and value their positive attributes.

TABLE 16-4

CATEGORIES OF ADOLESCENTS' STRENGTHS

TYPE	DESCRIPTION
Health	Being in general good health, promoting and maintaining health, and having energy and vitality.
Aesthetic strengths	The ability to enjoy and recognize beauty in nature, objects, or people.
Special aptitudes or resources	Special abilities or capacities such as skill for repairing things; the ability to make things grow, or a "green thumb"; and ability in mathematics or music.
Employment satisfaction	Enjoyment of work or duties, the ability to get along with coworkers, pride in work, and great satisfaction with work.
Social strengths	Having sufficient friends of both sexes, using humor in social relations, and having the ability to entertain others.
Spectator sports	Attending or being interested in football or baseball games, for example. The researchers included reading books and plays in this category.
Strengths through family and others	Getting along with brothers, sisters, and parents; being able to talk over problems with the father or mother; feeling close or loyal to the family.
Imaginative and creative strengths	Use of creativity and imagination in relation to school, home, or the family, and expression of creative capacity, through writing, for example.
Dependability and responsibility	Being able to keep appointments, being trusted by other people, keeping promises, and persevering in bringing a task to its conclusion.
Spiritual strengths	Attending activities and meetings of church, synagogue, etc.; being a member of a religious organization; relying on religious beliefs; feeling close to God; using prayer or meditation.
Organizational strengths	Being able to lead clubs, teams, or organizations and to give or carry out orders; having long- or short-range plans.
Intellectual strengths	Interest in new ideas from people, books, or other sources; enjoyment of learning; interest in the continuing development of the mind.
Other strengths	The ability to take risks, liking adventure or pioneering, and the ability to grow through defeat or crisis, for example.
Emotional strengths	The ability to give and receive warmth, affection, or love; the capacity to "take" anger from others and to be aware of the feelings of others; the capacity for empathy.
Expressive arts	Participating in plays, ballroom dancing, and other types of dancing; sculpting; or playing a musical instrument.
Relationship strengths	Getting along well with most teachers; being patient and understanding with people; helping others; accepting people as individuals regardless of sex, beliefs, or race; being confided in by other people.
Education, training, and related areas	Getting good grades and acquiring special skills, such as typing, selling, or mechanical drawing.
Hobbies and crafts	Having hobbies or interests such as stamp or coin collecting, sewing or knitting, or hairstyling.
Sports and activities	Participation in swimming, football, tennis, or basketball, for example, and enjoyment of or skill in these activities or outdoor activities such as camping and hiking.

Source: Adapted from Otto & Healy, 1966.

Researchers who gave blank sheets of paper to 100 high school students and asked them to list their own strengths found that out of a total of 19 categories (see Table 16-4, above), the average student listed only 7 strengths (Otto & Healy, 1966).

BOX 16-5 ▪ PROFESSIONAL VOICES

ERIK ERIKSON

Erik Erikson talks about ego strengths.

ERIKSON: I think the potential for the development of ego strength comes out of the successful completion of all the earlier developmental processes. I would say that you could speak of a fully mature ego only after adolescence, which means, after all, becoming an adult. I've personally learned most from my work with children and with adolescents and young adults. As [August] Aichhorn has taught us in working with late adolescents it isn't enough to interpret to adolescents what went wrong in their past history. The present is too powerful for much retrospection. In fact they often use that kind of interpretation to develop a florid ideology of illness, and actually become quite proud of their neuroses. Also, if everything "goes back" into childhood, then everything is somebody else's fault, and trust in one's power of taking responsibility for oneself may be undermined.

QUESTION: Was this not satirized in the Broadway musical *West Side Story,* in the Officer Krupke song, where the ostensible juvenile delinquents were singing, "We're not responsible for our acts, social conditions are"? The poverty-stricken person says, "I'm not responsible for my poverty. It's society's fault." The delinquent says, "It's my mother's fault."

ERIKSON: That's right. In fact, *West Side Story* has another vary insightful theme. I don't remember the exact words, but these young people are dancing and singing. "They say we're bums. All right, that's what we're going to be." We meet something similar in other sections of rebellious youth. They tell us, "You say we have an identity crisis. All right, an identity crisis is what we're going to have." So what we once gingerly diagnosed as sexual identity confusion is now represented almost mockingly by otherwise rather wholesome-looking young people.

Source: R. I. Evans, 1967, pp. 31–32; *photo:* UPI/Bettmann Newsphotos.

These researchers say:

> This indicates a limited self-perception of personality strengths not too markedly different from that of adults. In similar studies which have been conducted, adults have listed an average of six strengths, but at the same time were able to fill one or more pages with listings of their "problems" or "weaknesses." (Otto & Healy, 1966, p. 293)

Most of the young people listed strengths in relationships, intellectual strengths, or emotional strengths; more girls listed strengths in social functioning and dependability, while more boys listed strengths in sports and other activities. Although the listings by boys and girls differed somewhat, they were more alike than unlike.

These researchers gave adolescents more credit for personality strengths than the young people gave themselves, listing several "personality resources or strengths" of adolescents which differ qualitatively from those of adults and which appear in unique and distinctive patterns:

1 Adolescents have considerable energy, or drive, and vitality.
2 They are idealistic and have a real concern for the future of this country and the world.
3 They frequently exercise their ability to question contemporary values, philosophies, theologies, and institutions.
4 They have heightened awareness and perceptivity.

BOX 16-6 ■ A CHILD'S WORLD AND YOU

WHAT DO YOU THINK?

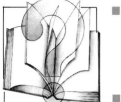

■ When teenagers complain that their parents "don't understand" them, do you think that they mean that their parents do not comprehend them or do not sympathize with them? Give reasons.

■ Men used to defend the double standard of sexual morality by pointing out that only women get pregnant. Since this is still true and since pregnancy among teenagers is a national problem, should teenage girls still be urged to follow a stricter standard of behavior than teenage boys?

■ Which of the following choices do you think is usually best for a teenage girl who discovers that she is pregnant: marry the father and raise the child, stay single but raise the child, give the baby to adoptive parents, or have an abortion?

■ What should a judge do with a first-time juvenile offender who has committed a felony: let the offender off with a warning, investigate the offender's family background before deciding, investigate the offender's socioeconomic status before deciding, sentence the offender to a term in a penal institution, or take some other action?

5 They are courageous, able to take risks themselves or stick their neck out for others.

6 They have a feeling of importance.

7 They possess a strong sense of fairness, and dislike intolerance.

8 More often than not, they are responsible and can be relied on.

9 They are flexible and adapt to change readily.

10 They are usually open, frank, and honest.

11 They have an above-average sense of loyalty to organizations and causes.

12 They have a sense of humor, which they often express.

13 More often then not, they have an optimistic and positive outlook on life in general.

14 They often think seriously and deeply.

15 They have great sensitivity to, and are considerably aware of, other people's feelings.

16 They are engaged in a sincere and ongoing search for identity.

If we can help more young people recognize and build on their strengths as they are about to enter adult life, adolescents' search for identity can turn up greater riches.

The normal developmental changes in the early years of life are obvious and dramatic signs of growth. The infant lying in the crib becomes an active, exploring toddler; the young child enters and embraces the worlds of school and society; the adolescent, with a new body and new awareness, prepares to step into adulthood. But growth and development do not stop with adolescence. People change in many ways throughout early, middle, and late adulthood. Some capacities, in fact, emerge relatively late in life, and human beings continue to shape their own development, as they have been doing since birth. What occurs in a child's world is important, but it is not the whole story. The narrative that follows is open-ended: each of us writes his or her own story of human development.

Summary

1   G. Stanley Hall viewed adolescence as a time of storm and stress, marked by turbulent, variable emotions.

2   Margaret Mead concluded from her studies of South Pacific cultures that much of the stress adolescents experience in western societies may be the result of cultural pressures.

3   According to Sigmund Freud, before adolescents enter the genital stage, the stage of mature adult sexuality, they must overcome their unresolved sexual feelings toward their parents. This process can produce temporary hostility. Freud, like Hall, considered adolescence a time of storm and stress.

4   Anna Freud considered adolescence more important for personality development than Sigmund Freud did. Two defense mechanisms that she found particularly important at this time are intellectualization (use of abstract thought to avoid unpleasant emotions) and asceticism (self-denial).

5   Erik Erikson's fifth psychosocial crisis is the conflict between identity and identity confusion. Finding an occupational identity is a key task of this stage. The "virtue" that should arise from this identity crisis is fidelity.

6   Research by James Marcia, based on Erikson's theory, examined the presence or absence of crisis and commitment in a person's identity formation. On the basis of these factors, Marcia identified four categories of identity formation: identity achievement (crisis leading to commitment), foreclosure (commitment with no crisis), confusion (no commitment, crisis uncertain), and moratorium (crisis, no commitment).

7   Marcia, Gilligan, and other researchers have found differences in the ways males and females define themselves. Intimate relationships appear to be more important for women; achieving a separate identity, for men.

8   Although the relationships between adolescents and parents are not always smooth, there is little evidence that full rebellion characterizes most of these relationships. Parents and their teenage children often hold similar values. Most arguments are about everyday matters.

9   Adolescents need a measure of independence, but too early separation or emotional independence from the family (or other significant adults) can cause alienation, susceptibility to negative peer influence, and physically or socially unhealthy behaviors.

10 Adolescents spend most of their time with peers. Friendships become more intimate, and romantic relationships with people of the other sex develop.

11 Adolescent sexuality strongly influences developing identity. Masturbation and occasional early homosexual experiences are common.

12 Sexual attitudes and behaviors are more liberal than in the past. There is more acceptance of premarital sexual activity, and there has been a decline in the double standard for males and females. Because of social pressure, many adolescents become sexually active earlier than they feel they should. A majority have had intercourse by the age of 17.

13 Although many parents are more accepting of teenage sexual behavior than in the past, many adolescents have difficulty discussing sexual matters with their parents.

14 Pregnancy is a major problem among adolescents today. The adolescent pregnancy rate in the United States is one of the highest in the world. Most pregnant teenagers have abortions. Ninety percent of those who have their babies keep them. Teenage pregnancy often has negative consequences for mothers, fathers, children, and society.

15 Comprehensive sex education programs and more communication between parents and their adolescents can encourage teenagers to delay sexual activity and to use contraceptives.

16 Juvenile delinquents fall into two categories. Status offenders commit acts that are not considered criminal for adults. The second kind of juvenile delinquent has committed an act that is considered a crime no matter what the age of the offender.

17 Young people under 18 account for more than their share of crimes, particularly crimes against property. The strongest predictor of delinquency is the family's level of supervision and disciplining of children. The poorest predictor is socioeconomic status.

18 Even with all the difficulties of establishing a personal, sexual, social, and vocational identity, adolescence—the threshold of adulthood—is typically interesting, exciting, and positive.

Key Terms

storm and stress (page 561)
genital stage (562)
libido (562)
reaction formation (562)
intellectualization (563)
asceticism (563)
identity versus identity confusion (564)
crisis (566)

commitment (566)
adolescent rebellion (569)
masturbation (580)
sexual orientation (580)
heterosexual (580)
homosexual (580)
status offender (590)

Suggested Readings

Bell, R., et al. (1988). *Changing bodies, changing lives.* New York: Vintage. A practical, reliable guide containing up-to-date information for teenagers on such issues as sex, AIDS, and social concerns.

Csikszentmihalyi, M., & Larson, R. (1984). *Being adolescent: Conflict and growth in the teenage years.* New York: Basic Books. A detailed, readable portrait of the day-to-day world of typical American middle-class teenagers: what they do, how they feel, and what they think about.

Erikson, E.H. (1968). *Identity: Youth and crisis.* New York: Norton. Erikson's classic discussion of the development of identity during adolescence.

Glenbard East Echo (Compilers). (1984). *Teenagers themselves.* New York: Adama. Over 9000 teenagers talk about their lives and values. The teenagers' own words destroy the idea that teenagers are apathetic about the world beyond their private concerns.

Hyde, J. (1986). *Understanding human sexuality* (3d ed.). New York: McGraw-Hill. An exceptionally readable textbook on sexuality covering a wide range of topics: physical and hormonal factors; contraception; sex research; variations in sexual behavior; sexual dysfunction; and sex in relation to religion, the law, and education.

Offer, D., Ostrov, E., & Howard, K.L. (1981). *The adolescent: A psychological self-portrait.* New York: Basic Books. A discussion of normal adolescents, focusing on feelings about sexual relations, their families, their friends, and themselves. This book challenges the view that adolescence is a time of storm and stress.

GLOSSARY

accommodation In Piaget's terminology, changes in existing cognitive structures to include new experiences. (page 29)

acquired adaptation Change in behavior to accommodate a new situation. (210)

acting-out behavior Misbehavior (for example, lying or stealing) spurred by emotional difficulties. (489)

adaptation In Piaget's terminology, the complementary processes of assimilation and accommodation. (29)

adolescence Developmental transition period between childhood and adulthood. (504)

adolescent growth spurt Sharp increase in height and weight that precedes sexual maturity. (509)

adolescent rebellion Break with parental and societal values undergone by some but not all adolescents. (569)

adoption Taking a child into one's family through legal means and accepting the child as one's own. (117)

affective disorder Disorder of mood, such as depression. (491)

allele One of a pair of genes affecting a trait; the genes may be identical or different. (61)

alpha fetoprotein (AFP) Blood test used to indicate the possibility of a defect in the formation of the brain or spinal cord of a fetus. (72)

ambivalent attachment Attachment style in which an infant becomes anxious before the primary caregiver leaves but both seeks and resists contact on the caregiver's return. (260)

amniocentesis Prenatal diagnostic procedure for examining the chromosomes of a fetus; sample cells are withdrawn from the amniotic fluid, in which the fetus floats, and are examined for signs of birth defects. (72)

anal stage In Freud's theory, the psychosexual stage of toddlerhood (12–18 to 36 months), in which the child receives pleasure through anal stimulation; toilet training is the most important gratifying situation. (242)

androgens General term for the male sex hormones. (355)

androgynous Having characteristics considered typical of males and other characteristics considered typical of females. (360)

anorexia nervosa Eating disorder, seen mostly in young women, characterized by self-starvation. (517)

anoxia Oxygen deprivation. (143)

Apgar scale Standard measurement of a newborn's condition that assesses appearance, pulse, grimace, activity, and respiration. (147)

apnea Temporary cessation of breathing. (189)

artificial insemination Nonsexual introduction of sperm into a woman's body with the intent to cause pregnancy. (116)

asceticism In Anna Freud's terminology, a defense mechanism characterized by self-denial in response to the fear of loss of control over one's impulses. (563)

assimilation In Piaget's terminology, the incorporation of a new object, experience, or concept into existing cognitive structures. (29)

attachment Active, affectionate, reciprocal relationship between two people; their interaction reinforces and strengthens the bond. The term often refers to an infant's relationship with parents. (259)

attention-deficit hyperactivity disorder (ADHD) Syndrome characterized by inattention, impulsivity, and considerable activity at inappropriate times and places. (445)

auditory-recognition memory Ability to remember and recognize sounds. (216)

authoritarian parents In Baumrind's terminology, parents whose primary child-rearing values are based on control and obedience. (376)

authoritative parents In Baumrind's terminology, parents whose primary child-rearing values blend respect for the child's individuality with a desire to instill social values in the child. (376)

autobiographical memory Memory of specific events in one's own life. (323)

autonomy Independence. (243)

autonomy versus shame and doubt In Erikson's theory, the second critical alternative of psychosocial development (18 months to 3 years), in which the child achieves a balance between self-determination and control by others. (243)

avoidant attachment Attachment style in which an infant rarely cries when the primary caregiver leaves and avoids contact upon his or her return. (260)

basic trust versus basic mistrust In Erikson's theory, the first critical alternative of psychosocial development, in which infants (birth to 18 months) develop a sense of how reliable people in their world are. (243)

battered child syndrome Syndrome of child abuse and neglect first identified in 1962. (303)

Bayley Scales Standardized test of infants' intelligence. (206)

behaviorism School of psychology that emphasizes the study of observable behaviors and events and the role of the environment in causing behavior. (23)

behavior therapy Treatment approach using principles of learning theory to alter behavior; also called *behavior modification*. (492)

birth trauma Injury sustained by an infant at birth. (143)

Brazelton Neonatal Behavioral Assessment Scale Measure of a newborn's behavioral ability that assesses interactive behaviors, motor skills, self-control, and response to stress. (148)

breech position Misalignment of a fetus in the uterus causing the feet or buttocks to emerge before the head. (131)

bulimia nervosa Eating disorder in which a person regularly eats huge quantities of food (binges) and then purges the body by taking laxatives or inducing vomiting. (518)

carrier In genetics, a person with an allele which is not expressed but can be passed on to future generations. (66)

case studies Studies of a single case or individual life. (33)

castration anxiety Part of the Oedipus complex in Freud's theory: a boy's fear of castration by the father, which leads to repression of sexual feelings for the mother and identification with the father. (349)

categorization Process of organizing material in one's mind into related groupings to aid in remembering. (428)

centrate In Piaget's terminology, to think about one aspect of a situation while neglecting others. (316)

cephalocaudal principle Principle that development proceeds in a "head-to-tail" direction: the upper body parts develop before the lower parts. (159)

cerebral cortex Upper layer of the brain. (162)

cesarean delivery Surgical removal of the baby from the uterus. (131)

child abuse Maltreatment of children involving physical injury, neglect, or psychological maltreatment. (303)

child development Scientific study of normal changes in children over time. (10)

childhood depression Affective disorder characterized by inability to have fun or to concentrate, and by an absence of normal emotional reactions. (491)

chorionic villus sampling (CVS) Prenatal diagnostic procedure for obtaining sample villi from the membrane surrounding the embryo and then examining the embryo's chromosomes for birth defects. (72)

chromosome Rod-shaped particle found in every living cell; it carries the genes. (57)

circular reaction In Piaget's theory, a simple behavior that is repeated often. (209)

classical conditioning Learning in which a previously neutral stimulus (conditioned stimulus) acquires the power to elicit a response (conditioned response) by association with an unconditioned stimulus that ordinarily elicits a particular response (unconditioned response). (23, 197)

clinical method Technique of observation in which questioning is flexible and the interviewer asks additional questions in response to particular answers. (35)

cognitive development Changes in mental powers and qualities that permit understanding; *see intellectual development.* (206)

cognitive play Play that reflects the level of the child's intellectual development. (372)

commitment Personal investment in an occupation or a system of beliefs. (566)

concordance Probability of agreement; used to measure the relative importance of hereditary and environmental factors in development. (82)

concrete operations Piaget's third stage of cognitive development, during which children develop the ability to think logically about the here and now, but not about abstractions. (419)

conditioned response (CR) In classical conditioning, a response to a conditioned stimulus; also known as *conditioned reflex.* (24, 198)

conditioned stimulus (CS) In classical conditioning, an originally neutral stimulus that, after repeated pairing with an uncondi-

tioned stimulus, provokes a conditioned response. (24, 197–198)

conservation Piaget's term for awareness that two stimuli which are equal (in length, weight, or amount, for example) remain equal in the face of perceptual alteration, so long as nothing has been added to or taken away from either stimulus. (316, 419)

control group In an experiment, people who are similar to people in the experimental group but do not receive the treatment whose effects are to be measured; results obtained with this group are compared with results obtained with the experimental group to assess cause and effect. (37)

convergent thinking Thinking that is aimed at finding the one "right" answer to a problem. (450)

coregulation Transitional stage in the control of behavior: parents exercise general supervision and children exercise moment-to-moment self-regulation. (474)

correlational study Study that assesses the direction and extent of a relationship between variables. (36)

creativity Ability to see things in a new light, to see problems that others may fail to recognize, and to come up with new, unusual, and effective solutions. (450)

crisis Period of conscious decision making related to identity formation. (566)

critical period Specific time during development when an event has its greatest impact. (15, 98, 164)

cross-sectional study Research that assesses groups of people of different ages at the same time. (40)

cross-sequential study Research assessing people in a cross-sectional study twice or more. (41)

crying Innate nonlinguistic form of communication that in newborns and infants expresses a

need for attention or a strong emotion; basic infants' cries include the rhythmic cry of need, the angry cry, the cry of pain, and the cry of frustration. (248)

data Information that is obtained through research. (18)

day care Program designed to care for young children outside the home. (328)

decenter In Piaget's terminology, to think simultaneously about several aspects of a situation. (316)

deduction Reasoning that shows a particular conclusion to be implied by a general premise. (317)

defense mechanism Unconscious distortion of reality to protect the ego against anxiety. (21)

deferred imitation Ability to observe an action and imitate it after a passage of time. (212, 314)

Denver Developmental Screening Test Screening test given to children (1 month to 6 years old) to identify abnormal development; it assesses personal-social, fine motor–adaptive, language, and gross motor behavior. (177)

dependent variable In an experiment, the variable that may or may not change as a result of changes in the independent variable. (37)

depression Emotional disturbance characterized by feeble responses to stimuli, low initiative, and sullen or despondent attitude. (85)

design stage Period in artistic development (commonly at age 3) in which children combine basic shapes into more complex patterns. (302)

developmental behavioral genetics Study of interactions of heredity and environment which create differences between people. (77)

difficult child Child who has an irritable temperament, irregular biological rhythms, and intense responses to situations. (253)

discipline Teaching children character, self-control, and moral behavior. (473)

divergent thinking Creative thinking; the ability to discover new, unusual answers to a problem. (450)

dizygotic twins Two people who are conceived by the mother and born at approximately the same time as a result of the fertilization of two ova; fraternal twins. (60)

DNA (deoxyribonucleic acid) Chemical carrying the instructions that tell all the cells in the body how to make the proteins that enable them to carry out their various functions. (58)

dominance hierarchy System of social ranking, recognized by all the members of a group, in which some members have power over all other members, some have power over certain other members and are subordinate to others, and some are subordinate to all other members. (368)

dominant inheritance Mendel's law that when an offspring receives genes for contradictory traits, only one of the traits—the dominant trait—will be expressed. (62)

Down syndrome Disorder caused by an extra twenty-first chromosome; it is characterized by mental retardation and often heart defects and other physical abnormalities. (69)

drug therapy Administration of drugs to treat emotional disorders. (493)

dyslexia Inability or difficulty in learning to read. (444)

easy child Child with a generally happy temperament, regular biological rhythms, and a readiness to accept new experiences. (253)

ego In Freud's theory, the representation of reason or common sense; it operates on the "reality principle." (19, 242)

egocentrism As used by Piaget, a child's inability to consider another person's point of view. (315)

elaboration Linking items to be remembered by creating a story about them or a visual image of them. (428)

Electra complex In Freud's theory, the process—involving sexual feelings for the father, fear of the mother, and repression of these emotions—by which a girl comes to identify with her mother. (349)

electronic fetal monitoring Use of machines to monitor the fetal heartbeat during labor and delivery. (128)

embryonic stage Second stage of pregnancy (2 to 8–12 weeks), characterized by differentiation of body parts and systems and ending when the bone cells begin to appear. (98)

emotion Psychological response to a situation; although the response can lead to altered behavior, the primary characteristic is a change in subjective feeling rather than in objective action. (245)

enuresis Bed-wetting. (299)

environment Combination of outside influences such as family, community, and personal experience that affect development. (52)

equilibration Striving for cognitive balance. (29)

estrogen Female sex hormone. (508)

experiment Highly controlled, replicable (repeatable) procedure in which a researcher assesses the effect of manipulating variables; an experiment provides information about cause and effect. (36)

experimental group In an experiment, people who receive the treatment under study; changes in these people are compared with changes in a control group. (37)

extinction Process whereby a response that is no longer reinforced stops or returns to its original (baseline) level. (25)

fallopian tube Either of two slender ducts connecting the ovaries to the uterus; a fallopian tube is normally the site of fertilization. (57)

family therapy Treatment technique in which the whole family is treated together and is viewed as the client. (492)

fetal alcohol syndrome (FAS) Combination of mental, motor, and developmental abnormalities affecting the offspring of some women who drink heavily during pregnancy. (105)

fetal death in utero Death of a fetus while in the uterus. (143)

fetal stage Final stage of pregnancy (8–12 weeks to birth), characterized by increased detail of body parts and greatly enlarged body size. (99)

fetoscopy Medical procedure permitting direct viewing of the fetus in the uterus. (72)

fetus Conceptus between 8 to 12 weeks and birth. (99)

field experiment Experiment performed in a setting familiar to the subject, such as a day care center. (39)

follicle Small sac containing an ovum, or female gamete. (56)

formal operations In Piaget's terminology, the final stage of cognitive development, characterized by the ability to think abstractly. (537)

gamete Sex cell. (56)

gender constancy Awareness that one will always be male or female. (361)

gender difference Psychological difference between the sexes. (354)

gender identity Awareness of one's own sex and the sex of others. (355)

gender roles Behaviors and attitudes that a culture deems appropriate for males and females. (354)

gender-schema theory Theory that children socialize themselves in their gender roles by developing the concept of what it means to be male or female. (362)

gender-typing Process by which a person learns a gender role. (267,354)

gene Functional unit of heredity; genes determine the traits that are passed from one generation to the next. (58)

genetic counseling Clinical service that advises couples of their probable risk of having a child with a particular hereditary disorder. (71)

genital stage In Freud's terminology, the psychosexual stage of mature sexuality; it occurs during adolescence. (562)

genotype Pattern of alleles carried by a person. (63)

gentle birth Delivering babies in dimly lit, quiet rooms, without forceps and with only local anesthesia or none; sometimes called the *Leboyer method*. (130)

germinal stage First 2 weeks of development of a conceptus, beginning at fertilization, characterized by rapid cell division and increasing complexity, and ending when the conceptus attaches to the wall of the uterus. (95)

gestation Period of time from conception to birth; normal full-term gestation is 266 days. (95, 124)

giftedness One or more of the following: superior general intellect, superiority in a single domain (like mathematics or science), artistic talent, leadership ability, or creative thinking. (447)

habituation Simple type of learning in which familiarity with a stimulus reduces, slows, or even stops a response. (173, 196)

handedness Preference for using one hand rather than the other; determination may be difficult, because not everyone prefers one hand for every task. (411)

heredity Inborn factors inherited from parents that affect development. (52)

heterosexual Sexually interested in members of the other sex. (580)

heterozygous Possessing different alleles for a trait. (62)

holophrase Single word that conveys a complete thought; the typical speech form of children aged 12 to 18 months. (222)

homosexual Sexually interested in members of the same sex. (580)

homozygous Possessing identical alleles for a trait. (62)

horizontal decalage In Piaget's terminology, the development of different types of conservation at different ages; thus a child can conserve substance before weight, and substance and weight before volume. (420)

humanistic perspective View of humanity that sees people as able to foster their own development in healthy, positive ways. (30)

hypothesis Possible explanation for an observation; a hypothesis is used to predict the outcome of an experiment. (18)

id In Freud's theory, the unconscious source of motives and desires; it operates on the ''pleasure principle.'' (19, 242)

ideal self Person's concept of what he or she wishes to be like; compare *real self*. (459)

identification Process by which a person acquires the characteristics of another person or a group; one of the most important personality developments of early childhood. (352)

identity versus identity confusion In Erikson's theory, the fifth crisis of psychosocial development, in which an adolescent must determine his or her own sense of self (identity), including the role he or she will play in society. (564)

imaginary audience Observer who exists only in the mind of an adolescent and is as concerned with the adolescent's thoughts and behaviors as the adolescent is. (540)

imprinting Instinctive form of learning in which, after a single encounter, an animal recognizes

and trusts one particular individual. (257)

independent segregation Mendel's law that individual traits are transmitted separately. (61)

independent variable In an experiment, the variable that is directly controlled and manipulated by the experimenter. (37)

induction Reasoning which asserts that a general rule can be made on the basis of one or more particular examples. (318)

industry versus inferiority In Erikson's theory, the fourth crisis that children face; they must learn the skills of their culture or risk developing feelings of inferiority. (462)

infantile autism Rare developmental disorder involving the inability to communicate with and respond to other people. (83)

infant mortality rate Proportion of babies who die within the first year of life. (185)

infertility Inability to conceive after 1 year of trying to have a baby. (116)

information-processing approach Study of intellectual development based on the mental capacities and processes that support thought. (202)

initiative versus guilt Third of Erikson's psychosocial crises, in which the child must balance the desire to pursue goals with the moral reservations that prevent carrying them out; successful resolution leads to the virtue of purpose. (351)

instrumental conditioning See *operant conditioning*. (25, 198)

intellectual development Changes in mental abilities, activities, or organization over time; also called *cognitive development*. (11)

intellectualization In the terminology of Anna Freud, a defense mechanism characterized by participating in abstract intellectual discussions to avoid unpleasant, anxiety-producing feelings. (563)

intelligence Ability to adapt, or appropriately alter behavior, in pursuit of a goal. (202)

intelligence quotient (IQ) Score calculated by dividing a person's mental age by his or her chronological age and multiplying the result by 100. (203)

interview method Research technique in which people are asked to state their attitudes, opinions, or histories. (36)

invisible imitation Imitation of an action with a part of the body that cannot be seen by oneself, such as imitation of facial expressions. (213)

in vitro fertilization Conception outside the body. (117)

isolette Crib which permits full temperature regulation under antiseptic conditions; formerly called an *incubator*. (140)

karyotype Photograph made through a microscope showing the chromosomes when they are separated and aligned for cell division; the chromosomes are displayed according to a standard array. (71)

kindergarten Traditional introduction to school for 5-year-olds, an optional year of transition between the relative freedom of home or preschool and the structure of formal schooling. (328)

laboratory experiment Experiment performed in a psychological laboratory setting that is subject to the experimenter's control. (38)

language Communication system that uses words and grammar. (220, 314)

language acquisition device (LAD) In nativist linguistics, the inborn ability to learn a language. (226)

lanugo Fine, soft prenatal hair; present on some neonates at birth, but soon lost. (145)

latency period In Freud's terminology, a period of relative sexual calm that occurs during mid-

dle childhood after the Oedipus complex has been resolved. (462)

learning Relatively permanent change in behavior that results from experience. (195)

learning disabilities (LDs) Disorders that interfere with specific aspects of learning and school achievement. (444)

learning theory Theory that most behavior is learned from experience. (225)

libido In Freud's terminology, the basic energy that fuels the sexual drive. (562)

linguistic speech Spoken use of language; besides words and grammar, it relies on pronunciation, intonation, and rhythm to convey meaning. (222)

longitudinal study Research that follows the same people over a period of time. (40)

long-term memory Stored memories; the capacity seems unlimited and the duration of a memory may be permanent. Compare *short-term memory*. (428)

low-birthweight baby General term used for both preterm and small-for-date babies; formerly called *premature babies*. (137)

mainstreaming Integration of handicapped and nonhandicapped children in the same classroom. (446)

masturbation Sexual self-stimulation. (580)

matching Sampling technique in which the members of the control group and the experimental group are selected by comparing and matching certain characteristics. (38)

maturation Unfolding of patterns of behavior in a biologically determined age-related sequence. (195)

mean length of utterance (MLU) Average length of a child's utterance, measured in morphemes. (224)

mechanistic perspective View of humanity which assumes that all change is a reaction to external

events; purpose, will, and intelligence are ignored or given little weight. (23)

meconium Fetal waste matter. (146)

medicated delivery Childbirth in which the mother receives anesthesia. (128)

meiosis Type of cell division in which the gametes receive one of each pair of chromosomes. (58)

menarche Girl's first menstruation. (396, 512)

mental age (MA) Assessment of a person's intellectual ability, determined by administering an intelligence test and matching the test taker's score with the average age of those who have scored similarly. (203)

mental retardation Below-average intellectual functioning. (443)

metacommunication Knowledge of communication processes. (438)

metamemory Knowledge of the process of memory. (428)

mitosis Process by which a cell divides in half, over and over again. (58)

monozygotic twins Two people with identical genes, arising from the formation of one zygote that divided; identical twins. (60)

morality of autonomous moral principles Third level in Kohlberg's theory of moral reasoning, in which people follow internally held moral principles and decide between conflicting moral standards. (424)

morality of constraint In Piaget's theory, the first stage of moral reasoning, in which a child thinks rigidly about moral concepts; also called *heteronomous morality*. (421)

morality of conventional role conformity Second level in Kohlberg's theory of moral reasoning, in which children want to please other people and have internalized the standards of authority figures. (424)

morality of cooperation In Piaget's theory, the second stage of moral reasoning, in which a child has moral flexibility; also called *autonomous morality*. (422)

morpheme Smallest meaningful unit of speech. (224)

motherese Simplified, slow, repetitive, high-pitched speech used by most adults and slightly older children when speaking with an infant. (228)

mother-infant bond Mother's feeling of attachment to her child. (257)

multifactorial inheritance Interaction of both genetic and environmental factors to produce certain traits. (64)

multiple alleles Genes that exist in three or more allelic states. (63)

mutation Change in a gene that leads to the production of a new, often harmful trait. (111)

nativism Theory that behavior is inborn; nativist linguistics holds that speech arises from an inborn capacity. (225)

natural childbirth Method of childbirth developed by Dr. Grantly Dick-Read that seeks to prevent pain by eliminating the mother's fear of childbirth. (130)

natural experiment Comparison of a person or a group of people who were exposed to some naturally occurring event (such as hospitalization or malnutrition) with a person or a group of people who were not exposed to the event. (39)

naturalistic observation Study of people in a real-life setting with no attempt to manipulate behavior. (34)

nature-versus-nurture controversy Dispute over the relative importance of hereditary and environmental factors in influencing human development; since both factors interact continuously, debate is widely seen as futile. (52)

neglect Withholding of adequate care, usually referring to such physical care as food, clothing, and supervision. (303)

neonatal jaundice Yellowing of the skin and eyeballs that is common among newborns and seldom serious. (146)

neonatal period First 4 weeks after birth. (144)

neonate Newborn in the first 4 weeks of life. (124)

neurotransmitter Chemical that transmits signals between neurons (nerve cells). (85)

neutral stimulus Stimulus that does not ordinarily evoke a reflex response. (24, 197–198)

nightmare Frightening dream, occurring toward morning and often vividly recalled. (298)

night terror Common sleep disorder of childhood in which a child suddenly awakens from a deep sleep in a state of panic. (298)

nonnormative life event Unusual event that may have a major effect on a person's life. (12)

nonorganic failure to thrive Emotional neglect resulting in a baby's failure to grow and gain weight at home despite adequate nutrition. (303)

norm Average performance, with which a person's score on a test is compared. (203)

normative age-graded influence Influence on development that is highly similar for all people in a given age group. (12)

normative history-graded influence Biological or environmental influence on development that is common to people of a particular generation. (12)

nurse-midwife Certified nurse who has been specially trained to assist at births. (133)

obesity Overweight condition marked by a skin-fold measurement in the 85th percentile. (399, 516)

object permanence In Piaget's theory, awareness that a person or thing continues to exist when out of sight. (207)

obstetrician Physician who specializes in delivering babies. (133)

Oedipus complex In Freud's theory, the process—involving sexual feelings for the mother, fear of the father, and repression of these emotions—by which a boy comes to identify with his father. (349)

operant conditioning Learning in which a response continues to be made because it has been reinforced; also called *instrumental conditioning*. (25, 198)

oral stage In Freud's theory, the psychosexual stage of infancy (birth to 12–18 months), characterized by gratification of the area around the mouth; feeding is the most common gratifying situation. (242)

organismic perspective View of humanity that sees people as active agents in their own development, focuses on qualitative changes, and sees development as discontinuous, or occurring in stages. (27)

Otis-Lennon School Ability Test Group intelligence test for children. (431)

penis envy Idea in Freud's theory that a young girl envies the male's penis and wishes that she had a penis herself. (350)

permissive parents In Baumrind's terminology, parents whose primary child-rearing values are self-expression and self-regulation. (376)

personal fable Conviction, typical in adolescence, that one is special, unique, and not subject to the rules that govern the rest of the world. (541)

personality Person's unique way of behaving, feeling, and reacting. (240–241)

personality-social-emotional development Changes in a person's unique style of responding, feeling, and reacting. (11)

phallic stage Stage of the preschool child in Freud's theory of psychosexual development, in which gratification is centered on the genital area. (349)

phenotype Observable characteristics of a person. (63)

Phenylketonuria (PKU) Hereditary abnormality which, if not discovered and treated with a special diet, leads to mental retardation; with special diet, development is normal. (148)

phobia Irrational, involuntary fear that is inappropriate to the situation and interferes with normal activities. (365)

physical development Changes in body, brain, sensory capacity, and motor skills over time. (11)

Piagetian approach Study of intellectual development based on describing qualitative changes in thinking that are typical of children at particular stages; named after its founder, Jean Piaget. (202)

pictorial stage Period of artistic development (between ages 4 and 5) in which drawing becomes less abstract and more representational. (302)

pleasure principle In Freud's theory, the attempt to gratify needs immediately; the operating principle of the id. (242)

polygenic inheritance Interaction of a number of different genes to produce certain traits. (64)

population All the members of a group to be studied. (38)

preconventional morality Kohlberg's first level of moral reasoning, in which the emphasis is on external control, obedience to the rules and standards of others, and the desire to avoid punishment. (424)

prejudice Negative attitudes toward certain groups. (468)

prelinguistic speech Communicative use of sounds by infants without using words or grammar. (221)

preoperational stage In Piaget's theory, the second major period of cognitive development (approximately age 2 to age 7), in

which children are able to think in symbols but are limited by their inability to use logic. (313)

prepared childbirth Method of childbirth developed by Dr. Fernand Lamaze that uses instruction, breathing exercises, and social support to eliminate fear and pain. (130)

preschool Program designed to provide educational experiences for young children. (328)

preterm (premature) baby Baby born less than 37 weeks after the mother's last menstrual period. (137)

primary circular reaction Simple repetitive act, centered on the baby's own body, to reproduce a pleasant sensation first achieved by chance. (210)

primary sex characteristics Organs directly related to reproduction, which enlarge and mature in early adolescence; compare *secondary sex characteristics.* (510)

private speech Talking aloud to oneself with no intent to communicate with anyone else. (341)

Project Head Start Compensatory preschool educational program begun in 1965. (335)

prosocial behavior Altruistic behavior; selflessness. (366)

proximodistal principle Principle that development proceeds in a near-to-far manner: the parts of the body near its center (spinal cord) develop before the extremities. (159)

psychoanalytic perspective View of humanity concerned with the unconscious forces motivating behavior. (18)

psychological maltreatment Action or failure to act that damages children's behavioral, cognitive, emotional, or physical functioning; emotional abuse. (494)

psychometric approach Study of intellectual development based on attempts to measure the quantity of intelligence. (201)

psychosexual development In

Freudian theory, the different stages of development in which gratification shifts from one body zone to another. (19)

psychosocial development Erikson's theory of personality development through the life span, stressing societal and cultural influences on the ego at eight stages. (21)

psychotherapy Treatment technique in which a therapist generally helps patients gain insight into their personalities and relationships and helps them interpret their feelings and behaviors. (492)

puberty Process that leads to sexual maturity and the ability to reproduce. (505)

punishment Stimulus that follows a behavior and decreases the likelihood that the behavior will be repeated. (25)

qualitative change Change in kind, as in the nature of intelligence. (10)

quantitative change Change in amount, such as in height, weight, or size of vocabulary. (10)

random sample Sampling technique in which the members of the control group and the experimental group are randomly selected from the larger population. (38)

reaction formation Defense mechanism characterized by replacement of an anxiety-producing feeling with the expression of its opposite. (562)

reaction range In genetics, a potential variability in the expression of a hereditary trait, depending on environmental conditions. (75)

reality principle In Freud's theory, the search for acceptable and realistic ways to obtain gratification; the operating principle of the ego. (242)

real self Person's concept of what he or she is like; compare *ideal self.* (459)

recall Ability to reproduce material from memory; compare *recognition*. (323)

recessive inheritance Expression of a recessive trait, which occurs only if a person (or an animal or a plant) is homozygous for the trait (has two alleles carrying it). (63)

recognition Type of memory that enables a person to correctly identify a stimulus as something previously known; compare *recall*. (322)

reflex behavior Involuntary reaction to stimulation. (164)

rehearsal Strategy to keep an item in short-term memory through conscious repetition. (428)

reinforcement Stimulus that follows a response and increases the likelihood that the response will be repeated. (25)

reliability (test-retest reliability) Constancy of scores when a person is tested more than once. (203)

representational ability Capacity to represent objects and actions in memory, largely through the use of symbols. (208)

resilient children Children who bounce back from unfortunate circumstances that would have a highly negative impact on the emotional development of most children. (495)

Rh factor Protein substance found in the blood of most people; when it is present in the blood of a fetus but not in the blood of the mother, death of the fetus can result. (110)

role-taking In Selman's terminology, assuming another person's point of view. (423)

sample In an experiment, a group of people who are used to represent the total population. (38)

schema In Piaget's terminology, the basic cognitive unit; a schema is generally named after the behavior involved. (29)

scheme Organized pattern of behavior. (208)

schizophrenia Psychological dis-

order marked by a loss of contact with reality; symptoms include hallucinations and delusions. (85)

school phobia Unrealistic fear of school, probably reflecting separation anxiety. (490)

scientific method Means of inquiry that depends on observation to establish findings, uses further observations to test alternative explanations for the findings, and then uses new observers to demonstrate the continuing validity of the observations. (32)

scribble Early form of drawing (appearing by age 2) in which the chief distinctions are the nature and placement of the line. (302)

secondary circular reaction Repetition of an action to see results outside the body. (210)

secondary sex characteristics Physiological signs of sexual maturation (such as breast development and growth of body hair) that do not involve the sex organs; compare *primary sex characteristics*. (511)

secular trend Trend noted by observing several generations; in child development, a trend toward earlier attainment of adult height and sexual maturity, which began a century ago and appears to have ended in the United States. (508)

secure attachment Attachment style in which an infant separates readily from the primary caregiver and actively seeks out the caregiver when he or she returns. (259)

self-awareness (1) Ability to recognize one's own actions, intentions, states, and abilities. (2) Realization, beginning in infancy, of separateness from other people, eventually allowing reflection on one's own actions in relation to social standards. (247, 459)

self-concept Sense of self, which guides one in deciding what to do in the future. (459)

self-definition Physical and psychological characteristics one considers important to describe oneself. (459)

self-esteem Favorable self-evaluation or self-image. (460)

self-fulfilling prophecy Prediction of behavior that biases people to act as though the prophecy were already true. (142, 442)

self-recognition Ability to recognize one's own image. (257, 459)

self-regulation Control of behavior in order to conform with social expectations. (278)

self-schema According to the information-processing approach, a set of "knowledge structures" which guide and organize the processing of information about the self and help children decide how to act. (463)

sensorimotor stage In Piaget's theory, the first stage in human cognitive development (birth to about age 2), during which infants acquire knowledge through sensory experience and motor activity. (207)

sensory memory Awareness of images and sensations that disappears quickly unless it is transferred into short-term memory. (428)

separation anxiety Distress shown by an infant when a familiar caregiver leaves. (271)

separation anxiety disorder Condition involving excessive anxiety for at least 2 weeks, concerning separation from people to whom a child is attached. (490)

sex difference Actual biological difference between the sexes. (354)

sex-linked inheritance Process by which certain recessive genes are transmitted differently to male and female children. (64)

sexual abuse Sexual contact between a child and an older person. (303)

sexually transmitted disease (STD) Disease spread by sexual contact; also called *venereal disease*. (524)

sexual orientation Whether a person is heterosexual or homosexual. (580)

shape stage Period in artistic development (at about age 3) when children begin drawing basic shapes—circles, squares, triangles, crosses, X's, and odd forms. (302)

shaping Bringing about a new response by reinforcing responses that are progressively like the desired one. (26)

short-term memory Working memory, which has a limited capacity; the content fades rapidly unless it is stored or actively preserved through rehearsal. Compare *long-term memory*. (428)

sign In Piaget's terminology, a conventional mental representation—such as a word—of a concept. (313)

significate Term used by Piaget for the real-world object or event represented by a signifier. (313)

signifier Term used by Piaget for symbols and signs. (313)

slow-to-warm-up child Child whose temperament is generally mild and who is hesitant about accepting new experiences. (253)

small-for-date baby Baby whose birthweight is less than that of 90 percent of all babies born at the same gestational age. (137)

smiling Innate form of communication that begins as a reflex and soon expresses pleasure, trust, and contentment. (249)

socialization Learning of behaviors deemed appropriate by one's culture. (256)

social-learning theory Theory proposed by Bandura that behaviors are learned by observing and imitating models. (26–27)

social play Play in which children interact with other children. (372)

social referencing Understanding an ambiguous situation by seeking out another person's perception of it. (273)

social speech Speech intended to be understood by a listener. (343)

spontaneous abortion Natural expulsion from the uterus of a conceptus that cannot survive outside the womb; also called *miscarriage*. (98)

standardization sample Large, representative group of people used in developing a statistical standard against which other people will be compared. (203)

Stanford-Binet Intelligence Scale Individual intelligence test that includes verbal, nonverbal, quantitative, and memory items. (325)

state Periodic variation in an infant's cycle of wakefulness, sleep, and activity. (148)

status offender Juvenile charged with committing an act that is considered criminal only because the offender is a minor (for example, truancy, running away from home, or engaging in sexual intercourse). (590)

stillbirth Delivery of a dead infant. (143)

storm and stress In Hall's terminology, the idea that adolescence is necessarily a time of strong and variable emotions; from the German *Sturm und Drang*. (561)

stranger anxiety Wariness of strange people and places often shown by infants in the second half of the first year. (271)

strange situation Experimental procedure used to assess the attachment between a mother and her infant. (259)

stuttering Involuntary repetition or prolongation of syllables. (404)

sudden infant death syndrome (SIDS) Sudden and unexpected death of an apparently healthy infant; also known as *crib death*. (188)

superego In Freud's theory, the representation of social values, communicated by parents and other adults. (19, 350)

symbol In Piaget's terminology, a personal mental representation of a sensory experience. (313)

symbolic function Ability, described by Piaget, to use mental representation, shown in language, symbolic play, and deferred imitation. (313)

symbolic play Play in which an object stands for something else. (314)

syntax Way in which words are organized into phrases and sentences. (437)

systematic desensitization Gradual exposure to a feared object for the purpose of overcoming the fear. (365)

System of Multicultural Pluralistic Assessment (SOMPA) Battery of measures designed to take environmental factors into account in assessing intelligence. (435)

tabula rasa Philosophical metaphor implying that at birth a baby is a blank slate with no inborn predispositions, a position espoused by John Locke. (73)

telegraphic speech Children's speech with an average of three morphemes per utterance, conveying a complete idea but not including extra ideas or using complex grammar. (224)

temperament Person's style of approaching other people and situations. (252)

teratogenic Capable of causing birth defects. (102)

tertiary circular reaction Deliberate varying of actions to see what will happen. (211)

testosterone Male sex hormone. (355)

theory Set of related statements about data; the goal of a theory is to integrate data, explain behavior, and predict behavior. (18)

tic Involuntary, repetitive muscular movement; also called *stereotyped movement disorder*. (405)

Torrance Tests of Creative Thinking Test battery developed for use with schoolchildren that measures creativity with words, pictures, and sounds and words. (450)

trait Hereditary characteristic such as shortness or tallness. (61)

transduction In Piaget's terminology, a child's method of thinking about two or more experiences without relying on abstract logic. (318)

transitional object Object—commonly a soft, cuddly one—used repeatedly by a child as a bedtime companion. (297)

transverse position Misalignment of a fetus that causes it to lie crosswise in the uterus. (131)

treatment In an experiment, a controlled form of manipulation; a treatment is the cause of any effects observed during the experiment. (37)

trimester First, second, or third 3-month period of pregnancy. (98)

Type A Personality type which includes traits such as aggressiveness, impatience, anger, hostility, and competitiveness and when present in adults is correlated with coronary disease. (405)

Type B Personality type that is easy-going and relaxed. (406)

ultrasound Medical procedure using high-frequency sound waves to detect the outlines of a fetus and determine whether the pregnancy is progressing normally. (72)

unconditioned response (UCR) In classical conditioning, an automatic, unlearned response to an unconditioned stimulus; also called an *unconditioned reflex*. (24, 197–198)

unconditioned stimulus (UCS) In classical conditioning, a stimulus that automatically elicits an unlearned response. (24, 197–198)

uterus Organ of gestation where the fertilized ovum develops until ready for birth; the womb. (57)

validity Extent to which a test measures what it is designed to measure. (203)

vernix caseosa Oily substance on a neonate's body that dries within a few days after birth. (145)

visible imitation Imitation of an action with a part of the body, such as the hands or feet, that can be seen by oneself. (213)

visual cliff Apparatus for testing depth perception. (171)

visual-recognition memory Remembrance of a visual stimulus. (216)

Wechsler Intelligence Scale for Children (WISC-R) Individual intelligence test for children that includes verbal and performance subtests. (431)

Wechsler Preschool and Primary Scale of Intelligence (WPPSI) Individual intelligence test for use with preschool children that includes separate verbal and performance subtests. (326)

weight conservation Understanding that an object will continue to weigh the same if nothing is added to it or taken away from it, even though its appearance may change. (215)

zygote Single cell formed through fertilization. (56)

BIBLIOGRAPHY

Abbott, D. A., & Brody, G. H. (1985). The relation of child age, gender and number of children to the marital adjustment of wives. *Journal of Marriage and the Family, 47*(1), 77–84.

Abramovitch, R., Corter, C., & Lando, B. (1979). Sibling interaction in the home. *Child Development, 50,* 997–1003.

Abramovitch, R., Corter, C., & Pepler, D. (1980). Observations of mixed-sex sibling dyads. *Child Development, 51,* 1268–1271.

Abramovitch, R., Corter, C., Pepler, D. J., & Stanhope, L. (1986). Sibling and peer interaction: A final follow-up and a comparison. *Child Development, 57,* 217–229.

Abramovitch, R., Pepler, D., & Corter, C. (1982). Patterns of sibling interaction among preschool-age children. In M. E. Lamb (Ed.), *Sibling relationships: Their nature and significance across the lifespan.* Hillsdale, NJ: Erlbaum.

Abrams, B., & Viederman, M. (1988, Spring). Pregnancy and childbirth: Normal and abnormal reactions. *Outlook* [Newsletter of the Department of Psychiatry, New York Hospital–Cornell Medical Center], p. 7.

Abravanel, E., & Sigafoos, A. D. (1984). Exploring the presence of imitation during early infancy. *Child Development, 55,* 381–392.

Abroms, K., & Bennett, J. (1979). *Paternal contributions to Down's syndrome dispel maternal myths.* ERIC.

Abroms, K. I., & Bennett, J. W. (1981). Changing etiological perspectives in Down's syndrome: Implications for early intervention. *Journal of the Division for Early Childhood, 2,* 109–112.

Abt Associates. (1978). *Children at the Center: Vol. 1. Summary findings and policy implications of the National Day Care Study.* Washington, DC: U.S. Department of Health, Education, and Welfare.

Acredolo, L., & Goodwyn, S. (1988). Symbolic gesturing in normal infants. *Child Development, 59,* 450–466.

Action for Children's Television. (undated). *Treat TV with T.L.C.* One-page flyer. Newtonville, MA: Author.

Adler, A. (1928). *Understanding human nature.* London: Allen & Unwin.

Ainsworth, M. D. S. (1969). Object relations, dependency, and attachment: A theoretical review of the infant-mother relationship. *Child Development, 40,* 969–1025.

Ainsworth, M. D. S. (1979). Infant-mother attachment. *American Psychologist, 34*(10), 932–937

Ainsworth, M. D. S. (1982). Attachment: Retrospect and prospect. In C. M. Parkes & J. Stevenson-Hinde (Eds.), *The place of attachment in human behavior*. New York: Basic Books.

Ainsworth, M. D. S., & Bell, S. (1970). Attachment, exploration, and separation: Illustration by the behavior of one-year-olds in a strange situation. *Child Development, 41*, 49–67.

Ainsworth, M. D. S., & Bell, S. (1977). Infant crying and maternal responsiveness: A rejoinder to Gewirtz and Boyd. *Child Development, 48*, 1208–1216.

Ainsworth, M. D. S., Blehar, M. C., Waters, E., & Wall, S. (1978). *Patterns of attachment: A psychological study of the strange situation*. Hillsdale, NJ: Erlbaum.

Alan Guttmacher Institute. (1981). *Teenage pregnancy: The problem that hasn't gone away*. New York: Viking.

Alemi, B., Hamosh, M., Scanlon, J. W., Salzman-Mann, C., & Hamosh, P. (1981). Fat digestion in very low-birth-weight infants: Effects of addition of human milk to low-birth-weight formula. *Pediatrics, 68*(4), 484–489.

Alford, B., & Boyle, M. (1982). *Nutrition during the life-cycle*. Englewood Cliffs, NJ: Prentice-Hall.

Allore, R., O'Hanlon, D., Price, R., Neilson, K., Willard, H. F., Cox, D. R., Marks, A., & Dun, R. J. (1988). Gene encoding the B subunit of S100 protein is on chromosone 21: Implications for Down syndrome. *Science, 239*, 1311–1313.

Almy, M., Chittenden, E., & Miller, P. (1966). *Young children's thinking: Some aspects of Piaget's theory*. New York: Teachers College Press.

Altemeir, W. A., O'Connor, S. M., Sherrod, K. B., & Vietze, P. M. (1985). Prospective study of antecedents for nonorganic failure to thrive. *Journal of Pediatrics, 106*, 360–365.

Altman, L. K. (1988a, June 5). Pregnant women's use of VDT's is scrutinized. *The New York Times*, p. 22.

Altman, L. K. (1988b, May 27). U.S. orders curbs on drug linked to birth defects. *The New York Times*, pp. Al, D19.

Alvarez, W. F. (1985). The meaning of maternal employment for mothers and their perceptions of their three-year-old children. *Child Development, 56*, 350–360.

Amabile, T. M. (1983). *The social psychology of creativity*. New York: Springer-Verlag.

American Academy of Pediatrics. (1989, March 6). AAP releases circumcision statement. News release.

American Academy of Pediatrics. (1973). The ten-state nutrition survey: A pediatric perspective. *Pediatrics, 51*(6), 1095–1099.

American Academy of Pediatrics. (1978a). Breast–feeding, a commentary in celebration of the International Year of the Child. *Pediatrics, 62*, 591–601.

American Academy of Pediatrics. (1978b). Juice in ready-to-use bottles and nursing bottle caries. *News & Comment, 29*, 1.

American Academy of Pediatrics. (1982). The promotion of breast-feeding. *Pediatrics, 69*, 654–661.

American Academy of Pediatrics. (1983). Growth hormone treatment of children with short stature. *Pediatrics, 72*(6), 891–894.

American Academy of Pediatrics. (1985, September 11). *Getting your child fit*. Elk Grove Village, IL: Author.

American Academy of Pediatrics. (1986a). *Day care facts and figures*. Elk Grove Village, IL: Author.

American Academy of Pediatrics. (1986b). *How to be your child's TV guide: Guidelines for constructive viewing*. Elk Grove Village, IL: Author.

American Academy of Pediatrics. (1986c). *Positive approaches to day care dilemmas: How to make it work*. Elk Grove Village, IL: Author.

American Academy of Pediatrics Committee on Adolescence. (1980). Teenage suicide. *Pediatrics, 66*(1), 144–146.

American Academy of Pediatrics Committee on Adolescence. (1986). Sexuality, contraception, and the media. *Pediatrics, 78*(3), 535–536.

American Academy of Pediatrics Committee on Adolescence. (1987a). Alcohol use and abuse: A pediatric concern. *Pediatrics, 79*(3), 450–453.

American Academy of Pediatrics Committee on Adolescence. (1987b). Tobacco use by children and adolescents. *Pediatrics, 79*(3), 479–481.

American Academy of Pediatrics Committee on Adolescence. (1988). Suicide and suicide attempts in adolescents and young adults. *Pediatrics, 81*(2), 322–324.

American Academy of Pediatrics Committee on Drugs. (1978). Effects of medication during labor and delivery on infant outcome. *Pediatrics, 62*(3), 402–403.

American Academy of Pediatrics Committee on Drugs. (1980). Marijuana. *Pediatrics, 65*(3), 652–656.

American Academy of Pediatrics Committee on Drugs. (1982). Psychotropic drugs in pregnancy and lactation. *Pediatrics, 69*(2), 241–243.

American Academy of Pediatrics Committee on Fetus and Newborn. (1986). Use and abuse of the Apgar score. *Pediatrics, 78*(6), 1148–1149.

American Academy of Pediatrics Committee on Fetus and Newborn. (1987). Neonatal anesthesia. *Pediatrics, 80*(3), 446.

American Academy of Pediatrics Committee on Nutrition. (1981). Nutritional aspects of obesity in infancy and childhood. *Pediatrics, 68*(6), 880–883.

American Academy of Pediatrics Committee on Nutrition. (1983). Toward a prudent diet for children. *Pediatrics, 71*(1), 78–80.

American Academy of Pediatrics Committee on Nutrition. (1986). Prudent life-style for children: Dietary fat and cholesterol. *Pediatrics, 78*(3), 521–525.

American Academy of Pediatrics Committee on Pediatric Aspects of Physical Fitness, Recreation, and Sports. (1981). Competitive athletics for children of elementary school age. *Pediatrics, 67*(6).

American Academy of Pediatrics Task Force on Blood Pressure Control in Children. (1987). Report of the second task force on blood pressure control in children. *Pediatrics, 79*(1), 1–25.

American Academy of Pediatrics Task Force on Infant Mortality. (1986). Statement on infant mortality. *Pediatrics, 78*(6), 1155–1160.

American Cancer Society. (1985). *1985 cancer facts and figures*. Pamphlet. Washington, DC: Author.

American Cancer Society. (1988). Cancer Statistics, 1988. *Cancer Journal of Clinicians, 38*(1), 21.

American Foundation for the Prevention of Venereal Disease, Inc. (1986). *Sexually transmitted disease [venereal disease]: Prevention for everyone* (13th rev. ed.). New York: Author.

American Heritage dictionary of the English language. (1971). Boston: Houghton Mifflin.

American Humane Society. (1987). Child abuse statistics. Denver: Author.

American Psychological Association. (1985, February 22). *Psychologists warn of potential dangers in TV violence*. Position statement. Washington, DC: Author.

Anand, K. J. S., & Hickey, P. R. (1987). Pain and its effect in the human neonate and fetus. *New England Journal of Medicine, 317*(21), 1321–1329.

Anastasi, A. (1958). Heredity, environment, and the question "How?" *Psychological Review, 65*, 197–208.

Anastasi, A. (1976). *Psychological testing* (4th ed.). New York: Macmillan.

Anastasi, A. (1988). *Psychological testing* (6th ed.). New York: Macmillan.

Anastasi, A., & Schaefer, C. E. (1971). Note on concepts of creativity and intelligence. *Journal of Creative Behavior, 3*, 113–116.

Anders, T., Caraskadon, M., & Dement, W. (1980). Sleep and sleepiness in children and adolescents. In I. Litt (Ed.), Adolescent medicine. *Pediatric Clinics of North America, 27*(1), 29–44.

Anderson, J. N. (1972). Attachment behavior out of doors. In N. Blurton Jones (Ed.), *Ethological studies of child behavior*. London: Cambridge University Press.

Andrews, S. R., Blumenthal, J. B., Johnson, D. L., Kahn, A. J., Ferguson, C. J., Lasater, T. M., Malone, P. C., Wallace, D. B. (1982). The skills of mothering: A study of Parent Child Development Centers. *Monographs of the Society for Research in Child Development, 47*(6, Serial No. 198).

Angier, N. (1982, March). Helping children reach new heights. *Discover,* pp. 35–40.

Annas, G. J. (1987). Protecting the liberty of pregnant patients. *New England Journal of Medicine, 316*(19), 1213–1214.

Anthony, E. J., & Koupernik, C. (Eds.). (1974). *The child in his family: Children at psychiatric risk* (Vol. 3). New York: Wiley.

Apgar, V. (1953). A proposal for a new method of evaluation of the newborn infant. *Current Researches in Anesthesia and Analgesia, 32*, 260–267.

Arend, R., Gove, R., & Sroufe, L. A. (1979). Continuity of individual adaptation from infancy to kindergarten: A predictive study of ego-resiliency and curiosity in preschoolers. *Child Development, 50*, 950–959.

Aries, P. (1962). *Centuries of childhood.* New York: Vintage.

Arnon, S., Midura, T., Damus, K., Wood, R., & Chin, J. (1978, June 17). Intestinal infection and toxin production by *Clostridium botulinum* as one cause of SIDS. *The Lancet,* pp. 1273–1276.

Aronson, E., & Bridgeman, D. (1979). Jig-saw groups and the desegregated classroom: In pursuit of common goals. *Personality and Social Psychology Bulletin, 5*, 438–446.

Aronson, E., Stephan, C., Sikes, J., Blaney, N., & Snapp, M. (1978). *The jigsaw classroom.* Beverly Hills, CA: Sage.

Asberg, M., Traskman, L., & Thoren, P. (1976). 5-HIAA in the cerebrospinal fluid: A biochemical suicide predictor? *Archives of General Psychiatry, 33*, 1194–1197.

Ash, P., Vennart, J., & Carter, C. (1977, April). The incidence of hereditary disease in man. *The Lancet,* pp. 849–851.

Asher, J. (1987). Born to be shy? *Psychology Today, 21*(4), 56–64.

Asher, S. (1978). Children's peer relations. In M. Lamb (Ed.), *Social and personality development* (pp. 91–113). New York: Holt.

Asher, S., Hymel, S., & Renshaw, P. D. (1984). Loneliness in children. *Child Development, 55*, 1456–1464.

Asher, S., Renshaw, P., Geraci, K., & Dor, A. (1979, March). Peer acceptance and social skill training: The selection of program content. Paper presented at the meeting of the Society for Research in Child Development, San Francisco.

Aslin, R. N., Pisoni, D. B., & Jusczyk, P. W. (1983). Auditory development and speech perception in infancy. In P. H. Mussen (Ed.), *Handbook of child psychology* (4th ed.) (pp. 573–687). New York: Wiley.

Associated Press. (1987, November 30). Infant survives on chips when family dies. *The New York Times,* p. A16.

Atkinson, R. C., & Shiffrin, R. M. (1968). Human memory: A proposed system and its control processes. In K. W. Spence & J. T. Spence (Eds.), *The psychology of learning and motivation: Advances in research and theory* (Vol. 2). New York: Academic.

Atkinson, R. C., & Shiffrin, R. M. (1971). The control of short-term memory. *Scientific American, 225*, 82–90.

Azrin, N., & Foxx, R. M. (1981). *Toilet training in less than a day.* New York: Pocket Books.

Babson, S. G., & Clarke, N. G. (1983). Relationship between infant death and maternal age. *Journal of Pediatrics, 103*(3), 391–393.

Baillargeon, R. (1987). Object permanence in 3½ and 4½-month-old infants. *Developmental Psychology, 23*(5), 655–670.

Baird, P. A., & Sadovnick, A. D. (1987). Life expectancy in Down syndrome. *Journal of Pediatrics, 110,* 849–854.

Baird, D. D., & Wilcox, A. J. (1985). Cigarette smoking associated with delayed contraception. *Journal of the American Medical Association, 253,* 2979–2983.

Bakwin, H. (1970, August 29). Sleepwalking in twins. *The Lancet,* pp. 446–447.

Bakwin, H. (1971a). Car-sickness in twins. *Developmental Medicine and Child Neurology, 13,* 310–312.

Bakwin, H. (1971b). Constipation in twins. *American Journal of Diseases of Children, 121,* 179–181.

Bakwin, H. (1971c). Enuresis in twins. *American Journal of Diseases of Children, 121,* 222–225.

Bakwin, H. (1971d). Nail-biting in twins. *Developmental Medicine and Child Neurology, 13,* 304–307.

Baldwin, W., & Cain, V. S. (1980). The children of teenage parents. *Family Planning Perspectives, 12,* 34.

Baltes, P. B., Reese, H. W., & Lipsitt, L. (1980). Life-span developmental psychology. *Annual Review of Psychology, 31,* 65–110.

Bandura, A. (1960). *Relationship of family patterns to child behavior disorders* (Progress report, USPHS, Project No. M-1734). Stanford, CA: Stanford University.

Bandura, A., Grusec, J. E., & Menlove, F. L. (1967). Vicarious extinction of avoidance behavior. *Journal of Personality and Social Psychology, 5,* 16–23.

Bandura, A., & Huston, A. (1961). Identification as a process of incidental learning. *Journal of Abnormal and Social Psychology, 63*(12), 311–318.

Bandura, A., Ross, D., & Ross, S. A. (1961). Transmission of aggression through imitation of aggressive models. *Journal of Abnormal and Social Psychology, 63,* 575–582.

Bandura, A., Ross, D., & Ross, S. A. (1963). Imitation of film-mediated aggressive models. *Journal of Abnormal and Social Psychology, 66*(1), 3–11.

Bane, M. J. (1980). A profile of the family in the 1980's. In *Focus on the family: New images of parents and children in the 1980's.* Boston: Wheelock College Center for Parenting Studies.

Barker, P. (1979). *Basic child psychiatry* (3d ed.). Baltimore: University Park Press.

Barnes, A., Colton, T., Gunderson, J., Noller, K., Tilley, B., Strama, T., Townsend, D., Hatab, P., & O'Brien, P. (1980). Fertility and outcome of pregnancy in women exposed in utero to diethylstilbestrol. *New England Journal of Medicine, 302*(11), 609–613.

Barnes, K. E. (1971). Preschool play norms: A replication. *Developmental Psychology, 5*(1), 99–103.

Barr, H. M., Streissguth, A. P., Martin, D. C., & Herman, C. S. (1984). Infant size at 8 months of age: Relationship to maternal use of alcohol, nicotine, and caffeine during pregnancy. *Pediatrics, 74*(3), 336–341.

Barrett, D. E., Radke-Yarrow, M., & Klein, R. E. (1982). Chronic malnutrition and child behavior: Effects of early caloric supplementation on social and emotional functioning at school age. *Developmental Psychology, 18*, 541–556.

Baruch, G., Barnett, R., & Rivers, C. (1983). *Lifeprints.* New York: McGraw-Hill.

Baruch, G. K., & Barnett, R. C. (1986). Fathers' participation in family work and children's sex role attitudes. *Child Development, 57*, 1210–1223.

Bass, M., Kravath, R. E., & Glass, L. (1986). Death-scene investigation in sudden infant death. *New England Journal of Medicine, 315*, 100–105.

Bassuk, E., & Rubin, L. (1987). Homeless children: A neglected population. *American Journal of Orthopsychiatry, 57*(2), 279–286.

Battelle, P. (1981, February). The triplets who found each other. *Good Housekeeping*, pp. 74–83.

Bauer, D. (1976). An exploratory study of developmental changes in children's fears. *Journal of Child Psychology and Psychiatry, 17*, 69–74.

Baughman, E. E. (1971). *Black Americans.* New York: Academic.

Baumrind, D. (1968). Authoritarian vs. authoritative control. *Adolescence, 3*, 255–272.

Baumrind, D. (1971). Harmonious parents and their preschool children. *Developmental Psychology, 41*(1), 92–102.

Baumrind, D. (1977). Some thoughts about childrearing. In S. Cohen & T. Comiskey (Eds.), *Child development: Contemporary perspectives.* Itasca, IL: Peacock.

Baumrind, D., & Black, A. E. (1967). Socialization practices associated with dimensions of competence in preschool boys and girls. *Child Development, 38*(2), 291–327.

Bayer, A. E. (1967). Birth order and attainment of the doctorate: A test of an economic hypothesis. *American Journal of Sociology, 72*, 540–550.

Bayley, N. (1949). Consistency and variability in the growth of intelligence from birth to 18 years. *Journal of Genetic Psychology, 75*, 165–196.

Bayley, N. (1965). Research in child development: A longitudinal perspective. *Merrill-Palmer Quarterly of Behavior and Development, 11*, 184–190.

Bayley, N. (1969). *Bayley scales of infant development.* New York: Psychological Corporation.

Beautrais, A. L., Fergusson, D. M., & Shannon, F. T. (1982). Life events

and childhood morbidity: A prospective study. *Pediatrics, 70*(6), 935–940.

Becker, B. J. (1983). *Item characteristics and sex differences on the SAT-M for mathematically able youths.* Paper presented at the annual meeting of the American Educational Research Association, Montreal.

Becker, R. F., King, J. E., & Little, C. R. D. (1968). Experimental studies in nicotine absorption during pregnancy: 4. The postmature neonate. *American Journal of Obstetrics and Gynecology, 101*, 1109–1119.

Behrman, R. E. (1985). Preventing low birth weight: A pediatric perspective. *Journal of Pediatrics, 107*(6), 842–854.

Behrman, R. E., & Vaughan, V. C. (Eds.). (1983). *Nelson textbook of pediatrics* (12th ed.). Philadelphia: Saunders.

Beit-Hallahmi, B., & Rabin, A. I. (1977). The kibbutz as a social experiment and as a child-rearing laboratory. *American Psychologist, 32*, 532–541.

Bell, A. P., Weinberg, M. S., & Hammersmith, S. K. (1981). *Sexual preference: Its development in men and women.* Bloomington: Indiana University Press.

Bell, G. D. (1963). Processes in the formation of adolescents' aspirations. *Social Forces, 42*, 179–195.

Bell, R. R. (1981). Friendships of women and men. *Psychology of Women Quarterly, 5*(3), 402–417.

Bell, S., & Ainsworth, M. D. S. (1972). Infant crying and maternal responsiveness. *Child Development, 43*, 1171–1190.

Bellinger, D., Leviton, A., Waternaux, C., Needleman, H., & Rabinowitz, M. (1987). Longitudinal analysis of prenatal and postnatal lead exposure and early cognitive development. *New England Journal of Medicine, 316*(17), 1037–1043.

Belmont, L. (1977). Birth order, intellectual competence and psychiatric status. *Journal of Individual Psychology, 33*, 97–103.

Belmont, L., & Marolla, A. F. (1973). Birth order, family size, and intelligence. *Science, 182*, 1096–1101.

Belsky, J. (1979). Mother-father-infant interaction: A naturalistic observational study. *Developmental Psychology, 15*, 601–607.

Belsky, J. (1980). A family analysis of parental influence on infant exploratory competence. In F. A. Pederson (Ed.), *The father-infant relationship: Observational studies in a family setting.* New York: Praeger.

Belsky, J. (1984). Two waves of day care research: Developmental effects

and conditions of quality. In R. Ainslie (Ed.), *The child and the day care setting.* New York: Praeger.

Belsky, J. (1985). Exploring individual differences in marital change across the transition to parenthood: The role of violated expectations. *Journal of Marriage and the Family, 47*(4), 1037–1044.

Belsky, J., Lang, M. E., & Rovine, M. (1985). Stability and change in marriage across the transition to parenthood: A second study. *Journal of Marriage and the Family, 47*(4), 855–865.

Belsky, J., & Rovine, M. J. (1988). Non-maternal care in the first year of life and the security of infant-parent attachment. *Child Development, 59*, 157–167.

Belsky, J., Spanier, G. B., & Rovine, M. (1983). Stability and change in marriage across the transition to parenthood. *Journal of Marriage and the Family, 45*(3), 567–577.

Beltramini, A. U., & Hertzig, M. E. (1983). Sleep and bedtime behavior in preschool-aged children. *Pediatrics, 71*(2), 153–158.

Bem, S. L. (1974). The measurement of psychological adrogyny. *Journal of Consulting and Clinical Psychology, 42*, 155–162.

Bem, S. L. (1976). Probing the promise of androgyny. In A. G. Kaplan & J. P. Bean (Eds.), *Beyond sex-role stereotypes: Readings toward a psychology of androgyny.* Boston: Little, Brown.

Bem, S. L. (1983). Gender schema theory and its implications for child development: Raising gender-aschematic children in a gender-schematic society. *Signs, 8*, 598–616.

Bem, S. L. (1985). Androgyny and gender schema theory: A conceptual and empirical integration. In T. B. Sonderegger (Ed.), *Nebraska Symposium on Motivation, 1984. Psychology and gender.* Lincoln: University of Nebraska Press.

Benacerraf, B. R., Gelman, R., & Frigoletto, F. D. (1987). Sonographic identification of second-trimester fetuses with Down's syndrome. *New England Journal of Medicine, 317*, 1371–1376.

Benn, R. K. (1986). Factors promoting secure attachment relationships between employed mothers and their sons. *Child Development, 57*, 1224–1231.

Bennett, F. C., Robinson, N. M., & Sells, C. J. (1983). Growth and development of infants weighing less than 800 grams at birth. *Pediatrics, 71*(3), 319–323.

Benson, J. B., & Uzgiris, I. C. (1985).

Effect of self-inflicted locomotion on infant search activity. *Developmental Psychology, 21*(6), 923–931.

Berenda, R. W. (1950). *The influence of the group on the judgments of children.* New York: King's Crown.

Bergman, A. B., Larsen, R. M., & Mueller, B. A. (1986). Changing spectrum of serious child abuse. *Pediatrics, 77*(1), 113–116.

Berk, L. E. (1986). Private speech: Learning out loud. *Psychology Today, 20*(5), 34–42.

Berk, L. E., & Garvin, R. A. (1984). Development of private speech among low-income Appalachian children. *Developmental Psychology, 20*(2), 271–286.

Berman, P. W., & Goodman, V. (1984). Age and sex differences in children's responses to babies: Effects of adult caretaking requests and instructions. *Child Development, 55,* 1071–1077.

Berman, S. M., MacKay, H. T., Grimes, D. A., & Binkin, N. J. (1985). Deaths from spontaneous abortion in the United States. *Journal of the American Medical Association, 253,* 3119–3123.

Bernard, J., & Sontag, L. W. (1947). Fetal reactivity to sound. *Journal of Genetic Psychology, 70,* 205–210.

Bernbaum, J. C., Pereira, G., Watkins, J. B., & Peckham, G. J. (1983). Nonnutritive sucking during gavage feeding enhances growth and maturation in premature infants. *Pediatrics, 71*(1), 41–45.

Berndt, T. J. (1982). The features and effects of friendship in early adolescence. *Child Development, 53* 1447–1460.

Bernstein, A. C., & Cowen, P. (1977). Children's concepts of how people get babies. In E. M. Hetherington & R. D. Park (Eds.), *Contemporary readings in child psychology.* New York: McGraw-Hill.

Bernstein, G. A., & Garfinkel, B. D. (1988). Pedigrees, functioning, and psychopathology in families of school phobic children. *American Journal of Psychiatry, 145,* 70–74.

Berscheid, E., Walster, E., & Bohrnstedt, G. (1973). The happy American body: A survey report. *Psychology Today, 7*(6), 119–131.

Bertenthal, B. I., & Campos, J. J. (1987). New directions in the study of early experience. *Child Development, 58,* 560–567.

Bertenthal, B. I., Campos, J. J., & Barrett, K. C. (1984). Self-produced locomotion: An organizer of emotional, cognitive, and social development in infancy. In R. N. Emde & R. J. Harmon (Eds.), *Continuities and disconti-*

nuities in development. New York: Plenum.

Bettelheim, B. (1987). *A good enough parent.* New York: Knopf.

Bickerton, D. (1981). *Roots of language.* Ann Arbor, MI: Karama.

Bierman, K. L., & Furman, W. (1984). The effects of social skills training and peer involvement on the social adjustment of preadolescents. *Child Development, 55,* 151–162.

Biller, H. B. (1981). The father and sex role development. In M. E. Lamb (Ed.), *The role of the father in child development.* New York: Wiley.

Biller, H. B., & Bahm, R. (1971). Father absences, perceived maternal behavior, and masculinity of self-concept among junior high school boys. *Developmental Psychology, 4,*178–181.

Bingol, N., Fuchs, M., Diaz, V., Stone, R. K., & Gromisch, D. S. (1987). Teratogenicity of cocaine in humans. *Journal of Pediatrics, 10,* 93–96.

Birnholz, J. C., & Benacerraf, B. R. (1983). The development of human fetal hearing. *Science, 222,* 516–518.

Birns, B. (1976). The emergence and socialization of sex differences in the earliest years. *Merrill-Palmer Quarterly, 22,* 229–254.

Bitman, J., Wood, D. L., Hamosh, M., Hamosh, P., & Mehta, N. R. (1983). Comparison of the lipid composition of breast milk from mothers of term and preterm infants. *American Journal of Clinical Nutrition, 38,* 300–312.

Black, J. K. (1981, September). Are young children really egocentric? *Young Children,* pp. 51–55.

Blakeslee, S. (1984, November 11). Brain studies shed light on disorders. *The New York Times,* Sec. 12, p. 45.

Blakeslee, S. (1986, October 7). Fetus returned to the womb following surgery. *The New York Times,* p. C1.

Blank, M., & Solomon, F. (1968). A tutorial language program to develop abstract thinking in socially disadvantaged preschool children. *Child Development, 39,* 379–389.

Blauvelt, H. (1955). Dynamics of the mother-newborn relationship in goats. In B. Schaffner (Ed.), *Group processes.* New York: Macy Foundation.

Blechman, E. A., McEnroe, M. J., Carella, E. T., & Audette, D. P. (1986). Childhood competence and depression. *Journal of Abnormal Psychiatry, 95*(3), 223–227.

Block, J. H. (1978). Another look at sex differentiation in the socialization behaviors of mothers and fathers. In F. Wenmark & J. Sherman (Eds.), *Psychology of women: Future direction of re-*

search. New York: Psychological Dimensions.

Bloom, B. S. (1985). *Developing talent in young people.* New York: Ballantine.

Bloom, B. S., & Sosniak, L. A. (1981, November). Talent development vs. schooling. *Educational Leadership.*

Blue Cross and Blue Shield Association (BCBSA). (1988). *No-nonsense AIDS answers.* Chicago: Author.

Blum, R. (1987). Contemporary threats to adolescent health in the United States. *Journal of the American Medical Association, 257*(24), 3390–3395.

Blumstein, P., & Schwartz, P. (1983). *American couples: Money, work, sex.* New York: Morrow.

Blyth, D. A., et al. (1981). The effects of physical development on self-image and satisfaction with body-image for early adolescent males. In R. G. Simmons (Ed.), *Research on community and mental health* (Vol. 2). Greenwich, CT: JAI.

Blyth, D. A., Simmons, R. G., & Carlton-Ford, S. (1983). The adjustment of early adolescents to school transitions. *Journal of Early Adolescence, 3*(1–2), 105–120.

Bogatz, G., & Ball, S. (1971). *The second year of Sesame Street: A continuing evaluation.* Princeton, NJ: Educational Testing Service.

Bolles, E. B. (1982). *So much to say.* New York: St. Martin's.

Bolles, E. B. (1984). *The Penguin adoption handbook.* New York: Viking.

Bonney, M. E. (1946). A sociometric study of the relationship of some factors to mutual friendships on the elementary, secondary, and college levels. *Sociometry, 9,* 21–47.

Bornstein, M. H. (1985a). Habituation of attention as a measure of visual information processing in human infants. In G. Gottlieb & N. A. Krasnegor (Eds.), *Development of audition and vision in the first year of postnatal life: A methodological overview.* Norwood, NJ: Ablex.

Bornstein, M. H. (1985b). How infant and mother jointly contribute to developing cognitive competence in the child. *Proceedings of the National Academy of Science, 82,* 7470–7473.

Bornstein, M. H., & Sigman, M. D. (1986). Continuity in mental development from infancy. *Child Development, 57,* 251–274.

Bornstein, M., Kessen, W., & Weiskopf, S. (1976). The categories of hue in infancy. *Science, 191,* 201–202.

Boston Children's Medical Center. (1972). *Pregnancy, birth, and the newborn baby.* New York: Delacorte.

Boston Women's Health Book Collective. (1976). *Our bodies, ourselves.* New York: Simon & Schuster.

Boswell, D., & Williams, J. (1975). Correlates of race and color bias among preschool children. *Psychological Reports, 36,* 147–154.

Bower, B. (1985). The left hand of math and verbal talent. *Science News, 127*(17), 263.

Bower, T. G. R. (1976). Repetitive processes in child development. *Scientific American, 235*(5), 38–47.

Bowlby, J. (1951). *Maternal care and mental health.* Geneva: World Health Organization.

Bowlby, J. (1958). The nature of the child's tie to his mother. *International Journal of Psychoanalysis, 39,* 1–23.

Bowlby, J. (1960). Separation anxiety. *International Journal of Psychoanalysis, 41,* 89–113.

Bowman, J. A., Sanson-Fisher, R. W., & Webb, G. R. (1987). Interventions in preschools to increase the use of safety restraints by preschool children. *Pediatrics, 79*(1), 103–109.

Brackbill, Y., & Broman, S. H. (1979). *Obstetrical medication and development in the first year of life.* Unpublished manuscript.

Bracken, M., Holford, T., White, C., & Kelsey, J. (1978). Role of oral contraception in congenital malformations of offspring. *International Journal of Epidemiology, 7*(4), 309–317.

Bradley, R., & Caldwell, B. (1976). Early home environment and changes in mental test performance in children from 6 to 36 months. *Developmental Psychology, 12*(2), 93–97.

Brand, D. (1987, August 31). The new whiz kids. *Time,* pp. 42–51.

Brandt, E. N. (1982). The health consequences of smoking—A report of the surgeon general (Report to Congress from the U.S. Department of Health and Human Services).

Brazelton, T. B. (1973). *Neonatal behavioral assessment scale.* Philadelphia: Lippincott.

Brecher, E., & the Editors of *Consumer Reports.* (1972). *Licit and illicit drugs.* Mount Vernon, NY: Consumers Union.

Breslau, N., Weitzman, M., & Messenger, K. (1981). Psychological functioning of siblings of disabled children. *Pediatrics, 67*(3), 344–353.

Brewster, A. B. (1982). Chronically ill hospitalized children's concepts of their illness. *Pediatrics, 69,* 355–362.

Bridges, K. M. B. (1932). Emotional development in early infancy. *Child Development, 3,* 324–341.

Bringuier, J.-C. (1980). *Conversations with Jean Piaget* (B. M. Gulati, Trans.). Chicago: University of Chicago Press.

Brittain, C. (1963). Adolescent choices and parent-peer cross-pressures. *American Sociological Review, 28,* 385–391.

Brodbeck, A. J., & Irwin, O. C. (1946). The speech behavior of infants without families. *Child Development, 17,* 145–156.

Brody, E. B., & Brody, N. (1976). *Intelligence.* New York: Academic.

Brody, J. E. (1981, March 10). Sperm found especially vulnerable to environment. *The New York Times,* pp. C1 ff.

Brody, J. E. (1973, March 18). Most pregnant women found taking excess drugs. *The New York Times.*

Brody, L. R., Zelazo, P. R., & Chaika, H. (1984). Habituation-dishabituation to speech in the neonate. *Developmental Psychology, 20,* 114–119.

Bronfenbrenner, U. (1970). *Two worlds of childhood: U.S. and U.S.S.R.* New York: Russell Sage.

Bronfenbrenner, U., Alvarez, W. F., & Henderson, C. R. (1984). Working and watching: Maternal employment status and parents' perception of their three-year-old children. *Child Development, 55,* 1362–1378.

Bronfenbrenner, U., Belsky, J., & Steinberg, L. (1977). *Daycare in context: An ecological perspective on research and public policy* (Review prepared for Office of the Assistant Secretary for Planning and Evaluation, U.S. Department of Health, Education, and Welfare).

Bronfenbrenner, U., & Crouter, A. (1982). Work and family through time and space. In S. B. Kamerman & C. D. Hayes (Eds.), *Families that work: Children in a changing world.* Washington, DC: National Academy.

Bronson, F. H., & Desjardins, C. (1969). Aggressive behavior and seminal vesicle function in mice: Differential sensitivity to androgen given neonatally. *Endocrinology, 85,* 871–975.

Bronstein, P. (1988). Father-child interaction: Implications for gender role socialization. In P. Bronstein & C. P. Cowan (Eds.), *Fatherhood today: Men's changing role in the family.* New York: Wiley.

Brooke, J. (1988, April 26). Technology aids vaccination effort. *The New York Times,* pp. C3.

Brooks, J., & Lewis, M. (1976). Infants' responses to strangers: Midget, adult, child. *Child Development, 47,* 323–332.

Brooks-Gunn, J. (1988). Pubertal processes and the early adolescent transition. In W. Damon (Ed.), *Child devel-*

opment today and tomorrow. San Francisco: Jossey-Bass.

Brooks-Gunn, J., & Furstenberg, F. F. (1986). The children of adolescent mothers: Physical, academic, and psychological outcomes. *Developmental Review, 6,* 224–251.

Brooks-Gunn, J., & Lewis, M. (1984). The development of early visual self-recognition. *Developmental Review, 4,* 215–239.

Brophy, J. E., & Good, T. L. (1973). Feminization of American elementary schools. *Phi Delta Kappan, 54,* 564–566.

Brophy, J. E., & Good, T. L. (1974). *Teacher-student relationships.* New York: Holt.

Brown, B. B., Clasen, D. R., & Eicher, S. A. (1986). Perceptions of peer pressure, peer conformity dispositions, and self-reported behavior among adolescents. *Developmental Psychology, 22*(4), 521–530.

Brown, J., LaRossa, G., Aylward, G., Davis, D., Rutherford, P., & Bakeman, R. (1980). Nursery-based intervention with prematurely born babies and their mothers: Are there effects? *Journal of Pediatrics, 97*(3), 487–491.

Brown, J. D., Childers, K. W., & Waszak, C. S. (1988, June). *Television and adolescent sexuality.* Paper presented at the conference on "Television and Teens: Health Implications," Manhattan Beach, CA.

Brown, J. E. (1983). *Nutrition for your pregnancy.* Minneapolis: University of Minnesota Press.

Brown, J. L. (1987). Hunger in the U.S. *Scientific American, 256*(2), 37–41.

Brown, P., & Elliott, H. (1965). Control of aggression in a nursery school class. *Journal of Experimental Child Psychology, 2,* 103–107.

Brown, R. (1973a). Development of the first language in the human species. *American Psychologist, 28*(2), 97–106.

Brown, R. (1973b). *A first language: The early stages.* Cambridge, MA: Harvard University Press.

Brown, R., Cazden, C. B., & Bellugi, U. (1969). The child's grammar from I to III. In J. P. Hill (Ed.), *Minnesota Symposia on Child Psychology* (Vol. 2). Minneapolis: University of Minnesota Press.

Brown, S. S. (1985). Can low birth weight be prevented? *Family Planning Perspectives, 17*(3), 112–118.

Browne, A., & Finkelhor, D. (1986). Impact of child sexual abuse: A review of the research. *Psychological Bulletin, 99*(1), 66–77.

Brozan, N. (1981, February 2).

Childbirth is eased in a chair. *The New York Times*, p. A16.

Brozan, N. (1982, October 29). Studying how a child grows. *The New York Times*, p. B10.

Bryant, B. K. (1982). Sibling relationships in middle childhood. In M. E. Lamb & B. Sutton-Smith (Eds.), *Sibling relationships: Their nature and significance across the lifespan*. Hillsdale, NJ: Erlbaum.

Bryer, J. B., Nelson, B. A., Miller, J. B., & Krol, P. A. (1987). Childhood sexual and physical abuse as factors in adult psychiatric illness. *American Journal of Psychiatry, 144*(11), 1426–1430.

Buckwald, S., Zorn, W. A., & Egan, E. A. (1984). Mortality and follow-up data for neonates weighing 500 to 800 g at birth. *American Journal of Diseases of Children, 138*, 779–782.

Buie, J. (1987, April 8). Pregnant teenagers: New view of old solution. *Education Week*, p. 32.

Bullen, B. A., Skrinar, I. Z., von Mering, G., Turnbull, B. A., & McArthur, J. W. (1985). Induction of menstrual disorders by strenuous exercise in untrained women. *New England Journal of Medicine, 312*, 1349–1353.

Bumpers, D. (1984). Securing the blessings of liberty for posterity: Preventive health care for children. *American Psychologist, 39*, 896–900.

Burgess, A. W., Hartman, C. R., & McCormack, A. (1987). Abused to abuser: Antecedents of socially deviant behaviors. *American Journal of Psychiatry, 144*(11), 1431–1436.

Burke, B. S., Beal, V. A., Kirkwood, S. B., & Stuart, H. C. (1943). Nutrition studies during pregnancy. *American Journal of Obstetrics and Gynecology, 46*, 38–52.

Bustillo, M., Buster, J. E., Cohen, S. W., Hamilton, F., Thorneycroft, I. H., Simon, J. A., Rodi, I. A., Boyers, S., Marshall, J. R., Louw, J. A., Seed, R., & Seed, R. (1984). Delivery of a healthy infant following nonsurgical ovum transfer. *Journal of the American Medical Association, 251*(7), 889.

Butler, F. (1973, December 16). "Over the garden wall/I let the baby fall." *The New York Times Magazine*, pp. 90–95.

Butterfield, E., & Siperstein, G. (1972). Influence of contingent auditory stimulation upon non-nutritional suckle. In J. Bosma (Ed.), *Oral sensation and perception: The mouth of the infant*. Springfield, IL: Thomas.

Calderone, M. S., & Johnson, E. W. (1981). *The family book about sexuality*. New York: Harper & Row.

California Department of Health, Maternal and Child Health Branch. (1977). *Nutrition during pregnancy and lactation*. Author.

Calvert, S. L., & Huston, A. C. (1987). Television and children's gender schemata. In L. S. Liben & M. L. Signorella (Eds.), *Children's gender schemata*. San Francisco: Jossey-Bass.

Campbell, F. L., Townes, B. D., & Beach, L. R. (1982). Motivational bases of childbearing decisions. In G. L. Fox (Ed.), *The childbearing decision: Fertility, attitudes, and behavior*. Beverly Hills, CA: Sage.

Campos, J., Bertenthal, B., & Benson, N. (1980, April). *Self-produced locomotion and the extraction of form invariance*. Paper presented at the meeting of the International Conference on Infant Studies, New Haven.

Campos, J. J., Langer, A., & Krowitz, A. (1970). Cardiac responses on the visual cliff in prelocomotor human infants. *Science, 170*, 196–197.

Cantor, P. (1977). Suicide and attempted suicide among students: Problem, prediction and prevention. In P. Cantor (Ed.), *Understanding a child's world*. New York: McGraw-Hill.

Capute, A. J., Shapiro, B. K., & Palmer, F. B. (1987). Marking the milestones of language development. *Contemporary Pediatrics, 4*(4), 24.

Card, J. J., & Wise, L. L. (1978). Teenage mothers and teenage fathers: Impact of early childbearing on the parents' personal and professional lives. *Family Planning Perspectives, 10*, 199.

Carlson, B. E. (1984). The father's contribution to child care: Effects on children's perceptions of parental roles. *American Journal of Orthopsychiatry, 54*(1), 123–136.

Carpenter, M. W., Sady, S. P., Hoegsberg, B., Sady, M. A., Haydon, B., Cullinane, E. M., Coustan, D. R., & Thompson, P. D. (1988). Fetal heart rate response to maternal exertion. *Journal of the American Medical Association, 259*(20), 3006–3009.

Carrera, M. A. (1986, April 11). *Future directions in teen pregnancy prevention*. Talk presented to the annual meeting of the Society for the Scientific Study of Sex, Eastern Region.

Carroll, J. L., & Rest, J. R. (1982). Moral development. In B. Wolman (Ed.), *Handbook of developmental psychology*. Englewood Cliffs, NJ: Prentice-Hall.

Carter, D., & Welch, D. (1981). Parenting styles and children's behavior. *Family Relations, 30*, 191–195.

Casey, P. H., Bradley, R., & Wortham, B. (1984). Social and nonsocial home environment of infants with nonorganic failure-to-thrive. *Pediatrics, 73*(3), 348–353.

Casey, R. J., & Berman, J. S. (1985). The outcome of psychotherapy with children. *Psychological Bulletin, 98*(2), 388–400.

Cassell, C. (1984). *Swept away*. New York: Simon & Schuster.

Cassidy, J. (1986). The ability to negotiate the environment: An aspect of infant competence as related to quality of attachment. *Child Development, 57*, 331–337.

Center for Educational Statistics. (1987). *Who drops out of high school? From high school and beyond*. Washington, DC: Office of Educational Research and Improvement, U.S. Department of Education.

Centers for Disease Control. (1983). *CDC Surveillance Summaries* (Vol. 32). Atlanta: Author.

Centers for Disease Control (1986). *Statistical information*. Atlanta: Author.

Chance, P., & Fischman, J. (1987). The magic of childhood. *Psychology Today, 21*(5), 48–58.

Chapman, A. H. (1974). *Management of emotional problems of children and adolescents* (2d ed.). Philadelphia: Lippincott.

Chasnoff, I. J., Burns, W. J., Schnoll, S. H., & Burns, K. A. (1985). Cocaine use in pregnancy. *New England Journal of Medicine, 313*, 666–669.

Chasnoff, I., Hunt, C., Kletter, R., & Kaplan, D. (1986). Increased risk of SIDS and respiratory pattern abnormalities in cocaine-exposed infants. *Pediatric Research, 20*, 425A.

Chasnoff, I. J., Lewis, D. E., & Squires, L. (1987). Cocaine intoxication in a breast-fed infant. *Pediatrics, 80*, 836–838.

Chervenak, F. A., Isaacson, G., & Mahoney, M. J. (1986). Advances in the diagnosis of fetal defects. *New England Journal of Medicine, 315*(5), 305–307.

Chess, S. (1983). Mothers are always the problem—or are they? Old wine in new bottles. *Pediatrics, 71*(6), 974–976.

Chess, S., & Thomas, A. (1982). Infant bonding: Mystique and reality. *American Journal of Orthopsychiatry, 52*(2), 213–222.

Child Care Action News. (1985). 2(1).

Child Welfare League of America. (1986). *Born to run: The status of child abuse in America*. Washington, DC: Author.

Children's Hospital of Pittsburgh. (1987, November). Depression in children. *Kidstuff*, p. 1.

Childs, D. (1983). *The GDR: Moscow's German ally.* London: Allen.

Chilman, C. S. (1980). *Adolescent sexuality in a changing American society: Social and psychological perspectives* (NIH Publication No. 80-1426). Bethesda, MD: U.S. Department of Health, Education, and Welfare, Public Health Service, National Institute of Health.

Chira, S. (1988, July 27). In Japan, the land of the rod, an appeal to spare the child. *The New York Times*, pp. Al, A10.

Chisholm, J. S. (1983). *Navajo infancy: An ethnological study of child development.* New York: Aldine.

Chomsky, C. S. (1969). *The acquisition of syntax in children from five to ten.* Cambridge, MA: Massachusetts Institute of Technology (MIT) Press.

Chomsky, N. (1972). *Language and mind* (2d ed.). New York: Harcourt Brace Jovanovich.

Chown, S. (1972). The effect of flexibility-rigidity and age on adaptability in job performance. *Industrial Gerontology*, *13*, 105–121.

Chumlea, W. C. (1982). Physical growth in adolescence. In B.B. Wolman (Ed.), *Handbook of developmental psychology*. Englewood Cliffs, NJ: Prentice-Hall.

Cicirelli, V. G. (1976a). Family structure and interaction: Sibling effects on socialization. In M. F. McMillan & S. Henao (Eds.), *Child psychiatry: Treatment and research*. New York: Brunner/Mazel.

Clark, R. A., & Gecas, V. (1977). *The employed father in America: A role competition analysis.* Paper presented at the Annual Meeting of the Pacific Sociological Association.

Clarke-Stewart, A. (1977). *Child care in the family: A review of research and some propositions for policy.* New York: Academic.

Clarke-Stewart, A. (1978). And daddy makes three: The father's impact on mother and young child. *Child Development*, *49*, 466–478.

Clausen, J. A. (1978). Adolescent antecedents of cigarette smoking: Data from the Oakland growth study. *Social Science and Medicine*, *1*, 357–382.

Clement, J., Schweinhart, L. J., Barnett, W. S., Epstein, A. S., & Weikart, D. P. (1984). *Changed lives: The effects of the Perry Preschool Program on youths through age 19.* Ypsilanti, MI: High-Scope.

Clifford, E. (1971). Body ratification in adolescence. *Perceptual and Motor Skills*, *33*, 119–125.

Cobrinick, P., Hood, R., & Chused, E. (1959). Effects of maternal narcotic addiction on the newborn infant. *Pediatrics*, *24*, 288–290.

Cohn, V. (1975, November 5). New method of delivering babies cuts down "torture of the innocent." *Capital Times*.

Coie, J. D., & Kupersmidt, J. B. (1983). A behavioral analysis of emerging social status in boys' groups. *Child Development*, *54*, 1400–1416.

Colao, F., & Hosansky, T. (1982). *The key to having fun is being safe.* New York: Safety and Fitness Exchange.

Colby, A., Kohlberg, L., Gibbs, J., & Lieberman, M. (1983). A longitudinal study of moral development. *Monographs of the Society for Research in Child Development*, *48*,(1-2, Serial No. 200).

Cole, C., & Rodman, H. (1987). When school-age children care for themselves: Issues for family life educators and parents. *Family Relations*, *36*, 92–96.

Cole, S. (1980). Send our children to work? *Psychology Today*, *14*(2), 44.

Coles, R., & Stokes, G. (1985). *Sex and the American teenager.* New York: Harper & Row.

Collins, J. A., Wrixon, W., Janes, L. B., & Wilson, E. H. (1983). Treatment-independent pregnancy among infertile couples. *New England Journal of Medicine*, *309*, 1201–1206.

Collins, R. C., & Deloria, D. (1983). Head Start research: A new chapter. *Children Today*, *12*(4), 15–19.

Collins, W. A. (Ed.). (1984). *Development during middle childhood: The years from six to twelve.* Washington, DC: National Academy.

Colman, A., & Colman, L. (1971). *Pregnancy: The psychological experience.* New York: Herder & Herder.

Condon, W., & Sander, L. (1974). Synchrony demonstrated between movements of the neonate and adult speech. *Child Development*, *45*, 456–462.

Condry, J., & Condry, S. (1974). *The development of sex differences: A study of the eye of the beholder.* Unpublished manuscript, Cornell University, Ithaca, NY.

Condry, J. C., Siman, M. L., & Bronfenbrenner, U. (1968). *Characteristics of peer- and adult-oriented children.* Unpublished manuscript, Cornell University, Department of Child Development, Ithaca, NY.

Conger, J. J., & Peterson, A. C. (1984). *Adolescence and youth.* New York: Harper & Row.

Conners, C. K. (1988). Does diet affect behavior and learning in hyperactive children? *Harvard Medical School Mental Health Letter*, *5*(5), 7–8.

Cooke, S. (1979). *A comparison of identity formation in preadolescent girls and boys.* Unpublished master's thesis, Simon Fraser University.

Coons, S., & Guilleminault, C. (1982). Development of sleep-wake patterns and non rapid eye movement sleep stages during the first six months of life in normal infants. *Pediatrics*, *69*(6), 793–798.

Coopersmith, S. (1967). *The antecedents of self-esteem.* San Francisco: Freeman.

Corbin, C. (1973). *A textbook of motor development.* Dubuque, IA: Brown.

Corrigan, S. A., & Moskowitz, D. S. (1983). Type A behavior in preschool children: Construct validation evidence for the MYTH. *Child Development*, *54*, 1513–1521.

Corter, C. M. (1976). The nature of the mother's absence and the infant's response to brief separation. *Developmental Psychology*, *12*(15), 428–434.

Corter, C. M., Rheingold, H. L., & Eckerman, C. O. (1972). Toys delay the infant's following of his mother. *Developmental Psychology*, *6*, 138–145.

Costanzo, P. R., & Shaw, M. E. (1966). Conformity as a function of age level. *Child Development*, *37*, 967–975.

Courchesne, E., Yeung-Courchesne, R., Press, G. A., Hesselink, J. R., & Jernigan, T. L. (1988). Hypolasia of cerebellar vermae lobules VI and VII in autism. *New England Journal of Medicine*, *318*, 1349–1354.

Cowan, M. W. (1979). The development of the brain. *Scientific American*, *241*, 112–133.

Cramer, D. W., Schiff, I., Schoenbaum, S. C., Gibson, M., Belisle, S., Albrecht, B., Stillman, R. J., Berger, M. M., Wilson, E., Stadel, B. V., & Seibel, H. (1985). Tubal infertility and the intrauterine device. *New England Journal of Medicine*, *313*, 941–947.

Cranley, M. S., Hedahl, K. J., & Pegg, R. J. (1983). Woman's perspectives of giving birth: A comparison of vaginal and cesarean deliveries. *Nursing Research*, *32*, 10–15.

Cratty, B. (1979). *Perceptual and motor development in infants and children* (2d ed.). Englewood Cliffs, NJ: Prentice-Hall.

Croake, J. W. (1973). The changing nature of children's fears. *Child Study Journal*, *3*(2), 91–105.

Crockett, L. J., & Peterson, A. C. (1987). Pubertal status and psychosocial development: Findings from the Early Adolescent Study. In R. M. Lerner & T. T. Foch (Eds.), *Biological-psychosocial interactions in early adolescence: A life-span perspective.* Hillsdale, NJ: Erlbaum.

Crumley, F. (1979). Adolescent suicide attempts. *Journal of the American Medical Association, 241*(22), 2404–2407.

Csikszentmihalyi, M., & Larson, R. (1984). *Being adolescent: Conflict and growth in the teenage years.* New York: Basic Books.

Cuckle, H. S., Wald, N. J., & Lindenbaum, R. H. (1984). Maternal serum alpha-fetoprotein measurement: A screening test for Down's syndrome. *The Lancet,* 926–929.

Cunningham, N., Anisfeld, E., Casper, V., & Nozyce, M. (1987, February 14). Infant carrying, breast feeding, and mother-infant relations. *The Lancet,* p. 379.

Daling, J. R., Weiss, N. S., Metch, B. J., Chow, W. H., Siderstrom, R. M., Moore, D. E., Spadone, L. R., & Stadel, B. V. (1984). Primal tubal infertility in relation to the use of an intrauterine device. *New England Journal of Medicine, 312,* 937–941.

Damon, W. (1977). *The social world of the child.* San Francisco: Jossey-Bass.

Damon, W. (1984). Peer education: The untapped potential. *Journal of Applied Developmental Psychology, 5,* 331–343.

Daniels, D., & Plomin, R. (1985). Origins of individual differences in infant shyness. *Developmental Psychology, 21*(1), 118–121.

Davidson, J. E., & Sternberg, R. J. (1984). The role of insight in intellectual giftedness. *Gifted Child Quarterly, 28*(2), 58–64.

Deaux, K. (1985). Sex and gender. *Annual Review of Psychology, 36,* 49–81.

DeCasper, A., & Fifer, W. (1980). Newborns prefer their mother's voices. *Science, 208,* 1174–1176.

DeCasper, A. J., & Spence, M. J. (1986). Prenatal maternal speech influences newborns' perception of speech sounds. *Infant Behavior and Development, 9,* 133–150.

Decker, M. D., Dewey, M. J., Hutcheson, R. H., & Schaffner, W. (1984). The use and efficacy of child restraint devices. *Journal of the American Medical Association, 252*(18), 2571–2575.

DeFrain, J., & Ernst, L. (1978). The psychological effects of sudden infant death syndrome on surviving family members. *Journal of Family Practice, 6*(5), 985, 989.

DeFrain, J., with Masters, L., Stork, J., & Stork, W. (1986). *Stillborn.* Lexington, MA: Lexington.

DeFrain, J., Taylor, J., & Ernst, L. (1982). *Coping with sudden infant death.* Lexington, MA: Heath.

DeFries, J. C., Fulker, D. W., & LaBuda, M. C. (1987). Evidence for a genetic etiology in reading disability of twins. *Nature, 329,* 537–539.

DeLoache, J. S. (1987). Rapid change in the symbolic functioning of very young children. *Science, 238,* 1556–1557.

Denney, N. W. (1972). Free classification in preschool children. *Child Development, 43,* 1161–1170.

Dennis, W. (1936). A bibliography of baby biographies. *Child Development 7,* 71–73.

Dennis, W. (1960). Causes of retardation among institutional children: Iran. *Journal of Genetic Psychology, 96,* 47–59.

Denny, F. W., & Clyde, W. A. (1983). Acute respiratory tract infections: An overview. In W. A. Clyde & F. W. Denny (Eds.), Workshop on acute respiratory diseases among children of the world. *Pediatric Research, 17,* 1026–1029.

Denny, F. W., & Loda, F. A. (1986). Acute respiratory infections are the leading cause of death in children in developing countries. *American Journal of Tropical Medicine, 35*(1), 1–2.

deRegt, R. H., Minkoff, H. L., Feldman, J., & Schwartz, R. H. (1986). Relation of private or clinic care to the cesarean birth rate. *New England Journal of Medicine, 315,* 619–624.

DeVries, R. (1969). Constancy of generic identity in the years three to six. *Monographs of the Society for Research in Child Development, 34*(3, Serial No. 127).

Deykin, E. Y., Alpert, J. J., & McNamara, J. J. (1985). A pilot study of the effect of exposure to child abuse or neglect on adolescent suicide behavior. *American Journal of Psychiatry, 142,* 1299–1303.

Diagnostic and statistical manual of mental disorders (3d ed., rev.) (DSM III-R). (1987). Washington, DC: American Psychiatric Association.

Dickson, W. P. (1979). Referential communication performance from age 4 to 8: Effects of referent type, context, and target position. *Developmental Psychology, 15*(4), 470–471.

Dickstein, S., & Parke, R. D. (1988). Social referencing in infancy: A glance at fathers and marriage. *Child Development, 59,* 506–511.

Dien, D. S. F. (1982). A Chinese perspective on Kohlberg's theory of moral development. *Developmental Review, 2,* 331–341.

Dietz, W. H., & Gortmaker, S. L. (1985). Do we fatten our children at the television set? Obesity and television viewing in children and adolescents. *Pediatrics, 75,* 807–812.

DiMaio, M. S., Baumgarten, A., Greenstein, R. M., Saal, H. M., & Mahoney, M. J. (1987). Screening for fetal Down's syndrome in pregnancy by measuring maternal serum alphafetoprotein levels. *New England Journal of Medicine, 317,* 342–346.

Dion, K. K., Berscheid, E., & Walster, E. (1972). What is beautiful is good. *Journal of Personality and Social Psychology, 24,* 285–290.

Doctors rule out transplant from organs of hanged boy. (1984, November 23). *The New York Times,* p. A26.

Dodge, K. A. (1983). Behavioral antecedents of peer social status. *Child Development, 54,* 1386–1399.

Dodge, K. A., Coie, J. D., & Brakke, N. P. (1982). Behavior patterns of socially rejected and neglected pre-adolescents: The roles of social approach and aggression. *Journal of Abnormal Child Psychology, 10,* 389–410.

Donaldson, M. (1979). *Children's minds.* New York: Norton.

Dorfman, C. (1987). *Japanese education today* (Pamphlet No. 065-000-00275-2). Washington, DC: U.S. Government Printing Office.

Dornbusch, S. M., Carlsmith, J. M., Bushwall, S. J., Ritter, P. L., Leiderman, H., Hastorf, A. H., & Gross, R. T. (1985). Single parents, extended households, and the control of adolescents. *Child Development, 56,* 326–341.

Dornbusch, S. M., Ritter, P. L., Leiderman, P. H., Roberts, D. F., & Fraleigh, M. J. (1987). The relation of parenting style to adolescent school performance. *Child Development, 58,* 1244–1257.

Dove, J. (undated). *Facts about anorexia nervosa.* Bethesda, MD: National Institutes of Health, Office of Research Reporting, National Institute of Child Health and Human Development.

Dreyer, P. H. (1982). Sexuality during adolescence. In B. B. Wolman (Ed.), *Handbook of developmental psychology.* Englewood Cliffs, NJ: Prentice-Hall.

Dunn, J. (1983). Sibling relationships in early childhood. *Child Development, 54,* 787–811.

Dunn, J. (1985). *Sisters and brothers.* Cambridge, MA: Harvard University Press.

Dunn, J., & Kendrick, C. (1982). *Siblings: Love, envy and understanding.* Cambridge, MA: Harvard University Press.

DuPont, R. L. (1983). Phobias in children. *Journal of Pediatrics, 102*(6), 999–1002.

Durden-Smith, J., & DeSimone, D. (1982, April). The sex signals. *Playboy,* pp. 144–146, 226–242.

Dyer, E. (1963). Parenthood as crisis: A re-study. *Marriage and Family Living, 25,* 196–201.

Easterbrooks, M. A., & Goldberg, W. A. (1984). Toddler development in the family: Impact of father involvement and parenting characteristics. *Child Development, 55,* 740–752.

Eckerman, C. O., & Stein, M. R. (1982). The toddler's emerging interactive skills. In K. H. Rubin & H. S. Ross (Eds.), *Peer relationships and social skills in childhood.* New York: Springer-Verlag.

Edwards, C. P. (1977). The comparative study of the development of moral judgment and reasoning. In R. Monroe, R. Monroe, & B. B. Whiting (Eds.), *Handbook of cross-cultural human development.* New York: Garland.

Egbuono, L., & Starfield, B. (1982). Child health and social status. *Pediatrics, 69*(5), 550–557.

Egeland, B., & Farber, E. A. (1984). Infant-mother attachment: Factors related to its development and changes over time. *Child Development, 55,* 753–771.

Egeland, B., & Sroufe, L. A. (1981). Attachment and early maltreatment. *Child Development, 52,* 44–52.

Ehrhardt, A. A., & Money, J. (1967). Progestin induced hermaphroditism: I. Q. and psychosocial identity. *Journal of Sexual Research, 3,* 83–100.

Eiger, M. S., & Olds, S. W. (1987). *The complete book of breastfeeding.* New York: Bantam.

Eimas, P., Siqueland, E., Jusczyk, P., & Vigorito, J. (1971). Speech perception in infants. *Science, 171,* 303–306.

Eimas, P. D. (1985). The perception of speech in early infancy. *Scientific American, 252*(1), 46–52.

Eisen, M., & Zellman, G. L. (1987). Changes in incidence of sexual intercourse of unmarried teenagers following a community-based sex education program. *Journal of Sex Research, 23*(4), 527–544.

Eisenberg, A., Murkoff, H. E., & Hathaway, S. E. (1984). *What to expect when you're expecting.* New York: Workman.

Eisenson, J., Auer, J. J., & Irwin, J. V. (1963). *The psychology of communication.* New York: Appleton-Century-Crofts.

Elardo, R., Bradley, R., & Caldwell, B. (1975). The relation of infants' home environments to mental test performance from six to thirty-six months: A longitudinal analysis. *Child Development, 46,* 71–76.

Elkind, D. (1981). *The hurried child.* Reading, MA: Addison-Wesley.

Elkind, D. (1984). *All grown up and no place to go.* Reading, MA: Addison-Wesley.

Elkind, D. (1988). *Miseducation.* New York: Knopf.

Elkind, D., & Bowen, R. (1979). Imaginary audience behavior in children and adolescents. *Developmental Psychology, 15*(1), 38.

Emmerich, W., Goldman, K. S., Kirsh, B., & Sharabany, R. (1976). *Development of gender constancy in economically disadvantaged children.* Princeton, NJ: Educational Testing Service.

Emmerick, H. (1978). The influence of parents and peers on choices made by adolescents. *Journal of Youth and Adolescence, 7*(2), 175–180.

Epstein, J. L. (1984, May). Single parents get involved in children's learning [Summary]. *CSOS Report.* Baltimore, MD: Johns Hopkins University Center for Social Organization of Schools (CSOS).

Epstein, L. H., & Wing, R. R. (1987). Behavioral treatment of childhood obesity. *Psychological Bulletin, 101*(3), 331–342.

Erikson, E. H. (1950). *Childhood and society.* New York: Norton.

Erikson, E. H. (1963). *Childhood and society* (2d ed.). New York: Norton.

Erikson, E. H. (1968). *Identity: Youth and crisis.* New York: Norton.

Eron, L. D. (1980). Prescription for reduction of aggression. *American Psychologist, 35*(3), 244–252.

Eron, L. D. (1982). Parent-child interaction, television violence, and aggression in children. *American Psychologist, 37*(2), 197–211.

Eskenazi, G. (1988, June 8). Girls' participation in sports improves. *The New York Times,* pp. A29, A33.

Espenschade, A. (1960). Motor development. In W. R. Johnson (Ed.), *Science and medicine of exercise and sports.* New York: Harper & Row.

Evans, E. D. (1975). *Contemporary influences in early childhood education* (2d ed.). New York: Holt.

Evans, G. (1976). The older the sperm. . . . *Ms., 4*(7), 48–49.

Evans, R. I. (1967). *Dialogue with Erik Erikson.* New York: Harper & Row.

Eveleth, P. B., & Tanner, J. M. (1976). *Worldwide variation in human growth.* London: Cambridge University Press.

Eysenck, H. J., & Prell, D. B. (1951). The inheritance of neuroticism: An experimental study. *Journal of Mental Science, 97,* 441–466.

Fagen, J. W. (1973). Infant's delayed recognition memory and forgetting. *Journal of Experimental Child Psychology, 16,* 424–450.

Fagen, J. W. (1982). Infant memory. In T. M. Field, A. Huston, H. Quay, L. Troll, & G. Finley (Eds.), *Review of human development.* New York: Wiley.

Fagen, J. W. (1984). Infant's long-term memory for stimulus color. *Developmental Psychology, 20*(3), 435–440.

Fagen, J. W., Morrongiello, B. A., Rovee-Collier, C., & Gekoski, M. J. (1984). Expectancies and memory retrieval in three-month-old infants. *Child Development, 55,* 936–943.

Falbo, T., & Polit, D. F. (1986). Quantitative review of the only child literature: Research evidence and theory development. *Psychological Bulletin, 100*(2), 176–189.

Fallot, M. E., Boyd, J. L., & Oski, F. A. (1980). Breast-feeding reduces incidence of hospital admissions for infection in infants. *Pediatrics, 65*(6), 1121–1124.

Fantuzzo, J. W., Jurecic, L., Stoval, A., Hightower, A. D., Goiins, C., & Schachtel, D. (1988). Effects of adult and peer social initiations on the social behavior of withdrawn, maltreated preschool children. *Journal of Consulting and Clinical Psychology, 56*(1), 34–39.

Fantz, R. L. (1963). Pattern vision in newborn infants. *Science, 140,* 296–297.

Fantz, R. L. (1964). Visual experience in infants: Decreased attention to familiar patterns relative to novel ones. *Science, 146,* 668–670.

Fantz, R. L. (1965). Visual perception from birth as shown by pattern selectivity. In H. E. Whipple (Ed.), New issues in infant development. *Annals of the New York Academy of Science, 118,* 793–814.

Fantz, R. L., Fagen, J., & Miranda, S. B. (1975). Early visual selectivity. In L. Cohen & P. Salapetek (Eds.), *Infant perception: From sensation to cognition: Vol. 1. Basic visual processes* (pp. 249–341). New York: Academic.

Fantz, R. L., & Nevis, S. (1967).

Pattern preferences and perceptual-cognitive development in early infancy. *Merrill-Palmer Quarterly, 13,* 77–108.

Farrow, J. A., Rees, J. M., & Worthington-Roberts, B. S. (1987). Health, developmental, and nutritional status of adolescent alcohol and marijuana abusers. *Pediatrics, 79,* 218–223.

Feagans, L. (1983). A current view of learning disabilities. *Journal of Pediatrics, 102*(4), 487–493.

Fein, G. (1981). Pretend play in childhood: An integrative review. *Child Development, 52,* 1095–1118.

Feinberg, M., Smith, M., & Schmidt, R. (1958). An analysis of expressions used by adolescents at varying economic levels to describe accepted and rejected peers. *Journal of Genetic Psychology, 93,* 133–148.

Feinman, S., & Lewis, M. (1983). Social referencing at ten months: A second-order effect on infants' responses. *Child Development, 54,* 878–887.

Feldman, R. D. (1982). Whatever happened to the quiz kids: Perils and profits of growing up gifted. Chicago: *Chicago Review Press.*

Feldman, W., Feldman, E., & Goodman, J. T. (1988). Culture versus biology: Children's attitudes toward thinness and fatness. *Pediatrics, 81,* 190–194.

Fenton, N. (1928). The only child. *Journal of Genetic Psychology, 35,* 546–556.

Ferber, R. (1985). *Solve your child's sleep problems.* New York: Simon & Schuster.

Fergusson, D. M., Horwood, L. J., & Shannon, F. T. (1986). Factors related to the age of attainment of nocturnal bladder control: An 8-year longitudinal study. *Pediatrics, 78*(5), 884–890.

Fetterly, K., & Graubard, M. S. (1984, March 23). Racial and educational factors associated with breastfeeding—United States, 1969 and 1980. *Morbidity and Mortality Weekly Report* (MMWR), pp. 153–154.

Field, D. (1981). Can preschool children really learn to conserve? *Child Development, 52,* 326–334.

Field, T. (1987). Interaction and attachment in normal and atypical infants. *Journal of Consulting and Clinical Psychology, 55*(6), 853–859.

Field, T., Sandberg, D., Garcia, R., Vega-Lahr, N., Goldstein, S., & Guy, L. (1985). Pregnancy problems, postpartum depression, and early mother-infant interactions. *Developmental Psychology, 21*(6), 1152–1156.

Field, T. M. (1978). Interaction behav-iors of primary versus secondary caretaker fathers. *Developmental Psychology, 14,* 183–184.

Field, T. M. (1986). Interventions for premature infants. *Journal of Pediatrics, 109*(1), 183–190.

Field, T. M., & Roopnarine, J. L. (1982). Infant-peer interaction. In T. M. Field, A. Huston, H. C. Quay, L. Troll, & G. Finley (Eds.), *Review of human development.* New York: Wiley.

Field, T. M., Widmayer, S., Greenberg, R., & Stoller, S. (1982). Effects of parent training on teenage mothers and their infants. *Pediatrics, 69*(6), 703–707.

Field, T. M., Woodson, R., Greenberg, R., & Cohen, D. (1982). Discrimination and imitation of facial expressions by neonates. *Science, 218,* 179–181.

Fitness Finders. (1984). *Feelin' good.* Spring Arbor, MI: Author.

Fivush, R., Hudson, J., & Nelson, K. (1983). Children's long term memory for a novel event: An exploratory study. *Merrill-Palmer Quarterly, 30,* 303–316.

Flavell, J. H. (1963). *The developmental psychology of Jean Piaget.* New York: Van Nostrand.

Flavell, J. H. (1977). *Cognitive development.* Englewood Cliffs, NJ: Prentice-Hall.

Flavell, J. H. (1986). The development of children's knowledge about the appearance-reality distinction. *American Psychologist, 41*(4), 418–425.

Flavell, J. H., Beach, D., & Chinsky, J. (1966). Spontaneous verbal rehearsal in a memory task as a function of age. *Child Development, 37,* 283–299.

Flavell, J. H., Green, F. L., Wahl, K. E., & Flavell, E. R. (1987). The effects of question clarification and memory aids on young children's performance on appearance-reality tasks. *Cognitive Development, 2,* 127–144.

Flavell, J. H., Speer, J. R., Green, F. L., & August, D. L. (1981). The development of comprehension monitoring and knowledge about communication. *Monographs of the Society for Research in Child Development, 46*(5, Serial No. 192).

Flavell, J. H., Zhang, X.-D., Zou, H., Dong, Q., & Qi, S. (1983). A comparison between development of the appearance-reality distinction in the People's Republic of China and the United States. *Cognitive Development, 15,* 459–466.

Fleisher, L. D. (1987). Wrongful births: When is there liability for prenatal injury? *American Journal of the Diseases of Children, 141,* 1260–1265.

Fletcher, A. B. (1987). Pain in the neonate. *New England Journal of Medicine, 317*(21), 1347–1348.

Fomon, S. J., Filer, L. J., Anderson, T. A., & Ziegler, E. E. (1979). Recommendations for feeding normal infants. *Pediatrics, 63*(1), 52–59.

Ford, J., Zelnik, M., & Kantner, J. (1979, November). *Differences in contraceptive use and socioeconomic groups of teenagers in the United States.* Paper presented at the meeting of the American Public Health Association, New York.

Forehand, R., Long, N., Brody, G. H., & Fauber, R. (1986). Home predictors of young adolescents' school behavior and academic performance. *Child Development, 57,* 1528–1533.

Forman, M. R., Graubard, B. I., Hoffman, H. J., Beren, R., Harley, E. E., & Bennett, P. (1984). The Pima infant feeding study: Breast feeding and gastroenteritis in the first year of life. *American Journal of Epidemiology, 119*(3), 335–349.

Fox, L. H., & Washington, J. (1985). Programs for the gifted and talented: Past, present, and future. In F. D. Horowitz & M. O'Brien (Eds.), *The gifted and talented: Developmental perspectives.* Washington, DC: American Psychological Association.

Franceschi, B. (1985). Personal communication to the authors.

Francoeur, R. T. (1985). Reproductive technologies: New alternatives and new ethics. *SIECUS Report, 14,* 1–5.

Frank, A. (1952). *The diary of a young girl* (B. H. Mooyaart-Doubleday, Trans.). Garden City, NY: Doubleday.

Frankenburg, W. K. (1978). *Denver developmental screening test.* Denver: University of Colorado Medical Center.

Frankenburg, W. K., Dodds, J. B., Fandal, A. W., Kazuk, E., & Cohrs, M. (1975). *Denver developmental screening test: Reference manual.* Denver: University of Colorado Medical Center.

Frankenburg, W. K., Fandal, A. W., Sciarillo, W., & Burgess, D. (1981). The newly abbreviated and revised Denver developmental screening test. *Journal of Pediatrics, 99*(6) 995–999.

Freedman, D. G. (1979, January). Ethnic differences in babies. *Human Nature,* pp. 15–20.

Freeman, D. (1983). *Margaret Mead and Samoa.* Cambridge, MA: Harvard University Press.

Freud, A. (1946). *The ego and the mechanisms of defense.* New York: International Universities Press.

Freud, S. (1959). An autobiographical study. In J. Strachey (Ed. and Trans.),

The standard edition of the complete psychological works of Sigmund Freud (Vol. 20). London: Hogarth. (Original work published 1925)

Freud, S. (1953). *A general introduction to psychoanalysis* (J. Riviere, Trans.). New York: Permabooks. (Original work published in 1935)

Fried, P. A. (1982). Marijuana use by pregnant women and effects on offspring: An update. *Neurobehavioral Toxicology and Teratology, 4,* 451–454.

Fried, P. A., Watkinson, B., & Willan, A. (1984). Marijuana use during pregnancy and decreased length of gestation. *American Journal of Obstetrics and Gynecology, 150,* 23–27.

Friedman, E. A. (1986). How much fetal monitoring and Cesarean section is enough? *New England Journal of Medicine, 315*(10), 641–643.

Friedman, M., & Rosenman, R. H. (1974). *Type A behavior and your heart.* New York: Knopf.

Friedrich, L. K., & Stein, A. H. (1973). Aggressive and prosocial television programs and the natural behavior of preschool children. *Monographs of the Society for Research of Child Development, 38*(Whole No. 4).

Frisch, H. (1977). Sex stereotypes in adult-infancy play. *Child Development, 48,* 1671–1675.

Frisch, R. E., Wyshak, G., & Vincent, L. (1980). Delayed menarche and amenorrhea in ballet dancers. *New England Journal of Medicine, 303,* 17–19.

Frueh, T., & McGhee, P. (1975). Traditional sex role development and amount of time spent watching television. *Developmental Psychology, 11*(1), 109.

Fuchs, D., & Fuchs, L. S. (1986). Test procedure bias: A meta-analysis of examiner familarity effects. *Review of Educational Research, 56,* 243–262.

Fuchs, F. (1980). Genetic amniocentesis. *Scientific American, 242*(6), 47–53.

Fuchs, L. S., & Fuchs, D. (1986). Effects of systematic formative evaluation of student achievement: A metaanalysis. *Exceptional Children, 53,* 199–205.

Furman, W. (1982). Children's friendships. In T. M. Field, A. Huston, H. C. Quay, L. Troll, & G. E. Finley (Eds.), *Review of human development.* New York: Wiley.

Furman, W., & Bierman, K. L. (1983). Developmental changes in young children's conceptions of friendship. *Child Development, 54,* 549–556.

Furman, W., & Buhrmester, D. (1985). Children's perceptions of the personal relationships in their social networks. *Developmental Psychology, 21*(6), 1016–1024.

Furstenberg, F. F. (1976). The social consequences of teenage parenthood. *Family Planning Perspectives, 8*(4), 148–164.

Gaensbauer, T., & Hiatt, S. (1984). *The psychobiology of affective development.* Hillsdale, NJ: Erlbaum.

Gamble, T. J., & Zigler, E. (1986). Effects of infant day care: Another look at the evidence. *American Journal of Orthopsychiatry, 56*(1), 26–42.

Gamer, E., Thomas, J., & Kendall, D. (1975). Determinants of friendship across the life span. In F. Rebelsky (Ed.), *Life: The continuous process.* New York: Knopf.

Garai, J. E., & Scheinfeld, A. (1968). Sex differences in mental and behavioral traits. *Genetic Psychology Monographs, 77,* 169–299.

Garcia-Coll, C., Kagan, J., & Reznick, J. S. (1984). Behavioral inhibition in young children. *Child Development, 55,* 1005–1019.

Gardner, H. (1979, March 29). Exploring the mystery of creativity. *The New York Times,* pp. C1, C17.

Gardner, H. (1983). Frames of mind: The theory of multiple intelligences. New York: Basic Books.

Gardner, R. (1973). *Understanding children.* New York: Aronson.

Garland, J. B. (1982, March). *Social referencing and self-produced locomotion.* Paper presented at the meeting of the International Conference on International Studies, Austin, TX.

Garmezy, N. (1983). Stressors of childhood. In N. Garmezy & M. Rutter (Eds.), *Stress, coping and development in children.* New York: McGraw-Hill.

Garn, S. M. (1966). Growth and development. In E. Ginzberg (Ed.), *The nation's children* (pp. 24–42). New York: Columbia University Press.

Garrison, E. G. (1987). Psychological maltreatment of children: An emerging focus for inquiry and concern. *American Psychologist, 42*(2), 157–159.

Garrison, W. T., & Earls, F. J. (1986). Epidemiological perspectives on maternal depression and the young child. In E. Z. Tronick & T. Field (Eds.), *Maternal depression and infant disturbances.* San Francisco: Jossey-Bass.

Garvey, C., & Hogan, R. (1973). Social speech and social interaction: Egocentrism revisited. *Child Development, 44,* 562–568.

Gath, A. (1985). Down's syndrome in the first nine years. In A. R. Nicol (Ed.), *Longitudinal studies in child psychology and psychiatry.* New York: Wiley.

Gavotos, L. A. (1959). Relationships and age differences in growth measures and motor skills. *Child Development, 30,* 333–340.

Geber, M. (1962). Longitudinal study and psychomotor development among Baganda children. *Proceedings of the Fourteenth International Congress of Applied Psychology, 3,* 50–60.

Geber, M., & Dean, R. F. A. (1957). The state of development of newborn African children. *The Lancet,* pp. 1216–1219.

Geffner, R. (1978). *The effects of interdependent learning on self-esteem, interethnic relations, and intra-ethnic attitudes of elementary school children: A field experiment.* Unpublished doctoral dissertation, University of California, Santa Cruz.

Geller, E., Ritvo, E. R., Freeman, B. J., & Yuwiler, A. (1982). Preliminary observations of the effect of fenfluramine on blood serotonin and symptoms in three autistic boys. *New England Journal of Medicine, 307*(3), 165–169.

Gelman, R., Bullock, M., & Meck, E. (1980). Preschoolers' understanding of simple object transformations. *Child Development, 51,* 691–699.

Gelman, R., Spelke, A., & Meck, E. Work on animism in children, in press.

General Mills, Inc. (1977). *Raising children in a changing society.* Minneapolis, MN: Author.

General Mills, Inc. (1981). *The General Mills American family report 1980–81: Families at work: Strengths and strains.* Minneapolis, MN: Author.

Geshwind, N., & Galaburda, A. M. (1985). Cerebral lateralization. Biological mechanisms, associations and pathology: I. A hypothesis and a program for research. *Archives of Neurology, 42,* 428–459.

Gesell, A. (1929). Maturation and infant behavior patterns. *Psychological Review, 36,* 307–319.

Getzels, J. W., & Jackson, P. W. (1963). The highly intelligent and the highly creative adolescent: A summary of some research findings. In C. W. Taylor & F. Baron (Eds.), *Scientific creativity: Its recognition and development.* New York: Wiley.

Gil, D. G. (1971). Violence against children. *Journal of Marriage and the Family, 33*(4), 637–648.

Gilligan, C. (1982). *In a different voice: Psychological theory and women's development.* Cambridge, MA: Harvard University Press.

Gilligan, C. (1987). Adolescent development reconsidered. In C. E. Irwin (Ed.), *Adolescent social behavior and health.* San Francisco: Jossey-Bass.

Ginott, H. (1965). *Between parent and child*. New York: Macmillan.

Ginsburg, H., & Miller, S. M. (1982). Sex differences in children's risk-taking behavior. *Child Development, 53,* 426–428.

Ginsburg, H., & Opper, S. (1979). *Piaget's theory of intellectual development* (2d ed.). Englewood Cliffs, NJ: Prentice-Hall.

Gintzler, A. R. (1980). Endorphin-mediated increases in pain threshold during pregnancy. *Science, 210,* 193–195.

Ginzberg, E., et al. (1951). *Occupational choice: An approach to a general theory.* New York: Columbia University Press.

Gladue, B. A., Green, R., & Hellman, R. E. (1984). Neuroendocrine response to estrogen and sexual orientation. *Science, 225,* 1496–1499.

Gleitman, L. R., Newport, E. L., & Gleitman, H. (1984). The current status of the motherese hypothesis. *Journal of Child Language, 11,* 43–79.

Glick, P. C. (1980). Remarried: Some recent changes and variations. *Journal of Family Issues, 1,* 455–478.

Glick, P. C. (1984). American household structure in transition. *Family Planning Perspectives, 16*(5), 205–211.

Golbus, M., Loughman, W., Epstein, C., Halbasch, G., Stephens, J., & Hall, B. (1979). Prenatal genetic diagnosis in 3000 amniocenteses. *New England Journal of Medicine, 300*(4), 157–163.

Gold, D., & Andres, D. (1978a). Developmental comparison between adolescent children with employed and non-employed mothers. *Merrill-Palmer Quarterly, 24,* 243–254.

Gold, D., & Andres, D. (1978b). Relations between maternal employment and development of nursery school children. *Canadian Journal of Behavioral Science, 10,* 116–129.

Gold, D., Andres, D., & Glorieux, J. (1979). The development of Francophone nursery-school children with employed and nonemployed mothers. *Canadian Journal of Behavioral Science, 11,* 169–173.

Gold, M., & Yanof, D. S. (1985). Mothers, daughters, and girlfriends. *Journal of Personality and Social Psychology, 49*(3), 654–659.

Golden, M., Birns, B., & Bridger, W. (1973, March). *Review and overview: Social class and cognitive development.* Paper presented at the meeting of the Society for Research in Child Development, Philadelphia.

Golden, N. L., Sokol, R. J., Kuhnert, B. R., & Bottoms, S. (1982). Maternal alcohol use and infant development. *Pediatrics, 70,* 931–934.

Goldschmid, M. L., & Bentler, P. M. (1968). The dimensions and measurement of conservation. *Child Development, 39,* 787–815.

Goldsmith, M. F. (1985). Possible herpes virus role in abortion studies. *Journal of the American Medical Association, 251,* 3067–3070.

Goldsmith, M. F. (1988). Trial appears to confirm safety of chorionic villus sampling procedure. *Journal of the American Medical Association, 259*(24), 3521–3522.

Goldstein, H., & Tanner, J. (1980, March 15). Ecological considerations in the creation and the use of child growth standards. *The Lancet,* pp. 582–585.

Goodman, G. S. (1984). The child witness: An introduction. *Journal of Social Issues, 40,* 1–7.

Gopnik, A., & Meltzoff, A. N. (1986). Relations between semantic and cognitive development in the one-word stage: The specificity hypothesis. *Child Development, 57,* 1040–1053.

Gopnik, A., & Meltzoff, A. N. (1987). The development of categorization in the second year and its relation to other cognitive and linguistic developments. *Child Development, 58,* 1523–1531.

Gordon, D., & Young, R. (1976). School phobia: A discussion of etiology, treatment, and evaluation. *Psychological Bulletin, 39,* 783–804.

Gordon, S. (1982, March 13). Speech to the American Association of Sex Educators, Counselors, and Therapists. New York.

Gordon, S., & Everly, K. (1985). Increasing self-esteem in vulnerable students: A tool for reducing pregnancy among teenagers. *Impact '85,* Syracuse, NY: Ed-U Press.

Gortmaker, S. L., Dietz, W. H., Sobol, A. M., & Welher, C. A. (1987). Increasing pediatric obesity in the United States. *American Journal of the Diseases of Children, 141,* 535–540.

Gottesman, I. I. (1962). Differential inheritance of the psychoneuroses. *Eugenics Quarterly, 9,* 223–227.

Gottesman, I. I. (1963). Heritability of personality: A demonstration. *Psychology Monographs, 77*(9, Whole No. 572).

Gottesman, I. I. (1965). Personality and natural selection. In S. G. Vandenberg (Ed.), *Methods and goals in human behavior genetics* (pp. 63–80). New York: Academic.

Gottesman, I. I., & Shields, J. (1966). Schizophrenia in twins: 16 years consecutive admission to a psychiatric clinic. *British Journal of Psychiatry, 112,* 809–818.

Gottman, J. M., Gonso, J., & Rasmussen, B. (1975). Social interaction, social competence, and friendship in children. *Child Development, 46,* 709–718.

Gould, M. S., & Shaffer, D. (1986). The impact of suicide in television movies. *New England Journal of Medicine, 315,* 690–694.

Graubard, S. G. (1988, January 29). Why do Asian pupils win those prizes? *The New York Times,* p. A35.

Gray, J. A., Lean, J., & Keynes, A. (1969). Infant androgen treatment and adult open-field behavior: Direct effects and effects of injections of siblings. *Physiology and Behavior, 4*(2), 177–181.

Graziano, A. M., & Mooney, K. C. (1982). Behavioral treatment of "nightfears" in children: Maintenance and improvement at 2½ to 3-year follow-up. *Journal of Counseling and Clinical Psychology, 50*(4), 598–599.

Greenberg, M., & Morris, N. (1974). Engrossment: The newborn's impact upon the father. *American Journal of Orthopsychiatry, 44*(4), 520–531.

Greenberger, E., & Steinberg, L. (1986). *When teenagers work.* New York: Basic Books.

Greenfield, P. (1966). On culture and conservation. In J. S. Bruner, R. R. Olver, & P. Greenfield (Eds.), *Studies in cognitive growth.* New York: Wiley.

Greenough, W. T., Black, J. E., & Wallace, C. S. (1987). Experience and brain development. *Child Development, 58,* 539–559.

Gregory, D. (1964). *Nigger.* New York: Dutton.

Grief, E. B., & Ulman, K. J. (1982). The psychological impact of menarche on early adolescent females: A review of the literature. *Child Development, 53,* 1413–1430.

Gross, S. J., Geller, J., & Tomarelli, R. M. (1981). Composition of breast milk from mothers of preterm infants. *Pediatrics, 68,* 490–493.

Grotevant, H., & Durrett, M. (1980). Occupational knowledge and career development in adolescence. *Journal of Vocational Behavior, 17,* 171–182.

Grotevant, H., Scarr, S., & Weinberg, R. 1977). Intellectual development in family constellations with adopted and natural children: A test of the Zajonc and Markus model. *Child Development, 48,* 1699–1703.

Gruen, G., Korte, J., & Baum, J. (1974). Group measure of locus of control. *Developmental Psychology, 10*(5), 683–686.

Guidubaldi, J., & Perry, J. D. (1985).

Divorce and mental health sequelae for children: A two year follow-up of a nationwide sample. *Journal of the American Academy of Child Psychiatry,* 24(5), 531–537.

Guilford, J. P. (1967). *The nature of human intelligence.* New York: McGraw-Hill.

Guttmacher, A. F. (1973). *Pregnancy, birth, and family planning.* New York: Viking.

Hadley, J. (1984, July-August). Facts about childhood hyperactivity. *Children Today,* pp. 8–13.

Hagman, R. R. (1932). A study of fears of children of preschool age. *Journal of Experimental Education, 1,* 110–130.

Haire, D. (1972). The cultural warping of childbirth. *International Childbirth Education Association News,* p. 35.

Haith, M. M. (1986). Sensory and perceptual processes in early infancy. *Journal of Pediatrics, 109*(1), 158–171.

Hall, C., & Lindzey, G. (1978). *Personality* (3d ed.). New York: Wiley.

Hall, E. (1970). A conversation with Jean Piaget and Bärbel Inhelder. *Psychology Today, 4,* 27–28.

Hall, E. (1984). Sandra Scarr: What's a parent to do? *Psychology Today, 18*(5), 59–63.

Hall, E. G., & Lee, A. M. (1984). Sex differences in motor performance of young children: Fact or fiction? *Sex Roles, 10,* 217–230.

Hall, G. S. (1916). *Adolescence.* New York: Appleton. (Original work published 1904)

Hamilton, S., & Crouter, A. (1980). Work and growth: A review of research on the impact of work experience on adolescent development. *Journal of Youth and Adolescence, 9*(4), 323–338.

Hanley, R. (1988a, February 4). Surrogate deals for mothers held illegal in Jersey. *The New York Times,* pp. A1, B6.

Hanley, R. (1988b, February 4). Legislators are hesitant on regulating surrogacy. *The New York Times,* p. B7.

Hanson, S. M. H. (1988). Divorced fathers with custody. In P. Bronstein & C. P. Cowan (Eds.), *Fatherhood today: Men's changing role in the family.* New York: Wiley.

Hardy-Brown, K., & Plomin, R. (1985). Infant communicative development: Evidence from adoptive and biological families for genetic and environmental influences on rate differences. *Developmental Psychology, 21*(2), 378–385.

Hardyck, C., & Petrinovich, L. F. (1977). Left-handedness. *Psychological Bulletin, 84,* 385–404.

Harlow, H. F., & Harlow, M. K. (1962). The effect of rearing conditions on behavior. *Bulletin of Menninger Clinic, 26,* 213–224.

Harlow, H. F., & Zimmerman, R. R. (1959). Affectional responses in the infant monkey. *Science, 130,* 421–432.

Harmon, R., Suwalsky, J., & Klein, R. (1979). Infant's preferential response for mother versus unfamiliar adult. *Journal of the American Academy of Child Psychiatry, 18*(3), 437–449.

Harris, B. (1979). Whatever happened to little Albert? *American Psychologist, 34*(2), 151–161.

Harris, L., & Associates. (1986). *American teens speak: Sex, myths, TV, and birth control. The Planned Parenthood poll.* New York: Planned Parenthood Federation of America.

Harris, V. A., Katkin, E. S., Lick, J. R., & Haberfield, T. (1976). Paced respiration as a technique for the automatic response to stress. *Psychophysiology, 13,* 386–391.

Harrison, M. R., Golbus, M. S., Filly, R. A., Nakayama, D. K., & Delorimier, A. A. (1982). Fetal surgical treatment. *Pediatric Annals, 11*(11), 896–903.

Hart, S. N., & Brassard, M. R. (1987). A major threat to children's mental health: Psychological maltreatment. *American Psychologist, 42*(2), 160–165.

Hartmann, E. (1981). The strangest sleep disorder. *Psychology Today, 15*(4), 14–18.

Hartshorne, H., & May, M. A. (1928–1930). *Studies in the nature of character* (Vols. 1–3). New York: Macmillan.

Hartup, W. W. (1970). Peer relations. In T. D. Spencer & N. Kass (Eds.), *Perspectives in child psychology: Research and review.* New York: McGraw-Hill.

Hartup, W. W. (1984). The peer context in middle childhood. In W. A. Collins (Ed.), *Development during middle childhood.* Washington, DC: National Academy.

Harvey, E. B., Boice, J. D., Honeyman, M., & Flannery, J. T. (1985). Prenatal x-ray exposure and childhood cancer in twins. *New England Journal of Medicine, 312,* 541–545.

Haryett, R. D., Hansen, R. C., & Davidson, P. O. (1970). Chronic thumbsucking: A second report on treatment and its physiological effects. *American Journal of Orthodontics, 57,* 164.

Hass, A. (1979). *Teenage sexuality: A survey of teenage sexual behavior.* New York: Macmillan.

Haswell, K., Hock, E., & Wenar, C. (1981). Oppositional behavior of preschool children: Theory and intervention. *Family Relations, 30,* 440–446.

Haugh, S., Hoffman, C., & Cowan, G. (1980). The eye of the very young beholder: Sex typing of infants by young children. *Child Development, 51,* 598–600.

Hay, D. F., Pedersen, J., & Nash, A. (1982). Dyadic interaction in the first year of life. In K. H. Rubin & H. S. Ross (Eds.), *Peer relationships and social skills in children.* New York: Springer.

Hayden, A., & Haring, N. (1976). Early intervention for high risk infants and young children: Programs for Down's syndrome children. In T. D. Tjossem (Ed.), *Intervention strategies for high risk infants and young children* (pp. 573–607). Baltimore: University Park Press.

Hayes, L. A., & Watson, J. S. (1981). Neonatal imitation: Fact or artifact? *Developmental Psychology, 17*(5), 655–660.

Hayghe, H. (1986, February). Rise in mothers' labor force activity includes those with infants. *Monthly Labor Review,* pp. 43–45.

Helmreich, R. (1968). Birth order effects. *Naval Research Reviews, 21.*

Henly, W. L., & Fitch, B. R. (1966). Newborn narcotic withdrawal associated with regional enteritis in pregnancy. *New York Journal of Medicine, 66,* 2565–2567.

Herbst, A. L., Kurman, R. J., Scully, R. E., & Poskanzer, D. D. (1971). Clear-cell adenocarcinoma of the genital tract in young females. *New England Journal of Medicine, 287*(25), 1259–1264.

Herrmann, H. J., & Roberts, M. W. (1987). Preventive dental care: The role of the pediatrician. *Pediatrics, 80*(1), 107–110.

Herold, E. S., & Goodwin, M. S. (1981). Premarital sexual guilt and contraceptive attitudes and behavior. *Family Relations, 30,* 247–253.

Hess, R. D., & Holloway, S. D. (1984). Family and school as educational institutions. In R. D. Parke (Ed.), *Review of Child Development Research 7: The family.* Chicago: University of Chicago Press.

Heston, L. L. (1966). Psychiatric disorders in foster-home-reared children of schizophrenic mothers. *British Journal of Psychiatry, 112,* 819–825.

Hetherington, E. M. (1965). A developmental study of the effects of sex of the dominant parent on sex role preference, identification and imitation in children. *Journal of Personality and Social Psychology, 2,* 188–194.

Hetherington, E. M. (1980). Children and divorce. In R. Henderson (Ed.), *Parent-child interaction: Theory, research and prospect.* New York: Academic.

Hetherington, E. M. (1986). Family relations six years after divorce. In *Remarriage and parenting today: Research and theory*. New York: Guilford.

Hetherington, E. M., Cox, M., & Cox, R. (1975). *Beyond father absence: Conceptualizing of effects of divorce*. Paper presented at the meeting of the Society for Research in Child Development, Denver.

Hetherington, E. M., & Parke, R. (1979). *Child psychology: A contemporary viewpoint* (2d ed.). New York: McGraw-Hill.

Heyns, B., & Catsambis, S. (1986). Mother's employment and children's achievement: A critique. *Sociology of Education, 59*, 140–151.

Hier, D. B., & Crowley, W. F. (1982). Spatial ability in androgen-deficient men. *New England Journal of Medicine, 20*, 1202–1205.

Hiernaux, J. (1968). Ethnic differences in growth and development. *Eugenics Quarterly, 15*, 12–21.

Hill, C. R., & Stafford, F. P. (1980). Parental care of children: Time diary estimate of quantity, predictability, and variety. *Journal of Human Resources, 15*, 219–239.

Hill, J. P. (1980). The family. In *Yearbook of National Society for Study of Education*. Chicago: University of Chicago Press.

Hill, J. P. (1987). Research on adolescents and their families: Past and prospect. In C. E. Irwin (Ed.), *Adolescent social behavior and health*. San Francisco: Jossey-Bass.

Hingson, R., Alpert, J. J., Day, N., Dooling, E., Kayne, H., Morelock, S., Oppenheimer, E., & Zuckerman, B. (1982). Effects of maternal drinking and marijuana use on fetal growth and development. *Pediatrics, 70*(4), 539–546.

Hirsch, H. V., & Spinelli, D. N. (1970). Visual experience modifies distribution of horizontally and vertically oriented receptive fields in cats. *Science, 168*, 869–871.

Hirsch, J. (1972). Can we modify the number of adipose cells? *Postgraduate Medicine, 51*(5), 83–86.

Hobbs, D., & Cole, S. (1976). Transition to parenthood: A decade replication. *Journal of Marriage and the Family, 38*(4), 723–731.

Hobbs, D., & Wimbish, J. (1977). Transition to parenthood by black couples. *Journal of Marriage and the Family, 39*(4), 677–689.

Hofferth, S. L. (1979). Day care in the next decade: 1980–1990. *Journal of Marriage and the Family, 41*(3), 649–658.

Hoff-Ginsberg, E. (1985). Some contributions of mothers' speech to their children's syntactic growth. *Journal of Child Language, 12*, 367–385.

Hoff-Ginsberg, E. (1986). Function and structure in maternal speech: Their relation to the child's development of syntax. *Developmental Psychology, 22*(2), 155–163.

Hoff-Ginsberg, E., & Shatz, M. (1982). Linguistic input and the child's acquisition of language. *Psychological Bulletin, 92*(1), 3–26.

Hoffman, L. W. (1979). Maternal employment. *American Psychologist, 34*(10), 859–865.

Hoffman, L. W. (1984). Work, family, and the socialization of the child. In R. D. Parke (Ed.), *The family*. Chicago: University of Chicago Press.

Hoffman, L. W. (1986). Work, family, and the child. In M. S. Pallak & R. O. Perloff (Eds.), *Psychology and work: Productivity, change, and employment*. Washington, DC: American Psychological Association.

Hoffman, L. W. (1989). Effects of maternal employment in the two-parent family: A review of recent research. *American Psychologist, 44*(2), 283–292.

Hoffman, M. L. (1970). Moral development. In P. H. Mussen (Ed.), *Carmichael's manual of child psychology*. New York: Wiley.

Hoffman, M. L., & Hoffman, L. W. (Eds.). (1964). *Review of child development research*. New York: Russell Sage.

Hogge, W. A., Schonberg, S. A., & Golbus, M. S. (1986). Chorionic villus sampling: Experience of the first 1000 cases. *American Journal of Obstetrics and Gynecology, 154*, 1249–1252.

Holmes, L. (1978). Genetic counseling for the older pregnant woman: New data and questions. *New England Journal of Medicine, 298*(25), 1419–1421.

Holmes, L. D. (1987). *Quest for the real Samoa: The Mead-Freeman controversy and beyond*. South Hadley, MA: Bergin & Garvey.

Honigfeld, L. S., & Kaplan, D. W. (1987). Native-American post-neonatal mortality. *Pediatrics, 80*(4), 575–578.

Honzik, M. P., Macfarlane, J. W., & Allen, L. (1948). The stability of mental test performance between two and 18 years. *Journal of Experimental Education, 17*, 309–323.

Hooker, E. (1957). The adjustment of the male overt homosexual. *Journal of Projective Techniques, 21*, 18–31.

Horn, J. (1983). The Texas Adoption Project: Adopted children and their intellectual resemblance to biological and adoptive parents. *Child Development, 54*, 268–275.

Horney, K. (1939). *New ways in psychoanalysis*. New York: Norton.

Horowitz, F. D., & O'Brien, M. (1986). Gifted and talented children: State of knowledge and directions for research. *American Psychologist, 41*(10), 1147–1152.

Householder, J., Hatcher, R., Burns, W., & Chasnoff, I. (1982). Infants born to narcotic-addicted mothers. *Psychological Bulletin, 92*, 453–468.

Howard, M. (1983, March). Postponing sexual involvement: A new approach. *SIECUS Report, 11*(4), 5–6, 8.

Howe, M. (1988, August 20). Lawyer must wait to take exam. *The New York Times*, p. 31.

Hoyenga, K. B., & Hoyenga, K. T. (1979). *The question of sex differences*. Boston: Little, Brown.

Hsu, L., Crisp, A., & Harding, B. (1979, January 13). Outcome of anorexia nervosa. *The Lancet*, pp. 61–65.

Huang, L. J. (1982). Planned fertility of one-couple one-child policy in the People's Republic of China. *Journal of Marriage and the Family, 44*, 775–784.

Hudson, J. L., Pope, H. G., & Jonas, J. M. (1983). Treatment of bulimia with antidepressants: Theoretical considerations with clinical findings. In A. J. Stunkard & E. Stellar (Eds.), *Eating and its disorders*. New York: Raven.

Hughes, M. (1975). *Egocentrism in preschool children*. Unpublished doctoral dissertation, Edinburgh University, Edinburgh.

Humphrey, L. L. (1986). Structural analysis of parent-child relationships in eating disorders. *Journal of Abnormal Psychology, 95*(4), 395–402.

Hunt, C. E., & Brouillette, R. T. (1987). Sudden infant death syndrome: 1987 perspective. *Journal of Pediatrics, 110*(5), 669–678.

Huston, T. L. (1983). Power. In H. H. Kelley, E. Berscheid, A. Christensen, J. H. Harvey, T. L. Huston, G. Levinger, E. McClintock, L. A. Peplau, & D. R. Peplau, *Close relationships*. New York: Freeman.

Hutt, C. (1972). *Males and females*. Middlesex, England: Penguin.

Hyde, J. (1986). *Human sexuality* (3d ed.). New York: McGraw-Hill.

Hyde, J., & Linn, M. C. (1988). Gender differences in verbal abilities: A meta-analysis. *Psychological Bulletin, 104*(1), 53–69.

Ianni, F. A. J. (1983). *Home, school, and community in adolescent education*. ERIC/CUE Urban Diversity Series, No. 84.

Immunizing the world's children.

(1986, March-April). *Population Reports* (Series L; No. 5. L154-L192).

Ingram, D. D., Makuc, D., & Kleinman, J. C. (1986). National and state trends in use of prenatal care, 1970–1983. *American Journal of Public Health, 76*(4), 415–423.

Inhelder, B., & Piaget, J. (1964). *The early growth of logic in the child.* New York: Norton.

Inouye, E. (1965). Similar and dissimilar manifestations of obsessive-compulsive neuroses in monozygotic twins. *American Journal of Psychology, 121,* 1171–1175.

Institute for Social Research. (1985). How children use time. In *Time, goods and well-being.* Ann Arbor: University of Michigan.

Interagency Committee on Learning Disabilities. (1987). *Learning disabilities: A report to the U. S. Congress.*

Ioffe, F., Childiaeva, R., & Chernick, V. (1984). Prolonged effect of maternal alcohol injection on the neonatal electroencephalogram. *Pediatrics, 74*(3), 330–335.

Iosub, S., Bamji, M., Stone, R. K., Gromisch, D. S., & Wasserman, E. (1987). More on human immunodeficiency virus embryopathy. *Pediatrics, 80,* 512–516.

Istvan, J. (1986). Stress, anxiety, and birth outcomes: A critical review of the evidence. *Psychological Bulletin, 100*(3), 331–348.

Iwanaga, M. (1973). Development of interpersonal play structures in 3, 4, and 5 year old children. *Journal of Research and Development in Education, 6,* 71–82.

Izard, C. E. (1971). *The face of emotions.* New York: Appleton-Century-Crofts.

Izard, C. E. (1977). *Human emotions.* New York: Plenum.

Izard, C. E. (Ed.). (1982). *Measuring emotions in infants and children.* London: Cambridge University Press.

Izard, C. E., Huebner, R. R., Resser, D., McGinness, G. C., & Dougherty, L. M. (1980). The young infant's ability to produce discrete emotional expressions. *Developmental Psychology, 16*(2), 132–140.

Jacobson, J. L., Jacobson, S. W., Fein, G. G., Schwartz, P. M., & Dowler, J. K. (1984). Prenatal exposure to an environmental toxin: A test of the multiple effects model. *Developmental Psychology, 20*(4), 523–532.

Jacobson, J. L., & Wille, D. E. (1984). Influence of attachment and separation experience on separation distress at 18 months. *Developmental Psychology, 20*(3), 477–484.

Jacobson, J. L., & Wille, D. E. (1986). The influence of attachment pattern on developmental changes in peer interaction from the toddler to the preschool period. *Child Development, 57,* 338–347.

Jacobson, S. W., Fein, G. G., Jacobson, J. L., Schwartz, P. M., & Dowler, J. K. (1985). The effect of intrauterine PCB exposure on visual recognition memory. *Child Development, 56,* 853–860.

Janos, P. M., & Robinson, N. M. (1985). Psychosocial development in intellectually gifted children. In F. D. Horowitz & M. O'Brien (Eds.), *The gifted and talented: Developmental perspectives.* Washington, DC: American Psychological Association.

Jaslow, C. K. (1982). *Teenage pregnancy* (ERIC/CAPS Fact Sheet). Ann Arbor, MI: Counseling and Personnel Services Clearinghouse.

Jay, M. S., DuRant, R. H., Shoffitt, T., Linder, C. W., & Litt, I. F. (1984). Effect of peer counselors on adolescent compliance in use of oral contraceptives. *Pediatrics, 73*(2), 126–131.

Jeffcoate, J. A., Humphrey, M. E., & Lloyd, J. K. (1979). Disturbance in the parent-child relationship following preterm delivery. *Developmental Medicine and Child Neurology, 21,* 344–352.

Jelliffe, D., & Jelliffe, E. (1974). *Fat babies: Prevalence, perils and prevention.* London: Incentive Press.

Jelliffe, D. B., & Jelliffe, E. F. P. (1983). Recent scientific knowledge concerning breastfeeding. *Rev. Epidem. et Sante Publ., 31,* 367–373.

Jensen, A. R. (1969). How much can we boost IQ and scholastic achievement? *Harvard Educational Review, 39,* 1–123.

Jersild, A. T. (1946). Emotional development. In L. Carmichael (Ed.), *Manual of child psychology.* New York: Wiley.

Jersild, A. T., & Holmes, F. (1935). Children's fears. *Child Development Monographs, 6*(20).

Jiao, S., Ji, G., & Jing, Q. (1986). Comparitive study of behavioral qualities of only children and sibling children. *Child Development, 57,* 357–361.

Johnston, J., & Ettema, J. S. (1982). *Positive images: Breaking stereotypes with children's television.* Newbury Park, CA: Sage.

Johnston, L. D., O'Malley, P. M., & Bachman, J. G. (1988). National trends in drug use and related factors among American high school students and young adults. National trends through 1987. Rockville, MD: National Institute on Drug Abuse.

Jones, E. (1961). *The life and work of Sigmund Freud* (Edited and abridged by L. Trilling & S. Marcus). New York: Basic Books.

Jones, E. F., Forrest, J. D., Goldman, N., Henshaw, S. K., Lincoln, R., Rosoff, J. I., Westoff, C. F., Wulf, W., & Wulf, D. (1985). Teenage pregnancy in developed countries: Determinants and policy implications. *Family Planning Perspectives, 17,* 53–63.

Jones, K. L., Smith, D. W., Ulleland, C., & Streissguth, A. P. (1973). Pattern of malformation in offspring of chronic alcoholic mothers. *The Lancet,* pp. 1267–1271.

Jones, M. C. (1957). The late careers of boys who were early—or late—maturing. *Child Development, 28,* 115–128.

Jones, M. C. (1958). The study of socialization patterns at the high school level. *Journal of Genetic Psychology, 93,* 87–111.

Jones, M. C., & Mussen, P. H. (1958). Self-conceptions, motivations, and interpersonal attitudes of early- and late-maturing girls. *Child Development, 29,* 491–501.

Jost, H., & Sontag, L. (1944). The genetic factor in autonomic nervous system function. *Psychosomatic Medicine, 6,* 308–310.

Justice, B., & Duncan, D. F. (1977). Child abuse as a work-related problem. *Journal of Behavior Technology, Methods and Therapy, 23,* 53–55.

Justice, E. M. (1985). Categorization as a preferred memory strategy: Developmental changes during elementary school. *Developmental Psychology, 21*(6), 1105–1110.

Kagan, J. (1958). The concept of identification. *Psychological Review, 65*(5), 296–305.

Kagan, J. (1971). *Personality development.* New York: Harcourt Brace Jovanovich.

Kagan, J. (1979). Overview: Perspectives on human infancy. In J. Osofsky (Ed.), *Handbook of infant development.* New York: Wiley.

Kagan, J. (1982a). The emergence of self. *Journal of Child Psychology and Psychiatry, 23,* 363–381.

Kagan, J. (1982b). The ideas of spatial ability. *New England Journal of Medicine, 306,* 1225–1226.

Kagan, J. (1984). *The nature of the child.* New York: Basic Books.

Kagan, J., Reznick, J. S., Clarke, C., Snidman, N., & Garcia-Coll, C. (1984). Behavioral inhibition to the unfamiliar. *Child Development, 55,* 2212–2225.

Kagan, J., Reznick, J. S., & Snidman, N. (1988). Biological bases of childhood shyness. *Science, 240,* 167–171.

Kahn, A. J., & Kamerman, S. B. (1984, September 25). For whom preschool education is unattainable [Letter to the editor]. *The New York Times*, p. A26.

Kallman, F. J. (1953). *Heredity in health and mental disorder*. New York: Norton.

Kamin, L. J. (1974). *The science and politics of IQ*. Potomac, MD: Erlbaum.

Kamin, L. J. (1981). Commentary. In S. Scarr (Ed.), *Race, social class, and individual differences in I.Q.* Hillsdale, NJ: Erlbaum.

Kandel, D. B., Davies, M., Karus, D., & Yamaguchi, K. (1986). The consequences in young adulthood of adolescent drug involvement. *Archives of General Psychiatry, 43*, 746–754.

Kaplan, H., & Dove, H. (1987). Infant development among the Ache of eastern Paraguay. *Developmental Psychology, 23*(2), 190–198.

Kaplan, M., Eidelman, A. I., & Aboulafia, Y. (1983). Fasting and the precipitation of labor. *Journal of the American Medical Association, 250*(10), 1317–1318.

Kappas, A., Drummond, G. S., Manola, T., Petmezaki, S., & Valaes, T. (1988). Sn-protoporphyrin use on the management of hyperbilirubinemia in term newborns with direct Coombs-positive ABO uncompatibility. *Pediatrics, 81*(4), 485–497.

Karnes, M. B., Teska, J. A., Hodgkins, A. S., & Badger, E. D. (1970). Educational intervention at home by mothers of disadvantaged infants. *Child Development, 41*, 925–935.

Katz, P., & Zalk, S. (1978). Modification of children's racial attitudes. *Developmental Psychology, 14*(5), 447–461.

Katz, P. A. (1987). Variations in family constellation: Effects on gender schemata. In L. S. Liben & M. L. Signorella (Eds.), *Children's gender schemata*. San Francisco: Jossey-Bass.

Kaufman, J., & Zigler, E. (1987). Do abused children become abusive parents? *American Journal of Orthopsychiatry, 57*(2), 186–192.

Kearsley, R. B. (1981). Cognitive assessment of the handicapped infant: The need for an alternative approach. *American Journal of Orthopsychiatry, 51*(1), 43–54.

Keeney, T. J., Cannizzo, S. R., & Flavell, J. H. (1967). Spontaneous and induced verbal rehearsal in a recall task. *Child Development, 38*, 953–966.

Kellogg, R. (1970). Understanding children's art. In P. Cramer (Ed.), *Readings in developmental psychology today*. Delmar, CA: CRM.

Kelly, J. B. (1987, August). *Longer-term adjustment in children of divorce: Converging findings and implications for practice*. Paper presented at the annual meeting of the American Psychological Association, New York.

Kempe, C. H., Silverman, F. N., Steele, B. N., Droegemueller, W., & Silver, H. K. (1962). The battered child syndrome. *Journal of the American Medical Association, 181*(Pt. 1), 17–24.

Keniston, K. (1977). *All our children*. New York: Harcourt Brace Jovanovich.

Kenyatta, J. (1965). *Facing Mt. Kenya*. New York: Vintage.

Kirkley-Best, E., & Kellner, K. R. (1982). The forgotten grief: A review of the psychology of stillbirth. *American Journal of Orthopsychiatry, 52*, 420–429.

Kitchen, W., Ford, G., Orgill, A., Rickards, A., Astbury, J., Lissenden, J., Bajuk, B., Yu, V., Drew, J., & Campbell, N. (1987). Outcome in infants of birth weight 500-to-900 g: A continuing regional study of 5-year-old survivors. *Journal of Pediatrics, 111*, 761–766.

Kirkley-Best, E., & Kellner, K. R. (1982). The forgotten grief: A review of the psychology of stillbirth. *American Journal of Orthopsychiatry, 52*, 420–429.

Kirshenbaum, J. (1976, July 12). Assembly line for champions. *Sports Illustrated*, pp. 56–65.

Klaus, M. H., & Kennell, J. H. (1976). *Maternal-infant bonding*. St. Louis: Mosby.

Klaus, M. H., & Kennell, J. H. (1982). *Parent-infant bonding* (2d ed.). St. Louis: Mosby.

Klein, R. P., & Durfee, J. T. (1975). *Infants' reactions to strangers versus mothers*. Paper presented at the meeting of the Society for Research in Child Development, Denver.

Kleinberg, F. (1984). Sudden infant death syndrome. *Mayo Clinic Proceedings, 59*, 352–357.

Kline, M., Tschann, J., Johnston, J., & Wallerstein, J. (1988, March 30). *Child outcome in joint and sole custody families*. Paper presented at the annual meeting of the American Orthopsychiatry Association, San Francisco.

Klinnert, M. D., Emde, R. N., Butterfield, P., & Campos, J. J. (1986). Social referencing: The infant's use of emotional signals from a friendly adult with mother present. *Developmental Psychology, 22*(4), 427–432.

Knitzer, J. (1984). Mental health services to children and adolescents. *American Psychologist, 39*, 905–911.

Koff, E., Rierdan, J., & Sheingold, K. (1982). Memories of menarche: Age, preparation, and prior knowledge as determinants of initial menstrual experience. *Journal of Youth and Adolescence, 11*, 1–9.

Kohlberg, L. (1966). A cognitive-developmental analysis of children's sex-role concepts and attitudes. In E. E. Maccoby (Ed.), *The development of sex differences*. Stanford, CA: Stanford University Press.

Kohlberg, L. (1968). The child as a moral philosopher. *Psychology Today, 2*(4), 25–30.

Kohlberg, L. (1969). Stage and sequence: The cognitive-developmental approach to socialization. In D. A. Goslin (Ed.), *Handbook of socialization theory and research*. Chicago: Rand McNally.

Kohlberg, L. (1976). Moral stage and moralization. In T. Lickona (Ed.), *Moral development and behavior* (pp. 31–53). New York: Holt.

Kohlberg, L., & Gilligan, C. (1971, Fall). The adolescent as a philosopher: The discovery of the self in a postconventional world. *Daedalus*, pp. 1051–1086.

Kohlberg, L., Yaeger, J., & Hjertholm, E. (1968). Private speech: Four studies and a review of theories. *Child Development, 39*, 691–736.

Kohn, M., & Rosman, B. L. (1973). Relationship of preschool social-emotional functioning to later intellectual achievement. *Developmental Psychology, 6*(3), 445–452.

Kolata, G. (1986). Obese children: A growing problem. *Science, 232*, 20–21.

Kolata, G. (1988a, January 5). New treatments may aid women who have repeated miscarriages. *The New York Times*, p. C3.

Kolata, G. (1988b, March 29). Fetuses treated through umbilical cords. *The New York Times*, p. C3.

Kolder, V. E. B., Gallagher, J., & Parsons, M. T. (1987). Court-ordered obstetrical interventions. *New England Journal of Medicine, 316*, 1192–1196.

Kopp, C. B. (1982). Antecedents of self-regulation: A developmental perspective. *Developmental Psychology, 18*(2), 199–214.

Kopp, C. B., & McCall, R. B. (1982). Predicting later mental performance for normal, at-risk, and handicapped infants. In P. B. Baltes & O. G. Brim (Eds.), *Life-span development and behavior* (Vol. 4). New York: Academic.

Korner, A. F., Zeanah, C. H., Linden, J., Berkowitz, R. I., Kraemer, H. C., & Agras, W. S. (1985). The relationship between neonatal and later activity and temperament. *Child Development, 56,* 38–42.

Kotelchuck, M. (1973, March-April). *The nature of the infant's tie to his father.* Paper presented at the meeting of the Society for Research in Child Development, Philadelphia.

Kotelchuck, M. (1975, September). *Father caretaking characteristics and their influence on infant-father interaction.* Paper presented at the meeting of the American Psychological Association, Chicago.

Kraemer, H. C., Korner, A., Anders, T., Jacklin, C. N., & Dimiceli, S. (1985). Obstetric drugs and infant behavior: A re-evaluation. *Journal of Pediatric Psychology, 10,* 345–353.

Kramer, J., Hill, K., & Cohen, L. (1975). Infants' development of object permanence: A refined methodology and new evidence for Piaget's hypothesized ordinality. *Child Development, 46,* 149–155.

Krauss, R., & Glucksberg, S. (1977). Social and nonsocial speech. *Scientific American, 263*(2), 100–105.

Kreutzer, M., & Charlesworth, W. R. (1973). *Infant recognition of emotions.* Paper presented at the meeting of the Society for Research in Child Development, Philadelphia.

Kreutzer, M., Leonard, C., & Flavell, J. (1975). An interview study of children's knowledge about memory. *Monographs of the Society for Research in Child Development, 40*(1, Serial No. 159).

Kropp, J. P., & Haynes, O. M. (1987). Abusive and nonabusive mothers' ability to identify general and specific emotion signals of infants. *Child Development, 58,* 187–190.

Kuntzleman, C. T. (1984). Personal communication to S. W. Olds.

Kuhl, P. K., & Meltzoff, A. N. (1982). The bimodal perception of speech in infancy. *Science, 213,* 1138–1141.

Kupfersmid, J., & Wonderly, D. (1980). Moral maturity and behavior: Failure to find a link. *Journal of Youth and Adolescence, 9*(3), 249–261.

Kurinij, N., Shiono, P. H., & Rhoads, G. G. (1988). Breast-feeding incidence and duration in black and white women. *Pediatrics, 81*(3), 365–371.

Labbok, M. H., & Hendershot, G. E. (1987). Does breastfeeding protect against malocclusion? An analysis of the 1981 child health supplement to the National Health Interview Survey. *American Journal of Preventive Medicine, 3,* 4.

Lagercrantz, H., & Slotkin, T. A. (1986). The "stress" of being born. *Scientific American, 254*(4), 100–107.

Lamb, M. E. (1977). Father-infant and mother-infant interaction in the first year of life. *Child Development, 48,* 167–181.

Lamb, M. E. (1978). Influence of the child on marital quality and family interaction during the prenatal, perinatal, and infancy periods. In R. Lerner & G. Spanier (Eds.), *Child influences on marital and family interaction: A life-span perspective.* New York: Academic.

Lamb, M. E. (1981). The development of father-infant relationships. In M. E. Lamb (Ed.), *The role of the father in child development* (2d ed.). New York: Wiley.

Lamb, M. E. (1982a). The bonding phenomenon: Misinterpretations and their implications. *Journal of Pediatrics, 101*(4), 555–557.

Lamb, M. E. (1982b). Early contact and maternal-infant bonding: One decade later. *Pediatrics, 70*(5), 763–768.

Lamb, M. E. (1987). Predictive implications of individual differences in attachment. *Journal of Consulting and Clinical Psychology, 55*(6), 817–824.

Lamb, M. E., Campos, J. J., Hwang, C. P., Leiderman, P. H., Sagi, A., & Svejda, M. (1983). Maternal-infant bonding: A joint rebuttal. *Pediatrics, 72*(4), 574–575.

Landesman-Dwyer, S., & Emanuel, I. (1979). Smoking during pregnancy. *Teratology, 19,* 119–126.

Landwirth, J. (1987). Fetal abuse and neglect: An emerging controversy. *Pediatrics, 79,* 508–514.

Lawson, A., & Ingleby, J. D. (1974). Daily routines of preschool children: Effects of age, birth order, sex and social class, and developmental correlates. *Psychological Medicine, 4,* 399–415.

Leahy, R. (1976). Development of preference and processes of visual scanning in the human infant during the first three months of life. *Developmental Psychology, 12*(3), 250–254.

Leakey, R. E., & Lewin, R. (1977). *Origins.* New York: Dutton.

Leary, W. E. (1988a, June 22). Survey finds sharp drop in tooth decay. *The New York Times,* p. A1.

Leary, W. E. (1988b, January 16). Young adults show drop in cocaine use. *The New York Times,* p. A 24.

Leboyer, F. (1975). *Birth without violence.* New York: Random House.

Lee, R. V. (1973, September 16). What about the right to say "no"? *The New York Times Magazine.*

Lee, V. E., Brooks-Gunn, J., & Schnur, E. (1988). Does Head Start work? A 1-year follow-up comparison of disadvantaged children attending Head Start, no preschool and other pre-school programs. *Developmental Psychology, 24*(2), 210–222.

Lefty liberation. (1974, January 7). *Time,* p. 85.

Lehtovaara, A., Saarinen, P., & Jarvinen, J. (1965). *Psychological studies of twins: 1. GSR reactions.* Helsinki: University of Helsinki, Psychological Institute.

LeMasters, E. E. (1957). Parenthood as crisis. *Marriage and Family Living, 19,* 352–355.

Lennard, H. L., & Associates. (1971). *Mystification and drug misuse.* San Francisco: Jossey-Bass.

Lenneberg, E. H. (1967). *Biological functions of language.* New York: Wiley.

Lenneberg, E. H. (1969). On explaining language. *Science, 164*(3880), 635–643.

Lerner, J. V., & Galambos, N. L. (1985). Maternal role satisfaction, mother-child interaction, and child temperament: A process model. *Child Development, 21*(6), 1157–1164.

Lerner, R., & Lerner, J. (1977). Effects of age, sex, and physical attractiveness on child-peer relations, academic performance, and elementary school adjustment. *Developmental Psychology, 13*(6), 585–590.

Lester, B. M. (1979). A synergistic process approach to the study of prenatal malnutrition. *International Journal of Behavioral Development, 2,* 377–394.

Lester, B. M. (1987). Developmental outcome prediction from acoustic cry analysis in term and preterm infants. *Pediatrics, 80*(4), 529–534.

Lester, R., & Van Theil, D. H. (1977). Gonadal function in chronic alcoholic men. *Advances in Experimental Medicine and Biology, 85A,* 339–414.

Levano, K. J., et al. (1986). A prospective comparison of selective and universal electronic fetal monitoring in 34,995 pregnancies. *New England Journal of Medicine, 315,* 615–619.

Levine, M. D. (1987). *Developmental variation and learning disorders.* Cambridge, MA: Educators Publishing.

Levy, D. M. (1966). *Maternal overprotection.* New York: Norton.

Lewin, T. (1988, March 22). Despite criticism, fetal monitors are likely to remain in wide use. *The New York Times,* p. 24.

Lewis, D. O., Pincus, J. H., et al. (1988). Neuropsychiatric, psychoeducational and family characteristics of 14 juveniles condemned to death in the United States. *American Journal of Psychiatry, 145,* 584–589.

Lewis, M., & Brooks, J. (1974). Self, other, and fear: Infants' reactions to people. In H. Lewis & L. Rosenblum (Eds.), *The origins of fear: The origins of behavior* (Vol. 2). New York: Wiley.

Lickona, T. (1973). *An experimental test of Piaget's theory of moral development.* Paper presented at the meeting of the Society for Research in Child Development, Philadelphia.

Lickona, T. (Ed.). (1976). *Moral development and behavior.* New York: Holt.

Liebenberg, B. (1969). Expectant fathers. *Child and Family, 8,* 265–278.

Liebert, R. M. (1972). Television and social learning: Some relationships between viewing violence and behaving aggressively. In J. P. Murray, E. A. Rubinstein, & G. A. Comstock (Eds.), *Television and social behavior* (Vol. 2). Washington, DC: U. S. Government Printing Office.

Liebert, R. M., & Poulos, R. W. (1976). Television as a moral teacher. In T. Lickona (Ed.), *Moral development and behavior* (pp. 284–298). New York: Holt.

Light, R. J. (1973). Abused and neglected children in America: A study of alternative policies. *Harvard Educational Review, 43,* 556–598.

Lindsey, R. (1988, February 1). Circumcision under criticism as unnecessary to newborn. *The New York Times,* pp. A1, A20.

Linn, M. C., & Petersen, A. C. (1985). Emergence and characterization of gender differences in spatial ability: A meta-analysis. *Child Development, 56,* 1479–1498.

Linn, S., Schoenbaum, S. C., Monson, R. R., Rosner, B., Stubblefield, P. G., & Ryan, K. J. (1982). No association between coffee consumption and adverse outcomes of pregnancy. *New England Journal of Medicine, 306*(3), 141–145.

Lipsitt, L. (1982). Infant learning. In T. M. Field, A. Huston, H. Quay, L. Troll, & G. Finley (Eds.), *Review of human development.* New York: Wiley.

Lipsitt, L. P. (1986). Learning in infancy: Cognitive development in babies. *Journal of Pediatrics, 109*(1), 172–182.

Lipsitt, L. P., & Werner, J. S. (1981). The infancy of human learning processes. In E. S. Gollin (Ed.), *Developmental plasticity.* New York: Academic.

Livson, N., & Peskin, H. (1980). Perspectives on adolescence from longitudinal research. In J. Adelson (Ed.), *Handbook of adolescent psychology.* New York: Wiley.

Locke, R. (1979, January 7). Preschool aggression linked to TV viewing. *Wisconsin State Journal,* p. 2.

Loda, F. A. (1980). Day care. *Pediatrics in Review, 1*(9), 277–281.

Loeber, R., & Dishion, T. (1983). Early predictors of male delinquency: A review. *Psychological Bulletin, 94,* 68–99.

Loehlin, J., Lindzey, G., & Spuhler, J. (1975). *Race differences in intelligence.* San Francisco: Freeman.

Long-term outlook for children with sex chromosome abnormalities. (1982, July 3). *The Lancet,* p. 27.

Looft, W. R. (1971). *Toward a history of life-span developmental psychology.* Unpublished manuscript, University of Wisconsin, Madison.

Lorenz, K. (1957). Comparative study of behavior. In C. H. Schiller (Ed.), *Instinctive behavior.* New York: International Press.

Lorenz, K. (1971). *Studies in animal and human behavior* (Vol. II). Cambridge, MA: Harvard University Press.

Lott, I. T., Bocian, M., Pribram, H. W., & Leitner, M. (1984). Fetal hydrocephalus and ear anomalies associated with maternal use of isotretinoin. *Journal of Pediatrics, 105,* 597–600.

Loucopoulos, A., Ferin, M., & VandeWiele, R. L. (1984). Cervical mucus-related infertility treated by pulsatile administration of gonadotropin-releasing hormone. *Fertility and Sterility, 41,* 139–141.

Louis Harris & Associates. *See* Harris, L., & Associates.

Lowman, C., Verdugo, N., Malin, H., & Aitken, S. (1983, July 8). Patterns of alcohol use among teenage drivers in fatal motor vehicle accidents—United States, 1977–1981. *Morbidity and Mortality Weekly Report (MMWR),* pp. 344–347.

Lowrey, G. H. (1978). *Growth and development of children* (7th ed.). Chicago: Year Book Medical.

Lozoff, B., Wolf, A. W., & Davis, N. S. (1985). Sleep problems seen in pediatric practice. *Pediatrics, 75,* 477–483.

Lutjen, P., Trounson, A., Leeton, J., Findlay, J., Wood, C., & Renou, P. (1984). The establishment and maintenance of pregnancy using in vitro fertilization and embryo donation in a patient with primary ovarian failure. *Nature, 307,* 174–175.

Lynn, R. (1982). IQ in Japan and the United States shows a growing disparity. *Nature, 297,* 222–223.

Maccoby, E. (1980). *Social development.* New York: Harcourt Brace Jovanovich.

Maccoby, E., & Jacklin, C. (1974). *The psychology of sex differences.* Stanford, CA: Stanford University Press.

Maccoby, E. E. (1984). Middle childhood in the context of the family. In W. A. Collins (Ed.), *Development during middle childhood.* Washington, DC: National Academy.

Macey, T. J., Harmon, R. J., & Easterbrooks, M. A. (1987). Impact of premature birth on the development of the infant in the family. *Journal of Consulting and Clinical Psychology, 55*(6), 846–852.

Macfarlane, A. (1975). Olfaction in the development of social preferences in the human neonate. In *Parent-infant interaction* (CIBA Foundation Symposium, 33). Amsterdam: Elsevier.

Maeroff, G. I. (1984, October 29). Interest in learning foreign languages rises. *The New York Times,* pp. A1, A17.

Mahoney, E. R. (1983). *Human sexuality.* New York: McGraw-Hill.

Main, M., & Solomon, J. (1986). Discovery of an insecure disorganized/disoriented attachment pattern: Procedures, findings, and implications for the classification of behavior. In M. Yogman & T. B. Brazelton (Eds.), *Affective development in infancy.* Norwood, NJ: Ablex.

Malmquist, C. P. (1983). Major depression in childhood: Why don't we know more? *American Journal of Orthopsychiatry, 53*(2), 262–268.

Maloney, M. J., & Klykylo, W. M. (1983). An overview of anorexia nervosa, bulimia, and obesity in children and adolescents. *Journal of the American Academy of Child Psychiatry, 22,* 99–107.

Mamay, P. D., & Simpson, P. L. (1981). Three female roles in television commercials. *Sex Roles, 7*(12), 1223–1232.

Mannuzza, S., Klein, R. G., Bonagura, N., Konig, P. H., & Shenker, R. (1988). Hyperactive boys almost grown up: II. Status of subjects without a mental disorder. *Archives of General Psychiatry, 45,* 13–18.

Manosevitz, M., Prentice, N. M., & Wilson, F. (1973). Individual and family correlates of imaginary companions in preschool children. *Developmental Psychology, 8*(1), 72–79.

Maratsos, M. (1973). Nonegocentric communication abilities in preschool children. *Child Development, 44,* 697–700.

March of Dimes Birth Defects Foundation. (1983a). *Drugs, alcohol, tobacco abuse during pregnancy.* White Plains, NY: Author.

March of Dimes Birth Defects Foundation. (1983b). *Genetic counseling.* White Plains, NY: Author.

March of Dimes Birth Defects Foundation. (undated). *Low birthweight.* Public health education information sheet. White Plains, NY: Author.

Marcia, J. E. (1966). Development and validation of ego identity status. *Journal of Personality and Social Psychology*, 3(5), 551–558.

Marcia, J. E. (1979, June). *Identity status in late adolescence: Description and some clinical implications.* Address given at a symposium on identity development, Rijksuniversitat Groningen, Netherlands.

Marcia, J. E. (1980). Identity in adolescence. In J. Adelson (Ed.), *Handbook of adolescent psychology.* New York: Wiley.

Marion, R. W., Wiznia, A. A., Hutcheon, G., & Rubinstein, A. (1986). Human T-cell lymphotropic virus type III (HTLV-III) embryopathy. *American Journal of the Diseases of Children*, 140, 638–640.

Markus, H. (1980). The self in thought and memory. In M. Wegner & R. R. Vallacher (Eds.), *The self in social psychology.* New York: Oxford University Press.

Markus, H. J., & Nurius, P. S. (1984). Self-understanding and self-regulation in middle childhood. In W. A. Collins (Ed.), *Development during middle childhood.* Washington, DC: National Academy.

Marquis, K. S., & Detweiler, R. A. (1985). Does adopted mean different? An attributional analysis. *Journal of Personality and Social Psychology*, 48, 1054–1066.

Marshall, S. P. (1984). Sex differences in children's mathematic achievement: Solving computations and story problems. *Journal of Educational Psychology*, 76, 194–204.

Martin, G. B., & Clark, R. D. (1982). Distress crying in neonates: Species and peer specificity. *Developmental Psychology*, 18(1), 3–9.

Martin, J., Martin, O., Lund, C., & Streissguth, A. (1977). Maternal alcohol ingestion and cigarette smoking and their effects on newborn conditioning. *Alcoholism: Clinical and Experimental Research*, 1, 243–247.

Martinez, G. A., & Kreiger, F. W. (1985). The 1984 milk-feeding patterns in the United States. *Pediatrics*, 76, 1004–1008.

Marwick, C., & Simmons, K. (1984). Changing childhood disease pattern linked with day-care boom. *Journal of the American Medical Association*, 215(10), 1245–1251.

Marzano, R. J., & Hutchins, C. L. (1987). *Thinking skills: A conceptual framework.* (ERIC Document Reproduction Service No. ED 266436).

Maslow, A. (1954). *Motivation and personality.* New York: Harper & Row.

Maslow, A. (1968). *Toward a psychology of being.* Princeton, NJ: Van Nostrand.

Masnick, G., & Bane, M. J. (1980). *The nation's families, 1960–1990.* Cambridge, MA: Joint Center for Urban Studies of MIT and Harvard University.

Masson, J. M. (1984). *The assault on truth: Freud's suppression of the seduction theory.* New York: Farrar, Straus & Giroux.

Masten, A. S. (1986). Humor and competence in school-aged children. *Child Development*, 57, 461–473.

Masters, W. H., & Johnson, V. E. (1966). *Human sexual response.* Boston: Little, Brown.

Masters, W. H., & Johnson, V. E. (1979). *Homosexuality in perspective.* Boston: Little, Brown.

Matas, L., Arend, R., & Sroufe, L. A. (1978). Continuity of adaptation in the second year: The relationship between quality of attachment and later competence. *Child Development*, 49, 547–556.

Matlin, M. W. (1987). *The psychology of women.* New York: Holt, Rinehart, & Winston.

Matthews, K. A., & Angulo, J. (1980). Measurement of the type A behavior pattern in children: Assessment of children's competitiveness, impatience-anger, and aggression. *Child Development*, 51, 466–475.

Matthews, K. A., & Volkin, J. I. (1981). Efforts to excel and the type A behavior pattern in children. *Child Development*, 52, 1283–1289.

Maurer, D., & Salapatek, P. (1976). Developmental changes in the scanning of faces by young children. *Child Development*, 47, 523–527.

Maxwell, L. (1987). *Eight pointers on teaching children to think.* Washington, DC: Office of Educational Research and Improvement, U. S. Department of Education.

May, K. A., & Perrin, S. P. (1985). Prelude: Pregnancy and birth. In S. M. H. Hanson & F. W. Bozett (Eds.), *Dimensions of fatherhood.* Beverly Hills, CA: Sage.

Mayer, J. (1973). Fat babies grow into fat people. *Family Health*, 5(3), 24–26.

Maynard, J. (1973). *Looking back: A chronicle of growing up old in the sixties.* Garden City, NY: Doubleday.

Maziade, M., Boudreault, M., Cote, R., & Thivierge, J. (1986). Influence of gentle birth delivery procedures and other perinatal circumstances on infant temperment: Developmental and social implications. *Journal of Pediatrics*, 108(1), 134–136.

McAlister, A. L., Perry, C., & Maccoby, N. (1979). Adolescent smoking: Onset and prevention. *Pediatrics*, 63(4), 650–658.

McCall, R. B., Appelbaum, M. I., & Hogarty, P. S. (1973). Developmental changes in mental performance. *Monographs of the Society for Research in Child Development*, 38 (Serial No. 150).

McCarthy, J., & Menken, J. (1979). Marriage, remarriage, marital disruption, and age at first birth. *Family Planning Perspectives*, 11(27).

McCartney, K. (1984). Effect of quality of day care environment on children's language development. *Developmental Psychology*, 20(2), 244–260.

McCary, J. L. (1975). *Freedom and growth in marriage.* Santa Barbara, CA: Hamilton.

McCaskill, C. L., & Wellman, B. A. (1938). A study of common motor achievements at the preschool ages. *Child Development*, 9, 141–150.

McClelland, D., Constantian, C., Regalado, D., & Stone, C. (1978). Making it to maturity. *Psychology Today*, 12(1), 42–53, 114.

McDaniel, K. D. (1986). Pharmacological treatment of psychiatric and neuro-developmental disorders in children and adolescents (Part 1, Part 2, Part 3). *Clinical Pediatrics*, 25(2,3,4), 65–71, 198–224.

McEwan, K. L., Costello, C. G., & Taylor, P. J. (1987). Adjustment to infertility. *Journal of Abnormal Psychology*, 96(2), 108–116.

McGraw, M. B. (1940). Neural maturation as exemplified in achievement of bladder control. *Journal of Pediatrics*, 16, 580–589.

McKenry, P. C., Walters, L. H., & Johnson, C. (1979). Adolescent pregnancy: A review of the literature. *Family Coordinator*, 23(1), 17–28.

McKinley, D. (1964). *Social class and family life.* New York: Free Press.

McKinney, K. (1987). *A look at Japanese education today.* Washington, DC: Office of Educational Research and Improvement, U. S. Department of Education.

McKinnon, D. W. (1968). Selecting students with creative potential. In P. Heist (Ed.), *The creative college student: An unmet challenge.* San Francisco: Jossey-Bass.

McNeill, W. H. (1976). *Plagues and peoples.* Garden City, NY: Doubleday.

Mead, M. (1928). *Coming of age in Samoa.* New York: Morrow.

Mead, M. (1935). *Sex and temperament in three primitive societies.* New York: Morrow.

Mead, M. (1949). *Male and female: A study of the sexes in a changing world.* New York: Morrow.

Mednick, B. R., Baker, R. L., & Sutton-Smith, B. (1979). *Teenage pregnancy and perinatal mortality.* (Contract No. 1-117-82807). Unpublished report.

Medrich, E. A., Roizen, J. A., Rubin, V., & Buckley, S. (1982). *The serious business of growing up.* Berkeley: University of California Press.

Melnick, S., Cole, P., Anderson, D., & Herbst, A. (1987). Rates and risks of diethylstilbestrol-related clear-cell adenocarcinoma of the vagina and cervix. *New England Journal of Medicine, 316*, 514–516.

Melton, G. B., & Davidson, H. A. (1987). Child protection and society: When should the state intervene? *American Psychologist, 42*(2), 172–175.

Meltzoff, A. N. (1985). Immediate and deferred imitation in fourteen- and twenty-four-month-old infants. *Child Development, 56*, 62–72.

Meltzoff, A. N. (1988). Infant imitation and memory: Nine-month-olds in immediate and deferred tests. *Child Development, 59*, 217, 225.

Meltzoff, A. N., & Moore, M. K. (1977). Imitation of facial and manual gestures by human neonates. *Science, 198*, 75–78.

Meltzoff, A. N., & Moore, M. K. (1983). Newborn infants imitate adult facial gestures. *Child Development, 54*, 702–709.

Meredith, N. V. (1969). Body size of contemporary groups of eight-year-old children studied in different parts of the world. *Monographs of the Society for Research in Child Development, 34*(1).

Metzger, B. E., Ravnikar, V., Vileisis, R. A., & Freinkel, N. (1982, March 13). "Accelerated starvation" and the skipped breakfast in late normal pregnancy. *The Lancet*, pp. 588–592.

Miller, B., & Gerard, D. (1979). Family influences on the development of creativity in children: An integrative review. *Family Coordinator, 28*(3), 295–312.

Miller, B. C., & Myers-Walls, J. A. (1983). Parenthood: Stresses and coping strategies. In H. I. McCubbin & C. R. Figley (Eds.), *Stress and the family: Vol. 1. Coping with normative transitions.* New York: Brunner/Mazel.

Miller, C. A. (1987). A review of maternity care programs in western Europe. *Family Planning Perspectives, 19*(5), 207–211.

Miller, E., Cradock-Watson, J. E., & Pollock, T. M. (1982, October 9). Consequences of confirmed maternal rubella at successive stages of pregnancy. *The Lancet*, pp. 781–784.

Miller, G. A. (1956). The magical number seven, plus or minus two: Some limits on our capacity to process information. *Psychological Review, 63*, 81–97.

Miller, J. F., Williamson, E., Glue, J., Gordon, Y. B., Grudzinskas, J. G., & Sykes, A. (1980). Fetal loss after implantation: A prospective study. *The Lancet*, pp. 554–556.

Miller, L. B., & Bizzel, R. P. (1983). Long-term effects of four preschool programs: Sixth, seventh, and eighth grades. *Child Development, 54*, 727–741.

Miller, P. H. (1983). *Theories of developmental psychology.* San Francisco: Freeman.

Miller, V., Onotera, R. T., & Deinard, A. S. (1984). Denver developmental screening test: Cultural variations in southeast Asian children. *Journal of Pediatrics, 104*(3), 481–482.

Mills, J., Harlap, S., & Harley, E. E. (1981). Should coitus in late pregnancy be discouraged? *The Lancet*, p. 136.

Mills, J. L., & Graubard, B. I. (1987). Is moderate drinking during pregnancy associated with increased risk for malformations? *Pediatrics, 80*, 309–314.

Mills, J. L., Graubard, B. I., Harley, E. E., Rhoads, G. G., & Berendes, H. W. (1984). Maternal alcohol consumption and birth weight: How much drinking is safe during pregnancy? *Journal of the American Medical Association, 252*, 1875–1879.

Mills, J. L., Shiono, P. H., Shapiro, L. R., Crawford, P. B., Rhoads, G. G. (1986). Early growth predicts timing of puberty in boys: Results of a 14-year nutrition and growth study. *Journal of Pediatrics, 109*, 543–547.

Milne, A. M., Myers, D. E., Rosenthal, A. S., & Ginsburg, A. (1986). Single parents, working mothers, and the educational achievement of school children. *Sociology of Education, 59*, 125–139.

Minde, K., Shosenberg, N., Marton, P., Thompson, J., Ripley, J., & Burns, S. (1980). Self-help groups in a premature nursery: A controlled evaluation. *Journal of Pediatrics, 96*, 933–940.

Miranda, S., Hack, M., Fantz, R., Fanaroff, A., & Klaus, M. (1977). Neonatal pattern vision: Predictor of future mental performance? *Journal of Pediatrics, 91*(4), 642–647.

Mittler, P. (1971). *The study of twins.* Baltimore: Penguin.

Money, J., & Ehrhardt, A. (1972). *Man and woman, boy and girl.* Baltimore: Johns Hopkins University Press.

Money, J., Ehrhardt, A., & Masica, D. N. (1968). Fetal feminization induced by androgen insensitivity in the testicular feminizing syndrome: Effect on marriage and maternalism. *Johns Hopkins Medical Journal, 123*, 105–114.

Montemayor, R. (1983). Parents and adolescents in conflict: All families some of the time and some families most of the time. *Journal of Early Adolescence, 3*, 83–103.

Moore, A. U. (1960). *Studies on the formation of the mother-neonate bond in sheep and goats.* Paper presented at the meeting of the American Psychological Association.

Moore, N., Evertson, C., & Brophy, J. (1974). Solitary play: Some functional reconsiderations. *Developmental Psychology, 10*(5), 830–834.

Morbidity and Mortality Weekly Report (MMWR). (1986, December 12). Update: Acquired immunodeficiency syndrome—United States.

Morbidity and Mortality Weekly Report (MMWR). (1987), August 14). Update: Acquired immunodeficiency syndrome—United States.

Morland, J. (1966). A comparison of race awareness in northern and southern children. *American Journal of Orthopsychiatry, 36*, 22–31.

Morris, R., & Kralochwill, T. (1983). *Treating children's fears and phobias: A behavioral approach.* Elmsford, NY: Pergamon.

Mortimer, J. T. (1975). Occupational value socialization in business and professional families. *Sociology of Work and Occupations, 2*, 29–53.

Mortimer, J. T. (1976). Social class, work, and the family. Some implications of the father's occupation for familial relations and sons' career decisions. *Journal of Marriage and the Family, 38*, 241–256.

Moskowitz, B. A. (1978). The acquisition of language. *Scientific American, 239*(5), 92–108.

Murphy, C. M., & Bootzin, R. R. (1973). Active and passive participation in the contact desensitization of snake fear in children. *Behavior Therapy, 4*, 203–211.

Murphy, D. P. (1929). The outcome of 625 pregnancies in women subjected to pelvic radium roentgen irradiation. *American Journal of Obstetrics and Gynecology, 18*, 179–187.

Murray, A. D., Dolby, R. M., Nation, R. L., & Thomas, D. B. (1981). Effects of epidural anesthesia on newborns and their mothers. *Child Development, 52*, 71–82.

Mussen, P. H., Conger, J. J., & Kagan, J. (1969). *Child development and personality.* New York: Harper & Row.

Mussen, P. H., & Eisenberg-Berg, N. (1977). *Roots of caring, sharing and helping: The development of prosocial behavior in children*. San Francisco: Freeman.

Mussen, P. H., & Jones, M. C. (1957). Self-conceptions, motivations, and interpersonal attitudes of late- and early-maturing boys. *Child Development, 28*, 243–256.

Mussen, P. H., & Rutherford, E. (1963). Parent-child relations and parental personality in relation to young children's sex role preferences. *Child Development, 34*, 589–607.

Myers, J. K., Weissman, M. M., Tischler, G. L., Holzer, C. E., Leaf, P. J., Orvaschel, H., Anthony, J. C., Boyd, J. H., Burke, J. D., Kramer, M., & Stoltzman, R. (1984). Six-month prevalence of psychiatric disorders in three communities. *Archives of General Psychiatry, 41*, 259–267.

Myers, N., & Perlmutter, M. (1978). Memory in the years from 2 to 5. In P. Ornstein (Ed.), *Memory development in children*. Hillsdale, NJ: Erlbaum.

Nadi, N. S., Nurnberger, J. I., & Gershon, E. S. (1984). Muscarinic cholinergic receptors on skin fibroblasts in familial affective disorder. *New England Journal of Medicine, 311*, 225–230.

Naeye, R. L., & Peters, E. C. (1984). Mental development of children whose mothers smoked during pregnancy. *Obstetrics and Gynecology, 64*, 601.

National Assessment of Educational Progress. (1981, October). *Reading, thinking and writing: Results from the 1979–80 national assessment of reading and literature* (Report No. 11-L-01). Denver: Education Commission of States.

National Center for Education Statistics (NCES). (1983). High school dropouts: Descriptive information from high school and beyond. *NCES Bulletin*. Washington, DC: U.S. Department of Education.

National Center for Education Statistics (NCES). (1984). *The condition of education* (Publication No. NCES-84-401). Washington, DC: U.S. Government Printing Office.

National Center for Education Statistics (NCES). (1985). *The relationship of parental involvement to high school grades* (Publication No. NCES-85-205b). Washington, DC: U.S. Government Printing Office.

National Center for Education Statistics (NCES). (1986). *Education statistics: A pocket digest* (Publication No. CS-86-401). Washington, DC: U.S. Department of Education Center for Statistics.

National Center for Health Statistics. (1984a). *Annual summary of births, deaths, marriages, and divorces: U.S., 1983* (DHHS Publication No. PHS 84-1120). Hyattsville, MD: Public Health Service.

National Center for Health Statistics. (1984b). *Trends in teenage childbearing. United States 1970–1981* (Series 21, No. 41, Stock No. 01702200-851-3). Washington, DC: U.S. Government Printing Office.

National Center for Health Statistics. (1987). Final mortality statistics, 1985, advance report. *Monthly Vital Statistics Report, 36*(5, supplement).

National Clearinghouse for Alcohol Information. (undated). *Drinking and pregnancy*. Rockville, MD: Author.

National Coalition on Television Violence. (undated). *Action alert: War toys/cartoons more violent*. Champaign, IL: Author.

National Commission on Excellence in Education. (1983, April). *A nation at risk: The imperative for educational reform* (Stock No. 065-000-00177-2). Washington, DC: U.S. Government Printing Office.

National Commission for the Protection of Human Subjects of Biomedical and Behavioral Research. (1978). Report.

National Foundation/March of Dimes. (1972, January). *Science News*.

National Institute on Alcohol Abuse and Alcoholism (NIAAA). (1986). *Media alert: FAS awareness campaign: My baby . . . strong and healthy*. Rockville, MD: National Clearinghouse for Alcohol Information.

National Institute of Child Health and Human Development. (1978). Smoking in children and adolescents. *Pediatric Annals, 7*(9), 130–131.

National Institute on Drug Abuse (NIDA). (1987). Cocaine use remains steady, other drug use declines among high school seniors. *NIDA Notes, 2*(2), 1.

National Institute of Mental Health (NIMH). (1981). *Plain talk about adolescence*. Washington, DC: U.S. Government Printing Office.

National Institute of Mental Health (NIMH). (1982). *Television and behavior: Ten years of scientific progress and implications for the eighties, Vol. 1: Summary report* (DHHS Publication No. ADM 82-1195). Washington, DC: U.S. Government Printing Office.

National Institutes of Health (NIH). (1979). NIH Consensus Development Conference. *Clinical Pediatrics, 18*(9), 535–538.

National Institutes of Health (NIH). (1984, February 6–8). The use of diagnostic ultrasound imaging in pregnancy. Consensus Development Conference Statement.

National Institutes of Health (NIH). (1987). Newborn screening for sickle cell disease and other hemoglobinopathies. Consensus Development Conference Statement, *6*(9), 1–8.

National SIDS Clearinghouse (undated). Leaflet.

Neal, J. H. (1983). Children's understanding of their parents' divorces. In L. A. Kurdek (Ed.), *Children and divorce: New directions for child development* (No. 19). San Francisco: Jossey-Bass.

Nelson, K. (1973). Structure and strategy in learning to talk. *Monographs of the Society for Research in Child Development, 38*(1–2).

Nelson, K. (1981). Individual differences in language development: Implications for development and language. *Developmental Psychology, 17*(2), 170–187.

Nelson, K. (1989). Remembering: A functional developmental perspective. In P. R. Solomon, G. R. Goethels, C. M. Kelley, & B. R. Stephens (Eds.), *Memory: An interdisciplinary approach*. New York: Springer-Verlag.

Nelson, N., Enkin, M., Saigal, S., Bennett, K., Milner, R., & Sackett, D. (1980). A randomized clinical trial of the Leboyer approach to childbirth. *New England Journal of Medicine, 302*(12), 655–660.

New Medico Head Injury System. (1987). *Childhood head injury prevention safety tips for children and parents*. Printed handout.

New York Times, The (1987, November 25). Bureau of Labor Statistics, p. B9.

Newson, J., Newson, E., & Mahalski, P. A. (1982). Persistent infant comfort habits and their sequelae at 11 and 16 years. *Journal of Child Psychology and Psychiatry, 23*, 421–436.

Nieberg, P., Marks, J. S., McLaren, N. M., & Remington, P. L. (1985). The fetal tobacco syndrome. *Journal of the American Medical Association, 253*, 2998–2999.

Nisan, M., & Kohlberg, L. (1982). Universality and variation in moral judgment: A longitudinal and cross-sectional study in Turkey. *Child Development, 53*, 865–876.

Nordlicht, S. (1979). Effects of stress on the police officer and family. *New York State Journal of Medicine, 79*, 400–401.

Norton, F. C., Placek, P. J., & Taffel, S. M. (1987). Comparisons of national cesarean-section rates. *New*

England Journal of Medicine, 316, 386–389.

Nussbaum, M., Shenker, I. R., Baird, D., & Saravay, S. (1985). Follow-up investigation in patients with anorexia nervosa. *Journal of Pediatrics, 106,* 835–840.

Oates, R. K., Peacock, A., & Forrest, D. (1985). Long-term effects of nonorganic failure to thrive. *Pediatrics, 75,* 36–40.

O'Bryant, S. L., & Corder-Boltz, C. R. (1978). The effects of television on children's stereotyping of women's work roles. *Journal of Vocational Behavior, 12,* 233–244.

O'Connor, M. J., Cohen, S., & Parmelee, A. H. (1984). Infant auditory discrimination in preterm and full-term infants as a predictor of 5-year intelligence. *Developmental Psychology, 20,* 159–165.

O'Connor, M. J., Sigman, M., & Brill, N. (1987). Disorganization of attachment in relation to maternal alcohol consumption. *Journal of Consulting and Clinical Psychology, 55*(6), 831–836.

Offer, D. (1969). *The psychological world of the teenager: A study of normal adolescent boys.* New York: Basic Books.

Offer, D., & Offer, J. B. (1974). Normal adolescent males: The high school and college years. *Journal of the American College Health Association, 22,* 209–215.

Offer, D., Ostrov, E., & Marohn, R. C. (1972). *The psychological world of the juvenile delinquent.* New York: Basic Books.

Olds, S. W. (1985). *The eternal garden: Seasons of our sexuality.* New York: Times Books.

Olds, S. W. (1986). *The working parents' survival guide.* New York: Bantam.

Olds, S. W. (1989). *The working parents' survival guide.* Rocklin, CA: Prima.

Oliner, S. P., & Oliner, P. M. (1988). *The altruistic personality: Rescuers of Jews in Nazi Europe.* New York: Free Press.

Ornstein, P. (1978). Introduction: The study of children's memory. In P. Ornstein (Ed.), *Memory development in children* (pp. 1–19). Hillsdale, NJ: Erlbaum.

Osofsky, J. (Ed.). (1979). *Handbook of infant development.* New York: Wiley.

Ostrea, E. M., & Chavez, C. J. (1979). Perinatal problems (excluding neonatal withdrawal) in maternal drug addiction: A study of 830 cases. *Journal of Pediatrics, 94*(2), 292–295.

Oswald, P. F., & Peltzman, P. (1974). The cry of the human infant. *Scientific American, 230*(3), 84–90.

Otis, A. S., & Lennon, R. T. (1967). *Otis-Lennon Mental Ability Test* (Primary Levels I and II). New York: Harcourt Brace.

Otto, H., & Healy, S. (1966). Adolescents' self-perception of personality strengths. *Journal of Human Relations, 14*(3), 483–490.

Page, D. C., et al. (1987). The sex-determining region of the human Y chromosome encodes a finger protein. *Cell, 51,* 1091–1104.

Palkovitz, R. (1985). Fathers' birth attendance, early contact, and extended contact with their newborns: A critical review. *Child Development, 56,* 392–406.

Paltrow, L. M. (1988, Winter). Court forces dying woman to undergo cesarean. *Civil Liberties, 363,* 12.

Papalia, D. (1972). The status of several conservation abilities across the life-span. *Human Development, 15,* 229–243.

Papousek, H. (1959). A method of studying conditioned food reflexes in young children up to age six months. *Pavlovian Journal of Higher Nervous Activity, 9,* 136–140.

Papousek, H. (1960a). Conditioned motor alimentary reflexes in infants: 1. Experimental conditioned sucking reflex. *Ceskoslovenska Pediatrie, 15,* 861–872.

Papousek, H. (1960b). Conditioned motor alimentary reflexes in infants: 2. A new experimental method of investigation. *Ceskoslovenska Pediatrie, 15,* 981–988.

Papousek, H. (1961). Conditioned head rotation reflexes in infants in the first months of life. *Acta Paediatrica, 50,* 565–576.

Paris, S. G., & Lindauer, B. K. (1976). The role of inference in children's comprehension and memory for sentences. *Cognitive Psychology, 8,* 217–227.

Parke, R. (1977). Some effects of punishment on children's behavior—Revisited. In P. Cantor (Ed.), *Understanding a child's world.* New York: McGraw-Hill.

Parke, R. D., & Tinsley, B. R. (1981). The father's role in infancy: Determinants of involvement in caregiving and play. In M. E. Lamb (Ed.), *The role of the father in child development* (2d ed.). New York: Wiley.

Parker, J. G., & Asher, S. R. (1987). Peer relations and later personal adjustment: Are low-accepted children at risk? *Psychological Bulletin, 102*(3), 357–389.

Parkes, J. D. (1986, September 1). The parasomnias. *The Lancet,* pp. 1021–1025.

Parmelee, A. H. (1986). Children's illnesses: Their beneficial effects on behavioral development. *Child Development, 57,* 1–10.

Parmelee, A. H., Wenner, W. H., & Schulz, H. R. (1964). Infant sleep patterns: From birth to 16 weeks of age. *Journal of Pediatrics, 65,* 576.

Parten, M. (1932). Social play among preschool children. *Journal of Abnormal and Social Psychology, 27,* 243–269.

Patterson, D. (1987). The causes of Down syndrome. *Scientific American, 257*(2), 52–60.

Patterson, G. R., Chamberlain, P., & Reid, J. B. (1982). A comparative evaluation of a parent-training program. *Behavior Therapy, 13*(5), 638–650.

Patterson, G. R., & Stouthamer-Loeber, M. (1984). The correlation of family management practices and delinquency. *Child Development, 55,* 1299–1307.

Pearlin, L. I., & Kohn, M. L. (1966). Social class, occupation, and parental values: A cross-national study. *American Sociological Review, 31,* 466–479.

Pebly, A. R. (1981). Changing attitudes toward the timing of first birth. *Family Planning Perspectives, 13*(4), 171–175.

Pedersen, F. A., Cain, R., & Zaslow, M. (1982). Variation in infant experience associated with alternative family roles. In L. Laosa & I. Sigel (Eds.), *The family as a learning environment.* New York: Plenum.

Pedersen, F. A., Rubenstein, J. L., & Yarrow, L. J. (1973, March–April). *Father absence in infancy.* Paper presented at the meeting of the Society for Research in Child Development, Philadelphia.

Pedersen, F. A., Rubenstein, J. L., & Yarrow, L. J. (1979). Infant development in father-absent families. *Journal of Genetic Psychology, 135,* 51–61.

Pederson, E., Faucher, T. A., & Eaton, W. W. (1978). A new perspective of the effects of first-grade teachers on children's subsequent adult status. *Harvard Educational Review, 48,* 1–31.

Peel, E. A. (1967). *The psychological basis of education* (2d ed.). Edinburgh: Oliver & Boyd.

Pepler, D., Corter, C., & Abramovitch, R. (1982). Social relations among children: Siblings and peers. In K. Rubin & H. Ross (Eds.), *Peer relationships and social skills in childhood.* New York: Springer-Verlag.

Perrin, E. C., & Gerrity, P. S. (1981). There's a demon in your belly: Children's understanding of illness. *Pediatrics, 67,* 841–849.

Persson-Blennow, I., & McNeil, T. F.

(1981). Temperament characteristics of children in relation to gender, birth order, and social class. *American Journal of Orthopsychiatry, 51,* 710–714.

Peskin, H. (1967). Pubertal onset and ego functioning. *Journal of Abnormal Psychology, 72,* 1–15.

Peskin, H. (1973). Influence of the developmental schedule of puberty on learning and ego functioning. *Journal of Youth and Adolescence, 2,* 273–290.

Petri, E. (1934). Untersuchungen zur Erbedingtheir der Menarche. *Z. Morph. Anthr., 33,* 43–48.

Pettigrew, T. F. (1964). Negro American intelligence. In T. F. Pettigrew (Ed.), *Profile of the Negro American* (pp. 100–135). Princeton, NJ: Van Nostrand.

Phillips, D., McCartney, K., & Scarr, S. (1987). Child-care quality and children's social development. *Developmental Psychology, 23*(4), 537–543.

Phillips, D. P., & Carstensen, L. L. (1986). Clustering of teenage suicides after television news stories about suicide. *New England Journal of Medicine, 315*(11), 685–689.

Phillips, D. P., & Paight, B. A. (1987). The impact of televised movies about suicide. *New England Journal of Medicine, 317*(13), 809–811.

Piaget, J. (1932). *The moral judgment of the child.* New York: Harcourt Brace.

Piaget, J. (1951). *Play, dreams, and imitation* (C. Gattegno & F. M. Hodgson, Trans.). New York: Norton.

Piaget, J. (1952a). *The child's conception of number.* London: Routledge.

Piaget, J. (1952b). *The origins of intelligence in children.* New York: International Universities Press.

Piaget, J. (1955). *The child's construction of reality.* London: Routledge.

Piaget, J. (1962). Comments on Vygotsky's critical remarks concerning *The language and thought of the child,* and *Judgment and reasoning in the child.* In L. S. Vygotsky, *Thought and language.* Cambridge, MA: Massachusetts Institute of Technology (MIT) Press.

Piaget, J., & Inhelder, B. (1967). *The child's conception of space.* New York: Norton.

Pines, M. (1977, February 13). St-st-st-st-st-st-stuttering. *The New York Times Magazine,* pp. 261.

Pines, M. (1979). Superkids. *Psychology Today, 12*(8), 53–63.

Pines, M. (1983, November). Can a rock walk? *Psychology Today,* pp. 44–54.

Pines, M. (1984, March). PT conversa-

tion: Michael Rutter, resilient children. *Psychology Today,* pp. 57–65.

Placek, P. J. (1986). Commentary: Cesarean rate still rising. *Statistical Bulletin, 67,* 9.

Plomin, R. (1983). Developmental behavioral genetics. *Child Development, 54,* 253–259.

Pollock, L. A. (1983). *Forgotten children.* Cambridge, MA: Cambridge University Press.

Pope, H. G., Hudson, J. I., Jonas, J. M., & Yurgelun-Todd, D. (1983). Bulimia treated with imipramine: A placebo-controlled, double-blind study. *American Journal of Psychiatry, 140,* 554–558.

Porter, N. L., & Christopher, F. S. (1984). Infertility: Towards an awareness of a need among family life practitioners. *Family Relations, 33,* 309–315.

Power, T. G., & Chapieski, M. L. (1986). Child-rearing and impulse control in toddlers: A naturalistic investigation. *Developmental Psychology, 22*(2), 271–275.

Poznanski, E. O. (1982). The clinical phenomenology of childhood depression. *American Journal of Orthopsychiatry, 52*(2), 308–313.

Prager, K., Malin, H., Graves, C., Spiegler, D., Richards, L., & Placek, P. (1983). Maternal smoking and drinking behavior before and during pregnancy (DHHS Publication No. PHS 84-1232). Washington, DC: U.S. Government Printing Office.

Prechtl, H. F. R., & Beintema, D. J. (1964). *The neurological examination of the full-term newborn infant: Clinics in developmental medicine* (No. 12). London: Heinemann.

Pugh, D. (1983, November 11). Bringing an end to mutilation. *New Statesman,* pp. 8–9.

Pugh, W. E., & Fernandez, F. L. (1953). Coitus in late pregnancy. *Obstetrics and Gynecology, 2,* 636–642.

Pugliese, M. T., Weyman-Daum, M., Moses, N., & Lifschitz, F. (1987). Parental health beliefs as a cause of nonorganic failure to thrive. *Pediatrics, 80*(2), 175–182.

Pulaski, M. A. S. (1971). *Understanding Piaget: An introduction to children's cognitive development.* New York: Harper & Row.

Purnick, J. (1984, November 26). City tries to keep young mothers in school. *The New York Times,* p. B1.

Putallaz, M. (1987). Maternal behavior and children's sociometric status. *Child Development, 58,* 324–340.

Pynoos, R. S., Frederick, C., Nader, K., Arroyo, W., Steinberg, A., Eth, S., Nunez, F., & Fairbanks, L. (1987).

Life threat and post-traumatic stress in school-age children. *Archives of General Psychiatry, 44,* 1057–1063.

Quay, H. (1987). Intelligence. In H. C. Quay (Ed.), *Handbook of juvenile delinquency.* New York: Wiley.

Questions, Science Times. (1988, June 7). *The New York Times,* p. C11.

Quinby, N. (1985, October). On testing and teaching intelligence: A conversation with Robert Sternberg. *Educational Leadership,* pp. 50–53.

Rachal, J. V., Guess, L. L., Hubbard, R. L., Maisto, S. A., Cavanaugh, E. R., Waddell, R., & Benrud, C. H. (1980). *Adolescent drinking behavior: Vol. 1. The extent and nature of adolescent alcohol and drug use.* Research Triangle Park, NC: Research Triangle Institute.

Radin, N. (1981a). Child rearing in intact families. *Merrill-Palmer Quarterly, 27,* 489–514.

Radin, N. (1981b). The role of the father in cognitive, academic, and intellectual development. In M. E. Lamb (Ed.), *The role of the father in child development.* New York: Wiley.

Radin, N. (1988). Primary caregiving fathers of long duration. In P. Bronstein & C. P. Cowan (Eds.), *Fatherhood today: Men's changing role in the family.* New York: Wiley.

Rafferty, C. (1984, April 23). Study of gifted from childhood to old age. *The New York Times,* p. B5.

Rassin, D. K., Richardson, J., Baranowski, T., Nader, P. R., Guenther, N., Bee, D. E., & Brown, J. P. (1984). Incidence of breast-feeding in a low socioeconomic group of mothers in the United States: Ethnic patterns. *Pediatrics, 73,* 132–137.

Rauh, J. L., Schumsky, D. A., & Witt, M. T. (1967). Heights, weights, and obesity in urban school children. *Child Development, 38,* 515–530.

Ravitch, D. (1983). The education pendulum. *Psychology Today, 17*(10), 62–71.

Read, M. S., Habicht, J.-P., Lechtig, A., & Klein, R. E. (1973, May). *Maternal malnutrition, birth weight, and child development.* Paper presented at the International Symposium on Nutrition, Growth and Development, Valencia, Spain.

Reese, H. W. (1961). Relationships between self-acceptance and sociometric choices. *Journal of Abnormal and Social Psychology, 62,* 472–474.

Reese, H. W. (1977). Imagery and associative memory. In R. V. Kail & J. W. Hagen (Eds.), *Perspectives on the development of memory and cognition.* Hillsdale, NJ: Erlbaum.

Reeves, R. (1984, October 1). Journey

to Pakistan. *The New Yorker*, pp. 39–105.

Reid, J. R., Patterson, G. R., & Loeber, R. (1982). The abused child: Victim, instigator, or innocent bystander? In D. J. Berstein (Ed.), *Response structure and organization*. Lincoln: University of Nebraska Press.

Reiss, I. L. (1986). *Journey into sexuality: An exploratory voyage*. Englewood Cliffs, NJ: Prentice Hall.

Rendina, I., & Dickerscheid, J. D. (1976). Father involvement with first born infants. *Family Coordinator, 25*, 373–379.

Resnick, M. B., Eyler, F. D., Nelson, R. M., Eitzman, D. V., & Bucciarelli, R. L. (1987). Developmental intervention for low birth weight infants: Improved early developmental outcome. *Pediatrics, 80*(1), 68–74.

Rest, J. R. (1975). Longitudinal study of the Defining Issues Test of moral judgment: A strategy for analyzing developmental change. *Developmental Psychology, 11*(16), 738–748.

Restak, R. (1984). *The brain*. New York: Bantam.

Reznick, J. S., Kagan, J., Snidman, N., Gersten, M., Baak, K., & Rosenberg, A. (1986). Inhibited and uninhibited children: A follow-up study. *Child Development, 57*, 660–680.

Rheingold, H. L. (1956). The modification of social responsiveness in institutionalized babies. *Monographs of the Society for Research in Child Development, 21*(Whole No. 63).

Rice, B. (1979). Brave new world of intelligence testing. *Psychology Today, 13*(4), 27–41.

Richards, M. P. M. (1971). Social interaction in the first week of human life. *Psychiatria, Neurologia, Neurochirugia, 74*, 35–42.

Richardson, D. W., & Short, R. V. (1978). Time of onset of sperm production in boys. *Journal of Biosocial Science, 5*, 15–25.

Ridenour, M. V. (1982). Infant walkers: Developmental tool or inherent danger. *Perceptual and Motor Skills, 55*, 1201–1202.

Rieder, M. J., Schwartz, C., & Newman, J. (1986). Pattern of walker use and walker injury. *Pediatrics, 78*(3), 448–493.

Rieser, J., Yonas, A., & Wilkner, K. (1976). Radial localization of odors by human newborns. *Child Development, 47*, 856–859.

Rindfuss, R. R., & St. John, C. (1983). Social determinants of age at first birth. *Journal of Marriage and the Family, 45*, 553–565.

Ritvo, E. R., Freeman, B. J., Mason-Brothers, A., Mo, A., & Ritvo, A. M. (1985). Concordance for the syndrome of autism in 40 pairs of afflicted twins. *American Journal of Psychiatry, 142*, 74–77.

Roberts, E. J., Kline, D., & Gagnon, J. (1978). *Family life and sexual learning: A study of the role of parents in the sexual learning of children*. New York: Project on Human Sexual Development, Population Education.

Roberts, G. C., Block, J. H., & Block, J. (1984). Continuity and change in parents' child-rearing practices. *Child Development, 55*, 586–597.

Robinson, R. (1972). Low-birthweight babies. In R. Robinson (Ed.), *Problems of the newborn*. London: British Medical Association.

Robson, K. S. (1967). The role of eye-to-eye contact in maternal-infant attachment. *Journal of Child Psychology and Psychiatry, 8*, 13–25.

Roche, A. F. (1981). The adipocyte-number hypothesis. *Child Development, 52*, 31–43.

Rock, D. A., Ekstrom, R. B., Goertz, M. E., Hilton, T. L., & Pollack, J. (1985). *Factors associated with decline of test scores of high school seniors, 1972 to 1980*. Washington, DC: U.S. Department of Education, Center for Statistics.

Rodman, H., & Cole, C. (1987). Latchkey children: A review of policy and resources. *Family Relations, 36*, 101–105.

Rogers, C. C., & O'Connell, M. (1984). Childspacing among birth cohorts of American women: 1905–1959. *Current Population Reports*, Ser. P-20, No. 385.

Rohn, R., Sarles, R., Kenny, T., Reynolds, B., & Heald, F. (1977). Adolescents who attempt suicide. *Journal of Pediatrics, 90*(4), 636–638.

Roopnarine, J., & Field, T. (1984). Play interaction of friends and acquaintances in nursery school. In T. Field, J. Roopnarine, & M. Segal (Eds.), *Friendships in normal and handicapped children*. Norwood, NJ: Ablex.

Roopnarine, J., & Honig, A. S. (1985, September). The unpopular child. *Young Children*, pp. 59–64.

Rose, R. J., & Ditto, W. B. (1983). A developmental-genetic analysis of common fears from early adolescence to early adulthood. *Child Development, 54*, 361–368.

Rose, R. M., Gordon, T. P., & Bernstein, I. S. (1972). Plasma testosterone levels in the male rhesus: Influences of sexual and social stimuli. *Science, 178*(4061), 643–645.

Rose, S. A., & Wallace, I. F. (1985). Visual recognition memory: A predictor of later cognitive functioning in preterms. *Child Development, 56*, 843–852.

Rosenberg, M. S. (1987). New directions for research on the psychological maltreatment of children. *American Psychologist, 42*(2), 166–171.

Rosenthal, M. K. (1982). Vocal dialogues in the neonatal period. *Developmental Psychology, 18*(1), 17–21.

Rosenthal, P. A., & Rosenthal, S. (1984). Suicidal behavior by preschool children. *American Journal of Psychiatry, 141*, 520–525.

Rosenthal, R., & Jacobson, L. (1968). *Pygmalion in the classroom*. New York: Holt.

Rosenzweig, M. R. (1984). Experience, memory, and the brain. *American Psychologist, 39*(4), 365–376.

Rosenzweig, M. R., & Bennett, E. L. (Eds.). (1976). *Neural mechanisms of learning and memory*. Cambridge, MA: Massachusetts Institute of Technology (MIT) Press.

Rosetti-Ferreira, M. C. (1978). Malnutrition and mother-infant asynchrony: Slow mental development. *International Journal of Behavioral Development, 1*, 207–219.

Ross, J. B., & McLaughlin, M. (Eds.). (1949). *A portable medieval reader*. New York: Viking.

Rovee-Collier, C., & Fagen, J. W. (1976). Extended conditioning and 24-hour retention in infants. *Journal of Experimental Child Psychology, 21*, 1.

Rovee-Collier, C., & Fagen, J. W. (1981). The retrieval of memory in early infancy. In L. P. Lipsitt (Ed.), *Advances in infancy research* (Vol. 1). Norwood, NJ: Ablex.

Rovee-Collier, C., & Lipsitt, L. (1982). Learning, adaptation, and memory in the newborn. In P. Stratton (Ed.), *Psychobiology of the human newborn*. New York: Wiley.

Rubin, A. (1977, September). Birth injuries. *Hospital Medicine*, 114–130.

Rubin, D. H., Krasilnikoff, P. A., Leventhal, J. M., Weile, B., & Berget, A. (1986, August 23). Effects of passive smoking on birth-weight. *The Lancet*, pp. 415–417.

Rubin, K. (1982). Nonsocial play in preschoolers: Necessary evil? *Child Development, 53*, 651–657.

Rubin, K., Maioni, T. L., & Hornung, M. (1976). Free play behaviors in middle-class and lower-class preschoolers: Parten and Piaget revisited. *Child Development, 47*, 414–419.

Rubin, K., Watson, K., & Jambor, T. (1978). Free-play behaviors in preschool and kindergarten children. *Child Development, 49*, 534–536.

Rubin, K. H., Daniels-Beirness, T., &

Hayvren, M. (1982). Social and social-cognitive correlates of sociometric status in preschool and kindergarten children. *Canadian Journal of Behavioral Science, 14,* 338–349.

Ruble, D. N., & Brooks-Gunn, J. (1982). The experience of menarche. *Child Development, 53,* 1557–1566.

Rule, S. (1981, June 11). The battle to stem school dropouts. *The New York Times,* pp. A1, B10.

Russell, C. (1974). Transition to parenthood: Problems and gratifications. *Journal of Marriage and the Family, 36*(2), 294–302.

Russell, G. F. M., Szmukler, G. I., Dare, C., & Eisler, I. (1987). An evaluation of family therapy in anorexia nervosa and bulimia nervosa. *Archives of General Psychiatry, 44,* 1047–1056.

Russell, L. B., & Russell, W. L. (1952). Radiation hazards to the embryo and fetus. *Radiology, 58*(3), 369–376.

Rutter, M. (1971). Parent-child separation: Psychological effects on the children. *Journal of Child Psychology and Psychiatry, 12,* 233–260.

Rutter, M. (1974). *The qualities of mothering: Maternal deprivation reassessed.* New York: Aronson.

Rutter, M. (1979a). Maternal deprivation, 1972–1978: New findings, new concepts, new approaches. *Child Development, 50,* 283–305.

Rutter, M. (1979b). Separation experiences: A new look at an old topic. *Pediatrics, 95*(1), 147–154.

Rutter, M. (1983). Stress, coping, and development: Some issues and some questions. In N. Garmezy & M. Rutter (Eds.), *Stress, coping, and development in children.* New York: McGraw-Hill.

Rutter, M. (1984). Resilient children. *Psychology Today, 18*(3), 57–65.

Ryerson, A. J. (1961). Medical advice on child rearing, 1550–1900. *Harvard Educational Review, 31,* 302–323.

Sachs, B. P., McCarthy, B. J., Rubin, G., Burton, A., Terry, J., & Tyler, C. W. (1983). Cesarean section. *Journal of the American Medical Association, 250*(16), 2157–2159.

Sadowitz, P. D., & Oski, F. A. (1983). Iron status and infant feeding practices in an urban ambulatory center. *Pediatrics, 72*(1), 33–36.

Sagi, A., & Hoffman, M. (1976). Empathic distress in newborns. *Developmental Psychology, 12*(2), 175–176.

Salapatek, P., & Kessen, W. (1966). Visual scanning of triangles by the human newborn. *Journal of Experimental Child Psychology, 3,* 155–167.

Salk, L., Lipsitt, L. P., Sturner, W. Q., Reilly, B. M., & Levat, R. H. (1985, March 16). Relationship between maternal and perinatal conditions and eventual adolescent suicide. *The Lancet,* pp. 624–627.

Sameroff, A. (1971). Can conditioned responses be established in the newborn infant? *Developmental Psychology, 5,* 1–12.

Sandler, D. P., Everson, R. B., Wilcox, A. J., & Browder, J. P. (1985). Cancer risk in adulthood from early life exposure to parents' smoking. *American Journal of Public Health, 75,* 487–492.

Santrock, J. W., Sitterle, K. A., & Warshak, R. A. (1988). Parent-child relationships in stepfather families. In P. Bronstein & C. P. Cowan (Eds.), *Fatherhood today: Men's changing role in the family.* New York: Wiley.

Sarrel, L. J., & Sarrel, P. M. (1984). *Sexual turning points.* New York: Macmillan.

Scales, P. (1977). Males and morals: Teenage contraceptive behavior amid the double standard. *Family Coordinator, 26*(3), 211–222.

Scarf, M. (1975, October 19). The fetus as guinea pig. *The New York Times Magazine.*

Scarr, S., & Weinberg, R. (1983). The Minnesota Adoption Study: Genetic differences and malleability. *Child Development, 54,* 260–267.

Schaffer, D. L. (1971). *Sex differences in personalities.* Belmont, CA: Brooks/Cole.

Schaffer, H. R., & Emerson, P. (1964). The development of social attachments in infancy. *Monographs of the Society for Research in Child Development, 29*(3).

Schanberg, S. M., & Field, T. M. (1987). Sensory deprivation stress and supplemental stimulation in the rat pup and preterm human neonate. *Child Development, 58,* 1431–1447.

Schiro, A. (1988, August 25). Parents agree to detente in the clothes wars. *The New York Times,* pp. C1, C6.

Schmeck, H. M., Jr. (1976, June 10). Trend in growth of children lags. *The New York Times,* p. 13.

Schmitt, B. D., & Kempe, C. H. (1983). Abusing neglected children. In R. E. Behrman & V. C. Vaughn (Eds.), *Nelson textbook of pediatrics* (12th ed.). Philadelphia: Saunders.

Schmitt, M. H. (1970). Superiority of breast-feeding: Fact or fancy? *American Journal of Nursing, 1488–1493.*

Schor, E. L. (1987). Unintentional injuries: Patterns within families. *American Journal of the Diseases of Children, 141,* 1280.

Schuckit, M. A. (1985). Genetics and the risk for alcoholism. *Journal of the American Medical Association, 254*(18), 2614–2617.

Schuckit, M. A. (1987). Biological vulnerability to alcoholism. *Journal of Consulting and Clinical Psychology, 55*(3), 301–309.

Schulman, S. (1986). Facing the invisible handicap. *Psychology Today, 20*(2), 58–64.

Schwebel, M. (1982). Effects of the nuclear war threat on children and teenagers: Implications for professionals. *American Journal of Orthopsychiatry, 52*(4), 608–617.

Schweinhart, L. J., Weikart, D. P., & Larner, M. B. (1986). A report on the High/Scope preschool curriculum comparison study: Consequences of three preschool curriculum models through age 15. *Early Childhood Research Quarterly, 1,* 15–45.

Scott, J. P. (1958). *Animal behavior.* Chicago: University of Chicago Press.

Sears, P., & Barbee, A. (1978). Career and life satisfaction among Terman's gifted women. In *The gifted and the creative: A fifty-year perspective.* Baltimore: Johns Hopkins University Press.

Sears, R. R., Maccoby, E. E., & Levin, H. (1957). *Patterns of child rearing.* New York: Harper & Row.

Seibel, M. M. (1988). A new era in reproductive technology. *New England Journal of Medicine, 318*(13), 828–834.

Selman, R. L. (1973, March). *A structural analysis of the ability to take another's social perspective: Stages in the development of role-taking ability.* Paper presented at the meeting of the Society for Research in Child Development, Philadelphia.

Selman, R. L., & Selman, A. P. (1979). Children's ideas about friendship: A new theory. *Psychology Today, 13*(4), 71–80.

Selye, H. (1980). The stress concept today. In I. L. Kutash, L. B. Schlesinger, & Associates (Eds.), *Handbook on stress and anxiety* (pp. 127–143). San Francisco: Jossey-Bass.

Sexton, M., & Hebel, R. (1984). A clinical trial of change in maternal smoking and its effect on birth weight. *Journal of the American Medical Association, 251*(7), 911–915.

Shangold, M. (1978, May 14). Female runners advised to follow common sense. *The New York Times,* Sec. 5, p. 2.

Shannon, D. C., & Kelly, D. H. (1982a). SIDS and near-SIDS (Part 1). *New England Journal of Medicine, 306*(16), 959–965.

Shannon, D. C., & Kelly, D. H. (1982b). SIDS and near-SIDS (Part 2). *New England Journal of Medicine, 306*(17), 1022–1028.

Shannon, L. W. (1982). *Assessing the relationship of adult criminal careers to juvenile careers*. Iowa City: University of Iowa, Iowa Urban Community Research Center.

Shatz, M., & Gelman, R. (1973). The development of communication skills: Modifications in the speech of young children as a function of listener. *Monographs of the Society for Research in Child Development, 38*(5, Serial No. 152).

Shaywitz, S., Cohen, D., & Shaywitz, B. (1980). Behavior and learning difficulties in children of normal intelligence born to alcoholic mothers. *Journal of Pediatrics, 96*(6), 978–982.

Sheps, S., & Evans, G. D. (1987). Epidemiology of school injuries: A 2-year experience in a municipal health department. *Pediatrics, 79*(1), 69–75.

Sherman, A., Goldrath, M., Berlin, A., Vakhariya, V., Banoom, F., Michaels, W., Goodman, P., & Brown, S. (1974). Cervical-vaginal adenosis after in utero exposure to synthetic estrogen. *Obstetrics and Gynecology, 44*(4), 531–545.

Sherman, L. W., & Berk, R. A. (1984, April). The Minneapolis domestic violence experiment. *Police Foundation Reports*, pp. 1–8.

Shinn, M. (1978). Father absence and children's cognitive development. *Psychological Bulletin, 85*, 295–324.

Shipp, E. R. (1988, February 4). Decision could hinder surrogacy across nation. *The New York Times*, p. B6.

Shneidman, E. (1985). *The definition of suicide*. New York: Wiley.

Short, R. V. (1984). Breast feeding. *Scientific American, 250*(4), 35–41.

Siegel, O. (1982). Personality development in adolescence. In B. B. Wolman (Ed.), *Handbook of developmental psychology*. Englewood Cliffs, NJ: Prentice-Hall.

Siegler, R. S., & Richards, D. (1982). The development of intelligence. In R. Sternberg (Ed.), *Handbook of human intelligence*. London: Cambridge University Press.

Signorielli, N., Gross, L., & Morgan, M. (1982). Violence in television programs: Ten years later. In D. Pearl, L. Bouthilet, & J. Lazar (Eds.), *Television and behavior: Ten years of scientific progress and implications for the eighties: Technical reviews* (Vol. 2). Washington, DC: National Institute of Mental Health.

Silverstein, B., Perdue, L., Peterson, B., et al. (1986). The role of the mass media in promoting a thin standard of bodily attractiveness for women. *Sex Roles, 14*(9/10), 519–532.

Silverstein, B., Peterson, B., & Perdue, L. (1986). Some correlates of the thin standard of bodily attractiveness for women. *International Journal of Eating Disorders, 5*(5).

Simmons, R. G., Blyth, D. A., & McKinney, K. L. (1983). The social and psychological effects of puberty on white females. In J. Brooks-Gunn & A. C. Petersen (Eds.), *Girls at puberty: Biological and psychological perspectives*. New York: Plenum.

Simmons, R. G., Blyth, D. A., Van Cleave, E. F., & Bush, D. M. (1979). Entry into early adolescence: The impact of school structure, puberty, and early dating on self-esteem. *American Sociological Review, 44*(6), 948–967.

Simmons, R. G., Burgeson, R., Carlton-Ford, S., & Blyth, D. A. (1987). The impact of cumulative change in early adolescence. *Child Development, 58*, 1220–1234.

Simner, M. L. (1971). Newborn's response to the cry of another infant. *Developmental Psychology, 5*(1), 135–150.

Simons, C. (1987, March). They get by with a lot of help from their *kyoiku* mamas. *Smithsonian*, pp. 44–52.

Singleton, L., & Asher, S. (1979). Racial integration and children's peer preferences: An investigation of developmental and cohort differences. *Child Development, 50*, 936–941.

Siqueland, E. R., & Lipsitt, L. P. (1966). Conditioned head-turning in human newborns. *Journal of Experimental Child Psychology, 3*(4), 356–376.

Skeels, H. M. (1966). Adult status of children with contrasting early life experiences. *Monographs of the Society for Research in Child Development, 31*(Whole No. 3).

Skeels, H. M., & Dye, H. B. (1939). A study of the effects of differential stimulation on mentally retarded children. *Program of the American Association of Mental Deficiency, 44*, 114–136.

Skinner, B. F. (1938). *The behavior of organisms: An experimental approach*. New York: Appleton-Century.

Skinner, B. F. (1957). *Verbal behavior*. New York: Appleton-Century-Crofts.

Slater, E., with Shields, J. (1953). *Psychotic and neurotic illnesses in twins* (Medical Research Council Special Report, Ser. No. 278). London: H. M. Stationery Office.

Slater, P. (1958). Parental role differentiation. In R. L. Closer (Ed.), *The family: Its structure and functions*. New York: St. Martin's.

Slobin, D. I. (1971). Universals of grammatical development in children. In W. Levelt & G. B. Flores d'Arcais (Eds.), *Advances in psycholinguistic research*. Amsterdam: New Holland.

Smilansky, S. (1968). *The effects of sociodramatic play on disadvantaged preschool children*. New York: Wiley.

Smith, T. E. (1981). Adolescent agreement with perceived maternal and paternal educational goals. *Journal of Marriage and the Family, 43*(1), 85–93.

Snarey, J. R. (1985). Cross-cultural universality of social-moral development: A critical review of Kohlbergian research. *Psychological Bulletin, 97*, 202–232.

Snarey, J. R., Reimer, J., & Kohlberg, L. (1985). Development of social-moral reasoning among kibbutz adolescents: A longitudinal cross-cultural study. *Development Psychology, 21*, 3–17.

Snow, C. E. (1972). Mother's speech to children learning language. *Child Development, 43*, 549–565.

Snow, C. E. (1977). Mother's speech research: From input to interaction. In C. E. Snow & C. A. Ferguson (Eds.), *Talking to children: Language input and acquisition*. London: Cambridge University Press.

Snow, C. E., Arlman-Rupp, A., Hassing, Y., Jobse, J., Joosten, J., & Verster, J. (1976). Mothers' speech in three social classes. *Journal of Psycholinguistic Research, 5*, 1–20.

Snow, M. E., Jacklin, C. N., & Maccoby, E. E. (1983). Sex-of-child differences in father-child interaction at one year of age. *Child Development, 54*, 227–232.

Solantaus, T., Rimpela, M., & Taipale, V. (1984). Threat of war in the minds of 12- to 18-year-olds in Finland. *The Lancet*, p. 784.

Solomons, H. (1978). The malleability of infant motor development. *Clinical Pediatrics, 17*(11), 836–839.

Song, M., & Ginsburg, H. P. (1987). The development of informal and formal mathematical thinking in Korean and U.S. children. *Child Development, 58*, 1286–1296.

Sontag, L. W. (1966). Implications of fetal behavior and environment for adult personality. *Annals of the New York Academy of Science, 134*, 782–786.

Sontag, L. W., & Richards, T. W. (1938). Studies in fetal behavior: Fetal heart rate as a behavioral indicator. *Child Development Monographs, 3*(Whole No. 4).

Sontag, L. W., & Wallace, R. I. (1934). Preliminary report of the Fels fund: A study of fetal activity. *American Journal of Diseases of Children, 48*, 1050–1057.

Sontag, L. W., & Wallace, R. I. (1936). Changes in the heart rate of the human fetal heart in response to vibratory stimuli. *American Journal of Diseases of Children, 51*, 583–589.

Sorce, J. F., Emde, R. N., Campos, J., & Klinnert, M. D. (1985). Maternal emotional signaling: Its effect on the visual cliff behavior of 1-year-olds. *Developmental Psychology, 21*(1), 195–200.

Sorensen, R. C. (1973). *Adolescent sexuality in contemporary America.* Tarrytown, NY: World.

Sorensen, T., Nielsen, G., Andersen, P., & Teasdale, T. (1988). Genetic and environmental influences on premature death in adult adoptees. *New England Journal of Medicine, 318*, 727–732.

Spezzano, C. (1981, May). Prenatal psychology: Pregnant with questions. *Psychology Today*, pp. 49–57.

Spiro, M. E. (1954). Is the family universal? The Israeli case. *American Anthropologist, 56*, 839–846.

Spiro, M. E. (1958). *Children of the kibbutz.* Cambridge, MA: Harvard University Press.

Spitz, M. R., & Johnson, C. C. (1985). Neuroblastoma and paternal occupation: A case-control analysis. *American Journal of Epidemiology, 121*(6), 924–929.

Spitz, R. A. (1945). Hospitalism: An inquiry in the genesis of psychiatric conditioning in early childhood. In D. Fenschel et al. (Eds.), *Psychoanalytic studies of the child* (Vol. 1, pp. 53–74). New York: International Universities Press.

Spitz, R. A. (1946). Hospitalism: A follow-up report. In D. Fenschel et al. (Eds.), *Psychoanalytic studies of the child* (Vol. 1, pp. 113–117). New York: International Universities Press.

Spock, B. (1976). *Baby and child care.* New York: Pocket Books.

Spock, B., & Rothenberg, M. B. (1985). *Baby and child care.* New York: Pocket Books.

Sroufe, L. A. (1977). Wariness of strangers and the study of infant development. *Child Development, 48*, 731–746.

Sroufe, L. A. (1979). Socioemotional development. In J. Osofsky (Ed.), *Handbook of infant development.* New York: Wiley.

Sroufe, L. A. (1983). Individual patterns of adaptation from infancy to preschool. In M. Perlmutter (Ed.), *Proceedings of Minnesota symposium on child psychology.* Hillsdale, NJ: Erlbaum.

Sroufe, L. A., Fox, N. E., & Pancake, V. R. (1983). Attachment and dependency in a developmental perspective. *Child Development, 54*, 1615–1627.

Sroufe, L. A., & Waters, E. (1976). The ontogenesis of smiling and laughter: A perspective on the organization of development in infancy. *Psychological Review, 83*, 173–189.

Sroufe, L. A., & Wunsch, J. (1972). The development of laughter in the first year of life. *Child Development, 43*, 1326–1344.

Stacey, M., Dearden, R., Pill, R., & Robinson, D. (1970). *Hospitals, children and their families: The report of a pilot study.* London: Routledge.

Stainton, M. C. (1985). The fetus: A growing member of the family. *Family Relations, 34*, 321–326.

Stamps, L. (1977). Temporal conditioning of heart rate responses in newborn infants. *Developmental Psychology, 13*(6), 624–629.

Stang, H. J., Snellman, L., Condon, L. M., & Kastenbaum, R. (1988). Local anesthesia for neonatal circumcision. *Journal of the American Medical Association, 259*(10), 1507–1511.

Stangor, C., & Ruble, D. N. (1987). Development of gender role knowledge and gender constancy. In S. Liben & M. L. Signorella (Eds.), *Children's gender schemata.* San Francisco: Jossey-Bass.

Stanton, A. N. (1984, November 24). Overheating and cot death. *The Lancet*, pp. 1199–1201.

Starfield, B. (1978). Enuresis: Focus on a challenging problem in primary care. *Pediatrics, 62*, 1036–1037.

Starfield, B., Katz, H., Livingston, G., Benson, P., Hankin, J., Horn, S., & Steinwachs, D. (1984). Morbidity in childhood—A longitudinal view. *New England Journal of Medicine, 310*, 824–829.

Stark, E. (1984, April). East meets west. *Psychology Today*, p. 20.

Stark, R., & McEvoy, J. (1970). Middle-class violence. *Psychology Today, 4*, 52–65.

Starkey, P., Spelke, E. S., & Gelman, R. (1983). Detection of intermodal numerical correspondences by human infants. *Science, 10*, 179–181.

Staub, S. (1973). *The effect of three types of relationships on young children's memory for pictorial stimulus pairs.* Unpublished doctoral dissertation, Harvard University Graduate School of Education, Cambridge, MA.

Stein, A., & Friedrich, L. (1975). Impact of television on children and youth. In E. M. Hetherington (Ed.), *Review of Child Development Research* (Vol. 5). Chicago: University of Chicago Press.

Steinberg, L. (1981). Transformations in family relations at puberty. *Developmental Psychology, 17*, 833–840.

Steinberg, L. (1985). *Adolescence.* New York: Knopf.

Steinberg, L. (1986a). Latchkey children and susceptibility to peer pressure: An ecological analysis. *Developmental Psychology, 22*(4), 433–439.

Steinberg, L. (1986b). Stability (and instability) of Type A behavior from childhood to young adulthood. *Developmental Psychology, 22*(3), 393–402.

Steinberg, L. (1987a). Impact of puberty on family relations: Effects of pubertal status and pubertal timing. *Developmental Psychology, 23*(3), 451–460.

Steinberg, L. (1987b). Single parents, stepparents, and the susceptibility of adolescents to antisocial peer pressure. *Child Development, 58*, 269, 275.

Steinberg, L. (1987c). Bound to bicker. *Psychology Today, 21*(9), 36–39.

Steinberg, L. (1988). Reciprocal relation between parent-child distance and pubertal maturation. *Developmental Psychology, 24*(1), 122–128.

Steinberg, L., & Silverberg, S. B. (1986). The vicissitudes of autonomy in early adolescence. *Child Development, 57*, 841–851.

Steiner, J. E. (1979). Human facial expressions in response to taste and smell stimulation. *Advances in Child Development and Behavior, 13*, 257.

Stenchever, M. A., Williamson, R. A., Leonard, J., Karp, L. E., Ley, B., Shy, K., & Smith, D. (1981). Possible relationship between in utero diethylstilbestrol exposure and male fertility. *American Journal of Obstetrics and Gynecology, 140*(2), 186–193.

Stern, M., & Hildebrandt, K. A. (1986). Prematuring stereotyping: Effects on mother-infant interaction. *Child Development, 57*, 308–315.

Sternberg, R. J. (1984, September). How can we teach intelligence? *Educational Leadership*, pp. 38–50.

Sternberg, R. J. (1985a). *Beyond IQ: A triarchic theory of human intelligence.* New York: Cambridge University Press.

Sternberg, R. J. (1985b, November). Teaching critical thinking, Part I: Are we making critical mistakes? *Phi Delta Kappan*, pp. 194–198.

Sternberg, R. J. (1986). *Intelligence applied: Understanding and increasing your intellectual skills.* San Diego: Harcourt Brace.

Sternberg, R. J. (1987, September 23). The uses and misuses of intelligence testing: Misunderstanding meaning, users over-rely on scores. *Education Week*, pp. 28, 22.

Sternglanz, S., & Serbin, L. (1974). Sex role stereotyping in children's television programs. *Developmental Psychology, 10*, 710–715.

Stevens, J. H., & Bakeman, R. (1985). A factor analytic study of the HOME scale for infants. *Developmental Psychology, 21*(6), 1196–1203.

Stevenson, H. W., Stigler, J. W., Lee, S., Lucker, G. W., Kitamura, S., & Hsu, C. (1985). Cognitive performance and academic achievement of Japanese, Chinese, and American children. *Child Development, 56*, 718–734.

Stevenson, M., & Lamb, M. (1979). Effects of infant sociability and the caretaking environment on infant cognitive performance. *Child Development, 50*, 340–349.

Stewart, M. A., & Olds, S. W. (1973). *Raising a hyperactive child.* New York: Harper & Row.

Stewart, R. B. (1983). Sibling attachment relationships: Child-infant interactions in the strange situation. *Developmental Psychology, 19*(2), 192–199.

Stigler, J. W., Lee, S., & Stevenson, H. W. (1987). Mathematics classrooms in Japan, Taiwan, and the United States. *Child Development, 58*, 1272–1285.

Stjernfeldt, M., Berglund, K., Lindsten, J., & Ludvigsson, J. (1986, June 14). Maternal smoking during pregnancy and risk of childhood cancer. *The Lancet*, pp. 1350–1352.

Stone, L. J., Smith, H. T., & Murphy, L. B. (1973). *The competent infant: Research and commentary.* New York: Basic Books.

Strauss, M., Lessen-Firestone, J., Starr, R., & Ostrea, E. (1975). Behavior of narcotics-addicted newborns. *Child Development, 46*, 887–893.

Streissguth, A. P., Martin, D. C., Barr, H. M., Sandman, B. M., Kirchner, G. L., & Darby, B. L. (1984). Intrauterine alcohol and nicotine exposure: Attention and reaction time in 4-year-old children. *Developmental Psychology, 20*(4), 533–541.

Strickland, D. M., Saeed, S. A., Casey, M. L., & Mitchell, M. D. (1983). *Science, 220*, 521–522.

Stringham, J. G., Riley, J. H., & Ross, A. (1982). Silent birth: Mourning a stillborn baby. *Social Work, 27*, 322–327.

Stuart, M. J., Gross, S. J., Elrad, H., & Graeber, J. E. (1982). Effects of acetylsalicylic-acid ingestion on maternal and neonatal hemostasis. *New England Journal of Medicine, 307*, 909–912.

Stunkard, A. J., Foch, T. T., &

Hrubec, Z. (1986). A twin study of human obesity. *Journal of the American Medical Association, 256*, 51–54.

Sullivan, H. S. (1953). *The interpersonal theory of psychiatry.* New York: Norton.

Sullivan, M. W. (1982). Reactivation: Priming forgotten memories in infants. *Child Development, 53*, 516.

Sullivan-Bolyai, J., Hull, H. F., Wilson, C., & Corey, L. (1983). Neonatal herpes simplex virus infection in King County, Washington. *Journal of the American Medical Association, 250*(22), 3059–3062.

Suomi, S., & Harlow, H. (1972). Social rehabilitation of isolate-reared monkeys. *Developmental Psychology, 6*(3), 487–496.

Sutton-Smith, B. (1982). Birth order and sibling status effects. In M. E. Lamb & B. Sutton-Smith (Eds.), *Sibling relationships: Their nature and significance across the lifespan.* Hillsdale, NJ: Erlbaum.

Swan, H., & Huston, V. (1985). *Alone at home: Self-care for children of working parents.* Englewood Cliffs, NJ: Prentice-Hall.

Sweetland, J. D., & DeSimone, P. A. (1987). Age of entry, sex, and academic achievement in elementary school children. *Psychology in the Schools, 24*, 406–412.

Tabor, A., Philip, J., Madsen, M., Bang, J., Obel, E., & Norgaard-Petersen, B. (1986, June 7). Randomised controlled trial of genetic amniocentesis in 4606 low-risk women. *The Lancet*, pp. 1287–1292.

Tanfer, K., & Horn, M. C. (1985). Contraceptive use, pregnancy and fertility patterns among single American women in their 20's. *Family Planning Perspectives, 17*(1), 10–19.

Tanner, J. M. (1964). The adolescent growth-spurt and developmental age. In G. A. Harrison, J. S. Werner, J. M. Tannert, & N. A. Barnicot (Eds.), *Human biology: An introduction to human evolution, variation, and growth* (pp. 321–339). Oxford: Clarendon.

Tanner, J. M. (1982). *Growth at adolescence* (2d ed.). Oxford: Scientific Publications.

Tautermannova, M. (1973). Smiling in infants. *Child Development, 44*, 701–704.

Taylor, A. R., Asher, S. R., & Williams, G. A. (1987). The social adaptation of mainstreamed mildly retarded children. *Child Development, 58*, 1321–1334.

Teach a child's first teacher. (1988, January 26). *The New York Times*, p. A22.

Tellegen, A., Lykken, D. T., Bouchard,

T. J., Wilcox, K. J., Segal, N. L., Rich, S. (in press). Personality similarity in twins reared apart and together. *Journal of Personality and Social Psychology.*

Teller, D. Y., & Bornstein, M. H. (1987). Infant color version and color perception. In P. Salapatek & L. B. Cohen (Eds.), *Handbook of infant perception: Vol. 1. From sensation to perception* (pp. 185–236). Orlando, FL: Academic.

Terman, L. M., & Oden, M. H. (1959). *Genetic studies of genius: Vol. 5. The gifted group at mid-life.* Stanford, CA: Stanford University Press.

Thomas, A., & Chess, S. (1977). *Temperament and development.* New York: Brunner/Mazel.

Thomas, A., & Chess, S. (1984). Genesis and evolution of behavioral disorders: From infancy to early adult life. *American Journal of Psychiatry, 141*(1), 1–9.

Thomas, A., Chess, S., & Birch, H. G. (1968). *Temperament and behavior disorders in children.* New York: New York University Press.

Thomas, D. (1985). The dynamics of teacher opposition to integration. *Remedial Education, 20*(2), 53–58.

Thomas, R. (1979). *Comparing theories of child development.* Belmont, CA: Wadsworth.

Thompson, R. A., Lamb, M. E., & Estes, D. (1982). Stability of infant-mother attachment and its relationship to changing life circumstances in an unselected middle-class sample. *Child Development, 53*, 144–148.

Thompson, S. K. (1975). Gender labels and early sex-role development. *Child Development, 46*, 339–347.

Tiger, L., & Shepher, J. (1975). *Women in the kibbutz.* New York: Harcourt Brace.

Timiras, P. S. (1972). *Developmental physiology and aging.* New York: Macmillan.

Tisdale, S. (1988). The mother. *Hippocrates, 2*(3), 64–72.

Tomasello, M., Mannle, S., & Kruger, A. C. (1986). Linguistic environment of 1- and 2-year-old twins. *Developmental Psychology, 22*(2), 169–176.

Toner, B. B., Garfinkel, P. E., & Garner, D. M. (1986). Long-term follow-up of anorexia nervosa. *Psychosomatic Medicine, 48*(7), 520–529.

Tonkova-Yompol'skaya, R. V. (1973). Development of speech intonation in infants during the first two years of life. In C. A. Fergusin & D. Slobin (Eds.), *Studies of child language development.* New York: Holt.

Tronick, E. (1972). Stimulus control and the growth of the infant's visual field. *Perception and Psychophysics, 11,* 373–375.

Tronick, E. Z., & Field, T. (Eds.). (1986). Maternal depression and infant disturbance. In W. Damon (Ed.), *New directions for child development.* San Francisco: Jossey-Bass.

Tronick, E. Z., & Gianino, A. F. (1986). The transmission of maternal depression to the infant. In E. Z. Tronic & T. Field (Eds.), *Maternal depression and infant disturbance.* San Francisco: Jossey-Bass.

Trotter, R. J. (1983). Baby face. *Psychology Today, 17*(8), 14–20.

Trotter, R. J. (1987). You've come a long way, baby. *Psychology Today, 21*(5), 34–45.

Tsai, M., & Wagner, N. (1979). Incest and molestation: Problems of childhood sexuality. *Resident and Staff Physician,* 129–136.

Tuddenham, R. D. (1951). Studies in reputation: 3. Correlates of popularity among elementary school children. *Journal of Educational Psychology, 42,* 257–276.

Ungerer, J., Brody, L. R., & Zelazo, P. R. (1978). Long-term memory for speech in 2- to 4-week-old infants. *Infant Behavioral Development, 1,* 127.

UNICEF. (1984). *The state of the world's children 1985.* London: Author.

U.S. Bureau of the Census. (1984). *Marital status and living arrangements: March 1983* (Current Population Reports: Population characteristics, Series P-20, No. 389). Washington, DC: U.S. Government Printing Office.

U.S. Bureau of the Census. (1985). *Household and family characteristics: March 1984* (Current Population Reports, Series P-20, No. 398). Washington, DC: U.S. Government Printing Office.

U.S. Bureau of the Census. (1987, May). *Who's minding the kids? Child care arrangements: Winter 1984–1985* (Current Population Reports, Series P-70, No. 9). Washington, DC: U.S. Government Printing Office.

U.S. Bureau of the Census. (1988a). *Americans' marital status and living arrangements.* Washington, DC: U.S. Government Printing Office.

U.S. Bureau of the Census. (1988b). *Fertility of American women: June 1987* (Current Population Reports, Series P-20, No. 427). Washington, DC: U.S. Government Printing Office.

U.S. Department of Justice. (1988). Statistics.

U.S. Department of Health, Education, and Welfare. (1976). *Health, United States, 1975* (DHEW Publication No. HRA 76-1232). Rockville, MD: National Center for Health Statistics.

U.S. Department of Health and Human Services (USDHHS). (1980a). *Preterm babies* (DHHS Publication No. ADM 80-792). Washington, DC: U.S. Government Printing Office.

U.S. Department of Health and Human Services (USDHHS). (1980b). *Smoking, tobacco, and health* (DHHS Publication No. PHS 80-50150). Washington, DC: U.S. Government Printing Office.

U.S. Department of Health and Human Services (USDHHS). (1980c). *The status of children, youth, and families, 1979* (DHHS Publication No. OHDS 80-30274). Washington, DC: U.S. Government Printing Office.

U.S. Department of Health and Human Services (USDHHS). (1981). Statistics on the incidence of depression.

U.S. Department of Health and Human Services (USDHHS). (1982). *Prevention '82* (DHHS PHS Publication No. 82-50157). Washington, DC: U.S. Government Printing Office.

U.S. Department of Health and Human Services (USDHHS). (1984). *Child sexual abuse prevention: Tips to parents.* Washington, DC: Office of Human Development Services, Administration for Children, Youth, and Families. National Center on Child Abuse and Neglect.

U.S. Department of Health and Human Services (USDHHS). (1986). *Head Start: A child development program.* Washington, DC: U.S. Government Printing Office.

U.S. Department of Health and Human Services (USDHHS). (1987). *Project Head Start.* Washington, DC: U.S. Government Printing Office.

U.S. Department of Health and Human Services (USDHHS). (1988, January). Project Head Start statistical fact sheet. Washington, DC: U.S. Government Printing Office.

U.S. Department of Justice, Federal Bureau of Investigation (FBI). (1987, July 25). Press release on crimes in 1986.

U.S. Department of Justice, Federal Bureau of Investigation (FBI). (1983). Crime in the United States. *Uniform Crime Reports—1982.*

U.S. Public Health Service. (undated).

University of California. (1988). Small kids, small foods. *Berkeley Wellness Letter, 4*(6), p. 7.

University of Michigan News and Information Services. (1988, January 12). Summary of 1987 drug study results. Ann Arbor, MI: Author.

University of Texas Health Science Center at Dallas. (1983, May 4). *Radiation biologist works to protect fetus from chromosome damage.*

Upjohn Company. (1984). *Writer's guide to sex and health.* Kalamazoo, MI: Author.

Uzgiris, I. C. (1972). *Patterns of cognitive development in infancy.* Paper presented at the Merrill-Palmer Institute Conference on Infant Development, Detroit.

Uzgiris, I. C., & Hunt, J. (1975). *Assessment in infancy.* Urbana: University of Illinois Press.

Valdes-Dapena, M. (1980). Sudden infant death syndrome: A review of the medical literature, 1974–1979. *Pediatrics, 66*(4), 597–614.

Valentine, D. P. (1982). The experience of pregnancy: A developmental process. *Family Relations, 31*(2), 243–248.

Vandenberg, S. G. (1967). Hereditary factors in normal personality traits (as measured by inventories) (1965). In J. Wortes (Ed.), *Recent advances in biological psychiatry* (Vol. 9, pp. 65–104). New York: Plenum.

Vaughan, V., McKay, R. J., & Behrman, R. (1979). *Nelson textbook of pediatrics* (11th ed.). Philadelphia: Saunders.

Veroff, J., Douvan, E., & Kulka, R. (1981). *The inner American.* New York: Basic Books.

Visher, E., & Visher, J. (1983). Stepparenting: Blending families. In H. I. McCubbin & C. R. Figley (Eds.), *Stress and the family: Vol. 1. Coping with normative transitions.* New York: Brunner/Mazel.

Vuillamy, D. G. (1973). *The newborn child.* Edinburgh: Churchill Livingstone.

Vuori, L., Christiansen, N., Clement, J., Mora, J., Wagner, M., & Herrera, M. (1979). Nutritional supplementation and the outcome of pregnancy: 2. Visual habituation at 15 days. *Journal of Clinical Nutrition, 32,* 463–469.

Vygotsky, L. S. (1962). *Thought and language.* Cambridge, MA: Massachusetts Institute of Technology (MIT) Press.

Wachs, T. (1975). Relation of infants' performance on Piaget's scales between 12 and 24 months and their Stanford Binet performance at 31 months. *Child Development, 46,* 929–935.

Wald, E. R., Dashevsky, B., Byers, C., Guerra, N., & Taylor, F. (1988). Frequency and severity of infections in day care. *Journal of Pediatrics, 112,* 540–546.

Walk, R. D., & Gibson, E. J. (1961). A comparative and analytical study of visual depth perception. *Psychology Monographs, 75*(15).

Walker, L. (1984). Sex differences in the development of moral reasoning: A critical review. *Child Development, 55,* 677–691.

Walker, L. (1987, August). *A longitudinal study of moral stages.* Paper presented at the annual meeting of the American Psychological Association, New York.

Wallach, M. A., & Kogan, N. (1965). *Modes of thinking in young children: A study of the creativity-intelligence distinction.* New York: Holt.

Wallach, M. A., & Kogan, N. (1967). Creativity and intelligence in children's thinking. *Transaction, 4*(1), 38–43.

Wallerstein, J. S. (1983). Children of divorce: The psychological tasks of the child. *American Journal of Orthopsychiatry, 53*(2), 230–243.

Wallerstein, J. S. (1987). Children of divorce: Report of a ten-year follow-up of early latency-age children. *American Journal of Orthopsychiatry, 57*(2), 199–211.

Wallerstein, J. S., & Kelly, J. B. (1980). *Surviving the break-up: How children actually cope with divorce.* New York: Basic Books.

Warren, K. S. (1988, March 19). Protecting the world's children: An agenda for the 1990s. *The Lancet,* p. 659.

Wasserman, A. L. (1984). A prospective study of the impact of home monitoring on the family. *Pediatrics, 74,* 323–329.

Waters, E., Wippman, J., & Sroufe, L. A. (1979). Attachment, positive affect, and competence in the peer group: Two studies in construct validation. *Child Development, 50*(3), 821–829.

Watson, J. B. (1919). *Psychology from the standpoint of a behaviorist.* Philadelphia: Lippincott.

Watson, J. B. (1958). *Behaviorism* (rev. ed.). New York: Norton.

Watson, J. B., & Rayner, R. (1920). Conditioned emotional reactions. *Journal of Experimental Psychology, 3,* 1–14.

Webb, W. B., & Bonnet, M. (1979). Sleep and dreams. In M. E. Meyer (Ed.), *Foundations of contemporary psychology.* New York: Oxford University Press.

Wegman, M. E. (1986). Annual summary of vital statistics—1985. *Pediatrics, 78*(6), 983–994.

Wegman, M. E. (1987). Annual summary of vital statistics—1986. *Pediatrics, 80*(6), 817–827.

Weiffenback, J., & Thach, B. (1975). *Taste receptors in the tongue of the newborn human: Behavioral evidence.* Paper presented at the meeting of the Society for Research in Child Development, Denver.

Weinstein, R. S., Marshall, H. H., Sharp, L., & Botkin, M. (1987). Pygmalion and the student: Age and classroom differences in children's awareness of teacher expectation. *Child Development, 58,* 1079–1093.

Weisman, S. R. (1988, July 20). No more guarantees of a son's birth. *The New York Times,* pp. A1, A9.

Weiss, L., & Lowenthal, M. (1975). Life-course perspectives on friendship. In M. Lowenthal, M. Thurner, & D. Chiriboga (Eds.), *Four stages of life.* San Francisco: Jossey-Bass.

Weissman, M. M., Gammon, D., John, K., Merikangas, K. R., Warner, V., Prusoff, B. A., & Sholomskas, D. (1987). Children of depressed parents: Increased psychopathology and early onset of major depression. *Archives of General Psychiatry, 44,* 847–853.

Weitkamp, L., & Schacter, B. Z. (1985). Transferrin and HLA: Spontaneous abortion, neural tube defects, and natural selection. *New England Journal of Medicine, 313,* 925–932.

Wellman, H., & Lempers, J. (1977). The naturalistic communicative abilities of two-year-olds. *Child Development, 48,* 1052–1057.

Wells, A. S. (1988a, September 7). For those at risk of dropping out, an enduring program that works. *The New York Times,* p. B9.

Wells, A. S. (1988b, January 3). The parents' place: Right in the school. *The New York Times Education Supplement,* p. 63.

Werner, E., Bierman, L., French, F. E., Simonian, K., Connor, A., Smith, R., & Campbell, M. (1968). Reproductive and environmental casualties: A report on the 10-year follow-up of the children of the Kauai pregnancy study. *Pediatrics, 42*(1), 112–127.

Werner, E. E. (1985). Stress and protective factors in children's lives. In A. R. Nichol (Ed.), *Longitudinal studies in child psychology and psychiatry.* New York: Wiley.

Werner, J. S., & Siqueland, E. R. (1978). Visual recognition memory in the preterm infant. *Infant Behavior and Development, 1,* 79–94.

Werts, C. E. (1966). Social class and initial career choice of college freshmen. *Sociology of Education, 39,* 74–85.

Werts, C. E. (1968). Paternal influence on career choice. *Journal of Counseling Psychology, 15,* 48–52.

Whisnant, L., & Zegans, L. (1975). A study of attitudes toward menarche in white middle class American adolescent girls. *American Journal of Psychiatry, 132*(8), 809–814.

White, B. L. (1971, October). *Fundamental early environmental influences on the development of competence.* Paper presented at Third Western Symposium on Learning, Western Washington State College, Bellingham, WA.

White, B. L. (1975). *The first three years of life.* Englewood Cliffs, NJ: Prentice-Hall.

White, B. L., Kaban, B., & Attanucci, J. (1979). *The origins of human competence.* Lexington, MA: Heath.

White, K. R. (1982). The relation between socio-economic status and academic achievement. *Psychological Bulletin, 91*(3), 461–481.

Whitehurst, G. J., Falco, F. L., Lonigan, C. J., Fischel, J. E., DeBaryshe, B. D., Valdez-Menchaca, M.D. & Caulfield, M. (1988). Accelerating language development through picture book reading. *Developmental Psychology, 24*(4), 552–559.

Wideman, M. V., & Singer, J. F. (1984). The role of psychological mechanisms in preparation for childbirth. *American Psychologist, 34,* 1357–1371.

Wilcox, A. J., Weinberg, C. R., O'Connor, J. F., Baird, D. D., Schlatterer, J. P., Canfield, R. E., Armstrong, E. G., & Nisula, B. C. (1988). Incidence of early loss in pregnancy. *New England Journal of Medicine, 319*(4), 189–194.

Williams, E. R., & Caliendo, M. A. (1984). *Nutrition: Principles, issues, and applications.* New York: McGraw-Hill.

Williams, J., Best, D., & Boswell, D. (1975). The measurement of children's racial attitudes in the early school years. *Child Development, 46,* 494–500.

Williams, T. M. (1978). *Differential impact of TV on children: A natural experiment in communities with and without TV.* Paper presented at the meeting of the International Society for Research on Aggression, Washington, DC.

Wilson, G., McCreary, R., Kean, J., & Baxter, J. (1979). The development of preschool children of heroin-addicted mothers: A controlled study. *Pediatrics, 63*(1), 135–141.

Wilson, R. S. (1983). The Louisville Twin Study: Developmental synchronies in behavior. *Child Development, 54,* 298–316.

Winer, G. A. (1982). A review and analysis of children's fearful behavior in dental settings. *Child Development, 53,* 1111–1133.

Winick, M. (1981, January). Food and the fetus. *Natural History*, pp. 16–81.

Winick, M., Brasel, J., & Rosso, P. (1972). Nutrition and cell growth. In M. Winick (Ed.), *Nutrition and development*. New York: Wiley.

Wittrock, M. C. (1980). Learning and the brain. In M. C. Wittrock (Ed.), *The brain and psychology*. New York: Academic.

Wolf, M. (1968). *The house of Lim.* Englewood Cliffs, NJ: Prentice-Hall.

Wolf, T. M., Sklov, M. C., Wenzl, P. A., Hunter, S. MacD., & Berenson, G. S. (1982). Validation of a measure of type A behavior pattern in children: Bogalusa heart study. *Child Development, 53*, 126–135.

Wolfe, D. A. (1985). Child-abusive parents: An empirical review and analysis. *Psychological Bulletin, 97*(3), 462–482.

Wolff, P. H. (1966). The causes, controls, and organizations of behavior in the newborn. *Psychological Issues, 5*(1, Whole No. 17), 1–105.

Wolff, P. H. (1969). The natural history of crying and other vocalizations in early infancy. In B. M. Foss (Ed.), *Determinants of infant behavior* (Vol. 4). London: Methuen.

Wright, J. T., Waterson, E. J., Barrison, I. G., Toplis, P. J., Lewis, I. G., Gordon, M. G., MacRae, K. D., Morris, N. F., & Murray Lyon, I. M. (1983, March 26). Alcohol consumption, pregnancy, and low birthweight. *The Lancet*, pp. 663–665.

Yamamoto, K., Soliman, A., Parsons, J., & Davies, O. L. (1987). Voices in unison: Stressful events in the lives of children in six countries. *Journal of Child Psychology and Psychiatry, 28*(6), 855–864.

Yarrow, L. (1961). Maternal deprivation: Toward an empirical and conceptual reevaluation. *Psychological Bulletin, 58*, 459–490.

Yarrow, M. R. (1978, October 31). *Altruism in children.* Paper presented at program, Advances in Child Development Research, New York Academy of Sciences, New York.

Yogman, M. J. (1984). Competence and performance of fathers and infants. In A. MacFarlane (Ed.), *Progress in child health.* London: Churchill Livingston.

Yogman, M. J., Cooley, J., & Kindlon, D. (1988). Fathers, infants, and toddlers: A developing relationship. In P. Bronstein & C. P. Cowan (Eds.), *Fatherhood today: Men's changing roles in the family.* New York: Wiley.

Young, K. T., & Zigler, E. (1986). Infant and toddler day care: Regulations and policy implications. *American Journal of Orthopsychiatry, 56*(1), 43–55.

Yudkin, M. (1984). When kids think the unthinkable. *Psychology Today, 18*(4), 18–25.

Zabin, L. S., & Clark, S. D. (1983). Institutional factors affecting teenagers' choice and reasons for delay in attending a family planning clinic. *Family Planning Perspectives, 15*(1), 25–29.

Zabin, L. S., Hirsch, M. B., Smith, E. A., & Hardy, J. B. (1984). Adolescent sexual attitudes and behavior: Are they consistent? *Family Planning Perspectives*, pp. 16, 181.

Zabin, L. S., Kantner, J. F., & Zelnik, M. (1979). The risk of adolescent pregnancy in the first months of intercourse. *Family Planning Perspectives, 11*(4), 215–222.

Zacharias, L., Rand, W. M., & Wurtman, R. J. (1976). A prospective study of sexual development and growth in American girls: The statistics of menarche. *Obstetrical and Gynecological Survey, 31*(4), 323–337.

Zacharias, L., & Wurtman, R. J. (1969). Age at menarche. *New England Journal of Medicine, 260*, 868–875.

Zajonc, R. B. (1976). Family configuration and intelligence. *Science, 197*(4236), 227–236.

Zajonc, R. B. (1983). Validating the confluence model. *Psychological Bulletin, 93*(3), 457–480.

Zakariya, S. B. (1982, September). Another look at the children of divorce: Summary report of the study of school needs of one-parent children. *Principal*, pp. 34–37.

Zelazo, P. R. (1981). An information-processing approach to infant cognitive assessment. In *Developmental disabilities in preschool children.* Englewood Cliffs, NJ: Spectrum.

Zelazo, P. R., & Kearsley, R. (1980). The emergence of functional play in infants: Evidence for a major cognitive transition. *Journal of Applied Developmental Psychology, 1*(2), 95–117.

Zelazo, P. R., Kotelchuck, M., Barber, L., & David, J. (1977, March). *Fathers and sons: An experimental facilitation of attachment behaviors.* Paper presented at the meeting of the Society for Research in Child Development, New Orleans.

Zelnik, M., Kantner, J. F., & Ford, K. (1981). *Sex and pregnancy in adolescence.* Beverly Hills, CA: Sage.

Zeknik, M., & Shah, F. K. (1973). First intercourse among young Americans. *Family Planning Perspectives, 15*(2), 64–72.

Zeskind, P. S., & Iacino, R. (1984). Effects of maternal visitation to preterm infants in the neonatal intensive care unit. *Child Development, 55*, 1887–1893.

Zeskind, P. S., & Marshall, T. R. (1988). The relation between variations in pitch and maternal perceptions of infant crying. *Child Development, 59*, 193–196.

Zeskind, P. S., & Ramey, C. T. (1981). Preventing intellectual and interactional sequelae of fetal malnutrition: A longitudinal, transactional, and synergistic approach to development. *Child Development, 52*, 213–218.

Zigler, E. F. (1987). Formal schooling for four-year-olds? *North American Psychologist, 42*(3), 254–260.

Zimmerman, I. L., & Bernstein, M. (1983). Parental work patterns in alternate families: Influence on child development. *American Journal of Orthopsychiatry, 53*(3), 418–425.

Zuckerman, B. S., & Beardslee, W. R. (1987). Maternal depression: A concern for pediatricians. *Pediatrics, 79*(1), 110–117.

Zuckerman, D. M., & Zuckerman, B. S. (1985). Television's impact on children. *Pediatrics, 75*, 233–240.

RESOURCES

A LARGE NUMBER OF ORGANIZATIONS, both public and private, exist to help people obtain information, counseling, or other help for specific conditions. The following list is just a small sample of such agencies, which are concerned with various medical and psychological issues and disorders discussed in this book.

Some organizations distribute literature or offer counseling directly. Others, including those listed here for which only a telephone number is given, provide referrals to local resources.

If a topic in which you are interested is not included here, look in the telephone directory (in the yellow pages, under "Associations," "Social Service Organizations," or "Human Services Organizations") or in the Encyclopedia of Associations in the reference room of your local library.

Numbers and addresses listed here are subject to change or disconnection without notice. To obtain information on toll-free numbers, dial 800-555-1212.

ALCOHOL AND DRUG INFORMATION AND TREATMENT

Alcoholics Anonymous
P.O. Box 459, Grand Central
Station
New York, NY 10163
Information: 212-686-1100
Hot line: 212-473-6200

Local phone numbers are given in the white pages of telephone directories of communities around the world.

The largest and most successful organization in the world for recovery from alcoholism, through meetings and peer support. All services are free.

Al-Anon Family Group Headquarters
P.O. Box 459, Grand Central
Station
New York, NY 10163
212-481-6565

Local phone numbers can be obtained from local AA chapter or telephone directory.

Offers information and help to family and friends of people with drinking and drug problems.

Hazelden Educational Materials
Pleasant Valley Road
Box 176
Center City, MN 55012-0176
800-328-9000 (United States
except Minnesota)
800-257-0070 (Minnesota)
612-257-4010 (Alaska and outside
United States)

Nonprofit organization which publishes and sells a wide range of books, pamphlets, and video and audio cassettes about chemical dependency, both for users and for those close to them. Free catalog.

Drug Information and Treatment Hotline
800-662-HELP

A 24-hour hotline sponsored by the federal government and affiliated with the National Institute of Drug Abuse.

National Clearinghouse for Alcohol and Drug Information
P.O. Box 2345
Rockville, MD 20852
301-468-2600

Government-sponsored source of literature.

BIRTH DEFECTS AND DISEASES

Muscular Dystrophy Association
810 Seventh Avenue
New York, NY 10010
212-586-0808

Supplies general information about the disease and services offered.

National Multiple Sclerosis Society
205 East 42d Street
New York, NY 10017
212-986-3240

Gives information about research and treatment.

National Down Syndrome Society
141 Fifth Avenue
New York, NY 10010
212-460-9330

Gives information about parent support groups, publications, and special programs.

Spina Bifida Information and Referral
343 South Dearborn
Chicago, IL 60604
800-621-3141
312-663-1562 (in Illinois)

Provides general information and referrals.

Spinal Cord Society
2410 Lakeview Drive
Fergus Falls, MN 56537
800-328-8253
800-862-0179 (in Minnesota)

Offers general information and monthly newsletter.

CANCER

American Cancer Society
4 West 35th Street
New York, NY 10001
800-ACS-2345
212-736-3030

For free information on almost any concern about cancer, this number will aid you in finding local resources.

Cancer Information Service
National Cancer Institute, National
Institute of Health
Bethesda, MD 20892
800-4-CANCER

Persons at this number will answer cancer-related questions in addition to providing free information on cancer prevention.

CHILD ABUSE

Incest Survivors Anonymous
P.O. Box 5613
Long Beach, CA 90805
213-422-1632

Provides information to help people who have experienced incest adjust psychologically and socially.

National Child Abuse Hotline
Child Help USA
Woodland Hills, CA 91370
800-422-4453

Provides information and referrals to both parents and children to prevent and deal with consequences of child abuse.

Parents Anonymous Hotline
2230 Hawthorne Boulevard
Suite 210
Torrance, CA 90505
800-421-0353

Makes referrals to self-help groups of parents who want to prevent themselves from or stop abusing their children.

CHILD ADVOCACY

Children's Defense Fund
520 New Hampshire Avenue NW
Washington, DC, 20036
800-424-9602
202-628-8787 (in Washington, DC)
Provides information and resources on a wide range of issues concerning children.

EATING DISORDERS

National Association of Anorexia Nervosa and Associated Disorders
Box 7
Highland Park, IL 60033
312-831-3438
Provides referrals to local therapists.

EDUCATION AND CHILD CARE

ChildCare Action Campaign
99 Hudson Street
Suite 1233
New York, NY 10013
212-334-9595
This national coalition of leaders from various institutions and organizations serves as an advocacy group offering information on many aspects of child care through individual information sheets, a bimonthly newsletter, and audio training tapes for family day care providers.

National Association for the Education of Young Children
1834 Connecticut Avenue NW
Washington, DC, 20009
202-232-8777 or 800-424-2460
This professional association accredits child-care centers and preschools around the country, holds regional and national meetings, and distributes publications for both professionals and parents.

National Black Child Development Institute
1463 Rhode Island Avenue NW
Washington, DC, 20005
202-387-1281
This national nonprofit organization focuses on child care, health, education, and welfare. It holds conferences, conducts tutorial programs, and helps homeless children find adoptive families.

FAMILY SUPPORT

Family Resource Coalition
230 North Michigan Avenue
Suite 1625
Chicago, IL 60601
Gives information on free or low-cost programs offering child development classes, hot lines, and support groups.

Parents without Partners
7910 Woodmont Avenue
Bethesda, MD 20814
800-638-8078
301-654-8850 (in Maryland)
Provides information on local chapters of support groups for single parents.

Single Parent Resource Center
225 Park Avenue South
New York, NY 10003
Provides information and resources for single parents.

GENERAL HEALTH

National Health Information Clearinghouse
U.S. Office of Disease Prevention and Health Promotion
800-336-4797
Government service answering almost any health-related concern.

National Women's Health Network
224 Seventh Street SE
Washington, DC, 20003
202-543-9222
Provides information relating to women's health topics.

INFANT MORTALITY

Compassionate Friends, Inc.
P.O. Box 3696
Oak Brook, IL 60522
312-323-5010
Offers support to bereaved parents and siblings of infants and older children through 460 chapters in the United States.

National Sudden Infant Death Syndrome Clearinghouse
3520 Prospect Street NW
Ground Floor Suite 1
Washington, DC, 20057
202-625-8410
Provides resources and information.

MEDICAL HELP

American Trauma Society
1400 Mercantile Lane
Suite 188
Landover, MD 20785
800-556-7890
Offers literature on accident prevention.

Orton Dyslexia Society
724 York Road
Baltimore, MD 21204
800-222-3123 (except Maryland)
Provides information about reading and writing disorders.

MENTAL HEALTH

National Institute of Mental Health
Public Inquiries Branch
5600 Fishers Lane
Room 15C-05
Rockville, MD 20857
301-443-4517

Federally sponsored agency which answers questions about depression and other psychological disorders.

MISSING CHILDREN

Child Find
P.O. Box 277
New Paltz, NY 12561
800-I AM LOST

Hotline to report disappearances or sightings.

National Center for Missing and Exploited Children
1835 K Street NW
Suite 700
Washington, DC, 20006
800-843-5678

Hotline to report disappearances or sightings.

PREGNANCY AND CHILDBIRTH

American Society for Psychoprophylaxis in Obstetrics/Lamaze
1840 Wilson Boulevard
Suite 204
Arlington, VA 22201
800-368-4404

Makes referrals to local Lamaze chapters, which help prospective parents prepare for childbirth and infant care.

International Childbirth Education Association
P.O. Box 20048
Minneapolis, MN 55420
800-624-4934

Offers a free catalog of materials on pregnancy, childbirth, and child care.

National Clearinghouse for Family Planning Information
Health and Human Services Department
P.O. Box 12921
Arlington, VA 22209
703-558-7932

Federally sponsored agency which provides information on publications about birth control.

SLEEP PROBLEMS

Association of Sleep Disorders Center
P.O. Box 2604
Del Mar, CA 92014
619-755-6556

Provides a listing of sleep disorder centers in the United States and Canada.

SPEECH AND HEARING

National Center for Stuttering
200 East 33d Street
New York, NY 10016
800-221-2483
212-532-1460 (in New York)
Provides information and literature on treatment programs.

SUICIDE

National Adolescent Suicide Hotline
2210 North Halsted
Chicago, IL 60614
800-621-4000

Provides help and counseling to prevent suicide and to help surviving family and friends.

SEXUALLY TRANSMITTED DISEASES AND AIDS

AIDS Hotline
800-342-AIDS

Provides sources to contact with questions.

V.D. National Hotline
800-227-8922

Provides sources to contact with concerns and questions about sexually transmitted diseases.

ACKNOWLEDGMENTS

COVER PHOTOGRAPHS

Top row, left to right: Suzanne Szasz/ Photo Researchers; Nancy Durrell McKenna/Photo Researchers; Jim Pozarik/Gamma-Liaison; Richard Hutchings/Photo Researchers.
Second row, left to right: Stephen Becker; Fern Logan; Stephen Becker; Fern Logan.
Third row, left to right: Fern Logan; Sally Olds; Fern Logan; Larry Nicholson/Photo Researchers.
Bottom row, left to right: John Annerino/Gamma-Liaison; Valerie Campbell; John Annerino/Gamma-Liaison; Fern Logan.

PART-OPENING ART

Beginnings: *Baby in Red High Chair;* Abby Aldrich Rockefeller Folk Art Center, Williamsburg, Virginia.
Infancy and Toddlerhood: Mary Cassatt, *Mother and Child,* 1890; Wichita Art Museum, Roland P. Murdock Collection; photo by Henry Nelson.
Early Childhood: Bernique Longley, *Hermanos,* 1958; from the collection of Philip R. Johnsson; provided by Santa Fé East.
Middle Childhood: Robert Henri, *Eva Green;* Wichita Art Museum, Roland P. Murdock Collection; photo by Henry Nelson.
Adolescence: Daniel Garber, *Orchard Window;* © Philadelphia Museum of Art, given by the artist's family.

INTRODUCTION

Opening photograph: © Erika Stone, 1987.

Opening quotation: Hartford, John. (1971). "Life Prayer" form *Work Movies.* Copyright © 1971 by Ensign Music Corporation. Reprinted by permission.

CHAPTER 1

Opening photograph: © Mimi Cotter/ International Stock.

Quotations in text:
Page 24: Watson, J. B. (1958). *Behaviorism* (revised edition). Copyright 1924, 1925 by The People's Institute Publishing Company, Inc. Copyright 1930 by W. W. Norton & Company, Inc. Copyright renewed 1952, 1953, 1958 by John B. Watson. Reprinted by permission of W. W. Norton & Company, Inc.
Page 35: Piaget, Jean (1952a). *The child's conception of number.* First published in Switzerland from the French, 1941. Translated by C. Gattegno and F. M. Hodgson. Reprinted by permission of Routledge & Kegan Paul Limited and Basic Books, Inc.
Page 41: Ross, J. B., & McLaughlin, M. (Eds.). (1949). *A portable medieval reader.* Copyright 1949 by The Viking Press, Inc. Copyright renewed © 1976 by James Ross and Mary Martin McLaughlin. All rights reserved. Reproduced by permission of Viking Penguin, a division of Penguin Books USA, Inc.

CHAPTER 2

Opening photograph: © Jeffry W. Myers 1988/Stock, Boston.

Opening quotation: Leonard, William Ellery. (1923). *Two Lives.* © 1923 by B. W. Huebsch, Inc. © 1951 Charlotte Charlton Leonard, Viking-Penguin. Reprinted by permission of the author's heirs.

Box 2-3: Adapted from Hall, E. (1984). Sandra Scarr: What's a parent to do? *Psychology Today, 18*(5), 62–63. © 1983 by PT Partners, L. P. Reprinted by permission.

Figure 2-10: Adapted from Anastasi, A. (1958). Heredity, environment, and the question "how?" *Psychological review, 65,* 197–208. Copyright 1958 by the American Psychological Association. Adapted by permission of the publisher and author.

Figure 2-11: Adapted from Tellegen, A., et al. (1988). Personality similarity in twins reared apart and together. *Journal of Personality and Social Psychology, 54*(6), 1031–1039. Copyright 1988 by the American Psychological Association. Adapted by permission of the publisher and author.

Table 2-1: Adapted from Vaughan, V., McKay, R. J., & Behrman, R. (1979). *Nelson textbook of pediatrics,* 11th edition. Adapted by permission of W. B. Saunders.

Table 2-2: Tisdale, S. (1988, May/June). The mother. *Hippocrates: The Magazine of Health and Medicine, 2*(3), 64–72. Researched by Valerie Fahey. Copyright © 1988 Hippocrates Partners. Reprinted by permission.

CHAPTER 3

Opening photograph: © Taeke Henstra/ Photo Researchers.

Opening quotation: Sexton, Anne. (1966). "Little Girl, My String Bean, My Lovely Woman" from *Live or Die.* Copyright © 1966 by Anne Sexton. Reprinted by permission of Houghton-Mifflin Company.

Box 3-4: Eisenberg, A., Murkoff, H. E., & Hathaway, S. E. (1984). *What to expect when you're expecting.* Copyright © 1984 by Arlene Eisenberg, Heidi Eisenberg Murkoff, and Sandee Eisenberg Hathaway. Reprinted by permission of Workman Publishing, Inc.

Figure 3-3: Bellinger, D., et al. (1987). Longitudinal analysis of prenatal and postnatal lead exposure and early cognitive development. *New England Journal of Medicine, 316*(17), 1037–1043. Reprinted by permission.

Table 3-1: Eisenberg, A., Murkoff, H. E., & Hathaway, S. E. (1984). *What to expect when you're expecting.* Copyright © 1984 by Arlene Eisenberg, Heidi Eisenberg Murkoff, and Sandee Eisenberg Hathaway. Reprinted by permission of Workman Publishing, Inc.

Quotation in text: Page 101, Weisman, S. R. (1988, July 20). No more guarantees of a son's birth. *The New York Times,* pp. A1 & A9. Copyright © 1988 by The New York Times Company. Reprinted by permission.

CHAPTER 4

Opening photograph: © David R. Austen/Stock, Boston.

Opening quotation: Fraiberg, Selma. (1959). *The Magic Years.* Copyright 1959 Selma H. Fraiberg, copyright renewed. Reprinted by permission of Charles Scribner's Sons, an imprint of Macmillan Publishing Company.

Figure 4-2: Norton, F. C., Placek, P. J., & Taffel, S. M. (1987). Comparisons of national cesarean-section rates. *New England Journal of Medicine, 316,* 387. Reprinted by permission.

Table 4-1: Adapted from Brown, S. S. (1985). Can low birth weight be prevented? *Family Planning Perspectives, 17*(3), 112–118. © 1985 The Alan Guttmacher Institute. Reprinted by permission.

Table 4-2: Timiras, P. S. (1972). *Developmental physiology and aging.* Copyright © 1972 by P. S. Timiras. Reprinted by permission of Macmillan Publishing Company.

Table 4-3: Apgar, V. (1953). A proposal for a new method of evaluation of the newborn infant. *Current Researches in Anesthesia and Analgesia.* Reprinted by permission of the International Anesthesia Research Society.

CHAPTER 5

Opening photograph: © Erika Stone 1987.

Figure 5-5: Wegman, M. E. (1987). Annual summary of vital statistics . . . (1986). *Pediatrics 86*(6), 817–827. Copyright 1986 by *Pediatrics.* Reprinted by permission.

Table 5-2: Martin, E. A. (1987). How to tell if a baby is well nourished. *Roberts' nutrition work with children,* 4th edition. Reprinted by permission of the author and the University of Chicago Press.

Table 5-3: Bolles, E. B. (1982). *So much to say.* Copyright © 1982 by Edmund Blair Bolles. Published by St. Martin's Press, Inc. Reprinted by permission.

Table 5-4: Adapted from Frankenburg, W. K. (1978). Denver Developmental Screening Test. © 1978 by W. K. Frankenburg. Adapted by permission of the author.

Quotation in text: Page 169, Eiger, M. S., & Olds, S. W. (1986). *The complete book of breastfeeding,* 2d edition. Copyright © 1972, 1987 by Sally Wendkos Olds and Marvin S. Eiger, M.D. Reprinted by permission of Workman Publishing, Inc.

CHAPTER 6

Opening photograph: © Erika Stone 1987.

Figure 6-1: Fagen, J. W. (1982). Infant memory. In T. M. Field, et al. (Eds.), *Review of human development.* Copyright © John Wiley & Sons. Reprinted by permission.

Table 6-2: Adapted in part from Capute, A. J., Shapiro, B. K., & Palmer, F. B. (1987, April). Marking the milestones of language development. *Contemporary Pediatrics, 4*(4), 25. Copyright 1987 by *Contemporary Pediatrics.* Adapted by permission of the publisher and author. Adapted in part from Lenneberg, E. H. (1969, May 9). On explaining language. *Science, 164*(3880), 635–643. Copyright 1969 by the American Association for the Advancement of Science. Reprinted by permission.

Table 6-3: Acredolo, L., & Goodwyn, S. (1988). Symbolic gesturing in normal infants. *Child Development, 59,* 450–466. © The Society for Research in Child Development, Inc. Reprinted by permission.

CHAPTER 7

Opening photograph: © Suzanne Szasz/Photo Researchers.

Table 7-1: Sroufe, L. A. (1979). Socioemotional development. In J. Osofsky

(Ed.), *Handbook of infant development.* Copyright © 1979 by John Wiley & Sons. Reprinted by permission.

Table 7-2: Adapted from Trotter, R. J. (1983). Baby face. *Psychology Today, 17*(8), 14–20. © 1983 by PT Partners, L. P.

Table 7-3: Adapted from Thomas, A., & Chess, S. (1984). Genesis and evolution of behavioral disorders: From infancy to early adult life. *American Journal of Psychiatry, 141*(1), 1–9. Adapted by permission.

CHAPTER 8

Opening photograph: © Erika Stone 1988.

Opening quotation: Sandburg, Carl. (1936). No. 8 from *The People, Yes.* Copyright © 1936 by Harcourt Brace Jovanovich, Inc., renewed © 1964 by Carl Sandburg. Reprinted by permission of the publisher.

Figure 8-1: Ferber, R. (1985). *Solve your child's sleep problems.* Copyright © 1985 by Richard Ferber, M.D. Reprinted by permission of Simon & Schuster, Inc.

Figure 8-2: Kellogg, R. (1970). Understanding children's art. In P. Cramer (Ed.), *Readings in developmental psychology today,* 35, 36, 39. Reprinted by permission of Mayfield Publishing Company.

Figure 8-3: American Association for Protecting Children. (1987). *National estimates of child abuse and neglect reports, 1976–1986.* Reprinted by permission.

Table 8-1: Lowrey, G. H. (1978). *Growth and development of children,* 7th edition. Copyright © 1978 by Year Book Medical Publishers, Inc., Chicago. Reproduced by permission.

Table 8-2: Beautrais, A. L., Fergusson, D. M., & Shannon, F. T. (1982). Life events and childhood morbidity: A prospective study. *Pediatrics, 70*(6), 935–940. Reprinted by permission.

Table 8-3: Corbin, C. (1973). *A textbook of motor development,* pp. 118–119. Copyright © 1973 by William C. Brown, Publishers, Dubuque, Iowa. Reprinted by permission.

Quotation in text: Pages 302, 303, Kellogg, R. (1970). Understanding children's art. In P. Cramer (Ed.), *Readings in developmental psychology today,* 35, 36, 39. Reprinted by permission of Mayfield Publishing Company.

CHAPTER 9

Opening photograph: © George Ancona/International Stock.

Table 9-2: Adapted from Berk, L., & Garvin, R. (1984). Development of private speech among low income Appalachian children. *Developmental Psychology, 20*(2), 271–284. Copyright 1984 by the American Psychological Association. Adapted by permission.

Table 9-3: Bolles, E. B. (1982). *So much to say.* Copyright © 1982 by Edmund Blair Bolles. Published by St. Martin's Press, Inc. Reprinted by permission.

CHAPTER 10

Opening photograph: © Tim Davis/Photo Researchers.

Opening quotation: Smith, Stevie. (1972). "Papa Love Baby" from *Stevie Smith: Collected Poems.* Copyright © 1972 by Stevie Smith. Reprinted by permission of New Directions Publishing Corporation.

Table 10-1: Morris, R., & Kralochwill, T. (1983). *Treating children's fears and phobias: A behavioral approach.* Copyright © 1983 by Pergamon Press, Inc., Elmsford, NY. All rights reserved. Reprinted by permission.

Quotation in text: Page 380, McClelland, D., et al. (1978). Making it to maturity. *Psychology Today, 12*(1), 42–53, 114. © 1987 by PT Partners, L. P.

CHAPTER 11

Opening photograph: © Richard Hutchings/Photo Researchers.

Opening quotation: Olds, Sharon. (1983). "Size and Sheer Will" from *The Dead and the Living.* Copyright © 1983 by Sharon Olds. Reprinted by permission of Alfred A. Knopf, Inc.

Figure 11-1: Adapted from Gortmaker, S. L., et al. (1987). Increasing pediatric obesity in the U.S. *American Journal of the Diseases of Children, 141,* 535–540. Copyright 1987 by the American Medical Association. Adapted by permission.

Figure 11-3: Schor, E. L. (1987). Unintentional injuries: Patterns within families. *American Journal of the Diseases of Children, 141,* 1280. Copyright 1987 by the American Medical Association. Reprinted by permission.

Table 11-1: Adapted from Rauh, J. L., Schumsky, D. A., & Witt, M. T. (1967). Heights, weights and obesity in urban school children. *Child Development, 38,* 515–530. © 1967 by The Society for Research in Child Development, Inc. Adapted by permission.

Table 11-2: Adapted from Cratty, B. J. (1979). *Perceptual and motor development in infants and children,* 2d edition. © 1979. Adapted by permission of Prentice-Hall, Inc.

CHAPTER 12

Opening photograph: © Ellis Herwig/Picture Cube.

Opening quotation: Ionesco, Eugene. (1967). *Fragments of a Journal.* Trans. by Jean Stewart. Reprinted by permission of Grove Press.

Box 12-1: Hall, E. (1970). A conversation with Jean Piaget and Bärbel Inhelder. *Psychology Today, 4,* 27–28. Copyright © 1970 by PT Partners, L. P.

Figure 12-1: Otis, A. S., & Lennon, R. T. (1967). *Otis-Lennon Mental Ability Test, Primary I and Primary II Levels.* Copyright © 1967 by Harcourt Brace Jovanovich, Inc. All rights reserved. Reprinted by permission.

Figure 12-2: Wallach, M. A., & Kogan, N. (1967). Creativity and intelligence in children's thinking. *Transaction, 4*(1), 38–43. Copyright © 1967 by Transaction Publishers. Reprinted by permission.

Table 12-1: Adapted in part from Hoffman, M. L. (1970). Moral development. In P. H. Mussen (Ed.), *Carmichael's manual of child psychology.* Copyright © 1970 by John Wiley & Sons. Adapted by permission. Adapted in part from Kohlberg, L. (1964). The development of moral character and moral ideology. In M. Hoffman & L. Hoffman (Eds.), *Review of child development research,* Vol. I, pp. 396–398. Copyright © 1964 by the Russell Sage Foundation. Reprinted by permission of the Russell Sage Foundation.

Table 12-2: Selman, R. L. (1973). *A structural analysis of the ability to take another's social perspective: Stages in the development of role-taking ability.* Paper presented at the meeting of the Society for Research in Child Development. Reprinted by permission.

Table 12-3: Kohlberg, L. (1969, 1976). Moral stage and moralization. In T. Lickona (Ed.), *Moral development and behavior.* Published by Holt, Rinehart & Winston. Reprinted by permission of Thomas Lickona.

Table 12-4: Adapted from Chomsky, C. (1969). *The acquisition of syntax in children from five to ten.* Copyright © 1969 by The Massachusetts Institute of Technology. All rights reserved. Adapted by permission.

Quotation in text: Page 424, Kohlberg, L. (1969). Stage and sequence: The cognitive developmental approach to socialization. In D. A. Goslin (Ed.), *Handbook of socialization theory and research.* Published by Rand McNally. Reprinted by permission of David A. Goslin.

CHAPTER 13

Opening photograph: © Erika Stone 1985.

Opening quotation: Crawford, Karen. (1968). "Being Nobody" from *Miracles* by Richard Lewis. Published by Simon & Schuster. Reprinted by permission of the author.

Box 13-5: Pines, M. (1984, March). PT conversation: Michael Rutter, resilient children. *Psychology Today, 21*(5), 57–65. © 1987 by PT Partners, L. P.

Table 13-1: Chance, P., & Fischman, J. (1987). The magic of childhood. *Psychology Today.* © 1987 by PT Partners, L. P. Reprinted by permission.

CHAPTER 14

Opening photograph: © Ronnie Kaufman/Stock Market.

Opening quotation: McGinley, Phyllis. (1956). "A Certain Age" from *Times Three.* Copyright © 1956 by Phyllis McGinley. Copyright renewed © 1984 by the Estate of Phyllis McGinley. All rights reserved. Reprinted by permission of Viking-Penguin, a division of Penguin Books USA, Inc.

Box 14-1: Kenyatta, J. (1965). *Facing Mt. Kenya: The tribal life of the Gikuyu.* All rights reserved under International and Pan American copyright conventions. Reprinted by arrangement with Martin Secker & Warburg, Ltd., by permission of Random House, Inc.

Box 14-2: Gordon, Sol. (1982, March 13). Acceptance speech upon receiving the 1982 award for distinguished service in the field of human sexuality from the American Association of Sex Educators, Counselors and Therapists in New York City. Reprinted by permission of Sol Gordon, Syracuse University.

Quotation in text: Page 512, Frank, A. (1952). *Anne Frank: The diary of a young girl.* Translated by B. H. Mooyaart-Doubleday. Copyright © 1952 by Otto H. Frank. Copyright © 1967 by Doubleday & Company, Inc. All rights reserved. Reprinted by permission.

CHAPTER 15

Opening photograph: © 1987 Will & Deni McIntyre/Photo Researchers.

Opening quotation: Waugh, Evelyn. (1976). *The Diaries of Evelyn Waugh.* Michael Davie, editor. Copyright © 1976 by the Estate of Evelyn Waugh. Reprinted by permission of Little, Brown and Company and A.B. Peters Ltd.

CHAPTER 16

Opening photograph: Ed Galluci © 1981/Stock Market.

Opening quotation: Merriam, Eve. (1964). "Conversation with Myself" from *It Doesn't Always Have to Rhyme* in *A Sky Full of Poems.* Copyright © 1964, 1970, 1973 by Eve Merriam. All rights reserved. Reprinted by permission of Marian Reiner for the author.

Box 16-3: Jones, E. F., et al. (1985, March/April). Teenage pregnancy in developed countries: Determinants and policy implications. *Family Planning Perspectives, 17*(2), 53–63. © 1985 The Alan Guttmacher Institute. Reprinted by permission.

Box 16-4: Quotation from Gordon, S., & Everly, K. (1985). Increasing self-esteem in vulnerable students: A tool for reducing pregnancy among teenagers. *Impact '85, 8.* Published by Ed-U Press, Syracuse University. Reprinted by permission of Sol Gordon, Syracuse University.

Box 16-5: Evans, R. I. (1967). *Dialogue with Erik Erikson,* 31–32. Copyright © 1967 by Richard I. Evans. Reprinted by permission of Harper & Row, Publishers, Inc.

Figures 16-1, 16-2, and 16-3: Csikzentmihalyi, M., & Larson, R. (1984). *Being adolescent: Conflict and growth in the teenage years.* Copyright © 1984 by Basic Books, Inc., Publishers. Reprinted by permission.

Table 16-2: Adapted from Marcia, J. E. (1966). Development and validation of ego identity status. *Journal of Personality and Social Psychology, 3*(5), 551–558. Copyright 1966 by the American Psychological Association. Adapted by permission.

Table 16-3: Montemayor, R. (1983). Parents and adolescents in conflict: All families some of the time and some families most of the time. *Journal of Early Adolescence, 3,* 83–103. Reprinted by permission of Sage Publications, Inc.

Table 16-4: Adapted from Otto, H., & Healy, S. (1966). Adolescents' self-perception of personality strengths. *Human Relations, 14*(3), 483–490. Adapted by permission.

Quotation in text: Page 562, Mead, M. (1928). *Coming of age in Samoa.* Reprinted by permission of the Institute for Intercultural Studies, New York.

INDEXES

NAME INDEX

Middle childhood (*Cont.*):
   emotional problems in, 489–493
   Erikson on, 462–463
   everyday life in, 464–466
   family in, 472–489
   Freudian theory on, 462
   peer groups in, 466–472
   self-concept in, 459–464
   stress and resilience in, 493–497
   physical development during, 394–395
     handedness and, 411–412
     health and safety during, 401–409
     height and weight during, 395–397
     motor skills during, 409–411
     nutrition and growth during, 397–401
   reactions to divorce in, 481
Milestones in motor development, 177–181
   culture and, 182
Minority groups:
   self-fulfilling prophecies involving, 442–443
   [*See also* Blacks; Culture(s); Ethnic groups; Socioeconomic influences]
Miscarriages (spontaneous abortions), 98–99
Missing children, resources on, R4
Mister Rogers' Neighborhood, 367
Mistrust in Erikson's theories, 243
Mitosis, 58, G6
Modeling, 365
Monozygotic (identical) twins, 60, G6
   intelligence of, 80
   physical similarities among, 79
   studies of, 77
Montessori, Maria, 333
Montessori method, 333–335
Moral development, G6–G7
   in adolescence, 542–544
   in middle childhood, 421–427
Morality:
   of autonomous moral principles, 424
   of constraint, 421
   of conventional role conformity, 424
Moro reflex, 164
Morphemes, 224, G7
Mother-child relationships:
   in animal studies, 257
   attachment, 259–264
   in development of competence, 231–232
   Erikson on, 243
   language development and, 228–229
Mother-infant bond, 257–258, G7
"Motherese," 228–229, 266, 343, G7
Mothers:
   breastfeeding by, 166–168
   childbirth and:
     of low-birthweight babies, 138–139
     maternity care for, in Europe, 141
     medicated deliveries and attitudes of, 128–135
     prenatal environment in, 101–112

Mothers (*Cont.*):
   surrogate, 117
   (*See also* Childbirth; Pregnancy)
   depression in, 252
   in Freudian theory, 349
   in Israeli kibbutzim, 332
   in one-parent households, 485
   of rejected and isolated children, 385
   remarriage of, 484
   role in personality and social development of infants and toddlers of, 256–264
   sexual identity of children and, 357–359
   temporary separations between infants and, 275–276
   unmarried adolescents as, 584–590
   working, 329, 476–478
Motor development:
   in early childhood, 300–301
     artistic development, 301–303
   of infants:
     crawling, 180
     culture and milestones in, 182
     environmental influences on, 183–185
     infant walkers for, 184
     milestones in, 177–181
     reflex behaviors, 164–166, 176–177
     repetitive processes in, 177–178
   during middle childhood, 409–411
     handedness in, 411–412
   (*See also* Physical development)
Multifactorial inheritance, 64, G7
Multiple alleles, 63, G7
Multiple births, 59–60, 64
Muscles, early childhood growth of, 287
Muscular Dystrophy Association, R2
Mutations, G7
Mutual-regulation model, 252
Myelin, 162–163

National Adolescent Suicide Hotline, R4
National Association of Anorexia Nervosa and Associated Disorders, R3
National Association for the Education of Young Children, R3
National Black Child Development Institute, R3
National Center for Missing and Exploited Children, R4
National Center for Stuttering, R4
National Child Abuse Hotline, R2
National Clearinghouse for Alcohol and Drug Information, R2
National Clearinghouse for Family Planning Information, R4
National Commission for the Protection of Human Subjects of Biomedical and Behavioral Research, 42, 43
National Committee for Citizens in Education, 551
National Down Syndrome Society, R2
National Health Information Clearinghouse, R3

National Institute on Drug Abuse, 520–523
National Institute of Mental Health, 106, R4
National Institutes of Health (NIH), 75, 446
National Multiple Sclerosis Society, R2
National Sudden Infant Death Syndrome Clearinghouse, R3
National Women's Health Network, R3
Nativism, 225–226, G7
Natural childbirth, 130, G7
Natural experiments, 39, G7
Naturalistic observations, 34–35, G7
Nature-versus-nurture controversy, 52–53, 73–78, G7
   in sexual identity, 355–357
   visual cliff experiments and, 171
Negative reinforcement, 25
Negativism, 244
Neglect, 303–308, G7
   of adolescents, 527–528
Nelson, Katherine, 323–324
Neonatal jaundice, 146, G7
Neonatal period, 144, G7
Neonates (newborns), 124, 144–145, G7
   body systems of, 145–147
   classical conditioning of, 198
   emotions in, 245
   in Erikson's theories, 243
   health of, 147–148
   hearing by, 173–174
   mother-infant bond in, 257
   oral stage in, 242
   pattern vision of, 173
   reflex behaviors in, 164–166
   senses of smell, taste and pain in, 174–176
   sensorimotor stage in, 209–210
   smiling by, 249–250
   states of, 148–151
   visual-recognition memory in, 216
   (*See also* Infants)
Nervous system of infants, 162–163
Neural stimuli, 197, G7
Neurotic school phobia, 490
Neurotransmitters, 85, G7
Newborns (*see* Neonates)
New York Longitudinal Study (NYLS), 252–255
Nicotine (*see* Smoking)
Night terrors, 298, G7
Nightmares, 298, G7
Nighttime fears, 298–299
Nocturnal emissions (wet dreams), 511
Nonnormative life events, 14, G7
Nonorganic failure to thrive (NFT), 303, G7
Nonsocial play, 373, 374
Normal development, 5
Normative age-graded influences, 13, G7
Normative history-graded influences, 13–14, G7
Norms, 203, G7
Novelty preference, 217